P9-DOF-532
3 0379 10053 2680

Dictionary of the Middle Ages

AMERICAN COUNCIL OF LEARNED SOCIETIES

The American Council of Learned Societies, organized in 1919 for the purpose of advancing the study of the humanities and of the humanistic aspects of the social sciences, is a nonprofit federation comprising forty-five national scholarly groups. The Council represents the humanities in the United States in the International Union of Academies, provides fellowships and grants-in-aid, supports research-and-planning conferences and symposia, and sponsors special projects and scholarly publications.

MEMBER ORGANIZATIONS

AMERICAN PHILOSOPHICAL SOCIETY, 1743
AMERICAN ACADEMY OF ARTS AND SCIENCES, 1780
AMERICAN ANTIQUARIAN SOCIETY, 1812
AMERICAN ORIENTAL SOCIETY, 1842
AMERICAN NUMISMATIC SOCIETY, 1858
AMERICAN PHILOLOGICAL ASSOCIATION, 1869
ARCHAEOLOGICAL INSTITUTE OF AMERICA, 1879
SOCIETY OF BIBLICAL LITERATURE, 1880
MODERN LANGUAGE ASSOCIATION OF AMERICA, 1883
AMERICAN HISTORICAL ASSOCIATION, 1884
AMERICAN ECONOMIC ASSOCIATION, 1885
AMERICAN FOLKLORE SOCIETY, 1888
AMERICAN DIALECT SOCIETY, 1889
AMERICAN PSYCHOLOGICAL ASSOCIATION, 1892
ASSOCIATION OF AMERICAN LAW SCHOOLS, 1900
AMERICAN PHILOSOPHICAL ASSOCIATION, 1901
AMERICAN ANTHROPOLOGICAL ASSOCIATION, 1902
AMERICAN POLITICAL SCIENCE ASSOCIATION, 1903
BIBLIOGRAPHICAL SOCIETY OF AMERICA, 1904
ASSOCIATION OF AMERICAN GEOGRAPHERS, 1904
HISPANIC SOCIETY OF AMERICA, 1904
AMERICAN SOCIOLOGICAL ASSOCIATION, 1905
AMERICAN SOCIETY OF INTERNATIONAL LAW, 1906
ORGANIZATION OF AMERICAN HISTORIANS, 1907
AMERICAN ACADEMY OF RELIGION, 1909
COLLEGE ART ASSOCIATION OF AMERICA, 1912
HISTORY OF SCIENCE SOCIETY, 1924
LINGUISTIC SOCIETY OF AMERICA, 1924
MEDIAEVAL ACADEMY OF AMERICA, 1925
AMERICAN MUSICOLOGICAL SOCIETY, 1934
SOCIETY OF ARCHITECTURAL HISTORIANS, 1940
ECONOMIC HISTORY ASSOCIATION, 1940
ASSOCIATION FOR ASIAN STUDIES, 1941
AMERICAN SOCIETY FOR AESTHETICS, 1942
AMERICAN ASSOCIATION FOR THE ADVANCEMENT OF SLAVIC STUDIES, 1948
METAPHYSICAL SOCIETY OF AMERICA, 1950
AMERICAN STUDIES ASSOCIATION, 1950
RENAISSANCE SOCIETY OF AMERICA, 1954
SOCIETY FOR ETHNOMUSICOLOGY, 1955
AMERICAN SOCIETY FOR LEGAL HISTORY, 1956
AMERICAN SOCIETY FOR THEATRE RESEARCH, 1956
SOCIETY FOR THE HISTORY OF TECHNOLOGY, 1958
AMERICAN COMPARATIVE LITERATURE ASSOCIATION, 1960
AMERICAN SOCIETY FOR EIGHTEENTH-CENTURY STUDIES, 1969
ASSOCIATION FOR JEWISH STUDIES, 1969

Moses and the Brazen Serpent. Detail from an English ivory cross of the Romanesque period (*ca.* 1150). THE METROPOLITAN MUSEUM OF ART, THE CLOISTERS COLLECTION, 1963 (63.112)

Dictionary of the Middle Ages

JOSEPH R. STRAYER, *EDITOR IN CHIEF*

Volume 10

POLEMICS—SCANDINAVIA

CHARLES SCRIBNER'S SONS • NEW YORK

Library of Congress Cataloging in Publication Data
Main entry under title:

Dictionary of the Middle Ages.

Includes bibliographies and index.
1. Middle Ages—Dictionaries. I. Strayer,
Joseph Reese, 1904–1987

D114.D5 1982 909.07 82-5904
ISBN 0-684-16760-3 (v. 1) ISBN 0-684-18274-2 (v. 8)
ISBN 0-684-17022-1 (v. 2) ISBN 0-684-18275-0 (v. 9)
ISBN 0-684-17023-X (v. 3) ISBN 0-684-18276-9 (v. 10)
ISBN 0-684-17024-8 (v. 4) ISBN 0-684-18277-7 (v. 11)
ISBN 0-684-18161-4 (v. 5) ISBN 0-684-18278-5 (v. 12)
ISBN 0-684-18168-1 (v. 6) ISBN 0-684-18279-3 (v. 13)
ISBN 0-684-18169-X (v. 7) ISBN 0-684-19073-7 (set)

Published simultaneously in Canada
by Collier Macmillan Canada, Inc.

7 9 11 13 15 17 19 Q/C 20 18 16 14 12 10 8

PRINTED IN THE UNITED STATES OF AMERICA.

The *Dictionary of the Middle Ages* has been produced with
support from the National Endowment for the Humanities.

The paper in this book meets the guidelines for
permanence and durability of the Committee on
Production Guidelines for Book Longevity of the
Council on Library Resources.

Maps prepared by Patricia A. Rodriguez and Sylvia Lehrman.

Editorial Board

Advisory Committee

Editorial Staff

Contributors to Volume 10

HÉLÈNE AHRWEILER
Université de Paris I
POLITICAL THEORY, BYZANTINE

GUSTAVE ALEF
University of Oregon
PRIMARY CHRONICLE, RUSSIAN

THEODORE M. ANDERSSON
Stanford University
REGINSMÁL AND FÁFNISMÁL; REYKDŒLA SAGA; SAGA

GREGORY PETER ANDRACHUK
University of Victoria
RODRÍGUEZ DEL PADRÓN, JUAN

RHIAN M. ANDREWS
Queen's University of Belfast
RHYS OF DEHEUBARTH

GRACE MORGAN ARMSTRONG
Bryn Mawr College
PROVERBS AND SENTENTIAE

ANI P. ATAMIAN
RUBEN I; RUBENIDS

SUSAN M. BABBITT
American Philosophical Society
ROBERT DE CLARI; ROGER DE FLOR

ROGER S. BAGNALL
Columbia University
ROMAN EGYPT, LATE

TERENCE BAILEY
University of Western Ontario
PROCESSIONS, LITURGICAL; PSALM TONES

CARL F. BARNES, JR.
Oakland University, Rochester, Michigan
REGNAULT DE CORMONT; RHEIMS CATHEDRAL; RIB;

CARL F. BARNES (*cont.*)
ROBERT DE COUCY; ROBERT DE LUZARCHES; ROSE WINDOW; ST. DENIS, ABBEY CHURCH; ST. SERNIN, TOULOUSE; STE. CHAPELLE, PARIS

ROBERT BARRINGER
St. Michael's College, University of Toronto
POPE

ÜLKÜ Ü. BATES
Hunter College, City University of New York
QARAGŪZ FIGURES; QAYṢARĪYA; RAHLE; SARĀY

SILVIO A. BEDINI
Smithsonian Institution
PORTOLAN CHART; RICHARD OF WALLINGFORD

JEANETTE M. A. BEER
Purdue University
PROVENÇAL LANGUAGE; RENAUT DE BEAUJEU; ROMAN DE LA ROSE

GHAZI I. BISHEH
Jordan Archaeological Museum
RIWĀQ

THOMAS N. BISSON
University of California, Berkeley
RAMON BERENGUER IV

JONATHAN BLACK
SARUM USE

JONATHAN M. BLOOM
Harvard University
QAᶜA

C. E. BOSWORTH
University of Manchester
SAFFARIDS

CALVIN M. BOWER
University of Notre Dame
PROLATIO; PROPRIETAS; QUADRIVIUM; RHYTHM

MARJORIE N. BOYER
York College, City University of New York
ROADS AND BRIDGES, WESTERN EUROPEAN

GERARD J. BRAULT
Pennsylvania State University
ROLAND, SONG OF

MICHAEL BRETT
University of London
QAYRAWĀN, AL-

CYNTHIA J. BROWN
University of California, Santa Barbara
RHÉTORIQUEURS

ROBERT BROWNING
Dumbarton Oaks Research Center
RHETORIC: BYZANTINE

KEVIN BROWNLEE
Dartmouth College
ROBERT D'ARBRISSEL

LESLIE BRUBAKER
Wheaton College, Norton, Massachusetts
POLYPTYCH; PREPENDULIA; PROSKYNESIS; PYXIS; RAVENNA; RELIQUARY; REREDOS; SACRAMENTARY, ILLUMINATION OF

LANCE W. BRUNNER
University of Kentucky
PRECENTOR; RESPONSORY; SANCTUS

CONTRIBUTORS TO VOLUME 10

RICHARD W. BULLIET
Columbia University
Roads in the Islamic World

GLYN S. BURGESS
University of Liverpool
Romulus

JAMES F. BURKE
University of Toronto
Ruiz, Juan

DAVID BURR
Virginia Polytechnic Institute and State University
Richardus de Mediavilla

DANIEL CALLAM
St. Thomas More College, University of Saskatchewan
Purgatory, Western Concept of

AVERIL CAMERON
King's College, University of London
Procopius

ERIC G. CARLSON
State University of New York at Purchase
Romanesque Architecture

JOHN CARSWELL
University of Chicago
Sa^{c}d

JAMES E. CATHEY
University of Massachusetts, Amherst
Rán

HENRY CHADWICK
Magdalene College, Cambridge
Priscillian

GRETEL CHAPMAN
Rainer of Huy; Roger of Helmarshausen

YVES CHARTIER
University of Ottawa
Regino of Prüm; Remigius of Auxerre

JEROME W. CLINTON
Princeton University
Rhetoric: Persian; Rūmī (Jalāl al-Dīn)

FRANK M. CLOVER
University of Wisconsin, Madison
Roman Empire, Late

SIDNEY L. COHEN
Louisiana State University
Scandinavia: Before 800

CHARLES W. CONNELL
University of West Virginia
Propaganda

LAWRENCE I. CONRAD
Wellcome Institute for the History of Medicine
Quraysh

JOHN J. CONTRENI
Purdue University
Priscian

WILLIAM J. COURTENAY
University of Wisconsin, Madison
Roscelinus

EDWARD J. COWAN
University of Guelph
Robert II of Scotland

EUGENE L. COX
Wellesley College
Provence; Savoy, County of

WENDY DAVIES
University College, London
St. David's

MICHAEL T. DAVIS
Mt. Holyoke College
Resurrection Cycle

JAMES DOYNE DAWSON
Boston University
Primitive Church, Concept of

ALICIA DE COLOMBÍ-MONGUIÓ
State University of New York at Albany
Razón de Amor

PETER F. DEMBOWSKI
University of Chicago
St. Patrick's Purgatory

WALTER B. DENNY
University of Maryland
Qibla; Rugs and Carpets

LUCY DER MANUELIAN
Ptłni; Sanahin; Sargis Picak

JAMES DICKIE
Rauḍa

WILLIAM J. DIEBOLD
Prie-Dieu; Rohan Master; St. Philibert, Tournus

JERRILYNN D. DODDS
Columbia University
Santiago de Compostela

MARTHA WESTCOTT DRIVER
Pynson, Richard

LAWRENCE G. DUGGAN
University of Delaware
Representative Assemblies, German

A. A. M. DUNCAN
University of Glasgow
Robert I of Scotland; St. Andrews

MANUEL DURAN
Yale University
Santillana, Marqués de

FRANCIS A. DUTRA
University of California, Santa Barbara
Portugal

STEVEN N. DWORKIN
University of Michigan
Portuguese Language

ANDREW S. EHRENKREUTZ
University of Michigan
Postal and Intelligence Services, Islamic; Saladin

MARCIA J. EPSTEIN
University of Calgary
Quodlibet; Rondeau; Rondellus; Rota; Rotrouenge

DAVID B. EVANS
St. John's University, New York
Pseudo-Dionysius the Areopagite

ROBERT FALCK
University of Toronto
Salvatoris Hodie

CONTRIBUTORS TO VOLUME 10

ANN E. FARKAS
Brooklyn College
RUBLEV, ANDREI; RUSSIAN AND SLAVIC ART

STEPHEN C. FERRUOLO
Stanford University
RUFINUS

JOHN V. A. FINE, JR.
University of Michigan
SAMUIL OF BULGARIA; SANDALJ HRANIĆ KOSAČA; SAVA, ST.

SEYMOUR L. FLAXMAN
City University of New York
RUUSBROEC, JAN VAN

JOHN F. FLINN
University of Toronto
RENARD THE FOX

PETER G. FOOTE
University College, London
SCANDINAVIA: POLITICAL AND LEGAL ORGANIZATION

CLIVE FOSS
University of Massachusetts, Boston
ROADS AND COMMUNICATIONS, BYZANTINE

ANDRÉ FOURÉ
Archevêché de Rouen
ROUEN, USE OF

JOHN B. FREED
Illinois State University
RAINALD OF DASSEL; SAXON DYNASTY; SAXONY

EDWARD FRUEH
Columbia University
QUEROLUS; RADULFUS TORTARIUS; RATPERT OF ST. GALL; RICHER OF ST. REMI

RICHARD N. FRYE
Harvard University
SAMANIDS

JOACHIM E. GAEHDE
Brandeis University
PRE-ROMANESQUE ART

STEPHEN GARDNER
Sackler Museum, Harvard University
RAMSEY, JOHN; RAMSEY, WILLIAM; SALISBURY CATHEDRAL

NINA G. GARSOÏAN
Columbia University
ṘAMIK; QIRMIZ; SAHAK, ST.

ADELHEID M. GEALT
Indiana University
PREDELLA; ST. CECILIA MASTER; SASSETTA; ROSSELLO DI JACOPO FRANCHI

CHRISTIAN J. GELLINEK
University of Florida
ROLANDSLIED

STEPHEN GERSH
University of Notre Dame
REALISM

MOSHE GIL
Tel-Aviv University
SAMARITANS

JAMES L. GILLESPIE
Notre Dame College of Ohio, Ursuline College
RICHARD II; RICHARD III

PETER B. GOLDEN
Rutgers University
QARAKHANIDS; QARA QOYUNLU; RUM; RUSSIA, NOMADIC INVASIONS OF; SARMATIANS

OLEG GRABAR
Fogg Art Museum, Harvard University
QUBBA

JAMES A. GRAHAM-CAMPBELL
University College, London
RINGERIKE STYLE

KATHRYN GRAVDAL
Columbia University
RAOUL DE HOUDENC

JAMES GRIER
Queen's University, Ontario
ST. MARTIAL SCHOOL; SANTIAGO DE COMPOSTELA, SCHOOL OF

MARY GRIZZARD
University of New Mexico
POTTERY: REPOUSSÉ; REXACH, JUAN; RODRIGO DE OSONA

ARTHUR GROOS
Cornell University
REINFRID VON BRAUNSCHWEIG; RUDOLF VON EMS

PIERRE-MARIE GY, O.P.
Institut Supérieur de Liturgie, Paris
RITUAL

ANDRAS HAMORI
Princeton University
RHETORIC: ARABIC, HEBREW

NATHALIE HANLET
RADOLF OF LIÈGE; RANGERIUS OF LUCCA; RHETICIUS OF AUTUN, ST.; RUDOLF OF FULDA; SAMPIRUS OF ASTORGA

PRUDENCE OLIVER HARPER
Metropolitan Museum of Art
SASANIAN ART

RALPH HATTOX
Emory University
SAMARKAND

EINAR HAUGEN
RÍGSÞULA

ROBERT K. HAYCRAFT
RETABLE

EDWARD R. HAYMES
Cleveland State University
ROSENGARTEN

THOMAS HEAD
Claremont College
RELICS

LOTTE HELLINGA
The British Library
PRINTING, ORIGINS OF

ROBERT H. HEWSEN
Glassboro State College
PONTUS

BENNETT D. HILL
St. Anselm's Abbey
SACK, FRIARS OF THE; SAVIGNY

JOHN HOWE
Texas Tech University
RICHARD DE BURY

PETER HUENINK
Vassar College
PRE-ROMANESQUE ARCHITECTURE; SAXON ARCHITECTURE

ANDREW HUGHES
University of Toronto
PSALTER; RHYMED OFFICES

CONTRIBUTORS TO VOLUME 10

SHAUN F. D. HUGHES
Purdue University
RIMUR; SCANDINAVIA IN ARABIC SOURCES

MICHAEL H. IMPEY
University of Kentucky
ROMANIAN LANGUAGE AND LITERATURE

OLGA TUDORICA IMPEY
Indiana University
ROMANIAN LANGUAGE AND LITERATURE

EPHRAIM ISAAC
Institute of Semitic Studies, Princeton, New Jersey
PRESTER JOHN

ALFRED L. IVRY
Brandeis University
SAADIAH GAON

WILLIAM E. JACKSON
University of Virginia
REINMAR DER ALTE

W. T. H. JACKSON
Columbia University
RADBOD OF UTRECHT; RAGIMBOLD OF COLOGNE; REGINALD OF CANTERBURY; RIMBERT, ST.; SALOMO OF CONSTANCE

MICHAEL JACOFF
Brooklyn College
PSEUDO-NICCOLÒ

PETER JEFFERY
University of Delaware
SARUM CHANT

JENNIFER E. JONES
PRESENTATION IN THE TEMPLE; PSYCHOPOMP; RAYMOND DE MUR; ROBERT OF JUMIÈGES

WILLIAM CHESTER JORDAN
Princeton University
PRINCE; PROVOST

PETER JORGENSEN
University of Georgia
SAMSONS SAGA FAGRA

WALTER EMIL KAEGI, JR.
University of Chicago
PRONOIA; PROTOSPATHARIOS

MARIANNE E. KALINKE
University of Illinois
RÉMUNDAR SAGA
KEISARASONAR; RIDDARASÖGUR

HOWARD KAMINSKY
Florida International University
PRAGMATIC SANCTION OF BOURGES; PROVISIONS, ECCLESIASTICAL

EDWARD J. KEALEY
College of the Holy Cross
ROGER OF SALISBURY

THOMAS E. KELLY
Purdue University
RUTEBEUF

MARILYN KAY KENNEY
RHODRI MAWR

HERBERT L. KESSLER
The Johns Hopkins University
PSALTER, ILLUMINATION OF

RICHARD KIECKHEFER
Northwestern University
REFORM, IDEA OF

DALE KINNEY
Bryn Mawr College
RAINALDUS; SAN MARCO, VENICE

ALAN E. KNIGHT
Pennsylvania State University
PUY

LINDA KOMAROFF
Metropolitan Museum of Art
SAMANID ART AND ARCHITECTURE

ELLEN KOSMER
Worcester State College
PUCELLE, JEAN

MARYANNE KOWALESKI
Fordham University
POLL TAX, ENGLISH

DENNIS M. KRATZ
University of Texas at Dallas
RUODLIEB

HENRY KRATZ
University of Tennessee
PÜTERICH VON REICHERTSHAUSEN, JAKOB III

RICHARD LANDES
University of Pittsburgh
RADULPHUS GLABER

JACOB LASSNER
Wayne State University
SAMARRA

RICHARD LEMAY
City University of New York
ROMAN NUMERALS

KEITH LEWINSTEIN
Princeton University
RĀḌĪ, AL-

P. OSMUND LEWRY, O. P.
Pontifical Institute of Mediaeval Studies, Toronto
QUAESTIONES

RUDI PAUL LINDNER
University of Michigan
QAYKHOSRAW I; QILIJ ARSLĀN II

JOHN LINDOW
University of California, Berkeley
RAGNARǪK

LESTER K. LITTLE
Smith College
SALIMBENE

LARS LÖNNROTH
Göteborgs Universitet
RÓMVERJA SAGA

BRYCE LYON
Brown University
PROVISIONS OF OXFORD; RICHARD I THE LIONHEARTED

R. D. McCHESNEY
Hagop Kevorkian Center for Near Eastern Studies, New York University
QARĀ MUḤAMMAD; YUSUF

MICHAEL McCORMICK
Dumbarton Oaks/The Johns Hopkins University
PRICKINGS; PUNCTUATION; QUIRE; RUDOLF OF ST. TROND; RULING; RUPERT OF DEUTZ

MICHAEL McVAUGH
University of North Carolina
REGIMEN SANITATIS SALERNITANUM

CONTRIBUTORS TO VOLUME 10

PAUL MAGDALINO
University of St. Andrews
Postal and Intelligence Services, Byzantine

MICHAEL S. MAHONEY
Princeton University
Ptolemaic Astronomy

CLARK MAINES
Wesleyan University
Renaissances and Revivals in Medieval Art

GEORGE P. MAJESKA
University of Maryland
Prokhor of Gorodets; Rurik; Russian Architecture

J. RUSSELL MAJOR
Emory University
Representative Assemblies, French

STEPHEN MANNING
University of Kentucky
Reverdie

RICHARD C. MARKS
The Royal Pavilion, Art Gallery, and Museums, Brighton
Prudde, John

LOUISE MARLOW
Princeton University
Sasanian History

MICHAEL E. MARMURA
University of Toronto
Rāzī, al-; Rushd, Ibn (Averroës)

JOAQUÍN MARTÍNEZ-PIZARRO
State University of New York at Stony Brook
Roskilde Chronicle; Saxo Grammaticus

THOMAS F. MATHEWS
New York University
Presbyterium

RALPH WHITNEY MATHISEN
University of South Carolina
Polemius Silvius; Prosper of Aquitaine; Salvian of Marseilles

CHRISTOPHER MELCHERT
University of Pennsylvania
Saffāḥ, Abū 'l-ᶜAbbās al-

DANIEL FREDERICK MELIA
Study Center of the University of California, London
St. Mary's Abbey, Dublin

GUY MERMIER
University of Michigan
Quinze Joies de Mariage, Les

BRIAN MERRILEES
University of Toronto
Robert of Greatham; Roman de Toute Chevalerie; Romance of Horn; Scalacronica; Sanson de Nanteuil

JOHN MEYENDORFF
Fordham University
Russian Orthodox Church

ROBERT P. MULTHAUF
Smithsonian Institution
Salt Trade

MARINA MUNDT
Universitetet i Bergen
Ragnars Saga Loðbrókar

JAMES J. MURPHY
University of California, Davis
Rhetoric: Western European

FAUZI M. NAJJAR
Michigan State University
Political Theory, Islamic; Ramadan

JOHN T. NOONAN, JR.
University of California, Berkeley
Rolandus

BARBARA OEHLSCHLAEGER-GARVEY
University of Illinois
Prependulia; Proskynetarion

RICHARD O'GORMAN
University of Iowa
Robert de Boron; Robert le Diable

THOMAS H. OHLGREN
Purdue University
St. Chad, Book of

NICOLAS OIKONOMIDES
Université de Montréal
Porphyrogenitos; Procheiros Nomos; Pseudo-Kodinos

BERNARD O'KANE
American University in Cairo
Sahn

PÁDRAIG P. Ó NÉILL
University of North Carolina
Saltair na Rann

ERIC L. ORMSBY
McGill University
Purgatory, Islamic Concept of

LEAH OTIS
Prostitution

ROBERT OUSTERHOUT
University of Illinois
Polycandelon; Prothesis

WALTER PAKTER
University of California, Berkeley
Rogerius

PETER PARTNER
Winchester College
Rome

OLAF PEDERSEN
University of Aarhus
Quadrant

MOSHE PERLMAN
University of California, Los Angeles
Polemics, Islamic-Jewish

EDWARD PETERS
University of Pennsylvania
Prisons

CARL F. PETRY
Northwestern University
Qāᵓitbāy, al-Ashraf; Qalāᵓūn, al-Manṣūr; Qānṣūh al-Ghawrī

PETER POGGIOLI
University of Melbourne
Rouen

VENETIA PORTER
The British Council
Samarkand Ware

JAMES M. POWELL
Syracuse University
Robert Guiscard; Roger I of Sicily; Roger II of Sicily

CONTRIBUTORS TO VOLUME 10

MICHAEL R. POWICKE
University of Toronto
PREROGATIVE

THOMAS RENNA
Saginaw Valley State College
QUAESTIO IN UTRAMQUE PARTEM

ROGER E. REYNOLDS
Pontifical Institute of Mediaeval Studies, Toronto
PONTIFICAL; ROSARY; SACRAMENTARY; ST. PETER, LITURGY OF

THEODORE JOHN RIVERS
SACHSENSPIEGEL

PHYLLIS B. ROBERTS
PREACHING AND SERMON LITERATURE, WESTERN EUROPEAN

TIMOTHY R. ROBERTS
RATRAMNUS OF CORBIE

IAN S. ROBINSON
Trinity College, Dublin
POLITICAL THEORY, WESTERN EUROPEAN: TO 1100

ELAINE GOLDEN ROBISON
PRUDENTIUS; PTOLEMY OF LUCCA; RAHEWIN; RAIMON DE CORNET; RAIMON DE MIRAVAL; ROBERT OF MELUN; ROFFREDUS DE EPIPHANIIS OF BENEVENTO

EDWARD H. ROESNER
ST. VICTOR MS

LINDA C. ROSE
PRAETORIAN PREFECT; RHODES; ROMANOS I LEKAPENOS; ROMANOS II; ROMANOS IV DIOGENES

TEOFILO F. RUIZ
Brooklyn College
RECONQUEST, THE

JAMES R. RUSSELL
Columbia University
ŠĀBUHR I; ŠĀBUHR II; ŠĀHANŠĀH; SASANIAN CULTURE

IRINA RYBACEK
PRAGUE

PAULA SANDERS
Harvard University
QĀHIR BI'LLĀH, AL-; QAᵓIM, AL-; SANA

V. J. SCATTERGOOD
Trinity College, Dublin
PROPHECY, POLITICAL: MIDDLE ENGLISH

NICOLAS SCHIDLOVSKY
PSALTIKON

JANICE L. SCHULTZ
Canisius College
RICHARD OF ST. VICTOR

SIMON SCHWARZFUCHS
Bar-Ilan University
RABBINATE

EDWARD A. SEGAL
Yale University
ST. GALL, MONASTERY AND PLAN OF

DANUTA SHANZER
University of California, Berkeley
RUTILIUS CLAUDIUS NAMATIANUS

ALEXANDER M. SHAPIRO
Oheb Shalom Congregation
RESPONSUM LITERATURE, JEWISH

LON R. SHELBY
Southern Illinois University
RIED, BENEDIKT; RORICZER, CONRAD; RORICZER, MATHES

CARL D. SHEPPARD
University of Minnesota
ROMANESQUE ART

JOHN R. SHINNERS, JR.
St. Mary's College, Notre Dame, Indiana
RELIGIOUS INSTRUCTION

IAN SHORT
Birkbeck College
PSEUDO-TURPIN

CHARLES R. SHRADER
RATHER OF VERONA

MICHAEL A. SIGNER
Hebrew Union College
PREACHING AND SERMONS, JEWISH

GIULIO SILANO
Pontifical Institute of Mediaeval Studies, Toronto
RAYMOND OF PEÑAFORT, ST.; RESCRIPTS

LARRY SILVER
Northwestern University
RIEMENSCHNEIDER, TILMAN; ST. BARTHOLOMEW, MASTER OF; ST. VERONICA, MASTER OF

ECKEHARD SIMON
Harvard University
RABER, VIGIL; ROSENPLÜT, HANS

BARRIE SINGLETON
University of London
POPPEHOWE, THOMAS; PRENTYS, THOMAS; ROLF, THOMAS

KENNETH SNIPES
Manhattan College
PSELLOS, MICHAEL

ROBERT J. SNOW
University of Texas
SANTIAGO DE COMPOSTELA

HAYM SOLOVEITCHIK
Hebrew University, Jerusalem
RASHI (RABBI SOLOMON BEN ISAAC)

PRISCILLA P. SOUCEK
New York University
RAQQAH

ERNST H. SOUDEK
PROSE LANCELOT

GABRIELLE M. SPIEGEL
University of Maryland
RIGORD

YEDIDA K. STILLMAN
State University of New York at Binghamton
QALANSUWA

MELVIN STORM
Emporia State University, Kansas
RIDDLES

JOSEPH R. STRAYER
Princeton University
PROVINCE, ECCLESIASTICAL

CONTRIBUTORS TO VOLUME 10

RONALD GRIGOR SUNY
University of Michigan
QMA

SANDRA CANDEE SUSMAN
RAVERTI, MATTEO

DONALD W. SUTHERLAND
University of Iowa
SAC AND SOC

MERLIN SWARTZ
Boston University
PREACHING AND SERMONS, ISLAMIC

JAMES ROSS SWEENEY
Pennsylvania State University
ROMANIAN PRINCIPALITIES

FRANK TALMAGE
University of Toronto
POLEMICS, CHRISTIAN-JEWISH

JOHN TAYLOR
University of Leeds
ROBIN HOOD

ROBERT TAYLOR
Victoria College, University of Toronto
RAIMBAUT D'AURENGA; RAIMBAUT DE VAQUEIRAS; RAIMON VIDAL DE BESALÚ

WILLIAM H. TeBRAKE
University of Maine
RECLAMATION OF LAND

CLAIBORNE W. THOMPSON
RUNES

KARL UITTI
Princeton University
PROVENÇAL LITERATURE

JOHN VAN ENGEN
University of Notre Dame
PRESENTATION, RIGHT OF

MILOŠ VELIMIROVIĆ
University of Virginia
ROMANOS MELODOS

ELISABETH VODOLA
PRAEMUNIRE; POSTGLOSSATORS

F. W. VON KRIES
University of Massachusetts, Amherst
REINMAR VON ZWETER

CHRYSOGONUS WADDELL
Abbey of Gethsemani
PREMONSTRATENSIAN RITE; PREMONSTRATENSIANS

STEPHEN L. WAILES
Indiana University
RAPULARIUS

JEANETTE A. WAKIN
Radcliffe College
QADI

SETH WARD
University of Haifa
POLL TAX, ISLAMIC

MORIMICHI WATANABE
Long Island University
POLITICAL THEORY, WESTERN EUROPEAN: AFTER 1100

RUTH HOUSE WEBBER
University of Chicago
RONCESVALLES

ELLEN T. WEHNER
Centre for Medieval Studies, University of Toronto
POLISTORIE; QUATRE LIVRE DES REIS, LI

BERNARD G. WEISS
University of Toronto
RESURRECTION, ISLAMIC

ESTELLE WHELAN
QAṢR; SABĪL

KEITH WHINNOM
University of Exeter
SAN PEDRO, DIEGO DE

GREGORY WHITTINGTON
New York University
PORTCULLIS; QUATREFOIL; REFECTORY; SACRISTY

JOHN WILLIAMS
University of Pittsburgh
SANCTIUS; SARRACINUS

KENNERLY M. WOODY
ROMUALD OF RAVENNA, ST.

RONALD JOHN ZAWILLA, O. P.
RESERVATION OF THE SACRAMENT

RONALD EDWARD ZUPKO
Marquette University
POUND, MONEY; POUND, WEIGHT; QUARTER; REEVE; SACK

Dictionary of the Middle Ages

Dictionary of the Middle Ages

POLEMICS, CHRISTIAN-JEWISH—SCANDINAVIA

POLEMICS, CHRISTIAN-JEWISH. The Jewish-Christian debate in the Middle Ages may be characterized as a continual reiteration of stock themes, varying in accordance with prevailing concerns determined by particular historical conditions. Its objectives were several. On the Christian side, the proselytization of the Jews was ostensibly the chief motive, although Jews frequently appear as straw men in doctrinal or apologetic tracts against heterodox Christian sects or other groups. For historical reasons, Jews generally avoided attempts at proselytization. Yet they often entered debate because they were obliged to or because they wished to demonstrate the superiority of their religion to others, or, more frequently, to apostates or would-be apostates in order to bring them back to the fold. A major question to be considered in analyzing any disputation or polemical treatise is whether it is academic or intended for practical use or both. One indication of the often academic character of these works is the fact that they were most generally written in literary languages (Latin for Christians and Hebrew for Jews). Vernacular treatises were rare—although they did appear with increasing frequency in the thirteenth century—but even these were subsequently translated and circulated in the literary language, which limited them to internal use only.

The chief arguments were based on Scripture, appeals to reason and logic, and social critique. Questions raised included those of whether the Messiah had come in the person of Jesus or whether the messianic age could be said to have commenced at all; the abrogation of the Old (pentateuchal) Law and its subsequent rabbinic development (halakah) and its replacement by the spiritual law of the Gospel; the identity of the true Israel (*verus Israel*)—whether the election of the Old Israel (the Jews) had been superseded by that of the New (the church). One of the chief proofs advanced by Christians that the Jews were no longer the elect of God was their loss of political sovereignty, while Jews maintained that such loss of sovereignty was not complete since Jewish rulers and nobles were still to be found (for instance the Khazar kings from the eighth to the tenth centuries, Jewish nobles in Spain, and the geonim in the Near East). Another criterion for the determination of the true Israel was that of moral superiority, claimed by both sides. It was in this context that the issue of Jews engaging in usury was frequently raised. Beyond these issues, open to discussion were particular elements of theology and practice; for Christians, the Incarnation, the Virgin Birth, the sacraments and most especially the Eucharist, the Trinity, clerical celibacy, and the adoration of saints; for Jews, the rabbinic interpretations of Scripture and the development of Jewish law.

Both sides used the Old Testament to argue their case. Classic texts were: Genesis 49:10, the "Shiloh" passage, an obscure verse interpreted in a variety of ways over the centuries but understood by the church to refer to loss of dominion by the Jews with Jesus' advent; Isaiah 7:14, which, following the Vulgate, was said to predict the Virgin Birth of Jesus; Isaiah 52 and following, the "suffering servant" passages, which the church understood christologically but which the Jews interpreted as a reference to Israel, the Jewish Messiah, or the prophet himself; and many passages from the Psalter. While Christians could rarely use the New Testament on their behalf since it was not recognized as authoritative by Jews, the latter felt free on occasion to attack it on various grounds. Similarly, Christians would condemn rabbinic literature (Talmud and Midrash) for its alleged blasphemies and promotion of incredulity. At the same time, however, Christians would employ selected passages of

POLEMICS, CHRISTIAN-JEWISH

that literature to prove that the rabbis of antiquity actually believed in the basic principles of Christianity and that therefore contemporary Jews should do so as well. This approach was predicated on the notion of Jewish obstinacy, according to which the Jews knew the truth all along but refused to admit it. In the classic formulation of Joachim of Fiore in the thirteenth century, "The Jews have not wished to be able to change." Finally, arguments drawn from the currents of philosophical thought in vogue in their day were a major instrument in demonstrating the basic irrationality of an opponent's doctrines and the rationality of one's own.

The Jewish-Christian debate was conducted in a variety of literary and artistic genres: the dialogue—following classical and patristic models—between a Jew and a Christian, of which a characteristic feature was the disproportionate amount of space granted the representative of the author's own religion and the much more restricted allotment of the opponent; the formal theological treatise (which at times could also be couched in the form of a dialogue); drama (miracle plays and the like, such as the twelfth-century *Jeu d'Adam*); liturgical and other poetry; arguments included within biblical commentaries and within more general philosophical and theological treatises; the graphic and plastic arts (sculptures of the Church Triumphant, upright with cross and chalice, and Synagogue, blindfolded and downcast with broken staff and tables of the law falling from her left hand; caricatures of Christian themes in Hebrew manuscript illuminations). A variety of rhetorical devices including satire and parody were frequently employed.

EARLY MEDIEVAL POLEMICS

The format of medieval Christian anti-Jewish polemic was inherited from the church fathers. The first writings were *testimonia,* chains of biblical passages in support of Christianity, which gave way to highly sophisticated treatises such as the second-century *Dialogue with Trypho* by Justin Martyr and the somewhat later (*ca.* 400) *Discussion Concerning the Law Between Simon a Jew and Theophilus a Christian.* Central for the writings of the late Middle Ages was the *On the Catholic Faith from the Old and New Testaments Against the Jews* of the sixth-century encyclopedist and bishop of Seville, Isidore. Reacting to the harsh treatment of the Jews by Sisebut, the Visigothic king of Spain, Isidore noted that Sisebut had "compelled by force those whom he ought to have incited by the arguments of the true faith." Although this is a somewhat bookish treatise, Isidore demonstrates his knowledge of actual Jewish argumentation, particularly apologetics about the loss of Jewish sovereignty. Less academic and more vituperative are the letters of the ninth-century Agobard of Lyons, who denounced Jewish beliefs, labeled them superstitions, and—following decisions of church councils, particularly various councils at Toledo, in 633, in 638, and in the 680's—stressed the necessity of avoiding the society of Jews because of their rejection of Christianity. In this period, ecclesiastics at the court of Louis the Pious of France were scandalized by the conversion of a Frankish noble and deacon, Bodo-Eleazar, to Judaism, which was partly facilitated by the liberal atmosphere of the court itself, the scene of much free discussion. Bodo fled to Saragossa and there defended his new faith in a correspondence with Pablo Álvaro of Córdoba, himself of Jewish origin. This conversion was an important factor in prompting Agobard's successor to the see of Lyons, Amulo, to denounce the "abominable craftiness" of the Jews in even stronger terms. Shifting location from France to Italy, one immediately feels a shift in mood. Much milder is the eleventh-century treatise of Peter Damian, active at the papal court, who tried to convince practitioners of Judaism of the mystical meaning of the Old Testament commandments.

In surveying early medieval Jewish polemics, it must be recalled that outside the Hellenistic world, Jewish thought was articulated not in discursive fashion, but, in characteristic Oriental style, in the form of parable and exemplum. Talmudic and midrashic anti-Christian polemic is often ironic and tends to parody. With the rise of the antitalmudic Karaite movement in ninth-century Iraq, Islamic modes of discursive thought and philosophy were adopted. The early Karaite thinker Dāwūd ibn Marwān al-Muqammiṣ (late ninth century) devoted part of his *Twenty Treatises* to a refutation of Christianity. He was followed by Jacob al-Kirkisānī (second quarter of the tenth century), who maintained in his *Book of Lights and Watchtowers* that Christianity had little to do with Jesus but was an invention of Paul and, in its final form, the creation of the Council of Nicaea (325), which disregarded the teachings of both Peter and Paul. Other leading Karaite authors, such as Daniel al-Qūmisī, Salmon ben Jeroham, Japheth ben Eli, and Judah Hadassi, routinely included anti-Christian

 POLEMICS, CHRISTIAN-JEWISH

polemical sections in their biblical commentaries and writings. Rabbinite or normative Judaism quickly followed suit, and in his theological magnum opus, the *Book of Beliefs and Opinions,* Saadiah ben Joseph Gaon (882–942) set forth in the fashion of the prevailing *kalām* a refutation of all disbelievers, including Christians. Saadiah maintained that he was not interested in engaging crass anthropomorphists among the Christians but only more sophisticated Trinitarians. It is noteworthy that he himself espoused a philosophical theory of the threefold nature of God's essence, denying, of course, that there was any Trinitarianism involved.

The pre-Crusade period seems to have been rich in public and private oral disputations. In 581, the Merovingian king Chilperic convened a disputation between the Jewish merchant Priscus and Bishop Gregory of Tours. Recorded in the latter's *Histories,* the debate employed scriptural stock arguments. In the seventh century, Alcuin reported a debate he witnessed in Pavia between the Jew Lullus (Julius?) and Peter of Pisa. Less routine was the ninth-century discussion, noted in the eleventh-century southern Italian *Chronicle of Ahimaaz,* between the Byzantine emperor Basil I and Shephatiah ben Amittai of Oria on the subject of which was the more beautiful structure—Solomon's Temple or the Church of Hagia Sophia in Constantinople.

ELEVENTH TO THIRTEENTH CENTURIES

The eleventh and twelfth centuries marked an increasing sophistication in interreligious polemics on the part of both Jews and Christians. In his sermons, Fulbert of Chartres (*ca.* 970–1028) emphasized a positive exposition of Christianity rather than attacking Judaism, although he too stressed the Jewish loss of temporal power. Of great influence was the *Dialogue* of Peter Alfonsi (1062–*ca.* 1140), a converted Spanish Jew formerly known as Moses the Spaniard, between his former and new selves, Peter and Moses. One of the first Christian authors to employ rabbinic literature in the refutation of Judaism, Peter used his knowledge of Hebrew to prove that the Trinity had been revealed in the ineffable name of God, the tetragrammaton YHWH. The use of rabbinic literature would now become ever more widespread and is found, albeit from secondary sources, in the writings of Alan of Lille, Peter Comestor, and others. Unusual for its urbane tone was the *Disputation* of Gilbert Crispin (*ca.* 1046–1117), abbot of Westminster, allegedly a discussion between Gilbert and a Jew from Mainz who came to conduct business, a frequent pretext for such encounters. Both announce their intention to have a "tolerant" and "patient" discussion. Much more academic in tone are the *Dialogue of a Philosopher with a Christian and a Jew* by Peter Abelard (*ca.* 1079–*ca.* 1142), and the treatise of William of Champeaux (*ca.* 1070–1122), which stresses ethical values. Rupert of Deutz (*ca.* 1075–1129) devoted a considerable portion of his *Anulus* to an elaboration of two commandments repeatedly discussed in contemporary Jewish literature, the Sabbath and circumcision, taken to be the minimal defining elements of Judaism, as well as an exposition refuting the contention that Christian Trinitarianism was a form of polytheistic idolatry. Stressing the Christian experience over theology, Rupert seems to be addressing a far more concrete situation than some of his more academic contemporaries. His approach may well stem from his close physical proximity to the convert Herman of Scheda, who in his discussions with Christian theologians in Mainz came to profess Christianity from experiential and not theological motivations. Other twelfth-century treatises made greater use of rational argumentation, which seems to have led to increased vituperation. Representative are Peter the Venerable's *Treatise Against the Chronic Obstinacy of the Jews* (before 1143) and Peter of Blois's *Against Jewish Disbelief* (*ca.* 1200). In the former, the author reasons that since man is a rational animal, and since Jews do not listen to reason, Jews are little more than beasts.

The *Kuzari* of Judah Halevi (*ca.* 1075–1141), a major defense of what the author terms "a despised religion," was couched in the form of a fictitious dialogue between a Jewish sage and the king of the Khazar empire who converts to Judaism. While not primarily an anti-Christian work, Christianity is dealt with both implicitly and explicitly. More pivotal are the Hispano-Provençal works, the first Hebrew polemics written in Europe, the *Wars of the Lord* (1170) of Jacob ben Reuben and the *Book of the Covenant* of Joseph Ḳimḥi (*ca.* 1105–*ca.* 1170). Jacob ben Reuben refutes Christianity in twelve chapters with philosophical proofs, scriptural exegesis, and a critique of the Gospels and the Book of Acts, passages from which he translated into Hebrew. Kimḥi's work is less structured and more resembles a natural dialogue. Stress is laid on the still unredeemed character of the world—a constant theme in Jewish writings—and a social cri-

POLEMICS, CHRISTIAN-JEWISH

tique of Christianity. Attributing both good works and faith to the Jews (note the interpenetration of Christian fideism), Kimḥi enumerated Jewish observance of the Ten Commandments:

> "I am the Lord." The Jews declare God's unity. "You shall have no other Gods." The Jews do not make idols. "You shall not take the name of the Lord in vain." There is no nation in the world that avoids vain oaths as does Israel. "You shall not murder. . . ." There are no murderers or adulterers among them. Oppression and theft are not as widespread among Jews as among Christians who rob people on the highways and hang them and gouge out their eyes. Jewish girls, with modesty, are not to be seen about nor found wanton like the daughters of the Gentiles, who go out everywhere to streetcorners.

Kimḥi's contemporary, Gilbert Crispin, responds to such charges, as does the Christian of the *Book of the Covenant,* with an extolling of Christian asceticism: "There are many among us who abstain not only from eating pork but from meat altogether. . . . There are many men of war and wrath who have abandoned fighting and temporal riches and have turned to serving God in poverty."

The transition to the thirteenth century saw an intensity of polemical activity in the northern Franco-German region. The debates that took place are reflected in the *Book of Joseph the Zealot,* which represents the argumentation of a family of polemicists named Official. The work is a manual arranged according to passages from the Old and New Testaments for ready reference. Striking is the openness of the Christian clergy as it appears here and the unrestrained frankness of the Jews. Some of this material is of a technical nature and would be useful only for internal consumption or for use against apostates. Of a similar character was the anonymous *Book of Contention,* which, in addition to the scriptural section, includes a critique of Christian doctrine and cult. Much of Franco-German Jewish culture had Italian roots and here too the apparent influence of Moses of Salerno's *Arguments* on the *Contention* can be seen. Of Italian provenance too was the *Testimony of the Lord Is Faithful* of Solomon ben Moses de Rossi, who prefaces his work with a discourse on the proper mode of debate and a warning not to overantagonize Christian interlocutors.

The Franco-German treatises cited above deal with the frequently raised question of usury. Interest taking was a fact of life for some medieval Jews, and Christians advanced the argument that Jews were not allowed by their own law to do so. The *Contention* goes on the offensive and challenges priests who collect prebends. Two Narbonnese Jewish writers attack this question also. David Kimḥi, the son of the author of the *Covenant,* maintains in his biblical commentaries that Jews will lend without interest to their Christian "brothers" when Christians start treating them as brothers. The subject is dealt with at length in Meir ben Simeon's *War in Fulfillment of a Commandment,* which records a debate with the bishop of Narbonne. This still unpublished manuscript contains a wealth of material relevant to Provence of that period.

DISPUTATIONS AT PARIS AND BARCELONA

Thirteenth-century France was the scene of the first of the three great medieval disputations, that of Paris at the court of Louis IX in 1240, between Nicholas Donin, a converted Jew, and Jehiel ben Joseph, Moses ben Jacob of Coucy, and others. It was not truly a disputation but a trial in which the Talmud was accused, on the basis of argumentation taken from Karaite anti talmudic propaganda, of blaspheming the Christian faith, scoffing at Jesus, and encouraging contempt for Christians. The Jews argued that the Jesus mentioned in the Talmud could not have been the Jesus of the Gospels, and that the gentiles discussed in the Talmud are not Christians but pagan idolators. Despite this defense, the Talmud was condemned and burned in Paris two years later. Meanwhile, in Spain, the growing strength of the Dominicans set the stage for the Disputation of Barcelona in 1263. Under the direction of Raymond of Peñafort, a school had been established for the teaching of Hebrew, Arabic, and Aramaic for missionary purposes. In this context, in the presence of James I of Aragon, a converted Jew named Pablo Christiani (Pau Christià) was called upon to debate Moses ben Nahman (Naḥmanides), the leader of Aragonese Jewry, and to argue on the basis of rabbinic literature the issues of whether (1) the Messiah had come, (2) the Messiah is God or man, and (3) the Jews or the Christians are in possession of the true faith. The outcome was a foregone conclusion, however, since it was declared that "the truth of Christianity because of its certainty cannot be subject to dispute." Naḥmanides provided ad hoc refutations of Pablo's christological interpretations of Jewish writings. Yet in the course of the debate he made a much more far-reaching declaration: the nonlegal pronouncements of rabbinic lore were not of binding character but were to be treated as sermons to be accepted or not as one chose. Whether or not Naḥmanides fully believed this, this stance would prove an effective polemical ploy in the centuries to come. Rather than debate whether Jesus was the Messiah or not, Naḥmanides preferred to play down the issue of the Messiah altogether, claiming that the king of Aragon was indeed more important to him than the Messiah, since it is more meritorious to observe the commandments under the yoke of a gentile monarch than under a Jewish messianic ruler. Besides Naḥmanides' own replies, this debate prompted Pablo's cousin, Jacob ben Elijah of Valencia, to reply to Pablo in a series of letters, thus showing the increased use of the epistolary medium.

Present at the Disputation of Barcelona was Ramón Martí (Raimond Martini), a Dominican scholar and disciple of Raymond of Peñafort, who later wrote the *Dagger of the Faith* (1278), a compendious work in Latin, Hebrew, and Aramaic, which expanded on the Dominican techniques in proving Christianity from Jewish sources and became paradigmatic for works of this kind. Milder in tone were the anti-Jewish writings of the Mallorcan mystic, Ramon Lull, whose polemics may be found in such major works as the *Blanquerna* and the *Book of the Gentile and the Three Wise Men* as well as in the specialized tracts the *Scourge of the Jews* and the *Book of Preaching Against the Jews.*

FOURTEENTH AND FIFTEENTH CENTURIES

In the fourteenth century, the writings of the Franciscan biblical exegete Nicholas of Lyra (*ca.* 1270–*ca.* 1349) were influential. Nicholas, whose knowledge of Hebrew and Jewish literature was impressive (although later criticized by Pablo de Santa María), composed two anti-Jewish treatises. One is a more or less conventional treatment of the Incarnation, while the other refutes Jewish critiques of the Gospel of Matthew such as those found in Jacob ben Reuben's *Wars of the Lord.* More curious is the *Epistle* of Rabbi Samuel the Moroccan, a translation or more likely a fabrication by Alphonsus Bonihominis of a letter by an eleventh-century convert to Christianity, which stresses that the length of the Jews' exile is proof that they are being punished for their sins. Among Spanish polemics, Bernard (Bernat) Oliver's *Against Jewish Blindness* is a learned but dry scholastic treatise. By far the most interesting fourteenth-century advocate of Christianity was the former Jew Abner of Burgos (Alfonso of Valladolid, *ca.* 1270–1340), who underwent a profound conversion experience. He remained dedicated to demonstrating the truth of Christianity to his former coreligionists and wrote several works in Hebrew; the most important among them is *Teacher of Righteousness,* which survives in a Spanish translation. Abner used much the same line of argument as his predecessors, but, because of his comprehensiveness, his writing in Hebrew, and increased sensitivity on the part of his Jewish opponents, he provoked a plethora of responses. Directly or indirectly he was answered in the compendious *Touchstone* of Shem Tov ben Isaac Shaprut (which was based on the *Wars* of Jacob ben Reuben and which records a debate between the author and Peter Luna, later Benedict XIII, in Pamplona); the *Support of the Faith* of Moses ha-Cohen of Tordesillas; and, in the next century, the *Shield and Spear* of Ḥayyim ibn Musa, directed primarily against Nicholas of Lyra, and Isaac Pulgar (Pollegar) in the *Support of Religion.*

In the late fourteenth century, after the wave of forced conversions instigated in Spain by the anti-Jewish preaching of the Dominican friar Vincent Ferrer, a Jew who had been forcibly baptized but continued to profess Judaism, Profiat Duran of Perpignan (*ca.* 1345–*ca.* 1414) produced two significant anti-Christian writings. In his short letter "Be Not Like Thy Fathers," he satirically encouraged an acquaintance who had embraced Christianity not to follow a rational and coherent Judaism but to espouse an irrational and illogical Christianity. Less witty but more systematic was his *Reproach of the Gentiles,* a treatise attacking the dogmas of Christianity, the sacraments, and, like Jacob al-Kirkisānī, the very underpinnings of the faith, maintaining that Jesus was a misguided cabalist and that the Christian faith was the fabrication of later theologians. He presented the most detailed textual critical analysis of the New Testament to date and showed familiarity with and exploited dissident views within the church similar to those expressed by Wyclif and Marsilius Ficino (who was himself involved in refutations of Judaism). The *Reproach* had been commissioned by Duran's associate, Ḥasdai Crescas (*ca.* 1340–1412), the leader of Aragonese Jewry and a distinguished thinker, who then prepared his own adaptation in Catalan, which now survives in Hebrew translation under the title *Refutation of the Principles of the Christians.* The *Reproach* left its very visible mark also on the treatise known as the *Bow*

POLEMICS, CHRISTIAN-JEWISH

and Shield of Duran's kinsman, Simeon ben Ẓemah Duran of Algiers.

At the time of the forced conversions of 1391, a cultured Jew by the name of Solomon Halevi was baptized under the name of Pablo de Santa María. As the protégé of Peter of Luna (Benedict XIII), he received a doctorate from the Sorbonne and then succeeded to the see of Burgos. Among his writings is the *Scrutiny of the Scriptures,* a lengthy refutation of Judaism on the model of the *Dagger of the Faith.* Following his conversion, an interchange took place between him and his former associate Joshua Lorki. Lorki addressed an epistle to him in Hebrew, maintaining that, on the basis of the Hebrew Scriptures, the Messiah could not be said to have come, and prodded Pablo to tell him why he had converted to Christianity. He observed that the motivations for conversion are a desire for pleasures of the flesh and wealth, despair over Israel's exile, and acceptance of the Christian claim that the election of the old Israel had been abrogated, or a true religious experience. Paul replied, ironically apologizing for his rusty Hebrew, but unfortunately the apology for his conversion has not survived. Lorki apparently was trying less to rebuke Paul than to find his own bearings, for he shortly thereafter embraced Christianity himself under the name of Gerónimo de Santa Fé. As Gerónimo, he was the leading Christian contender at the last of the great medieval disputations, held at Tortosa in 1413–1414. The disputation was initiated by the soon-to-be-deposed Benedict XIII, who wanted to win support for his right to the papacy by converting Spanish Jews to Christianity. Representatives of all the leading Aragonese Jewish communities were present, but because of the absence of truly gifted debaters (Ḥasdai Crescas was now deceased and Profiat Duran, because of his forced baptism, could not openly defend Judaism) and because of the inability of the Jewish delegation to present a united front, the disputation was little less than a disaster for the Jews. A number of the Jewish participants themselves apostatized and this in turn had a demoralizing effect upon the rank and file of Aragonese Jewry. The disputation ultimately produced several literary polemics.

The last distinguished philosopher of Iberian Jewry, Joseph Albo (*d. ca* 1444), who was present at the debate, included a refutation of Christianity in his *Book of Roots.* Another figure present at the debate and active behind the scenes, the aged poet Solomon ben Reuben Bonafed, addressed a rhymed prose epistle to Francesc de Sant Jordi, the former Jew Astruc Rimoch, chiding him for his conversion in terms strongly reminiscent of the satirical epistle of Profiat Duran. Despite the irony, the letter sharply reflects the demoralization of the author in the face of recent events. On the Christian side, Gerónimo de Santa Fé set forth his views in a two-part treatise, the *Refutation of Jewish Disbelief,* eventually translated into Hebrew, Catalan, and Portuguese. In the first part, he essentially summarizes Martí's *Dagger of the Faith,* using rabbinic literature to prove the truth of Christianity, while in the second part he vehemently denounces rabbinic literature for its blasphemies and vilification of the Christian faith. This treatise was answered later in the century by the son of Simeon ben Ẓemaḥ Duran, Solomon, in his *Holy War,* and by the author-statesman and Spanish exile Isaac Abrabanel.

Once again, the contrast in tone between Spain and the more liberal Italy may be seen in the friendlier disputation, reflecting the urbane atmosphere of the Renaissance, recorded in the *Disputation* of Elijah Ḥayyim ben Benjamin of Genazano between the author and the Franciscan monk Francis of Aquapendente, under papal auspices in Orvieto (second half of the fifteenth century). In central Europe, noteworthy is the debate of the baptized Jew Peter Niger (Schwartz) in 1474 at Regensburg and, at the end of the preceding century, that of an apostate, Pesaḥ-Peter, at Prague; he denounced the Jews as calumniators of Christianity and had many imprisoned. Among them was the Prague jurist and theologian Yom Tov Lipmann Muelhausen, who recorded this incident in his *Book of Contention.* A general defense of Bohemian Jewish orthodoxy, which incorporated both mystical and rationalistic traditions, the *Contention* criticizes Christianity much along the lines of the old German *Contention* but in a spirit reflecting the atmosphere of the times and with an awareness of the new developments in Bohemian Christian thought as advanced by the Hussites.

Prominent among fifteenth-century Christian treatises was the *Fortress of the Faith* of Alfonso de Espina, one of the chief agitators for the establishment of the Spanish national Inquisition. Using the techniques of Ramon Martí and Gerónimo, the work propounds a plan for the evangelizing of the Jews and a program for their eschatological conversion. Written in 1459, it foreshadows the Spanish expulsion as the author rehearses the various expulsions of the Jews from Christian countries. It

POLEMICS, ISLAMIC-JEWISH

was particularly vitriolic in its repetition of the charges of ritual murder and host desecration, frequent in earlier anti-Semitic writings. In contrast to Espina's *Fortress* are the more humanistic apologetics of such thinkers as Nicholas of Cusa (1401–1464) and Francisco Suárez (1548–1617), which reflect Renaissance attitudes. In Cusa's *On the Peace of the Faith,* he explored the common ground of all creeds. Although he saw Jewish refusal to accept the messiahship of Jesus as an obstacle to the unity of mankind, he wishfully had the Jewish participant in his discussion take a compromise position on this issue.

The history of Jewish-Christian disputation in the Middle Ages no doubt represents one of the more negative aspects of crosscultural contact. Yet it must not be forgotten that it often produced—directly or indirectly—much fruitful stimulation and interpenetration of ideas, on both sides, in biblical exegesis, theology, and virtually every area of cultural endeavor.

BIBLIOGRAPHY

Salo W. Baron, *Social and Religious History of the Jews,* V (1957), 82–137, 326–352, IX (1965), 97–134, 287–307; Bernhard Blumenkranz, *Les auteurs chrétiens latins du moyen âge sur les juifs et le judaïsme* (1963); Daniel J. Lasker, *Jewish Philosophical Polemics Against Christianity in the Middle Ages* (1977); Arthur Lukyn Williams, *Adversus Judaeos: A Bird's-eye View of Christian Apologiae Until the Renaissance* (1935). Bibliographies are in "Index polemicus," in *Patrologia latina,* CCXIX (1879), 439–444; Judah Rosenthal, "Anti-Christian Polemical Literature Until the End of the Eighteenth Century: A Bibliography" (in Hebrew), in *Areshet,* 2 (1960); Frank Talmage, "Judaism on Christianity—Christianity on Judaism," in *The Study of Judaism: Bibliographical Essays* (1972).

FRANK TALMAGE

[See also **Abelard, Peter; Abrabanel, Issac ben Judah; Agobard; Anti-Semitism; Crescas, Ḥasdai; Fulbert of Chartres; Gregory of Tours, St.; Isidore of Seville, St.; Jeu d'Adam; Jews and the Catholic Church; Jews in Christian Spain; Jews in Europe; Jews in the Papal States; Judah Halevi; Lull, Ramon; Naḥmanides, Moses; Nicholas of Cusa; Nicholas of Lyra; Peter of Blois; Peter of Pisa; Peter the Venerable; Raymond of Peñafort; Rupert of Deutz; Saadiah Gaon; Sisebut; William of Champeaux.**]

POLEMICS, ISLAMIC-JEWISH. The rise of Islam, the claims of Muḥammad that he was the Prophet restoring the primeval faith of Abraham and that the Koran supersedes earlier scriptures, inevitably displaced in the eyes of Muslims both Judaism and Christianity and reduced their followers to the status of misguided infidels. Furthermore, as the Prophet was disappointed at being repudiated by the Jews of Medina, and as the Jewish tribes that were settled there joined the opposition to his growing power, suffering defeat, expropriation, and extermination, the Koran resounds with the echoes of this conflict. Islam thus inherited from its early days a certain anti-Jewish animus, which was rekindled from time to time, and was kept alive in literature, especially in polemics.

With the emergence of the Islamic empire, great masses embraced Islam and brought into it the attitudes and prejudices prevailing among earlier ethnic and religious groups (especially Near Eastern Christianity, with its legacy and lore of anti-Jewish notions reflected in Hellenistic sources and sharpened in the course of the rise and entrenchment of the church in the Roman Empire).

As Arabic became the idiom of the vast literature of Islamic peoples and their civilization, this literature (to which non-Muslims also contributed), especially in works on history and geography, discussed Jews, their history and tenets. Later, with the rise of theological discussions, polemics directed against Jews appeared.

Apparently Jewish converts to Islam played the role of informants. From this source notions on Jewish Scriptures, sometimes Hebrew passages in transliteration and translation, were obtained, duly commented upon, "exposed," and ridiculed. Jewish customs were mentioned only to be rejected and decried. As against these, Koran passages were adduced and Islamic practices praised. Some converts claimed visions indicating heavenly guidance to abandon their ancestral community and embrace the faith of Islam. Conversions sometimes turned into solemn festive occasions at the mosque.

The theologians took up from there, fitting the earlier faiths into a system in which they appeared as aberrations or distortions of the human mind and of divine injunctions, on the road toward the ultimate truth of Islam.

Islamic polemics against the non-Muslims are mostly directed against Christians, and only a small fraction of them are concerned with the Jews. Curiously, nothing substantial of the early writings seems to have reached us from the East. The earliest work comes from Spain, from the pen of the

 POLEMICS, ISLAMIC-JEWISH

eminent man of letters Ibn Ḥazm (994–1064). He seems to have returned to the subject more than once. In his major theological work and in a separate pamphlet he turns against the Jews and their writings as well as against a contemporary Jewish dignitary in Granada, Samuel ha-Nagid.

Ibn Ḥazm goes into a detailed textual critique of the Bible, mostly the Pentateuch, in particular Genesis. He points out contradictions, illogical statements, absurdities, anthropomorphisms, and the revolting crudity of certain passages (such as incest and fornication in the stories of Noah and his daughters, Jacob and his eldest son). According to him, the Jewish Scriptures are unreliable distortions and Ezra was a contemptible forger. Only quite late did the law spread as a new faith, the work of the rabbis.

Ibn Ḥazm finds these conclusions consistent with his view of the Jews as a mendacious, prevaricating lot. Yet he also quotes a few passages from the (abrogated) Scriptures as announcements of Muḥammad's advent.

His information on other biblical books is less solid. Presumably he had a list of passages supplied to him. The same is true for the short section devoted to the Talmud: old wives' tales of God moaning about the destruction of the Temple. The Jews bribed Paul to mislead the early Christians, just as they later tried to foment the Shīʿa schism among Muslims. Ibn Ḥazm wonders at the Jewish leaders' blind fidelity to their ancestors, group loyalty, and the desire to perpetuate their worldly position and mastery over their people.

From the East comes the tract of a Jewish convert (of Spanish antecedents), a native of Baghdad, the distinguished physician-mathematician Samau'al al-Maghribī (*ca.* 1125–1175). His *Silencing the Jews* had a great impact for at least two centuries. It is the earliest preserved compendium of Islamic polemics against Judaism. It includes an autobiography and visions depicting meetings with the prophet Samuel (the author's namesake) and the prophet Muḥammad. He explains that his mind was trained since his youth in mathematics, and this made him also ponder religious problems logically. Reason should be the supreme judge in evaluating tradition. Historical relativism is hailed and imputed to deity.

Jews believe in a tradition based on Scripture. But, according to Samau'al, the Scripture is replete with contradictions. One passage abrogates another. The minutiae of Jewish observance reflect illogical rabbinic interpretation of scriptural passages, not divine intent.

It is also contrary to reason to repudiate a prophet whose tenets meet with wide acceptance and to believe another. Either all the monotheistic prophets must be accepted or none. The Jews claim that the transmission by their ancestors is reliable, but this argument can be used by any group. The Jews have no record of scientific achievements. They had better accept Jesus and Muḥammad. Hebrew quotations are presented to show that the prayers are postbiblical.

Samau'al also mentions the folklore concerning Jesus and Muḥammad, and says that a number of scriptural passages point to Muḥammad. The Torah was falsified by Ezra and the priests. To illustrate how the rabbis hold sway over the masses and mislead the people, Samau'al tells the story of a recent messianic movement: the Jews waited on the rooftops to be carried to their homeland.

The Muslim argument against Judaism thus centers on (1) abrogation (*naskh*); (2) the distortion or forgery of Scripture (*taḥrīf*), as proved by the critique and confrontation of passages; what remained problematic was whether the text itself had been changed or whether the construction put on it was wrong; (3) anthropomorphism (*tajsīm*) and unacceptable utterances; and (4) announcements (*aʿlām*) of the advent of Muḥammad and Islam (preserved even in the debunked Scripture, by the grace of God).

There are other pamphlets, in addition to those of Ibn Ḥazm and Samau'al, with varying degrees of vehemence, level, and learning. But they offer merely variations on the theme.

While in Christian lands Jews produced a number of works against Christianity and its anti-Jewish polemics, in the Islamic empire Jews generally abstained from retorts to Islamic polemics and from a critique of the dominant faith.

In thirteenth-century Baghdad, under the Mongols before they embraced Islam (when for a few decades Islam ceased to be the rulers' religion), the Jewish philosopher Ibn Kammūna penned a treatise (in 1280) about the three faiths, their respective claims and counterclaims. The chapters on Judaism and Islam are superb expositions. Dispassionateness notwithstanding, after the *Examination of the Three Faiths* was reviewed during a Friday service in a mosque, the author had to be hidden in a coffin to save him from an irate Muslim mob.

A century earlier Maimonides in his *Epistle to Yemen* offered a summary of the Jewish case, for synagogue use, with a warning about the necessity to keep a low profile.

In a sense, the Islamic anti-Jewish literature was used, along with anti-Jewish poems, sermons, and tracts directed against all non-Muslims serving in governmental offices or as physicians, to bedevil from time to time the lot of the Jewish population in Islamic societies. This literature did not determine the status and position of the infidel but it reflected and sometimes contributed to shaping them.

BIBLIOGRAPHY

Camila Adang, "Ibn Ḥazm on Jews and Judaism" (Ph.D. diss., Catholic Univ., Amsterdam, 1985); Moshe Perlmann, "The Medieval Polemics Between Islam and Judaism," in S. D. Goitein, ed., *Religion in a Religious Age* (1974).

MOSHE PERLMANN

[See also **Ḥazm, Ibn; Jews in Muslim Spain; Jews in North Africa; Jews in the Middle East; Philosophy and Theology, Jewish: Islamic World.**]

POLEMIUS SILVIUS (*fl.* 430–448), a Gallic author said to have been mentally deranged, who held a post in the imperial civil service until the late 430's. He was a friend of Hilary of Arles and wrote some religious works, now lost. He also wrote a *Laterculus,* or *Register,* the following sections of which survive: (1) a dedicatory letter to Eucherius of Lyons, (2) *The Names of All the Roman Emperors,* to 448, (3) *The Names of the Provinces,* (4) *The Names of All the Animals,* (5) *A Description of Rome,* (6) *A Summary of History,* to 449, (7) *The Various Sounds of Animals,* and (8) *The Names of Weights and Measures.*

BIBLIOGRAPHY

Text of the *Laterculus* is in *Monumenta Germaniae historica, Auctorum antiquissimorum,* IX, Theodore Mommsen, ed. (1892), 511–551. See also Elegius Dekkers, ed., *Clavis patrum latinorum,* 2nd ed. (1961), no. 2256; Arnold H. M. Jones, *The Prosopography of the Later Roman Empire,* II, John R. Martindale, *A.D. 395–527* (1980), 1,012–1,013; Martin von Schanz, Carl Hosius, and Gustav Krüger, *Geschichte der römischen Literatur,* IV, pt. 2 (1920), 130.

RALPH W. MATHISEN

POLISTORIE, a chronicle in Anglo-Norman French prose recounting the political and ecclesiastical history of England from Brutus on, completed in 1314. Although it is based largely on Latin chroniclers such as Geoffrey of Monmouth, its latter portion contains much original material. The author, John, was a clergyman at Canterbury; he moralizes frequently, incorporates a religious history of the world from the Creation, and concentrates on ecclesiastical affairs concerning Canterbury.

BIBLIOGRAPHY

An edition is "Jehan de Caunterbire, *Polistorie:* A Critical Edition," William N. Ferris, ed. (diss., North Carolina, 1963). See also William N. Ferris, "The Amorphous John of Canterbury," in *Romance Notes,* **11** (1969–1970).

ELLEN T. WEHNER

[See also **Anglo-Norman Literature; Chronicles.**]

POLITICAL THEORY, BYZANTINE. When Constantine I founded the city of Constantinople on 11 May 330, no one could have imagined that he was also founding an empire. Constantine and his successors considered themselves Roman emperors, and the empire was called Roman by contemporaries; it was only in the seventeenth century that the term "Byzantine" began to be used. Constantinople was soon called New Rome or Second Rome, which indicated the role it was to play.

Thus, the Byzantine Empire was an organic continuation of imperial Rome. Unlike its predecessor, however, from its inception Byzantium was under the standard of the Christian religion. Accepted shortly before by Constantine, Christianity counted its followers mainly among the peoples of the eastern provinces. The terms "Christian" and "Roman" became joined in respect to Byzantium: the Byzantine people identified themselves with the "new chosen people"; Constantinople, already the New Rome, became "New Jerusalem." The emperor's official title was the "very holy emperor [of

Romans] faithful in Christ," and his state was the "very Christian state protected by God."

Rome bequeathed to Byzantium the state and its workings, its civil and military institutions, its law and justice. As the sole heir of the Roman emperor, the emperor of Constantinople was the supreme magistrate, the administrative chief of state, and the head of the army. He was the source of power and of law, and guarantor of the functioning of imperial institutions.

According to Eusebius of Nicomedia, as a Christian the Byzantine emperor was the representative of Christ on earth. The Christian empire of Byzantium was formed in the image of the heavenly empire of Christ. On earth this empire was to cover the entire civilized Christian world. According to this principle of uniqueness of the empire, Byzantium added the Christian ecumenical dimension to the universalist Roman one. The Christian emperor of Byzantium was to be the defender of Christendom in its entirety and the protector of humanity.

Uniqueness, universality, and ecumenism of the empire are the fundamental characteristics of Byzantine political theory. They are complemented by another important principle, the eternity of the empire. This principle, worked out in the sixth century (it is explained clearly in Cosmas Indicopleustes), is based on the belief that Byzantium would remain invincible until the end of time because its empire was the first to adopt Christianity. Fed by omens and prophecies, the idea of the empire's perpetuity within its universal boundaries was profoundly and solidly rooted in the popular consciousness.

Since the Byzantine emperor was acknowledged to be the master and defender of the civilized world—Christendom in its entirety—all his undertakings were justified, and the notion of "just and pure war" was applied to all wars waged by the Byzantines. Placed under the Virgin's protection and with the cry "The cross conquers," the Byzantine army was on a "crusade" everywhere it fought. This may explain Byzantium's lack of understanding of the crusades the Westerners waged from the twelfth century on, which aimed solely to free the Holy Land.

Another important concept of Byzantine political theory is the absolute respect for ancestral traditions (*patria*). Throughout its history Byzantium sought to defend the "Roman order," the Pax Romana having become the Pax Byzantina; to deviate from that order was to disturb the harmony of the world, as Constantine VII Porphyrogenitos expressed it. Byzantium was thus averse to any radical reforms, and only slow and progressive adaptation of the legislative and administrative machinery of state to new realities was capable of responding to the demands of the times. Devotion to the greatness was considered a major political virtue, as well as a moral and aesthetic one.

The Roman-Christian Byzantine Empire regrouped the populations of the Roman East around Constantinople. They were the only ones who had been capable of resisting the upheaval caused by the arrival of the barbarians, who had established themselves in the western provinces of the empire. Diverse traditions motivated the Byzantine population: some were strongly Hellenized and urbanized, notably those in Alexandria, Antioch, and Beirut, whereas the rural populations of the interior, excluded from the Greco-Roman culture, were attached to Oriental traditions. The harmonious and peaceful coexistence of these elements—Roman, Christianized, Hellenized, and Oriental—was a major preoccupation of the Byzantine government, and its political theory therefore had to take all these multiple legacies into account.

The Byzantine world expected the emperor to assure its well-being, security, and peace. To achieve this, the emperor drew strength and virtue from divine protection. Thus aided and protected, the emperor took care of the world entrusted to him, expressing his solicitude (*pronoia*) by applying adequate measures for the welfare of the Byzantine world. He acted "economically," in the image of God. The principle of "economy" practiced by the emperor constituted a fundamental notion of responsibility and justice, attributes of the imperial function. It expressed the emperor's duty to draw as near as possible to God, his "archetype," so as to establish the best government in the world. Completed by the Christian notion of perfectibility, "imperial economy" embodied the Hellenistic notion of the prince as imitator of God. According to the Hellenistic political thought inherited by Byzantium, the prince had all the qualities that drew him to God: he was merciful, just, philanthropic. It is mainly the quality of philanthropy, of Hellenistic origin but also part of Christian teaching, that characterizes Byzantine humanism. It is the basis for the principle of respect for others in Byzantium's relations not only with its own citizens but also with the outside world. "Roman philanthropy" was practiced by the emperor toward his enemies.

Hellenistic political thought is seen in treatises on forms and methods of government. These treatises, in the form of advice to the sovereign, were widely circulated. *Basileia* (from *basis laou,* foundation of the people), or *imperium,* is the best government. Its opposite is tyranny, just as the opposite of aristocratic government (oligarchy) is democracy. The latter term had a strongly pejorative meaning in Byzantium: it signified the power of the rabble. Nevertheless, the humanistic virtues of the emperor were those of the prince of the Hellenistic period. Christian teaching had augmented these qualities with the typically Byzantine notion of "economy," which meant the distance (the margin of imperfection) separating imperial action from God's perfect action.

Thus, near perfection, the emperor, summit and source of power, assumed the appearance of a providential man for those he ruled. Imperial imagery and the symbols of power emphasized this character by conferring the traits of an Oriental monarch upon him. The sophisticated and complicated ceremonial of the Byzantine court, the luxury and ostentation of the imperial finery, the sumptuousness of the objects related to aulic life, and certain actions, such as prostration before the emperor, emphasized the quasi-sacred character of the veneration surrounding the imperial person. Clothing, jewels, and all sorts of luxury goods stressed the inaccessible character of the imperial function.

These articles, like the end they pursued, bear witness to the Oriental origin and inspiration of these practices. They have been considered proof of the theocratic character of Byzantine power. It seems, however, more reasonable to see them as an effort to make evident to all the splendor of the imperial function, and thus to provoke fear, admiration, and wonder. In political theory, the idea that directed the elaboration of Byzantine aulic habits aimed, through material means, at impressing the imagination and assuring the widest diffusion of the message of the greatness of the emperor.

The Byzantines sought to spread the basic principles of the greatness and the perpetuity of the Roman Empire and to make the surrounding world share them. They pursued this effort relentlessly, often with success. It was the dominant characteristic of Byzantine foreign policy even at the time of the empire's greatest reverses, and accounts for the desperate efforts exerted by Byzantium to preserve for itself alone the title "Roman Empire" when confronted by Carolingian, Slavic, and Norman ambitions. Byzantine diplomats and the imperial chancellery, when considering the formal hierarchy of the rulers of the world, placed their emperor as the supreme chief, the father of the family of rulers. Each of the other rulers was called, according to his importance, brother, son, nephew, or friend of the Byzantine emperor.

Besides revealing Byzantine political theory in international relations, this notion of the family of rulers is the application of another fundamental principle of Byzantine political theory: proximity or vicinity. According to it, Byzantine protocol, and thus the relations of the emperor with his people and those he administered, was ordered. Each person's importance was measured by the proximity of his rank to the emperor. Both the aulic hierarchy and the civil and military hierarchy depended on this principle. The summit was occupied by the emperor, since all the dignities were conferred by him or in his name, and all offices and duties were exercised by delegation or subdelegation of the imperial power.

Thus the principle of vicinity was an example of the principle of delegation practiced by the emperor. These two principles emphasized the fact that the emperor was source and summit of power. His authority was stronger than the law because it was the law's source. The only limitation on the emperor's authority was with regard to God, from whom it proceeded. The indispensable presence of the patriarch at the coronation ceremony was a perfect illustration of this.

Good relations between the Christian emperor and the Byzantine patriarch (the highest ecclesiastical authority) were an absolute necessity for the peace of the empire. The patriarch of Constantinople claimed to be the living image of Christ, entrusted with the spiritual salvation of his flock, just as the emperor, as Christ's delegate, was charged with the physical well-being of his subjects. Empire and priesthood had to coexist harmoniously to guarantee the welfare of the Byzantine people. This belief was recorded in the civil law texts (the ninth-century *Epanagoge*) and was proclaimed by Emperor John I Tzimiskes (*r.* 969–976) and repeated by Theodore II Laskaris (*r.* 1254–1259). Attempts by strong emperors or ambitious patriarchs to introduce caesaropapism or papocaesarism were exceptions that did not alter the character of the relations between *imperium* and priesthood, founded in Byzantium upon a tacit parallelism between the two. The church had its own hierarchy and its own laws consistent with the interests of the state. The state defended the interests of the church, if need be by the intervention of its military forces. The disturbance of this equilibrium led to crises that shook the Byzantine world. Only unimpeded collaboration between church and state could assure Byzantium of the working of the institutions upon which the life of the empire depended.

In this manner, the political theory of Byzantium, even though it sought historical justification for its principles (such as the universality and perpetuity of the empire), was based on the interaction of factors that formed the social fabric of the Byzantine world, the dynamics that carried the objectives of Byzantium. State and church were there to bind the certitudes of the past to the hopes of the future, and upon their agreement depended the prosperity of the whole empire.

BIBLIOGRAPHY

Hélène Ahrweiler, *L'idéologie politique de l'empire byzantin* (1975); Ernest Barker, *Social and Political Thought in Byzantium* (1957); Norman H. Baynes, *Constantine the Great and the Christian Church* (1930, repr. 1972); Alexander Kazhdan and Giles Constable, *People and Power in Byzantium* (1982), chap. 6.

HÉLÈNE AHRWEILER

[See also **Basileus; Byzantine Empire; Caesaropapism; Constantine I, the Great; Constantinople; Diplomacy, Byzantine; Patriarch; Pronoia; Roman Empire, Late.**]

POLITICAL THEORY, ISLAMIC. There is in Islam a relationship between religion and politics that is paralleled in no other religion, with the possible exception of Judaism. "Islam is a religion and a state," goes a Muslim saying. Religion is viewed as necessary for the organization and integration of society; this is the divine purpose in sending prophets. Islam is, therefore, not only a faith but also a law or set of rules (*sharīᶜa,* literally, path) that finds its ideal expression in a political community (*umma*). The Islamic state is, in theory, a theocracy or a nomocracy within which there is no separation between church and state, the spiritual and the temporal. Adherence to the faith means immediate admission to membership in a political community with corollary rights and privileges.

It follows that Islamic political theory falls within the scope of canonical jurisprudence (*fiqh*) and dialectical theology (*kalām*), the two traditional Muslim sciences concerned with the theoretical and practical parts of divine law. *Fiqh* is primarily concerned with ascertaining prescribed commands regarding practical matters, just as *kalām* is primarily concerned with the defense of dogma. The principles of jurisprudence are the fundamentals of the Islamic polity. Islamic political theory is thus closely tied and subordinated to theological and juristic considerations. There are three main schools of Islamic political theory.

TRADITIONAL POLITICAL THEORY

In a rudimentary form, traditional political theory in Islam developed around the controversy of succession to the temporal office of the Prophet. No other issue stirred early Muslim life and thought as did that of succession to the Messenger of God. As long as the Prophet lived, Hitti says, he "performed the functions of prophet, lawgiver, religious leader, chief judge, commander of the army and civil head—all in one." With his death in 632, divine revelation ceased, necessitating a new definition of the relationships of the community and the faith. The Prophet left no heir apparent; neither did he leave any directions about the future course his community should follow in the eventuality of his death. It was this controversy that generated the most serious political discussions and brought about enough bloodshed to split the community into two main sects: Sunni and Shīᶜa.

The Sunnis, the overwhelming majority of Muslims, are the followers of the orthodox path ordained by the Koran, the prophetic traditions, and the usage of the community. Unlike the Shiites, Sunnis believe in the validity of the historic caliphate and reject the notion that the imam is the mediator of the Muhammadan revelation, without whom its relevance cannot be known. According to Sunni political theory, the caliph is a political functionary, a guardian of the divine law, but he is in no sense an authority in doctrine. The caliph is to be elected by the community and must rule and manage its affairs according to divine law.

The Shiites claim that the caliphate belongs to ᶜAlī, cousin and son-in-law of the Prophet, and his offspring. Although Shiism originated as an Arab political movement, it was later adopted in Iran as the official religion, developing an articulate doctrinal basis for its political aspirations. Like Sunnis, Shiites give their allegiance to the Koran and the *sunna* (custom) of the Prophet, but hold the subsequent conduct of the community to have been illegal.

The succession controversy directed traditional Islamic political theory to be primarily concerned with the caliphate or imamate, its necessity, the qualities of the ruler, and the obligations of the believers. The concept of individual freedom did not attain the abstraction of a political principle. All jurists agree that the head of state must have certain leadership qualities: knowledge of the religious law, piety, courage in the defense of the community, administrative ability, and membership in the Quraysh tribe, to which the Prophet belonged. Although both Sunnis and Shiites agree on the necessity of the imamate, there is disagreement as to whether it is required by reason or by law. While Sunni theory recognizes consensus as the most important single basis for choosing a caliph, Shiites hold that the imamate is established by designation from God, and that it devolves from ᶜAlī to his descendants.

Muslim political theory was articulated more than two centuries after Muḥammad established his theocracy at Medina. In other words, when Muslims began to theorize about the caliphate, the Islamic state had already reached the zenith of its power and had started on the road to decline. From the middle of the tenth century on, the Abbasid caliph found himself the ward and puppet of Turkish sultans, exercising no political power beyond investing the real rulers with office—an investiture that was deemed necessary to legitimate their rule. This explains the highly apologetic character of Islamic theories of state. The greater the decline in the political power of the Islamic state, the more diligently the jurists labored to defend its legitimacy.

MIRRORS OF PRINCES

The decline in the power of the caliphate and the ascendancy of military leaders of Turkish or Iranian origin gave rise to a new genre of political literature known as the "mirror of princes." In the spirit of the Florentine statesman and political theorist Niccolò Machiavelli (1459–1527), the "mirror" consists chiefly of advice to rulers and their ministers on how to establish, maintain, and conduct the affairs of state. While the "mirror" stresses pragmatic and prudential policies and measures based on political theory, it, unlike *The Prince* and the *Discourses,* pays more than lip service to religious principles and morality. To some extent, it represents an integration of early Persian literature into Islamic teachings. For example, justice, not as an abstract principle or value but as a guarantee of government stability, is stressed in all treatises on advice to princes; it is also enjoined by religion. Much of the literature is in the form of anecdotes and political aphorisms.

An example of the "mirror" genre well known in the West is the *Book of Government* (*Siyāsat-nāma*) of Niẓām al-Mulk (1018–1092), the famous prime minister of the Seljuk sultan Malikshāh (1072–1092), in which he stresses the religious and ethical duties that the ruler must perform for his own salvation and for the welfare of the state. In addition to piety and moral integrity, the ruler must have the qualities of physical beauty, good character, justice, and courage; he should possess military abilities and a taste for the arts and sciences. He must also ensure the rule of law, choose the right counselors, and always consult with the judges of the court. Advice on many other details in the conduct of state is also provided, based on religious principles as much as on practical experience.

POLITICAL PHILOSOPHY

It was the declining condition of the Islamic state as much as the influence of Greek philosophy and science that directed the minds of Muslim philosophers (*falāsifa*) to political science or political philosophy. Having accepted the intention, methods, and possibility of political philosophy from the Greeks, they sought to introduce it into their culture and adapt it to an Islamic milieu. The problem centered around the relationship between philosophy and a society governed by revealed law. Just as philosophy investigates the principles of being, so political philosophy investigates the nature or principles of all human affairs or political things—Islamic theology and jurisprudence included. While the traditional Islamic disciplines are concerned with practical matters in the life of the Muslim polity, political philosophy probes into the principles of all kinds of polity. The founder of political philosophy in Islam was al-Fārābī (*d.* 950), followed by such other eminent philosophers as Ibn Sīna (*d.* 1037), Ibn Rushd (*d.* 1198), and Ibn Khaldūn (*d.* 1406).

The deterioration in the position of the Islamic state, coupled with confusion in theological and juridical questions, prompted the Muslim philosophers to attempt to bring rational order into Muslim life and thought. What facilitated their task is a certain parallelism between the role of the imam or caliph in Islam and that of the philosopher-king in Plato's political philosophy. By identifying Plato's philosopher-ruler with the head of the Muslim community, they could subordinate religion and divine law to philosophical analysis, without rejecting their role as instruments of social and moral control for the masses. The intimation is obvious: while philosophy and the attainment of wisdom guarantee true happiness for the elite, religion is sufficient for the masses. No wonder the ideas of these philosophers were rejected by the established orthodoxy and their books banned or burned. Their influence on the life of the Muslim community was minimal. But they left a legacy worthy of serious study and reconsideration.

BIBLIOGRAPHY

Leonard Binder, "Al-Ghazālī's Theory of Islamic Government," in *The Muslim World,* **45** (1955); Louis Gardet, *La cité musulmane: Vie sociale et politique,* 3rd ed. (1969); Hamilton A. R. Gibb, "Some Considerations on the Sunni Theory of the Caliphate" and "Al-Māwardī's Theory of the Caliphate," in his *Studies on the Civilization of Islam,* Stanford Shaw and William R. Polk, eds. (1962, repr. 1982); Philip Hitti, *History of the Arabs,* 5th ed. (1951); Yusuf Ibish, *The Political Doctrine of al-Bāqillānī* (1966); Ralph Lerner and Muhsin Mahdi, eds., *Medieval Political Philosophy: A Sourcebook* (1963); George Makdisi *et al.,* eds., *La notion d'autorité au moyen âge: Islam, Byzance, Occident* (1982), 57–68, 83–126, 163–187, 211–226; Nizām al-Mulk, *The Book of Government; or, Rules for Kings,* Hubert Darke, trans., 2nd ed. (1978); Erwin I. J. Rosenthal, *Political Thought in Medieval Islam* (1968); W. Montgomery Watt, *Islamic Political Thought: The Basic Concepts* (1968).

FAUZI M. NAJJAR

[See also **Caliphate; Imam; Islam, Religion; Law, Islamic; Mirror of Princes; Sunna; Shīʿa;** and individual political philosophers.]

POLITICAL THEORY, WESTERN EUROPEAN: TO 1100. The political vocabulary and stock of political exempla of intellectuals between 500 and 1100 derived from the Vulgate. Their political assumptions came, usually without elaboration, from the church fathers. Above all they inherited the patristic idea of a sharp distinction between human society in its natural, primitive state and the political realities of the present day. "Nature brought forth all men equal; but a secret dispensation placed some in authority over others," according to Pope Gregory I (*Moralia* XXI.15). According to Augustine, God "did not wish the rational man made in his own image to have dominion over any save irrational creatures . . . our ancestors are remembered not as kings of men but as shepherds of flocks" (*De civitate Dei* XIX.15).

The idea of natural equality was regularly evoked in the reforming councils of the Carolingian age and of the tenth century. Jonas of Orléans (*d.* 842/843) warned the lay nobility against taking differences of worldly dignity and wealth for differences in nature (*De institutione laicalis* II.22) and admonished the king to appoint as dukes and counts only such men as understood that their subjects were by nature their equals (*De institutione regia* 5). Smaragdus, abbot of St. Mihiel (*d.* after 825), alone among early medieval authors, used the idea of natural equality as an argument against the owning of slaves (*Via regia,* 30). The reforming bishop Rather of Verona used the idea to argue (*ca.* 935) that "very often men have dominion over their betters" (*Praeloquia* I.10).

Dominatus (lordship) in all its aspects—the institutions of slavery, civil government, and private property—was alien to what Ambrose and Augustine described as the natural law written in the heart of all men; it was a product of man's fall. Political institutions originated in man's intolerable pride and appetite for subjecting others (Augustine, *De doctrina christiana* I.23). Nevertheless, *dominatus* was to be accepted as a divinely ordained punishment, intended to correct those very sins which first produced it. The function of government was to terrorize evildoers and so repress the bestial tendency in mankind. The encyclopedist Isidore of Seville (*ca.* 560–636) provided an influential summary of this doctrine: "God so ordered the life of men, making some slaves, others lords, so that the slaves' inclination to behave badly may be restrained by the power of their rulers. . . . So also princes and kings were appointed among the nations so that they might coerce the people from evil by their terror and force them to live righteously by their laws" (*Sententiae* III.47).

Hence Carolingian authors would regard a subject who rebelled against his king and a slave who escaped from his master as equally guilty of sacrilege (see, for example, Hrabanus Maurus, *Epistolae* XV.3, XXX.5). Similarly, private property was a divinely ordained remedy for human avarice. Nature had originally bestowed all things on men for the common use; but fallen man must respect property rights. Therefore, the doctrine "I do not sin if I take from the rich to give to the poor" is the suggestion of the devil (Pseudo-Augustine, *Sermones suppositiții* 287, c.2-Caesarius of Arles). The idea of the original *communis omnium possessio* (Isidore, *Etymologiae* V.4) exercised its greatest influence on the religious life, elaborated in the ninth-century Pseudo-Isidorean decretals using the example of the "common life" of the apostles. The idea also survived in early medieval canon law, which regarded theft for need (*per necessitatem*) as a slight offense, requiring a light penance (Regino of Prüm, *De synodalibus causis* II.437; Burchard of Worms, *Decretum* XI.56).

"MIRRORS OF PRINCES"

The format and subject matter of the political writings of this period were most strongly influenced by the *Regulae pastoralis* (Pastoral care) of Gregory I. Gregory's political thought, as expressed in this work, is concerned exclusively with the moral problems implicit in the subject-ruler relationship—especially the tendency of rulers to forget humility and natural equality. Although the *Regulae pastoralis* was written for the instruction of bishops, its teachings were understood to be equally valid for secular rulers. Gregory did not differentiate between spiritual and temporal government; he cited the conduct of St. Peter as a model for secular officeholders and warned bishops against imitating the example of King Saul. Hence Smaragdus, one of Gregory's Carolingian imitators, could issue what was substantially the same book as both a treatise on secular government (*Via regia*) and a treatise on the monastic life (*Diadema monachorum*). Under the all-pervasive influence of St. Gregory, medieval political thought came to focus not on the political community or "body politic," but on the moral qualities of the individual, ruler or ruled. Characteristic of Gregorian political thought is his definition of the term "tyrant." A tyrant is any man who exercises dominion without humility, whether in the state, the province, the congregation, his own house, or in himself; for God is concerned not with the scope which a man has for evildoing, but with a man's evil intentions. It was not until the investiture controversy of the late eleventh century that polemicists rediscovered the purely political sense of "tyrant," using Isidore's definition: a wicked ruler who cruelly oppresses the people (*Etymologiae* IX.3).

The political literature produced by the disciples of St. Gregory took the form of treatises of moral instruction for secular rulers—"mirrors of princes" (*specula principum*). This genre continued to flourish throughout the Middle Ages and Renaissance, even when more sophisticated forms of political analysis were current, but in the early medieval period "mirrors of princes" provided the unique medium of political speculation. The first identifiable "mirror" was a Frankish work of about 645, addressed by an unknown bishop to a Merovingian king (Clovis II or Sigibert III), advising him to imitate the examples of the good kings David and Solomon, listening to the advice of churchmen, just as they had obeyed the prophets. Already this little work displays the main characteristics of the Carolingian *specula principum*—the writings of Cathwulf and Alcuin (whose "mirrors" are contained in letters to Charlemagne); of the Aquitanian authors of the reign of Louis the Pious—Smaragdus, Ermoldus Nigellus, and Jonas of Orléans; of the later ninth-century authors Lupus of Ferrières (Servatus Lupus), Sedulius Scottus, and Hincmar of Rheims.

Above all, the "mirrors of princes" focused on exempla from the Old Testament. "Read the Book of Kings to learn what reverence is due to a brother king," wrote Hincmar (*ca.* 806–882) to Charlemagne's grandson, Louis the German (*Epistola synodi carisiacensis* 15); while the latter's elder brother, Pepin I of Aquitaine, was advised by Jonas of Orléans to read Deuteronomy to learn "what a king ought to be and what he must beware" (*De institutione regia* 3). This preoccupation with Old Testament kingship, especially as presented in the Books of Samuel, was influenced partly by St. Gregory, partly by the seventh-century Irish work *De XII abusivis saeculi* of Pseudo-Cyprian, whose ninth chapter, on the virtues and duties of kings, was a source of many Carolingian *specula*. Sedulius' *Liber de rectoribus christianis* (*ca.* 850) is recognizably a synthesis of these elements—biblical, Gregorian, and insular. Sedulius' Christian king must be a warlord like Moses, Hezekiah, Jehosophat, and Judas Maccabeus, his warfare directed to the conversion of the heathen and the defense of the church. In addition, the king must imitate David, who as God's minister destroyed "tyrants"—"tyrant" being defined as a ruler dominated by pride (*superbia*). The cult of David and Solomon promoted by Alcuin (*ca.* 730–804) at the court of Charlemagne survived to exalt the kingship of the Ottonians (for example, Hrotswitha von Gandersheim, *Gesta Ottonis*) and the Salians (for example, Berno von Reichenau, letters to Henry III; Benzo of Alba, *Libri ad Heinricum IV*).

The Carolingian authors' emphasis on the moral qualities of kings was echoed in the early tenth century in the *Praeloquia* of Rather of Verona and in the early eleventh century in the *Institutes of Polity* of Wulfstan of York and the *Tetralogus* addressed by the imperial chaplain Wipo of Burgundy to Henry III. Discussion of the duties of kingship is also found in eleventh-century royal biographies, which are slightly disguised "mirrors of princes," for example, Wipo's *Deeds of the Emperor Conrad* (*ca.* 1047). The most remarkable of these biographical *specula* is the *Life of St. Edmund, English King and Martyr* of Abbo of Fleury (*ca.* 945–1004), which, with its portrait of a king prepared to die for the Christian faith, anticipated the political ideas of the papal reform movement.

KINGSHIP AS DIVINE "MINISTERIUM"

The principal writers on kingship in the early Middle Ages were monks, brought up on the writings of the great monk-pope Gregory I; inevitably their royal ideology drew on ideas of abbatial or episcopal authority. Their starting point was the exhortation of St. Paul to the faithful to submit to the secular ruler as a divinely ordained minister of wrath against the evildoer (from the Vulgate, Rom. 13:4). Much early medieval discussion of kingship is encapsulated in commentaries on chapter 13 of the Epistle to the Romans, many of which cited or were influenced by the commentary of "Ambrosiaster" (*ca.* 380). Carolingian scholars, and equally their Ottonian and Salian successors, accepted Ambrosiaster's opinion that the king was, by virtue of his divine *ministerium* (office), "vicar of God." A Carolingian court poet summarized the idea thus: "There is only one who is enthroned in the kingdom of the air, the thunderer. It is fitting that there should only be one ruler under him on earth, through his merit an example to all men" ("Hibernicus exsul" [Dungal?]). This parallel system of monarchical rule, God, "the highest and true emperor," as Pope Gelasius I called him, ruling in heaven, while his *vicarius* ruled on earth, is evoked by the Carolingian *laudes regiae,* the liturgical acclamations of the kings. Here the kingship of God and that of the prince are fused together in a celebration of the qualities of triumphant war leadership: "our invincible arms," "our impregnable wall," "our defense and exaltation." The divine nature of royal authority is likewise emphasized in the *intitulationes* (superscriptions) of *diplomata* (state documents), in which, from the Carolingian period onward, chancery officials recorded their lords' titles: "Charles, king by the grace of God," "great and peace-loving emperor, crowned by God," "Louis, emperor augustus by the ordination of divine providence." To the illiterate layman the royal ceremony of crown-wearing conveyed something of these ideas. The king was enthroned in majesty, while the choir sang the *laudes regiae;* and the spectator might be moved to cry out (as happened at a crown-wearing of William the Conqueror), "Behold, I see God!"

The crucial ceremony of this divine kingship was the royal anointing (the act of coronation being of secondary importance). This initiation rite—an ecclesiastical ritual into which secular symbols of office, crown, sword, lance, and scepter became absorbed—again illustrates the influence of the Old Testament, especially the exemplum of David (1 Sam. 16:1–13), on early medieval ideas of kingship. Introduced into the Visigothic kingdom of Spain in 672 and into the Frankish kingdom—apparently by papal initiative—in 751, the ceremony had become indispensable throughout Western Christendom by the tenth century; when the German king Henry I refused unction in 919, the clergy of his kingdom regarded him as "a sword without a handle." The significance of royal consecration did not, however, remain constant in this period; the emphasis changed according to the needs of the consecrators. The need of the papacy at the time of the consecration of Pepin III as king of the Franks in 751 and 754 was for a military protector for the lands of St. Peter. The ceremony of 751 replaced an ineffective ruler with a vigorous warlord, albeit a warlord lacking royal blood. The consecration of 754, performed on the king and his sons, demonstrated that anointing could create not only a king but also a royal dynasty, "a holy race and a royal priesthood" (*Liber pontificalis: Life of Stephen II*).

The ninth-century Frankish episcopate came to regard kings as their creatures and agents, "because kings are consecrated by bishops, but bishops cannot be consecrated by kings" (Hincmar, *Ad. Episc. de Inst. Carol.* 2). The more successful and more confident German rulers of the tenth and eleventh centuries drew a different conclusion from the fact of their consecration: "I have been anointed similarly [to priests] with holy oil, and power of ruling before all others has been given to me" (Anselm, *Gesta episcorum Leodiensiam,* 66). Thus spoke Henry III, whose clerical courtiers acclaimed him as "head of the church," and "lord of lords." In contemporary France churchmen attributed to the anointed Capetian king the miraculous power of healing scrofula. This transference of Christ's power to his *vicarius,* the Capetian king, is the theme of an early-eleventh-century work of royal hagiography, Helgaud's *Life of King Robert the Pious.*

RESISTANCE

If the king was the divinely ordained minister of God, it was surely sacrilegious to oppose him. This was the invariable conclusion of early medieval commentators on Romans 13. For example, the reforming bishop Atto of Vercelli (*d.* 961) wrote that it was impious to resist royal authority "even if it seems unjust. . . . For it is profane to violate what God ordains" (*Epistolae* I). In support of this opinion he cited the synodal legislation of seventh-century Visigothic Spain. Even more influential was the insistence of St. Gregory on the obedience due to kings, here summarized by Wenrich, master of the cathedral school of Trier, about 1080: "Pope Gregory . . . addresses persons in high places, however useless or even infamous, with their titles of dignity . . . and does not refrain from aggrandizing their power" (*Epistola* in *Monumenta Germaniae historica, Libelli* I.291). St. Gregory, like David, knew how "to soothe the raging Saul by playing the harp," a reference to the use of David in *Regulae pastoralis* III.4 as an exemplum of the good subject who does not resist an evil ruler.

The context of this summary of Gregorian thought was the investiture controversy in Germany. Wenrich of Trier wrote as a supporter of King Henry IV, using the authority of Gregory I to rebuke Pope Gregory VII, who was sanctioning rebellion against the divinely ordained king. The reign of Henry IV of Germany witnessed a revolution in political thought—prompted first by the Saxon rebellion of 1073 and subsequently by the conflict of pope and king—which overturned the political assumptions of the Carolingian and Ottonian age. The Saxons (whose attitudes were recorded by the chroniclers Lambert of Hersfeld and Bruno of Merseburg) justified their rebellion by reviving Isidore's distinction between king and tyrant: "You will be a king if you act rightly; if you do not so act, you will be no king." Henry IV was a tyrant because he was not "restrained by the laws and customs of his predecessors" and acted "with barbarous cruelty" toward the Saxons (Lambert of Hersfeld, *Annales* [1076]). The ideological basis of the opposition of the reforming papacy to Henry IV was stated by Peter Damian as early as 1065: "A king must be revered while he obeys the Creator; but when a king opposes the divine commands, he is rightly held in contempt by his subjects" (*Epistolae* VII.3). Gregory VII was more specific about his reasons for deposing Henry IV: "Unless he is as obedient, as humbly devoted and useful to holy church as a Christian king ought to be . . . beyond doubt holy church will not only not favor him, but will oppose him" (*Register* IX.3).

The various theories of resistance current in the late eleventh century were summarized in the pro-papal polemic of Manegold of Lautenbach (*Liber ad Gebehardum, ca.* 1085), an incoherent, plagiaristic, but also innovatory work. Manegold defended rebellion against Henry IV by means of three arguments: (1) that there are many historical precedents for the excommunication of wicked and unjust kings (a favorite argument of Gregory VII); (2) that "'king' is not the name of a natural quality but the title of an office" (chap. 30), and as kingship is the most responsible of secular offices, it demands commensurate moral qualities of its holder (also an argument of Gregory VII); and (3) that the king rules according to a contract (*pactum*) with his subjects and, if he breaks that contract, he automatically dissolves the oaths of allegiance sworn to him at his accession (a refinement of the Saxons' justification for rebellion).

EMPIRE AND PAPACY

The investiture controversy witnessed not only the first attack on sacred kingship but also the opening of the contest of empire and papacy for theoretical supremacy in Western Christendom, a contest which would dominate the political thought of the later Middle Ages. The Fathers had conceived of "the sacred authority of bishops and the royal power" as a duality, divinely ordained to govern the world side by side. According to the influential definition of Pope Gelasius I (492–496) (*Duo quippe sunt Epistolae* XII.2), it was the emperor's task to "rule over the human race"; but, as a faithful son of the church, he was subject to the bishops in matters respecting his salvation.

Carolingian and Ottonian intellectuals echoed this idea of a single Christian society governed by two powers with separate roles. The precise division of labor was spelled out in the letter of Charlemagne to Pope Leo III on the latter's election in 795. The king's duty was "to defend holy church outwardly from the attack of pagans and from devastation by the arms of infidels and to fortify her inwardly through the enforcement of the acceptance of the catholic faith" (Alcuin, *Epistola* 93). The pope's duty was to pray "that the Christian people may always have the victory everywhere." The Western emperors of the early Middle Ages were above all preoccupied with *dilatatio* (the expansion of the Christian faith), obedient to the precept of Augustine: "We say that emperors are fortunate . . . if they put their power at the disposal of God's majesty, to extend his worship far and wide" (*De civitate Dei* V.24). Hence an Ottonian emperor, waging constant wars against the Slavs on his frontiers, would call himself in his diplomata "most devout and most faithful *dilatator* of holy churches" (Otto III).

In early medieval Rome an alternative view of emperorship developed, according to which the emperor was the pope's subordinate, entrusted with his defense and that of the lands of St. Peter. The traditional papal protector, the Byzantine emperor, ceased in the early eighth century to be a true Christian emperor when he embraced the policy of iconoclasm. This breach with Constantinople perhaps produced the forgery on which later papal claims to supremacy in temporal affairs was often to be based: the "Donation of Constantine." The Donation contained a vision of papal territorial independence which it became the duty of the pope's Carolingian allies to realize. The official biographer of Pope Leo III expressed the papal political theory in his account of the imperial coronation of Charlemagne on 25 December 800. The Romans designated Charles emperor "seeing how great was the defense which he gave and the love which he bore the holy Roman church and her vicar" (*Liber pontificalis* XCVIII.20, 23–24). It was a promotion which he had earned by the effectiveness of his defense of papal interests.

Papal emperor-making in the later ninth and early tenth centuries fostered the theory that the imperial coronation was a constitutive act, intended to create a papal defensor. However, the coronation of Emperor Otto I in 962 initiated a century of imperial control in Rome, when, in the words of Pope Gregory VII, "the rule of our church was given to the Germans." The great champion of papal independence, Gregory VII declared that the pope was supreme in temporal as in spiritual matters and claimed the right to depose emperors by virtue of the power of binding and loosing. His opponents denounced him for having "unsurped *regnum* and *sacerdotium* [priestly office] and thereby shown contempt for the ordination of God, who wished government to consist principally not in one but in two" (Henry IV, Letter 3)—a violation of Gelasian duality.

BIBLIOGRAPHY

Werner Affeldt, *Die weltliche Gewalt in der Paulus-Exegese* (1969); Robert W. Carlyle and Alexander J. Carlyle, *A History of Medieval Political Theory in the West,* I–IV (1903–1932); C. Erdmann, *Forschungen zur politischen Ideenwelt des Frühmittelalters* (1951); Robert Folz, *The Concept of Empire in Western Europe from the Fifth to the Fourteenth Century,* Sheila Ann Ogilvie, trans. (1969); Ernst H. Kantorowicz, *Laudes Regiae* (1946); Karl F. Morrison, *The Two Kingdoms: Ecclesiology in Carolingian Political Thought* (1964); J. Nelson, *Rituals of Royal Inauguration in Early Medieval Europe* (diss., Cambridge Univ., 1967); Ian S. Robinson, *Authority and Resistance in the Investiture Contest* (1978); Percy E. Schramm, *Kaiser, Rom und Renovatio,* 2 vols. (1929), and *Der König von Frankreich* (1939); Walter Ullmann, *Principles of Government and Politics in the Middle Ages* (1961); John M. Wallace-Hadrill, *Early Germanic Kingship in England and on the Continent* (1971).

IAN S. ROBINSON

[See also **Anointing; Carolingians and the Carolingian Empire; Decretals, False; Deposition of Rulers; Donation of Constantine; Ecclesiology; Investiture and Investiture Conflict; Kingship, Rituals of; Kingship, Theories of; Laudes; Mirror of Princes; Papacy, Origins and Development of; Pepin III and the Donation of Pepin;** and individual personalities.]

POLITICAL THEORY, WESTERN EUROPEAN: AFTER 1100. Among the dominant themes of political theory during the period from 1100 to 1485 are the nature of kingship and law, the correct relationship between ecclesiastical and temporal authority, and the proper structure of government, both religious and secular. These issues were addressed from a variety of changing perspectives throughout this period.

At the outset of the period stands the learned, urbane Englishman John of Salisbury (*ca.* 1115–

1180), who is regarded as one of the most important of the medieval political theorists writing before the rediscovery and spread of Aristotelianism. A close friend of Adrian IV (*r.* 1154–1159), the only English pope, John is known for his support of the supremacy of the ecclesiastical over the temporal power, his organic theory of the state, and his doctrine of tyrannicide that he expounded in his *Policraticus* (1159).

TWELFTH-CENTURY DISCOVERIES

Two revivals of ancient thought had a great impact on late medieval political thought: the revival of the study of Roman law in the late eleventh century and the rediscovery of Aristotle's works in the twelfth century. Roman law had ceased to be widely taught sometime before 1000. One of the most important results of its revival was the evolution of a scientific jurisprudence and of legal methods. Irnerius (*ca.* 1055–*ca.* 1130), a master of arts in Bologna, began the formal study of Roman law and made the first glosses on Justinian's *Corpus iuris civilis*. The school of glossators, founded by Irnerius, attempted to discover the exact meaning of the Justinian texts and to introduce Roman law unadulterated into medieval practice. The glossators' approach, which did not take into account the real, existing laws of their own times, inevitably proved inadequate. Its eclipse began at about the middle of the thirteenth century.

The school of postglossators, or commentators, represented a strong reaction to the practice and teaching of law by the glossators. Founded in the second half of the thirteenth century by Jacques de Révigny, professor at Toulouse and later at Orléans, the new method of legal science was introduced into Italy by Cino da Pistoia (*ca.* 1270–1336/1337) and had as its most famous advocate Bartolo da Sassoferrato (1313/1314–1357). Going beyond merely glossing the texts of Justinian's codes, which was the essence of the glossators' method, the Italian postglossators tried to adapt Roman law texts to the sources of medieval law as practiced in the courts. The new school reached its peak in the fourteenth century, and its influence continued to be felt well into the fifteenth.

The development of Roman legal studies after the eleventh century greatly influenced the law of the church. Some attempts had been made to arrange and harmonize the divergent, often contradictory authorities and precedents of church law, but it was Gratian, a Camaldolese monk of Bologna, who used the dialectical method to solve numerous contradictions found in papal decrees, patristic statements, and royal and imperial laws, and around 1140 compiled the *Concordia discordantium canonum* (The concord of discordant canons). Gratian was certainly influenced by the revival of the study of Roman law and its impact on legal studies.

Almost as important as the revival of the study of Roman law for the development of late medieval political theory was the rediscovery of Aristotle's political ideas. The metaphysical and scientific works of Aristotle, most of which were not known in the early Middle Ages, were gradually translated into Latin toward the end of the twelfth century. It was the translation of his *Politics* (*ca.* 1260) by William of Moerbeke that marked a high point in the reception of the works of the Stagirite. As a result, the Aristotelian, naturalistic notion of the state as a perfect society (*societas perfecta*), independent of any other entity, including the church, and sufficient unto itself, gained acceptance in the later Middle Ages and weakened the traditional, essentially negative conception of the state advanced by church fathers, especially St. Augustine: that the state came into being as a result of and as a remedy for the Fall of Man. At first the Roman church tried unsuccessfully to restrain the spread of Aristotelianism. Yet the vitality of Aristotle's ideas manifested itself as an increasing number of theologians, philosophers, and political theorists turned to the study of Aristotle.

The triumph of Aristotle in the thirteenth century was to a large extent due to the influence of Thomas Aquinas (1224–1274). Since Thomas was not a political theorist in the modern sense of the term, his political ideas must be culled from his various works, especially *De regimine principum* and *Summa theologiae*. Following Aristotle closely, Thomas stated that man is "naturally a social being." The state is a natural entity whose goal and justification is the good life. This naturalistic view of the state was tempered and modified in accordance with the teaching of his Christian philosophy. The ultimate purpose of social life is not merely to enjoy the good life, but to attain spiritual salvation. Thomas' greatest accomplishment was to synthesize Christianity and Aristotelianism.

Thomas followed Aristotle in classifying the forms of government into good types and bad types. He thought the best form of government was monarchy not only because "in the whole universe there is one God," but also because he identified unity with peace. In his famous analysis of law, which is more Stoic and Scholastic than Aristotelian, Thomas distinguished four forms: eternal law, natural law, divine law, and human law. He insisted that human law, which is defined as an "ordinance of reason for the common good, made by him who has care of the community, and promulgated," must be in accord with some rule of reason.

It has been suggested that Thomas, the greatest and the most moderate of all medieval Aristotelians, who tried with great success to "baptize Aristotle," contributed unconsciously to the weakening of the medieval, hierarchical synthesis that constituted the Christian commonwealth (*respublica Christiana*) by introducing a secular element into the synthesis.

GROWTH OF THE HIEROCRATIC THEORY

The so-called Gelasian theory, which since the early Middle Ages was regarded as the guiding principle concerning the relationship between the spiritual and the temporal hierarchy within the *respublica Christiana,* was first expressed in a letter of Pope Gelasius I (*r.* 492–496) to the Byzantine emperor Anastasius I (*r.* 491–518). While clearly admitting the dualistic, parallel existence of the pope's sacred authority (*auctoritas*) and the imperial power (*potestas*), the pope advocated the essential superiority of the spiritual power over the temporal power and laid the foundation for the later development of the monistic theory of papal supremacy. Most canon lawyers after the eleventh century accepted the Gelasian doctrine.

After the investiture controversy of the eleventh century, which was an attempt by Pope Gregory VII (*r.* 1073–1085) to restore the "right order" in the *respublica Christiana,* the curialist, essentially monistic doctrine concerning the two powers began to be advocated more forcefully. Gratian's work, which was popularly called *Decretum,* became the standard work on church law less than a century after its compilation. Like Gratian, most Decretists, who were commentators on the *Decretum,* regarded the pope as the legitimate holder of the "keys of the Kingdom of Heaven" that Christ had entrusted to St. Peter, although they did not assert that the papal power was unrestricted. We find in Decretists both a strong emphasis on the papal fullness of power (*plenitudo potestatis*) and at the same time a great respect for the indefectibility of the community. There were also many Decretists who held that a general council, which symbolized the universal consent of the whole church, was superior to the pope.

Since there were many ambiguous statements in the *Decretum* about the question of the two powers, Gratian has been regarded both as a monistic and as a dualistic thinker. That is why canon lawyers after Gratian could all appeal to and invoke him even though they were split into two camps concerning the question. Huguccio (*d.*1210), the most famous Decretist, clearly upheld the dualistic interpretation of the problem. Johannes Teutonicus (*d.* 1245), author of the influential *Glossa ordinaria,* essentially agreed with Huguccio, although he often vacillated. It can be said that Gratian in the *Decretum* and the Decretists in general stood for the traditional dualistic notion of two powers that were distinguished as to origin and field of action.

Pope Innocent III (*r.* 1198–1216) occupied a very important place in the development of the theory of two powers. Although the pope, who was a faithful pupil of Huguccio, supported a carefully delineated, dualistic theory of two powers, he certainly contributed to the later growth of the "hierocratic" theory of papal supremacy by regularly using *plenitudo potestatis* (fullness of power) as a description of papal governmental power, although it had been used in canonical writings since the fifth century. The hierocratic theory signifies the theory of direct power for the pope in temporal affairs.

Pope Innocent IV (*r.* 1243–1254), who was one of the foremost Decretalist lawyers of the thirteenth century, further strengthened the hierocratic tendencies seen in the views of Innocent III. According to Innocent IV, the jurisdiction of the pope, who is the highest competent judge of all men (*iudex ordinarius omnium*), extended not only to Christians but also to pagans. Since there was no legitimate authority outside the church, it was right to wage a crusade against Islam and Islamic countries. Other Decretalists, especially Hostiensis (*d.* 1271), developed similarly extreme ideas on papal *plenitudo potestatis.*

It is not accurate to think, however, that the so-called hierocratic theorists, such as Innocent IV and Hostiensis, completely rejected the dualistic theory of Gelasius. There is no denying that both Innocent III and Innocent IV advocated extension of papal powers. But contrary to the older view, which held that these popes were extreme hierocrats, recent studies tend to accept the theory that they were essentially dualistic thinkers who were aware of the existence of two hierarchies of government in medieval life. What is important in examining the political theorists of the later Middle Ages is to know, first, if they attributed direct or indirect power in temporal affairs to the pope, and second, if they gave him the power normally (*regulariter*) or only in cases of necessity (*casualiter*).

POPE BONIFACE VIII AND PHILIP THE FAIR

It was the dispute between Pope Boniface VIII (*r.* 1294–1303) and King Philip IV the Fair (*r.* 1285–1314) of France that produced an outburst of treatises and pamphlets dealing with the problem of papal power in temporal affairs. The adherents of the pope strongly supported his authority in all affairs of life, whether spiritual or temporal. The papal claims made in the bulls *Clericis laicos* (1296), *Ausculta fili* (1301), and *Unam sanctam* (1302) contained words and phrases that could be interpreted to support the doctrine of direct papal power in temporal affairs. King Philip's supporters, many of whom were trained in Roman law, argued for his independence in temporal affairs within the boundaries of his realm. The dispute was essentially a conflict of two principles: the hierocratic conception of Christian society and the emerging doctrine of national sovereignty.

It is noteworthy that three of the most important papal supporters—James of Viterbo (*d.* 1308), Egidius Colonna (*ca.* 1247–1316), and Augustinus Triumphus (*ca.* 1275–1328)—were members of the Augustinian order. In place of the canonists, who had set the pace in the thirteenth century, it was now a group of Augustinian friars who actively supported the papal claims. In his *De regimine christiano* (1301/1302), James of Viterbo advocated a system within which the church was superior in both spiritual and temporal affairs. But the *De ecclesiastica potestate* (1302) of Egidius Colonna was no doubt the most noteworthy defense of the illimitable direct power of the pope in temporal as well as spiritual spheres. In this work the Aristotelian-Thomist conception of the state as a natural community, which Egidius had expounded in the *De regimine principum* (*ca.* 1285), was replaced by a strong emphasis on the Augustinian view of the sinful condition of human nature and of the negative origin of the state. All legitimate lordship (*dominium*) is derived from the pope and is subject to his control. The pope is the ultimate owner of all the material goods in the world, and men who are alien to God cannot exercise any rightful dominion. No one can be lord of anything unless he is baptized by the church and in a state of grace. Although Egidius admitted that as a general rule the pope's *plenitudo potestatis* is to be exercised according to common law, he said that where any kind of spiritual issue is involved, the pope can exercise jurisdiction in temporal affairs and judge any case if he chooses to exercise his *plenitudo potestatis*.

Augustinus Triumphus is another important and well-known papalist of the fourteenth century. Of his no fewer than thirty-six works, the enormous *Summa de ecclesiastica potestate* (1328) best represents his mature thinking on political theory. To Augustinus the term *ecclesia* was synonymous with society at large and embraced both the spiritual and the temporal spheres. The powers of Christ, both *potestas ordinis* (sacramental power) and *potestas iurisdictionis* (jurisdictional power), were inherent in the *ecclesia*, which was the Mystical Body of Christ (*corpus Christi mysticum*). In terms of the *potestas ordinis*, the pope was not different from other bishops. But in regard to the *potestas iurisdictionis* there was only one vicar of Christ: the pope.

Stressing Christ's commission of governmental power to St. Peter alone in Matthew 16:18–19, Augustinus noted that the pope was the source of all governmental power exercised in a Christian society. Its holder was *caput ecclesiae* in place of Christ. As *vicarius Christi* the pope was in actuality Christ and had the *plenitudo potestatis* in both spheres, but it was the pope's possession of *potestas iurisdictionis* that made him *caput ecclesiae*. Some writers have asserted that Augustinus' logic led to a denial of the secular power. But his emphasis on the jurisdictional nature of the pope's powers had a considerable moderating influence on his otherwise strongly hierocratic theory. It was always necessary for Augustinus to distinguish between the infallible papal office and the fallible officer. According to him, the pope who became a heretic was no longer a true pope but a tyrant. A general council, acting on behalf of the entire body of the faithful (*congregatio fidelium*), could always replace the pope when necessary. Thus Augustinus, an ardent supporter of papal supremacy, becomes almost indistinguishable from an antihierocratic supporter of conciliar supremacy. It is nowadays generally acknowledged that of the foremost representatives of the papal hierocratic theory, Augustinus was a more moderate thinker than Egidius Colonna. In general, most papal apologists did not really advocate a doctrine of absolute papal supremacy in all spheres.

In response to the writings of the extreme papalists, many pro-royal pamphlets were written. But the most lucid and comprehensive reply to the papalist supporters was the *De potestate regia et papali* (1302/1303) of the French Dominican John of Paris (*d.* 1306), which was written to counter the works of Egidius Colonna and James of Viterbo.

Although John admitted that the *sacerdotium* was qualitatively superior in dignity to the *regnum,* he insisted that the spiritual power was not superior in all respects and was not entitled to claim supremacy in temporal affairs. Both take their power immediately from God. Hence the spiritual power was supreme in spiritual matters, while the temporal power was superior in temporal matters. His aim was clearly to argue for the independence of the *regnum Franciae.* But his position was not completely dualistic, for he allowed the emergency, or extraordinary, right of interference. There are cases, he said, where either power can take action in the other's sphere if negligence or misgovernment makes it necessary. John thus differed from real dualists, such as Dante, but his essentially dualistic theory was a response to the hierocratic theory of papal direct power in temporal affairs.

Clearly manifesting the influence of the corporation theory of the Decretalists, John stated that the church as a whole was a corporation and that the supreme authority of the church was spread throughout all its members. Because the pope was the vicar of Christ, he had *plenitudo potestatis,* but as *universalis dispensator* of ecclesiastical property, he did not possess *dominum* over church goods. He derived his authority as *dispensator* from the *congregatio fidelium.* Therefore, a pope could be deposed not only for heresy or notorious crime, but also for incompetence by the college of cardinals or a general council. John was not really a radical in temper and outlook; he essentially wished to restore a balance between the two powers that had been tipped inordinately in favor of papal power by hierocratic papalists.

Opposition to the papalist doctrine of *plenitudo potestatis* was also voiced by the great Italian poet Dante Alighieri (1265–1321). Studies have shown that Dante was quite abreast of the canonistic studies of his time despite his strong denunciations of the Decretalists in Book III of the *Monarchia* (*ca.* 1311/1313). There he argued that the world should be united under one sovereign ruler, that the Roman Empire was constituted and guided by God, and that the temporal world ruler came directly from God and not from the papacy. A world monarch was needed for the development of what he called "human civilization" (*humana civilitas*), which could not be attained without peace. His discussion on the relationship of the two powers has been long and hotly debated. Some writers have spoken of his essentially dualistic and moderate position; others have maintained that his position is contradictory, especially because of his sudden turnabout in the final section of Book III. It seems clear, however, that his manifest intention was to establish the principle that both spiritual and temporal powers derive directly from God.

MARSILIUS OF PADUA AND WILLIAM OF OCKHAM

Of all medieval political thinkers, probably no one has been more often praised, criticized, or vilified than Marsilius of Padua (*ca.* 1278–1342). His *Defensor pacis* (1324) was dedicated to Louis IV the Bavarian, who was then in the thick of his struggle with Pope John XXII (*r.* 1316–1334). A student of medicine rather than of theology, Marsilius apparently had no systematic knowledge of Scholastic theology. But he regarded Aristotle as almost infallible. Although he referred to Justinian's code a few times in the *Defensor pacis,* he did not cite a single civilian. His doctrine of a functioning community of citizens (*universitas civium*) may have been derived from his experience in and observation of the structure of northern Italian communes such as Padua.

Marsilius' central concern was to discredit any divinely granted papal primacy over the church. According to him, there was no *plenitudo potestatis* of the pope, no vicariate of Christ, and no Petrine succession. He discussed the problem of the state in general terms in *Dictio* I of the book, then proceeded to examine the essence and nature of the church in *Dictio* II. In discussing the nature of the state, Marsilius followed Aristotle closely, saying that the state was an organism composed of six parts. The priesthood was merely a part of the state. As the source of all political authority and the "efficient cause" of the laws in the Aristotelian sense, he discussed the *legislator humanus,* which meant the people or whole body of citizens, or the weightier part (*valentior pars*) thereof. In *Dictio* II, Marsilius' fundamental principle that the whole structure of the body politic depended on the will of the *legis-*

lator humanus was applied to the church, which was "the whole body of the faithful who believe in and invoke the name of Christ" (*universitas fidelium credentium et invocantium nomen Christi*). As the *universitas civium* must be the legislator in the political community, so in the church the *universitas fidelium* must define articles of faith, elect the pope, the priesthood, and the general council, and control excommunication.

The functions of the priesthood in the church were those of teaching and preaching the Word of God and administering the Sacraments. The priests had no coercive authority, spiritual or temporal, over either clergy or laymen. Only the civil government had coercive authority. Where there was, as a result of a new element unknown to Aristotle, civil discord, the chief disturber of the peace of Christendom was the *plenitudo potestatis* of the bishop of Rome. Having the final jurisdiction over church and papacy, the *legislator humanus* was to be the final judge in matters of heresy. The pope, if he erred and was accused of heresy, was to be judged by a rightly constituted general council composed of important men, both lay and clerical, who are the *pars valentior* of the Christian people.

The sweeping powers that Marsilius conferred on temporal authority and the coherence of the general argument in the *Defensor pacis* have impressed many commentators, some of whom have called his system "totalitarian." The *Defensor pacis* can certainly be called "one of the real landmarks not alone in the history of the struggle between church and state, but in the development of political thought as a whole."

It is remarkable how such different writers as Marsilius of Padua and William of Ockham (*ca.* 1285–1347) have often been grouped together as chief critics of the papacy. As the polemical and ecclesiastical works of Ockham have been more intensively studied, there has arisen a greater realization than before that Ockham, who was essentially Scholastic and traditional in his ecclesiological thought, was a more moderate thinker than the radical Marsilius.

Unlike Marsilius, Ockham does not devote any portion of his works to the theory of the state. His political ideas are expressed in theological terms. Following Johannes Teutonicus and Huguccio, Ockham, who cited canon law frequently, distinguished between the Universal Church and the Roman church. The former was the *corpus Christi mysticum* and the *congregatio fidelium;* the latter was not identical with the former. Only the Universal Church was the unfailing guardian of the truth, while the existing, institutionalized Roman church could err. In discussing the general council, Ockham departed from the canonical tradition. In contrast with the Universal Church, which was inerrant, the general council, which was merely a part of the Universal Church, could err. The Universal Church can be perfectly represented only by the sum total of its members.

Ockham's depreciation of the established ecclesiastical authorities and his essentially anticonciliar attitudes were due to his conviction that he and his friends belonged to a tiny minority holding fast to the faith when almost the whole of the Roman church had abandoned it. He fought as dangerous enemies the hierocrats and their exaggerated doctrine of papal *plenitudo potestatis* in both spiritual and temporal matters. According to him, a pope who persisted in heresy ceased to be pope. Not only a general council but any Christian who knew the pope to be a heretic could take action against him. Yet William always supported the autonomy and dignity of the pope. Thus he, like John of Paris and Dante, sought to restore the balance between the two powers that had been lost as a result of the doctrine of papal *plenitudo potestatis.*

THE CONCILIAR MOVEMENT

The political theory of the late fourteenth and fifteenth centuries was deeply influenced by the momentous events that took place in the Roman church. Shortly after the return of the papacy from Avignon to Rome in 1377, the church entered the period of the Great Schism (1378–1415), in which there were at first two opposing popes. When confronted with the difficult question of how to solve the Great Schism, two theorists, Conrad of Gelnhausen (*ca.* 1320–1390) and Henry of Langenstein (1325–1397), argued that the crisis should be resolved by a general council. When advocated by John of Paris and Marsilius, the doctrine of conciliar supremacy was merely an academic theory. But when it became clear that all other suggested proposals and solutions were unworkable or impossible, it began to assume a great significance as the only practical method of ending the Great Schism.

Meeting in 1408, thirteen cardinals decided to call a general council at Pisa the next year. The Council of Pisa elected Alexander V as pope in June 1409, but matters were made worse because of the refusal of the other two popes to step down. The

Council of Constance was summoned in 1414 and was attended by some of the leading conciliar theorists: Cardinals Pierre d'Ailly (1350–1420) and Francesco Zaberella (*ca.* 1360–1417), the German Dietrich of Niem (*d.* 1418), and the Frenchman John Gerson (1363–1429). On 6 April 1415 the council adopted the decree *Haec sancta,* which asserted the doctrine of conciliar supremacy. On 7 October 1417 the decree *Frequens* was proclaimed; it stated that it would be necessary to hold general councils on a regular basis. Only one month thereafter the council brought the Great Schism to an end by electing Martin V (*r.* 1417–1431) as undisputed pope.

The Council of Basel, which was opened by Pope Eugenius IV in 1431, was almost at once involved in troubles with him. As the influence of the lower clergy increased, the council took a series of antipapal measures. In 1437 the council split into a majority and a minority over the question of reunion with the Greek church. The majority party, which remained in Basel, chose the antipope Felix V in 1439, adhering tenaciously to the doctrine of conciliar supremacy. Thus that doctrine, which had enabled the Council of Constance to effect the reunion of the two churches, brought about a breakup of the church once more and began to lose its popularity.

Nicholas of Cusa (1401–1464) was the theorist who presented the most impressive synthesis of conciliar ideas. In *De concordantia catholica,* which he presented to the Council of Basel late in 1433 or early in 1434, he strongly defended the theory of conciliar supremacy. He is famous for his emphasis on consent in legislation and government: "[S]ince all men are by nature free," he wrote, "every rulership whether it is by written law or by living law . . . can only come from the agreement and consent of the subjects." But one of the main tasks of the work was to consider the problem of the church from the viewpoint of the relationship between the pope and the general council. In Book I of the work, Nicholas discussed the church, which meant the whole union of believers (*congregatio fidelium*). Book II was on the priesthood (*sacerdotium*), or the "soul" of the church; Book III treated the empire (*sacrum imperium*) as the "body" of the church.

In describing the organization of the church, Nicholas said that no assembly is rightfully called a general council unless it includes the pope or his legate. He also carefully distinguished among different kinds of councils. The general council, which represents the universal church, is above the pope and is less infallible than the pope alone, although it is not always inerrant. But the patriarchical general council (*concilium universale patriarchale*), which is presided over by the pope, is always inerrant because the *sedes Romana* is never wrong. These ideas of Nicholas of Cusa indicate that he was not an advocate of extreme popular sovereignty in the church.

After the split of the Council of Basel into two factions, Nicholas sided with the propapal, minority party. Rejecting the radical position of the majority party that the choice was "either the pope or the council," he took a more moderate position of "the pope and the council." His change of position from conciliarism to papalism showed unmistakably that he now preferred the more hierarchical, Neoplatonic conception of the church that was at the heart of the pro-papal hierocratic theory. Indeed, it can be said that the restoration of unity in the church in 1416 had weakened the theory of conciliar supremacy and hastened the return of the hierocratic theory of the church. Nicholas' move over to the papal camp was certainly not an isolated case, and perhaps reflected a general change in mood and attitude among some prominent leaders of the church from the conciliar movement to conservative papal absolutism.

The monumental *Summa de ecclesia* (1449–1453) of John of Turrecremata (1388–1468), which defended papal absolutism against the claims of the Council of Basel, and the *De ortu et auctoritate imperii Romani* (1446) of Aeneas Sylvius Piccolomini (later Pope Pius II), which stressed the absolute authority of the political ruler, demonstrate that a shift was taking place from the conciliar movement as a manifestation of late medieval constitutionalism to a period of modern absolutism. It may be said that history was moving from a period in which the theory of conciliar supremacy had emerged as an antithesis to the theory of papal absolutism to a period in which the principle of absolutism was to rise as a reaction to the theory of conciliar supremacy.

BIBLIOGRAPHY

Sources. The modern editions and translations of the main works by authors cited in the article are Aeneas Sylvius Piccolomini, *De ortu et auctoritate imperii Romani,* Rudolf Wolkan, ed., in *Der Briefwechsel des*

Eneas Silvius Piccolomini, II (*Fontes rerum Austriacarum,* 67) (1912), 6–24, German translation by Gerhard Kallen (1939); Augustinus Triumphus, *Tractatus brevis de duplici potestate,* Richard Scholz, ed., in his *Die Publizistik zur Zeit Philipps des Schönen und Bonifaz VIII* (1903), 486–501; Dante Alighieri, *Monarchia,* Pier Giorgio Ricci, ed. (1965), trans. by Donald Nicholl (1954) and by Herbert W. Schneider, 2nd ed. (1957); Dietrich von Niem, *De modis uniendi et reformandi ecclesiam in concilio universali,* Hermann Heimpel, ed. (1933, repr. 1969); Egidius Colonna, *De ecclesiastica potestate,* Richard Scholz, ed. (1929); John Gerson, *Oeuvres complètes,* Palémon Glorieux, ed., 10 vols. (1960–1973); James of Viterbo, *De regimine Christiano,* Henri-Xavier Arquillière, ed. (1926); John of Paris, *Tractatus de potestate regia et papali,* Jean Leclercq, ed., in his *Jean de Paris et l'ecclésiologie du XIIIe siècle* (1942), 171–260, trans. by John A. Watt (1971) and by Arthur P. Monahan (1974), German translation by Fritz Bleienstein (1969); John of Salisbury, *Policraticus,* Clement C. J. Webb, ed. (1909), trans. by John Dickinson (1927); Marsilius of Padua, *Defensor pacis,* Charles W. Previté-Orton, ed. (1928), and Richard Scholz, ed., 2 vols. (1932–1933), English translation by Alan Gewirth (1956); Nicholas of Cusa, *De concordantia catholica,* Gerhard Kallen, ed. (Lib. I, 2nd ed. 1964; Lib. II, 2nd ed. 1965; Lib. III, 2nd ed. 1959; indices, 1968); Thomas Aquinas, *Selected Political Writing,* Alexander Passerin d'Entrèves, ed., with trans. by J. G. Dawson (1948); William of Ockham, *Opera politica,* J. G. Sikes, ed. (1960–).

Studies. Works that deal with general political theory during the period from 1100 to 1485 include Robert W. Carlyle and Alexander J. Carlyle, *Mediaeval Political Theory in the West,* 6 vols. (1903–1936); Alexander Passerin d'Entrèves, *The Medieval Contribution to Political Thought* (1939, repr. 1959); Otto Gierke, *Political Theories of the Middle Age,* Frederic W. Maitland, trans. (1900, repr. 1958); Georges de Lagarde, *La naissance de l'esprit laïque au déclin du moyen âge,* 6 vols. (1934–1946), new ed., 5 vols. (1956–1970); Ewart Lewis, *Medieval Political Ideas,* 2 vols. (1954); Charles H. McIlwain, *The Growth of Political Thought in the West* (1932); John B. Morrall, *Political Thought in Medieval Times,* 3rd ed. (1971); Walter Ullmann, *A History of Political Thought: The Middle Ages* (1965).

The following is a select list of publications organized according to the sections of this essay.

Twelfth-century discoveries. Quirinus Breen, "The Twelfth-century Revival of Roman Law," in his *Christianity and Humanism* (1968); Stanley Chodorow, *Christian Political Theory and Church Politics in the Mid-twelfth Century* (1972); Thomas Gilby, *Principality and Polity: Aquinas and the Rise of State Theory in the West* (1958); Stephan G. Kuttner, *Harmony from Dissonance: An Interpretation of Medieval Canon Law* (1960); Gaines Post, *Studies in Medieval Legal Thought: Public Law and the State 1100–1322* (1964).

The growth of the hierocratic theory. Michele Maccarone, *Chiesa e stato nella dottrina di Papa Innocenzo III* (1940); William D. McCready, "Papal Plenitudo Potestatis and the Source of Temporal Authority in Late Medieval Papal Hierocratic Theory," in *Speculum,* **48** (1973); James Muldoon, "Extra ecclesiam non est imperium: The Canonists and the Legitimacy of Secular Power," in *Studia Gratiana,* **9** (1966); Brian Tierney, *Origins of Papal Infallibility 1150–1350* (1972); Walter Ullmann, *Medieval Papalism: The Political Theories of the Medieval Canonists* (1949), and *The Growth of Papal Government in the Middle Ages,* 3rd ed. (1970); John A. Watt, *The Theory of Papal Monarchy in the Thirteenth Century* (1965).

Pope Boniface VIII and Philip the Fair. Alexander Passerin d'Entrèves, *Dante as a Political Thinker* (1952); Jean Leclercq, *Jean de Paris et l'ecclésiologie du XIIIe siècle* (1942); William D. McCready, "The Papal Sovereignty in the Ecclesiology of Augustinus Triumphus," in *Mediaeval Studies,* **39** (1977); J. Rivière, *Le problème de l'église et de l'état au temps de Philippe le Bel* (1926); Paul Saenger, "John of Paris, Principal Author of the *Quaestio de potestate papae (Rex pacificus),*" in *Speculum,* **56** (1981); Michael J. Wilks, *The Problem of Sovereignty in the Later Middle Ages* (1963).

Marsilius of Padua and William of Ockham. Charles C. Bayley, "Pivotal Concepts in the Political Philosophy of William of Ockham," in *Journal of the History of Ideas,* **10** (1949); Philotheus Boehner, "Ockham's Political Ideas," in *Review of Politics,* **5** (1943); Alan Gewirth, *Marsilius of Padua,* I (1951); Helmar Junghans, *Ockham im Lichte der neueren Forschung* (1968); Arthur S. McGrade, *The Political Thought of William of Ockham* (1974); Gregorio Piaia, *Marsilio da Padova nella riforma e nella controriforma* (1977); Carlo Pincin, *Marsilio* (1967); Friedrich Prinz, "Marsilius von Padua," in *Zeitschrift für bayerische Landesgeschichte,* **39** (1976); Jeannine Quillet, *La philosophie politique de Marsile de Padoue* (1970).

The conciliar movement. Remigius Bäumer, ed. *Die Entwicklung des Konziliarismus* (1976); Antony J. Black, *Monarchy and Community* (1970) and *Council and Commune: The Conciliar Movement and the Council of Basel* (1979); C. M. D. Crowder, ed., *Unity, Heresy and Reform, 1378–1460* (1977); Ernest. F. Jacob, *Essays in the Conciliar Epoch,* 3rd ed. (1963); Erich Meuthen, *Nikolaus von Kues, 1401–1464,* 5th ed. (1982); John B. Morrall, *Gerson and the Great Schism* (1960); Thomas E. Morrissey, "Emperor-elect Sigismund, Cardinal Zabarella, and the Council of Constance," in *Catholic Historical Review,* **69** (1983); Francis Oakley, *The Political Thought of Pierre d'Ailly* (1964), Louis B. Pascoe, *Jean Gerson: Principles of Church Reform* (1973); Paul E. Sigmund, *Nicholas of Cusa and Medieval Political*

Thought (1963); Joachim W. Stieber, *Pope Eugenius IV, the Council of Basel, and the Secular and Ecclesiastical Authorities in the Empire* (1978); Brian Tierney, *Foundations of the Conciliar Theory* (1955) and *Religion, Law and the Growth of Constitutional Thought 1150–1650* (1982); Walter Ullmann, *The Origins of the Great Schism* (1948, repr. 1967); Morimichi Watanabe, *The Political Ideas of Nicholas of Cusa, with Special Reference to His "De concordantia catholica"* (1963).

Karl Binder, *Konzilsdenken bei Kardinal Juan de Torquemada O.P.* (1976); Thomas M. Izbicki, *Protector of the Faith: Cardinal Johannes de Turrecremata and the Defense of the Institutional Church* (1983); Gerhard Kallen, *Aeneas Silvius Piccolomini als Publizist in der "Epistola de ortu et auctoritate imperii Romani"* (1939); Morimichi Watanabe, "Authority and Consent in Church Government: Panormitanus, Aeneas Sylvius, Cusanus," in *Journal of the History of Ideas,* 33 (1972); Berthe Widmer, *Enea Silvio Piccolomini in der sittlichen und politischen Entscheidung* (1963).

MORIMICHI WATANABE

[See also **Aristotle in the Middle Ages; Bologna, University of; Church, Latin: 1305 to 1500; Conciliar Theory; Corpus Iuris Civilis; Councils, Western (1311–1449); Decretists; Decretum; Defensor Pacis; Glossators; Investiture and Investiture Conflict; Law, Canon: After Gratian; Papacy, Origins and Development of; Plenitudo Potestatis; Postglossators; Schism, Great;** and individual personalities.]

POLL TAX, ENGLISH. Poll taxes were levied in 1377, 1379, and 1381 on all adults in England, except for those in the exempt jurisdictions of Cheshire and Durham, in order to finance the country's war against the French. The first poll tax was granted in February 1377 by the last Parliament of Edward III. One groat (four pence) was collected from all lay persons fourteen years of age or older, with the exception of those who regularly begged for a living. A separate tax was exacted from the clergy; beneficed clergy paid one shilling and the unbeneficed paid four pence. The mendicant clergy were exempt from the tax. This tax, the first in England to be assessed per head rather than on the basis of property or wealth, was a financial success; about £20,000 was raised for war expenditures.

The second poll tax was awarded in May 1379 by Parliament to Richard II, but was collected on a graduated scale of assessment, according to rank and income, from the clergy and all lay persons sixteen years of age or older. Beggars were again free of the tax and married women were assessed with their husbands. The tax ranged from four pence levied from the poorest lay and clerical inhabitants to as much as ten marks (£6. 13s. 4d.) assessed on archbishops and the dukes of Lancaster and Brittany.

The third poll tax was granted in November 1380 by Parliament and in 1381 was levied on all persons fifteen years of age or older, with the exception of genuine beggars. Like the 1377 tax, the 1381 poll tax was imposed at a flat rate per head, but at the rate of one shilling per person, it was three times the 1377 tax. Wealthier inhabitants within each community, however, were encouraged to shoulder a larger share of the tax burden, provided that no man paid more than twenty shillings, or less than four pence, for himself and his wife.

The 1377 poll tax has often been used by historians to estimate medieval populations, since the returns listed either the numbers taxed or the sums collected (from which the numbers taxed may be easily calculated). The 1379 poll tax, however, cannot be used to estimate populations because of widespread evasion and the gradation of the tax, which makes it impossible to derive population figures from the sums noted in the returns. But, in contrast to the 1377 tax, the 1379 returns list each taxpayer by name and, frequently, by occupation and therefore provide a valuable outline of household and occupational structure in medieval English communities. Similarly, the 1381 returns also contain names, but the recording of occupations is less common. Furthermore, evasion of the 1381 tax was even more widespread; there were only two-thirds as many taxpayers in 1381 as in 1377. Unmarried females were especially underenumerated. The 1381 poll tax, which came at the end of a decade of heavy taxation in England and fell most heavily upon the poorest classes, has also been singled out by historians as one of the immediate causes of the 1381 Peasants' Rebellion in England.

BIBLIOGRAPHY

Maurice W. Beresford, "The Poll Taxes of 1377, 1379, and 1381," in *The Amateur Historian,* 3, no. 7 (1958), reprinted with some changes in his *The Lay Subsidies: The Poll Taxes of 1377, 1379, and 1381* (1963); Carolyn C. Fenwick, "The English Poll Taxes of 1377, 1379, and 1381: A Critical Examination of the Returns" (diss., Univ. of London, 1983); Charles Oman,

The Great Revolt of 1381 (1906), 22–31, 158–185; Josiah C. Russell, *British Medieval Population* (1948), 118–146; Thomas F. Tout, *Chapters in the Administrative History of England,* III (1928), 348–368.

MARYANNE KOWALESKI

[See also **England (1216–1485); Peasants' Rebellion; Taxation, English.**]

POLL TAX, ISLAMIC. Non-Muslim residents of Islamic states (dhimmis) were required to pay the tax or tribute known as the *jizya,* as the Koran legislates: "Fight those to whom the Book has come who believe not in God and the Last Day . . . until they pay the *jizya* out of hand, in humility" (9:29).

In the early days of Islam, there was no uniform policy for taxation on non-Muslims in either theory or practice. Wide variations appear to reflect differing types of conquest and especially the various Byzantine and Sasanian practices previously in force in the conquered areas. From at least the ninth century, Islamic law held that the *jizya* applied to all sane, healthy, male adult non-Muslims, except the old and indigent. The amount was fixed by jurists at either a fixed rate, usually one dinar or twelve dirhams per year, or a graduated rate, one dinar for the poor, two for the middle class, and four for the wealthy. The poll tax was often set as a lump sum for an entire town or community. Dhimmis who converted to Islam were freed from the *jizya,* although they became subject to the tithe and alms tax.

BIBLIOGRAPHY

C. Cahen, "Djizya," in *Encyclopedia of Islam,* II (1965); Daniel C. Dennett, *Conversion and the Poll Tax in Early Islam* (1950); Frede Løkkegaard, *Islamic Taxation in the Classic Period* (1950); both of these are reprinted in *Islamic Taxation: Two Studies* (1973).

SETH WARD

[See also **Taxation, Islamic.**]

POLO, MARCO (1254–1324), merchant and explorer, was born in Venice. He made his journey to China with his father Niccolo and his uncle Maffeo at the age of seventeen. They left Italy in 1271 and by May 1275 had reached Chandu (Xanadu, K'ai-p'ing-fu), north of the Great Wall of China. This was the summer residence of Kublai Khan, emperor of China and the overlord of all the vast Mongol domains. Marco entered the service of the great khan, while his father and uncle continued their commercial activities. As an important Mongol inspector, the young Venetian took part in missions to Yunnan and to Indochina, and for three years governed a Chinese town. In 1292 he was ordered to accompany a Mongol princess to Persia, where she was to marry Arghun Khan, the Mongol ruler of that country. From Persia he continued his journey to the West and in 1295 returned to Venice, after an absence of twenty-four years. In 1296 he was captured in the naval battle of Curzola, during a war between Venice and Genoa and was imprisoned in Genoa, where he was held three years. There he dictated the story of his travels to Rusticello, a Pisan. Freed in May 1299, at the age of forty-five, he returned to Venice, where he lived for twenty-five years more.

Marco Polo's account, *Il milione* or, as originally titled, *Divisament dou Monde* (The description of the world; better known in English as *The Travels of Marco Polo*), was written down in a mixture of Italian and French, very like the *lingua franca* spoken in the Latin East after the establishment of the Latin Empire of Constantinople in 1204. The use of this language gave his story a large audience. It told how, after leaving Asia Minor, Marco crossed Mesopotamia and the Persian Gulf and reached Hormuz. Then, going through Persia and the Pamir plateau, he arrived at Cambaluc (Peking), residence of the grand khan Kublai, who had become emperor of China. He remained in Cathay (medieval China) for seventeen years, and traveled widely through the country. Marco also mentioned Japan—although he never visited that country—and told some fantastic stories about it. These stories, however, made a great impression because he claimed that the country was full of gold and pearls. In the last centuries of the Middle Ages the mirage of Japanese gold dazzled the minds of many readers of the "Book of Marvels," as it was soon called. In 1428 Prince Pedro of Portugal acquired a copy at Venice, so it seems likely that his brother, Henry the Navigator, also read it. When Columbus left Spain in 1492 he hoped to find the golden roofs of Cipangu (the Chinese name for Japan).

Marco Polo, on his return journey to Europe through southern Asia, crossed India. This country, like Japan and China, seemed to inhabitants of the West a land of wealth and spices. Thus, Marco's book became a sort of catalogue of the riches of Asia. What he said of the spice trade at Zayton (now Ch'üan-chou), the great port of south China, also had an almost hypnotic influence on the minds of later European explorers. His description of Java made it seem a paradise of spices, while the Malabar Coast (southwest India) appeared to be a paradise of precious stones and other treasures.

Medieval readers were also struck by Marco Polo's account of the size and magnificence of the cities he had visited, above all, those of China. He visited Hangchow (which he called Kinsai) several times. This city, the capital of southern China, which was conquered by the Mongols in 1279, was much larger than any European city. For Marco Polo it was a symbol of the enormous power of the great khan.

On the whole the "Book of Marvels" is a collection of curiosities—geographic, historical, physical, economic, and technical. Of its 234 chapters there are only eighteen on the journey itself. It is the work of a good observer, but of an observer who has a lively imagination and a head full of fantasies. Marco Polo was writing about the most picturesque countries in the world, writing with enthusiasm and without much sense of order. Nevertheless, he has charmed and continues to charm all those who love stories of adventure. This is what has made Marco Polo the most famous explorer of the Middle Ages, far better known than his thirteenth-century predecessors, John of Plano Carpini and William of Rubruck, both monks and diplomatic envoys of the pope and the king of France, who wrote in Latin about their travels through the deserts of central Asia.

BIBLIOGRAPHY

Marco Polo, *Il milione,* Luigi Foscolo Benedetto, ed. (1928); Henry Yule, ed. and trans., *The Book of Ser Marco Polo,* 3rd ed. rev. and enl. by Henri Cordier, 2 vols. (1903); Paul Pelliot, *Notes on Marco Polo,* 3 vols. (1959–1973).

CHARLES VERLINDEN

[See also **Exploration by Western Europeans; John of Plano Carpini; Khan; Mongol Empire; Travel and Transport; Venice.**]

POLOVTSIANS. See **Russia, Nomadic Invasions of.**

POLYCANDELON, a type of Byzantine chandelier. The standard form was a flat metal disc decorated with openwork, which held glass oil lamps and, less often, both oil lamps and candles, and was suspended by chains. Sometimes the base was cruciform, and an unusual type was in the form of a church. Surviving examples of polycandela are of bronze or silver, but none preserves the original glass lamps. Polycandela apparently came into use between the fourth and sixth centuries and were common lighting devices in Byzantine churches. They were also used in a secular context.

Bronze polycandelon from Constantinople. COURTESY OF THE BYZANTINE COLLECTION, DUMBARTON OAKS, ACC. NO. 40–19, Trustees of Harvard University, Washington, D.C.

BIBLIOGRAPHY

Laskarina Bouras, "Byzantine Lighting Devices," in *Jahrbuch der österreichisches Byzantinistik,* **32,** pt. 3 (1982), 480, plates 3, 4, 6; Kurt Weitzmann, ed., *Age of Spirituality: Late Antique and Early Christian Art, Third to Seventh Century* (1979), 595, 622–623.

ROBERT OUSTERHOUT

[See also **Lighting Devices.**]

POLYPTYCH (1), literally, any object with many folds. First used to describe folding or hinged documents, the term now normally refers to paintings or sculptural reliefs made up of two or more panels, which may or may not be hinged to fold, and which are most commonly used as altarpieces. Works composed of two panels (often ivories or devotional images) are called diptychs; three-panel works (usually ivories or altarpieces), triptychs. From the fourteenth century, the term "polyptych" may include altarpieces with a narrow painted strip called a predella that extends across the base. Notable examples are Duccio di Buoninsegna's *Maestà* (originally with a predella, 1308–1311) and Hubert and Jan van Eyck's *Ghent Altarpiece* (*ca.* 1425/1426–1432).

BIBLIOGRAPHY

Donald L. Ehresmann, "Some Observations on the Role of Liturgy in the Early Winged Altarpiece," in *Art Bulletin,* **64** (1982); H. Hager, *Die Anfänge des italienischen Altarbildes* (1962); Otto Pächt, "The 'Avignon Diptych' and Its Eastern Ancestry," in *De artibus opuscula XL: Essays in Honor of Erwin Panofsky,* Millard Meiss, ed., I (1961). For works dealing with Early Christian ivory diptychs, see the bibliography under "Diptych."

LESLIE BRUBAKER

[See also **Altarpiece; Diptych; Duccio di Buoninsegna; Ghent Altarpiece; Marzal de Sax; Orcagna, Andrea; Panel Painting; Retable; Triptych** (most with illustrations).]

POLYPTYCH (2), a land book containing an inventory of all or part of the lands of an estate or seigniory, together with the names of the men as well as the payment and service obligations attached to these lands, the information having been gathered through a formal inquisition with sworn witnesses. The name comes from the many-leaved tablet (Greek: *polyptychon*) on which the earliest of these books were written, and it was applied to books with other contents as well. Although this term was in use from late Roman times and at least from the eighth to the fourteenth century to describe land books, the content of these books underwent evolution as the nature of landlord-tenant relations changed and as the purposes served by the books became more economic than political. Among many other terms used for these books are terrier, *censier* (favored by French scholars), *liber censualis* or *censuum, Urbar* (favored by German scholars), and *urbarium.* The relation of the Carolingian polyptych to the Roman *cadastre* or tax lists is a matter still under debate. Famous polyptychs include that of the Parisian abbey of St. Germain-des-Prés commissioned by Abbot Irminon (806–829) and the Domesday Book of William the Conqueror. Several considerations limit the value of polyptychs as bases for historical generalization: For example, from the earlier Middle Ages relatively few survive and they come from a rather narrow region of Western Europe and deal almost exclusively with church property; they may overlook the lands on the manor reserved to the lord or be incomplete in other ways; they may describe the ideal rather than the actual; and only large estates tended to have them. Nevertheless, they remain the best available source of demographic information for the earlier Middle Ages. They are fundamental, especially after 1300, for examining the structure of the seigniory, and they are vital to the study of the rural economy and society.

BIBLIOGRAPHY

The basic work is Robert Fossier, *Polyptyques et censiers* (1978). See also Georges Duby, *The Early Growth of the European Economy* (1974), 78–83; Walter Goffart, "From Roman Taxation to Mediaeval Seigneurie: Three Notes," note 3, "Flodoard and the Frankish Polptychs," in *Speculum,* **47** (1972); Benjamin Guérard, ed., *Polyptyque de l'abbé Irminon; ou, Dénombrement des manses, des serfs, et des revenus de l'abbaye de Saint-Germain-des-Prés sous le règne de Charlemagne,* 2 vols. (1844) (also edited by Auguste Honoré Longnon, 2 vols. [1886–1895]); Paul Lehmann, "Mittelalterliche Büchertitel," in *Sitzungsberichte der Bayerischen Akademie der Wissenschaften,* IV (1948); Émile Lesne, *Histoire de la propriété ecclésiastique en France,* III, *L'inventaire de la propriété: Églises et trésors des églises du commencement du VIIIe à la fin du XIe siècle* (1936), 1–83; Wolfgang Metz, "Zur Geschichte und

Kritik der frühmittelalterlichen Güterverzeichnisse Deutschlands," in *Archiv für Diplomatik,* 4 (1958); Charles H. Taylor, "Note on the Origin of the Polyptychs," in *Mélanges d'histoire offerts à Henri Pirenne,* II (1926), 475–481.

JAMES J. JOHN

[See also **Demography; Domesday Book; Estate Management.**]

PONTIFICAL, a book, for use by a bishop or pontiff, of noneucharistic ceremonial *ordines* or directions with formularies corresponding to the sacramentary. Before the development of the pontifical, texts for use by the bishop, such as those used for the dedication of churches or the ordination of clergy, were kept in separate *libelli* or booklets with one or more *ordines* and in sacramentaries (which were and still are occasionally called pontificals when made for a bishop). Gradually these texts were combined, sometimes with didactic treatises on the liturgy, to form a single book, which could easily be consulted by a bishop. The earliest pontificals, dating back to the ninth century, are often poorly arranged and at times include doublets in their texts, thereby demonstrating their origins in older collections of *libelli.* Moreover, in the early pontificals there is a great deal of material incorporated that could be used by *sacerdotes* in either the episcopal or presbyteral orders.

Besides the Roman rite, whose pontifical eventually came to dominate, other early liturgical rites had their own pontificals. For the Old Spanish or Mozarabic rite there existed the episcopal *Liber ordinum,* whose texts go back to the seventh century and earlier, but whose only witness now is in an eleventh-century codex (MS 4) from the northern Spanish monastery of Silos. The Milanese rite had its own pontifical at least by the tenth century, but it is clearly romanized. In the British Isles the churches had their own pontificals at least by the tenth century, reflecting in part older rites used in Ireland and England. Among these Insular pontificals is the famous *Claudius Pontifical* (London, British Library, Cotton Claudius A. iii, s. X).

By the middle of the tenth century a new pontifical had been compiled at Mainz, which was to provide the basis for the Roman pontifical used in large parts of Europe throughout the remainder of the Middle Ages and into modern times. This pontifical, now called the *Pontificale romano-germanicum,* contained ceremonial Ordines, texts from the sacramentaries, didactic treatises, and texts of canon law. It spread quickly into France, England, Poland, and Italy, and was accepted in Rome by the eleventh century.

By the end of the eleventh century and the period of the so-called Gregorian Reform this pontifical was undergoing modifications to remove its more Germanic elements, such as rituals for trial by ordeal. This simplified pontifical, now called the *Pontificale romanum XII saeculi,* was rapidly diffused outside of Rome as the church attempted to suppress other rites, such as the Old Spanish, and to impose its own books and liturgical uses throughout the Western church.

During the pontificate of Innocent III a new version of the Roman pontifical was created especially for ceremonies at the Lateran, and this book goes under the name of *Pontificale romanae curiae.* This pontifical, which is found in at least three major recensions, spread rapidly throughout Europe, and there are many manuscripts of it either in a fairly pure form or in forms adapted to local usage.

According to Vogel, about 1292 the great legal and liturgical scholar Guillaume Durand of Mende began to compile a beautifully ordered new pontifical, now called the *Pontificale Guilelmi Durandi.* Using earlier versions of the Roman pontificals and elements of local usage, Durand ordered his material into three parts concerning persons, places, and the liturgical year and offices. A particularly important feature of this pontifical was that functions of a simple priest that had been included in older Roman pontificals were omitted by Durand, thereby resulting in a pure pontifical. This enormously popular pontifical provided the basis for the first printed edition of the Roman pontifical by Agostino Patrizzi Piccolomini and Johannes Burchard in 1485.

Together with their obvious value as witnesses to episcopal ceremonial practice, medieval pontificals are especially noted for their illuminations. As books made for some of the most important and influential ecclesiastical officers in Western Christendom, pontificals were often handsomely illustrated, and among the most frequently illustrated ceremonies are those showing clerical ordinations (whose texts often came first in the manuscripts) and regal and imperial coronations.

BIBLIOGRAPHY
Richard W. Pfaff, *Medieval Latin Liturgy: A Select Bibliography* (1982), 36; N. K. Rasmussen, *Les pontificaux du haut moyen âge,* 3 vols. (diss., Paris, 1978); Roger E. Reynolds, "The Portrait of the Ecclesiastical Officers in the *Ragnaldus Sacramentary* and Its Liturgico-Canonical Significance," in *Speculum,* **34** (1972), "The *De officiis vii graduum:* Its Origins and Early Medieval Development," in *Mediaeval Studies,* **34** (1972), *The Ordinals of Christ from Their Origins to the Twelfth Century* (1978), "'At Sixes and Sevens'—and Eights and Nines: The Sacred Mathematics of Sacred Orders in the Early Middle Ages," in *Speculum,* **54** (1979), "The 'Isidorian' *Epistula ad Leudefredum:* An Early Medieval Epitome of the Clerical Duties," in *Mediaeval Studies,* **41** (1979), "Image and Text: The Liturgy of Clerical Ordination in Early Medieval Art," in *Gesta,* **22** (1983), "The Ordination Rite in Medieval Spain: Hispanic, Roman, and Hybrid," in Bernard F. Reilly, ed., *Santiago, Saint-Denis, and Saint Peter: The Reception of the Roman Liturgy in Leon-Castile in 1080* (1985), and "The Ordination of Clerics in Toledo and Castile After the Reconquista According to the 'Romano-Catalan' Rite," in *II. Congreso Internacional de Estudios Mozarabes: IX. Centenario de la Reconquista de Toledo 1085–1985,* R. Gonzálvez-Ruiz, ed. (1987); Cyrille Vogel, *Introduction aux sources de l'histoire du culte chrétien au moyen âge* (1975).

ROGER E. REYNOLDS

[See also **Collectarium; Gallican Rite; Liturgy, Treatises on; Manuscripts, Celtic Liturgical; Mass, Liturgy of the; Milanese Rite; Missal; Mozarabic Rite; Ordinale; Ordines Romani; Sacramentary.**]

PONTUS (Greek: Pontos), originally Cappadocia-on-the-Pontus, referring to the Black Sea. In antiquity it was the name for the mountainous region of northeastern Anatolia lying along the southeast coast of the Black Sea. Geographically Pontus consisted of a narrow but fertile coastal lowland south of which lay parallel mountain ranges separated by trenchlike river valleys. On the west it was bounded by the watershed between the Scylax River (Çekerek) and the valley of the Halys (Kizil Irmak), and on the east by the mouth of the Acampsis (Çoruh), that is, on the west by Paphlagonia and on the east by Colchis. Inland it extended across the coastal mountains (the Paryadres or Pontic Alps) to the parallel range that separated it from Cappadocia proper. Between the two ranges lay the fertile valleys of the Iris (Yesil Irmak) and its tributary, the Lycus (Kelkit). A land of rugged grandeur and beautiful forests (oak, beech, and, in the uplands, fir), Pontus possessed a lush, Riviera-like coast, whose mild climate yielded rich crops of grain and fruit. The chief wealth of the region, however, lay in the rich mineral deposits of the mountains (iron, copper, silver, and salt), as well as in the ample timber used for shipbuilding.

Originally a part of Cappadocia proper, Pontus was annexed by Rome as a province in A.D. 64. In the reorganization of Justinian (536) Polemoniac Pontus—the greater part of ancient Pontus—was divided between the Byzantine provinces of Armenia I and Armenia II (the former renamed Greater Armenia in 591). Later, under Heraklios (610–642), all of Pontus was included in the large Armeniac theme, reflecting the considerable and growing Armenian population of the region. This entity was then dissolved into four smaller themes, of which the Armeniac included western Pontus; the Khaldian, eastern Pontus; and the Koloneian, the Pontic hinterland. In 1204, Pontus became the independent Greek Empire of Trebizond under the Komnenoi dynasty. With its prosperity based both upon trade and the Pontic mineral wealth, Trebizond flourished until conquered by the Ottoman Turks in 1461.

BIBLIOGRAPHY
Nicholas Adontz, *Armenia in the Period of Justinian,* Nina G. Garsoïan, trans. (1970); J. G. C. Anderson *et al., Studia pontica,* 3 vols. (1903–1910); David Magie, *Roman Rule in Asia Minor,* 2 vols. (1950), 177–231, 1066–1110; William M. Ramsay, *The Historical Geography of Asia Minor* (1890, repr. 1972), 317–329.

ROBERT H. HEWSEN

[See also **Alexios I of Trebizond; Anatolia; Andronikos I Komnenos; Armenia: Geography; Byzantine Empire: History; Fairs; Themes; Trebizond.**]

POPE. Elements of a papal definition assumed their medieval shape from the time of Leo I (*ca.* 400–461). While the title "pope" (Greek: *papas;* Latin: *papa*) conveyed by itself only a general sense of spiritual fatherhood and was not, in Western practice, finally restricted to bishops of Rome before the late ninth century, Leo placed new emphasis on the pope as "heir" of St. Peter. This title, according to Roman legal understanding, implied spiritual and juridical identity between Peter and each one who successively became bishop of Rome. Consequently, the popes exercised that same function which Christ had accorded to Peter within the church, and necessarily took on Peter's rights and responsibilities in their entirety. Thus, to the established canonical identity of the pope as the bishop of Rome, metropolitan of the Italian region and sole patriarch within the Western church, there was added (in Western Christian understanding) his role as bearer of the Petrine power and primacy in every age.

The papal definition grew in two ways. New titles accrued to the office. Some expressed a personal dimension of papal experience, as, for example, the adoption of the name "servant of the servants of God" (*servus servorum Dei*) by Gregory I to underscore the role of the papacy as a service rendered to other bishops. Others, such as "vicar of Christ" and "vicar of God," which emerged in the fifth and seventh centuries, were later used to develop theological and juridical ideas latent in the Leonine conception of the Petrine primacy. A second way of augmenting the papal definition was by the direct claims and teachings of the popes themselves. The "Dictates of the Pope" (*Dictatus papae*), a document in the register of Gregory VII, claimed for the pope a name, a holiness, and a universal significance unique in the church and brought all other canonical and conciliar authority under his own. The bull *Unam sanctam* (1302) of Boniface VIII interpreted the papal fullness of power (*plenitudo potestatis*—a term traditional since Leo I) to mean that all authority under God, secular as well as sacred, had been entrusted to Peter and therefore to his successors. Boniface also explicitly "defined" the teaching that subjection to the Roman pontiff was necessary to salvation for every human creature. The fact that from the thirteenth century the universal jurisdiction and infallibility of the pope were topics of debate for canonists and theologians suggests that they cannot be said to have been formally defined.

A formal conciliar definition of the papacy might seem to have emerged at the Council of Ferrara-Florence (1438–1447), which described the Roman pontiff as holding the primacy in the whole world, as being the successor of Peter, the true vicar of Christ, the head of the entire church, and the father and teacher of all Christians. It further stated that to the pope in blessed Peter was given by Christ the full power (*plenam potestatem*) of feeding, ruling, and governing the universal church. The presence, however, of a saving clause guaranteeing all the rights and privileges of the Eastern patriarchs has enabled the Greek tradition to treat this definition as a canonical statement only, whereas for the Christian West these same terms have been understood as part of the doctrine of the church, not merely of its discipline.

BIBLIOGRAPHY

Joseph Gill, "The Definition of the Primacy of the Pope in the Council of Florence," in *Heythrop Journal,* **2** (1961); Jean-Marie Roger Tillard, *The Bishop of Rome* (1983); Walter Ullmann, "Leo I and the Theme of Papal Primacy," in *Journal of Theological Studies,* n.s. **11** (1960), and *Principles of Government and Politics in the Middle Ages* (1961).

ROBERT BARRINGER

[See also **Boniface VIII, Pope; Bull, Papal; Dictatus Papae; Ferrara-Florence, Council of; Gregory I the Great, Pope; Gregory VII, Pope; Leo I, Pope; Papacy, Origins and Development of; Plenitudo Potestatis.**]

POPPEHOWE, THOMAS (*fl.* early fifteenth century), Thomas Colyn, and Thomas Holewell made a large alabaster tomb for Queen Joan of England's first husband John the Valiant IV, duke of Brittany (*d.* 1399), around 1408. In that year these craftsmen were shipped to Brittany with the tomb, presumably for its erection in St. Peter's, Nantes. The tomb was destroyed in the French Revolution but is known through an eighteenth-century drawing.

BIBLIOGRAPHY

Lawrence Stone, *Sculpture in Britain: The Middle Ages,* 2nd ed. (1972); Frederick Herbert Crossley, *English Church Monuments, A.D. 1150–1550* (1921), 26–27.

BARRIE SINGLETON

[See also **Holewell, Thomas.**]

PORETE, MARGARET. See **Mysticism, Christian: Continental (Women).**

PORPHYROGENITOS, "the one who is born in the purple," that is, the son or daughter of a Byzantine emperor born during his or her father's

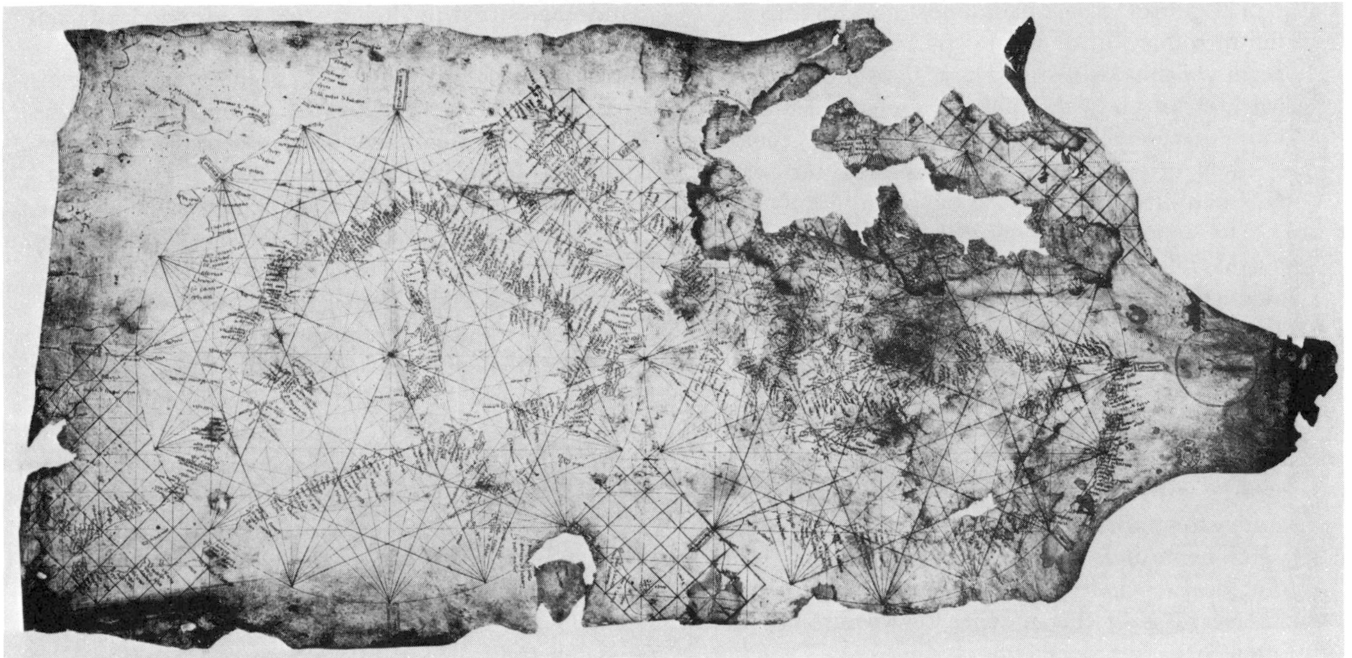

The *Carta Pisana,* the oldest known portolan chart. Possibly Genoese, 1290–1300. PARIS, BIBLIOTHÈQUE NATIONALE, RES. GE B 118

reign. The condition of "porphyrogenitos" did not assure any special constitutional rights, but it undoubtedly had prestige and was often added as an epithet to the name of a prince, even when he himself eventually became an emperor. The best known instance of this practice is the emperor and writer Constantine VII Porphyrogenitos (*r.* as sole emperor 945–959).

NICOLAS OIKONOMIDES

[See also **Byzantine Empire; Constantine VII Porphyrogenitos.**]

PORTCULLIS (from the French *porte-coulisse,* sliding door or gate), a strong frame or door, usually a heavy grating of iron or timber bars with the lower ends pointed, set in grooves in the side walls of a fortified gateway and let down quickly as a defense against assault.

GREGORY WHITTINGTON

[See also **Castles and Fortifications** (with illustration).]

PORTOLAN CHART, in common use between about 1300 and 1500, is a coastal chart or map graphically depicting harbors, prominent features such as promontories that could serve as landmarks for taking bearings, as well as reefs, shoals, and other navigational hazards. Its content was based entirely upon the experience of seafarers and was intended to assist navigators and shipmasters. It was generally drawn on parchment, utilizing a whole skin or sections glued on boards. It was carefully drawn with sharp lines and bright colors. The coloring followed a conventional scheme, with black, red, green, blue, yellow, and sometimes gold and silver having each their special places. Place-names were usually lettered in black, while a few were marked in red to indicate not size or importance but the presence of a safe harbor and availability of shipstores and water supply. Certain features, such as islands and coastal cliffs were sometimes drawn in perspective and exaggerated for emphasis. Inland topographical characteristics were simply sketched or else omitted altogether, while important towns were featured with small scenes. Sovereign states might be indicated by coats of arms. Bodies of water remained uncolored or shown with blue or green wavy lines, except for the Red Sea, which was generally colored red. The language appearing on the chart was almost invariably Latin, although examples written in Catalan and Italian dialects are known.

PORTOLAN CHART

The portolan emerged almost concurrently with the introduction of the magnetic compass in Europe, which is believed to have been brought to the Mediterranean in the tenth or eleventh century by the Normans. The place of origin of the compass is often given as Amalfi, which was part of the Norman kingdom founded in southern Italy.

The portolan was almost invariably oriented north, reflecting the earliest application of the magnetic compass to navigation and mapmaking. The advent of the compass changed the appearance of sea charts by featuring "the rose of the winds," or windrose, with its rays indicating the winds. The network of loxodrome lines, known also as rhumbs or windrays, radiating from the windrose, crisscrossed all major bodies or water and served as guides for transferring the geographical outlines to parchment, and a grid of squared lines was added outside the circle of rays for this purpose. The intersections of the network of loxodromes were often formed into subsidiary windroses. They bore no relation to the drawing of the geographical content and varied from one chart to another. When used with a magnetic compass the rhumbs enabled a navigator to lay a course from one harbor to another, and he utilized one or more rhumbs to direct his ship to a landfall.

The typical portolan included no graduations, parallels, or meridians, and instead of degrees, as in later nautical charts, directions were marked in terms of winds with which every experienced seaman was familiar. At first the twelve primary winds known in ancient times were used, and the early medieval compass card was divided into twelve directional points. In time they were reduced to eight, corresponding with the primary winds, N, NE, E, SE, S, SW, W, NW. As greater precision was required, eight "half-winds" and sixteen "quarter-winds" were added. When drawn, the thirty-two points resembled flower petals, with the consequence that the compass card became known as "the rose of the winds," or windrose.

The portolan is believed to have developed as a supplement to the ancient Greek written manuscript books known as *peripli,* or coast pilots, which summarized the accumulated knowledge of generations of seagoers. The earliest examples were probably compiled from cruder smaller charts of coastlines sketched by fishermen and coastal traders. As trade increased it was no longer possible to provide required detailed information by written language alone, particularly to unlettered seamen, and this situation led to the production of the portolan.

Renewed maritime activity in the Mediterranean region by Europeans by the second half of the thirteenth century greatly increased the need for nautical charts and gave birth to the trade of the chartmaker. Their shops sprang up in important north Italian and Catalonian ports. As well as can be determined, these were the only cartographers prior to the mid fifteenth century. They studied written descriptions of ports and coasts and examined the frequently traveled routes and crude charts made by mariners. Meeting incoming ships, these early chartmakers recorded itineraries obtained from pilots and shipmasters and combined the data thus acquired to make their sailing charts.

The portolan originated in one of the northern Italian maritime republics, probably Genoa or Venice, where mathematics and mensuration were already known to and used by the mercantile class. As the demand for nautical charts spread beyond Italy, portolans were also produced in the Catalan communities of Barcelona and on Majorca. With the intermingling of Muslims and Jews in southern Spain and on Majorca came new ideas and knowledge of eastern and northern African geography that supplemented information about the Mediterranean's northern and western shores and the North Atlantic geography.

Although there is no documentary evidence that the portolan existed prior to the late thirteenth century, the appearance of several copies of a chart of the Mediterranean and Black seas at about that time has been judged to be too accurate and detailed to have been the work of a single individual or group of navigators, suggesting an earlier development. The earliest known portolan charts were of the Mediterranean. Subsequently the Black Sea was added. Later, coastal charts of the British Isles were produced and eventually the peninsula of Scandinavia was included.

Portolan makers often pursued additional vocations, such as shipmaster, astrologer, or maker of mathematical instruments, perhaps from need as much as from opportunity. As an example, the notable Catalan portolan maker of Palma Abraham Cresques, who described himself as "a master of mappa mundi and compasses," produced navigational instruments as well as charts. Also attributed to him was the Catalan Atlas, commissioned by Charles V of France and completed in 1375.

In time the craft of the chartmaker evolved into

the profession of the cartographer, following the rediscovery in the fifteenth century of Ptolemy's geographical atlas among the Greek manuscripts brought to Florence from Constantinople. This new profession required competence in mathematical cartography as well as sophisticated artistic skills, and consequently the early cartographers were frequently recruited from the arts. The advent of the printing press in the fifteenth century enabled the cartographer's maps and charts to be reproduced with greater consistency and accuracy and made possible wider distribution. A few printed portolan charts produced before 1500 have survived; but evidence suggests that at first navigators and shipmasters considered hand-drawn charts to be more accurate and preferred manuscript charts to printed ones.

Portolan charts were also compiled into atlases in the fourteenth and fifteenth centuries and often contained a world map, usually oval in shape, charts of local regions, such as particular harbors and stretches of coastline, separate charts of the Adriatic, Aegean, and occasionally the Caspian seas, and a chart of the Mediterranean. Additions might include sketchy sailing directions, astronomical and astrological calendars, and tables of lunar cycles. The noted Laurentian Portolano of 1351 consisted of eight sheets covering the known world from the Canary Islands and the British Isles to the middle of the western coast of India.

The exploration of the African coast by the Portuguese followed by the discovery of the New World brought increased importance to the work of the cartographer and an increased and immediate need for nautical charts and maps incorporating the latest information. Portugal and Spain responded promptly to meet the need. In Lisbon the Casa da India added a cosmographic department by 1508, supervised by a junta for the purpose of charting the New World. In Spain a similar effort was made to maintain government control over the charting of new territories by creating a master chart supervised by a government commission. Shipmasters were required to use only copies of the official government chart, which was revised periodically to include the latest information received from returning seafarers.

BIBLIOGRAPHY

Leo Bagrow, *History of Cartography,* D. L. Paisey, trans., rev. and enl. by R. A. Skelton (1964, repr. with corrections 1966); Lloyd A. Brown, *The Story of Maps* (1949); Giuseppe Gino Guarneri, *Geografia e cartografia nautica nella loro evoluzione storia e scientifica* (1956); Michel Mollat du Jourdin *et al., Sea Charts of the Early Explorers,* L. le R. Dethan, trans. (1984); Attilio Mori, "La cartografia dell'Italia dal secolo XIV al XVIII," in *Bollettino della reale società geografica italiana,* 7 (1930); Raleigh A. Skelton, *Maps: A Historical Survey of Their Study and Collecting* (1972); Edward L. Stevenson, *Portulan Charts: Their Origin and Characteristics* (1911); Eva G. R. Taylor, *The Haven-finding Art* (1957); Ronald V. Tooley, *Maps and Map-makers,* 6th ed. (1978); John Noble Wilford, *The Mapmakers* (1981).

SILVIO A. BEDINI

[See also **Compass, Magnetic; Exploration by Western Europeans; Geography and Cartography; Mappa Mundi; Navigation.**]

PORTUGAL: TO 1279

THE ORIGINS OF PORTUGAL

During the centuries when Iberia was under Roman, Germanic, and Muslim domination, the part of the peninsula that eventually became the kingdom of Portugal was largely on the periphery of events, especially compared to the prominent position of the southern and eastern coastal regions under the Romans and the Muslims and that of the central meseta under the Visigoths. Nonetheless, many of the cultural and material innovations introduced into Iberia during these three great conquests took firm root in the western region, from which Portugal would emerge. There was also much continuity in civil and ecclesiastical administration during the years of Roman, Germanic, and Muslim rule.

The Iberian tribes that occupied the lands of the future Portugal put up a strong resistance to Rome's efforts at conquest. By the time Caesar Augustus' reign drew to a close in A.D. 14, however, the region was firmly under Roman rule and its inhabitants integrated into the Roman way of life. Roads, aqueducts, and bridges appeared, as did monuments, walls, amphitheaters, and temples. Commerce was stimulated, money coined, and mineral wealth exploited. A municipal system in which towns exercised authority over the surrounding countryside became an important institution and formed the basis of many future Portuguese cities. Latin was adopted as the common language, the basis of modern Portuguese. The inhabitants of

PORTUGAL: TO 1279

western Iberia shared in the Christianity that Rome had brought to the peninsula. Braga (Bracara) became one of its major centers.

During the reign of Diocletian (284–305), the Iberian Peninsula was divided into five provinces, three of which included parts of modern Portugal: Gallaetia—with its capital at Braga—encompassed what is now Portugal north of the Douro River; Lusitania—centered at Mérida (Emerita)—included the area south of the Douro River and west of the Guadiana River; and Baetica contained the small slice of territory to the east of the Guadiana. Several important road systems were constructed: one led from Lisbon (Olisipo) to Mérida, and another connected Lisbon with Braga via Santarém (Scallabis), Coimbra (Aeminium), and Porto (Cale). These road systems eventually helped integrate the kingdom of Portugal by breaking down the dichotomy that existed between its northern and southern regions. In addition, Braga had good communications with the rest of the province of Gallaetia. In Lusitania important cities were also connected by a network of roads.

It is estimated that more than one million people lived in what is now Portugal on the eve of the Germanic invasions. Roman rule had brought about much stability in the peninsula, but a certain decline was becoming apparent as early as the fourth century. According to some scholars the Roman legacy to Iberia also included a stagnant, stratified society and a decadent economy.

In 409, the Alans, two branches of the Vandals, and the Suevi entered the Iberian Peninsula in search of exploitable land. They were followed five or six years later by the Visigoths, who eventually gained control over most of the peninsula. The Suevi kingdom was confined to the old Roman province of Gallaetia in the northwest after attempts to dominate a larger area failed. The two chief cities of the Suevi kingdom were Lugo and Braga, the latter being the capital. Agriculture dominated and animals were raised. Coins were minted in almost a dozen towns. Although the heathen Suevi were converted to orthodox Christianity during the reign of Rechiarius (448–457) while Balconio was metropolitan, they lapsed into Arianism shortly thereafter. About 558, largely through the efforts of St. Martin of Dume (*d.* 579), the Arian Suevi were reconverted to Christianity. St. Martin, often called the apostle to the Suevi, founded churches and monasteries. The monastery and, later, diocese at Dume, a short distance from Braga, became an important religious and cultural center with St. Martin as its first bishop. St. Martin also became bishop of Braga, around 569.

Although the Suevi built on the ecclesiastical organization established under the Roman rule, some important changes occurred. Under the Romans Braga had authority only over dioceses north of the Douro River. But by the sixth century the dioceses of Lamego, Viseu, Coimbra, and Idanha, formerly under the jurisdiction of Mérida, came under the control of Braga. They were all located south of the Douro and north of the Tagus rivers in the old Roman province of Lusitania. Braga was one of the six metropolitan sees in the Iberian Peninsula.

In 561 the first Council of Braga was convened by the Suevi monarch, Theodemir. The council attacked Priscillianism and Arianism and concerned itself with disciplinary matters and the liturgy. A second council, held at Braga in 572, further confirmed the see's prestige. St. Martin took part in the first council and presided over the second. He was also active in efforts to eradicate pagan beliefs, many varieties of which he described in his *De correctione rusticorum.*

In 585, following more than a century of conflict between the Suevi in the northwest and the Visigoths, the latter, led by King Leovigild, overran the Suevi and incorporated their kingdom. For more than fifty years after the Suevi were absorbed by the Visigoths, Braga remained in control of the dioceses south of the Douro. This authority served as the precedent for the later claims of bishops of Braga and early Portuguese monarchs to jurisdiction over lands south of the Douro. In the mid seventh century the Visigoths reduced Braga's authority, limiting it once again to the old Roman province of Gallaetia.

Leovigild was Arian and initially the Christian Suevi were persecuted. It was not until the reign of Leovigild's son, Recared, that orthodox Christianity became the religion of the entire peninsula. In 589 Recared, who had been converted two years earlier, made a solemn profession of faith at the Third Council of Toledo. At that council representatives from eleven dioceses in what later became Portugal were present. During the period of Visigothic rule, Toledo, the capital, became the primatial see for the entire peninsula.

Monasticism continued to flourish in the see of Braga after the Visigothic conquest. One of the most important figures in the history of Iberian

PORTUGAL: TO 1279

monasticism was St. Fructuosus (*d.* 665/667), the son of a Visigothic nobleman. Bishop of Dume and, later, bishop of Braga, St. Fructuosus wrote two important monastic rules: *Regula monachorum* and *Regula communis,* the latter including his famous pact that outlined the relationship between monk and abbot. The monasteries he helped to found became important centers of culture. In fact, for several centuries Braga was one of the chief centers of Christian thought and culture in all of Europe. After the Muslim conquest Braga was the only metropolitan see in Iberian Christendom until the reign of Alfonso VI.

In 711 Muslim forces overran most of the peninsula. In the part that would become Portugal, Beja and Faro fell in 713, soon followed by Évora, Coimbra, Santarém, and other towns. The Muslim presence in the northwestern part of the peninsula, however, was a small one. A series of Berber revolts in the 740's, along with dissension among the newcomers, further weakened Muslim control of what had been the Roman province of Gallaetia. At the same time, a Christian kingdom, Asturias, was taking shape in the remote northern mountain districts. Soon the slow reconquest of the peninsula from the Muslims was under way. Christians made significant headway against the Muslims under the leadership of Alfonso I of Asturias (739–757). During Alfonso I's reign, Christians recaptured the lands that became Galicia and the lands that became Portugal north of the Douro River, including the cities of Braga, Porto, Viseu, and Chaves. However, on a number of occasions during the next hundred years Muslim forces took the counteroffensive, and much of the area between the Minho and Douro rivers was devastated. Bishops and other Christian leaders of the region fled to the court of Asturias at Oviedo. Braga and other cities were seriously damaged and partially abandoned. Castles and monasteries were demolished. The region became a frontier area that separated Christians and Muslims. Although the extent of the Christian depopulation continues to be debated by historians, some of the countryside, at least, remained in the hands of Christian peasants, especially in the region near the coast. Alfonso II of Asturias (791–842), who tried to restore the civil and ecclesiastical heritage of the Visigoths in his kingdom, took advantage of continued dissension among the Muslims. He raided as far south as Lisbon in 798. But it was not until the middle part of the ninth century, during the reign of Ordoño I (850–866), that a strong effort was made to reorganize and resettle the region around the Minho River. Ordoño's son and successor, Alfonso III of Asturias (866–910), continued that policy and pushed southward. Muslim Coimbra was captured and destroyed in 868. That same year Portucale (Porto) began to be repopulated, partly with the refugee Mozarabic population of Coimbra. Porto and, to the north, Chaves became important centers of administration. Viseu and Lamego were also resettled, and bishops were named to them. Braga, which had suffered a number of raids, was rebuilt between 905 and 910. To the east, Alfonso III continued colonizing the Douro River valley in León and in what eventually became the kingdom of Castile. By 900, in spite of Muslim counterattacks, the Christian frontier in the western part of the peninsula had moved to the Mondego River.

During the tenth century, as the various monarchs of Asturias-León partitioned their realm among their children, Galicia, as the old Gallaetia was now called, was given the status of a kingdom. A crucial ingredient in the development of an autonomous sentiment in that part of the northwest which was to become Portugal were the officials whom the monarchs appointed to oversee the affairs of lands recaptured from the Muslims. These officials provided for their regions' defense and helped consolidate the new territories by promoting settlement. They held a variety of titles, the most important being count. The crown gave these local barons important privileges, and the barons, with their increasingly powerful families, slowly increased their autonomy. This was not a process exclusive to the region south of the Minho. The same type of pattern was also occurring in Castile.

In 868 Porto was placed in charge of a knight by the name of Vímara Peres. As the region grew in importance it was detached from the kingdom of Galicia and given a governor. Before long there were references to a "territorio portucalense," the limits of which expanded with the passage of time. One of the earliest important leaders of this territory was Diogo Fernandez, a Castilian warrior, who had married the granddaughter of Vímara Peres. The daughter of this union, Mumadona Dias, the most powerful woman in northwest Iberia in the tenth century, married Count Mendo Gonçalves in 926. Mumadona was a great patron of the church. Among her many benefactions was the founding of the monastery of São Mamede in Guimarães. One of Mumadona's sons was the

PORTUGAL: TO 1279

count Gonçalo Mendes, who ruled the region from 950 to 999. He was succeeded by five or six governors from the same family, one of whom, Mendes Gonçalves, was tutor and father-in-law of Alfonso V of León, the first Asturian monarch to use the title of king of León. For almost two hundred years, the geographic nucleus of the future kingdom of Portugal, separated from Galicia, was in the hands of this family. In addition, these leaders intervened on several occasions in the affairs of the kingdom of León.

Increased autonomy was becoming the rule in the western part of the peninsula. Knights who had distinguished themselves in victories over the Muslims often were absorbed into important families in the region below the Minho. The nobility in the region from the Minho River southward, although divided regarding politics in León and Castile, were united in the face of Viking attacks and the Muslim threat. This was another important bond in promoting autonomy. In addition, common interests based on Atlantic location engendered an awareness that problems in the west differed greatly from those of León or Castile. The Muslim threat was the most severe. Several centuries of Christian gains were wiped out in a decade as the frontier rapidly receded from the Mondego to the Douro River. Almanzor (al-Manṣūr), the powerful Muslim dictator, and his troops made a number of incursions into the western part of the peninsula. He sacked and destroyed Coimbra in 987. It was not until seven years later that he resettled it with both Muslims and Mozarabs and began to rebuild. Coimbra soon became an important Muslim city, and its Mozarabic population would play an important role later on in the region's history. Almanzor also devastated much of the territory between the Mondego and the Douro rivers. Lamego and Viseu were captured and the countryside ravished. In 997, in one of the great humiliations Iberian Christendom experienced at the hands of the Muslims, Almanzor sacked Compostela. He destroyed the cathedral and carried off its bells to Córdoba to hang them in the great mosque.

Vikings frequently raided the western part of the peninsula in this period, with respect for neither Christian nor Muslim territory. The raids of 968, 1008, and 1015 were particularly devastating. On the last-mentioned occasion, the region between the Douro River and the Ave River to the north was ravaged. Part of the population was held captive during the Norsemen's nine-month sojourn there.

The Christians in the western part of the peninsula tried to rebound from these disasters, but the initial efforts were not successful. Alfonso V (994–1027) was killed attempting to free Viseu from Muslim rule. However, the collapse of the caliphate of Córdoba in 1031 and the fragmentation of Muslim Spain into *taifa* kingdoms, coupled with the resolution of dynastic problems in Castile, provided a golden opportunity for the Christians to regain their lost territories. The land of Santa María, later known as Feira, below the Douro River, was captured. A new nobility began to play an important role in recapturing this region. Gonçalo Trastemires captured Montemor in 1034. Others, with the encouragement of Ferdinand I of León and Castile (1037–1065), moved into the region of Paiva. Soon the monarch himself began campaigning in what is now the Portuguese province of Beira. In 1055 he seized Seia and Gouveia. Lamego was recaptured in 1057. In the following years so was Viseu, the latter with the help of the Cid. Tarouca, Travanca, and Penalva soon followed. In 1064, after a six-month siege, Coimbra fell to the forces of Ferdinand I. A new county with the same name was formed south of the Douro and entrusted to a wealthy rural proprietor from that region, the Mozarabic leader Sesnando Davídiz, who governed the province until his death in 1091. He, in turn, was succeeded by his son-in-law, Martim Monis. The Mondego River was once again the region's border, and the valley was securely in Christian hands.

In this same period Ferdinand I tried to rein in the centrifugal forces in his realm. He removed Mendo Nunes from his post in the province of Portugal and replaced him with subordinates. He also separated the "terra de Santa María" (Feira) from Terra Portucalense. But he did recognize the region's other administrative divisions. At the Council of Coyanza (1050), Portugal was referred to in the same terms as the kingdoms of León, Galicia, and Asturias.

The death of Ferdinand I in 1065 and the subsequent division of his kingdom among his children set the wheels in motion for an eventually successful separatist movement that would result in the kingdom of Portugal.

TERRA PORTUCALENSE

When Ferdinand I died in 1065, his domains were divided among his three heirs. Sancho, the eldest, received Castile and Navarre. The future

PORTUGAL: TO 1279

Alfonso VI was given the governance of the kingdom of León and Asturias. García inherited Galicia and Terra Portucalense. Sancho was dissatisfied with this division and was soon warring against his brothers. The northern part of the Iberian Peninsula was plunged into civil war.

The death of Sancho I in 1072 gave Alfonso VI the opportunity to take over the kingdom of Castile. Later he annexed parts of Galicia and Terra Portucalense to his kingdom of León and thus brought together once again the lands ruled by Ferdinand I. In addition, Alfonso pushed southward against the Moors. He captured Toledo in 1085 and made it the new capital of his realm. But next year Alfonso was unable to halt an Almoravid offensive, and the Muslim forces reoccupied many of their former territories.

In the late eleventh century, in response to Alfonso VI's pleas for help against continuing Almoravid invasions, several contingents of French knights arrived in the Iberian Peninsula. Many of these land-hungry younger sons hoped to obtain fame, fortune, and properties on this new frontier while they pursued the Christian goals of the crusades. Two of the most important of these adventurers were Raymond and Henry, countrymen of Alfonso's Burgundian wife, Queen Constance. Raymond, who was the son of Guillaume I of Burgundy, married Urraca, Alfonso VI's daughter and heiress. Alfonso entrusted his son-in-law with the administration of the county of Galicia as well as that of Terra Portucalense and Coimbra as far south as the Muslim frontier along the Tagus River. But Raymond's authority over the region to the south of Galicia was short-lived. In a new wave of attacks, Muslim forces soon overran the Christians' southernmost boundaries.

In the meantime, Henry, grandson of Robert I of Burgundy, had arrived in Iberia and had distinguished himself in battle against the Almoravids. In 1095 he married the young Teresa, Alfonso VI's favorite, albeit illegitimate, daughter. Alfonso VI now awarded this son-in-law the governance of Terra Portucalense. By the end of the year Henry was being addressed as lord of Coimbra, and by 1097 he was referred to as count of Portucale. Henry established his capital at Guimarães and stimulated settlement in the territory under his administration. Although he continued to take part in Alfonso VI's campaigns against the Muslims and to advise Alfonso at court, he also sought opportunities to exert greater independence from the monarch. In this endeavor he was aided by the isolation of Terra Portucalense from the other Christian territories in the Iberian Peninsula. Mountains formed barriers, and there was scant communication by water. With the exception of the Douro, none of the rivers that flow through northern Portugal originate to the east, in what is now Spain. Political factors, such as internal problems in the kingdom of León and Muslim threats to the Spanish kingdoms, strengthened this isolation. Thus, local identity and self-reliance were encouraged. The attention of Terra Portucalense was directed to the southwest and to the Atlantic Ocean.

Succession problems in León prompted a pact of friendship and mutual assistance between Henry and Raymond. Henry was promised Toledo, or at least Galicia, for backing his brother-in-law's claims to the succession of the kingship of León. But the death of Raymond in 1107, followed closely in 1108 by that of young Sancho, Alfonso VI's son and new heir by the Moorish princess Zaida, and by that of Alfonso himself in 1109, ended these plans and threw the succession into wide dispute.

During the years of civil war that followed, Henry, and later his widow, Teresa, attempted to gain greater independence for the county of Portucale. Teresa, like her husband before her, encouraged the establishment of new settlements. She also tried to expand her authority beyond the Minho River by allying herself with a faction of Galician nobles headed by Fernando Peres. Some of the wealthiest and most powerful Portuguese nobles opposed Teresa's Galician adventures and rallied around Afonso Henriques, the son of Teresa and Henry, a youth who had been only three years old at the time of his father's death. At the Battle of São Mamede in 1128, Afonso Henriques' forces defeated those of his mother and her supporters. Afonso Henriques exiled Teresa and took over the rule of the county of Portucale. During his long reign Afonso Henriques firmly established his line on the Portuguese throne; Portugal's first ruling house came to be known as the Burgundian dynasty.

AFONSO I, PORTUGAL'S FIRST KING (1128–1185)

Afonso Henriques (also known as Afonso I of Portugal) and his successors had four chief aims: (1) to assert Portugal's independence from León and Castile by establishing a separate kingdom, (2) to drive out the Muslims to the south and carve out the boundaries of what would become the Portu-

PORTUGAL
0 100 Miles
0 100 Kilometers
ATLANTIC OCEAN
Lugo
Santiago de Compostela
GALICIA
Minho R.
León
Lima R.
Chaves
Bragança
ENTRE DOURO E MINHO
Braga
TRAS-OS-MONTES
Ave R.
Guimarães
Tordesillas
Portucale (Porto)
Douro R.
Feira
Lamego
Paiva R.
Tarouca
Castelo Rodrigo
Viseu
BEIRA ALTA
Almeida
Penalva do Castelo
Celórico de Basto
Seia
Gouveia
Vilar Maior
Coimbra
Sabugal
Montemor-o-Velho
Travanca
Mondego R.
BEIRA BAIXA
Leiria
Idanha
Batalha
Tomar
Tagus R.
Torres Novas
Belver
Toledo
Óbidos
Castelo de Vide
Cáceres
Santarém
Portalegre
Marvão
Trujillo
Torres Vedras
Crato
Albuquerque
Avis
Arronches
Guadiana R.
Sintra
Salvaterra de Magos
Monforte
Mérida
Lisbon
Elvas
Almada
Palmela
Montemor-o-Novo
Badajoz
Sesimbra
Setubal
Évora
Juromenha
Alconchel
Alcácer do Sal
Mourão
Sado R.
ALENTEJO
Moura
Beja
Serpa
Aroche
Aljustrel
Aracena
Ourique
Guadalquivir R.
Córdoba
Mértola
ALGARVE
Seville
ANDALUSIA
Castro Marim
Alvor
Silves
Ayamonte
Granada
Lagos
Albufeira
Tavira
Faro
Gibraltar
Strait of Gibraltar
Tangiers
Ceuta

PORTUGAL: TO 1279

guese nation, (3) to firmly establish the position of monarch with its accompanying sovereign power, (4) to organize a church independent of León and Castile and then keep this increasingly powerful church in line by subordinating it to the monarchy. By 1383, when the death of Ferndinand I of Portugal marked the end of the Burgundian dynasty, the first two goals had been achieved and the latter two were close to fulfillment.

Afonso Henriques made gains steadily in his move toward independence from León and Castile. After Urraca's death in 1126, Urraca's son by Raymond of Burgundy, Alfonso Raimúndez, assumed power as Alfonso VII, king of León. In 1135 he was crowned by the cortes of León emperor of the "whole Spain." Afonso Henriques refused to recognize the sovereignty that his cousin claimed over Portugal and was in almost constant revolt. The Portuguese leader took advantage of Alfonso VII's problems with Aragon by allying himself to that kingdom and waging war on the frontiers of León and Castile. After four armed conflicts with Alfonso VII, during which Afonso Henriques invaded Galicia four times (1130, 1135, 1137, and 1139) and Alfonso VII invaded Portugal, peace was worked out between the two leaders. In 1143, in the Treaty of Zamora, Afonso Henriques promised to stay out of Galician territory and affairs and, in return, Alfonso VII recognized his cousin as king of Portugal. Afonso Henriques had already taken this title for himself in 1140 and had commended his kingdom to the Holy See, declaring himself a vassal of the pope. The papacy of Lucius II accepted this offer in 1144 following the pact between Afonso Henriques and Alfonso VII. (However, it was not until 1179 that a pope would address Afonso Henriques as "king.")

The threat to Portuguese independence greatly diminished with the death of Alfonso VII in 1157, the subsequent division of his realm between his two sons, Sancho (III of Castile) and Ferdinand (II of León), and the death of Sancho the following year, which threw Castile into chaos. By 1185, the year when Afonso Henriques died, the task of asserting Portugal's independence from León and Castile was virtually complete. Although the successors of Afonso Henriques came into intermittent conflict with Portugal's Christian neighbors to the east and the north, it was not until the reign of Ferdinand I of Portugal in the late fourteenth century (the last Burgundian monarch), when Castilian forces invaded Portugal three times, that Spanish power seriously threatened Portugal's autonomy.

The second major goal of the Burgundian dynasty—to drive the Muslims farther and farther south—was not achieved as readily as the assertion of Portuguese independence. But Afonso Henriques did take some important steps in that direction by making significant inroads into Muslim territory. Early in his reign, he secured the region around Coimbra and transferred his capital there. In 1135 he gave further attention to his southern borders by fortifying Leiria. In 1139 he won an important skirmish at Ourique during one of his raids into Muslim regions. This enabled him to exact tribute from Muslims living near his southern borders. Afonso Henriques was aided in his ventures against the Muslims by the chaos in Islamic Spain, which resulted from the breakdown of Almoravid rule and the corresponding Almohad revolt in North Africa that was spreading to Muslim Iberia.

Soon, Afonso Henriques began a big push against the Muslim forces along his Tagus River frontier. In the next two decades major territorial gains were achieved. In 1147 Afonso Henriques captured the important city of Santarém. This conquest opened the way to Lisbon, which was taken later the same year after a seventeen-week siege, carried out with the aid of several thousand northern European knights, participants in the Second Crusade, who interrupted their journey to the Holy Land to help Afonso Henriques. Neighboring Muslim strongholds in Sintra and Palmela also surrendered to the Christian forces. The capture of Lisbon was Afonso Henriques' greatest victory against the Muslims during his long reign.

With the aid of the Knights Templar and the orders of Santiago and Avis, three clerico-military orders that had been introduced into Portugal during the second and third quarters of the twelfth century, and with the derring-do of adventurers like the famed Geraldo "Sem Pavor" (the Fearless), Afonso Henriques advanced further into Muslim territory. The Portuguese were able to gain control—at least temporarily—of such Muslim strongholds as Alcácer do Sal on the Sado River south of Lisbon and a number of important towns in the Alentejo and across the Guadiana River in what is now Spanish Estremadura. These victories owed much to surprise attacks led by Geraldo, a man whose exploits were soon putting fear into the hearts of Muslims inhabiting the region. Between 1165 and 1168 he captured strongholds such

PORTUGAL: TO 1279

as Évora, Moura, Serpa, Juromenha, Alconchel, Trujillo, Cáceres, and part of Badajoz and turned them over to Afonso Henriques. But when Geraldo and Afonso Henriques were attempting to capture the citadel at Badajoz, the Portuguese king was thrown from his horse. Crippled by a broken leg, Afonso Henriques was taken prisoner by his son-in-law, Ferdinand II of León, who had temporarily allied himself with the Muslims when he saw the Portuguese moving into territory he considered to be Leonese. The price Afonso Henriques paid for his freedom was the relinquishment of his claims to Badajoz and his conquests on the east bank of the Guadiana River, as well as to those in Galicia north of the Minho River. The monarch's injuries, for all practical purposes, brought Afonso Henriques' illustrious military career to a close.

After the Almohads gained ascendancy in the southern part of the Iberian Peninsula, the Muslims recaptured many of the strongholds they had lost to Afonso Henriques during the 1160's. Even though the future Sancho I of Portugal led a raid to the outskirts of Seville in 1178, the Almohads pushed the Portuguese back to the Tagus. Although Sancho claimed a few victories later on during his reign, it would be up to Afonso Henriques' grandson and great-grandsons to drive the remaining Muslim forces from southern Portugal.

Afonso Henriques initiated a strong royalist tradition in Portugal. In doing so, he was imitating León. He was aided in his endeavor by the territorial compactness of his kingdom. The great length of Afonso Henriques' reign was an important factor in the development of royal ascendancy. Also, Afonso Henriques' decision to have his son and heir, Sancho I, rule jointly with him during the last fifteen years of his reign eliminated succession disputes that could have weakened the crown's position. Thus the sovereignty of the crown over the three estates of nobility, clergy, and commoners was established early in Portugal, although it was not unchallenged.

As part of the effort to create an independent Portugal, Afonso Henriques was anxious to establish a church in his kingdom separate from that in Santiago de Compostela and separate also from the church in Toledo, which had been awarded the status of primatial see during the Visigothic domination of Iberia. Afonso Henriques' father, Henry of Burgundy, had backed the archbishop of Braga in his assertion of independence from Toledo. In 1103 the papacy gave Braga control not only over dioceses in Galicia, but also over those of Coimbra, Viseu, and Lamego in Portugal. A decade and a half later, however, Braga was stripped of its control over dioceses south of the Douro River. When Afonso Henriques came to power, he managed to recover the lost dioceses for Braga. However, the conquest of Lisbon and other cities in southern Portugal caused new problems because dioceses in this region had never been subordinate to Braga. Ironically, when the efforts to establish a Portuguese church succeeded, it was the church that offered the crown the fiercest rivalry. Of all the internal struggles for power in Portugual during the Middle Ages, those between crown and church were the most bitter.

THE REIGN OF SANCHO I (1185–1211)

When Sancho I succeeded his father as king of Portugal, the Almohads were approaching the apogee of their power in the southern part of the Iberian Peninsula. In 1184, the year before Afonso Henriques' death, an Almohad offensive had threatened Santarém. In 1189 Sancho I, with the aid of two fleets of crusaders from the Third Crusade, managed to capture Alvor and the important Muslim city of Silves, the latter after a lengthy siege. But the Portuguese success was short-lived. The following year the Almohad leader, Abū Yūsuf Ya^{c}qūb, avenged these losses by a two-pronged attack on Christian Portugal. One army besieged Silves and the other swept through the Alentejo, destroying part of Évora, capturing Torres Novas, and besieging the Knights Templar at Tomar. In 1191, Ya^{c}qūb I led an even stronger force, which captured Alcácer do Sal as well as the fortresses of Palmela, Sesimbra, and Almada across the Tagus River from Lisbon. Shortly thereafter, Silves fell to the Almohads. Sancho was forced to sign a five-year truce with the Muslims.

Given the stalemate with the Muslims, Sancho I turned his attention to resettling those areas conquered by the Portuguese during the reign of his father that Portugal had retained. He developed municipal institutions to attract settlers to abandoned zones. During his reign almost fifty charters were awarded, most of them in the central and eastern regions of his kingdom. Settlers on the frontier received additional privileges, such as dispensations from certain labor and tax requirements. Sancho I also encouraged immigration from outside the Iberian Peninsula and promoted agri-

 PORTUGAL: TO 1279

culture. The king was well aware of the importance of the clerico-military orders in guarding against invasions by the Muslims, or by the Leonese and Castilians, and he granted large concessions to the Knights Templar and the orders of Santiago and Avis.

During the first half of Sancho I's reign, although Portugal's independence was not seriously threatened, there were almost continual skirmishes between Portugal and the neighboring Christian kingdoms. Between 1185 and 1189, Sancho I fought with his brother-in-law, Ferdinand II of León, whose forces invaded Beira before they were finally defeated at Celórico. In the early 1190's Portugal joined Aragon and León as part of an anti-Castile pact. Between 1196 and 1199 Portugal engaged in hostilities with Alfonso IX of León, occasioned by that king's repudiation of his marriage with Sancho's daughter Teresa, after Pope Celestine III annulled their marriage because they were first cousins. In addition, there were frequent clashes along Portugal's northern border. Thanks to the mediation of Pope Innocent III, peace with León and Castile was concluded in 1200.

Although Sancho I's share of the royal patrimony had included few properties and few monies, Sancho was able, by his astuteness and energy, to accumulate substantial wealth, which he deposited in strongholds such as Évora, Coimbra, and Belver. Sancho I also continued his father's policy of promoting royal authority.

A harbinger of the problems that would bedevil future Portuguese monarchs was Sancho I's conflict with the papacy. The first dispute concerned the annual tribute of two marks of gold that Afonso Henriques had promised he and his successors would pay the papacy. After some bitter exchanges and the arrival in Portugal of a papal legate of Pope Innocent III, the twenty years of back payments were made. This issue was relatively minor compared to Sancho's conflicts with the bishops of Porto and Coimbra—the first of a series of church-state conflicts that would result in excommunications and interdicts for Sancho and his successors. The bishops claimed that the Portuguese king was not respecting their ecclesiastical immunities. Although Sancho I challenged their charges and enjoyed considerable support from his subjects, Pope Innocent III excommunicated him and placed Portugal under interdict. Only when the end of his life approached did Sancho I submit to Rome and ask forgiveness.

THE TURBULENT RULE OF AFONSO II (1211–1223)

The reign of Afonso II, Portugal's third monarch and Sancho I's son and successor, was relatively short, but it was far from uneventful. Afonso II did much to consolidate the various gains of his predecessors, particularly by seeking to augment royal power. In 1211 Afonso II promulgated the first corpus of Portuguese law. This legislation had four chief purposes: (1) to guarantee the rights of royal as well as private property, (2) to regularize the administration of civil justice, (3) to defend the material interests of the crown, and (4) to eliminate abuses by both the clergy and the nobility. Afonso II also developed two institutions to strengthen royal prerogatives: the *inquirições gerais* (general inquiries) to investigate the legitimacy of earlier grants; and the *confirmações* (confirmations). He sent teams of investigators out into the country to check on the legitimacy of claims and grants, and to take testimony. Sometimes the inquiries resulted in an annulment of grants and loss of property or privileges. Predictably, this action to improve public administration and to strengthen royal control caused some turmoil, resented as it was by the higher clergy and nobles, jealous of their prerogatives and immunities. Serious disruptions often limited the scope of the inquiries. However, the investigations did improve public administration and were a model for future kings of Portugal, especially Afonso III and Dinis.

In his will, Sancho I had left part of the royal patrimony to Afonso II's brothers and sisters. Afonso II deemed this a challenge to his sovereignty. He argued that the royal patrimony was indivisible and that he should have jurisdiction over all crown properties. Rather than face the restrictions that their brother, the king, was putting on their goods and persons, Afonso's brothers left the kingdom for voluntary exile. However, the king's sisters, two of whom (Teresa and Mafalda) had been queens in Castile, refused to accept Afonso II's authority over their grants. When Afonso applied force to get his way, the princesses protested to Pope Innocent III, who reacted in August 1212 by placing Portugal under an interdict that lasted for a year and a half. In the meantime, Afonso paid the pope the annual tribute, which had been in arrears since Sancho I's lump-sum payment late in the preceding century. Finally, a papal bull published by Innocent III in 1216 provided the foundations for a settlement to the quarrel. It asserted that

 PORTUGAL: TO 1279

Sancho I had intended that his daughters have the revenue from, but not jurisdiction over, the towns he had willed them. But because of a new conflict involving Afonso II—this time with the archbishop of Braga—which resulted in the king's excommunication, the issue of the royal patrimony was not definitively settled until the beginning of Sancho II's reign in 1223.

In the process of investigating the grants that were claimed by the church in Portugal, Afonso II annulled a number of them. Estêvão Soares da Silva, the archbishop of Braga, convoked an assembly of clergy and condemned the actions of the king, accusing him not only of abuses against the church, but of living an adulterous life. The king redoubled his efforts against the church in northern Portugal. When the archbishop excommunicated Afonso and his chief advisers and put Portugal under interdict, the monarch ordered his forces to destroy the properties of the archbishop, including his granaries, vineyards, and orchards. The archbishop then appealed to Rome, and Pope Honorius III intervened. Afonso II, with an heir only twelve years old and faced with a papal threat of deposition, began negotiations with the archbishop of Braga. But before they were concluded, the king died, an excommunicate.

When Afonso II assumed power in 1211, Portugal's independence was fairly well established, although there still were occasional threats from neighboring Christian kingdoms. In 1212 Alfonso IX of León used the clash between the Portuguese king and his brothers and sisters as an excuse to invade northern Portugal. With help from some Portuguese nobles, including one of Afonso II's brothers, the Leonese defeated the supporters of Afonso II at the battle of Valdevez. Fortunately for the Portuguese, the threat of hostilities with Alfonso VIII of Castile forced the Leonese king to withdraw from Portugal, and Afonso II was able to recover the occupied territory.

There was relatively little fighting against the Muslims on Portugal's borders during the reign of Afonso II. The Portuguese monarch did, however, send troops to aid his father-in-law, Alfonso VIII of Castile, in the famous Battle of Las Navas de Tolosa in 1212, in which the Christians decisively defeated the Almohad forces. Las Navas de Tolosa was the gateway to Andalusia, and the Almohads never recovered from this defeat. The Portuguese distinguished themselves by their bravery in this encounter, the outcome of which is considered by many to be the greatest Christian victory of the Reconquest.

Five years later, when Afonso II was at Coimbra, the bishop of Lisbon convinced knights from the Fifth Crusade to aid the Portuguese in an attempt to regain the important stronghold of Alcácer do Sal. The crusaders, together with the Templars, Hospitalers, and Knights of Santiago, captured Alcácer after a two-month siege. This victory opened up the Sado River basin to Portuguese settlement and commerce.

SANCHO II: REIGN AND DEPOSITION (1223–1248)

Conditions in Portugal did not presage a quiet reign when Sancho II, barely into his teens, ascended the Portuguese throne. His father had died while under the penalty of excommunication, and the kingdom was still under interdict. In addition, Portugal was seething with discontent in the aftermath of royal efforts to consolidate the crown's authority. Clergy, nobility, and to a lesser extent commoners, were each nursing a set of grievances. The higher clergy charged that their ecclesiastical immunities were being violated. The nobility were upset by the crown's efforts to recover royal lands, income, and jurisdictions. Members of both estates, in turn, were abusing the monasteries and the populace.

Soon a series of compromises were worked out in an attempt to salve the wounds festering since the days of Afonso Henriques. At a meeting between crown, clergy, and nobility, guarantees were agreed upon that defined ecclesiastical and noble rights and privileges on the one hand, and royal prerogatives on the other. In exchange for lifting the many excommunications and the countrywide interdict imposed during the reign of Afonso II, the archbishop of Braga was indemnified with a cash grant and reconstruction of buildings damaged during the previous decade. To help strengthen this modus vivendi, Sancho II visited much of the northern part of his kingdom shortly after his coronation.

Next, Sancho II turned his attention to the struggle against the Muslims, a task that had been a lesser priority for his father. In his efforts to consolidate Portuguese power in the Alentejo, Sancho II profited from the existing disunity in Muslim Iberia and North Africa, which was the result of a disputed succession. He was also aided by Alfonso IX of León's renewed crusade against the Almohads. Sancho II took a personal interest in the fighting and distinguished himself in battle. He was soon leading Portuguese troops against Muslim strongholds on the west bank of the Guadiana River, and he took measures to fortify the upper Alentejo. By granting charters to a variety of towns and by moving his court temporarily to Beira Baixa, Sancho also encouraged the repopulation of lands bordering the upper reaches of the Guadiana.

Military activity was most intense in two phases: 1226–1230 and 1234–1240. The clerico-military orders played major roles in both series of campaigns. Elvas changed hands several times. It was given a charter (*foral*) by the Portuguese monarch in May of 1229. The following year, Juromenha fell to Sancho's forces while Castilian troops captured neighboring Badajoz. During this first phase of fighting, Sancho II received considerable help from the Knights Hospitaler. In return, they were given Crato, the future headquarters of their order in Portugal, and much of the region surrounding it. In the second phase, the Order of Santiago played a major role. Bolstered by a papal bull of Gregory IX, which granted indulgences to those who aided the Portuguese Reconquest, Sancho II and his forces pushed further south, capturing Aljustrel in 1234 and Mértola and Ayamonte in 1238, all of which were entrusted to the Order of Santiago. With the help of a nascent Portuguese navy, Sancho's forces also captured Tavira. These conquests, in addition to augmenting Portuguese territory and to providing a southern corridor to the Atlantic, isolated the important Moorish stronghold of Silves in southwestern Portugal from the Muslim kingdoms in Andalusia.

Although the Portuguese military campaign against the Muslims was achieving success, and the more mundane tasks of settlement and administrative organization were proceeding effectively, law and order were breaking down in other parts of Portugal, especially in the north. Sancho II proved unable to restrain and pacify restless nobles and clergy. The Portuguese clergy, seeking an ally in an increasingly activist papacy, constantly complained to Rome about violations of ecclesiastical immunities, rights, and privileges. While grounds did exist for these charges, the clergy themselves were not without blame. Some prelates were permitting large numbers of men to receive the tonsure—which enabled these men to avoid military service and to seek juridical shelter in the more lenient ecclesiastical courts—for dubious motives, possibly to increase the number of clerical supporters. Pope Gregory IX sent his legate, Jean d'Abbeville, cardinal of S. Sabina, to mediate the conflict. The legate attempted to take an impartial stance in the conflict. He criticized the intrigues of the bishops and encouraged Sancho II's crusading efforts. After the legate's departure, however, the conflict flared anew. In 1237, when the crown's candidate for bishop failed to receive ecclesiastical approval, the crown, in the person of Sancho II's younger brother, Fernando, resorted to force in an effort to intimidate the Lisbon clergy. To the north, the king's uncle played a similar role in Porto. Another interdict was placed on the kingdom, but rapid royal repentance and submission to church authority soon led to the lifting of the penalties.

In 1241 Sancho II married his distant cousin, Mécia López de Haro, widow of a Castilian noble. The king's enemies used this occasion to claim that Sancho had become "lazy and sensual." Others, including his brother Afonso, the count of Boulogne, charged that the marriage was uncanonical. Eventually, Pope Innocent IV ordered Sancho II to leave Dona Mécia.

In the meantime, conditions in Portugal had deteriorated. Murder, theft, rape, and arson were rampant. Churches were sacked and clergy assassinated. By 1242 the disorders seemed to many to be approaching a state of civil war.

On a number of occasions the papacy had informed Sancho II of its displeasure over Portugal's unsettled conditions. At the Council of Lyons, 1244–1245, which was attended by Portuguese bishops and by royal envoys as well, the alleged anarchy in Portugal was debated. Although the bishop of Lisbon defended his monarch by blaming conditions in Portugal on "rebellious and malcontent vassals," and by praising Sancho's crusade against the Muslims, Pope Innocent IV, in a bull of 24 July 1245, accused Sancho of "indolence and pusillanimity." The pope cited the need for an active and prudent ruler to restore order in Portugal, and he effectively deposed Sancho II by reducing him to king in name only and by turning over the government to his brother Afonso, count of Boulogne. Innocent IV instructed the Portuguese to receive and obey Afonso as soon as he arrived in Portugal and to ignore the orders of Sancho II.

Since 1238 Afonso had been residing in France, where he was influential at the court of his maternal aunt, Queen Blanche, wife of Louis VIII and mother of Louis IX. After Pope Innocent IV issued his deposition of Sancho II, a delegation of Portu-

PORTUGAL: TO 1279

guese—a number of whom had testified at the Council of Lyons—visited Paris, where they swore obedience to Afonso. They also exacted a series of promises from the future monarch to respect the church, to honor the privileges and customs of Portugal, and to promote justice.

Early in 1246, Afonso arrived in Lisbon, where he was well received by many of the nobility and clergy, as well as some merchants and commoners. Sancho II sought aid from Castile. He promised his throne, in the event he died childless, to his cousin, Ferdinand III of Castile. Although a contingent of Leonese and Castilian nobility came to Sancho's aid, the future Afonso III prevailed. Afonso argued that he was following papal orders, was backed by the French crown, and was supported by a majority of Portuguese. He also promised that those who opposed him would be excommunicated. Sancho II, along with a few of his most loyal supporters, and the Leonese and Castilian forces, eventually retreated to Toledo, where he died in January of 1248.

THE REIGN OF AFONSO III (1248–1279)

Afonso III was crowned king of Portugal following notification of his brother's death. He renewed the policies of Portugal's earlier monarchs by asserting royal authority wherever possible, and by taking a hard line with the privileged classes when their immunities and prerogatives interfered with the royal treasury or administration.

Early in his reign, Afonso III took up the task of driving the Muslims from their isolated strongholds in southwestern Portugal. The time was propitious for such a move. Ferdinand III of Castile, with the aid of the Portuguese military orders and some Portuguese nobles, had been campaigning successfully against the Muslim kingdoms in Andalusia. Seville would fall to Christian forces in November of 1248.

Afonso III personally led the drive to oust the Muslims from the Algarve. In March of 1249 he captured Faro. Soon, Albufeira and Silves, along with a number of lesser towns and fortresses, fell to the Portuguese. This completed the ouster of Muslim military forces from what was to be the limits of modern Portugal. In 1251, Afonso III continued his campaign—this time to the east of the Guadiana River in territory that the Castilians regarded as their preserve. Castile, in the meantime, claimed parts of the Algarve. Armed conflict soon broke out between Portugal and Castile over these disputed territories.

In 1252 Alfonso X "El Sabio" (the Wise) ascended the Castilian throne. A year later, a truce was arranged between the two kings. It was resolved that Afonso III would marry Beatrice of Castile, the illegitimate daughter of Alfonso X. The marriage took place in 1253. In addition, it was decided that the administration of the newly conquered kingdom of the Algarve and the lands east of the Guadiana River would be Portugal's, but the usufruct of these territories would remain in the hands of Alfonso X until the first-born son of the marriage between Afonso III and Beatrice reached the age of seven.

Unfortunately, there were three seemingly insurmountable difficulties to implementing this marital arrangement. First, Beatrice was only six years old; second, she was related to Afonso III within the fourth degree of consanguinity; third, and most importantly, Afonso III was already married to Matilda, countess of Boulogne, who was living in France. Indeed, Matilda was soon complaining to the pope about her husband's bigamous marriage. Although Pope Alexander IV placed under interdict those parts of Portugal where the king was residing, he was unable to persuade Afonso III to leave his young bride.

Matilda's death in 1258 helped resolve some of the Portuguese monarch's difficulties. But papal opposition to the marriage continued, as did the interdict. The bishops and cathedral chapters of Portugal came to the king's defense. In 1260—by which time the thirteen-year-old Beatrice had already borne two children to Afonso—they pleaded with Pope Urban IV to lift the interdict and legitimize the children. They argued that the abandonment of Beatrice by Afonso would lead to war with Castile, and they claimed that ecclesiastical penalties were causing spiritual harm and scandal in Portugal. Finally, in 1263, after a visit to Rome by a delegation of Portuguese bishops, and after much lobbying by European leaders such as Louis IX of France and the duke of Anjou, the request for the necessary dispensations and legitimizations was granted.

The birth in 1261 of Dinis, Afonso III's third child by Beatrice (the first was a girl, the second a boy who died in infancy), provided the necessary ingredient for the resolution of the controversy between Castile and Portugal. By the Treaty of Badajoz in 1267 Alfonso X of Castile renounced his rights to the kingdom of the Algarve, while Afonso III gave up Portuguese claims to the territories

PORTUGAL: TO 1279

between the Guadiana and Guadalquivir rivers. Portugal, however, would have authority over the territory to the west of the mouth of the Guadiana and its confluence with the Caia River.

In addition to the reconquest of the Algarve and the resolution of Portugal's boundaries with Castile, several other major accomplishments marked Afonso III's reign. Afonso promoted greater participation by towns and their officials in Portuguese national life. At Leiria in 1254, for the first time in the nation's history, representatives of the cities participated in the cortes along with the nobility and the higher clergy. Laws were also enacted to protect commoners from abuse at the hands of the privileged classes. Furthermore, Afonso III restructured the country's monetary system. Charters issued during his reign show that a moneyed economy was replacing barter. Fixed monetary taxes replaced the custom of paying in kind. At the cortes of Coimbra in 1261, Afonso III agreed to devalue the currency only once during a reign instead of every seven years, as was becoming the practice. The monarch favored Lisbon over Coimbra as the kingdom's chief commercial and administrative center, and he increased the royal treasury by promoting the country's economy.

Afonso III continued his predecessors' policy of strengthening royal prerogatives. This was accomplished chiefly through the use of the *inquirições gerais* and *confirmações.* In 1258, in response to complaints from royal officials as well as commoners, the crown sent investigative teams into the *comarcas* (districts) of Entre Douro e Minho, Tras-os-Montes, and Beira Alta to examine titles to lands claimed by nobility and clergy. Sworn testimony was taken to determine if the rights of the crown were being respected. Afonso III was anxious to curb the power of the old nobility and the higher clergy, especially those in the *comarca* of Entre Douro e Minho, the oldest and most populous region of Portugal. These investigations revealed a wide range of violations, including the usurpation of the royal patrimony, evasion of taxes, and abuses of commoners by the privileged estates, both secular and clerical. Laws were promulgated to deal with these infractions and they soon sparked fresh opposition from clergy and nobility.

In 1267 a number of Portuguese prelates traveled to Rome and presented Pope Clement IV with an extensive list of grievances. They accused Afonso III of condoning, even encouraging, violence in civil administration, of using unfair practices in his business dealings, and of infringing on ecclesiastical liberties. The Portuguese monarch answered these charges with testimonials from the towns of the kingdom that defended his actions and praised his administration. In addition, in 1273, during the meeting of the cortes at Santarém, Afonso III established a commission to investigate his acts and those of his officials. But the papacy was not impressed by the results of this investigation, which maintained that there had been little wrongdoing. In 1275 Pope Gregory X ordered that the king correct abuses and promise not to repeat them under pain of a series of penalties. These penalties would be invoked in stages, beginning in 1277, and would progress from local interdict, to excommunication, to a general interdict for the kingdom, to freeing the Portuguese from obedience to their king. And, indeed, by the end of 1277, Afonso III had been excommunicated and the kingdom placed under interdict. Soon, minor revolts broke out against the king in which Afonso III's son and successor, Dinis, took part. In January of 1279, a month before his death, Afonso III made his peace with the church and with his son.

BIBLIOGRAPHY

Useful overviews for understanding Portugal's origins during 400–1000 are Torquato de Sousa Soares, *Contribuição para o estudo das origens do povo português* (1970); Jaime Cortesão, *Os factores democráticos na Formação de Portugal* (1930, repr. 1964, 1966); José Leite de Vasconcelos, *Religiões da Lusitania,* 3 vols. (1897–1913, facsimile ed. 1981).

The Roman experience in what is now Portugal is studied in Jorge de Alarcão, *Portugal romano,* 3rd rev. ed. (1983). To date there is no general history of the Suevi in the Iberian Peninsula, but useful materials can be found in Pierre David, *Études historiques sur la Galice et le Portugal de VIe au XIIe siècle* (1947). Mário Tavares Chicó, *A arquitectura gótica em Portugal* (1954, 2nd ed. 1968), and José Augusto Correia de Campos, *Monumentos da antiguidade árabe em Portugal* (1970), provide a better understanding of the Germanic and Moslem presence in what became the kingdom of Portugal.

For the centuries immediately preceding Portuguese independence, a key study is Damião Peres, *Como nasceu Portugal,* 7th ed. (1970), and several important essays by Manuel Paulo Merêa collected in his *História e direito* (1967).

The classic study for the period 1095–1279 is Alexandre Herculano de Carvalho e Araujo, *História de Portugal: Desde o começo da monarchia até o fim do reinado de Afonso III,* 4 vols. (1980–1983); this edition, with preface and critical notes by José Mattoso, is the best of the many editions since the work first appeared (1846–1853). Also essential are articles in Joel Serrão, ed., *Dicionário de história de Portugal,* 4 vols. (1961–1971). The best recent overview is José Mattoso, *Identificação de um país: Ensaio sobre as origens de Portugal, 1096–1325,* 2 vols. (1985). Other good overviews are António Henrique R. de Oliveira Marques, *História de Portugal desde os tempos mais antigas . . . ,* I, 9th ed. (1981), which covers the years before 1557, and Joaquim Veríssimo Serrão, *História de Portugal,* I (1977), which covers the years 1080–1415. See also Fortunato de Almeida, *História de Portugal,* I (1922); Luíz Gonzaga de Azevedo, *História de Portugal,* 5 vols., 2nd ed. (1954); and Damião Peres, ed., *História de Portugal: Edição monumental,* I (1928). A useful shorter study is António Baião, Hernani Cidade, and Manuel Múrias, eds., *História de expansão portuguesa no mundo,* I (1937).

The best treatment on the role of the church is Fortunato de Almeida, *História da igreja em Portugal,* I, 2nd ed. (1967). Also useful is José Mattoso, *Religião e cultura na idade média portuguesa* (1982), which gathers many of the author's earlier published essays. In his *The Shadow King: "Rex Inutilis" in Medieval Law and Literature, 751–1327* (1970), Edward M. Peters includes a chapter entitled "Sancho II of Portugal and Thirteenth-century Deposition Theory."

Landholding patterns, society, economy, and political aspects of medieval Portugal are analyzed in Henrique da Gama Barros, *História da administração publica em Portugal nos séculos XII a XV,* 11 vols., 2nd ed. (1945–1954). Armando Castro in his *A evolução económica de Portugal dos séculos XII a XV,* 11 vols. (1964–1979), relies heavily on Gama Barros as he analyzes the economy of the period. Food production is studied by António Henrique de Oliveira Marques, *Introdução a história da agricultura em Portugal: A questão cerealífera durante a idade média,* 2nd ed. (1968). Although much of it deals with a later period, António Henrique R. de Oliveira Marques, *A sociedade medieval portuguesa: Aspectos de vida quotidiana* (1964), is valuable for the social history of the Middle Ages. There is an English translation by Sharon Wyatt, *Daily Life in Portugal in the Late Middle Ages* (1971). The nobility is studied by José Mattoso, *A nobreza medieval portuguesa: A familia e o poder* (1981), and *Ricos-homens, Infanções e cavaleiros: A nobreza medieval portuguesa nos séculos XI e XII* (1982). A good overview of Portuguese foreign policy during the Middle Ages is in Pedro Soares Martínez, *História diplomática de Portugal* (1986); also useful is Marcelo Caetano, *História do direito português,* I (1981), which deals with the years 1140–1495 and discusses law in medieval Portugal.

The chief chronicler of the period was António Brandão; his four works listed below have all been edited by A. de Magalhães Basto: *Crónica do Conde D. Henrique, D. Teresa e Infante D. Afonso* (1944); *Crónica de D. Afonso Henriques* (1945); *Crónicas de D. Sancho I e de D. Afonso II* (1945); and *Crónicas de D. Sancho II e de D. Afonso III* (1946). Basto has also edited the *Crónica de Cinco Reis de Portugal* (1945). A contemporary account of the conquest of Lisbon from the Muslims in 1147, *De expugnatione Lyxbonensi,* has been published in Latin and English on opposite pages by Charles Wendell David (1936).

For those doing research on the history of medieval Portugal, António Henrique R. de Oliveira Marques, *Guia do estudante de história medieval portuguesa* (1964), is essential. There have been several new editions.

Unfortunately, there is little on medieval Portugal for those who read only English. Roger Collins, *Early Medieval Spain: Unity in Diversity, 400–1000* (1983), raises a number of interesting questions but fails to take advantage of excellent Portuguese scholarship on a number of important points. The best brief account in English of Portugal in the eleventh, twelfth, and thirteenth centuries is Bailey W. Diffie, *Prelude to Empire: Portugal Overseas Before Henry the Navigator* (1960). Portugal's origins as a nation from a geographer's viewpoint are discussed by Dan Stanislawski, *The Individuality of Portugal: A Study in Historical-Political Geography* (1959). Harold Livermore has published several editions of his *A History of Portugal,* but the first edition (1947) is the best for those interested in Portugal's early history. Still useful is Henry Morse Stephens' colorful account *The Story of Portugal* (1891). António Henrique R. de Oliveira Marques, *History of Portugal,* I (1972, 2nd ed. 1976), is the most detailed and sophisticated account in English. Joseph F. O'Callaghan, *A History of Medieval Spain* (1975), includes much information on Portugal.

FRANCIS A. DUTRA

[See also **Agriculture and Nutrition; Almohads; Almoravids; Anthony of Padua, St.; Asturias-León; Aviz, Order of; Barbarians, Invasions of; Castile; Chivalry, Orders of; Cortes; Deposition of Rulers; Excommunication; Interdict; Islam, Conquests of.**]

PORTUGAL: 1279–1481

REIGN OF DINIS I

During the long reign of Dinis I (1279–1325) Portugal reached in many respects its high-water mark in the Middle Ages. The monarch's actions generated significant internal growth within his kingdom and also did much to ensure the viability of Portugal as an independent entity in the Iberian Peninsula. With the Muslim threat largely neutralized, Dinis was free to turn his attention to Portugal's boundaries with Castile. Towns, castles, and strongholds in three areas were of particular con-

 PORTUGAL: 1279–1481

cern: (1) those on the east bank of the Guadiana, (2) those of the Ribacoa district in the region of Beira Baixa, and (3) those near the Castilian border which were under the control of Dinis' younger brother, Dom Afonso.

Through shrewd alliances and the judicious use of military force, Dinis took advantage of the dynastic problems in Castile following the death of Sancho IV in 1295. The Portuguese monarch first gained undisputed authority over the towns of Moura, Serpa, and Mourão. Then, in the 1297 Treaty of Alcañices, which definitively fixed Portugal's borders with Castile, Portugal gained the towns and fortresses it desired in the Ribacoa district. The treaty was sealed by marriage alliances between Ferdinand IV of Castile and Constança, Dinis' daughter, and between Ferdinand's sister Beatriz and Dinis' heir, the future Afonso IV.

Dinis also resolved the problems inherent in his younger brother's control of a number of towns on the Castilian border, which Prince Afonso used as staging points to intervene in Castilian affairs. Dinis was determined to bring Afonso's towns under royal authority and surrounded his brother's fortresses. In 1299 an accord was reached in which Afonso received privileges over Sintra, Ourém, and other places closer to Lisbon in exchange for his rights over the towns near Castile's borders. This action not only helped secure Dinis' borders, but also removed an irritant to Portugal's relations with Castile.

To further strengthen his kingdom's borders, Dinis undertook a large-scale program of renovation and repair, constructing forty-four new strongholds and castles and repairing many old ones. Also, because many of the border towns were underpopulated, Dinis promoted resettlement. The Ribacoa district and the east bank of the Guadiana River received the greatest attention. But the region north of the Douro was not neglected. Walls were built to strengthen Guimarães and Braga as well as several smaller towns. In addition, Dinis had a wall constructed along the banks of the Tagus River to protect Lisbon from attacks by sea.

Related to these activities were Dinis' efforts to separate from Castilian influence and authority the four clerico-military orders active in Portugal: the Templars, the Hospitalers, Santiago, and Avis. The first two were international orders with headquarters in the Holy Land and branches throughout Europe; the latter two had their origins in the Iberian Peninsula. All four had played important roles in driving out the Muslims, holding the frontiers, and reclaiming the newly won lands. For these activities, the orders had been given extensive spiritual and temporal privileges.

Portugal's conflicts with Castile, especially during the reign of Sancho IV (1284–1295) and his son, Ferdinand IV (1295–1312), convinced Dinis that his kingdom's security was threatened by the fact that the clerico-military orders in Portugal were under the jurisdiction of non-Portuguese leaders. Castilian interference in the political and military life of the monk-knights living in Portugal was an ever-present danger, especially in the Order of Santiago. During the Portuguese Reconquest much land and many strongholds had been given to the order. As boundary disputes became more intense during the reign of Sancho IV, Dinis sought to obtain from the papacy a measure of independence for the order. In 1288, Pope Nicholas IV issued the bull *Pastoralis officii,* which authorized commanders and knights of the Order of Santiago in Portugal to select one of their own members to be in charge of temporal and spiritual administration. The master-general, who resided in Castile, would only conduct visitations. Strong protests from Castile convinced both Pope Celestine V and his successor, Boniface VIII, to revoke Nicholas IV's concession. In late 1318 or early 1319 Dinis' agents argued Portugal's case before Pope John XXII, who then turned the dispute over to the archbishops of Braga and Compostela for resolution. These prelates decided that the Portuguese members of the order should elect and obey their own provincials, in effect placing that order under Portuguese control.

In the meantime the Templars had fallen on hard times. The loss of the Holy Land in 1291 was one of two main factors that led to the demise of the order. The other was the ultimately successful personal campaign of Philip IV the Fair of France and his advisers to destroy the order and gain control of its valuable and extensive holdings. In 1312 Pope Clement V suppressed the Templars and shortly afterward ordered their holdings to be distributed to the Templars' archrivals, the Knights Hospitalers. Dinis of Portugal, like a number of the other European monarchs, had sequestered all the Templar properties in his kingdom and put its knights under his protection. The Portuguese monarch's agents at the papal court argued that the annexation of the Templars' properties in Portugal by the Knights Hospitalers would be prejudicial to the Portuguese crown and the Portuguese people. As an

 PORTUGAL: 1279–1481

alternative, they proposed the foundation of a new order of monk-knights that would incorporate the property of the Templars and, with headquarters in the Algarve, would protect the Portuguese frontier from the Muslims. Clement V's successor, John XXII, agreed with this proposal and on 14 March 1319 by the bull *Ad ea ex quibus* established the Military Order of Our Lord Jesus Christ, which soon became the premier order in Portugal.

During the reign of Dinis the economic foundations of Portugal were greatly strengthened. So energetic were the monarch's agricultural reforms that he was given the epithet "O Lavrador" (the Farmer). Dinis cut back on large landholdings by the church and the higher nobility. He improved landholding patterns on a regional basis and affirmed the nobility of farming one's own land. He promoted the reclamation of marshes and swamps and ordered the planting of pine forests near Leiria to prevent the encroachment of coastal sand and salt as well as to provide needed timber. Dinis' agricultural reforms ranged from the division of uncultivated lands into groups of ten, twenty, or thirty *casais* with lifetime leases in Entre Douro e Minho, to cooperatives (communal enterprises) in Tras-os-Montes, to an emphasis on repopulating the Alentejo by founding towns, hampering the wealthy from unproductively monopolizing large tracts of property, and granting land to those who would cultivate it. In this way, Dinis increased the number of small proprietors and rural workers, who paid a rent to the crown. During the thirteenth century, Portugal's population probably numbered between 800,000 and a million inhabitants.

Dinis also took note of Portugal's foreign trade. He encouraged the export of agricultural produce, salt, and salted fish to Flanders, England, and France in exchange for textiles and metals. He increased Portugal's foreign contacts as well and encouraged maritime development in the Algarve. In 1293 he supported the creation of a *bolsa de comércio* by Portuguese merchants for their legal defense in foreign ports. The monarch promoted trade fairs and gave the towns that held them privileges and exemptions. Dinis also reformed the kingdom's coinage. Further, he promoted the mining industry by encouraging the extraction of silver, tin, sulphur, and iron.

Although Portuguese shipping had played a role in the kingdom's defense, as well as in the offensive against the Muslims, it was not until the reign of Dinis that a Portuguese navy was officially established. In 1317 the Portuguese monarch signed a contract with the Genoese Manuele Pessagno (Manuel Peçanha) that made him and his heirs admirals of Portugal and gave him many important rights and privileges. Pessagno was to provide twenty Genoese captains and build up the king's fleet. He was obliged to defend Portugal's coast, but at the same time was free to engage in commerce between his native Italy and England and Flanders.

Dinis ordered the exclusive use of Portuguese as the nation's language. Works of history and law were translated into Portuguese, including the *Siete partidas* of Dinis' grandfather, Alfonso X. In 1290 papal approval was received for the University of Lisbon, which Dinis had founded several years earlier. In 1308 the university was transferred to Coimbra, where it remained until 1338. Between 1354 and 1377 it was again at Coimbra; then it returned to Lisbon and remained there until 1537.

By promoting royal justice and by cracking down on the usurpation of royal prerogatives, Dinis also greatly increased royal authority. He reinstituted the *inquirições* of his predecessors, especially in the regions of Beira Baixa and Entre Douro e Minho. Further, he gradually resolved the kingdom's problems with the papacy, ending the twenty-two year struggle with Rome that had left his father and him excommunicates and Portugal under interdict. In 1289 a compromise, the "Concordat of the Forty Articles," was signed. Although the church did not give up any of its ideas regarding the immunity of its holdings and its jurisdiction, it did agree to obey royal authority.

An important figure in Portugal during Dinis' reign was his wife, Isabel—the future St. Isabel—whom he married in 1288. The daughter of Pedro III of Aragon, the Portuguese queen played an important role as a mediator in the feuds between her husband and his brother Afonso, and between the king and his son, the future Afonso IV. In addition, her skill as a conciliator was of major significance in the negotiations leading to the Treaty of Alcañices, which fixed the definitive boundaries between Portugal and Castile.

FROM AFONSO IV TO FERDINAND I

Dinis' long reign was followed by another lengthy one, that of his son. Afonso IV (*r.* 1325–1357), an austere ruler, continued his father's policies of augmenting the crown's patrimony, strengthening royal authority, and promoting justice. His reign, however, was marked by numerous

PORTUGAL: 1279–1481

internal revolts, conflicts with Castile, and dislocations in the wake of the Black Death.

During the early part of his reign, Afonso IV was preoccupied with the struggle against his bastard half-brother, Afonso Sanches. After the latter's death in 1329, Portugal became embroiled in a conflict with Castile over Afonso IV's daughter Maria, wife of Alfonso XI of Castile (*r.* 1312–1350). After Alfonso XI abandoned her, Portugal gave its support to Juan Manuel, Alfonso XI's cousin and a perpetual thorn in the Castilian monarch's side, and to others who contested Alfonso XI's power. In fact, Afonso IV married off his son and heir, Pedro, to Constanza, daughter of Juan Manuel. Alfonso XI then refused to allow Constanza to leave Castile, and Portugal, in alliance with Aragon, invaded Castile in 1336.

These disputes among the Christian kingdoms gave the Muslims the opportunity to recover some of the territory they had earlier lost to the Christians. The Marinids were in the ascendancy in North Africa and allied with the Muslims in Granada. Gibraltar was seized in 1333. In 1340 the Marinids invaded the peninsula after destroying an Aragonese and Castilian fleet in the Strait of Gibraltar. Castile and Portugal temporarily put their differences aside and signed a peace treaty at Seville in July of 1340. A Portuguese, Genoese, and Castilian armada was organized near the Strait of Gibraltar, but storms scattered it. Portuguese forces, led by Afonso IV and accompanied by the archbishop of Braga, the bishop of Évora, and knights from the Portuguese military orders, however, played an important role in the victory at Salado (30 October 1340), a major event in the Christian reconquest of the Iberian Peninsula.

The Black Death struck Portugal late in September of 1348 and continued its devastation for the remainder of the year. The pestilence claimed at least one-third of Portugal's population. Some villages and small towns completely disappeared, while others became greatly depopulated. There was an exodus to the cities by many of the survivors, which further aggravated the problem of rural depopulation. Because the epidemic often wiped out entire families, some shifts occurred within the social strata as distant relatives and the poor came into vast sums of money or substantial properties. The church also benefited greatly from the many deathbed grants of estates and goods. A shortage of labor led to higher wages and prices. Famine and food shortages became regular occurrences in many parts of the kingdom as the Black Death was followed by new plagues and epidemics. There were frequent devaluations. Abandoned agricultural lands were turned into vineyards, olive groves, pasturage, or hunting preserves. Social instability and famine led to discontent, unrest, and an increasing number of riots. Afonso IV and his successors used iron-handed methods trying to control these upheavals: they fixed wages, cracked down on vagrancy, and bound workers to their traditional occupations. The cortes was called in 1352 and 1361 in hopes of solving some of the problems.

Meanwhile, Prince Pedro's wife, Constanza, who had arrived in Portugal in 1340, gave birth to three children, including Ferdinand (Fernando), the future king of Portugal. Pedro, however, had fallen in love with Inés de Castro, his wife's maid-in-waiting and a member of a powerful Galician family. Although Afonso IV banished Inés from his kingdom, she returned to Portugal after Constanza's death in 1345 and gave birth to four illegitimate children by Pedro. Afonso IV believed that his son Pedro was setting a bad example, neglecting his royal duties and compromising Portugal's security by falling under the influence of Galician and Castilian nobles, headed by Inés' brothers. In 1355, apparently at Afonso IV's orders, Inés was murdered. Prince Pedro, aided by Castilian forces led by the brothers of Inés de Castro, mounted a full-scale revolt against his father, but in 1356 peace returned.

Next year, the thirty-seven-year-old Pedro (*r.* 1357–1367) ascended the Portuguese throne. Chroniclers emphasize his love of hunting, his extensive travel throughout his kingdom, and his obsession with justice and administration. Pedro the Cruel to some, and Pedro the Just to others, the monarch frequently dispensed personal and summary justice during his travels. Although he had promised his father that he would not harm the executioners of Inés de Castro, he exchanged them for some Castilian refugees and had them brutally executed in his presence. In 1360 Pedro tried to prove that he had been secretly married to Inés de Castro and he had her remains exhumed and entombed at the monastery of Alcobaça. Pedro also began the process of "royalizing" the military orders by naming his bastard son João (born 1358) master of Avis, a policy that the son continued when he became King João I.

During Pedro's reign there were ten years of peace with Castile. Pedro continued to centralize

PORTUGAL: 1279–1481

authority to deal with the aftermath of the Black Death. In 1361 he established the *Beneplacito régio,* which prohibited the publication or divulgation of any papal document in Portugal without the express approval of the monarch, ostensibly in order to avoid forgeries and counterfeits. However, according to some scholars, its purpose was to impress the authority of the king over the church, and according to others, Pedro probably wished to keep to himself any news from Rome regarding his efforts to legitimize his children by Inés de Castro. Although there was a strong negative reaction to the law on the part of the higher clergy, they and the nobility were too weak in the aftermath of the Black Death to seriously challenge Pedro's will. Also, by the 1360's the papacy had lost the aggressiveness it had displayed in the previous century.

In 1367 the twenty-two-year-old Ferdinand (*r.* 1367–1383) became the ninth king of Portugal. The wealthiest by far of the Portuguese monarchs to that date, Ferdinand did much to promote commerce and shipbuilding, and his economic legislation has justly been praised. But the positive achievements during Ferdinand's reign generally have been obscured by his three disastrous wars with Castile and by his marriage to the controversial Leonor Teles.

Pedro I of Castile was assassinated in 1369 by his bastard half-brother, Enrique of Trastámara, who then became the new king of Castile, Enrique II (1369–1379). Ferdinand of Portugal, the great-grandson of Sancho IV of Castile and the nearest legitimate male heir of Pedro I, also claimed the Castilian throne and enjoyed the support of a number of Castilian border towns. In June of 1369 Ferdinand entered Galicia, where he was well received, but Enrique II counterattacked by invading Portugal and seizing a number of towns in Tras-os-Montes, including Braga and Bragança. Papal intervention brought the war to a close in September of 1370. Ferdinand agreed to give up his claim to the Castilian throne and promised to marry Enrique's daughter, Leonor. Soon, however, he reneged on his marriage promise by wedding instead the already married Dona Leonor Teles.

In 1372 Ferdinand entered into an English-Portuguese alliance against the Trastámaras. By the Treaty of Tagilde, the Portuguese monarch allied himself with John of Gaunt, the duke of Lancaster, who had married an illegitimate daughter of Pedro I of Castile. This pact was followed in 1373 by the Treaty of Westminister, in which Ferdinand promised to defend the duke of Lancaster's claim to the Castilian throne. In the meantime, the second of Ferdinand's three wars with Castile had begun. Enrique II of Castile again invaded Portugal, taking and sacking Lisbon in February of 1373 and occupying the Portuguese capital for two months. Once more the papal legate fashioned a peace, with a treaty signed in March of 1373. This temporarily put Portugal in the French-Castilian camp in the Hundred Years War against England. Portugal was forced to give up her shipping and a number of her towns to Castile for three years.

In 1379 Enrique II of Castile died and was succeeded by his son Juan I (1379–1390). Portugal renewed the alliance with England and preparations began for a third war against Castile. Some 3,000 English troops arrived in Lisbon in July of 1381, but soon they were out of hand, killing and robbing the city's inhabitants; they continued their depredations against the Portuguese populace in the Alentejo, where they were sent to fight the Castilians. In the meantime Juan I's Castilian forces attacked Lisbon and its environs. The following year, 1382, peace was arranged and the Castilians provided ships to return the unruly English troops to their homeland.

This same period witnessed the beginning of the Great Western Schism. Portugal initially backed Clement VII in Avignon and received many benefits from the Avignon papacy. But because England backed Pope Urban VI in Rome, the Portuguese switched their allegiance to the popes of Rome.

The death in September of 1382 of the wife of Juan I of Castile prompted the widowed monarch to undertake a new marriage with Beatriz, daughter of Ferdinand of Portugal and Leonor Teles. This union was favored by the pro-Castilian party in Portugal, which included Leonor Teles, the bishop of Lisbon, and many nobles. The marriage contract was signed at Salvaterra de Magos in May of 1383. Ferdinand was seriously ill at the time and died five months later, naming in his will the widowed Queen Leonor Teles as regent and governor of Portugal.

JOÃO I AND HIS SUCCESSORS

The actions of the Castilian faction met with opposition from many Portuguese, especially those of the lower and middle classes. The devastation and suffering that resulted from the three wars with Castile, wars fought mainly on Portuguese soil, had produced much hostility toward Castile. In Decem-

PORTUGAL: 1279–1481

ber of 1383 João, the master of Avis and illegitimate son of Pedro I, killed the chief negotiator for the Castilian faction, and the Castilian-born bishop of Lisbon was thrown to his death from the tower of his cathedral, as the Lisbon populace revolted and proclaimed João regent and defender of the realm. Leonor Teles, who had the support of many of the nobility and the higher clergy, fled to Santarém, where she invited her new son-in-law, Juan I of Castile, to invade Portugal. When he arrived, she turned over the government of Portugal to him and her twelve-year-old daughter Beatriz. In March 1384 Juan I besieged Lisbon by land while a Castilian fleet from Seville blockaded the Portuguese capital by sea. An outbreak of plague, however, forced Juan to raise the siege and return to Castile.

The Portuguese cortes that met at Coimbra in 1385 included three main factions: (1) a pro-Castilian faction that supported the rule of Beatriz and Juan I; (1) pro-legitimist representatives who proposed as ruler Dom João, the oldest son of Pedro I and Inés de Castro; (3) a nationalist group that wanted Dom João, master of Avis, as king. A key figure in the cortes' debate was Doctor João das Regras, a recent graduate of the University of Bologna. He disputed Juan I's claim on the grounds that the Castilian king had invaded Portugal and had failed to comply with the marriage agreement at Salvaterra de Magos. Furthermore, Juan I was accused of violating Portuguese privileges (*foros*), as well as pledging allegiance to the antipope at Avignon. The same arguments were applied to young Beatriz. In addition her legitimacy was questioned on the basis of her mother's reputation.

João das Regras also opposed the claims to the throne of Dom João and Dom Dinis, the sons of Pedro I and Inés de Castro. He argued that he had documentary evidence that the papacy had refused to recognize the "secret" marriage of Pedro I and Inés de Castro and had declined to legitimize their sons.

João das Regas maintained that the empty throne would best be filled by João of Avis, despite his illegitimacy and the fact that he was younger than the two sons of Inés de Castro. The threat of a Castilian invasion and the perilous state of the kingdom required a capable leader such as the regent and defender of the realm had proved himself to be. Largely due to the energetic efforts of João das Regras, João of Avis was elected king by the Portuguese cortes on 6 April 1385.

An attack by Juan I appeared imminent, and the new Portuguese king and his constable, Nuno Álvares Pereira, prepared to meet it. In June 1385, Portuguese forces defeated a Castilian contingent at the Battle of Trancoso. Juan I of Castile then launched a major invasion, hoping to cut Portugal in two and to capture Lisbon. On 14 August 1385 the Castilians met the Portuguese forces, and although the latter were greatly outnumbered, they managed to rout the invaders in the famous Battle of Aljubarrota.

Clearly the revolution of 1383–1385 brought some political changes to Portugal, but their number and significance are still debated. The fifteenth-century chronicler Fernão Lopes wrote that there was "a new world and a new generation of people of rank." Despite this observation, however, there was no sweeping renovation of society. The traditional landed nobility was not destroyed, and the highest posts continued to belong to the families who held them before the revolution of 1383. What did change to a certain extent were their effective political power and privileges. After the revolution their power was limited. João I promoted legists and bureaucrats and favored merchants. Artisans gained significance in several urban areas, particularly in Lisbon. At the same time a new landed nobility was becoming powerful. Portugal's constable, Nuno Álvares Pereira, became one of the most important of this group. After signing a peace treaty with Castile in 1411, João began preparations to capture Ceuta in North Africa. In 1415 the Muslim stronghold fell to the Portuguese.

Much of Portugal's history in the fifteenth century revolves around the legitimate and illegitimate children of João I of Avis and their heirs. Duarte, João's eldest son, succeeded his father on the throne in 1433. Pedro, the second son, famous for his travels throughout Europe between 1425 and 1428, served as regent from 1439 to 1446 for Duarte's young son, Afonso V. João I continued the royalization of the Portuguese military orders by making another of his sons, Henrique (Henry the Navigator), the master of the Order of Christ. Henry and the order played important roles in Portugal's North African campaigns as well as in her overseas exploration and colonization. The fourth legitimate son, João, was named master of Santiago and constable of Portugal. Ferdinand, the youngest of João I's sons, was named master of Avis. He was captured during Portugal's disastrous effort to capture Tangiers in 1437 and died a captive in Muslim

PORTUGAL: 1279–1481

hands in 1443. João I's daughter, Isabel, married Philip, duke of Burgundy, in 1429, thereby helping to strengthen Portugal's commercial ties with Flanders. Afonso, illegitimate, but the oldest son of João I, became count of Barcelos and later first duke of Bragança. Afonso's two sons played important roles during the fifteenth century in the struggle between the powerful landed aristocracy and those who worked to promote greater centralization and royal power.

Duarte had been entrusted with a number of royal responsibilities during the last years of his father's life. His own reign, however, was a short one, lasting a mere five years and one month (1433–1438). He worked closely with the cortes, convoking it at least four or five times during his years in power. Like his father, Duarte was alarmed at the number of crown lands that had been alienated into the hands of the landed nobility. Along with his brother Pedro, Duarte energetically attempted to centralize government and recover those lands. An important instrument for this was the *Lei mental,* promulgated at the cortes meeting at Santarém in 1434. The *Lei mental* declared that it had been in the mind of João I, when he gave out grants of crown land, that the grants would be confirmed at the beginning of each reign and that they could be inherited only by legitimate males. It was retroactive, though lands in the hands of his half-brother, Afonso, count of Barcelos, were exempt.

Duarte also promoted overseas exploration. In 1434 the Portuguese Gil Eanes rounded Cape Bojador. During Duarte's reign 100 leagues of African coast were explored. However, the monarch's North African policy was disastrous. The attempt to take Tangiers in 1437 resulted not only in a humiliating loss for the Portuguese but the turning over of Prince Ferdinand as a hostage.

Six-year-old Afonso V was acclaimed king shortly after his father's death in 1438. Although Duarte's will left both the regency and the education of his children to his widow, Queen Leonor, there was much sentiment in Portugal, especially in the larger towns and cities, for a regency by Duarte's brother, Pedro. In December of 1439 the cortes at Lisbon elected Pedro as regent, and several weeks later entrusted him also with the education of Duarte's children.

Pedro was a strong ruler, placing many of his retainers in important posts and continuing his brother Duarte's policy of centralization. However, the death in 1442 of Pedro's younger brother and strong supporter, João, master of Santiago and constable of Portugal, weakened his position. At the same time Pedro was losing support from the elements who had named him regent in 1439, and he alienated the duke of Bragança's older son, the count of Ourém.

When fourteen-year-old Afonso V's majority was proclaimed in January of 1446, Pedro continued to act in an advisory capacity to the young king. But although Afonso V married Pedro's daughter, Isabel, in 1447, relations between him and his father-in-law were deteriorating. Afonso, count of Barcelos, and after 1442 first duke of Bragança, along with disaffected landed nobility mostly from Beira and Entre Douro e Minho, soon had the confidence of the youthful monarch. In 1448 Pedro was forced to relinquish his authority and retire to his estates at Coimbra. Soon he was charged with being a rebel and disloyal to the king. A year later, at the Battle of Alfarrobeira between the forces of Afonso V and the greatly outnumbered forces of Pedro, the former regent was killed. Many of Pedro's supporters also lost their lives and their properties, although six years later Afonso V issued a general pardon to Pedro's supporters.

Alfonso V was very active in crusading against the Muslims in North Africa. Because of this, he is sometimes called "the African." Alcácer Ceguer (El-Ksar es-Seghir), one of the wealthiest cities in the Magrib, fell to the Portuguese in 1458. During the next dozen years the Portuguese continued to campaign in North Africa, but without much success. In 1471, however, Portuguese forces captured Arzila. Several days after this victory, Tangiers was abandoned to the Portuguese as, soon, was Larache. These strongholds in North Africa were, however, like Ceuta (captured by João I in 1415), a drain on Portugal's manpower and supplies.

As long as Prince Henry, Afonso V's uncle, was alive, the Porguguese continued to explore down the coast of western Africa and began colonizing the Atlantic islands of Madeira and the Azores. After Henry's death in 1460 the efforts at exploration abated somewhat. During the latter years of Afonso V's reign, overseas activity and exploration down the west coast of Africa were once again stepped up under the direction of the king's son and heir, the future João II.

Afonso V moved away from the policy of centralization promoted by his uncles Duarte I and the regent Pedro. Afonso was almost profligate in giving lands and privileges to the landed nobility,

PORTUGAL: 1279–1481

especially to the count of Barcelos and first duke of Bragança and his family, at the expense of the royal patrimony. New rankings of the nobility—the baronetcy and the marquisate—were introduced. In 1451 the count of Ourém, the elder son of the first duke of Bragança, was given the additional title of marquis of Valença. Despite criticism of the king's extravagance by the cortes meeting in Lisbon in 1460, it was clear that the landed nobility increasingly dominated Portugal.

In the latter years of his reign, Afonso V was preoccupied with Castile as he tried to marry his thirteen-year-old niece, Juana, called "La Beltraneja" by her enemies, daughter of Enrique IV of Castile and Afonso's sister Joana. Enrique's death in 1474 had left Juana heiress to the throne of Castile although her claim was challenged by Enrique's half-sister, Isabel, the latter having married Ferdinand of Aragon in 1469. Initially a significant part of the Castilian nobility backed Juana's cause and that of Afonso V, who was proclaimed king of León and Castile in 1475. Afonso was counting on an earlier alliance with Louis XI of France to turn the tide in his favor. But Portugal's French alliance came to naught and the Portuguese loss at the Battle of Toro in 1476, combined with papal refusal to grant the needed dispensations for Afonso's marriage to his niece, doomed Afonso V's and Juana's cause. In 1479 the Treaty of Alcáçovas was signed; it recognized Isabel as queen of Castile and ceded the Canary Islands to her kingdom.

The years of Afonso's rule have been viewed by some as the last flowering of chivalry and the political power of the wealthy landed nobility. In many respects, Afonso V was an anachronism in fifteenth-century Portugal. At the same time, the monarch did promote the new European humanism and was the patron of Mateus of Pisa, Fernão Lopes, Gomes Eanes de Zurara, the painter Nuño Gonsalves, and the legist Vasco Fernandes de Lucena.

The virtual abdication by Afonso V of his royal responsibilities during the last ten years of his reign made his son, the future João II, the de facto ruler of Portugal during much of the period between 1476 and 1481. When João II ascended the throne in 1481, he had the backing of the cortes that met at Évora that same year to restore centralized royal authority. João II was said to have remarked that his father had left him only the royal highways.

With João II, the Renaissance monarchy began in Portugal. Considered one of the ablest European monarchs of the fifteenth century, João was determined to subordinate the landed nobility to the crown. Before long, evidence turned up that allegedly implicated Ferdinand, third duke of Bragança, one of the wealthiest and most powerful men in the entire Iberian Peninsula, in a conspiracy with Ferdinand of Aragon and Isabel of Castile to overthrow the rule of João II. The duke of Bragança was brought to trial, found guilty as charged, and publicly beheaded in Évora in 1483. The following year João II's cousin (and brother-in-law), Diogo, fourth duke of Viseu, who had continued to plot against the monarch, was stabbed to death by João II's own hand. Others involved in the conspiracies were executed or imprisoned, or sought refuge in Castile. With the support of the cortes, the extension of royal law and administration was greatly increased. Although the high social and economic status of the nobility remained, any threat the nobility posed to the crown was extinguished.

BIBLIOGRAPHY

In addition to the works mentioned in the preceding article, see the overview of Portuguese history for the years 1279–1481 in vol. III of José Hermano Saraiva, ed., *História de Portugal* (1983).

The reign of D. Dinis is chronicled by Rui de Pina, *Crónica de D. Dinis.* Rui de Pina also wrote chronicles of *Dom Duarte, Dom Afonso V,* and *Dom João II.* The works of Pina have been united in a new edition by Manuel Lopes de Almeida as *Crónicas de Rui de Pina* (1977). A contrasting view of the regent D. Pedro is Gaspar Dias de Landim, *O Infante D. Pedro.* Luís Filipe Lindley Cintra, ed., *Crónica Geral de Espanha de 1344,* 3 vols. (1951), has an excellent introduction. The greatest of Portugal's chroniclers was Fernão Lopes, a reading of whom is essential for an understanding of the fourteenth and early fifteenth centuries. There are editions of his *Crónica de D. Pedro, Crónica de Dom Fernando,* and *Crónica de D. João I.,* 2 vols. Fernando, brother of Pedro and Henry is described by Frei João Álvares in *Crónica do Infante Santo D. Fernando.* For overseas expansion, see Gomes Eanes de Zurara, *Crónica da Tomada de Ceuta* and *Crónica dos Feitos de Guiné.* A new critical edition of Damião de Gois is *Crónica de Principe D. João* (1977), Graça Almeida Rodrigues, ed. The same monarch is treated by Garcia de Resende, *Chrónica de D. João II e Miscelanea.*

There are several important collections of documents that often go far beyond the limits suggested by their titles: *Monumenta Henricina,* 15 vols. (1960–1974), with introd. and notes by António Joaquim Dias Dinis; João Martins da Silva Marques, *Descobrimentos portugueses,* 3 vols. (1944–1971); Alberto Iria, *Descobri-*

mentos portugueses: O Algarve e os Descobrimentos, 2 vols. (1956); Vitorino Magalhães Godinho, *Documentos sobre a expansão portuguesa,* 3 vols. (1945).

For social and economic history, see Antonio de Sousa e Silva Costa Lobo, *História da sociedade em Portugal no século XV* (1904); Humberto Baquero Moreno, *Tensões sociais em Portugal na idade média* (1976), and *Marginalidade e conflitos sociais em Portugal nos séculos XIV e XV: Estudos de história* (1985); Virginia Rau, *Feiras medievais portuguesas: Subsídios para o seu estudo,* 2nd ed. (1982), and *Sesmarias medievais portuguesas* (1946).

The Jews in Portugal are studied by María José Pimenta Ferro, *Os judeus em Portugal no século XIV.* The 1970 edition includes an appendix with seventy-five documents that are not included in the 1979 edition. The same author also published *Os judeus em Portugal no século XV,* 2 vols. (1982–1984), which attempts to identify all the Jews living in Portugal in the fifteenth century.

In 1984 the Fundação Calouste Gulbenkian published a facsimile reproduction of the 1792 edition of the *Ordenações Afonsinas,* 5 vols. Another important study for the Middle Ages as well as the Renaissance is Martim de Albuquerque, *O poder político no renascimento* (1968).

For the historiography of the period, see José Verissimo Serrão, *A historiografia portuguesa,* I (1972), and *Cronistas de século XV posteriores a Fernão Lopes* (1977). For the crisis and revolution of 1381–1385, see Salvador Dias Arnaut, *A crise nacional dos Fins do século XIV: A sucessão de D. Fernando,* I (1959); Joel Serrão, *O caracter social da revolução de 1383,* 2nd ed. (1976); Antonio Borges Coelho, *Revolução de 1383,* 4th ed. (1981). Two important articles on the subject by Marcello Caetano have been reprinted under the title *A crise nacional de 1383–1385* (1985). Also useful is Valentino Viegas, *Cronologia da revolução de 1383–1385* (1985).

There is an excellent psychological profile of João I by A. H. de Oliveira Marques in *Dicionário de história de Portugal,* II, 607–611. The role of Prince Henry and the events surrounding him are best discussed in António Joaquim Dias Dinis, *Estudos Henriquinos,* I (1960). For the Regent D. Pedro, see Humberto Baquero Moreno, *A batalha de alfarrobeira: Antecedentes e significado histórico,* 2nd ed., 2 vols. (1979–1980). J. T. Montalvão Machado has studied *Dom Afonso, Primeiro duque de Bragança: Sua vida e obra* (1960).

A few English studies are valuable: Peter E. Russell, *The English Intervention in Spain and Portugal in the Time of Edward III and Richard III* (1955); Francis M. Rogers, *The Travels of the Infante Dom Pedro of Portugal* (1961); and Bailey W. Diffie, *Prelude to Empire: Portugal Overseas Before Henry the Navigator* (1960). An excellent summary of early Portuguese overseas expansion is Bailey W. Diffie and George D. Winius, *Foundations of the Portuguese Empire, 1415–1580* (1977). See also A. C. de C. M. Saunders, *A Social History of Black Slaves and Freedmen in Portugal, 1441–1555* (1982); Elaine Sanceau, *The Perfect Prince: A Biography of the King Dom João II* (1959), which also covers the reign of Afonso V; and William D. Phillips, Jr., *Enrique IV and the Crisis of Fifteenth-century Castile, 1425–1480* (1978). A general account of Portugal's development within the context of the entire peninsula is Stanley Payne, *A History of Spain and Portugal,* I (1973).

FRANCIS A. DUTRA

[See also **Castile; Dinis; Exploration by Western Europeans; Gonsalves, Nuño; Reconquest.**]

PORTUGUESE LANGUAGE. In the centuries following the disintegration of the Western Roman Empire, the spoken Latin of the west and northwest of the Iberian Peninsula gradually evolved into the linguistic systems known as Galician and Portuguese. At the outset Portuguese and Galician must have displayed a high degree of linguistic unity. Most scholars agree that the major sound changes which characterize the history of Portuguese—the loss of *-l-* (*salīre* > *sair* [to leave]), of *-n-*, with subsequent nasalization of the preceding vowel (*lūna* > Old Portuguese *lũa* [moon]), and the alteration of *pl-*, *cl-*, and *fl-* to *ch-* (*plānu* > *chão* [flat], *clamāre* > *chamar* [to call], *flamma* > *chama* [flame])—originated in the north and were brought southward with the reconquest. The northern dialects ultimately displaced the varieties of Romance spoken by the Christians who had lived under Muslim domination since the early eighth century. In 1139 the county of Portugal broke away from the kingdom of León and formed an independent political entity with its political and commercial center at Lisbon, which was recaptured from the Arabs in 1147. The territory north of the Minho remained under the political and linguistic influence of León and later of Castile. With the passing of time, the linguistic divergences between Galician and Portuguese widened.

The first complete Old Portuguese texts extant go back to the first decade of the thirteenth century. (Recent research has cast doubt on the authenticity of the *Auto de partilhas,* a division of inheritance dated 1192, and the will of Elvira Sanchez from 1193, long considered the oldest Portuguese texts.)

Old Portuguese orthography presents a confusing picture, as scribes sought to adapt the Latin alphabet to the sounds of the vernacular. Double vowels first developed through the fall of an intervocalic consonant (*populu* > *poboo* [people]) and continued to be written double after the vowels had contracted and shortened in pronunciation. Double vowels came to replace single vowels to indicate nasalization (*maao* = *mão* [hand]), which was also marked indiscriminately by the use of *m*, *n*, a tilde, or acute accents on a double vowel (*cimco* = *cinco* [five], *poner* = *põer* [modern *pôr*], *tẽpo* = *tempo* [time], *úú* = *um* [one]). The graphs *g* and *j* were both employed for [g] and [dʒ] as in *fugo* = *fujo* [I flee] and *gisa* = *guisa* [way]; *quo-* and *guo-* stood for [kw] and [gw] and in *quoall* = *qual* [which], *linguoa* = *lingua* [language, tongue]. The letters *i*, *j*, and *y* were often interchanged (*iulgar* = *julgar* [to judge], *oye* = *hoje* [today], *mujto* = *muito* [many], and *ydade* = *idade* [age]. An *h* denoted vowel hiatus (*sahir* = *sair*) and came to be used unetymologically in word-initial position (*honde* = *onde* [where], *hir* = *ir* [to go]); *h* could also stand for postconsonantal [İ] (*sabha* = *sabia* [I used to know], *mha* = Old Portuguese *mĩa* [modern *minha*] [my, mine]). Early documents employ *ll* and *nn* for the lateral and nasal palatals today spelled *lh* and *nh*. Older texts contain instances of initial *ff-*, *ll-*, *ss-*, and *rr-* for their single counterparts. It is believed that syllable-final *-ll* (*mortall* [mortal], *malldade* [illness]) marked the velar liquid.

The pronunciation of medieval Portuguese differed in several respects from that of the modern language. Rhyme discloses that the language rigorously kept apart the [ɛw] of such forms as *meu* [my], *teu* [your], *seu* [his, her], and *deus* [god] from the [ew] of the preterit ending *-eu;* modern Portuguese has merged these sounds as [ew]. The diagraph *ou* represents [ow], today [o]. The spelling does not indicate to what extent (if any) unstressed vowels had been weakened or reduced before 1500. If Old Portuguese practiced metaphony, that is, the raising of tonic [ɛ] and [ɔ] to [e] and [o] under the influence of a final high vowel (witness such rhymes as *medo:cedo* with [e]), one must assume that *-o* denoted [u]. Nasalization was much more widespread in the older language (Old Portuguese *arẽa* [sand], *bõa* [good], *lũa* [moon], *põer* [to put], *tẽer* [to have], *vẽir* [to come] versus modern *areia, boa, lua, pôr, ter, vir*). In the Old Portuguese vowel sequences *ĩo* and *ĩa*, a palatal nasal developed between the vowels and replaced the nasal resonance; in this way Old Portuguese *galĩa* [hen], *vĩo* [wine], and the suffix *-ĩo* became *galinha, vinho,* and *-inho*.

Statements by sixteenth-century grammarians and the evidence furnished by the conservative dialects of northern Portugal provide reliable information concerning the value to be assigned to Old Portuguese consonants. The pronunciation of *c* + *e*, *c* + *i*, or *ç* as [ts]; of *z* as [dz]; of *ch* as [tʃ]; and of *g* + *e*, *i*, and *j* as [(d)ʒ] constitute the main differences between medieval and modern consonantism. Sporadic instances of such spellings as *Lixboa* may indicate that some speakers already pronounced syllable final *-s* as [ʃ].

The old language displayed more form variation than does the modern language. Alongside *o* and *a*, Old Portuguese employed, *el*, *lo*, and *la* as definite articles. Beside direct object *te* appear scattered examples of *che*, prevalent in Galician, as an indirect object pronoun; in like fashion, *xe* flanks *se*. The medieval pronominal inventory also included *y* or *hi* [to there] and *ende* [from there, about it] (*cf.* French *y* and *en*). In addition to the stressed series of possessive pronouns and adjectives that have come down into the modern language, Old Portuguese had possessives that evolved as unstressed forms (*mha, ta,* and *sa*). The medieval demonstratives included *aqueste, aquesta, aquesse, aquessa, aquesto,* and *aquisto*. Worthy of mention here is *medês* [same] alongside *me(e)smo*.

Old Portuguese verbs differed in several key respects from their modern counterparts, clinging, for example, to a number of etymological forms: *arço* [I burn]←*arder*, *menço* [I lie]←*mentir*, *moiro* [I die]←*morrer*, *perço* [I lose]←*perder*, and *senço* [I feel]←*sentir*, as well as so-called inchoatives in *-sco* (*gradesco, paresco*); compare modern *ardo, minto, morro, perco, sinto,* and *pareço*. Until the fifteenth century the second-person plural retained *-d-* (present indicative *falades, comedes,* present subjunctive *faledes, comades,* imperfect *falávades, comíades*). The first person of strong preterits often ended in *-i* rather than *-e* (*dixi, estivi, pudi, quigi, ouvi, soubi*), while the third singular showed *-o* (*ouvo, soubo*). Many *-er* verbs displayed a past participle in *-udo*, as in *atrevudo*←*atrever* [to dare], *teudo*←*teer*, *vençudo*←*vencer* [to conquer], versus modern *atrevido, tido,* and *vencido*. Old Portuguese futures which differ from the modern forms are *ferrei*←*ferir*, [to wound], *jarei*←*jazer* [to lie], *marrei*←*mãer* [to remain], *porrei*←*pôr*, *querrei*←*querer* [to want], *terrei*←*tẽer*, and *verrei*←*vẽir*.

One additional feature of medieval Portuguese that straddles the boundary between phonology and morphology deserves mention here. The older language carefully distinguished the results of the Latin sequences *-ane, -ant; -one, -unt, -udine;* and *-ānu;* note *cane* > Old Portuguese *cam* [dog], *amant* > *amam; vīsiōne* > *visom* [vision], *sunt* > *som* [they are], *-(it)udine; -idõe* (*certidõe* [certainty]); *germānu* > *irmão* [brother]. By the end of the Middle Ages these endings had merged as diphthongal *-ão* (although the unstressed verb endings retained the spelling *-am*): *cão, visião, são, certidão* versus *amam.*

In regard to syntax, the older language displayed greater freedom of usage in such matters as the use of the definite article, prepositions, relative pronouns, simple past tenses, and the collocation of object pronouns. The medieval language favored *haver* over *tẽer* both as a main verb meaning "to have" and as the auxiliary verb in compound past tenses. It preferred by a wide margin the inherited simple pluperfect *falara* [I had spoken]. The use of *seer* and *estar* with predicate adjectives and locatives appeared more fluid than it is today.

By the end of the sixteenth century the major shifts that mark the transition from the medieval to the modern language had taken place.

BIBLIOGRAPHY

The best histories are Serafim da Silva Neto, *História da língua portuguêsa,* 3rd ed. (1979), and Paul Teyssier, *Histoire de la langue portugaise* (1980). See also Kurt Baldinger, "El gallego-portugués y sus relaciones de substrato con la Aquitania," in his *La formación de los dominios lingüísticos en la península ibérica,* 2nd ed. (1972); Francisco da Silveira Bueno, *A formação histórica da língua portuguêsa,* 3rd ed. (1967); William J. Entwistle, *The Spanish Language, Together with Portuguese, Catalan, and Basque* (1936), 278–312; Fernando V. Peixoto da Fonesca, *Noções de história da língua portugesa,* 2nd ed. (1964); Harri Meier, *Ensaios da filologia românica* (1948), 5–30.

The standard historical grammars are Joseph Huber, *Altportugiesisches Elementarbuch* (1933); José Joaquim Nunes, *Compêndio de gramática histórica portuguesa,* 3rd ed. (1945); Edwin B. Williams, *From Latin to Portuguese,* 2nd ed. (1962).

There exists no adequate descriptive grammar of Old Portuguese. Useful outlines can be gleaned from José Leite de Vasconcellos, *Lições de filologia portuguesa,* 3rd ed. (1959), and Carolina Michaëlis de Vasconcellos, *Lições de filologia portuguesa, segundo as prelecções feitas aos cursos de 1911/12 e de 1912/13,* 2nd ed. (1956). Samples of Old Portuguese are in José Leite de Vasconcellos, *Textos arcaicos,* 5th ed. (1970); José Joaquim Nunes, *Crestomatia arcaica,* 7th ed. (1970); Kimberly S. Roberts, *An Anthology of Old Portuguese* (n.d.).

STEVEN N. DWORKIN

[See also **Latin Language.**]

POSTAL AND INTELLIGENCE SERVICES, BYZANTINE. As a continuation of the later Roman Empire, the Byzantine Empire relied heavily on overland communications, inheriting a superb road network and an elaborate public postal and transport system, the *cursus publicus* or *demosios dromos.* Its operation in the fourth, fifth, and sixth centuries is documented by a number of sources, notably the *Codex Theodosianus,* the pilgrim itineraries, the sixth-century treatises of John (Ioannes Laurentii) Lydus, and Procopius' *Secret History.* The express service (*cursus velox / oxys dromos*) used saddlehorses (*veredi*), packhorses (*parhippi*), light two-wheeled carriages (*birotae*) drawn by teams of three mules, and four-wheeled carts (*raedae*) drawn by teams of mules eight strong in summer and ten strong in winter. There were weight limits of 30 pounds (11 kg) for a rider (raised by Justinian to 60 pounds), 200 pounds (75 kg) for a *birota,* and 1,000 pounds (373 kg) for a *raeda.* The normal, slow post (*cursus clabularis / platys dromos*) employed wagons (*angariae*), each with a weight limit of 1,500 pounds (560 kg) and drawn by two pairs of oxen; it transported the *annona* or food supply levied for the army, military equipment, and building materials. Along the stretches of public road between cities were staging posts at eight-to-fifteen-mile (13–24 km) intervals that kept fed and rested animals at the ready—according to Procopius these included as many as forty horses. The posts were managed by contractors (*mancipes*); some were merely relay stations (*mutationes / allagai*), while others (*mansiones / stathmoi*) provided accommodations.

The system was maintained by the praetorian prefectures at enormous public expense, and repeated efforts were made to restrict its use to persons with official business. But the rich and powerful could usually obtain the requisite passport or warrant (*evectio / synthēma*) without much trouble. It was to prevent abuses of this kind that the *cursus* was brought, in the mid fourth century,

POSTAL SERVICES, BYZANTINE

under the control of the master of the offices (*magister officiorum*). From the *agentes in rebus* or *magistrianoi* subordinate to him were appointed inspectors (*curiosi;* literally, spies), charged with investigating cases of unauthorized use. Inevitably, these officials found their own way of abusing the system. It must have been ripe for reform when Justinian's hated praetorian, prefect John of Cappadocia, took an axe to it, reducing both the number of stations and the number of animals kept at each. Whether this measure really affected strategic communications with the eastern frontier as adversely as it hit the profits of the landowners who sold provender to the *mancipes* is impossible to tell from the biased accounts of Procopius and John Lydus. In any case, the invasions that already disrupted provincial life in Europe and, from the beginning of the seventh century, affected the Asian provinces began to create new priorities, as travelers and stations were increasingly exposed to attack. The post undoubtedly shared in the process of change that transformed the pattern of defense, administration, and settlement throughout the Balkans and Asia Minor during the Byzantine "dark ages" of the seventh and eighth centuries. It is likely that efforts were made to reduce traffic, especially in bulky goods, to close stations that invited attack or were difficult to defend, to encourage greater local initiative, and to devise alternative routes and methods of communication, such as the famous "telegraph system" of beacons from the Taurus Mountains to Constantinople that was instituted under Theophilos I (829–842) to give early warning of Arab invasions from Cilicia.

There is nevertheless ample evidence that the express service was maintained until the eleventh century. Although the staging posts now kept no more than four to six horses each, the system was costly enough to require its own source of income and the labor services of peasants, the *exkoussatoi tou dromou,* who were exempted from all other corvées. Its staff included couriers and intendants and was subordinate to the bureau of the logothete of the drome. His office had evolved from that of the chief inspector of the post, the *curiosus cursus publici praesentalis,* in the *officium* of the master of the offices, whom the logothete had effectively replaced by the mid ninth century, when the title of *magistros* became purely honorific. He was thus responsible not only for the postal service but also for foreign affairs and the reception of foreign ambassadors.

The logothete of the drome may also have been in charge of government intelligence. Intelligence services are by nature impenetrable and hard to define in neat bureaucratic terms, especially in a monarchy where every loyal or ambitious subject was a potential informant, and all the emperor's intimates were potential secret agents. However, there is some evidence that at least until the eleventh century the Byzantines treated intelligence gathering as a function of government to be approached in a systematic, professional way. Treatises like the *Strategikon* attributed to Emperor Maurice (582–602), and Constantine VII Porphyrogenitos' (905–959) *On the Administration of the Empire* (*De administrando imperio*) reveal a concern to collect information on neighboring peoples and file it away for reference. According to Procopius, the empire maintained a large number of professional, salaried spies (*kataskopoi*), until Justinian "went to no expense, and eradicated the very name of spies from the land of the Romans." However, Justinian can take some credit for a successful piece of industrial espionage, the introduction of silkworms to Byzantine territory around 550. It is unlikely that his economy measures were of long-term significance, since Byzantium could hardly have survived the "dark ages" without reliable information on enemy movements. The case of the *patrikios* David of Sinope, who was sent to the caliph in 714, ostensibly to discuss peace terms, but in reality to learn the extent of Arab war preparations, cannot have been an isolated occurrence.

In any case, important espionage was directed by field commanders. The authors of military handbooks from the sixth to the eleventh century stress that spies and lookouts were an essential part of every army. Maurice mentions two categories of spies: *sculcatores,* or scouts, who watched for defectors, observed enemy movements, and were trained to assess numbers at a glance; and *exploratores,* who went behind enemy lines in disguise. The *Taktika* of Emperor Leo VI (*d.* 912) adds little to this, but later military treatises break new ground, as is clear from the new words that they use for spies. The *De velitatione bellica,* attributed to Nikephoros II Phokas (963–969), reveals the existence on the eastern frontier of an elaborate early warning and espionage network, which employed not only professional spies but also merchants who were going to Cilicia on business. The *De castrametatione,* which seems to reflect the concerns of a commander in the western provinces, distinguishes three groups: guides (*ducatores*), with good knowledge of the terrain; "*chōsarioi,* called *trapezitai* by the eastern troops," who forayed into enemy territory to capture potential informers or collaborators; and "spies proper," who were to be sent "not only among the Bulgarians, but also among other neighboring nations, *viz.*, Patzinakia and Hungary." It adds that "men who are taken prisoner with their wives and children are often more useful than spies; for, receiving pledges that they will be set free with their wives and children, they too are sent out to spy, and having learned what their people are about, they return and tell the truth." Finally, one should not neglect to mention naval espionage, of the kind practiced during the preparations for an expedition against Crete in 911, when the naval commander based at Attaleia was instructed to send galleys to Syria, "that they might bear news and accurate report of all that was being prepared and done there."

Counterintelligence was certainly not neglected. Visitors to the capital were closely supervised, and, according to Liutprand of Cremona (*d.* 972), a curfew was maintained to guard against foreign infiltrators. Saints' lives record several instances of traveling holy men being arrested by government agents simply because they looked suspicious. St. Basil the Younger, in the reign of Leo VI, was actually charged with being a Saracen spy (*dēlatōr*) and brought to Constantinople for interrogation. The men who arrested him are described, interestingly, as *magistrianoi,* which suggests that the *agentes in rebus* had survived as a kind of security police. In this case they appear to have been subordinate not to the logothete of the drome, as might have been expected, but to Leo VI's chamberlain (*parakoimōmenos*), the Muslim eunuch Samonas. Samonas, who also exposed the treasonable plotting of Patriarch Nikolaos I Mystikos and foiled the coup of Andronikos Doukas, seems to have been at the head of a very effective counterintelligence network.

BIBLIOGRAPHY

Sources. Maurice [Maurikios], *Das Strategikon,* George T. Dennis, ed., and E. Gamillscheg, trans. (1981); "Traité de castramétation," Ch. Gaux, ed., in *Notices et extraits des manuscrits de la Bibliothèque Nationale et autres bibliothèques,* **36** (1899).

Studies. Francis Dvornik, *Origins of Intelligence Services* (1974), chap. 3; Friedrich Held, *Das byzantinische Strassensystem in Kappadokien* (1977); Michael F. Hendy, *Studies in the Byzantine Monetary Economy* (1985); R. H. J. Jenkins, "The 'Flight' of Samonas," in *Speculum,* **23** (1948); Arnold H. M. Jones, *The Later Roman Empire, 284–602,* 2 vols. (1964); Vitalien Laurent, *Le corpus des sceaux de l'empire byzantin,* II, *L'administration centrale* (1981); D. A. Miller, "The Logothete of the Drome in the Middle Byzantine Period," in *Byzantion,* **36** (1966); Nicolas Oikonomidès, *Les listes de préséance byzantines des IXe et Xe siècles* (1972), 311–312; Philip Pattenden, "The Byzantine Early Warning System," in *Byzantion,* **53** (1983).

PAUL MAGDALINO

[See also **Byzantine Empire: Bureaucracy; Byzantine Empire: History; Codex Theodosianus; Diplomacy, Byzantine; Historiography, Byzantine; Law, Byzantine; Leo VI the Wise, Emperor; Logothete; Lydus; Maurice, Emperor; Nikolaos I Mystikos, Patriarch; Procopius; Roads and Communications, Byzantine; Roman Empire, Late.**]

POSTAL AND INTELLIGENCE SERVICES, ISLAMIC (Barīd). In medieval Arabic nomenclature *barīd* was applied to the official post and intelligence service of the Islamic states, as well as to the mount, the courier, and the post "stage." Although medieval Muslim writers derived this term from the custom of shortening the tails of the government mounts (*burīdan,* "cutting" in Persian), its etymological origin most probably stems from the Latin *veredus, veredarius* and Greek *beredos,* which under the form *beldār* is commonly used in talmudic literature and is found also in Syriac.

Following their conquest of the Near East and during their early organization of an administrative system, the Arabs instituted the state postal service that had been known to the vanquished Byzantine and Sasanian empires. The vast extension of the Islamic "empire"—from Spain in the west to the steppes of Central Asia and India in the east—dictated the establishment of an efficient *barīd,* the strengthening of which was included in the centralizing reforms of the fifth Umayyad ruler, ᶜAbd al-Malik (*r.* 685–705). The Abbasid dynasty continued to attach great importance to this institution, so that by the middle of the ninth century it covered all lands of the caliphate.

According to reliable medieval sources, the system of *barīd* involved no fewer than 930 "stages," theoretically situated 12 kilometers (7.5 miles) apart in Iran, and 24 kilometers (15 miles) in the Western provinces. Special officials were held responsible for the movement of the post according to schedule. The movement of the relays could not have been particularly fast; except for special occasions, when horses were used, the messengers (Arabic singular: *fayj;* Persian singular: *buranīq*) rode mainly on mules in Iran and camels in the West. Only in times of political or military emergencies did the caliphs, the viziers, or the provincial governors speed up the postal service in the affected area.

Since the *barīd* included the gathering and passing on of information regarding the operations of governmental agencies (provincial governors and treasurers not excepted), the provincial postmasters (singular: *ṣāḥib al-barīd*) were directly responsible to the head of the Department of the Post (*ṣāḥib diwān al-barīd*) in the capital of the caliphate. There the reports were communicated directly to the caliph. Although there also existed the office of a director of intelligence (*khabar*), the *barīd* constituted one of the most sensitive governmental services and was entrusted to close associates of the caliph or to palace eunuchs.

In the tenth century the decline of the central government and the proliferation of petty regional dynasties caused a disorganization of the *barīd.* The Buyids allegedly cut off the *barīd* to secure their control over the caliph. Under the Seljuks and in the wake of the invasion of the crusaders, the governmental postal organization further decayed, but even then there seems to have been maintained a more or less regular service performed by the bearers of government messages, known as the *rusul.* The Zangids and Ayyubids resorted to the use of runners, swift cameleers, and pigeons.

Under the powerful Mamluk sultans the postal service experienced a period of resurgence mainly because of its vital importance for waging wars against the crusaders and the Mongols. Its chief reorganizer, Sultan Baybars (*r.* 1260–1277), relied not only on the Abbasid model but also on that operated by his Mongol antagonists. The Mamluk *barīd,* which first operated in Egypt and on the Cairo-Damascus route, was later extended to Syrian coastal towns and the castles on the Taurus borders. It involved both couriers (singular: *barīdī*) commanded by a *muqaddam al-barīdīya* and the stages for changing horses, first established in public caravanserais and later in special buildings erected for the purpose. A pigeon post and a system of visual signaling were also used.

At the turn of the fifteenth century, the invasion of Syria by Tamerlane terminated the operations of the medieval *barīd,* variants of which existed in Muslim Spain, in the Hafsid state in eastern Barbary, and in the Ottoman sultanate. The *barīd* also influenced the medieval Near Eastern mail service run by private enterprise.

BIBLIOGRAPHY

Francis Dvornik, *Origins of Intelligence Services* (1974), chap. 4, with bibliography; S. D. Goitein, "The Commercial Mail Service in Medieval Islam," in *Journal of the American Oriental Society,* **84** (1964); D. Sourdel, "Barīd," in *Encyclopaedia of Islam,* new ed., I (1960), 1,045–1,046, with detailed bibliography.

ANDREW S. EHRENKREUTZ

[See also **Animals, Draft; Baybars al-Bunduqdārī; Buyids; Caliphate; Travel and Transport, Islamic.**]

POSTGLOSSATORS, or commentators, were the jurists who wrote on Roman law from about 1250 to the early sixteenth century; that is, between the publication of the *Glossa ordinaria,* the standard gloss on Justinian's *Corpus iuris civilis* by Accursius, and the inauguration of the new textual approach to legal literature by the humanists. The most famous of the postglossators was Bartolo da Sassoferrato (1313/1314–1357), who so dominated his profession that it became a maxim that "no one is a jurist unless he is a Bartolist" (*nemo iurista nisi sit Bartolista*). Not far behind in reputation were Bartolo's teacher, Cino da Pistoia (*ca.* 1270–1336/1337), a poet as well as a lawyer, and a friend of Dante and Petrarch, and Bartolo's student Baldus (1327–1400), who was also an expert in canon law. The postglossators transformed Roman law into a living legal system that could be applied in courts of law throughout Europe, and so prepared the way for the wholesale "reception" of Roman law in many European countries in the early sixteenth century, when the Roman law as interpreted by the postglossators became "common law" in Germany, the Netherlands, Spain, Scotland, and elsewhere.

Up to the time of the publication of the *Glossa ordinaria,* the jurists were mainly concerned with simply understanding the texts of Roman law—no small task, since the details of so ancient and highly sophisticated a legal system was (and is) very arcane, and the texts themselves needed careful

POSTGLOSSATORS

study and rehabilitation. The *Glossa ordinaria* consolidated this research. With a standard interpretation of the texts at hand, the postglossators could turn to the challenge of modifying this academic system so that it would be of practical value. The influence of Roman law on medieval and modern law would doubtless have been substantial even without their work, for the solutions worked out over a period of time by the great jurists of Roman law were bound to attract study and imitation. But the influence would have been confined to individual areas in which Roman law was especially adaptable to medieval needs. As a result of the postglossators' accomplishment, Roman law dominated virtually every European legal system except the English, and with the export of legal systems that followed colonization, it survives as a major source of law on several continents.

In order to make Roman law usable, the postglossators had to expand it in areas that had been largely ignored by earlier Romanists. In particular, they virtually created the science of criminal law, a central concern of the modern state but a neglected area of both Roman and medieval law. Albertus Gandinus (*d. ca.* 1310) initiated this study, and authors like Lucas de Penna (*d. ca.* 1390) developed it along very modern lines, emphasizing that criminal law must be public rather than private and must focus on reform of the criminal rather than revenge for the victim. In other areas the postglossators were able to exploit traditionally strong aspects of Roman law that had fallen into desuetude during the early Middle Ages but were well suited to the expanding economy of the High Middle Ages. Thus the Roman expertise on contracts formed the basis of the commercial law introduced by the postglossators. Their contempt for feudal law and their Romanist analysis of ownership were vital for the transition from medieval to modern society. Perhaps even more vital were their political views, which still, in the medieval fashion, were couched in legal terms. The postglossators emancipated the secular ruler from his theoretical dependence on the pope, and portrayed the state as a positive, divinely ordained entity rather than a mere remedy for sin. They helped to demonstrate the usefulness for the medieval monarch of the Roman doctrine of sovereignty, which portrayed the emperor as supreme legislator rather than simply as supreme judge. Similarly, their development of the foundations of statutory law was to be of great practical significance. Most famous of all their contributions to public and private law is the perfection of the concept of the corporation as a fictitious person, possessing a will of its own and susceptible to civil and criminal rights and liabilities.

The literary form from which the postglossators take their name is the commentary, an often voluminous work of legal exegesis that developed from lectures given in law courses. Although the postglossators are closely identified with Italy, it was in France, especially Orléans, that the commentary took root, during a period in which legal studies in Italy were rather stagnant. Jacques de Révigny (*d.* 1296) and Pierre de Belleperche (*d.* 1308) launched the commentary, and Cino da Pistoia, who had studied in France, brought it to Italy.

The lecture began with the reading of the text—a passage from one of the works in Justinian's *Corpus*—and of its accompanying gloss. Some of the postglossators wished to free themselves from this rigid textual orientation, and universities found it necessary to prescribe the readings of text and gloss by statute. The lectures and the commentaries based on them were often rambling and diffuse, incorporating digressions that developed their own literary formats. The *repetitio* rehearsed all the legal ramifications of a given text; the *tractatus* discursively expanded a special topic; *quaestiones,* usually drawn from real cases, debated the validity of a certain legal principle. Publication of these lectures often took the form of students' notes, called *reportationes* or *recollectae.* These were not unlike the lecture notes that can be purchased in university bookstores, except that the medieval ones are usually more interesting because they include the personal notes and sketches by means of which the medieval student beguiled the tedium of his courses. Sometimes this was as far as the "publication" of the work went, and we have manuscripts that record the lectures as given by the same professor on the same topics in various years, or as given at one time but reported by various students. The published—that is, printed—commentaries of certain authors are nothing more than printed versions of these student lecture notes. Other professors, however, were careful to work up their lecture notes into authoritative commentaries.

The postglossators did not aim at a careful elucidation of the history and textual meaning of their Roman sources. It was only by freeing themselves from this often antiquarian sort of research that they could create a practical legal system. The humanists were contemptuous of the postglossators' methods and of their style: "verbose on easy topics, silent on hard ones, and prolix on matters of narrow scope" was how the French humanist Jacques Cujas described them. The scientific approach to legal scholarship was equally opposed to the postglossators' methods, and it was the great nineteenth-century scholar Savigny who gave them the dismissive label "postglossators."

This attitude is now a thing of the past. The postglossators are studied not only, and perhaps not chiefly, for their legal doctrines, but for their political views and their value as historical sources. Their literary form, now in the forefront of research, is the *consilium,* an attorney's opinion advising a judge, written at the behest of the judge or litigants in a court case. *Consilia* were especially important in the Italian communes, where they supplemented the often scanty legal knowledge of the *podestà,* who presided as judge. In the later Middle Ages communal statutes increasingly required judges to seek *consilia* in difficult cases, though without obligating them to follow the advice.

Consilia evolved from "disputed questions," classroom debates on legal problems usually based on real cases. Both have the same pattern: They begin with a description of the case (*casus*), then pose the question that arises from it, debate the pros and cons in the familiar Scholastic way, and close with a solution. But while "disputed questions" were only training exercises, *consilia* influenced real decisions.

Though not used in all law courts—they were mainly for magistrates who were not trained jurists—*consilia* over time affected legal procedures and the concept of legal evidence. The readiness of communal courts to revise earlier judgments on the basis of a new and "better" *consilium* contributed to the doctrine that legal decisions rested on probability rather than certainty, since jurists increasingly saw judgments as susceptible to revision on the basis of "more expert" evidence in the future, as Mario Ascheri has shown.

The scope of *consilia* was not narrowly legal. Political views were often expressed in legal forms. Hence, *consilia* (sometimes when in this guise called "allegations") can be studied as archives of historical information. By their nature they convey historical details with great immediacy, and they are often signed and dated.

Consilia survive by the thousands, and organizing them to make them accessible is one of the main problems of scholarship on the postglossators. Another is the uncertainty in text transmission and attribution. As often happens in other periods, works circulating anonymously or with varying attribution tended to be fathered on particularly famous authors. Moreover, postglossators often built upon or expanded earlier works, the results often being incorporated into the original text as "additions," perhaps carefully signed and designated as such, perhaps not. It is not unusual for the author of the additions to have been passed down in the text tradition as the author of the work itself. The enormous bulk of the literature, and the invention of printing during the period of the postglossators' dominance, add to the confusion, which for some authors is so considerable as to hinder analysis of their doctrines.

BIBLIOGRAPHY

Mario Ascheri, "'Consilium sapientis,' perizia medica e 'res iudicata': Diritto dei 'dottori' e istituzioni comunali," in *Monumenta iuris canonici,* ser. C, VI (1980); Enrico Besta, *Fonti del diritto italiano,* 2nd ed., rev. (1950); Gero Dolezalek and Hans van de Wouw, *Verzeichnis der Handschriften zum römischen Recht bis 1600,* 4 vols. (1972); Otto Gierke, *Das deutsche Genossenschaftsrecht,* III (1881), 351–501; Harold D. Hazeltine, "Roman and Canon Law in the Middle Ages," in *Cambridge Medieval History,* V (1926, repr. 1957); Norbert Horn, "Die legistische Literatur der Kommentatoren und der Ausbreitung des gelehrten Rechts," in Helmut Coing, ed., *Handbuch der Quellen und Literatur der neueren europäischen Privatrechtsgeschichte,* I (1973); T. M. Izbicki, "Problems of Attribution in the *Tractatus Universi Iuris,*" in *Studi senesi,* **92** (1980); Domenico Maffei, *La donazione di Constantino nei giuristi medievali* (1964); Lauro Martines, *Lawyers and Statecraft in Renaissance Florence* (1968); Peter Riesenberg, "The Consilia Literature: A Prospectus," in *Manuscripta,* **6** (1962); Walter Ullmann, *The Medieval Idea of Law as Represented by Lucas de Penna* (1946, repr. 1969); Paul Vinogradoff, *Roman Law in Medieval Europe,* P. Stein, ed., 3rd ed. (1961, repr. 1968); Hans J. Wolff, *Roman Law* (1951), 183–206; Cecil N. S. Woolf, *Bartolus of Sassoferrato* (1913).

The publications of *Ius romanum medii aevi* (1961–), and the bibliographies published annually in the *Bulletin of Medieval Canon Law* (1971–) and *Medioevo Latino* (1978–), are useful for keeping up with current literature.

ELISABETH VODOLA

[See also **Baldus; Bartolo da Sassoferrato; Cino da Pistoia; Corpus Iuris Civilis; Glossators; Justinian I; Law, Civil; Law, Schools of.**]

Surrey jug with animal-headed tubular spout and incised lines. Green glaze on buff ground, 15th century. MUSEUM OF LONDON, INV. NO. A.27544

POTTERY. At the time of the fall of the Roman Empire, three classes of pottery were being made: unglazed earthenware, red-gloss pottery, and lead-glazed pottery.

Red-gloss pottery, also known as Samian ware, was made throughout the Roman Empire wherever suitable clay existed: in Italy, France, Spain, Hungary, England, and Germany. There were both ornamental and functional vessels, but the shapes continued to be those of the late classical period, with little variation. The ware was bright red with a fine gloss. Decorations were in relief, and consisted of human, animal, vegetal, or geometric motifs pressed into the clay with an intaglio mold. It was wheel-made pottery, produced in bulk. The fine gloss was similar to a modern casting slip and was not a true glaze.

The most common type of early medieval pottery, which continued to be produced throughout the Middle Ages in Europe, was an unglazed common earthenware. It varied according to the color of the local clay and was usually buff or gray. Vessels were frequently decorated by making scored lines or indentations in the soft clay surface. Less common was the sgraffito technique of decoration, where lines were scratched through the slip, which differed in color from the clay of the pot, to result in an engraved pattern of either light on a dark ground or vice versa. A great number of earthenware vessels were decorated with relief patterns, usually produced by applying a stamp made of wood or baked clay directly to the surface or to a pad of clay previously laid upon it. The great variety of relief decorations includes geometric forms, coats of arms, and stylized motifs from the plant and animal kingdoms.

Utilitarian vessels were the most common type of unglazed earthenware, with jugs and pitchers the chief surviving articles. Other common ware included unglazed cooking pots with convex sides and a slight indentation below the flaring mouth. There were also flat frying pans and saucepans with single handles (pipkins). Cups were rare until the end of the Middle Ages. Wine vessels (or amphorae) continued to be very common throughout the Middle Ages.

Several centers manufactured very fine unglazed earthenware. Noteworthy were the early medieval German pottery towns of Badorf and Pingsdorf. Badorf ware, dating from the eighth and ninth centuries, was buff or yellowish, and included cooking pots with sagging bases, open basins, pitchers, and loop-handled amphorae. Pingsdorf ware, made from the ninth through the late twelfth century or afterward, had a similar buff or yellowish ground but was painted with red or purple decorations. The motifs were simple forms such as commas, dribbles, and wavy or slanting lines. Pingsdorf ware was an extremely hard-fired earthenware or stoneware. Later medieval German pottery continued to be stoneware but was gray. Stoneware, which is fired to the point of semivitrification, was the great contribution made by Germany to the evolution of pottery.

Though less common than unglazed earthenware, lead-glazed vessels were made throughout most of Europe during the Middle Ages. They had the same shapes as the unglazed ware but also included other forms, such as the aquamanile (horizontal jug), made for the frequent hand washing that was necessary before the invention of forks. Most had the shape of a standing animal, such as a lion, deer, goat, or horse. Occasionally other metal vessels were imitated, as in a Surrey jug in the London Museum, with a spout resembling a serpent's head with open jaws. In other glazed pitchers, the tubular spout is a sign of the influence of metalware.

Lead glaze, as transparent as glass, could be stained with metal oxides. From the thirteenth century a green color was given to the wares by mixing copper filings into the glaze. The color varied according to the amount of copper, from a yellowish green to a deep, bright green. A yellow or buff-toned ware resulted when a transparent galena glaze was oxidized in the firing. The yellow changed to a warm brown when the fabric fired to red or when there was a strong iron content in the clay. Lead-glazed ware, also known as semi-faience (half-majolica), had a limitation in the possibilities of decoration, for it had a tendency to run, and pigments laid upon it with a brush had a tendency to shift or blur. Therefore, apart from the stained glaze, much of the decoration was incised or stamped. Motifs were geometric, coats of arms, or human, animal, or vegetal forms.

A major technical change was achieved wherever true faience was introduced. True faience, which used white tin glaze (commonly called enamel), was invented in the Middle East, probably in Mesopotamia; although the use of tin glaze in the preparation of tiles was known earlier, its first application to pottery vessels was in the ninth century, in order to imitate the appearance of the white porcelain being exported to the Middle East from China. It was never more than superficially imitative of porcelain, however, for porcelain is distinguished from pottery by its dense, impermeable, vitrified, translucent character. The presence of tin in the composition of the faience glaze renders it opaque and white; thus it provides an excellent surface for the ordinary buff or red earthenware to receive the painted colors of decoration. The art of painting earthenware in colors (which included metallic luster pigments) spread from the Middle East through the Islamic lands to Spain and eventually to Italy.

The long presence of Islamic civilization in Spain was decisive in the formation of its important ceramic industry. With Moorish Spain came the importance of tiles, which were used especially to cover the lowest part of the walls. Those of the fourteenth century, from the Alhambra, are small polygonal shapes of a single color, which are set into bands of mosaiclike patterns of green, blue, white, brown, and black. Each small piece was either sawed into shape after firing or was set into a mold before firing. The manufacture and use of tiles continued to be important in Christian Spain as well as in other European countries, but patterns were usually painted directly on each tile.

In the early thirteenth century, after the Christian conquest of Manises, Paterna, and Teruel, ceramic production continued to bear the Muslim imprint. The pottery from these centers bore predominantly Islamic motifs in turquoise and brown, blue, or blue and gold. Mainly, shallow bowls, *botas* (various sorts of jars), candelabra, and tiles were made. By the fourteenth century, a significant influence on these centers would be that of Moorish lusterware (earthenware painted with metallic pigments).

Probably the most celebrated example of Hispano-Moorish lusterware is the "Alhambra vase" of the fourteenth century. It is one of several similarly shaped vessels from this period with a narrow base, swelling body, and slender neck. It is covered with arabesques, inscriptions, and a pair of stylized antelopes, and originally had two wing-shaped handles.

By the middle of the fourteenth century, Spain became famous for its export of lusterware. Some of the primary centers of manufacture were Málaga, Calatayud, Manises, Paterna, and Teruel. Gothic motifs were added to the repertory of Middle Eastern decorations. Prominent shapes of Spanish lusterware were shallow and deep dishes, as well as the albarello. The latter was a drug jar with a cylindrical shape, slightly concave in the center. A shape of Middle Eastern origin, it may have derived from a section of bamboo cane; hence its name in Italian was *alberello* (little tree), which was later corrupted to albarello. The shape passed with little variation to Spain as well as to Italy.

The ceramic production of medieval Italy featured lead-glazed earthenware until the fourteenth century, when there was a change to the manufacture of faience in Orvieto, Siena, and Florence. From there, the production of faience spread to many other centers, such as Gubbio, Deruta, and Urbino. It was called *maiolica* in Italian, that is, from the island of Majorca, from where Valencian faience was shipped to Pisa. Individual styles were developed in many places in Italy; and at first, designs were simple, with only two colors, usually green and brown. In modern usage the term "majolica" usually signifies the distinctive type of earth-

The "Alhambra vase." Hispano-Moorish lusterware from Málaga, 14th century. MUSEO ARQUEOLÓGICO, GRANADA. FOTO MAS, BARCELONA

enware painted with mainly pictorial decorations that flourished in Italy in the second half of the fifteenth century and the beginning of the sixteenth century.

BIBLIOGRAPHY

Otto von Falke, *Das rheinische Steinzeug* (1908); Édouard Garnier, *Dictionnaire de la céramique* (1893); Manuel González Martí, *Cerámica del Levante español,* I (1944); Manuel Gómez Moreno, *Cerámica medieval española* (1924); Emil Hannover, *Pottery and Porcelain,* Bernard Rackham, ed. and trans., I (1925); Giuseppi Liverani, *Five Centuries of Italian Maiolica* (1960); Concepción Pinedo and Eugenia Vizcaino, *La cerámica de Manises en la historia* (1977); Bernard Rackham, *Medieval English Pottery* (1948, 2nd ed., rev. 1972), and *Italian Maiolica* (1952); Louis M. Solon, *Ancient Art Stoneware of the Low Countries and Germany* (1892).

MARY F. GRIZZARD

[See also **Azulejo; Ceramics; Faience; Lusterware; Majolica.**]

POUND, MONEY. The history of the English monetary pound as a money of account began with the introduction of the silver penny during the eighth century. The penny dominated local, regional, and interregional transactions for the next five centuries, until the issuance of larger silver denominations and the reintroduction of gold coinage during the later thirteenth century. During the era of the penny, and for a long time afterward, both the pound and the shilling were monetary units used solely in keeping accounts. They were not minted as coins until the early modern era. The shilling was the first to appear as a circulating coin during the reign of Henry VII.

Several distinct methods of computation for the money pound of account (£ standing for Latin *libra,* French *livre*) were used during the Middle Ages in England. The pound was either twelve ounces of twenty pence (*d.* standing for denarius or denier) each, or twenty shillings (*s.* standing for solidus or shilling) of twelve pence each, or forty-eight shillings of five pence each, or sixteen ounces of sixteen pence. In each case the penny weighed thirty wheat corns.

Payment by pounds of account for major transactions became more frequent after the ninth century, even though the actual coins exchanged were pennies. In time these pounds of pure silver were reckoned as equal to 240 silver pennies, especially after the Norman Conquest. The original intention was that the pound weight of silver and the pound of money should be the same.

After 1066, when the Norman or Frankish method of taking twelve pence or denarii to the shilling or solidus was adopted officially, the convenience of a pound that would divide into twenty shillings of twelve pence was sufficient to stabilize what was already widely accepted as a special English method of reckoning.

William I established his mint in the Tower of London, even though more than sixty provincial mints continued to operate. He also adopted a pound weight that had probably been used before the Conquest, but which he named the tower pound and which was 6.25 percent lighter than the troy pound, the official coinage system of weight.

The Domesday Book distinguished between the pound *ad numerum,* or by tale; the pound *ad pensum,* or by weight; and the pound *ad scalam,* which was a pound by tale with an allowance of six pennies extra to make up for the loss of weight in the coins by wear, clipping, and other activities. The *ad scalam* system recognized that coins in circulation were lighter than they should have been, not that there was any legal difference between money from the mint and a pound weight of silver.

Etymologically both the pound by weight and the money pound of account derive from the Middle English *pound(e), pond(e), pownd(e),* and *pund(e),* from the Old English *pund,* from the Latin *pondo,* pound, originally "in weight," and akin to the Latin *pondus,* a weight. Its abbreviations £, l., lb., and lib. all derive from the Latin *libra,* which also means pound.

RONALD EDWARD ZUPKO

[See also **Domesday Book; Ducat; Florin; Mints and Money, Western European; Nomisma; Penny; Shilling; William I of England.**]

POUND, WEIGHT, a weight in the British Isles in the apothecary, avoirdupois, mercantile, tower, troy, and Scots tron systems. The apothecary pound contained 5,760 grains (373.242 grams), or 288 scruples of 20 grains each, or 96 drams of 60 grains each, or 12 troy ounces of 480 grains each. The avoirdupois pound contained 7,000 grains (453.592 grams), or 256 drams of 27.344 grains each, or 16 ounces of 437.5 grains each, and was used for all products not subject to apothecary or troy weight. The mercantile pound contained 6,750 troy grains (437.400 grams), or 15 mercantile ounces of 450 troy grains each. It was used in England for all goods except electuaries, money, and spices until sometime in the fourteenth century, when it was replaced by the avoirdupois pound. The tower pound, also called the Saxon or moneyer's pound, contained 5,400 troy grains (349.920 grams), or 12 tower ounces of 450 troy grains each. It was used in England generally for electuaries, money, and spices until 1527, when it was replaced by the troy pound. The English troy pound contained 5,760 troy grains (373.242 grams), or 240 pennyweights of 24 troy grains each, or 12 troy ounces of 480 troy grains each, while the Scots troy pound contained 7,609 troy grains (493.063 grams), or 256 drops of 29.72 troy grains each, or 16 troy ounces of 475.5 troy grains each. The Scots tron pound, used for home productions (such as butter, cheese, hides, tallow, wool, coal, and hay), contained 9,520 troy grains (616.896 grams), or 320 drops of 29.75 troy grains each, or 20 troy ounces of 476 troy grains each.

RONALD EDWARD ZUPKO

[See also **Livre; Weights and Measures, Western European.**]

PRACHATITZ, PETER VON. See **Peter von Prachtatitz.**

PRAEMUNIRE usually refers to the English statutes of 1353, 1365, and 1393, which strengthened the royal courts' penalties against those who appealed their judgments in other courts. The papal court in Rome was the main rival with which the statutes were concerned, and papal provision (appointment) to English ecclesiastical offices, widely felt to be the right of English patrons, was the chief object of the penalties. (More broadly, "praemunire" comes from the Latin name of one of the writs that enforced the royal courts' supremacy.)

The statutes were a result of institutional developments of the preceding centuries. As part of the settlement of the Constitutions of Clarendon (1164), disputes over the ownership of churches (advowson) were to be tried by the royal courts, rather than by the ecclesiastical courts, which handled such cases in other countries, including France. By the middle of the thirteenth century the royal courts had full control over such litigation, wresting cases from the church courts when necessary by means of writs of prohibition. But papal assumption of control over ecclesiastical benefices in the later thirteenth century eroded this arrangement. The royal writ was of no use against litigants in the papal court in Rome. During the early fourteenth century the royal courts forbade appeals to Rome, not only in advowson cases but also in the other cases traditionally excluded from the church courts by writs of prohibition, though the issue was dominated by the question of benefices. But existing procedures for penalizing such appeals were weak. Although in Parliament the Commons often pressed for stronger measures, the royal interests were divided, the king often finding papal patronage the most efficient way of securing appointments for his own candidates.

Public sentiment called for stronger legislation. The statute of Praemunire (1353) complemented that of Provisors (1351) by increasing the existing impediments against appeals to Rome. Such appellants would be issued a writ of warning of two months. If the defendant failed to appear within that period, his possessions would be forfeited to the king, and a writ of arrest would be issued against him. A defendant who continued to evade the sheriff would be outlawed.

Thus the statute of Praemunire concerned contumacious defendants, most usually those at the papal court, and its procedures did not apply to those whose presence in court the sheriff was able to ensure by other means. Nor did it affect the penalties for conviction in these cases of illegal appeal, which remained forfeiture and imprisonment. Like many acts that eventually came to be of constitutional significance, Praemunire addressed itself to a narrow area of legal procedure.

The statutes of Provisors and Praemunire were renewed in 1365, now at the royal behest; but this legislation was again weak. In the next decades, activity focused on attempts to achieve a concordat with the papacy. The attempt having failed, Provisors was renewed in a stiff form in 1390. In the following year Pope Boniface IX annulled it and the earlier statutes, and sent a legate to England to try to have them repealed. The great statute of Praemunire of 1393 was a retaliation against these papal acts. It forbade anyone to bring into England documents in which the pope impeded bishops from executing a royal judgment, on pain of the procedures of Praemunire outlined above. In other words, it short-circuited papal attempts to prevent bishops—subjects of the pope but usually also servants of the crown—from executing the royal courts' decisions. This narrow interpretation is doubtless the appropriate one; for negotiations for a concordat, eventually reached in 1398, were proceeding. But the statute enunciated the important doctrine that the English crown was subject not to the pope but to God in temporal matters.

The statute was largely ignored for a generation. When it was taken up again in the 1430's, it was by those who wished to use it to curtail not only the papal but also the English ecclesiastical courts, and the feudal courts, in favor of royal jurisdiction. Thus it was with a certain bizarre logic that in 1530 Henry VIII, to complete the ecclesiastical courts' subordination to the king, sued every cleric in England on charges of Praemunire. After accepting a massive fee for "pardon," the king placed himself at the head of the church courts, allowing them to continue as jurisdictions delegated from the crown.

BIBLIOGRAPHY

Source. Record Commission, ed., *Statutes of the Realm,* I (1810), 329, 385, and II (1816), 84–86.

Studies. G. B. Flahiff, "The Writ of Prohibition to Court Christian in the Thirteenth Century," in *Mediaeval Studies,* 6 (1944), *Mediaeval Studies,* 7 (1945); Edgar B. Graves, "The Legal Significance of the Statute of Praemunire of 1353," in Charles H. Taylor and John L. La Monte, eds., *Anniversary Essays in Mediaeval History, by Students of Charles Homer Haskins* (1929); May McKisack, *The Fourteenth Century 1307–1399* (1959); Frederic W. Maitland, "Church, State, and Decretals," in his *Roman Canon Law in the Church of England* (1898); Guillaume Mollat, *The Popes at Avignon, 1305–1378,* 9th ed., Janet Love, trans. (1963); William A. Pantin, *The English Church in the Fourteenth Century* (1955), and "The Fourteenth Century," in Clifford H. Lawrence, ed., *The English Church and the Papacy in the Middle Ages* (1965); J. J. Scarisbrick, *Henry VIII* (1968); William Templeton Waugh, "The Great Statute of Praemunire," in *English Historical Review,* 37 (1922).

ELISABETH VODOLA

[See also **Benefice, Ecclesiastical; Benefice, Lay; Clarendon, Constitutions of; Concordat; Law (various articles); Parliament, English; Presentation, Right of.**]

PRAETORIAN PREFECT, the senior civilian official of the early Byzantine Empire, a position created by Constantine I. The praetorian prefects held supreme authority over the administration of their prefectures and were answerable to the emperor alone. There were four praetorian prefectures, with the prefect of the East and the prefect of Italy being of higher rank than those of Illyricum and Gaul. The prefects had administrative, financial, and judicial functions, but they had no military authority. Provincial governors were appointed at their recommendation, and they had the right to dismiss them subject to the emperor's approval. The prefects received reports from the vicars and governors, had their own treasuries, and were responsible for the pay and victuals of the army. They were also the final appeal judges, and important imperial edicts were addressed to them. Praetorian prefects present in Constantinople were ex officio members of the imperial council or *consistorium*. This office seems to have survived until the seventh century, when the prefectures were replaced (in the territory that still remained within the empire) by a new administrative unit, the theme.

BIBLIOGRAPHY

A. H. M. Jones, *The Later Roman Empire, 284–602,* 2 vols. (1964).

LINDA C. ROSE

[See also **Byzantine Empire: Bureaucracy; Constantine I the Great.**]

PRAGMATIC SANCTION OF BOURGES, the title given to an ordinance of King Charles VII of France, 7 July 1438, promulgating the decisions of a council of the French clergy held at Bourges in the two previous months, for the purpose of reforming the church of France (the "Gallican Church") in accord with the reform decrees of the Council of Basel. The unusual term "pragmatic" was drawn from Roman law and was intended to signify that the king was deliberately establishing public law in an area not generally recognized as coming under royal jurisdiction, inasmuch as the papacy had claimed the sole right to govern the European church.

The Pragmatic Sanction included the conciliar decrees of Constance and Basel asserting the supreme authority of general councils in the church and providing that such councils be held periodically. It picked up the Basel prohibitions of clerical concubinage, of abusive excommunications and interdicts, and of appointments as cardinals of those who were not qualified or who were related to the pope or other cardinals. It also included the Basel stipulations designed to ensure that the Mass and other ceremonies be properly celebrated; that the clergy duly read their canonical hours each day; and that the churches not be profaned by fairs, secular festivals, or dancing in the churchyards. Basel's suppression of papal taxation was repeated, with some exceptions for the benefit of the reigning pope, Eugenius IV, and with extra stipulations making benefices conferred by lay patrons immune from all papal taxation. Cases in church courts were to proceed within the realm in the normal order of appeals, and no appeals were to go directly to the papacy.

Above all, the Pragmatic Sanction repeated the Basel decrees suppressing the pope's right to confer benefices and restoring the older common law of the church in this matter. Thus, all dignitaries were to be elected by the appropriate bodies of electors (for example, bishops were to be elected by the cathedral chapters). In contrast to Basel, however, the Sanction allowed the king and princes to suggest candidates. There were to be no general reservations of benefices to the pope's own collation, except in the lands of the papacy or in cases of benefices vacated at the papal court. The pope would, however, be allowed to name dignitaries in some special cases (thus the king could have his candidates appointed by the pope if he wished). The Basel provision that one-third of all vacancies be filled by univesity graduates was developed into a system by which the universities of the realm could submit lists of candidates to the regular electors, collators, or patrons.

While the Sanction was never strictly applied, and was indeed several times revoked and restored by Louis XI and subsequent kings, it retained its importance as a monument of Gallicanism, that is, the territorialization of the French church under royal control. In this respect it picked up previous tendencies beginning in the 1390's, and it was to be cited frequently in later centuries by Gallicanists opposing papal claims to sovereignty over the clergy. The Protestant Reformation, and Gallicanism and its counterparts in the Catholic realms, caused the papacy to lose much of the control over church personnel and revenues that it had won in the Avignon period.

BIBLIOGRAPHY

Source. Louis-Guillaume de Vilevault and Louis-George O. F. de Bréquigny, eds., *Les ordonnances des rois de France de la troisième race,* XIII (1782).

Studies. Étienne Delaruelle, Edmond-René Labande, and Paul Ourliac, eds., *L'église au temps du Grand Schisme et de la crise conciliaire, 1378–1449* (1962), 352–368; Victor Martin, *Les origines du gallicanisme,* 2 vols. in 1 (1939); Noël Valois, *Histoire de la Pragmatique Sanction de Bourges sous Charles VII* (1906).

HOWARD KAMINSKY

[See also **Annates; Benefice, Ecclesiastical; Benefice, Lay; Conciliar Theory; Concordat; Councils, Western; Praemunire; Provisions, Ecclesiastical; Schism, Great; Simony; Taxation, Church.**]

PRAGUE (Czech: Praha). Archaeological evidence attests Slavic settlements in the Prague basin from the fourth century. The origins of the medieval town may be dated to 870–890, when the Přemyslid dynasty (which was to rule Bohemia until 1306) established its seat at the Prague castle, Hradčany, on the left bank of the river Vltava (German: Moldau). In the second half of the tenth century, another castle, Vyšehrad, rose on the right bank of the Vltava several miles to the south. The first written record about Prague appeared in 929, in the work of the Saxon chronicler Widukind of Corvey, and around 965 the Jewish merchant Ibrāhīm ibn Yaᶜqūb of Tortosa described "Fraga" as a busy city built of stone, where Slavs, Russians, Muslims, Jews, and Turks exchanged their goods.

Following the Christianization of Bohemia, Prague became the religious center of the country: the bishopric dates from 973, a Benedictine abbey at Břevnov was founded by St. Adalbert in 993, and a Latin cathedral school opened about 1000. The town was also an economic, political, and cultural hub. German and Jewish merchant communities are documented from the eleventh century, and the first record of regular fairs is from 1105. One of the first stone bridges in central Europe, the Judith's Bridge across the Vltava, was completed in 1172, and the Old Town, a market center on the right bank, was surrounded by fortified walls during the 1230's. Around 1287 the Old Town adopted a legal code based on the so-called Swabian Mirror. Meanwhile, King Přemysl Otokar II founded a predominantly German town on the left bank, around Hradčany, in 1257; this community, which came to be known as the Lesser Side (Malá strana), adopted the Magdeburg urban code.

With the accession of Charles IV to the Czech throne in 1346, Prague entered one of its most glorious periods. In 1348 Charles founded the New Town, adjacent to the Old Town and populated mostly by Czechs; the same year he founded a university (Charles University, the oldest in central Europe); he also built new churches, monasteries, and fortifications, expanded the Lesser Side, and spanned the Vltava with a stone bridge that carries his name. Intending to make Prague a "second (Slavic) Rome," Charles attracted to his court famous European artists, architects, sculptors, and writers, among them Peter Parler, Mathieu d'Arras, Cola di Rienzo, and Petrarch. The cultural flourishing was accompanied by growth in trade and the increasing importance of artisans' guilds. When Charles IV died in 1378, Prague was the largest European city east of the Rhine, with about 40,000 inhabitants.

In the ensuing decades Prague turned into a religious, nationalist, and military battlefield. John Hus began to preach in the Bethlehem Chapel in 1402, not only calling for a religious reform but also articulating a Czech national program vis-à-vis the Germans; in 1409 the participation of German "nations" at Charles University was decreased from three votes to one, and about 1,000 German students and teachers left the city in protest; and after 1419 Prague witnessed popular risings of Hussites against churches, monasteries, and the patriciate, and two battles between the Hussite army and Emperor Sigismund's crusaders. The radical Hussites were defeated in 1434 and the city then became the main center of Czech Utraquism, but the physical and economic damage suffered during the upheavals took long to heal. It was not until the late sixteenth century that Prague regained prominence as the cosmopolitan residence of Emperor Rudolf II.

BIBLIOGRAPHY

Götz Fehr, *Prag: Stadt an der Moldau* (1979); Josef Janáček, *Malé dějiny Prahy,* 3rd ed. (1983), trans. into German as *Das alte Prag,* 2nd ed. (1983); Kamil Novotný and Emanuel Poche, *The Charles Bridge of Prague,* Norah Robinson-Hronková, trans. (1947); Alois Svoboda, *Prague: An Intimate Guide,* Roberta Finlayson-Samsour, trans. (1965); Joseph Wechsberg, *Prague: The Mystical City* (1971).

IRINA RYBACEK

[See also **Bohemia-Moravia; Cosmas of Prague; Hus, John; Hussites; Mathieu d'Arras; Přemyslid Dynasty; Parler Family.**]

PREACHING AND SERMONS, ISLAMIC. As a specialized form of oratory concerned with the proclamation of the truth revealed by God to Muḥammad, preaching has been an inseparable part of Islam from the beginning. This truth, recorded in the Koran and reflected in the traditions (*aḥādith;* sing., *ḥadīth*), of the Prophet, was held to be essential for the salvation of humankind and therefore universal in its claims. While the dissemination of this truth was taken in some sense to be the responsibility of the community of believers as a whole, Islam did not hesitate, already at an early period, to make a special place for a distinct class of persons whose task it was to communicate the divine message in the form of sermons and religious discourses to the gathered assembly. The beginnings of such a class cannot be given a precise date. There is reason to believe, however, that preachers were active already during the Medinan period of Muḥammad's life (622–632). Although few details of the activity of these early preachers have been preserved, these latter appear to have played a not insignificant role in the establishment and propagation of Islam. Since specimens of their public utterances have not survived, little can be said about the precise content of their preaching or its form or stylistic features.

As a documentable historical phenomenon, preaching emerges into the light of day only in the period after the death of the Prophet in 632. The period of the *rāshidūn* and Umayyad caliphates (632–750) was a time of rapid evolutionary development for the nascent tradition of Islamic preaching. Probably already in the *rāshidūn* period (632–660), the phenomenon of preaching began a process of internal differentiation that led to the formation of two quite distinct forms or traditions of Muslim preaching.

On the one hand, particularly in connection with the prayers of Friday noon, it evolved into a clearly defined, officially regulated institution with a highly marked ritual character. During the first century, the Friday sermon (*khuṭba*) was frequently given by the caliph himself and by his provincial governors. However, by the end of the Umayyad period, the function of giving the Friday sermon had been delegated to a special class of preachers (*khuṭabāʾ*; sing., *khaṭīb*), usually appointed by the caliph or a highly placed caliphal representative. The principal function of this class was to exhort the faithful, to pronounce on important issues facing the larger community, especially those that affected the interests of the state, and, above all, to represent the caliph as the head of the community. Although not formalized by Islamic usage, it became the practice in the Umayyad period to include in the Friday *khuṭba* a brief invocation in which the name of the reigning caliph was mentioned. The sermon itself was divided into two separate parts and was in general composed in a highly stylized form of Arabic. The length of the sermon, which could and did vary, in general was relatively brief, lasting no longer than ten or fifteen minutes. By the early Abbasid period (beginning 750) it became the general practice to restrict the *khuṭba* to congregational mosques (*jāmiʿ*) located in those towns or cities where a caliphal representative was present. While there undoubtedly was some variation in practice on the local level, by the beginning of the Abbasid period the Friday *khuṭba* had become, in all important respects, a clearly delineated institution and, apart from Egypt during the Fatimid period, appears to have evolved little during the subsequent centuries.

Alongside the institution of the Friday *khuṭba,* which was in some respects a part of the religious arm of the state, another form of preaching emerged that was distinctly popular in outlook and largely independent of the state. Although some of the popular preachers, already in the early period, were appointed by governmental authorities to specific pulpits, the majority of them appear to have carried on their activities without any kind of official designation. Indeed, the sources give us the distinct impression that many, if not most, chose to maintain a discreet distance between themselves and the authorities. While the latter did on occasion attempt to establish some control over the activities of these preachers by banning them from the mosques of particular cities or regions, such efforts on the whole proved futile since popular preachers—in contrast to the Friday *khuṭabāʾ*—were not restricted either by law or by precedent to the mosque and could always carry on their preaching in settings less amenable to control by the authorities. Unlike the Friday preacher, who was confined to a fixed weekly schedule, preachers of the popular sort could preach freely at times of their own choosing.

The Arabic word used most commonly in the sources to designate these early lay preachers is *qāṣṣ* (pl., *quṣṣāṣ*), literally meaning a narrator or teller of stories. Its use as the principal designation for popular preachers suggests that narratives of a religious or devotional character played a significant role in their sermons and public discourses. This fact is amply borne out by specimens of early Muslim preaching that have come down to us in the works of medieval authors. The narrative tendency

 PREACHING, ISLAMIC

of early Muslim preaching, together with a predominantly prose style, is, of course, not surprising given the fact that a very substantial portion of the Koran itself consists of stories of a devotional and admonitory character. In addition to the term *qāṣṣ*, *wāᶜiẓ* (one who admonishes) and *mudhakkir* (one who reminds) gradually came into use and, from the tenth century on, largely displaced *qāṣṣ*, which by then tended to be reserved for heterodox and unprincipled preachers.

Judging from the information to be found in the Arabic sources for the period and on the basis of sermons and fragments of sermons that have been preserved, the *quṣṣāṣ* as a class appear to have had a fairly well-defined view of themselves and of their place within the Muslim community. In the first place, they quite naturally regarded it as one of their principal duties to look after the religious well-being of the community, a duty that included exhorting believers to greater devotion and obedience, explicating a text of the Koran, and providing instruction on matters of doctrine and practice. Second, as the sources indicate in some detail, the preachers of the Umayyad and early Abbasid periods also thought of themselves as "revivalists" who were entrusted with the renewal and reform of the Muslim community. They did not hesitate to subject the community and its leaders to severe criticism where deviation from the teachings of the Koran and the example of the Prophet was evident. Eschatological themes, which played such a prominent part in the preaching of the period, served to infuse their pronouncements with a sense of urgency and provided their preaching with an effective sanction. The ascetic movement that came into its own in the eighth century gave strong reinforcement to the reformist and revivalist tendencies among the *quṣṣāṣ*. Finally, the *quṣṣāṣ* regarded the conversion of non-Muslims as an important part of their mission. Since Muslims remained a distinct minority within their own empire as late as the ninth century, there was naturally ample opportunity for missionary preaching. While it would be going too far to credit the *quṣṣāṣ* with being the only or even principal agents of conversion, they did play an increasingly significant role in that process. More than one medieval chronicler reports that the *quṣṣāṣ* frequently accompanied Muslim armies on military campaigns to exhort the troops and to help maintain morale. Enemy soldiers taken captive on such campaigns must have been the object of the missionary efforts of the *quṣṣāṣ*.

Although there is evidence from as early as the Umayyad period that uninformed, deceitful, or unscrupulous persons had entered the ranks of preachers, the *quṣṣāṣ* on the whole remained an influential and respected class. Among them were to be found persons of genuine devotion and high moral character, not to mention persons of outstanding learning and intellectual achievement. The highly literate and sophisticated al-Jāḥiẓ, a native of Basra and an admirer of the early *quṣṣāṣ*, records in his *Al-Bayān al-tabyīn* the names of the leading preachers of the Umayyad and early Abbasid period along with selections from their sermons. Among the preachers mentioned by him in a list that includes such figures as al-Ḥasan al-Basrī (*d.* 728), Ṣāliḥ al-Murrī (*d.* 788/789), and Abū ᶜAlī al-Uswārī (*d. ca.* 815), we find the names of men who were also renowned as exegetes, traditionists, philologists, reciters of the Koran, and theologians. At least one, Mūsā ibn Sayyār al-Uswārī (*fl.* eighth century), is said to have been fluent in both Arabic and Persian and to have delivered sermons in each with equal ease. By the ninth century the Muᶜtazilite school of Basra and Baghdad, which championed doctrines of a decidedly rationalist character, reckoned among its members a number of preachers noted for their eloquence and learning.

Despite the fact that individuals of a high caliber continued to be found among the *quṣṣāṣ*, by the tenth century and perhaps already somewhat earlier preachers as a class had come under increasingly severe criticism, and apparently not without some justification. While criticism of the *quṣṣāṣ* was not entirely new, the legitimacy of preachers as a class had never been seriously called into question. Now, however, a sustained attempt, undertaken in the main by orthodox sufis (mystics) and by religious scholars (*ᶜulamāᵓ*), especially traditionists, was made to scrutinize the practices of the preachers. Among other things, they were accused of exploiting their audiences for material gain, of introducing into their sermons apocryphal traditions and materials derived from non-Islamic sources, and of espousing views that were contrary to established doctrine. Although it is difficult to gauge the impact of this criticism, it does appear to have prompted a number of efforts at reform. Perhaps the most significant of these was an attempt, encouraged in some cases by preachers themselves, to establish greater control over the activities of preachers by requiring them to be "licensed" by the authorities as a precondition for preaching in public. While this practice was not adopted universally, by the eleventh century it had become fairly widespread, especially in the larger cities. It was apparently in the context of these efforts at reform that the term *qāṣṣ*, tarnished by its association with unscrupulous preachers, was gradually replaced by the terms *wāᶜiẓ* and *mudhakkir*.

Although preachers continued to be the object of criticism, particularly in *ᶜulamāᵓ* circles, throughout the remainder of the medieval period, the tradition of the popular preacher does not appear to have suffered irreparable damage. Our sources for the eleventh and twelfth centuries indicate that preachers were active in all important segments of the Muslim community, Sunni and Shiite alike, and in all the great urban centers of the Muslim world, with the possible exception of North Africa and Spain, where they continued to be opposed by the well-entrenched Malikite school of law. From the end of the tenth century to the middle of the thirteenth, it was at Baghdad that the tradition of the popular preacher appears to have achieved its greatest success. In Baghdad the tradition was linked closely, though not exclusively, with the Hanbalite school, which, from its inception in the ninth century, had maintained a strong populist orientation. It is hardly surprising, therefore, that Hanbalism should have produced an inordinately large number of preachers. It was the Hanbalite preachers, among whom were such names as al-Barbahārī (*d.* 941), Ibn Samᶜūn (*d.* 997), ᶜAbd al-Qādir al-Jīlānī (*d.* 1166), and Ibn al-Jawzī (*d.* 1200), who played a leading role in the reaction against both rationalism and Shiism, and who, in the process, laid the groundwork for the revival of Sunni traditionalism and the reestablishment of Abbasid power.

Ibn al-Jawzī, a leading Hanbalite scholar of the twelfth century, may rightly be regarded as one of the most successful Muslim preachers of the medieval period. His great eloquence and learning were acknowledged even by his detractors. During the peak of his career his audiences are reported by his contemporaries to have numbered in the tens of thousands and he himself claimed to have converted a hundred thousand persons to Islam during his lifetime. Even if this figure is taken as exaggerated, the impact of his preaching was enormous. The Spanish traveler Ibn Jubayr, who visited Baghdad in 1184 and who attended three separate rallies at which Ibn al-Jawzī preached, describes him as "the wonder of all time." As a preacher and a teacher of the art of preaching, Ibn al-Jawzī's influence was felt well beyond the confines of Baghdad or even Iraq. In addition to those who came to hear him preach from other parts of the Muslim world, he was personally responsible for training a number of younger preachers who eventually assumed preaching posts in such cities as Cairo, Damascus, Mosul, and Haran, as well as in a number of lesser centers.

While preaching continued to flourish during the first half of the thirteenth century, by the middle of the fourteenth century it was clearly on the decline (partly because it came to be increasingly confined to the Friday *khuṭba*) and appears to have played at best only a modest role in the religio-political history of Islam until the rise of the great revivalist movements of the modern period.

BIBLIOGRAPHY

Thomas W. Arnold, *The Preaching of Islam,* 2nd rev. and enl. ed. (1913); Clifford E. Bosworth, *The Mediaeval Islamic Underworld,* pt. 1 (1976); Ignác Goldziher, *Muslim Studies,* II, S. M. Stern, ed., C. R. Barber and S. M. Stern, trans. (1967); ᶜAbd al-Raḥman ibn ᶜAlī Ibn al-Jawzī, *Kitāb al-quṣṣāṣ w'al-mudhakkirīn,* Merlin L. Swartz, ed. and trans. (1971); Muḥammad ibn Aḥmad Ibn Jubayr, *The Travels of Ibn Jubayr,* R. J. C. Broadhurst, trans. (1952); George Makdisi, *Ibn ᶜAqīl et la résurgence de l'Islam traditionaliste au XIe siècle* (1963); Louis Massignon, *Essai sur les origines du lexique technique de la mystique musulmane,* new rev. and enl. ed. (1954); Adam Mez, *The Renaissance of Islam,* Salahuddin Khuda Bukhsh and D. S. Margoliouth, trans. (1937, repr. 1979); Johannes Pedersen, "The Islamic Preacher," in Samuel Löwinger and Joseph Somogyi, eds., *Ignace Goldziher Memorial Volume,* I (1948), "The Criticism of the Islamic Preacher," in *Die Welt des Islams,* n.s. 2 (1953), and "Khaṭīb," in *Encyclopaedia of Islam,* 2nd ed.; Charles Pellat, *Le milieu baṣrien et la formation de Ǧāḥiẓ* (1953), and "Ḳāṣṣ," in *Encyclopaedia of Islam,* 2nd ed.; Merlin L. Swartz, "The Rules of Popular Preaching in Twelth-century Baghdad, According to Ibn al-Jawzi," in George Makdisi, Dominique Sourdel, and Janine Sourdel-Thomine, eds., *Predication et propagande au moyen âge: Islam, Byzance, Occident* (1983).

MERLIN SWARTZ

[See also **Islam, Religion; Rhetoric, Arabic.**]

PREACHING AND SERMONS, JEWISH. The classical sermonic literature of the Jews is known as *derush* or *derashah,* which means to inquire after or

PREACHING, JEWISH

seek out the intention of the biblical text. Much of this literature has been preserved, but little systematic study has been undertaken. The sermon was delivered in the synagogue and associated with the weekly lectionary from the Five Books of Moses. Sermons were also delivered during festivals and at weddings. Sermons were preached orally and usually in the vernacular. When they were committed to writing, often pains were taken to make the sermon more erudite, and aesthetics were subordinated to intellectual aspects.

The literary form of the Hebrew sermon was influenced by the exegetical and legal literature of the Talmud. The sermon began with a proem utilizing a verse from Scripture or a quotation from rabbinic legal literature that seemed to be unrelated to the occasion. The art of the *darshan* (preacher) was to relate the seemingly unrelated quotation to the lesson from Scripture. After the proem the sermon explained several verses from the lectionary and concluded with a message of hope or consolation. The sermon was thus an amalgam of the author's ideas, rabbinic literature, and Scripture. The preacher's goal was to demonstrate that his conclusion flowed from and was in full harmony with the classical biblical and rabbinic literature.

A most important consideration of the sermon literature in Judaism was that the audience generally had access to the same texts as the preacher. Thus the rhetorical aesthetic was designed to surprise the audience by developing a connection or an insight that they had not previously considered. Stories, parables, even jokes were introduced as illustrative material; grammar and etymologies helped the preacher reinforce his point. Devices such as *gematria,* assigning numerical values to letters of the Hebrew alphabet and demonstrating that the numbers were equivalent to the idea advanced in the sermon, were also used. Acrostics, acronyms, and puns were other tools of the medieval *darshan.*

From the seventh through twelfth centuries the major focus of Hebrew sermonic literature was on collecting the exegetical and homiletic teaching of the rabbis of the first four centuries. These anthologies were organized either according to the weekly pentateuchal portion (for example, *Deuteronomy Rabbah*) or according to the festival and special sabbath cycle of the Jewish calendar (*Pesikta*). These anthologies do not provide a complete text of the sermon but are collections of proems. From the Jews who lived under Islamic rule in the eighth century we have a homiletic work known as *She'iltot* (Questions) from Aḥai of Shabha (680–752). The structure of the *She'iltot* involved the raising of a legal question and its answer, which was then expanded into a sermon. Evidence of Jewish sermons being preached in contemporary northern Europe comes from the letters of Agobard of Lyons (769–840) as well as from the eleventh-century "Chronicle of Ahimaaz," which mentions a preacher who came from Israel to southern Italy with sermons in rhymed prose. The title *darshan* begins to be attributed to individuals in eleventh-century Narbonne, but little is known about the sermons of these preachers.

Even during the thirteenth and fourteenth centuries sermonics never developed into an independent literary genre. We have only anthologies or encyclopedic works such as the *Lekaḥ Tov* of Tovia ben Eliezer (*fl.* eleventh century) or the *Yalkut Shimoni,* ascribed to Simon of Frankfurt (*fl.* thirteenth century). These anthologies seem to have been handbooks for preaching, since they are organized according to the weekly pentateuchal reading and refer almost exclusively to the rabbinic homiletic literature of the first four centuries. The most original "encyclopedia" from northern Europe is the *Sefer Ḥasidim* (Book of the pious), attributed to Rabbi Judah he-Ḥasid ("the Pietist," *d.* 1217). This book was not compiled as a sermonic collection but does contain homiletic passages and exempla material.

The sermonic literature that developed as an original and independent genre in Provence and Spain during the twelfth and thirteenth centuries evinced a growing interest in philosophic literature. The rise of philosophic literature occasioned efforts to harmonize philosophic ideas with traditional rabbinic sources. Rooted in Aristotle are the sermons of Abraham bar Ḥiyya (*d. ca.* 1136) on repentance and the immortality of the soul. Jacob ben Abba Mari Anatoli (*d.* 1256), who was active in the translation of Arabic philosophic writings and lived at the court of Emperor Frederick II in Naples, composed his *Malmad ha-Talmidim* (Goad to the disciples) to popularize the philosophic ideas in Maimonides' *Guide of the Perplexed.*

Homiletic tradition continued in Spain during the thirteenth century in the form of popular preaching. Moses Nahmanides (*d. ca.* 1270) and his disciple Jonah of Gerona (*d.* 1263) wrote sermons on penitential themes. Baḥya ben Asher (*d.* 1340) composed a homiletic collection, *Kad ha-Kemaḥ*

(Bushel of flour), comprising sixty sermons arranged in a alphabetical order. *Kad ha-Kemaḥ* reflects both theological themes and social criticism of religious laxity. Similar themes are echoed in the homiletic portions of Moses of Coucy's *Sefer Mitzvot ha-Gadol* (The great book of the commandments), describing his travel from France to Spain (1236–1240), where he preached against the lax religious observance and against marriages between Jews and Christians.

In the fifteenth century the sermon became a major genre of religious expression in Spain. The last great medieval homiletic collection seeking a harmony of philosophy and rabbinic Judaism is to be found in the *Aqedat Yitzḥaq* (Binding of Isaac) of Isaac Arama (*d.* 1494). These sermons reveal the tensions of a Jewish community forced to listen to Christian sermons and criticism from the upper classes of Spanish society. Other sermonic productions, for instance by Isaac Abrabanel (*d.* 1508) and Joseph Jabetz (*d.* 1507), set aside philosophic discourse and brought messianism into the center of Jewish aspiration as a consolation for the tragic expulsion of the Jews from Spain and Portugal.

The sixteenth century witnessed a growth of sermonic literature in the new or revived areas of Jewish settlement: Italy, Safed, and Poland. In each area an indigenous tradition developed. Focus on philosophy and aesthetics was characteristic of sixteenth- and seventeenth-century collections of sermons from Italy. Jewish preachers in sixteenth-century Poland reflected upon the social problems of the burgeoning Jewish population. In the Ottoman Empire, and particularly in the Galilean center of Safed, the popularization of Jewish mystical literature was a dominant theme.

BIBLIOGRAPHY

S. Bäck, "Die Darschanim vom 15. bis Ende des 18. Jahrhunderts," in Jakob Winter and August Wünsch, eds., *Geschichte der rabbinischen Litteratur während des Mittelalters* (1894); Salo W. Baron, *A Social and Religious History of the Jews,* VI (1958), 152–175, 399–412; Israel Bettan, *Studies in Jewish Preaching* (1939); Joseph Dan, *Sifrut ha-musar veha-derush* (1975); Simon Gliksberg, *Ha-Derashah be-Yisrael* (1940), 40–170; Leopold Zunz, *Die gottesdienstlichen Vorträge der Juden* (1892).

MICHAEL A. SIGNER

[See also **Abrabanel, Isaac Ben Judah; Abraham bar Ḥiyya; Agobard; Exegesis, Jewish; Expulsion of Jews; Jews (various articles); Judaism; Maimonides, Moses; Naḥmanides, Moses; Philosophy and Theology, Jewish; Talmud, Exegesis and Study of.**]

PREACHING AND SERMON LITERATURE, WESTERN EUROPEAN. The development of preaching and sermon literature played an important role in the history of the church in Western Europe. In a society where large numbers of people were illiterate, sermons were the primary means of instruction of the laity. The duties of a priest included preaching, which meant not only exhorting people to the better life but also instructing them in the tenets of the faith. Indeed, as the Middle Ages progressed, the importance of preaching was emphasized all the more. On all levels of the clergy, from parish priest to university master, preaching was recognized as an important aspect of Christian communal life.

PREACHING TO CLERICS

The growth of the preaching art in medieval Europe occurred in several stages. Although the tradition of preaching was as old as Christianity and its Jewish roots, the early Middle Ages contributed relatively few noteworthy preachers. The fathers of the church recognized the importance of preaching. They had before them Jesus and Paul as models, and numerous parables, stories, and examples drawn from the Bible. St. Augustine (354–430) wrote one of the early guides to preaching in book IV of his *De doctrina Christiana,* and Pope Gregory I (590–604) emphasized the close relationship of biblical interpretation, teaching, and preaching.

The history of the medieval sermon may be seen as the transition from the simple patristic homily to the more complex sermon of the High and later Middle Ages. That transition had to take into account the distinction (which already existed in the early Middle Ages) between preaching to clerical audiences (*ad cleros*) and preaching to popular audiences (*ad populum*).

The distinguishing mark of early medieval preaching, however, was that it was essentially preaching by clerics for audiences of clerics, the language being Latin. Preaching in the tenth and eleventh centuries, for example, mainly took the form of the monastic sermon that was delivered daily by either abbot or ordinary monk. These early sermons were simple in style and content. Sermons were preached in the morning (*mane*) and later in

PREACHING, WESTERN

the day, usually at vespers (*collation*). In Benedictine monasteries the sermon as a whole might be divided into two parts and delivered in the morning and at vespers.

The simple style that was so characteristic of these monastic sermons influenced the form of sermons in the early twelfth century. A theme drawn from Scripture, generally based on the daily liturgy, was the point of departure. The theme was not, however, followed by the *protheme,* which was a creation of the thirteenth century. Changes in terminology reflect this development of the medieval sermon. The term *homilia* or homily was generally reserved for the kind of preaching where a biblical passage, normally read during the Mass, was explained phrase by phrase and was, therefore, a commentary on the Gospel of the Mass. The term *sermo* or sermon, which replaced it by the thirteenth century, was applied to the type of preaching where a short quotation, also taken from the liturgy for the day, was divided at length and developed according to the rule of the *ars praedicandi.*

Because sermons of this period were still largely for clerical audiences, they concentrated on theological themes, such as grace, the sacraments, and redemption. The major preachers of the era included regular clergy (those who lived by the monastic rule) and secular clergy (including bishops and archbishops). St. Bernard of Clairvaux (*d.* 1153) was one of the best of twelfth-century sermon makers. Other regulars whose preaching was noteworthy, and whose sermons reflect the life of the cloister, include the Benedictines Guibert of Nogent (*d. ca.* 1125) and Peter of Celle (*d.* 1183), the Cluniac Peter the Venerable (*d.* 1156), the Cistercians Alan of Lille (*d.* 1202/1203) and Adam of Perseigne (*d.* 1208 or later), and from the Abbey of St. Victor, Hugh (*d.* 1141), Richard (*d.* 1173), and Peter Comestor (*d. ca.* 1179). Some of the most distinguished scholars in twelfth-century intellectual history were noteworthy preachers: Anselm, archbishop of Canterbury (*d.* 1109), Ivo of Chartres (*d.* 1115), Peter Abelard (*d.* 1142), Hildebert, bishop of Le Mans and archbishop of Tours (*d.* 1133), Peter Lombard (*d.* 1160), and Peter of Blois (*d.* 1212).

RISE OF POPULAR PREACHING

By the last part of the twelfth century, sermons had entered a distinctive stage influenced by the increasing importance given to popular preaching. This is not to say that popular audiences were ignored earlier. There was, in fact, legislation in the capitularies of Charlemagne (813) urging that sermons be preached to the people in the language they would understand. The real impetus to popular preaching, however, coincided with the offensive taken by the church against two principal enemies: the Saracens abroad and heretics in the Christian community at home.

The importance attached to popular preaching can be seen in several measures taken by the church in the early thirteenth century. For example, the Fourth Lateran Council (1215) adopted as canon 10 a statement that emphasized the responsibility of the bishop to name men suited to fulfill the important task of instructing the people by word and example. Pope Innocent III (1198–1216), who was also a renowned preacher, was an example to an age when the sermon was coming into its own not only as a weapon against the enemies of the church but also in winning popular support for his plans of church reform. Masters in the cathedral schools in Paris who were trained in theology, such as Stephen Langton, later archbishop of Canterbury (*d.* 1228), Peter the Chanter (*d.* 1197), and Robert of Courson (*d.* 1219), responded to this call. They were interested in the reinvigoration of Christian teaching and therefore attached great importance to popular preaching. The founding of the Franciscan and Dominican orders also occurred in the early years of the thirteenth century. Their rapid spread throughout the cities of Western Europe in the course of the thirteenth century may be seen as a continuation and extension of this effort by the church to educate and persuade the laity.

MEDIEVAL AUDIENCES

By the late twelfth and early thirteenth centuries, then, we see clearly emerging a dual tradition of preaching in response to the changing needs of the medieval church. There was, on the one hand, the growing importance of popular preaching, which was to affect the nature and character of sermons to lay audiences. On the other hand, preaching to clerical audiences did not decline in importance. In fact, these sermons took on an even greater significance, since clerics were also potential preachers to the laity. The university sermon addressed to clerics, for example, became an important feature of medieval preaching in the thirteenth and fourteenth centuries. A more elevated and "polished" style was generally reserved for these clergy, while familiar

PREACHING, WESTERN

and practical explanations were features of those sermons addressed to predominantly lay audiences. Since the preaching of the period was primarily instructive, sermons were highly colored by including allegorical and symbolical interpretations, satire, elegy, and rhymes. These were effective teaching devices in all kinds of sermons.

The dual character of this preaching can be seen further in the descriptions of medieval audiences. Clerical audiences were made up of relatively small groups of listeners who were seated either in the church choir or on stone benches that ran the length of the side walls of the chapel. Audiences of clerics that generally heard sermons preached in Latin included secular clergy gathered at church synods or councils, or in the schools and universities, and regular clergy gathered in the cloister or monastic chapel.

Popular audiences were generally larger and appear to have been enthusiastic listeners as they surrounded their preachers. Grouped separately, men on one side and women on the other (as dictated by traditional practice), lay audiences usually sat during the preaching of the sermon—the majority on benches, though noble ladies sat on chairs and cushions brought by their servants. There is also evidence that audiences stood during the preaching of the sermon, although this view has been disputed by some authors. The practice probably varied. Nobles often had their own chapels, but church authorities urged them to attend parish churches. In special circumstances when there was an especially large crowd, the sermon might deliberately be moved from the church and preached in a public place. However, preaching outside the church was later forbidden in France; the Council of Angers (1448) condemned it.

We know about specific groups of medieval audiences from such twelfth- and thirteenth-century preachers as Alan of Lille, Jacques de Vitry (*d.* 1240), Humbert of Romans (*d.* 1277), and Guibert of Tournai (*d.* 1284), whose sermon collections include preaching to princes, nobles, burghers, students, workers, merchants, peasants, sailors, regular and secular clergy, women, and children.

It was not unusual for a preacher to be interrupted by questions or objections from his audience. The practice was a reminder of the early days of the church, when homilies and lessons were given by the bishop, who interrogated the people and responded to their questions. The sermon was not only a theological exercise to mark an occasion in the church calendar, it was also an important teaching device.

SERMON TEXTS

It is now commonly accepted that sermons addressed to the laity or to mixed audiences of clergy and laity were preached in the vernacular. Nevertheless, the language of the sermons in the manuscripts is Latin. In the view of most scholars, this practice reflects the dual nature of medieval preaching and the special requirements of medieval "publication." For example, the sermons of the bishop of Paris, Maurice de Sully (*d.* 1196), were preached in French, but the Latin texts were prepared by Maurice himself for the use of the clergy in his diocese. Similarly, popular sermons given in English were written down in Latin. Latin was the language of publication, and it had long been the tradition of the church to publish in Latin sermons that had been composed and preached in the vulgar tongue. Thus Bernard of Clairvaux in the twelfth century addressed his monks in Latin and the people in the vernacular. Preachers spoke to their congregations in the common language they understood. In an era when the formal study of Latin was restricted to monastic or cathedral schools, the general population could be expected to understand preaching only in the vulgar tongue.

The problem of the transmission of the sermons (how the sermons came to be written down in the form we find them in the manuscripts) is closely related to that of language. The course of finally rendering the sermon into Latin, whether by another cleric or by the author himself, is not always clear. The text might, in its final appearance, be the whole of the sermon or only a digest. Even if the spoken sermon was in the vernacular, this does not mean that the written Latin sermon was always a direct translation of the sermon as delivered. The intervention of a time interval and/or a reporter must be taken into account. In the thirteenth century, "publication" of a sermon meant giving it orally or writing it down. Although the second ordinarily followed the first, the two forms were not necessarily joined.

Sermons were generally classified into four types: improvised, prepared, recited (from memory), and read. Improvised sermons, though given quite frequently, were not often preserved or reproduced. A listener, or sometimes the speaker himself, might record such sermons, but in all likelihood the written version would be a summary of the actual text. The prepared sermon, on the other hand, is much more frequently found to have survived in the manuscripts. Its method, general appearance, citations of texts, and commentaries indicate the great pains taken in its preparation. In this instance the manuscript is much more likely to contain the actual sermon as delivered.

Sometimes the author himself may have brought together a collection of his sermons, translating them into Latin, possibly to serve as a manual for other preachers. The book of sermons that comes down to us under the name of Maurice de Sully, bishop of Paris, is an example of this practice. Other well-known preachers who collected their sermons in similar fashion, introduced by a preface addressed to colleagues, include Jacques de Vitry, John of Abbeville (*d.* 1237), and Guibert of Tournai.

Most frequently, however, it appears that the sermon was written down by a listener, either as it was given or afterward. Certain priests carried notebooks or tablets with them when they listened to the preaching of their colleagues, taking notes either for their own use or for the benefit of others. These copies by a second hand are often the only ones we have. This writing down of the sermon by a listener, called *reportatio,* had close connections with the teaching of the schools. As Beryl Smalley has noted, it was an established university practice for masters to correct reports of their lectures personally before their publication. The University of Paris, for example, appointed scribes specially charged with noting down the sermons of its members. Hence it is according to their notes that so many of the collections of diverse origin and authorship were formed.

Collections of sermon texts of many known and anonymous authors are typical of what we find in the scores of manuscripts of the twelfth to the fourteenth centuries. The intermingling of texts, so often rendered homogeneous by an unknown reporter-copyist, creates untold difficulties for students of medieval sermon literature. These sermons look very much alike in the manuscripts, beginning with a theme drawn from Scripture and perhaps identified by an appropriate rubric that notes the occasion for the sermon. The sermon often goes on to draw upon a common stock of examples and similitudes. One has to go beyond the externals of the sermon texts and begin to identify them by author. This is facilitated by a careful study of the collections, since many bear attributions (correct or incorrect) to a particular author.

There are, then, four steps in the transmission of sermon texts: (1) delivery of the sermon; (2) recording of the text and its translation, where necessary, by author or clerk; (3) collections of the texts of various masters, sometimes, but not always, arranged according to the liturgical calendar; (4) gathering together of a group of sermons of a prominent preacher, again frequently arranged according to the ecclesiastical calendar, possibly to be used as a handbook for other preachers.

SERMONS AND LITURGY

The ecclesiastical year formed a continuous drama during which the faithful were instructed in the tenets of religion. Preachers preached on Sundays and on the feast days of the church calendar, but sermons were not limited to these occasions. Prelates frequently preached to the clergy in synod and on pastoral visits. Bishops preached during their visitation to monasteries and churches. Special sacred ceremonies, such as ordinations, dedications, consecrations, elections, coronations, and pilgrimages, were frequently highlighted by the preaching of a sermon.

Preaching to the laity on Sundays and feast days, or on extraordinary occasions, was an important function of the clergy. The duty to instruct the people in the principles of the faith had been articulated by the church in canon 19 of the Council of Constantinople (692). Scripture provided the basis of preaching, and the early sermon was, in fact, little more than an exposition on Scripture, specifically on the daily Gospel reading. The preaching of the sermon took place in the course of the Mass, following the Gospel reading. These "sacred sermons" generally contained some exposition of the particular Gospel. There were also sermons given on special occasions that were usually relegated to the end of the Mass. These were called "extraordinary sermons."

The juxtaposition of the Gospel reading and the preaching of the sermon raises the question of the connections between the sermon and the liturgy. The history of the liturgy has been treated in some detail by Josef A. Jungmann, who has described the pre-Christian origins of the delivery of the sermon, preached in the vernacular. It had been the custom in the ancient synagogue to follow the Sabbath Bible reading with some clarifying explanation. Early medieval sermons reflected this homiletic character, and the subsequent history of the medieval sermon is, in effect, a history of its increasing complexity and independence from the Mass. By the High and later Middle Ages, the sermon not only had come into its own as an independent genre but also had come more and more to leave the confines of the Mass. This is most evident in the preaching of the mendicants, who preached wholly apart from the Mass to any assembly of willing listeners in towns and villages.

Sacred sermons, however, were part of the service prescribed in the regulations and service books of the church. Although the Roman liturgical rite in its entirety was not uniformly accepted in Western Europe until the sixteenth century (with the promulgation of the papal bull *Quo primum tempore* by Pope Pius V in 1570), it nonetheless was the basis of much of the liturgy in various parts of medieval Europe from the sixth to the sixteenth century. The *Ordines Romani* contain the rules that determine the conduct of the service and appropriate Gospel readings from which a preacher might select his sermon theme.

INSTRUCTION IN PREACHING

Medieval preachers could draw upon other kinds of aids to assist their preaching. The fresh emphasis on popular preaching led to the development of the *artes praedicandi,* which reflected the side of preaching that could be guided by rules and formal instruction. By the thirteenth century, the art of preaching had come under the same tendencies of specialization that we see elsewhere in medieval society. Preaching, therefore, required more formalized techniques. Its practitioners included not only bishops and parish priests but also university masters and doctors of theology, who dealt with the instruction of the Christian community as well as with the education of clerics.

The widespread availability of preaching handbooks and collections of model sermons was an important factor in the attempt to upgrade the level of preaching. Preaching manuals increased in number and diffusion in the thirteenth and fourteenth centuries. Their contents varied. While their main intent was to outline the choice of theme and various subdivisions of the sermon according to certain conventional rules, the manuals came to include other materials as well. Handbooks of themes, distinctions, authorities, concordances, and examples undoubtedly formed a useful reference library for the preacher. Most of the treatises considered the technique and composition of the sermon; some also gave attention to voice, gesture, and delivery.

The development of the preaching art and the widespread availability of preaching manuals obviated the necessity for separate instruction in the schools in the art of preaching. Although the masters in the schools did not devote much time in their lectures to instruction on preaching per se (this apparently was the function of the preaching handbook), there are important connections among preaching, sermon making, and the study of Scripture in the medieval schools and universities.

The education of the clergy had reached a critical stage by the twelfth and thirteenth centuries. The increasing concentration in major centers such as Paris deprived the general ranks of the clergy of adequate leadership and instruction. The Third and Fourth Lateran councils (1179 and 1215) moved to correct this situation by providing stipends for teaching masters who would give free instruction to clerics and poor scholars. Initially directed at cathedral churches, the ruling was extended in 1215 to include other churches.

Medieval schools from their earliest days emphasized the close ties between teaching and preaching. Practices in the schools came to be formalized later in university statutes. C. E. Bulaeus, in his history of the University of Paris, mentions the custom of preaching sermons to masters and scholars in the schools of twelfth-century Paris on all major feast days, during Advent and Lent, and on the feasts of the patrons and saints of the nations. The statutes of the university contain references to the importance of preaching. Newly admitted students in the faculty of theology, for example, were required to preach. Students in theology had to preach at least once a year, and preaching competence was required for the granting of the license (doctorate) in theology.

Masters who were also preachers participated in the direct instruction of the surrounding community. University regulations explicitly directed that theological masters preach on certain days and in specified churches in the capital. Masters and students at the faculty of theology were also expected to attend university sermons. After 1231 morning sermons at Paris were followed in the evening by the *collatio,* a sermon in which the preacher often took the theme of the morning sermon and expanded on it. Paris statutes of 1335 were even more precise in calling for sermons to be given in the

PREACHING, WESTERN

presence of masters and students in the church of the Dominicans or Franciscans, the College of Navarre, or some other church, such as St. Germain-des-Prés. Our sources also mention that students of grammar and arts went with their masters to hear university sermons.

The University of Paris furnished the model for theological studies throughout medieval Europe. From the thirteenth to the fifteenth century, other universities came to include provisions for preaching in their statutes. At Oxford, where university sermons appear as early as 1170, candidates for the license in theology were required to preach in Latin at the Church of St. Mary the Virgin. Such preaching occurred every Sunday during full term, done by a bachelor or doctor of theology. An additional sermon was added by statute in the fifteenth century, and there is evidence that candidates sometimes wanted to preach in English at St. Peter's in the East, instead of in Latin at St. Mary's. Oxford students were required to attend university sermons.

Theological instruction arrived later in Italian universities. It was not until the fourteenth century that a faculty of theology was introduced at Bologna and statutes relating to preaching drafted. Earlier ecclesiastical studies at Bologna emphasized canon law. Preparation for the work of preacher and confessor was left to the schools of the friars before the fourteenth century. Statutes introduced at the University of Padua in 1331 borrowed largely from the current statutes at Bologna. Apparently, regular university sermons were preached at the Dominican church in Padua as well as in other Italian universities.

Elsewhere in Europe, universities followed these examples as they developed their own theological faculties. The statutes of the University of Salamanca, where a chair of theology was endowed in 1355, included provisions for the regular preaching of university sermons. The regulations of the German universities of Prague, Vienna, and Heidelberg also required such preaching. Established by royal charter of Charles IV in 1348, Prague had been granted a theological faculty from the outset and generally held the monopoly on theological teaching in the German lands until the Hussite troubles in the fifteenth century, when Vienna (founded in 1365) came to dominate the German universities. Heidelberg, founded in 1386, followed the Paris model for sermons and preaching in its faculty of theology.

THE SERMON IN FULL DEVELOPMENT

The form of the sermon itself when it reached its fullest development was as follows: The preacher took his place in the pulpit and, following ancient custom, made the sign of the cross. Before addressing the faithful in their own tongue, he pronounced in Latin the theme or text to be explicated. Having announced his theme, the preacher invited his listeners to pray for the good result of the preaching. A section sometimes called the *protheme* or *antetheme,* or more accurately the exordium, introduced this prayer and frequently contained some excuse relating to the preacher's unworthiness. In the manuscripts, the prayer that was repeated simultaneously by the preacher and his audience is indicated by the opening words "Pater Noster" or "Ave Maria."

Once the initial prayer had been pronounced, the preacher restated the theme, a repetition possibly motivated by the arrival of latecomers. After developing the theme by the use of examples and similitudes, the preacher concluded the sermon with a new prayer (indicated in the manuscripts by "Rogabimus" or by the patristic formula "Quod nobis prestare qui vivit et regnat Deus per omnia secula seculorum" [to which may He lead us Who lives and reigns forever]) that invoked divine blessing on all. This form was characteristic of most sermons by the end of the twelfth century.

A more complex *protheme* was introduced in the course of the thirteenth century. The fully developed *protheme* served as a kind of introduction and summary of the theme and was normally based on a different biblical passage from the sermon itself. It usually contained a reference to the characteristics of the good preacher. Though relatively brief, the *protheme* had its own divisions of the theme and a short synopsis of the points that would be developed later in the sermon by citing various authorities. By the end of the thirteenth century, the *protheme* had become virtually a sermon within a sermon.

After the *protheme,* the preacher reintroduced and developed his theme and discussed it fully by introducing scriptural or patristic authorities, classical sources, popular proverbs, or some appropriate ideas of his own. The division of the theme into parts facilitated the preacher's organization and presentation of the sermon, and enabled his audience to follow the argument and understand the points made by the speaker with greater ease. It was

PREACHING, WESTERN

also possible to subdivide these divisions as a method of expanding upon the theme.

The means by which sermons could be developed were rather elaborate by the later Middle Ages. A late medieval tractate on preaching listed nine methods of expanding a sermon: (1) through concordance of authorities, (2) through discussion of words, (3) through explanation of the properties of things, (4) through a multiplication of senses, (5) through analogies and natural truths, (6) through marking of an opposite, (7) through comparisons, (8) through interpretation of a name, and (9) through multiplication of synonyms.

THE STUDY OF SERMON TEXTS

The importance of sermons to scholars as sources of knowledge about the Middle Ages is now widely acknowledged. Sermons can tell us much about religious, social, intellectual, and literary history. Sermons are important sources for the history of manners and popular fables. The French scholar Ch.-V. Langlois compared them to the popular press as reflective of the spiritual state of the age. In his studies on medieval preaching in England, Gerald Owst emphasized how sermons can contribute to our knowledge of social life and thought. In addition, where the preacher can be positively identified, his sermons are significant biographical sources, since they may contain clues to his thinking and/or references to contemporary issues and events.

For all their potential as sources, however, and despite their availability in great numbers, relatively few scholars have studied sermons in a systematic and thorough way. Some comments on the problems of sermon research may help to explain why. The first problem is bibliographical. Prior to the publication, beginning in 1969, of J. B. Schneyer's *Repertorium,* there was no single listing of the manuscripts in European libraries that contain sermon collections. The sermons themselves present formidable difficulties to the scholar. Sermons attributed to a particular preacher appear among thousands of medieval sermons in the manuscripts of the High and later Middle Ages. Most are unpublished, and in their present state in the manuscripts it is difficult to disentangle one preacher's sermons from another's. Moreover, as Charles H. Haskins put it, many of these medieval sermons in the condensed and desiccated form in which they have come down to us do not make very interesting reading.

Nor can we overlook other limitations of the genre. Sermons are by nature hortatory. They tend to exaggerate good and evil in order to make a point. They often include borrowed anecdotes, examples, and similitudes. Only occasionally are there direct comments on the preacher's personal experiences. Nevertheless, while the mirror is not perfectly flat (what historical source is without the blemish of bias or abridgment?), sermons do reflect the thought and mores of the society and give insight into its preachers and its audiences.

Students of the Middle Ages can use the sermon texts fruitfully. Their use as sources, however, requires application of professional standards of historical criticism, consideration of the sermon in the light of medieval rhetorical theory and practice, attention to the relationship between the spoken and written sermon, and the question of the vernacular versus the Latin sermon. Consideration of these special problems, especially as they relate to the transmission of the sermon, is necessary to any meaningful historical study of sermons and their preachers. The pitfalls are many, but the glimpse into the society that the preacher mirrors in his sermons makes the venture rewarding.

BIBLIOGRAPHY

This bibliography is selective. For more detailed listings see Roberts (1968), Rouse and Rouse (1979), and Murphy (1971). Current bibliographies on all aspects of medieval sermon studies appear in *Medieval Sermon Studies Newsletter* (1977–). Johannes B. Schneyer, *Repertorium der lateinischen Sermones des Mittelalters für die Zeit von 1150 bis 1350,* 9 vols. (1969–1980), contains volumes devoted to individual preachers, anonymous sermons, university and conciliar sermons, and sermons of the various religious orders. Included are bibliographies, the scriptural theme and incipit (opening lines), occasion of the sermon, and references to manuscripts and printed editions.

General studies on sermons and preaching include Charles S. Baldwin, *Medieval Rhetoric and Poetic (to 1400)* (1928, repr. 1959), 228–257; Louis J. Bataillon, "Approaches to the Study of Medieval Sermons," in *Leeds Studies in English,* n.s. **11** (1980); John W. Blench, *Preaching in England in the Late Fifteenth and Sixteenth Centuries* (1964); Louis Bourgain, *La chaire française au XIIe siècle d'après les manuscrits* (1879, repr. 1973); Ch.-V. Langlois, "L'éloquence sacrée au moyen âge," in *Revue des deux mondes,* **115** (1893); Jean Leclercq, "Recherches sur d'anciens sermons monastiques," in *Revue Mabillon,* **36** (1946); Albert Lecoy de la Marche, *La chaire française au moyen âge, spécialement au XIIIe siècle,* 2nd ed., rev. and enl. (1886); Milton McCormick

Gatch, *Preaching and Theology in Anglo-Saxon England* (1977); Gerald R. Owst, *Preaching in Medieval England* (1926, repr. 1965), and *Literature and Pulpit in Medieval England,* (1933, 2nd rev. ed. 1961, repr. 1966); Homer G. Pfander, *The Popular Sermon of the Medieval Friar in England* (1937); Durant W. Robertson, Jr., "Frequency of Preaching in Thirteenth-century England," in *Speculum,* **24** (1949); Johannes B. Schneyer, *Wegweiser zu lateinischen Predigtreihen des Mittelalters* (1965), and *Geschichte der katholischen Predigt* (1969); Beryl Smalley, *English Friars and Antiquity in the Early Fourteenth Century* (1960); Jennifer Sweet, "Some Thirteenth-century Sermons and Their Authors," in *Journal of Ecclesiastical History,* **4** (1953); Michel Zink, *La prédication en langue romane avant 1300* (1976).

On the connections between preaching and medieval schools and universities, see John W. Baldwin, *Masters, Princes, and Merchants: The Social Views of Peter the Chanter and His Circle,* 2 vols. (1970); Caesar Egassius Bulaeus (César Égasse du Boulay), *Historia universitatis Parisiensis* (1665–1673), II, III; Marie-Magdeleine Davy, *Les sermons universitaires parisiens de 1230–1231* (1931); Heinrich Denifle and Émile Chatelain, eds., *Chartularium universitatis Parisiensis,* II (1891), nos. 1185, 1188, 1189, 1192; Astrik L. Gabriel, *Garlandia: Studies in the History of the Mediaeval University* (1969); Palémon Glorieux, "Sermons universitaires parisiens de 1267–68," in *Recherches de théologie ancienne et médiévale,* **16** (1949); Charles H. Haskins, "The University of Paris in the Sermons of the XIIIth Century," in *American Historical Review,* **10** (1904).

Jean Leclercq, "Le magistère du prédicateur au XIIIe siècle," in *Archives d'histoire doctrinale et littéraire du moyen âge,* **21** (1946); Andrew G. Little and Franz Pelster, *Oxford Theology and Theologians c. A.D. 1282–1302* (1934), 147–215; Jean Longère, *Oeuvres oratoires de maîtres parisiens au XIIe siècle,* 2 vols. (1975); Pierre Mandonnet *et al., Saint Dominique* (1938), II, 83–100, on the preaching office and the role of masters in preaching; Hastings Rashdall, *The Universities of Europe in the Middle Ages,* F. M. Powicke and A. B. Emden, eds., 3 vols., new ed. (1936); Beryl Smalley, "Oxford University Sermons 1290–1293," in J. J. G. Alexander and M. T. Gibson, eds., *Medieval Learning and Literature: Essays Presented to Richard William Hunt* (1976), and *The Study of the Bible in the Middle Ages,* 2nd ed., rev. (1952, repr. 1964).

For studies of particular sermons or preachers, see Marie-Thérèse d'Alverny, *Alain de Lille: Textes inédits* (1965); Bernard of Clairvaux, *On the Song of Songs,* Kilian Walsh, trans., 2 vols. (1971–1976); Mary Aquinas Devlin, ed., *The Sermons of Thomas Brinton, Bishop of Rochester 1373–1389,* 2 vols. (1954); Marcel Dickson and Christiane Dickson, "Le cardinal Robert de Courson: Sa vie," in *Archives d'histoire doctrinale et littéraire du moyen âge,* **9** (1934); Guerric of Igny, *Liturgical Sermons,* 2 vols., monks of Mount St. Bernard Abbey, trans. (1971); Nicholas M. Haring, "The Liberal Arts in the Sermons of Garnier of Rochefort," in *Mediaeval Studies,* **30** (1968); Patrick J. Horner, "John Paunteley's Sermon at the Funeral of Walter Froucester, Abbot of Gloucester (1412)," in *American Benedictine Review,* **28** (1977), and "A Sermon on the Anniversary of the Death of Thomas Beauchamp, Earl of Warwick," in *Traditio,* **34** (1978), a Latin edition; Anne Hudson, ed., *Selections from English Wycliffite Writings* (1978); Isaac of Stella, *Sermons on the Christian Year,* I, H. McCaffery, trans. (1979); John of La Rochelle, *Eleven Marian Sermons,* Kilian F. Lynch, ed. (1961); John, Abbot of Ford, *Sermons on the Final Verses of the Song of Songs,* I, *Sermons 1–14,* Wendy M. Beckett, trans. (1977); Peggy Ann Knapp, *The Style of John Wyclif's English Sermons* (1977).

Phyllis B. Roberts, *Studies in the Sermons of Stephen Langton* (1968), "Stephen Langton and St. Catherine of Alexandria: A Paris Master's Sermon on the Patron Saint of Scholars," in *Manuscripta,* **20** (1976), "Master Stephen Langton Preaches to the People and Clergy: Sermon Texts from Twelfth-century Paris," in *Traditio,* **36** (1980), in Latin, and *idem,* ed., *Selected Sermons of Stephen Langton* (1980); Charles A. Robson, *Maurice of Sully and the Medieval Vernacular Homily* (1952).

For related studies, see T. M. Charland, ed., *Artes praedicandi* (1936); Josef A. Jungmann, *The Mass of the Roman Rite: Its Origins and Development,* Francis A. Brunner, trans., 2 vols. (1951–1955, rev. ed. in 1 vol. 1959); James Jerome Murphy, *Medieval Rhetoric: A Select Bibliography* (1971), 71–81, and *Rhetoric in the Middle Ages* (1974), 269–355; Richard H. Rouse and Mary A. Rouse, *Preachers, Florilegia, and Sermons: Studies on the 'Manipulus florum' of Thomas of Ireland* (1979); Jean Thiébaut Welter, *L'exemplum dans la littérature religieuse et didactique du moyen âge* (1927, repr. 1973); Siegfried Wenzel, *Verses in Sermons: 'Fasciculus morum' and Its Middle English Poems* (1978).

PHYLLIS B. ROBERTS

[See also **Abelard, Peter; Alan of Lille; Anselm of Canterbury; Ars Praedicandi; Bernard of Clairvaux, St.; Church, Early; Courson, Robert of; Dominicans; Exemplum; Florilegia; Franciscans; Guibert of Nogent; Hugh of St. Victor; Innocent III, Pope; Ivo of Chartres, St.; Jacques de Vitry; Langton, Stephen; Latin Literature; Paris, University of; Peter Comestor; Peter Lombard; Peter of Blois; Peter the Chanter; Peter the Venerable; Rhetoric: Western European; Richard of St. Victor.**]

PRECENTOR, the director of a church choir and the person generally responsible for matters concerning music in churches, cathedrals, and monasteries. His responsibilities usually included conducting the choir, organizing the performing forces, training and disciplining the singers, and supervising the compilation and care of the musical books. The specific list of duties varied with the institution; when the ceremony was elaborate or the choir large, the precentor often delegated some of his responsibilities to others, the succentor being his principal deputy.

The term "precentor" used in the sense of a well-delineated office within the organization of the church is found from the ninth century on, particularly in French and English sources. It was used synonymously with the term "cantor." Before the eleventh century the leader of the choir was referred to by such titles as archicantor, *cantor primus, primicerius schola cantorum*, or simply *primicerius*.

BIBLIOGRAPHY

Charles Du Cange, "Praecentor" and "Primicerius," in *Glossarium mediae et infimae latinitatis,* V (1845 and later editions); Frank L. Harrison, *Music in Medieval Britain* (1958); Erich Reimer, "Musicus—cantor," in Hans H. Eggebrecht, ed., *Handwörterbuch der musikalischen Terminologie* (1972–); Manfred Schuler, "Zur Geschichte des Kantors im Mittelalter," in *Bericht über den internationalen musikwissenschaftlichen Kongress Leipzig 1966* (1970).

LANCE W. BRUNNER

[See also **Cantor; Music,** various articles.]

PREDELLA (Italian for "step" or "kneeling stool") generally denotes the base of an altarpiece upon which the main panels rest. This base was frequently painted with small narrative scenes, a practice that developed in the fourteenth century and lasted in various regions well into the fifteenth and even sixteenth centuries. These paintings were often small, intimate, and charming scenes drawn from biblical texts, such as Duccio's paintings of the Birth, Infancy, and Childhood of Christ (combined with representation of Old Testament Prophets) on the front predella of the *Maestà* (1308–1311), one of the first painted predellas and the earliest to survive. A later example is the predella of Michael Pacher's *St. Wolfgang Altarpiece* (1471–1481).

BIBLIOGRAPHY

A. Preiser, *Das Entstehen und die Entwicklung der Predella in der italienischen Malerei* (1973); Roberto Salvini and Leone Traverso, *The Predella from the XIIIth to the XVIth Centuries* (1960); Ruth Wilkins Sullivan, "The Anointing in Bethany and Other Affirmations of Christ's Divinity on Duccio's Back Predella," in *Art Bulletin,* **67** (1985), and "Some Old Testament Themes on the Front Predella of Duccio's *Maesta,*" in *Art Bulletin,* **68** (1986).

ADELHEID M. GEALT

[See also **Altar–Altar Apparatus; Altarpiece; Duccio di Buoninsegna; Hagenauer, Nikolaus; Marzal de Sax; Orcagna, Andrea; Pacher, Michael; Rossello di Jacopo Franchi** (most with illustrations).]

PREMONSTRATENSIAN RITE. Any attempt to sketch a genetic history of the medieval phase of the Premonstratensian (or Norbertine) rite confronts two obstacles: the nonexistence of primary sources for the early decades of the Premonstratensian order's existence, and the de facto divergence in liturgical practice despite reiterated insistence by popes, abbots general, and general chapters on liturgical uniformity. It is certain, however, that the original form of the rite was determined by St. Norbert's initial adoption of the severe *Ordo monasterii* or *Regula secunda* attributed (wrongly) to St. Augustine, and by his dependence on the customary of the canons regular of Springiersbach (former diocese of Trier). Among the novel features of this much-criticized proto-Premonstratensian practice was the variable number of psalms, antiphons, and readings of the night Office, which differed in the three periods of the year: November through February; March and April, September and October; May through August. There was no prime or compline. Lauds, terce, sext, and none had three psalms; vespers, six. A bull of Pope Honorius II, issued probably in 1126 or 1127, after the departure of Norbert for Magdeburg, directed the canons of the church of Prémontré to follow the practice of other brethren regular (*secundum aliorum regularium fratrum consuetudinem*). From this time on, the basic structure of the Office was that of the standard Roman Office as celebrated by other groups of canons and by diocesan clergy at large. Under Hugh of Fosse (*d.* 1164), immediate successor of Norbert and first abbot of Prémontré, a complete liturgical code was elaborated. Cistercian legislation and institutions had indeed heavily influenced the Premonstratensian counterparts, but this influence did not extend decisively to either the form or the content of the Office and Mass books. Manuscript sources extant from the latter half of the twelfth century on reflect, in general, Rhenish liturgical traditions characteristic of the milieu in which the White Canons first flourished. This in no way rules out the existence of elements derived from particular reform groups of canons regular, Carthusians, and Benedictine and Cistercian monks. The unified rite elaborated at Prémontré won orderwide acceptance—more or less—only in the mid thirteenth century. This slowness of diffusion was due in part to the rapid spread of the order throughout geographically disparate regions, and to difficulties in acquiring completely new books and in abandoning familiar local usages.

The chant melodies recoverable from the earliest manuscripts represent no more than a local development of the standard chant called "Gregorian," though with a preference for Teutonic particularities (substitution of *fa* and *do* for *mi* and *ti*).

The calendar, basically the traditional Roman one, included saints popular in the regions of France and Germany that first welcomed Norbert and his reform; but it also kept pace with the evolution of the Roman calendar at large. There were five degrees of feasts—*duplex, celeber, IX lectionum, III lectionum, antiphona*—and double feasts had still further divisions. To the canonical Office were added the Office of Our Lady and the daily Office for the Dead. The two daily conventual masses (*missa matutinalis* after prime, *missa summa* after terce or sext) were supplemented, in the thirteenth century, by the daily Mass of Our Lady. The Mass order was derived from the Cistercian *ordo missae*. Especially characteristic were the emphasis on the eucharistic cult and the solemnization of Christmas (exclusion of all feasts in Christmastide except those of Stephen, John, and the Holy Innocents) and of Easter (daily solemn vespers with procession during the octave). The use of pontifical rites by abbots became general only in the fourteenth century.

BIBLIOGRAPHY

Archdale King, *Liturgies of the Religious Orders* (1955), 157–234; Placide Lefèvre, *L'ordinaire de Prémontré d'après des manuscrits du XIIe et du XIIIe siècle* (1941), *La liturgie de Prémontré* (1957), and, as editor, *Coutumiers liturgiques de Prémontré du XIIIe et du XIVe siècle* (1953); Boniface Luykx, *Essai sur les sources de l' "Ordo missae" Prémontré,* Analecta praemonstratensia, XXIII (1947).

CHRYSOGONUS WADDELL

[See also **Augustine of Hippo, St.; Cistercian Rite; Clergy; Divine Office; Mass.**]

PREMONSTRATENSIANS. Founded by St. Norbert of Xanten in the solitude of Prémontré, near Laon, France, in 1120, the Premonstratensians have also been variously designated Canons Regular of Prémontré, Norbertines, and—chiefly in England—White Canons (after the color of their habit).

Born around 1180 to noble parents at Xanten, near the border between the present-day Netherlands and Germany, Norbert's early life was that of a rather worldly and wealthy subdeacon and canon of St. Victor, first at the court of Archbishop Frederick I of Cologne and later at the court of Emperor Henry V. After his dramatic conversion in 1115, he was ordained a priest in December of that year. Norbert's first attempts at preaching and at reforming his fellow canons at Xanten resulted in his denunciation to the synod of Fritzlar (1118) as a hypocrite, an innovator, and an unauthorized preacher. Divesting himself of his several benefices and considerable possessions, Norbert journeyed south, and at St. Gilles in Languedoc received from Pope Gelasius II authorization to serve the church at large as itinerant preacher. Norbert's missionary activity and miracles soon attracted an entourage of disciples and associates. Encouraged by the recently elected Pope Calixtus II at the Council of Rheims (October 1119) and aided by his principal patron, Bartholomew de Vir (or de Jur), bishop of Laon, Norbert installed the nucleus of his nascent order in the valley of Prémontré, in the diocese of Laon, in 1120.

As canon of St. Victor and later as itinerant preacher, Norbert had become well acquainted with every form of canonical and monastic life. His intention was now to give shape to a form of religious life that would provide something of a transition between monks of the classic Benedictine stamp and the mendicant orders of the thirteenth century, an order both contemplative and active, in which evangelical poverty and simplicity, preaching and pastoral activity, manual work and a strict ascetic program would combine to express the perfection of the apostolic life. Moreover, this life was to be open to virtually all comers. The canons, who constituted the first order, had as their associates lay brothers religious after the Cistercian model of the lay brotherhood; the second order was made up of nuns (later, canonesses), who, like the canons, had as their associates lay sisters who were religious under the same title as the lay brothers; finally, there was the third order, comprised of laymen and laywomen tertiaries affiliated with the community in a way of life midway between cloister and world. This structure was later to serve as the model for Dominicans and Franciscans. The composition of this new religious family, however, was to undergo a considerable evolution. Patterned on the infant church at Jerusalem, the typical Norbertine community was originally made up of an essential core of clerics surrounded by a numerically much larger group of lay brothers and nuns, much as the New Testament "multitude of believers" had once been grouped around the apostles. The proportions rapidly reversed as the number of lay brothers and canonesses decreased to the point that the average Norbertine community was a community of canons only.

The expansion of the order began even before the profession of the first members at Prémontré. In 1121, while passing through Namur, Norbert received from Ermensinde, wife of Count Gottfried of Namur, the nearby villa of Floreffe with its two churches. Floreffe was destined to become one of the major abbeys of the order, with twenty-two parishes, seven daughterhouses, and three convents.

The religious profession of Norbert's disciples at Prémontré—some forty clerics and an even larger number of laymen and laywomen—took place on Christmas of 1121. The terms of the profession formula, preserved in the writings of Adam Scotus, specified that the profession was being made *secundum evangelia* (according to the Gospels, that is, the life of evangelical poverty imposed by Christ on the apostles as he sent them on their missionary preaching tours), *et dicta apostolorum* (and according to the sayings of the apostles, the organization of the infant church as described in the first chapters of Acts), and *et propositum sancti Augustini* (and according to the program of St. Augustine, as expressed in the Rule of St. Augustine).

The implicit reference to the Rule of St. Augustine in the profession formula is less clear than it might appear to be. Which Rule of St. Augustine? Three forms of the Rule were accessible to Norbert: (1) the "feminine" version addressed to the nuns of Hippo, (2) the "masculine" version accepted in general as the standard text, and (3) the "masculine" version preceded by an *Ordo monasterii* or monastic directory attributed to Augustine but more likely written by Augustine's friend and disciple Alypius after his return from a voyage to Palestine. Severe in its exigencies and markedly archaic in its liturgical prescriptions, this third version of the Rule had been adopted only in a few centers of canonical reform (Springiersbach, diocese of Trier; the cathedral chapter at Salzburg; the abbey of Rolduc; the congregation of Arrouaise). Norbert and his community opted for the severe version of the Augustinian Rule, which called for daily fasting, abstinence from meat, manual labor, and a stringent practice of silence. Special importance was attached to three traditional observances: (1) divine worship, which admitted of a certain splendor in vestments and church appointments; (2) the daily chapter of faults; and (3) generous hospitality and care of the poor. The original habit was a poor man's garb consisting of tunic, cincture, and cape, all of unbleached wool, which repeated washing tended to leave off-white.

The abbey of Prémontré was built originally along the lines of a double monastery with a common church and with buildings for men and women within the same enclosure, kept separate by dividing walls. The exact canonical status of the first community of women at Prémontré is uncertain. Were they nuns who had taken vows, or simply a group of devout women who, under the direction of Ricvère de Clastres, lived in total material and spiritual dependence on Norbert and his community of men, rendering them material services in return?

Norbert's genius was that of reformer rather than of organizer and administrator, and his own personal charisma and mission as wandering preacher engaged him almost uninterruptedly in miracle-filled missionary journeys. These resulted in an influx of aspirants at Prémontré and at the foundations that soon began multiplying with astonishing rapidity. In 1122 community life was inaugurated at Floreffe (near Namur) and at Cappenberg (Westphalia); and in the same year the canons of Cuissy (Laon) were aggregated to Prémontré. A new series of aggregations and fundations began in 1124, when St. Martin of León and St. Michael of Antwerp joined the Norbertine reform. The tempo of foundations and aggregations soon accelerated and was to slow only after 1150. On 28 May 1124 Norbert obtained at Noyon the approbation of his reform from the papal legates Peter of León and Gregory of Sant'Angelo; and in

1126 he obtained directly from Pope Honorius II a further confirmation in a papal bull issued on two separate occasions, once from Como and once from the Lateran.

Meanwhile, at Prémontré the rigors of the observance and the peculiarities of the pseudo-Augustinian *Ordo monasterii* had occasioned criticism from friend and foe alike. While the main lines of Norbert's reform and the spiritual values emphasized by the founder were carefully preserved, the structures and institutions of the new order now underwent a considerable evolution. This evolution was carried out chiefly under the direction of Norbert's successor, Hugh of Fosse, first abbot of Prémontré and first abbot general of the order (1128–1161). In 1126 Norbert accepted his election as archbishop of the still largely pagan see of Magdeburg—ideal territory for a zealous missioner—and it was there that his activity as missionary bishop and reformer centered until his death on 6 June 1134.

Though he was far removed from Prémontré, Norbert's influence remained considerable. At Magdeburg he installed canons of his reform in six of the city's parishes and in fourteen others in the region; and it was from Magdeburg that the Norbertine reform spread rapidly throughout Teutonic and Slavic regions. This created tensions within the order at large, for Norbert, ever inclined toward the more active and apostolic aspect of canonical life, easily admitted of local adaptations and maintenance of regional customs in matters of liturgy and observance, whereas west of the Rhine the ideal of uniformity of observance after the Cistercian model enjoyed far greater credit. Moreover, Hugh of Fosse by temperament and by personal conviction emphasized the "monastic" values of canonical life, so that, almost from its earliest period, the reform manifested a fruitful tension between the complementary values of action and contemplation—but a tension that could also become a cause of conflict and disunity.

The organization of the order after the pattern of the Cistercians began almost immediately with Hugh's election as abbot of Prémontré. Anxious to preserve unity, charity, and a high level of observance in a religious family hitherto united only by the personal authority of the founder, Hugh convoked the first Premonstratensian general chapter in 1128. The capitulants numbered only six, but there were nine in 1129, twelve in 1130, eighteen in 1131; and by the time of Hugh's death in 1161, the annual chapter, held on the feast of St. Denis (9 October), was bringing as many as 120 abbots to Prémontré. Since its evolution soon rendered the earliest legislation obsolete in points of detail, it is hardly surprising that manuscript sources from this early period are no longer extant. The earliest recoverable twelfth-century collections of statutes and customaries make it clear, however, that the constitutional basis of the new order was patterned directly on Cistercian models, with the system of filiations and the annual general chapter corresponding to those of the White Monks.

The organizational efforts of Hugh and his fellow capitulants met with resistance chiefly from the houses in Saxony, where Norbert's apostolate-oriented policies had made the greatest impact. But by 1177, with the expedition of Pope Alexander III's bull *In apostolicae sedis,* the definitive organization of the order under the general direction of the abbot of Prémontré, and with a system of annual general chapters, filiations, and visitations borrowed largely from Cîteaux, had long since become standard practice sanctioned by tradition. A development particular to the order, and canonized by the general chapter of 1290, was the grouping of the houses into *circaria* or circaries. By 1320 there were thirty such provinces. As early as 1126 the abbey of Steinfeld became a center for the diffusion of the order in Bohemia; and in east Germany the abbey of Magdeburg (1129) proved even more prolific. Crusaders brought the order to Palestine, where three foundations were established before 1145. By the mid thirteenth century at least 500 abbeys or priories could be listed, extending from Ireland in the west to Palestine in the east, and including Greece, Hungary, Poland, and Scandinavia.

Even during Norbert's lifetime the religious habit was modified by the addition of surplice and black cape, according to the model of other groups of canons. Pastoral needs in regions surrounding many of the abbeys soon involved members of the order in a parochial ministry of the sort excluded by the early statutes, which allowed Premonstratensians to serve only parishes attached to their abbey. This parish administration received Pope Clement III's formal authorization in 1188. Though a few of the early abbeys had maintained schools from the time of their foundation, the emergence of abbeys as schools for clerics and for the study of the humanities became generalized chiefly in those regions where emphasis was on the active apostolate of the White Canons. The Collegium Norbertinum was established in Paris in 1252, but the rise of colleges attached to the greater European universities was a postmedieval development.

As early as 1137 a general chapter decree had called for the separation of communities of men from those of women; and with this physical distancing came both relative autonomy and decline for most of the communities of women, whose status was now officially that of canonesses. Despite sporadic gestures at providing a minimum of spiritual and material help for the monasteries of women, the canons made little effort to ensure the continued existence of these once populous abbeys. The few houses of women that managed to survive, or that were newly founded, had only tenuous relations with the communities of men.

Though only Norbert received the distinction of formal canonization—and this not until 1582—the history of the order teems with saintly figures venerated in particular regions or throughout the order at large. Premonstratensians led the way in ecclesiastical reform, and many of the abbeys became training grounds for future bishops. Between 1130 and 1560, no fewer than thirty-two Norbertines held the see of Brandenburg; and at Havelberg there were twenty-five Premonstratensian bishops between 1129 and 1548.

Intellectual life flourished in the abbeys, and hundreds of writers contributed to the intellectual tradition of the order. Two of special importance were Philip of Harvengt (or of Bonne Espérance, *d.* 1183), whose synthesis of Norbertine spirituality stresses the apostolic concerns central in the life of St. Norbert, and Adam Scotus (of Dryburgh, *d.* 1213/1214), whose synthesis is more in line with the contemplative ideal of Hugh of Fosse, and who passed from the Premonstratensians to the Carthusians. A third influential writer was Hermann Joseph, canon of Steinfeld (*d.* 1241), whose Marian poetry and devotional writings crystallized the affective tendencies of thirteenth-century piety.

With the waning of the Middle Ages came the waning of the order. The wealth of certain houses, the practice of personal proprietorship of funds, (*peculium*), overextension in the field of pastoral activity, the Black Death, the effects of decadent Scholasticism—all these were factors leading to the collapse subsequent to the Great Schism, the Reformation, and the wars of religion. Only with the Counter-Reformation was the order born anew.

BIBLIOGRAPHY

H. M. Colvin, *The White Canons in England* (1961); Cornelius Kirkfleet, *The White Canons of St. Norbert* (1943); François Petit, *La spiritualité des Prémontrés aux XIIe et XIIIe siècles* (1947), and *Norbert et l'origine des Prémontrés* (1981); Micheline Pontenay de Fontette, *Les religieuses à l'âge classique du droit canon* (1967), 13–25.

CHRYSOGONUS WADDELL

[See also **Alexander III, Pope; Augustine of Hippo, St.; Augustinism; Cistercian Order; Mendicant Orders; Philip of Harvengt.**]

PŘEMYSLID DYNASTY. The rulers belonging to the Přemyslid dynasty, which originated sometime in the eighth century, became dominant in central Bohemia (inhabited by Czechs) at the end of the ninth century; by the 990's they had extended their rule over all of Bohemia, and from the beginning of the eleventh century they also ruled neighboring Moravia. Their first recorded residence was at Levý Hradec, west of Prague; between roughly 870 and 890 they moved their seat to Prague, which was becoming a busy trading settlement on a new west–east trade route.

The legendary Přemysl the Plowman, who by marrying the prophetess Libuše became the ruler of the Czechs, is considered to be the founder of the dynasty. This legend first appeared in the early-twelfth-century *Chronica Boemorum* of Cosmas of Prague, and shortly afterward it was attested in depictions in the Katharine Church at Znojmo. The first historical figure is Prince Bořivoj (*d. ca.* 894), who reportedly was baptized by Archbishop Methodios at the court of the Great Moravian ruler Svatopluk, and who, according to legend, built the first Christian church in Bohemia, at Levý Hradec. Bořivoj and his wife, Ludmila, later venerated as a saint, initiated the conversion of Bohemia to Christianity.

Bořivoj's grandson Václav (Wenceslaus) began to rule in the 920's, but in 929 or 935 he was murdered by his brother Boleslav, possibly because the latter opposed Wenceslaus' submission to the Saxon king Henry I. As early as the end of the tenth century, Wenceslaus began to be venerated as a martyr-saint, and by the eleventh century he became a dominant figure of the Přemyslid dynasty and a patron saint of Bohemia. Gradually St. Wenceslaus came to be viewed as an "eternal ruler"

PŘEMYSLID DYNASTY

of the Czechs, and the reigning dukes were considered his temporal representatives.

Under the rule of Boleslav I (*d.* 967/973?) the political unification of the country proceeded. In 995 the Přemyslids eliminated their most powerful rivals by massacring all male members of the Slavnik family at their seat at Libice, and by the early eleventh century Bohemia was so consolidated that attempts by the Polish ruler Bolesław I to subjugate it, in 1003–1004, proved unsuccessful. The Czechs thus established themselves as a nation clearly set off from neighboring Poland. Under Duke Oldřich (*r.* 1012–1033) the Přemyslids conquered Moravia, which since then has been united with Bohemia. Until the thirteenth century Moravia was often ruled by the younger sons of the Přemyslid dynasty.

Soon the relationship of Bohemia to the Holy Roman Empire began to loom large. The arguments about the extent of German sovereignty over medieval Bohemia and the degree of Czech autonomy have had special relevance for modern Czech history, particularly in the period after 1848. Bohemia and Moravia were indeed part of the empire, and that fact was never disputed by the Czechs. Even the bishoprics of Prague and Olomouc belonged to the archbishopric of Mainz until 1344. Just as indisputable, however, is the special position of the Bohemian rulers, who had to be elected by the Bohemian nobility before being invested as kings and/or emperors in the empire. Bohemia had a special position in other respects as well; for instance, there were no imperial properties in the country.

From the mid eleventh century, Přemyslid dukes strove to obtain the title of king. In 1059–1060 Duke Spytihněv probably petitioned Pope Nicholas II for the crown, but was given only a bishop's miter (for an annual fee). His heir, Vratislav II, was more successful: he was crowned king in 1085, even though the royal dignity was granted to him personally, not to his successors. Finally, Přemysl Otokar I (1197–1230) was crowned king by Philip of Swabia in 1198 and the hereditary royal title was confirmed by the Golden Bull of Frederick II in 1212. Henceforth, the Boehmian rulers were kings, the only ones in the empire besides the kings of Germany.

Power struggles and disputes over the throne within the Přemyslid dynasty strengthened the position of the Bohemian nobility, which formed its own association, had its own jurisdiction, and at times had its own seal. In the thirteenth century this union of nobles, the "land community" (*obec* in Czech, *Landgemeinschaft* in German), had its own roll in the land register (*tabulae terrae*), which recorded the judicial decisions of the land court and formed the basis of the developing legal system. The nobility, particularly the large southern Bohemian noble families such as the Vitkovci, thus became the most important rivals of the kings.

To counteract this adversary power, the kings began to establish royal towns, which by the second half of the thirteenth century had become their most important power base. Another policy intended to expand royal possessions was German colonization, encouraged by the Přemyslids during the thirteenth century. Particularly important was the influx of immigrants to the new mining centers, such as Kutná Hora, thirty miles east of Prague.

The rule of Václav I (1230–1253) marked the beginning of the Přemyslids' expansionist policies, which culminated during the reign of Přemysl Otokar II (1253–1278). Přemysl took advantage of the weakening central power in the empire and tried to expand his sphere of influence in neighboring regions, first in Austria by claiming the so-called Babenberg inheritance, and then in Silesia, Poland, and Hungary, where in 1260 he defeated the Hungarian army at Kressenbrunn. The next thirteen years represented the apex of Přemysl's power. In 1273 the German electors chose Rudolf of Habsburg as the new German king and Přemysl (who aspired to the German royal title) turned against him, but soon Rudolf allied himself with some of the Czech nobility; the conflict ended in 1278 at the Battle of Moravské Pole (Dürnkrut), where Přemysl was defeated and killed. Rudolf then invaded Bohemia and the country plunged into anarchy. After a five-year interregnum, Václav II (*r.* 1283–1305), Přemysl's son, established his position and launched a vigorous foreign policy, becoming king of Poland in 1300 and securing the crown of Hungary for his son in 1301. Přemyslid rule in Poland, however, was soon seriously challenged. After the death of Václav II, his son Václav III set out on a campaign to assert his power in Poland; but before he could cross the border, he was murdered (4 August 1306) at Olomouc. With him the male line of the dynasty died out. The murder was never solved.

Václav II's daughter Elizabeth (Eliška) married John of Luxemburg (son of the German king Henry VII), who was elected king of Bohemia in 1310. Their son, Holy Roman Emperor Charles IV (*r.* 1346–1378), was the most important medieval Czech king.

BIBLIOGRAPHY

The basic historical works are Václav Novotný, *České dějiny,* I, pts. 1–4 (1912–1937); František Palacký, *Dějiny národu českého v Čechách a na Moravě,* I–II (1848–1875), new ed., Olga Svejkovská, ed. (1968); Josef Šusta, *Soumrak Přemyslovců a jejich dědictví* (1935). See also Karl Bosl, *Handbuch der Geschichte der böhmischen Länder,* I (1967); Československá akademie věd, *Přehled dějin Československa,* I, pt. 1 (1980); Zdeněk Fiala, *Přemyslovské Čechy,* 2nd ed. (1975); František Graus, *Die Nationenbildung der Westslawen im Mittelalter* (1980), and "Böhmen," in *Lexikon des Mittelalters,* II, pt. 1 (1983); Friedrich Prinz, *Böhmen in mittelalterlichen Europa* (1984).

[See also **Bohemia-Moravia; Cosmas of Prague; Germany: Electors; Habsburg Dynasty; Holy Roman Empire; Hungary; Poland; Prague.**]

PRENTYS, THOMAS (*fl.* early fifteenth century), English owner of an alabaster quarry and workshop in Chellaston, Derbyshire. According to one surviving document, dated 1414, he sold the raw material to certain French masons, who were to carve a now unknown object for Fécamp Abbey. In 1420 he and Robert Sutton together made a large tomb for Ralph Greene and his wife at Lowick, Northamptonshire. Both the contract and the tomb survive.

BIBLIOGRAPHY

W. St. J. Hope, "On the Early Working of Alabaster in England," in *Archaeological Journal,* **61** (1904); Lawrence Stone, *Sculpture in Britain: The Middle Ages,* 2nd ed. (1972), 179–180.

BARRIE SINGLETON

[See also **Gothic Art: Sculpture; Sutton, Robert.**]

PREPENDULIA (*pendilia, pendulia*), hanging pieces or pendant ornaments on the Byzantine imperial crown. Most often they were long strings of pearls or other jewels ending in a triad of pearls that hung to the shoulders. Empresses, as exemplified by the image of Theodora in the apsidal mosaic at S. Vitale in Ravenna (*ca.* 547), wore them throughout the Byzantine period. Emperors, such as Justinian in the same mosaic, also wore *prependulia,* though imperial portraits on coins suggest that they were less common for men during the seventh, eighth, and ninth centuries. A tenth-century example is found in the portrait of Co-emperor Alexander (later sole ruler and regent, 912–913, for his nephew Constantine VII Porphyrogenitos), in the mosaic of the north gallery of Hagia Sophia, İstanbul.

BIBLIOGRAPHY

John Beckwith, *Early Christian and Byzantine Art* (1970, 2nd ed. 1979), 193, 375; Paul A. Underwood and Ernest J. W. Hawkins, "The Mosaics of Hagia Sophia at Istanbul: The Portrait of Emperor Alexander," in *Dumbarton Oaks Papers,* **15** (1961). For the portraits of Emperor Justinian and Empress Theodora, see Giuseppe Bovini, *Mosaici de Ravenna* (1956).

LESLIE BRUBAKER
BARBARA OEHLSCHLAEGER-GARVEY

[See also **Byzantine Art, 843–1453; Costume, Byzantine; Mosaic and Mosaic Making; Paludamentum (with illustration); Ravenna.**]

PREROGATIVE. The term "prerogative" was not to occupy a central place in political and legal history until early modern times. It has been used somewhat loosely, however, to describe certain aspects of the authority of medieval, notably English, rulers.

It is found as an aspect of Carolingian royal power, for instance in a charter of Charles III (the Simple, *r.* 893–923). But for extensive use in the early Middle Ages one must turn to English common law. A crucial example cited by Maitland from the Year Book for 1292–1293 states that "the King is prerogative." This royal quality protects him from suit by a subject. A particular example of this shows a suitor's effort to claim certain ancestral privileges (for example, to hold pleas, have a gallows and a pillory) being overthrown by a more recent royal grant, because a king is such that his acts override seemingly better established rights. Similarly, if a tenant has both king and lesser lord as landlord, the rights of the king will always prevail in case of a conflict.

In the fourteenth century prerogative begins to expand a little. The Year Books of Kings Edward II and III of England show prerogative changing the tenure of advowson from ascendant to gross; that is, it no longer reverted to the lord on death of the holder (Year Book 5 Edward II). A right of presentation to a benefice acquired by the king during an abbatial vacancy would not come to the new abbot

PREROGATIVE

unless specifically applied for (Year Book 12 Edward II). Further legal record studies would probably produce a variety of additional extensions, or at least elaborations of this technical-seeming quality. (It is well summed up in Maitland's phrase, adopted by many subsequent writers, describing prerogative as intensifying those rights of kings that otherwise are similar to those of other feudal persons of authority.)

The term has been used by editors of a list of certain royal rights set down in the later thirteenth century ("*prerogativa regis*" in *Statutes of the Realm*). One such right was *primer seisin*, the enjoyment of a year's revenue from the lands of a deceased tenant.

Constitutional and administrative historians frequently project a modern notion of prerogative into the Middle Ages. Henry Hallam argues that the king has a rightful prerogative accepted by all, and also a whole set of illicit ones that provoked protest and revulsion: the purveyance of victuals, the impressment of troops and labor, the arbitrary acts of forest judges, and above all, the employment of irresponsible seals and offices of government—the Privy Seal, the Signet, the Wardrobe, the Chamber. In matters of law the king's prerogative involved the dispensation of subjects from certain laws and the exercise of justice on request (where the claimant had no right). Altogether, Hallam projected the notion from the sixteenth century into medieval usage, although some of these issues appear in pronouncements of Lancastrian judges and kings and in the reign of Edward IV. The broader view is usefully summed up by Julius Hatschek.

Thomas F. Tout's exploration of household departments and of the lesser royal seals did much to correct the excessively Whig notions of constitutionalists, showing that convenience, not malevolent principle (or lack of it!), often lay behind their development. But his depiction of Edward II (*r.* 1307–1327) and Richard II (*r.* 1377–1399) does put their "prerogative" at the heart of their conflicts with their subjects. Indeed, if it is simply a term to describe excessive royal power it may stand, but only rarely does it reflect contemporary sources. Edward II used his Wardrobe and his Privy Seal to advance "prerogative" powers over men and goods. Foiled by baronial opposition, he developed new "prerogative" instruments, notably the Chamber and the Chamber Lands, to protect his powers. These were to peak in the period of Edward III's wars with France, serving England well. If challenged by older traditions, as by the Chancery in 1340–1341, they triumphed handily.

Richard II's reign produced the high point in this clash of principle. In 1387 the royal judges made, according to Tout, "the first definite formulation of the theory of royal prerogative" in response to Richard II's query whether the statute of the previous year infringed on his regality and prerogative. This formulation was countered, the following year, by a reassertion of parliamentary sovereignty. The overthrow of this in turn by Richard's infamous trio of parliamentary knights (Bushy, Bagot, Green) gave "prerogative" its last dangerous twist: the management, rather than blunt repression, of parliamentary lords and knights. The deposition and death of Richard opened the gate to a more democratic solution.

Fifteenth-century kings were becoming more conscious of their prerogative as such. Many royal replies to parliamentary requests reserved their prerogative. It was also reserved in concessions by treaty to foreign kings. The distinction stated by many modern constitutional historians between "legal" and "illegal" prerogative begins to claim attention. Could prerogative refer at once to a defined power (for example, to license, or to exempt) and to a reserve of unspecified sovereignty? Writers such as Sir John Fortescue were raising the question, and they saw that absolutism loomed. Similar issues inherent in the growth of royal authority are to be found in France and Spain, but the peculiar role of prerogative in their discussion and attempted resolution is rarely found.

BIBLIOGRAPHY

Sources. Year Book 20–21 Edward I, in Rolls Series (1866), 57; *Year Book 5 Edward II,* in Selden Society, Yearbook Series, **10** (1947), xxv; *Year Book 12 Edward II, ibid.*, **23** (1950), 51, 52; Great Britain, *The Statutes of the Realm,* I (1810), 226, and II (1816), 102.

Studies. Henry Hallam, *View of the State of Europe During the Middle Ages,* 2 vols. (1818 and subsequent editions); Julius Hatschek, *Englische Verfassungsgeschichte bis zum Regierungsantritt der Königin Victoria* (1913); Frederick Pollock and Frederic W. Maitland, *The History of English Law Before the Time of Edward I,* 2nd ed., 2 vols. (1968); Thomas F. Tout, *Chapters in the Administrative History of Mediaeval England,* 6 vols. (1920–1933), see index in vol. VI.

MICHAEL R. POWICKE

[See also **Edward II of England; Edward III of England; England: 1216–1485; Fortesque, Sir John; Law, English Common; Richard II.**]

 PRE-ROMANESQUE ARCHITECTURE

PRE-ROMANESQUE ARCHITECTURE

CAROLINGIAN ARCHITECTURE

Carolingian architecture forms the first body of monumental art since Roman times in the north of Europe. The revival of large-scale churches in stone took place in a broad landscape of selective scholarship, the assembly of learned men from all parts of Latin Europe, and the renewal and strengthening of connections with the Mediterranean world. Churches of the empire, from the last quarter of the eighth century down to about 900, were resonant with the energy and aspirations of the royal court, both in the models they chose and in the programs they set. Although few Carolingian churches can be seen today, archaeological excavations provide evidence upon which to base reconstructions of ground plans. Certain churches can be firmly dated, and sometimes the purposes and circumstances of their construction are known from documents of the period. On this evidence the churches can be classified into fairly coherent groups.

The best-known monument of the period is the palace (palatine) chapel at Aachen (Aix-la-Chapelle). Built in the decade of the 790's, it is centrally planned with a vaulted gallery encircling a domed spatial core. Charlemagne's chapel constituted an architectural school of its own: It spawned many copies largely known from excavated plans and the writings of various medieval authors. Churches built on the palace chapel plan, a type usually destined for special purposes, are situated mainly in the Carolingian heartland of present-day Belgium and Holland. Other important examples are Bishop Theodulf's oratory (806) at Germigny-des-Prés near Orléans and the church of St. Mary in the monastic complex of St. Riquier in northeastern France.

The majority of Carolingian churches are simple, longitudinally planned buildings. They are small and less original in design than the basilican state churches of the same period. The basic plan is a hall nave with a squared chancel or, in some variations, with three contiguous apses. The hall church was widely dispersed in territories of the empire and used in rural areas long after the Carolingian period. Remains dating mostly from the eighth century have been found under Ste. Gertrude at Nivelles, St. Willibrord at Echternach, St. Maria at Mittelzell, and the Abdinghof church at Paderborn. There is a grouping of hall churches in the region of present-day Switzerland, where examples still intact include St. Sylvester at Goldbach, St. Peter at Müstail, St. Johann at Münstair, and St. Benedetto at Malles (*ca.* 800).

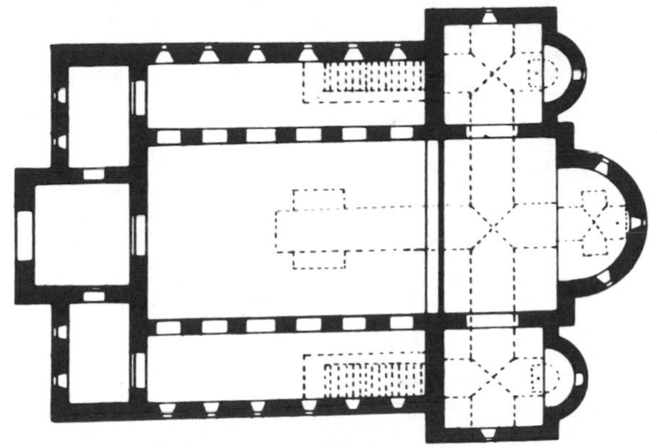

St. Michael's Church, Steinbach, 821–827. Ground plan showing crypt passages. Reproduced from Donald Bullough, *The Age of Charlemagne* © 1965 PAUL ELEK PRODUCTIONS LTD., LONDON

Another plan widely adopted in the period had an aisled nave on piers and a transept with projecting longitudinal chapels, all with apsidal terminations. In this triapsidal plan, interior space is articulated by structure and there is a build-up of mass at the east end, no doubt to emphasize in architectural terms the focal point of the liturgy and to provide more space for the clergy. The church at Steinbach (821–827), built by Charlemagne's former chancellor and biographer, Einhard, is an important example of this type, but with a transept lower in elevation than the nave. The diversity of Carolingian plans depended on special circumstances peculiar to each religious foundation and on formal choices urged by purposes of the program, but the real energy of the school lay in the transformation of the Early Christian basilican plan.

The axial disposition of space in the basilica was best suited to the processional liturgy of the Roman rite instituted by the Frankish church and to the display of relics. The basilican plan also retained strong associations with the Roman Empire and, in particular, with the Constantinian past. The return to this plan in the last decades of the eighth century suggests that its role in the new order of Carolingian government was political as well as ecclesiastical. The degree of freedom and invention by Carolingian builders when resorting to tradition can be seen in the increasing complexity of the east

 PRE-ROMANESQUE ARCHITECTURE

Westwork of the former Benedictine abbey church at Corvey on the Weser, 873–885. PHOTO: BRUNO BALESTRINI. COURTESY OF EDIZIONI ELECTA, MILAN

and west ends of the plan. Space is treated as something to be blocked off into liturgically distinct parts. At the east, transepts—sometimes with crossing squares and raised choirs, sometimes with a chancel bay between transept and apse—articulate ritual space.

Particular architectural emphasis was given to the crypt, which became an integral part of the east body of the church. A rich variety of crypts were used. In some churches, for instance, there is an annular crypt, with a semicircular vaulted passage surrounding the tomb of the venerated saint; in others, however, tunnel crypts were used, with parallel vaulted cells cut through by a connecting passage; and, finally, there is the hall crypt, a somewhat later type that was essentially a lower church with three aisles of equal height on columns. A variant of this type, the outer crypt, ran outside the body of the upper church. Outstanding examples of the last type, all dating from the mid to late ninth century, are Hildesheim Cathedral, the abbey church at Corvey, St. Philibert-de-Grandlieu, and St. Germain at Auxerre. A hall crypt forms the core of an extensive crypt development at Auxerre. Early-ninth-century tunnel crypts appear in St. Peter near Fulda, Echternach, and St. Médard in Soissons. At Steinbach, the crypt passages form three successive crosses. Annular crypts of the mid eighth to late ninth centuries occur in St. Emmeram at Regensburg, St. Lucius in Chur, and the abbey churches of Vreden, Werden, and Nivelles.

The program at the west end of the basilica often assumed that of a separate ecclesia, with the addition of a counter-choir, sometimes with a transept and a tower block in vaulted stories called a westwork. The westwork functioned variously as a station in the processional liturgy, an imperial loggia, a chancellery, and a martyrium complex. It was also used for defense—real or implied. The westwork of Corvey on the Weser, added between 873 and 885, has survived virtually intact. Westworks and crypts were both important preliminaries to the fully vaulted churches of the later eleventh century.

Abbot Fulrad's church of St. Denis, consecrated in 775, is an early example of a Carolingian state church, one that directly concerned both Pepin the Short and Charlemagne. The texts and archaeological remains prove that Carolingian St. Denis was an elongated three-aisled basilica with a single semicircular apse to the east and a small transept. An annular crypt existed under the apse. In 832 Abbot Hilduin (*ca.* 775–*ca.* 855) added an outer crypt. The basic plan of St. Denis, which had not been used on either side of the Alps since the fifth century, is shared by a number of similar churches built *romano more* (in the manner of Rome). The phrase is usually taken to mean the survival of Roman building techniques, especially masonry techniques. It may refer, as well, to the orientation of churches defined by the liturgical reform of the eighth and ninth centuries. Carolingian masonry emphasizes articulation of surface more than the mass of the wall. Examples may still be seen in Notre-Dame-de-la-Basse-Oeuvre at Beauvais (eighth or tenth century) and in the gatehouse (*Torhalle*) at Lorsch, a structure noteworthy for its pattern-work masonry and revival of antique decorative vocabulary. The basilica at Fulda (819), modeled on Old St. Peter's in Rome, is a documented example of a plan in the Roman manner. The west apse opened into a transept of enormous dimensions, equivalent in space to a transverse nave. The plan suggests that the liturgical focus was at the west end of the basilica. Fulda was also a

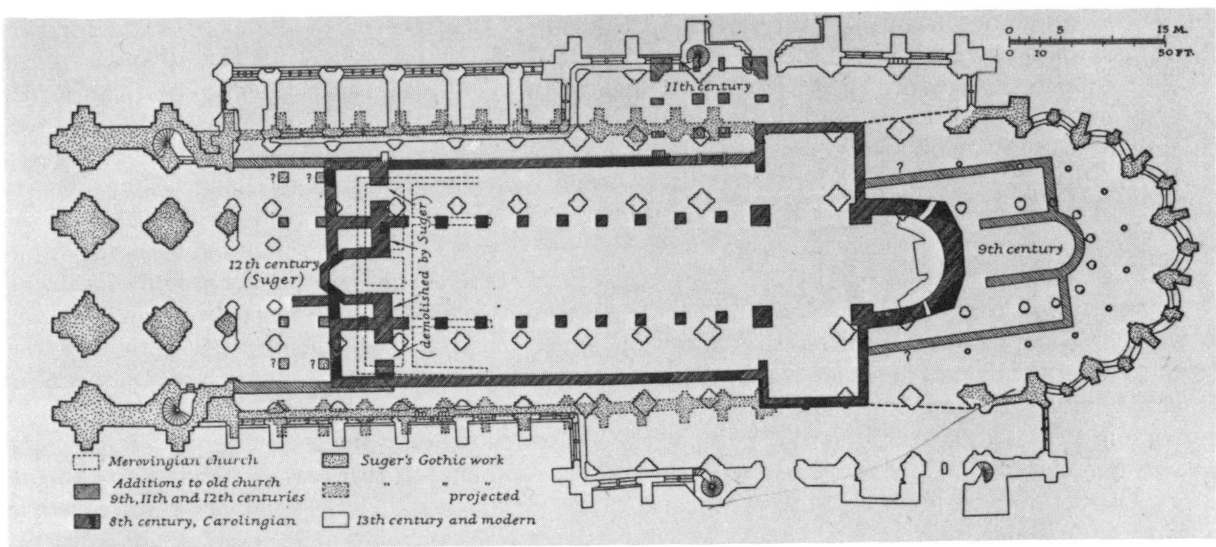

St. Denis, abbey church. Ground plan showing the original 8th-century basilica, the outer crypt (832), and the later Gothic construction. © 1959 KENNETH JOHN CONANT

St. Riquier Abbey. 17th-century engraving copied from a miniature in the *Chronicle of St. Riquier* by Hariulf (*ca.* 1088). PARIS, BIBLIOTHÈQUE NATIONALE

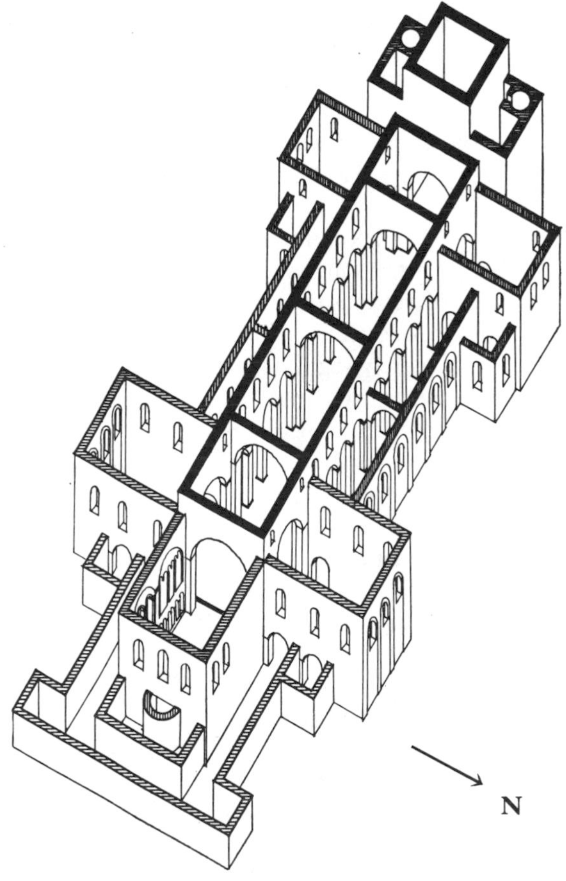

St. Gertrude, Nivelles (1046). Reproduced from Louis Grodecki, *L'architecture ottonienne* © 1958 MAX LECLERC AND CO., PARIS

 PRE-ROMANESQUE ARCHITECTURE

double-ended church. It had two facing apses, one at each end of the axial vessel. The earliest example of the Carolingian double-ended plan is possibly the basilica of St. Maurice d'Agaune, from the end of the eighth century. Notable examples of the eighth and ninth centuries include the Salvatorkirche at Paderborn, St. Willibrord at Echternach, St. Remi at Rheims, Auxerre Cathedral (St. Étienne), and Oberzell at Reichenau (836).

The famous parchment tracing of about 820 from St. Gall (Chapter Library) depicts a layout designed to order the lives of monks living together in a paradigmatic Benedictine monastery. The St. Gall plan may be based on multiples of a modular prime unit that control the dimensions and proportions of the structures within the claustral complex. It appears that modular construction methods were also used in the layout of the palace grounds at Aachen. Both examples indicate that theoretical principles of design were employed from an early period in the medieval West. The provenance of the St. Gall scheme came from sources close to the Court School. It is thought that Bishop Hildebold's early-ninth-century cathedral at Cologne served as a model for the church on the plan of St. Gall.

The most celebrated architectural statement of the Carolingian period is St. Riquier. The abbey church, built between 790 and 799, is known from accounts by Abbot Angilbert (*r.* 781–814) and later (1088) by the monk-chronicler Hariulf that tell of a vast wealth of relics and liturgical furnishings and of elaborate processionals whose itinerary and stations were carefully regulated. An eleventh-century drawing of the church by Hariulf survives in two seventeenth-century copies. They show a series of architectural masses that hem in the basilican nave along the main axis. The west transept was incorporated in the westwork and contained galleries, as did its counterpart at the eastern end. In its spatial concept and balance of exterior masses and vertical accents, St. Riquier anticipates Ottonian principles of design.

OTTONIAN ARCHITECTURE

The Frankish monumental tradition gained new life in the Ottonian period. Ottonian architecture, which takes its name from a succession of Saxon emperors named Otto, is the architecture of the German empire of the late tenth and the greater part of the eleventh centuries. The revival of Europe in the eleventh century, which elsewhere is associated with the Romanesque, was marked in Germany by the renewal of the empire and contacts with Italy and Byzantium. The domain of the empire had lessened considerably, but its territories were prodigiously fertile in new churches and renovated older structures after the year 1000. Church building was supported by the reigning dynasty and, in particular, by prince-bishops, with the result that many churches are linked to the personalities of high-ranking churchmen. Ottonian architecture acquired from the empire the aims and ambitions as well as the forms of state and thus was rarely separated from the great impetus of Germany.

Few churches of the period retain their essential structure, and for that reason architectural historians are unable to determine precise dates, except in a very few cases. Ottonian architecture is usually discussed in terms of the continuation of Carolingian traditions. For example, following the practice at Aachen and St. Riquier, Otto I brought marble columns from Italy for his cathedral in Magdeburg. Indeed, the basic compositional and structural features of the style—basilican plans, twin transepts, raised choirs, hall crypts, and westworks—reveal the persistence of Carolingian formulas far into the eleventh century. Nevertheless, although these forms were not new, they were employed by Ottonian builders to their limits within the tradition—that is, using traditional elements in innovative ways—and in a rich repertory of design.

The great achievement of Ottonian builders was the clear statement of the relationship between mass and space. The divisions and separations of longitudinal space are defined in both massing and plan. Exterior masses grow logically from the plan. They are both additive and agglomerative. Complex massing announces hieratic programs for the enactment of ritual or the presentation and display of relics, as in St. Michael's at Hildesheim (completed 1033), with its balanced masses on the double-ended plan, or in St. Gertrude at Nivelles (after 1046), with its subtly graduated composition at the east end. Spatial composition is easily grasped from exterior masses that enclose each unit of the structure. Ottonian architecture is not noted for plastic treatment of walls or for a great richness of mural decoration. The mass of the wall is usually emphasized, but it might be articulated into compartments and registers by pilaster strips and roundheaded arches, blind arcades, and niches, as at Hersfeld Abbey (*ca.* 1037), Nivelles, and Speyer. Interiors were plastered and painted, but the sense of a

 PRE-ROMANESQUE ARCHITECTURE

chromatic spatial concept has been lost in most churches.

Interior space is a sharply differentiated gradation of cubes and rectangular volumes. Space is not divided by bays, as in Romanesque architecture. Walls and deep arches cut off broad or high areas of the interior from each other, especially in churches that use the low transept. Subgroups of churches have been classified in terms of the kinds of transepts that were used. In one group, the transept cuts across the nave and forms a continuous transverse volume. The Lower Saxon churches at Gernrode (St. Cyriakus, begun in 961) and Hersfeld and the small collegiate church at Walbeck (before 1000) are examples of this type. In another group, of which St. Michael's at Hildesheim is the classic example, the crossing square is separated from the nave, transept, and choir by four equal arches. Churches with such regular crossings include the cathedrals at Trier, Metz, and Verdun, and the abbey church of Limburg an der Haardt (1025–1045) in upper Lorraine; Swiss churches grouped around Einsiedeln (1031–1039) and Reichenau; and certain examples in the bishopric of Utrecht, such as St. Peter's (begun *ca.* 1050). Finally, there is the group in which the nave cuts through the transept—which is usually lower than the nave and forms separate compartments. A principal example, without aisles, is St. Pantaleon at Cologne (after 953), although its chief interest lies in its perfectly preserved westwork (by 1005). Outside the Rhineland, the low transept is more general in the region of the Meuse that falls within the diocese of Liège.

The greatest eleventh-century churches of the Meuse, a group that includes Bishop Notger's Cathedral of Liège, St. Truiden (St. Trond), Tongeren (Tongres), and the abbey church at Stavelot (Stablo, 1030), no longer stand. Only the collegiate church at Nivelles survives as the exemplar of this innovative school, with a host of smaller churches such as at Lobbes, Celles, and Hastière-par-Delà. In these churches diaphragm arches are inserted at the junction of nave and low transept. The cathedral of St. Lambert at Liège (1015) was possibly the first imperial church to have twin transepts, preceding both Hildesheim and Nivelles. St. Servatius at Maastricht (consecrated 1039) still retains Ottonian features. Susteren, in Dutch Limburg, preserves its outer crypt. Of the cathedrals on the Rhine (including those at Mainz, Worms, and Strasbourg), only the cathedral of Speyer (*ca.* 1031–1061) preserves considerable parts of its Ottonian fabric. There, a vast crypt lies beneath the choir and runs the full length of the transept. In the upper church, a giant order of half-round columns and cubic capitals enclosed the clerestory windows under the flat wood covering. The church underwent extensive Romanesque rebuilding in the years following 1081.

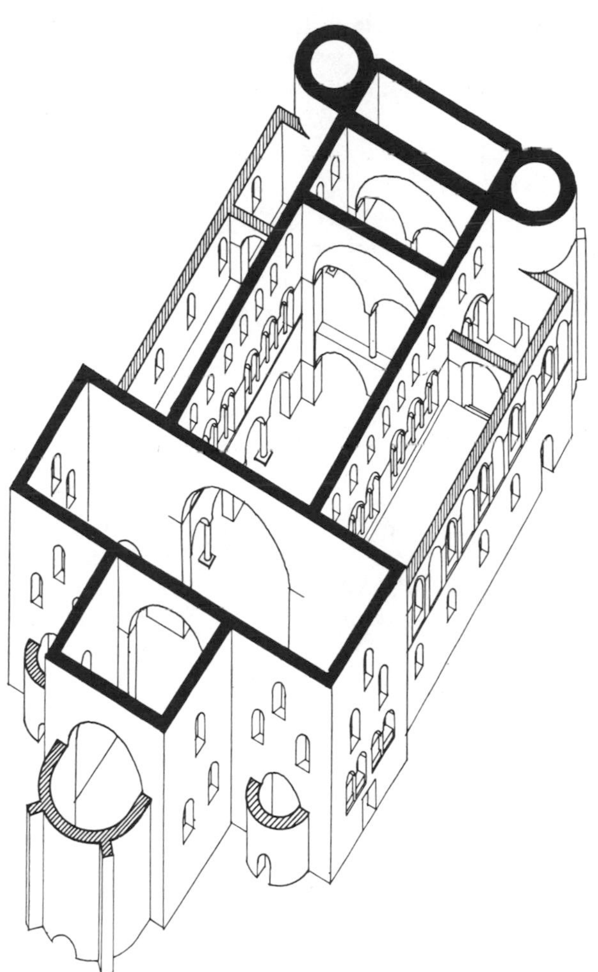

St. Cyriakus, Gernrode (begun 961). Reproduced from Louis Grodecki, *L'architecture ottonienne* © 1958 MAX LECLERC AND CO., PARIS

The creative impulse of the Ottonian school is not to be underrated. Builders were prepared to propose new architectural solutions to meet the needs of liturgical evolution and the requirements of the relic cult. The acceptance of monastic reform in Lorraine, for example, has been tied to the development of the outer crypt in that region. In another case, the exceptional pilgrimage program of the east end at Nivelles is a response to the popular cult of St. Gertrude. Churches of the period frequently had vaulted choirs and aisles. That naves were not vaulted is perhaps due more to tradition than to lack of ability to cover spaces in stone. Certain features associated with the Romanesque style were in place by an early date: nave galleries at St. Cyriakus, Gernrode (from 961); pier alternation at Gernrode, Hildesheim, Echternach (1031), and Lobbes (pre-eleventh century?); ambulatories at Stavelot (Stablo, 1040) and St. Maria im Capitol at Cologne (before 1048); and the paired west towers at Strasbourg (from 1015).

BIBLIOGRAPHY

Hartwig Beseler and Hans Roggenkamp, *Die Michaeliskirche in Hildesheim* (1954); Kenneth J. Conant, *Carolingian and Romanesque Architecture, 800–1200,* 3rd ed. (1973); Sumner McKnight Crosby, *The Abbey of St. Denis, 475–1122* (1942); Luc-Francis Genicot, *Les églises mosanes du XIe siècle* (1972); Louis Grodecki, *L'architecture ottonienne* (1958); Carol Heitz, *Recherches sur les rapports entre architecture et liturgie à l'époque carolingienne* (1963), "More romano: Problèmes d'architecture et liturgie carolingiennes," in *Roma e l'età carolingia* (1976), and *L'architecture religieuse carolingienne* (1980); Pierre M. L. Héliot, *Du carolingien au gothique: L'évolution de la plastique murale dans l'architecture religieuse du nord-ouest de l'Europe* (1966); Walter W. Horn and Ernest Born, *The Plan of St. Gall,* 3 vols. (1979); Jean Hubert, Jean Porcher, and Wolfgang F. Volbach, *Carolingian Art* (1970); Richard Krautheimer, "The Carolingian Revival of Early Christian Architecture," in *Art Bulletin,* **24** (1942); Hans E. Kubach and Albert Verbeek, *Romanische Kirchen an Rhein und Maas* (1971); Hans E. Kubach, *Romanesque Architecture* (1975); Edgar Lehmann, "Die Architektur zur Zeit Karls des Grossen," in *Karl der Grosse,* Wolfgang Braunfels, ed., III (1965), 301–319; Albrecht Mann, "Grossbauten vorkarlischer Zeit und aus der Epoche von Karl dem Grossen bis zu Lothar I," *ibid.,* 320–335; Friedrich Oswald, L. Schaefer, and Hans Sennhauser, *Vorromanische Kirchenbauten* (1966); David Parsons, "The Pre-Romanesque Church of St. Riquier: The Documentary Evidence," in *Journal of the British Archaeological Association,* **130** (1977); *Rhin-Meuse: Art et civilisation 800–1400* (catalog of the exhibition, 1972); Warren Sanderson, *Monastic Reform in Lorraine and the Architecture of the Outer Crypt, 950–1100* (1971), 3–36; May Vieillard-Troiekouroff, "L'architecture en France du temps de Charlemagne," in *Karl der Grosse,* Wolfgang Braunfels, ed., III (1965), 336–368; Willy Weynes, "Der carolingische Dom zu Köln," *ibid.,* 384–423.

PETER HUENINK

[See also **Aachen, Palace Chapel; Angilbert, St.; Apse; Arch; Architecture, Liturgical Aspects; Basilica; Bernward; Carolingians and the Carolingian Empire; Charlemagne; Church, Types of; Crypt; Germany: 843–1137; Hariulf; Hilduin of St. Denis; Masons and Builders; Notger of Liège; Otto I the Great; Otto III; Renaissances and Revivals in Medieval Art; St. Gall, Monastery and Plan of; Strasbourg Cathedral; Theodulf of Orléans; Westwork.**]

PRE-ROMANESQUE ART. "Pre-Romanesque" is a term of convenience. It refers to a period of Western European art which set forth many of the elements that were to contribute to the rise of the monumental Romanesque style of the twelfth century. The spread of Christianity from the fifth century onward had advanced the dissemination of the late antique legacy to the barbarians settled within and beyond the borders of the defunct Western Roman Empire. The art of the Frankish kingdom under the Merovingian rulers, for instance, or the art of the Lombards in Italy and the Visigoths in what is now Spain and southern France, as well as the Hiberno-Saxon art in the British Isles, by and large absorbed late antique forms into native idioms rather than reconstituting them to new purpose and effects. It was not before Charlemagne's revival of the Roman Empire under Frankish leadership that a lasting recovery of Mediterranean figural art in the north was set in motion.

CAROLINGIAN ART

As visual tokens of his *renovatio,* Charlemagne had marbles, columns, and capitals brought from Rome and Ravenna to his palace at Aachen (Aix-la-Chapelle). He caused ancient bronzes to be set up there to vie with the authority of monuments kept at the papal palace, the Lateran, in Rome. For example, a she-bear from southern Gaul was to emulate the Roman she-wolf and an equestrian statue from Ravenna—then thought to represent Theodoric—was to parallel the equestrian statue of Marcus Aurelius—then believed to depict Constantine the Great.

Mosaics. Beyond the use of spoils, Charlemagne revived large-scale bronze casting and mosaic decoration. A foundry at Aachen cast the doors and gallery railings for the palace (palatine) chapel in imitation of Roman design, while mosaics in the chapel's dome recalled representations in Early Christian churches of Rome with an image of Christ

 PRE-ROMANESQUE ART

adored by the Twenty-four Elders of the Apocalypse. This mosaic is lost; but still extant is one in the apse of the oratory at Germigny-des-Prés built about 806 by Theodulph, bishop of Orléans (*d.* 821). Instead of more common Early Christian subjects, for instance Christ in Majesty, it shows the Ark of the Covenant adored by angels. This choice reflects the Visigoth Theodulph's opposition to Byzantine image worship as stated in the *Libri carolini,* probably authored by him.

Paintings. Written sources tell of wall paintings in palaces and churches. At Aachen Charlemagne's palace contained depictions of the Liberal Arts as well as scenes from Charles's war in Spain. The palace of Louis I the Pious (*r.* 814–840) at Ingelheim boasted historical images from antiquity to the conquests of Charlemagne, while the palace church was decorated with pictorial sermons arranged in typological juxtaposition, Old Testament scenes on one side and Gospel scenes on the other. A few fragmentary paintings have survived north of the Alps, at Auxerre, Coblenz, Lorsch, Cologne, Fulda, Corvey, and Trier, and in the Alpine region and northern Italy, at Malles, Naturno, Cividale, Brescia, and Milan. In the church of St. John the Baptist at Müstair (Switzerland), however, an extensive cycle of paintings has come to light. The nave walls were originally covered with episodes from the story of David and Absalom (now Zürich, Landesmuseum) and scenes from the life of Christ. In the three apses are scenes of the lives of the saints surmounted by images of Christ, and on the western wall is the oldest preserved monumental composition of the Last Judgment. The style of the paintings, although provincial, points to Italian influence.

Illuminations. The most numerous and instructive witnesses to the scope and success of the Carolingian renaissance are illuminated manuscripts. On Charlemagne's directives, revised Bibles, Gospels, and liturgical books were prepared for reforms of the divine service, while literacy and learning were propagated by the copying of historical, literary, and scientific works of ancient authors. "Correct" content and text were the paramount concern, but the codices issuing from Charlemagne's Court School at Aachen were intended to set an example by the order of their layout and the beauty of their decoration.

The earliest known illuminated Carolingian manuscript is a Gospel lectionary written between 781 and 783 by the court scribe Godescalc (Paris,

St. John. Miniature from the Godescalc Gospels, 781–783. PARIS, BIBLIOTHÈQUE NATIONALE, MS NOUV. ACQ. LAT. 1203, fol. 2v

Bibliothèque Nationale, nouv. acq. lat. 1203). Clear Roman capital letters stand side by side with interlace initials of Hiberno-Saxon origin, while portraits of Christ, the Evangelists, and an image of the Fountain of Life enunciate the Carolingian ambition to recapture late antique pictorial traditions in order to make the sacred figures and their message tangible. A lingering attachment to two-dimensional expression in the Godescalc miniatures was overcome in later manuscripts of Charlemagne's Court School, such as the early-ninth-century Gospels of St. Médard of Soissons (Paris, Bibliothèque Nationale, lat. 8850), whose evangelists are rendered as firmly corporeal figures placed into arches that, however ambiguously, invite a view into depth.

Carolingian art depended on models of various age, origin, and style. Whereas the ornate gravity of the evangelist portraits of the Court School proper is reminiscent of sixth-century mosaics and ivories

Above: Christ with nine angels, the sun, and the moon. *Below*: The Psalmist receiving a crown from an angel; Moses and the Children of Israel. Illumination of Psalm 102 from the Utrecht Psalter, School of Rheims, 820–830. UTRECHT, BIBLIOTHEEK DER RIJKSUNIVERSITEIT, COD. 32, fol. 59r

at Ravenna, the evangelists of the late-eighth-century Coronation Gospels (Vienna, Weltliche Schatzkammer), also produced in the ambience of the court, appear like antique authors. Probably the work of Italian or Greek artists, they are painted in an illusionistic style that reaches back to the Hellenistic traditions of late antiquity.

While works of the Court School influenced later miniature painting mainly in the monastic centers of the East Frankish Empire, the illusionistic technique of the Coronation Gospels and its few early-ninth-century descendants was taken up and transformed by the illuminators assembled by Archbishop Ebo at Hautvillers near Rheims. The Evangelists of the Ebo Gospels (Épernay, Bibliothèque Municipale, MS 1), dating between 816 and 835, are painted with swift, vehement brushstrokes that evoke their inspired exaltation to a degree unknown in late antique art. (See illustration at 'Ebo of Rheims.") The same turbulent fervor pervades the bister drawings of the contemporary Psalter now at Utrecht (University Library, cod. 32), which, in most instances, illustrate the text by word images. The Rheimsian artists must have had a Mediterranean model for this work, just as they had models for their illustrated editions of the plays of Terence (Paris, Bibliothèque Nationale, lat. 7899) and of the *Physiologus* (Berne, Bürgerbibliothek, cod. 318). But the high-strung expressive force of the Utrecht Psalter drawings, with their multitudes of agitated little figures swarming over rapidly sketched hilly landscapes, is a Carolingian contribution that was to influence northern medieval art for centuries to come.

Another translation of southern models into still different forms and expressions was achieved in the monastery of St. Martin at Tours. It was here that the pattern for the illustration of Gospelbooks with a *majestas Domini* and Evangelist portraits was perfected to last for hundreds of years. It was here also that large pandect Bibles began to receive narrative pictures based on late antique Bible illustrations. The last and finest of three illustrated Touronian Bibles preserved was made about 845/846 on the order of the lay abbot Count Vivian for Charles II the Bald (Paris, Bibliothèque Nationale, lat. 1). Besides many decorated initial letters combining classical perspicuity with vine, beast, and figure motives, the manuscript contains six full-page miniatures heading biblical books, a frontispiece with scenes from the life of St. Jerome, and a page depicting the presentation of the codex to the West Frankish king. The hand of the best of the three painters who collaborated on the Vivian Bible is found again in a Gospelbook made for the emperor Lothair between 849 and 851 (Paris,

PRE-ROMANESQUE ART

Bibliothèque Nationale, lat. 266). While in debt to the style of Rheims, the painter tempered its verve by firmly constructed surfaces owed to late antique example. The eminence of Tours was cut short by Norman devastation in 853. By then, however, Touronian illumination had left an indelible mark on other important centers of the Carolingian Empire.

The diocese of Metz added still another dimension to Carolingian art. A sacramentary made for Archbishop Drogo between 850 and 855 (Paris, Bibliothèque Nationale, lat. 9428) is decorated with initial letters that are entwined with acanthus vines of classical derivation and enclose New Testament and liturgical scenes executed in an illusionistic style. Taking up an idea already announced in eighth-century Insular illumination as well as in manuscripts of the Court School of Charlemagne, the "historiated" initial was to find its most imaginative realization in the Romanesque. Nonetheless, the initials of the Drogo Sacramentary remain unique in their harmonious union of classical lettering, acanthus tendrils, and figural scenes. (See illustration at "Initials, Decorated.")

Developments during the second half of the century largely fed on and elaborated the achievements of the first. The most richly decorated Carolingian Bible known was made at Rheims for Charles II the Bald around 870 (Rome, Abbazia di S. Paolo fuori le Mura). Its sumptious full-page initials present the apogee of Rheimsian calligraphy, while about half of the twenty-four frontispiece miniatures are indebted to Touronian models and the other half to late antique sources. The style of the miniatures presents a fusion of late antique form with the lessons of Rheims and Tours.

Another Bible made for Charles II the Bald between 871 and 873 at St. Amand (Paris, Bibliothèque Nationale, lat. 2) is the finest example of the so-called Franco-Saxon style, which made its appearance in the north of France during the second quarter of the ninth century and outlasted all other Carolingian styles into the next century. Like most Franco-Saxon manuscripts, this Bible is decorated only with initials that integrate Hiberno-Saxon interlace and beast motives into a design of lucid order and sober elegance. (See illustrations at "Codex Aureus" and "Franco-Saxon School.")

Like his grandfather, Charles II the Bald established a Court School. Although its location is uncertain, several manuscripts can be attributed to it. These are distinguished by an eclectic ornamental vocabulary consisting of motives gleaned from the Court School of Charlemagne, from Rheims, Tours, and Metz. The *Codex Aureus* (Golden Codex) of St. Emmeram (Munich, Staatsbibliothek, Clm. 14000) is its last and most spectacular work. Written by the brothers Beringar and Liuthard in 870, this Gospelbook displays lavish full-page initials in which the letters are submerged in a carpet-like weave of golden interlace and leaf scrolls. The miniatures combine Touronian and Rheimsian elements but infuse them with a courtly ostentation that emulates the luster of Charlemagne's Court School manuscripts.

Initial page of Genesis (fol. 10r) from the Bible of S. Paolo fuori le Mura. Court School of Charles the Bald, *ca.* 870. ROME, ABBAZIA DI S. PAOLO FUORI LE MURA

The loss of Charles II the Bald's patronage at his death in 877 signals the decline of the Carolingian revival, although several centers remained active, particularly in the East Frankish domains. The most notable of these was the monastery of St. Gall, which had developed its own initial style from

PRE-ROMANESQUE ART

diverse West Frankish contacts. The Folchard Psalter, produced sometime before 872 (St. Gall, Stiftsbibliothek, cod. 23), shows this style at its height, while the *Psalterium Aureum* (Golden Psalter), begun before 883 (St. Gall, Stiftsbibliothek, cod. 22), added narrative illustrations to the repertory of St. Gall. These, however, are colored outline drawings without the materiality that Carolingian art had reconquered for the north.

Sculpture and metalwork. Goldsmiths and ivory carvers provided book covers. A small number of surviving ivories belonged to codices of the Court School of Charlemagne. Their subject matter and style was largely derived from late antique diptychs. A sixth-century design evocative of imperial triumph was, for instance, adapted to portray the triumph of Christ and the Virgin on the front and rear covers of the Lorsch Gospels, dating about 810 (front: London, Victoria and Albert Museum; rear: Vatican—the manuscript itself is divided between the Vatican Library [Pal. lat. 50] and Biblioteca Documentara Batthyaneum, Alba Julia, Romania).

Another group of ivories reflects the style of Rheims, especially that of the Utrecht Psalter, which also provided the subject matter for the covers of the Psalter of Charles II the Bald, written between 842 and 869 by the court scribe Liuthard (Paris, Bibliothèque Nationale, lat. 1152). While the location of the atelier is unknown, several other ivories of this so-called Liuthard group belonged to manuscripts of the Court School of Charles the Bald. The largest, affixed to the Pericopes of Emperor Henry II in the early eleventh century (Munich, Staatsbibliothek, Clm. 4452), may once have adorned the back of the *Codex Aureus* of St. Emmeram, which still retains its original golden front cover depicting Christ in Majesty, the evangelists, and scenes of Christ's miracles in repoussé relief framed by pearls and precious stones. The figure style of the *Codex Aureus* gold cover, of a closely related front cover of the Lindau Gospels in the Pierpont Morgan Library in New York, and of the small gold-sheathed portable altar of King Arnulf in the Munich Residence represent refined versions of that confluence of elements from various Carolingian schools also found in the miniatures of the Court School of Charles II the Bald.

Ivory carving also flourished at Metz. Late antique lessons underlie the reliefs of the Drogo Sacramentary, portraying liturgical scenes and scenes from the life of Christ, and, even more so, a plaque with scenes from the Passion on a Gospel-book made for Drogo (Paris, Bibliothèque Nationale, lat. 9388). Numerous later ivories, classified as the "Younger Metz School," however, betray contacts with the "Liuthard" style, while displaying more blocklike forms. To this group belongs the throne Charles II the Bald brought to Rome on the occasion of his coronation as emperor in 875. Now kept at St. Peter's as the so-called throne of St. Peter (*Cathedra S. Petri*), it is covered with ivory reliefs of acanthus scrolls containing, besides a bust portrait of Charles, images of cosmic symbols, and constellations derived from Carolingian copies of late antique astronomical manuscripts, as well as combat groups traceable to the Utrecht Psalter.

Courtly display of precious materials is manifest also in a number of engraved rock crystals probably made in an atelier in Lorraine. They either served as seals, such as that of King Lothair II (*r.* 855–869), which was fastened around 1000 to the Ottonian Lothair (Lothar) Cross (Aachen, Dom), or they had liturgical use, as for instance a crystal engraved with scenes from the story of Susannah and the Elders for Lothair II around 865 (London, British Museum).

Later ninth-century ivories show a turn toward compact figures, restrained action, and compositions governed by stricter symmetry. Among the finest works of this phase are the two tablets carved by Tuotilo (Tutilo) of St. Gall toward the end of the ninth century and later used as book covers (St. Gall, Stiftsbibliothek, cod. 53). Inspirations from the Court School of Charles II the Bald are cast into a firm two-dimensional order in the *majestas Domini* of the front and the Assumption of Mary and scenes from the life of St. Gall on the back. (See illustration at "Tuotilo.")

The chef d'oeuvre of Carolingian goldsmith work is the Paliotto, or Golden Altar, of S. Ambrogio in Milan, commissioned between 824 and 859 by Archbishop Angilbert II from the goldsmith Wolvinus (Wolvinius or Vuolvinus). The altar's four sides are decorated with images in gold and silver repoussé framed by borders of filigree, precious stones, and enamel. The golden front, indebted to early Byzantine art for subject matter and style, preserves an extensive New Testament cycle. The silver and silver-gilt panels on the sides and back—the latter portraying scenes from the life of St. Ambrose and two dedicatory medallions with images of Angilbert and Wolvinus—exhibit the simpler but more coherent forms then in the making in northern miniature painting, especially at Tours.

PRE-ROMANESQUE ART

It is not impossible that Angilbert called northern artists to Milan to work side by side with southern goldsmiths. (See illustration at "Metalsmiths, Gold and Silver.")

The disintegration of Carolingian rule disrupted artistic production for nearly three generations. Its recovery during the later tenth century was sustained by monastic reform movements, particularly that of Cluny. The reforms spread throughout Europe, and different pre-Romanesque styles were created in Germany, England, France, Italy, and Spain.

GERMANY

The consolidation of the empire under the Saxon dynasty (919–1024) gave a powerful stimulus to pre-Romanesque German art, called Ottonian after three Saxon emperors named Otto, although the term "Ottonian" includes the art of the time of the first Franco-Salian emperors: Conrad II (*r.* 1024–1039) and Henry III (*r.* 1039–1056). Imperial commissions as well as the patronage of the princes of the church and noble abbesses were responsible for the most splendid manuscripts produced in the great Ottonian monasteries. Books used for church services were now preferred, especially Gospelbooks and evangeliaries, which, from about 980 onward, were often illustrated with narrative cycles.

Illuminations. Corvey in the Saxon heartlands was one of the first centers to produce illuminated manuscripts. A mid-tenth-century Gospelbook (New York, Pierpont Morgan Library, MS 755) is still limited to stately initial pages that set Franco-Saxon forms and foliage motives derived from the Court School of Charles II the Bald onto purple grounds embellished with patterns borrowed from Eastern textiles. Portraits of the Evangelists and Christ were soon added, however, taking up either types from Charles's Court School (New York, Public Library, MS Astor 1) or types transmitted by those rare Franco-Saxon manuscripts containing images. The Evangelists of a late-ninth-century Franco-Saxon Gospels (Prague, Kapitulni Knihova, Cim. 2) served as models for two surviving leaves from a Corvey codex of the last quarter of the tenth century (Helsinki, Finland National Museum; Leipzig, Staatsbibliothek).

After about 1000, Weser-Corvey was overshadowed by Hildesheim, which owed its renown to the patronage of St. Bernward, bishop from 993 to 1022. The manuscripts commissioned by him echo Carolingian models similar to those used at Corvey; but the miniatures of the Bernward Gospels (Hildesheim, Dom, MS 18) are more ornate, with strong colors and heavily delineated figures on textilelike background patterns.

A less stiffly decorative translation of Carolingian sources was made at Fulda. The Evangelists of the so-called *Codex Wittekindeus* (Widukind Gospels), dating from the 970's (Berlin, Deutsche Staatsbibliothek, MS theol. lat. fol. 1), are based on the images of a Gospelbook from the Court School of Charlemagne, although they are painted in a technique reminiscent of court manuscripts of Charles II the Bald. Close in time is a richly illustrated sacramentary (Göttingen, Staats- und Universitatsbibliothek, cod. theol. fol. 231), whose short figures with eloquently exaggerated gestures are characteristic of Fulda painting into the first quarter of the eleventh century, until contacts with Mainz, center of the diocese, brought a more sophisticated figure style—as exemplified by a sacramentary of about 1020 (Vatican Library, cod. lat. 3548).

The island monastery of Reichenau on Lake Constance held the most famed of all Ottonian scriptoria. Its first phase of illumination is represented by two distinct groups of manuscripts. One, called the "Eburnant group" after the name of a scribe appearing in several books, is represented by an evangeliary written before 969 for the sacristan Gero, later (969–976) archbishop of Cologne (Darmstadt, Landesbibliothek, cod. 1948). The elegant initials of the Gero Codex take up late Carolingian forms from nearby St. Gall, while the miniatures derive directly from Charlemagne's Lorsch Gospels.

The initial pages of the other group are permeated by the restless energy of tightly knotted tendrils, and their purple grounds are enlivened by geometric design or by dragons and other beasts finely drawn in gold. This group is named after Ruodpreht (Roudprecht), the scribe of a Psalter made about 980 for Egbert, archbishop of Trier from 977 to 993 (Cividale, Museo Archeologico, cod. 136). The rendition of figures as linear surface patterns in the Psalter's miniatures bears relation to late-tenth-century murals with scenes of Christ's miracles in the church of St. George at Oberzell on the Reichenau, and it points to connections with the art of Italy.

The "Ruodpreht" style is also found in the Evangelist portraits and the dedication page of an evangeliary written about 985 for Archbishop

PRE-ROMANESQUE ART

The Annunciation. Miniature from the *Codex Egberti* by the Master of the Registrum Gregorii, School of Reichenau, *ca.* 985. TRIER, STADTBIBLIOTHEK, COD. 24, fol. 9v

Egbert by the Reichenau monks Kerald and Heribert (Trier, Stadtbibliothek, cod. 24). The narrative New Testament miniatures of the manuscript, on the other hand, recall the style and illusionistic technique of early-fifth-century illumination to a degree not even matched by Carolingian adaptations of late antique sources at Tours. Some late antique model must have been available to the Ottonian painters, but the treatment of subject matter also betrays their knowledge of a tenth-century Byzantine manuscript.

Seven of the *Codex Egberti*'s miniatures are by a master with an extraordinary comprehension of late antique art. His firmly modeled figures deployed within logically constructed spaces also distinguish two single leaves remaining from a manuscript of the Epistles of St. Gregory written about 984 for Egbert at Trier, one representing Otto II flanked by personifications of the empire's provinces (Chantilly, Musée Condé), the other depicting St. Gregory inspired by the Holy Spirit (Trier, Stadtbibliothek). This Master of the Registrum Gregorii, that is, the Gregory Master (*fl. ca.* 980–990), also produced the so-called Gospels of Ste. Chapelle (Paris, Bibliothèque Nationale, lat. 8851), which contain Evangelists developed from Carolingian types and a Majesty page combining a Touronian scheme with gold ground, the first use of this Byzantine device in the West. The codex was given to the monastery of Echternach, where its images had a somewhat hardened reflection in the *Codex Aureus Epternacensis* (Nuremberg Golden Gospels), dating before 1039 (Nuremberg, Germanisches National Museum, Hs. 2° 156142). Another Gospelbook made by the Gregory Master (Manchester, John Rylands Library, MS 98) found its way to Cologne, where it contributed to the rise of the scriptorium of that archdiocese.

Reichenau illumination, however, went another way. While the influence of the *Codex Egberti* is evident in a Gospelbook dedicated about 990 by the monk Liuthar to Otto III (Aachen, Dom), Byzantine elements were now favored over late antique ones. Besides an image signifying Otto's theocratic rule, the manuscript contains full-page miniatures with christological scenes often placed without foothold onto a golden ground enframed by finely wrought arches. Reduced plastic volume, linearity, and eloquent gesture announce tendencies consummated in later codices of the so-called Liuthar group, especially in the Gospels illuminated for Otto III around 1000, famed for "visionary" Evangelists (Munich, Staatsbibliothek, cod. lat. 4453), and even more so in the Book of Pericopes made for Emperor Henry II in either 1007 or 1012 (Munich, Staatsbibliothek, cod. lat. 4452). Pictorial narration here turns into poignant drama. Nearly disembodied large figures, painted in luminous cool hues, interact by expressive gesture and intense glance on expanses of shimmering gold evoking realms beyond time and space. The initial pages, while maintaining the vocabulary of the "Ruodpreht" group, complement the miniatures by the grand sweep of their letters. In the last great Reichenau codex, an Apocalypse manuscript dating before 1020 (Bamberg, Staatsbibliothek, MS Bibl. 140), fervor is calmed by stiffened linearity. Thereafter the Reichenau style went into eclipse, although activity continued until the middle of the century.

Miniature painting in Cologne came into its own at the very end of the tenth century. A Gospels written perhaps in 999 for the church of St. Gereon (Cologne, Historisches Archiv, cod. W 312) is one of the earliest of a series following the decorative program of the (Manchester) Gospels by the Gregory Master. The miniatures, however, are executed in a broadly coloristic technique owed to some tenth-century Byzantine court manuscript. A sacramentary also produced for St. Gereon (Paris, Bibliothèque Nationale, lat. 817) and a Gospels commissioned by the abbess Hitda of Meschede (Darmstadt, Landesbibliothek, cod. 1640) repre-

PRE-ROMANESQUE ART

sent the height of this expressive painterly style, which spiritualizes imagery just as much as the linear mode of Reichenau. When, between 1021 and 1035, the cathedral canon Hillinus had a Gospelbook made by two visiting Reichenau monks, Purchadus and Chuonradus (Conrad) (Cologne, Dombibliothek, cod. 12), gold ground and linearity were introduced to Cologne. A rich mid-eleventh-century Gospels (Bamberg, Staatsbibliothek, MS Bibl. 94), with miniatures stressing symbolic over narrative content, shows a blend of painterly and linear forms on golden grounds. The last third of the century brought a progressively simpler and harder style, which spelled the end of Ottonian painting at Cologne.

One source for Ottonian illuminators at Regensburg was the late Carolingian *Codex Aureus* (Golden codex), given by Emperor Arnulf to the monastery of St. Emmeram during the last decade of the ninth century. A sacramentary made before 1012 for Henry II (Munich, Staatsbibliothek, cod.

Christ in the house of Martha and Mary. Miniature from the Book of Pericopes of Henry II. School of Reichenau, 1007 or 1012. MUNICH, BAYERISCHE STAATSBIBLIOTHEK, COD. CLM. 4452, fol. 162r

Christ with Life and Death. Miniature from the Uta Gospels, School of Regensburg, 1002–1025. MUNICH, BAYERISCHE STAATSBIBLIOTHEK, COD. CLM. 13601, fol. 3v

lat. 4456) contains a portrait of the emperor directly copied from the image of Charles II the Bald in the *Codex Aureus* but translated into two-dimensional patterns sparkling with brighter colors and gold. The heads of the figures, however, have a Byzantine cast, and the impact of a Byzantine source is also evident on a page depicting the emperor crowned by Christ, a Byzantine concept articulated, for instance, by the portrait of Basil II in his Psalter of about 1017 (Venice, Biblioteca Marciana, gr. 17). A Gospelbook produced for Abbess Uta of Niedermünster (Munich, Staatsbibliothek, cod. 13601) added another component to the Regensburg synthesis of Carolingian and Byzantine form, namely a complex theological content. A representation of the Crucified Christ as victor over death, placed against a schematic golden framework with explanatory verses, links the four phases of man's redemption to the four basic figures of Geometry, the four elements of Music, and other quaternities; while the facing page, depicting St.

PRE-ROMANESQUE ART

Henry III and Queen Agnes offering the codex to the Virgin. Miniature from the Gospels for Speyer Cathedral. School of Echternach, 1043–1046. EL ESCORIAL, REAL BIBLIOTECA DE SAN LORENZO, COD. VITR. 17, fol. 3r. Foto MAS, Barcelona

Erhard celebrating Mass, evokes the trifold ecclesiastical hierarchy and three degrees of access to God. This intellectual imagery was based on interpretations by the Regensburg monk Hartwic of the writings of the sixth-century Pseudo-Dionysios in the Latin translation of the Carolingian scholar John Scottus Eriugena.

Other Bavarian scriptoria flourished. A fine Book of Pericopes was, for instance, illuminated for Henry II before 1014 at Seeon (Bamberg, Staatsbibliothek, MS Bibl. 95), but Salzburg gained preeminence during the second third of the eleventh century and became the only major Ottonian scriptorium to evolve a Romanesque style. The agent of this continuity was the Byzantine influence already felt at Regensburg and steadily increasing at Salzburg, perhaps due to the monastery's situation on the Eastern trade route. The miniatures of an evangeliary dedicated about 1070 by the sacristan Berthold to St. Peter's at Salzburg (New York, Pierpont Morgan Library, MS 780) announce the Romanesque drapery style of simplified linear rhythms, which defines the figures' movements and substantial forms.

Long overshadowed by nearby Trier, the monastery of Echternach entered the last phase of Ottonian illumination during the second third of the eleventh century with many manuscripts. The first luxury production was the already mentioned *Codex Aureus Epternacensis* in Nuremberg, made before 1039 for the use of the monastery. In addition to motifs derived from the Gregory Master's Ste. Chapelle Gospels, the codex contains decorative pages simulating Byzantine textiles and a christological cycle which surpasses that of the *Codex Egberti* in scope, while advancing a harder, more hieratic style. The patronage of the Salian emperor Henry III (*r.* 1039–1056) was responsible for several splendid books. The most extensive Ottonian New Testament cycle known is contained in a Book of Pericopes given to Henry and his mother, the empress Gisela (*d.* 1043), on occasion of their visit to Echternach in 1039 (Bremen, Staatsbibliothek, MS b. 21). An even more ornate Gospels was commissioned by the emperor between 1043 and 1046 for Speyer Cathedral (Escorial, cod. vit. 17). Facing dedication pages depict Henry's parents, Conrad II and Gisela, kneeling before Christ in Majesty, and Henry III and his wife, Agnes of Poitou, offering the codex to the Virgin enthroned below an image of Speyer Cathedral. The miniatures are painted in the Echternach style, but the carefully modeled faces of Christ and the Virgin as well as Christ's blessing hand are certainly by a Byzantine artist. No other traces of his hand or influence are found in this or later Echternach manuscripts. Indeed, the more frigid style and diminished pictorial program of the Gospels of Henry III, dedicated about 1050 to the Cathedral of Goslar (Uppsala, Universitetsbiblioteket, MS c. 93), evince the waning of Byzantine tutelage and portend the decline of Echternach as one of the last guardians of Ottonian painting.

Sculpture and metalwork. As in Carolingian times, metalwork and ivory carving furnished imperial regalia and precious works for church services. Attributions to specific workshops are often difficult because craftsmen now developed their styles largely independent from manuscript illumination.

Unknown, for instance, is the provenance of sixteen ivory panels with scenes from the life of Christ, which survive in several collections and are thought to have belonged to an antependium given by Otto I to the cathedral of Magdeburg (after 955). The compact and clearly delineated figures have variously called for attribution to Reichenau, Einsiedlen, or Lorraine, but are also related to a plaque and two ivory *situlae* made about 980 at Milan (Milan, Castello Sforzesco; Milan Cathedral; London, Victoria and Albert Museum). (See illustration at "Chairete.")

Also uncertain is the origin of the imperial crown (Vienna, Schatzkammer). Its ring of eight hinged plates decked with jewels and pearls was made for Otto I during the third quarter of the tenth century; the frontal cross is of the period of Otto III, and the bow was added for Conrad II. The emperor's role as God's vicar on earth, *rex et sacerdos,* is proclaimed by the cloisonné enamels on four of the plates depicting Christ as king of kings and three Old Testament kings. The figure types as well as the technique are indebted to Byzantine art, an influence perhaps transmitted through Italy.

Direct Byzantine contact is exemplified by an ivory of 982/983 representing Otto II and his wife, the Greek princess Theophano (955?–991), crowned by Christ (Paris, Musée de Cluny). Probably by a Byzantine artist, the ivory may once have adorned the cover of a manuscript. Ottonian esteem for things Byzantine led to the incorporation of near-contemporary Byzantine works on several book covers, for example that of the Gospels of Otto III at Munich, that of the Bernward Gospels at Hildesheim (MS 18), and on a cover made about 1020 for a Carolingian Gospels (Aachen, Dom). Byzantine enamels of Christ and eleven of the apostles were reused on the cover of the Pericopes of Henry II to enframe the Carolingian ivory, probably taken from the *Codex Aureus* of St. Emmeram, both preserved in Munich.

The best Ottonian ivories of the decades around 1000 were produced in the area between the Moselle, the Meuse, and the lower Rhine. Their styles differ, however. Liège carvers, for instance, translated Carolingian examples into subtly rounded, animated reliefs, as exemplified by a book cover made for the Gospels of Bishop Notger (Liège, Musée Curtius). A more ornate and elegantly linear style distinguishes work from Cologne, such as a relief representing Christ blessing Sts. Victor and Gereon (Cologne, Schnütgen Museum). The most original work is owed to a master active at Trier. A *majestas Domini* relief and a diptych representing Moses Receiving the Law and the Doubting Thomas (both in Berlin, Staatliche Museen), as well as a plaque depicting St. Paul (Paris, Musée de Cluny), show gruff, earthy figures carved with a singular power of expression. By his hand is also the Crucifixion ivory on the cover of the *Codex Aureus Epternacensis* in Nuremberg. Effigies of the empress Theophano and her son Otto III among the gold repoussé figures surrounding the ivory—executed in a different style—prove the cover to be about forty to fifty years earlier than the manuscript. It may originally have belonged to the Ste. Chapelle Gospels of the Gregory Master.

The enamels bordering the *Codex Aureus* cover connect it with the portable reliquary altar of St. Andrew, foremost among the few surviving works of Archbishop Egbert's atelier at Trier (Trier, Dom). The rectangular box on four recumbent lions incorporates into its enamel and jewel decoration a seventh-century Frankish brooch enclosing a sixth-century gold medallion of the emperor Justinian I, and it supports a gold-covered foot, one of the first preserved examples of many medieval reliquaries shaped in a form appropriate to the relic contained.

In fact, the earliest known medieval sculptures in the round were reliquaries. A relic was contained in a gold-sheathed wooden Virgin and Child made for Abbess Mathilde of Essen during the last quarter of the tenth century, perhaps at Cologne (Essen, Minster). Although fully rounded, the brittle surface glitter of the folds still denies the sense of solidity and structural clarity of a later wooden Virgin, long stripped of its gold, which was made for Bishop Imad of Paderborn (*ca.* 1060, Paderborn, Diozesanmuseum).

Crucifixes could also serve as reliquaries, as mentioned already in a late Carolingian document. Among a number of surviving wooden reliquary crucifixes, Christ's human suffering is most movingly evoked by the crucifix given between 969 and 976 to Cologne Cathedral by Archbishop Gero (Cologne, Dom).

Ateliers in the archbishopric of Cologne produced a series of jeweled golden crosses. Of four preserved in the treasury of Essen Minster, three were gifts of Abbess Mathilde (973–1011) and a fourth of Abbess Theophano (1039–1056). Gold, filigree work, enamels, and jewels irradiate their fronts, while the backs are engraved with leaf scrolls, evangelist symbols, and the *Agnus Dei,* or an image of Christ Blessing. To this group belongs the Lothair (Lothar) Cross of the end of the tenth century (Aachen, Dom), so called because the decoration of the front includes a Carolingian crystal

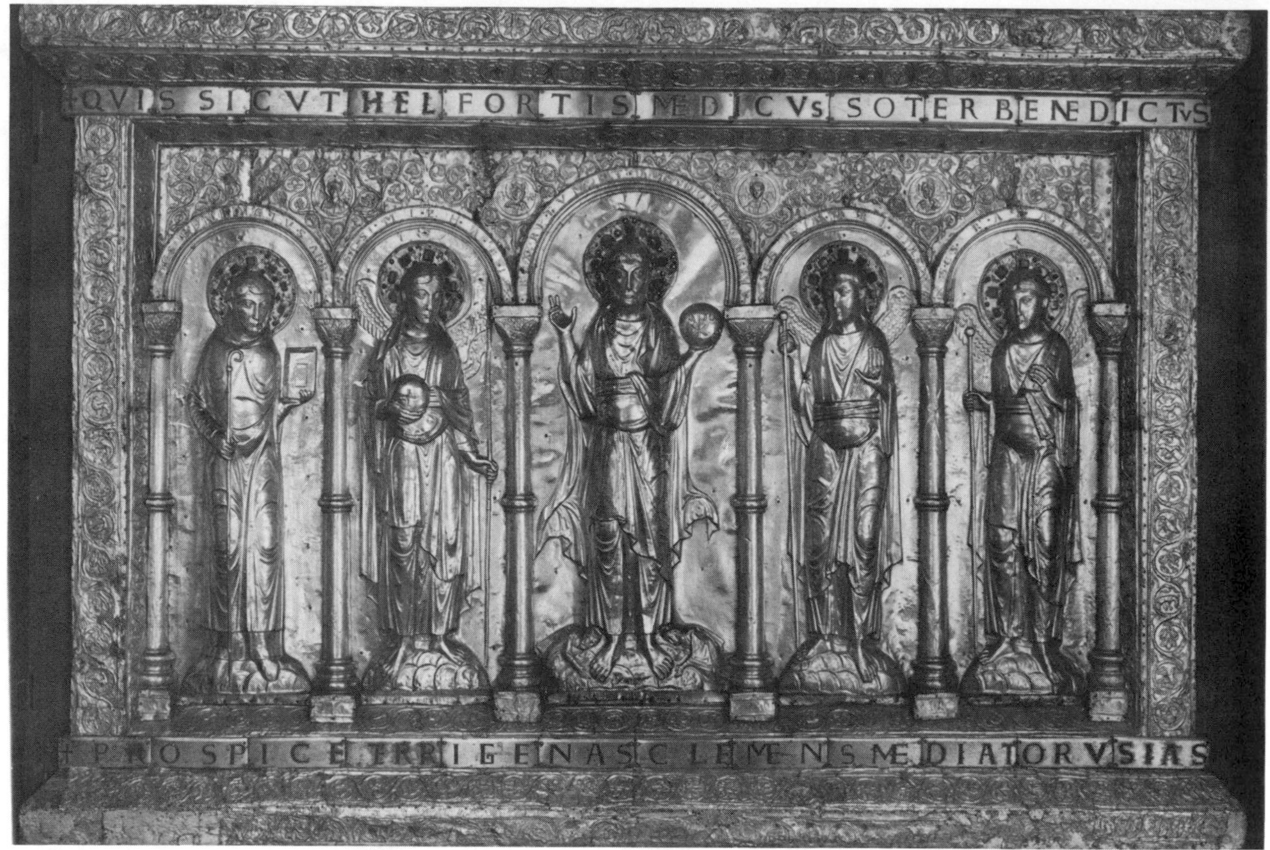

Basel antependium, depicting Christ with Sts. Benedict, Michael, Gabriel, and Raphael. Silver gilt, with repoussé relief and niello work, *ca.* 1019. MUSÉE DE CLUNY, PARIS, INV. NR. CL. 2350

with a portrait of King Lothair II (*r.* 855–869). An antique cameo portraying Augustus is placed in the center to signify Christ *imperator,* while the back is engraved with a superb image of the crucified dead Christ. Of still undetermined west German origin is the large cross containing a particle of the True Cross and the Holy Lance that Conrad II added about 1030 to the imperial treasure (Vienna, Schatzkammer). The niello engravings on the back are stylistically related to those of a portable altar dedicated between 1014 and 1024 by Henry II to Bamberg Cathedral (Munich, Residenz).

Henry's generosity also enriched the cathedrals of Aachen and Basel. A golden pulpit dating between 1002 and 1014 and a golden altar antependium of about 1020 are still preserved at Aachen (Dom), whereas the Basel antependium, made about 1019 at Mainz or Fulda, is now in Paris (Musée de Cluny). Less restored than the works at Aachen, the golden altar of Basel shows Christ, St. Benedict, and three archangels standing below arches. Tiny figures of Henry II and his wife, Kunigunde (*d. ca.* 1039), kneel at Christ's feet. Above the arches are personifications of the Four Cardinal Virtues contained in medallions surrounded by delicate scrolls of foliage. Although the serene and elegantly elongated golden figures with jeweled halos are executed in high repoussé relief, their radiance joins with that of the golden ground. They are not conceived as sculptures in their own right.

This sense of monumental yet impalpable existence also pervades a work made in the early eleventh century at Regensburg, the golden container for the Uta Gospels (Munich, Staatsbibliothek). A powerfully modeled Christ in Majesty is firmly held by a framework decked with enamels, pearls, and precious stones. Also from Regensburg is a reliquary cross made about 1006 for the sister of Henry II, Queen Gisela of Hungary (Munich, Residenz). Encrusted with jewels and pearl-framed enamels, it holds a strongly abstracted figure of Christ solidly cast in gold.

Adam and Eve reproached by God after the Fall. Detail from the bronze doors originally from St. Michael, Hildesheim. 1015. FOTO MARBURG/ART RESOURCE

The most important center for metal casting flourished at Hildesheim under Bishop Bernward. Still kept in the cathedral treasury are a silver crozier, a pair of tall silver candlesticks, and a small silver-gilt crucifix, all cast in the lost-wax technique between 996 and 1008. Bernward's most ambitious commissions were the more than twelve-foot-high bronze column, variously dated to the first or second decade of the eleventh century, and the large bronze doors, made before 1015, now both at Hildesheim Cathedral. (See illustration at "Metallurgy.")

The bronze column, cast in a single hollow piece, recalls the triumphal columns of Rome, which Bernward had seen on a visit. Once surmounted by a crucifix, it proclaims the Triumph of Christ by its helical band of reliefs depicting in twenty-four scenes the Lord's ministry on earth from the Baptism at the bottom to the Entry into Jerusalem at the top. The bronze doors, originally for the abbey of St. Michael, now at the cathedral, bear reliefs with eight scenes from Genesis in a descending sequence on one wing and the same number of New Testament scenes in an ascending order on the other. Typological juxtapositions pair, for instance, the Fall of Adam and Eve with the Crucifixion, or Eve nursing Cain with the Virgin and Child, thus alluding to redemption through Christ. The pictorial sources have been traced to Carolingian and Anglo-Saxon illuminated manuscripts. On the Ottonian reliefs, however, the story of the Fall and Salvation is translated into human drama, grippingly enacted by figures which lean out from the background so that every head is fully modeled in the round.

Such condensation of religious emotion and typological content in near-three-dimensional form seems to anticipate Romanesque portal sculpture. But monumental Romanesque sculpture was to evolve from the interaction of sculptors and architects. While there is some evidence of Ottonian architectural sculpture, for instance in fragments of large stone figures preserved from St. Pantaleon at Cologne, the Hildesheim doors, like most other works of pre-Romanesque sculpture, remain essentially autonomous pictorial expressions.

ENGLAND

Danish invaders had devastated Anglo-Saxon monasteries and churches for nearly two generations before King Alfred the Great (849–899)

 PRE-ROMANESQUE ART

checked their inroads by a victory in 878 and a peace negotiated in 885. Thus, he was able to initiate a recovery of culture and art in the south of England, which was expanded by the growing power of his successors to the kingdom of Wessex and—from King Athelstan in 924/925—to "all England." Animal ornament, the artistic contributions of the Scandinavians, remained restricted to the north except for a few instances during the reign of the Danish king Cnut the Great over England from 1016 to 1035. Although he had embraced Anglo-Saxon culture, Scandinavian motives appear, for example, on a tomb relief found in the cemetery of Old St. Paul's Cathedral in London (Museum of London) and in the initial decoration of a few manuscripts.

Illuminations. The Anglo-Saxons looked to the Continent for guidance and acquired Carolingian models whose influence has been traced in such work as the late-ninth-century "Alfred Jewel" (Oxford, Ashmolean Museum) or the stole and maniple embroidered between 909 and 916 at Winchester (Durham Cathedral). Manuscripts of the first phase of Anglo-Saxon art have initials which combine denatured Carolingian leaf scrolls with interlace and human or animal forms derived from southern English manuscripts of the later eighth century. The earliest figural illuminations of the second quarter of the tenth century are based on either Carolingian or seventh- to eighth-century Italo-Byzantine work. The former is reflected in the dedication pages of a copy of Bede's *Life of St. Cuthbert* (Cambridge, Corpus Christi College, MS 183) and a copy of Hrabanus Maurus' (*ca.* 780–856) *De laudibus sanctae crucis* (Cambridge, Trinity College, MS B.16.3), and the latter in miniatures added at Winchester to the so-called Athelstan Psalter between 924/925 and 940 (London, British Library, Cotton MS Galba A. xviii).

The most spectacular phase of Anglo-Saxon art began in the mid tenth century after the reforms launched by Sts. Dunstan, Ethelwold, and Oswald had brought about a rapid renewal of monastic life and opened fresh contacts with the Continent. Scriptoria at Winchester, Canterbury, Glastonbury, Ely, and other centers developed a new and original style of manuscript illumination which is conveniently but inaccurately known as the "Winchester style."

"Winchester" illumination is distinguished by the vibrant flicker and swirl of calligraphic drapery formulae and by foliate borders composed of richly colored acanthus vines proliferating under and over trellislike golden bands. It appears first in the dedication miniature of the foundation charter for New Minster at Winchester granted by King Edgar in 966 (London, British Library, Cotton MS Vespasion A.viii) and, developed to baroque exuberance, in the Benedictional of St. Aethelwold dating between 971 and 984 (London, British Library, add. MS 49598). While indebted to various Carolingian inspirations—the foliate patterns have precedent in manuscripts from Metz, the structure of the initial pages is frequently based on Franco-Saxon example, and the figure style recalls work of Charlemagne's Court School—the Anglo-Saxon artists created entirely new effects by fusing frames and figures into scintillating surface patterns invested with the sense of incessant motion that had been the essence of Hiberno-Saxon illumination centuries earlier.

Around the year 1000 the Carolingian Utrecht Psalter was copied at Canterbury (London, British Library, Harley MS 603). The copyists captured the restless vivacity of their model, although, favoring rhythmic coloristic patterns, they substituted polychrome lines for the monochrome of the Carolingian drawings. To be sure, there exist earlier Anglo-Saxon pen drawings, for instance, a drawing of St. Dunstan prostrate before Christ made at Glastonbury between 960 and 970 (Oxford, Bodleian MS Auct. F.4.32), but the illusionistic, sketchy Utrecht Psalter style was to have a strong impact on subsequent "Winchester" work, such as the delicate polychrome drawing of the Crucifixion in a Psalter probably from Ramsay Abbey dating around 1000 (London, British Library, Harley MS 2904) or the fully colored miniatures of the "Missal" (sacramentary) of Robert of Jumièges, possibly painted at Ely between 1016 and 1030 (Rouen, Bibliothèque Municipale, MS 374 [Y.6.]). (See illustration at "Robert of Jumièges.")

Anglo-Saxon originality and increasing independence from Carolingian example is particularly manifest in Psalter illustration. In a Psalter from Bury St. Edmunds dating from the second quarter of the eleventh century (Vatican Library, Reg. lat. 12), often newly invented word images are drawn in an expressive and volatile style into the text margins instead of heading each psalm, as in the Utrecht and Harley Psalters. Another innovation in Psalter illustration was the use of full-page frontispieces with scenes from the lives of David and Christ, as exemplified by the dramatic polychrome drawings

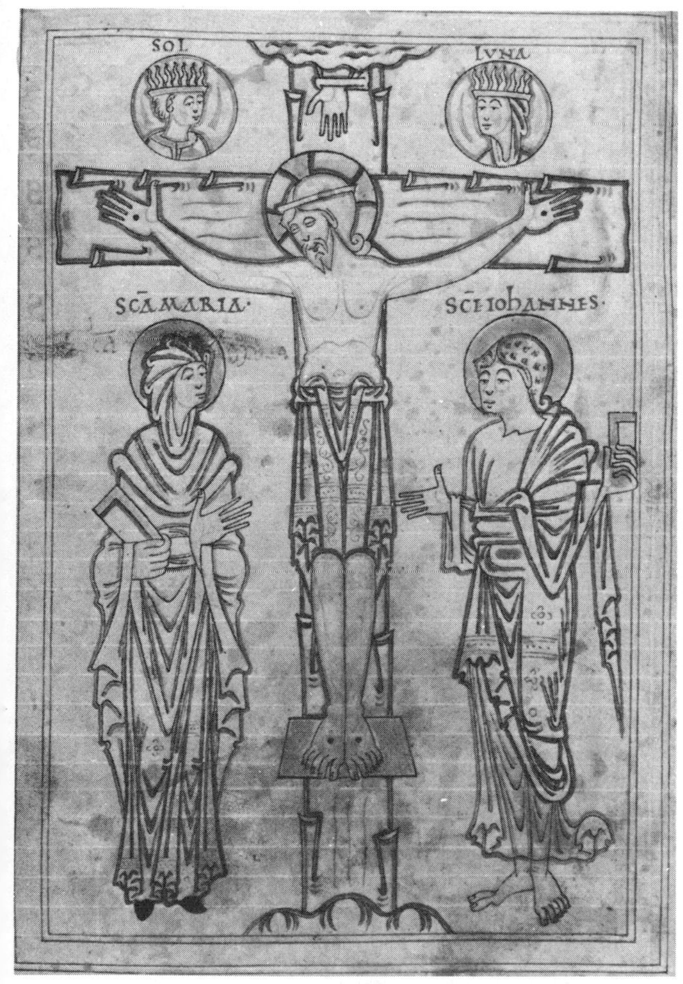

Crucifixion pages from a Psalter written at Winchester: *ca.* 1060 (left); *ca.* 1087 (right). BY PERMISSION OF THE BRITISH LIBRARY, LONDON, ARUNDEL MS 60, fols. 12v and 52v

of a mid-eleventh-century Psalter from Winchester (London, British Library, Cotton MS Tiberius C.vi).

The manuscripts of vernacular texts written and illuminated at Canterbury in the late tenth and early eleventh centuries are unique: Aelfric's (*fl.* 980's–1010) *Metrical Paraphrase of the Pentateuch and Joshua* (London, British Library, Cotton MS Claudius B.iv) and Caedmon's (*fl. ca.* 675) Old English poetic version of Genesis (Oxford, Bodleian MS Junius 11). Their narrative illustrations, partly indebted to late antique Old Testament cycles but direct and naive in style, may have served as visual guides for the exposition of scripture to laymen.

The "Winchester" tendency toward ornamental stylization reached its height on the eve of the Norman Conquest. In the Gospels of Judith of Flanders, dating between 1050 and 1065 (New York, Pierpont Morgan Library, MS 709), elegantly attenuated figures convey emotional fervor by the thrust of gesture and the vigor of drapery patterns. The change from Anglo-Saxon to English Romanesque illumination is most strikingly exemplified by two Crucifixion pages in a Psalter written at Winchester about 1060 (London, British Library, Arundel MS 60). The first (fol. 12v) presents a stiffened version of the mid-eleventh-century polychrome drawing style; the second (fol. 52v), added about 1087 and reflecting Norman influence, segments a firmly delineated and colored design into rhythmic patterns informed by a new sense of surface relief.

Sculpture and metalwork. The styles of manuscript illumination were adapted for ivories and metalwork. Of the wealth recorded in contempo-

PRE-ROMANESQUE ART

rary inventories, only a small number of precious objects have survived. Among the most outstanding are a late-tenth-century reliquary cross adorned with gold filigree, enamel medallions, and a figure of Christ carved from walrus tusk, which is closely related to the drawing of Christ in the Ramsey Psalter (London, Victoria and Albert Museum), and, more hardened in style, the front cover of the Gospels of Judith of Flanders dating before 1066, which displays a Christ in Majesty between two seraphim and a Crucifixion group cast in gold and set on a ground covered with gold filigree and jewels (New York, Pierpont Morgan Library).

There also exist fragments of large-scale sculpture in stone which betray the influence of the manuscript medium, such as a pair of angels in the late-tenth-century church at Bradford-on-Avon, whose style parallels that of the New Minster Charter, or a mid-eleventh-century relief representing the Harrowing of Hell in Bristol Cathedral that recalls the drawing of the same subject in the Cotton Psalter Tiberius C.vi. The decoration of walls with elaborate reliefs was undertaken in the train of the reforms responsible for the repair and building of numerous abbeys and churches and seems to anticipate Romanesque architectural sculpture. The Anglo-Saxon work, however, is distinguished from Romanesque by the technique of cutting and incising rather than sculpting in the round.

FRANCE

The demise of the Carolingian Empire had left France splintered into feuding provinces beyond the control of impotent kings. Lacking the patronage of imperial or episcopal courts enjoyed by Ottonian artists or the sense of common endeavor fostered by the Anglo-Saxon monasteries, French art of the tenth and eleventh centuries depended on the efforts of local ecclesiastical patrons to revive piety and learning. Numerous manuscripts, some of them illustrated, of lives of local saints were to stimulate the cult of their relics; an example is the *Life of St. Wandregisil,* written at St. Bertin in the tenth century (St. Omer, Bibliothèque Municipale, MS 764). Their primitive style, however, shows no trace of the accomplished techniques of Carolingian painting, just as the ornamental decoration of tenth-century French manuscripts generally reverted to those pre-Carolingian zoomorphic forms which, except for the Franco-Saxon works, the Carolingian *renovatio* had eschewed.

Illuminations. Regional stylistic traditions based on chance availability of Carolingian and other models, on itinerant artists, and on contacts with trends outside France began to emerge around the year 1000. The old monastery of St. Bertin once more became an important center of manuscript production under its abbot, Odbert (986–1007), who, an illuminator himself, created a new style from lessons learned from Anglo-Saxon artists invited to St. Bertin and from Carolingian exemplars. A Carolingian manuscript of Aratus' *Phainomena* (Leiden, Bibliotek der Rijksuniversiteit, Voss. lat. Q.79) was copied twice at St. Bertin (Boulogne, Bibliothèque Municipale, MS 188; Bern, Burgerbibliothek, MS 88), and an Anglo-Saxon hand is, for instance, discernible in the illustrations of a late-tenth-century Gospels (Boulogne, Bibliothèque Municipale, MS 11). Its Majesty page was copied in another Gospels by a French artist who tempered the "Winchester" style into harder, more firmly contained outlines (St. Omer, Bibliothèque Municipale, MS 56). Carolingian and Anglo-Saxon inspirations are fused into new coherence in a Psalter written about 1000 and signed "Odbertus decoravit" (Boulogne, Bibliothèque Municipale, MS 20). The ornamental decoration recalls St. Bertin's own Franco-Saxon past, the historiated initials of the Drogo Sacramentary, and the figure style of the "Winchester" translation of the Carolingian idiom of Rheims, even though the whole is disciplined by the firm structure of its design. This is equally true of a splendid Gospelbook also illuminated by Odbert (New York, Pierpont Morgan Library, MS 333). Its full-page initials on purple ground are historiated with figures bending to the shape of the letter, and they are firmly set off by frames decorated with foliate scrolls inhabited by pairs of beasts and hunting scenes, which approach Romanesque form.

During the second quarter of the eleventh century the nearby Abbey of St. Vaast embarked on a three-volume Bible, a format common to later Romanesque Bibles (Arras, Bibliothèque Municipale, MS 559 [435]). Its surviving illuminations blend Anglo-Saxon and Franco-Saxon motives into crisply executed complex forms. On the other hand, a sacramentary produced at St. Vaast in the middle of the century for the church of St. Denis (Paris, Bibliothèque Nationale, lat. 9436) betrays knowledge not only of manuscripts of the Court School of Charles II the Bald but also of Ottonian works from Cologne by its expressively elongated figures and a

PRE-ROMANESQUE ART

broad painterly style. Similar coloristic effects mark the miniatures in a *Life and Miracles of St. Amand* written at St. Amand in the second half of the century (Valenciennes, Bibliothèque Municipale, MS 502).

Other influences and models guided the developments in the southwest of France at St. Martial, Limoges, and other monasteries in Aquitaine. The most outstanding of a group of manuscripts produced at Limoges around 1000 is a lectionary containing initial letters that loosely combines Touronian palmette motives, pre-Carolingian beasts, and some figures of Byzantine derivation (Paris, Bibliothèque Nationale, lat. 5301). A particularly elegant decorative style of playfully woven linear plaits with interspersed palmette terminals on variously colored grounds distinguishes an eleventh-century gradual from Albi (Paris, Bibliothèque Nationale, lat. 776) and a sacramentary from Figeac (Paris, Bibliothèque Nationale, lat. 2293). From St. Sever in the Gascogne comes the only French copy of the Commentary on the Apocalypse, composed about 776 by the Asturian monk Beatus of Liébana (Paris, Bibliothèque Nationale, lat. 8878). The illustrations of this mid-eleventh-century Apocalypse of St. Sever are based on the same picture cycle used in tenth-century Spanish manuscripts. Instead of the flat shapes of the Spanish images with their strident colors, however, the French miniatures are executed in a linear style that advances to the threshold of the Romanesque by acknowledging rounded forms.

A very different approach to Romanesque concreteness is found in a series of manuscripts produced about the middle of the eleventh century at the abbey of St. Germain-des-Prés in Paris. A psalter and hymnal (Paris, Bibliothèque Nationale, lat. 11550) and a *Life and Miracles of St. Germanus* (Paris, Bibliothèque Nationale, lat. 12610) contain some delicately modeled drawings against purple or green grounds. While based on the expressive idiom of Carolingian Rheims, they have a linear coherence tentatively suggestive of forms in relief.

Finally, Normandy—especially the abbey of Mont-Saint-Michel—developed its own characteristic style from about 975 onward, first from Carolingian and Anglo-Saxon sources and, later, from northern French and Ottonian inspirations. The most extensively illuminated Norman manuscript preserved is a sacramentary dating between 1050 and 1065 (New York, Pierpont Morgan Library, MS 641). It contains numerous historiated initials

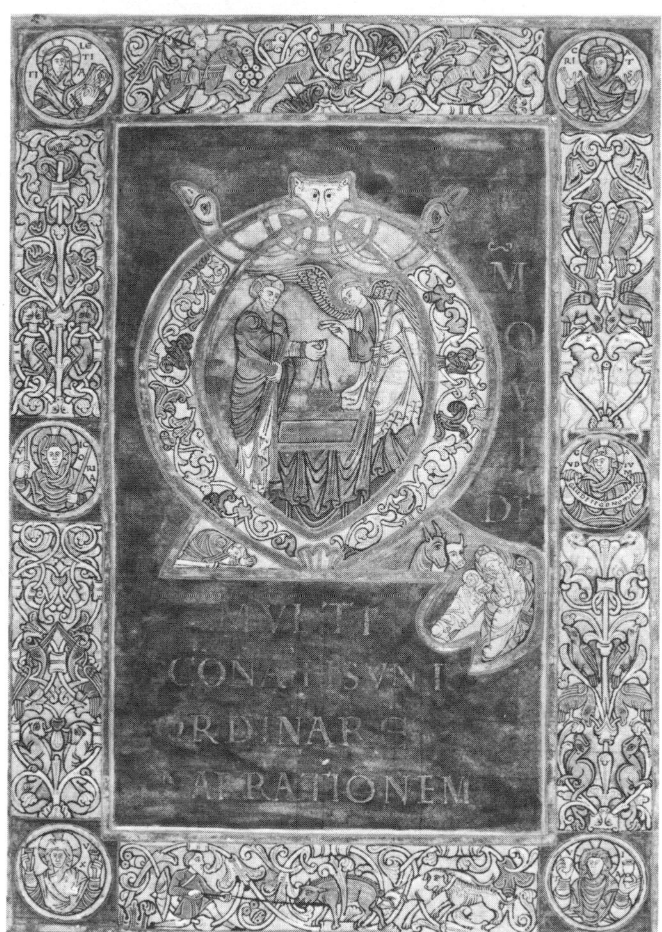

Initial page of Matthew from the Gospelbook illuminated by Abbot Odbert of St. Bertin, 990–1012. NEW YORK PIERPONT MORGAN LIBRARY, MS 333, fol. 51

as well as pages with figurative scenes. The frames of two full-page initials are of "Winchester" origin, while all others have a simpler design combining Franco-Saxon decorative schemes with a running acanthus motive of Ottonian type. Ottonian influence also underlies certain pictorial formulas, but the figure style is derived from late-tenth-century Anglo-Saxon painting, although the contours are hardened and the draperies are cast into repetitive patterns.

Sculpture and metalwork. Various tenth- and eleventh-century accounts tell of the existence of metal-sheathed reliquary statues of the Virgin and of saints, particularly in the regions of Rouergue, Auvergne, and Languedoc. Only the famous statue of the enthroned St. Fides (St. Foy) at Conques has survived to testify to a tradition reaching back to Carolingian times and forward to the Romanesque

PRE-ROMANESQUE ART

wooden Madonnas of France. After the translation of the saint's head to Conques between 856 and 882, a late antique head was joined to a rough wooden core in gold casing. The present appearance of the work is, however, mainly the result of a renovation made probably after 984 and certainly before Bernard of Angers described the statue in his *Liber miraculorum sancte fidis,* written between 1007 and 1029. Later centuries added further details. Centuries of devotion also left their traces on another reliquary at Conques. A small house-shaped shrine associated with either Pepin the Short (le Bref), duke of Aquitaine (751–768), or Pepin I, king of Aquitaine (817–838), contains eighth- as well as ninth-century embossed gold plaques, gems, and enamels to which filigree decoration and a Crucifixion group in gold repoussé were added in the early eleventh century. (See illustration at "Reliquary.")

Figurative architectural sculptures, still rare in eleventh-century France, deserve mention as preludes to the Romanesque. The crudely carved monster capitals of about 1018 at St. Bénigne, Dijon, for instance, or the mid-eleventh-century capitals with biblical and christological scenes from St. Germain-des-Prés and at St. Benoît-sur-Loire initiated the vast repertoire of subjects on Romanesque capitals. Romanesque portal sculpture has antecedents in the marble lintel of 1019–1020 at St. Génis-des-Fontaines in the eastern Pyrenees with Christ in Majesty between six apostles carved in low relief. A somewhat later lintel at St. André-de-Sorède combines a similar composition with a window frame showing the symbols of the Evangelists, the seraphim, and angels blowing horns, the whole forming an abridged representation of the Last Judgment, the first one known in architectural sculpture.

ITALY

While a source and a conduit of late antique and Byzantine inspirations to the north, pre-Romanesque Italy remained an artistic backwater, its local traditions subject to external influences or conquests. The south was occupied in turn by the Byzantines, the Arabs, and the Normans, while the north was largely controlled first by the Carolingians and then by the Ottonians.

Mosaics and paintings. The Frankish alliance with the papacy encouraged artistic activity in Rome, where old churches were restored and received new mosaics or wall paintings. In 799 Pope Leo III (*r.* 795–816) commissioned mosaics in the Triclinium of the old Lateran Palace, which contained an image of St. Peter giving the pallium to Pope Leo and the banner of Rome to Charles, king of the Franks. Under Pope Pascal I (*r.* 817–824) Sta. Prassede, Sta. Cecilia, and Sta. Maria in Domnica, and under Gregory IV (*r.* 827–844) S. Marco, received mosaic decorations that deliberately took up Early Christian compositions, while their hardened style betrays the ninth-century date. Frescoes in the lower church of S. Clemente show early Byzantine influence. The most powerful of these ex-voto images is an Ascension flanked by the donor, Pope Leo IV (*r.* 847–855), and St. Vitus. The contrast between the frontal stillness of the two framing figures and the Apostles' violent gestures heightens the impact of the painting, whose sacred aspect was made manifest by a relic embedded in the center of the scene, a stone said to have come from the actual site of the Ascension. Related in style are the mid-ninth-century frescoes, representing scenes from the life of St. Zacharias, in Sta. Sofia at Benevento as well as the paintings in the crypt of Sta. Maria in Insula in the Benedictine monastery of S. Vincenzo al Volturno. Built by Abbot Epiphanius (824–842), the cruciform vaulted crypt contains the most extensive pre-Romanesque fresco cycle surviving in southern Italy.

By the end of the ninth century, artistic vitality in Italy was spent, as it was in the north. It was only with the arrival of the Ottonians on the Italian stage that activity resumed, particularly in Lombardy. Among the few preserved monuments reflecting the quality of Milanese art, the frescoes of S. Vincenzo a Galliano are the most impressive. The church, consecrated in 1007, was a donation of Aribert, whom Emperor Henry II appointed archbishop of Milan in 1018. The apse contains Christ in Glory flanked by two archangels and the prophets Jeremiah and Ezechiel, while remains below show episodes from the life of St. Vincent. Painted in luminous cool colors, the figures have a monumentality and a passionate sweep of gesture that recalls the art of the Reichenau, a connection already mentioned in regard to a group of Ottonian ivories. Indeed, the style of these ivories is related to the figural compositions in gilded and painted stucco which adorn the early-eleventh-century ciborium above the altar in S. Ambrogio, Milan.

The revival of monumental painting and other arts in southern Italy was launched from St. Benedict's monastery at Monte Cassino by Abbot Desiderius (1058–1086). The frescoes of the Cassinensian church of S. Angelo in Formis, dating between 1072 and 1087, belong, however, already to the history of Romanesque art in their new fusion of Western and mid-Byzantine elements.

Illuminations. Monasteries associated with Monte Cassino developed in the second half of the tenth century a uniquely south Italian version of illustrated manuscripts—liturgical rolls for the Easter ritual: the benediction of the baptismal font and the blessing of the Paschal candle with the hymn "Exultet iam angelica turba caelorum . . ." (Let the angelic heavenly host rejoice). The miniatures, executed as colored outline drawings, are inverted in the text, which allowed the congregation to see them while the deacon read and unrolled the parchment over the edge of the pulpit. Twenty-eight Exultet Rolls have been preserved either whole or in fragment. The earliest, its figural style close to the frescoes of S. Vincenzo al Volturno, was made between 981 and 987 at Benevento (Vatican Library, lat. 9820), while the latest dates from the thirteenth century. Apart from some subjects which appear in nearly all the rolls, for instance Christ's Descent into Limbo, the choice of images differs from roll to roll as determined by the text. There are narrative scenes from the Old and New Testaments, liturgical scenes such as the lighting of the Paschal candle, genre scenes illustrating the Praise of the Bees who provide wax for the candle, as it appears, for example, in a roll made at Bari around 1000 (Bari, Cathedral, MS 1). There are allegorical images showing personifications of the Earth or the Church and illustrations to prayers for intercession with portraits of emperors, princes, donors, and benefactors. The chronological sequence of the Exultet Rolls charts the stylistic development of south Italian illumination, which came under increasing Byzantine influence. This influence reached its height after the middle of the century, as exemplified by a roll produced about 1060 at Monte Cassino during the abbacy of Desiderius (London, British Library, Add. MS 30337).

Except for the Exultet Rolls, Italian pre-Romanesque scriptoria had neither the continuity of output nor the quality of contemporary production as found in northern Europe. Of some interest, however, is a south Italian herbarium and treatise on surgery, whose rude outline drawings of medical operations depend on a late antique model (Florence, Biblioteca Laurenziana, MS Plut. 73, 41), or the early-eleventh-century *Codex legum Langobardorum* and *Capitula regum Francorum* with rustic colored drawings of scenes and personages referring to the Lombard and Carolingian dynasties (Cava dei Tirreni, MS 4). Unique is the manuscript of Hrabanus Maurus, *De universo aut rerum naturis,* produced in 1023 at Monte Cassino. Its 361 illustrations present a compendium of the encyclopedic knowledge of the early Middle Ages, but the primitive style of the colored drawings has little merit (Monte Cassino, MS 132). North Italian illumination reflects transalpine influences that are translated into various provincial versions: a Psalter probably produced at Milan during the last quarter of the tenth century (Vatican Library, lat. 83); a gradual of 1039 from Nonantola (Rome, Biblioteca Angelica); and the Sacramentary of Bishop Warmund of Ivrea of about 1000 (Ivrea, Chapter Library, cod. 82,2).

SPAIN

The Iberian Peninsula, cut off from the rest of Europe by geography and with most of her lands occupied by Muslim invaders, remained outside the mainstreams of pre-Romanesque Western art.

Paintings. Late antique and Visigothic traditions and a preference for nonfigural imagery underlie the art of the kingdom of Asturias during the late eighth and the first half of the ninth centuries. Wall paintings in Asturian churches, for example that of S. Julián de los Prados (Santullano) in Oviedo, built by King Alfonso II (791/792–842), consist only of architectural tableaux reminiscent of celestial palace images in Early Christian mosaics at Ravenna and Thessaloniki. Similarly, the decoration of a singular early(?)-ninth-century Bible (Cava dei Tirreni, MS 1) is restricted to crisply executed ornamental initials and crosses.

Remains of figurative frescoes exist in Catalonia, which was less insulated from Europe than other parts of Spain. Three churches at Tarrasa, variously dated to the early ninth or the early eleventh century, have paintings whose rustic linearity has been compared to drawings in manuscripts. Two surviving eleventh-century Catalan Bibles, the Ripoll Bible (Vatican Library, lat. 5729) and the Roda Bible (Paris, Bibliothèque Nationale, lat. 6), are of great interest for their unprecedented number of illustrations that preserve parts of Early Christian cycles.

Illuminations. Spanish art came into its own in the train of the *Reconquista,* launched by Alfonso III (*r.* 866–911), which fostered renewed activity in

 PRE-ROMANESQUE ART

the monastic scriptoria of Asturias and León during the first half of the tenth century. A Bible written and illuminated in 920 (León, Cathedral, cod. 6) represents an early phase of the style known as Mozarabic, meaning arabicized, although Muslim features are not prevalent. The Gospel frontispieces show angels enclosed in a circle, each bearing the symbol of an evangelist on its shoulder, the whole forming patterns of multicolored bands. (See illustration at "John of S. Martín de Albares.") In miniatures of a copy of St. Gregory's *Moralia in Job,* produced in 945 in the monastery of Valeránica by the scribe Florentius (Madrid, Biblioteca Nacional, cod. 80) and in a Bible of 960 containing portraits of Florentius and his disciple Sanctius congratulating each other upon completion of their work (León, Colegiata de S. Isidoro, cod. 2), the figures present themselves more coherently as flatly silhouetted shapes with staring eyes. An artistic naiveté in drawing is offset by the striking effect of harsh color combinations. (See illustration at "Sanctius.") The initials of the *Moralia in Job,* on the other hand, recall the Carolingian Franco-Saxon style.

The Bible of 960 contains numerous Old Testament illustrations largely derived from a late antique narrative cycle, possibly through the intermediary of a lost Visigothic Bible. The most original Spanish contribution to medieval art, however, was the cycle of illustrations to the Commentary on the Apocalypse compiled around 776 by the Asturian monk Beatus of Liébana, to which was often added St. Jerome's commentary to the Book of Daniel. The apocalyptic visions of strife and final victory over malevolent powers were of particular relevance to the continuing struggle against Islam and internal heresy. More than twenty surviving Beatus manuscripts, from the tenth to the thirteenth century, attest to their popularity.

It is thought that Beatus' text was accompanied by illustrations already during his lifetime (*ca.* 798), but the earliest preserved copy dates to the middle of the tenth century. It was produced by the painter and scribe Maius (Magius) in a monastery of St. Michael's, perhaps S. Miguel de Escalada (New York, Pierpont Morgan Library, MS 644). The colophon of another Beatus manuscript from the monastery of S. Salvador de Tábara mentions that the *archipictor* Maius died there in 968 and that his disciple, the monk Emeterius, completed the task in 970 (Madrid, Archivo Histórico Nacional, cod. 1240). Emeterius' name appears again, this time in collaboration with the monk Senior and a *pintrix,* a nun named Ende, in the Gerona Beatus which, dated 975, was probably also made at Tábara (Gerona, Cathedral, MS 7). (See illustration at "Ende.")

The range of themes illustrated goes far beyond that in Carolingian, Ottonian, or even later Apocalypses. Beginning and ending with decorative full-page renderings of the letters Alpha and Omega, the manuscripts contain, besides images depicting the visions of St. John, illustrations of the Book of Daniel and Beatus' commentary. To these are added portraits of the Evangelists with Witnesses; genealogical tables of the four pre-Christian ages; sometimes a bird killing a serpent, signifying Christ's defeat of the Devil; and the Victory Cross of Oviedo, symbol of the *Reconquista.* The miniatures, repeatedly spread over two facing pages, translate the text into a powerfully direct imagery. Without any concession to natural appearances, the painters evoked the visions of the "last events" by intense colors, flatly applied in startling juxtapositions, and by the raw force of simply drawn shapes. In the last Beatus manuscript painted in the Mozarabic style, begun in 1091 and completed in 1109 at the monastery of S. Domingo de Silos (London, British Library, add. MS 11695), color and pattern are still the prime means of expression, but the miniatures display a new sense of abstract order in composition as well as in the strictness of figural design. Some paintings in the later portion of the manuscript hint at the artist's knowledge of French Romanesque art.

Sculpture and metalwork. Spain's artistic isolation came to an end as a result of the expansive policies set in motion by Ferdinand I the Great, king of León and Castile (*r.* 1037–1065), and his ties with the Burgundian abbey of Cluny. While the Beatus manuscript made by Facundus for Ferdinand and his wife, Sancha, in 1047 (Madrid, Biblioteca Nacional, cod. Vit. 14-2) shows a particularly elegant version of Mozarabic art, their prayer book of 1055 (Santiago de Compostela, Bibliotheca de la Universidad, Res. 1) contains a dedication page which reveals northern influence in iconography and style. (See illustration at "Fructuosus.") Works in metal and ivory donated by Ferdinand and Sancha to S. Isidoro at León also testify to the impact of northern examples. While the great Victory Cross presented in 908 by Alfonso III (*r.* 866–910) to the cathedral of Oviedo displays Mozarabic taste by the brilliant chromatic effect of

PRE-ROMANESQUE ART

its precious stones and colored glass paste inlays, the large ivory cross given by Ferdinand I and Sancha to S. Isidoro in 1063 (Madrid, Museo Arqueológico) relates by the style of its carvings as much to the earlier prayer book as it anticipates the forms of Romanesque sculpture. One source of this development is intimated by the reliquary shrine of St. Isidor, part of the donation of 1063 (León, Treasury of S. Isidoro). Its partly gilt silver repoussé reliefs with scenes from Genesis bear a remarkable resemblance to the reliefs of Bishop Bernward's bronze doors at Hildesheim. Drapery patterns, however, are more tightly organized and compositions more strictly related to their frames, both features of the nascent Romanesque.

Indeed, Spanish metalwork and ivories of the second half of the eleventh century—including the ivory plaques of standing Apostles of the reliquary of Sts. John the Baptist and Pelagius of 1059 (León, Treasury of S. Isidoro), as well as the carvings of the shrine of St. Millán dating between 1053 and 1067 (abbey of S. Millán de la Cogolla, Rioja)—are striking witnesses of Spain's entry into the world of the European Romanesque.

The Ancient of Days with Vision of the Four Beasts. Miniature from Beatus' *Commentary on the Apocalypse.* S. Domingo de Silos, 1091–1109. BY PERMISSION OF THE BRITISH LIBRARY, LONDON, ADD. MS 11695, fol. 240r

BIBLIOGRAPHY

General works. John Beckwith, *Early Medieval Art* (1964); Caecilia Davis-Weyer, *Early Medieval Art, 300–1150* (1971); C. R. Dodwell, *Painting in Europe, 800 to 1200* (1971); Victoria H. Elbern, ed., *Das erste Jahrtausend: Kultur und Kunst im werdenden Abendland an Rhein und Ruhr,* 3 vols. (1962–1964); André Grabar and Carl Nordenfalk, *Early Medieval Painting* (1957); Ernst Kitzinger, *Early Medieval Art in the British Museum* (1940, 2nd ed. 1955, repr. 1960, 1963, 1969); Peter Lasko, *Ars Sacra, 800–1200* (1972); Percy Ernst Schramm and Florentine Mütherich, *Denkmale der deutschen Könige und Kaiser* (1962), and Schramm, *Die deutschen Kaiser und Könige in Bildern ihrer Zeit* (1983); Hans Swarzenski, *Monuments of Romanesque Art* (1954, 2nd ed. 1967).

Carolingian art. Wolfgang Braunfels, *Die Welt der Karolinger und ihre Kunst* (1968); Adolf Goldschmidt, *Die Elfenbeinskulpturen aus der Zeit der karolingischen und sächsischen Kaiser,* I (1914, repr. 1969); Roger Hinks, *Carolingian Art* (1935, repr. 1962); Jean Hubert, Jean Porcher, and Wolfgang F. Volbach, *The Carolingian Renaissance* (1970); *Karl der Grosse: Lebenswerk und Nachleben,* Wolfgang Braunfels, ed., 4 vols. (1965–1967); Herbert L. Kessler, *The Illustrated Bible from Tours* (1977); Wilhelm Koehler, *Die karolingischen Miniaturen,* I–III (1930–1960), and, with Florentine Mütherich, IV–V (1971–1982), and *Buchmalerei des frühen Mittelalters: Fragmente und Entwürfe aus dem Nachlass,* Ernst Kitzinger and Florentine Mütherich, eds. (1972); Florentine Mütherich and Joachim E. Gaehde, *Carolingian Painting* (1977); Julius von Schlosser, *Schriftquellen zur Geschichte der karolingischen Kunst* (1892, repr. 1974); *Utrecht Psalter: Vollständige Faksimile-Ausgabe im Originalformat der Hanschrift 32 aus dem Besitz der Bibliothek der Rijksuniversiteit te Utrecht,* Koert van der Horst and Jacobus H. A. Engelbregt, eds. (1984).

Ottonian art. Peter Bloch and Hermann Schnitzler, *Die ottonische Kölner Malerschule,* 2 vols. (1967–1969); Adolf Goldschmidt, *Die Elfenbeinskulpturen aus der Zeit der karolingischen und sächsischen Kaiser,* II (1914, repr. 1970); Louis Grodecki, Florentine Mütherich, Jean Taralon, and Francis Wormald, *Le siècle de l'an mil* (1973), 87–188, 261–308, 339–348; Hans Jantzen, *Ottonische Kunst* (1947, repr. 1959); Otto Lehmann-Brockhaus, *Schriftquellen zur Kunstgeschichte des 11. und 12. Jahrhunderts für Deutschland, Lothringen und Italien,* 2 vols. (1938); Carl Nordenfalk, "Der Meister des Registrum Gregorii," in *Münchner Jahrbuch der bildenden Kunst,* 3rd ser., **1** (1950), 61–77, and "The Chronology of the Registrum Master," in *Kunsthistorische Forschungen: Otto Pächt zu seinem 70. Geburtstag* (1972), 62–70; Georg Swarzenski, *Die Regensburger Buchmalerei des 10. und 11. Jahrhunderts* (1901), and *Die Salzburger Malerei von den erstan Anfängen bis zur Blütezeit des romanischen Stils,* 2 vols. (1908–1913); R. Wesenberg, *Bernwardische Plastik, zur ottonischen Kunst unter Bischof Bernward von Hildesheim* (1955).

Anglo-Saxon art. Louis Grodecki *et al., Le siècle de l'an mil* (1973), 227–254, 317–320; Otto Homburger, "L'art carolingien de Metz et l'école de Winchester," in *Gazette des Beaux-Arts,* **62** (1963); Thomas D. Kendrick, *Late Saxon and Viking Art* (1949); David Talbot Rice, *English Art 871–1100* (1952); Elzbieta Temple, *Anglo-Saxon Manuscripts, 900–1066,* II (1976).

French art. Jonathan J. G. Alexander, *Norman Illumination at Mont St. Michel, 966–1100* (1970); Louis Grodecki *et al., Le siècle de l'an mil* (1973), 189–208, 321–330; Jean Porcher, *French Miniatures from Illuminated Manuscripts* (1960).

Italian art. Myrtilla Avery, *The Exultet Rolls of South Italy,* II (1936); Hans Belting, *Studien zur beneventanischen Malerei* (1968); Geza de Francovich, "Arte carolingia ed ottoniana in Lombardia," in *Römisches Jahrbuch für Kunstgeschichte,* **6** (1942–1944); Louis Grodecki *et al., Le siècle de l'an mil* (1973), 221–225, 309–313; Janine Wettstein, *Sant'Angelo in Formis et la peinture médiévale en Campagne* (1960).

Spanish art. Jesús Domínguez Bordona, *Spanish Illumination,* 2 vols. (1930, repr. 1969); Jacques Fontaine, *L'art préroman hispanique,* 2 vols. (1973–1977); Louis Grodecki *et al., Le siècle de l'an mil* (1973), 209–220, 331–337; Peter K. Klein, *Der ältere Beatus-Kodex Vitr. 14–1 der Biblioteca Nacional zu Madrid,* 2 vols. (1976); Wilhelm Neuss, *Die katalanische Bibelillustration um die Wende des ersten Jahrtausends und die altspanische Buchmalerei* (1922), and *Die Apokalypse des Hl. Johannes in der altspanischen und altchristlichen Bibelillustration,* 2 vols. (1931); Pedro de Palol and M. Hirmer, *Spanien: Kunst des frühen Mittelalters vom Westgotenreich bis zum Ende der Romanik* (1965), 34–35, 44–46; Helmut Schlunk, *Arte visigodo, arte asturiano* (1947); John Williams, *Early Spanish Manuscript Illumination* (1977).

JOACHIM E. GAEHDE

[See also **Aachen Palace Chapel; Anglo-Saxon Art; Beatus Manuscripts; Bernward; Bible; Bronze and Brass; Carolingians and the Carolingian Empire; Codex Aureus; Crucifixion; Emeterius of Tábara; Enamel; Evangeliary; Exultet Roll; Fulda; Germany: 843–1137; Gospelbook; Ivory Carving; Liuthard; Lombard Art; Maius; Manuscript Illumination, European; Metalsmiths, Gold and Silver; Migration and Hiberno-Saxon Art; Mozarabic Art; Obeco; Paliotto of S. Ambrogio; Pericope; Psalter; Reliquary; Renaissances and Revivals in Medieval Art; Repoussé; Romanesque Art; Sacramentary; Tuotilo; Utrecht Psalter; Wolvinius of Milan.**]

PRESBYTERIUM designates, first of all, the gathering of the priests of a diocese insofar as they share the jurisdictional and liturgical responsibilities of their bishop. But the term also has an architectural use, referring to the separate area of the church building, screened off or separated by means of railing, curtains, or other barrier from the laity, for the accommodation of the priests. In the Early Christian period the presbyterium was located behind the altar, in that part of the basilica more commonly called the apse, where a synthronon, or semicircular bench, often raised on steps, provided seating for the priests on either side of the bishop's throne. The grouping of the priests around their bishop was seen as parallel to the community of the apostles with Christ. In later medieval architecture the presbyterium was assimilated into the choir.

BIBLIOGRAPHY

Johannes Jahn, *Wörterbuch der Kunst* (1957), 31; Richard Krautheimer, *Early Christian and Byzantine Architecture* (1965).

THOMAS F. MATHEWS

[See also **Apse; Architecture, Liturgical Aspects (with illustration); Basilica; Choir; Church, Early; Clergy; Early Christian and Byzantine Architecture; Synthronon.**]

PRESENTATION IN THE TEMPLE. According to Jewish custom, the firstborn child is dedicated to Yahweh (Exod. 13). Jesus was taken by his parents for such a dedication, where a sacrifice of doves was made to release him from service in the temple (Luke 2:22–40).

Iconographically, the scene of the Presentation in the Temple is often combined with two other biblically related incidents: the purification of the Mother (Lev. 12) and the meeting of the Holy Family and Simeon (Luke 2:25). In the fourth century, Hypapante, a special feast dedicated to the Presentation in the Temple, was established in the Eastern church. The Hypapante type, or a scene including Simeon, is popular in Byzantine depictions of the presentation scene. By the late fifth or early sixth century, this feast was also celebrated in

PRESENTATION, RIGHT OF

the Western church. Charlemagne also declared the observation of the Purification of Mary in the Western church. This celebration concerns the blessing of candles, hence the name Candlemas. By the twelfth and thirteenth centuries, all three scenes were depicted in one: the Christ Child in the temple meeting with Simeon attended by witnesses holding candles. In the West, the Presentation generally takes place at an altar at which Mary hands the Christ Child to Simeon. This sacrificial altar may serve as a prefiguration of Christ's expiatory death.

BIBLIOGRAPHY

André Grabar, *Christian Iconography: A Study of Its Origins* (1967); Frederick Hartt, *History of Italian Renaissance Art* (1969); Ernst Kitzinger, *The Art of Byzantium and the Medieval West* (1976); Gertrud Schiller, *Iconography of Christian Art,* 2nd ed., Janet Seligman, trans., 2 vols. (1971–1972).

JENNIFER E. JONES

The Presentation in the Temple. Panel by Ambrogio Lorenzetti for Siena Cathedral, 1342; now in the Uffizi, Florence. PHOTO: ALINARI/ART RESOURCE

PRESENTATION, RIGHT OF, the key element in the canon law of patronage (*ius patronatus*) developed during the twelfth and thirteenth centuries in the aftermath of the Gregorian reform of the church. It conferred upon the patron (either an individual or a corporate person such as a monastery or cathedral chapter the right to present a candidate for the collation of a benefice. This right of presentation was tantamount to a right of appointment.

The steep decline of urban civilization in the late Roman Empire and the concurrent spread of Christianity throughout the countryside fostered the foundation of churches and chapels on local initiative. Bishops and monks played a role in this, but most churches sprang from the generosity of great lay magnates, who in turn considered them their own and appointed clerics to serve in them with little concern for episcopal authority. The devolution of nearly all political and military power upon the incoming Germanic peoples hastened this process, for these peoples had little understanding of the old Roman notion of public office. Indeed one of the first historians to study this matter systematically, Ulrich Stutz, regarded such private ownership of churches (*Eigenkirche*) and the consequent lordship (*dominium*) over them as essentially a Germanic feature rooted in pagan times, when Germanic lords acted as priests in their own houses and temples. But recent historians suggest it may be more accurate to say that the entire West, to varying degrees at different times and places, lost nearly all conception of a public law or public office, so that lordship eventually became all, a lordship exercised at once over persons and property with little sense of distinction between them.

Several Carolingian prelates (notably Agobard of Lyons and Hincmar of Rheims) protested the resulting abuses, and Carolingian conciliar legislation insisted that country priests be examined and installed by their bishops, but extensive and genuinely effective protest had to await the Gregorian reform movement. The reformers could not overturn centuries of ingrained custom, especially at the local level, although many lords in an act of piety donated their churches to religious houses. The reformers did insist, however, that all lay investiture cease and that clerics be installed through ecclesiastical channels. Henceforth bishops alone, in most instances, could appoint clerics to a particular benefice (this word is itself a reminder of how office had become almost inextricably confused with property), but the founding or controlling lords and religious houses retained the right to present candidates to the bishop.

The pertinent canon law was worked out most extensively by Pope Alexander III (*r.* 1159–1181) and the canonists of the later twelfth century; the form they had given it by the early thirteenth century held with remarkably little variation down through the Middle Ages and beyond. The patron's right was based theoretically upon his act of foundation. In response to the reformers, lords spoke first of electing their candidates, but from about 1160, with the support of Pope Alexander, the term "presentation" gained general usage. Pope Alexander insisted that bishops reject unsuitable candidates, especially the sons of priests, and the *Glossa ordinaria* says they may do so without proving any specific fault. But the presumption remained that the patron's right of presentation was in effect a right of selection which would only rarely be overturned. To accommodate such necessary changes, a right of variation permitted the patron to present an alternate candidate. From the time of Pope Innocent III (*r.* 1198–1216), canon law forbade self-presentation, but it permitted the presentation of sons and nephews. In sum, the reformers managed to gain mastery of the church in principle, a notable legal and ecclesiastical achievement, but they could not radically alter the underlying social realities.

BIBLIOGRAPHY

Peter Landau, *Ius patronatus: Studien zur Entwicklung des Patronats im Dekretalenrecht und der Kanonistik des 12. and 13. Jahrhunderts* (1975); Ulrich Stutz, "Patronat" and "Eigenkirche, Eigenkloster," in *Real-Encyklopädie für protestantische Theologie und Kirche,* 3rd ed., XV (1904) and XXIII (1913), and "The Proprietary Church as an Element of Mediaeval Germanic Ecclesiastical Law," in Geoffrey Barraclough, ed., *Mediaeval Germany, 911–1250,* II (1938); Paul Thomas, *Le droit de propriété des laïques sur les églises et le patronage laïque au moyen âge* (1906).

JOHN VAN ENGEN

[See also **Agobard; Benefice; Church, Latin: 1054 to 1305; Hincmar of Rheims; Investiture and Investiture Conflict; Law, Canon: After Gratian; Reform, Idea of.**]

PRESTER JOHN (Presbyter Johannes, Presbyter Joannes, Prestre Johan, Prete Gianni, Prestre Jehan, Pretre Jean, King Johannes, John the Priest), a legendary Christian potentate who, during the Middle Ages, was believed to have ruled in the Far East, India, or Ethiopia. There was speculation that he had broken up and brought under his dominion various Muslim forces in his area and was ready to come to the rescue of the crusaders. In the middle of the twelfth century, when European international prospects seemed rather gloomy and depressing, this sensational story flashed a ray of hope for the Christian world.

The first known medieval writer to acknowledge the power and prestige of Prester John was Otto of Freising, whose *Chronicon* (*ca.* 1145) gives a summary of a report made by Hugh, bishop of Jabala, who was visiting Europe in 1145, concerning a certain Nestorian priest-king called John. This John was said to be a descendant of the Magi, ruler of a land on the other side of Armenia in the Far East, who had led his army to victory over the Persians and neighboring peoples and was proceeding to Jerusalem when he was stopped by unfavorable climatic conditions.

About this time there appeared a fabulous letter attributed to the priest-king himself, allegedly written around 1165, and first mentioned by Alberich of Trois Fontaines in his 1241 chronicle. The letter was written to Manuel I Komnenos but was also addressed to the German emperor Frederick I Barbarossa, Louis VII of France, the king of Portugal, and other European princes. Beyond its original political intent, parts of the letter were turned into medieval rhyme and sung by ubiquitous minstrels all over Europe. The message itself depicts Prester John as a mighty and ideal ruler over a colorful and utopian state where everyone was well-to-do and where law reigned; a land of enchanted castles, vast wealth, pepper forests, crystal-clear emerald waters, monstrous animals, and other marvels. Most significantly, it affirms the king's intention to visit Jerusalem in the near future. Whether in a supposed response to this message or because of his own initiative, Pope Alexander III wrote a letter to the king of Ethiopia on 27 September 1177 expressing the desire for an alliance with the fabled priest-king and sent it with his own personal physician, who never returned.

This utopian state and mighty Christian empire was first thought to be in Asia, with Genghis Khan as priest-king. But the devastation of Eastern Europe by the Mongol forces destroyed this belief. The idea of a Nestorian Christian ruler in the Far East persisted, however, with its accompanying exaggerated stories.

For example, Marco Polo, the Franciscan William of Rubruck, and the historian Bar Hebraeus identified the priest-king as Un-Khan, whom Genghis Khan had in fact overthrown.

But after almost two centuries of fruitless search for the priest-king from Georgia to Mongolia to India, the eyes of Europe turned toward Africa. John of Plano Carpini, and even Marco Polo, unintentionally pointed to Ethiopia as the home of Prester John.

The earliest known message of a European monarch to Ethiopia was written about 1400 by Henry IV of England and addressed to "King of Abyssinia, Priest John," who most probably was the emperor David (1382–1412). The letter refers to the latter monarch's intended second visit to the Holy Land and his desire to free the Holy Land from its Muslim domination. While there is yet no evidence that this particular letter was received by Emperor David, Ethiopian sources do indicate the arrival of friendly European letters of appeal about this time. In fact, in 1402, an Ethiopian delegation arrived in Europe, guided by Antonio Bartoli, an Italian who had actually then been living in Ethiopia. From this time onward, throughout the period of the reigns of Emperors Yishaq (1413–1430), Zar^ca Ya^cqob (1434–1468), and Ba^ceda Maryam (1468–1478), communication between Ethiopia and Europe accelerated: in 1430, the embassy of Jean, duke of Berry; in 1439–1441, the Ethiopian delegation at the Council of Florence; in 1448, the letter of Jean de Lastic, grand master of Rhodes; and other similar letters and missions took place until the discovery of the Cape of Good Hope, which opened the channels of communication even wider, culminating in the first accurate information about Ethiopia and the land of Prester John by Francisco de Almeida and Francisco Alvares.

That Ethiopia is the land of Prester John may not have been a novel idea. In the ninth century, for instance, Eldad ha-Dani popularized the view that there existed in the region of Ethiopia independent and powerful Jewish kingdoms of the ten lost tribes. The Jewish traveler Benjamin of Tudela, who was in the vicinity of Ethiopia in the second half of the twelfth century, also wrote of the existence of a mythical Jewish king, a ruler of utmost splendor over a realm situated somewhere in the midst of a vast desert. For the Jews, the news about the ten lost tribes was of course extremely exciting because it indicated the nearness of the coming of the long-expected Messiah. On the other hand, to Muslims and Christians, who believed that the Jews would never again be independent because they were destined to live under foreign rule forever, such news was foreboding. There is, in fact, a good possibility that the myth of Prester John may have been a Christian response to the Jewish legend; such apologetics may in turn have been translated into the hope for assistance by the crusaders in the Holy Land.

With the advent of actual European contact with Ethiopia, the legend of Prester John gradually disappeared.

BIBLIOGRAPHY

Marcus N. Adler, ed., *The Itinerary of Benjamin of Tudela* (1907); Francisco Alvares, *The Prester John of the Indies,* Lord Stanley of Alderley, trans., C. F. Beckingham and G. W. B. Huntingford, eds., 2 vols. (1961); John Buchan, *Prester John* (1910); Osbert G. S. Crawford, ed., *Ethiopian Itineraries, Circa 1400–1524* (1958); Francis C. Hingeston-Randolph, ed., *Royal and Historical Letters During the Reign of Henry the Fourth, King of England and France and Lord of Ireland* (1860, repr. 1964); Charles A. Kohler, "Documents relatifs à Guillaume Adam, archevêque de Sultanieh, puis d'Antivari, et son entourage (1318–1346)," in *Revue de l'orient latin,* **10** (1903–1904); Hiob Ludolf, *Historia aethiopica* (1681); Elaine Sanceau, *The Land of Prester John* (1944); Robert Silverberg, *The Realm of Prester John* (1972); Vsevolod Slessarev, *Prester John: The Letter and the Legend* (1959); William Woodville Rockhill, ed. and trans., *The Journey of William of Rubruck to the Eastern Parts of the World 1253–55, as Narrated by Himself, with Two Accounts of the Earlier Journey of John of Pian de Carpine* (1900); Henry Yule, ed. and trans., *The Book of Ser Marco Polo,* 3rd ed., rev. (1903).

EPHRAIM ISAAC

[See also **Abyssinia; Bar Hebraeus; Benjamin of Tudela; Exploration by Western Europeans; John of Plano Carpini; Nestorianism; Otto of Freising; Polo, Marco.**]

PRÉVÔT. See **Provost.**

PRICKINGS, the technical term for regular series of small perforations which usually appear in the margins of ancient and medieval books. Book producers punched these holes through several sheets simultaneously and then used them as the reference points between which guide lines could be drawn. In this way the writing lines appear in the same place on all the pages of one gathering or quire of a manuscript. Another kind of pricking seems to have guided the folding of sheets into quires. The type of instrument used and the patterns of both kinds of prickings provide useful clues as to the assembly and origin of manuscripts. Because prickings typically lie close to edges of pages, they have sometimes disappeared from books which have been trimmed and rebound.

BIBLIOGRAPHY

Léon Gilissen, *Prolégomènes à la codicologie* (1977), 107–114, 242–244; Leslie W. Jones, "Pricking Manuscripts: The Instruments and Their Significance," in *Speculum,* **21** (1946), and "Where Are the Prickings?" in *Transactions and Proceedings of the American Philological Association,* 75 (1944).

MICHAEL MCCORMICK

[See also **Manuscript Books, Production of; Pecia; Quire; Ruling.**]

PRIE-DIEU (French: pray [to] God). A piece of furniture used for private prayer, the prie-dieu comprises a lecternlike shelf set at an angle and a small padded strip for the knees. Depictions of the prie-dieu in late medieval manuscripts indicate that it was often draped with cloth. See, for example, the manuscript of the *Belles heures* of Jean, duke of Berry (New York, The Cloisters, fols. 91 and 91v).

BIBLIOGRAPHY

The Belles Heures of Jean, Duke of Berry, facsimile (1958); Millard Meiss and Elizabeth H. Beatson, *The Belles Heures of Jean, Duke of Berry* (1974).

WILLIAM J. DIEBOLD

[See also **Furniture, Liturgical.**]

PRIEST. See **Clergy.**

PRIMARY CHRONICLE, RUSSIAN. The *Primary Chronicle,* also known as *The Tale of Bygone Years,* is the earliest extant native narrative source for the history of the early Russian state. The opening lines state its purpose: to unfold the origins, formation, and history of the land of Rus. In the true biblical fashion it traces the origin of the Slavs to Japhet, Noah's third son, and quickly turns to the Slavic tribes, particularly those dwelling on the southern European steppe, who will become subject to the princes residing at Kiev, on the lower Dnieper River. The bulk of the narration deals with military, political, and religious developments until the early twelfth century.

The chronicle exists in two principal redactions—the Laurentian, dating from 1377, and the Hypatian, a compilation of the fifteenth century. Earlier scholars attributed the authorship of the original version to Nestor, a monk living in Kiev's famous Monastery of the Caves (Pecherskaya Lavra) during the late eleventh and early twelfth centuries. Twentieth-century opinion, founded upon careful textual examination, considers the chronicle to be the product of a succession of authors.

Given its importance for the history of the early Russian state, the chronicle has been a constant source of study and debate. There are obvious errors in the dating of events, particularly for the earlier period; internal inconsistencies; and factual mistakes. Tales, some of local origin and others modeled after foreign prototypes, particularly Scandinavian and Byzantine, were clothed in Russian dress and presented as unique historical events. Notable among these are the stories of Kiev's origin, the coming of the Vikings, Oleg's death, Olga's revenge, and the charming narration of Vladimir's conversion to Christianity. A lively, though not always edifying, debate has swirled around the so-called invitation theory. The chronicle alleged that the Varangians (Vikings) came and imposed tribute (around 860–862) on the Slavic tribes living in the Russian north near the Baltic Sea. These tribes soon rose in revolt and expelled the overlords, but then they could not live in peace with one another. So they invited three Varangian princes to rule over them. These three, Rurik and his younger brothers Sineus and Truvor, migrated to northern Russia with their retinues. After the death of his brothers, Rurik ruled alone, and from him the major princely lines descended.

In 1876 Vilhelm Thomsen delivered a series of lectures at Oxford stressing the Scandinavian origins of the early Russian state and the essential Nordic (Normanist) contribution to the development of Kievan political government, thereby touching off a controversy seemingly without end.

Russian nationalists and their Soviet counterparts have particularly resented the implications of Slavic backwardness in political, social, and cultural life. The "Normanists" and "anti-Normanists" do not dispute the Viking invasion, but rather the level of early Russian political and cultural organization and the contributions made by the invaders.

Despite its faults, the *Primary Chronicle* makes a unique contribution to the history of Kievan politics, wars, invasions, and connections with Byzantium. For most problems in Kiev's history the chronicle remains the only source.

BIBLIOGRAPHY

Sources. Povest vremennych let, Varvara P. Adrianova-Peretts, ed. (1950), containing the Laurentian text and modern Russian translation (vol. I) and the commentaries (vol. II); *Polnoe sobranie russkikh letopisei,* II (1843, 3rd ed. 1923), containing the Hypatian text; "The Russian Primary Chronicle," Samuel H. Cross, trans. and ed., in *Harvard Studies and Notes in Philology and Literature,* **12** (1930), the Laurentian text, revised in *The Russian Primary Chronicle: Laurentian Text,* Samuel H. Cross and Olgerd O. Sherbowitz-Wetzer, trans. and eds. (1953); Serge A. Zenkovsky, ed. and trans., *Medieval Russia's Epics, Chronicles, and Tales,* 2nd ed. (1974), which includes fragments from the *Primary Chronicle.*

Studies. Norah K. Chadwick, *The Beginning of Russian History* (1946); Henryk Paszkiewicz, *The Origin of Russia* (1954); Andrzej Poppe, "The Political Background to the Baptism of Rus: Byzantine-Russian Relations Between 986–89," in *Dumbarton Oaks Papers,* 30 (1976); Adolf Stender-Peterson, *Varangica* (1953); Vilhelm L. P. Thomsen, *The Relations Between Ancient Russia and Scandinavia and the Origin of the Russian State* (1877, repr. 1965); George Vernadsky and Michael Karpovich, *A History of Russia,* II, George Vernadsky, *Kievan Russia* (1948).

GUSTAVE ALEF

[See also **Kievan Rus; Rurik; Vladimir, St.**]

PRIMAS. See **Hugh (Primas) of Orléans.**

PRIMITIVE CHURCH, CONCEPT OF. The phrases *ecclesia primitiva* (primitive church) and *vita apostolica* (apostolic life) expressed the practice of the early church, conceived as a model for the perfect Christian life. During the early centuries, the life of the first Christian community at Jerusalem, described in Acts 2:42–47 and 4:32–37, was often cited as an example of Christian unity and generosity in almsgiving, but with emphasis on the continuity of apostolic tradition, and with little notion of the apostolic age as a distinct period. Nor were these passages usually thought to imply literal communism, which had pagan and heretical associations. But in the fourth century Eusebius (*Ecclesiastical History* 2.16–17) popularized the idea that the Christians of apostolic times had been communistic. The spread of monasticism gave rise to the belief that the cenobites imitated the way of life of the early church, principally in renouncing all private property. Thereafter, these passages in Acts and related New Testament passages were generally interpreted so as to suggest a literal communism that was no longer practiced by the church as a whole, except for monastic and other religious communities. This theme was canonized in the writings of Basil and other Greek fathers. It was supported by the pagan philosophical theory of communism as the state of nature, a state that Christians identified with Eden.

Latin Christianity developed the theme of the primitive church in distinct monastic and clerical versions. John Cassian (*ca.* 360–*ca.* 432/435) presented to Gallic monks the theory, based on Acts 15:28–29, that the common life had been abandoned by the apostles as a concession to the Gentile Christians; those who continued the *ecclesia primitiva* (a phrase coined by Cassian) withdrew into the cenobitic life, while the anchoritic life arose later, in the time of Anthony. Cassian thus created a myth of the primitive church that emphasized the decline of standards after the apostolic age, and established the notion of a primitive perfection that should serve as an ideal for later reforms.

At the same time, Augustine introduced the common life among his African clergy. Like Cassian he emphasized the imitation of Acts and thought the spread of Christianity to Gentiles had ended the primitive common life (*On Christian Doctrine* 3.6.10–11); but he saw the primitive church as a model for clergy as well as monks. During the early Middle Ages the two traditions were propagated by the houses of monks and of canons respectively, though the full common life was rarely enforced in houses of canons.

Certain Pseudo-Isidorian decretals, attributed to Popes Clement I (92–101), Urban I (222–230), and Miltiades (311–314), fixed these ideas in canon law and attempted to rationalize them. It was explained that the primitive church lived from alms until it accepted landed property in the time of Constantine. The primitive church was thus identified with the pre-Constantinian age and was associated not only with the common life but with the absence of endowments. As the acceptance of wealth was assumed to be a necessary result of the success of the church, the idealization of the primitive church did not denigrate the later church.

The Gregorian reform revived both the clerical and monastic versions of the theme. Augustine's program of the full common life for clergy was enforced by the papacy. A dossier of decretals compiled by Anselm of Lucca (*d.* 1086), including the Pseudo-Isidorian decretals described above, demonstrated the antiquity of the "regular canons," whose vita it traced through Augustine to the primitive church. (These decretals passed into Gratian's *Decretum, causa* 12.) It was supposed that the clerical common life had been relaxed after Augustine and had been revived in the time of Gregory VII.

At the same time the reformed monastic tradition, represented chiefly by the Cistercians, reaffirmed the traditional concept of monastic history, stressing continuity with the primitive church, the desert fathers, and the Benedictine Rule. The return to manual labor and rejection of tithes and other clerical revenues were the main points of the reform. The Cluniac and other traditional houses opposed the revival of manual labor, holding that the assumption of clerical status and revenues by monks was a necessary consequence of the endowment of the church by Constantine. This position, which became dominant as the reformers modified their original austerity, resembled the canonists' views in implying an acceptance of change in ecclesiastical institutions, as against the reformers' insistence on unqualified conformity to the primitive church.

In the early twelfth century several deviant movements appeared, eremitic rather than monastic, marked by mendicant poverty and itinerant preaching, and claiming to follow the Gospel precepts rather than the traditional common life. Most were quickly absorbed by the revived Benedictinism of the Cistercians. But at the end of the century, this tradition was revived in the Franciscan movement. The primitive Franciscans conceived their *religio* (order) as a direct imitation of the Gospel and arrogated the terms *primitiva ecclesia* and *vita apostolica* to their new way of life, which was distinguished by poverty, individual and common, and by mendicancy. This conception was early adopted by the Dominicans, who originally had considered themselves an order of regular canons with limited property, and was also adopted by the later orders of mendicant friars.

A clear mendicant "ideology" was not developed until the controversies with the secular clergy in the later thirteenth century. At the University of Paris in the 1250's, Bonaventure and Aquinas developed the doctrine of a double profession of poverty in the primitive church: one was for the perfect, consisting in renunciation of property both individual and common and in mendicancy, and had been established in the Gospel precepts; the other, the common life, was established in Christ's possession of a purse (John 12:6) and in the apostolic church of Acts. Mendicancy, it was claimed, prevailed during the period of the *ecclesia primitiva,* which ended when the church accepted landed property in the time of Constantine. The primitive standard had been continued by hermits, and in the thirteenth century it had been revived by Francis and Dominic.

There soon appeared a Franciscan variant of this theory, made official in the Friars Minor by Bonaventure's *Apologia pauperum* (1269). According to this theory, Christ and the apostles had rejected all legal ownership of goods, accepting only the "use" of goods; this was the legal situation of the Franciscan order established by the bull *Quo elongati* in 1230. The common life, entailing corporate possession of property, was practiced by the ordinary faithful in the primitive church and later by the cenobite monks and by all later orders except the Franciscans. Thus all orders could be traced to the primitive church, but only the Franciscans to the Apostles. This theory, to which Nicholas III gave official sanction in the bull *Exiit qui seminat* (1279), naturally led to polemics between the Franciscans and the other mendicant orders, all of which accepted some property.

The later disputes over Franciscan observance led Pope John XXII, in 1323, to reinterpret Franciscan poverty. He forced the order to accept legal ownership and declared that Christ and the apostles had held property in some degree. The earlier Franciscan belief in a primitive church completely devoid of juridical rights or property was continued by small groups of heretical Franciscans (Fraticelli). This belief inspired much criticism of the church by such thinkers as Marsilius of Padua, William of

Ockham, and John Wyclif. Through this channel, the conflicts over the nature of the primitive church deeply influenced speculation about church polity and property in the fourteenth and fifteenth centuries.

BIBLIOGRAPHY

The earlier Middle Ages (to 1250). Pier Cesare Bori, *Chiesa Primitiva: L'immagine della communità delle origini (Atti 2, 42–47, 4, 32–37) nella storia della chiesa antica* (1974); James Doyne Dawson, "The Tradition of the Apostles" (diss., Princeton, 1974); Gerhart Ladner, *The Idea of Reform* (1959); Jean Leclercq, *The Life of Perfection,* Leonard J. Doyle, trans. (1961); Giovanni Miccoli, "Ecclesiae primitivae forma," in his *Chiesa Gregoriana: Richerche sulla riforma del secolo xi* (1966); Glenn Olsen, "The Idea of the Ecclesia Primitiva in the Twelfth-century Canonists," in *Traditio,* **25** (1969), "Reference to the *Ecclesia Primitiva* in Eighth-century Irish Gospel Exegesis," in *Thought,* **54** (1979), "St. Boniface and the *Vita apostolica,*" in *American Benedictine Review,* **31** (1980), "Reform After the Pattern of the Primitive Church in the Thought of Salvian of Marseilles," in *Catholic Historical Review,* **68** (1982), "Bede as Historian: The Evidence from His Observations on the Life of the First Christian Community at Jerusalem," in *Journal of Ecclesiastical History,* **33** (1982), "The Image of the First Community of Christians at Jerusalem in the Time of Lafranc and Anselm," in France, Centre National de la Recherche Scientifique, Colloques Internationaux, *Les mutations socio-culturelles au tournant des XIe–XIIe siècles* (1984), "Reference to the Ecclesia Primitiva in the Decretum of Burchard of Worms," in Sixth International Congress of Medieval Canon Law, *Proceedings* (1980), and "From Bede to the Anglo-Saxon Presence in the Carolingian Empire," in Centro Italiano di Studi sull'Alto Medioevo, *Angli e Sassoni al di qua e al di là del mare nell'alto medioevo,* Settimane de Studio, **32** (1986); John Van Engen, "The 'Crisis of Cenobitism' Reconsidered: Benedictine Monasticism in the Years 1050–1150," in *Speculum,* **61** (1986); Marie-H. Vicaire, *The Apostolic Life,* W. De Naple, trans. (1966).

The later Middle Ages (after 1250). Yves M.-J. Congar, "Aspects ecclésiologiques de la querelle entre mendiants et séculiers dans la seconde moitié de XIIIe siècle et le debut de XIVe siècle," in *Archives d'histoire doctrinale et littéraire du moyen âge,* **36** (1961); James Doyne Dawson, "Richard FitzRalph and the Fourteenth-century Poverty Controversies," in *Journal of Ecclesiastical History,* **34** (1983); Cajetan Esser, *The Origins of the Franciscan Order,* Aedan Daly and Irina Lynch, trans. (1970); Malcolm D. Lambert, *Franciscan Poverty* (1961); Gordon Leff, *Heresy in the Later Middle Ages,* 2 vols. (1967); Louis B. Pascoe, "Jean Gerson: The Ecclesia Primitiva and Reform," in *Traditio,* **30** (1974).

JAMES DOYNE DAWSON

[See also **Benedictine Rule; Church, Early; Decretals, False; Dominicans; Franciscans; Friars; Heresies, Western European; Hermits, Eremitism; Mendicant Orders; Monasticism, Origins; Reform, Idea of;** and individual personalities.]

PRINCE (Latin: *princeps*) was second only to lord (*dominus*) as the most general term for a ruler or supervisor of a territory, a fortification, or a people in the Middle Ages. In the early days of the Roman Empire, the word, which we might loosely translate as "first citizen," was a euphemism designed to make palatable the assumption of absolute authority by Augustus, but as the real power of the emperor became a constitutionally accepted fact, the word lost the weak meaning of "first citizen." The following usages in medieval Latin are well attested: *princeps* could designate a king, a chieftain of a barbarian tribe (*princeps populi*), the Merovingian mayor of the palace, a duke, a count, a castellan (*princeps castri*), a bishop (*princeps civitatis*), or an abbot (*princeps monasterii*). In the plural, *principes* signified the more powerful or influential people (*proceres*) of a region or, especially, the imperial princes of the German nation (*Reichsfürstenstand*).

The abstract noun, *principatus,* designated suzerainty, rule, rulership, or the dignity of rulership, again especially as it pertained to the Holy Roman Empire; and it was widely used in these senses throughout the Middle Ages. On the other hand, the use of prince and princess (*principissa*) for the (legitimate) children of a reigning monarch became common only in the very late Middle Ages.

The word prince enjoyed a special place in the vocabulary of medieval political theory. The Renaissance treatises of Niccolò Machiavelli and Sir Walter Raleigh that bear the word in their titles recall a long tradition of medieval discussions of good and bad *principatus* exemplified in a number of works known as "mirrors of princes." The preference among writers for discussing good and evil rulership with a vocabulary based on the word *princeps* owes something, perhaps, to the liturgical formula for Jesus as the *Princeps Pacis* (Prince of Peace; Isa. 9:6) and for Satan as the *Princeps hujus mundi* (Prince of this world; John 12:31); but it certainly owes much more to the fact that a number of important maxims drawn from Roman law employed the word. Among these were two "absolutist" maxims that were extensively glossed, namely, "What pleases the prince has the force of law" (*Quod principi placuit legis habet vigorem;* cf. *Digest* 1, 4, 1) and "All the laws are in the secret place of the prince's breast" (*Omnia iura in scrinio pectoris principis est;* cf. *Code* 6, 23, 19, 1).

BIBLIOGRAPHY

On the genre known as "mirrors of princes," see the introduction to Jean-Philippe Genet, ed., *Four English Political Tracts of the Later Middle Ages* (1977). For a revealing explication of medieval discussions of the maxims quoted, see Ernst H. Kantorowicz, *The King's Two Bodies* (1957), 28, 95, 105, 106, 153, 455.

WILLIAM CHESTER JORDAN

[See also **Kingship, Theories of; Mirror of Princes; Political Theory.**]

PRINCE OF PRINCES. See **Archon ton Archonton.**

PRINTING, ORIGINS OF. The first press in Europe to produce printing with movable type was situated in Mainz and operated by Johannes Gutenberg. This press started printing around the year 1450, and by the end of 1455 it had probably completed the production of its first major work, a Latin Bible in two volumes. The activities in Mainz did not go unnoticed in the wider world, yet it was years before printing began to spread geographically. Printing outside Mainz was first carried out in the city of Bamberg by a former associate of Gutenberg, and possibly by Gutenberg himself.

The exact circumstances surrounding the spread of printing presses to new locations are often as obscure as those of the invention itself. It is clear, however, that in the first decade after 1455 Mainz was the center from which a band of experienced printers dispersed. They must have learned the craft in the workshop of Gutenberg and Johann Fust, or from either of them after the partners had gone their separate ways.

Printing was soon introduced into two cities, Strasbourg and Cologne, both of which were to make a great impact on the history of printing. In Strasbourg, Johannes Mentelin introduced printing by 1460; Ulrich Zel introduced printing to Cologne after he settled there in 1464. Later, as an old man, Zel reminisced about his early years in Mainz. His memories are recorded in the Cologne *Chronicle* (printed in 1499) and are a valuable source for the early spread of printing.

German printers soon introduced printing into Italy, which was to become the most prolific area of printing in the fifteenth century. In 1465, Conrad Sweynheym and Arnold Pannartz established a press in the Benedictine monastery of S. Scolastica in Subiaco, not far from Rome. It seems likely that Italy's first typographical enterprise was established on the initiative of one or more cardinals. Nicholas of Cusa, cardinal of S. Pietro in Vincoli, has been mentioned in particular.

The press in Rome differed in character and taste from the first Mainz press. It did not produce Bibles or liturgies but showed a definite humanistic influence. Classical and patristic texts were prepared for publication by its editor, Giovanni Andrea Bussi, bishop of Aleria. In prefaces to his work, Bussi expressed the wish to spread throughout the world texts which had so far remained unknown, and to make them accessible to people at every social level, as part of the new education of man. Perhaps the influence of Nicholas of Cusa can be detected here; he had been educated by the Brethren of the Common Life. Bussi edited the texts in order to make them acceptable to a wide readership. He emended the manuscripts available to him and rid them of obvious mistakes. He was the first editor who stated that he was conscious of a responsibility to his readers for the mass-produced text. This was a very significant step in the development of publishing in print. It should not be confused—as has been done by later scholars—with a sense of responsibility for the authenticity of the words of the ancient authors.

In 1469 production of printed books began in Venice, the next Italian city to harbor printing. The first press, that of the brothers de Spira (or von Speier), printed mainly classical authors. This was an enterprise on a purely commercial basis, without patronage of any kind.

Venice rapidly became the most important center of printing in Europe, both for production and for distribution. It was in Venice that printing established itself as a truly international trade. The lead was taken once again by German printers, Johannes de Spira and his brother Vindelinus (or Windelin), and also Johannes de Colonia and Johannes Manthen. They were soon followed by the Frenchman Nicolas Jenson, by native printers, by many

PRINTING, ORIGINS OF

other Germans, Frenchmen, and Dutchmen, and by a Cretan.

Venice overshadowed all other towns in the fifteenth century, both in production and as a center of trade. Initially, however, trade did not keep pace with production. In the early 1470's, Venice suffered from overproduction of classical texts, and there was a brief crisis in the industry. Ten years later a much larger production could find its way to remote corners of the reading world without apparent difficulty, thanks to the network of trade channels which had developed by that time.

Around 1470 printing was still confined to a few centers, ten in the German-speaking countries, five in Italy, perhaps one in the Netherlands, and one in France, where a flourishing press was established at the Sorbonne in 1470 with the enthusiastic support of the humanist scholar Guillaume Fichet. But soon afterward printing began to spread rapidly, and the map became dotted with many places that could boast of one or more presses—or at least of having harbored them for some time.

The map of printing during the fifteenth century, sprinkled with no fewer than 252 places where some form of printing took place, can be both instructive and misleading. It shows how printing spread after 1470 to Spain (Barcelona, 1473), the Low Countries (Utrecht, Alost, and Bruges, 1473), Hungary (Budapest, 1473), England (Westminster, 1476), and the outer corners of Europe—Cracow (1475), Stockholm (1483), Copenhagen (about 1489), Danzig (1499), and, in southern Europe, Reggio di Calabria (1475), Lisbon (1489), and Cagliari (1493).

Two concentrations are found on the map, in northern Italy and in southwest Germany. Other large areas were not served directly by printing presses but were nevertheless provided plentifully with printed books. For example, in the British Isles (which saw besides Westminster and London only short-lived and modest presses in Oxford and St. Albans), books in Latin were imported on a large scale from most major continental centers of printing. By 1480 the book trade had been organized so efficiently that no English printer found it worth his while to produce books that could be obtained elsewhere. English printers concentrated almost exclusively on English material. Even if England may present an extreme case, it illustrates very well the importance of the trade channels. Of the 252 recorded places of printing in the fifteenth century, only 11 were to produce more than a thousand editions. The 11—all of them major commercial centers—were Strasbourg, Cologne, Nuremberg, Augsburg, and Basel in the German-speaking countries; Venice, Milan, Florence, and Rome in Italy; and Paris, later followed by Lyons, in France.

Yet figures based on bibliographical enumeration can give a false impression. Information on the size of press runs is scarce indeed. Records of early Venetian books mention editions of 300 to 500 copies; there is, however, much to suggest that the number of copies printed could vary considerably. And then, naturally, the product itself could range from a small pamphlet or a single sheet to a multivolume work. If, therefore, modern bibliographers estimate that around 30,000 editions were printed in the fifteenth century, any figure is meaningless as an indication of the quantity, let alone the impact, of printed output in that period.

In addition to these considerations, one has to take the rate of survival into account. Each category of printing was affected in a different way. Generally speaking, Latin texts had a better rate of survival than books in the vernacular, with the exception of Latin liturgies and schoolbooks. Large books stood a better chance than small books, and most of what once served an ephemeral purpose disappeared. A beautiful and large illustrated book, like the famous *Nuremberg Chronicle,* printed in 1493 in Nuremberg, survives in hundreds of copies. But the majority of fifteenth-century books are extant in only one or two copies.

We can be certain that what has come down to us is only a small proportion of what was produced. It will therefore be almost impossible to overestimate the impact of the invention of printing on fifteenth-century Europe, as, inevitably, any estimate is based on our knowledge of what survives.

Initially, printing affected an exclusive circle of high ecclesiastical officials. Very rapidly it was realized that this was a medium with which to reach a wider public, as we have seen with the first printers in Italy. Soon printed material spread through universities, churches and monasteries, secular governments, schools, the feudal nobility, and the professional classes (lawyers and physicians). For each of these categories highly specialized material was produced. However, printers were rapidly to realize that the economics of the trade demanded expansion of their markets. This meant not only geographical spread, but also penetration into new layers of society. Printers (or at least some printers) made a conscious effort to create new classes of book owners and, ultimately, new classes of readers. Known classics were produced in more popular versions; devotional texts were printed in appealing form, with illustrations; popular texts in the vernacular found a wider dissemination. Book illustration, as well as layout and clearly legible typefaces, could help the inexperienced reader.

Having found a greater variety of users, the printed book began to appear in a greater variety of forms than its predecessor, the manuscript codex. The printed book, cheaper and more readily available, was owned by individuals rather than by institutions, and therefore became smaller in size. Bindings became less solid (and less durable), and layout was adapted to quick reference, with indexes, clear titles and headings, and other features to guide the user. But the most rapid and dramatic development was in the design of the letters that appeared on the page. Typography, compared with handwriting, is a depersonalized form; the medium encourages simplification and standardization of graphic forms, which were pioneered by some influential designers in the 1470's and 1480's and which became current by the 1490's.

The majority of books in the fifteenth century—estimated at about three-quarters of the total—were printed in Latin, at that time still the general language for all who used the written word, script, or print. Directly under the influence of printing and the new readership it created, the role of the vernacular languages became much more important, and this affected the languages themselves. Larger-scale distribution of texts in the vernacular led to the standardization of vernacular languages. Archaic language and regional peculiarities were trimmed off in favor of modern, metropolitan forms. Unlike the scribe of a manuscript, every printer had to satisfy more than one customer at a time. No one expressed this better than William Caxton in the preface to his translation of the *Aeneid:* "Certainly it is harde to playse every man by cause of dyversite and chaunge of langage."

The most essential feature of printed material is that it is produced in a large number of copies that are, in principle at least, identical. Incidents during production could and did cause variations between copies, which nowadays have to be studied if one wishes to establish a text exactly as the printer intended it. But to the contemporary reader these variations were largely irrelevant, or at worst no more annoying than errors in typesetting that could be found throughout all the copies of an edition. The marvel of printing was that a text had to be copied only once by setting it in type, in order to obtain a large number of uniform copies.

The advantage of having multiple copies of identical texts was seized in many situations where a standard text was required: in church services, in the schoolroom, in universities, and in law. The flood of legal books, of both canon and civil law, is a manifestation of the conscious attempt to achieve uniform and authoritative texts. Unlike the earlier experience with printing in the Far East, Western printing appears not to have been applied at once to civic administration. Such few instances as we have for the fifteenth century are remarkable in their realization of the principle of uniformity.

With the multiplication of uniform texts, for whatever purpose they were printed, came a sense of responsibility for the quality of the text. This realization was first of all manifest in liturgy and other sacred texts, which were usually produced under supervision of the clergy. Successive editions of legal texts, with corrections, may bear testimony to attempts at greater perfection. Ecclesiastical and secular powers could exercise some form of control, although this found no official form until the sixteenth century. It was in the first place the growing competition among printers, and the demands from their public, that served to increase the awareness of the need to provide products of high quality. Behind each printing house, however, stands an individual with his own interpretation of what constitutes quality. It is therefore impossible to generalize.

Some printers offer outstanding examples of the realization of new possibilities and obligations. Their names have rightly acquired a patriarchal ring: Friburger, Gering, and Crantz, the first printers at the Sorbonne; Koberger, who built an international emporium in Nuremberg; Ratdolt, the superb technician who reformed scientific books; Jenson, who pioneered the Roman typeface; William Caxton, the enterprising merchant who enthusiastically shared his experience of the Continent with his English public; and Aldus Manutius, the scholar-printer who in his choice of texts and the form he gave his books opened up a new era that led into sixteenth-century scholarship. They, however, are only a handful among the hundreds who each, in the early decades of printing, interpreted the medium as would fit their individual circumstances. In their joint work, more than in any individual effort, lies the immense significance the introduction of printing had for society.

PRINTING, ORIGINS OF

We can sometimes perceive how readers responded to more readily accessible material by examining annotated copies of books. Annotators might compare the texts in various editions and use the result of this collation to improve the text of one copy. Printers and editors responded to this critical spirit by attempting to bring together superior sources, querying the accuracy of manuscripts and generally striving to improve their editions. This phenomenon is best known in literary texts, but in fact it took place on every intellectual level, wherever there was demand for accurate information, appertaining to any form of knowledge. The critical spirit of the early sixteenth century—the age of the Reformation and also of Erasmus, when Western thinking was transformed—was partly the result of the experience with printed books.

Early printing has been studied since the late sixteenth century, with interest centered initially on the controversy over who produced the first printed book. The first author to pay attention to the spread of printing was Petrus Scriverius in his *Laure-crans voor Laurens Coster van Haerlem,* published in 1628. The spread of printing was also the focal point for the first bibliographies proper of the subject, which appeared in the eighteenth century: Michael Maittaire, *Annales typographici* (1719–1741), and Georg Wolfgang Panzer, *Annales typografici* (1793–1803).

Books printed before the year 1501 are called "incunabula." The term was first used in 1639/1640 by Bernardus à Mallinckrodt in a refutation of the work of Scriverius with the title *De ortu ac progressu artis typographicae.* Incunabula are usually listed in separate bibliographies and catalogs; the demarcation of printing before and after the year 1501 is essentially arbitrary and may sometimes lead to unfortunate divisions.

Many incunabula do not bear an imprint providing information about the place of printing, printer, and date. Since the middle of the nineteenth century, students of incunabula have considered that their most important tasks are to identify editions, to ascribe them to printers and places of printing, and to arrange them in chronological order. A full inventory in alphabetical sequence of all incunabula then known was published by Ludwig Hain in his *Repertorium bibliographicum* (1826–1838). Stimulated by this publication, a method of identification based on the classification of typographical material was devised by Henry Bradshaw and Jan Willem Holtrop and perfected by Robert Proctor and Konrad Haebler. Recently, satisfactory results for identification and chronological arrangement have come from new and accurate methods for recording paper, including beta-radiography and electron-radiography.

Early printed books can be studied for many reasons other than the purely bibliographical tasks of identification and chronology. They are sources for studying the technical development of the craft of printing. Their graphic design and illustrations are the subjects of separate branches of scholarship. The study of the book trade is revealing for the economic history of Europe. Incunabula are important links in textual transmission, and therefore in the transmission of two millennia of Western knowledge. They survive as important witnesses to a period of transition in European culture.

BIBLIOGRAPHY

Bibliographies. Catalogue of Books Printed in the XVth Century Now in the British Museum (1908–); S. Corsten and K. H. Staub, eds., *Der Buchdruck im 15. Jahrhundert: Eine Bibliographie* (1987); *Gesamtkatalog der Wiegendrucke* (1972–); Frederick R. Goff, *Incunabula in American Libraries* (1964, rev. repr. 1973, with 1972 suppl.).

Classification. Konrad Haebler, *Typenrepertorium der Wiegendrucke,* 5 vols. (1905–1924, repr. 1968); Wytze Hellinga and Lotte Hellinga, *Henry Bradshaw's Correspondence on Incunabula with J. W. Holtrop and M. F. A. G. Campbell,* 2 vols. (1968–1978); Robert Proctor, *An Index to the Early Printed Books in the British Museum,* 2 vols. (1898–1903).

The development of printing. Luigi Balsamo, "The Origins of Printing in Italy and England," in *Journal of the Printing Historical Society,* **11** (1976–1977); Curt F. Bühler, "Incunabula," in Bühler *et al., Standards of Bibliographical Description* (1949), 3–60, and *The Fifteenth-century Book* (1960); Lotte Hellinga and Wytze Hellinga, "Notes sur une ancienne Bible 'imprimée en l'an 1450,'" in *Studia bibliographica in honorem Herman de la Fontaine Verwey* (1966), 240–260; Massimo Miglio, ed., *Giovanni Andrea Bussi: Prefazioni alle edizioni di Sweynheym e Pannartz, prototipografi romani* (1978); Ernst Schulz, *The Study of Incunables,* Bernhard Bischoff, trans. (1977).

The spread of printing. Colin Clair, *A Chronology of Printing* (1969); Elizabeth L. Eisenstein, *The Printing Press as an Agent of Change,* 2 vols. (1979); Lucien Febvre and Henri-Jean Martin, *The Coming of the Book,* David Gerard, trans. (1976); Ernst P. Goldschmidt, *Medieval Texts and Their First Appearance in Print* (1943); Lotte Hellinga and Helmar Härtel, eds., *Buch und Text im 15. Jahrhundert/Book and Text in the Fifteenth Century* (1981); Rudolf Hirsch, *Printing, Selling, and Read-*

ing, 1450–1550, 2nd rev. ed. (1974); Robert Teichl, "Der Wiegendruck im Kartenbild," in *Bibliothek und Wissenschaft,* I (1964).

LOTTE HELLINGA

[See also **Bois Protat; Brethren of the Common Life; Caxton, William; Carthusians; Engraving; Gutenberg, Johannes; Manuscript Books, Production of; Nicholas of Cusa; Paleography; Paper, Introduction of; Technology, Western; Wynkyn de Worde.**]

PRINTS AND PRINTMAKING. See **Engraving; Woodcut.**

PRIOR AND PRIORESS. See **Clergy.**

PRISCIAN (*fl.* sixth century A.D.) was one of the most important teachers of the Middle Ages. Born in Caesarea in North Africa late in the fifth century, he was called to Constantinople, capital of the Byzantine Empire, where he taught under the patronage of Emperor Anastasius (491–518). Learned circles in Rome during the Ostrogothic period called upon Priscian to write grammatical manuals which, it was hoped, would improve knowledge of Latin. The works Priscian contributed to the teaching of grammar ensured his reputation and influence long after his death. The *Institutiones grammaticae,* his most important pedagogical treatise, exists in hundreds of extant manuscript copies.

The *Institutiones* was commissioned by Julian, a Roman consul and patrician, who wanted a Latin grammar based on Greek authorities. Priscian adapted the works of Apollonius Dyscolus and Herodianus for his new, Roman audience. His manual consists of eighteen major subdivisions that treat of grammar and language. It begins with a description of the human voice, letters, and other rudiments, proceeds through the parts of speech, and concludes with syntax. Priscian illustrated his teachings with numerous examples taken from Greek and Latin authors, some of whom are known today only through his book. Many later medieval writers who cited classical authorities owed their knowledge of them to their reading of Priscian and not to direct contact with the authors. Priscian was also an important conduit of Greek learning, vocabulary, and concepts to the West. The *Institutio de nomine et pronomine et verbo* is a condensation of parts of the *Institutiones grammaticae.*

Priscian wrote three other, shorter grammatical works for his Latin patrons. The *De figuris numerorum* treated the Greek origins of Roman numbers, weights, and measures. The *De metris fabularum Terentii* attempted to demonstrate the Latin debt to Greek meter. Priscian's *Praeexercitamina* is a close translation of Hermogenes' *Progymnasmata,* supplemented by a few Roman examples and references to Latin authors. It was an attempt to introduce Romans to Greek rhetorical principles. The *Partitiones duodecim versuum Aeneidos principalium,* on the other hand, was intended for Greek students as an aid in their study of Latin grammar. Arranged in master-student dialogue format, the *Partitiones* taught Latin grammar by asking the student to scan, identify, and explain grammatical forms used in the *Aeneid.*

Priscian also wrote two poems. The *De laude Anastasii imperatoris* is a panegyric. The *Periegesis* is a translation of the like-named work of Dionysius. A *Liber de accentibus* and other poems have been attributed to Priscian, but they are not his.

Priscian's works, especially the grammatical manuals, inspired many medieval commentaries, particularly during the Carolingian period. What was difficult for sixth-century Roman students to grasp became even more so in later centuries. Commentators had to explain Priscian's terminology and also to work through confusion wrought when Priscian misunderstood his Greek sources or when Greek and Latin grammatical structures were incompatible.

BIBLIOGRAPHY

Source. Heinrich Keil, *Grammatici latini,* II, III (1855, 1859, repr. 1961).

Studies. Alan Cameron, "The Date of Priscian's *De laude Anastasii,*" in *Greek, Roman, and Byzantine Studies,* **15** (1974); Pierre Paul Courcelle, *Late Latin Writers and Their Sources,* Harry E. Wedeck, trans. (1969), 325–330; Rudolf Helm, "Priscianus," in *Paulys Realencyclopädie der classischen Altertumswissenschaft,* XXII, pt. 2 (1954), 2,328–2,346; R. W. Hunt, "Studies on Priscian in the Eleventh and Twelfth Centuries," in *Mediaeval and Renaissance Studies,* **1** (1941–1943) and **2** (1950); Reginald O'Donnell, "Alcuin's Priscian," in John J. O'Meara and Bernd Naumann, eds., *Latin Script and Letters, A. D. 400–900* (1976); Maciej Salamon, "Priscianus und sein Schülerkreis in Konstantinopel," in *Philologus,* **123** (1979).

JOHN J. CONTRENI

[See also **Classical Literary Studies; Grammar; Schools, Grammar; Trivium.**]

PRISCILLIAN (*d.* 386), bishop of Ávila in Roman Hispania from 381, executed on charges of sorcery and Manichaeanism. From about 370, as a layman of high education and social standing, he led a movement of ascetic discipline and renewal in Spain and Aquitaine. His interest in the occult and encouragement of nocturnal meetings of men and women who studied apocryphal scriptures to inspire celibacy led to accusations. A council at Saragossa (October 380) expressed alarm at some practices. But Priscillian had supporters among the bishops, and by two of them, Instantius and Salvianus, he was consecrated bishop of Ávila in 381. This election was offensive to Hydatius, bishop of Emerita (Mérida), who, with the support of Ambrose of Milan, won a rescript from the emperor Gratian exiling "pseudo-bishops and Manichees." Priscillian unsuccessfully bid for papal support, but won reinstatement from Gratian. Gratian's murder (383) was fatal to Priscillian's cause. The new Western emperor, Maximus, sent the case to a synod at Bordeaux (384), from which Priscillian unwisely appealed to Maximus at Trier. There he was accused by his brother bishop Ithacius of Ossonuba (Estoi) on the capital charge of sorcery, as well as Manichaeanism, praying naked, and unseemly relations with women. Under torture he confessed and with at least six supporters was executed.

Maximus' fall (388) resulted in a reaction in favor of Priscillian. His remains were taken to Galicia, where he was venerated as a martyr, conceivably at Compostela. Galicia remained fervently Priscillianist until the sixth century. Priscillianist Gospel prefaces ("Monarchian Prologues") and canons on the Pauline epistles were devotedly copied in Vulgate manuscripts. Eleven anonymous, certainly Priscillianist, tractates in a fifth-century Würzburg manuscript, first printed in 1889, illuminate his ascetic principles and declare his abhorrence of Manichaeanism. They also set forth an esoteric doctrine directed at vegetarian celibate ascetics of both sexes, seeking to enable them to discern the powers of evil and to transcend the narrow-mindedness of humdrum church life. He passionately defends the right to read apocrypha because of their emphasis on asceticism and because it is a principle of his that there are more things in heaven and earth than ordinary clergy and laity guess from the canonical Scriptures. His execution by the civil power after accusations by a brother bishop led Ambrose and Martin of Tours to refuse recognition to those who held communion with his accuser. The case was not (as represented by Gibbon) an anticipation of the Inquisition handing over heretics to the secular arm.

BIBLIOGRAPHY

Sources. Georg Schepss, *Corpus scriptorium ecclesiasticorum latinorum,* XVIII (1889), contains the Würzburg tracts, the canons on the Pauline epistles, and Orosius' *Commonitorium de errore Priscillianistorum et Origenistorum,* which quotes from a letter written by Priscillian. A Priscillianist tract on the Trinity is found in G. Morin, *Études, textes, découvertes* (1913), 178. All except the Orosius work are reprinted in *Patrologia latina,* supplement II (1960), 1,391–1,507. The canons can also be found in John Wordsworth and Julian White, *Novum testamentum Domini nostri Iesu Christi latine* (Oxford Vulgate) II (1889, 2nd ed. 1938), 20–32. The Monarchian Prologues are in John Chapman, *Notes on the Early History of the Vulgate Gospels* (1908), 217–222.

Studies. Adhémar d'Alès, *Priscillien et l'Espagne chrétienne à la fin du IVe siècle* (1936); Ernest C. Babut, *Priscillien et le priscillianisme* (1909); Henry Chadwick, *Priscillian of Ávila* (1976); Benedikt Vollmann, *Studien zum Priszillianismus* (1965), and *idem,* in Pauly-Wissowa, *Realencyclopädie,* supplement XIV (1974), 485–559, with full bibliography.

HENRY CHADWICK

[See also **Ambrose, St.; Astrology; Church, Early; Dualism; Heresies; Manichaeans; Magic and Folklore, Western European; Witchcraft.**]

PRISONS. Modern penology distinguishes between custodial, punitive, and coercive prisons. It has become conventional wisdom that medieval law knew the first and third of these, but not the second. In fact, medieval law knew and used all three kinds. According to classical Roman law the head of a household might maintain a domestic prison (*ergastulum*) for his own slaves, but punitive or coercive imprisonment of free citizens was forbidden. The jurist Ulpian (*d.* 228) stated that "prison ought to be used for confining men, not punishing them" (Justinian's *Digest* 48.19.8.9), and this penological doctrine was known to medieval civil lawyers.

The folklaws of early medieval Europe made few provisions for imprisonment, although powerful people did confine their personal enemies and prisoners of war, and, in a few instances, both Lombard and Anglo-Saxon law recognized punitive imprisonment as an alternative to stiffer punishments, particularly blood sanctions. From the late ninth century there emerged the practice of custodially confining certain classes of accused criminals pending trial or sentence, and, to a far lesser extent, coercive imprisonment pending the payment of a fine or the fulfillment of a legal obligation. From the thirteenth century on, the latter included imprisonment for debt. In these cases confinement varied widely, since imprisonment was thought to be chiefly apprehension and control of someone, not necessarily strict confinement. Prisoners might be confined simply within a region or a town or part of a particular building, which was generally termed *murus largus;* confinement in cramped rooms, cages, stocks, or fetters was known as *murus strictus.* Prison escapes were frequent and punishment was severe. Prisoners had to pay for their own maintenance, and in England until the end of the Middle Ages franchisal jails were sources of income for those who held them.

The contribution of alms for prisoners was a large part of medieval charitable enterprise, and sympathy for the plight of prisoners was also reflected in saints' cults, notably that of St. Leonard, which focused on the saint's function as a liberator of prisoners. The injunctions of Scripture, the image of the imprisoned Boethius, and familiarity with prison conditions supported both sympathy and charity.

A distinctive influence was exercised by the church, which, prohibited by its doctrine from shedding blood, was not able to exercise the most widely used sanctions of medieval criminal law. Monasteries and bishops maintained prisons, chiefly for clerical discipline, since canon law most commonly aimed at the correction, rather than the punishment, of offenders. From the late twelfth century on, however, the large number of heresy convictions led to the construction of more ecclesiastical and secular prisons as well as to an ecclesiastical doctrine of punitive imprisonment, laid out in the decretal *Quamvis* of Pope Boniface VIII, in 1298 (*Liber sextus* 5.9.3).

Although doctrines of imprisonment varied widely throughout Europe and within individual territories, one may discern a generally common pattern. From the eleventh through the late thirteenth century, prison was chiefly custodial, with (in England, at least) the institutions of bail and jail (gaol) delivery prominent. From the late thirteenth century on, punitive imprisonment was more widely used, often as an alternative to blood sanctions and often ending with the payment of a fine. Even though custodial and coercive imprisonment dominated until the eighteenth century, punitive imprisonment was well known and used from the thirteenth.

BIBLIOGRAPHY

Most general histories are not reliable for the medieval period. For England, see Ralph B. Pugh, *Imprisonment in Medieval England* (1968); Barbara Hanawalt, *Crime and Conflict in English Communities, 1300–1348* (1979); Christopher Harding *et al.*, *Imprisonment in England and Wales: A Concise History* (1985). For France, see Annik Porteau-Bitker, "L'emprisonnement dans le droit laïque du moyen âge," in *Revue historique de droit français et étranger,* 4th ser., **46** (1968). For the cult of St. Leonard, see Steven D. Sargent, "Religious Responses to Violence in Eleventh-century Aquitaine," in *Historical Reflections / Reflexions Historiques,* **12** (1985); for papal Avignon, see Jacques Chiffoleau, *Les justices du pape* (1984). There is a mine of information for the Italian city-republics in Gotthold Bohne, "Die Freiheitsstrafe in den italienischen Stadtrechten des 12.–16. Jahrhunderts," in *Leipziger rechtswissenschaftliche Studien,* **4** (1922) and **9** (1925). On imprisonment for debt, see Jay Cohen, "The History of Imprisonment for Debt and Its Relation to the Development of Discharge in Bankruptcy," in *The Journal of Legal History,* **3** (1982).

EDWARD PETERS

[See also **Châtelet; Inquisition; Jail Delivery; Law,** various articles.]

PROBST. See **Provost.**

PROCESSIONS, LITURGICAL. Liturgical processions were both prominent and frequent in the

Middle Ages. The definitive shape of the practice was provided by Rome, for the West, and by Constantinople, for the Byzantine church, but it had roots in the primitive church, and even in biblical and pagan antiquity. The early Christians seem to have taken up processions as soon as such public demonstrations were tolerated by civil authorities. A procession in Milan in 388 was mentioned by St. Ambrose, and processions in Jerusalem about the same time by Egeria; and in both cases the customs seem already to have been well established. It is not surprising that processions should be taken up quickly; the early Christians inherited a taste for them from their pagan forebears, and found sanction for them in Scripture.

If justification was found in the biblical processions before the Ark or to the Temple, only one Christian procession, on Palm Sunday, can be said to derive directly from Scripture. In this respect the more immediate pagan practices had a greater influence. It is not far in spirit or time from the imperial triumphs in which torches were carried, images borne, incense burned, and hymns of praise sung on the way to the Capitol, to the processions organized by St. John Chrysostom (348–407) in which lighted candles were carried, silver crosses borne, and psalms sung on the way to the cathedral. And there was a continuity in more than external features.

On 25 April the ancient Romans had observed the Robigalia, a festival in honor of the deities believed to control the appearance of rust or mildew; and on this occasion processions were held, during which prayers were offered for the protection of the crops. The Christian Romans, following a custom already well established in the sixth century, held a procession, the Major Litany, on the same day, for the same purpose, and even over much the same route. Similar circumstances surround the Rogation days (Minor Litany, or Gallican Rogations). From the fifth century these days were observed in Gaul with processions on the three days preceding Ascension to seek protection for the harvest. A pagan observance, the Ambarvalia, with similar processions through the fields, had been held alternately on 17 to 20 and 27 to 30 May. For still another example there is the Purification (Candlemas) procession. The old arrangements for it present a curious anomaly: penitential trappings for a feast day. The pope went on foot, not as usual on horseback, with bare feet and in black vestments. It seems that the procession and feast were originally distinct, and that the former was a Christian carryover from the pagan Amburbale or Lupercalia. Both were occasions of purification and expiation, and the first, at least, involved a procession.

In times of public calamity processions played a conspicuous part in communal prayer. Emperor Theodosius ordered processions in the year 394 to plead for divine help in his imminent attack on Eugenius and Arbogast. St. John Chrysostom mentioned others held in April of 399, when heavy rains were endangering the harvest. Mamertus, bishop of Vienne in Gaul, instituted Rogation processions about the year 470 after an earthquake and the destruction of the royal palace by lightning. Processions were held during the siege of Saragossa by Childebert I (*d.* 558). Other processions in the face of impending disaster are reported for Rheims in 546, Limoges about 580, Sicily in 601, and Rome in 590 and 603. Processions of this kind were frequent enough that Justinian in 527 found it necessary to lay down regulations for them. They remained customary throughout the Middle Ages.

While Rogation processions did customarily terminate with Mass, they can be considered essential features of the liturgy. The Mass processions, however, were accessory. Although the reason for them came later to be obscured, they had, originally, a practical purpose. They served to conduct the celebrant and his ministers to the site of the service. As early as the middle of the second century the site of a saint's martyrdom or burial was considered especially sanctified to his cult and was the ideal location for the principal celebration of the local Christian community on his feast day. After the end of the persecutions, churches were built over or near such places and to house important relics. Before the end of Constantine's reign (337) the basilicas of the Holy Sepulcher and Martyrium in Golgotha had been built in Jerusalem; and in Rome, a shrine over the tomb of St. Lawrence and the basilica of the Holy Cross to house the newly recovered relics of the Passion. It was customary for the local bishop or abbot to preside in such holy places at especially solemn celebrations. This custom was observed not only on the feasts of the saints whose shrines they were, but, for the more important churches, even on the anniversaries of the dedication.

From Egeria, in the fourth century, we learn of processions in which the bishop made his way to celebrations and commemorations in churches built over the holy places of Jerusalem. Similar processions were certainly widespread at the time. In Rome the episcopal Mass was celebrated away from the cathedral especially frequently. The *Liber pontificalis* mentions a circuit of "stations" in the reign of Pope Hilary (461–468). If it was not so in Hilary's time, this circuit, as it was enlarged by successive popes, became something more than a round of the local martyria for their respective anniversaries. Fifty-nine station days are specified in the earliest surviving list from about the beginning of the seventh century. The Gregorian Sacramentary, which represents the practice of about the end of the eight century, lists sixty-eight. Later documents bring the total to eighty-nine, including all the Marian feasts, Christmas, Epiphany, Septuagesima, Sexagesima, and Quinquagesima Sundays, all the Sundays and weekdays of Lent, Easter, and Pentecost and all the days of their octaves, the Sundays of Advent, and the Ember Days. Only a very few of these stations took place at St. John Lateran (the cathedral of Rome); the others were distributed among all the great churches of the city.

The locations of some of the stations, for example that at S. Maria Maggiore on Christmas and that at Sta. Croce in Gerusalemme on Good Friday, were clearly chosen for being especially appropriate to the occasion. But most of the stations could have been held just as acceptably—with respect to the liturgy—as well in one church as another. The Roman arrangement was made necessary by that city's growing Christian population. The episcopal Mass attended by the whole Christian community had been a primitive ideal of the church. The stational masses in Rome and elsewhere served as a substitute for this ideal. They were another way of maintaining unity in a Christian body grown too large to meet in any one place. The bishop made his way to these stations in solemn processions that, owing to their frequency, were a very prominent feature of the local liturgies. They remained so in Rome at least until the Avignon exile, and in Constantinople until the Islamic conquest in 1453.

In smaller centers, processions commonly played a part comparable in importance to their role in Rome or Constantinople. Indeed, they are often similar in significant details. But although processions were natural enough in the great cities to bring together large Christian communities, in most localities they were largely unnecessary and were often awkwardly arranged. Of course there were always some processions that did keep their original function and served to conduct the local bishop or abbot, or his representative, to stations in parish churches on certain feasts and Sundays. In most of these cases, however, it can be argued that the whole arrangement was extraneous. Except for the Rogation days, which traditionally united the whole community in a common petition and—what were almost as rare in most centers—feasts of saints with local shrines, there could be little advantage, liturgical or practical, for a bishop or abbot to celebrate Mass away from his own church.

To be sure, there was always some ostensible purpose; processions were never aimless wanderings. But most accomplished nothing that was necessary. The occasion that at first sight appears to be their immediate prompting is usually only a pretext. Consider, for example, that in some places the participants walked in silence, and without ceremony, to a neighboring church, where a blessing was read over the palms or candles or the final morning Office recited, and began there a procession back to Mass in their own church. According to another arrangement, the procession set out from its home church to another for some brief commemoration, only to return immediately for Mass. The most frequent arrangement everywhere had processions follow a circuitous route entirely within the church or church grounds, pausing for remembrances at certain fixtures.

It is clear from the Gregorian Sacramentary that the pope presided at vespers on some of the great feasts, and that the Office was held in the appropriate Roman churches. The procession to the vespers station at S. Maria Maggiore for the Feast of the Assumption is described in one of the *Ordines Romani.* There must have been other processions like this one for similar occasions. In Jerusalem, among those processions seen by Egeria in the fourth century, were ones held regularly after vespers from the main church to the sanctuary that housed Christ's cross. Amalarius in 812 knew of short Offices in Rome, held at "various altars," "at the cross," and "at the font." Many of these short Offices called for processions, even within a church. Processions were often mounted for ceremonies if a ceremony was to take place at some distance from the main altar and choir, or even within this area if the transit was of sufficient duration—from the main altar to the ambo, for example, with the Gospelbook at Mass. These formal processions varied from simple to solemn, according to the occasion and the resources of the church or cathedral. Such ceremonies, in keeping with the general elaboration of the liturgy in all but the severe monastic houses, were increasingly common in the later Middle Ages.

Processions for the reception of eminent visitors into the church were provided for everywhere. Bede reports that in 597 St. Augustine, the missionary sent by Pope Gregory I to Britain, received the local king in such a ceremony, and this is by no means the earliest example. In Rome such processions were customarily held by the regional clergy for the pope when he reached the stational churches.

Even locally, such processions would be frequently called for. Monasteries everywhere received not only official visits from patrons, visiting abbots, other prelates, and so forth, but also—being bound by the obligations of Christian charity to extend hospitality to strangers—visits from many other distinguished people, often of the highest ranks of the nobility, who used the monastic houses as places of rest in their travels. The ceremonial reception was given, as well, to the bishop or abbot on his return to his own church after a journey.

The principal participants in the liturgical processions were, of course, the celebrant (or chief dignitary) and the clergy. The crosses, which were universally carried in the processions, were originally episcopal insignia, but by the sixth century at least the original strictness in this respect was relaxed and crosses were carried even when clergy of lower rank were officiating. The water, candles, incense, and Gospelbooks that were so often part of the processions were probably, in the beginning, intended to furnish the necessities for the Mass (or whatever Office) at the site of the station. In the earliest centuries, many of the sites were normally left unattended, and in any case could hardly have been expected to provide vessels and other paraphernalia appropriate to the episcopal dignity. The vestments, in the earliest stational processions, seem to have been carried in chests, the robing, a more or less formal ceremony depending on circumstances, taking place at the site. But in later centuries, the vestments worn in the processions were those called for by the Office to be performed, but with the significant addition of the *pluviale* (originally, "rain-cape"), even when the entire procession was to take place indoors.

The earliest writers to refer to Christian processions make no reference to special chants. We read, as for fourth-century Jerusalem, only of psalms, and of hymns and antiphons "appropriate for the day." The importance of psalm recitation in the early processions should not be overlooked; it must be supposed that most of their length—often very considerable—was taken up in this manner. Special chants, at least not known to have been used for any other purpose, are found in the earliest chant books. These pieces vary greatly in style, but are often lengthy and melismatic. Special processional hymns appear somewhat later, these often characterized by a refrain, perhaps to be sung by all the participants in the procession. The other chants were usually sung by a small *schola* (choir) reading from a processional book or, in the earliest years, a few pages detached from the antiphoner.

BIBLIOGRAPHY

Michel Andrieu, ed., *Ordines romani du haut moyen âge,* 5 vols. (1931–1961); Terence Bailey, *The Processions of Sarum and the Western Church* (1971); Victor D. Boissonnet, *Dictionnaire alphabético-méthodique des cérémonies et des rites sacrés,* 3 vols. (1846–1847); D. de Bruyne, "L'origine des processions de la chandleur et des rogations," in *Revue bénédictine,* **34** (1922); M.-N. Colette, *Le répertoire des rogations d'après un processionnal de Poitiers (XVIe siècle)* (1976); Louis Duchesne, ed., *Liber pontificalis,* 2 vols. (1886–1892); Etheria, "Peregrinatio," in Louis Duchesne, *Christian Worship: Its Origin and Evolution,* M. L. McClure, trans. (5th ed., 1919), 490–523; P.-M. Gy, "Collectaire, rituel, processionnal," in *Revue des sciences philosophiques et théologiques,* **44** (1960); Michel Huglo, "Processional," in *The New Grove Dictionary of Music and Musicians* (1980), and "Les antiennes de la procession des reliques," in *Revue grégorienne,* **31** (1952); R. Janin, "Les processions religieuses à Byzance," in *Revue des études byzantines,* **24** (1966); *Processionale ad usum Sarum* (1502, repr. 1980); Geoffrey Willis, *Further Essays in Early Roman Liturgy* (1968), 1–87; F. Wormold, "A Medieval Processional and Its Diagrams," in Arthur Rosenmauer and Gerold Weber, eds., *Kunsthistorische Forschungen Otto Pächt* (1972); F. Yates, "Dramatic Religious Processions in Paris in the Late Sixteenth Century," in Société de Musique d'Autrefois, *Annales musicologiques,* II (1954), 215–262.

TERENCE BAILEY

[See also **Divine Office; Litany; Liturgy, Stational; Mass, Liturgy of the; Ordines Romani; Pontifical; Sacramentary.**]

PROCHEIROS NOMOS, the code of civil, public, and penal law in forty titles, issued by the Byzantine emperor Basil I and by his sons and co-emperors

Constantine and Leo (later Leo VI) between the years 870 and 879 (possibly 872). Mainly based on Justinian's legislation and its commentaries, it was also influenced by the Isaurian *Eclogue* and by constitutions of later emperors, including Basil himself. In its present form, the *Procheiros nomos* seems to have been interpolated by the inclusion of tenth-century legislation (according to Andreas Schminck, it would have been issued by Leo VI in the tenth century). Concise and well organized, this code circulated widely within Byzantium, was translated into Slavonic, and influenced the Serbs, Bulgarians, and Russians.

BIBLIOGRAPHY

The text is readily available in the reprint by Panagotes and Ioannes Zepos, *Jus graecoromanum,* II (1931), 108–228. An English translation is Edwin H. Freshfield, *A Manual of Eastern Roman Law: The Procheiros Nomos* (1927). For the date see D. Ginis, in *Epeteris Hetaireias Byzantinon Spoudon,* 30 (1960–1961), 351. For the interpolations, see Nicolas Oikonomides, "Leo VI's Legislation of 907 Forbidding Fourth Marriages: An Interpolation in the Pocheiros Nomos (IV, 25–27)," in *Dumbarton Oaks Papers,* 30 (1976); J. N. Scapov, "Prohiron v vostochnoslavyanskoy pismennosti," in *Vizantysky Vremennik,* n.s. 38 (1977); Andreas Schminck, *Studien zu mittelbyzantinischen Rechtsbüchern* (1986).

NICOLAS OIKONOMIDES

[See also **Basil I the Macedonian; Basilics; Corpus Iuris Civilis; Eclogue; Epanagoge; Law, Byzantine; Leo VI the Wise, Emperor.**]

PROCOPIUS (*ca.* 500–after 554), the major historian of the reign of the Byzantine emperor Justinian (*r.* 527–565). Born in Caesarea, in Palestine, he became secretary (later assessor) to the general Belisarios in 527 and accompanied him on the Persian, African, and Italian campaigns. He was in Constantinople during the plague of 542, after which time his movements are unclear. *Wars,* books I through VII, covered the campaigns on all three fronts up to 550. In the same year Procopius wrote the *Secret History,* a pamphlet violently hostile to Belisarios and his wife, Antonina, as well as to Justinian and his wife, Theodora. It professed to give the true explanation of events described already in the *Wars.* In 554 Procopius added *Wars* VIII, rounding off the narrative to date on all fronts, and about the same time he composed the *Buildings,* a panegyrical record of Justinian's building activity.

The opposing bias of the works is usually explained in terms of Procopius' life—his experiences and personality—but the works themselves are the only evidence for his life. Their differing characteristics must be explained in terms of their genres and the constraints which these genres imposed.

The *Wars* was much copied and used by historians of the next generations (for example, Agathias, Evagrius, Theophanes Confessor), but the *Secret History* may not have been known until the tenth century, when it is mentioned in the *Suda.*

The *Wars* was written from a conservative and aristocratic viewpoint; it is a classicizing military and political history, duly embellished with digressions and speeches. In books I through VII the subject matter is divided geographically (I–II, Persian War; III–IV, Vandalic War; V–VII, Gothic War), but book VIII covers events on all fronts from 550 to about 554. Procopius was an eyewitness to much that he relates, yet many of his descriptions of places have been shown to be deficient in detail. A staunch supporter of Justinian's early imperialist policy, he does not much criticize either its practicality or the methods Justinian used. And despite the *Buildings,* Procopius was not much interested in the economies or societies of the areas in which Justinian made war. His merits are those of the reporter, and for much of his narrative he is the only source. He collected a vast mass of information, much of which we are in no position to check. The *Wars* is written in a clear and straightforward Greek, imitating classical authors (especially Thucydides and Polybius); like Thucydides, Procopius sometimes figures in his own history and allows his work to be highly colored by his own opinions. He generally excludes purely ecclesiastical matters and is sometimes uneasy about Christian vocabulary, yet there are enough unselfconscious passages to show that he accepted the truth of Christianity, even though he preferred to couch his comments on causality in the language of fortune or fate. He is noteworthy, however, for his disapproval of doctrinal dispute, an attitude which he shared with Agathias.

The *Secret History,* discovered in the Vatican Library in the seventeenth century, is such a scurrilous attack on Belisarios and Justinian and their wives that its authorship has often been doubted. Yet stylistic analysis and cross references to the

Wars make Procopius' authorship certain, and internal references indicate a date of 550. Procopius was by then thoroughly disillusioned with Belisarios as well as the whole imperial endeavor; his former hero had refused to take a stand against Justinian when the chance had been offered. Procopius writes as a disappointed man. Many of the "true" reasons he now gives for earlier actions are purely scurrilous and must be treated with caution, but the work also contains some more serious criticism of Justinian's policies. In form the *Secret History* is an invective, but when Procopius claims that Justinian and Theodora were demons in human form, this is no mere literary topos but a serious opinion revealing Procopius' adherence to contemporary religious attitudes.

The *Buildings,* commissioned by the emperor, is a panegyrical description of Justinian's buildings, arranged area by area. The six books begin with Constantinople and proceed geographically, but as their literary quality is variable, and Italy is omitted altogether, it is clear that the work is unfinished. There are many problems of sources and purpose, and if Procopius had access to official lists for some areas, he did not have them for all. The principles of inclusion are not clear either, but it is certain from other evidence that this account is not a complete record. The discrepancy between this work of flattery and the vituperation of the *Secret History* has caused much difficulty for students of Procopius, but a more sympathetic approach to panegyric now allows a higher valuation of the *Buildings* for the remarkable amount of evidence it presents. It is a prime text for the growing field of Byzantine archaeology. Interesting for the ideology of imperialism is its focus on fortifications and churches, and it is worth noting that Procopius here depicts Justinian as directly inspired by God.

BIBLIOGRAPHY

Edition and translations. Opera omnia, Jacobus Haury, ed., rev. by Gerhard Wirth, 4 vols. (1962–1964); *History of the Wars, Secret History, and Buildings,* Averil Cameron, trans. and ed. (1967); *Secret History,* Richard Atwater, trans. (1927, repr. 1961); *Secret History,* G. A. Williamson, trans. (1966).

Studies. Averil Cameron, "The 'Scepticism' of Procopius," in *Historia* (Wiesbaden), **15** (1966), and *Procopius and the Sixth Century* (1985); J. A. S. Evans, *Procopius* (1972); Berthold Rubin, *Prokopios von Kaisareia* (1954), repr. in *Pauly's Realencyclopädie der classischen Altertumskunde,* XXIII.1 (1957), 273–599.

AVERIL CAMERON

[See also **Agathias; Belisarios; Byzantine Empire: History; Byzantine Literature; Historiography, Byzantine; Justinian I; Suda; Theodora I, Empress; Theophanes Confessor.**]

PROKHOR OF GORODETS (*fl.* late fourteenth and early fifteenth century) was a Russian painter. He is thought to have been the teacher of the great Russian painter Andrei Rublev. The two worked with the Byzantine painter Theophanes the Greek on the frescoes (no longer extant) and iconostasis of the cathedral of the Annunciation (1405) in the Moscow Kremlin.

BIBLIOGRAPHY

Victor N. Lazarev, *Andrei Rublev i ego shkola* (1966), 14–23, plates 23–38; Arthur Voyce, *The Art and Architecture of Medieval Russia* (1967), 214.

GEORGE P. MAJESKA

[See also **Iconostasis; Moscow Kremlin, Art and Architecture; Rublev, Andrei; Russian Art; Theophanes the Greek.**]

PROLATIO, a term used in mensural notational theory since the early fourteenth century to designate the nature of the subdivision of the semibreve into minims. "Prolation" came to be described as *maior prolatio* (or *prolatio perfecta*) or *minor prolatio* (or *prolatio imperfecta*), depending on whether the semibreve was divided into three or two minims. The term *prolatio* with respect to the semibreve served as analogue to the terms *tempus* (time) with respect to breve and the *modus* (mood) with respect to long. The three levels of rhythmic organization were defined as such in Jehan des Murs's *Libellus cantus mensurabilis* (*ca.* 1340).

In the fifteenth century *prolatio* also came to designate musical meter, especially the *quatre prolacions* defining the four possible combinations of *tempus* and *prolatio.*

BIBLIOGRAPHY

Willi Apel, *The Notation of Polyphonic Music 900–1600* (5th ed., 1961); Margaret Bent, "Notation, pt. III," in *The New Grove Dictionary of Music and Musicians,* XIII (1980), 362–373; Rudolf Bockholdt, "Semibrevis minima und Prolatio temporis," in *Die Musikforschung,* **16** (1963). See also Wolf Frobenius, "Prolatio," in *Handwörterbuch der musikalischen Terminologie,* Hans Heinrich Eggebrecht, ed., II (1972).

CALVIN M. BOWER

[See also **Ars Nova; Jehan des Murs; Ligature; Musical Notation, Western; Musical Treatises; Rhythm.**]

PRONOIA (plural, *pronoiai*), an important Byzantine legal instrument for granting revenues that belonged to the empire. Originally these grants were temporary and revocable; the revenues normally derived from land, such as a village or an estate, although they also could include fishing rights, mines, or other sources of income. The monetary value (*posōtēs*) of a *pronoia* therefore varied. A *pronoia* could involve the transfer to its holder of administrative rights over peasants (*paroikoi*) who worked the land.

Pronoiai first appeared in the eleventh century, but it is unlikely that there was any customary use of them to pay for the services of soldiers before 1204. In the Nicene and early Palaiologan periods (between 1204 and the 1320's), however, the empire did use substantial numbers of *pronoiai* to recruit and finance its armies. Military *pronoia* holders often were called *stratiotai* (soldiers). Open to question, though, is the degree to which (if at all) the *pronoiai* were used to support soldiers in the reigns of the Komnenoi and the Angeloi (1081–1185 and 1185–1204, respectively), and whether it is appropriate to identify the granting of *pronoiai* with feudalism. The latest research questions the existence of feudalism in the Byzantine Empire before 1204 and the ascription of the origins of Byzantine feudalism to the granting of *pronoiai*. Despite the use of the term "feudalism" in both the East and the West, the *pronoia* should not be identified or confused with the Western European fief.

The recipient of a *pronoia,* who could be either a Byzantine or a foreigner, was given an imperial chrysobull, or authorization, that described the property and the attendant rights and immunities, and could be diminished, augmented, or altered only by the emperor. He took it to an official of the relevant local imperial administration—in the thirteenth century, for example, to the *dux* of a theme. The next steps were an examination of any conflicting claims; a survey of the land and establishment of its boundaries; registration of the *paroikoi;* the listing of their taxes, dues, and services; and an inventory of objects of value associated with the property, such as livestock.

No reliable statistics exist regarding the total number of *pronoiai* or the percentage of imperial manpower they theoretically supported. It is generally believed that *pronoia* holders supplied important numbers of the military manpower that helped to check the Turks in Anatolia in the early and mid thirteenth centuries. Military *pronoia* holders did not always provide military service in person; when they did not, they were expected to supply qualified soldiers, fully equipped and mounted, in their stead. When they performed the services themselves, however, they received rations in kind (*siteresia*) and perhaps a cash payment in addition to their *pronoia* revenues.

The imperial government gradually lost control of the *pronoiai,* which originally had been revocable but in many cases had become hereditary by the fourteenth century. In the late thirteenth and early fourteenth centuries, the emperors decided to increase their reliance on foreign mercenaries, which led to a decrease in the importance of *pronoiai* as a means of financing their armies.

Many scholars argue that the *pronoia* was a weak and dangerous source of military manpower, and that it contributed to the decentralization and disintegration of the empire. Whatever the case may be, the decline of the *pronoiai* did parallel the weakening of central authority in the empire. The *pronoia* affected late Byzantine social and economic conditions; in particular the granting of them contributed to the reduction of rural farmers to the condition of dependent serfs.

Sources of information on the *pronoia* include the *praktika* (inventories of dependent villages drawn up for purposes of taxation) of monasteries—although many scholars believe that monasteries were not supposed to receive *pronoiai*—the histories of Niketas Choniates and George Pachymeres, and the Chronicle of the Morea.

BIBLIOGRAPHY

Michael Angold, *A Byzantine Government in Exile: Government and Society in Exile Under the Lascarids* (1975); Angeliki E. Laiou-Thomadaki, *Peasant Society in the Late Byzantine Empire* (1977); George Ostrogorsky, *Pour l'histoire de la féodalité byzantine,* Henri Grégoire, trans. (1954).

WALTER EMIL KAEGI, JR.

[See also **Byzantine Empire: Economic Life and Social Structure; Paroikoi; Taxation, Byzantine.**]

PROPAGANDA. Medieval (like modern) propaganda refers to the attempt to influence human attitudes and actions by controlling representations in spoken, written, pictorial, or even musical form. Prior to 1622, when Pope Gregory XV founded the Congregation for the Propagation of the Faith to direct the foreign missionary effort, the term "propaganda" was unknown in the Latin West. Although medieval propaganda is most often associated with the era of church reform and the crusades of the eleventh and twelfth centuries, it had a much longer period of development. The most current research reveals that it often reflects more positive connotations regarding psychological and social changes than one usually associates with the modern use of the term. Moreover, though lacking the sophistication and organization of their modern counterparts, medieval propagandists struggled, often successfully, with the same basic issues and problems of content, audience, technique, and media of communication.

There were basically two types of propaganda in the Middle Ages. First, as exemplified by many forms of written works, sermons, and the plastic arts throughout the period, there was the positive, integrative propaganda directed toward the development of a more unified medieval culture. Second, there was the negative, antagonistic propaganda, most typically characteristic of the treatises and letters of the eleventh-century investiture controversy of the pro- and anticrusade treatises, sermons, and poetry of the twelfth and thirteenth centuries. More careful review of the forms of medieval propaganda reveals much about the specific features of these categories.

FORMS OF PROPAGANDA

One of the earliest and most persistent forms was the saint's life or hagiography. Most of these documents were written to provide a model of the good life for others to emulate. They also reflect changing social structures, societal and generational conflict, and the longer tradition of saintly lives going back to the early Christian era. The Life of Radegunde in the sixth century and of St. Guthlac in the eighth century provide fruitful early examples, while the *vita* of Mary d'Oignies was used productively by Jacques de Vitry in the thirteenth century. Another form, which often embellished the hagiographical sources, was visions and prophecies. Visions were often used purposefully to show the continuing miraculous power of saints whose cults might be waning and thereby restore the trade of pilgrims.

Miracles, exempla, and fables served a similar purpose but would likely be used as broader reminders of God's power in a region waning in its adherence to the faith. Thus, the reports of extra-powerful accomplishments, whether divine or human, were used over the entire medieval period, peaking perhaps with the development of the cult of the Virgin as fostered by visions of the twelfth and thirteenth centuries, or with the promotion of the life of the mystic as reported in fourteenth-century hagiography.

More concrete, iconographic forms of propaganda were developed early in the period and continued to evolve into the fifteenth century. Vivid portrayals of scriptural truths and classical tables kept the message of Christian life in the foreground of the worship of the largely illiterate faithful. Decoration of the Romanesque windows, doors, and tympana gave way to more realistic or human-like forms in the portals and stained glass of the monumental Gothic cathedrals. The evolution of architectural forms became a form of propaganda. The power of the church or the secular community was reflected in the achievement of structures whose height bespoke more complex and costly solutions of technical problems and also represented some forms of spiritual unity. Thus, by various artistic and architectural means, the medieval church became a dramatic propaganda platform from which to proclaim the goals and stages of Christian life: by the external towers; the multiple messages on the west facade that reminded the faithful of the Last Judgment; the apse facing eastward, where the ultimate sacrifice of Christ took place; or the internal sculptures, mosaics, and painted walls.

Coins, relics, and even the crown of the king or the crosier and ring of the bishop were utilized to remind individuals of their respective places or duties in the medieval universe. Relics were used to promote the cults of saints and to attract pilgrims, as witnessed by the case of Ste. Foy in southern France. Coins, on the other hand, propagandized the power and authority of the secular monarchs.

By the tenth century, some of the earlier forms of propaganda had begun to develop more specialized uses in behalf of narrower causes. Whereas earlier histories, such as Bede's *Ecclesiastical History of England,* and various other chronicles and annals were written to portray a broader divine plan, these forms now produced justification of the development of the new religious orders. Foundation documents, another form of history, were written to underline the uniqueness of a particular house or order, and monastic charters were written and rewritten to validate the continued possession of a particular abbey or monastery by an existing order. The introductions to these charters (known as harangues) were also used to remind the laity of its responsibility to forgo claims to ecclesiastical properties.

The written word assumed many propagandistic forms and purposes in the medieval world. The Bible itself was, of course, the main vehicle. The *Chanson de Roland* was another. Some of the medieval examples that resemble more acerbic forms of modern propaganda are found in the eleventh-century collection known as the *Libelli de lite,* which contains a number of works produced to castigate the opposition in the investiture contest. Many of these were in letter form, another important genre of propaganda, particularly from the eleventh through the thirteenth century. The letters of Bernard of Clairvaux, Peter the Venerable, and Berengar of Poitiers serve as prime examples in the monastic struggles of the twelfth century. The letters of Pope Gregory VII and Emperor Henry IV illuminate the medieval notion of propaganda in the eleventh century, as do the letters of Innocent III, Gregory IX, and Frederick II in the thirteenth century.

Speeches and sermons were among the other forms of medieval rhetoric used as propaganda. Preachers exercised great propagandistic freedom, whether they were advocating crusades or the values of a particular monastic order. The speeches of Urban II at Clemont in 1095, of Bernard in the twelfth century, and of Jacques de Vitry in the thirteenth century stand out as prime examples. Given the oral nature of the culture, these two remained the primary vehicles of medieval propaganda.

The legends of patron saints and the myths of the French chansons de geste provide still further examples. The early epic heroes of the Germanic world were transformed into models of the Christian warrior, which in turn became exemplars for the *athleti Christi* praised by Bernard in his advocacy for the monastic military orders of the twelfth century.

Medieval crusade propaganda provides the best example of antagonistic literature of the type associated with war propaganda in the modern era. Sermons, speeches, and songs were all critical in persuading the knights of Europe to embark on the great pilgrimage to the Holy Land. But by the thirteenth century many of the same forms, especially the sirventes, plus such special treatises as the *Collectio de scandalis,* document the propaganda of a developing anticrusade sentiment.

Special occasions, such as coronations and investments, as well as several aspects of the regular church liturgy, can also be considered as forms of medieval propaganda. The work of Ernst Kantorowicz on the *Laudes regiae* (liturgical acclamations of the Latin West) deserves special attention as documentation of the most general propagation of the medieval world view of Christ as king and emperor that modeled the parallel view of the emperor or king as the agent of Christ.

Finally, there is the example of church councils and canon law. What began as a project of papal reform in the eleventh century soon became a weapon of propaganda in the *Dictatus papae* of Gregory VII. This outline of papal primacy continued to be used as such through the more frequent codifications of canon law in the church councils called by the popes of the twelfth and thirteenth centuries, culminating in the symbolic climax of the Fourth Lateran Council of 1215. A different propaganda potential was exploited by Innocent IV and Gregory X in issuing the summones to the First and Second Councils of Lyons in 1245 and 1274, respectively. Both tried to use the occasion of the calling of a council to propagandize their particular goals for a renewal of the crusade.

The relative effectiveness of each of these approximately two dozen forms of medieval propaganda is difficult to assess because of their great variety of purposes and audiences. Furthermore, the limitations placed on their transmission by conditions of transportation, language, and media development made medieval propaganda less effective than the skill of individual practitioners might otherwise suggest.

TECHNIQUES AND PURPOSE

Medieval propaganda operated in an essentially protoliterate culture. Thus, the more effective techniques were visual and oral: church sculpture, for example, reached a broad audience. But the scope was limited and the message was simple. Letters were often read aloud in monasteries, as were chronicles. Speeches and sermons were delivered in various locations: in cloisters, in cathedrals, and in open urban squares or rural fields. As we have already noted, although many primary propaganda instruments—speeches, rumors, insignia (for example, the crusader's cross), and architecture—were available, the secondary instruments, the means of distribution, were significantly limited. Medieval propaganda was therefore always constrained by the fragmentation of audiences that resulted from the natural or man-made barriers and lack of technology to overcome them. Nevertheless, it is surprising how rapidly news could travel under the typical conditions of poor roads, highway robbers, and lack of centralized government control.

Given conditions of general illiteracy and lack of intellectual sophistication, much of medieval propaganda was directed to the elite groups and not to the masses. Speeches were presented to the knightly classes, letters were read to the cloistered monks or literate clerks, and sermons were often similarly directed. The media of architecture and sculpture were not flexible enough to persuade many to be crusaders, so sermons were used. Rumors and insignia, too, could be used quite effectively to that end. The propagandists, therefore, presented their rational (and nonrational) appeals to audiences that they knew and understood. They were less effective at controlling and targeting the various other segments of their broad and diverse audiences.

PROPAGANDA AND CULTURAL CHANGE IN THE WEST

Medieval propaganda, reflecting other cultural changes, demonstrated a relatively high level of flexibility and adaptability over the centuries. Early forms defended the church against paganism and carried forward the apologetic lines of argument first developed by Augustine, Origen, and Ambrose. By the sixth and seventh centuries, however, more positive tones were characteristic of the works of hagiography and history, and Germanic laws and monastic rules became the accepted, codified behavioral models. Gregory of Tours argued the need to preserve Christian values in the face of a general deterioration of the Merovingian civilization; Pope Gregory I wrote hymns and other propaganda for the expansion of Christianity into the wilds of England; and Benedict of Nursia produced the standard rule of monastic culture for centuries to come. Thus, in the West, propaganda sought to preserve civilization through the integration of Christian, pagan, and Germanic elements.

During the eighth and ninth centuries, propaganda in many forms was employed to promote the development of the Carolingian Empire, as an embodiment of a renewed Roman Empire on the one hand, and as the protector of the Roman church on the other. The Carolingians used various means to promote the image of a new, holy, and Roman Empire: proclamations of the popes; the coronation of Charlemagne in 800; the imperial court trappings at Aachen, including the chapel and the throne; the use of the *missi dominici* (agents of the king); the exchange of envoys with the Islamic court; the development of a new script and the palace school culture; and more typical forms such as coins and, later, manuscript illuminations. It was deemed necessary to show that the emperor's authority was ubiquitous and that he enjoyed divine favor at least as much as his counterpart in Byzantium, whom he had replaced in the West as defender of the church against all of its barbarian and Islamic enemies.

By the tenth and eleventh centuries, the propaganda needs had shifted again. There were several key themes, including the ongoing *translatio imperium* (translation of the empire) that had begun in Charlemagne's era, but its tenth-century proponents were in the Germanic portion of the now-divided Carolingian Empire. The defense of Rome was in the hands of the Ottonian emperors, who were successful against the Magyars. But they were not able to protect the papacy against the family quarrels in Rome itself to determine which family would control the selection of the popes. Thus, church reform became another major theme of propaganda, which argued for the elimination of the abuses of simony, lay investiture, and clerical marriage in particular. The Cluniacs established both a model for monastic reform and a new network for the dissemination of propaganda. By means of letter and visitation to the daughter houses, Cluny could be very persuasive and influential on behalf of papal causes as well.

Although in the eleventh century church reform continued to draw much attention, there was also a need to focus more on issues of centralization of both papal and imperial authority. We find the emergence of a major campaign between popes and emperors over rights of investiture. The letter was one of the most prominent forms of propaganda in this war. There are numerous collections, including those of the *Libelli de lite;* of the popes and emperors (especially those of Gregory VII and

Henry IV); and of numerous adherents to both sides, such as Meinhard of Bamberg and the so-called Hildesheim Collection. There were other vehicles as well, such as the *Dictatus papae* of Gregory VII and the *Collection in Seventy-four Titles* of canon law formulation, that promoted the papal view of centralized authority.

Another focus of eleventh-century Western propaganda was the promotion of peace in the troubled feudal society. In the absence of a central protective authority, which had been enjoyed to some extent in the Carolingian world, there was an attempt to develop a means to fill that role: the Peace of God and the Truce of God. In the first case, sanctions were issued by the bishops instead of the king against those who did not protect the clergy and church lands, as well as nuns, widows and orphans, and the poor, against the ravages of feudal warfare. The violators were subject to excommunication, another powerful propaganda weapon of the medieval church. The Truce of God strove to prevent all violence during certain times, as exemplified by its first issuance at the Council of Toulouges (1027), whereby "no one should attack his enemy between Saturday evening and Monday morning." By the eleventh century the Truce also attempted to extend the number of days, regarding which there is extensive evidence drawn from the works of Ralph Glaber and Adhemar of Chabannes, as well as hagiography, relics, chronicles, church councils, and sermons. All testify that the bishops were the chief promoters in this case. Based upon their own local needs, the bishops claimed that the Peace of God was merely a renewal of the peace of Christ that had been bestowed broadly upon the Christian people; and they claimed that the Truce reflected the understanding that "no Christian should kill another Christian." The Truce was first applied only to the Lord's day per se, but the propaganda was increasingly extended to the logical conclusion that one should never shed the blood of another Christian.

The explosion of Western propaganda in the twelfth century, operating on many fronts and utilizing numerous forms simultaneously in behalf of a variety of causes, reflects the dynamics of cultural change in that era. Histories, chronicles, annals, and foundation charters, for example, were used to rationalize and promote the newly developing monastic reform orders as well as particular aspects of their respective creeds. Letters were also used for this purpose, as were hagiographies, art, and architecture. One notes here the contrast between the starker simplicity of the Cistercian monastic church and the increasing splendor of Cluny, a prominent theme in the writings of Bernard of Clairvaux. At the same time emperors and popes, in their continuation of the investiture struggle, used treatises, letters, and poems.

Of course it was the crusade that consumed the greatest amount of the propagandists' attention and energy. The speech of Urban II at Clermont in 1095 marked only the beginning of a long series of speeches, sermons, chronicles, treatises, poems, and symbols to promote first the pilgrimage and then the holy war to save the Holy Land from the infidel. In addition, the popes promoted the expeditions by means of church councils and synods, tithes, indulgences, and excommunications. Papal letters to bishops, abbots, and secular leaders alike often reflect how far the popes were prepared to extend themselves in this effort; and the rhetoric of Bernard's sermons and letters probably best catches the dramatic spirit of the twelfth-century procrusade propaganda. However, an anticrusade propaganda continued to develop as well, despite the regular issuance of papal crusade encyclicals following that of Eugenius III (*Quantum predecessores*) and the appearance of some centralized media control through the use of various networks to read letters and preach sermons.

The propaganda of the thirteenth century featured a definite anticrusade component in several forms, including the treatises known as the *Collectio de scandalis,* the poetry of the sirventes, and the collection of anecdotal views contained in the works of Humbert of Romans and others who provided information for Gregory X prior to the commencement of the Second Council of Lyons in 1274. However, there were other aspects to consider, even beyond the continued procrusade sermons and letters. The mendicants and the secular orders, for example, waged a significant battle against one another over such issues as the control of education at Paris and the right to preach in local parishes. Much of the debate was apparently carried out in public discourse, rumor, and quasi-legal forums, but it was often recorded in the chronicles and poetry of individuals like Matthew Paris and Rutebeuf. The popes, in addition to promoting the crusades, were also propagandizing in letter, treatise, and council against the Hohenstaufen emperors, particularly Frederick II. He in turn pleaded his case before the heads of the developing European centralized monarchies.

In the fourteenth century, propagandists were busy with several major issues. The court of the French monarchs employed several skilled individuals, such as Pierre Dubois, in behalf of antipapal and pro-French, or at least promonarchy, positions. The developing hostility toward the clerical establishment was proclaimed in sermons, treatises, and chronicles, culminating in the works of John Wyclif in England and John Hus in Bohemia. Church reform was further debated in the matter of the indulgence, which had been so abused in the crusade era, and of the mendicants, who had been first attacked in the thirteenth-century. Furthermore, with the movement of the papacy to Avignon, the very essence of papal authority was brought into question. Much propaganda spilled out in the subsequent schism and the advocacy of a conciliar form of church rule. Many serious ecclesiastical reformers became proponents of the mystical perspective of Christian life as the only alternative to the chaos of the fourteenth century. The hagiography of the period clearly reflected this perspective.

Finally, a significant new strain of secular criticism of the estalishment emerged in the strikes of workers (*ciompi*) at Florence and in the revolt of peasants in England in the last decades of the century. The voice of "every man" was heard in a new way, if only as a whimper, and its tone was found in Chaucer, in *Piers Plowman,* and in the fabliaux.

By the fifteenth century, with the Hundred Years War and the Wars of the Roses, the natural proclivity for the propaganda of antagonism reemerged, apparently at a much higher emotional pitch. Fifteenth-century propaganda treatises are characterized by a greater degree of slander and ridicule of opponents than is found in earlier treatises. In the case of France at least, it would appear also that the propagandists were better known and perhaps better qualified than their earlier counterparts. Jean de Montreuil, Noël de Fribois, and Robert Blondel, for example, all provide political pieces from the perspective of having served at the court of the king or of being friends of those holding key positions. The propaganda of this era is also noteworthy for reflecting the movement toward national monarchy and, therefore, a sense of national identity. This enthusiasm for promoting the individual state, whether the early civic humanism of Italy or the emergence of the French and English nations, overshadowed the issue of papal universality although the issues of church reform still remained, and would remain until well after the Reformation.

BYZANTINE PROPAGANDA

In Byzantium propaganda was used to promote imperial power. The forms were as varied as those in the Latin West, but the written word was most significant. During Justinian's reign (527–565), there were acclamations, official speeches, inscriptions, panegyrics, and the legislation recorded in the *Corpus iuris civilis*. Speeches of the emperor—for example, that of Justin II (*r.* 565–578) on the occasion of the appointment of Tiberius as caesar—developed the thesis that imperial power was a gift of God. In addition, coinage, monumental architecture such as Hagia Sophia, mosaics, and even color were all part of the scheme to promote the imperial image as an ideal of eternity, piety, generosity, and victory. Purple and gold were the symbols for life and power, and were reserved for imperial use. The gold of coins was meant to reflect the splendor of the imperial court. Monumental art and illuminated manuscripts portrayed the emperor as a victor presiding over his court or as having more than human powers, an embodiment of the very notion of empire itself.

Concurrently, two central propaganda themes were dominant in the Byzantine East: first, the anti-Islamic and anti-Carolingian campaigns to rally the Eastern Roman Empire around the emperor in Constantinople for the preservation of the empire itself; and second, the propaganda of the iconoclastic struggle. The elevation of Charlemagne in 800 was treated as an act of usurpation, a political parallel to the developing split between East and West that was already apparent in the iconoclastic struggle. In the East the religious struggle was fierce, especially following the appointment of the historian Nikephoros as patriarch in 806. The propaganda of the opposition group of monks, who were angered because of his defense of icons and because he was not one of them, was bitter. Included among the range of forms that propagandists used were the colorful miniatures of the *Chronicle* of John Skylitzes depicting the revolt of the iconodule Thomas against Emperor Michael II (820–829); the acts of various ecclesiastical synods; and even the cruel public acts of persecution and martyrdom that marked the iconoclastic era to the very end in the early 840's. For example, around

837 the patriarch John Grammaticus used red-hot irons to inscribe iconoclastic verses on the foreheads of two Palestinian brothers who opposed what proved to be the last thrust of iconoclasm.

In the eleventh century, in contrast with the Western interest in the Peace of God and the Truce of God, the Byzantines sought to promote a more militant image of the emperor. The primary means were once again coinage and manuscript illumination. Particularly illustrative is the gold nomisma of Isaac I (1057–1059) that shows the emperor, for the first time since the reign of Leo III (717–741), wearing military rather than civil costume and holding a sword. Contemporary interpretation understood this to mean that the emperor claimed success based on his own power and not God's.

Byzantine imperial propaganda of the twelfth century is marked by attempts to justify violent coups d'état. For example, Isaac II (1185–1195) ordered "posterlike" images of himself displayed above the portals of churches. These showed him becoming emperor by a miracle. In fact he had deposed and executed his predecessor, Andronikos. Ironically, the latter had used a large painted panel near the church of the Forty Martyrs for similar ends: to alter impressions about the tragedy of his murder of the empress Xena and to portray himself as a peasant. Finally, the twelfth century saw extensive use of court ritual and rhetoric at occasions such as funerals and weddings in an attempt to render the emperor more solemn, more in harmony with heaven, and more admirable to his subjects. One of the most prominent publicists of the period, Eustathios Kataphloros of Thessaloniki, used funeral orations to praise Emperor Manuel I as God's coruler and earthly deity, and to support his overall political goals as well.

From the thirteenth through the fifteenth century much of Eastern propaganda continued to revolve around familiar themes. There was, in addition, more of an anti-Western focus, which resulted from the failure of the crusades and, in particular, the diversion of the Fourth Crusade to capture Constantinople. There were also polemics in the continuing dispute between Eastern and Western forms of orthodoxy that lasted until the fall of Constantinople to the Turks in 1453. With the increasing pressures on the imperial structure after the Byzantine recapture of Constantinople in 1261, much propaganda was often utilized to woo opponents such as the popes toward church union or to rationalize or even whitewash imperial actions. An example of the latter is John VI Kantakouzenos (1347–1354), who wrote his memoirs to present his role in the civil wars from 1321 to 1354 in a more favorable light. The panegyric also remained an important form of imperial propaganda.

ISLAMIC PROPAGANDA

In contrast with Byzantine and European Christian works of the seventh century, poetry was the most effective form of early Islamic propaganda. Strident poetry was used to promote Islam in the bedouin culture as the new religion fought first for its survival and then for its ascendancy among the Arabs. Poetry had an important place in Arab culture: poets were the tribal spokesmen. Muḥammad himself employed three poets to promote the new creed. The most famous was Ka^{c}b ibn Zuhayr, who composed the *Burda* (Mantle ode) that eulogized the Prophet as a sayyid of an Arab tribe. However, the Koran itself, established by Muḥammad, was the most significant of all Islamic propaganda. Throughout the medieval period it remained the chief means of propagation of the Islamic creed, the main symbol and source of Islamic law, theology, and way of life.

In the eighth and ninth centuries, there were significant changes in the focuses of Eastern and Western propaganda alike. In the Islamic world a long-standing propaganda campaign preceded the physical battle between the Umayyads and the Abbasids. Recorded largely in anecdotal stories rather than poetry, it can be found in both the *ḥadith* (anecdotes relating deeds or sayings of the Prophet) and *akhbar* (the deeds and sayings of the Prophet's companions and men of later periods). The works of the Hanbalites in the ninth century, particularly that of the collector of anecdotes who was best known as Ibn Abi ᵓl-Dunya in Baghdad, represent the Umayyad side. Though there are some anecdotes that reflect unfavorably on them, most extol the virtues, piety, compassion, justness, and generosity of the Umayyad caliphs. Even when the Abbasids emerged as successors in the long struggle, they did not suppress the Umayyad anecdotes, perhaps because they encouraged a virtuous life without presenting any real challenge to the Abbasids.

In contrast with this view of the Islamic world as one dominated by conflict, there was that of splendid court life presented in the *Thousand and One Nights*. In depicting the social order of urban private life, the institutionalized relations of men and women, and the personal aspects of human conflict, these tales popularized Islam to non-Muslims from another perspective.

Within Islam itself the debates over religious law and custom marked the Shiite and Sunnite propaganda, which appeared regularly with the advent of a new caliph or the outbreak of a revolt. Although the Islamic world had become calmer with the establishment of the Abbasid court at Baghdad, the battle between caliphs and provincial governors over the exercise of absolute power continued. Earlier, in the ninth century, there had been an attempt at theological resolution by reference to the Islamic notion of authority. But now the Fatimid caliphs, for example, in their propaganda to win over their subject peoples presented themselves as favored by God.

The high degree of individual freedom enjoyed in the Islamic world is reflected in the early-eleventh-century Islamic campaigns of the "Pure Brethren" (Ikhwan al-Safaᵓ) at Basra and Baghdad. This group was dedicated to personal enlightenment and spiritual purification, but chose to propagate its ideals among others as well, producing a handbook or encyclopedia of the sciences of rational philosophy that remained popular in Islamic society throughout the Middle Ages.

By the thirteenth century Islamic propaganda was in a state of relative abeyance because of the fall of Baghdad to the Mongols in 1258. Even after that event, however, propaganda in the environs was directed toward reminding the local sultans of their duties to promote the public welfare. One of the better examples is that of Ali al-Harawi of Syria, who had the local reputation of being a "vagabond Sufi" but was respected because of his experience and wise counsel. He used this influence in particular on al-Malik al-Ẓāhir to provide a model of the ideal Muslim prince in the face of opposition from the pro-Shiite propagandists. Whereas the propaganda of the Mongol conquerors was directed toward affirming the monumental achievement of their conquest, the Islamic world itself was able to continue its international Muslim institutions. In practical terms, this left much of the propaganda in the hands of the Sufis or the *ᶜulamāᵓ* of the Shiite and Sunnite sects, on the one hand, and the Arab or Persian poets, on the other. This control was reinforced by the Muslim ban on icons as idolatry and by the lack of political dynasties to legitimize the myths and symbols of heraldry that marked the West in this period.

MEDIEVAL PROPAGANDA CONTRASTED WITH MODERN PROPAGANDA

Medieval propaganda shares a number of characteristics with its modern counterpart, and in other ways it differs. The medieval propagandists, for example, had good instincts regarding the detection of public opinion and a sense of audience. Yet their efforts to influence action were not well centralized by the machinery of a modern state; thus, the propaganda was not often well designed or even organized. The dominant problem remained that of the primitive means of communication. Unable to overcome this, medieval propaganda was essentially directed toward diverse elite constituencies with different purposes; it was not a campaign that could affect the masses as we understand them.

By the thirteenth century, the multiplication of forms and their simultaneous use in key situations, such as the crusades, suggest that the medieval world understood the necessity of reaching several audiences simultaneously, and that each audience might respond better to a given medium. It is less clear, however, that the propagandists understood the need to translate their messages into simple, direct symbols or stereotypes in order both to simplify and to orchestrate the desired outcomes. Nor does it appear that the messages were often intended to influence more than the elite: perhaps to rationalize to posterity or the masses after the fact, but not to influence. The symbols were too complex and not readily translatable for them. Even Muḥammad, for example, was not sufficiently well known to serve as a ready-made bête noir in the West.

Medieval propaganda is, in other ways, comparable with the modern. It exhibited an understanding of the same general goals; it was concerned with society's central issues; and while there were positive elements to it, still other examples lend support to our modern bias regarding propaganda, namely, that it is the epitome of the "big lie" technique. Even Vincent of Beauvais and Peter the Venerable, for example, were careless with their facts in the creation of anti-Islamic polemics in the twelfth and thirteenth centuries. Similarly, from time to time one finds other examples from the investiture contest in the West, from the imperial misrepresentations by the Byzantine usurpers, and from the various attacks by Shiite or Sunnite advocates. It is also true that medieval propagandists wanted to inculcate ideas, not explain them; and thus they frequently disseminated conclusions of doubtful validity.

In contrast with modern, medieval propaganda seems to possess elements of conflict between what Jacques Ellul calls "vertical propaganda," which is designed by a leader to influence the crowd, and "horizontal propaganda," the attempt to utilize the principle of group dynamics, to influence the crowd from within. Because of medieval networks of monastic communities, circles of bishops, feudal courts, and the like, the propaganda that was directed to a similar group (such as the monks or mendicants) was more effective than that which tried to cross group lines (the vertical model).

The most difficult aspect of the study of medieval propaganda is that of assessing its real impact. Often we cannot determine the influence of anything so abstract as ideas, particularly conflicting ideas about a controversial issue. Moreover, some of our most interesting evidence has been preserved because it was found useful for an entirely different reason. For example, it is fairly clear now that the *Codex Udalrici* of the eleventh-century investiture contest was preserved for its examples of rhyming prose and was used by the German masters of Latin style in the twelfth century—not because it had any measured influence on the outcome of the contest. In general, the tests of numbers, audience size, and number of surviving manuscripts or artifacts cannot be applied in any scientific way.

Yet it can be reasonably argued that medieval propaganda had influence. The propaganda of Augustine, the Bible, the Koran, and Bernard of Clairvaux may be regarded as outstanding examples. Yet, one cannot envision the success of the monastic orders in the East and West, the crusades, or the Sufis, or the survival of the Byzantine imperial mystique or the Holy Roman Empire, without the lesser-known vehicles of propaganda that were employed to sustain them over time.

In conclusion, there do appear to be a number of aspects of the study of propaganda in general that help us understand medieval propaganda better, particularly why it appears to reflect social and political change so clearly. First, propaganda can succeed only where there is an audience that has a psychological need for it. The developing state, for example, uses propaganda to allay people's anxieties, to provide justification. There is a sense that latent public opinion drives the need for propaganda, an audience anxiety that demands information, particularly in times of rapid social transformation. This certainly was the case in the Europe of the twelfth to fourteenth centuries.

Second, propaganda serves to crystallize prejudices and to intensify conflict in response to a group need to stereotype and to form images that represent unexpressed anger and hostility. The propagandist responds to that need and makes a public symbol out of previously private opinions.

Third, propaganda can "immortalize" a concept by providing an "irrational, external, and collective tenet that provides a scale of values, rules of behavior, and a principle of social integration" (Ellul, pp. 166–167). In a rapidly changing society such as that of the West in the late Middle Ages, propaganda derived from that same need to promote action with little thought. The process of secularization was in conflict with ecclesiastical and religious standards of long standing. To rally support for the papal centralized model of control, the propagandists preached a crusade, using the symbol of the cross.

A fourth generalization about propaganda seems also to apply to the medieval situation: the more you use propaganda, the more you divide the audience and weaken the impact. This may well explain the failure of much of the procrusade propaganda of the thirteenth century.

Finally, the difficulties of measuring the effects of propaganda in the Middle Ages have not been overcome today. People generally have two opinions on a subject, one publicly expressed and one held privately. One can best measure the potential impact of propaganda by examining preexisting attitudes, general societal trends, and special interests of those to whom the propaganda will be addressed. And it has been demonstrated that propaganda is most effective among the more elite segments of society. Education makes men more favorably disposed to propaganda because they are more interested in and better able to understand facts, problems, and choices, and more willing to learn new attitudes.

Medieval propaganda of both the East and the West seems to demonstrate understanding of these principles. It was thus used to appeal to the elites to facilitate and support change in medieval society.

BIBLIOGRAPHY

Thomas W. Arnold, *The Preaching of Islam* (1913, repr. 1956); Josef Benzinger, "Zum Wesen und zu den Formen von Kommunikation und Publizistik im Mittelalter," in *Publizistik,* 15 (1970); Robert Brentano,

"Western Civilization: The Middle Ages," in Harold D. Lasswell, Daniel Lerner, and Hans Speier, eds., *Communication and Propaganda in World History,* I (1979); Hanns Buchli, *Sechstausend Jahre Werbung: Geschichte der Wirtschaftswerbung und der Propaganda* (1962); Charles W. Connell, "Pro- and Anti-Crusade Propaganda: An Overview," in Patricia W. Cummins, Patrick W. Conner, and Charles W. Connell, eds., *Literary and Historical Perspectives of the Middle Ages* (1982); Giles Constable, *Letters and Letter-Collections* (1976), and "Papal, Imperial, and Monastic Propaganda in the Eleventh and Twelfth Centuries," in George Makdisi, Dominique Sourdel, and Janine Sourdel-Thomas, eds., *Prédication et propagande au moyen âge: Islam, Byzance, Occident* (1983); H. E. J. Cowdrey, "The Peace and the Truce of God in the Eleventh Century," in *Past and Present,* **46** (1970); Norman Daniel, *Islam and the West: The Making of an Image* (1960).

Jacques Ellul, *Propaganda: The Formation of Men's Attitudes,* Konrad Kellen and Jean Lerner, trans. (1973); Carl Erdmann, "Die Anfänge der staatlichen Propaganda im Investiturstreit," in *Historische Zeitschrift,* **154** (1936), and *The Origin of the Idea of Crusade,* Marshall W. Baldwin and Walter Goffart, trans. (1977); Patrick Geary, *Furta Sacra: Thefts of Relics in the Central Middle Ages* (1978); Clifford Geertz, "Ideology as a Cultural System," in David E. Apter, ed., *Ideology and Discontent* (1964); J. T. Gilchrist, "Canon Law Aspects of Eleventh-century Gregorian Reform Programme," in *Journal of Ecclesiastical History,* **13** (1962); Jocelyn N. Hillgarth, "Coins and Chronicles: Propaganda in Sixth-century Spain and the Byzantine Background," in *Historia,* **15** (1966); C. J. Holdsworth, "Visions and Visionaries in the Middle Ages," in *History,* n.s. **48** (1963); Ernst H. Kantorowicz, *Laudes regiae* (1946); Gerhart Ladner, *Theologie und Politik vor dem Invertiturstreit* (1936, repr. 1968), 42–59; P. S. Lewis, "War Propaganda and Historiography in Fifteenth-century France and England," in *Transactions of the Royal Historical Society,* 5th ser., **15** (1965).

J. W. McKenna, "Popular Canonization as Political Propaganda: The Cult of Archbishop Scrope," in *Speculum,* **45** (1970); Karl Mirbt, *Die Publizistik in Zeitalter Gregors VII* (1894); Colin Morris, "Propaganda for War: The Dissemination of the Crusading Ideal in the Twelfth Century," in W. J. Sheils, ed., *The Church and War* (1983); George Makdisi, Dominique Sourdel, and Janine Sourdel-Thomas, eds., *Prédication et propagande au moyen âge: Islam, Byzance, Occident* (1983); William Patt, "Early 'Ars Dictaminis' as Response to a Changing Society," in *Viator,* **9** (1978); Terence Qualter, *Propaganda and Psychological Warfare* (1962); I. S. Robinson, "The Friendship Network of Gregory VII," in *History,* **63** (1978); Richard Scholz, *Die Publizistik zur Zeit Philipps des Schönen und Bonifaz VIII* (1903, repr. 1962); André Seguin, "Bernard et la seconde croisade," in *Bernard de Clairvaux* (1953); Palmer A. Throop, *Criticism of the Crusade: A Study of Public Opinion and Crusade Propaganda* (1940).

CHARLES W. CONNELL

[See also **Acclamations; Bernard of Clairvaux, St.; Byzantine Empire: History; Carolingians and the Carolingian Empire; Cistercian Order; Clermont, Council of; Cluny, Order of; Crusade, Concept of; Crusade Propaganda; Crusades and Crusader States; Dictatus Papae; Gothic Architecture; Gothic Art; Hagiography; Historiography; Hundred Years War; Iconoclasm, Christian; Investiture and Investiture Conflict; Islam, Conquests of; Islam, Religion; Laudes; Peace of God, Truce of God; Pilgrimage, Western European; Preaching and Sermon Literature, Western European; Preaching and Sermons, Islamic; Prophecy, Political; Wars of the Roses.**]

PROPHECY, POLITICAL: MIDDLE ENGLISH. According to the author of *The Complaint of Scotland* (1529), "The inglismen gifis ferme credit to diuerse prophane propheseis of Merlyne, and til vthir ald corruppit vaticinaris" (chap. 10, l. 21). The general truth of this statement is borne out by most of the surviving evidence. Books like "les propheties de Merlyn," owned by Sir Simon Burley in 1388, are regularly encountered in medieval libraries. Some people, like John de Courcy, the Anglo-Norman conqueror of Ulster, who always carried his book with him, were inveterate consulters of prophecies. What is more, the government was sufficiently convinced of the propagandist value of political prophecy that it banned this sort of writing from time to time, as in 1402, when prophecies were used by the Welsh, and in 1406, when they were exploited by the Lollards. The authority which was felt to attach to political prophecies seems to have derived as much from their biblical and classical antecedents as from their occasionally successful predictions.

The object of the political prophecy is to influence the course of future events. Naturally, prophecies appear most frequently at times of crisis and potential change. Most prophecies are of a relatively vague, nonspecific sort—presumably to leave the maximum amount of scope for their predictions to come true. They often contain a certain amount of verifiable historical fact—presumably to contextualize their predictions and lend them some credibility—and then an extrapolation, wishful or fearful, toward likely future events. Many political prophecies are attributed, without foundation, to some famous person such as Gildas or Bede or Thomas Becket, or to an imaginary seer such as Merlin.

Many prophecies deal with the destinies of nations, but occasionally smaller social and political groups or even individuals claim their attention. Sometimes direct reference is made to named groups or persons, but more frequently prophecies refer by means of cryptic allusions or symbols. Two methods were principally used: the "Galfridian" method (so called because it was given popularity by Geoffrey of Monmouth) used animal or plant symbolism; the "Sibylline" method used the initial letters of names. But practically anything could serve the prophetic poet's turn (there are prophecies, for example, using the numbers on dice), and sometimes more than one method is used in the same poem. None of this makes it easy to interpret prophecies—nor does the propensity of many writers for reusing old material, with little alteration, in new contexts.

MERLIN AND RELATED PROPHECIES

The best known of all prophecies are those made by Merlin in part VII of Geoffrey of Monmouth's *Historia regum Britanniae* (finished about 1136). Prophecies of Merlin, Geoffrey tells the reader, were so popular in the British (that is, Welsh) language and created so much interest in England that he was persuaded by Alexander, bishop of Lincoln, to turn aside from his main history and put them into Latin.

Geoffrey's prophecy is long and does not hang together particularly well; it was almost certainly assembled from disparate sources. There are recognizable allusions to historical incidents—such as the wreck of the *White Ship* off Barfleur in 1120, in which William, son of Henry I, drowned. The incident which prompts the prophecy, however, is a battle between two dragons in a drained pool. Merlin interprets this incident in terms of the relations between the Britons and the Saxons:

> Alas for the Red Dragon, for its end is near. Its cavernous dens shall be occupied by the White Dragon, which stands for the Saxons whom you [*i.e.*, King Vortigern] have invited over. The Red Dragon represents the people of Britain, who will be overrun by the White One: for Britain's mountains and valleys shall be levelled, and the streams in its valleys shall run with blood.

The prophecy goes on wishfully to predict the regaining of Britain by Cadwalader and Conan.

Though there is no extant Middle English version of Merlin's prophecy as a whole, parts of it are frequently reused—usually to express a hope for the recovery of Britain. One stanza from the version in Oxford, Bodleian Library, MS Rawlinson K 42, p. 104, reads:

> Then schal Cadwaladre Conan calle,
> And gadre Scotlonde vn-to hys flocke;
> Þanne in Ryueres blode schall falls,
> And þanne schal perysche braunche & stocke

—the "braunche and stocke" presumably being those of the English, who shall "be deposyde for euer and aye." Another version, in Oxford, All Souls College, MS 33, fol. 136v, substitutes Owan for Conan, but is essentially a similar wish for a Welsh conquest of England:

> Cadwalladyre sall Owan call.
> And Walys sall busk þaim forto ryse.
> And Allbayn sall to þaim fall.

There are, in fact, many prophecies which hope for a reestablishment of a sort of pan-Celtic hegemony over Britain. One such, an unpublished item from Dublin, Trinity College, MS 516, fol. 16r, begins conventionally enough:

> This is the propheci þat thai have in Wales
> When Walsch, Scotes and Irisch flittith þair fane,
> & cum vnto London by dovnes eke & dales

but ends with specific predictions of good fortune for "Sir Lyonil the Mortimer." This is particularly appropriate because in 1378 the Welsh royal title passed to the Mortimer family. And it was by virtue of his connection with the Mortimers that Edward IV's claims to the throne were so frequently urged by reference to prophecies favoring a return to Welsh rule of Britain. The supporters of Henry VII, because the Tudors were a Welsh family, also adduced this type of prophecy in his support. Henry appears, for example, to be the "grete gentilman" of "the blode of Cadwalidus" for whom great things are predicted in the year 1484 in some verses from London, British Museum, Lansdowne MS 76, fol. 63v.

THOMAS OF ERCELDOUNE AND HIS INFLUENCE

Scarcely less famous than Merlin was Thomas of Erceldoune, or Thomas Rymour. There is evidence that Thomas was a historical person in thirteenth-century Scotland. His eminence as a prophet was established by what was taken to be a prediction of the death of King Alexander III of Scotland in 1286; but he also derived credit from having predicted, possibly in 1296 or 1297, a glorious career for Wallace.

Much is attributed to Thomas of Erceldoune, but nothing which is certainly of his composition has survived. The lengthiest item—*The Romance and Prophecies of Thomas of Erceldoune*—appears to date from the late fourteenth century, or even the early fifteenth.

In the *Romance,* a beautiful lady appears to Thomas, and after he has fallen in love with her, she takes him away to her enchanted country. He stays for seven years and is shown visions of heaven, purgatory, and hell. On his return to the real world he asks, as a token of their love, that she will tell him of "som farley." In the form of a lengthy prediction she reviews the events of fourteenth-century Scottish history, paying particular attention to the struggle for supremacy between the Bruce family and the Baliols, and ending with the invasion of England by James Douglas, second earl of Douglas, in 1388 and the battle of Otterburn.

As the lady then tries to depart, Thomas asks for further information:

> Telle me, ȝif it thi willis bee,
> Of thyes Batells, how þay schall ende,
> And whate schalle worthe of this northe countre?
> (490–492, Thornton version)

The lady complies, starting with what appears to be a reference to Henry IV's invasion of Scotland and siege of Edinburgh in 1400. But then she predicts three battles for which there is no basis in historical fact—between "Seton and the sea," at "Gladsmoor," and at "Sandyford." She also speaks of a bastard who will come out of the west, will become leader of all Britain, and will eventually die in the Holy Land. But Thomas ends with a question that belongs to history:

> Lufly lady, tel þou me
> Off blake Agnes of Don[bar].
> (659–660, Cambridge version)

This refers to Agnes, wife of Patrick, earl of March, who in her husband's absence successfully held the castle of Dunbar against the English for five months in 1338.

The prophecies of Thomas of Erceldoune were extremely popular, and many historical battles came to be identified with the three mentioned in the final fit of *The Romance and Prophecies.* Some Scots saw the English victory at Pinkie in 1547 as fulfillment of the predictions about "Seton." In 1471 some Englishmen referred to the battle of Barnet as "Gladsmoor," perhaps because of the large numbers of dead there; but in 1745 the victorious Highlanders identified Prestonpans as "Gladsmoor."

What is more, Thomas' prophecies as a whole were revised and updated. An English version from MS Lansdowne 762 refers to events as late as the battle of Flodden and the sieges of Thérouanne and Tournai in 1513. The prophecy attributed to Thomas in Robert Waldegrave's *Whole Prophesie of Scottlande* (1603) has a definite allusion to 1547:

> At Pinkin Cleuch their shal be spilt
> Much gentle blood that day.

and a possible one to 1558 in the lines on the "French wife," which may refer to the marriage of Queen Mary to the Dauphin in that year.

The Cock in the North, in the version from London, British Museum, Cotton Rolls ii.23, twice mentions Thomas as a prophet (along with Bridlington, Bede, Banaster, and Merlin) and twice alludes to the battle at "Sandyford." But, in this particular form, the poem appears to have little to do with Scottish history. It seems to review one particular aspect of English history—the Percy rebellions against Henry IV—and to allude to Yorkist hopes for victory over the Lancastrians—if, that is, the Mole represents the earl of Westmoreland and the Mermaid is Queen Margaret:

> The molle and the mermayden mevith in mynd—
> Criste that is oure creature hath cursid hem by mouthe!

The Cock in the North seems clearly to derive some of its ideas from sources other than Thomas. The famous opening:

> When the cocke in the Northe hath bilde his nest,
> And buskith his briddis and becenys hem to fle . . .

appears to derive from John of Bridlington:

> Tempore brumali gallus nido boreali
> Pullos unabit, et se volitare parabit.

There are also Scottish prophecies, such as the so-called *Second Scottish Prophecy,* which owe virtually nothing to Thomas. In fact, much of the symbolism of the *Second Scottish Prophecy* appears to derive from Geoffrey of Monmouth. The prophecy itself deals in generalities and was frequently updated. Various versions of it are dated 1382, 1385, 1387, 1482, 1535, and 1642.

THE LAST KING OF ROME

Several medieval prophecies are based, in whole or in part, on the so-called Last King of Rome story (first found in the writings of Pseudo-Methodius and in the apocryphal apocalypses of Daniel). This story tells how the last king of Rome will undertake a pilgrimage or crusade to Jerusalem to defeat the forces of Antichrist and reestablish Christian rule and government. Although the prophecy is basically about the unification and extension of Christendom, it was given, in its several retellings, nationalistic variations. In the tenth century, for example, the monk Adso of Montier-en-Der, in a letter to Queen Gerberga, predicted that the last king would be of the Frankish dynasty.

In 1307–1308, Adam Davy, basing his sequence of dreams on this sort of story, predicted a glorious future for Edward II, culminating in his being "corouned myd gret blis" as "Emperour in cristianete" (verses 80–82), followed by a "pilerinage . . . to bien awreke of oure fon" (verses 103–104).

In 1349, the Minorite friar John of Ruspescissa predicted that an Englishman would win the Holy Sepulcher. At this date he must have had in mind Edward III, and, indeed Edward III is the king for whom glory is foretold in one Latin version of *The Lion, the Lily, and the Son of Man,* according to a note in London, British Museum, MS Cotton Cleopatra D iii, referring to the prediction: "Filius hominis mare transibit, et portabit signum mirabile ad terram promissionis." This prophecy almost always ends with the prediction of a crusade, but the symbolism of the title refers to European politics. A couplet version in London, British Museum, MS Lansdowne 762, for example, tells how the Lily (the king of France) will spread into the Land of the Lion (Flanders) until defeated by the Man's Son (the king of England) and the Eagle out of the East (the emperor). In the manuscript the Man's Son is identified with "Kynge Henry of England" and the date 1524 appears; but the poem appears to be older and may have been updated from 1424.

THE SIX KINGS

Scarcely less popular is the prophecy of the Six Kings, which appears to derive from Geoffrey of Monmouth. In the versions of this prophecy dating from the late fourteenth and early fifteenth centuries, the Six Kings are usually interpreted as Henry III (the Lamb of Winchester), Edward I (the Dragon), Edward II (the Goat), Edward III (the Lion or the Boar), Richard II (the Ass), and Henry IV (the Mole).

According to a story reported by Edward Halle in the sixteenth century, this is the prophecy used for their own encouragement by the enemies of Henry IV:

> A certayne writer writeth that this earle of Marche, the Lorde Percy and Owen Glendor wer vnwisely made belieue by a Welsh Prophecier, that Kyng Henry was the Moldwarpe, cursed of Goddes owne mouthe, and that they thre were the Dragon, the Lion and the Wolffe, whiche shoulde deuide this realme betwene theim, by the deuiacion and not deuinacion of that mawmet Merlin.

In London, British Museum, MS Cotton Galba E.ix, there is a couplet version of this prophecy of the sort this writer may have had in mind, though it is not identical with his description. Henry IV, according to the poet, is a "grete wretche" who is "weried with Goddes mowth" and who will be "casten down with sin & with pride" by a "dragon" and a "wolf þat sall cum out of the west" (presumably Percy and Glendower). The Dragon and the Wolf will receive help from Ireland:

> Out of Yreland þan sall cum a liown
> And hald with þe wolf and with þe dragown

—perhaps a reference to Glendower's request for Irish help in 1401. The poet also alludes to the tripartite division of England that the rebels proposed to carry out after their hoped-for victory:

> Þan sall all Ingland on wonder wise,
> Be euyn partid in thre parties.

Another English version of this prophecy, beginning, "He shall convert the cursed Sarasines," predicts that the reign of the Mole will be short and that the Ass will return—no doubt a product of the belief, held by some particularly in 1402, that Richard II was still living and would reclaim his kingdom.

OTHER PROPHECIES

Several prophecies touched on the relations between Richard II and Henry IV, and one of them, dealing with an ampulla of sacred oil, appears to have had a profound effect on Richard II. According to the story, Thomas Becket, while exiled from

England, was presented with an ampulla of sacred oil by the Virgin Mary, who told him that future kings of England, if anointed with this oil, would invariably be successful in war and drive the pagans from the Holy Land. On her instructions, Becket gave the oil to a monk, who hid it in a church. But the ampulla eventually came to England with Edward III. The story enters history when Richard II finds an ampulla in the Tower of London, with a Latin prophecy attached to it. Richard wished for a second coronation with the oil, but this was refused. Ironically, the oil was later used for the anointing of Henry IV. With certain additions and alterations this story appears in Latin, French, and Welsh.

Two fragmentary pieces in Middle English alliterative verse called *Thomas à Becket's Prophecies* have also survived. In the version in Cambridge, University Library, MS Kk.I.5, the prophecy is evoked by a revelation inscribed on a stone, which is discovered by workmen in Poitiers as they are building a tower:

It sayd, "Masterles men, yhe this tour make;
A Bayre sall come out of Berttane wytht so brode tuskis,
He sall trauyll up yhour towre, and your towne þer efter,
And dycht his den in þe derrest place þat euer aucht kynge charl[es.]"

The prophecy goes on to state that the Boar will conquer France, Lombardy, and Milan, and then sail to the Holy Land "To convert the cateffes þat noȝtt one Crystis lewys." Since there is no mention of his return he will presumably die there. The rest of the poem predicts how England will be ruled by women and how pestilences and torments will occur until the people know Christ. The boar in this prophecy is probably meant to represent Edward III, as in the Six Kings prophecy, and the two boars who are mentioned in the Hatton MS version of *Thomas à Becket's Prophecies* are probably meant to be Edward III and the Black Prince.

Political prophecies had a considerable vogue in the Middle Ages, and prophetic elements sometimes appear in poems of a basically different sort. At the end of *Piers Plowman* B VI, for example, there are some lines predicting that "er fyue yer be fulfilled . . . famyn shal aryse" and that through "flood and foule wedres fruytes shul faile" (321–331). The vogue lasted beyond the Middle Ages too. The Fool in *King Lear* (3.2.80–95), in the course of some predictions about dire future events to happen in England, quotes two lines from a medieval prophecy attributed to Merlin:

Then shall the realm of Albion
Come to great confusion

and he adds, prophesying the prophecy as it were, "This prophecy Merlin shall make, for I live before his time."

With Shakespeare, however, the time of prophecies was coming to an end. As an indication of this, Hotspur, in *I Henry IV* (3.1.148–155), gives a scathing account of the prophecies Glendower used to encourage himself. Hotspur lists the symbols—"moldwarp," "ant," "dragon," "finless fish," "clip-winged griffon," and so on—and describes them as "skimble-skamble stuff." Prophecies continued to be invoked and to be written, but the evidence is that they came increasingly to be treated with skepticism and scorn.

BIBLIOGRAPHY

Sources. F. J. Furnivall, ed., *Adam Davy's 5 Dreams About Edward II* (1878); Geoffrey of Monmouth, *Historia regum Britanniae,* Jacob Hammer, ed. (1951); Joseph Hall, ed., *The Poems of Laurence Minot* (1897); J. Rawson Lumby, ed., *Bernardus de cura rei famuliaris, with Some Early Scottish Prophecies* (1870); James A. H. Murray, ed., *The Complaynt of Scotlande,* 2 vols. (1872), and *The Romance and Prophecies of Thomas of Erceldoune* (1875); Clifford Peterson, "John Harding and Geoffrey of Monmouth: Two Unrecorded Poems and a Manuscript," in *Notes and Queries,* **225** (1980); Rossell H. Robbins, ed., *Historical Poems of the XIVth and XVth Centuries* (1959); Thomas Wright, ed., *Political Poems and Songs Relating to English History,* 2 vols. (1859–1861).

Studies. The basic study remains Rupert Taylor, *The Political Prophecy in England* (1911). See also Alison Allan, "Yorkist Propaganda: Pedigree, Prophecy, and the 'British History' in the Reign of Edward IV," in Charles Ross, ed., *Patronage, Pedigree, and Power in Later Medieval England* (1979); Morton W. Bloomfield, *Piers Plowman as a Fourteenth-century Apocalypse* (1962); Margaret Enid Griffiths, *Early Vaticination in Welsh* (1937); V. J. Scattergood, *Politics and Poetry in the Fifteenth Century* (1971); Glanmor Williams, "Prophecy, Poetry, and Politics in Medieval and Tudor Wales," in H. Hearder and H. R. Loyn, eds., *British Government and Administration: Studies Presented to S. B. Chrimes* (1974).

V. J. SCATTERGOOD

[See also **Allegory; Anglo-Norman Literature; Anglo-Saxon Literature; Antichrist; Arthurian Literature;**

Astrology; Beast Epic; England; Geoffrey of Monmouth; Ludus de Antichristo; Magic and Folklore, Western European; Matter of Britain, Matter of France, Matter of Rome; Middle English Literature; Propaganda; Scotland; Scottish Literature, Gaelic; Wales; Welsh Literature.]

PROPRIETAS, a term used in mensural notational theory since the last half of the thirteenth century to describe the proper written form of a ligature and, more specifically, the form and rhythmic value of the first note of a ligature. Among earlier modal rhythmic theorists, such as John of Garland, *proprietas* referred to the proper written form of ligated notes, that is, the form inherited from plainsong notation. With the rise of mensural theory, especially after Franco of Cologne's *Ars cantus mensurabilis* (*ca.* 1280), a ligature was described as *cum proprietate, sine proprietate,* or *cum opposita proprietate,* with reference to the written form and rhythmic value of the first note of the ligature. A ligature with no altered first note (*cum proprietate*) was rendered with the first note a breve. A ligature with a downward stem added to or subtracted from the first note (*sine proprietate*) was rendered with the first note a long. A ligature with an upward stem added to the first note (*cum opposita proprietate*) was rendered with the first two notes both semibreves.

BIBLIOGRAPHY

Margaret Bent and David Hiley, "Notation," pt. III, in *The New Grove Dictionary of Music and Musicians,* XIII (1980), 358–359 and 362–373; Wolf Frobenius, "Proprietas," in *Handwörterbuch der musikalischen Terminologie,* Hans Heinrich Eggebrecht, ed., II (1972); Fritz Reckow, "Proprietas und Perfectio: Zur Geschichte der Rhythmus, seiner Aufzeichnung und Terminologie im 13. Jahrhundert," in *Acta musicologica,* 39 (1967); William G. Waite, *The Rhythm of Twelfth-century Polyphony* (1954).

CALVIN M. BOWER

[See also **Ars Nova; Franco of Cologne; John of Garland; Ligature; Musical Notation, Western; Musical Treatises; Rhythm.**]

PROSA. See **Sequence.**

PROSE LANCELOT. The term "Prose Lancelot" has been applied by modern scholars to a trilogy of Old French prose romances, written about 1215–1230, which form the nucleus of the so-called Vulgate Cycle, the most widely read and most influential body of Arthurian material throughout the Middle Ages, and one of the most powerful monuments of all of French prose.

The three romances are *Le livre de Lancelot del lac* (The book of Lancelot of the Lake, commonly referred to as *Lancelot* proper), *La queste del Saint Graal* (The quest of the Holy Grail), and *Mort Artu* (The death of Arthur). They were compiled and unified by at least two persons, probably Cistercian monks from Champagne or Burgundy, who used the technique of *entrelacement* (interlacement) to create a continuous narrative. Together, the three romances, of which the *Lancelot* proper is three times as long as the other two combined, constitute a gargantuan artistic effort. (They occupy 1,200 folio pages in Heinrich O. Sommer's diplomatic edition.)

The authors of the Prose Lancelot used as their sources probably not only everything that was known about Lancelot (as, for example, Ulrich von Zatzikhoven's *Lanzelet* and Chrétien de Troyes's *Chevalier de la charrette*), but apparently everything transmitted in written or oral form revolving around King Arthur and his more illustrious knights. The name "Prose Lancelot" was given to the romances because they form an extended biography of Lancelot, a relative latecomer to Arthurian romance, and trace the hero's fate from his *enfances* (childhood) to his saintly death.

The *Lancelot* proper introduces the hero at his birth and gives a detailed account of a calamitous youth who loses both parents and is reared by the semisupernatural Lady of the Lake (whose surname Lancelot acquires). It goes into great detail, expounding his glorious career as King Arthur's most valiant knight but also illuminating his fateful yet illicit love of Queen Guenevere. The first tryst between Lancelot and the queen—later alluded to by Dante in an immortal part of his *Inferno*—ends innocently, and it is not until the author, who is Lancelot's most successful apologist, has a chance to prove King Arthur himself false to his marriage vows that Lancelot and the queen consummate their love, thereby setting the stage for a series of events that culminates in the dissolution of the Arthurian fellowship.

Among the subsequent descriptions of countless

PROSE LANCELOT

tournaments and strange encounters, as well as the introduction of many illustrious knights, such as Lancelot's best friend, Galehaut, one crucial event stands out: the begetting of Galahad (Galaad) by Lancelot upon the daughter of the Grail King. Lancelot, the victim of trickery who did not knowingly betray Guenevere, nevertheless fulfills the prophecy that he was to father the knight who would succeed in the quest of the Holy Grail. Further adventures set the stage for this quest, in which Lancelot plays a prominent, though not dominant, role.

The *Lancelot* proper is a meandering yet majestic work written by a pious, compassionate man. Next to passages that seem irrelevant or trivial to a modern reader, there are others that make for a relatively smooth transition to the more ascetic, less compromising *Queste del Saint Graal.*

This part of the trilogy begins with Lancelot's knighting of Galahad and the latter's being recognized during a Pentecostal gathering at Camelot as the long-awaited hero sent by God to deliver the land from great wonders and strange adventures. After a brief appearance of the Holy Grail during the same gathering, Arthur's knights recognize their mission and swear to go in search of the vessel. Lancelot, Galahad, Gauvain, Bors (Bohort), Lionel, Hector, and others of prominence depart together but soon go their separate ways to meet adventures that are in accordance with their respective degrees of knightly merit. Lancelot, for one, soon recognizes that his quest is leading nowhere, and it is not until he repents his sinful ways that he is able to reach the Grail castle, where he is granted a partial vision of the mystery within the Grail. Perceval and Bors, less stained than Lancelot, join up with Galahad and, after sundry adventures, reach the Grail castle, where, in a scene of great solemnity, they are initiated into the rite of the Grail, at the height of which Galahad is invited to anoint the Maimed King with the blood from the Bleeding Lance. The three elect knights then journey to the land of Sarras (Palestine), where Galahad has the supreme vision of the Holy Grail and dies in ecstasy. Perceval also passes away soon thereafter, and only Bors returns to Camelot to tell of the wondrous events he has witnessed.

The *Quest,* though disjointed and patched in places, is elevated in spirit and sublime in tone. It is consistent in its moral tone and less forgiving than the *Lancelot* proper. Its message centers on a Cistercian ascetic ideal, and it is filled with a mystical vision of man's role in the world. The author of this part of the Prose Lancelot was clearly a different person from the one who wrote the *Lancelot* proper. In the next section, however, the latter seems to have taken over again, because in the *Mort Artu* there is a return to the more conciliatory, less severe tone of the *Lancelot* proper.

The *Mort Artu* begins with Bors's return to Camelot and Lancelot's relapse into his old sin. It describes the discovery of Lancelot and Guenevere's secret, as well as Lancelot's various rescue missions of his lover, during one of which he unwittingly kills Gauvain's favorite brother, Gaheriet, and thus turns a staunch friend into an implacable enemy. It is Gauvain's rancorous hatred that determines the subsequent chain of events. Arthur lays siege to Lancelot's castle and, through the intervention of the pope, gets his wife back from Lancelot, who all along wants to be reconciled with his lord and friend. Arthur at this point is also ready to forgive and forget, but Gauvain succeeds in rekindling his animosity. A number of indecisive battles ensue, and it is only after Gauvain is mortally injured by Lancelot that Arthur withdraws his forces from Lancelot's realm. Meanwhile, inexorable fate has moved everybody closer to doom. In Arthur's absence, his bastard son Mordret has usurped the crown. In addition to the treachery at home, Arthur is threatened by a Roman invasion of Gaul. After a quick campaign against the Romans, he crosses over to Dover and in spite of ill omens leads his forces against Mordret. On a day of great carnage on Salisbury Plain, the best of Arthur's remaining knights die, and the king and his son kill each other. Guenevere takes the veil and shortly thereafter dies. Lancelot returns to Logres (Britain) to avenge Arthur's death on the sons of Mordret. This accomplished, he becomes a hermit and, four year later, dies in peace.

The magnificent cycle of a noble but all too human hero's life has closed and the message which the authors of the Prose Lancelot wanted to convey has emerged in all clarity. It is a reminder of mortality and a warning against the desecration of the marriage vows, as well as an exhortation to the performance of spiritually valuable deeds. Emanating from a period whose perception in spiritual matters was keener than our own, the Prose Lancelot offered its readers a clear notion of what constituted right living. Its popularity throughout the Middle Ages was practically unrivaled. Soon after its compilation in France, a Dutch translation ap-

Emperor Leo VI prostrating himself before Christ. Mosaic above the imperial door of the inner narthex of Hagia Sophia, İstanbul, *ca.* 920. COURTESY OF THE BYZANTINE PHOTOGRAPH COLLECTION.

peared, which in turn served as the source of a Middle High German prose romance of Lancelot. In Italy, the *Tavola ritonda* owes its existence to the Prose Lancelot, and in Portugal and Spain the *Demanda de Santo Grial* and *Amadís de Gaula,* respectively, were affected by it. In Scotland, it inspired the *Lancelot of the Laik;* in England, the stanzaic *Le Morte Arthur* and Malory's great *Le Morte Darthur.* Both Dante and Chaucer knew the Prose Lancelot, which even today survives in a great number of handwritten manuscripts as well as in early printed versions. It retained its popularity well into the sixteenth century, when such authors as du Bellay and Ronsard expressed their admiration for it.

BIBLIOGRAPHY

Editions. The best available critical edition is that of Alexandre Micha, *Lancelot: Roman en prose du XIIIe siècle,* 9 vols. (1978–1983). Heinrich O. Sommer's pioneer edition, *The Vulgate Version of the Arthurian Romances,* 8 vols. (1908–1916), was the standard text for most of the studies on the Prose Lancelot, which is contained in volumes III–VI. This edition is not very reliable because it is in essence only a diplomatic transcription of one manuscript. Lucy A. Paton's translation into English, *Sir Lancelot of the Lake* (1929), is compacted but offers all the essential elements of the *Prose* Lancelot.

Studies. James D. Bruce, *The Evolution of Arthurian Romance,* 2 vols., 2nd ed. (1928, repr. 1958); Jean Frappier, "The Vulgate Cycle," in *Arthurian Literature in the Middle Ages,* Roger S. Loomis, ed. (1957, 5th repr. 1979); Elspeth Kennedy, "Social and Political Ideas in the French Prose *Lancelot,*" in *Medium aevum,* **26** (1957); Roger S. Loomis, *The Development of Arthurian Romance* (1963, 1970), 92–111; Ferdinand Lot, *Étude sur le Lancelot en prose* (1918, repr. 1954); Alexandre Micha, "Les manuscrits du *Lancelot en Prose,*" in *Romania,* **81** (1960) and **84** (1963), and "Sur la composition du *Lancelot en prose,*" in *Études de langue et de littérature du moyen âge: Offertes à Félix Lecoy* (1973); Jessie L. Weston, *The Legend of Sir Lancelot du Lac* (1901).

ERNST H. SOUDEK

[See also **Arthurian Literature; Chrétien de Troyes; French Literature: After 1200; French Literature: Romances; Matter of Britain, France, Rome.**]

PROSKYNESIS, literally, "to worship," to prostrate oneself in an act of submission, supplication, adoration, veneration, penitence, or respect. *Proskynesis* was practiced by the Greeks and Romans and continued by the Byzantines. As described at the court of Justinian by Procopius (*Secret History,*

XXX), subjects routinely "fell on their faces to the floor, stretching their hands and feet out wide, kissed first one foot and then the other of the Augustus, and then retired" when admitted to the presence of the emperor. Visual expressions of such acts of submission usually involve conquered peoples kneeling with arms extended and heads bowed down to the ground before or beneath the emperor, as the conquered Bulgars are depicted in one of the frontispiece miniatures of the Psalter of Basil II (*r.* 976–1025; Venice, Biblioteca Marciana, cod. gr. 17).

A more common use of *proskynesis* in art was as an indication of veneration, supplication, or adoration. The earliest known Christian example, a wall painting dating from about 390 at SS. Giovanni e Paolo in Rome, shows a martyr venerated by two prostrate figures. It was, however, apparently only after definitions of proper degrees of veneration were formulated during and after iconoclasm that *proskynesis* became fully accepted and standard in Byzantine religious imagery. In the narthex mosaic at Hagia Sophia of about 920, for example, the penitent emperor Leo VI (886–912) prostrates himself before Christ; and *proskynesis* is rampant in posticonoclastic biblical and liturgical illustrations.

BIBLIOGRAPHY

Anthony Cutler, *Transfigurations: Studies in the Dynamics of Byzantine Iconography* (1975), 53–110, with extensive bibliography; Nicolas Oikonomides, "Leo VI and the Narthex Mosaic of Saint Sophia," in *Dumbarton Oaks Papers,* 30 (1976).

LESLIE BRUBAKER

[See also **Basil II the "Killer of Bulgars"; Byzantine Art; Icon, Theology of; Leo VI the Wise, Emperor; Procopius; Proskynetarion.**]

PROSKYNETARION, Byzantine Greek for "a place of worship," is—in an Orthodox church—an elaborate frame, shrine, tabernacle, or ciborium within which a portable icon is placed. On any given feast day, the appropriate icon is taken from its location elsewhere in the church, carried in procession, and fastened on a hook in this tabernacle. The icon is then kissed, and *proskynesis* is performed before it; hence its name.

BIBLIOGRAPHY

Constantinus VII Porphyrogenitus, *De administrando imperio,* Gyula Moravcsik, ed., Romilly J. H. Jenkins, trans., rev. ed. (1967), 82–83.

BARBARA OEHLSCHLAEGER-GARVEY

[See also **Icon, Theology of; Proskynesis.**]

PROSPER OF AQUITAINE (Prosper Tiro) (*ca.* 390–*ca.* 460) is best known as one of the strongest defenders of the doctrines of Augustine, even though he seems to have remained a layman all his life. He was born in southern Gaul. Two poems written around the year 415 about the miseries caused by the barbarian invasions of Gaul, the *Carmen de divina providentia* (The song of the divine providence) and the *Poema coniugis ad uxorem* (Poem of a husband to his wife), have been attributed to him.

While in Marseilles in 427, Prosper became involved in doctrinal controversy when Augustine's work *On Reproof and Grace* was unfavorably received in Gaul; indeed, contemporary Gallic sources refer to Augustine's "heresy of predestination." Prosper and his friend Hilary of Marseilles, therefore, wrote to Augustine on the matter, and at about the same time, Prosper wrote his own *Epistula ad Rufinum de gratia et libero arbitrio* (Letter to Rufinus on grace and free will), as well as a poem, *De ingratis* (On those without grace), in 1,002 hexameters on the same topic. In 431 Prosper and Hilary traveled to Rome seeking support for Augustine's doctrine, and Celestine I addressed a favorable response to the bishops of southern Gaul. In the next year Prosper wrote his *De gratia et libero arbitrio contra collatorem* (On grace and free will, a book against the "Conferencer"), an attack upon one of the *Conferences* of John Cassian, in which Prosper, wrongly, attempted to taint the southern Gallic churchmen with Pelagianism. Other works of Prosper in this same vein include the *Pro Augustino responsiones* (Responses on behalf of Augustine), the *Epitaphium Nestorianae et Pelagianae haereseon* (Epitaph of the heresies of Pelagianism and Nestorianism), the *Epigrammator in obtrectatorem Augustini* (Epigrams against the detractor of Augustine), and the *De vocatione omnium gentium* (On the summoning of all the nations). All of Prosper's efforts, however, were in vain, and the anti-Augustinians, often misleadingly called the semi-Pelagians, were to prevail in Gaul until the Council of Orange in 529. Prosper, perhaps realizing his defeat, settled in Rome and entered the chancery of Pope Leo I. There, according to some sources, he authored some of Leo's most important tracts, such as the *Epistula ad Flavianum* (Letter to Flavianus), or *Tome* (449), which outlined Leo's policy against the Monophysites.

Under the name of Prosper Tiro—Prosper "the Recruit"—there has been preserved a very useful *Epitoma Chronicon* (Abridged chronicle), a summary of world history from Adam to A.D. 455. There seems to be no good reason not to identify this Prosper with Prosper of Aquitaine. The *Chronicle,* based until 378 on those of Jerome and Eusebius, is a valuable independent source especially for the years after 425, and is particularly valuable for its material on the history of church doctrine and heresies, especially Pelagianism.

BIBLIOGRAPHY

Sources. The writings of Prosper of Aquitaine are in *Patrologia latina,* XVII (1879), XLV (1865), and LI (1861). Also, *Epistula ad Augustinum,* A. Goldbacher, ed., in *Corpus scriptorum ecclesiasticorum latinorum,* LVII (1911), 454–468; *Poema coniugis,* Wilhelm von Hartel, ed., *ibid.,* XXX, pt. II (1894), 344–348; *Epitoma chronicon* in *Monumenta Germaniae historica: Auctores antiquissimi,* IX (1892, repr. 1981), 341–499.

Translations. Prudentius de Letter, ed. and trans., *Prosper of Aquitaine: Defense of St. Augustine* (1963); Michael P. McHugh, ed. and trans., *The "Carmen de Providentia Dei" Attributed to Prosper of Aquitaine* (1964); J. Reginald O'Donnell, ed. and trans., *Prosper of Aquitaine: Grace and Free Will* (1949).

Studies. Nora K. Chadwick, *Poetry and Letters in Early Christian Gaul* (1955); Eligius Dekkers, ed., *Clavis patrum latinorum,* 2nd ed. (1961), nos. 516–528, 2257; J. R. Martindale, *The Prosopography of the Later Roman Empire,* II (1980), 926–927; Martin Schanz, Carl Hosius, and Gustav Kruger, *Geschichte der römischen Literatur,* IV, pt. II (1920, repr. 1959), 112, 114, 491–501; Louis Valentin, *St. Prosper d'Aquitaine* (1900).

RALPH W. MATHISEN

[See also **Augustine of Hippo, St.; Cassian, John; Celestine I, Pope; Heresies, Western European; Leo I, Pope; Patrick, St.; Pelagius.**]

PROSTITUTION. The prostitute, as defined by Ulpian in a passage of the *Digest* later paraphrased by medieval canonists and civilians, was a woman who dealt in commerce of her body with numerous partners (literally, "without choosing" her partners).

A fully accepted aspect of Roman life, prostitution was considered by the early church to be an inevitable social phenomenon; Augustine judged it necessary in an imperfect world (*De ordine*). The church took strong measures against procuring (Council of Elvira, *ca.* 300), however, and rejected the Roman notion of a permanent stigma attached to women who had once been prostitutes (several of the female saints of the early church were former prostitutes).

The Germanic peoples seem not to have had a distinct notion of what constituted a prostitute, and the Latin term *meretrix,* as used in several Frankish texts (*Lex salica,* Jonas of Orléans's *De institutio laicali*), would seem to indicate nothing more precise than a woman of questionable sexual conduct. This imprecise use of the term *meretrix* may well explain the introduction in the eleventh and twelfth centuries of a new expression, *publica meretrix,* to designate a public prostitute and to distinguish her from other women of "deviant" sexual conduct. The widespread use (by canonists, civilians, and town archivists) of the term in the High Middle Ages may be linked to the revival of commerce and urban life during this period, a situation propitious to the existence of a socially identifiable group of women earning their living principally or exclusively from the indiscriminate commerce of their bodies.

It was mainly the towns that regulated prostitution in this period; their policy was rudimentary and negative, forbidding prostitutes to ply their trade in town centers (Toulouse, 1201; Padua, 1236). Gradually a more elaborate policy developed; dress and behavior codes were imposed on prostitutes, and, crucially, their workplaces came not only to be recognized but to be guaranteed by municipal and seigneurial or royal authority (Montpellier, 1285). Some towns began to restrict prostitution to municipally owned houses in the 1360's and 1370's, and by the fifteenth century several of these brothels enjoyed the French royal safeguard. Institutionalized prostitution, which seems to have originated in the Mediterranean world, had spread to most of Western Europe by the fifteenth century.

The legal status of the prostitute in the later Middle Ages was relatively favorable. In southern

France, for instance, public women could marry, bequeath property, testify in municipal courts, and bring charges of assault and rape against their aggressors. Convents of repentant women, founded largely in the thirteenth and fourteenth centuries, facilitated the prostitute's possible retreat to the religious life, simple retirement, or "reinsertion" into society. Although many women turned to prostitution because of poverty (some were placed in brothels as pawns on debts, notably in Italy), well-to-do and propertied prostitutes were not rare.

As prostitution became institutionalized, municipal and royal repression of procuring intensified (although Italian towns remained tolerant of procuring longer than French and German ones). Fifteenth-century institutionalized prostitution fitted into a context of increasing moral rigor, and itself became the object of reforming fervor in the sixteenth century when, both in lands of the Reformation and those of the Counter-Reformation, measures were taken to dismantle the whole system of institutionalized prostitution. When condemnation of "simple" fornication (that is, fornication uncomplicated by incest or adultery), largely tolerated in medieval society, became general, the social justification for the town brothel disappeared.

BIBLIOGRAPHY

Iwan Bloch, *Die Prostitution,* 2 vols. (1912–1925); Pierre Dufour, *Histoire de la prostitution chez tous les peuples du monde,* 6 vols. (1851–1853); Bronislaw Geremek, *Les marginaux parisiens aux XIV*[e] *et XV*[e] *siècle* (1976); Leah Otis, *Prostitution in Medieval Society* (1985), with extensive bibliography; Auguste Rabutaux, *De la prostitution en Europe depuis l'antiquité jusqu'à la fin du XVI*[e] *siècle* (1865); Jacques Rossiaud, "Prostitution, jeunesse, et société dans les villes du sud-est au XVe siècle," in *Annales: Économies, sociétés, civilisations,* 31 (1976).

LEAH OTIS

[See also **Concubinage, Western; Family and Marriage, Western European.**]

PROTHESIS, a chamber in a Byzantine church normally located on the north side of the bema. It served as the site of the preparation and storage of the species of the Eucharist.

BIBLIOGRAPHY

Richard Krautheimer, *Early Christian and Byzantine Architecture* (1965, repr. 1975).

ROBERT OUSTERHOUT

[See also **Apse; Diaconicon; Early Christian and Byzantine Architecture; Pastophory** (with illustration).]

PROTOSPATHARIOS, a Byzantine term meaning "the first swordholder." It referred to the highest-ranking member of the *spatharioi* (imperial bodyguards). It became, around 700, an honorific title bestowed by insignia on both eunuchs and non-eunuchs, including important military officers such as the strategos and domesticos. The title became widespread in the ninth and tenth centuries and then decreased in importance. There also was a special function or office of *protospathar* for the leader of palace-eunuch *spathars,* who guarded the emperor in his palace. A special *protospathar* was in charge of a maritime court. Those holding the title of *protospatharios* served as a special escort of the emperor in the palace at Constantinople, in court ceremonial, at the hippodrome, at church, at banquets, and on campaign expeditions. They sometimes were entrusted with special missions. The title of *protospatharios* was sometimes granted to esteemed foreign rulers.

BIBLIOGRAPHY

Rodolphe Guilland, "Le protospathaire," in *Byzantion,* 25–27 (1955–1957), repr. in his *Recherches sur les institutions byzantines,* II (1967), 99–131; Nicolas Oikonomides, *Les listes de préséance byzantines des IX*[e] *et X*[e] *siècles* (1972), 297.

WALTER EMIL KAEGI, JR.

[See also **Byzantine Empire: Bureaucracy.**]

PROVENÇAL LANGUAGE. Provençal generally designates the totality of medieval dialects in those regions south of the Loire that once constituted Provincia Narbonensis. "The Province," as it was familiarly known in Rome, had been assigned to Julius Caesar by the Senate in 59 B.C. The Romance language that developed there was known as *lenga romana.* It was characterized also as the *lenga (langue) d'oc* (see Dante's *De vulgari eloquentia,* I, 8) because of its distinctive pronunciation of the

PROVENÇAL LANGUAGE

affirmative particle *hoc;* compare northern French *oïl* and Italian *sì.* A less satisfactory medieval term for it was, synecdochically, *lemosi* (Limousin). Raimon Vidal de Besadún (or Besalú, 1160–1210) characterized it thus in his treatise *Rasos de trobar:* "La parladura francesca val mais et [es] plus avinenz a far romanz e pasturellas; mas cella de Lemozin val mais per far vers et cansons et serventes; et per totas las terras de nostre lengage son de major autoritat li cantar de la lenga lemosina que de negun' autra parladura." (The French language is better and more suited to the composition of romances and pastourelles, but Limousin is better for verses, songs, and *sirventes*; and throughout all our language region, songs in the Limousin tongue have more importance than those of any other dialect.)

There were many reasons for the divergence of *lenga d'oc* and *langue d' oïl.* Even before the Roman occupation of Gaul the populations of the two regions had been different. The south had been populated in turn by Iberian, Ligurian, and then Celtic races, whereas the north was inhabited primarily by Celts at the time of Caesar's invasion. He described them in his *Bellum gallicum* as being of two main types: *Celtae* and *Belgae.* Differences in the population base were reinforced by differences in geography. Natural boundaries like the Massif Central automatically separated south from north. As a result, Provence's trade and commerce was normally with the Mediterranean countries of Italy and Spain rather than with the rest of Gaul.

Colonization of the two regions did not proceed at the same pace. The south was acquired earlier by Rome (121 B.C.), and Roman domination was eventually absolute. It was only in 58–51 B.C. that Julius Caesar subdued the north in the Gallic Wars. Subsequent patterns were no less diverse. In 419 A.D. Honorius allowed the Visigoths to settle in Toulouse, Agen, Bordeaux, Périgueux, Saintes, Angoulême, and Poitiers. Their mini-kingdom survived for eighty years and added certain words (chiefly place-names) to the southern language. However, the linguistic impact of the Visigoths in the south was slight compared with that of the Germanic invaders in the north, whose inroads culminated in the Frankish takeover at the end of the fifth century.

It was Frankish influence that caused several major phonetic changes. *W* was introduced and survived as a bilabial in the northern regions of Gaul, where Frankish influence was strongest. The phoneme *h* was reintroduced (compare northern French *hauberc* and Provençal *osberc*). Lexical borrowings were extensive. Even such drastic changes as the diphthongization of stressed vowels and weakening of unstressed syllables in northern Gaul have been attributed to Germanic influence. Despite the conjectural nature of such hypotheses, there is no doubt that the relative stability of southern Gaul protected its language from the rapid changes that characterized the much-invaded north.

As a literary vehicle Provençal was the first Romance language to achieve excellence. Its first substantial extant piece is an eleventh-century manuscript of the *Boecis.* The work itself was composed around 1000, and it is reasonable to assume that other poems had preceded this fictionalized life of the Roman philosopher Boethius (*ca.* 480–*ca.* 524). The text has features that imply an evolving literary tradition: it comprises 257 decasyllabic lines complete with a conventional caesura after the fourth syllable; it is arranged in laisses of varying length; and it appears to be modeled upon existing poetic traditions.

Phonetically speaking, the text is already unmistakably Provençal. It maintains tonic free *a* (*jutgar* from Vulgar Latin *judicare;* compare Old French *jugier*). It has no spontaneous diphthongization (*valor* from VL *valorem;* compare OF *valeur*). The *au* derived from Vulgar Latin is retained (*causa* from VL *causam;* compare OF *chose*).

Certain features, like the loss of final *n,* seem dialectal (*bo* from VL *bonum;* compare OF *bon*). And the fluctuating treatment of [*k*] before *a* and of intervocalic *d* suggests contamination from the *langue d'oïl.* The consensus on the dialectal origin of the *Boecis* is that it was Limousin, perhaps from the abbey of St. Martial in Limoges.

The second Provençal text to have survived was written at some time in the middle of the eleventh century and was hagiographic: the *Chanson de sainte Foi d'Agen.* Its 593 octosyllabic lines, arranged in monorhymed laisses of varying length, describe the martyrdom of St. Fides (third century). The poem contains the enigmatic claim that the author was writing it "in the French way" (*a lei francesca*). The sixteenth-century French scholar Claude Fauchet interpreted this to mean "in rhyme," then used the phrase as evidence that rhyme was a French invention. Since both the *Boecis* and the *Chanson de sainte Foi d'Agen* predate the rhymed literature of all other Romance languages, the meaning of this (and several other authorial claims) remains unclear. Dialectally

PROVENÇAL LANGUAGE

speaking, the text is unlike the Limousin *Boecis,* retaining final *n* (*man,* from VL *manum*) and *n* before final *s* (*razons* from VL *rationes*). Archaisms and rare morphological occurrences complicate the linguistic evidence, but it seems likely that the *Chanson de sainte Foi d'Agen* originated in Narbonne.

During the eleventh century Provençal took a new direction. The literary language was artificially divested of many dialectal features and was transformed by the troubadours into the koine that we now understand by the phrase "Old Provençal." The benefits of artificial standardization were obvious: poets who came from diverse regions and backgrounds could nevertheless travel from patron to patron and from court to court without problems of comprehension. Their literature influenced the whole of Western Europe until it was destroyed by the Albigensian Crusade, which effectively removed its patrons.

The language of the troubadours preserved much of the Vulgar Latin sound system. The vowels of Provençal were

[ą̣] [ạ] [ę] [ẹ] [ǫ] [ọ] [ị] [ü]

The conservatism of this vowel system may be seen from the following table, in which the tonic free vowels of Provençal may be compared with their Vulgar Latin source and with the northern French developments:

Provençal	Vulgar Latin	Old French
cantar	*cantare*	*chanter*
pe	*pedem*	*pied*
tela	*telam*	*toile*
mola	*molam*	*muele*
flor	*florem*	*fleur*
mil	*mille*	*mil*
dur	*durum*	*dur*
aur	*aurum*	*or*

Diphthongs and triphthongs did exist in Provençal (for example, *ai, ei, oi, au, eu, iu, ou, iei, ioi, iau, ieu, iou*). Such groups had been created by the influence of palatals that characteristically combined with a preceding vowel—Provençal *pieitz* from VL *pectus,* compare northern French *piz;* Provençal *nuoit* from VL *noctem,* compare northern French *nuit.* Each letter of these groups had its own sound, and in triphthongs the middle sound was stressed.

Thus, although there was no spontaneous diphthongization and no overall development of nasalized vowels as there was in the north (for example, VL *bene* became *bien* in the north but *be* in the south), palatalization was responsible for many sound changes. The phenomenon had begun in the Vulgar Latin period and was widespread in Gaul. The shift of [u] to [ü] was undoubtedly complete in Provençal by the eleventh century. So too were most of the consonantal modifications (the evolution of *c* before *e* or *i* as [ts] and later [s], *g* before *e* or *i* as [dʒ], and the development of palatal *l,* palatal *n,* and *ch* [tʃ]). However, the *lenga d'oc* retained some features in the twelfth century that the northern language had long left behind, for example the voicing of intervocalic *p* and *t* to *b* and *d,* respectively.

The orthographical renderings of the Provençal sound system were varied. Without the necessity for a standardized spelling (which would be imposed only later, with the invention of printing), Provençal's composite koine was inevitably rendered differently by scribes of different regions. An idiosyncratic, regional orthography cannot therefore be interpreted as evidence of an author's provenance, but only of the scribe's.

In its morphology Provençal, like all the Romance languages, showed a simplified case system—the six Latin cases had been replaced by two: subject and oblique. The first fulfilled the role of the Latin nominative; the second served in place of all the other cases Latin had used.

The five declensions of Latin were so modified that the new system cannot be regarded as a direct development from Classical Latin. The dominant model for the declension of substantives was provided by the following two types (derived from Latin's first and second declensions):

Masculine Nouns

	Singular	Plural
Subject	*sers*	*ser*
Oblique	*ser*	*sers*

Feminine Nouns

	Singular	Plural
Subject	*causa*	*causas*
Oblique	*causa*	*causas*

This analogical pattern influenced even anomalies like the masculines without a terminal *s* (*paire*

PROVENÇAL LANGUAGE

from Latin *pater*), the feminines with a terminal *s* (*naus* from Latin *navis*), the indeclinables, and the imparisyllabics.

Adjectives followed a similar masculine-feminine declension. Some synthetic comparatives and superlatives (adjectival and adverbial) survived into Provençal, but the more usual method of expressing comparative and superlative ideas was analytic: by the composite forms *plus* or *mais* preceding adjective or adverb.

Adverbs were most usually formed by the addition of *-men* to the feminine singular of the adjective, for example *belamen* (beautifully).

Ille when unstressed and used adjectivally provided Provençal with its forms for the definite article:

Definite Article

	Masculine	Feminine
Singular		
Subject	*lo, le (sers)*	*la (causa)*
Oblique	*lo (ser)*	*la (causa)*
Plural		
Subject	*li (ser)*	*las (causas)*
Oblique	*los (sers)*	*las (causas)*

Provençal's pronouns derived from Latin in a double set, depending on whether they had developed in accented or unaccented position, for example *me, mi* (me) and the possessive *tos, tieus* (your), formed by analogy with *mieus* (my) from Latin *meus*.

Phonetic erosion of interrogatives and relatives, which had begun in Vulgar Latin, resulted in a paradigm of three forms: *qui* (subject case), *que* (object case), and *cui* (dative case). The possibility of ambiguity was reduced by the use of the composite relative pronoun *loquals,* the use of *dont* as the genitive of the relative pronoun, and the use of a pronominal form peculiar to the south: *quina* or *quinha* (feminine), which was the source of an analogical masculine *quin* or *quinh*.

Composition had produced demonstratives like the pronoun/adjectives *cest* (*ecce iste*), *cil* (*ecce ille*), *aquest* (*atque iste*), and *aquel* (*atque ille*), which were successful over such vulnerable monosyllables as *is* or *hic*.

The verb system had lost the Latin deponents, passive voice, past infinitive, future participle, and the supine. The present participle had merged phonetically with the gerundive. On the other hand, new composite verb formations like the conditionals, composite perfect and pluperfect, future, and future anterior had developed to meet new needs of expression.

The two productive conjugations of Provençal were the *-ar* (for example, *cantar*) and *-ir* (inchoative, for example *fenir*) types, and it was upon their pattern that new formations were modeled rather than upon the inherited *-ir* (non-inchoative, for example *dormir*), *-re* (*rendre*), and *-er* (*voler*).

Syntactically, Provençal retained many of the advantages of the Classical Latin system. Its case system was still flexible enough to accommodate variations in word order, and the subjunctive mood continued to serve a wide range of functions. Patterns of coordination that characterized everyday speech were, however, encroaching upon the traditional Latin system, and there were consequent changes in the use of conjunctions and prepositions.

It was in vocabulary that the troubadours' influence was most dramatic. Utilizing feudal and religious terminology, they effectively altered the connotations of scores of words to serve their sophisticated analyses of the nature of *fin'amors.* The poets of *fin'amors* did not, however, long survive the destruction of the southern courts by the Albigensian Crusade (1209–1244). In the thirteenth and fourteenth centuries dialectal differences became more pronounced, and the koine that had once been the dominant literary language of Europe was dealt a final blow in 1539. In that year the political edict of Villers-Cotterets made Francien the official language of Francis I's kingdom. That language thus became both tool and symbol of the political unification of north and south.

BIBLIOGRAPHY

Joseph Anglade, *Grammaire de l'ancien provençal* (1921); Édouard Bourciez, *Éléments de linguistique romane,* 5th ed. (1967); W. D. Elcock, *The Romance Languages* (1960, rev. ed. 1975); Åke Grafström, *Étude sur la graphie des plus anciennes chartes languedociennes, avec un essai d'interprétation phonétique* (1958); Charles H. Grandgent, *An Outline of the Phonology and Morphology of Old Provençal,* rev. ed. (1905, repr. 1973); Robert A. Hall, Jr., *External History of the Romance Languages* (1974); Frank Hamlin, Peter T. Ricketts, John Hathaway, *Introduction à l'étude de l'ancien provençal* (1967); Mildred K. Pope, *From Latin to Modern French,* rev. ed. (1952, repr. 1956); D. R.

Sutherland, "Flexions and Categories in Old Provençal," in *Transactions of the Philological Society* (1959).

JEANETTE M. A. BEER

[See also **Catalan Language; Cathars; Courtly Love; French Language; Languedoc; Latin Language; Raimon Vidal de Besalú; Troubadour, Trouvère; Vulgar Latin.**]

PROVENÇAL LITERATURE: TO 1200

THE LANGUAGE

The term traditionally used to designate one of the two principal languages of medieval Gallo-Romance literature—"Old Provençal"—is largely a misnomer. Provence is only one of the territories and Provençal but one of the dialects covering the area reaching roughly from the Alps to the Atlantic and from the Mediterranean (as well as from south of the Pyrenees) to approximately north of the Massif Central. Furthermore, "Old Provençal" can hardly be construed as the dialect of the centralizing power of a developing national state. The literary language of the south, or Midi, of what we today call France corresponded, in the Middle Ages, to no real, or even incipient, single area of political strength—as did, for example, the language of Île-de-France (*langue d'oïl* in its "Francien" form) in the north or, eventually, Castilian in Spain.

The outstanding characteristic of "Old Provençal" literature is that though it was composed and understood over a period of centuries in territories easily as extensive as the largest Western European kingdom of the day, circumstances of history rendered the building of an analogous political unity impossible. In fact, the cultural coherence expressed in this literature, particularly during the twelfth and thirteenth centuries, was of a type that not only did not favor, or lead to, political coherence but very possibly contributed to hindering any such development. The kind of poetic universality striven for by the major poets of the time precluded emphasis upon the creation of a militarily and politically powerful center (though, for a time, Toulouse came close). Indeed, by stressing courts and courtliness, not *a* court, the Midi opened itself to exploitation by more militaristic neighbors even as those neighbors were increasingly subjected to its cultural and literary influence. Ironically, "Old Provençal" claims to poetic universality were employed, in the name of certain universals of doctrine, against the Midi by powers engaged in the process of constructing for themselves a national, even particularist, identity.

Generally speaking, then, for its twelfth- and thirteenth-century inhabitants, what we call the Midi referred to a kind of idealized space: it existed in opposition to "France." Many modern historians write of Occitania or, following a late-thirteenth-century tradition, of Languedoc, the country (and language) of *oc* (yes), as opposed to *oïl* (*oui*, "yes" in French). (Defining the three branches of *ydioma tripharium* in his *De vulgari eloquentia* [1303–1304], Dante designated "Old Provençal" as *lingua oc,* contrasting it with *lingua oïl* and *lingua si* [Italian]. However, for Dante, *oc, oïl,* and *si* stood for a specificity both linguistic and literary: *oc* was the language of lyric poetry, *oïl* that of narrative.) In reality, Occitania was a highly decentralized patchwork of duchies, counties, principalities, and towns that included Aquitaine, Gascony, Béarn, Foix, Toulouse (Languedoc proper), Limousin, Auvergne, Venaissin, Provence, and such border areas as Poitou, Roussillon, Nice, and even Catalonia, each with its idiosyncratic dialect and, of course, with constantly changing borders and regimes.

Yet, despite this flux, William IX, duke of Aquitaine, the first known troubadour, is typical of his time (early twelfth century) when he distinguishes between the vernacular and Latin by referring to the former as *romans* (<ROMANICE, spoken tongue, Romance), not as a language to be associated with any specific place or province (for instance, Poitou): "E ieu prec en Jesu del tron / Et en romans et en lati" (And I pray the enthroned Lord Jesus / In Romance and in Latin [that is, in "total," unrestricted language], Alfred Jeanroy, ed., XI, lines 23–24). The same poem betrays an equally characteristic Occitanian consciousness of place in the first stanza: "Pos de chantar m'es pres talenz, / Farai un vers, don sui dolenz: / Mais non serai obedienz / En Peitau ni en Lemozi" (Since a desire to sing has overcome me / I shall make a poem concerning what saddens me: / I shall no longer pledge [love] fealty / In the lands of Poitou and the Limousin [that is, where love poetry is composed, Occitania]).

Poets were aware, then, of a vernacular, a spoken language different from the learned, universal Latin. And their vernacular—a vehicle of poetry—was something other than vernaculars spoken outside Occitania, such as *frances, franses* (French).

For the troubadours what we call "Old Provençal" today denoted essentially a widespread language of poetry—a set of dictions regulated according to the rules of given verse forms (*vers, canso, sirventes,* and so on) and of styles (*trobar leu, clus, ric*). For them Occitania was, quite literally, first and foremost the land of poetry. And, as such, its borders were flexible. In a very genuine sense the Midi was to be found wherever troubadours composed and sang—in Italy, in Spain, at the court of Henry II and Eleanor, even in the Holy Land.

Not until the later Middle Ages would regionalism (Gascon, Toulousan, or Provençal particularism) be stressed over and above the idealized poetic place of Occitania. Even the bloody depredations carried out by the crusading armies of Simon de Montfort and the French kings are frequently depicted as efforts to destroy poetry. Or, rather, the ravages perpetrated on the society and the civilization of the Midi, as well as on its relative independence, are symbolized by thirteenth-century poets in their accounts as being the death, or exile, of Love, of Courtesy, and of Song. Consequently, we must consider "Old Provençal" to be what modern scholars call a literary koine, a fairly standardized, very stylized artistic vehicle, rooted in the spoken dialects of Occitania yet distinct from them.

Around 1200 the Catalan troubadour Raimon Vidal de Besalú (or Bezaudun) summarized the situation very well. In the *Rasos de trobar* (Rules for composing verse) he declares: "Whoever wishes to compose or understand poetry must first learn that no speech [*parladura*] of our language [*nostre lengatge*] is natural and correct but that speech of France [that is, *oïl*] and of Lemosi, or of Provence, or of Auvergne, or of Quercy [the dialects upon which the medieval Occitanian koine rests]; for that reason I tell you that when I speak of Lemosi, all these lands [*terras*] are included as well as all their neighbors and the lands in between." As a group—separate but linked—these dialects together are opposed to, and are the equivalent of, the "parladura . . . de Franza." Not only does Raimon Vidal foreshadow Dante's classification, but he tells us virtually all we need to know concerning the status and meaning of "Old Provençal."

THE BEGINNINGS

Very few Provençal texts composed before the twelfth century have survived, and none of them is a secular troubadour song. As was the case north of the Loire (and elsewhere in Romance Europe), Latin remained the essential vehicle of writing. Though men and women no doubt sang songs and told stories in their native vernacular, only clerkly, or pious, compositions were deemed fit to be written down. To be sure, Latin documents originating in Occitania as far back as the seventh century possess linguistic traits here and there that reflect rhythms and words characteristic of popular speech. By the tenth and eleventh centuries bilingual manuscripts, particularly charters, provide, alongside Latin, examples of early Provençal prose and verse. (A curious Latin alba, dating from the tenth or early eleventh century, contains a repeated two-line refrain that many scholars consider to be Provençal, though no two experts seem to agree as to what the refrain might mean.)

Two linguistically mysterious poems, known as the *Passion du Christ* and the *Vie de saint Legier* (Life of St. Leodegar), dating in all likelihood from the end of the tenth century and preserved in an eleventh-century codex discovered at Clermont-Ferrand, present a kind of hybrid language neither entirely *langue d'oïl* nor entirely *langue d'oc* but, rather, an interesting fusion of the two. Composed in assonanced octosyllabic couplets, the *Passion* (516 lines) and the *Saint Legier* (240 lines) are pious narratives. The former recounts Christ's trial, Crucifixion, Resurrection, and Ascension. The latter tells of the martyrdom of Bishop Leodegar; it "translates" a late-seventh-century Latin *vita.* Both works, responding to the spirit of the injunction of the Council of Tours (813), which had prescribed the use of the vernacular in sermons, put sacred writ and hagiographic tradition into a language the "people" (the nonclerics) could understand.

Although most experts now believe that these texts probably originated in *oïl* territory and were copied by *oc*-speaking scribes (many imperfect assonances in Provençal can easily be corrected by retranslating the assonanced forms back into Francien), the "copying" is, to say the least, highly creative. In the case of the *Passion,* especially, one is tempted to conjecture that its language might well have been designed, in a de facto if not entirely intentional fashion, to demonstrate the possibilities of an open-ended, pan-Gallo-Romance literary vernacular—a language at once distinct from, but nevertheless related to, the spoken vernaculars of both *oïl* and *oc.* By 1000 the linguistic boundaries of the literary koines of *oïl* and *oc* had hardly been fixed. In any case, the language of the Clermont *Passion* and *Saint Legier* mirrors what, at the time, must have been the intense intellectual commerce between monastic institutions situated in the north and those in the Midi.

Monastic culture probably produced the two indisputably Occitanian poems that, along with fragments of a translation of the Gospel according to St. John (chaps. 13–17), have survived from the eleventh century. (In addition, two religious songs from *ca.* 1100 have been preserved.)

The first of these poems—a 257-line fragment—is known as the *Boecis;* it is (very freely) based on Boethius' *De consolatione Philosophiae* and is written in (mainly) rhyming decasyllabic laisses, stanzas of unequal length, inserted by a scribe, probably in the early eleventh century, into a tenth-century codex. (Guesses as to its date of composition vary widely, from 950 to 1050.) The metrical form of this text (four + six syllables) closely resembles that of what would subsequently become the Old French chanson de geste: *Coms fu de Roma / e ac ta gran valor* (He was a count of Rome and was highly prized [by the emperor]). Its reliance on a simple linking of clauses (parataxis) also recalls the Romance epic, but in eschewing assonance in favor of rhyme, the *Boecis* is prosodically idiosyncratic, even innovative, with regard to that tradition; rhyme suggests lyric song far more than does assonance. The poem renders Boethius' test, adding to it numerous popular motifs and fictions associated with the legend of this Christian thinker whom the age regarded as a saintly martyr. It is ostensibly directed to the moral improvement of young men overly tempted by the pleasures and vainglory of the world. The dialect shows pronounced Limousin coloration (for instance, *-en* < Latin -ENT, -ANT, -UNT).

The *Chanson de sainte Foy* (The song of St. Fides), possibly originating in the Narbonne area and usually dated in the period 1030–1070, comprises 593 octosyllabic verses deployed in 55 rhyming laisses of varying length. (The propensity of Old Provençal for rhyme at so early a date is quite remarkable.) The poem recounts the holy life, martyrdom, and miracles of a young girl from Agen who met her death at the hands of the Roman governor of the province during his campaign to enforce the anti-Christian policy of the pagan emperors Diocletian and Maximian (who reigned jointly from 286 to 305). But other materials, quite interestingly, are also pressed into service here. We witness, for example, the conflation of two hagiographic legends: the story of St. Fides and that of another local saint, St. Caprais, who bears witness to an angel's intervention on behalf of St. Fides at one point during the series of tortures inflicted upon her. Next, a lengthy section of text tells of Maximian's siege of Marseilles, a fief then ruled by his son-in-law Constantine, who would become the first Christian emperor. Maximian's army, which included Amazons, Saracens, Armenians, hermaphrodites, Jews, and (even) Pygmies—all typically chanson de geste–style "pagans"—is eventually defeated and the pagan emperor is hanged by order of his own daughter. Diocletian dies upon hearing of his colleague's demise.

Sainte Foy presents a number of baffling problems for the literary historian. The poet—or poets—relied on learned church Latin sources, to be sure, but the text alludes both explicitly and implicitly to what sounds very much like an active and rich set of vernacular poetic traditions. We have already mentioned the chanson de geste–like characteristics.

Laisse II of the poem, which may or may not have been a later interpolation within a hypothetical lost original, speaks of a "song" that the narrator heard (*audi*), a *canczon* that was "of Spanish theme" (*de razon espanesca*), well known, as laisse III puts it, to the countries of the Basques, the Aragonese, and the Gascons (peoples whose lands either bordered on or, in a sense, were part of Spain). The song was couched neither "in Greek words" nor "in the Saracen tongue." "Whoever should tell [*diz*] it well in the French-manner [*a lei francesca*] will gain, I think, great profit and fame in the world." This song may or may not really have existed; claims of this sort—the source topos—are routinely made in medieval narrative (see also laisse I). Yet, the fact of song, if not a particular song, seems more plausible than implausible. The narrator would appear, then, to describe himself as a professional poet or a *joglar* (French: *jongleur*), an entertainer capable of putting his talent and his experience of vernacular—even secular—poetry to work in order to present this "honeylike" sweet and soft song, the pious story of St. Fides, to the public of his time.

Many questions arise. For example, did *Sainte Foy* survive because of its religious inspiration while other formally similar texts, on secular themes, were consigned to oblivion? One is strongly tempted to think so. After all, books—particularly pre-twelfth-century books—were copied and preserved mainly in monasteries or other religious institutions (*Sainte Foy* and *Boecis* had been kept, presumably for several centuries, in the abbey of Saint-Benoît-sur-Loire). No definitive answer to questions of this sort can be forthcoming; however, one may be permitted at least to suspect the presence of a widespread and flourishing vernacular poetry in eleventh-century Occitania.

Also hinted at in *Sainte Foy* is what, within a more general medieval set of values, might be labeled a peculiarly Occitanian sense of time and place. Like *Boecis* (and other early vernacular hagiography), *Sainte Foy* constitutes a modernization and an adaptation to local conditions of an earlier Latin text, or texts. (In the opening verses the narrator speaks of having had read to him a "Latin book" about "olden times.") However, there is nothing school-like, or learned, in this adaptation. Agen is at once a particular town and a kind of emblem, the "world" viewed according to an Occitanian perspective: its citizens' "paganism" is depicted both as pre-Christian (that is, from the time before God sent his Son to deliver them from the devil's bondage) and as a taste for "Saracen"—non-Christian—practices (they serve an idol with Cordoban gold, as the Israelites once served Mammon). The geography of the poem includes Gascony, Aragon, and the Basque country; mention is made of the Greek and Saracen languages. Biblical imagery is found side by side with references to Roman history and to the city of Marseilles. The term *a lei francesca* implies a knowledge, on the poet's part, of something he considers to be other than his native literary manner.

When seen together, all these things suggest medieval Occitania, a time and place distinct from, yet related to (and seemingly tolerant of), France, Romanness, Spain, Greece, Islam, Hebrew tradition, and the Mediterranean. Even more important, perhaps, the "sweet and soft song" focuses upon and celebrates a young Occitanian lady; it amplifies her biography in poetico-historical terms, thereby imparting to it a definite spiritual meaning and a relevance of a general sort. The celebration of St. Fides' story in the Occitanian vernacular and within a characteristically Occitanian framework of reference by a poet who clearly identifies himself as such (and not, say, as a cleric, a mere transmitter) may be interpreted as constituting (1) the poetic and moral history of the people from whom the saint and her only slightly less holy witness, St. Caprais, issued; and (2) the fusion, which will come to epitomize the later literature of the Midi and will be its greatest gift to the literatures of other countries, of poet, language, and subject matter as coequal and equivalent terms in the poetic enterprise.

Of all this the *Sainte Foy* poet-narrator was highly conscious, as is shown in his closing, where he refuses to recount—sing—the extinction of Diocletian's lineage: "E si·s sun mort, vos nunqua·n calla, / Q'eu nonc'o prez una medalla! / Del lor cantar ja·m pren nualla" (And if they died out, do not care about it at all, / for I do not prize them a pennyworth! / I am starting to feel disgust at the idea of singing about them [lines 591–593]). There is nothing naive about this "subjective" tone; it is typically Occitanian: the concepts of worthiness and esteem inform Old Provençal poetry. Without *prez,* or *pretz,* no poetry is possible, or so the troubadours (such as Marcabru) will constantly remind us. The poet frequently views himself—his function—as sole custodian and judge of *pretz.* It is in this fashion that the poet's custodianship extends to and over his people.

One might well conclude that the rhetorical and technical framework of *Sainte Foy* borders closely on that of the lyric; the narrator's stress of his own, personalized authority as craftsman—his "subjectivity"—and the fact that the carefully wrought rhyming laisses are virtually stanzas (they vary only slightly in length) are traits rather more characteristic of lyric compositions than of French-style straight narrative. In any case, the great tradition of Occitanian verse—its artfulness, its special linking of poetry and civilization—is already remarkably well delineated in the *Chanson de sainte Foy.* It contains, in nonsecular form, the themes and values of the great twelfth-century *canso*; the "country" of *Sainte Foy* is the Occitanian language itself, the new "illustrious vernacular" of a poetry conceived in idiosyncratically lyric terms.

TROUBADOUR POETRY: THE CLASSICAL PERIOD

The lyric verse we call "troubadour poetry" emerged around 1100. Why it did at that time and in Occitania has been the object of countless studies and much conjecture. Possible classical, Christian, and Muslim influences have been cited to account for one or more important features of this poetry—for instance, the proximity of Muslim culture in Spain and the presence there of a love poetry, some of it partly in Romance, resembling in certain aspects the work of the troubadours; and also the fact that Occitanian noblemen, including William IX, visited Spain and even fought there, bringing back booty and slaves, some of whom were, apparently, minstrels and songstresses. Most scholars suppose the existence of a lost secular lyric tradition in Occitania antedating the close of the eleventh century, ascribing its loss to the tradition's profane character and consequent lack of prestige.

The first known troubadour—that is, the first whose compositions (eleven songs) were written down and survive to this day—was, by contrast, a most prestigious nobleman, William, ninth duke of Aquitaine and seventh count of Poitiers (1071–1127), whose station in life guaranteed the preservation of at least part of his oeuvre, scattered though this was in nine codices. The practice of composing secular verse acquired, as it were, its letters of nobility from so illustrious a personage. (It was observed above that several important characteristics of troubadour lyric poetry are found in *Sainte Foy,* and are not completely absent from the earlier *Boecis.* After all, Boethius loves Philosophy, a somewhat abstract "lady," to be sure, who nevertheless is depicted, quite sensuously, as strikingly feminine: beautiful, well dressed, and worthy).

No theory has yet come near to settling the myriad questions relating to the origins of the troubadour lyric. For our purposes it will suffice to note that political and social conditions, the presence, especially at Poitiers, where William held court, of a more or less refined and educated lay elite, and the existence, as evidenced by *Sainte Foy* and other texts, of an already remarkably developed *oc* literary koine encouraged the serious cultivation of what would become the Old Provençal lyric. Though doubtless a powerful lord, William IX was no king of France or of England; his repeated failures as a crusader could hardly inspire the development of a native Occitanian chanson de geste. Moreover, Occitania possessed no genuine—or aggressive—power center, as did northern France or Castile in Christian Spain. (Toulouse, at a later date, would most closely approach this ideal, especially subsequent to the diminution of Catalan influence, but the power of its extraordinary counts would be crushed by France and the papacy.)

In addition, feudal structures in the Midi were far less developed than in the north. By 1100 the social status and the political power of women were relatively more elevated in Occitania than in France or England: the *midons* (lady) of so much Provençal poetry was by no means entirely a lyric fiction. Women could inherit property and, in some cases, exercise effective suzerainty. (*Midons* derives from the Latin masculine *meus dominus,* my lord.) Some centers of learning existed in the south but, by and large, were of a character different from those established north of the Loire.

The twelfth century witnessed the establishment of the teaching of law and medicine at Montpellier, and, in keeping with its traditions of tolerance, Occitania sheltered a number of important centers of Jewish thought; cabalistic reflection, for example, underwent significant renewal at the hands of a school led by Moses of Narbonne. Nevertheless, in contrast to France proper, the study of pure philosophy never took root in Occitania. The cultivation of logic—the discourse of philosopy and theology—was subordinated to other kinds of intellectual concerns and discourse: the elaboration of a worldly ideal of life and of a language expressing this ideal. Spiritual values, too, claimed their share of attention.

Thus, significantly, at the time troubadour poetry was beginning to emerge at the court of Poitiers as the expression of the new ideal of refined aristocratic (though socially open-ended) behavior, we find present at that court Robert d'Arbrissel, a Cluniac who was spiritual adviser to numerous highborn women. He was influential in the founding of the abbey of Fontevrault, an exceptionally rich establishment designed for and run by noblewomen. (It was there that William IX's granddaughter, Eleanor of Aquitaine, and her husband, Henry II, were buried, side by side.) In Occitania, then, monastic culture came to be closely connected to—even to complement—court society. Many a nobleman, or noblewoman, and troubadour (some of very humble extraction) retired to a monastery in order to make peace with God. Also, it is believed, monasteries served as schools, preserving and teaching, formally or informally, the language and the art of poetry. In the Midi, at least for the aristocracy, art, life, spirituality, and courtly behavior were all facets of the same complex entity, blended in a new and unique fashion and accorded expression in the body of troubadour verse. No strong clerkly class was to emerge in Occitania as it did in *oïl* territory.

Meanwhile, though the aristocratic worldliness just described tended to undermine ecclesiastical authority, it ought not to be construed as an explicit attack on established orthodoxy. Conversely, twelfth-century Occitania witnessed the spread, at first among the middle and the lower classes, of what would eventually be branded as outright heresy, the Albigensian, or Cathar, movement. The Cathars rejected traditional baptism, denied the Old Testament, and, in general, adopted a Manichaean dualism according to which the world and its creatures are the work of the devil. Fasting, sexual abstinence, and simplicity of ritual characterized the Boni Homines (Good Men), who made up the Albigensian equivalent of the priestly class. Preaching was in the vernacular. The Good Men disdained the Roman ecclesiastical hierarchy and rejected its authority. The Cathars constituted, so to speak, the other side of the Occitanian spiritual coin, a kind of reversal of courtly worldliness, distinct from it, yet, as opposites often work, also related to it. By 1150 the Cathars were strongly implanted in Albi (hence "Albigenses"), Toulouse, Carcassonne, and Agen. Their impact in Provençal literature, though indisputable, is difficult to pinpoint. However, their presence in Occitania would have enormous and tragic consequences for the civilization and political status of the Midi.

To an astonishingly high degree, the complexities of Occitanian life in the early twelfth century are represented in the work of such early, "classical" troubadours as William IX and his immediate successors, Cercamon, Marcabru, and Jaufré Rudel. This is why, in my opinion, it is useless—even wrong—to attempt to reduce the content of their work to any clear-cut, easily defined "doctrine" (such as courtly love, *fin'amors*). But before we discuss the work of the first two generations of troubadours, some general remarks of a technical nature are in order.

The Old Provençal *trobador* (objective case; nominative: *trobaire*; French: *trouvère*) was formed on the basis of the verb *trobar* (French: *trouver*), which, according to most scholars, derives from the Latin *tropare* (to make music or verse, <TROPUS; Greek: *tropos*, tune or melody). A troubadour—the modern French, and English, adaptation of *trobador*—is consequently a maker of melodies, a songwriter, not merely a composer or "inventor" of verse. The poems and their music settings were meant to be publicly performed, most often with instrumental accompaniment, by professional entertainers known as *joglars* (compare Latin *joculatores*), who frequently prefaced their renditions with remarks concerning the life of the troubadour (these remarks have been collected and are known as *vidas* [biographies, lives]) or with brief explanations of the poems (*razos*).

The names, if not the works, of more than 100 troubadours—male and female—have been preserved; more than 900 stanza forms, or permutations, have been identified. Surviving musical settings, written down in Gregorian notation, number close to 275. These are exceedingly difficult to interpret, since troubadour verse and music are syllabic (one syllable could not, apparently, be held over more than one note, though several syllables could share the same note), in contrast to Gregorian chant. It seems certain, however, that musical rhythms and tropes both complemented and were played off against verbal rhythms and tropes for special and interesting effects. Given troubadours were known for their relative expertise in music (*sons*) or in words (*motz*)—for instance, Jaufré Rudel, who, according to his *vida,* produced "mains bons vers et ab bons sons, ab paubres motz" (many fine songs, with good melodies [but] with poor [uncomplicated, not rich?] words).

A number of fairly well-defined lyric genres came into being or were further developed during the twelfth century, the following being the most important: The *vers* (song, ode) eventually evolved into the *canso* or *chanso* (love song). The *sirventes,* formally very close to the *canso,* treated themes other than love, usually moral, political, and/or satirical. Poems in dialogue included the *tenso* (a kind of free argument or debate between two characters, each speaking in alternate stanzas); the partimen (French: *jeu-parti*; compare English "jeopardy"), in which the poet proposes a controversial issue for debate and allows his partner to choose the side he will argue for, with himself defending the other side, again in alternating stanzas; and the *pastorela* (French: *pastourelle*), in which a wandering knight meets a shepherdess, asks for her love, and either obtains it (by sweet words or by force) or is prevented from obtaining it (by the girl's steadfastness, sometimes by the intervention of her shepherd friends). The *alba* (dawn song), a very ancient genre present in embryonic form in the Song of Songs, tells of the lovers' sadness at having to separate at daybreak for fear of discovery. *Baladas* or *dansas* (dance songs) affected characteristics of greater simplicity and were sung probably in chorus; gaily celebrating the joys of love, they emphasize refrain structures and mark the tempos and the steps of dance.

Within each of these genres considerable variety

was cultivated. For example, in the *pastorela* the shepherdess is at times all too willing to grant her favors to the knight; at other times she is a pathetic victim (or, conversely, quite able to give the importunate knight a well-deserved comeuppance). Similarly, the diction of the *vers,* breathtaking in its air of transcendence in Jaufré Rudel's sublime "Lanquan li jorn son lonc en may . . ." (When the days are long, in May . . .), conveys a tone of obscene ribaldry in William IX's "Ferai un vers, pos mi somelh . . ." (I shall make a song, since I am asleep . . .) or of deliberately shocking crudity in Marcabru's moving "Bel m'es quan la rana chanta . . ." (It pleases me when the frog sings . . .). Eloquence and lyricism, passion and tenderness, humor and mockery, even skepticism and drollery find a place within the compass of troubadour verse.

Lack of space precludes any but the most summary discussion of these genres and of the immense prosodic and stanzaic variety to be found in the poems themselves. Proper analysis of rhyme schemes, stanzaic structure, distribution of line elements within stanzas, and the like would require a book-length treatment, as would such other important matters as imagery, poetic figures, theme, and, of course, music. On at least one level, troubadour poetic achievement must be measured in terms of poetic virtuosity—that is, with regard both to the poet's ability to "fit" into the rules of the Provençal lyric corpus viewed as a whole (each poet is a kind of participant in a general, ongoing process) and to his unique "voice" within that corpus. The notion of "voice" is, to a considerable degree, what is contained in the *vida[s]* and *razo[s]* devoted to a given troubadour. Thus, for example, William IX "was one of the greatest courtly men the world has ever seen and one of the greatest deceivers of women, as well as a fine knight-at-arms and very given to the courting of ladies; he was an expert writer of verse and singer; for a long time he went about the world, fooling women . . ." —the rest of the text speaks of his progeny, including Eleanor, wife of King Henry II of England and mother of kings.

In other words, poetic "voice" is, and yet is not, the equivalent of what we today call "originality." Essentially, it corresponds to an ability to work both meaningfully and recognizably—technically as well as thematically—within a universally understood tradition. The poet's "person" is synonymous with this work: it is his "variation" upon convention. Consequently, for us it makes sense to understand the lyric corpus at once as a collective achievement and as a set of individual articulations of (and within) that achievement.

Formal variety and play characterized both *vers* and *canso* (the latter term coming into more prominent use in the closing years of the twelfth century). The possibilities open to the genre, though too numerous for detailed summary here, nevertheless lend themselves, in a general way, to concise recapitulation. A typical *canso* may comprise five or six *coblas* (stanzas) of varying length (but of identical length in any given poem), followed by one or more *tornadas* (short stanzas; French: *envois* [envoys]) addressed, in many cases, to the poet's patron, lady, or audience (these individuals are often designated by a *senhal* [code name], as is, frequently, the poet himself). Within the *cobla* the lines are not necessarily of equal length, but one pattern is maintained throughout the poem. The rhyme scheme may be the same in all stanzas (*coblos unissonans*) or in two succeeding stanzas (*coblas doblas*), or, especially in older poetry, it may differ from stanza to stanza (*coblas singulars*).

Though stanza length may vary considerably (from two to more than forty lines), six or seven lines per *cobla* are not uncommon; a certain tripartition of the stanza is often superimposed upon an underlying bipartite structure, for instance, a rhyme pattern *ab/ba* (or *ab/ab*)—the *pedes*—followed by the coda, *ccd,* as in Jaufré Rudel's poem of *amor de lonh* (distant love):

Lanquan li jorn son lonc en may
M'es belhs dous chans d'auzelhs de lonh,
E quan mi suy partitz de lay
Remembra·m d'un' amor de lonh:
Vau de talan embroncx e clis
Si que chans ni flors d'albespis
No·n platz plus que l'yverns gelatz
(Jeanroy, ed., V, lines 1–7)

When the days are long, in May,
Sweet birdsong from afar pleases me.
And when I have turned away from that,
I remember a distant love;
Saddened, I go about with lowered head,
And neither birdsong nor hawthorn flower can
Cheer me, no more than would the frozen winter.

This little masterpiece, comprising seven identically rhyming *coblas* leading up to a three-line *tornada,* epitomizes the genre.

A sense of craft is necessarily built into the idea of the *canso;* by definition the troubadour is concerned with formal problems. Small wonder, then, that for Dante in the *De vulgari eloquentia,* all noble poetry must be based on the "song." Yet high seriousness is not always the ostensible goal of this concern. Craft and a certain poetic gamesmanship frequently go hand in hand, nowhere to better purpose than in several surviving texts by William IX. In "Ben veulh que sapchon li pluzor . . ." (I want people to know . . .), this prince of irony deliberately and punningly conjoins metaphors and images of poetry making, dicing, and copulation in such a way as to seem to praise these "equivalent" activities while mocking them. The poem starts with a string of workmanship images:

Ben vuelh que sapchon li pluzor
D'est vers si's de bona color,
Qu'ieu ai trag de mon obrador:
Qu'ieu port d'ayselh mestier la flor,
Et es vertaz,
E puesc ne traire·l vers auctor
Quant er lassatz.
(Jeanroy, ed., VI, lines 1–7)

I want people to know
Whether this little *vers* from my workshop
Is of good color;
For in this craft I win the prize [the flower],
And that's the truth,
And I can cite this poem, when it has been bound up,
As evidence of this.

Are these images as intentionally "unaristocratic" as the droll puns of the poem's ending? After all, the idea of the count of Poitiers being a (presumably lowborn) workman is at least as bizarre and as funny as his claiming master status because his girlfriend, after a night of dalliance, invariably wants him again the day after: "Qu'ieu suy d'aquest mestier, so·m va, / Tan ensenhatz / Que be·n sai guazanhar mon pa / En totz mercatz" (For I am, I brag, so well trained in this craft that I know well how to earn my bread from it, in any marketplace). Yet, who else but a lord so powerful (and politically so unsuccessful) as the count of Poitiers could have created for himself, and exploited, this kind of poetic persona? And in what better a fashion might such an individual proclaim—even meditate upon—the primacy of technique in the sort of poetic activity represented, for him, by the lyric mode? William's oeuvre, I believe, may be seen as an exemplary justification of the highly wrought, largely secular lyric—of a poetry or song that would be valued primarily for its own sake as well as for the range of possibilities open to a poetry so conceived.

William assumes here, at least in part, the character—the social and (a)moral mask—of the *joglar,* the frequently maligned professional entertainer who amuses and who, more rarely, instructs his audience with his songs and play. William downplays the sacred singer (for instance, the kind of *joglar* who narrates the history of St. Fides); indeed, it has been averred, many of his poems read like parodies of sacred verse. Though assuredly a prince, William was scarcely a saintly man; he was excommunicated at least once, and legends concerning his bawdy irreverence abound. This nobleman consciously played at being the kind of *joglar* who specialized not in songs about kings and saints but in obscene verses, though of course this is something he could not, socially speaking, have really been. William's kind of poetry encouraged him in that play, and this poetic gamesmanship allowed him to expand the frontiers of verse for himself as well as for the troubadours who followed in his footsteps, writing verse and, each one, adopting his own persona.

In this way, William's oeuvre paved the way for a poetic construction—the sum of troubadour poetic activity—that would parallel (partake of, yet differ from) the world of twelfth-century Occitanian life. William, the duke-count/*joglar,* emerges, then, as a complex set of personas in his verse, as a kind of vagabond king before his time—as, in other words, a freewheeling troubadour. These personas, in the dialectic regulating them, permitted an expanded kind of poetic exploration that would include and, to a certain degree, resolve immensely contradictory tendencies in human experience. William's "master," couched in amusingly ironic terms in "Ben vuelh . . . ," is a poetic mastery, authentically affirmed, no more and no less masterful than the expression he gave, on other occasions, to *joi,* to devoted love, or to spiritual concerns of disconcerting depth. In this sense William created the "troubadour"; in true medieval fashion his example constitutes his originality, his meaning.

Consequently, it is within the context just described that we must try to understand William's love poems. For the modes of love, including the modes of *fin'amors* (generally rendered in English as "courtly love"), are, like poems themselves, subject to technical play, virtuosity, and stylization. Indeed, one explanation for the predominance of certain kinds of love poetry within the troubadour corpus might well be that such poetry lends itself particularly well to the kinds of technical exploration—theme and variations—so characteristic of twelfth- and thirteenth-century Provençal verse. Lyric virtuosity, with its necessary emphasis upon the persona of the poet, and the experience of love complement each other. It is this complementarity that helps generate the meditations on *mezura* (measure, balance), *cortezia* (courtliness), *proeza* (prowess, value), *solatz* (pleasure, consolation), and so on, that we find in so many troubadour songs.

None of these terms should be construed as designating a clearly defined concept—no more than *fin'amors* denotes a doctrine; their meaning(s) can be approached only as the words themselves are employed in specific poems or in given bodies of formally related poems. Similarly, the sometimes ribald diction of the blue-blooded William IX serves purposes quite distinct, within his work, from the intentionally crude vocabulary of the lower-class Marcabru, whose professional mark, if we are to believe his *vida,* was his nasty tongue. Yet, just as William put on the mask of the *joglar,* so could Marcabru and Cercamon aspire to genuine troubadour standing and sing, when they so wished, with tenderness and noble love.

Old Provençal *joi* (<GAUDIUM), along with its congeners and variants (*joia, gaug, jai*), is one of the most complex and frequently recurring words within the troubadour vocabulary. Although it invariably designates a positive value, the precise meaning of *joi* depends almost entirely on the context of the individual poem in which it is used. The meanings range from "sexual satisfaction, pleasure, joy" to "ineffable value, highest earthly happiness, sense of perfection deriving from the practice of *cortezia.*" This polysemy, or attribution of multiple meanings to a single term, is well represented in the *vers* of William IX, who, even in this respect, set the tone for subsequent compositions. *Joi* is associated with *joven* (youth) in "Companho, faray un vers . . . convinen" (Companions, I shall make a proper *vers*); the first two stanzas have a deceptively courtly air about them (*vilans* are those who do not understand these lines), but the rest of the poem undercuts this courtliness: the poet's two lady friends are likened to two horses he had enjoyed riding and between which he is hard pressed to choose. In "Pus vezem de novelh florir" (Since we once again see the flowers bloom), a rather more idealized love song, *joi* (line 5) takes on a more abstract, general value: the "joy" of love, physical, perhaps, but also emotional and, even, with spiritual overtones.

"Farai chasoneta nueva" (I shall compose a new little song) depicts the courtly lover imploring the love of his demanding lady. He will die if she refuses to grant him what he wants, whereas if they give each other their love freely "Totz lo joys del mon es nostre" (All the joy of the world is ours). "Mout jauzens me prenc en amar" (With great happiness I give myself over to love) depicts *joi* simultaneously as the object of the poet's love and as something that emanates from his beloved (*mi dons*). This *joi* is all-powerful, greater than any other *joi,* and is capable of perpetuating life, of curing illnesses. It is what the poet feels—or wishes to feel—and it is objectified. (His art is what he can offer the lady in return for her love, as well as *his* love: "Si·m vol mi dons s'amor donar, / Pres suy . . . de son laus enavantir" [If my lady consents to give me her love, / I am ready . . . to proclaim her praise].) However sublime such *joi* may be, in "Pos de chantar m'es pres talenz" (Since the desire to sing has seized me), a poem in which William takes leave of love service, he explicitly renounces it (along with political power): "De proeza e de joi fui, / Mais ara partem ambedui" (I once belonged to prowess and to *joi* / But now I must relinquish these). *Proeza* and *joi,* along with *cavalairia* (chivalry) and *orgolh* (grandeur), must be abandoned by him who, one assumes, is preparing to meet his Maker.

Joi remains, then, of this world, at least for William. Thus, in his use of *joi* and in the various permutations this term undergoes in his work, William epitomizes the troubadour practice of imparting meanings within strictly poetic paramaters. The fact of his several personas, or stances, underlies everything else and substantiates the diverse rhetorical and dictional plays that constitute, along with his explicit sense of craft, the sense of his oeuvre.

William's example authenticated the freedom of the troubadour lyric, as well as the directions subsequently taken by the tradition he did so much to establish. We can understand, for instance, how *joi* (or *proeza,* or *pretz,* or, conversely, such antivalues as *malvestat* [wickedness] and *vilania* [villainy, loutishness]) was further modified in later works through metaphorical processes, addition of adjectives, or even personification.

The troubadour mode spread quickly from the courts of Poitiers and the Limousin. By the mid twelfth century it had reached all over Occitania and had begun to penetrate abroad, to France, Italy, Spain, and England. Kings, princes, counts, and clergymen composed *vers* and *cansos,* but the great majority of troubadours—fiefless noblemen, bourgeois, individuals from the lower classes—came from humbler walks of life. The earliest known, and mysterious, *trobairitz* (lady troubadour), the Comtessa de Dia, flourished around 1200. Her aristocratic love poetry is unmistakably and directly erotic: "Ben volria mon cavallier / tener un ser en mos bratz nut" (How I should like, one evening, to hold my knight, naked, in my arms).

Joglars and troubadours alike were wont to travel, some of them extensively, from court to court. This expansion of poetic activity led, on the one hand, to a kind of concentration on the *canso,* or love song, and, on the other, to the eventual creation of general styles—the *trobar leu* (plain, open style), the *trobar clus* (hermetic, closed style), and, later, the *trobar ric* (rich, or convoluted, style). Individual poets came to be associated with one or another of these styles.

Important to the civilization of the time and to the practice of poetry, at least up to the first third of the thirteenth century, was the fact that patronage could be, and often was, lavished on talented, though impecunious, poets. Rambaut de Vaqueiras, who began as the squire and *joglar* of Boniface of Montferrat, was dubbed a knight by his master and accompanied him to war. The Italian-born Sordello, despite a suspicious earlier career, was welcomed by Count Ramon Berenguer IV of Provence, a Catalan, who provided him with lands and a wife. Such social open-endedness—the possibility of upward social mobility—did a great deal to maintain and even to define the aristocratic character of the Old Provençal lyric, both in practice and in myth.

But good fortune was not the lot of every troubadour. Marcabru, perhaps the most profound Occitanian poet of his time, is described by one of the *vidas* devoted to him as having been "cast at the door of a powerful man, so that it is not known who he was nor whence he came." He was "very famous, listened to, and feared because of his tongue—indeed, he spoke so contemptuously of people that, finally, he was put to death by the castellans of Guyenne, about whom he had said bad things." He is spoken of as having, in his youth, accompanied the troubadour Cercamon, from whom he learned *trobar* and also, perhaps, with whom he explored certain moral and religious questions in his verse. First protected by Duke William X, son of William IX and father of Eleanor, he followed the latter to the French court when she married Louis VII. The journey was a failure. He returned to the Midi, then eventually went to Spain, where, at various courts, he experienced his usual disappointments.

Marcabru's poetic activity may be dated principally during the second quarter of the twelfth century and, largely in the *trobar clus* manner, includes *vers* and a wide variety of genres (*tenso, pastorela, planh* [lament], *gab* [boast], *sirventes,* crusade songs), many of them satiric in tone. A *vidas* in manuscript A, quoting one of his own poems, refers to him as a man who "never loved any woman and never was loved by one." Interestingly, this misogynistic moralist, whose diction at times displayed a crudity bordering on the obscene, felt deep affection and respect for his contemporary Jaufré Rudel, sometimes identified as the elegant and gentle prince of Blaye (or Blaja), one of the most delicate practitioners of *fin'amors.* Unlike Jaufré Rudel, who, so to speak, defended purity and *proeza* by exemplifying them, Marcabru did so by bitterly attacking their opposite counterparts: hypocrisy, *vilania,* and stinginess. (Nevertheless, it is to Marcabru that we owe the expression *fin joi* [pure, ideal joy].)

As was the case with William IX, a sense of self, of poetic voice, is built into the forty-odd surviving poems of Marcabru, but that voice may be described as a kind of transposition, or reversal, of the *joglar* mask so often affected by the noble duke. Poetry was Marcabru's only possession, his unique wealth and status. For this reason his place in the world could at best remain but tenuous, dependent on others (most of whom he despised) for recognition and material favor. Consequently, one finds in his verse an ideal courtly world of which only faint glimmers may be observed in real-life behavior: filth and baseness characterize reality. His poetry inhabits a universe of antitheses; in one of his *pastorelas* it is the shepherdess (described, positively, as *la vilana*) who speaks with authentic eloquence; the knight is sham. In another poem, Proeza (personified) is besieged, along with Jois and Jovens, by those whom Malvestat has corrupted, while knights and ladies indulge in wife and husband swapping. Such people, who pass for noble, are sterile, incapable of true generosity, and, it is suggested, their immoral illiberality will cause the demise of poetry. Marcabru assumes William's *joglar* mask in order to attain what, for him, is genuine aristocracy—an aristocracy of righteousness, to be achieved through proper poetic activity.

In "Per savi·l tenc ses doptanssa" (Without doubt I hold him to be wise), one of Marcabru's uncommon, relatively "simple" poems, the poet considers his art self-consciously and, even more important, far more extensively than William IX had ever done: A wise man is he "who guesses the meaning of each word in my singing and how the theme is worked out," for "myself I am hard-put to clear up an obscure word." In stanza II, troubadours with childish minds "turn into torment that which is granted by truth" and "compose words *per esmanssa*" (preciously, inappropriately) that "do not hold together" (*entrebeschatz de fraichura*). Such troubadours have no art; consequently, the poet says, they put false love on the same footing as *fin'amors* (lines 13–14); they lie, for the well-being of lovers is "Jois, Sofrirs [patient suffering] e Mesura." False love—love that seeks satisfaction in concupiscence—is to inadequate poetry what good poetry is to *fin'amors*; for Marcabru, as he states elsewhere, *mesura* is equivalent to speaking (as well as loving) nobly. Though his poems may not always be easy of access, neither is that which they are meant to express (or incarnate) authentic *fin'amors;* however, they are, Marcabru implies, true.

An understanding of *fin joi* (and of such congeners as *proeza, mesura,* and *amor*) depends on knowing how to recognize *malvestat, vilania,* and *fals'amor*. This understanding is worked out in purely lyric terms through the use of song and words, stanzaic form, rhyme scheme, images, and other devices (such as springtime/winter and other antitheses; allusions to Scripture and to the church fathers; personifications; invective; *senhal*). The complexity of Marcabru's "thought" constitutes a direct function of the complexity of his poetic virtuosity, his total association of (frequently hermetic) technique with the process of (a largely moral) intellection. To put it briefly, Marcabru thinks in verse; the words of his poems, as they are strung out in "sentences," obey a logic that is based no less on rhyme patterns and the like than on the requirements of Old Provençal syntax. In this way—to quote T. S. Eliot's phrase—he quite consciously "dislocates language into meaning." That is what renders so much of his work recalcitrant to analysis or to translation. And that is what lies at the heart of his *trobar clus* manner—surely his attempt to equate the false with the poetically hackneyed and vapid.

In illustration of the above, let us glance at the first stanza of poem XIV in Dejeanne's edition:

[Co]ntra [l'i]vern que s'e[n]ansa,
Ab cossi[ri]er que m'as[sa]ilh
M'es belh [q]ue del chant [m]'enans,
Ans [q]u'autre cossieriers m'assalha,
Pus per un cosselh descrec
No m'es ops qu'autre m'encresca.

Against the advancing winter,
With the trouble that assails me,
It pleases me that I should advance out of [profit from] song
Before another trouble assails me;
Since I am waning because of one plan,
I have no need that another cause me to wax.

(In the two *tornadas* of this *vers* the poem is likened to a dance.)

As can easily be seen, the translation is but the roughest approximation of the original; far more is left out than can be carried over into English prose paraphrase.

In traditional fashion, this opening stanza sets the poem's "season" (late fall), its tone, and its rhythm. Winter, the season of diminishment (antilyric), is coming—is "growing"—in, coincidentally with trouble assailing the poet. Parallel to the movement of winter is movement in line 3 of the poet himself, who, in a curious image, must "advance" (also "profit" from) his song before, again through parallelism with line 2 (the first four lines, with double parallels, constitute the *frons*—two *pedes*—the last two, the coda), another trouble comes to assail him. The final lines of the stanza are mysterious. Obviously they play on the poem's theme of antithesis: diminishment-in-growth versus growth-in-diminishment. The winter grows (diminishment), the poet undoes himself of (from) a song (growth). Also, the verb takes the first person in the initial line of the coda, whereas in the second it takes the third person, with *me* as the object; this corresponds to the stanza's overall structure. I decide to "decrease" (to "grow"? by writing, by eliminating trouble?) and therefore do not need to "increase" (to be the victim, or object, of some other purposefulness or design [*cosselh*]). The poet thus views himself as both subject and object and situates himself within the dialectic—the dance—of growth and diminishment.

Lack of space precludes further close reading of

this astonishing work. However, it is the first recorded poem written entirely in derivative rhymes; that is, the various rhymes, in their relationships, are tied to the respective words semantically and morphologically as well as phonetically. Also, all odd-numbered stanzas present one and the same rhyme scheme, whereas all even-numbered stanzas share another; the binary effect is all-pervasive. Marcabru identifies himself as both lover and poet; but clearly his "love" is refracted through the heavily emphasized prism of his virtuosity, his "dance." Moreover, the motion of the poem in all its rhythms is oppositional, or antithetical, like the to-and-fro movements of dancing partners—the dance even, one presumes, in the game, as well as in the poetry, of love.

This is the contrary of Jaufré Rudel's *trobar leu.* As Jaufré rose above the games of courtliness through his concentrated, absolute simplicity, so Marcabru seems laboriously to rise above them by techniques of systematic verbal undercutting. Is this not, then, a poem about poetry? But what is a poem about poetry? Much more than mere music, it seems to tell us, it is the dance, with its beat, that counts, an emphasis that, curiously, tends to intellectualize the work and render it still more opaque. With poetry of this sort Marcabru forges an instrument of moral, not mystic or spiritual, consciousness. Indeed, his work creates such a consciousness within the troubadour tradition and does so exclusively with the means—the poetic art—furnished him by that tradition: Marcabru exemplifies lyric "thought." And in so doing, he incorporates into the lyric the kinds of concern, the values, and the fervor expressed and treated in the *a lei francesca* manner by his great predecessor, the poet of the *Chanson de sainte Foy.*

During the years 1150–1180, approximately, the troubadour mode underwent still greater expansion. Stress was increasingly placed on the *canso,* and a certain codification of love themes occurred. Highly placed noblemen and noblewomen composed songs. With growing frequency, so did talented *joglars,* who, so to speak, earned themselves a place and privileges at court through the practice of ever more refined verse making and who came to be recognized as authentic troubadours. It is probable, though by no means certain, that Bernart de Ventadorn, who flourished during the third quarter of the twelfth century and whose biography is crammed full of more or less romantic legends (Was he—did he aspire to be—the lover of Eleanor of Aquitaine? Did he tire of a life dedicated to worldly pleasures and retreat to a monastery? At Dalon?), came from a relatively humble background and lived with, as well as wrote for, a series of noble patrons. Very little, then, is known concerning Bernart. However, a corpus of forty-four poems has survived in an impressive number of manuscripts and this, along with the numerous legends about him, testifies to the great esteem in which he was held by his contemporaries and successors. Consequently, we may properly choose him as representative of the best and most highly regarded singers of *fin'amors.* He is the classic troubadour, at the high-water mark of the Old Provençal lyric tradition, and he epitomizes the best-known features of that tradition.

One of the *vidas* devoted to Bernart speaks of the viscount of Ventadorn, Bernart's lord, as having been "charmed" by his "trobar e . . . cantar" and therefore showering honors upon him. The viscount "si avia moiller, joven e gentil e gaia" (had a wife who was young, well-bred, and joyful); she too was "charmed" by Bernart's songs, "so she fell in love with him and he with her." That is why he composed "chansos e . . . vers" about (and for) her, about the love he felt for her, and on the *valor* (great merits) of the lady (*dompna*). This situation is archetypal in Occitanian love poetry: a noble and generous patron, who admits the poet to his company; his wife, or another lady at court, beautiful and perfect in all ways, for love of whom the poet makes, as best he can, exquisite songs. The lady may return this love (or choose not to do so) and "reward" the poet in any one of a number of ways ranging from an affectionate glance to a kiss—to, in some cases, outright and total physical intimacy.

This poetic (and/or "real") "game of love," with its very possible dangers to all concerned, ostensibly involved intricate rules every bit as complicated (and arduous) as the rules for composing songs. (Compendia of such rules were set down in "codes," as were rules for writing poetry, particularly in Catalonia.) The lady also could withdraw her love (both *vidas* speak of this happening to Bernart), or she might never have accorded it in the first place, preferring to remain haughty and disdainful. Secrecy, or at least its outward forms, must be maintained, so flatterers, spies, and slanderers (*lauzengiers*) would somehow be circumvented.

Interestingly, seldom does the troubadour admit that he might be betraying his patron by "loving" his wife; the margin of love, or of poetically conceived love behavior, appears to have been great. When mentioned as such, the "husband" is usually referred to as the *gelos* (jealous [reprehensible] one), fit for the society of *lauzengiers*, upon whom any trick might legitimately be played. The prototype of the *gelos* is a certain legendary Raimon de Castel Rossillon, who, according to the *vida* of Guillem de Cabestaing, killed the poet-lover of his wife, cut out his heart, and, after having it cooked, served it to his wife for dinner. Upon hearing what she has eaten, the wife throws herself out of the balcony window and dies. The king of Aragon, depicted in this text as a true protector of troubadours and their ladies, avenges the luckless troubadour and his beloved by destroying Raimon's castles and tossing him into prison. It would seem, then, that within the *fin'amors* vocabulary, the categories "noble protector" and "jealous husband" were mutually exclusive.

Bernart de Ventadorn regularly equates love for his lady with the effort of writing songs. The two are inseparable. Both love and the making of poetry are enterprises of the highest nobility that together bring out the best in a man. Moreover, if poetry is to be genuine, it must be based on real love, authentically felt by a troubadour-lover capable of such feeling. The poet willingly gives his all to the lady; no sacrifice is too great on her behalf. He must suffer and overcome; the commitment is total:

Non es meravelha s'eu chan
melhs de nul autre chantador,
que plus me tra·l cors vas amor
e melhs sui faihz a so coman.
Cor e cors e saber e sen
e fors' e poder i ai mes.
Si·m tira vas amor lo fres
que vas autra part no·m aten.
(M. Lazar, ed., p. 60, lines 1–8)

It is no wonder that I sing
better than any other singer,
for my heart pulls me more toward love
and I am better suited to its command.
Heart and body, knowledge and mindfulness
and strength and power I have committed to it.
And the rein so draws me toward love
that I turn my attention nowhere else.

Out of the best commitment comes the best song. (This affirmation helps explain, I think, the proliferation of legends surrounding Bernart's life—tales recounted in the *vidas* and in the works of other poets.) All too numerous, implies Bernart, are those troubadours who merely go through the motions of love, cynically; despite possible temporary successes in court and with ladies, they must necessarily compose poorly: "Chanters no pot gaire valer, / si d'ins dal cor no mou lo chans" (Singing is useless unless the song comes from the heart). Genuine love seeks no recompense beyond itself, yet it has many virtues, such as an ability to protect the lover against the cold and to reassure him, even when the lady does not respond.

The poet, as Bernart depicts him, serves his lady in a fashion recalling the gestures and the duties of a feudal vassal: she is liege lord of his heart. From all this he gains a deeper comprehension of things and of *valor:* he sets himself apart from all others and achieves his own nobility. He becomes, as it were, his own lord. Looking at, touching, or even possessing the beloved are all forms, essentially, of contemplation that lead to the *joi* of understanding—or experiencing—*cortezia, pretz,* and *solatz.* In moments of despair, as when his beloved lady rewards his attentions with indifference (or worse), Bernart threatens to write no more, as in the famous "Can vei la lauzeta mover" (When I see the lark beat his wings), where, disappointed in love, he calls out to "Tristan" in the *tornada:* "Tristans, ges no·n auretz de me, / qu'eu m'en vau, chaitius, no sai on. / De chantar me gie e·m recre, / e de joi e d'amor m'escon" (Tristan, you will have nothing more from me, / for I, in misery, take my leave, whither I do not know. / I renounce and forswear making songs / and I seek shelter far from joy and love [lines 57–60]).

All of Bernart's *cansos* and *tensos* treat these themes, with the full panoply of images (seasons, birds, and so on), antitheses ("Per midons m'esjau no-jauzitz" [For my lady I rejoice without joy], line 9 of "Can lo boschatges es floritz" [When the wood is in flower]), and vocabulary that typifies the Old Provençal love song. His oeuvre is a highly wrought set of themes and variations, totally conventional and exemplary.

It is, of course, impossible to determine to what extent, if any, Bernart's work mirrors "real life" in late-twelfth-century Occitanian courts. To affirm that the troubadours were systematic and, as it were, professional (and more or less tolerated) adulterers—Bernart's ladies were married—would seem to be as foolish as to believe that these ladies were, for him, veiled stand-ins for the Virgin. Relationshps between poetry and life are always difficult to circumscribe: *A* never does quite equal *B*. Bernart's oeuvre brings together many different strands. First and foremost, he was a superb craftsman. And for him, as well as, presumably, for his courtly contemporaries, the craft of poetry was, at the very least, closely tied to a kind of behavior, of crafted sentiment—the analogies of poetry and behavior are striking. Through the exercise of his craft, a Bernart de Ventadorn could aspire to a noble status—a kind of social position—not without traits shared with the status of a nobleman like Count Eble of Ventadorn and his lady.

But just as the troubadour's love for a highborn lady was fraught with uncertainty, so his position at court must have been subject to many potential vicissitudes. What, finally, is interesting to observe is the outwardly "existential" character of the conventions governing the professional and personal situations of a troubadour like Bernart. He was no learned cleric, like Wace in Norman England or Chrétien de Troyes at the court of Champagne. Rather, he depicts himself as a person, participating fully—intimately—in at least a portion of the court's activities; indeed, he was central to these activities. Such was, one concludes, the nature of the "entertainment" he provided. In fact, what he and other troubadours symbolized in their poetic endeavors came to be viewed as indispensable to the kind of civilization the great courts of the Midi most prided themselves on. (One need only compare these courts with, say, the all too serious, poetically almost illiterate court of Eleanor's first husband, Louis VII of France, in order to articulate a sense of that civilization.)

Bernart brought the art of the *canso,* principally in the manner of *trobar leu,* to a high level of technical perfection. (Music accompanying some eighteen of his songs has been preserved.) Yet, as I have tried to show, there inheres in Bernart's work a significant dimension of—or capacity for—what might be called idealism. By attempting to fuse with his beloved, the poet participates in—he creates—*joi. Joi* can be many things: utter perfection is one of these. Bernard seeks *joi,* and that, by definition, implies that seldom, if ever, does he actually achieve it. Consequently, in some fundamental and characteristically lyric way, the poet must remain alone, ever isolated in his work and in his longing. Within a secular framework, yet genuinely just the same, Bernart bears a strong resemblance to the imprisoned Boecis of the eleventh-century poem, who sought out, and adored, the ineffably beautiful Lady Philosophy. Bernart's quest—and that of several of his contemporaries—possesses many attributes of the inner-directed, though "objectified," search for meaning undertaken by Boecis and celebrated by one of the very earliest Occitanian poets.

BIBLIOGRAPHY

Sources. Bernart de Ventadorn, *The Songs of Bernart de Ventadorn,* Stephen G. Nichols, Jr., *et al.,* eds. (1962, rev. ed. 1965), and *Bernard de Ventadour, troubadour de XIIe siècle: Chansons d'amour,* Moshe Lazar, ed. (1966); Bertran de Born, *The Poems of the Troubadour Bertran de Born,* William D. Paden, Jr., Tilde Sankovitch, and Patricia Stäblein, eds. and trans. (1986); Jean Boutière and A.-H. Schutz, eds., *Biographies des troubadours* (1950, rev. ed. 1964); Cercamon, *Les poésies de Cercamon,* Alfred Jeanroy, ed. (1922, repr. 1966); Margarita Egan, *The Vidas of the Troubadours* (1984); Jaufré Rudel, *Les chansons de Jaufré Rudel,* Alfred Jeanroy, ed., 2nd ed., rev. (1965), and *The Songs of Jaufré Rudel,* Rupert T. Pickens, ed. and trans. (1978); Gabrielle Kussler-Rayté, ed., "Les chansons de la contesse Béatrix de Dia," in *Archivum romanicum,* **1** (1917); René Lavaud and G. Machicot, eds., *Boecis: Poème sur Boèce (fragment)* (1950); Marcabru, *Poésies complètes du troubadour Marcabru,* Jean M. L. Dejeanne, ed. (1909, repr. 1971); Raimbaut de Vaqueiras, *The Poems of the Troubadour Raimbaut de Vaqueiras,* Joseph Linskill, ed. (1964); Raimon Vidal, *The Razos de Trobar of Raimon Vidal and Associated Texts,* J. H. Marshall, ed. (1972); Ste. Foy, *La chanson de sainte Foy,* Ernst Hoepffner and Prosper Alfaric, eds., 2 vols. (1926); St. Léger, "La vie de St. Léger," Gaston Paris, ed., in *Romania,* **2** (1873), and *Saint-Léger: Étude de la langue du manuscrit de Clermon-Ferrand, suivie d'une edition critique du texte . . . ,* Joseph Linskill, ed. (1937, repr. 1974); Sordello, *Sordello: Le poésie,* Marco Boni, ed. (1954); William IX, *Les chansons de Guillaume IX,* Alfred Jeanroy, ed., 2nd ed. rev. (1964), and *The Poetry of William VII, Count of Poitiers, IX Duke of Aquitaine,* Gerald A. Bond, ed. and trans. (1982).

Studies. Dictionaries and grammars include Joseph Anglade, *Grammaire de l'ancien provençal* (1921, repr. 1977); Frank Hamlin, Peter T. Ricketts, and John Hathaway, *Introduction à l'étude de l'ancien provençal* (1967), grammar, texts, glossary, bibliography; Emil Levy, *Provenzalisches Supplement-wörterbuch,* 8 vols. (1894–1924), and *Petit dictionnaire provençal-français,* 5th ed. (1973); Kurt Baldinger with Doris Diekmann-Sammet, *Complement bibliographique au Provenzalisches Supplement-wörterbuch de Emil Levy: Sources, datations* (1969).

Anthologies are Karl Bartsch, *Chrestomathie provençale,* 6th ed., rev. by Eduard Koschwitz (1904, repr. 1973), glossary in French; Frederick Goldin, ed. and trans., *Lyrics of the Troubadours and Trouvères* (1973); Raymond T. Hill and Thomas G. Bergin, *Anthology of the Provençal Troubadours,* 2nd ed., rev. by Bergin with

Susan Olson, William D. Paden, Jr., and Nathaniel Smith, 2 vols. (1973), introduction, map, chronology, notes, and glossary in English; René Lavaud and René Nelli, *Les troubadours,* 2 vols. (1960–1966), Old Provençal text and French translation; Alan R. Press, ed. and trans., *Anthology of Troubadour Lyric Poetry* (1971), selections from fifteen well-known troubadours, Old Provençal text and English translation; Jacques Roubaud, *Les troubadours: Anthologie bilingue* (1971).

Among bibliographies are Alfred Pillet and Henry Carstens, *Bibliographie der Troubadours* (1933, rev. 1968); Robert A. Taylor, *La littérature occitane du moyen âge* (1977); the yearly listings in *Publications of the Modern Language Association* (*PMLA*) and *Year's Work in Modern Language Studies.*

Critical studies include D'Arco Silvio Avalle, *La letteratura medievale in lingua d'oc nella sua tradizione monoscritta* (1961); Charles Camproux, *Histoire de la littérature occitane* (1953, repr. 1971); István Frank, *Répertoire métrique de la poésie des troubadours,* 2 vols. (1953–1957, repr. 1971); Alfred Jeanroy, *La poésie lyrique des troubadours,* 2 vols. (1934, repr. in 1 vol. 1973), and *Histoire sommaire de la poésie occitane, des origines à la fin du XVIIIe siècle* (1945, repr. 1973); Robert Lafont and Christian Anatole, *Nouvelle histoire de la littérature occitane,* I (1970); Linda M. Paterson, *Troubadours and Eloquence* (1975); L. T. Topsfield, *Troubadours and Love* (1975, repr. 1978); Hendrik Jan van der Werf, *The Chansons of the Troubadours and Trouvères: A Study of the Melodies and Their Relation to the Poems* (1972).

KARL UITTI

[See also **Alba; Bernart de Ventadorn; Canso; Catalan Literature; Catalonia; Cathars; Cercamon; Comtessa de Dia; Courtly Love; Eleanor of Aquitaine; French Language; French Literature; Jaufré Rudel; Jeu Parti; Joglar/Jongleur; Laisse; Languedoc; Marcabru; Partimen; Pastourelle; Raimbaut de Vaqueiras; Raimon Vidal de Besalú; Sirventes; Tenso; Tornada; Toulouse; Trobairitz; Troubadour, Trouvère; Vers; Vidas; William IX of Aquitaine.**]

PROVENÇAL LITERATURE: AFTER 1200

TROUBADOUR POETRY: APOTHEOSIS AND DECLINE OF THE *CANSO* (1200–1250)

The great historical watershed of Occitanian culture and, especially, of Occitanian poetry may be located in the period roughly from 1200 to 1250. This was the time of a series of wars known generally as the Albigensian Crusade (1209–1229); these wars coincided with the decay of the courtly lyric, as it had been practiced during the twelfth century, and culminated in the virtual destruction of the relatively autonomous Occitanian courtly society that had nurtured that poetry. The extent to which there may have existed a cause-and-effect relationship between, on the one hand, these wars and the depredations they brought about and, on the other hand, the increasingly formalistic (and narrow) troubadour poetry of approximately 1200–1220 is impossible to determine.

A great many scholars impute the decline of erstwhile favored troubadour styles to the wars and the persecutions suffered by Occitania: poetic values, they conclude, fell victim to French and papal "imperialism." However, by the same token, it ought to be pointed out that the political and military weakness of Occitania, which allowed the lands and the culture of the Midi eventually to be taken over by France (in conjunction with other powers, including England) during the thirteenth century, also characterized and helped define the climate that produced the kinds of poetry epitomized by William IX and his immediate successors. Something in the social, political, and intellectual structures of Occitania—their weaknesses as well as their strengths—favored the early taking root there of the type of poetry we associate with the troubadours, to the relative detriment of other kinds of literary expression (for instance, heroic narrative verse, as practiced in France and Castile).

The issues are extraordinarily complex. The period during which Occitania was politically subjugated and spiritually ravished was also the period in which the identification of Occitania with the poetic enterprise—in particular with the *canso*—was most lucidly and most emphatically articulated. It is this identification, with many of its concomitant paradoxes, that I propose to explore. But, before discussing the poetry itself and the implications of Occitania's self-identification with troubadour poetry, let us briefly recapitulate some of the major historical events of the first half of the thirteenth century.

During the twelfth century, the emergence in certain Occitanian centers of what came to be known as the Cathar heresy, coupled with the increasingly secular-minded courtly society that evolved in parallel fashion elsewhere in Occitania, prompted much criticism on the part of the papacy. The established church became increasingly suspicious of the typically Occitanian *convivencia* (living together) of worldliness, mystical asceticism (situated outside the church), and remarkable tolerance of Jewish culture and "usury." The Midi was slipping out from under orthodox ecclesiastical authority.

Meanwhile, two sets of events took place during the second half of the twelfth century that would finally enable the church and its temporal allies to take action against these "dangerous" trends. The stability achieved by certain Occitanian princes, both within the Midi and in regard to centers in France, England, the empire, and Spain, gave way to fratricidal war (Catalans against Toulousans) and increased interference in Occitanian affairs by northerners. Thus Henry II Plantagenet, husband of Eleanor of Aquitaine, laid claim to Toulouse subsequent to the assassination, in 1181, of Ramon Berenguer. During the same period a number of powerful Occitanian princes and such pro-Occitanians as Frederick I Barbarossa and Richard I of England died. The misled Fourth Crusade (1202–1204), the first that was turned against Christians, resulted in the sack of Constantinople. Thus the stage was set for a holy war against Occitanian heresy and weakness—for a French comeback in Occitanian affairs and for a solution to the Midi's heterodoxy.

On 14 January 1208, at St. Gilles, the papal legate Peter of Castelnau was assassinated; this murder was undoubtedly linked to the excommunication the preceding year of Count Raymond VI of Toulouse. The crusade that followed this assassination put an end to the relative independence enjoyed by many Occitanian lands and towns. Under the pretext of stamping out the Cathar heresy, and of restoring the spiritual authority of Rome as well as the temporal power of the king of France, crusaders from all over Europe (though principally from France) sacked, pillaged, and killed: great lords were murdered or deprived of their fiefs, literally thousands (a papal legate mentioned the hyperbolic figure 150,000) were put to the sword in the sack of Béziers (July 1209) or driven from their homes after the surrender of starving Carcassonne. Still other towns, such as Nîmes, perhaps prudently, welcomed the conquerors and were at least temporarily spared.

The establishment of the Dominican and Franciscan Inquisitions, designed to restore doctrinal orthodoxy, tended to foment a climate of doubt and fear. Though in fact the inquisitors were never quite so bloodthirsty as they often have been depicted (numerous Franciscans were sympathetic to the Occitanian cause), they viewed with utmost suspicion the very secular and freewheeling ways of many troubadours. The Occitanians fought back, sometimes with success, as in the taking of the castle of Beaucaire, near Marseilles, in 1216, by Raymond VII of Toulouse and in the battlefield slaying, in 1218, of the hated Simon de Montfort. In 1242 Raymond VII was able to join an anti-French alliance composed of Spanish and Occitanian lords as well as of such powerful sovereigns as the king of England and Emperor Frederick II. After some initial successes, however, the alliance disintegrated. Occitania had missed its chance for nationhood. Montségur, a stronghold of Cathar heretics, was captured in 1244; Quéribus, the last great Occitanian fortress, fell in 1255. Aquitaine remained attached to the English crown; the rest of the Midi was effectively incorporated into the French kingdom and ruled by French officials.

Such troubadours as lived and wrote during these tragic years composed bitter protests against the invaders and the horrors of these wars. Many gave vent to sentiments of despair, hatred, and rage. Some, like Guillem Figueira, inveighed against the Roman church, committing it to hellfire and damnation. Still others praised the Occitanian resistance in *cansos* and *sirventes,* defending what they perceived to be their country's cause. Large numbers of troubadours fled to Spain and Italy, where they wandered, composed songs, and took refuge at hospitable courts.

In much of the verse of the time, the ruin of Occitania is seen as the ruin of poetry. The world is out of joint, upside down because poetry—*cansos*—may no longer freely be composed, enjoyed, and rewarded. In short, the upheavals suffered by the "country" of Occitania—identified as the land of lyric song—are portrayed as upheavals in the conditions of poetry. During the period 1200–1250, poetry came to stand as an extraordinary metaphor for an entire civilization; and it was consciously understood as such. This metaphor, which has survived intact in much of the criticism and scholarship devoted in our own day to Old Provençal literature, is perhaps the last great creation of the Occitanian lyric. It is not quite identical with the very learned (and medieval) metaphor of the world-as-book, nor does it express exactly the equally traditional golden age (of the past) topos, although in a sense it is related to both. Rather, as befits the essential nature of lyric structure, the metaphor possesses a characteristically existential dimension: the time of poetry, now past, was a time of life (love); this time (this poetry) still exists in our memory; we live because we issue from a race of poets (lovers and warriors). Poetry thus achieves—indeed, incarnates—a special efficacy; it cannot be taken away from us.

In order to appreciate the power of this metaphor-myth of poetry as it acquired peculiar cogency during the sad years of the early thirteenth century, we must first look more closely at certain developments in troubadour verse during the period immediately preceding the Albigensian Crusade. This was the time of the most exuberant flowering of the troubadour lyric. Giraut de Bornelh, whose mysterious and extraordinarily moving alba "Reis glorios, verais lums e clartatz" (Glorious King, true light and brightness) is recognized as one of the masterpieces of Old Provençal verse; Bertran de Born, the warrior-poet and patriot, who brought the art of the *sirventes* to its peak; Peire Vidal, the servant and counselor of many great lords as well as the almost irresponsibly passionate poet-lover of numerous ladies; the rigorously conventional and very esteemed troubadour and companion of Richard Lionheart, Gaucelm Faidit, who was one of the Occitanian poets to sojourn in the Holy Land—these, and others too numerous to mention here, make up the generation active during the period immediately preceding the Albigensian Crusade. One of the most highly regarded troubadours of the late twelfth century was Arnaut Daniel, whom Dante places among the lustful in circle VII of Purgatory (*Purgatorio,* XXVI) and who speaks to Dante the pilgrim in Old Provençal. (Dante's guide, the poet Guido Guinizelli, refers to Arnaut as "miglior fabbro del parlar materno" [the best craftsman in the mother tongue]; and in the *De vulgari eloquentia,* Dante identifies him as the master love poet [II, ii, 8–9].) Arnaut had the good fortune to be protected by both Richard Lionheart and Alfonso of Aragon. He claims, moreover, to have attended the coronation of King Philip II Augustus of France in 1180. A brief review of his work sheds valuable light on this precrisis period. Arnaut epitomizes the values his time associated with poetic expertise—the myth of troubadour poetry.

Arnaut Daniel practiced the art of *trobar ric* (following the *clus* style of Marcabru and, especially, of the deliberately intricate and well-born Raimbaut d'Aurenga). Whereas Bernart de Ventadorn had insisted upon the link and the equilibrium between sincerely felt love and poetic accomplishment, Arnaut emphasizes poetic convention and stylistic mannerism as the sign of the aristocracy, or distinction, of love. Bernart's balance is disrupted. Arnaut's imagery and vocabulary, his syntax and his sound effects, are recherché in the extreme, designed to underscore techniques that are played with for their own sake. He seeks out the difficult in order to vanquish it; his poems are brilliant tours de force.

The success enjoyed by Arnaut Daniel provides stunning proof of the esteem accorded to sheer verbal virtuosity by the Occitanian court society of the time (as well as by later Italian emulators at least down to Petrarch). Within the *trobar ric* the content of the poem is of no intrinsic value; its structurings are, in and of themselves, the raison d'être to the exclusion of virtually everything else. Nevertheless, though it may be difficult for us to grasp this fact, Dante's testimony clearly indicates that Arnaut's procedures were understood as genuinely reflecting the meanings of the *canso*—the love song. What is significant, then, is not only Arnaut's poetic practice but also the fame and the glory that accrued to him as a troubadour.

Nowhere is Arnaut's "formalism" more evident than in his famous sestina, a poem made up of six six-line stanzas (plus a three-line *tornada*). The rhyme words are as distinct semantically from one another as possible: *intra* (enters), *ongla* (fingernail, claw, or talon), *arma* (soul), *verga* (rod), *oncle* (uncle), and *cambra* (bedroom). The last rhyme word of stanza I becomes the first of the second stanza, and so on, with each stanza separated from its predecessor by repeating in its initial rhyme the concluding word of the preceding stanza. Proselike "sense" is very much subordinated to the adequate working out of this tyrannical pattern, as well as to the subtle phonetic games involving liquids, nasals, and occlusives in the rhymes. Here are stanzas I and IV:

Lo ferm voler qu'el cor m'intra
no·m pot jes becs escoissendre ni ongla
de lausengier, qui pert per maldir s'arma;
e car non l'aus batr'ab ram ni ab verga,
sivals a frau, lai on non aurai oncle,
jauzirai joi en vergier o dinz cambra.

(Karl Bartsch, *Chrestomathie provençale,* 150)

The steadfast desire [love] that enters my heart
cannot be broken, either with his beak or with his claw,

by the flatterer who, by slandering, loses his soul;
And since I dare not beat him with branch or with rod,
in hiding, where I shall have no uncle [to spy on me],
I shall take my joy, in an orchard or a bedroom.

Anc la seror de mon oncle
non amei plus ni tant, per aquest'arma!
C'aitant vezis cum es lo detz de l'ongla,
s'a lei plagues, volgr'esser de sa cambra.
De mi pot far l'amors qu'inz el cor m'intra
mieills a son vol c'om fortz de frevol verga.

Never the sister of my uncle
did I more—or as much—love, by my soul!
As close as the finger is to the fingernail
—If it please her—would I be to her bedroom.
Love can do with me—he who enters my heart—
More easily what he wants than a strong man can
bend a supple rod.

By today's standards of taste this is hardly great poetry: the humor—"in" jokes, surely—lacks the robustness of William IX; the recondite language does not translate any moral fervor of the kind we find in Marcabru; and here *joi* is but a conceit compared with what we observe in the poems of Bernart de Ventadorn. It would almost seem that in seeking to renew or advance within the troubadour tradition by so sharply focusing upon technical mastery, Arnaut Daniel succeeds chiefly in delineating a certain capacity for emptiness—a potential sterility—within that tradition. The sestina is quite gratuitous. It leads nowhere; it is the end of its line. But that is precisely what it was meant to be. Why? Because, we must conclude, Arnaut wished to be the self-appointed and self-conscious exemplar of troubadour love poetry; and many of his contemporaries, as well as Dante and Petrarch, considered him to be just that.

Whereas for most of us Bernart is far more authentically exemplary of the tradition, Arnaut was understood in his own time as being the first poet to accord absolute primacy to pure technique, that is, to relationships of sound as these undermine relationships of sense in the poetic, or lyric, art—the art most intimately associated with (even confused with) *fin'amors*. It is no more and no less than this technical mastery that was singled out by Petrarch when he called Arnaut the *gran maestro d'amor*. Arnaut was the perfect lover because not only were his verses flawless, but they demonstrated that the poet (and/or lover) could overcome enormous difficulties with apparent effortlessness. With Arnaut, then, the status of the "perfect" troubadour and his craft—the poetic persona and the art—had come, in a very real sense, to be recognized as epitomizing the civilization to which, formerly, that status has been merely analogous. Lyric song thus became *fin'amors* incarnate, and *cortezis* and *valor* to boot—a standard to which, so to speak, "real life" could aspire only imperfectly. Arnaut's verse refines away the recalcitrant impurities of existence in a fashion heretofore never attempted. Subjected in this way to outrageous refinement, the very vocabulary of troubadour verse is subverted: it is pure clay in the poet's hands.

Not every poet shared Arnaut's high opinion of himself or, for that matter, the view that courtly lyric poetry of his kind invariably represented—or could be substituted for—the best of human values and accomplishments. In an amusing *sirventes* (*Pos Peire d'Alvernhe a Chantat, ca.* 1195), Peire de Vic, the Monk of Montaudon, satirizes his own career and that of fifteen late-twelfth- and thirteenth-century troubadours, including Arnaut Daniel. (Peire's style recalls Marcabru, especially when, in another poem, he wittily and crudely inveighs against women's use of cosmetics.) As for Arnaut, "a sa vida be no chantet" (he never sang well in his whole life); he uses "fols motz c'om non enten" (mad words that nobody understands). Peire de Vic is making light fun of a whole generation of troubadours—of their self-consciousness and their pretension. He does so by summarizing, one troubadour to a stanza, "what they say,"—that is, he reduces and "translates" their poems, providing a kind of miniature, comic *razo* for each. But the fact that Peire does this tends to demonstrate precisely what he criticizes, that the precedence accorded poetry by such as Arnaut Daniel and the peculiar formalism, or perfectionism, that resulted had gained wide currency and a large measure of acceptance by the early decades of the thirteenth century.

A kind of positive consciousness of the precedence, or absolute value, accorded to poetry by works like those of Arnaut Daniel—the equivalence established between formal, refined lyric song and the very sense of Occitanian civilization—is clearly articulated in the prose *vidas* and *razos*. These texts were composed during the thirteenth and fourteenth centuries (mainly 1250–1300, principally in Italy, though also in Languedoc and in Catalonia), that is, immediately subsequent to the disasters that befell Occitania. These largely fictional biographies and interpretations of the lives and works of some 101 troubadours tell the story of the collective troubadour experience as this was understood by a post-troubadour time. They do so, of course, as narrative in the third person, but in reference always to individual poets (thereby respecting the lyric character of that experience). The very considerable importance of these texts with regard to the development of vernacular prose narrative and biography in Western Europe is only now being properly recognized and evaluated. The fictions, as we shall presently see, are as revealing as—more revealing than—the anecdotal data contained in them. The *vidas* are poetic, too, and they tell their truth poetically. In them the myth of poetry assumes a legendary, and therefore lasting, form, a kind of history.

Interestingly, some of the lengthiest and most detailed *vidas* and *razos* are devoted to troubadours now relegated to the second or third rank, many of whom lived during the traumatic years 1200–1220. (Conversely, texts concerning such early and major figures as Jaufré Rudel and Marcabru are often disappointingly laconic.) For instance, Boutière and Schutz have collected and published one *vida* and four *razos* devoted to the minor troubadour Raimon de Miraval (one of the poets mocked by the Monk of Montaudon). Let me translate, in extenso, the last of these *razos,* a text meant to be spoken before a performance of Miraval's work. It illustrates and, I believe, confirms perfectly our preceding observations. Miraval's artistry is not at issue here so much as the fact of his troubadour status, the true center of interest for the one who composed the *razo*:

> After the count of Toulouse had been dispossessed by the church and the French, and he had lost Argence and Beaucaire; after the French had taken St. Gilles, the Albigeois, and the Carcassès; after the Biterrois had been devastated, the viscount of Béziers killed, and all the well-born people of these lands either killed or fugitive in Toulouse, Miraval was staying with the count of Toulouse, in the company of whom he called himself "Audiart." And he was living in great grief, for all the well-born people of whom the count was lord and master, both ladies and knights, had been killed or dispossessed; he had, moreover, lost his wife, as you shall hear, and his lady had betrayed and deceived him; he had also lost his castle.
>
> It came to pass that the king of Aragon visited Toulouse, in order to speak with the count and to see his sisters, Lady Elienor and Lady Sancha. He gave great comfort to his sisters, to the count his son-in-law, and to the nobility of Toulouse; and he promised to get Beaucaire and Carcassonne back for the count, and to recover Miraval's castle for him; and to act so that upper-class society would once again find the happiness it had lost.
>
> Miraval took great joy in the promises the king had made to the count and to himself to return to them what they had lost; and he rejoiced because of the summertime that had come—even though he had decided to compose no more songs until he had recovered the castle of Miraval that he had lost—and because he had fallen in love with Lady Elienor, the count's wife, the most beautiful and best lady in the world, to whom he had not yet declared his love, he composed this song, which says:
>
> It pleases me to sing and be sociable,
> Since the air is soft and the weather
> [time] is joyful.
>
> And when he had finished the song, he sent it to the king, in Aragon. That is why the king came with a thousand knights in order to help the count of Toulouse and to keep the promise he had made to him to recover the land that he had lost. And because of this the king was slain by the French outside Muret, with all the thousand knights he had brought with him, for not a single one escaped. (Boutière and Schutz, eds., pp. 404–405)

This *razo* purportedly is a commentary on a poem by Miraval; it is in fact a statement concerning the relationship of Miraval's status as a troubadour to the events leading to the Battle of Muret and the major defeat of what courtly Occitania stood for. Historical deeds are interpreted consistently with reference to the idealized, yet "factual," person Miraval, whose oeuvre is seen as reflecting, even determining, the course of these deeds: his love song inspired the king of Aragon's return, eventually "causing" the disaster at Muret. The loss of Miraval's castle (which, incidentally, he was wont to offer to his several poetic paramours) metonymically represents in concrete, individualized fashion the dispossession of Occitanian upper-class society. All this is depicted as though restoring Miraval's castle to him would signify the return of the time of lyric poetry (note the summer [time-of-lyric] imagery) and the restoration of the golden age that had flourished previous to the French invasion. Miraval's personal depression represents, even embodies, the despair of Occitania. A kind of tragic fatality pervades everything here: gone are the good old days, and efforts at restitution (to enable Miraval to compose songs anew) are doomed to failure. Miraval, it is suggested, will never love again nor indulge in *trobar* because of circumstances beyond his control—and despite the valiant efforts of the count of Toulouse and his ally, the king of Aragon.

Miraval's history is construed as englobing that of his country, as a metaphor for the history of Occitania. Thus, in a very meaningful way, Miraval's *joi* (or deprivation of it) constitutes an emblem of what we today might call Occitanian civilization and independence.

Vidas and *razos* such as this one function then as both a "study" of troubadour poetry and a profoundly creative historical investigation. They offer an evaluative statement concerning an entire people—or, at least, its upper classes—that is ostensibly based on a narrowly framed textual and biographical explication. These texts affirm the identity of late-thirteenth-century Occitanians and their Italian and Spanish emulators with the glories of their poetic past, which they are enjoined to remember and understand. That is why *vidas* and *razos,* in the guise of preludes, were performed by *joglas* before they sang the songs; they constitute the historical counterpart of these formalized compositions. Through these *vidas* and *razos* the meaning of courtly society, which had come to an end, was brought to others. Thanks largely to these texts the claims to universality of Old Provençal poetry—the myth of the troubadour—were given new substance and that poetry survived, though naturally it was to be much transformed. In a sense, then, the *vidas* and *razos* were designed, quite poetically, to overcome the difficulties wrought by the historical destructions they record.

Post-thirteenth-century Occitanian literature, with a few brilliant exceptions, may in general be described as evincing two main tendencies: assimilation into French (indeed, European) literature, on the one hand, and, on the other, an increased provincialism. Little by little the Old Provençal koine broke down into regional dialects, a few of which became literary vehicles in their own right (Provençal, *langue d'oc,* Gascon) while others carried on as patois, islands of rustic speech. *Langue d'oïl* gained ground in administration and in literature. A great lord like Gaston III of Foix welcomed at his court the French-language poet Froissart, Chaucer's contemporary. None of the fourteenth-century popes at Avignon protected Occitanian writers. The founding, at Toulouse in 1323, of the Consistori de la Subragaya Companhia del Gai Saber promoted the survival (or revival) of song writing in Occitan, but though interesting poets wrote at its behest (for instance, Raimon de Cornet, who blended love imagery and Franciscan mysticism), this was essentially a local phenomenon and led to the development of a Toulouse-based, fundamentally provincial, literary language.

By the middle of the fourteenth century Old Provençal had completely lost its former universality. Occitan had, so to speak, gone underground, as evidenced in the increasingly folkloric character of popular religious plays, songs, and confessional literature. However, Old Provençal did remain the language of a remarkable literature in prose, principally scientific handbooks and compendia of various sorts. In 1539, Francis I of France promulgated the Ordinance of Villers-Cotterets, which proclaimed the obligatory use of French in all official juridical and administrative "acts" within his kingdom. Thus, at the risk of only slight oversimplification, it may be said that with the destruction of the old-style twelfth-century courtly society during the first half of the thirteenth century, and subsequent to the composition of the prose *vidas* and *razos,* Old Provençal literature became a burnt-out case in its own territory. In more ways than one the *canso* (the love song) was a victim of its own success and of its too narrowly perfectionist view of itself. Its demise, rather than being directly caused by the deterioration of the society that created it, may be more accurately said to parallel and reflect that destruction.

NONLYRIC GENRES

The Old Provençal literary adventure was unique in the history of medieval Europe. Although the troubadour phenomenon and its antecedents constitute the best-known—even, perhaps, the most significant—elements of that great poetic adventure, other literary activities taking place during the period 1100–1400 (and especially after 1200) ought not to be entirely neglected. The *canso* and other forms of lyric are quintessentially Occitanian, yet the love song, even in its most formalized state, gains in meaning when situated within a broader context—a literary context from which it derived many of its values (for instance, *Boecis, Sainte Foy*) and to which, as we saw in the case of the prose *vidas* and *razos,* it made important contributions.

Just as the extraordinary devotional poetry (most of it of Franciscan inspiration) of the thirteenth and fourteenth centuries clearly owes a great deal to the *canso* tradition, so, it must be recognized, that tradition reflected and benefited from other kinds of poetic exploration, some of which came to flourish only during and after the Albigensian wars. Indeed, the increasing popularity in Occitania of certain narrative genres by the close of the twelfth century confirms the existence there of a variety of literary activities that led, perhaps, to a kind of generic specialization and, in consequence, favored the refinements we associate with lyric poets like Arnaut Daniel. The virtuosity of Arnaut represents a culmination (and "purification") of previous trends present in the *canso;* it also stands in relationship to other literary modes and possibilities contemporary with it. At the same time as Arnaut's *trobar ric* was endeavoring to eliminate "story elements" from the love song, narratives—many of them either French in origin or strongly influenced by French models—were being composed in Occitan. Interestingly, it was during the last quarter or so of the twelfth century that a significant penetration of troubadour styles into the literature of *langue d'oïl* began: the Old French trouvères emerged at that time. Occitanian acceptance of given French narrative models, albeit changing them to suit Occitanian tastes, was accompanied by the simultaneous implantation, in *oïl* territory, of *oc* lyric forms.

As did their *oïl* counterparts, but not nearly to the same extent, *oc* poets cultivated epic, or chanson de geste–type, narrative and, starting quite possibly earlier than in *langue d'oïl,* romance narrative. Unfortunately, many texts have been lost and scholars have frequently had to rely on external evidence in order to reconstruct the earliest history of these genres. Thus, allusions in the works of such troubadours as Cercamon and Bernart de Ventadorn to Arthurian materials prompt scholars to believe that stories concerning Arthur and his knights must have circulated at an early date in Occitania. Themes of Celtic and ancient Greek or Latin provenance occur over and over again in poems by twelfth-century troubadours; some of these themes have no French counterpart, leading historians to posit the existence of native, but now lost, Occitanian narrative poems. Even such authentically French materials as the Roland legend receive a characteristically Occitanian development (hinted at in troubadour songs, confirmed in later, surviving Old Provençal redactions). Finally, along with *Boecis* and *Sainte Foy,* such twelfth-century narrative works as have been preserved, either entire or in fragmentary form, prove the legitimacy of the claim that narrative was indeed practiced continuously from the very beginning of Occitanian literature down to the end of the Middle Ages, even though from about 1100 to 1220 its literary role was secondary to that of the lyric.

Two surviving narrative fragments antedate the last quarter of the twelfth century. One includes some 105 lines—the beginning—of a poem concerning Alexander the Great (a very popular hero in medieval Europe, about whom many subsequent vernacular romances would be composed, in French, Spanish, and German). Written by a certain Alberic (of Briançon?) around 1110–1120, the poem employs the same meter as *Sainte Foy* (rhyming octosyllabic laisses) and is composed in characteristically clerkly terms. (Note Solomon's proverb, or *sententia,* quoted in lines 3–4, a device recommended by rhetorical manuals for the exordium, or beginning, of a learned poem.) This very early *roman antique* portrays Alexander's prodigious childhood and early education: though but a child of three days, he was the equal of a four-month-old! He was well instructed "in all the arts" so as to enable him to display "dignity," "counsel," "goodness," "wisdom," and "honesty"—along with "prowess." He was taught his letters, and could write "on parchment" in Greek, Latin, and Hebrew. Fittingly, perhaps, the fragment ends with a description of Alexander's accomplishments as a musician. This then is the paragon of the generous nobleman—a hero gifted in the liberal arts, in war, and, presumably, in love, his life conceived, of course, in purely secular terms. Surely the character was designed to please the refined lords of certain Occitanian courts and to be emulated by them. Indeed, Alberic's Alexander constituted, first and foremost, a very Occitanian social ideal.

There have also survived about 700 lines of a "historical epic" entitled *Cançun d'Antiocha* by Grégoire Béchada (1126–1138), probably a recast of an older song recounting the story of the siege of Antioch (1097–1098), part of the First Crusade, in which many Occitanians participated. This text provides the model for subsequent poetic commentary, in epic form, upon important historical events (for instance, the Albigensian Crusade).

Among the narrative poems that may be dated with some certainty in the closing decades of the twelfth century, two are of particular importance: (1) the linguistically hybrid *Girart de Rosselhon* (*ca.* 1180), composed in decasyllabic (six + four syllables) rhyming laisses, and (2) an Arthurian romance, *Jaufré,* written, like the romances of Chrétien de Troyes, in rhyming octosyllabic couplets. Scholars have disputed the dating of the latter text; it was once thought to have been composed around 1225–1230, but opinion now favors a pre-1200 date.

The 10,000-line *Girart de Rosselhon,* based on a Burgundian legend, tells the tale of King Charles Martel and Girart, who, after saving Rome, marry the emperor's daughters, Elissent and Berte. Elissent loves Girart and is loved by him but is obliged to marry Charles, while Girart weds Berte. This provokes a falling-out of king and vassal, wars, exile for Girart and Berte, numerous adventures, and, eventually, a reconciliation. The love triangle of lord-lady-vassal is akin to that found in much troubadour poetry (Charles is certainly depicted as a king of *gelos,* "jealous husband"), but the resolution follows the *a lei francesca* mode rather than the lyric manner. Elissent and Girart renounce carnal passion; Berte is portrayed, sympathetically, as a loving and supportive wife. It is largely thanks to her that order is finally restored. In short, *Girart de Rosselhon* exemplifies what might be described as the interpenetration of ancient Old Provençal modes (*Sainte Foy*), stock troubadour situations, and the spirit of the chanson de geste.

In other words, northern French materials are reworked in a typically Occitanian fashion: the grandeur and stark sobriety of the Old French epic are suffused with the Occitanian spirit of meditation on such feminine qualities as fidelity, compassion, understanding, and capacity for transcendence. The salvation of men in this word is viewed as depending on Woman. The masculine world is violent and brutal—darkly tragic; spirituality and peace—civilization—are the gifts, precious and indispensable, of womanhood. All this is couched in the immensely moving heroic verse of the traditional decasyllabic epic, the verse associated with the telling of cataclysmic, even cosmically important, historical events. The effect is extraordinary, ranging from a sense of foreboding and of gloom to feelings of great tenderness and human dignity.

Jaufré is another matter. The story concerns the young knight Jaufré's pursuit of a certain Taulat de Rogimont, who, at Arthur's court one Whitsuntide, had killed a favorite of the queen. Many adventures ensue, including Jaufré's falling in love with, and eventually marrying, the noble Brunissen. The story is replete with mysteries and magic. Jaufré finally defeats Taulat, sending him back to Arthur with apologies; but before he does this, he has had repeatedly to demonstrate his prowess as a knight. He closely resembles such heroes of Chrétien de Troyes as Yvain and Perceval. The ambiance of *Jaufré* is entirely courtly, although, as with the French romances of the time, the text utilizes numerous folkloristic motifs.

Jaufré is, then, a chivalric romance of the purest kind. The hero "works out" his love by performing knightly deeds. His good works, as they accumulate, prove his great merit. But whereas Jaufré "progresses" in valor and in merit, there is, in another sense, no "progression." The knight's prowess simply *is;* his feats constitute a narrational procedure through which, as a kind of linear revelation, his merit is exemplified. Jaufré is the lover-knight of the Old Provençal *canso,* depicted by a storyteller, a witness other than himself who, perforce, refers to him in the third person. Jaufré's "inner" and "outer" worlds thus merge in this romance dimension that is neither entirely objective nor entirely subjective. (Herein lies the importance of magic and the marvelous in this text.)

The authorial ironies we associate with Chrétien de Troyes and his followers are essentially absent in *Jaufré.* The narrator here "tells it like it is," as though he were composing the idealized biography of a Bernart de Ventadorn. Once again, love service is all important; it stands as a metaphor—even, one might say, as a symbol—for what is best in a man. Thus, though Jaufré ostensibly wishes to defeat Taulat and marry Brunissen, his activity is chiefly concerned with repairing injustices, righting wrongs, and protecting the defenseless; that is his destiny, his being. (Analogously, Brunissen, having fallen in love with Jaufré, prays to God that he will seek out her love and that she will not fall victim to *deshonor;* her nobility is fully equal to his.) Exploring in this way—in narrative form—what might be called the "referential" aspects of *fin'amors,* what *fin'amors* may be said to stand for, *Jaufré* at least implicitly corresponds to the kind of association between *fin'amors* and purely technical virtuosity observed in the songs of Arnaut Daniel. And in so doing, this text, which was probably composed in *oc* territory south of the Pyrenees, helped pave the way for subsequent meditations on these matters—a tradition that would reach at least as far as Cervantes.

By the close of the twelfth century, what the *canso* is less and less willing to do is relegated to, or taken over by, newly popular narrative forms. The ethos of this narrative verse, though, remains essentially that of *trobar leu,* without, however, the sense of immediacy one finds in great lyric poetry. *Jaufré,* after all, is a fiction, despite its apparent unwillingness to regard itself as such (an unwillingness evidenced in its lack of the ironies with which, for instance, a text like Chrétien's *Cligès* is replete). Nevertheless, *Jaufré* is a poetic experiment of the highest importance. In many ways it foreshadows future developments like the biographical *vidas*. These, when performed along with the lyrics they were designed to introduce, restored immediacy—presence—to the "objectified," or witnessed, account of the troubadour experience and scheme of values. Here, the verse narrative of *Jaufré* conjoins prose third-person *vida* and first-person lyric verse.

Along with texts like *Girart de Rosselhon, Jaufré* illustrates the possibilities open to narrative verse on Occitanian territory—possibilities that, during the first half of the thirteenth century, would be put to very good use by the poets of the great *Chanson de la croisade contre les Albigeois*. Finally, it may at least be suggested that, in seeking to reconcile inner feeling and thought with the outer, overwhelmingly real truth of God, the thirteenth- and fourteenth-century Occitanian devotional poets responded poetically to some of the concerns addressed by the similarly subjective-objective text of *Jaufré*.

Thus, even before the advent of the tragic events of the thirteenth century, Old Provençal literature had begun to develop the resources that would be needed to express, and intellectually to cope with, the violence that would be perpetrated upon the culture it had grown to incarnate.

As was the case in northern France, vernacular prose came into its own in Occitania during the thirteenth century. (Some legal documents, including translations of the Justinian Code, antedate 1200; Raimon Vidal's grammatico-poetic treatise, the *Rásos de trobar* [Rules for composing verse], was written *ca.* 1200, in Catalonia.) The first known Old Provençal prose narrative (pre-1250) is the heavily fictionalized chronicle called the *Roman de Filomena* (or Chronicle of Notre-Dame-de-la-Grasse), the only surviving thirteenth-century prose romance in Occitan. This text recounts the founding and endowing by Charlemagne of a monastery that, with Roland's help, withstands Saracen attack. Much of the action takes place around Narbonne, whose Moorish king is presented as a particularly odious lout, fully meriting his wife's abjuration of her Muslim faith and of him, and whose Jewish population strongly supports Charlemagne. (Relatively tolerant and easygoing Occitania was a haven for many Jewish communities, at least before the Albigensian Crusade and the Inquisition that followed.) Other early prose texts are mainly of a religious nature—a few saints' lives, biblical versions, and the debris of Cathar writings.

The great monument of thirteenth-century Old Provençal prose remains the corpus of *vidas* and *razos*. However, concern with poetry and with its meanings (as well as with poetic techniques) was expressed in a number of prose works composed during the second half of the century and in the 1300's. Following and expanding upon the example of Raimon Vidal, a number of commentators studied and wrote about the language and modes of troubadour poetry from a theoretical and historical point of view. The *Donatz proensal* (Provençal "Donatus" or Primer), composed around 1240 by Uc Faidit for Italian admirers of Occitan, provides a Latin-based description of Old Provençal along with a rhyming dictionary. The *Leys d'amors* (Laws of love), dating from the mid fourteenth century and set down by a group of collaborators directed by Guilhem Molinier, have survived in three different redactions, two in prose and one in verse. The *Leys* constitute a kind of poetico-rhetorica-moral summa, including, along with precise descriptions of the various lyric genres and much linguistic commentary, smatterings of theology, bits of advice concerning proper manners, and such. (The work had been commissioned by the Toulouse Consistori de la Subragaya Companhia del Gai Saber.) The period 1250–1350 saw the rise of other kinds of didactic literature, in verse and prose. The nearly 35,000 octosyllabic rhymed couplets of the *Breviari d'amor* (*ca.* 1300) by Matfre Ermengaud, a Franciscan who attempted to reconcile Catholic orthodoxy and the Old Provençal obsession with love, synthesizes troubadour feminism and the Marian cult. This encyclopedic text is packed with lore of all sorts, as well as with shrewd and accurate observations on contemporary Occitanian society.

The spirit of learned inquiry and exegesis also pervades the work of another Franciscan, the Majorcan Ramon Lull, one of the most profound and prolific writers of all time, who flourished during the second half of the thirteenth century and the first decade of the fourteenth. For many years the victim of Dominican intellectual persecution, Lull and his work (as well as his strong influence on such thinkers as Montaigne and even Descartes) have only recently come to be recognized and adequately appraised. He is said to have composed poems in Occitan and, as well, to have learned

Arabic in order more easily to convince Muslims, through eloquence, of the error of their ways. In addition to Latin treatises Lull wrote several works in a rather heavily Catalanized *langue d'oc.* (It is probable, however, that at least some of the specifically Catalan traits in his writings are due to the later scribes whose copies have preserved his works.) Lull's thought manifests profound mistrust of what might be called the political view of mankind and an equally strong love for "natural," or moral, man, whose instincts, with the help of God, are basically good. In this sense his Franciscanism reflects certain traditional, even anarchical, Occitanian values.

Much religious poetry—lyric and narrative—was composed during the thirteenth and fourteenth centuries, partly in reaction to the events of the Albigensian Crusade, but also as an outgrowth of certain mystical trends present in earlier troubadour verse and in such texts as the *Boecis* poem. Poetic love service lent itself to adaptation in the service of God, particularly with regard to the Marian devotion, as in Guiraut Riquier's song to the Virgin (1289), which ends: "Sos amadors prec Midons que mantenha, / Si que quasqus son dezirier n'atenha" (I pray My Lady will protect her lovers, / And that each one will attain his desire). The oeuvre of several thirteenth- and fourteenth-century poets provides a mix of secular love songs and devotional poems, sometimes accompanied by violently satirical verse addressed, frequently, to the abuses of Rome and its clergy. Raimon de Cornet's famous *versa* (the feminine, hence "upside down," form of *vers*) deplores the corruption of the church and of the world, but this Franciscan-turned-Cistercian also predicts the regeneration of mankind through the intervention of Our Lady, whom he comes precariously close to identifying with *his* lady, a Beatrice-like figure he calls Rose. One of the greatest of all Occitanian troubadours, Peire Cardenal (*ca.* 1180–*ca.* 1278), wrote love poems, some sixty (surviving) *sirventes* (directed against, for instance, the clergy, thieves, the French), and a stunningly beautiful *canso* in praise of the Cross.

Piety and mysticism—orthodox and not so orthodox—inform Occitanian devotional poetry, as does a spirit of invective when the poet feels obliged to denounce the pillaging and destruction to which his country was subjected. (The combination reminds one of Dante.) Prose and verse saints' lives, prayers (including a recently discovered Cathar "ritual"), and theatrical works (such as the late-thirteenth-century *Mystery of the Passion,* the oldest extant vernacular Passion) testify to the vigor of postcrusade religious literature in Occitan. Though our investigation has shown that it would not be accurate to state, as some scholars have done, that subsequent to the crusade the troubadour lyric was, so to speak, "transformed" into a poetry of religious inspiration, "replacing" love poetry, it is certainly true that by the middle of the thirteenth century devotional poetry came to play a very major role in the Old Provençal literary canon, a role that would continue to increase in subsequent centuries.

The chanson de geste tradition is represented in the thirteenth century by the 5,000-line *Fierabras* (*ca.* 1240) and, in the fourteenth, by two fragments known, respectively, as *Roland at Saragossa* (1,410, mainly decasyllabic, lines) and *Ronsasvals* (1,802 decasyllables). These all derive from French models and are heavily influenced by courtly romance. *Fierabras* and *Roland at Saragossa* utilize the motif of the beautiful Saracen lady who, for love of a Christian warrior, converts to Christianity. (The prose *Roman de Filomena,* roughly contemporary with *Fierabras,* also tells of Roland's "friendship" with a Saracen queen who, upon her conversion, marries a Christian baron.)

Interesting and original though these texts are, they nevertheless pale in comparison with another kind of epic, the "historical" *Chanson de la croisade contre les Albigeois.* It is an unfinished chronicle-poem of 213 often lengthy, assonanced, and monorhymed laisses, like *Antiocha,* in alexandrines and with a six-syllable line concluding each laisse. In reality this work consists of two epico-historical chronicles, the first (2,768 lines) composed by Guilhem de Tudela (a cleric and professional *joglar*), the second (6,810 lines) anonymous (probably a *joglar* from the county of Foix). These together recount the story of the crusade from the time of Peter of Castelnau's murder (14 January 1208) to the siege of Toulouse by Louis, son of Philip Augustus, in 1219. (Guilhem's text stops in 1213, at the moment Pedro II of Aragon decides to support the beleaguered count of Toulouse—the decision that culminated in the battle of Muret.)

Except in most matters of exterior form and in their common attention to detail, the two parts are totally dissimilar. Although at times Guilhem blames the crusaders' excesses, he basically favors the French; he seems to be recording the events as they occurred. His hybridized language contains many French forms. His account is sober, even when he tells of the massacre following the fall of Béziers. He piously desires the conversion of heretics and the repentance of those who lend heretics their support. It has been plausibly suggested that Guilhem left off writing when his supposed patron, Baudouin, the pro-French brother of Raymond VII of Toulouse, was captured and put to death (March 1214), thus temporarily depriving the Occitanian pro-French party of their leader.

The *cobla capcaudada* form utilized by Guilhem (the final, six-syllable verse of the laisse furnishes the rhyme of the following laisse) gives way to the *cobla capfinida* (the final, six-syllable verse of the laisse provides, though usually in variant form, the first hemistich of the following laisse) at laisse 132, and with this prosodical change the poem takes on a new tonality, an entirely different point of view.

Written, in all likelihood, in 1228, the anonymous second part of the *Chanson* constitutes a stirring defense of the Occitanian cause, recounting events from the Battle of Muret down to 1219 and focusing particularly on the heroic Count Raymond VII, the victor at Beaucaire and the leader of a temporarily free Occitania. Values like *Paratge* (nobility), *Pretz,* and *Lialtatz* (loyalty) are allegorized and celebrated, rhetorically linked to the very soul of Occitania. The principal actors in this immense drama—Raymond, the pope, Simon de Montfort, and many others—are described in detail and carefully delineated, as in a well-constructed historical novel. The protagonists' deliberations are carefully "reproduced," as though the poet were witnessing and recording them. (This is a common device in medieval chronicles.) The pope is portrayed as an indecisive puppet, manipulated by the college of cardinals and the Roman bureaucracy. Simon de Montfort is depicted as the incarnation of epic *desmezura,* or hubris, and of *l'orgolh de França* (French pride). Occitanian *paratge* is painstakingly assimilated to the notion of authentic Christianity, to the extent that the two concepts are deemed indispensable to each other: without *paratge* true Christianity cannot subsist.

In this fashion and with consummate rhetorical skill, the civilizational system represented by the Old Provençal lyric—Marcabru and Bernart de Ventadorn—is narratively joined to and receives new life from an essentially Franciscan religious ideology. (Our poet has no fondness for the Dominicans. Furthermore, like Peire Cardenal and others, he stresses the Occitanian—especially Toulousan—devotion to Mary.) The anonymous *Chanson* is an especially complex and profound work.

The *Chanson de la croisade contre les Albigeois* represents the high-water mark of such Occitanian verse narrative as was placed at the service of authentic Occitanian values and meanings—values that increasingly came to be associated, in literary terms, with Franciscan-style devotion. Entirely poetic in its conception and structure—in its own way as technically perfect as any *canso* of Arnaut Daniel—the *Chanson* confronts and expresses reality. Yet its very perfection and the nature of its themes—what made it unique—rendered it literarily without influence. It fathered no progeny, initiated no new tradition. Like the *vidas* and the *razos,* it constituted a poetic response to an otherwise incomprehensibly tragic historical and literary situation. To be sure, later texts, such as the fourteenth-century *Légende de Barlaam et Josaphat,* which, according to some scholars, is replete with blends of Cathar and Franciscan thought, continued to couch peculiarly Occitanian values and conceptual schemes in poetic and narrative form. But these texts owe nothing to the thirteenth-century *Chanson.* The didactic tradition, exemplified by the *Leys d'amors* and *Breviari d'amor,* was far more influential and typical of post-1250 trends.

The other narrative masterpiece of thirteenth-century Occitania—a poem as different as one might find from the *Chanson*—is *Flamenca,* an extraordinarily sophisticated courtly romance diversely dated by scholars (1240–1250? 1272?). Surviving in but one manuscript, this text, sometimes referred to as a *nova* (compare Italian *novella,* English "novel"), comprises 8,096 octosyllabic lines (rhyming couplets). Its beginning and conclusion are missing, however, and the midsection is not without lacunae. Here is, very succinctly, the plot.

The incomparably beautiful Flamenca weds Archimbaut of Bourbon, a rich lord. They live happily until, subsequent to a long visit from the king, who is struck by Flamenca's beauty, Archimbaut becomes jealous and locks his wife, along with two female servants, in a tower; she is allowed to leave this prison only to attend Mass on Sundays and feast days. A young Burgundian knight, Guillem de Nevers, learns Flamenca's plight and promptly—sight unseen—falls in love with her. He goes to Bourbon and, disguising himself as a religious, serves at Mass in Flamenca's chapel. Each Sunday he manages to exchange one or two words with the lady. After three months of this he convinces Flamenca of his love and arranges a rendezvous with her at the baths. Alleging reasons of health, she convinces her husband to allow her to go. (Guillem has a tunnel dug between his apartments and the baths.) The lovers meet regularly and secretly for several months, until Flamenca obtains her freedom from the tower by promising Archimbaut that she will henceforth guard herself as well as he has guarded her. Flamenca returns to the court, but Guillem becomes sad at no longer being alone in enjoying her company. She enjoins him to leave Bourbon, at least for a while, which he does, earning himself a great reputation as a knight. Archimbaut hears of Guillem's prowess, wishes to meet him, and invites him to Bourbon for a tournament; the lovers are reunited. The manuscript stops in the midst of describing the jousts.

The dashing young knight, the beautiful lady, the *gelos*—these are the stock-in-trade of Old Provençal love poetry, here, however, recast in an entirely playful narrative frame. (The influence of certain *oïl* texts and authors, such as *Tristan,* Marie de France, Chrétian, is probable.) The fictional world in which love conquers all (even at the cost of profaning the Mass) is charming, despite its aura of scandal, precisely because it is a fictional world not to be taken seriously, where, in a sense, anything goes. Delightful though it may be, the story is secondary to what it allows the romancer to do: celebrate the game of *fin'amors*; explore the reasons and the psychological mechanisms of falling in love; provide a remarkably varied series of very real-sounding descriptions of court activities (for instance, the postprandial arrival of *joglars* on Flamenca's wedding day), of clothing, of tournaments, and such. Humor, light irony, and a gentle complicity with the protagonists pervade this romance, which, in striking contrast to the contemporary vogue for religious poetry in Occitania, is entirely secular in tone and values. No trace of clerkly pedantry disfigures the text's essentially aristocratic quality. Indeed, Guillem's assumption of the clerk's habit and the purposes he puts it to may well constitute a not-too-sly dig at the clergy.

Though not in all respects entirely anomalous within the Occitanian purview, *Flamenca* nevertheless expresses none of the transcendence characteristic of so much troubadour love poetry; nor does it allude in any fashion to the torments suffered by the Midi (unless its implicit anticlericalism may be construed as a veiled attack on the church). It is a work of pure entertainment, composed for the enjoyment of a leisure class in rapid process of secularization. As several scholars have pointed out, *Flamenca* conjoins certain attributes of Occitanian courtliness with the newer courtliness of such northern trouvères as Conon de Béthune and Jehan Renart; it assimilates to Old Provençal form a developing *esprit français.* Here the seriousness and the pretension of an Arnaut Daniel are, in a very real sense, amusingly trivialized; in contrast to *Jaufré, fin'amors* provides the pretext for a vain and pleasant—a charming—story.

EPILOGUE

Despite occasional spurts of activity (of which a few have been alluded to in the preceding pages), the fourteenth and fifteenth centuries mark a steady decline in Occitanian literature. Assimilation of writers to the French language and the increased provincialization of the Midi characterize this decline. The sapping of Occitanian cultural unity was accompanied by an apparently irreversible literary and linguistic fragmentation as the troubadours and what they stood for passed into history. Their teachings and their example were to take root and to flower in foreign lands, however. To a considerable degree, the causes of this decline had been present almost from the start in Occitania's political weakness and even in the peculiar coherence of troubadour culture, with its close and exclusivist identification of lyric poetry and civilization. The Albigensian Crusade, both in fact and in how it was understood by the poets of the time, dramatically confirmed these tendencies.

By the close of the fourteenth century, religious writing of various sorts had come to dominate the local vernacular(s). Saints' lives, mystery plays, and visionary literature are all represented. Of these, the fourteenth-century prose *Barlaam et Josaphat,* with its curious blend of Cathar Manichaeism and Franciscan popular piety, stands out as a minor masterpiece. This tale of religious conversion takes place in an atmosphere suffused with the marvelous and romance-type magic. Nevertheless, as Jeanroy put it, though somewhat unfairly, "Outside of numerous works of piety, which differ little from those of the preceding century and of which none deserves our attention today, the fifteenth century has bequeathed to us only a sizable collection of lyric pieces and two sets of mystery plays" (*Histoire sommaire de la poésie occitane,* p. 127). During the period 1350–1550, Occitanian literary culture reached its nadir. But, starting in the sixteenth century, a revived historical consciousness took shape in certain centers of the Midi; humanists and others began once again to study the past. Systematic philological inquiry, developed in post-Revolutionary France and elsewhere (chiefly in Germany and Italy), led to a new understanding of Old Provençal literature and also contributed to the Félibrige, or Modern Provençal, revival of the nineteenth century. The troubadour came to life again, in another time.

BIBLIOGRAPHY

For a summary listing of dictionaries and grammars, anthologies, English and modern French translations, bibliographies, and general critical works, see the bibliography for **Provençal Literature: To 1200.**

Sources. Joseph Anglade, ed., *Las leys d'amors,* 4 vols. (1919–1920); Arnaut Daniel, *Les poésies d'Arnaut Daniel,* René Lavaud, ed. (1910, repr. 1973), and *Canzoni,* Gianluigi Toja, ed. (1960); Karl Bartsch and Leo Wiese, eds., "Fragment de l'Alexandre d'*Albéric de Besançon,*" in *Chrestomathie de l'ancien français (VIIIe–XVe siècles),* 12th ed. (repr. 1969); Camille Chabaneau, ed., *Sainte Marie Madeleine dans la littérature provençale* (1885); *Chansons de la croisade contre les Albigeois,* Paul Meyer, ed., 2 vols. (1875–1879), also, Eugène Martin-Chabot, ed. and trans., 3 vols. (1931–1961), and Henri Gougaud, ed. and trans. (1984); Gaucelm Faidit, *Les poèmes de Gaucelm Faidit,* Jean Mouzat, ed. (1965); Giraut de Bornelh, *Sämtliche Lieder des Trobadors Giraut de Bornelh,* Adolf Kolsen, ed., 2 vols. (1910–1935); Guilhem Figueira, *Ein provenzalischer Troubadour,* Emil Levy, ed. (1880); Guiraut Riquier, *Guiraut Riquier: Las cansos,* Ulrich Mölk, ed. (1962); Ferdinand Heuckenkamp, ed. *Die provenzalische Prosa-Redaktion des geistlichen Romans von Barlaam und Josaphat* (1912); *Jaufré: Ein altprovenzalischer Abenteuerroman des XIII. Jahrhunderts,* Hermann Breuer, ed. (1925); Alfred Jeanroy, ed. *Les joies du Gai Savoir: Recueil de poésies couronnées par le Consistoire de la Gaie Science (1324–1484),* Jean-Baptiste Noulet, trans. (1914).

Ramon Lull, *Opera latina,* I–XV (1959–), *Poésies,* Josep Romeu i Figueras, ed. (1958), *The Book of the Lover,* Edgar Allison Peers, trans. (1923), *The Art of Contemplation,* Edgar Allison Peers, trans. (1925), and *The Tree of Love,* Edgar Allison Peers, trans. (1926); Matfre Ermengaud, *Le breviari d'amor de Matfre Ermengaud suivi de sa lettre à sa soeur,* Gabriel Azaïs, ed., 2 vols. (1862–1881), and *Le breviari d'amor de Matfre Ermengaud,* Peter T. Ricketts, ed., V (1976–); Peire de Vic, *Les poésies du moine de Montaudon,* M. Routledge, ed. (1977); John H. Marshall, ed., *The "Donatz Proensals" of Uc Faidit* (1969); Jean-Baptiste Noulet and Camille Chabaneau, eds., *Deux manuscrits provencaux du XIVe siècle contenant les poésies de Raimon de Cornet, de Pèire de Ladils et d'autres poètes de l'école toulousaine* (1888); Raimon de Miraval, *Les poésies du troubadour Raimon de Miraval,* L. T. Topsfield, ed. (1971); Paul Meyer, ed., "Fragment d'une *Chanson d'Antioche,*" in *Archives de l'Orient latin,* 2 (1884); Francisque Michel, ed., *Gérard de Rossillon: Chanson de geste ancienne* (1856); François Raynouard, extracts of *Fierabras,* in *Lexique roman,* I (1844); *Le roman de Flamenca: Nouvelle occitane du 13e siècle,* Ulrich Gschwind, ed. (1976), *Le roman de Flamenca,* Paul Meyer, ed. and trans., 2nd ed. (1901), and *The Romance of Flamenca,* Merton J. Hubert, trans. (1962); Mario Roques, ed., *Ronsasvals,* in *Romania,* 58 (1932), and *Roland à Saragosse* (1956); Friedrich E. Schneegans, ed., *Gesta Karoli Magni ad Carcassonam et Narbonam* (contains the *Roman de Filomena*) (1898).

Studies. Alberto Limentani, *L'eccezione narrativa: La Provenza medievale e l'arte del racconto* (1977); Edgar Allison Peers, *Ramon Lull* (1929, repr. 1969); Elizabeth Wilson Poe, *From Poetry to Prose in Old Provençal: The Emergence of the Vidas, the Razos, and the Razos de Trobar* (1984).

KARL UITTI

[See also **Arnaut Daniel; Arthurian Literature; Barlaam and Josaphat; Canso; Cathars; Chanson d'Antioche; Chanson de la Croisade Contre les Albigeois; Chansons de Geste; Chrétien de Troyes; Courtly Love; Ermengaud, Matfre; Flamenca, Romance of; French Literature: After 1200; Giraut de Bornelh; Guilhem de Tudela; Guiraut Riquier; Inquisition; Jaufré Rudel; Joglar/Jongleur; Laisse; Languedoc; Leys d'Amors; Lull, Ramon; Marcabru; Peire Cardenal; Peire Vidal; Raimbaut d'Aurenga; Raimon de Cornet; Raimon de Miraval; Raimon Vidal de Besalú; Sirventes; Troubadour, Trouvère; Vers; Vidas.**]

PROVENCE. The term "Provence" varies in application, depending upon whether the concern is political or cultural. For medieval troubadours "la Proenza" comprised the whole of southern France from Poitou to Nice, wherever some form of Provençal was spoken. For the Romans "Provincia" meant the first of the provinces in Gaul, the region south of Lyons between the Pyrenees and the Alps, later Gallia Narbonensis, centering on Narbonne and linking Roman Spain with Italy. In the third century this province was reorganized, the lands east of the Rhône forming a separate jurisdiction that included what would become medieval Provence—the region bounded on the south by the Mediterra-

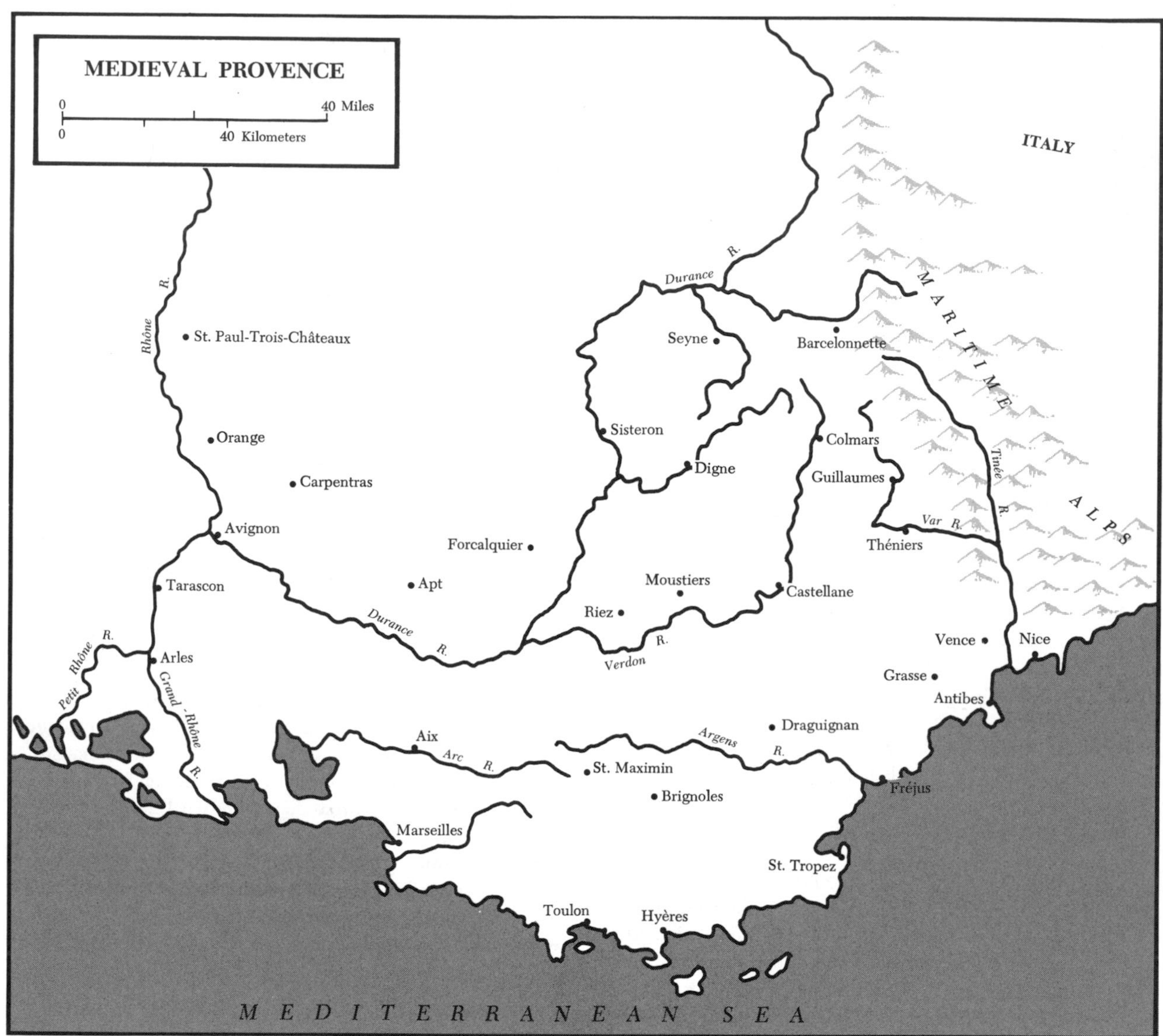

nean, on the north by the Dauphiné, and on the east by the Maritime Alps.

In upper Provence an Alpine herding economy prevailed, the richer agricultural land being in lower Provence; but the large network of river valleys permitted relatively easy communication between the interior and the littoral, which, with the Durance Valley route to Italy, fostered commerce and travel. After the tenth century Provence's location between the Mediterranean and northwestern Europe promoted a growth of trade and of towns that was later favored by the Angevin conquest of southern Italy and by the establishment of the papacy at Avignon.

Provence was conquered in the sixth century by the Franks, who soon faced the task of protecting it from the Muslims. The campaigns of Charles Martel in 736–739 may have been as destructive as the invasions themselves, but the long wars against the infidel provide the only unifying theme in the history of the region for the next 250 years. The invaders established a powerful base at Le Freinet in the Gulf of St. Tropez, from which for more than a century they raided as far north as Switzerland. Resistance depended largely upon local resources, and the exploits of local war leaders during this period furnished the historical and legendary material from which a large body of important epic literature was formed (for instance, the cycle of William of Orange). Finally, in the 970's, Count

William "the Liberator" of Provence, aided by Marquis Arduin of Turin, succeeded in driving the Muslims out of the region permanently.

Since the Treaty of Verdun (843) Provence had formed part of the empire of Charlemagne's grandson Lothair I, and under his successors it was included in the various kingdoms of Burgundy that came into existence during the late ninth and early tenth centuries. The last king of an independent upper Burgundy, Rudolf III (*d.* 1032), bequeathed his rights to Emperor Conrad II "the Salian," who made some effort to establish his influence in Provence by constituting himself protector of the church there. Imperial sovereignty was rarely more than theoretical, however, as the dynasty of William the Liberator strengthened its position by marriages with the Capetians and the counts of Toulouse, Gévaudan, Urgel, and Barcelona.

The counts of Toulouse, descendants of Roubaud, adopted the title "marquis of Provence" and contested the authority of Ramon Berenguer I, count of Barcelona-Provence (*r.* 1113–1131), who was a descendant of William the Liberator. In 1125 Berenguer reached a settlement with Alphonse Jourdain of Toulouse by which the latter received a marquisate of Provence consisting of the territories north of the Durance and west of the Rhône, with Avignon, Pont-de-Sorgues, Caumont, and Le Thor to be administered jointly. After the county of Toulouse passed to the Capetian royal line in 1271 on the death of Louis IX's brother Alphonse, the part of the marquisate known as the Comtat Venaissin was ceded (1274) to the papacy. Thus Avignon, in the Comtat, was a logical choice of residence for Pope Clement V in 1309, and in 1348 the city was purchased from Queen Joanna of Naples.

In effect the treaty of 1125 marks the creation of the medieval county of Provence, which until 1245 was ruled by members of the house of Barcelona, although their authority was contested by the princes of Les Baux in lower Provence and by the counts of Forcalquier in upper Provence. On the death of Ramon Berenguer III without male heirs in 1166, Provence was seized by his cousin, the count of Barcelona, who in 1162 had become King Alfonso II of Aragon. Alfonso designated Provence for his second son, also Alfonso (*r.* 1196–1209), whom he married to Garsende, heiress of Forcalquier, thus preparing the annexation of that important region to the county of Provence during the reign of their son, Ramon Berenguer V (*r.* 1209–1245). The latter, having no sons, bequeathed his county to his youngest daughter, Beatrice. Her marriage in 1246 to Charles I of Anjou, the youngest of Louis IX's brothers, marked the advent of a new comital dynasty, the first of two Angevin lines (1246–1382, 1382–1481).

With the conquest of the kingdom of Sicily by Charles in 1266 came a new Mediterranean connection to replace that of Catalonia, which now became an enemy and rival of Provence, especially after the Sicilian Vespers (1282) delivered Sicily into the hands of Pedro III of Aragon. Under the Angevin rulers Provence became part of a much larger political entity with problems of its own. Although Provençal commercial interests were favored by the kings of Naples, the loss of Eastern markets after the fall of Acre in 1291, the loss of Sicily, the rivalry of the Genoese, and incessant warfare with the Aragonese all contributed to a period of economic decline. In 1382 Queen Joanna I was murdered at the orders of her cousin Charles of Durazzo. A majority of the towns in Provence accepted him as her successor, despite Joanna's having named as her heir her adopted son, Louis of Anjou, brother of Charles V of France. Louis' efforts to secure his Neapolitan inheritance ended with his death in 1384, but his widow, Marie of Blois, established herself in Provence. Although she was forced to cede the county of Nice to Count Amadeus VII of Savoy as the price of Savoyard assistance, she did succeed in driving out the partisans of Charles of Durazzo and in rallying the Provençals behind her son, Louis II.

Once Provence was secured, recovery of the throne of Naples became the central concern of the rulers of Provence until, with the death of his son John in 1470, King René (*r.* 1434–1480) abandoned all practical efforts to make good his claims. "Good King René" was succeeded briefly by his nephew Charles of Maine, then in late 1481 by another nephew, Louis XI of France, who easily defeated the forces of René's grandson, René II, duke of Lorraine, thus opening the way for the annexation of Provence to the kingdom of France in 1486.

During the early period of Catalan rule, Provence was governed by a multitude of virtually independent local rulers—lay, ecclesiastical, municipal—whose loyalty to the comital house varied with local interests. It was not until the reign of Ramón Berenguer V that a comprehensive organization of comital government occurred. Charles I of

Anjou carried centralization still further; he increased the number of *vigueries* and placed at the head of government a seneschal, a *juge mage,* and a treasurer assisted by special agents. The earliest known meeting of an Estates of Provence occurred in 1286, following the death of Charles I. The Estates of Provence met frequently to provide for security and defense during the fourteenth century by levying taxes and raising troops.

According to legend, the earliest Christians in Provence were Mary Magdalen and a group of companions who were miraculously transported across the sea from Palestine on a raft, and who converted the population: St. Martha at Tarascon, St. Lazarus at Marseilles, St. Maximin and Mary Magdalen at Aix, St. Trophime at Arles. The earliest known bishop was Marcian at Arles in 254. In 314 the first of many church councils convened at Arles. But the actual proofs of a Christian presence in the region are even earlier: funerary monuments from the early second century.

Monasticism made its appearance with John Cassian, who founded the abbey of St. Victor at Marseilles (*ca.* 416) and produced the first set of instructions for monastic life in the West. St. Victor later was influenced by Cluny, acquired special privileges from the Holy See like those of Cluny, and by the 1080's had become the motherhouse of an order of reformed houses scattered throughout Provence, Languedoc, and northern Spain. St. Caesarius of Arles (*d.* 542) composed a rule for monks and one of the earliest rules for nuns in the West. Other important indigenous foundations were the Augustinian abbey of St. Ruf, established about 1039 near Avignon, from which other foundations spread widely in southern France and Spain. The Cistercian order made its appearance notably at Le Thoronet, Sénanque, and Silvacane in the mid twelfth century. As early as 1221 St. Dominic designated "Provence" as one of the five provinces of the Order of Preachers, whose principal concern was to combat heresy in Languedoc. In 1248 Salimbene visited Franciscan houses of wide repute at Hyères and at Aix.

In architecture there was a Provençal Romanesque style that drew from Languedoc, northern Italy, and the heritage of Roman monuments everywhere in view. Major examples were the early cathedrals of Arles, Marseilles, Aix, and Avignon, with notable Romanesque sculpture at St. Trophime in Arles, Montmajour, and St.-Paul-de-Mausole. Remarkable examples of Cistercian style are represented by the abbeys mentioned above; and from Avignon in the fourteenth century a school of "papal Gothic" developed (St. Pierre at Avignon, St. Siffrein at Carpentras). The papal court was also responsible for introducing Italian artists, who created a French "Avignon school" of painting, of which surviving masterpieces include the *Burning Bush* by Nicolas Froment and the *Coronation of the Virgin* by Enguerrard Charonton.

In literature the advent of the troubadours in the early twelfth century inaugurated a new era for practitioners of the *langue d'oc,* introducing new poetic forms and new conceptions of love. The movement began in Aquitaine but soon reached Provence, where Raimbaut d'Aurenga (*d.* 1173) was the earliest known poet. The courts of Les Baux at Orange and Marseilles were great centers of patronage for troubadours, as were those of Alfonso II of Aragon-Provence and Ramon Berenguer V. Although Provence was largely spared the destructive effects of the Albigensian Crusade, the wars in Languedoc and the enmity between the houses of Anjou and Aragon promoted a movement toward northern Italy, where troubadour traditions began to take root in the thirteenth century. In the fifteenth century King René's patronage fostered a short-lived revival of Provençal art and literature that came to an end with the French annexation.

BIBLIOGRAPHY

Édouard Baratier, *La démographie provençale du XIII*^e^ *au XVI*^e^ *siècle* (1961) and, as editor, *Histoire de la Provence* (1969), and *Documents de l'histoire de la Provence* (1971); Robert H. Bautier and Janine Sornay, *Les sources de l'histoire économique et sociale du moyen âge, I, Provence, Dauphiné, et états de la maison de Savoie* (1968); V. L. Bourrilly and Raoul Busquet, *La Provence au moyen âge: Histoire politique l'église, les institutions 1112–1481* (1924); André Compan, *Histoire de Nice et de son comté* (1973); Paul-Albert Février, *Le développement urbain en Provence de l'époque romaine à la fin du XIV*^e^ *siécle* (1964); Joseph Fornery, *Histoire du Comté Venaissin et de la ville d'Avignon,* 3 vols. (1909); Albert Lecoy de la Marche, *Le roi René: Sa vie, son administration, ses travaux artistiques et littéraires,* 2 vols. (1876, repr. 1969); Guillaume Mollat, *The Popes at Avignon, 1305–1378,* Janet Love, trans. (1963); Thérèse Sclafert, *Cultures en Haute-Provence: Déboisements et pâturages au moyen âge* (1959); André Villard, *Art de Provence* (1957).

EUGENE L. COX

[See also **Angevins; Aragon, Crown of; Avignon; Burgundy, Kingdom of; Caesarius of Arles, St.; Charles Martel; Charonton, Enguerrand; Consuls, Consulate; Courtly Love; Froment, Nicolas; Islam, Conquests of; Languedoc; Marseilles; Provençal Literature; Raimbaut d'Aurenga; Ramon Berenguer IV; Romanesque Architecture; Romanesque Art; Troubadour, Trouvère.**]

PROVERBS AND SENTENTIAE. Proverbs (Latin: *pro* + *verbum,* word) and *sententiae* (from Latin: *sentire,* to feel, have an opinion) belong to the category of wisdom, or gnomic, literature. Proverbs express a general truth in pithy fashion. They are easily isolated from the context in which they appear, although, according to the eminent paroemiologist Archer Taylor, they are not easily defined: "The definition of a proverb is too difficult to repay the undertaking." Recent studies, often of a semiotic nature, for example by Greimas, Meleuc, Barthes, and Rodegem, have called attention to the formal properties of proverbs and *sententiae.* Proverbs have been shown to function denotatively and connotatively (Greimas); to use a limited grammar of structures (Dundes); to present a nonoppositional or, more usually, binary oppositional character, that is, to contain two contrasting elements (Dundes).

Both proverbs and *sententiae* are expressions of an undefined, general *auctoritas* (authority), which they typically assert in affirmative sentences of an impersonal nature in the present tense. The *sententia*—maxim, or apothegm—differs from the proverb, according to Marie-Louise Ollier, by its more restricted, that is, relative, expression of a truth. Whereas the proverb functions tersely by analogy, identifying the general category to which a particular behavior belongs, the *sententia* is syllogistic in nature and perforce lengthier. Compare, for example, the following proverb and *sententia* from the *Yvain* of Chrétien de Troyes:

> *Mieux vault courtois mort que villain vif.*
> Better a dead gentleman than a live peasant.
> (vv. 31–32)

> *Qui pert sa joie et son solaz*
> *Par son mesfet et par son tort,*
> *Molt se doit bien hair de mort.*
> He who loses his joy and pleasure
> By his misdeed and wrong
> Must hate himself to death.
> (vv. 3,536–3,538)

A usual distinction between proverb and *sententia* is that the former springs from popular, that is, oral, tradition, whereas the latter often proceeds from clerkly, or written, culture. This traditional and generally correct view of proverbs as the crystallization of folk wisdom should, however, not obscure the fact that vernacular funds of proverbs were occasionally enriched by borrowings from learned sources. Such appears to be the case for the proverb that it is an ill bird which fouls its own nest; John Kunstmann has traced the source of this adage through medieval ecclesiastical and scientific writers back to Aristophanes' description of the hoopoe.

According to Ollier, proverbs and *sententiae* are considered by Aristotle in his *Rhetoric* to be proofs; the former are *probationes inartificiales* (natural proofs), the latter, *probationes artificiales* (artificial proofs) attached to the *inventio* (discovery of the argument). Later they were shifted to the *elocutio* (considerations of style), and medieval *artes poeticae* (poetic arts) assign the proverb most often to the *dispositio* (organization of arguments). The early-twelfth-century *Poetria nova* of Geoffrey of Vinsauf suggests various ways of including proverbs in introductions and conclusions of literary compositions. Pons le Provence, the author of a thirteenth-century *Summa dictaminis,* urges the use of proverbs as the most appropriate *captatio benevolentiae* (that is, way of "seizing" the hearer's goodwill) in a petition and catalogues them according to the situations envisaged: for example, son to father, debtor to creditor, minor clergy to prelates.

Compendia of Latin and vernacular proverbs were made as early as the twelfth century but especially during the thirteenth and fourteenth centuries, periods that were marked by the encyclopedic effort to catalogue knowledge, as in Vincent de Beauvais's *Speculum maius,* and by the flourishing of preaching. Twelfth-century collections of French proverbs with Latin translations include the *Fecunda ratis* of Egbert of Liège (*fl.* late tenth century) and the *Proverbia* of Master Serlo (*fl. ca.* 1024). It is important to note that of the twenty-seven manuscript collections of proverbs extant in Old French—dated from the thirteenth and fourteenth centuries and described by Joseph Morawski in his edition—ten include allegorical glosses or biblical concordances. One of these (Paris, Bibliothèque Mazarine, MS 1030) completes the list of *proverbes moralisés* (moralizing proverbs) by the *Principia quorundam sermonum* (fol. 151), a text that dem-

PROVERBS AND SENTENTIAE

onstrates how to use proverbs as the starting point for the sermon. The link between nonsecular proverbs and sermon composition is confirmed by Jean Welter, who, in studying the use of the exemplum, notes the presence of vernacular proverbs in sermons of Guibert de Tournai, the Provençal Armand de Belvézer, and Jacques de Lausanne, who used them to catch and hold the attention of the congregation before developing the exemplum.

The *Tabula exemplorum secundum ordinem alphabeti* (*ca.* 1270–1285), compiled by a French Franciscan, contains, among more traditional Latin material, French proverbs and expressions as well as exempla dealing with legendary or historical French figures. The collection of exempla in Auxerre, Bibliothèque Municipale, MS 35, divides each rubric into a section devoted to authorities and proverbs and one to the exemplum itself. For his *Summa predicaentium,* the fourteenth-century English Dominican John of Bromyard compiled a collection of about 200 Latin exempla, to some of which he appended proverbs in English as well as in French. He is, according to Welter, the first of the English moralists to attach importance to proverbs in his vernacular. The presence of the proverb in sermonaries is evidence of the frequency with which profane material penetrated the sacred domain. The fact that preachers made frequent use of the proverb, either in the vernacular or in Latin translation, underscores the importance of popular, oral culture to the clerkly, didactic enterprise. As already indicated, vernacular proverbs sometimes existed side by side with Latin translation in collections intended for preachers. (We may speculate that, depending on the class of the lay audience addressed, preachers may have preferred to pronounce the entire sermon in Latin rather than interrupt it with vernacular quotations of proverbs.) Of the twenty-seven manuscript collections collated by Morawski, four contain the vernacular proverbs next to the Latin translation ascribed to Master Serlo; three other manuscripts join anonymous Latin translations to the vernacular aphorisms.

The fund of local folk wisdom upon which preachers could draw for inspiration or development of ideas was also enriched by the infusion of classical or Hebraic proverbs, in translation or in the original. The biblical Book of Proverbs was first translated into the vernacular in the last half of the twelfth century by the Anglo-Norman Sanson of Nanteuil, under the title *Proverbes de Salomon.* The so-called Proverbs of Seneca were current in the twelfth century; St. Bernard quoted one in support of the Crusade. Thanks to Priscian's grammar, which contained ten thousand lines of quotations from the ancients, as well as to the flourishing of florilegia from Carolingian times on, classical proverbs and *sententiae* were available to clerk or preacher. One such anthology (Rome, Vatican Library, MS Pal. Lat. 957, fol. 97–184 v), dating from the late twelfth century, includes proverbs and *sententiae* of classical philosophers along with fragments of Macrobius' *Saturnalia* and extracts from St. Jerome, Pliny, Apuleius, Cicero, Seneca, Aulus Gellius, and Ennodius.

What accounts for this considerable appeal of the proverb to preachers and theoreticians of the sermon? Indeed, in a larger context, why does the proverb—of oral and popular provenance—enjoy such appeal as well as prestige among learned and unlearned alike? Grace Frank stressed that the disdain with which modern writers treat aphorisms, equating them with platitudes and poverty of thought and/or vocabulary, is the antithesis of the medieval attitude toward them. A variety of factors—the medieval veneration for tradition and for *auctoritas,* the custom of settling arguments of all kinds by citation of texts, the tendency to understand things hierarchically and to proceed from categories to general truths—probably explain the frequency with which proverbs were used in the Middle Ages and the respect accorded them. The Old French manuscripts collated by Morawski show not only the importance of proverbs to sermonaries but also a link between proverbs and the judicial system. Two fifteenth-century manuscripts (Paris, Bibliothèque Nationale, lat. 10360, and Rome, Vatican Library, Reg. 1429) gloss the vernacular aphorisms with juridical commentaries, from Gratian's *Decretum* and the *Digest* in the first case and from canon and civil law generally in the second. The relationship implied by such glosses permits us to ask if the proverb was invoked in court cases in much the same way that it is used in modern African judicial procedures, although in the latter case the proverb appears to play the role of legal precedent.

In the same way that the proverb of popular and oral origin was frequently cited as an authority in sermons and law, it also penetrated vernacular literature. Frank has shown the importance of understanding the proverb in its literary context in order to appreciate the writer's genius in using the aphorism to his own ends. Thus, the proverb "Qui bien aime a tart oblie" (Morawski no. 1835: Who loves well takes long to forget), when placed in the mouth of Tristan in the Oxford *Folie,* takes on a poignancy not present in what Frank calls the proverb's "pedestrian presentation of the commonplace." Since Tristan has disguised himself to be near Yseut, his citing the proverb becomes a rich reminder of his faithfulness in concocting the disguise scheme and his consequent frustration at Yseut's otherwise understandable failure to recognize her physically changed lover. Frank also examines various literary contexts in which there appear variants of the proverbial expression "Boire ses hontes" (Drink or swallow one's shame). Huon de Méry used it metaphorically: shame, compared to a drink, permits the sinner to swallow quantities of sin. The same expression is uttered by Jesus in the fourteenth-century *Miracle de Saint Geneviève* in regard to the iniquities of the French when he says, "Let them drink their follies."

Charles of Orléans uses it in a *Rondeau* to describe a man of effrontery: "Qui a toutes ses hontes bues / Il ne lui chault que l'en lui die" (Whoever has swallowed all his shame / Does not care what may be said to him). François Villon turns the same proverb to an apparently self-deprecating remark on his own experience in the opening lines of the *Testament:* "En l'an de mon trentiesme aage / Que toutes mes hontes j'eus bues" (In my thirtieth year / When I have drunk all my shame). By incorporating the popular proverb into this critically important passage of the poem he captures our attention and then directs it to the poet's attitude toward his checkered past. He thus assures himself of the reader's complicity from the outset.

The twelfth-century French romancer Chrétien de Troyes regularly invokes popular proverbs (despite the clearly clerkly identity of his narratives), probably for their value as authorities rather than their popular appeal. The prologue to his last romance, the *Conte du Graal* or *Perceval,* invokes the adage "Who sows little reaps little." This aphorism, accompanied by references to the romancer's artistic efforts and to the fruit he expects them to bear, alerts the medieval listening audience and reader alike to a similar theme: the cultivation of the hero's own hidden talents, which are to be developed in the body of the romance. Ollier has studied Chrétien's use of proverbs and *sententiae* in another romance, *Yvain,* or the *Chevalier au lion.* She draws a conclusion also suggested by the evidence cited above, namely, that the proverb is so obviously an extratextual generalization or truth that when Chrétien inserts it in the narrative context, he introduces an anonymous, public voice of authority. It complements his own and allows him to objectify and universalize his narrator's opinions. Chaucer's taste for, and frequent citation of, common proverbs has been attributed by B. J. Whiting to his knowledge of French fabliaux and the poetry of Eustache Deschamps.

It is not surprising, given the popular character of medieval semiliturgical and secular drama, that proverbs should appear therein. Adam de la Halle's *La jeu de la feuillée* (1276) is a virtuoso development of several elements, among them the proverb that one can never be so fully the victim of a spell that one cannot regain one's senses. Whiting's study of proverbs in English biblical plays of the fourteenth and fifteenth centuries shows that, contrary to our expectations, proverbs are not frequently cited for their didactic value. Rather, they are included for their contribution to comic dialogue. The four major play cycles (Chester, York, Towneley, and Coventry) contain nearly 7,000 more lines than Chaucer's works and yet fewer than one-fourth as many proverbs and *sententiae.* Whiting also notes that the English morality plays make similar use of proverbs, assigning them principally to characters representing Vices, most often to the Merry Jester figure. The citations serve the interests of humor or realistic characterization rather than didacticism. In contrast, Whiting notes that in the French mystery, passion, and miracle plays of the fourteenth and fifteenth centuries, the proverbs are more often associated with a lesson than with comedy or realistic characterization. The *Mystère des actes des apostres,* attributed to the Gréban brothers, contains two proverb-capping scenes, in one of which two priests try to outdo each other in citing proverbs appropriate to the death of St. James.

The relationship between proverbs and vernacular literature transcends invocation of an extratextual authority or the creation of character and/or humor. In the lyric the proverb is often an integral element of the poem's structure. Most important in this regard is the development of a lyric genre in which each stanza ends in a different proverb. Early examples are the Old French *Proverbe au vilain* and the monk Hélinand de Froidmont's *Vers de la mort,* both dating from the late twelfth century. The genre survived in the thirteenth century with the *Proverbes au comte de Bretaigne* and the *Proverbes ruraux et vulgaux.* It became more elaborate in the fourteenth century in poetry of fixed form when Deschamps used proverbs in refrains of his ballads. He was imitated in such experimentation by Guillaume de Machaut, Christine de Pizan, and Charles of Orléans. Villon composed a ballad entirely of proverbs. Frank points out that this poetry dominated by proverbs was eventually accompanied in the manuscripts by pictures intended probably to dramatize the didactic import of the aphorism. Often, however, as in Grace Frank and Dorothy Miner's edition of the fifteenth-century *Proverbes en rimes,* the images depict only the literal meaning of the rhymed proverb; as such, they served as models for artisans like glassworkers and tapestry weavers. The verse occupied proportionally little space; as one manuscript indicates, they were *bons dictz moraulx pour tapis ou verrieres de fenestres* (good moral sayings for tapestry and window-glass makers). The marriage between rhymed proverb and image was probably the forerunner of the Renaissance emblem books.

In other vernacular literatures as well, the lyric was occasionally associated with the proverb. In the German didactic lyric (*Spruchdichtung*), the stanzas present general moral concepts, which they appropriately elaborate in a generalizing syntax that is characterized by "pithy, proverbial or *sententia*-like utterances, often in initial or final position," according to Olive Sayce. In the didactic lyric, at times *sententiae* are at the beginning of stanzas, and proverbs are at the end. Peire Cardenal, a Provençal troubadour, used proverbs as an instrument of satiric judgment in his *sirventes* (a Provençal poetic genre).

With few exceptions, studies of axiomatic sayings in medieval literature have directed more attention to proverbs than to *sententiae,* the use of which is considered usually marginal. Ollier, in her examination of authority statements in Chrétien de Troyes's *Yvain,* however, draws an interesting distinction: *sententiae* are more often invoked than proverbs in this romance and, with a few exceptions that issue from the narrator, are found in the direct discourse of romance characters. According to Ollier, the greater frequency of their use occurs because characters in this aristocratic genre are less likely to speak in the low style associated with the proverb. The proverb is cited as an extratextual, public authority to which the narrator subscribes, whereas the *sententia* exists within the text and represents a character's best effort to draw general conclusions about his situation. Chrétien is clearly exploiting the implicit tension between popular and learned culture in proverbs and *sententiae,* often at the expense of his characters. The discrepancy between the learned-sounding *sententia* and fictive reality can generate humor or irony.

Much work remains to be done in the study of proverbs and *sententiae.* The use to which proverbs are put in specific genres of vernacular literature—the possibility that they serve different or similar purposes in romance, drama, and poetry—remains largely unexplored. The particular circumstances in which proverbs are cited in Latin or vernacular is a subject that ought to appeal to students of the *translatio studii* (transfer of knowledge from antiquity to the Middle Ages) and *clergie* (clerkliness). Although theoretical studies have addressed the semiotics of the proverb, further inquiry is undoubtedly called for. Equally important would be contributions to the anthropological and sociological understanding of the proverb's use.

BIBLIOGRAPHY

Grace Frank, "Proverbs in Medieval Literature," in *Modern Language Notes,* **48** (1943); Grace Frank and Dorothy Miner, eds., *Proverbes en rimes* (1937), 2–4; Charles H. Haskins, *The Renaissance of the Twelfth Century* (1933, repr. 1957), 113; Wolfgang Mieder, *Proverbs in Literature: An International Bibliography* (1978); Wolfgang Mieder and Alan Dundes, eds., *The Wisdom of Many: Essays on the Proverb* (1981), esp. 21–28, 44; Joseph Morawski, ed., *Proverbs français antérieurs au XV*[e] *siècle* (1925); Marie-Louise Ollier, "Proverbe et sentence: Le discours d'autorité chez Chrétien de Troyes," in *Revue des sciences humaines,* **163** (1976); Olive Sayce, *The Medieval German Lyric 1150–1300* (1982), 38, 415; Archer Taylor, *The Proverb* (1962); Jean T. Welter, *L'exemplu dans la littérature religieuse et didactique du moyen âge* (1927), and *La tabula exemplorum secundum ordinem alphabeti* (1926, repr. 1973); Bartlett J. Whiting, *Proverbs in the Earlier English Drama* (1938), 4, 56–61, 65–66, and *Proverbs, Sentences, and Proverbial Phrases from English Writings, Mainly Before 1500* (1968).

GRACE MORGAN ARMSTRONG

[See also **Adam de la Halle; Alphabetization, History of; Anglo-Norman Literature; Anglo-Saxon Literature; Anthologies; Ars Poetica; Chrétien de Troyes; Deschamps, Eustache; Egbert of Liège; Exemplum; Fabliau and Comic Tale; French Literature; Gnomic Literature; Gréban, Arnoul; Latin Literature; Miracle Plays; Mystery Plays; Passion Plays, French; Peire Cardenal; Preaching and Sermon Literature, Western European; Rhetoric, Western European; Sanson de Nanteuil; Sirventes; Villon, François.**]

PROVINCE, ECCLESIASTICAL. In its early years Christianity was largely an urban religion; it spread from city to city (as the letters of St. Paul demonstrate). The chief cities of Roman provinces were naturally the main targets for this missionary activity. Smaller towns in the province would receive Christianity from the capital, and the clergy in these smaller towns accepted the leadership of the church of the capital city. Thus a distinction arose between the bishop of the chief town and the bishops who were established, little by little, in outlying places. The bishop of the capital city was called the archbishop or the metropolitan; he was to see that the faith was kept pure, and that competent and orthodox men were chosen as bishops of towns in his province. He was supposed to hold a meeting with the leading clergy of his province (bishops and abbots) at least once a year. This system was fairly well established by the time of the Council of Nicaea (325), which in effect formalized it.

The early ecclesiastical province was thus modeled geographically on the old Roman province, the basic administrative unit of the empire. There were some attempts to go further and create higher units based on the Roman diocese, composed of a large group of provinces, but these efforts failed; and by a curious shift the word "diocese" in church administrative language was applied to the district of the ordinary bishop, which was only part of a province.

The spread of Christianity to regions that had never been Roman or in which invaders had wiped out the Roman administrative system forced the papacy to create purely ecclesiastical provinces that were usually larger than the old Roman ones. Thus England had only two provinces, the very large province of Canterbury and the much smaller (and poorer) province of York. In northern Germany and Scandinavia, the provinces, on the whole, were large.

The pope was free to create new provinces or to divide existing ones. For example, in 1317 John XXII decided that the great city of Toulouse should have an archbishop and become the center of an ecclesiastical province. He accomplished this by separating Toulouse from the province of Narbonne (of which it had been a part) and by creating six new dioceses in small towns around Toulouse, which were made subject to the new archbishop of Toulouse.

European settlement of the Americas forced the creation of many new provinces, and the process still goes on.

BIBLIOGRAPHY

There is no history of the creation, growth, and division of ecclesiastical provinces. The entry on the subject in *Dictionnaire de droit canonique* explains the rules for provincial synods and the powers of the archbishop. Also useful is "Divisions, administratives et ecclésiastiques," in *Dictionnaire d'archéologie chrétienne et de liturgie,* for the early period, and the entries "Conciles" and "Diocèse" in *Dictionnaire de théologie catholique.* Otherwise one must turn to the numerous histories of individual provinces.

JOSEPH R. STRAYER

[See also **Church, Latin: Organization; Diocese, Ecclesiastical; Metropolitan; Parish.**]

PROVISIONS, ECCLESIASTICAL. An ecclesiastical provision was an action by which a person was provided with a church benefice. There were other terms for this as well, and "provision" usually refers to a grant by the papacy or to the papal bull by which the grant was made. Since papal provisions became frequent only in the thirteenth century, and became normal for all major and many minor benefices only under the Avignon popes in the fourteenth century (when hundreds of thousands were granted), modern use of the term usually indicates the latter period and its immediate sequel in the Great Schism, and less often the fifteenth century.

There were two main kinds of papal provisions. The overwhelming majority were granted to clerics who were not rich, noble, or well-connected, and who "supplicated" the papacy for them either in person or through a proctor, specifying the benefice or type of benefice requested. The supplication was signed by the pope and submitted to one set of officials who passed it on to others; the latter examined the candidate for his suitability to the requested benefice. If he passed, the supplication was approved by the pope and redacted into a papal rescript written on parchment. This was compared with the original supplication, assessed a certain fee, and sometimes submitted to possible contestation in the office of contested letters (*audiencia literarum contradictarum*); emerging from this, it was given the papal seal (*bulla*). Apart from gratuities, the supplicant had to pay the assessed fee and the cost of having the bull registered. A supplicant without other benefices who was too poor to pay the full fee could get a letter of provision (*in formam pauperum*), either gratis or at a reduced fee; such a letter was not registered.

Provisions of the type thus far discussed did not convey a title to a benefice but only a "right to [claim] the property" (*ius ad rem [petendam]*); this right was limited to what had been originally requested: a particular vacant benefice or a benefice of a certain sort that might become vacant—an "expectancy." The sort of benefice was defined by its yearly value, by whether it involved the cure of souls, and by its location in a particular diocese or province. Almost all benefices granted in this way were "minor"—worth not more than 200 livres a year if with cure of souls, 100 livres if without. In the case of an expectancy, it was up to the provision holder to watch for an appropriate vacancy and present his bull to the local judges; other candidates would probably be on hand, some of them named by local patrons, others also holding papal provisions. The decision was supposed to go to the papal providee of earliest date. The winner would then be "instituted" in the benefice at the command of the judges; he thereby acquired "right in the property" (*ius in re*), entitling him to receive the benefice's revenues. Finally, he would be physically installed in the benefice. Three years of uncontested "real possession" of *ius in re* made it immune to challenge. It has been estimated that only half the supplications submitted at Avignon resulted in bulls of provision, and only half the providees actually got benefices by means of their bulls.

Far better off were those few of high estate or with high patronage who received the other kind of provision mentioned above. These were actual grants of particular major benefices, made (allegedly) "at [the pope's] own initiative" (*motu proprio*), with formulaic clauses overriding all rights to the contrary and all other claims, and naming local judges-executors to institute the providee in the benefice without further judicial cognizance (*execucio parata*), and to install him in physical possession, seeing to it that he was accepted by the relevant church dignitaries and duly received his revenues. Provisions in this form also were granted when papal confirmation was obtained by those who had originally received their benefices by ordinary means.

BIBLIOGRAPHY

Geoffrey Barraclough, *Papal Provisions* (1935, repr. 1971), remains the basic work in English. For the routine of papal chancery, see Bernard Guillemain, *La politique bénéficiale du pape Benoît XII, 1334–1342* (1952), 11–14. Guillaume Mollat, "Bénéfices ecclésiastiques en occident," in *Dictionnaire de droit canonique,* II (1937), 416–428, provides the most exact definition of the legalities in the matter. See also Mollat, *La collation des bénéfices ecclésiastiques sous les papes à Avignon (1305–1378)* (1921), and William A. Pantin, *The English Church in the Fourteenth Century* (1955), chap. 4, "Papal Provisions." Francis Oakley, *The Western Church in the Later Middle Ages* (1979), is useful for background and contains a good bibliography.

HOWARD KAMINSKY

[See also **Babylonian Captivity; Benefices, Ecclesiastical; John XXII, Pope.**]

PROVISIONS OF OXFORD (1258). The Provisions of Oxford were a group of resolutions submitted to Henry III (1216–1272) by the English baronage at a great council assembled at Oxford on 11 June 1258. Sometimes called the "Mad Parliament," this assembly had been summoned to settle differences between Henry and the barons. Henry had enraged the barons by demanding financial support for his so-called "Sicilian Adventure." This was an attempt to help the pope in his struggle against the Hohenstaufen in Sicily and to make Henry's second son, Edmund, king of Sicily. Even before the Sicilian Adventure, which ended as a fiasco, the barons had been unhappy with Henry for relying upon his Poitevin relatives to staff key departments of the government and to give him counsel. The barons, who saw themselves as the natural advisers of the king, mistrusted both the Poitevins and Henry's reliance on them.

Forced by the barons to come to terms, Henry agreed to the expulsion of the Poitevin favorites from England and to the institution of a committee of twenty-four, equally representing royal and baronial interests, to reform the government. The proposals of this committee as accepted by the king and great council were the Provisions of Oxford. They established a council of fifteen to be appointed jointly by the king and barons. The council of fifteen was to advise the king on all political and government matters and redress royal abuses of government. A committee of twelve from the baronial ranks was to supervise this council and meet with it three times a year.

In addition, such principal organs of government as the Chancery and the Exchequer were henceforth to be independent of the royal household, specifically of the wardrobe, which had been controlled by the Poitevins and had exercised many functions of the Chancery and Exchequer. The heads of these offices were to be appointed by the council, to be solely responsible to it, and to hold office only for one year. Moreover, the chancellor should seal without conciliar authorization only routine writs, and the treasurer was to ensure that all royal revenues were paid directly into the Exchequer and not diverted to the household treasuries of the wardrobe and chamber.

The office of justiciar, which had not functioned since 1234, was resurrected with the thought that a principal royal officer from the baronial ranks concerned with policy, finance, and law would guarantee even tighter control over the king. As for local government, sheriffs were to be landholders in the counties they served and to hold office for only one year; keepers of royal castles were to be screened by the council and to be closely supervised; and all royal officials were to be closely scrutinized. There was provision also for a committee of twenty-four to consider the possibility of granting an extraordinary aid or tax, a circumstance that never occurred.

The Provisions of Oxford represented a determined effort of the barons to curb the royal prerogative and to secure some control over royal government and policy. Essentially they stemmed from chapter 61 of Magna Carta, which provided that King John should be responsible to a baronial council. The Provisions of Oxford envisaged control of the executive arm of government by means of the justiciar and the council of fifteen, but even when confirmed and spelled out in more detail in the Provisions of Westminster in 1259 they were too complicated to be implemented effectively by the barons.

Recognizing the Provisions as a major threat to his royal prerogative, Henry III immediately set about to circumvent baronial control. Seven years of tension and war ultimately ended with the royal cause prevailing. The Provisions of Oxford were nevertheless an interesting constitutional experiment that served as a model for the Ordinances of 1311, designed to reform the government of Edward II (1307–1327) and to place him under baronial control. Yet baronial inability to cooperate and a too narrow political base doomed these attempts at aristocratic or oligarchic government to failure. Effective and enduring control of the king would come only with the development of parliament.

BIBLIOGRAPHY

For the text of the Provisions of Oxford and related documents see I. J. Sanders, ed., *Documents of the Baronial Movement of Reform and Rebellion, 1258–1267* (1973).

Of numerous studies the following works are among the most valuable: Ernest F. Jacob, *Studies in the Period of Baronial Reform and Rebellion, 1258–1267* (1925); William Stubbs, *The Constitutional History of England,* 4th ed. (1896), II, 69–84; Thomas F. Tout, *Chapters in the Administrative History of Mediaeval England* (1920), I; Reginald F. Treharne, *The Baronial Plan of Reform* (1932).

BRYCE LYON

[See also **Barons' War; Chancery; England; Exchequer; Henry III of England; Justiciar; Parliament.**]

PROVOST. Two variant medieval Latin words, *propositus* and *praepositus,* account for the alternative vowels found in the French and German forms of the term "provost" (German: *Probst*; French: *prévôt*). The most inclusive definition of the term would be "person set above others, supervisor." The number of specialized meanings of "provost," however, is enormous.

In ecclesiastical usage, "provost" was employed to denominate an abbot, a prior, or an abbot's assistant for administration (especially of finances and estates). In the High Middle Ages it was used for the head of a mendicant convent. The term was more widely applied to any member of the church hierarchy whose supervisory authority was being emphasized. From the time of Cyprian (mid third century), for example, its use for a bishop is attested; there are subsequent uses of the word for dean of a cathedral chapter, head of a collegiate church, and chief priest. Lay administrators of ecclesiastical estates were sometimes given the title, as were the monastic overseers of nunneries and the clerical supervisors of episcopal households.

An outgrowth of the ecclesiastical usages of the word "provost" was its application to officials in educational administration. The term is attested from the late Middle Ages for the head of a school or for someone executing important duties within the administration of a school.

In military usage the term could be employed for

any officer who exercised supervisory responsibilities, for example the provost marshal. Although that term is not attested in this precise form in English until the late seventeenth century, the phrase reflects similar medieval uses of the word "provost" in compounds (such as the English "propheest marshal" and the Latin *praepositus guerrae* and *praepositus militum*). The archangel Michael was, in this military sense, the provost of heaven, the head of the heavenly host.

The word "provost" could be used for various classes of public officials. In early medieval Latin it was applied to those officials who represented ranks from the Roman imperial administration, such as the head of the lime supply. It also became a term for municipal magistrates, as in the Scottish burghs (compare the English "mayor") and in many towns on the Continent, such as Bruges, Valenciennes, and Tournai.

The heads of guilds sometimes bore the title. The most important example is the provost of the merchants of Paris, whose duties as overseer of commercial activity in the city were varied and whose authority was considerable.

A distinct office for the head of the merchants of Paris goes back to the early or central Middle Ages. The title "provost," however, was not associated formally with that office until the publication of the *Livre des métiers,* the guild regulations of the various crafts of Paris (*ca.* 1260). The provost was counseled by four aldermen who represented the interests of various sectors of the merchant community. The court of the provost of the merchants had jurisdiction over commercial activities in the city. There is some reason to believe, too, that this court exercised seigneurial jurisdiction over certain thoroughfares in the city, as the owner or representative of the owners of these thoroughfares. The provost of the merchants also had cognizance over public works in the commericial sector of the city and some, though limited, authority over the watch, or guards, of the commercial sector. Finally, the provost of the merchants was the person responsible for the execution of politices, such as the levying of municipal taxes and the regulation of commerce with other cities, that were necessary to the commercial well-being of the merchants. This does not mean that Paris enjoyed municipal self-government, for, as we shall see, there were significant limitations imposed on the provost of the merchants.

Lords throughout Western and Central Europe administered their estates with men called provosts. This was not the exclusive designation. In Germany, for example, words like *ministerialis,* advocate, and so on, were used as well. The main function of these men was to oversee the collection of revenue and produce, regulate local markets, and make sure that the estates could support the itinerant court of the lord whenever it took up residence there.

In royal or central government, the word "provost" had additional meanings. In the Carolingian period *praepositus palatii* was used as a synonym for the better-known "mayor of the palace." But other high household officials might bear the name too, such as the seneschal and the chamberlain. In the eleventh century the group of royal estate managers and collectors of revenue in France, known usually though not exclusively as *praepositi,* underwent an evolution to public officials that is one of the most important developments in the emergence of the medieval state. This evolution was not especially spectacular. Men who were collectors of domain revenue gradually, sometimes imperceptibly, took on functions that in hindsight seem "governmental"—the suppression of riots and the protection of the king's regalian rights, for example. With the aid of important men in the district in which they worked, they might also exercise the king's justice. Such men were never, perhaps, endowed with the dignity that we associate with the delegates of the royal court (baillis) who were sent out to supervise them, but they carried much of the burden of provincial government on their shoulders.

The provosts were, on the whole, remunerated through revenue farms for which they bid competitively. This gave an acquisitive edge to their administrative functions that soured their relationship with the governed. So far as is known, a great many of the provostships were hereditary in the twelfth and thirteenth centuries (not legally so, perhaps), but there was an informal network of agreements that kept certain provostships in the hands of particular families over several generations.

The provosts usually operated out of the larger towns in the royal domain. If these towns were near Paris, the provosts would come to the capital periodically to render account of their farms. If their towns were at a distance from the capital, groups of provosts would render their accounts to baillis delegated by the royal court to receive them. In the later Middle Ages new officials were created and the duties of the provost were attenuated. This was especially true in the area of finance, where "receivers" emerged as the preparers of local accounts. In many regions the provosts became minor judicial officials.

The one great exception to the estate-manager type of official described thus far was the provost of Paris (not to be confused with the provost of the merchants of the city). In the late twelfth century there were in Paris, serving the king's interest, two officials—one, a delegate of the royal court, called a bailli; the other, a farmer of royal revenue, called a provost. The bailli's power was severely restricted in Paris in the time of Philip Augustus (1180–1223)—that is, at a time when the office of bailli in the royal administration was being transformed into the principal focus of adminstrative expertise and of military and judicial authority in the countryside. The office of bailli of Paris was circumscribed probably because of the sensibilities of the king, who did not want a person with too much power in control of the capital. Whatever the reason, the petty bailli of Paris came to be called "provost" in recognition of his realtive lack of authority.

By the time of the death of Philip Augustus, then, Paris may be said to have had two provosts. One was the administrative descendant of the old bailli and still bore the aura of having been a delegate of the royal court. His judicial competence, his supervision of minor officials in the city, and his remuneration by salary reflected this stature. The other provost was the farmer of royal income. For simplicity, we may call the former bailli the judicial provost, and the other official the financial provost. They ruled the city for the king—but not the entire city, for the merchants had their own organization that, to a great extent, supervised commerce in Paris.

The size and importance of Paris made the two provosts, despite the presumed desires of Philip Augustus, men of wealth and power. They were not rivals to the throne, but neither were they images of mere provincial authorities. The court of the judicial provost (called the Châtelet) was one of the most powerful in the kingdom. Its original jurisdiction (leaving aside matters of commerce) extended to Paris and its hinterland, the viscounty of Paris. It had appellate jurisdiction over the castellanies in the viscounty and over seigneurial jurisdictions in the city and hinterland. Appeals from the Châtelet were heard at the central court of the kingdom, the Parlement of Paris. Eventually the Châtelet gained some jurisdiction over the crime of treason, a good measure of the importance of the court, and of the man who ran it.

Sometime around 1260 the anomaly of two provosts was remedied. Louis IX appointed Étienne Boileau, who combined the duties of both offices and who regulated the relations of the now unique royal provost with the provost of the merchants. It is to him that we owe publication of the *Livre des métiers*.

BIBLIOGRAPHY

Julia Barrow, "Cathedrals, Provosts, and Prebends: A Comparison of Twelfth-century German and English Practice," in *Journal of Ecclesiastical History,* **37** (1986); Léon-Louis Borrelli de Serres, *Recherches sur divers services publics du XIIIe au XVIIe siècle,* 3 vols. (1895–1909); Raymond Cazelles, *Nouvelle histoire de Paris de la fin du règne de Philippe Auguste à la mort de Charles V, 1223–1380* (1972); Henri Gravier, "Essai sur les prévôts royaux du XIe au XIVe siècle," in *Nouvelle revue historique de droit français et étranger,* **27** (1903); William Chester Jordan, *Louis IX and the Challenge of the Crusade* (1979); Philibert Schmitz, *Geschichte des Benediktenordens,* 4 vols. (1947–1960); Arie Serper, "L'administration royale de Paris au temps de Louis IX," in *Francia,* VII (1979).

In addition to the above, material on ecclesiastical provosts is scattered through the institutional histories of the various monastic orders and on lay provosts, for the most part, through histories of estate management and national institutions.

WILLIAM CHESTER JORDAN

[See also **Bailli; Châtelet; Mayor; Mayor of the Palace; Paris; Parlement of Paris; Seneschal; Taxation, French.**]

PRUDDE, JOHN (*d.* by 20 November 1473), was one of the most important English glass painters of the fifteenth century. Between 1440 and 1461 he was king's glazier, and during this period he glazed windows in several royal palaces and foundations. He also undertook other commissions, of which the most important (and the only one which survives) was the glazing of the Beauchamp Chapel, in the Church of St. Mary, Warwick, begun in 1447. In its greater range and quantity of colored glass than had hitherto been seen in fifteenth-century England, and its use on an unprecedented scale of colored glass inserts to represent jewels, the Beauchamp

St. Alban. Stained glass by John Prudde from the east window of Beauchamp Chapel, St. Mary's Church, Warwick, 1447–1450. REPRODUCED FROM TRANSACTIONS AND PROCEEDINGS OF THE BIRMINGHAM ARCHAEOLOGICAL SOCIETY, 53 (1928)

Chapel was very influential on other wealthy patrons and fellow glaziers.

BIBLIOGRAPHY

Philip B. Chatwin, "Some Notes on the Painted Windows of the Beauchamp Chapel, Warwick," in *Transactions and Proceedings of the Birmingham Archaeological Society,* 53 (1928); Herbert Chitty, "John Prudde, 'King's Glazier,'" in *Notes and Queries,* 12th ser., **3** (1917), 419–421; Charles Winston, *Memoirs Illustrative of the Art of Glass Painting* (1865).

Faith, having conquered Idolatry, crowns the martyrs; Chastity battles Lust. Pen drawings on vellum from a 10th-century copy of the *Psychomachia* of Prudentius. BERN, BURGERBIBLIOTHEK, COD. 264, fol. 35v

RICHARD C. MARKS

[See also **Glass, Stained; Glass, Western European.**]

PRUDENTIUS (Aurelius Prudentius Clemens) (348–after 404), a Christian-born, classically educated Roman magistrate who became for medieval men the archetypal Christian Latin poet. He afforded a powerful stimulus to the development of allegorical poetry with his *Psychomachia,* a battle between personified Virtues and Vices. Also noteworthy is his view that Christianity did not abrogate the imperial mission of Rome but rather ennobled it.

BIBLIOGRAPHY
Marion M. van Assendelft, *Sol ecce surgit igneus: A Commentary on the Morning and Evening Hymns of Prudentius* (1976); Johann Bergman, ed., *Aurelii Prudentii Clementis Carmina* (1926); Roy J. Deferrari and James M. Campbell, *A Concordance of Prudentius* (1932); Kenneth R. Haworth, *Deified Virtues, Demonic Vices, and Descriptive Allegory in Prudentius' Psychomachia* (1980); Bernard M. Peebles, *The Poet Prudentius* (1951); Edward K. Rand, "Prudentius and Christian Humanism," in *Transactions and Proceedings of the American Philological Association,* **51** (1920); H. J. Thomson, ed. and trans., *Prudentius,* 2 vols. (1949–1953, repr. 1962, 1969, 1979).

ELAINE GOLDEN ROBISON

[See also **Allegory; Drama, Western European; Early Christian Art; Eulalie, La Séquence de Ste.; Hymns, Latin; Latin Literature; Morality Play; Virtues and Vices.**]

PSALM TONES, any musical formulas for the recitation of the psalms and canticles, whether ornate or simple, solo or choral; the term most often designates the simple formulas used for the choral recitation of the Psalter in the Daily Office.

The 150 psalms were sung in the course of each week in the Gregorian cursus; even spread over two weeks, as in the Ambrosian, the amount of text to be completed by a choir not restricted to trained singers made complexity impractical, and simple musical figures a necessity. The basis of the simple tones is recitation on one note, although a psalmody restricted to this was not found in the medieval liturgy. An inflection marking the conclusion of each psalm verse was always employed, and additional inflections, in accordance with local usage and liturgical circumstances, were usual. The forms of the Gregorian psalmody were fully developed by the beginning of the tenth century, when an attempt was made to treat them systematically in the anonymous *Commemoratio brevis de tonis et psalmis modulandis.* Complete uniformity in all details was not found until the nineteenth century and the general acceptance of standard editions of the chant.

At its most complex the psalm tone might have six parts: (1) the intonation, a rising figure introducing (2) the recitation tone, (3) the median cadence at the caesura, (4) a second intonation, set to the first syllables of the second half of the verse and leading again to the recitation note, (5) the cadence, and (6) the termination.

The first intonation was normally sung for the first verse only, and by the cantor alone to set the pitch for the choir. The choice of recitation tone depended on the antiphon assigned; in later times it was simply dictated by the mode of this chant. The median cadence and the second intonation were also determined by the mode of the antiphon. They seem not to have been part of the primitive psalmody (they are lacking in the early Ambrosian books), and until modern times there was a great deal of local variation in their use. The choice of cadence depended on the family of chants to which the antiphon belonged. The decision was not merely a matter of mode (there are as many as fourteen cadences for a single mode in some books), nor was it simply to ensure the smooth transition from the end of the psalm tone to the repetition of the antiphon (the usual explanation), for several in the same mode end on the same note.

The earliest practice seems to have been to sing the inflections to the appropriate syllables without regard for the word accent. But even in the earliest Gregorian books some of the cadences, median and final, have been adjusted by means of inserted notes so that the last, or the last two, accented syllables are reinforced by the musical accent. Rarely, even the intonation figures seem to have been "accentual."

The canticle tones and those used for the antiphons of the Mass became slightly more decorated than the tones for the Psalter; and in the first case, the intonation came to be sung for all verses. The invitatory tones, although not elaborate, are much less systematic, and retain many archaic features.

Very elaborate solo psalm tones were also used, for the tracts, for example, and for most of the verses of the great responsories, respond graduals, and alleluias. At first sight such verses might seem rather to employ independent melodies than formulas that have been adapted to many texts.

BIBLIOGRAPHY
Willi Apel, *Gregorian Chant* (1958); Terence Bailey, "Ambrosian Psalmody: An Introduction," in *Rivista internazionale di musica sacra,* **1** (1980), and *idem,* ed., *Commemoratio brevis de tonis et psalmis modulandis* (1979); Thomas Connolly, "Psalm, II," in *The New Grove Dictionary of Music and Musicians,* XV (1980); J. Smits van Waesberghe, "L'évolution des tons psalmodiques au moyen âge," in *Atti del Congresso internazi-*

onale di musica sacra, 1950 (1952); S. J. P. Van Dijk, "Medieval Terminology and Methods of Psalm Singing," in *Musica disciplina,* 6 (1952).

TERENCE BAILEY

[See also **Antiphon; Cadence; Cantor; Gregorian Chant; Psalter; Responsory.**]

PSALTER. The Psalter contains 150 psalms, although a short apocryphal text, Psalm 151, is found in a number of manuscripts throughout the Middle Ages. The division of psalms into verses may differ from source to source because the "title" of the psalm is counted or because of a rearrangement of paragraphs.

Two early translations of the Bible are significant for the Psalter. The first, made from the Septuagint in 384, became known as the Roman text. It was used everywhere except northern Italy and Spain until the ninth century. At St. Peter's in Rome, it was in use until the mid sixteenth century, having been superseded elsewhere by Jerome's translation of the Hexapla, made in 389. This translation, used in the reforms of Charlemagne, is known as the Gallican Psalter. It was intended as a working copy for reference rather than for use in the services; and in the course of numerous revisions during the Middle Ages it was contaminated from earlier Psalters, thereby becoming inferior to the Roman Psalter. The Itala Psalter, so called by St. Augustine, is not a separate work but either the Gallican or Roman text used in the Vulgate, Jerome's last translation of the Bible, made from the Hebrew in 393. With respect to the invitatory psalm, however, Itala has come to refer to the Roman version of the text. Because the Authorized Version uses later Hebrew sources than were used for the Vulgate, its numbering of the psalms and the distribution of verses in them differs, as in Table 1. In this article Vulgate numbering is used.

Table 1. Numbering of the psalms

Vulgate	Auth. Ver.	Vulgate	Auth. Ver.
1–8	1–8	114	116:1–9
		115	116:10–end
9:1–21	9	116–145	117–146
9:22–end	10	146	147:1–11
10–112	11–113	147	147:12–end
113:1–8	114	148–150	148–150
113:9–end	115		

Because its texts are the foundation for the ferial course of the Offices, the Psalter is often singled out as a special book to which other material relating to the liturgical services, including chant, is added. Such books, bound either separately or as a distinct section in a Breviary, are best described as Ferial or Liturgical or Choir Psalters.

The Psalter is divided in several ways. In the biblical Psalter, traditional divisions are unrelated to the use of psalms within the services. They may be retained in the Choir Psalter, where other practical divisions result from the way the psalms are distributed over the week. Psalms 1–108 are mostly assigned to matins, 109–147 to vespers, and 148–150 and others to lauds; the Little Hours use psalms from here and there in the numerical sequence. Psalm 94 is always assigned as the daily invitatory text. Artwork and the use of large initials at the beginning of each section highlight four arrangements. First is the fivefold, or biblical. This is a division into five books, each ending with a psalm stressing the text *Benedicamus Domino* in its final verses, and thus having a function similar to that of the doxology. It is said to be rare in France. Second is the eightfold, or liturgical. This is a division according to the secular distribution of psalms in matins for the seven days of the week, with an eighth section devoted to vespers, and it is presumably the one also called the Roman division. Psalms for lauds and the other hours are interspersed numerically according to the cursus of the use to which the Psalter belongs. Third is the threefold. Said to be of Irish origin, this arrangement is rare in France and more common in Germany. It has no relation to the distribution of psalms in the services. Fourth is the tenfold. This appears later in France and combines the threefold and eightfold. As well as these four large divisions, some books identify the fifteen Gradual Psalms (119–133) and the Penitential Psalms (6, 31, 37, 50, 101, 124, 142) with special initials. The various divisions of the Psalter are shown in Table 2.

Victor Leroquais identified several kinds of Choir Psalter according to what is contained other than the psalms themselves, but the contents are sufficiently varied for even these categories to be inadequate. The Choir Psalter, providing the texts and chants that are to be performed every day of the year when nothing proper is assigned, underpins the Temporale in the same way that the Ordo does for Mass books and the Common of Saints for the Sanctorale. It thus should provide the common or

Table 2. Divisions of the Psalter

	Biblical	Liturgical	Threefold	Tenfold
1	Beatus vir	Beatus vir	Beatus vir	Beatus vir
26		Dominus illuminatio mea		Dominus illuminatio mea
41	Quemadmodum			
38		Dixi custodiam		Dixi custodiam
51			Quid gloriaris	Quid gloriaris
52		Dixit insipiens		Dixit insipiens
68		Salvum me fac		Salvum me fac
72	Quam bonus			
80		Exulatate Deo		Exulatate Deo
89	Domine refugium			
97		Cantate Domino		Cantate Domino
101			Domine exaudi	Domine exaudi
106	Confitemini Domino quoniam bonus			
109		Dixit Dominus Domino		Dixit Dominus Domino

ferial texts (often with their chants) of the numerous genres discussed below. This additional material and the order in which it appears can differ widely from source to source, though the number of items and their texts that are common to all daily services does not vary as much from use to use as the variety of presentations would suggest. The discrepancy arises from the willingness or reluctance of the scribe to include material that is only seasonally or partly common. In order to accommodate more easily the requirements of the services, the psalms may appear not in biblical order but in the order they are used, so that dislocations of the numerical sequence may give the appearance of error or misbinding in some books. Often, an incipit may indicate the presence of a text given in full elsewhere, out of its numerical position, or rubrics may explain the situation.

Ferial or common antiphons, dialogues, and doxologies occur in all the Office Hours and therefore appear regularly throughout the Choir Psalter, in the place they are required. The doxology is often abbreviated to its first word or two. Antiphons are given complete, after the psalm or group of psalms with which they are associated, but commonly their incipits, needed by the soloist for the intonation, also appear beforehand. A characteristic sequence of texts and initial letters is thus set up, separating the long texts of the psalms themselves. In manuscripts that transmit the chant, the antiphons and their incipits will also be distinguished by the presence of notation. Items such as chapters, hymns, and short responsories, used in some services, appear only at those places in the Psalter where they are required.

After the psalm texts themselves, Choir Psalters usually continue with other material that is common but not assigned to a particular weekday: the lesser canticles at lauds, the major (New Testament) canticles (Magnificat, Benedictus, and Nunc dimittis), the Athanasian creed for prime, the Te Deum. A monastic Psalter will transmit the monastic canticles. Monastic books sometimes include even the Preface and Canon of Mass, perhaps indicating that the book was for use by clergy away from their monastery. The numerous prayers and preces that frequently follow prime may also be included. The litany is given near the end of the Choir Psalter, and following it there may be various votive offices, the daily Office of the Dead, and the daily Office of the Virgin. Commemorations and the benedictions for the lessons of matins will often appear, together with rubrics explaining how they are distributed. In books that have the chants, the tone for dialogues and readings will usually appear; it is not uncommon to find some information regarding the psalm tones and the modal system of chants, and perhaps even a complete Tonary.

Because the principal contents are the same in all examples, Leroquais regards Psalters as particularly difficult to assign to a place of use. When the various divisions and methods of highlighting them and the format and organization of all the additional items are taken into consideration, it may be possible to discern families of Psalters, making localization a possibility.

BIBLIOGRAPHY

Andrew Hughes, *Medieval Manuscripts for Mass and Office* (1982), esp. paragraphs 873–885; Victor Leroquais, *Les psautiers manuscrits latins des bibliothèques publiques de France,* 3 vols. (1940–1941).

ANDREW HUGHES

[See also **Antiphon; Benedicamus Domino; Bible; Breviary; Canticle; Divine Office; Jerome, St.; Mass, Liturgy of the; Psalm Tones; Tonary; Vulgate.**]

PSALTER, ILLUMINATION OF. Used in both private and public prayer by Jews and then Christians, the Psalter comprises the Old Testament psalms and, usually, odes excerpted from other biblical books. In the Eastern church, the Septuagint translation was used; in the West, three versions circulated, all attributed to St. Jerome (*d.* 419/420): Roman, Gallican, and a translation from Hebrew. Sometimes two or three translations were written in parallel columns in the same manuscript.

Four principal means of illustrating the Psalter evolved during the Middle Ages. One, the "aristocratic Psalter," consists of biographical images of David, the author of the psalms, and of the authors of the odes, such as Moses and Isaiah (an example is the early-tenth-century Byzantine Paris Psalter, Bibliothèque Nationale, cod. gr. 139). The second, or "monastic Psalter," contains illustrations of the actions described or alluded to in the text, usually in the margins of the manuscript (for example, the ninth-century Chludov Psalter, Moscow, Historical Museum, cod. 129D). The third comprises literal depictions of the allusive language in the psalm verses (for example, the Utrecht Psalter). And the fourth appends biblical narrative sequences at the front of the book (see Paris, Bibliothèque Nationale, cod. lat. 8846).

BIBLIOGRAPHY

John A. Lamb, *The Psalms in Christian Worship* (1962); Johan Jakob Tikkanen, *Die Psalterillustration in Mittelalter,* 2 vols. in 1 (1895–1900, repr. 1903).

HERBERT L. KESSLER

[See also **Anglo-Norman Literature; Anglo Saxon Literature; Arundel Psalter; Bible; Bible, French; Bible, Old and Middle English; Byzantine Art; Catalan Literature; Divine Office; Paris Psalter; Pre-Romanesque Art; Utrecht Psalter; Vulgate.**]

PSALTIKON, Byzantine liturgical manual for the solo singer (*psaltes*) and companion volume to the *Asmatikon* of the choral ensemble in the Hagia Sophia of Constantinople. Both the Office and the Mass are represented in a florid chant for the skilled musician. Like the *Asmatikon,* this collection forms the background for the arrival of the larger "orders of service," the *Akolouthiai,* and the highly melismatic (*kalophonic*) compositional style of the fourteenth and fifteenth centuries.

BIBLIOGRAPHY

Dimitri E. Conomos, *The Late Byzantine and Slavonic Communion Cycle: Liturgy and Music* (1985); Gisa Hintze, *Das byzantinische Prokeimena-Repertoire* (1973); Christian Thodberg, *Der byzantinische Alleluiarionzyklus* (1966); Oliver Strunk, *Essays on Music in the Byzantine World* (1977), 45–54, 157–161.

NICOLAS SCHIDLOVSKY

[See also **Asmatikon; Hymns, Byzantine; Music, Byzantine.**]

PSELLOS, MICHAEL (1018–*ca.* 1078), Byzantine scholar, statesman, and historian. Born in Constantinople to parents of modest means, he early attracted the attention of imperial patrons. Beginning with Michael IV (1034–1041), he held high offices under each succeeding emperor. He fell into disfavor briefly in the last year of the reign of Constantine IX Monomachos (1042–1055) and retired to a monastery on Mt. Olympus, changing his name from Constantine to Michael. After a few months, the empress Theodora recalled him to Constantinople, and he played a leading role in the intrigues which culminated in the deposition of Michael VI Stratiotikos and the accession of Isaac I Komnenos in 1057. He was at the height of his political power at the beginning of the reign of his former pupil Michael VII Doukas (1071–1078), but appears soon to have been dismissed by that emperor. His final years are shrouded in obscurity, and the place and date of his death are uncertain.

Most of what we know about Psellos comes from his most important work, the *Chronographia,* a remarkable history of the Byzantine imperial court from 976 to 1077. Psellos himself is often at the center of his narrative, and his information must be interpreted with the greatest care. He also composed lengthy and elaborately rhetorical funeral orations for a number of his leading contemporaries, including John Mauropous and the patriarchs Michael Keroularios, Constantine Leichoudes, and John VIII Xiphilinos. These very difficult orations, along with about 500 of his highly rhetorical letters, are fundamental but virtually unexplored sources for the internal history of the Byzantine Empire in the eleventh century.

Psellos was one of the most important scholars of the Byzantine period, if only for the amazing breadth of his encyclopedic knowledge. The number of works attributed to him in Byzantine and Renaissance manuscripts is enormous, and many of these works still remain unpublished, or are available only in careless, uncritical early editions. There are considerable problems of disputed or false attribution, and even the authorship of his famous dialogue *De operatione daemonum* has recently been questioned. He wrote scientific and philosophical treatises on mathematics, music, astronomy, physics, metaphysics, theology, ethics, alchemy, medicine, and law. Many of his treatises are little more than paraphrases or epitomes of ancient authors, but he made these works accessible to a considerably wider audience. He was in a sense the first great Byzantine popularizer of ancient Greek learning and literature, and his works helped to stimulate a revival of interest in ancient philosophy and science. His excerpts from ancient authors are also of great historical value, sometimes preserving portions of their works which have otherwise been lost (scholars had scarcely begun to extract and identify the wealth of such fragments embedded in his treatises and commentaries by the second half of the twentieth century).

Psellos was often cited in the later Byzantine period, along with Demosthenes and Gregory of Nazianzus, as a master of the Attic style, and some of his shorter works were occasionally included as models in later handbooks of rhetoric. The *Chronographia,* his most popular work today, survives in a single manuscript and seems to have been little read until its rediscovery in the nineteenth century.

BIBLIOGRAPHY

Sources. J. F. Boissonade, ed., *Michael Psellus De operatione daemonum* (1838, repr. 1964); *The Chronographia,* Edgar R. A. Sewter, trans. (1953, repr. 1979); Eduardus Kurtz and Franciscus Drexl, *Michaelis Pselli Scripta minora,* 2 vols. (1936–1941); *De omnifaria doctrina,* L. G. Westerink, ed. (1948); *Patrologia graeca,* CXXII (1864); Konstantine N. Sathas, *Bibliotheca graeca medii aevi* [in Greek], IV and V (1874–1875).

Studies. Gertrud Böhlig, *Untersuchungen zum rhetorischen Sprachgebrauch der Byzantiner, mit besonderer Berücksichtigung der Schriften des Michael Psellos* (1956); Paul Gautier, "Le *De daemonibus* du Pseudo-Psellos," in *Revue des études byzantines,* **38** (1980); Herbert Hunger, *Die hochsprachliche profane Literatur der Byzantiner,* I (1978), 372–382; E. Kriaras, "Psellos," in *Paulys Realencyclopädie der classischen Altertumswissenschaft,* suppl. XI (1968); Yakov N. Liubarskii, *Michail Psell: Lichnost i tvorchestvo* (1978); Émile Renauld, *Étude sur la langue et du style de Michel Psellos* (1920), and *Lexique choisi de Psellos* (1920); Bruno Rhodius, *Beiträge zur Lebensgeschichte und zu den Briefen des Psellos* (1892); Kenneth Snipes, "A Newly Discovered History of the Roman Emperors by Michael Psellos," in *Jahrbuch der österreichischen Byzantinistik,* **32,** pt. 3 (1982); Günter Weiss, *Oströmische Beamte im Spiegel der Schriften des Michael Psellos* (1973).

KENNETH SNIPES

[See also **Biography, Secular; Byzantine Empire: History; Byzantine Literature; Classical Literary Studies; Constantine IX Monomachos; Doukas; Gregory of Nazianzus, St.; John VIII Xiphilinos, Patriarch; Michael Keroularios; Theodora the Macedonian, Empress.**]

PSEUDO-DIONYSIUS THE AREOPAGITE (*fl. ca.* 500), perhaps more properly known as Dionysius the Pseudo-Areopagite. Dionysius is the pseudonym of a Christian Platonist author who wrote in Greek four treatises and ten letters, the *corpus dionysiacum,* and who fraudulently claimed to be Dionysius the Areopagite, an Athenian converted to Christianity by the apostle Paul (Acts 17:34). None of the many modern attempts to discover the true identity of this later Dionysius have succeeded. We know only that he wrote in the Byzantine Christian East (perhaps in Syria) and that he was immersed in the teachings of the later Neoplatonic school of Athens and especially of Proclus (*d.* 485). This pagan philosophy was employed by Dionysius to expound a Christian "mystagogy," that is, initiation into the "mysteries" leading to the union of the soul with the divine.

The first and longest work of the *corpus dionysiacum, On the Divine Names,* classifies and interprets the names given to God. Dionysius claims to have found these names in the Christian Scriptures, but has in fact borrowed them from the Neoplatonist tradition, in accord with which he describes them as moments of the "processions" or outpourings of the divine energy from the "thearchy" or divine principle. The divine thus manifests itself in a given order as, for example, "the Good," "Being," "Life," and "Intellect." The brief *Mystical Theology* explains the two ways of approaching the divine. The cataphatic or positive way (from *kataphatikos*) affirms its attributes, descending from the highest, while the apophatic way (the *via negativa,* or way of negation, from Greek *apophatikos*) ascends towards the divine by denying its attributes, attaining it only in "the truly mystical cloud of unknowing," beyond which God resides in a "divine darkness." *The Ecclesiastical Hierarchy* describes and interprets symbolically the visible "mysteries" or sacraments of the church. Finally, *The Celestial Hierarchy* organizes the angels immediately above the ecclesiastical hierarchy into three orders; each rank, as assigned, effects the purification, illumination, and perfection, in that sequence, of the ranks below.

The *corpus dionysiacum* mentions other works by Dionysius, (for example, *The Theological Outlines* and *The Symbolic Theology*); these are perhaps lost but more probably fictitious. Dionysius claims to have received his doctrine from his master, a certain Hierotheos (otherwise unknown), like Dionysius one of Paul's converts and so a member of the original circle around the apostles.

Pseudo-Dionysius' works first surfaced in the Byzantine East in the early sixth century, but were generally accepted as authentic and authoritative only after being interpreted in an orthodox Christian sense by John of Scythopolis (early sixth century) and Maximus the Confessor (*d.* 662). In later Byzantine Orthodoxy their influence remained substantial. In the West, the first of some fifteen translations into Latin was made by Hilduin around 832 and revised with commentary by John Scottus Eriugena around 862. Dionysius' influence on Thomas Aquinas is evident in the Neoplatonic concepts of the *Summa theologiae,* and Bonaventure referred to him as the *doctor mysticus.* In the Renaissance and Reformation his reputation sharply declined. Finally, in 1895, Hugo Koch and Joseph Stiglmayr, working independently, confirmed the later dating of the *corpus dionysiacum;* their conclusions are the basis of all current scholarly studies.

BIBLIOGRAPHY

Sources. Patrologia graeca, III (1889), IV (1889); *La hiérarchie céleste,* René Roques *et al.,* eds. (1958). Translations are *On the Divine Names and The Mystical Theology,* Clarence E. Rolt, trans. (1920); *The Divine Names, and Mystical Theology,* John D. Jones, trans. (1980).

Studies. Philippe Chevalier, ed., *Dionysiaca,* 2 vols. (1937–1949); Hyacinthe François Dondaine, *Le corpus dionysien de l'Université de Paris au XIIIe siècle* (1953); Stephen Gersh, *From Iamblichus to Eriugena: An Investigation of the Prehistory and Evolution of the Pseudo-Dionysian Tradition* (1978); Hugo Koch, *Pseudo-Dionysius Areopagita in seinen Beziehungen zum Neoplatonismus und Mysterienwesen* (1900); René Roques, "Contemplation, extase, et ténèbre chez le Pseudo-Denys," in *Dictionnaire de spiritualité,* II (1953), 1,885–1,911, *L'univers dionysien* (1954), "Denys l'Areopagite (Le Pseudo-)," I–III, in *Dictionnaire de spiritualité,* III (1957), 244–286; "Denys . . . ," in *Dictionnaire de l'histoire et de géographie ecclésiastique,* XIV (1958), 265–286, and *idem,* with L. Lemaître and M. Viller, 'Le Pseudo-Denys l'Areopagite," in *Dictionnaire de spiritualité,* II (1953), 1,785–1,787.

DAVID B. EVANS

[See also **Angel/Angelology; Hilduin of St. Denis; Maximus the Confessor, St.; Mysticism, Christian; Neoplatonism; Philosophy and Theology, Western European.**]

PSEUDO-KODINOS, an anonymous treatise on Byzantine court titles, offices, hierarchy, and ceremonies, written before 1368, probably between 1347 and 1354, and falsely attributed in one manuscript to a certain *curopalates,* George Kodinos. It is a systematic exposition divided into twelve chapters describing: (1) the hierarchical order of titles and offices; (2) the costumes and the insignia of each title and office; (3) the services performed by each official, in court as well as in the administration and the army, with a special chapter devoted to the attributions of the grand domestic as head of the armed forces; (4) the ceremonies held throughout the year in the presence of the emperor, including those of his marriage and of his mourning; and (5) the ceremonies of promotion to the highest ranks in the empire (crowning of the emperor, consecration of the patriarch, elevation to the rank of despot, *sebastokrator,* and caesar). The text is preserved in a considerable number of manuscripts, some of which contain further additions and modifications.

Pseudo-Kodinos is an important source for our knowledge of the Byzantine court and administration during the Palaiologan period. The information it provides can be completed by comparing it to several anonymous short lists of titles and offices dating from the fourteenth and fifteenth centuries. All these texts are now conveniently published in one volume with French translation and commentary.

BIBLIOGRAPHY
Jean Verpeaux, ed. and trans., *Pseudo-Kodinos: Traité des offices* (1966).

NICOLAS OIKONOMIDES

[See also **Byzantine Bureaucracy; Caesar; Clergy, Byzantine; Curopalates; Despot; Encyclopedias and Dictionaries, Byzantine; Palaiologoi; Patriarch; Sebastokrator.**]

PSEUDO-NICCOLÒ (also called l'Illustratore, *fl.* mid fourteenth century), a leading Bolognese illuminator, so named because his work was earlier confused with that of Niccolò da Bologna, whom he strongly influenced. His miniatures, found mainly in legal texts, display compact, energetic figures, strong colors, and forceful characterizations often drawing vividly upon contemporary life.

BIBLIOGRAPHY
Helena C. Cassee, *The Missal of Cardinal Bertrand de Deux: A Study in Fourteenth-century Bolognese Miniature Painting,* Michael Hoyle, trans. (1980); Mario Rotili, *La miniatura gotica in Italia,* I (1968), 70–72; Mario Salmi, *Italian Miniatures* (1954), 20–21.

MICHAEL JACOFF

[See also **Manuscript Illumination, European; Niccolò da Bologna.**]

PSEUDO-TURPIN. One of the most successful and influential of medieval forgeries, this Latin prose history was spuriously attributed to the archbishop of Rheims who in the *Chanson de Roland* dies in the Battle of Roncesvalles. It is an incongruous amalgam of homiletic and popular epic material compiled about 1140, perhaps at the Abbey of St. Denis. Incorporated into the fraudulently authoritative *Liber sancti Jacobi* (Codex Calixtinus), the *Pseudo-Turpin* was rapidly established as an authentic, eyewitness account of Charlemagne's legendary Spanish campaigns, in particular the epic Battle of Roncesvalles. It long commanded a preeminent place in medieval historiography, both learned and secular. Its survival in more than 170 Latin manuscripts attests to its popularity, as does its translation into a great variety of vernaculars, including at least fifteen independent versions in medieval French alone.

BIBLIOGRAPHY
Sources. For the Latin text, see C. Meredith-Jones, ed., *Historia Karoli Magni et Rotholandi ou Chronique du Pseudo-Turpin* (1936). For recent editions of various French versions of the text, see Claude Buridant, ed., *La traduction du Pseudo-Turpin du manuscrit Vatican Regina 624* (1976); Ian Short, ed., *The Anglo-Norman Pseudo-Turpin Chronicle of William de Briane* (1973); Ronald N. Walpole, ed., *The Old French Johannes Translation of the Pseudo-Turpin Chronicle,* 2 vols. (1976), *An Anonymous Old French Translation of the Pseudo-Turpin Chronicle* (1979), and *Le Turpin français, dit le Turpin I* (1985).
Studies. Ian Short, "The Pseudo-Turpin Chronicle: Some Unnoticed Versions and Their Sources," in *Medium aevum,* **38** (1969), and "A Study in Carolingian Legend and Its Persistence in Latin Historiography (XII–XVI Centuries)," in *Mittellateinisches Jahrbuch,* 7 (1972); Ronald N. Walpole, *Philip Mouskés and the Pseudo-Turpin Chronicle* (1947).

IAN SHORT

[See also **Chronicles, French; Forgery; Grandes Chroniques de France; Historiography, Western European; Philippe Mousket; Roland, Song of, Roncesvalles.**]

PSYCHOMACHIA. See **Allegory; Prudentius; Virtues and Vices.**

PSYCHOPOMP, one who leads souls to another world. In ancient Greek mythology, Hermes acts as psychopomp by leading shades to their subterranean or extraterrestrial abodes. In medieval Christian iconography, Christ is the psychopomp who guides souls to heaven, for only through him can one enter the Kingdom of Heaven. In Byzantine iconography, Christ is often depicted as a psychopomp in scenes of the death of the Virgin as he transports her soul to heaven. In the Arian sect, the cow is believed to perform the role of psychopomp.

BIBLIOGRAPHY
Franz Cumont, *After Life in Roman Paganism* (1922); Alessandro della Seta, *Religion and Art* (1914).

JENNIFER E. JONES

[See also **Arianism; Death and Burial; Koimesis.** Illustrations at **Kariye Djami; Koerbecke, Johann; Paolo Veneziano.**]

PTŁNI, a large Armenian church constructed in the sixth or seventh century, possibly by Prince Manuel Amatuni, who is shown in a hunting scene carved on the south wall. Now in ruins, Ptłni is significant as one of the oldest surviving domed hall churches of Armenia and the prototype for many others constructed from the ninth century on (Marmašen, Širakawan). The central dome, now collapsed, rested on a drum supported by engaged piers and was buttressed by lateral niches.

Ptłni is notable for its figured reliefs (Christ and the Apostles, Daniel, hunting scenes, wine pitchers), which are among the earliest on the exterior of a Christian church.

BIBLIOGRAPHY

Lucy Der Manuelian, "Armenian Sculptural Images, Fifth to Eighth Centuries," in T. J. Samuelian, ed., *Classical Armenian Culture* (1982), 176–207; Sirarpie Der Nersessian, *Armenian Art,* Sheila Bourne and Angela O'Shea, trans. (1978), and *The Armenians* (1970); G. Hovsepian, "The Monastery Church of Budghoons (Budghavank) and the Doming of Ancient Armenian Churches," in *Materials for the Study of Armenian Art and Culture,* fasc. III (1944).

LUCY DER MANUELIAN

[See also **Armenian Art.**]

PTOLEMAIC ASTRONOMY

HISTORICAL DEVELOPMENT

The astronomy of Claudius Ptolemy's *Mathematical Compilation* synthesized some 500 years' effort to account for the observed motions of the fixed stars, sun, moon, and planets on the assumption that their proper motions were uniform and circular, and that the earth lay immobile at the center of a rotating universe. Composed around A.D. 150 and known later to Arabic readers as *al-Majisti* and to Latin readers as the *Almagest,* Ptolemy's grand system had neither successor nor rival until the publication of Nicolaus Copernicus' *De revolutionibus orbium coelestium* in 1543. The bulk of the technical astronomy during the intervening 1,400 years, both in the Middle East and Europe, was devoted to the computation of tables and the design of instruments that translated Ptolemy's theorems and calculations into almanacs, horoscopes, and planetaria. While Islamic astronomers carried out some systematic observations aimed at filling gaps left in Ptolemy's work, especially in his treatment of such long-term motions as precession, Europeans concentrated on making the system accessible and useful to a variety of users.

Before the establishment of the university curriculum in Europe, Ptolemaic astronomy circulated separately from the geocentric world picture on which it was predicated and from which it had initially taken its task. In the *Timaeus* (*ca.* 350 B.C.) Plato had first sketched out the kinetic model of a spherical earth resting immobile at the center of a vast rotating sphere containing the fixed stars and encompassing a nested series of concentric spheres, each carrying one of the "wandering stars"—that is, the planets and the sun—along its own path through the stars. Although each sphere rotated uniformly, the combination of their separate gyrations gave rise to the appearance of irregularity in the motions of the sun and planets as viewed from the earth. Able to give a rough, qualitative account of the sun's combined daily and annual motions, Plato left to astronomers the task of articulating the model for all the planets and of fitting it mathematically to the data that Babylonian and Greek observers had already been accumulating over several centuries. That was the task that Ptolemy finally completed.

Yet, from Plato's time on, practically no one doubted the geocentric model itself, whatever its precise fit with observational data. As Aristotle showed in greater detail in his *De caelo* (On the heavens), reason and common experience confirmed it. Philosophers, poets, church fathers, educators, and encyclopedists all spoke of the universe much as Plato had described it, on occasion embellishing his picture with the nomenclature and simpler mathematical features of technical astronomy as it was developing. Although such embellishments pointed to the astronomers' more intricate version of the model, they did not provide sufficient detail to supplant the technical literature. They did, however, make access to that literature necessary for a full understanding of the general accounts.

A socially fragile enterprise, mathematical and observational astronomy did not survive the ferment of the late empire in the West. Until the

PTOLEMAIC ASTRONOMY

translation of the *Almagest* into Latin—from the Greek in 1160, from the Arabic in 1175—European readers drew their picture of the world from the encyclopedists and the poets—and hence, in the absence of any ongoing technical tradition, had neither the need for a work as sophisticated as Ptolemy's nor the basis for understanding it. After its translation into Latin, the *Almagest* itself circulated among a quite small number of mathematicians, while simplified versions of its contents served the wider learned audience, especially at the universities. These versions took two basic forms: *De spera* (On the sphere) and *Theorica planetarum* (Theory of the planets).

TREATISES "ON THE SPHERE"

Treatises on the sphere, of which John of Sacrobosco's (*ca.* 1220) became the standard, set out for students the structural elements of the geocentric universe and the rudiments of the mathematical model that accounted for its astronomical phenomena.

Although the texts varied in detail, they generally opened with mathematical definitions of the sphere and with the basic metaphysical and empirical arguments that made it the shape of the earth and heavens. They turned then to the major circles, lines, and points of reference in the sky: equator or equinoctial circle, celestial poles, zodiacal or sign-bearing circle (actually a band, bisected by the ecliptic), *coluri* (meridians through the equinoctial and solstitial points), horizon, zenith, and so on.

As might be expected in a university text, the definitions were accompanied by synonyms and etymologies, the expounding of which accomplished one of the evident tasks of the sphere literature: exegesis of passages in classical literature where the various terms appear or are alluded to. For example, before explaining the rising and setting of the zodiacal constellations (and hence of the sun with them) in terms of a uniformly rotating sphere cut by a fixed, oblique horizon, Sacrobosco briefly treated three other measures of the phenomenon "according to the poets," and even in his main discussion quoted frequently from Vergil, Ovid, and Lucan.

According to writers on the sphere, the motion of the sun eastward along the ecliptic combined with the rotation of the stars westward along the equator to account for seasonal changes in the length of daylight, while moving the circle of the sun's motion slightly off center toward Gemini adjusted for the unequal length of the seasons. The resulting extremes of apogee and perigee of the sun also explained why the arctic regions are too cold, and the intertropical zone is too hot, to be habitable; the intermediate region of habitation was divided into seven climes according to half-hour differences in the length of the solstitial day.

A very slow motion of the celestial sphere about the poles of the ecliptic produced the gradual drift, or precession, of the equinoctial and solstitial points eastward along the zodiac. In some accounts—for instance, Robert Grosseteste's (*ca.* 1215–1230)—this Ptolemaic device was supplanted by Thābit ibn Qurra's more intricate mechanism for nonuniform precession, or trepidation.

With the kinetic model established for the sun and stars, treatises on the sphere turned briefly to the moon and planets, the several different cycles of which required more sophisticated arrangements of moving spheres and the use of two new devices, the epicycle and the equant. These lay at the heart of Ptolemaic astronomy, constituting both the basis of its precision and the point of its departure from strict geocentrism. Yet, precisely here writers on the sphere hurried through their presentations. "Every planet except the sun has an epicycle," wrote Sacrobosco, "and an epicycle is a small circle along the circumference of which the planet is borne, and the center of the epicycle is always carried along the circumference of the deferent." Simply introducing the names of the devices and their components in this manner, he could do no more than suggest vaguely how they were related to the phenomena they saved, in particular to the retrograde motion of the planets and to eclipses of the moon and sun.

TRACTS ON THE "THEORY OF THE PLANETS"

As part of the arts curriculum, the tracts *De spera* represent what most educated people knew—or were supposed to know—about Ptolemaic astronomy. They set out the vocabulary and conveyed a general, qualitative sense of how the basic mathematical devices explained the celestial appearances. But they provided neither demonstrations of the mathematics nor instructions for linking the devices to the observational data contained in the various astronomical tables. For mathematical demonstrations the curious student of the thirteenth or fourteenth century still had to seek out the *Almagest* itself; for the links between theory and data he could turn to readily accessible abridgments

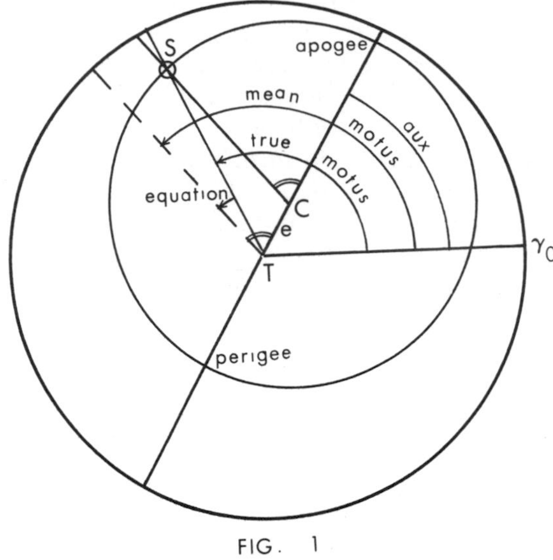

FIG. 1

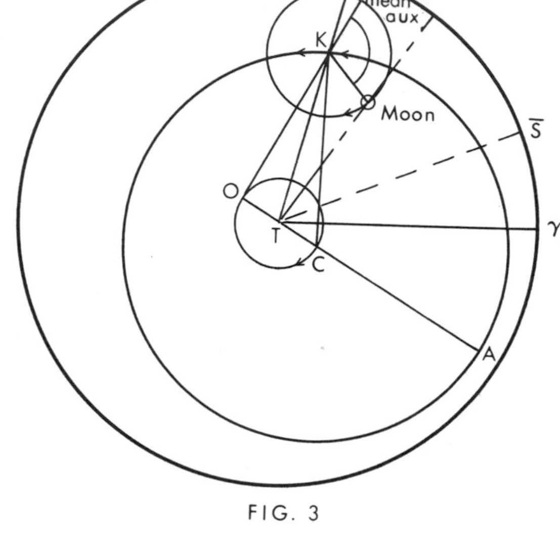

FIG. 3

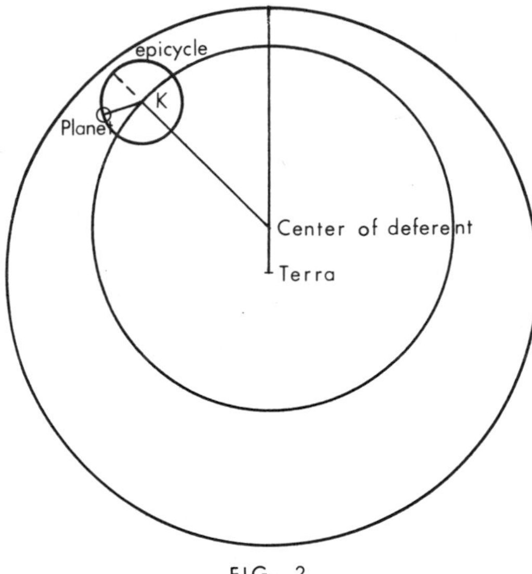

FIG. 2

Legend:

T = *terra*
S = *sol*
γ_0 = 0° Arietis (vernal equinox)
C = center of deferent
E = eccentricity
$\underline{K}$ = center of epicycle
$\bar{S}$ = mean sun
A = aux
O = *oppositio augis*
P = planet
E = equant

generically titled *Theorica planetarum* (Theory of the planets).

Theorica planetarum texts generally began with the model of the sun's motion familiar from *De spera* (Fig. 1). The sun moves uniformly in the plane of the ecliptic along the circumference of a circle, the center of which is displaced from the center of the world along the apsidal line joining apogee and perigee (the points of slowest and fastest motion, called here the *aux* and *oppositio augis*, respectively). The two centers of reference give rise to two measures of the sun's *motus*, or longitude along the ecliptic from the conventional starting point of 0° Arietis (vernal equinox). The mean *motus* about the center of the eccentric increases uniformly at a rate fixed by dividing 360° by the length in days of the solar year. The true *motus* about the earth differs from the mean by an amount called the "equation of the sun," which varies over the year as a function of the mean *motus* and depends as well on the eccentricity (the distance *e* between the two centers) and on the longitude of the apsidal line. Values for

FIG 4

the mean *motus* and the equation were contained in the astronomical tables, and their sum (or, at times, difference) gave the true *motus*.

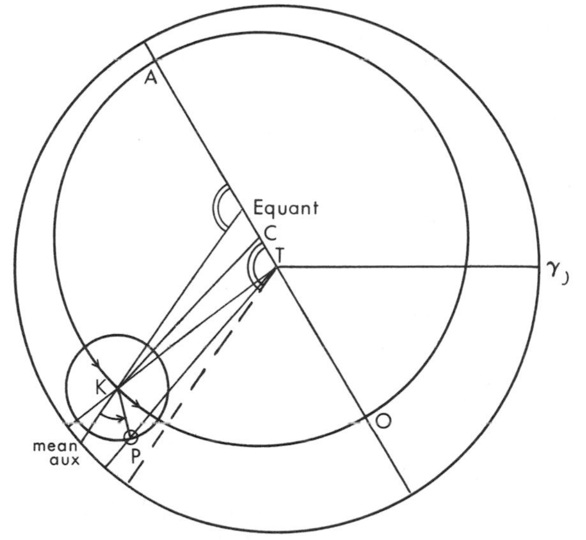

The moon and planets required much more intricate arrangements, fundamental to which was the epicycle (Fig. 2). The body was taken to move on a small circle, the epicycle, the center of which itself moved on a circle, the deferent, around the center of the world. In most cases the deferent was an eccentric circle like that of the sun. In the case of the moon (Fig. 3), the eccentric deferent itself constituted a large epicycle turning on a smaller deferent centered on the earth. From a starting position of conjunction with the sun, the center of the deferent revolved from east to west at about 11° a day, the center of the epicycle from west to east at about 13° a day (with respect to the earth), and the moon on the epicycle in the same direction as the deferent at about 24° a day. (As a result of the first two motions, the mean sun always lay midway between the center of the moon's epicycle and the apogee of its deferent.)

Uniform motion on the epicycle (mean argument) was measured from its mean *aux,* a point determined by a line drawn from a point opposite the deferent's center on its small circle. When added to (or, during half the cycle, subtracted from) the "equation of center," or difference between mean *aux* and true *aux* (determined by a line from the earth through the center of the epicycle), the mean argument was transformed into the true argument. The true argument then led to an "equation of argument," that, added to the mean *motus* of the epicycle's center, in turn yielded the true *motus* of

PTOLEMAIC ASTRONOMY

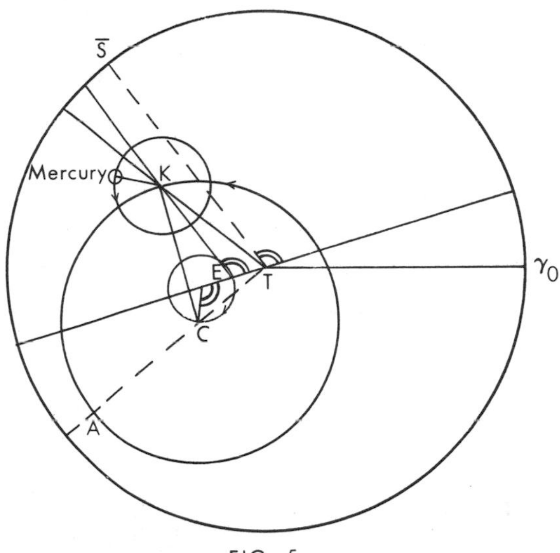

FIG. 5

the moon. Again, mean values and equations, which depended on mathematical calculations using the moon's fixed parameters, could be found in the tables.

The three "outer" planets (Mars, Jupiter, Saturn) each had a fixed eccentric deferent, but the motion of the epicycle's center from west to east along it was made uniform with respect to the center of another circle, the equant. That center lay on the apsidal line joining the earth and the center of the deferent (Fig. 4). The line from the equant's center through the epicycle's center determined the latter's mean *aux,* from which the mean argument of the planet was measured, increasing from west to east. Otherwise, the parameters of the planet's motion were defined as in the moon's model, except that the equation of argument and the equation of center were always equal. Two additional points on the planet's epicycle required special identification: the points on the bottom half between which the planet's speed eastward counteracted the epicycle's westward swing along the deferent, thus making the body, as seen from earth, stop, move eastward, stop, and then resume its normal westward motion. These "points of station" bounded the arc of retrograde motion.

To account for the fact that Mercury and Venus (the "inner" planets) always remain within fixed distances from the sun, the center of each epicycle was taken to move about the equant with the mean *motus* of the sun. Revolving about the epicycle at a uniform rate determined by the period of conjunction with the sun, each planet moved away from the sun to a fixed limit and then moved toward it again,

PTOLEMAIC ASTRONOMY

first to one side, then to the other, in an exaggerated form of retrograde motion. Although Venus' model otherwise looked like that of an outer planet, Mercury's had a moving eccentric like the moon's; the center of the deferent revolved about a circle centered on the line of apsides and passing through the center of the equant (Fig. 5).

Ptolemy's needlessly intricate mechanism for dealing with variations in planetary latitude north and south of the ecliptic received scant attention in medieval theory. The plane of the moon's deferent and epicycle was inclined to that of the ecliptic, and the line of intersection joining the nodes (called the "head and tail of the dragon") was rotated in the ecliptic by a separate motion of the moon's heaven. In the planetary models, the deferent was inclined to the ecliptic at a fixed angle, while the epicycle's inclination to the deferent varied from a minimum at the nodes (where the epicycle lay in the plane of the ecliptic) to a maximum at quadrature.

Equally problematical to medieval writers was the phenomenon of precession, in which a minute difference between the lengths of the solar and sidereal years causes a very slow motion of the equinoctial points, and consequently of the planets' *auges,* along the ecliptic. Ptolemy had explained it by giving the sphere of the stars a motion, in consequence, about the pole of the ecliptic, thus producing a steady eastward drift of the *auges.* But in a study widely available in translation as *De motu octave spere,* the ninth-century astronomer Thābit ibn Qurra proposed an oscillating model to account for what he thought was a periodic variation in precession, called "trepidation." The *Theorica planetarum* texts cited both theories, leaving the choice to the reader.

TABLES AND INSTRUMENTS

Following the pattern of the *Almagest,* then, each *Theorica planetarum* analyzed the "true" appearances from the earth into a composite of mean motions and compensating equations, and, conversely, showed how such parameters translated into actually observable measurements. But while the *Almagest* also provided the apparatus for calculating those parameters from the observational data combined with the mathematics of the models (and thus, incidentally, for tinkering with the models), the *Theorica planetarum* texts assumed that readers had access to one of the various tables that by the Middle Ages circulated separately from their prototype in the *Almagest* and that reflected in the mixed provenance of their data the subsequent touch of Indian and Islamic hands.

Belonging to an independent genre, a set of tables (Arabic: *zīj*) had its own accompanying instructions, or canons, and could be used without reference to the models. The first tables to enter Europe stemmed from the ninth-century Arabic astronomer and mathematician al-Khwārizmī; rendered into Latin by Adelard of Bath in 1126, they were subsequently adjusted for the dating of the Christian era and for various European meridians. Somewhat later they were joined by another set, the Toledan Tables by the eleventh-century astronomer al-Zarqālī, whose translated canons were particularly popular. In the 1260's Alfonso X of Spain ordered the compilation of tables designed to be universal; preliminary calculations allowed the user to adjust for meridian and epoch. Extant only in the form given them by John of Lignères, Jehan des Murs, and John of Saxony in Paris in the 1320's, and generally accompanied by the canons of one or another editor, the Alfonsine Tables remained the standard for European astronomy until the sixteenth century.

Using the tables with an understanding of the models behind them was made easier by versions of the *Theorica planetarum* that translated the models directly into calculating instruments. The earliest such instrument in the Latin West was Campanus of Novara's equatorium.

In his *Theorica planetarum* (*ca.* 1260), Campanus gave instructions for assembling sets of graduated disks into physical models of the planets' circles (ecliptic, equant, epicycle). With each disk then set from the tables to the appropriate mean *motus,* a planet's true place appeared under a string stretched from the center of the instrument, through the point marking the planet on the epicycle disk, and onto the ecliptic scale etched on the rim. Inspired perhaps by Arabic instruments, the equatorium underwent improvement in the fourteenth and fifteenth centuries; in particular, Campanus' separate models were brought together into a single mechanism allowing for all possible combinations of circles.

PTOLEMY'S PLACE IN THE MIDDLE AGES

The replacement of mathematics by mechanics in medieval Europeans' general understanding and use of Ptolemaic astronomy placed an emphasis on its coherence as a total structure, an emphasis reinforced by knowledge of Ptolemy's own attempt at unification in his *Planetary Hypotheses* and of similar efforts by Arab cosmologers such as al-Farghānī (Alfraganus) and al-Biṭrūjī (Alpetragius). Of a piece with such structural concerns, but generally critical of them, were the writings of later European cosmologers who worried about the incompatibility of Ptolemy's eccentrics, equants, and epicycles with Aristotle's universe of nested spheres rotating uniformly about a common center. Among the better-known critiques was Henry of Langenstein's *De reprobatione ecentricorum et epiciclorum,* referred to in some manuscripts as simply *Contra theoricam planetarum.*

Ptolemaic astronomy in the Middle Ages served practical and pedagogical ends rather than theoretical ones. Writers aimed at designing tables and instruments rather than at carrying out systematic observations aimed at articulating and improving the system. For the most part, it was only the astrologer who needed astronomy at the time, in order to be free of the vagaries of weather and location in determining the positions of the planets. Not until the later fifteenth century, with the work of Johannes Regiomontanus (in particular his completion of Georg Peurbach's *Epitome Almagesti*), did theoretical mathematical astronomy begin to attract scholarly interest for its own sake and bring a return to the *Almagest* itself. When it did, the Ptolemaic system, pressed perhaps precisely by the mechanical and cosmological concerns noted above, had only a short future.

BIBLIOGRAPHY

Recent surveys of medieval astronomy (with bibliography) may be found in Olaf Pedersen and Mogens Pihl, *Early Physics and Astronomy* (1974), and in David C. Lindberg, ed., *Science in the Middle Ages* (1978). Olaf Pedersen's *A Survey of the Almagest* (1974) sets out the elements of Ptolemy's system. For a recent translation of the *Almagest,* see G. J. Toomer, *Ptolemy's Almagest* (1984). Abridged translations of various primary sources may be found in Edward Grant, ed., *A Source Book in Medieval Science* (1974).

An edition of Robert Grosseteste's *De spera* appears in Ludwig Baur, *Die philosophischen Werke des Robert Grosseteste* (1912). Sacrobosco's treatise receives full scholarly treatment and an English translation in Lynn Thorndike, *The Sphere of Sacrobosco and Its Commentators* (1949). Until Pedersen's definitive edition of the most popular *Theorica planetarum* appears, readers can turn for a Latin text of this treatise to Francis J. Carmody's *Theorica planetarum Gerardi* (1942). For a discussion of the various treatises called *Theorica planetarum,* see Olaf Pedersen, "The *Theorica planetarum* Literature of the Middle Ages," in *Classica et mediaevalia,* **23** (1962).

Emmanuel Poulle provides a detailed survey of the tools of medieval planetary theory in *Les sources astronomiques (textes, tables, instruments)* (1981), *Les instruments de la théorie des planètes selon Ptolémée: Equatoires et horologerie planétaire du XIIIe au XVIe siècle,* 2 vols. (1980), and *Les tables alphonsines, avec les canons de Jean de Saxe* (1984). Other studies include G. J. Toomer, "A Survey of the Toledan Tables," in *Osiris,* **15** (1968); and John D. North, "The Alfonsine Tables in England," in Yasukatsu Maeyama and Walter Gabriel Saltzer, eds., *Prismata* (1977). Owen Gingerich and Barbara Welther have used the computer to analyze "The Accuracy of the Toledan Tables," also in *Prismata.*

For Campanus of Novara's discussion of the equatorium, see Francis S. Benjamin, Jr., and G. J. Toomer, *Campanus of Novara and Medieval Planetary Theory: Theorica planetarum* (1971), which contains the Latin text and an English translation of Campanus' *Theorica planetarum.* Later versions of the equatorium are presented in Derek J. Price, ed., *The Equatorie of the Planetis* (1955).

On precession the basic text is Thābit ibn Qurra's *De motu octave spere,* which has been edited by Francis J. Carmody in *The Astronomical Works of Thabit b. Qurra* (1960); for a translation, see O. Neugebauer, "Thâbit ben Qurra 'On the Solar Year' and 'On the Motion of the Eighth Sphere,' " in *Proceedings of the American Philosophical Society,* **106** (1962). For discussions of trepidation, see Bernard R. Goldstein, "On the Theory of Trepidation," in *Centaurus,* **10** (1965); and Willy Hartner, "Trepidation and Planetary Theories," in *Oriente e occidente nel medioevo: Filosofia e scienze* (Accademia Nazionale dei Lincei, Atti dei Convegni, **13** [1971]).

On Henry of Langenstein's criticism of Ptolemaic astronomy, see Claudia Kren, "Homocentric Astronomy in the Latin West," in *Isis,* **59** (1968).

MICHAEL S. MAHONEY

[See also **Adelard of Bath; Alfonsine Tables; Aristotle in the Middle Ages; Armillary Sphere; Astrolabe; Astronomy; Calendars and Reckoning of Time; Clockwork, Planetary; Computus; Equatorium; Gerard of Cremona; Grosseteste, Robert; Henry of Langenstein; Jehan des Murs; Mathematics; Paris, University of; Physics; Sundials; Toledan Tables.**]

PTOLEMY OF LUCCA (*ca.* 1236–*ca.* 1326), a Dominican student of Thomas Aquinas and later bishop of Torcello. He was a historian and political theorist who developed his theories along two divergent lines. First, he was a republican. Starting

Queen Jeanne praying near the tomb of St. Louis. Miniature by Jean Pucelle from the *Hours of Jeanne d'Évreux,* early 14th century. THE METROPOLITAN MUSEUM OF ART, NEW YORK, CLOISTERS COLLECTION MS 54.1.2, fol. 102v

from the Aristotelian definition of governments as either despotic or nondespotic (the latter being either royal or political), Ptolemy advanced to classify royal government as despotic. The crucial contrast is between a political regime with a ruler limited by laws, and one in which the ruler is above positive law and cannot be called to account. Second, Ptolemy was a convinced papal hierocrat and believed that all lordship comes from God. Since Christ's advent temporal power has been invested in the popes, his successors. The common threads in these two theoretical elaborations are Ptolemy's anti-imperialism and his Italian patriotism, both of which are revealed throughout his writings.

BIBLIOGRAPHY

Sources. Historia ecclesiastica, Ludovicus Muratori, ed. (1727, repr. 1977), 754–1,242; *Tractatus de iurisdictione ecclesiae super regnum Apuliae et Siciliae,* Stephanus Baluze, ed., in J. D. Mansi, ed., *Miscellanea,* I (1761), a work attributed by Baluze to Cardinal Nicholas of Aragon; *Exaemeron,* T. Masetti, ed. (1880); *Determinatio compendiosa de iurisdictione imperii,* Marius F. Krammer, ed. (1909); *Die Annalen des Tholomeus von Lucca,* Bernhard Schmeidler, ed. (1930); *De regimine principum,* a work begun by Thomas Aquinas and, from bk. II, chap. 4, completed by Ptolemy, in *Divi Thomae Aquinatis Opuscula philosophica,* Raimondo M. Spiazzi, ed. (1973).

Studies. Robert W. Carlyle and Alexander J. Carlyle, *A History of Mediaeval Political Theory in the West,* V, *The Political Theory of the Thirteenth Century* (1928, repr. 1953); Charles T. Davis, "Ptolemy of Lucca and the Roman Republic," in *Proceedings of the American Philosophical Society,* **118** (1974), and "Roman Patriotism and Republican Propaganda: Ptolemy of Lucca and Pope Nicholas III," in *Speculum,* **50** (1975).

ELAINE GOLDEN ROBISON

[See also **Aquinas, St. Thomas; Political Theory, Western European.**]

PUCELLE, JEAN (*d.* 1334), a major figure of Parisian manuscript illumination from about 1320 to his death. Pucelle was the first French artist to incorporate Italian spatial and pictorial concepts into his work in a major way. The basic elements of his style persist throughout his career: clarity of expression, graceful elegance, refined but lively decoration, and a concern for three-dimensional spatial representation.

His manuscripts are customarily divided into two groups, those preceding his contact with Italian art and those of his maturity, which show strong Italian influence. Of his youthful works the best known is the Franciscan Breviary (Vatican Library, MS urb. lat. 603) made for Blanche of France, a collaborative effort of which Pucelle painted only a small portion. The three works most securely attributed to him are works of his maturity: the Billyng Bible (Paris, Bibliothèque Nationale, MS lat. 11935), the Belleville Breviary (Paris, Bibliothèque Nationale, MS lat. 10483–10484), and the *Hours of Jeanne d'Évreux* (New York, The Metropolitan Museum of Art, Cloisters Collection, MS 54.1.2), this last the first major work of French illumination painted in grisaille (tones of gray) rather than in color. Two other works usually attributed to Pucelle are the Breviary of Jeanne d'Évreux (Chantilly, Musée Condé, MS 51) and the *Miracles de Notre Dame* of Gautier de Coinci

(Paris, Bibliothèque Nationale, MS nouv. acq. fr. 24541). Despite the relative brevity of his artistic activity, Pucelle is a major figure whose style dominated Parisian art long after his death. His stylistic influence not only appears in manuscript illumination but also has echoes in metalwork, embroidery, and ivory carving.

BIBLIOGRAPHY

François Avril, "Trois manuscrits de l'entourage de Jean Pucelle," in *Revue de l'art,* **9** (1970), and *Manuscript Painting at the Court of France: The Fourteenth Century (1310–1380)* (1978), 11–23; Françoise Baron, "Enlumineurs, peintres et sculpteurs parisiens du XIVe et XVe siècles d'après les archives de l'Hôpital Saint-Jacques," in *Bulletin archéologique du Comité des travaux historiques et scientifiques* (1971); Florens Deuchler, "Jean Pucelle—Facts and Fictions," in *Metropolitan Museum of Art Bulletin,* n.s. **29** (1971); Kathleen Morand, *Jean Pucelle* (1962); Carl Nordenfalk, "Maître Honoré and Maître Pucelle," in *Apollo,* **79** (1964); Lilian Randall, "Games and the Passion in Pucelle's Hours of Jeanne d'Évreux," in *Speculum,* **47** (1972); J. J. Rorimer, *The Hours of Jeanne d'Évreux* (1957).

ELLEN KOSMER

[See also **Book of Hours; Breviary (with illustration); Gothic Art; Manuscript Illumination, European.**]

PULGAR, HERNANDO DEL. See **Spanish Literature: Biography.**

PUMPKIN DOME. See **Dome.**

PUNCTUATION (Medieval Latin: *punctuatio,* application of points or marks, punctuation). The history of punctuation in Latin script may be conceived as a slow and incomplete shift from systems of rhetorical distinctions within a text to systems of syntactical distinctions. The various signs or punctuation marks that implement these systems developed and changed in meaning. While the period is attested as early as the second century A.D., the exclamation point occurs only in the sixteenth. The books of classical antiquity contained little punctuation in the modern sense. Since the classical world was primarily concerned with the auditory effect of the spoken word, rhetorical considerations of oral delivery shaped attempts at punctuation. The two best-known types of visual distinction between members of a phrase that survived into the very early Middle Ages were the use of a blank space to mark a pause (most ancient books favored the *scriptura continua,* handwriting in which words directly followed one another without intervening space) and the system *per cola et commata,* in which the various rhetorical sense units of a text were laid out line by line, each unit beginning a new line. Theoreticians nonetheless developed a threefold system that distinguished punctuation by points placed at three different levels (lower, median, and raised), marking brief, medium, and long pauses.

The disappearance of Latin as a living language entailed a greater need for punctuation that distinguished the syntactical and semantic elements of a sentence; early medieval manuscripts display a great variety of usages. The Carolingian renaissance brought with it new and incomplete efforts at systematization, including the relatively common use of periods or points and slanted strokes for short stops, and combinations of points and hooks or commas for long stops—roughly comparable with our modern commas and periods, respectively. A simplified system widely attested in liturgical manuscripts of the tenth and eleventh centuries used a lowered point for short stops and a raised point for full stops. The introduction of an early form of the modern sign for a question mark around the eleventh century provided a relatively complete system of signs that seems to have gained general currency thanks to its systematic application in manuscripts copied by Cistercian monks for the texts that were read aloud during meals. Punctuation continued to develop through the late Middle Ages, the Renaissance, and well into modern times. Certain types of punctuation signs are characteristic of certain regions or book-producing centers at certain periods, and thus aid the paleographer in determining the origins of manuscripts. However, changing practice often led medieval readers to add or adapt punctuation in the books they used, so that manuscript punctuation may be presumed original only after careful scrutiny.

BIBLIOGRAPHY

Bernhard Bischoff, *Paläographie des römischen Altertums und des abendländischen Mittelalters* (1979), 214–219; J. Moreau-Maréchal, "Recherches sur la ponctuation," in *Scriptorium,* **22** (1968); Jean Vézin, "Le point d'interrogation, un élément de datation et de localisation des manuscrits: L'exemple de Saint-Denis au IXe siècle," *ibid.,* **34** (1980); Donatella Frioli, "Grafia e interpunzione del latino nel medioevo," in *Studi medievali,* 3rd ser., **25** (1984).

MICHAEL MCCORMICK

[See also **Latin Language; Paleography, Western European.**]

PURGATORY, ISLAMIC CONCEPT OF. In Islamic tradition, the closest parallel to the Roman Catholic doctrine of purgatory is expressed by the term *barzakh,* a word of Persian origin that denotes both the abode of the dead prior to Judgment Day and the indefinite period of time between death and resurrection. The word *barzakh* occurs in three passages of the Koran, where it signifies a barrier between the living and the dead (suras 23:100; 25:53), as well as an isthmus between two seas (sura 55:20). From this early sense, there developed the notion of an intermediary realm where the dead await judgment. There is a rich literature on the subject in Arabic.

The dead in *barzakh* do not practice atonement for unexpiated sins in order to purify their souls for the ascent to heaven, as in Catholic doctrine. Rather, in Islam the soul's ultimate destiny is sealed at death, in accordance with the primordial decree of God. *Barzakh* represents a period and a place of waiting; it accommodates the righteous as well as the wicked. In this respect the doctrine has more affinity with ancient notions of the underworld than with Catholic conceptions. Nevertheless, for the virtuous, *barzakh* is a foretaste of paradise, and their period of waiting is pleasant. The wicked, however, are shown their future torments and suffer the pains of hellfire in anticipation. This is comparable in some respects to the belief of the Eastern Orthodox Church.

Barzakh, which in some accounts is described as a place shaped like a mortar with a narrow base and flaring sides, is one of the three realms made by God. There is, first, the realm of this world (*dār al-dunyā*), then the realm of *barzakh,* and, finally, "the realm of everlastingness" (*dār al-qarār*). These realms exist along a continuum, and there is a hidden affinity among them. Just as in the realm of this world, it is the body that is manifest and that conveys sensations of pain and pleasure to the spirit, so, in the realm of *barzakh,* the spirit becomes manifest and acts as the conduit for sensations of torment or felicity to the body, now hidden in its grave.

Accordingly, the so-called "torment of the tomb" (*ᶜadhāb al-qabr*) is inseparably linked to the doctrine of *barzakh.* Originally, it was held that all the dead, including the righteous—and even the prophet Muḥammad—had to undergo the torments of the tomb. These torments are various and are described in graphic and chilling detail in the literature. There is, for example, the dreadful suffering known as *ḍaghṭa,* or "pressure," in which the walls of the grave compress and constrict the deceased intolerably. These torments are possible because death betokens not annihilation, but merely the severance of body and spirit; and the dead are endowed with a curiously attenuated sentience. Thus, they can hear but are mute, or they can speak, but their voices are inaudible or audible only to animals. A corpse knows who is washing it, but it cannot communicate. The newly buried dead can hear the footsteps of their kinfolk slowly quitting the graveside but are unable to call them back with their cries.

Inside the grave, the two interrogating angels, Munkar and Nakīr, question the dead on matters of belief. If the replies of the deceased are inadequate, the angels proceed to torture him, but if he can answer to their satisfaction, they leave him in peace. At this point, the dead are afforded a glimpse of their future, irrevocable destinies: the saved gaze upon paradise; the damned suffer a vision of hell.

Certainly early sects, most notably the Muᶜtazilites, questioned this indiscriminate mingling of wicked and righteous in the ordeals of the grave. Certain theologians, such as the Muᶜtazilite Abu 'l-Hudhayl al-ᶜAllāf (*fl. ca.* 840), in the desire to uphold God's justice, denied that any but unbelievers underwent the torment of the tomb. The accepted belief that innocent children might suffer in the grave came under particular scrutiny. Such reactions seem gradually to have modified the doctrine; later discussions usually state that, whereas *barzakh* represents the pit of hell for unbelievers, for believers it represents paradise. The Hanbalite theologian Ibn Qayyim al-Jawzīyah (*d.* 1350) speaks, for example, of "the torments and the felicities of the grave."

To be sure, certain traditions allowed for intercession by the living on behalf of the dead. The

PURGATORY, WESTERN

great theologian al-Ghazālī (*d.* 1111) cites examples of sinners who repented and called on God's mercy and who were, as a result, removed from hell. In general, however, *barzakh* was viewed as the shadowy realm where the soul's fixed and eternal fate was prefigured.

BIBLIOGRAPHY

Ragnar Eklund, *Life Between Death and Resurrection According to Islam* (1941); Abū Ḥāmid al-Ghazālī, *Al-Durrah al-fakhira fī kashf ʿulūm al-ākhira,* Lucien Gautier, ed. and trans., *La perle précieuse de Ghazali: Traité d'eschatologie musulmane* (1878), and *The Precious Pearl,* Jane I. Smith, trans. (1979); Ibn Qayyim al-Jawzīya, *Al-Rūḥ . . . fiʾl-kalām ʿalā arwāḥ al-amwāt waʾl-aḥyāʾ* (1966); John Macdonald, "The Twilight of the Dead," in *Islamic Studies,* 4 (1965); Jane I. Smith "Concourse Between the Living and the Dead in Islamic Eschatological Literature," in *History of Religions,* **19** (1980); Jane I. Smith and Yvonne Y. Haddad, *The Islamic Understanding of Death and Resurrection* (1981); Jalāl al-Dīn al-Suyūtī, *Sharḥ al-ṣudūr bi-sharḥ ḥāl al-mawtā waʾl-qubūr* (1891).

ERIC L. ORMSBY

[See also **Islam, Religion; Paradise, Islamic; Philosophy and Theology, Islamic.**]

PURGATORY, WESTERN CONCEPT OF. The doctrine of purgatory developed mainly out of the ancient Christian custom of praying for the dead, a custom referred to as early as the second century in epitaphs and inscriptions from the catacombs, in Christian literature, and in liturgical sources. From such prayer, especially offering the Eucharist at the graveside and on the anniversary of death, arose the medieval practice of offering large numbers of masses for the dead. By the seventh century a remembrance of the dead had become common at all weekday masses, and by the fourteenth century, also at masses on Sundays and feast days. Prayer for the dead took on a special importance in the eighth century with the formation of special fraternities for this purpose. They received lavish support from all levels of society on the understanding that many masses would be offered for a donor after his death. These societies were often connected with a monastery, where there were large numbers of priests to offer the masses. An annual day of special prayers for the dead was observed in Spain during the seventh century. At the abbey of Cluny the day was 2 November which, in the eleventh century, began to be observed in other monasteries. From these it spread to the whole church as All Souls Day.

The doctrine of purgatory was greatly influenced by the form of public penance in the early church. After a grave sin had been committed the sinner was readmitted into the church only after years, or even a lifetime, of severe penances, although a penitent who had become seriously ill would be reconciled before the completion of his penance. It became accepted teaching that divine justice required every sin to be punished. Penances were performed to discharge this debt even for minor sins. The Rule of St. Benedict (*ca.* 540), for instance, exhorts the monk to direct his Lenten penances toward the remission of past negligence. The change from public penance to private confession did not eliminate the practice of expiating sins by means of bodily penances. Gradually, however, it became more and more common to reconcile penitents before they had completed their penance, to the point that by about 1000 the well-nigh universal practice was to forgive the sins at the time they were confessed. But the debt remained, even though the sins had been forgiven.

Prayers for the dead, coupled with the belief that satisfaction had to be made for every sin committed, led inevitably to the full doctrine of purgatory. Sinners who neglected, or who had had no chance to perform, voluntary penance in this life would have to expiate their sins after death, in purgatory.

In this, as in so many other matters, the writings of Augustine (*d.* 430) were a normative source for medieval theology. Although he believed that the eternal fate of an individual was determined by a particular judgment immediately after his death, Augustine cited I Corinthians 3:11–15 in support of the teaching that failings not expiated by good works in the present world are cleansed "by fire" in the next. He did not specify the precise nature of this purgative fire, but said that the pain involved would be intense.

He also taught that suffrages—prayers, alms, and the celebration of Mass performed by the living on behalf of the dead—were effective substitutes for the temporal punishment due to sin. Since the damned cannot be assisted by the prayers of the living, the existence of a state between heaven and hell is implied; it eventually received the name "purgatory," that is, "a place of cleansing." Augustine advanced II Maccabees 12:43–45 as scriptural evidence, but for him the universal observance of the church was sufficient justification.

PURGATORY, WESTERN

Augustine's hesitation with regard to the nature of the fire was later resolved by describing it as "real," similar to the fires of hell. Caesarius of Arles (*d.* 542), for example, stressed that the fires of purgatory were very painful and of long duration for those who had not made satisfaction for their sins in this life. Just as sinners being reconciled to the church had to expiate their sins by prayer and fasting, so the dead could be assisted by the same ascetical practices performed on their behalf by the living. His teaching was based explicitly on a distinction between mortal and venial sins: the former are serious faults by which a sinner merits hell if they remain unconfessed; the latter are minor faults that delay entrance into heaven. Caesarius justified this teaching from Scripture (Dan. 7:10; Ezek. 24:11; I Cor. 3:13), interpreted in the unpedantic style of the time.

The doctrine of purgatory was authoritatively confirmed and developed by Pope Gregory I (*d.* 604). He believed that because the end of time was near, a clearer view of the future life had been granted to the church. According to his teaching, the righteous entered heaven at death, and the wicked, hell. The imperfectly righteous, however, remained for a time "in certain mansions," to be cleansed by a purgatorial fire. Biblical texts were used in, or at least attached to, his dogmatic expositions. For example, he inferred from Jesus' statement that the sin against the Spirit would not be forgiven in this world or the next (Matt. 12:32) that there must be some sins which can be forgiven in the next life. Part of the purgatorial suffering was the pain of a continuing separation from God; that it was not permanent was used later to distinguish the pains of purgatory from those of hell.

Gregory reports visions of suffering souls who pleaded for prayers, including one of a monk who was released from purgatory after thirty masses had been celebrated for him on consecutive days. This string of masses, known as "Gregorian Masses," became a popular form of suffrage, first of all in monasteries and then, during the High Middle Ages, more generally.

The doctrine of purgatory continued to attract the attention of theologians, although nothing essentially new was said. Many stories were told illustrating the efficacy of prayers and penances by members of the church on earth in releasing the poor souls from their torments. A large number of these stories concerned visions or dreams in which a pathetic appeal for prayers was made by a soul suffering in purgatory. Often there was a second visitation, after the suffrages requested had been performed, in which the release of the soul from purgatory was announced. Accounts of these visions were widely circulated and formed an important part of medieval piety. The sufferings themselves were variously described. As comparable to those of hell they were believed to be more terrible than any earthly pain. The main scriptural evidence in discussions of purgatory continued to be I Corinthians 3:11–15. Purgatory is by definition a temporary state which will not continue after the general judgment. But without the prayers, alms, and penance of the church on earth it was expected that many souls would remain in purgatory until the end of time, especially those who had repented only on their deathbeds.

The great Scholastic theologians of the thirteenth century placed the traditional doctrine of purgatory in the overall context of the Christian faith. They accepted the doctrine itself unquestioningly for three reasons: it was a traditional and authoritative teaching of the church; it could be found in Scripture, especially in the ubiquitous I Corinthians 3:11–15; and it was reasonable that souls who were not bad enough to be condemned to hell and not good enough for heaven should be purified before entering God's presence. Purgatory was believed to be located near the center of the earth, beside hell and limbo.

The traditional teaching that the slightest pains of purgatory were more severe than the greatest suffering on earth was universally accepted. They were made more bearable, however, because the souls had a surety of entering heaven as soon as satisfaction for all their sins had been completed. This doctrine was proclaimed solemnly by Pope Benedict XII in 1336.

The subtlety of Scholastic reasoning is illustrated by the discussion about the possibility of guilt persisting in purgatory. One theory stated that venial sins would have been forgiven at death by an act of pure love for God. In purgatory, therefore, only the debt for these sins remains; because they have been forgiven, there is no guilt. The authority of Thomas Aquinas (*d.* 1274) was sufficient to ensure that this view would become the common teaching, despite the fact that Bonaventure (*d.* 1274) and Duns Scotus (*d.* 1308) taught the opposite—that guilt remained in purgatory for (venial) sins not forgiven before death.

Medieval theologians also accounted for differences in duration and intensity of suffering. The former was thought to depend on the number of sins, the latter on their gravity. But by far the greatest suffering was being prevented from entering heaven.

Aquinas recognized that indulgences were not intended for the souls in purgatory. Nevertheless, when the wording specifically allowed it, he accepted their being used as suffrages and so applied to the poor souls. The practice of suffrages in general was justified on the basis of the Communion of Saints. The belief was that all Christians were united as the Body of Christ, which was taken to be the visible church. Therefore, the prayers of the "church militant" (that is, on earth) could assist the "church suffering" (that is, in purgatory). The idea, however, that the souls in purgatory could, by their prayers, assist the living was a postmedieval development.

Dante (*d.* 1321) drew abundantly upon Scholastic theology in his *Divine Comedy*. The *Purgatory* can be viewed as an explication of the principle, found in Thomas Aquinas, that when the guilt of sin has been removed the love of God is restored to the sinner, who, therefore, freely wills to take upon himself the punishment for his past sins or, at least, to bear patiently the punishment God inflicts upon him. Thus, the sinners in the *Purgatory* gladly accept the purification by which they rise toward God. To emphasize this, Dante pictured purgatory not under the earth beside hell but on a mountain rising out of the ocean at the antipodes of Jerusalem. At the summit of the mountain is the garden of Eden, the primal earthly paradise where man's first innocence is regained and surpassed as the soul moves into heaven. Dante depicted the souls in purgatory still bearing the stain of sin. Each person prepares for the vision of God by eliminating the sinful attitudes that impede progress. Prayers for the dead, as the expression of Christian love, are welcomed as an aid in the cleansing that the souls eagerly pursue. The purgation is completed not by a divine pronouncement, but when the soul realizes that nothing in itself now hinders it from entering the presence of God. Similar ideas about purgatory, especially about the joy of the suffering souls, appear in the teachings of the mystic Catherine of Genoa (*d.* 1510).

During the Middle Ages only a few heretics, such as the Waldenses and Albigensians, denied the common teaching about purgatory. But at the Second Council of Lyons (1274) objections were made by the Greek bishops to the detailed Latin doctrine, especially on the reality of the fire of purgatory and the distinction between guilt and punishment. In consequence, the conciliar statement on purgatory is restrained, stating only that Christians who have not fully expiated for their sins will undergo purgative, purifying pains after death, and that they can be aided by the traditional suffrages. In 1439 another council attended by Greek bishops was held in Florence. Purgatory was again an important point of discussion. After extensive debate a general statement much the same as that of Lyons was accepted.

Despite the limited dogmatic formulations at these councils—counted as ecumenical in the West—the popular ideas of purgatory continued unaltered. The unsettled conditions during the fourteenth and fifteenth centuries, especially the ravages caused by the Black Death (1347–1350), focused the attention of the survivors on the needs of the dead. A heightened recourse to prayers, alms, and particularly to an abundance of masses for the dead led to abuses that were among the causes of the various reform movements of the fifteenth and sixteenth centuries.

BIBLIOGRAPHY

Adhémar d'Alès, "La question du purgatoire au concile de Florence en 1438," in *Gregorianum,* 3 (1922); Catherine of Genoa, *Purgation and Purgatory,* S. Hughes, trans. (1979), 69–87; Réginald Garrigou-Lagrange, *Life Everlasting,* P. Cummins, trans. (1952), 147–201; Jacques Le Goff, *The Birth of Purgatory,* Arthur Goldhammer, trans. (1984); John A. MacCulloch, *Medieval Faith and Fable* (1932, repr. 1973); A. Michel, "Purgatoire," in *Dictionnaire de théologie catholique,* A. Vacant, E. Mangenot, and É. Amann, eds., XIII (1936); Dorothy L. Sayers, "The Meaning of Purgatory," in her *Introductory Papers on Dante* (1954); Francis X. Shouppe, *Purgatory Explained by the Lives and Legends of the Saints* (1893, repr. 1973).

DANIEL CALLAM

[See also **Dead, Office of the; Death and Burial, in Europe; Espurgatoire St. Patrice; Indulgences; Paradise, Western Concept of; Penance and Penitentials.**]

PÜTERICH VON REICHERTSHAUSEN, JAKOB III (*ca.* 1400–1469), scion of a rich Munich patrician family that after the acquisition of the castle of Reichertshausen (between Munich and

Ingolstadt) was entitled to call itself part of the Bavarian nobility. He took part in the campaign against the Hussites and afterward occupied a number of high state offices under Duke Albrecht III. The culmination of his political career came with his appointment in 1466 to an advisory council to the young Albrecht IV and his brother Sigmund.

Püterich had strong antiquarian interests that led him to be an enthusiastic participant in jousting tourneys and to collect manuscripts of German poetry. We are well informed about his literary interests from his *Ehrenbrief* (1462), a poetic letter addressed to Archduchess Mechthild, the spouse of Albrecht VI of Austria. This little work is of some value as an indication of the extent to which the German works of the twelfth and thirteenth centuries were known and regarded in the fifteenth century.

The poem consists of 148 clumsily written seven-line strophes patterned after those in *Der jüngere Titurel.* It is composed in the traditional medieval epistolary form, with *salutatio* (1–29), *narratio* (30–144), and *conclusio* (145–148). Its purpose is to express extravagant gratitude to Mechthild, whose name appears in the work in the form of an acrostic, for having sent Püterich a list of the ninety-four manuscripts in her collection, twenty-three of which were of works he had never heard of before. In return he sends her a list of his 164 manuscripts, describing a number of them in his poem. Püterich furnishes the names of a number of authors and works unknown today, but also mentions such masters as Hartmann von Aue and Gottfried von Strassburg. Most of all he admired Wolfram von Eschenbach and Hadamar von Laber, the writers he sought to emulate. Püterich occupies a niche in Wolfram scholarship for having located his grave, as he narrates, in the town near Ansbach that is now known as Wolframs-Eschenbach.

BIBLIOGRAPHY

Editions. Arthur Goette, ed., *Der Ehrenbrief des Jakob Püterich von Reichertshausen* (1899); Theodor von Karajan, ed., "Der Ehrenbrief Jacob Püterichs von Reicherzhausen," in *Zeitschrift für deutsches Alterthum,* 6 (1848).

Studies. Gerhard Eis, "Püterich von Reichertshausen," in Karl Langosch, ed., *Die deutsche Literatur des Mittelalters, Verfasserlexikon,* V, *Nachträge* (1955); "Püterich," in *Allgemeine deutsche Biographie,* XXVI (1888).

Henry Kratz

[See also **Albrecht von Scharfenberg; Gottfried von Strassburg; Hadamar von Laber; Hartmann von Aue; Wolfram von Eschenbach.**]

PUY. Appearing in France in the twelfth century as a religious fraternity or mutual aid society, the *puy* soon became almost exclusively a literary society. There were *puys* in many French cities, each presided over by a prince of poets, who was elected each year and was obliged to give a banquet at the annual poetry contest. Occasionally plays were performed at these competitions.

BIBLIOGRAPHY

William Tydeman, *The Theatre in the Middle Ages* (1978), 201.

Alan E. Knight

[See also **Drama, Western European; French Literature: To 1200.**]

PYNSON, RICHARD (*d. ca.* 1530). Printer and contemporary of Wynkyn de Worde, Pynson was most likely born in Normandy and probably studied at the University of Paris. It is not known precisely when he set up shop in London, though there is evidence that he arrived sometime prior to 1492, the earliest date to appear in his colophons. About 1490 Pynson commissioned Guillaume Le Tailleur of Rouen to print two English law books, Sir Thomas Littleton's *Tenores novelli* and Nicolas Statham's *Abridgment of Cases,* to be sold in England. Around the same time he seems to have acquired the stock of books printed by William de Machlinia. In 1508 Pynson succeeded William Faques, also probably a Norman, as the king's printer.

Pynson was the first English printer to employ Roman type, and he was innovative in other respects as well. His printer's mark of about 1500 shows a deep bend in the border, evidence that it was printed from a metal block rather than the customary wood block. Like de Worde, Pynson was adept at appropriating book illustrations. The pilgrims in his undated edition of Chaucer's *Canterbury Tales* (*ca.* 1491) are crude copies of Caxton's, and the floral scroll borders first used by William de Machlinia in his English primer (*ca.* 1485) appear in several Pynson editions. The woodcuts of the French printer Antoine Vérard, the most influential and sophisticated publisher of books in the vernacular in the fifteenth century, were a main source for Pynson's illustrations.

Among the notable illustrated books produced by Pynson are Lydgate's *Fall of Princes* (1494), Pierre Gringore's *Castell of Laboure,* translated by Alexander Barclay (1505), *The Kalender of Shepherdes* (1506), and Alexander Barclay's translation of Sebastian Brant's *Shyp of Folys* (1509). The Morton Missal (1500), with several woodcut initials printed in red and elaborate branch and bird borders, is Pynson's finest effort. According to some art historians, it is the finest English missal produced at that time.

BIBLIOGRAPHY

Arthur M. Hind, *An Introduction to a History of Woodcut,* 2 vols. (1935, repr. 1963); Edward Hodnett, *English Woodcuts, 1480–1535* (1935, repr. 1973); Henry R. Plomer, *Wynkyn de Worde and His Contemporaries* (1925).

MARTHA WESTCOTT DRIVER

[See also **Caxton, William; Printing, Origins of; Woodcut; Wynkyn de Worde.**]

PYXIS (*pl.,* pyxides), a small, usually round, lidded container, normally made of ivory, bone, enamel, or—less commonly—silver. Many pyxides date from the early Christian period, but their original function is uncertain. The size, prevalence, and decoration of these pyxides suggest that they were used in the early liturgy, possibly as containers for the consecrated bread of the Eucharist or for incense; some may have functioned as reliquaries. In the medieval Latin West, the lidded box, now called the pyx (*pl.,* pyxes), was restricted to holding the host; these pyxes were used particularly to carry eucharistic wafers to the sick, as they still are today. An example is an ivory pyx (*ca.* 970) from Córdoba (New York, Metropolitan Museum, Cloisters Collection).

BIBLIOGRAPHY

Eucharistic Vessels of the Middle Ages (1975); Henri Leclerq, "Pyxide," in *Dictionnaire d'archéologie chrétienne et de liturgie,* XIV, pt. 2 (1948), 1,983–1,995; Kurt Weitzmann, ed., *Age of Spirituality: Late Antique and Early Christian Art, Third to Seventh Century* (1979), 596–598; Paul Williamson, *An Introduction to Medieval Ivory Carving* (1982).

LESLIE BRUBAKER

[See also **Altar–Altar Apparatus; Byzantine Minor Arts (with illustration); Coptic Art; Ivory Carving (with illustrations).**]

QĀᶜA, a lofty reception room in a traditional Egyptian urban house of a wealthy family. It consisted of a square sunken central space flanked by

View of a *qāᶜa* looking through the sunken central space into one of the two *eyvāns.* REPRODUCED FROM EDWARD W. LANE, *AN ACCOUNT OF THE MANNERS AND CUSTOMS OF THE MODERN EGYPTIANS* (1836)

two raised *eyvāns* (*līwān* in Egypt), which were large, deep alcoves. The *eyvāns* were usually covered with a flat wooden roof; the central space was roofed with a ventilator-skylight. The floor of the central space was paved and might be provided with a fountain; the *eyvāns*—one step higher—were also spread with mats in summer and rugs in winter. Cushions and mattresses placed around the perimeter of the *eyvāns* provided seating. The origins of the *qāᶜa* plan are unknown, yet it is generally supposed that it developed from a plan found in eleventh-century houses of Cairo, where two *eyvāns* flanked an open court. By the thirteenth century, the *qāᶜa* plan was well established, when it was adapted for use in Muslim religious buildings, particularly madrasas.

JONATHAN M. BLOOM

[See also **Eyvān; Islamic Art and Architecture.**]

QAᶜBA. See **Kaaba.**

QADI (or *qāḍī* or *cadi*), an Islamic judge. Qadis were first appointed under the Umayyads as legal assistants to the provincial governors in the Muslim urban centers that arose after the Arab conquests. During this period they gave judgments according to their own discretion, relying on customary practice and informal Islamic religious and ethical norms. Increasingly, under the Abbasids, the qadi became a specialist in religious law, appointed by the central government and subordinate to the chief qadi of the capital. After the systematization of the law, the qadi made his decisions according to the authoritative doctrine contained in the texts of the school of law to which he belonged. His jurisdiction extended to Muslims only; the non-Muslim communities retained their own legal institutions.

In theory the Muslim judiciary was independent and the qadi's duties applied to all matters of civil and criminal law. In practice, however, this broad competence varied. Because the qadi had to depend on the willingness and ability of the government to enforce his decisions, the qadi's tribunals soon were superseded in such spheres as criminal and fiscal law by other institutions for the administration of justice. In addition, the formalistic nature of court procedure and the stringent rules of evidence curtailed the freedom and personal discretion he could exercise.

The qadi sat in a single-judge tribunal. Attached to the court were assistants having a variety of functions and expertise. Although he, as well as the parties before him, could consult a mufti (a private scholar of high reputation) for his opinion (*fatwā*), the qadi was not bound by his views. The qadi's decisions were final. Besides giving judgments in civil suits, he had the right to impose discretionary punishments (*taᶜzīr*, "deterrence"). The qadi was an important and influential official and assumed administrative responsibilities extending far beyond matters adjudicated in his court. For example, he supervised the administration of mosques, pious endowments (*awqāf*), and estates of inheritance; he acted as guardian for orphans and others; and he had wide powers in many other functions that involved the public welfare.

BIBLIOGRAPHY

Noel J. Coulson, *A History of Islamic Law* (1964); Joseph Schacht, *Introduction to Islamic Law* (1964); Émile Tyan, *Histoire de l'organisation judiciaire en pays de l'Islam,* 2nd ed. (1960).

JEANETTE A. WAKIN

[See also **Law, Islamic.**]

QĀHIR BI'LLĀH, AL- (*r.* 929, 932–934), Abbasid caliph whose two short reigns were dominated by political intrigue and financial crisis. He first reigned in 929, after his brother al-Muqtadir was deposed briefly by a palace revolution. Al-Muqtadir was soon restored, but in 932, while fighting against the powerful general Muᵓnis, with whom his relations had remained strained, he was killed. Muᶜnis now proposed Abu'l-ᶜAbbās Aḥmad, the son of al-Muqtadir, as caliph, apparently in an attempt to retain the financial support of the late caliph's family. But Muᵓnis and his men raised to the caliphate Muḥammad, the son of the earlier caliph al-Muᵓtadid (*d.* 892), with the regnal title al-Qāhir bi'llāh (the Victorious by God). Al-Qāhir was beset from the beginning by overwhelming problems. Al-Muqtadir's extravagance had drained the treasuries, the troops were being paid late, and general fiscal and military instability followed. Al-Qāhir dealt with al-Muqtadir's family with ex-

QĀᵓIM, AL-

treme cruelty, beating his mother mercilessly in order to extract information about hidden funds. Then he appointed as vizier Ibn Muqla, who was involved in intrigues from the beginning to depose the caliph. For the remainder of his reign, al-Qāhir was preoccupied with both revenge against al-Muqtadir's former supporters and the intrigues of his own vizier, chamberlain, and emir against him.

In 933, Muᵓnis, Ibn Muqla, and Ibn Yalbaq, the chamberlain, conspired to depose al-Qāhir. In an episode that was entirely typical of its time, the caliph frustrated their plot by exploiting hostilities between rival factions in the army. He turned the Sājī, a contingent of palace guards upon whom Muᵓnis and Yalbaq depended, against them. They had not made good their promise to put the Sājī troops on an equal footing with the more prestigious (and better paid) Ḥujarī troops in Baghdad. Al-Qāhir now won their support by making these same promises. Muᵓnis and Yalbaq were arrested and executed, and Ibn Muqla went into hiding. Over the next year, two different viziers served al-Qāhir, while the financial problems of the caliphate continued unabated. In April 934, Ibn Muqla toppled the caliph by inciting both the Sājī and Ḥujarī guards against him. Al-Qāhir was imprisoned and then blinded on the order of the new caliph, al-Rāḍī (934–940).

The reigns of al-Qāhir and al-Rāḍī marked the nadir of Abbasid power. From this time on, the caliphs were to be completely at the mercy of the armies and a succession of powerful military commanders.

BIBLIOGRAPHY

"Ghulām," in *Encyclopedia of Islam,* II, new ed. (1965); Aḥmad ibn Muḥammad Ibn Miskawayhi, *The Experiences of the Nations,* in David S. Margoliouth and H. F. Amedroz, eds. and trans., *The Eclipse of the ᶜAbbasid Caliphate,* IV (1921), 217–223, 272–328.

PAULA SANDERS

[See also **Abbasids; Caliphate; Muqtadir, al- ; Seljuks.**]

QĀᵓIM, AL- (1031–1075), properly al-Qāᵓim bi-amr Allāh, Abbasid caliph whose rule bridged the Buyid and Seljuk periods. His long reign was characterized both by intense battles for political power between various emirs and by his largely successful efforts to restore the caliphate's prestige through the manipulation of symbols of authority, particularly titulature.

During the first part of his reign, the Buyid emirs Jalāl al-Dawla and Abū Kālījār, his nephew, constantly attempted to surpass each other by acquiring increasingly elaborate titles from the caliph. In 1038, al-Qāᵓim granted Jalāl al-Dawla the titles *shāhānshāh al-aᶜẓam* and *malik al-mulūk* (most exalted shāhānshāh, king of kings) over considerable public protest. Numerous Buyid emirs in the past had arrogated the titles to themselves, but none had ever obtained them from a caliph, and al-Qāᵓim took this step only after the leading jurists of Baghdad issued a *fatwā* (legal opinion) affirming legality. Al-Qāᵓim had refused several such requests previously, and his motive in granting the titles at this time seems to have been to reassert the traditional caliphal prerogative of legitimizing temporal power (albeit after the fact).

In 1044, the Seljuk Tughril Beg took Rayy (near modern Tehran), initiating a ten-year period of Buyid-Seljuk hostilities that ended in 1055, when Tughril Beg entered Baghdad. The advent of Sunni military power, however, did not mean increased political power for the Abbasid caliph, and his relations with Tughril Beg were, and remained, strained. Al-Qāᵓim was once again able to exercise his authority only by withholding or granting coveted titles and ceremonial privileges: he invested Tughril Beg with the titles (including sultan) he requested but refused to receive him in an audience at the palace until 1057. On the other hand, a very reluctant al-Qāᵓim was compelled to marry his daughter to Tughril Beg, who promptly took her away from Baghdad over her father's protests. Some years later, Tughril's successor, Alp Arslan, would return the daughter to Baghdad in an effort to gain the caliph's favor.

But al-Qāᵓim faced his most serious crisis in 1058, when the Turkish emir al-Basāsirī, who had acknowledged the Fatimid caliph in 1057, took Baghdad. Al-Qāᵓim was exiled from his capital, and for almost a year the *khuṭba* (the sermon given in the mosque on Fridays) in Baghdad was made in the name of the Fatimid caliph al-Mustanṣir. Tughril Beg put down the rebellion and returned al-Qāᵓim to Baghdad early in 1060.

The last years of al-Qāᵓim's reign, however, were far from peaceful. Though Sunni, the Seljuks disassociated themselves from traditional caliphal support of the Hanbalis by patronizing the Shāfiᶜī

QĀᵓITBĀY, AL-ASHRAF

school, leading to intense hostilities that rivaled the old Sunni-Shiite conflicts of the Buyid period. Moreover, the Seljuks showed no greater inclination than the Buyids had to relinquish any of their political or military power to the Abbasid caliph. In spite of this, al-Qāᵓim succeeded in consolidating the notion that the legitimation of political power was the exclusive prerogative of the Abbasid caliph. This position, formally articulated in his day by the jurist al-Māwardī, defined the character of the caliphate until the Mongol conquest.

BIBLIOGRAPHY

Wilferd Madelung, "The Assumption of the Title Shāhānshāh by the Būyids and 'The Reign of the Daylam (*Dawlat al-Daylam*),'" in *Journal of Near Eastern Studies,* 27 (1969); Hilāl ibn al-Muḥassin al-Ṣābīᵓ, *Rusūm dar al-khilāfah: The Rules and Regulations of the ᶜAbbāsid Court,* Elie A. Salem, trans. (1977).

PAULA SANDERS

[See also **Abbasids; Buyids; Caliphate; Seljuks; Tughril Beg.**]

QĀᵓITBĀY, AL-ASHRAF (the Illustrious), (1411/1412–1496), Mamluk sultan of Egypt and Syria (1468–1496), one of the foremost autocrats of the Burjī (Citadel) or Circassian line (1382–1517). Qāᵓitbāy was born in the Caucasus, but his exact birthdate is unknown. Purchased by Sultan Barsbāy (1422–1437), he was trained in the Citadel barracks of Cairo, manumitted as a mature soldier by Sultan Jaqmaq (1438–1453), and soon advanced to the status of *khāṣṣakī,* or bodyguard. Rising rapidly through the ranks of the imperial hierarchy, Qāᵓitbāy served as an assistant executive secretary (*nā'ib dawādār*) in the palace and was successively promoted as *amīr* (officer) of 10 and then 40 Mamluks, and commander of 1,000 (*muqaddam alf*). Ultimately, in 1467, he became captain of the royal guard in the Citadel (*raᵓs nawbat al-nuwāb*).

During the turmoil following Sultan Khushqadam's death (1467), Qāᵓitbāy supported the candidacy of a close associate, Timurbughā, who rewarded his ally by appointing him grand marshal (*atabeg, atābak*). When Timurbughā's bid for power faltered due to insufficient support from his troops and inadequate funds to buy it, Qāᵓitbāy accepted the throne in 1468 with studied reluctance, having shrewdly measured the strength of potential adversaries and hostile factions. Qāᵓitbāy sent Timurbughā off to honorable exile in the delta port of Damietta, establishing a precedent for deposed colleagues and their descendants that would last to the end of his sultanate.

Qāᵓitbāy's reign is significant for its military campaigns, which were on balance successful, and for its less auspicious domestic policies. On the foreign front, Qāᵓitbāy had to deal with a perennial threat from the Ottomans, who were expanding their influence throughout eastern Anatolia during the final decades of the fifteenth century. Whether active or latent, this menace troubled Qāᵓitbāy and accounts for his obsession with military preparedness. Qāᵓitbāy's Ottoman quandary was compounded by aggression on the part of two ambitious rulers in the districts east of Asia Minor: Shāh-Suwār of the Dhu'l-Qadr Turkomans, who ruled from Elbistan (southeastern Anatolia), and Uzun Ḥasan of Amida (Diyarbakir), chief of the Aq Qoyunlu Turkoman confederation. After two defeats at the hands of Shāh-Suwār, due to incompetent leadership, Qāᵓitbāy's army triumphed over its opponent in 1472. Shāh-Suwār was paraded through Cairo and executed. Qāᵓitbāy's officers never managed to check the western advance of Uzun Ḥasan on their own, but after his defeat by the Ottoman sultan Mehmed II the next year (1473), the Aq Qoyunlu prince lost his momentum and ceased to pose an active danger to Egypt or Syria.

Qāᵓitbāy's relations with the Ottomans worsened when he welcomed Jem, brother of Mehmed's successor, Bāyazīd II, to his court with covert partisan support in İstanbul. During the 1480's, Bāyazīd's armies crossed the Mamluk frontiers in southeastern Anatolia to besiege Adana, Malatya, and Tarsus. But Qāᵓitbāy's own forces countered the Ottomans successfully, and in 1490 the grand marshal Azbak defeated them at Qayṣarīya (Kayseri), deep in Anatolia itself. The Mamluk and Ottoman regimes elected to arrange a peace that lasted into the early sixteenth century.

Qāᵓitbāy's domestic policies may be assessed as short-term expedients to resolve long-term dilemmas. Similar to his precursors, Qāᵓitbāy failed to devise a sound tax strategy guaranteeing adequate funds for his regime. His expenses were enormous, consisting of campaign costs, special bonuses paid on demand to victorious soldiers, pensions to retired officers who had served previous sultans (necessary to forestall revolts), the budget of his vast household, and funds for his elaborate construction projects. To Qāᵓitbāy's credit, he recognized the potential revenues to be derived from international trade and took steps to promote good relations with European mercantile powers. Qāᵓitbāy freed the spice trade from state monopoly and granted Italian merchants new privileges in his realm—while also demanding the cessation of piracy against Egyptian coastal ports. Qāᵓitbāy's measures resulted in a renaissance of East-West commerce through Egypt that shored up the economy during his lifetime. But these tactics could not offset the endemic defects of his fiscal apparatus. Qāᵓitbāy was compelled to rely increasingly on forced payments, "voluntary" contributions from affluent notables, exactions from religious communities (Christians and Jews), confiscations from arrested officials, emergency taxes (often previously canceled to relieve pressure on merchants), and sequestration of endowed (*waqf*) properties—supposedly inviolate under religious law. According to his chronicler, Qāᵓitbāy spent more than seven million dinars on his campaigns. This huge sum, unequalled by any other contemporary ruler, included neither bonuses for troops nor amounts spent on defense building. Such figures explain the precarious state of the Egyptian economy at the end of the fifteenth century, but the capacity of Qāᵓitbāy to collect this money may suggest the existence of a hidden economy that remains marginally understood by modern scholars.

In spite of his financial excesses, for which he was rebuked by Muslim historians, Qāᵓitbāy was widely respected as the best of the Circassian sultans. Even of temper, pious of faith, generous to the needy, and effective with subordinates, Qāᵓitbāy managed to revive the Mamluk sultanate after a period of slack discipline. His monuments were unmatched by any of his contemporaries in Egypt for their scope and sumptuous decoration. They include Citadel expansions, fortresses in Alexandria and Aleppo, a vast mausoleum, a Sufi hospice (*khānqāh*), restoration of the Kaaba sanctuary in Mecca and the Prophet's Mosque in Medina, and an aqueduct to a mosque in Jerusalem. Qāᵓitbāy also donated lavish sums to college (madrasa) endowments, library funds, and a host of charities—many of which are recorded in his *waqf* deeds. Qāᵓitbāy died on 7 August 1496 at the age of about 84.

BIBLIOGRAPHY

Sources. Ibn Aja, *Tārīkh al-Amīr Yashbak al-Ẓāhirī,* ᶜAbd al-Qādir Tulaymāt, ed. (1974); Ibn al-Jīᶜān, *Al-Qawl al-mustaẓraf fī safar mawlānā al-Malik al-Ashraf,* R. Lanzone, ed. (1878); Ibn Iyās, *Badāᵓiᶜ al-zuhūr fī waqāᵓiᶜ al-duhūr,* Muḥammad Muṣṭafā, ed., III (1963), trans. by Gaston Wiet as *Histoire des Mamlouks circassiens,* II (1945); Leo Mayer, *The Buildings of Qaytbay as Described in His Endowment Deed* (1938); Muhammad M. Amīn, *Catalogue des documents d'archives du Caire de 239/853 à 922/1516* (in Arabic) (1981), 535 (index).

General. Peter M. Holt, *The Age of the Crusades: The Near East from the Eleventh Century to 1517* (1986); Gaston Wiet, *L'Egypte arabe* (1937).

Studies. Eliyahu Ashtor, *The Levant Trade in the Later Middle Ages* (1983); R. L. Devonshire, trans., "Relation d'un voyage du Sultan Qâitbây en Palestine et en Syrie," in *Bulletin de l'Institut français d'archéologie orientale,* 20 (1922); Jean Claude Garcin *et al., Palais et maisons du Caire,* I, *Époque mamelouke (XIIIᵉ–XVIᵉ siècles)* (1982); Christel Kessler, "The Fountain of Sultan Qāytbāy in the Sacred Precinct of Jerusalem," in Roger Moorey and Peter Parr, eds., *Archaeology in the Levant* (1978); Subhi Labib, "Ein Brief des Mamluken Sultans Qā'itbey en den Dogen von Venedig aus dem Jahre 1473," in *Der Islam,* **32** (1957), and *Handelgeschichte Ägyptens im Spätmittelalter* (1965); John Wansborough, "A Mamluk Commercial Treaty Concluded with the Republic of Florence, 894/1489," in Samuel M. Stern, ed., *Documents from Islamic Chanceries,* 1st ser. (1965), "A Mamluk Letter of 877/1473," in *Bulletin of the School of Oriental and African Studies,* **24** (1961), and "Venice and Florence in the Mamluk Commercial Privileges," *ibid.,* **28** (1965); Gaston Wiet, "Décrets mamlouks d'Égypte," in *Eretz-Israel,* **7** (1964), and "Deux princes ottomans à la cour d'Égypte," in *Bulletin de l'Institut d'Égypte,* **20** (1938); John E. Woods, *The Aqquyunlu* (1976), 114–117, 129–137.

CARL F. PETRY

[See also **Aq Qoyunlu; Circassians; Egypt, Islamic; Mamluk Dynasty; Ottomans.**]

QALĀMDAN. See **Dawāt.**

QALANSUWA, the name given to a type of brimless hat worn by men in the Muslim world. It was worn alone or with a winding cloth to form a turban. The word also seems to have designated a

Abū Zayd wearing a *qalansuwa*. Miniature from the *Māqamāt* of al-Harīrī. PARIS, BIBLIOTHÈQUE NATIONALE, MS ARABE 3929, fol. 69r

hood or cowl in early Islamic times, but this meaning was forgotten during the Middle Ages.

In early-seventh-century Arabia, the *qalansuwa* was a close-fitting cap. In time of war it was worn over a headcloth of mail. In the early Islamic empire it was one of the items forbidden to the conquered subjects by the Pact of ᶜUmar, under the general ban against dressing in Arab fashion.

During the Abbasid period, a Persian hat known as *qalansuwa ṭawīla* became popular. This high, conical hat resembling a miter was also called *dannīya* because it looked like an inverted amphora (*dann*). It consisted of a frame of reed or wood covered with fabric. According to a famous anecdote, Hārūn al-Rashīd wore a *qalansuwa* with "pilgrim" (*ḥājj*) emblazoned on one side and "holy warrior" (*ghāzī*) on the other, symbolizing the duties he undertook in alternate years: leading the pilgrimage to Mecca and leading warriors in the holy war against the Byzantines.

The *qalansuwa* is commonly depicted in illustrated manuscripts of al-Ḥarīrī's *Maqāmāt,* in which it is often worn by the hero Abū Zayd.

BIBLIOGRAPHY

Reinhart Dozy, *Dictionnaire détaillé des noms des vêtements chez les Arabes* (1845, repr. 1969), 365–371; Richard Ettinghausen, *Arab Painting* (1962), 82; Reuben Levy, "Notes on Costume from Arabic Sources," in *Journal of the Royal Asiatic Society* (April 1935), esp. 324–325.

YEDIDA K. STILLMAN

[See also **Costume, Islamic; Costume, Jewish; Hārūn al-Rashīd.**]

QALĀᵓŪN, AL-MANṢŪR (*d.* 1290), sultan of Egypt and Syria (1279–1290), an architect of the Mamluk state (dominated by Turkish or Circassian military slaves) along with his predecessor, al-Malik al-Ẓāhir Baybars (1260–1277). He was born in the Kipchak region north of the Black Sea; exactly when is unknown. Purchased as an adolescent, he was sent to Cairo, where he received his training from Al-Sunqur the Cupbearer, a senior officer in the Ayyubid court. Upon his patron's death in 1249, Qalāᵓūn entered the service of Sultan al-Malik al-Ṣālih ᶜAyyūb (*r.* 1240–1249). Throughout the turbulent years marking the transition from Ayyubid monarchy to Mamluk regime (1249–1259), Qalāᵓūn completed his training in the Rawḍa Island barracks on the Nile, and then fled to Syria from the new autocrat in Cairo, Aybak. Later, however, Aybak's successor, Quṭuz, welcomed him back to the capital. During this uncertain period, he developed an intimate relationship with Baybars that lasted until the latter's death.

Qalāᵓūn assisted Baybars in the Battle of ᶜAyn Jālūt in Palestine (1260), which checked the threat of a potential Mongol invasion of Syria and North Africa. After his assassination of Quṭuz, Baybars promoted Qalāᵓūn to the rank of *muqaddam alf* (commander of 1,000), the highest rung in the military hierarchy. Throughout Baybars' reign the two men worked closely together, sealing their personal tie with the betrothal of Baybars' older son, Baraka Khān, to Qalāᵓūn's daughter (1276). During the quarrels among competing Mamluk factions following Baybars' death, Qalāᵓūn initially refused the sultanate, allowing both of Baybars' sons to succeed. But when the second, Salāmish, was deposed while still a minor, Qalāᵓūn ascended the throne, convinced he could consolidate his position. In 1280 Qalāʾūn managed to quell rebellion by a rival in Syria who was supported by Baybars' disaffected Mamluks, and thus faced no further opposition to his authority.

Qalāʾūn's decade of unchallenged rule is memorable for his aggressive campaigns against the Mongols and Crusaders, and for his pragmatic policies designed to promote international trade through the Nile Valley. He led an expedition against the forces of Mangūtīmūr, brother of the Mongol Ilkhanids of Persia, defeating him at Ḥimṣ (Syria) in 1281. Because of dissension within the Mongol ruling elite over the ensuing years, no further penetrations of the Levant occurred. Qalāʾūn was thus able to focus his attention on the surviving Frankish coastal strongholds. In 1285 he captured the fortress of the Knights Hospitalers at Marqab after a thirty-eight-day siege. His greatest achievement came in 1289, when he occupied Tripoli, profiting from disputes over succession to its throne.

The next year Qalāʾūn laid plans for the siege of Acre, but he died in Cairo before he could depart. His son and successor, Khalīl, took the previously impregnable port city in 1291. Thus, Qalāʾūn, rather than the illustrious Saladin, succeeded in bringing the Crusader era to a close in the Levant. He also organized expeditions against the Christian Armenians and the pagan Nubians for the purpose of securing his extreme northern and southern frontiers. He thereby established the Mamluk state as the great power of the central Arab lands until the Ottoman conquest.

Qalāʾūn sought to ensure Egypt's prosperity by developing positive relations with foreign states, setting a precedent for his descendants. His chancery established ties with the Golden Horde of Russia, Byzantium, the rulers of Castile and Sicily, and the Habsburgs of Austria. He approved a commercial treaty with Genoa and promulgated a charter of safe conduct to attract merchants from south and east Asia. Copies of both documents have been preserved. Qalāʾūn left a legacy of monuments as testimony to his worldly success, the most impressive of which is his hospital-mausoleum complex located in the heart of medieval Cairo. Elaborately described by such writers as Maqrīzī and Nuwayrī, this imposing structure provided sophisticated medical care to patients, regardless of rank or wealth, financed by its extensive endowment (*waqf*).

Qalāʾūn died of a sudden illness on 11 November 1290, while preparing to set out for Acre. The eleven years of his administration witnessed the Mamluk regime's entrenchment in Egypt and Syria. Qalāʾūn's military and commercial achievements are undeniable. They set the stage for Egypt's extraordinary affluence that would last for half a century, until the death of al-Nāṣir Muḥammad in 1341. Indeed, Baybars' and Qalāʾūn's reigns should be interpreted jointly as the formative era of the Mamluk empire. These two rulers founded a military/bureaucratic system remarkable for its tenacity, though flawed by long-term defects. Its facade of power and wealth obscured problems of corrosive factionalism, exploitative feudalism, and economic predation that would ultimately sap the vitality of Egyptian and Syrian society, enabling the Ottomans to reduce these regions to provincial backwaters in the early sixteenth century.

BIBLIOGRAPHY

Arabic works include Muḥammad Amīn, *Catalogue des documents d'archives du Caire* (1981), 536 (in Arabic); Ibn Aybak al-Dawādārī, *Kanz al-durar wa-jāmiʿal-ghurar,* VIII, *Al-Durra al-zakīya fī akhbar al-dawla al-Turkīya,* Ulrich Haarmann, ed. (1971), 187, 197, 225, 231–307; Taqī al-Dīn al-Maqrīzī, *Khiṭaṭ* (1853–1854), II, 238, 379–380, 406–408; al-Qalqashandī, *Ṣubḥ al-aʿshā,* XIII (1918), 340–342; IbnʿAbd al-Ẓāhir, *Tashrīf al-ayyām wa'l-ʿuṣūr fī sīrat al-Malik al-Manṣūr,* Murād Kāmil, ed. (1961).

Studies in Western languages are David Ayalon, "The Circassians in the Mamlūk Kingdom," in *Journal of the American Oriental Society,* **69** (1949); Marius Canard, "Le traité de 1281 entre Michel Paléologue et le Sultan Qalāʾūn," in *Byzantion,* **10** (1935); Franz Dölger, "Der Vertrag des Sultans Qalāʾūn von Ägypten mit dem Kaiser Michael VIII Palaiologos (1281)," in *Serta Monacensia* (1952); Peter M. Holt, "Qalāwūn's Treaty with Acre in 1283," in *English Historical Review,* **91** (1976), "Qalāwūn's Treaty with Genoa in 1290," in *Der Islam,* **57** (1980), "The Treaties of the Early Mamluk Sultans with the Frankish States," in *Bulletin of the School of Oriental and African Studies* (University of London), **43** (1980), and *The Age of the Crusades: The Near East from the Eleventh Century to 1517* (1986), 99–107; Robert Irwin, *The Middle East in the Middle Ages: The Early Mamluk Sultanate* (1986), 62–84; M. Meinecke, "Das Mausoleum des Qalā'ūn in Kairo, Untersuchungen zur Genese der Mamlukischen Architekturdekoration," in *Mitteilungen des deutschen archäologischen Instituts,* Abt. Kairo, **26** (1970); Hassanein Rabie, *The Financial System of Egypt: A.H. 564–741/A.D. 1169–1341* (1972), 99, 114, 118, and "Ḳalāwūn," in *Encyclopaedia of Islam,* new ed., IV (1978); John Wansbrough, "The Safe-conduct in Muslim Chancery Practice," in *Bulletin of the School of Oriental and African Studies,* **34** (1971); Gaston Wiet, *L'Égypte arabe* (1937), 443–458.

CARL F. PETRY

[See also **Ayyubids; Baybars al-Bunduqdārī; Circassians; Emir; Golden Horde; Ḥimṣ; Mamluk Dynasty; Ottomans; Saladin; Slavery, Slave Trade; Sultan; Waqf; Warfare, Islamic.**]

QĀNṢŪH AL-GHAWRĪ (1440/1441–1516), Mamluk sultan of Egypt and Syria (1501–1516), the last significant ruler of the Circassian line (1382–1517). Purchased and manumitted by Sultan Qāʾitbāy (1468–1496), al-Ghawrī was trained in the barracks school of al-Ghawr, from which he derived his *nisba* title. Under his sovereign, al-Ghawrī held provincial executive posts (prefect of Upper Egypt, grand chamberlain of Aleppo) and was appointed governor of Malatya in southeastern Anatolia during the ephemeral sultanate of Qāʾitbāy's son, al-Nāṣir Muḥammad. He participated in the sultan's campaigns against the Ottomans, who were menacing Mamluk suzerainty along his northern frontier. Throughout the interregnum following Qāʾitbāy's death, al-Ghawrī served as captain of the royal guard (*raʾs nawbat al-nuwwāb*) and was designated senior court secretary (*dawādār kabīr*) by al-ʿĀdil Ṭūmān Bāy. Al-ʿĀdil's hold on the sultanate was precarious, and when a coterie of officers deposed him, they pressured al-Ghawrī to accept the throne (20 April 1501). Aware of his figurehead status, al-Ghawrī initially resisted their acclamation but managed to consolidate his authority over the next year and a half by transferring Mamluks of his precursor to Upper Egypt and arresting officers who had conspired against him. Yet, because of a chronic lack of treasury funds to pay bonuses, al-Ghawrī never managed to win the loyalty from his troops that Qāʾitbāy had enjoyed. He was compelled to extract periodic fealty oaths sworn by his officers and soldiers on the copy of Caliph ʿUthmān's (644–656) Koran, a holy relic held in the Citadel of Cairo.

Qānṣūh's reign witnessed a period of rapid transition in the central Islamic lands and the Indian Ocean. The Ottomans began once again to press eastward, the new Safavid monarch of Iran, Ismaʿil (1501–1524), nurtured grandiose dreams of imperial expansion, the bedouin tribes of Syria and western Arabia took advantage of Mamluk turmoil in Cairo to rebel, and the Portuguese began to threaten Mamluk hegemony in the Red Sea. Despite his dismal domestic situation, al-Ghawrī responded to these crises with remarkable alacrity. He managed to suppress the bedouin disturbances in Arabia by 1507 and parlayed an arrangement with his governor and rival, Sībāy of Damascus, who reduced tribal tensions in Syria. The sultan sent a major expedition under Amir Ḥusayn Mushrif al-Kurdī (November 1505) to fortify the Hejaz port of Jidda and to assist the prince of Gujarat in India against the Portuguese. He even secured naval supplies from the Ottoman sultan Bāyazīd II to construct a war fleet at Suez (1511) for the purpose of warding off the Europeans.

Al-Ghawrī took the unprecedented step of introducing firearms to his army, and organized a new Fifth Corps (*al-ṭabaqat al-khāmisa*) trained in their use. This unit was recruited from irregulars because of implacable resistance from the sultan's own soldiers to alternative weaponry. Yet al-Ghawrī's military and naval stratagems, taken at the last minute, came too late to salvage Mamluk fortunes. When the Portuguese attacked Aden in April 1513, al-Ghawrī planned a joint expedition with the Ottomans, headed by Ḥusayn Mushrif (now governor of Jidda) and Selmān Reʾīs (recently arrived at Suez with a naval contingent of 2,000 men). Engaged in the Yemen when al-Ghawrī was defeated, this combined force paved the way for Ottoman domination of southwestern Arabia.

Ottoman foreign policy had shifted abruptly with the accession of Selim I (1512–1520). Following his victory over Shah Ismaʿil at Chaldiran (23 August 1514), Selim defeated the Dhu'l-Qadirid ruler ʿAlaʾ al-Dawla, a Mamluk vassal. Alarmed by Selim's aggression, al-Ghawrī assembled an expedition he chose to lead personally (at the age of 78) and set out for Aleppo in May 1516. Upon his arrival at this provincial capital, al-Ghawrī attempted to negotiate a settlement. But Selim decided to eliminate his Mamluk rival to the south before pursuing Ismaʿil into Iran. The Mamluk-Ottoman confrontation took place north of Aleppo at Marj Dābiq (24 August 1516). Despite their technical disadvantage, the Mamluks fought bravely, but when a detachment broke ranks (probably arranged by a seditious officer), the Egyptian army was routed. Al-Ghawrī died of a stroke on the battlefield, and his body was never recovered.

Al-Ghawrī's domestic policies may be summarized as desperate expedients taken to secure his position and to garner funds for defense of the state. Al-Ghawrī presided over the Mamluk elite when it had degenerated into a predatory interest group demanding exorbitant cash payments for military service. Fiscal problems evolving within the regime throughout the preceding two centuries culminated during al-Ghawrī's reign. The sultan could rely on no systematic means of collecting money and was compelled to routinize the extortion, confiscation, and sequestration practiced on an ad hoc basis by his predecessors. His impounding of endowed (*waqf*) properties reached unprecedented levels. The Ottomans thus found a moribund, crisis-ridden state with minimal popular support when they arrived at the northern gates of Cairo in 1517.

The sources chronicling al-Ghawrī's reign report few public-works projects, yet the sultan did construct an impressive mausoleum-college complex near the Azhar mosque (but decorated with materials stripped from earlier monuments). He also enlarged and beautified the hippodrome (*maydān*) at the base of the Citadel, completed an aqueduct linking the Citadel to the Nile, constructed several caravansaries (*wikalas*) in Cairo and its environs, built a pavilion adjacent to the nilometer at the southern tip of Rawda Island, added to pious foundations in Mecca, and restored fortifications near the Red Sea ports.

BIBLIOGRAPHY

Sources. Najm al-Dīn al-Ghazzī, *Al-Kawākib al-sāʾira biaʿyān al-miʾa al-ʿāshira*, Jibrāʾīl Jabbūr, ed., I (1945), 294–297; Ibn Iyās, *Badāʾiʿ al-zuhūr fī waqāʾiʿ al-duhūr*, Muḥammad Muṣṭafā, ed., IV and V (1960–1961), 3–102, trans. by Gaston Wiet as *Journal d'un bourgeois du Caire*, I and II (1955–1960), 1–94; Shams al-Dīn Muḥammad ibn ʿAlī Ibn Ṭūlūn, *Iʿlām al-warā . . .*, Muḥammad Duhmān, ed. (1964), trans. by Henri Laoust as *Les gouverneurs de Damas sous les mamlouks et les premiers Ottomans (658–1156/1260–1744)* (1952), 77–143.

General. Peter M. Holt, *The Age of the Crusades: The Near East from the Eleventh Century to 1517* (1986); Gaston Wiet, *L'Égypte arabe* (1937).

Studies. Muḥammad Awad, "Sultan al-Ghawrī: His Place in Literature and Learning," in *International Congress of Orientalists, 20th* (1938); David Ayalon, *Gunpowder and Firearms in the Mamluk Kingdom* (1956); Hassanein Rabie, "Political Relations Between the Safavids of Persia and the Mamluks of Egypt and Syria in the Early Sixteenth Century," in *Journal of the American Research Center in Egypt,* **15** (1978); Robert Serjeant, *The Portuguese Off the South Arabian Coast* (1963); John Wansborough, "A Mamluk Ambassador to Venice in 913/1507," in *Bulletin of the School of Oriental and African Studies,* **26** (1963); G. Wickens, "Mamluk Egypt at the Eleventh Hour: Some Eyewitness Observations," in W. S. McCullough, ed., *The Seed of Wisdom: Essays in Honor of T. J. Meek* (1964); M. Mustafa Ziada, "The Fall of the Mamluks, 1516–17," in Jāmiʿat al-Qāhira, *Majalla Kulliyat al-adāb* (Cairo University, Bulletin of the Faculty of Arts), **6** (1942).

CARL F. PETRY

[See also **Circassians; Egypt, Islamic; Mamluk Dynasty; Marj Dābiq; Ottomans; Selim I; Warfare, Islamic.**]

QARA MUḤAMMAD (**Mehmed**) (*d.* 1389) was the second major leader of the Qara Qoyunlu (after Bayram Khōja, his uncle, who died in 1380). From 1380 to 1389 he led the Qara Qoyunlu, a confederation of Turkoman tribal groups that adhered to Mongol political and legal principles (as well as Islamic tenets) and inherited part of the Mongol (Ilkhanid) state in Iran.

Qara Muḥammad achieved considerable if somewhat ephemeral success leading the confederation in recurring struggles and alliances with other claimants to the Mongol legacy. The politics of legitimacy were complex. At Nakhchavan (Nakhichevan in the Azerbaijan SSR) he defeated a Jalayirid army (1382) but, in partial recognition of the then accepted legitimacy of that dynasty, agreed to support one of its members' claim to sovereignty. That alliance ended with the death of the Jalayirid; Qara Muḥammad went his own way, gradually acquiring the loyalty of the Turkoman tribes of eastern Anatolia, northwestern Iran, and parts of northern Iraq. He became strong enough to put up fierce resistance to the campaign of Tamerlane in Azerbaijan and eastern Anatolia in 1387 and to recapture the city of Tabriz from the Timurids in the following year.

Qara Muḥammad fell victim in 1389 to the consequences of a clan system of political alliances. One of the military leaders in his own service, the son of a man killed by Qara Muḥammad's uncle in his drive for power, exacted vengeance by assassinating Qara Muḥammad. As had happened at the beginning of his reign, the problem of indeterminate succession led to a period of bitter struggle, partly undoing the effects of Qara Muḥammad's military accomplishments.

The state over which Qara Muḥammad had had dominion was a classic example of the military patronage type bound by nomadic/clan principles of legitimacy. Sovereignty rested with Qara Muḥammad and his clan of the Qara Qoyunlu, but government and administration were somewhat dispersed through grants to adherents of the clan as well as to those whose military support was considered necessary or opportune. (Woods's paradigm of the state structure of the Aq Qoyunlu, a clan-state whose political principles were similar to those of the Qara Qoyunlu, is useful for understanding the political structure of the latter.)

BIBLIOGRAPHY

See Faruk Sümer, "Ḳara Ḳoyunlu," in *Encyclopaedia of Islam,* new ed., IV. John E. Woods, *The Aqquyunlu* (1976), provides much information on the Qara Qoyunlu and provides an important methodological approach to the study of the politics of the nomadic clan-state. It also contains an exhaustive list and description of sources from the fifteenth and sixteenth centuries, as well as a complete (to 1976) list of secondary materials.

R. D. McChesney

[See also **Qara Qoyunlu.**]

QARA QOYUNLU (Turkish, "black sheep"), a Turkoman tribal union, the ruling clan of which sprang from the Yiva Oghuz. The Qara Qoyunlu figured prominently in the affairs of eastern Anatolia, Azerbaijan, Iran, and Iraq from 1380 to 1468. Qara Yusuf ibn Qara Muḥammad (*d.* 1420) may be reckoned the founder of Qara Qoyunlu power. Driven to the Mamluks by Tamerlane, he returned in 1406 following a year of imprisonment in Damascus, the result of Tamerlane's pressure on the Mamluks. He then set about seizing Azerbaijan and Iraq, and defeating his neighbors. Jihānshāh (*d.* 1467) brought about the Qara Qoyunlu's greatest period of expansion. With his death in battle against the Aq Qoyunlu, their state crumbled and was largely absorbed by the Aq Qoyunlu and, later, by the Safavids.

BIBLIOGRAPHY

Abū Bakr Ṭihrānī, *Kitāb-i Diyārbakrīya,* 2 vols., N. Lugal and Faruk Sümer, eds. (1962–1964), text in Persian, introduction and notes in Turkish; Faruk Sümer, *Kara Koyunlular,* I (1967), with detailed bibliography; John E. Woods, *The Aqquyunlu* (1976).

Peter B. Golden

[See also **Aq Qoyunlu; Qara Muḥammad; Qara Yusuf; Timurids.**]

QARA YUSUF (*d.* 1420), who succeeded his father, Qara Muḥammad, after a bitter two-year struggle with the latter's assassin, is considered the third major leader of the Qara Qoyunlu confederation in northwestern Iran and eastern Anatolia. In terms of his military and political accomplishments, he was the most outstanding of the many capable men who led the Turkoman confederation in the late fourteenth and fifteenth centuries.

Qara Yusuf's activities fall into two distinct and equal periods: a freebooting period (1391–1405), during which he tried to establish himself as a regional force, and an expansionist period (1406–1420), in which he reassembled the military elements his father had welded together and then transformed the Qara Qoyunlu confederation into the main rival of the Timurids for control of western Iran.

In 1391 Qara Yusuf came to the leadership of the Qara Qoyunlu, but shortly afterward the campaigns of Tamerlane in Azerbaijan and eastern Anatolia broke his power. After a period of exile in Ottoman Anatolia, he moved to Iraq in 1402 and there formed an alliance with a Jalayirid leader (as his father had done). This venture was ended by Tamerlane when he conquered Baghdad. Qara Yusuf was imprisoned in Damascus and barely escaped execution. His imprisonment ended in 1405, and after a short and unsuccessful military adventure in Egypt, he returned to eastern Anatolia, where the second phase of his career began.

Between 1406 and 1408 Qara Yusuf regained much of the former Qara Qoyunlu territory at the expense of the Timurids. By 1409 the main contenders for political control of the triangle made up of eastern Anatolia, northern Iraq, northwestern Iran, through which the main east-west trade routes passed, were the Qara Qoyunlu under Qara Yusuf, the Timurids, and the Aq Qoyunlu confederation.

Despite repeated campaigns against the latter, Qara Yusuf was unable to dislodge them permanently from northern Iraq. Further, on his eastern flank he had to fight a two-front struggle with the Timurids, who were exerting continual pressure to regain Azerbaijan.

By the time of his sudden death in 1420, Qara Yusuf nonetheless had restored Qara Qoyunlu fortunes and had given the confederation control of the strategic trade corridor between the Caspian Sea and the upper Tigris River.

As in his father's time, the political entity over which Qara Yusuf ruled was a military-patronage state defined by personal loyalties and alliances rather than by territorial divisions. The right of succession remained indeterminate, a corporate right of the entire clan. Just as at the time of his father's death in 1389, a period of struggle for succession followed Qara Yusuf's death.

BIBLIOGRAPHY

S. Album, "A Hoard of Silver Coins from the Time of Iskandar Qara Qoyunlu," in *Numismatic Chronicle,* 7th ser., **16** (1976); Faruk Sümer, "Ḳara Ḳoyunlu," in *Encyclopaedia of Islam,* new ed., IV; John E. Woods, *The Aqquyunlu* (1976).

R. D. McChesney

[See also **Qara Muḥammad; Qara Qoyunlu; Timurids.**]

QARAGŪZ FIGURES (also Karagöz). Qaragūz is the name of one of the two main characters of the Turkish shadow theater and is also used to refer to the shadow theater itself, which, as a genre, is known as *hayal-i zill* (illusion or shadow).

The character Qaragūz represents the uneducated but humorous, vulgar but honest, quarrelsome but kind man of the street. His opponent in the plays, Hacivat, is educated and speaks in flowery language laden with Arabic and Persian words that Qaragūz does not—or pretends not to—understand. Hacivat is serious but self-centered. There are a number of secondary figures representing various classes and groups of Ottoman Turkey in the cast. Ethnic groups in the Ottoman Empire are stereotyped: the Persian carpet dealer, the European polka dancer, the Armenian jeweler, the Jewish moneylender, and so on. The women, lumped together, are devious and coquettish creatures. The heroes and heroines of folktales from Turkey, Iran, and Arab lands appear in subplots or vignettes.

The framework and the basic types have remained constant, and the stories are well known to both the performers and the audiences. The plots, however, are adapted to current issues and conditions. Ethnic jokes abound in the Qaragūz plays. Social ills are acted out, as are cultural and economic clashes among classes. The sultan, his government, and the religious institutions are rarely treated.

The shadow play "performers" are figures projected onto a cloth screen that is about 1.10 meter by .80 meter (3.6 feet by 2.6 feet). They are made of leather, usually of camel hide. The figures, painted with India ink and natural colors, are held against the back of the screen by persons who grasp the stick attached to each figure. The light source is behind the figures.

Each play starts with a prologue in which Hacivat tells the audience that the play they are about to see is only an illusion, and no appearance should be taken for reality. There follows a dialogue between Qaragūz and Hacivat, during which they display their personal characteristics amid much insult. The actual play then unfolds. The conclusion is often marked by another dialogue (although at times "secondary" voices join in).

The origin of Qaragūz shadow theater must have been the Far East. In the thirteenth century the Seljuks of Anatolia had shadow plays as entertainment. The character of Qaragūz apparently was introduced from Mamluk Egypt to Turkey in the early sixteenth century. We know that shadow plays were popular in Mamluk Cairo, and the *mamlūks,* or the "slaves" who constituted the ruling class, were largely from western and central Asia. The plays developed in Turkey according to local tastes and linguistic skills and became immensely popular at all levels of society. The number of plays was kept by convention to twenty-eight, one to be performed on each night of the holy month of Ramadan, save the last. The length of the individual play varied according to the improvisational skills of the performers and the reaction of the audience. Some lasted all night.

BIBLIOGRAPHY

Metin And, *Karagöz: Turkish Shadow Theatre* (1975); Cevdet Kudret, *Karagöz,* 3 vols. (1968–1970), in Turkish; Hellmut Ritter, ed. and trans., *Karagös: Türk-*

ische Schattenspiele, 3 vols. (1924–1953), play texts in German and Turkish.

ÜLKÜ Ü. BATES

[See also **Ottomans.**]

QARAKHANIDS, the ruling dynasty of a Turko-Islamic state (*ca.* late tenth–early thirteenth centuries, but having its origins in the mid ninth century) in eastern and western Turkestan. The term "Qarakhanid" (from the Turkic *qara,* "black" [symbolically "the North" or "great"], and *khan*), which figures as the highest title in the state, usually in conjunction with a totemic name, was created by modern scholars to replace the older and equally artificial ʾ"Ilek-khanid" (from the Turkic *ilig,* "prince," and *khan*). Contempory Islamic sources, including Maḥmūd al-Kāshgharī (who was of imperial Qarakhanid origin), refer to this dynasty as the "Khāqānīya" (from the Turkic *qaghan,* "emperor"), that is, the "imperial" Turks, or as the "Āl-i Afrāsiayāb" (dynasty of Afrāsiyāb, Turkic Alp Er Tonga, the legendary Turanian hero).

The origins of the dynasty are unclear. Some evidence, largely circumstantial, points to connections with the Ashina, the charismatic ruling clan of the first and second Turk empires in Mongolia (*ca.* 552–630, 680–741). Somewhat firmer evidence associates them with the Yaghma and Qarluq tribal confederations, vassals of the Turks, and with remnants of the western Turk empire and its successor, the Türgesh. In keeping with Turk tradition, the khanate was divided into eastern and western halves. The eastern, superior half was ruled by the Arslan Qara Qaghan (Lion khan of the north), and the western half by the Boghra Qara Qaghan (Camel kahn of the north). Beneath them was a tetrarchy bearing the titles Arslan Ilig, Boghra Ilig, Arslan Tegin, and Boghra Tegin. As members of the dynasty assumed different posts within the realm, their titles changed. Thus, the identification of different individuals in the written and numismatic sources is a formidable task.

Similarly, it is impossible to pinpoint the first appearance of the Qarakhanids in the sources. Modern scholarly opinion associates Bilge Kül Qadir Khan and his sons Oghulchaq and Bazir (last half of the ninth century), who warred with the Samanids in Kazakhstan, with the earliest Qarakhanids. The Samanids defeated them at Ispījāb (modern Sairam, near Chimkent, Kazakh SSR) in 840 and at Ṭarāz (or Talas; later Aulie-Ata; modern Dzhambul, Kazakh SSR) in 893. A grandson of Bilge Kül Qadir Khan, Satuq Boghra Khan (*d.* 955), influenced by a Bukharan *faqīh* (Muslim religious scholar), converted to Islam, taking the name ᶜAbd al-Karīm. The conversion of the tribesmen under Qarakhanid rule, undoubtedly accompanied by much internal turbulence, followed in the succeeding decades. In 960, the Muslim historian Ibn al-Athīr reports, "200,000 tents of the Turks" embraced Islam. The Islamization of these Turks, a goal of Samanid policy, was largely the result of the activities of Muslim missionaries.

The conversion to Islam, while providing a useful ideology for warfare with their pagan Turkic neighbors (Yimek/Kimeks, Basmils, Uighurs, and others), did not lessen Qarakhanid pressure on the declining Samanids. In 992 the Qarakhanid Hārūn (Boghra Khan) briefly held Bukhara, the Samanid capital. In 999 another Qarakhanid, Naṣr Ilig, having established an entente with Maḥmūd of Ghazna (998–1030), took Bukhara and divided the Samanid lands with his Ghaznavid ally. The Oxus served as the dividing line between the two realms. An attempt to restore Samanid fortunes by Ismāᶜīl II al-Muntaṣir (*r.* 1000–1005) failed, leaving the contest for central Asia to the two erstwhile allies, the Qarakhanids and Ghaznavids.

Following the failure of initial Qarakhanid encroachments on Ghaznavid territories, domestic strife erupted (perhaps promoted by Ghazna). The latter, exploiting Qarakhanid internal weakness, seized the collapsing Khwārizmshāh state in 1017, thereby outflanking its foes in the west and establishing Maḥmūd as the greatest power in the region. The Qarakhanids, plagued by internecine strife and defections to the Ghaznavids, were never able to answer this challenge. Adding to these domestic pressures were the disturbances set off in the Turkic steppe by tribal migrations (for instance, by the Qun and the Qay) and the breakup of the Kimek and Oghuz confederations.

Much of the Qarakhanid internal turmoil focused on the struggle between ᶜAlī Tegin (*d.* 1034), the master of Transoxiana, and his brother in the east, Yūsuf Qadir Khan (*d.* 1032), descendants of Hārūn, or Ḥasan (Boghra Khan, *d.* 992), who was a grandson of Satuq (Boghra Khan), the ally of Maḥmūd of Ghazna. With the passing of these figures and the Seljuk crushing of the Ghaznavids in

1040, the two halves of the khanate began to grow apart. The western khanate, under the sons of Naṣr (Ilig Khan) of the ᶜAlid line (descendants of ᶜAlī ibn Baytash Mūsā, another grandson of Satuq [Boghra Khan] who had retaken Transoxiana from the sons of ᶜAlī Tegin), consisted of Transoxiana, western Farghānā, and adjoining lands; the centers were Uzgand/Özkent, Samarkand, and Bukhara. After 1164 the western khanate again came under the rule of the sons of ᶜAlī Tegin. The eastern khanate, under the Hārūnids/Ḥasanids, encompassed eastern Turkistan, eastern Farghānā, and parts of the present-day Kazakh and Kirghiz SSRs. Its centers were Balasaghun and Kashghar.

The western Qarakhanids were conquered by the Seljuk Malikshāh in 1089, and the eastern khanate submitted shortly thereafter. Reduced to the status of vassals, and plagued by growing religious dissension (the western khans were accused of Shiism by the powerful Bukhara *ᶜulamāᵓ*) and tribal discontent, the khans became minor figures. Seljuk overlordship was replaced by that of the Qara Khitai (a somewhat sinicized dynasty of Mongol origin that had ruled northern China as the Liao dynasty from 947 to 1125, when they were ousted by the Jürchen), the new masters of central Asia by virtue of their victory over the Seljuk sultan Sanjar in 1141. The Qarakhanid dynasts remained significant but secondary factors in the growing struggle between the Khwārizmshāhs, also nominal vassals of the Qara Khitai Gür Khan, and their overlords. In 1212 the Khwārizmshāh Muḥammad (1200–1220) ended the western Qarakhanid state.

The eastern Qarakhanids succumbed to the general chaos that followed the attempted coup d'état by the Naiman prince Küchlüg against his father-in-law, the Gür Khan, in 1210/1211. Some Qarakhanids appear to have remained in Farghanā, but were soon submerged by the Mongol invasions.

The Qarakhanids played a significant role in the development of Turko-Islamic culture, building on the Turk and Uighur literary traditions, but with a strong Islamic component. Turkic was written in both the Arabic and the Uighur script. Among the literary works of the Qarakhanids are the *Qutadghu bilig* (Wisdom of royal glory), composed about 1069/1070 by Yūsuf Khāṣṣ Ḥājib, and the *Dīwān lughat al-Turk* (*ca.* 1074), a massive encyclopedia of Turkic philology, linguistics, history, and ethnography written in Arabic by Maḥmūd al-Kāshgharī.

BIBLIOGRAPHY

Wilhelm Barthold and V. V. Barthold, *Ocherk istorii Semirechia* (1898, 2nd ed. 1943), repr. in his *Sochinenia,* II.1 (1963), and *Turkestan Down to the Mongol Invasion,* 4th ed. (1977), with a complete list of sources; Elena Davidovich, "Numizmaticheskie materialy dlia khronologii i genealogii sredneaziatskikh Karakhanidov," in *Trudy Gosudarstvennogo Istoricheskogo Muzeia,* **26** (1957), "O dvukh karakhanidskikh kaganatakh," in *Narody Azii i Afriki* (1968), and "Voprosy khronologii i genealogii Karakhanidov vtoroi poloviny XII v," in *Sredniaia Aziia v drevnosti i srednevekove* (1977); *Kirgiziia pri Karakhanidakh,* Elena Davidovich, ed. (1983); Omeljan Pritsak, "Karachanidische Streitfragen 1–4," in *Oriens,* 3 (1950), "Die Karachaniden," in *Der Islam,* **31** (1954), with a complete list of sources, and "Von den Karluk zu den Karachaniden," in *Zeitschrift der deutschen morgenlädischen Gesellschaft,* **101** (1951); Yūsuf Khāṣṣ Ḥājib, *Wisdom of Royal Glory,* Robert Dankoff, trans. (1983).

PETER B. GOLDEN

[See also **Ghaznavids; Islam, Conquests of; Seljuks.**]

QAṢABA. See **Casbah.**

QAṢR (Arabic, from *qaṣara,* to "restrict" or "confine"), a building or part of a building that is not generally accessible, often because it serves to shelter women. In the Middle Ages the term was applied variously to private palaces, castles, pavilions, tomb chambers, and similar secluded architectural spaces. It denoted no specific architectural form.

BIBLIOGRAPHY

Edward W. Lane, *An Arabic-English Lexicon,* I, pt. 7 (1885), 2,534.

ESTELLE WHELAN

[See also **Harem.**]

QAYKHOSRAW I (Ghiyāth al-Dīn Kaykhosraw), Seljuk sultan of Rum in 1192–1197 and 1205–1211. The youngest of Qılıj Arslān II's sons, but also his designated successor, Qaykhosraw unsuccessfully attempted to defeat his brothers during his first reign. He spent his years of exile in Constantinople, where he married into a noble Byzantine family. After the Latin conquest of Constantinople in 1204, Qaykhosraw took refuge with his in-laws and, following his brother Rukn al-Dīn Sulaymānshāh's death, he led a successful coup against Konya (Ikonion) in March 1205.

The difficult Byzantine position allowed the Seljuks to extend their power: Qaykhosraw conquered Antalya on the Mediterranean coast in 1207 and brought pressure on the Cilician Armenian lands. In spring 1211, however, Qaykhosraw's army fought the Byzantines of Nicaea at Antioch on the Maeander, and although the Seljuk army did well at first, Qaykhosraw himself died at the hands of the enemy.

After the death of Qaykhosraw the frontier with Byzantium did not change, as the Seljuk amirs soon decided on the succession of ᶜIzz al-Dīn Qaykāᵓūs I, the eldest son, who negotiated a peace on the basis of the existing borders. For the time being, Byzantium in Nicaean exile had to deal with problems on its western flank, while the Seljuks' eastern enemies (Khwarazmians, Mongols, and border nomads) seemed a greater threat.

The significant processes in Anatolian history that began, or were strongly reinforced, during Qaykhosraw's years included the patronage of Persian literature and Sufi masters, a concern for interregional trade and the securing of routes, the establishment of a sound silver coinage, and an increasing (and increasingly disturbing) role for nomads in Anatolian life.

BIBLIOGRAPHY

Interpretations of Qaykhosraw's career differ; among the important views are those of Claude Cahen, *Pre-Ottoman Turkey* (1968); Osman Turan, *Selçuklular Zamanında Türkiye* (1971); and Alexis G. C. Savvides, *Byzantium in the Near East* (1981).

RUDI PAUL LINDNER

[See also **Byzantine History; Ikonion; Qılıj Arslan II; Seljuks of Rum.**]

QAYRAWĀN, AL- (**Kairouan**), was the capital of Ifrīqiya from the seventh to the eleventh century and thereafter a city noted for religious scholarship. The name is of Persian origin, meaning "resting-place," and was given to the camp established by the Arabs about 670 as their headquarters for the conquest of the Byzantine province of Africa. It was strategically situated about 80 miles (129 kilometers) south of the Byzantine capital, Carthage, on the natural frontier between the lower, drier lands to the south and east, across which the Arabs had advanced from Egypt, and the higher, wetter lands of the Atlas to the north and west. After the death of its founder, ᶜUqba ibn Nāfiᶜ, the camp was abandoned by the Arabs in the 680's, to be reoccupied in the 690's. When Byzantine Africa was finally conquered about 700, al-Qayrawān became the capital of the new Arab province of Ifrīqiya and the headquarters from which Mūsā ibn Nuṣayr undertook the conquest of western Algeria, northern Morocco, and Spain, 705–715. Thereupon it became the capital of the whole of the Arab West, until, following the Kharijite revolt at Tangier in 739, this huge dominion broke up in the civil wars surrounding the fall of the Umayyads in Damascus in 750. Reduced to the capital of Ifrīqiya, it was fought for by the Arabs and the largely Berber Kharijites until 772, when the province was finally reattached to the central Muslim lands, now ruled by the victorious Abbasids. In 800 it became the capital of the independent Aghlabid emirate of Ifrīqiya.

By then al-Qayrawān had turned from an army camp into a civilian city. A central area for administration, meeting, prayer, drill, and marketing was progressively enclosed, fortified, and reconstructed as a mosque with court and prayer hall, in 700–705, 724–727, and 774, each time larger to accommodate the growing population. The mosque, whose main axis points toward the southeast, continued to serve many purposes, including that of a fortress in which to take refuge. But the seat of government was transferred to a Dār al-Imāra or "Government House," opposite the south or *miḥrāb* wall. This separation of government from the mosque, accompanied by the development of a professional army distinct from the populace, was carried further by the Aghlabids when they abandoned the Dār al-Imāra for palaces outside the city altogether, first in al-ᶜAbbāsiya in 801, then in Raqqāda in 876–877. To prevent rebellion, they dismantled the walls of the city in 824. But between 836 and 863 they rebuilt the great mosque yet again, yet larger, and yet more heavily fortified with a massive tower. Beneath the pavement of the court was a large cistern fed by rainwater for public use; but the location of the big city on a semidesert site led to the building about 860 of two large circular reservoirs to the north of the city, filled by a winter stream and by an aqueduct from the hills. A broad main street ran through the city from north to south to the east of the great mosque. Streets may originally have been on a grid pattern, as at Tripoli (northern Africa), as late as the fourteenth century.

Al-Qayrawān remained a large metropolis under the Aghlabids, the Fatimids (909–972), and the first Zirids (972–1054). From 921 to 947–948 the Fatimids resided in Mahdia, a new city which they built on the coast; al-Qayrawān does not seem to have suffered. In 945 it briefly served as the capital of the rebel Abū Yazīd al-Nukkārī. After his defeat, the Fatimids returned to build a third palace, Ṣabra al-Manṣūrīya, as their principal abode, a mile or two away. Raqqāda was left as a park and place of muster for the army on campaign. Al-Qayrawān then grew to its greatest size, prospering from its position on the trade routes from Spain to the Middle East, within reach of the Mediterranean and ports in Sicily and Europe, as the terminus of a trans-Saharan route to the Sudan, and from the presence of a rich and powerful monarch. Among its different communities were Kharijite Berbers from the south and native Latin Christians. As a major center of the Malikite school of Islamic jurisprudence, the city was unfriendly to the Shiite court of the Fatimids. Their successors, the Zirids, while maintaining allegiance to the Fatimids, became more sympathetic to their subjects, and by the eleventh century the court at Ṣabra and the scholars of the city formed an intimate group of men of letters.

By then, al-Qayrawān was poorer, due to the departure of the Fatimids for Egypt in 972 and the consequent decline of trade. Eventually, in 1048, the Zirid sultan Mu^{c}izz attempted to revive the Fatimid empire in North Africa in his own name, but in so doing quarreled with the Arab nomadic tribes of the Banū Hilāl, who defeated him at the Battle of Ḥaydarān (in southeast Ifrīqiya) in 1052. Following this battle, Ṣabra was plundered and al-Qayrawān was twice besieged, in 1052 and 1053–1054. A city wall was built, but in 1054 the sultan made the decision to leave the city for Mahdia, where he went in 1057. The decision led to a massive emigration to the coastal cities, to Sicily, and to Spain. With so many people and the sultan himself gone, al-Qayrawān was plundered by the Arabs, who nevertheless then allied themselves with the remaining inhabitants, led now by the religious scholars of the city. Around their schools the city gradually changed, becoming much smaller and concentrating in the quarter southwest of the great mosque. Its political importance revived under the Almohads and their successors at Tunis from 1160 onward, when it became a strategically-placed provincial center.

Its fame as a holy city, however, was paramount. From the fourteenth century onward, the ^{c}*ulamā*$^{\supset}$ or scholars were joined by Sufi heikhs in their *zāwiya*s; particular sanctity came from Abū Zam^{c}a al-Balawī, a Companion of the Prophet, said to be buried nearby. Scholars and heikhs shared the same education and, with those of Tunis, came to form a powerful body in society during the rule of the Hafsids (1229–1574), with much influence in government. But Tunis, the political capital, tended eventually to predominate as the religious capital of the country, and when Tunisia finally recovered from the disasters of the sixteenth century, al-Qayrawān was clearly in second place.

BIBLIOGRAPHY

Robert Brunschvig, *La Berbérie orientale sous les Hafsides des origines à la fin de XVe siècle,* 2 vols. (1940–1947); Hady Roger Idris, *La Berbérie orientale sous les Zirides, X^{e}–XIIe siècles,* 2 vols. (1962); Alexandre Lézine, *Architecture d'Ifrīqiya* (1966), and "Notes d'archéologie ifriqiyenne," in *Revue des études islamiques,* 35 (1967); Mohamed Talbi, *L'émirat aghlabide* (1966).

MICHAEL BRETT

[See also **Aghlabids; Berbers; Fatimids; Ifrīqiya; Islamic Art and Architecture; Zirids.**]

QAYṢARĪYA, the core of a Muslim market or bazaar, consisted of a number of interconnected streets with shops lining both sides. The streets, which ended in gates that were locked at night, were often vaulted or covered with canvas. The word *qayṣarīya* possibly derives from the Roman and Byzantine imperial market (caesarian), since in the Islamic world this type of market was built or owned by an emir. In a *qayṣarīya* precious items were stored and sold.

BIBLIOGRAPHY

Solomon D. Goitein, *A Mediterranean Society,* I (1967), 191, 194, IV, 29; Ernst J. Grube *et al., Architecture of the Islamic World: Its History and Social Mean-*

Qibla wall and *miḥrāb* from the Great Mosque of Córdoba, 965. PHOTO: WIM SWAAN *ing,* George Michell, ed. (1978); Ira M. Lapidus, *Muslim Cities in the Later Middle Ages* (1984).

ÜLKÜ Ü. BATES

[See also **Bedestan.**]

QIBLA, the direction of the Kaaba in the Islamic holy city of Mecca, toward which Muslims orient themselves during prayer. In early Islam, evidence suggests that for a time the Prophet used Jerusalem as a qibla for the first mosque, his house in the town of Medina, but later changed the direction of prayer from north to south, toward the Kaaba.

The qibla wall of the mosque serves, therefore, as a focus of the communal prayers that constitute the bulk of the spare Islamic ritual of worship. The center of the qibla wall contains the *miḥrāb,* a niche that gives that wall its identity. Frequently the qibla is decorated with religious inscriptions, and the *miḥrāb* with carving, ceramics, polychromy, and calligraphy. In important mosques the minbar (pulpit) is placed against the qibla wall, to the right of the *miḥrāb.*

The computation of the direction of the qibla was often subject to error; the Great Mosque of Córdoba, for example, is oriented almost directly south rather than east-southeast toward Mecca. This explains the often baffling mixture of orientations the traveler encounters in Islamic cities with a long history of building, such as Cairo or Fēs.

BIBLIOGRAPHY

D. A. King, "Kibla," in *Encyclopaedia of Islam,* new ed., V (1986), and "Astronomical Alignments in Medieval Islamic Religious Architecture," in *Annals of the New York Academy of Sciences,* 385 (1982).

WALTER B. DENNY

[See also **Islamic Art and Architecture; Kaaba; Miḥrāb; Mosque.**]

QILIJ ARSLĀN II (*r.* 1151–1192), Seljuk sultan of Rum, the dominant Anatolian ruler of his century. His father, Mas'ūd I, placed him in charge of a southeast march against the crusaders (and his later rival Nūr al-Dīn). After Mas'ūd's death in 1155, Qılıj Arslān faced the additional rivalry of his brothers, the Byzantines, and the Danishmendids. Manuel I allied Byzantium with the Danishmendid rulers and forced the Seljuk sultan to seek peace. Qılıj Arslān accepted the independence of his brother Shāhānshāh, promised the Byzantines peaceful frontiers and a defensive alliance, and recognized the territorial annexations of Nūr al-Dīn and the Danishmendids. In 1162 the sultan visited Constantinople, where Manuel spent three months impressing on him the wealth and ceremonial opulence of his state. Peace with Byzantium, however, only freed the sultan to cement his authority in central and eastern Anatolia, while it did not lead to a cessation of nomad raids on Byzantine border possessions.

The fortuitous death of the Danishmendid ruler Yaghibasan in 1164 allowed Qılıj Arslān to begin stripping his Anatolian enemies of their lands and influence. The exiled rulers sought help from Nūr al-Dīn, whose attentions duly turned north in 1171 after the conquest of Egypt. Qılıj Arslān again, as with the Byzantines, relied on negotiations to save his position: Shāhānshāh retrieved his appanage in Ankara, the Danishmendid Dhū'l-Nūn retained a small area centered on Sivas, and Nūr al-dīn forced Qılıj Arslān to accept the responsibility for carrying on warfare against the Byzantines. This curious aspect of the agreement may have had less to do with a shared religious zeal than with a desire to define and secure the frontier separating Syrian and Anatolian claims.

The death of Nūr al-Dīn in 1174 destroyed the balance of power in Anatolia. Qılıj Arslān immediately annexed the lands of his immediate rivals. Manuel, troubled by the Seljuk revival and by the sultan's inability or unwillingness to control the border nomads, planned a campaign to recover the Byzantine lands. On 17 September 1176, however, the Seljuk army routed the Byzantine forces at the narrow pass of Myriokephalon/Kırkbaş, northwest of Yalvaç, thus guaranteeing unified Turkish control of the Anatolian plateau; Manuel's was the last great Byzantine offensive against the Turks. After Qılıj Arslān destroyed Malatya, the last Danishmendid principality, in 1178, through either his own efforts or those of the nomads nominally subject to him, a number of Byzantine towns on the western edge of the plateau came into the Seljuk orbit: Dorylaion/Şar Hüyük, near Eşkisehir; Kotyaion/Kütahya; and Sozopolis/Uluborlu.

During Qılıj Arslān's reign the rich and varied Seljuk silver coinage began to be struck, the result of the growth of long-distance trade, attested by

Byzantine sources, and of a related increase in silver mining in Anatolia.

Sometime around 1187 Qılıj Arslān partitioned his realm among (originally) ten sons, a brother, and a nephew.

While Qılıj Arslān retained Konya (Ikonion), his heirs ruled independently, and some of them struck coins in their own names. The sons of Qılıj Arslān soon warred against each other, as well as against their father, who had also to deal with the soldiers of the Third Crusade in 1190. A year later, the elderly sultan took flight and found refuge with Qaykhosraw I. Aided by a number of marcher lords, they reconquered Konya and were beginning to reunite the realm when the elderly sultan died in 1192, after nominating Qaykhosraw to succeed him.

BIBLIOGRAPHY

Claude Cahen, "Kilīdj Arslān II," in *Encyclopaedia of Islam,* V (1986), and a more detailed account in his *Pre-Ottoman Turkey,* J. Jones-Williams, trans. (1968); Osman Turan, *Selçuklular Zamanında Türkiye* (1971), 197–236. A Byzantine perspective is found in Speros Vryonis, Jr., *The Decline of Medieval Hellenism in Asia Minor* (1971).

RUDI PAUL LINDNER

[See also **Anatolia; Byzantine History; Danishmendids; Ikonion; Manuel I Komnenos; Qaykhosraw I; Seljuks of Rum.**]

QIRGHIZ. See **Kirghiz.**

QIRMIZ (kirmiz), a crimson dye produced from the crushed shells of aphids that cling to plants. It was found particularly in Armenia and was greatly prized in the Middle Ages. There are references to this dye in classical authors, but the name *qirmiz* (whence French *cramoisi* and English crimson) is known from, among others, the works of Arab geographers who describe and praise the dyed textiles that they call "Armenian goods (*aṣnāf armanīa*) . . . that do not have their equals in any part of the world." These goods seem to have been on sale in a number of cities, including Berdaᶜa/Partaw in Azerbaijan, and they circulated throughout the Muslim world. A number of centers of the dye works are known in the Middle Ages, but a major one may have been the town of Artašat in the valley of the Araks, if the historian al-Balādhurī's reference is to be read *Azdisāṭ . . . qaryat al-qirmiz* ("the chief village of *qirmiz*") and not *qaryat al-Hurmuz,* as has been suggested by some scholars.

BIBLIOGRAPHY

Al-Balādhurī, *Futūḥ al-buldān,* trans. by Philip K. Hitti as *The Origins of the Islamic State,* I (1916, repr. 1966), 314; Marius Canard in Joseph Laurent, ed., *L'Arménie entre Byzance et l'Islam depuis la conquête arabe jusqu'en 886,* rev. ed. (1980), 572, n. 44; Aram Ter Ghewondyan, *The Arab Emirates in Bagratid Armenia,* Nina G. Garsoïan, trans. (1976), 137–139, 140–141; Wilhelm von Heyd, *Histoire du commerce du Levant au moyen âge,* II (1886, repr. 1959), 607–609; Hakob Manandyan, *The Trade and Cities of Armenia in Relation to Ancient World Trade,* Nina G. Garsoïan, trans., 2nd rev. ed. (1965), 79, 143–144, 153; Robert Sergeant, *Islamic Textiles* (1972).

NINA G. GARSOÏAN

[See also **Dyes and Dying; Scarlet.**]

QMA (plural, *qmani*), a term in Georgian for "slave" or "serf," a subject of a lord (*patroni*). The term usually referred to dependent peasants, but vassals and even great nobles were *qmani* of their sovereigns. In the Georgian "feudal" hierarchy, a *qma,* even a peasant, could also be a *patroni* and have other *qmani* dependent on him. In general, *qma* denoted any subject who owed obedience to a *patroni,* who in turn was his protector or proprietor.

BIBLIOGRAPHY

William E. D. Allen, *A History of the Georgian People,* 2nd ed. (1971); Cyril Toumanoff, *Studies in Christian Caucasian History* (1963).

RONALD GRIGOR SUNY

[See also **Georgia: Political History.**]

QUADRANT, an astronomical instrument with a graduated arc of ninety degrees for measuring altitudes of the sun and stars. It originated in late antiquity, when it was described by Ptolemy in the *Almagest,* and was later developed by Arabic astronomers. In the West it had been known since the tenth century as a portable instrument that also had hour lines enabling its use as a sundial. The "old" quadrant (*quadrans vetus*) was first described in detail in the thirteenth century by Robert the Englishman in Montpellier and by others. It was developed by Jacob ben Machir Ibn Tibbon (Prophatius Judaeus, *ca.* 1236–1305) into a "new" quadrant (*quadrans novus*) that incorporated features of the astrolabe. In the Renaissance it became a large, stationary instrument (Copernicus), sometimes fixed to a wall (Tycho Brahe) as a meridian instrument.

BIBLIOGRAPHY

Giuseppe Boffito and C. Melzi d'Eril, eds., *Il quadrante d'Israel* (1922); Robert W. T. Gunther, *Early Science in Oxford,* II (1923), 154–174; José-María Millás-Vallicrosa, "La introducción del cuadrante con cursor en Europa," in *Isis,* 17 (1932); Paul Tannery, "Le traité du quadrant de maître Robert Anglès," in his *Mémoires scientifiques,* V (1922).

OLAF PEDERSEN

[See also **Astrolabe; Scientific Instruments; Sundials.**]

QUADRANT ARCH. See **Arch.**

QUADRIPARTITE VAULT. See **Vault.**

QUADRIVIUM, the part of the medieval seven liberal arts that followed the trivium in the curriculum and was composed of arithmetic, music, geometry, and astronomy. The word *quadruvium* first appears in the opening chapter of Boethius' *De institutione arithmetica,* probably written during the opening decade of the sixth century. (In manuscripts dating from the ninth century the spelling remains *quadruvium,* while *quadrivium* begins to appear in the tenth and eleventh centuries.) Although Boethius' arithmetical work is a translation of Nicomachus of Gerasa's *Eisagogē arithmetica,* no single word expressing the notion of the quadrivium appears in Nicomachus. The creation of the word and concept is thus accredited to Boethius.

For Boethius, the quadrivium represented a fourfold path whereby the soul of the student of philosophy is led away from the realm of sense perception and matter to the realm of pure, incorporeal knowledge. Each of these four paths is a mathematical discipline, and each discipline has its foundation in the ancient Pythagorean concept of quantity. According to the Neopythagoreans (especially those of the second century A.D.), quantity was subdivided into two genera: discrete and continuous. Discrete quantity is known through number. Continuous quantity, on the other hand, is known through line, and through forms created from lines.

To derive the four mathematical disciplines, each of these two genera is further subdivided. Discrete quantity in and of itself (for example, square numbers, triangular numbers, perfect numbers) is the subject of arithmetic, while discrete quantity in relationships (in ratios) is the subject of music. Continuous quantity that is fixed (that is, not in motion) is the subject of geometry, while quantity of this genus in motion is the subject of astronomy. The purpose of these four disciplines is to train the mind in manipulation of abstract truths as preparation for contemplation of the higher truths of philosophy.

At times during the Middle Ages and Renaissance, the quadrivium was reduced to a practical curriculum with no epistemological foundation, and at other times the philosophical impetus of its original formulation restored it to a purpose propaedeutic to philosophy.

BIBLIOGRAPHY

Boethius, *De institutione arithmetica . . . De institutione musica . . . ,* Gottfried Friedlein, ed. (1867, repr. 1966); Calvin M. Bower, "The Role of Boethius' *De institutione musica* in the Speculative Tradition of Western Musical Thought," in *Boethius and the Liberal Arts: A Collection of Essays,* Michael Masi, ed. (1981), 157–174; Pearl Kibre, "The Boethian *De institutione arithmetica* and the Quadrivium in the Thirteenth-century University Milieu at Paris," in *Boethius and the Liberal Arts: A Collection of Essays,* Michael Masi, ed. (1981), 67–80; Hans M. Klinkenberg, "Der Vervall des Quadriviums im frühen Mittelalter," in *Artes liberales von der antiken Bildung zur Wissenschaft des Mittelalters,* Josef Koch, ed. (1959), 1–32; Michael Masi, *Boethian Number Theory: A Translation of the "De institutione arithmetica"* (1983); Nicomachus Gerasenus, *Introduction to Arithmetic,* Martin Luther D'Ooge, trans., introduction by Frank E. Robbins and Louis C. Karpinski (1926); Leo Schrade, "Das propädeutische Ethos in der Musikanschauung des Boethius," in *Zeitschrift für Geschichte der Erziehung und des Unterrichts,* **20** (1930), and "Music in the Philosophy of Boethius," in

Musical Quarterly, **33** (1947); Alison White, "Boethius in the Medieval Quadrivium," in *Boethius: His Life, Thought, and Influence,* Margaret Gibson, ed. (1981), 162–205.

CALVIN M. BOWER

[See also **Arts, Seven Liberal; Boethius, Anicius Manlius Severinus; Fachschriftum; Trivium.**]

QUAESTIO IN UTRAMQUE PARTEM. This brief tract was written about 1302 in defense of King Philip IV the Fair of France. The anonymous author, perhaps a Parisian theologian, attacks the claims allegedly made by Pope Boniface VIII, which assert papal supremacy over secular matters. The *Quaestio* attempts to demonstrate that the spiritual power has no ordinary jurisdiction in temporal affairs. The arguments are drawn from Scripture, canon law, Roman law, history, and Aristotle. Christ did not give Peter both swords. Within the church the spiritual and temporal powers are separate and distinct, although the former possesses some indirect, incidental rights over the latter. The king of France is independent in his realm and not subject to emperor or pope in temporals; he is also granted implicit jurisdiction over some spirituals. Of particular significance is the *Quaestio*'s interpretations of recent canonist opinions. The work's moderate dualism anticipates the more thorough two-power system proposed by John of Paris.

BIBLIOGRAPHY

The text appears in Melchior Goldast, ed., *Monarchiae sancti romani imperii,* II (1614, repr. 1960), 95–107. For a discussion, see John Watt, "The *Quaestio in utramque partem* Reconsidered," *Studia Gratiana,* **13** (1967).

THOMAS RENNA

[See also **Boniface VIII, Pope; John of Paris; Philip IV the Fair; Political Theory, Western European; Two Swords, Doctrine of.**]

QUAESTIONES are a feature of Scripture study from the time of Jerome and Augustine. In his *In topica ciceronis,* I, Boethius defined a *quaestio* as a "doubtful proposition" (*dubitabilis propositio*). Such a problematic statement, admitting the question whether (*utrum*) it or its contradictory is true, became a characteristic artifice of twelfth-century philosophical and theological inquiry. Thirteenth-century university teachers continued to introduce *quaestiones* into the lectures of their textual commentaries but increasingly omitted the textual division and exposition that had preceded the question section. Specialized treatises and comprehensive summas also were often composed in this question form. Academic discussion too became a formal exercise with *quaestiones disputatae* and *quaestiones quodlibetales,* disputations conducted by the masters.

BIBLIOGRAPHY

Bernardo C. Bazán, "La *quaestio disputata,*" in *Les genres littéraires dans les sources théologiques et philosophiques médiévales* (1982); Martin Grabmann, *Die Geschichte der scholastischen Methode,* 2 vols. (1909–1911).

P. OSMUND LEWRY, O. P.

[See also **Biblical Interpretation; Dialectic; Exegesis, Latin; Philosophy and Theology, Western European; Scholasticism, Scholastic Method.**]

QUARTER, a measure of capacity and a weight, identical in size to the seam, used in the British Isles for dry products: chopped bark, Yorkshire, 9 heaped bushels (about 4.05 hectoliters); glass, generally 120 pounds (54.431 kilograms) or 24 stone of 5 pounds each, but occasionally 100 pounds (45.359 kilograms) or 20 stone of 5 pounds each; grain, generally 8 striked or leveled bushels (about 2.82 hectoliters) of 8 gallons each and equal to one-quarter chalder (hence the name *quarter*), but variations from 7 to 9 bushels were common; lime, Derbyshire, 8 striked bushels (about 2.82 hectoliters) at the wharves and 8 heaped bushels (about 3.60 hectoliters) at the kilns; salt, 4 hundredweight (203.208 kilograms); and Welsh coal, Devonshire, 16 heaped bushels (about 7.20 hecotliters).

RONALD EDWARD ZUPKO

[See also **Bushel; Chalder; Gallon; Pound; Weights and Measures, Western European.**]

QUARTON, ENGUERRAND. See **Charonton, Enguerrand.**

QUATRE LIVRE DES REIS, LI, a twelfth-century translation into Anglo-Norman French of the Four Books of Kings (Samuel 1–2 and Kings 1–2). Intended for a lay audience, the translation is based on the Vulgate with some interpolations from the older *Versio italica;* it also incorporates glosses from several commentaries, including the *Glossa ordinaria* and the *Glossa interlinea.* Written in elegant prose, the text is interspersed with short rhyming passages.

BIBLIOGRAPHY

An edition is Ernst R. Curtius, ed., *Li quatre livre des reis* (1911). Studies are M. Dominica Legge, *Anglo-Norman Literature and Its Background* (1963); and Wolf-Dieter Stempel, "Prosaübersetzung und Prosastil: Zur altfranzösischen Übersetzung der *Quatre livres des rois,*" in Erich von Richthofen *et al.,* eds., *Philologica romanica* (1975).

ELLEN T. WEHNER

[See also **Anglo-Norman Literature; Bible, French.**]

QUATREFOIL, an opening or ornamental frame in the shape of four radiating leaves or petals, widely used in Gothic art and architecture. The quatrefoil is composed of four lobes or foils arranged circularly. The points of intersection of these four segments of circles point inward and are called cusps.

GREGORY WHITTINGTON

[See also **Glass, Stained; Gothic Architecture; Rose Window; Tracery; Trefoil;** and the front cover of this volume.]

QUBBA, an Arabic word with several meanings. The primary meaning is that of cupola, as in Qubbat al-Sakhra, the Dome of the Rock in Jerusalem. The word's earlier meaning is that of tent, and it refers to a type of rounded tent that was not frequent in the Arabian Peninsula for dwellings, but that was used as a portable tent carried by camels, often serving to keep some tribal symbol. As a result, the domical shape seems to have acquired, if not always a specifically religious significance, at least an honorific one.

A third meaning of the word *qubba* is derivative but colloquially already frequent in the Middle Ages. It is that of mausoleum, of a monument built over someone's tomb. The reason for the use of this word is simply that a domical structure was the most common form for a mausoleum, as we know from early examples in Samarra (ninth century), the area of Baghdad (tenth century, known mostly from texts), and eventually the great tombs of medieval Cairo or the simpler mausoleums of well-known or obscure saints all over North Africa.

The main problem with these mausoleums is that, in a strict interpretation of Islam, it is not appropriate to emphasize after death such social or spiritual inequities as may have existed in life. As a result, many of the early mausoleums either reflected some pre-Islamic cult or folk practice or were the creation of splinter groups, especially the Shiites, who gave special emphasis to the line of descent from the Prophet. As time went on, however, the mausoleum often became simply a form of conspicuous consumption.

BIBLIOGRAPHY

E. Diez, "Ḳubba," in *The Encyclopaedia of Islam,* new ed., V (1986); Oleg Grabar, "The Earliest Islamic Commemorative Structures," in *Ars orientalis,* 6 (1966); E. Baldwin Smith, *The Dome* (1950).

OLEG GRABAR

[See also **Ayyubid Art and Architecture; Cupola; Dome; Dome of the Rock; Egypt; Fatimid Art; Islamic Art and Architecture; Samarra.**]

QUEROLUS, a Roman comedy of the late empire, probably dating from the early fifth century. The author may have been the fabulist Avianus. *Querolus* (The complainer) is the only extant Roman comedy aside from the plays of Plautus and Terence, and its plot has often been considered a reworking of the former's *Aulularia* (The pot of gold). However, even a cursory reading of the two plays reveals their independence.

In *Querolus,* Mandrogerus and his accomplices steal a pot of gold from Querolus, Euclio's son, but toss it back upon discovering only ashes, unaware that gold lies beneath the ashes. The play is dedicated to one Rutilius, possibly the poet Rutilius Claudius Namatianus.

During the Middle Ages, *Querolus* was attributed to Plautus, and indeed it seems to have been Plautus' greatest claim to fame. Sometime in the twelfth century Vital of Blois reworked the play, which is written in a kind of rhythmical prose, into elegiac verse. Vital called his version *Aulularia.*

BIBLIOGRAPHY

Two editions are Léon Herrmann, ed., *Avianus: Oeuvres* (1968); and Willi Emrich, ed., *Griesgram oder die Geschichte vom Topf: Querolus sive Aulularia* (1965). An English translation is available in George E. Duckworth, ed., *The Complete Roman Drama,* II (1942), 896–949. For an edition and French translation of Vital of Blois's *Aulularia,* see Gustave Cohen, ed., *La "comédie" latine en France au XIIe siècle,* I (1931), 59–106.

EDWARD FRUEH

[See also **Drama, Western European; Latin Literature; Vital of Blois.**]

QUINISEXT SYNOD. See **Councils (Ecumenical, 325–787).**

QUINZE JOIES DE MARIAGE, LES. As the taste for fabliaux in verse was fading away, the prose novella began to flourish as a genre. One of the most remarkable of these is the *Quinze joies de mariage,* an anonymous work from around the year 1400. Its themes are common to those found in the fabliaux. In fifteen chapters, it is the pitiful and at times mockingly amusing story of a husband duped and baited by his wife, her relatives, and her friends.

The work, frequently but falsely attributed to Antoine de la Sale, is probably from an unknown cleric of the end of the fourteenth or beginning of the fifteenth century. The place of composition is unknown. However, it has been suggested that it could be either the southwest of France or northern Poitou.

The characters of the story are the stock characters of the fabliaux: the henpecked, often simple-minded husband; the crafty, nagging wife; the conniving mother-in-law; the wife's lady friends and her lovers. The fifteen tales are well organized and make full use of dialogues to articulate the narrative into a lively and coherent unit. There is no doubt that in the *Quinze joies de mariage* we are dealing with a parody of the *Quinze joies de Nostre Dame,* a popular ladies' devotional.

We know little about the diffusion of the *Quinze joies de mariage.* There are four manuscripts extant, plus a fragment, all from the fifteenth century, and there are also several early editions printed in Lyons and in Paris.

BIBLIOGRAPHY

Editions. Joan Crow, ed., *Les quinze joyes de mariage* (1969); Jean Rychner, ed., *Les .XV. joies de mariage* (1963). For English translations, see Elisabeth Abbott, *The Fifteen Joys of Marriage* (1959), and Brent A. Pitts, *The Fifteen Joys of Marriage* (1985), with extensive bibliography.

Studies. Marcel Cressot, *Vocabulaire des "Quinze joies de mariage"* (1939); Guy Mermier, "La ruse féminine et la fonction morale des 'Quinze joies de mariage,'" in *Romance Notes,* **15** (1974).

GUY MERMIER

[See also **Antifeminism; Cent Nouvelles Nouvelles; Christine de Pizan; Courtly Love; Deschamps, Eustache; Fabliau and Comic Tale; Family, Western European; French Literature; Nouvelle; Romance of the Rose.**]

QUIRE (from Old French *quaer,* whence *cahier*), a gathering of leaves, the basic building block of the codex type of book. A quire comprises a series of double folios (bifolia or sheets) placed on top of one another and folded in the center to form a booklet. Alternatively, one large sheet might be folded several times to produce the same result. Quires of medieval manuscripts often contain four double folios, consituting gatherings of eight leaves or sixteen pages (a *quaternio*), but other formats were also used. Analyzing a manuscript's quires can reveal much about the book's origin and subsequent history.

BIBLIOGRAPHY

Bernhard Bischoff, *Paläographie des römischen Altertums und des abendländischen Mittelalters* (1979), 34–38; Léon Gilissen, *Prolégomènes à la codicologie: Recherches sur la construction des cahiers et la mise en page des manuscrits médiévaux* (1977).

MICHAEL MCCORMICK

[See also **Codex; Codicology, Western European; Manuscript Books, Binding of; Writing Materials.**]

QUIRE MARKS. See **Signatures.**

QUODLIBET (what you please). The disputation was a standard educational device in medieval universities. Normally the disputation would be on a specific topic, but on certain occasions the master would allow students to raise whatever questions they liked. These events were called *disputationes quodlibetales.*

Much later—in the sixteenth century—the term quodlibet migrated into music, where it was applied to compositions that combined familiar quotations from songs or instrumental works. Such combinative compositions were, however, composed as early as the thirteenth century. The concept of combinative music may have originated with the *cantus prius factus* techniques that formed the basis for much medieval polyphony.

Most notable among early examples of combinative music was the *motet enté* (grafted motet), whose tenor or refrain included quotations from popular vernacular songs. The French combinative chanson of the fifteenth and sixteenth centuries employed the technique of superimposing one popular song upon another, as well as that of successive quotation.

BIBLIOGRAPHY

Maria R. Maniates, "Quodlibet revisum," in *Acta musicologica,* 38 (1966), and "Combinative Chansons in the Escorial Chansonnier," in *Musica disciplina,* 29 (1975).

MARCIA J. EPSTEIN

[See also **Centonization; Chanson; Motet; Music, Western European; Quaestiones; Scholasticism; Scholastic Method; Universities.**]

QURĀN. See **Koran.**

QURAYSH, the tribe to which Muḥammad belonged and the dominant power in Mecca at his time. In late antiquity Quraysh seems to have consisted of some twelve seminomadic clans inhabiting the Hejaz in the general vicinity of Mecca, which at the time was an ephemeral encampment around the Kaaba, a shrine venerated by many Arabian tribes. The rise of Quraysh probably began under the leadership of Quṣayy in the early sixth century. By assembling a coalition of Quraysh clans, with the support of elements from the Syrian-based tribes of Kināna and Quḍāᶜa, Quṣayy was able to gain control of the lands surrounding the Kaaba. He then assigned residential tracts to the various clans, thus giving Quraysh a definite base of operations and transforming Mecca into a permanent town.

The prosperity of Quraysh at Mecca was made possible by trade through western Arabia and by the Kaaba's status as a religious sanctuary. Through a combination of trading stations, alliances with other Arab tribes, and general mercantile expertise, Quraysh organized much of the caravan traffic between Syria and Yemen, and eventually came to monopolize the important commercial routes through the Hejaz. This not only brought economic benefits but also served to enhance Mecca's religious status, for pilgrims as well as traders converged there from all over Arabia. Quraysh leaders encouraged this trend and promoted themselves as guardians of the Kaaba and providers for the pilgrims. Thus, as the economic and spiritual status of Mecca increased, so did the importance and prestige of Quraysh. By the time of Muḥammad, they were generally regarded as the most eminent tribe of western Arabia. More important, their commercial prosperity brought benefits to many tribes that participated in the Arabian trade; thus they had many potential allies in the event of military confrontation. Quraysh suffered from serious internal divisions; but its leaders were skilled and patient politicians, and managed not only to keep internal problems under control but also to bring numerous other tribes into a tenuous alliance for their mutual benefit.

Quraysh resisted the mission of Muḥammad, which it perceived as a threat, right up to the time of the Prophet's conquest of Mecca in 630. But religious affiliations did not nullify tribal ties in general, or the status enjoyed by Quraysh in particular. Muḥammad consistently proclaimed his Quraysh lineage, and even during the difficult days of nascent Islam in Medina, the members of Quraysh who had made the hegira with Muḥammad (*muhājirūn,* emigrants) were able to claim and hold dominant positions in the community, much to the chagrin of the early Medinan converts to Islam. After the fall of Mecca, and the death of the Prophet in 632, Quraysh consolidated its position in Medina through further emigration from Mecca, increased landholdings in the vicinity of Medina, and maintenance of its traditional neutrality among the tribes, which thus found themselves resolving their quarrels by handing power over to Quraysh.

The tribe played a leading role in the creation of the Islamic empire, which owed much to Quraysh political acumen, commercial contacts with neighboring regions, and diplomatic experience in dealing with other tribes. Quraysh leaders directed the early Arab conquests, organized the administration of the newly won lands, and comprised the dominant force in political affairs. The "elder statesmen" who convened to choose a caliph after the assassination of ᶜUmar ibn al-Khaṭṭāb in 644, for example, were all from Quraysh, and later Sunni political theory was simply codifying established custom when it stipulated that the caliph (or imam) must be from Quraysh.

Quraysh also made important contributions to the development of Islamic civilization. The Koran was collected under its auspices (at the behest of the caliph ᶜUthmān), and the disciplines of Koranic exegesis and prophetic tradition (*ḥadīth*) were initiated by Quraysh scholars. Law and history were represented by prominent schools of thought in Medina through the work of such Quraysh scholars as ᶜUrwa ibn al-Zubayr, Muḥammad ibn Muslim ibn Shihāb al-Zuhrī, and Mālik ibn Anas.

Though members of Quraysh would individually dominate the Islamic empire for centuries, the rapid expansion of Islam at the same time caused the tribe to break up and disperse throughout the Muslim world. In Arabia, Quraysh's economic strength was gradually but irrevocably undermined when the conquests erased old imperial frontiers and made it unnecessary for traders to detour along the difficult Arabian routes through Mecca and Medina, the centers of Quraysh power. Politically, the tribe suffered a disastrous setback when the seat of the caliphate left Arabia, never to return, after the assassination of ᶜUthmān ibn ᶜAffān in 656. ᶜAlī ibn Abī Ṭālib's transfer of the capital to Al-Kufa, in Iraq, emphasized the increasing importance of the new provinces, and further accelerated the decline of the position of Arabia. That Quraysh was unwilling to acquiesce in this reduced role was demonstrated by the revolt of Ṭalḥa ibn ᶜUbayd Allāh and al-Zubayr ibn al-ᶜAwwām, leaders of the clans of Taym and Asad, a few months after ᶜAlī's succession in 656. Under Umayyad rule from Syria, the Quraysh of Mecca and Medina were equally restless, and during the Second Civil War (684–692) they were enthusiastic partisans of ᶜAbd Allāh ibn al-Zubayr. Such conflicts served only to decimate the ranks of the tribe. Quraysh suffered heavy losses at the hands of the Umayyads at the Battle of al-Ḥarra in 683. By fighting against the Kharijites in late Umayyad times they also suffered severely; they were defeated with great slaughter at the Battle of Qudayd in 747, and those taken captive were killed unless they denied their Quraysh descent.

At the same time, the development of Islam itself worked against Quraysh. As the faith evolved into a religious system that transcended ethnic and tribal ties, it became increasingly difficult for the principles of Arab tribalism to justify the claims of clan notables (*ashrāf*) to power and privilege. The consequences of the Abbasid revolution ultimately made such claims untenable, and by the end of the eighth century the tribe was of little political consequence. Several Quraysh families were active on the Arabian political scene in later medieval times, but most were impoverished and of only local importance.

BIBLIOGRAPHY

Werner Caskel, *Ǧamharat an-nasab: Das genealogische Werk des Hišām ibn Muḥammad al-Kalbī* (1966); M. J. Kister, *Studies in Jāhilīya and Early Islam* (1980); Henri Lammens, *La Mecque à la veille de l'Hégire* (1924); W. Montgomery Watt, *Muhammad at Mecca* (1953), and *Muhammad at Medina* (1956). Doubts about the role of trade in the fortunes of Mecca generally, and Quraysh in particular, have been raised in Patricia Crone, *Meccan Trade and the Rise of Islam* (1987).

LAWRENCE I. CONRAD

[See also **Arabia; Caliphate; Mecca; Muḥammad.**]

RABANUS MAURUS. See **Hrabanus Maurus.**

RABBENU TAM. See **Jacob ben Meir.**

RABBINATE. The title rabbi appears in Palestine during the first century A.D. with the meaning "my master." It was then given only to those scholars who had been ordained. Since ordination (*semikhah*) could be granted only in Palestine, the title was in use only there. In Babylonia, therefore, sages used another title, that of *rav* (master). After the complete disappearance of the Palestinian ordination in the middle of the fourth century, the title fell into oblivion. It is therefore clear that despite the similarity of name, the medieval European rabbinate is completely different from the talmudic rabbinate and must be looked upon as an original creation of the new Franco-German Jewish settlements. The medieval rabbi, generally called *ha-Rav* (the rabbi), or later *morenu ha-rav* (our teacher the rabbi), emerges as a man of great talmudic knowledge who is able to expound and apply Jewish law and whose moral standards and punctiliousness in the fulfillment of his religious duties are beyond question. As such he takes charge of the judicial and ritual problems of his community and renders judgments, whether alone, as a *dayyan* (rabbinic judge), or as chairman of the rabbinic court (*ab bet din*). He must also teach the law (that is, the Talmud) and give instruction in its application.

With the emergence of an organized Jewish community in Europe during the late tenth and the early eleventh centuries, there arose a need to appoint a specific talmudic scholar who would be entrusted with the authority to resolve ritual and other problems. Until then such problems as arose among Jewish settlers had probably been dealt with on an individual basis by the notables sitting as a court of conciliation. But as the communities grew larger, first in the Rhine Valley and then in other German towns and in northern France, it became clear that Jewish life could no longer rely on the good services of some local scholars and community leaders who would be ready to devote part of their time to communal problems. The very growth of the community, the accumulation of bylaws and communal ordinances (*takkanot*), the accretion of local customs, and the accumulation of problems made it imperative to appoint some recognized scholar who enjoyed the community's confidence to deal with its problems.

The success of the community thus compelled it to create the rabbinate. The fact that medieval law recognized the validity of Jewish law for the Jews and therefore authorized the creation of a Jewish court made the emergence of the rabbinate possible: the scholar could also be a judge. In the first stage, the rabbi was not salaried, although it was soon recommended to take steps in order to enable him to support himself without having to give up his studies. Already in the thirteenth century the salaried rabbi appears. It seems that he received a basic salary from his community and some fees paid for services rendered to individuals. Nevertheless many rabbis of independent means continued some of their extrarabbinic activities, including occasional money-lending, while in the service of their community.

The medieval Jewish community was completely autonomous. In turn, its rabbi was completely independent, since there existed no rabbinic hierarchy except that which resulted from the personal influence and authority of some great rabbinic authority to whom others could turn with questions. In this way the responsum literature (*sheʾelot u-teshuvot*) flourished: a great authority would answer in writing the written questions that had been submitted to him. By contrast, the so-called chief rabbis of the period, including the *rab de la corte* in Castile, the *Arraby Moor* of Portugal, and the *Hochmeister* of Germany, were political appointees of the Christian rulers, who needed them mostly for taxation purposes. They were never recognized as heads of the rabbinic hierarchy by the reluctant Jewish communities.

The rabbi's jurisdiction applied to the city in which he lived and to its surroundings. Even in those German cities where there were two rabbis during the fourteenth and fifteenth centuries, the rabbinate was never confined to a synagogue but always had a territorial basis.

The Middle Ages never saw the development of a system or institution for the training of rabbis, although whenever possible a rabbi would set up and support a yeshiva (talmudic school) at his own expense and in his own home. In principle, a rabbi would authorize a pupil whom he deemed qualified to perform rabbinical functions and to assume the rabbinical title. This teacher-pupil relationship contributed to the revival during the fourteenth century of what was called the ordination "according to the usage of France and Germany," which had a mostly symbolic value. Very early on, rabbinic families appeared, the son succeeding the father in his position or being attached to another community. In view of the precarious conditions that prevailed then in Europe and the massacres and numerous migrations that took place during and after the Black Death, it soon became imperative to introduce some kind of rabbinical diploma that would enable its bearer to validate his title wherever he might move.

As a consequence of this method of bestowing the rabbinical title, some teachers felt that they were entitled not only to deliver diplomas but also to appoint their students as rabbis of a community;

they held that talmudic scholarship was the only necessary criterion for serving in that capacity. The community leaders, however, refused to accept this and insisted that the rabbi be elected. A compromise was eventually reached: the teachers maintained the exclusive right to deliver rabbinic diplomas; and the communities maintained the right to elect the rabbis, but only from the ranks of those who had received the diploma. As a result, many scholars were entitled to use the rabbinic title without assuming the office. The officiating rabbis, being rabbis of communites and not of synagogues, remained few.

The fact that rabbis were elected by the community or its leadership as well as the competition among the candidates did not enhance his authority in the eyes of the leadership, which tried to limit his influence. His authority in ritual matters, notably in those related to ritual food or divorces, was unquestioned. His judgments, whether he had rendered them alone or as chairman of a three-member rabbinic court, were generally accepted. But the overall communal leadership remained in the hands of the lay element, which even managed to limit the rabbis' right to proclaim an excommunication. Only very exceptional rabbinical personalities were able to impose their moral authority and assume political leadership.

On the other hand, Christian rulers often saw the rabbis as the Jewish counterpart of the Christian ecclesiastics (in England they even called them "bishops"!) and tried to influence or confirm their appointment. Their attempts were always rejected by the Jewish community, which steadfastly insisted on its exclusive right to appoint the rabbis.

Whereas in Slavic countries the Franco-German model of of the rabbinate was adopted with only minor, local changes, the situation was somewhat different in the Jewish communities of the Islamic world. There, although the institution existed more or less as it did in Western and Central Europe (with the occasional separation of the judicial and the purely rabbinical functions), the rabbinical title was generally not used, in order to avoid any possible confusion with the talmudic rabbinate that might give the impression of a revival of the suppressed ordination. This is why the religious leaders, particularly in Spain, generally used the title of *ḥakham* (scholar), the title of *dayyan* being reserved for the rabbinic judge, who was generally looked upon as superior to him in standing and in knowledge.

By the end of the Middle Ages, every sizable community in both the East and the West had established its rabbinate, which had become an essential part of its administrative and religious life.

BIBLIOGRAPHY

Simḥah Assaf, *Be-ᵓohale Yaᶜakov* (1943, repr. 1965), 27–65; Salo W. Baron, *The Jewish Community,* II (1948), 66–100; Roberto Bonfil, *Ha-rabanut be-italya be-tekufat ha-renesans* (1979); Mordechai Breuer, *Rabanut ashkenaz be-yeme ha-benayim* (1976); Simon Schwarzfuchs, *Études sur l'origine et le développement du rabbinat au moyen âge* (1957).

SIMON SCHWARZFUCHS

[See also **Exegesis, Jewish; Jewish Communal Self-government; Law, Jewish; Responsum Literature, Jewish; Talmud, Exegesis and Study of.**]

RABENSCHLACHT. See **Buch von Bern, Das.**

RABER, VIGIL (*ca.* 1480–1552), born in Sterzing, South Tirol (now Vipiteno, Italy), was the most important theater entrepreneur in German-speaking Central Europe. As regional play director in Tirol (working as far south as Trent), he was able to amass—in a lifetime of gathering and copying—the single largest collection of stage plays (over fifty-eight) known to have been assembled in medieval Europe.

Son of a Sterzing baker (the family house is still standing on Main Street), Raber is first attested in Bozen (Bolzano), the regional capital, in 1510. If he attended the Latin school in Sterzing (he wrote a good chancery cursive), he must have been an indifferent pupil. Manuscript entries by him are in a barbarous Latin.

Bozen and Sterzing records (mainly financial) indicate that Raber made his living both as a skilled craftsman (painting, gilding, wood carving, illuminating) and, less often, as an artist (altar panels). Bozen records refer to him frequently as *vilg maller* (Vigil the Painter). Much of this work was, however, connected to the theater. In 1514 we find him in Bozen charged with repairing the "dragon" (painted oilcloth over wood frame) used in the local Corpus Christi play, because it was regularly damaged by the spears of St. George and his squires.

Until 1522 Raber appears to have lived mainly in Bozen, where, in 1510, he began his collecting career by copying carnival plays available locally. In 1514 Raber worked for three months (at good pay) to design and build the stage and to rehearse the (lay) actors for the great seven-day performance of the Bozen Passion Play. Attentive to detail, he even purchased cows' tails (*khueschwäntz*) for the devils. In addition, he took on two of the roles, that of Judas (no volunteers) and Christ as Gardener. Not one to throttle ambition, he added a number of speeches to each part.

From 1533 on, Raber was the driving force behind theatrical activities in his native Sterzing, copying and directing plays, but also producing properties such as wooden masks for the devils. After charging him with writing out the Sterzing Passion in 1543, the church provost also commissioned him to repair the large angels' wings (gilded) and the wig of the Christ actor (restored).

When Raber died in December of 1552, his burial expenses were defrayed by the church provost, high tribute to a life spent in service to the church's most effective mass medium, the drama. The Sterzing town council moved quickly to acquire, from his widow, all play manuscripts (*alle vnnd jede geschribne spil*) and stage properties (*spil-ristungen*) Raber had assembled—for a bargain price of six florins (16 November 1553).

When Raber's collection, housed in the Sterzing town hall, was rediscovered in 1848, it contained some fifty-eight play books, most of them written by Raber himself. Raber's own inventory (9 November 1534) shows, however, that the collection was originally even larger. Aside from its size, the collection—which Raber operated like a lending library—is unique in its combination of religious drama and comedies (twenty-six) staged at carnival. The religious plays (longer, more comprehensive staging) are centered on the Easter season, from Palm Sunday to Whitsunday. Without parallel in medieval German are plays on David and Goliath, Dietrich von Bern (comedy), and a "Heavenly Parliament" in which the Virgin Mary presses suit to prevent Christ from becoming the Redeemer.

Since 1918 (when South Tirol was ceded to Italy), the Raber collection has figured in the local "cultural" politics involving Austria and Italy. Spirited away in 1941, it was returned only in 1984 to the Archiv der Gemeinde Sterzing.

BIBLIOGRAPHY

Editions. Oswald Zingerle, ed., *Sterzinger Spiele nach Aufzeichnungen des Vigil Raber,* 2 vols. (1886); Walther Lipphardt and Hans-Gert Roloff, eds., *Die geistlichen Spiele des Sterzinger Spielarchivs,* 6 vols. (1980–1986); Werner M. Bauer, ed., *Sterzinger Spiele* (1982).

Studies. Anton Dörer, "Vigil Raber," in Wolfgang Stammler and Karl Langosch, eds., *Die deutsche Literatur des Mittelalters: Verfasserlexikon,* III (1943), 951–992, V (1955), 925, and "Schicksale des Sterzinger Spielarchivs," in *Zeitschrift für deutsches Altertum und deutsche Literatur,* **94** (1965); Hans Schuhladen, "Vigil Raber und die Tiroler Fastnachtspieltradition," in *Deutsche Vierteljahrschrift für Literaturwissenschaft und Geistesgeschichte,* **51** (1977).

ECKEHARD SIMON

[See also **Drama, German.**]

RADBOD OF UTRECHT (*ca.* 850–917), Benedictine monk and bishop, educated at Cologne by his uncle, Archbishop Gunther, and at the court of Charles the Bald. He became bishop of Utrecht in 899 and remained there until he was driven by invading Danes to Deventer, where he died. He was the author of several homilies on saints and various poems, of which the most famous is that on the swallow, praising its intelligence and fellowship with man.

BIBLIOGRAPHY

Max Manitius, *Geschichte der lateinischen Literatur des Mittelalters,* I (1923), 603–604; *Radbodi Carmina,* Paul von Winterfeld, ed., in *Monumenta Germaniae historica: Poetae latini aevi carolini,* IV, pt. 1 (1899), 160–173; *Vita Radbodi,* O. Holder-Egger, ed., in *Monumenta Germaniae historica: Scriptorum,* XV, pt. 1 (1888), 568–571.

W. T. H. JACKSON

[See also **Carolingian Latin Poetry; Hagiography, Western.**]

RĀḌĪ, AL- (907–940), properly, al-Rāḍī bi'llāh Abu 'l-ᶜAbbās Aḥmad ibn al-Muqtadir, the twentieth Abbasid caliph. Although commonly praised by Muslim historians as the last caliph to rule independently, he was often little more than a tool in the hands of the powerful emirs and viziers of the day. Except intermittently, the authority of the caliph during his reign hardly extended beyond the confines of Baghdad; by al-Rāḍī's death the immediate political importance of the caliphate had become negligible. The events of al-Rāḍī's reign are thus taken by modern historians to symbolize the decline of the caliphate as a directly relevant factor in the politics of the Islamic world.

Al-Rāḍī came to power in April 934, after a rising of the Sājī faction of guards against his uncle, the caliph al-Qāhir. Unable to secure his uncle's legal abdication, al-Rāḍī had him blinded in prison, thereby rendering him unfit to rule. Upon assuming office, al-Rāḍī sought to appoint as vizier the famous ᶜAlī ibn ᶜĪsā, who asked to be excused on account of his great age. After a short-lived compromise that saw ᶜAlī's brother ᶜAbd al-Raḥmān as vizier in name (with ᶜAlī closely directing him), the office was finally given to Ibn Muqla. For most of his vizierate, Ibn Muqla was dominated by the chamberlain Ibn Yāqūt, appointed over Ibn Muqla's objections at the behest of Sīmā, chief of the Sājī guard. It was not until Ibn Yāqūt's death in 935 that Ibn Muqla gained real control of the administration, while the role of the caliph was largely eclipsed. Within a year Ibn Muqla was seized by supporters of Ibn Yāqūt's brother, and the powerless caliph had no choice but to dismiss him and appoint a successor.

As these political struggles wore on, the caliph, bankrupt and politically impotent, was forced to accept the offer of Ibn Rāᵓiq, the semi-independent governor of Wāsiṭ and Basra, to provide for the general expenses of government, including the army and court. In exchange for this, the caliph appointed him supreme commander (*amīr al-umarāᵓ*), a new title that not only asserted the primacy of the military commander of Baghdad over his colleagues elsewhere, but also served as the first formal recognition of a supreme temporal authority in Islam. The caliph was left only as formal head of state and symbol of the religious unity of Islam, while the practical business of government fell to Ibn Rāᵓiq. As supreme commander the latter's name was mentioned in the *khuṭba* (Friday sermon) along with that of the caliph. In 938 Ibn Raᵓiq was replaced as *amīr al-umarāᵓ* by Bajkam.

In addition to the political quarrels of emirs and viziers that dominate the sources for this period, al-Rāḍī's reign saw the continuing war with the Byzantines, struggles with the Hamdanid dynasty of Mosul, and the further advance of the Buyids, who a few years later succeeded in capturing Baghdad. In the capital al-Rāḍī was compelled to take measures against the Hanbalite mobs, led by al-Barbahārī, who were known to enter private homes, destroy musical instruments, assault female singers, and empty wine casks. They also attacked members of the Shāfiᶜī law school outside of mosques. Al-Rāḍī issued a pronouncement against them in 935, condemning the Hanbalite position on a number of important religious questions and ordering them to desist from their disruptive behavior. If the caliph was otherwise powerless, it was in this religiopolitical struggle with the Hanbalites that a wider sphere of independent political action was left open to him.

BIBLIOGRAPHY

A source is Muḥammad ibn Yaḥyā al-Sūlī, *Akhbār al-Rāḍī billāh w'al-Muttaqī billāh* (in French), Marius Canard, trans., 2 vols (1946–1950). The period 892–946 is covered in detail in Harold Bowen, *The Life and Times of ᶜAlī ibn ᶜĪsā* (1928). See also Dominique Sourdel, *Le vizerat ᶜabbaside de 749 à 936,* 2 vols. (1959–1960).

Keith Lewinstein

[See also **Abbasids; Buyids; Caliphate; Seljuks.**]

RADOLF OF LIÈGE (early eleventh century), monk, mathematician, and teacher. He exchanged numerous letters with Ragimbold of Cologne, who had been a fellow student at Chartres, arguing points of mathematics. He also corresponded with Fulbert of Chartres and constructed the first astrolabe in Liège.

BIBLIOGRAPHY

Max Manitius, *Geschichte der lateinischen Literatur des Mittelalters* II (1923), 690ff. and 778ff.; G. Schepss, "Geschichtliches aus Boethiushandschriften," in *Neues Archiv der Gesellschaft für ältere deutsche Geshichtskunde,* XI (1886), 139; Paul Tannery and Abbé Clerval, "Une correspondance d'écolâtres du XIe siècle," in *Notices et extraits des manuscrits de la bibliothèque nationale,* 36, (1899), 514–538.

Nathalie Hanlet

[See also **Astrolabe; Fulbert of Chartres; Mathematics; Ragimbold of Cologne.**]

RADULFUS TORTARIUS (**Raoul le Tourtier** or **Tortaire**) (*ca.* 1063–*ca.* 1114) was born at Gien, southeast of Orléans on the Loire. At an unknown time he entered the abbey of Fleury, where he wrote a continuation of the prose *Miracula sancti Benedicti* of André de Fleury, a verse work on the same subject, a book of epigrams, a translation of Valerius Maximus, and a *Translatio sancti Mauri* that includes an account of the saint's life and of the translation of his remains to Fleury.

BIBLIOGRAPHY
Radulfus' works are in *Patrologia latina,* CLX (1854), 1,171–1,244. See also Francis Bar, *Les epîtres latines de Raoul le Tourtier* (1937); and Max Manitius, *Geschichte der lateinischen Literatur des Mittelalters,* III (1931, repr. 1973), 872–877.

EDWARD FRUEH

[See also **Ami et Amile; French Literature.**]

RADULPHUS GLABER (Raoul Glaber) (*ca.* 985–*ca.* 1047), historian and epigraphist. Born out of wedlock in Burgundy, Radulphus entered the monastery of St. Germain of Auxerre when he was about twelve. By nature restive and averse to discipline, he sojourned in various monasteries, where, thanks to his literary talents, he was welcomed. From 1015 to 1030 he was the traveling companion of and historian for William of Volpiano, abbot of St. Bénigne-de-Dijon. At Cluny under Odilo, from 1030 to 1035, he eventually returned to Auxerre, where he continued his history up to 1047.

Radulphus Glaber's literary works include *Five Books of Histories,* the *Life of St. William,* parts of the *Acts of the Bishops of Auxerre,* and some epigraphy (now lost). His history, undertaken at William's request and dedicated to Odilo, began with the year 900 and presented an outline of French and imperial history, which, as it reached Radulphus' own time, became also a history of the world and of anonymous men. Several accounts of the same global material also appear in the contemporary history (*Historiae*) of Adémar of Chabannes. (An autograph copy of his *History* has been identified.)

Often criticized for inaccuracy, gossip, and prodigy mongering by political historians, he has proven a rich source for social history; and his theology of history prefigures some of the work of Hugh of St. Victor (*d.* 1141), Bishop Otto of Freising (*d.* 1158), and even Joachim of Fiore (*d.* 1202). Radulphus is best known for his apocalyptic interpretation of the two millennial dates since the Incarnation (1000 and 1033), which he linked to mass manifestations of popular piety (heresy, church building, pilgrimage, Peace of God councils). He has, accordingly, suffered from polemical treatment at the hands of modern historians opposed to the Romantic notion of the "terrors of the year 1000."

BIBLIOGRAPHY
Editions. For *Historiarum libri quinque,* see *Monumenta Germaniae historica: Scriptores,* G. Waitz, ed., VII (1846, repr. 1963), 51–72; *Patrologica latina,* CXLII (1853), 611–698; Marcel Prou, ed., *Raoul Glaber: Les cinq livres de ses histoires (900–1044)* (1886).

For a French translation, see Edmond Pognon, *L'an mille* (1947), 45–144. For Radulphus Glaber's life of William of Volpiano, see Neithard Bulst, "Rodulfus Glabers Vita domini Willelmi abbatis," in *Deutsches Archiv für Erforschung des Mittelalters,* **30** (1974); *Patrologica latina,* CLXII (1853), 703–720.

Studies. Paul E. Dutton, "Raoul Glaber's 'De divina quaternitate': An Unnoticed Reading of Eriugena's Translation of the *Ambigua* of Maximus the Confessor," in *Mediaeval Studies,* **42** (1980); J. France, "The Divine Quaternity of Radulphus Glaber," in *Studia monastica,* **18** (1975); Monique-Cecile Garand, "Un manuscrit d'auteur de Raoul Glaber?" in *Scriptorium,* **37** (1983); Julien Havet, "Note sur Raoul Glaber," in *Revue historique,* **40** (1889); Karl Leyser, *The Ascent of the Latin West* (1986); L. Musset, "Raoul Glaber et la balein: Les sources d'un racontar du XIe siècle," in *Revue du moyen âge latin,* **4** (1948); Stephen G. Nichols, *Romanesque Signs: Early Medieval Narrative and Iconography* (1983), chaps. 1–2; Ernest Petit, "Raoul Glaber," in *Revue historique,* **48** (1892); Paul Rousset, "Raoul Glaber, interprète de la pensée commune au XIe siècle," in *Revue d'histoire de l'église de France,* **36** (1950); Margarete Vogelgesang, "Der cluniacenische Chronist Radulfus Glaber," in *Studien und Mitteilungen zur Geschichte des Benediktiner-ordens und seiner Zweige,* **67** (1956), **71** (1960).

RICHARD LANDES

[See also **Adémar of Chabannes; Historiography, Western European; Millennialism; Odilo of Cluny, St.; Peace of God; William of Volpiano; Year 1000, The.**]

RAGIMBOLD OF COLOGNE (early eleventh century), famous teacher and mathematician at Cologne, conducted a correspondence about 1025 with Radolf of Liège on problems of geometry, for example the relation of the diagonal of a square to its sides, which throws considerable light on the state of knowledge in his time and on the availability of works on the subject.

BIBLIOGRAPHY

Epistolae, Paul Tannery, ed., in *Notices et extraits des manuscrits de la Bibliothèque Nationale,* **36** (1899), 514–536; Max Manitius, *Geschichte der lateinischen Literatur des Mittelalters,* II (1923), 778–781.

W. T. H. JACKSON

[See also **Fulbert of Chartres; Mathematics; Radolf of Liège.**]

RAGNARǪK, in Scandinavian mythology, the end of the order of the gods and the destruction of the world. The term literally means "fate of the gods." The form *ragnarøkkr,* "twilight of the gods," although incorrect, is attested in medieval manuscripts of *Snorra Edda* and has thus entered the literature. Details of *Ragnarǫk* are mentioned in many poetic sources, chief among them *Vafþrúðnismál* and *Vǫluspá.* The more complete account in the *Gylfaginning* of *Snorra Edda* is based on these and perhaps other (lost) sources.

Ragnarǫk begins with the *fimbulvetr,* three years of fierce winter without respite. The bonds of kinship, so important to Germanic society, are broken as brother kills brother, and adultery is rampant. A wolf swallows the sun and another the moon, making it impossible to reckon time, and all the creatures of evil break loose. Heimdallr sounds the alarm as the world tree Yggdrasill, symbolic of the universe, trembles with fear. The gods meet their enemies in individual combat. Odin battles and is swallowed by the wolf Fenrir, previously bound by Týr (but Odin's son Víðarr kills the wolf in revenge); Freyr falls before Surtr, who brings flame to burn the world and leads the sons of Muspell; Týr and the hound Garmr slay one another; Thor kills his archenemy, the Midgard serpent, but staggers back and falls dead from the serpent's poison; and Heimdallr and Loki kill one another. Surtr sets the world afire. The sun darkens, and the earth sinks into the sea as gods and men perish. The good and righteous will inhabit pleasant places, but the evil will be sent off for punishment.

The earth will rise again and unsown fields grow green. A new generation of gods will dwell where Asgard once stood: Víðarr and Váli, sons of Odin, and Móði and Magni, sons of Thor. Finally, the innocent Baldr and his guiltless slayer and half brother Hǫðr will be reconciled, and according to *Vǫluspá,* Hœnir will cast lots. Two of the race of men are also spared to repopulate the earth, and a daughter of the sun replaces her mother. The *Vǫluspá* poet adds that the "powerful, great one who rules all" will come to power.

Traditional scholarship has for the most part limited itself to seeking the origins of the motifs and to separating pagan from Christian components. Axel Olrik's studies are typical. They purport to identify Christian, Celtic, and Persian elements in the myth, but virtually no Germanic ones, as well as the date and routes whereby the Oriental material entered Germanic culture. The pattern was often followed by other scholars, with only details altered: Manichaean influence is often cited. A different course involves investigating the principal source, *Vǫluspá,* especially its historical context and the personality of its anonymous poet.

Neither of these courses is satisfactory. Notions of borrowing ignore the clearly defined role of *Ragnarǫk* in Old Scandinavian eschatology and fail to motivate the loan. The emphasis on *Vǫluspá* is more fruitful, but the myth is well attested in many other sources and craves explanation on its own terms. Given the Celtic and Iranian parallels, one may be dealing with an Indo-European inheritance incorporated into Germanic society and given special significance by the meeting with Christianity.

BIBLIOGRAPHY

Georges Dumézil, *Gods of the Ancient Northmen,* Einar Haugen *et al.,* trans. (1973); John S. Martin, *Ragnarok: An Investigation into Old Norse Concepts of the Fate of the Gods* (1972); Sigurður Nordal, ed., *Vǫluspá,* B. S. Benedikz and John McKinnell, trans. (1978); Axel Olrik, *Ragnarök: Die Sagen vom Weltuntergang,* Wilhelm Ranisch, ed. and trans. (1922); Will-Erich Peuckert, "Germanische Eschatologien," in *Arkiv für Religionswissenschaft,* **32** (1935); Richard Reitzenstein, "Weltuntergangsvorstellungen," in *Kyrkohistorisk Årsskrift* (1924), 129–212.

JOHN LINDOW

[See also **Eddic Poetry; Fenris Wolf; Fimbul Winter; Freyr; Hœnir; Midgard Serpent; Odin; Scandinavian Mythology; Snorra Edda; Thor.**]

RAGNARS SAGA LOÐBRÓKAR (Saga of Ragnarr Shaggy-Breeches) is an Old Norse *fornaldar-*

saga (legendary saga) by an unknown Icelandic writer, preserved in manuscripts from the fourteenth century and later. This type of saga has as a rule little or no historical authenticity. Although *Ragnars saga* is among the better ones in this respect, it too shows in exemplary fashion how in these legendary sagas historical facts can be overgrown by motifs from fairy tales and heroic legends. Thus we know from historical sources that Ragnarr and his sons all lived sometime in the ninth century, but none of them experienced the events precisely as recounted in the saga. Moreover, some of the saga characters were not Ragnarr's sons at all. Saxo Grammaticus' version in the ninth book of his *Gesta Danorum* also differs greatly from the account of the saga.

According to the saga, Ragnarr is king of the Danes. As a young man he goes to Gautland and kills a dragon whose size increases as its treasure grows; the motif of the little worm that grows to monstrous size is known from several countries and may well have originated in Persia, as A. H. Krappe has suggested, citing as a parallel the *Shāhnāma* by Firdawsī (or Ferdousi, *d. ca.* 1020). The dragon also guards the earl's daughter Þóra. Ragnarr returns to his country with her as his wife; she gives birth to two sons and dies soon afterward. Ragnarr's second wife is Áslaug, an otherwise unknown daughter of Sigurd and Brynhild who grew up as a foundling among poor people at Spangareid in southwestern Norway. The figure of Áslaug is easily recognized as that of the princess in poor clothing from fairy tales. In all probability she originated in a local folktale and serves in the saga to establish a genealogical connection between the Volsungs and King Harald Fairhair (*d. ca.* 930).

After a variety of adventures Ragnarr goes to Britain with only two ships. He is defeated and ends his life in the snake pit of King Ella. Characteristically, the weakest son makes revenge possible: Ívarr asks the English king to give him as wergild for his father a piece of soil in England such that it might be surrounded by one oxhide. This cunning trick (well known from Vergil's story of Dido) leads to the foundation of London (or, historically more probable, York); after some years Ívarr sends for his brothers and Ella is killed.

The origin of the tale is generally believed to lie in stories told in the Danish colonies in Northumbria about Ragnarr and, especially, about his sons' raids in England. Gradually these stories were linked together, and at the same time Ragnarr became the main character. In the twelfth-century lay *Krákumál,* Ragnarr is already said to have died in a snake pit, whereas the historical Viking leader Ragnarr perished of an epidemic disease brought back with him from a foray into France. The saga took its final shape when Áslaug was introduced. Striking features of the saga are the topics fetched from heroic legends and from fairy tales (for example, the peasant's clever daughter who is made queen after solving three riddles or the very helpful, weak child).

In the most important manuscript (Copenhagen, Royal Library, Ny kgl. saml. 1824b) *Ragnars saga* is presented as a continuation of *Vǫlsunga saga.* Because of its special mixture of motifs and because *Ragnars saga* is dependent on *Þiðreks saga,* it could hardly have been composed earlier than 1250.

BIBLIOGRAPHY

Bjarni Guðnason, "Gerðir og ritþróun Ragnars sögu loðbrókar," in *Einarsbók: Afmæliskveðja til Einars Ól. Sveinssonar, 12 desember 1969* (1969); Halldór Hermannsson, *Bibliography of the Mythical-Heroic Sagas* (1912), 34–39, and *The Sagas of the Kings (Konunga sögur) and the Mythical-heroic Sagas (Fornaldar sögur): Two Bibliographical Supplements* (1937), 60–62; Anne Holtsmark, "Heroic Poetry and Legendary Sagas," in *Bibliography of Old Norse-Icelandic Studies* (1965); Alexander H. Krappe, "Sur un épisode de la Saga de Ragnar Lodbrók," in *Acta philologica scandinavica,* **15** (1941–1942); Rory McTurk, "The Relationship of Ragnars saga loðbrókar to Þiðreks saga af Bern," in *Sjötíú Ritgerðir helgaðar Jakobi Benediktssyni,* II (1977); Marina Mundt, "Omkring dragekampen i Ragnars saga loðbrókar" in *Arv,* **27** (1971); A. H. Smith, "The Sons of Ragnar Lothbrok," in *Saga Book of the Viking Society,* **11** (1935); "Ragnars saga loðbrókar," in *Fornaldarsögur Norðurlanda,* Guðni Jónsson, ed., I (1950), 219–285; *Völsunga saga ok Ragnars saga loðbrókar,* Magnus Olsen, ed. (1906–1908).

MARINA MUNDT

[See also **Fornaldarsögur; Þiðreks Saga; Vǫlsunga Saga.**]

RAHEWIN (*d.* after 1170), secretary and chaplain to Bishop Otto of Freising (*d.* 1158). Upon receiving Otto's deathbed commission, which was endorsed by Emperor Frederick I Barbarossa (*r.* 1152–1190), Rahewin wrote the continuation of Otto's *Gesta Frederici* (books III and IV, covering the period from August 1157 to February 1160). He completed this work by June 1160 at the latest.

Rahle signed by Hasan, son of Suleiman of Isfahan (Persian or West Turkistani), 1360. THE METROPOLITAN MUSEUM OF ART, NEW YORK, ROGERS FUND 1910.218

Then, although he lived for another ten or more years, he never carried his chronicle past February 1160.

Rahewin suffers severely from comparison with Otto, perhaps the greatest historian of the Middle Ages; but he was a well-read man and a competent writer with some poetic talent. Moreover, he evidently enjoyed describing the particulars of history as fully as possible. In addition to the *Continuatio* and several poems, he may have written in 1162/1163 *Dialogus de pontificatu sanctae Romanae ecclesiae,* which favors Pope Alexander III (1159–1181) over Barbarossa's antipope Victor IV (F. J. Schmale casts some doubt on the ascription of the *Dialogus* to Rahewin).

BIBLIOGRAPHY

Sources. Otto, bishop of Freising, *Ottonis episcopi Frisingensis et Rahewini Gesta Frederici seu rectius,* F. J. Schmale, ed. (1965), ed. and trans. into English by Charles C. Mierow as *The Deeds of Frederick Barbarossa* (1953); Rahewin, "Dialogus de pontificatu sanctae Romanae ecclesiae," in *Monumenta Germaniae historica: Libelli de Lite,* III (1897), 526–546.

Studies. J. B. Gillingham, "Why Did Rahewin Stop Writing the Gesta Frederici?" in *English Historical Review,* **83** (1968); Max Manitius and Paul Lehmann, *Geschichte der lateinischen Literatur des Mittelalters,* III (1931, repr. 1974), 388–392; Peter Munz, "Why Did Rahewin Stop Writing the Gesta Frederici? A Further Consideration," in *English Historical Review,* **84** (1969).

ELAINE GOLDEN ROBISON

[See also **Historiography, Western European; Otto of Freising.**]

RAHLE, the Turkish term for a low lectern used for holding an open book, usually a Koran. (In some parts of the Muslim world, the term *kursī miṣḥaf,* meaning chair or throne of the Koran, is used.) The reader sits on the floor, keeping the *rahle* about chest level. Almost all *rahle*s (Turkish pl., *rahleler*) are of wood, some elaborately carved or inlaid with various colored woods and materials such as bone, shell, and mother-of-pearl. Other *rahle*s are collapsible, consisting of two interlocking rectangular pieces of wood. When opened, an X shape is formed: the book rests on the upper part, and the lower section forms the legs.

BIBLIOGRAPHY

Cevdet Çulpan, *Rahleler,* with German summary (1968); Hermann Schmitz, *The Encyclopedia of Furniture* (1957), pl. 311a.

ÜLKU Ü. BATES

[See also **Furniture, Islam; Kursī.**]

RAIMBAUT D'AURENGA (1144–1173), a powerful political figure as well as an esteemed troubadour from Provence. Raimbaut left forty-one poems, characterized by their difficult style, technical subtlety, and forceful images. He upheld the practice of *trobar clus* (obscure verse) in a debate poem with Giraut de Bornelh, pointing the way to the highly refined style of Arnaut Daniel.

BIBLIOGRAPHY
Walter T. Pattison, *The Life and Works of the Troubadour Raimbaut d'Orange* (1952).

ROBERT TAYLOR

[See also **Arnaut Daniel; Provençal Literature; Troubadour, Trouvère.**]

RAIMBAUT DE VAQUEIRAS (*ca.* 1155–1207), Provençal troubadour. Protected by his patron Boniface of Montferrat, Raimbaut fought in Sicily and on the Fourth Crusade. Twenty-six of his poems survive from the period 1175–1207. He is best known for his *estampida* called *Kalenda Maya* (May Day), a multilingual descort, a bilingual debate with a forthright Genoese lady, an allegorical poem called *Lo Carros* (The chariot), and an epic letter addressed to his patron.

BIBLIOGRAPHY
Joseph Linskill, *The Poems of the Troubadour Raimbaut de Vaqueiras* (1964).

ROBERT TAYLOR

[See also **Dance; Descort; Provençal Literature; Troubadour, Trouvère.**]

RAIMON DE CORNET (*d.* after 1349), Provençal troubadour whose father, also named Raimon de Cornet, had been a troubadour before him. He was educated for the church, probably at the University of Toulouse, and became a secular priest by 1324. Before 1327 he had briefly been a Franciscan and, more than that, a follower of the heretical Spiritual Franciscan Peter John Olivi. Raimon's flirtation with heresy seems to have placed him in some danger of death at the hands of the Inquisition at Avignon. Having returned to orthodoxy, his religious wanderings led him to become a "monge blanch," or White Monk of Cîteaux (the Cistercian Order), by 1341. His poetic career seems to have flourished between 1324 and 1340.

Raimon appears to have desired a close association with the Consistoire de Gai Saber (Gay Science), an academy established at Toulouse in 1323, and to have coveted the prizes it awarded. In the event, only once, in 1330, did one of his poems receive the annual Violette d'Or.

Approximately fifty of Raimon's poems have survived, belonging to all the genres except the *dansa.* He wrote religious and secular lyrics and love songs, social satires, epistolary poems, versified literary criticism, and didactic pieces. Concerning the quality of his poetry, opinion is remarkably divergent. Alfred Jeanroy devoted thirty pages to denouncing him: Raimon lacked imagination and originality, his ideas were jejune, his emotions superficial, his intellect disorganized, his spirit servile, and so on. Even where Jeanroy conceded Raimon real virtuosity—for example, in his use of rare and difficult rhymes—he could not refrain from calling their utilization "aussi puériles qu'inflexibles." J.-B. Noulet, on the other hand, declared that Raimon lacked neither originality nor talent and that he failed to win more prizes from the "Gai Consistoire" because he was not the sort of man who would constrain his inspiration in a servile manner in order to conform to the academy's canons.

BIBLIOGRAPHY
Alfred Jeanroy, "La poésie provençale dans le sud-ouest de la France et en Catalogne du début au milieu du XIVe siècle," in *Histoire littéraire de la France,* XXXVIII (1941), 1–11, 28–65; Robert Lafont and Christian Anatole, *Nouvelle histoire de la littérature occitane,* I (1970), 229–232; René Nelli and René Lavaud, eds. and trans., *Les troubadours,* II (1966), 772–793; J.-B. Noulet and Camille Chabaneau, eds., *Deux manuscrits provençaux du XIVe siècle* (1888).

ELAINE GOLDEN ROBISON

[See also **Provençal Literature; Troubadour, Trouvère.**]

RAIMON DE MIRAVAL (*ca.* 1165–*ca.* 1229) was one of the most colorful troubadours of the generation of 1200, although not a poet of the first rank. He was born into a noble Provençal family fallen on hard times, and his inheritance consisted of a one-quarter share in a castle in which there resided only forty men. Later achieving success in his career, he became a close friend of Count Raymond VI of Toulouse, the most important troubadour patron of his day. He was also on good terms with

King Pedro II of Aragon. In 1209 or 1211, during the Albigensian Crusade, Simon de Montfort seized the castle of Miraval, and Raimon took refuge, probably staying first with Count Raymond and later (after the battle of Muret, 1213) going to Spain, where he died.

What seized his contemporaries' imagination was Raimon's expertise in love: the troubadour Raimon Vidal said Miraval knew more of love than anyone. Medieval troubadour biographies recounted his many amorous adventures, but (even if some of these adventures were imaginary) his liaisons seem to have been repeatedly ill-starred. More impressive was his well-articulated elaboration of the theory of *fin'amors* (fine or courtly love). Of note is that his ideal relationship was marked less by passionate rapture than by contentment. He further envisioned this contentment as rendering the lovers ever more gracious to others, so that the courts in which they lived became ever more socially agreeable. For some troubadours, for example Raimbaut d'Aurenga and Arnaut Daniel, fulfillment in love conflicted with the imperatives of courtly behavior; for Raimon individual and social fulfillment were identical.

Stylistically, Raimon's commitment to social virtues was embodied in his preference for *trobar leu*, or easily comprehensible poetry, and his rejection of *trobar clus*, or obscure, "untamed" verse, which he said deserved neither "reputation nor praise." His poems, he declared, were easy to learn, with their fine, clear words and "sweet and graceful melodies" (Topsfield, number 31). It is noteworthy that for twenty-two of Raimon's approximately forty-five extant poems the music has survived.

BIBLIOGRAPHY

Paul Andraud, *La vie et l'oeuvre du troubadour Raimon de Miraval* (1902); Friedrich Gennrich, *Der musikalische Nachlass der Troubadours,* III (1958), 130–146; René Nelli, ed. and trans., *Raimon de Miraval: Du jeu subtil à l'amour fou* (1979); L. T. Topsfield, *Troubadours and Love* (1975), 219–237, and *idem,* ed., *Les poésies du troubadour Raimon de Miraval* (1971).

ELAINE GOLDEN ROBISON

[See also **Arnaut Daniel; Courtly Love; Provençal Literature; Raimbaut d'Aurenga; Simon de Montfort; Troubadour, Trouvère.**]

RAIMON VIDAL DE BESALÚ (*fl. ca.* 1200), Catalan author who wrote in Provençal. His prose *Razos de trobar* is one of the earliest vernacular treatises on grammar and rhetoric. Three verse novellas deal with courtly love (*So fo el temps . . .*), the decadence of poetry (*Abrils issi' . . .*), and the punishment of a jealous husband (the fabliau *Castia-gilos*).

BIBLIOGRAPHY

William H. Field, *Poetry and Prose: Raimon Vidal,* II (1971); John H. Marshall, ed., *The Razos de trobar of Raimon Vidal and Associated Texts* (1972); Raimon Vidal, *L'école des jaloux (Castia gilos): Fabliau du XIII*[e] *siècle par le troubadour catalan Raimon Vidal de Bezalu,* Irénée-Marcel Cluzel, ed. (1958).

ROBERT TAYLOR

[See also **Catalan Literature; Fabliau and Comic Tale; Provençal Language; Provençal Literature; Troubadour, Trouvère.**]

RAIMONDO DE' LIUZZI. See **Mondino dei Luzzi.**

RAINALD OF DASSEL (*ca.* 1120–1167), a noblemen, son of a Saxon count, was the cathedral provost of Hildesheim. He became Frederick I Barbarossa's archchancellor in 1156 and archbishop of Cologne in 1159. Rainald was the principal proponent of Frederick's antipapal policy. Rainald's hasty selection of a new antipope in 1164 prolonged the Alexandrian Schism. Rainald was also the patron of the Archpoet, whose "Imperial Hymn" presented Frederick's and Rainald's imperial doctrine in poetic language.

BIBLIOGRAPHY

Walther Föhl, "Studien zu Rainald von Dassel," in *Jahrbuch des kölnischen Geschichtsvereins,* **17** (1935), **20** (1938); Peter Munz, *Frederick Barbarossa: A Study in Medieval Politics* (1969).

JOHN B. FREED

[See also **Archpoet; Frederick I Barbarossa; Germany: 1138–1254; Goliards.**]

RAINALDUS (*fl.* 1260–1270), architect at Pisa. An inscription on the cathedral facade credits "this extraordinary work" (presumably the facade) to Rainaldus, "learned overseer and master craftsman." Some identify this Rainaldus with the homonymous *operaio* (overseer) and *sp*[eci?]*arius* (druggist, that is, a handler of precious powders) recorded in cathedral documents of 1264–1270; others date Rainaldus the architect a century earlier.

BIBLIOGRAPHY
Kenneth John Conant, *Carolingian and Romanesque Architecture* (1959), 232; Robert Papini, "La costruzione del Duomo di Pisa," in *L'arte,* **15** (1912); Piero Sanpaolesi, *Il Duomo di Pisa e l'architettura romanica toscana delle origini* (1975), 235–282; Christine Smith, "The Date and Authorship of the Pisa Duomo Facade," in *Gesta,* **19** (1980).

DALE KINNEY

[See also **Pisa Cathedral.**]

RAINER OF HUY (*fl.* early twelfth century), goldsmith. The "Reinerus aurifaber" who signed as witness a charter of 1125, given by Bishop Albero I of Liège to Notre-Dame de Huy, may be the "Reinerus aurifex" whose death is recorded (4 December) in the obituary of Neufmoustier Abbey near Huy. He has been identified as the artist who executed the baptismal font at St. Barthélemy in Liège, commissioned for Notre-Dame-aux-Fonts by Abbot Hellinus (1107–1118) and described in the *Chronicon rhythmicum* (1118).

Other works attributed to Rainer include an incense burner (Lille, Musée des Beaux-Arts, based unconvincingly on the name of the donor, Reinerus, given in the inscription) and a crucifix in the Schnütgen Museum in Cologne (*ca.* 1110/1120, based on stylistic parallels to the font).

BIBLIOGRAPHY
Canonici Leodiensis chronicon rhythmicum, in *Monumenta Germaniae historica: Scriptorum,* XII (1856), 419; *Chronique liègeoise de 1402,* Eugene Bacha, ed., (1900), 131; Gilles d'Orval, "Gesta episcoporum leodiensium," in *Monumenta Germaniae historica: Scriptorum,* XXV (1880), 95; Jean Lejune, "Renier, l'orfèvre, et les fonts de Notre Dame," in *Anciens pays et assemblées d'état,* fasc. 3 (1952); *Rhein und Maas: Kunst und Kultur 800–1400,* I (1972), 238, 241, 253, and II (1973), 194–196, 237–262, 396–397; Karl Hermann Usener, "Renier von Huy und seine künstlerische Nachfolge," in *Marburger Jahrbuch für Kunstwissenschaft,* 7 (1933).

John the Baptist preaching in the desert. Detail from the brass baptismal font by Rainer of Huy for St. Barthélemy, Liège, 1107–1118. PHOTO: A.C.L., BRUSSELS

GRETEL CHAPMAN

[See also **Bronze and Brass; Metalsmiths, Gold and Silver; Mosan Art** (with illustration).]

RAISING OF LAZARUS. See **Lazarus, Raising of.**

RAMADAN is the ninth month of the lunar Muslim calendar. According to E. W. Lane's *Arabic-English Lexicon,* when the names of the months were changed from the ancient language, they were then named according to the season in which they fell. This particular month happened to agree with the days of "vehement heat" (*ramiḍa*). The month of Ramadan, which was regarded as a sacred month in pre-Islamic Arabia, was designated as a month of fasting by the prophet Muḥammad, because during this month the Koran was first revealed to him. The revelation first mentioning Ramadan occurred in 624, the second year of the Prophet's migration from Mecca to Medina. Prior to that, Muḥammad and his followers observed the fast of ᶜĀshūrāᵓ, the Day of Atonement.

First regulations of the fast are to be found in the Koran (2:183–187 in A. Yusuf Ali's English edition). Fasting is prescribed to the Muslims "as it was prescribed to those before you," presumably referring to the Christians and Jews, "that ye may learn self-restraint." Fasting is the fourth "pillar" of Islam, and whoever denies the obligation to fast is considered infidel (*kāfir*). Intention (*nīya*) is a condition of the fast; it must be renewed each night, with the full formulation: To fast tomorrow to acquit my duty toward God of fasting Ramadan this year.

REGULATIONS OF THE FAST

Fasting during Ramadan is incumbent upon every Muslim in full possession of his senses and (if a woman) free from menstruation and the bleeding of childbed. It begins at the break of dawn when "a white thread is distinguishable to you from the black thread" (Koran 2:183) and lasts until sunset. Total abstinence from food, drink, and sexual intercourse is demanded, as is abstinence from indecent talk, slander, calumnies, lies, and insults. There are many traditions that stress this moral and spiritual value of fasting and the doing of good to humanity. What is prohibited during daylight is permitted during the hours of darkness.

Special dispensations in the case of illness, pregnancy, travel, and holy war are granted, provided restitution is made at a later time. The obligation must be renewed when the reason for exemption has disappeared. "For those who are able [yet do not perform] it, a redemption [is provided, viz.] the feeding of an unfortunate," but it is better to fast (Koran 2:184). The fast is not meant for self-torture. Islam does not enjoin asceticism; rather Muslims should in moderation and with gratitude avail themselves of God's bounty. "God intends every facility for you; He does not want to put you to difficulties. He wants you to complete the prescribed period and to glorify Him" (2:185).

The fast of Ramadan began with the sighting of the new moon. This was established with the testimony of trustworthy witnesses. The daily beginning and ending of the fast had to be announced to the people in a way settled by local custom. The traveler Ibn Jubayr, who visited Mecca as a pilgrim in 1183, described how the emir proclaimed the beginning of the fast by ordering the beating of drums the night before. In Egypt, the *missaḥarātī* roamed the streets before dawn, beating his drum to awaken the fasting Muslims to eat the *saḥūr,* the last meal before daybreak.

Special services and communal prayers (*ṣalāt al-tarāwīḥ* or *ṣalāt al-qiyām*) were performed during the nights of Ramadan. The Prophet seems to have held these prayers in high esteem. They consist of a series of bows (*rakᶜas*), ending with a single-bow prayer with a long set of supplication. As Ramadan drew to a close the religious aspect of the fast was intensified by strict adherence to the full program of night services. The last ten days of the month, the period during which the Night of Power (when Muḥammad received his first revelation) would fall, were and still are regarded the holiest. A *qiyām* service was added; it began about midnight and lasted, with long prostrations, several hours; the service ended with a long supplication (*duᶜāᵓ*) in which the congregation participated with repeated amens. Ibn Jubayr provides a vivid description of how such night services were conducted in twelfth-century Mecca. On the odd-numbered days of the last third of Ramadan, when the Koranic *tarāwīḥ* were concluded, the holy sanctuary was decorated with chandeliers and illuminated with numerous candles, lamps, and torches. The practice of repairing to the mosque during the last ten days of Ramadan is known as *iᶜtikāf,* meaning withdrawal for prayer and meditation. It was and continues to be considered meritorious and numbered among the good works.

The end of the month of fasting was again determined by the sighting of the crescent by dependable witnesses. Usually, the final decision was left to the qadis, or religious judges. The last day of the fast was followed by *ᶜid al-fiṭr,* or festival of the breaking of the fast. An early religious service—the festival of public prayer by the whole community—was followed by holidays and celebrations, lasting from three to four days, during which time new clothes were worn, sweets eaten, and gifts and visits of congratulations exchanged.

It is incumbent upon each Muslim, if able, to pay *zakāt al-fiṭr* before the end of the period of fasting or at least before the communal prayer that is celebrated on the day of the *ᶜid.* This particular deed of charity draws the believer nearer to God and unifies the Muslims, rich and poor, into one community. After having experienced hunger pains, Muslims would feel compassion for those who are in need. The *zakāt* is also meant to cleanse the believer's heart of the sins he may have committed during Ramadan. "A good deed erases a bad one," Muḥammad is reported to have said.

THE IMPORTANCE AND MEANING OF RAMADAN

Muslims usually celebrated Ramadan with elaborate preparations. Shops and bazaars were decorated with lights and flags. Mosques were brightly lit all night for the duration of the fast. Special lanterns (*fawānīs*) were lit in homes and carried through the streets by children who chanted traditional and religious hymns. In Cairo, as in many other Muslim cities, Ramadan was ushered out with pageantry. Shops were stocked with all kinds of food, fruits, nuts, and sweets, and people saved their colorful clothes for the occasion. (All of the practices discussed above continue to the present day.)

Muslim scholars stress the ethical and social sides of fasting. The fasting of Ramadan signifies the subjection of the passions, and the priority of the soul. The daily repetition of *nīya* emphasizes the conscious discipline of the soul; it is an assertion that the body is the servant, not the master, of man.

BIBLIOGRAPHY

Gustave von Grunebaum, *Muhammadan Festivals* (1951); "Ṣawm," in *Encyclopedia of Islam,* IV, 1st ed. (1934); John A. Williams, ed., *Islam* (1961), 112–113.

FAUZI M. NAJJAR

[See also **Fasting, Islamic; Islam, Religion.**]

RAMBAM. See **Maimonides, Moses.**

ṘAMIK (Pahlavi: **ramīk*), the lowest estate of Armenian medieval society, including both urban dwellers (traders and artisans) and the peasants (*šinakan*). Although they were *anāzat* (nonnoble) and subsequently taxable, the *ṙamik* were personally free and had some political rights; they are occasionally mentioned by the contemporary sources as participating in Armenian councils side by side with the nobles and clergy. They may even have served in special cavalry units known as *iamikspas,* mentioned in historical sources and conciliar canons.

BIBLIOGRAPHY

Hračya Ačaryan, *Hayeren Armatakan Baṙaran,* IV, 2nd ed. (1977), 140; R. Kherumian, "Esquisse d'une féodalité oubliée," in *Vostan* (1948–1949), 22, 27–30; Hakob Manandyan, *Feodalizme Hin Hayastanum* (1934), 118–119, 149, 188–189; Cyril Toumanoff, *Studies in Christian Caucasian History* (1963), 127.

NINA G. GARSOÏAN

[See also **Armenia, Social Structure; Šinakan.**]

RAMÓN DESTORRENTS. See **Destorrents, Ramón.**

RAMÓN LLULL. See **Lull, Ramon.**

RAMON BERENGUER IV (*ca.* 1113–1162), count of Barcelona (1131–1162) and prince of Aragon (1137–1162). He was the son of Ramon Berenguer III and Dolça of Provence, and older brother of Berenguer Ramon (*d.* 1144), who inherited Provence on their father's death. Ramon Berenguer IV's conquests at the expense of the Moors completed the territorial formation of Catalonia; his legal and administrative enterprises provided the new principality with concepts and institutions of regalian order; and his marriage to Petronilla, the heiress of Aragon, resulted in a dynastic union later to be known as the "Crown of Aragon."

Even before his father's death, Ramon Berenguer IV was active in the campaigns of the lower Ebro Valley, challenging the expansionist designs of Aragon in that zone. Upon the death of Alfonso the Battler (Alfonso I of Aragon) in 1134, Ramon was well placed to assume the preponderant role in the eastern Hispanic reconquest. Only Alfonso VII of Castile posed a threat to this preponderance, a threat which was parried by the recognition of Castilian suzerainty over the former Saracen kingdom of Saragossa. In a series of spectacular expeditions and campaigns, Ramon Berenguer IV attacked Alcolea (1141), Monzón (1142), Lorca (1144), Valencia (1146), and, jointly with the Genoese and Castilians, Almería (1147). In 1148–1149 came the decisive conquests of Tortosa, Lérida, and Fraga; toward 1152 fell Miravet, among numerous other Moorish strongholds of the lower Ebro; and with the clearing of the massif of Siurana in 1153 the occupation of New Catalonia was effectively completed.

In the same years Ramon Berenguer IV vigorously defended his younger brother's inheritance in Provence, and by intervening on behalf of the lord of Montpellier (1143), whose successor, Guillem VII, would be a faithful coadjutor in his Moorish campaigns, he laid the foundation of subsequent Aragonese-Catalonian lordship over Montpellier.

With the conquests of 1148–1153 Ramon Berenguer IV and his advisers quietly changed the political structure of the old Spanish March. The comital authority of Barcelona was redefined as a regalian principate in the *Usatges of Barcelona,* a code of customary law compiled from older materials toward 1150, while Tortosa and Lérida were partly retained in domain and partly enfeoffed, but were not erected into counties. In 1151 the count-prince ordered an administrative survey of Old Catalonia, and from that date may be traced the beginnings of regular territorial administration. Ramon Berenguer IV was thus the founder of the principality of Catalonia. He was represented toward 1180 as a conquering hero who fulfilled his dynastic destiny (*Deeds of the Counts of Barcelona*). His role in Aragon was hardly less important. By the terms of Ramon's marriage to Petronilla, his father-in-law Ramiro was to retain the title of king. But Ramiro's title was clouded by his father's astonishing will, by which the kingdom of Aragon was conveyed to the military orders; Ramon Berenguer IV had to negotiate the treaties with the Knights of the Hospital, of the Temple, and of the Holy Sepulcher to secure his wife's title and ultimately his own. Despite the urgings of some, the prince-count refused to assume the title of king in Aragon, leaving it to his eldest son, Alfonso II (*r.* 1162–1196), to consummate the union of the two inheritances. Negotiating effectively with King Henry II of England and with Emperor Frederick I Barbarossa, Ramon Berenguer IV stood out as the greatest ruler of Spain in his last years.

BIBLIOGRAPHY

See the bibliographies for "Aragon" and "Catalonia."

THOMAS N. BISSON

[See also **Alfonso I of Aragon; Aragon, Crown of (1137–1479); Barcelona; Catalonia (800–1137); Montpellier.**]

RAMSEY, JOHN (*fl.* 1297–1349), English master mason, was part of a large and influential family of builders active between the years 1300 and 1350 in London, Norfolk, and the West Country. Named master mason at Norwich Cathedral in 1304, he had worked there from about 1297, constructing parts of the cloister. He later worked also at Ely and London.

BIBLIOGRAPHY

Henning Bock, *Der Decorated Style* (1962), 40; Jean Bony, *The English Decorated Style: Gothic Architecture Transformed 1250–1350* (1979), 60–61; John Harvey, *English Medieval Architects: A Biographical Dictionary Down to 1550* (1954), 213–214, 2nd rev. ed. (1984), 240; D. J. Stewart, "Notes on Norwich Cathedral: The Cloisters," in *Archaeological Journal,* **32** (1875).

STEPHEN GARDNER

[See also **Gothic Architecture; Masons and Builders.**]

RAMSEY, WILLIAM (*fl.* 1325–1349), English master mason. Often considered the founder of the Perpendicular style, Ramsey was part of a large family of builders. His most notable works, apart from royal projects, were the influential cloister, chapter house, and choir screen at Old St. Paul's, London; St. Stephen's Chapel, Westminster; and perhaps the choir at Gloucester.

BIBLIOGRAPHY

Jean Bony, *The English Decorated Style: Gothic Architecture Transformed, 1250–1350* (1979), 58, 60–61; John Harvey, *English Medieval Architects: A Biographical Dictionary Down to 1550,* 2nd rev. ed. (1984), 242–245; John Harvey, *Gothic England: A Survey of National Culture 1300–1500,* 2nd rev. ed. (1948), 50–51, 57–58.

STEPHEN GARDNER

[See also **Gothic Architecture; Masons and Builders.**]

RÁN, a figure in Norse mythology, well known in later Icelandic tradition as the nautical goddess of death. As such she fulfills a function parallel to that of Hel. In *Eyrbyggja saga* (chap. 54), in *Friðþjófs saga* (chap. 6), and in the late *rímur,* it is said that the drowned at sea "go to Rán" and that the drowned who reappear as guests at their own

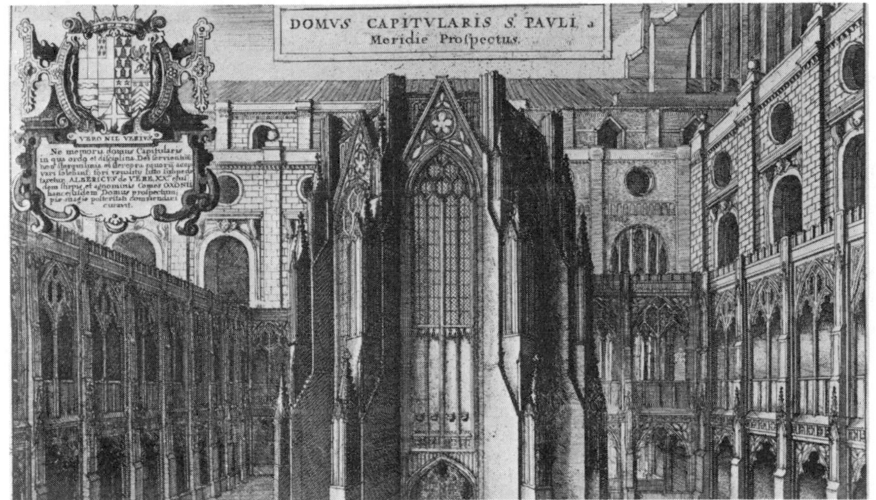

Old St. Paul's, London. Chapter house and cloister by William Ramsey, 1332–1349. Engraving by Wenceslas Hollar from William Dugdale, *The History of St. Paul's Cathedral in London* (1658). THE NEW YORK PUBLIC LIBRARY, ART, PRINTS & PHOTOGRAPHS DIVISION, ASTOR, LENOX & TILDEN FOUNDATIONS

funeral feasts have been well received by Rán. When his son is drowned, Egill mourns in *Sonatorrek* that Rán has hurt him deeply (*Egils saga Skallagrímssonar,* chap. 78).

The image of Rán with her net goes back to an older tradition. In the prose prologue to *Reginsmál* Loki borrows Rán's net in order to capture the dwarf Andvari, who lives as a pike under a waterfall.

Snorri in his *Edda* names the sea god Ægir as the husband of Rán. With him she has nine daughters who have the names of waves and who offer men at sea their embraces in hard weather. The name *Ægir* is clearly a reflex of the Proto-Germanic root **aXwa-* (compare Latin *aqua,* water). The word *Rán* has been linked with the verb *ræna* (plunder) or with *ráða* (determine, prevail), with a derivative nominal form **rāðn*—yielding *rán* (determiner, fate).

BIBLIOGRAPHY

Hilda R. E. Davidson, *Gods and Myths of Northern Europe* (1964), 128–130; *Egil's Saga,* Gwyn Jones, trans. (1960), 206; *Eyrbyggja Saga,* Paul Schach and Lee M. Hollander, trans. (1959), 114; Anne Holtsmark, "Rán," in *Kulturhistorisk leksikon for nordisk middelalder,* XIII (1968), 654–655; Snorri Sturluson, *The Prose Edda,* Arthur G. Brodeur, trans. (1916, repr. 1960), 137, 219; Jan de Vries, *Altgermanische Religionsgeschichte,* I (1956), 251–252.

JAMES E. CATHEY

[See also **Eddic Poetry; Egils Saga Skallagrímssonar; Eyrbyggja Saga; Hel; Loki; Reginsmál and Fáfnismál; Rímur; Scandinavian Mythology; Snorra Edda; Snorri Sturluson.**]

RANGERIUS OF LUCCA (late eleventh century), a monk, bishop of Lucca between 1097 and 1112. He wrote the life of St. Anselm of Lucca (*d.* 1086) began by the monk Donizo at the request of Matilda of Tuscany. Rangerius also completed another work begun by Donizo, *De anulo et baculo,* on the symbolism of the ring and the staff in marriage and church ritual.

BIBLIOGRAPHY

Rogerus Wilmans, ed., "Vita Anselmi," in *Monumenta Germaniae historica: Scriptores,* XII (1856), 13–35. See also Max Manitius, *Geschichte der lateinischen Literatur des Mittelalters,* III (1931), 48–49, 644.

NATHALIE HANLET

RAOUL DE HOUDENC (*fl.* late twelfth to early thirteenth century), poet from Île-de-France, considered by contemporaries to be the equal of Chrétien de Troyes. He is known for three works. *Méraugis de Portlesguez* (5,938 lines) is an Arthurian romance that transforms conventional material by its elaborate rhetorical style. *Le songe d'enfer* (678 lines) is of the vision genre and frames an allegorical voyage to the Infernal City. The didactic content is marked by an unusually satirical tone. *Le roman des ailes* (660 lines), an allegorical poem on the art of chivalry, sets forth the duties of the perfect knight. The two wings of *Prouesse* (prowess) symbolize *Largesse* (generosity) and *Courtoisie* (courtliness). Two works once thought to be by Raoul, *La vengeance Raguidel* and *La voie de paradis,* are no longer attributed to him.

BIBLIOGRAPHY

Sources. Various works can be found in Mathias Friedwagner, ed., *Sämtliche Werke,* I (1879); Achille Jubinal, ed., *Mystères inédits,* 2 vols. (1837); Philéas Lebesgue, ed., *Le songe de l'enfer, suivi de la voie de paradis* (1908); Auguste Scheler, ed., *Trouvères belges* (1879); Prosper Tarbé, ed., *Recherches sur l'histoire du langage et des patois de Champagne* (1851).

Studies. Alexandre Micha, "Raoul de Houdenc: Est-il l'auteur du *Songe du paradis* et de la *Vengeance Raguidel?*" in *Romania,* **68** (1944), and "Une source latine du *Roman des ailes,*" in *Revue du moyen âge latin,* **1** (1945); Ronald M. Spensley, "The Theme of *Meraugis de Portlesguez,*" in *French Studies,* **27** (1973).

KATHRYN GRAVDAL

[See also **Allegory, French; Arthurian Literature; French Literature; Troubadour, Trouvère.**]

RAOUL GLABER. See **Radulphus Glaber.**

RAPULARIUS. The original version of this Latin poem is transmitted virtually intact in four manuscripts; two others preserve a large part of it. Judging from the provenance of the manuscripts, and the distribution of the folkloric motif of a giant turnip, *Rapularius* comes from southern Germany. Mentioned in a literary catalog by Hugo von Trimberg about 1280, who wrote that it was a popular school text, it was likely composed early in the thirteenth century. Perhaps a century later a redaction was prepared in which only about a seventh of the original survives and the didactic passages are greatly expanded at the expense of the action. The original *Rapularius,* to which this article is devoted, consists of 221 elegiac distichs and tells the following story.

Two brothers of noble parentage have diverged in their fortunes: The one, wealthy and honored, serves the king as a knight, but the other is driven by poverty to working the land like a peasant. When among his crops a gigantic turnip grows, so large that twelve men could enjoy its shade together, he loads it onto a wagon drawn by four oxen and takes it to the king. Astounded and grateful, the king, when he learns of the farmer's noble origins and sorry condition, loads him with gifts and treasures. The high-placed brother learns of this good fortune and burns with envy. Reasoning that a king who gives such wealth for a huge turnip will surely give infinitely more for a genuinely valuable gift, he brings his own great treasure to the king as a present. But the king, following the advice of his perceptive wife, rewards this brother with . . . the turnip. Enraged, he lures his brother into an ambush. The hero is tied up in a sack and suspended from a tree, where his enemies leave him when they hear someone approaching on horseback. This proves to be a wandering scholar. The hero claims to have found the temple of wisdom within the sack; such marvelous understanding does he claim that the scholar eagerly takes his place, whereupon he rides off on the other's horse.

Rapularius (the word is a noun-agent formed on *rapula,* "turnip") is written with wit and rhetorical sophistication. No doubt it was valued in the schools for the quality of its verse and its pious or moralistic excurses (notably, against the envy of the rich brother), but students must also have been grateful for the lively story. Peasants and peasant diet were held in contempt by most educated persons of the Middle Ages, which made the hero's return to wealth and dignity by virtue of a turnip all the more ludicrous.

BIBLIOGRAPHY

Karl Langosch, *Waltharius, Ruodlieb, Märchenepen: Lateinische Epik des Mittelalters mit deutschen Versen* (1956), text with German trans., 308–331, notes and bibliog., 382–383; Stephen L. Wailes, "Fortuna and Social Anomaly: Principles of Mediaeval Humour in *Rapularius* and *Asinarius,*" in *Seminar,* **9** (1973).

STEPHEN L. WAILES

[See also **Hugo von Trimberg; Latin Literature.**]

RAQQAH (Rakka) is a city on the eastern bank of the Euphrates near its confluence with the Balikh. It was founded in 772 by the Abbasid caliph al-Manṣūr near the site of an earlier settlement, Kalinicos, which was an important trading center for the Byzantine and Sasanian empires. The Islamic city had a brick wall with several gates, a central mosque, and a palatial residence. Parts of the wall and one gate are probably from the eighth century, but the mosque and its minaret were rebuilt by the Zangid ruler Nūr al-Dīn Maḥmūd in 1165–1166.

Raqqah is also the reputed source of numerous glazed ceramic vessels with underglaze or luster-painted decoration that first reached the art market, probably via Aleppo, in the late nineteenth century. They are now preserved in many public and private collections. There is, however, no proof that these "Raqqah" vessels were actually made there. Comparable wares were made in Damascus and possibly also elsewhere in Syria.

BIBLIOGRAPHY

Keppel A. C. Creswell, *Early Muslim Architecture,* II (1940), 39–49; Ernst J. Grube, "Raqqa-Keramik in der Sammlung des Metropolitan Museum in New York," in *Kunst des Orients,* 4 (1963); Guy Le Strange, *The Lands of the Eastern Caliphate* (1905, repr. 1930), 86, 101–103, 124–125; Friedrich Sarre and Ernst Herzfeld, *Archaeologische Reise im Euphrat- und Tigris-Gebiet* (1911–1920), I, 3–6, 156–161, II, 349–364, III, pls. lxx, cxvi–cxx, IV, 9, 20–25.

PRISCILLA P. SOUCEK

[See also **Ayubbid Art and Architecture; Ceramics, Islamic; Lusterware.**]

RASHI (RABBI SOLOMON BEN ISAAC) (*ca.* 1040–1105), rabbinic exegete par excellence. Born in Troyes, he studied in his youth in the academies of Worms and Mainz, the major centers, indeed the fountainhead, of talmudic studies in Germany. He returned home apparently at an early age and quietly passed the rest of his life in his hometown, relentlessly engaged in an exegetical enterprise of awesome proportions—a commentary on the entire Talmud and Bible. He did not live to complete either of these projects.

Working off the interpretational traditions of the Rhineland academies, Rashi composed a commentary on most of the Talmud that for brevity and clarity has no equal. So definitive was his work that it drove all other commentaries from the field; works of figures no less than Abraham ben David of Posquières and Meir Abulafiah fell into desuetude, and the talmudic commentaries of Maimonides, written in Arabic, were deemed unnecessary to translate and were lost forever.

While many of Rashi's interpretations were challenged and alternative solutions proposed and widely accepted, it was Rashi's commentary that, within a century of his death, served as the point of departure of most talmudic discussions. The shift from exegesis to dialectic that took place in northern French and German thought in the twelfth century would have been impossible had not the prior problem of understanding each text in isolation been basically solved by Rashi's oeuvre. His older grandson and amanuensis, Samuel ben Meir, sought to complete those commentaries on talmudic tractates that Rashi had left unfinished, while his younger grandson, Jacob ben Meir (Rabbenu Tam), initiated the dialectical movement in talmudic thought, which entailed among other things a searching critique of Rashi's work.

Rashi's greatness as a commentator lies in the fact that he infiltrated the text as much as he commented upon it. Whereas most commentators focused upon explaining the difficult nub of an argument, Rashi sensed, as no commentator before or after, not only the central difficulty, but also the infinite minor lacunae of syntax, diction, and argument, in the stenographic-like text of the Talmud. And alongside of his more manifest remarks, he built, almost imperceptibly, hosts of minor bridges across these gaps. The end result, at its best, is that the text and commentary are so interwoven that in the reader's mind they are inseparable.

His biblical commentary is of sharply differing quality: that on the Prophets and Hagiographa is rudimentary, that on the Pentateuch (the Torah) a masterpiece that has stimulated over 200 supercommentaries. The differing density and quality most probably reflect the respective importance in Jewish life of the differing parts of the Bible. The Pentateuch is divided into fifty-two portions, and one portion is read publicly on each Saturday of the year. It is further incumbent upon each Jew to review the weekly portion of the Torah. Only scattered sections of the Prophets are read (as appendages to the weekly Torah readings), and no such duty of review is incumbent.

Rashi's achievement in his commentary on the Pentateuch does not lie in its definitiveness or unequaled lucidity but rather in its unique fusion of the literal sense of the text (as understood by Rashi) with rabbinic midrash (in the narrative portions of the Torah) and with the oral law (in its legal portions). The commentary had an incalculable impact upon the European Jewish mentality. It was taught to Jews from their earliest childhood as *the* interpretation of the Pentateuch, and the image of the biblical figures as well as the import and message of the biblical narrative were—in the Jewish imagination for close to a millennium—those drawn by Rashi. His grandson Samuel ben Meir argued for a more systematically literal interpretation and reported that Rashi in his later years was inclined in this direction but could not find the time to make the necessary revisions. Rashi's biblical commentary influenced Christian exegesis primarily through the medium of Nicholas of Lyra. Rashi often resorts to the vernacular to explain difficult words and passages. Thousands of Old French words are to be found in his commentary, and these have been studied by Arsène Darmesteter and David S. Blondheim.

Rashi's influence was overwhelmingly commentarial. He wrote responses, and his oral rulings were carefully noted by his students and then gathered in different collections, yet these works led a strange, checkered existence throughout the Middle Ages and until recent times. Almost all surviving manuscripts of one major collection, for example, are of Provençal rather than northern French or German (Ashkenazic) origin; and with one exception, all have been published only within the past century. Though not without impact, the practical legal decisions of the greatest talmudic commentator of all time never achieved the influence one might have easily expected. The reasons for this are not clear.

BIBLIOGRAPHY

"Rashi," in *Encyclopaedia judaica,* XIII (1972), with a good bibliography.

HAYM SOLOVEITCHIK

[See also **Bible; Exegesis, Jewish; Jacob ben Meir; Judeo-French; Law, Jewish; Nicholas of Lyra; Responsum Literature, Jewish; Talmud, Exegesis and Study of.**]

RATHER OF VERONA (**Rather of Liège**) (*ca.* 887–974), churchman and reformer, was educated at Lobbes, where he became a monk. His involvement in political affairs and his zeal for spiritual reform earned him such powerful supporters as the emperor Otto I (*r.* 936–973) as well as many enemies. Consequently, he alternately enjoyed power and acclaim and suffered exile and rejection. He was thrice bishop of Verona, bishop of Liège, abbot of Aulne-sur-Sambre, and abbot of Lobbes. His imprisonment at Pavia (934–936) sparked his greatest work, the *Praeloquia,* an intensely introspective guide to proper conduct for all levels of society. One of the most important pre-Gregorian reformers, Rather died at Namur.

BIBLIOGRAPHY

Sources. Rather's works are printed in *Patrologia latina,* CXXXVI (1853). See also Peter L. D. Reid, ed., *Ratherii Veronensis opera minora* (1976). The *Praeloquia* receives special attention in M. D. Metzger, "Selections from the *Praeloquia* of Ratherius of Verona: A Critical Edition with an Historical Introduction and Commentary" (diss., UCLA, 1975). Rather's letters have been edited by Fritz Weigle, *Monumenta Germaniae historica: Die Briefe der deutschen Kaiserzeit,* I (1949); and his sermons by Benny R. Reece, *Sermones Ratherii episcopi Veronensis* (1969). See also Peter L. D. Reid, *Tenth-century Latinity: Rather of Verona* (1981).

Studies. Erich Auerbach, *Literary Language and Its Public in Late Latin Antiquity and in the Middle Ages,* Ralph Mannheim, trans. (1965), 133–152; H. M. Klinkenberg, "Versuche und Untersuchungen zur Autobiographie bei Rather von Verona," in *Archiv für Kulturgeschichte,* 38 (1956); Louis F. Lumaghi, "Ratherius of Verona: Pre-Gregorian Reformer" (diss., Univ. of Colorado, 1975); A. Vogel, *Ratherius von Verona und das 10. Jahrhundert,* 2 vols. in 1 (1854). A useful brief discussion is in Max Manitius, *Geschichte der lateinischen Literatur des Mittelalters,* II (1923), 34–52.

CHARLES R. SHRADER

[See also **Church, Latin: To 1054; Germany: 843–1137; Latin Literature; Otto I the Great, Emperor; Reform, Idea of.**]

RATPERT OF ST. GALL (*d.* 25 October *ca.* 890), monk at St. Gall (in Switzerland), noted for his scholarly discipline, who studied with leading scholars of the time. Ratpert wrote *De casibus monasterii S. Galli,* about the origin, founding, and early years of the monastery. He was also the author of various poems.

BIBLIOGRAPHY

Max Manitius, *Geschichte der lateinischen Literatur des Mittelalters,* II (1923), 563, 566, 729; *Patrologia latina,* CXXVI (1879), 1,055–1,080; Peter Stotz, *Ardua spes mundi: Studien zu lateinische Gedichten aus Sankt Gallen* (1972).

EDWARD FRUEH

[See also **Monastery; St. Gall.**]

RATRAMNUS OF CORBIE (*fl.* 844–868) is known only through his writings. He discussed the presence of Christ's sacrificial body in the communion elements in *De corpore et sanguine domini* (*ca.* 844). He argued that the elect and the damned are both predestined in *De praedestinatione dei* (*ca.* 850). In *De nativitate Christi* (*ca.* 853) he asserted that the parturition of Christ was a normal physical occurrence instead of a miraculous event. He defended Latin church practices against those of the Greek church in *Contra Graecorum opposita* (*ca.* 868). Four other minor works of Ratramnus are extant.

BIBLIOGRAPHY

Ratramnus' works are in *Patrologia latina,* CXXI (1880), 12–102, 223–346, and in *Monumenta Germaniae historica: Epistolae,* VI (1902), 149–158. Other editions are: "De anima," in André Wilmart, ed., "Opuscule inédit de Ratramne sur la nature de l'âme," in *Revue Bénédictine,* 43 (1931); *De corpore et sanguine domini,* Jan. N. Bakhuizen van den Brink, ed. (1974); *Liber de anima ad Odonem bellovacensem,* Cyril Lambot, ed. (1951); "De nativitate Christi," in José M. Canal, ed., *La virginidad de María según Ratramno y Radberto, monjes de Corbie: Nueva edición de los textos* (1968).

See also Jean Paul Bouhot, *Ratramne de Corbie: Histoire litteraire et controverses doctrinales* (1976); Allen Cabaniss and George McCracken, "Ratramnus of Corbie: 'Christ's Body and Blood,'" in *Early Medieval Theology* (1957); John F. Fahey, *The Eucharistic Teaching of Ratramn of Corbie* (1951).

TIMOTHY R. ROBERTS

[See also **Berengar of Tours; Dialectic; Mass, Liturgy of the.**]

RAUḌA (plural, *riyāḍ*), "garden" (metaphorically, "tomb"), from the Arabic *rāḍa,* "to tame" or "to regulate," in this case a stream. It corresponds to the Persian *firdaws* (Greek: *paradeisos*), "garden," "vineyard," but essentially a "paradise"; that is, an enclosed park or royal demesne reserved for hunting and other forms of pleasure. Both terms are used synonymously with *janna,* the usual Arabic word for garden, which in the Koran is used eschatologically. More specifically, *jannāt al-na*ᶜ*īm*—the Gardens of Felicity (or of Grace, where one enjoys the grace of God)—means Heaven; and *sākin al-jannāt,* "dweller in the Gardens [of Felicity]," denotes, perhaps somewhat presumptuously, a deceased person. The Koranic descriptions lay stress on the presence of moisture, and it is interesting that water is in some ways the most important component in an Islamic garden, equally as—or even more important than—the soil. Detached from an eschatological framework, Koranic imagery merged with pre-Islamic landscape design in Persia to produce the characteristic garden of Islam. On Persian ceramics datable even as early as around 4000 B.C., the world or cosmos is depicted as divided symmetrically into four quadrants with a centrally placed pool or fountain, the waters of which flow out to fertilize all four quarters of the globe. Translated into a square or rectangular walled enclosure, this would provide a model to which Muslim landscape architects have remained faithful ever since. Islamic garden design thus rests both on cosmological premises (which account for the similarities) and on climatic factors (which account for the divergences), but the necessity in hot climates for artificial irrigation meant that one factor would always remain normative. This is a system of division by two axes intersecting at right angles so as to ensure an equitable distribution of water. When the plan is a simple—as opposed to a multiple—rectangle the principle axis alone carries water, while subordinate axes serve the purpose of communication. Thus a division into four, known by the Persian term *chārbāgh,* or fourfold plot, emerged as the basic unit of design, producing an extremely formal layout in the shape of a raised grid for the irrigation of large areas under gravitational pressure. The size of the plots varied according to the height of the grid and the dominant species in the planting scheme. Thus, the Islamic garden is designed to be looked down upon, from the vantage point of the paths, not unlike a carpet. In fact, artisans wove "garden" carpets, and these carpets are a better guide to how Persian gardens looked in their prime than any extant garden. The paths were lined with alternating cypresses and fruit trees, and

South Persian garden carpet from Amber, India, 1632. DEPARTMENT OF ARCHAEOLOGY AND MUSEUMS, JAIPUR, RAJASTHAN

the effect of the delicate blossoms against the somber trunks of the cypress can be gauged from contemporary miniatures.

In anticipation of postmortem bliss, the owners of these favored spots would sometimes elect to be buried in them. Thus *rauḍa* can also signify a tomb, even where no vestige of garden is present, as in the case of the Prophet's Rauḍa at Medina. The Septuagint uses *paradeisos* for the Garden of Eden; conversely, the Koran refers to paradise as "Gardens of Eden," from which it would seem that the telos envisaged is the restoration of the same condition of primal harmony as obtained prior to the Fall.

BIBLIOGRAPHY

Jonas Lehrman, *Earthly Paradise: Gardens and Courtyards in Islam* (1980); Elizabeth B. Macdougall and Richard Ettinghausen, *The Islamic Garden* (1976); Elizabeth B. Moynihan, *Paradise as a Garden in Persian and Mughal India* (1979); Constance M. Villiers Stuart, *Gardens of the Great Mughals* (1913); Donald N. Wilber, *Persian Gardens and Garden Pavilions* (1962).

JAMES DICKIE

[See also **Paradise, Islamic; Rugs and Carpets.**]

RAVENNA, approximately 75 miles (121 kilometers) south of Venice on the east coast of Italy, maintains one of the largest surviving bodies of fifth- and sixth-century monuments, most of them well preserved. It was made the capital of the Western emperors in 402 by Honorius and inhabited by Empress Galla Placidia (424–450) and Emperor Valentinian III (450–455) before being taken by the Ostrogoths (493), who made it their capital. In 540 the city was recaptured by Belisarios for Justinian and established as the see of the Byzantine viceroys. Due to Ravenna's geographical location and political significance, its fifth- and sixth-century products show a blending of Byzantine and Western forms.

The cathedral, a five-aisled basilica dedicated to the Anastasis (Resurrection), was built before 425, remodeled in the twelfth century, and destroyed in 1748. Early descriptions and engravings establish that the altar was in the center of the nave, a Constantinopolitan import, and that the walls were decorated with stucco, but a full reconstruction has never been attempted.

Only the nave (probably rebuilt) remains of S. Croce, commissioned by Galla Placidia, but excavations have revealed a cruciform plan similar to the Church of the Apostles in Milan (the previous capital), with a long narthex that seems to have been borrowed from Greece. Happily, the small cross-shaped building that originally abutted the narthex, the so-called Mausoleum of Galla Placidia, survives. This chapel, apparently constructed by workers from Milan around 424–425, houses the sarcophagi of Galla Placidia's half brother Honorius (*d.* 423), Galla Placidia (*d.* 450), and her husband Constantius III (*d.* 421 or 422). It was dedicated to the Roman St. Lawrence, and seems to have had a dual function as martyr's chapel and imperial mausoleum. Inside, the lower walls are revetted with marble, while above are mosaics representing St. Lawrence going to his martyrdom, Christ as Shepherd among a flock of sheep, deer drinking from the Fountain of Life, and pairs of apostles. The curved surfaces of the vaults show leafy scrolls and stars against a blue background. Galla Placidia was also responsible for the Church of S. Giovanni Evangelista (424–434). Though rebuilt or repaired in the seventh, twelfth, and twentieth centuries, portions of the original basilica showing Aegean features such as a polygonal apse remain; none of the mural decoration is preserved.

The Orthodox Baptistery, on the other hand, is one of the best-preserved examples of its kind. It was built around 400 as an octagonal, unvaulted structure with revetted lower walls; fifty years later under Bishop Neon it received a dome of hollow-tube construction and its remaining interior decoration. In the spandrels of the lowest zone prophets amid vine tendrils stand against a blue mosaic ground; directly above, stuccoed prophets(?) stand in niches; the dome, in mosaic, shows alternating *hetoimasiai* (an empty throne prepared for Christ's Second Coming) and altars in architectural frames ringing the twelve apostles, who in turn ring the central image of Christ's baptism. Bishop Neon was also responsible for a banquet hall with five niches that resembles more elaborate versions in Constantinople and Rome. The Ostrogoths, under the Arian Theodoric, entered Ravenna in 493 and built their own monuments. The Arian Baptistery (S. Maria in Cosmedin) of the late fifth century mimics the Orthodox Baptistery, especially in its dome mosaic. An archiepiscopal palace was also built for Archbishop Peter II (494–519), with a cruciform chapel decorated with mosaic, now heavily restored. Also during the last third of the fifth century, three additional basilicas—S. Spirito (adjoining the Arian Baptistery and contemporary with it), S. Agata (begun about 470), and S. Apollinare Nuovo—were built in Ravenna. The latter, the most important, was built by Theodoric around 493, and was dedicated to Christ. When Bishop Agnellus (556–569/570) converted it to Orthodox use the church was rededicated to St. Martin of Tours; it received its current appellation in the ninth century when the relics of Apollinaris (*ca.* 200) were translated from his church in the port of Classe. S. Apollinare Nuova is a simple basilica with a nave separated from two side aisles by an arcade.

Its details show the typical Ravennate blending of Italian, Aegean, and Byzantine features. The masonry technique is Milanese and the hollow-tube construction of the apse vault comes from southern Italy; the polygonal exterior of the apse is Aegean; the capitals seem to have been imported from Constantinople. Three zones of splendid mosaics are preserved in the nave. The top level shows scenes from the life of Christ (miracles on the north side, the passion on the south) arranged in liturgical order. The middle zone alternates windows with Old Testament prophets and patriarchs. The lowest level was reworked when the church was converted around 560. Of its scenes of Theodoric's court, there remain only the representations of the port of Classe (north wall, west end) and Theodoric's palace (south wall, west end)—both with all figures excised, though fingers overlapping columns bear witness to their former presence. Also remaining are the Virgin enthroned among four angels (north wall, east end) and an enthroned Christ (south wall, east end). The Orthodox additions to this zone were a procession of female martyrs on the north wall and male saints headed by St. Martin on the south.

Theodoric's final monument in Ravenna is his unfinished mausoleum, built around the time of his death in 526. This ten-sided and two-leveled building of massive ashlar blocks was probably meant to evoke imperial tombs in Rome and Constantinople. One of its more impressive features is a dome carved from a single huge piece of rock weighing approximately 230 tons.

The most celebrated church in Ravenna, S. Vitale, was begun after 525 by Bishop Ecclesius (521/522–531/532) on the site of an earlier church. Building continued under Bishop Ursicinus (533–536), but most of the church was erected and

The hospitality of Abraham and the sacrifice of Isaac, flanked by Jeremiah and Moses. Mosaics in the bema vault of S. Vitale, Ravenna, 546–548. ALINARI/ART RESOURCE

decorated under Victor (538–545). The mosaics were installed in 546–548 under Maximianus, who dedicated S. Vitale in 547. The church, financed by the banker Julianus, is a double-shelled octagon in plan and recalls Constantinopolitan churches such as SS. Sergios and Bakchos. The Byzantine connection is fitting, since most of S. Vitale was built after Justinian had taken Ravenna from the Ostrogoths in 540: the church might be seen as a showpiece of Byzantium in Italy. Columns and capitals were imported from the East and, though construction was entrusted to local workers (hollow-tube vaulting continues), the feeling of contemporary Constantinopolitan buildings was translated to the West. The famous mosaics are concentrated in the bema and apse. The heavily restored conch shows Christ, seated on a sphere, handing a martyr's crown to St. Vitalis and receiving a model of the church from Ecclesius. The bema vault depicts the Lamb of God in a wreath supported by angels; the walls have scenes from the Old Testament that prefigure the Christian Eucharist and, in the spandrels, two episodes from the life of Moses. On the walls of the apse are two imperial portraits, Justinian on the left and Theodora on the right. Symbolically, they may reenact the First Entrance of the Byzantine liturgy, imperial stand-ins for the Ravennate laity.

S. Apollinare in Classe (the port of Ravenna) was also financed by the banker Julianus. It was begun under Bishop Ursicinus and dedicated in 549. Before they were translated to S. Apollinare Nuovo in the ninth century, the remains of St. Apollinaris were held here. The church is a three-aisled, arcaded basilica; its mosaic decoration remains only in the apse. Here a symbolic Transfiguration incorporates St. Apollinaris interceding for his people above portraits of four archbishops of Ravenna.

BIBLIOGRAPHY

Ernst Kitzinger, *Byzantine Art in the Making* (1977); Richard Krautheimer, *Early Christian and Byzantine Architecture,* rev. ed. (1975); Kurt Weitzmann, ed., *The Age of Spirituality: Late Antique and Early Christian*

Art, Third to Seventh Century (1979). All three works provide syntheses of the vast bibliography.

LESLIE BRUBAKER

[See also **Apse; Baptistery; Basilica; Bema; Byzantine History (330–1025); Early Christian and Byzantine Architecture; Early Christian Art; Exarchate; Mosaic and Mosaic Making.**]

RAVERTI, MATTEO (early fifteenth century), Milanese sculptor and architect who is first documented as a fully trained and active sculptor in the workshops of Milan Cathedral shortly before 1404. He later worked in Venice on the decoration for the Ca' d'Oro and may have worked on the facade of S. Marco between 1418 and 1434, as well as on the Ducal Palace. It is also possible that the effigy of St. Simeon the Prophet in S. Simeone Grande in Venice (executed *ca.* 1410–1420) was produced by Raverti and his workshop, owing to the closeness in style to Raverti's St. George (1404) executed for Milan Cathedral.

BIBLIOGRAPHY

Costantino Baroni, "La scultura del primo Quattrocento," in *Storia di Milano,* VI (1955); Giovanni Mariacher, "Matteo Raverti nell'arte veneziana del primo quattrocento," in *Rivista d'arte,* **21** (1939); Ugo Nebbia, *La scultura nel Duomo di Milano* (1908), 61–62, 106–116; Charles Seymour, *Sculpture in Italy, 1400–1500* (1966), 21, 22, 271, and "Tomb of Saint Simeon the Prophet in San Simeone Grande, Venice," in *Gesta,* **15** (1976).

SANDRA CANDEE SUSMAN

[See also **Gothic Art: Sculpture; Milan Cathedral; S. Marco, Venice.**]

Gargoyle and *gigante* (giant), suggesting St. George and the dragon. Cast of sculpture by Matteo Raverti for facade of Milan Cathedral, 1404. MUSEO DEL DUOMO, MILAN

RAYMOND DE MUR (*fl.* early fifteenth century), Catalonian painter of the province of Lérida who worked in the International Gothic style. The Guimera altarpiece, representative of the artist's mature style, was executed between 1402 and 1412. Another extant work, the altarpiece of S. Pedro de Vinaixa, was commissioned in 1420. In his mature works, Raymond de Mur is noted for his use of rich, luxurious color and delicate figures. In addition his work shows an interest in overall surface patterns, often at the expense of creating a convincing pictorial space for his figures.

BIBLIOGRAPHY

Joseph Gudiol i Ricart, *Pintura gótica* (1955).

JENNIFER E. JONES

[See also **Altarpiece; Gothic, International Style.**]

The Nativity. Detail from the Guimera altarpiece by Raymond de Mur, 1402–1412. MUSEO EPISCOPAL DE VICH, BARCELONA/ FOTO MAS, BARCELONA

RAYMOND GAYRARD OF TOULOUSE. See **Gayrard, Raymond.**

RAYMOND LULLY. See **Lull, Ramon.**

RAYMOND OF PEÑAFORT, ST. (*ca.* 1180/85—6 January 1275), was born most probably in the tower of Peñafort, near Vilafranca del Penedes, in Catalonia. He spent the years 1210–1218 in Bologna, first as a student and then as a master in the school of law there. Tradition holds that, in 1219, his bishop called him back to Barcelona, where he was named canon penitentiary and provost of the cathedral chapter. He left these offices to enter the Dominican order between 1223 and 1229. It is also traditionally held that Raymond played a notable part in the foundation of the Mercedarians, in the compilation of their constitutions, and in obtaining papal approval for them.

Pope Gregory IX named Raymond papal confessor, chaplain, and penitentiary, and entrusted to him the compilation of the authentic book of decretals published on 5 September 1234; these remained in force as part of the law of the Roman Catholic church until 1917. As a member of the papal household, Raymond also assisted in the establishment of the Inquisition in Aragon in 1232. In 1238 he accepted unenthusiastically his election as master general of the Dominican order; in that capacity he compiled a redaction of the Dominican constitutions that fundamentally remained normative until 1924.

In 1240 Raymond renounced the office of master general in order to devote himself to the conversion of Jews and Muslims in Spain and Africa. At his behest, Dominican schools of Arabic and Hebrew were founded so that friars could be trained for missionary work; for similar purposes, he requested Thomas Aquinas to write the *Summa contra gentiles.* The great regard in which Raymond was held in his own country was attested by the presence of the kings of Aragon and of Castile at his burial. Requests for Raymond's canonization were continuous from the time of his death until the event, in 1601.

Among his many works, the most notable is perhaps the *Summa de poenitentia* or *Raymundina,* a guide for confessors that survives in hundreds of manuscripts and many printings (Rome 1603; Avignon 1715; Vienna 1744); it was also much imitated, summarized, and glossed. Notable also are his *Summa iuris canonici, Summa pastoralis,* and *Dubitabilia cum responsionibus.*

BIBLIOGRAPHY

Franciscus Balme and Ceslaus Paban, *Raymundiana: Seu documenta quae pertinent ad S. Raymundi de Pennaforti vitam et scripta,* 2 vols. in 1, in *Monumenta ordinis fratrum praedicatorum historica,* IV, fasc. 1–2 (1898–1901); Stephan Kuttner, "Raymond of Peñafort as Editor: The 'Decretales' and 'Constitutiones' of Gregory IX," in *Bulletin of Medieval Canon Law,* n.s. **12** (1982); José Rius Serra, *San Raimundo de Penyafort: Diplomatario (documentos, vida antigua, cronicas, procesos antiguos)* (1954); Amédée Teetaert, "La *Summa de poenitentia* de Saint Raymond de Penyafort," in *Ephemerides theologicae Lovanienses,* 5 (1928), and "La doctrine penitentielle de Saint Raymond de Penyafort,

O.P.," in *Analecta sacra Tarraconensia,* 4 (1928); Fernando Valls Taberner, *San Ramón de Penyafort* (1936), repr. with useful bibliographic and other notes in his *Literatura jurídica,* M. J. Peláez and J. Calvo González, eds. (1986), 61–182. See also the several studies in *Escritos del Vedat,* 7 (1977).

GIULIO SILANO

[See also **Decretals; Decretum; Dominicans; Inquisition; Law, Canon: After Gratian; Penance and Penitentials.**]

RĀZĪ, ABŪ BAKR MUḤAMMAD IBN ZAKARĪYA AL- (Rhazes) (*ca.* 854–925 or 935), a great physician of medieval Islam and one of its important philosophers. Born in Rayy (near modern Tehran), he first studied mathematics, astronomy, philosophy, and Arabic belles lettres. His devotion to the practice of medicine came later. Little is known about his teachers. Medieval Islamic sources mention a certain al-Balkhī among them and also note that al-Rāzī derived his philosophical views from a shadowy unorthodox thinker, Irānshahrī. Al-Rāzī practiced medicine first at a newly built hospital in Rayy and then at another newly built hospital, in Baghdad. Toward the end of his life his eyesight became very weak and he developed a cataract, but he refused to have it operated on, declaring that he had seen enough of the world.

His numerous medical writings include *al-Ḥāwī* (*Continens,* as it was translated into Latin), the medical diary published posthumously by his students. This work has often been wrongly identified with *Kitāb al-jāmiᶜ al-kabīr* (The great comprehensive book), the twelve-volume medical encyclopedia on which he labored during the last fifteen years of his life. (The confusion between the two works is due to the similarity in meaning of their respective Arabic titles.) His writings also include *al-Manṣūrī* (*Ad alma novem*) and the celebrated treatise on smallpox *Kitāb al-Jadarī wa al-ḥaṣba* (The book of smallpox and measles), where the difference between this disease and measles was defined for the first time. As a physician, he was very much the empiricist. This is shown by his careful recordings of case histories and by his criticism of Galen, in *Kitāb al-Shukūk ᶜalo Jālīnūs* (*Dubitationes in Galenium*). He also contributed to the development of alchemy through his careful classification of the substances known to him; and he is credited with helping develop pharmacy as a discipline independent of medicine.

Most of his philosophical writings (logic, physics, metaphysics, ethics, and criticism) are lost. The surviving works include the ethical treatise *Al-Ṭibb al-Rūḥānī* (The spiritual physick), the apologia *Al-Sīrat al-falsafīya* (The philosophic way of life), and the popular political essay *Fī amārāt al-iqbāl wa al-Dawla* (Portents of advancement and auspicious rule). An essay entitled *Maqāla fīmā baᶜd al-ṭabīᶜa* (Treatise on metaphysics) is also attributed to him. Another source of knowledge of his philosophical ideas consists of the discussion of them by medieval Islamic thinkers such as the Ismāᶜīlīya philosophers Abū Ḥātim al-Rāzī (*d.* 933), al-Kirmānī (*d.* 1021), and Nāṣir-i Khusraw (*d.* after 1072), the scientist-philosopher al-Bīrūnī (*d. ca.* 1050), and the theologian Fakhr al-Dīn al-Rāzī (*d.* 1209). It is true that most of these thinkers were opposed to al-Rāzī and highly critical of his views; nonetheless, their accounts of his ideas tend to complement not only each other, but also accounts that were less inimical, yielding a definite, discernible, philosophical position.

Al-Rāzī is noted for his cosmogony, which was greatly influenced by Plato's *Timaeus.* Similarly to Plato, he saw the world's creation as taking place at a finite moment in the past, but it was not ex nihilo. Rather, creation, for al-Rāzī, was the imposition of order on preexisting disorganized atomic matter. His metaphysics rested on the doctrine of the five eternal beings: atomic matter, absolute space, absolute time, the soul, and God. In answering the question of why God created the world, al-Rāzī resorted to myth, giving an answer that differs from Plato in *Timaeus.* The soul, according to al-Rāzī's myth, being ignorant, became enamored of matter and sought union with it. It thus strove to give matter the form needed to realize such a union. Matter, however, resisted this informing activity of the soul, leaving the latter in great misery. Then the creator, being compassionate, intervened on behalf of the soul, thus giving form to matter and instigating the creation.

The soul's union with matter meant its individuation, that is, the formation of particular living beings. God in his mercy endowed some of these living beings (humans) with reason, an emanation from himself, to awaken their souls to seek their original abode, away from matter. This awakening is achieved through philosophy, of which all men are capable, although many willfully refuse to pursue it. The end of the created world comes when reason prevails and all the individual souls disengage from matter, reuniting to form the one soul once again. When this takes place, matter reverts to its original state of disorganized floating atoms. The end of the created world is thus the return of the five eternal beings to their original state. The created world, which for al-Rāzī has a finite beginning in time, has also a finite end in time.

Related to this cosmogony are al-Rāzī's views on transmigration, the slaughter of animals, and prophetic revelation. Human souls that resist the call to reason, succumbing to bestial existence, occupy lower forms of life after death. There is also an upward movement of souls. The details of al-Rāzī's views on the upward movement, however, are lacking. He opposed cruelty to animals, maintaining that the creator never seeks man's harm and hence man in turn ought not to harm sentient beings. The slaughter of animals should be avoided, except when absolutely necessary. Such slaughter, however, may be justified in part because it may free the animal's soul to transmigrate to a higher form of life. As regards his views on prophethood, his stance was entirely antireligious. Salvation, he held, is achieved only through reason and philosophy, of which all sane men are capable. Hence there is no need for revelation. Furthermore, he argued, if the Creator were to reveal his truth to men, he would reveal it to all men. To favor one individual or one nation with his revelation would be totally inconsistent with his justice. It is the erroneous belief that such revelation took place, he maintained, that has caused so much strife in the world. Most wars, he held, are due to religion.

Al-Rāzī's greatest influence, both in the Islamic world and in Europe, was on the development of medicine and science. His philosophical views, particularly those on prophethood, hardly endeared him to the religious intellectuals. Nonetheless, his ideas were fiercely debated in medieval Islam and in this way contributed to the development of Islamic philosophy.

BIBLIOGRAPHY

Sources. Razis: Opera philosophica, Paul Kraus, ed. (1939); al-Rāzī, *A Treatise on the Small-pox and Measles,* William A. Greenhill, trans. (1847, repr. 1939).

Studies. Arthur J. Arberry, *The Spiritual Physick of Rhazes* (1950), and *Aspects of Islamic Civilization as Depicted in Original Texts* (1964), 120–130; Edward G. Browne, *Arabian Medicine* (1921); Donald Campbell, *Arabian Medicine,* 2 vols. (1926); Majid Fakhry, "A Tenth-century Arabic Interpretation of Plato's Cosmology," in *Journal of the History of Philosophy,* **6** (1968); Lenn E. Goodman, "Razi's Myth of the Fall of the Soul," in George F. Hourani, ed., *Essays in Islamic Philosophy and Science* (1975), and "The Epicurean Ethic of Muḥammad ibn Zakariyāʾ ar-Rāzī," in *Studia islamica,* **34** (1971); Albert Z. Iskandar, "The Medical Bibliography of al-Rāzī," in Hourani, *op. cit.;* Max Meyerhoff, "Science and Medicine," in Thomas Arnold and Alfred Guillaume, eds., *The Legacy of Islam* (1931); Salomon Pines, *Beiträge zur islamischen Atomenlehre* (1936).

MICHAEL E. MARMURA

[See also **Ismāʿīlīya; Medicine, History of; Pharmacopeia; Philosophy and Theology, Islamic; Science, Islamic.**]

RAZÓN DE AMOR (early thirteenth century) is the first lyric narrative poem in Spanish literature. The text (261 lines) by an anonymous poet, extant in a single manuscript (Paris, Bibliothèque Nationale, MS lat. 3576), is written in Spanish, with dialectalisms and archaisms. In *Razón de amor* appears the first poetic "I" in Spanish literature (excepting the Mozarabic *kharjas*). In a visionary *locus amoenus* (pleasant place), with two mysterious vases of water and wine, a *clerc* (cleric)-scholar drinks from a fountain, similar to the traditional *Fontefrida,* and wishes to sing of *fin'amor.* A beautiful maiden enters singing of her *amor de lonh* (love for a distant lover) for a courtly *clerc,* "not a knight." Several topics appear here for the first time in Spanish literature: *fin'amor, amor de lonh,* the *descriptio puellae* (description of a maiden), an embryonic *clerc*-chevalier debate, the dichotomy *vilain-courtois.* After a passionate mutual recognition, and a song of love from the maiden (recalling the Galician-Portuguese *cantigas de amigo*), she departs. A white dove enters and spills the water into the wine. Here begins the second part of the poem, quite different in tone, being a debate between the water and the wine similar to the *conflictus* (debate) *Denudata veritate,* a slightly earlier Latin poem. Its sacramental allusions are traditional, judging from a French debate. There is no consensus regarding the unity of *Razón de amor,* asserted by a majority. Critics have studied it within the courtly-love tradition and for its possible relationship to the *Song of Songs* or the *vidas* and *razos* of troubadours, or for its vague echoes from the *matière de Bretagne* and its kinship to the courtly *curialitas* (belonging to the clerical) of the medieval

Latin love lyrics. *Razón de amor* has been interpreted as Christian allegory and as permeated with Catharic elements; more likely is its relationship to the Spanish popular tradition in which short songs suggest a similar erotic enigma in the presence of water and wine. Despite all critical efforts *Razón de amor* remains ambiguous.

BIBLIOGRAPHY

Edition and translation. G. H. London, "The *Razón de amor* and the *Denuestos del agua y el vino:* New Readings and Interpretation," in *Romance Philology,* **19** (1965); translation of the first part only by Charles C. Stebbin, "The *Razón de amor*: An Old Spanish Lyrical Poem of the XIII Century," in *Allegorica,* **2** (1977).

Studies. Alicia C. de Ferraresi, *De amor y poesía en la España medieval: Prólogo a Juan Ruiz* (1976), 43–118, with bibliography, and "*Locus amoenus* y vergel visionario en *Razón de amor,*" in *Hispanic Review,* **42** (1974); Margo de Ley, "Provençal Bibliographical Tradition and the *Razón de amor,*" in *Journal of Hispanic Philology,* **1** (1976); Colbert Nepaulsingh, *The History of Literary Composition in Medieval Spain,* (1986); Arsenio Pacheco, "¿*Razón de amor* o *Denuestos del agua y el vino?*" in *Bulletin of Hispanic Studies,* **51** (1974); Margaret Van Antwerp, "*Razón de amor* and the Popular Tradition," in *Romance Philology,* **32** (1978).

ALICIA DE COLOMBI-MONGUIO

[See also **Cantigas de Amor, Amigo, and Escarnio; Courtly Love; Galician-Portuguese Poetry; Spanish Literature; Spanish Literature: Lyric Poetry.**]

REALISM is the philosophical theory that universals—terms truly predicated of a number of things—are independent of the human mind. In antiquity this doctrine was first formulated by Plato, who argued that universals existed separately from spatiotemporal objects, were perceptible by the mind alone, and were the causes of spatiotemporal things. This theory must be reformulated in a more complex manner when combined with the belief in a radical ontological disjunction between creative and created being. Thus, in the Middle Ages we find it argued (1) that universals as defined by Plato are contained in the mind of God: *universalia ante res*; and (2) that similar universals are immanent in the spatiotemporal realm: *universalia in rebus.* These teachings occur either together or singly.

UNIVERSALIA ANTE RES

This version of the realist theory of universals is primarily ontological but has certain epistemological implications. It was manifested in three basic forms, depending upon the kind of universal under discussion.

First, there are universals that are identified with the attributes of God: existence, life, intelligence, goodness, greatness, and the like. Among the classic discussions of these universals, the indirect descendants of Plato's moral Forms, are those in Boethius' *De Trinitate* and Anselm of Canterbury's *Monologion.*

The former takes its starting point from the notion that the Aristotelian categories can be applied to God only when transformed in meaning. In other words, if we declare that God is good (predication in the category of quality), we indicate that God is goodness itself (predication of quality transformed into predication of substance); or if we declare that God is great (predication in the category of quantity), we indicate that God is greatness itself (predication of quantity turned into predication of substance; *De Trinitate* 4.1–44).

The latter takes its starting point from the notion that that through which all things exhibit a certain attribute possesses that attribute to the highest degree. Thus, all things that are good derive their goodness from something that is good through itself, while all things that are great obtain their greatness from something that is great through itself, that which is good through itself necessarily being identical with that which is great through itself—namely, God (*Monologion* 1–4). Discussions such as these, explaining the nature of one important set of universals by equating them with the divine essence, recur in many medieval writers.

In the second place, there are universals that are identified with ideas in God's mind. Precise examples of these are not always provided, although they seem to be physical or cosmological in the main: universals corresponding to natural species like man and horse; to the elements of fire, air, water, earth; and so on. The notion that there are universals identical with divine ideas was transmitted to the Middle Ages by numerous sources.

Among the Christian ones Ambrose (*Hexameron* I.1.1–4) reports Plato's view that there are three principles of all things: "God" (*deus*), "the paradigm" (*exemplar*), and "matter" (*materia*), and that God looked toward the paradigm in making the world from matter.

Augustine (*De diversis quaestionibus LXXXIII*, qu. 46) provides an elaborate explanation of these universals. First, they may be called "Ideas" (*ideae*), "Forms" (*formae*), or "species" (*species*) with equal accuracy, although the description of them as "reasons" (*rationes*)—which the writer clearly favors—must be employed with greater caution, since this term would be more correctly applied to the Greek *logoi*, whose precise difference in relation to Ideas is not explained. Second, from the ontological viewpoint the Ideas are themselves not formed; they are eternal and, more precisely, do not come into being or perish; they are contained in the divine intellect; they are truly existent; they are immutable and, more precisely, self-identical; and they are sources of form to transitory things. Third, from the epistemological viewpoint the Ideas are perceived by the soul's rational part; they are perceived by a soul that is pure; they are perceived by the soul's eye; they are perceived by a soul that is similar to them. Finally, among examples of these Ideas are the species of man and horse, perhaps together with other natural species.

Boethius (*De consolatione philosophiae* III.m.9) versifies the Platonic theory that God is "the form of the supreme good" (*summi forma boni*) and produces all things "in accordance with a paradigm" (*ab exemplo*).

These teachings are reinforced by similar doctrines stated in the secular texts that formed the basis of the liberal arts curriculum in later times: Cicero, *Orator* (8ff.); Seneca, *Epistolae morales* (65.4–7); Apuleius, *De Platone et eius dogmate* (I.5.190–6.194); Calcidius, *In Timaeum* (307, 308.2–309.2); Macrobius, *Commentarii in somnium scipionis* (I.6.8–9); Servius, *In Aeneidem* (VI.289); Martianus Capella, *De nuptiis Philologiae et Mercurii* (I.68); and Priscian, *Institutiones grammaticae* (17.44).

The transmission to the Middle Ages of the notion that there are universals identical with divine ideas is easy to illustrate. Remigius of Auxerre (*Commentum in Martianum Capellam* I.32.7) comments upon Martianus Capella's text by identifying the Ideas of Platonism with the Divine Wisdom of Christian teaching; various medieval glossators interpret the verses of Boethius by invoking parallels from both scriptural and secular sources: the Anonymus Bruxellensis detects parallels with the teaching of the Gospel of John; Bovo II of Corvey—who suspects that Boethius' doctrine is largely secular in origin—compares the doxographers' threefold schema of God, paradigm, and matter in Ambrose and the Neoplatonists' three hypostases of God, intellect, and soul in Macrobius; the Anonymus Einsiedlensis finds parallels with the teachings of Calcidius' commentary on the *Timaeus;* Adalbold of Utrecht, who believes that Boethius is formulating a doctrine only partially comprehensible to non-Christians, interprets it with reference to the accounts of the creation of the world in Genesis and of the creative Word in John; William of Conches (*Glossae super Platonem* 56.125–126) elaborates on Calcidius' commentary by identifying the Platonic Ideas with the divine Wisdom of Christianity.

In the third place, there are universals that are identified with numbers in God's mind: the monad and the dyad, the first ten integers, geometrical shapes, and the like. Important discussions of these universals, the indirect descendants of Plato's mathematical Forms, occur in Boethius' *De institutione arithmetica* and Thierry of Chartres's *Commentum in Boethii de Trinitate.*

The former demonstrates that the sciences of arithmetic, geometry, music, and astronomy have a special epistemological function in elevating the human mind from the realm of the sensible to that of the intelligible. This is because number corresponds to the primary exemplar in God's thought, in accordance with which he produced the order and regularity of the physical cosmos (*De institutione arithmetica* I.1.10.1–19).

The latter provides something of a practical illustration of this theory by arguing that the sciences of arithmetic and geometry can be employed in delineating the nature of the triune God; thus the equation $1 \times 1 = 1$ indicates the equality of the Father's generation of the Son (arithmetical illustration), while the figure of a square indicates the perfection of that generation (geometrical illustration; *Commentum in Boethii de Trinitate* 2.30–34). Discussions of this kind, explaining the nature of one important set of universals by locating them in the divine mind, are quite common during the Middle Ages.

UNIVERSALIA IN REBUS

This version of the realist theory of universals is primarily epistemological but has certain ontological connotations. It was subject to continual formulation, criticism, and reformulation at the hands of philosophers.

An early version of the doctrine occurs in Remigius of Auxerre's *Commentum in Martianum Capellam,* where it is stated that every individual participates in a species, every species in a genus, and every genus in the supreme genus. Although the more generic is clearly prior ontologically to the more specific—hence the author's definition "'Man' is the substantial unity of many men" (*homo est multorum hominum substantialis unitas*)—the precise relation between the former and the latter is nowhere specified (*Commentum in Martianum Capellam* IV.157.17–18).

A reformulation of realism occurs in the *De eodem et diverso* of Adelard of Bath. Here it is argued that the Aristotelian doctrine that universals exist only in individual things and the Platonic teaching that they also exist outside individual things are not inconsistent with one another, "for if one considers objects, it is to the same thing that the names of genus, species, and individual are assigned, although in different respects" (*nam si res consideres, eidem essentiae et generis et speciei et individui nomina imposita sunt, sed respectu diverso; De eodem et diverso* 11.17–21). That Adelard is speaking of an individual thing in which generic and specific properties are actually existent rather than of an individual thing from which generic and specific notions are mentally abstracted is indicated clearly by his statement that minds contemplating the species "forget" (*obliviscuntur*) the individual and that minds contemplating the genus "do not notice the presence of" (*inesse non attendunt*) the species (11.29–32).

Another reformulation of realism occurs in the pseudo-Abelardian *De generibus et speciebus.* Here it is argued that the universal is not that which occurs in any given individual but "that whole collection assembled from other individuals of the same nature" (*totam illam collectionem ex singulis aliis huius naturae coniunctam*). That the author is concerned with an existent totality rather than a collective concept follows from the fact that the identity between individuals is based on "the similarity of their creation in both matter and form" (*similis creationis in materia et forma*).

Since the logical requirements of the universal cannot be satisfied by interpreting it either as contained in an individual or as the collection of individuals, it was inevitable that whenever the doctrine of *universalia in rebus* was formulated, it quickly attracted the attention of philosophical critics. The interpretation of Boethius' writings played a major role in such debates because he explicitly considered these problems but left no definitive solutions. Thus, his *In Isagogen Porphyrii commenta editio secunda* (I.10.158.21–164.2) discusses the three questions regarding universals noted by Porphyry—whether they subsist or are placed in bare concepts alone; whether, subsisting, they are corporeal or incorporeal; and whether they are separate from sensibles or are placed in sensibles and are in accordance with them (*sive subsistunt sive in solis nudisque intellectibus posita sunt sive subsistentia corporalia sunt an incorporalia et utrum separata a sensibilibus an in sensibilibus posita et circa ea constantia*)—and answers them along the lines of Alexander of Aphrodisias' conceptualism. On the other hand, in *De Trinitate* (2.42–58) and *Contra Eutychen et Nestorium* (2.1–3.101), solutions different from and perhaps conflicting with this are suggested. Although the doctrine of *universalia in rebus* was hardly accepted without reservations at any time in the Middle Ages, the crescendo of criticism reached its peak during the twelfth through fourteenth centuries in the writings of Peter Abelard and William of Ockham.

An early testimony to such controversies is provided by Ratramnus of Corbie's *De anima ad Odonem Bellovacensem.* Ratramnus replies to a theory regarding the nature of soul—expounded by a monk of St. Germer de Fly in accordance with the teaching of a certain Macarius Scottus—based on the interpretation of Augustine's *De quantitate animae.* On this view, of the three possibilities considered in this text—that soul is one, that it is one and many, and that it is many—Augustine gives support to the second, a fact necessitating a metaphysical doctrine that there is a single soul that is the source of the multiplicity of souls and corresponds to the universal "soul" to which individual souls are related (*De anima ad Odonem* 9.130.20–23). Ratramnus responds to this by arguing that of the three possibilities considered earlier, Augustine gives assent to none, since he is concerned with the concept "soul," which can be universal or particular, depending upon its application. Moreover, in the former case the concept of soul does not correspond to a single thing that is the source of the coordinate multiplicity (2.28.4–29.23).

The theory attacked by Ratramnus of Corbie is probably identifiable with the earlier realism of Remigius of Auxerre; it should be contrasted with the doctrines criticized in Abelard's *Logica ingredientibus,* whose affinities are more with the reformulated positions. Abelard responds to various interpretations of the nature of universals—their contemporary advocates are not actually named—that have arisen in the context of Prophyrian and Boethian commentary. One view maintains that all men are in themselves both many, because of their distinctness as persons, and one, because of their similarity of humanity; and that the selfsame thing is its own genus and species through having a difference in respect of itself (*Logica ingredientibus* 14.18–31). Abelard rejects this approach on the grounds that since everything affirmed regarding the universal would also have to be stated about the individual, the necessary distinction between universal and individual vanishes (15.23–35). Another view asserts that all men collected together represent the species "man," all animals collected together consitute the genus "animal," and so on (14.7–11). Abelard criticizes this theory on the grounds that whereas a universal must naturally be prior to the individuals coordinated with it, the collection of things is naturally posterior to the individuals of which it is composed (15.15–18).

As stated earlier, in the Middle Ages we find the teachings (1) that universals are contained in the mind of God and (2) that universals are immanent in the spatiotemporal realm asserted either together or singly. Both tenets are affirmed by writers such as Boethius, the commentators on Martianus Capella and Boethius, and Anselm of Canterbury; the first tenet but not the second is accepted by Abelard (see *Theologia Christiana* IV.138–139). A more radical rethinking of the problem is exemplified by certain medieval thinkers who—because of their emphasis upon the omnipresence of God in created things—permit the universals in the creator's mind and in the spatiotemporal realm to coincide. This position is persuasively expressed in John Scottus Eriugena's *Periphyseon* and in various writings of the school of Chartres.

BIBLIOGRAPHY

On the *universalia ante res* in general, see Gangolf Schrimpf *et al.*, "Idee II A," in *Historisches Wörterbuch der Philosophie,* IV, Joachim Ritter and Karlfried Gründer, eds. (1976). On specific questions see Fernand Brunner, "Creatio numerorum, rerum est creatio," in *Mélanges offerts à René Crozet,* II (1966); Kurt Flasch, "Der philosophische Ansatz des Anselm von Canterbury im Monologion und sein Verhältnis zum augustinischen Neuplatonismus," in *Analecta anselmiana,* **2** (1970); R. B. C. Huygens, "Mittelalterliche Kommentare zum 'O qui perpetua,'" in *Sacris erudiri,* **6** (1954); Giulio d'Onofrio, "Giovanni Scoto e Remigio di Auxerre: A proposito di alcuni commenti altomedievali a Boezio," in *Studi medievali,* 3rd ser., **22** (1981); H. Silvestre, "Le commentaire inédit de Jean Scot Erigène au mètre IX du livre III du *De consolatione philosophiae* de Boèce," in *Revue d'histoire ecclésiastique,* **47** (1952); Aimé Solignac, "Analyse et sources de la question 'De Ideis,'" in *Augustinus magister* (Congrès international augustinien, Paris, 21–24 septembre 1954), I (1954).

On the *universalia in rebus* in general, see Joseph Reiners, *Der aristotelische Realismus in der Frühscholastik* (1907). On specific questions see Philippe Delhaye, *Une controverse sur l'âme universelle au IXe siècle* (1950), 19–54; Tullio Gregory, *Platonismo medievale: Studi e ricerche* (1958), 31–51; Martin Tweedale, *Abailard on Universals* (1976), 53–132; Hans E. Willner, ed., *Des Adelard von Bath Traktat De eodem et diverso* (1903), 44–72.

STEPHEN GERSH

[See also **Abelard, Peter; Adelard of Bath; Adalbold of Utrecht; Ambrose, St.; Anselm of Canterbury; Augustine of Hippo, St.; Boethius; Bovo II of Corvey; Dialectic; John Scottus Eriugena; Macrobius; Martianus Capella; Philosophy and Theology; Plato in the Middle Ages; Ratramnus of Corbie; Remigius of Auxerre; Thierry of Chartres; Universals; William of Conches.**]

RECITING TONE. See **Psalm Tones.**

RECLAMATION OF LAND. Between the late 900's and the early 1300's, the landscape of Europe was transformed on a scale rarely seen in human history before or since. As late as the tenth century, large portions of the continent consisted of what might be termed wilderness, where the imprint of human culture was at most fleeting and slight. This was true particularly of temperate Europe, north of the Mediterranean basin, where vast areas remained untouched by human activity and were covered mostly by deciduous forest, as well as large tracts of swamp and marsh. By the early fourteenth century, this situation had changed dramatically. Only tiny patches of wilderness remained in a landscape characterized by fields, pastures, and villages. It was primarily reclamation, the deliberate restructuring of physical environments so that they conform to specific human purposes, that was responsible for this transformation.

RECLAMATION OF LAND

Reclamation is as old as civilization itself. Indeed, it may well qualify as one of those special kinds of behavior that help to make the human species distinct from all others. Over the millennia it has taken a wide variety of forms, depending not only upon the varying characteristics of physical environments but also upon the uses to which the land was to be put. Despite such diversity, however, reclamation has almost always been intimately associated with agriculture. By simplifying or completely eliminating existing flora and fauna, as well as by reshaping and contouring the landscape, it has created agricultural land where none existed before. This was especially true during the Middle Ages, when activities such as slashing, chopping, digging, grubbing, and burning were used to transform vast areas of woodland, marsh, and swamp into land suitable for agriculture.

That the landscape changes resulting from reclamation were considerable during the High Middle Ages is illustrated by an example from central Germany. In 1073, Emperor Henry IV, in danger of being captured by hostile Saxons along the northern fringe of the Harz Mountains near Harzburg, fled ninety kilometers (fifty-five miles) to the settlement at Eschwege. He reportedly journeyed for three days along a narrow path through what was described as primeval forest before arriving, exhausted, at his destination. Two hundred years later, Eschwege was entirely surrounded by a continuous expanse of fields, pastures, and villages.

Of course, not all regions were affected to exactly the same degree. Reclamation could take place only where there was land to be reclaimed—that is, land that could be exploited for agricultural purposes. In general, the Mediterranean world and the semi-arid regions of southwestern Asia had little potential agricultural land awaiting reclamation. Relatively high population densities had caused the extension of agriculture into virtually every possible nook and cranny long before the Middle Ages. Temperate Europe, in contrast, was only sparsely settled at the beginning of the Middle Ages, and contained huge, untapped reserves of potential agricultural land. Population densities had begun to increase in certain areas by the tenth century, particularly in the heartland of the early medieval Frankish territory, between the Loire and Rhine rivers, but the density of settlement dwindled dramatically east and north of the Rhine. It is not surprising, therefore, that most land reclamation during the High Middle Ages took place in the plentiful deciduous forests of western, central, and eastern Europe, as well as in the marshes and swamps of the coastal lowlands along the Atlantic Ocean, the North Sea, and the Baltic Sea.

Though it is impossible to show exactly how much of Europe was affected by reclamation during the High Middle Ages, there can be no doubt that it was extensive. A prime indicator of this is the large number of place-names, dating mostly from the eleventh through the thirteenth centuries, that refer to assarts, clearings, canals, dikes, and other aspects of the reclamation process. Further proof is seen in the establishment of numerous monasteries in wooded or waterlogged areas, in the extension of the church's network of parishes into those portions of the countryside where it previously had been lacking, and in the increasing importance of the tithes levied on newly reclaimed land (the *novales*).

The scale of reclamation was particularly impressive in central and eastern Europe, where Saxony, Thuringia, Franconia, Pomerania, Mecklenburg, Prussia, Bohemia, Transylvania, and other areas were reclaimed and settled by colonists from areas to the west. In Saxony, for example, the density of rural settlement is presently believed to have increased tenfold during the High Middle Ages. In the Alps and other mountainous regions, meanwhile, the edge of agriculture crept to ever higher elevations. Even in such a long-occupied and densely settled area as the vicinity of Cologne, however, there was a noticeable increase in *novales* collections during the eleventh and twelfth centuries. Estimates of the extent of wilderness reclaimed for agriculture between the tenth and fourteenth centuries—even in the long-settled areas of Europe—run as high as two-thirds of the presently occupied area. Not since the beginnings of agriculture, during the Neolithic era, had temperate Europe seen landscape change of such magnitude.

This transformation of the face of Europe had a profound impact on all aspects of life. In general, it stimulated the rural economy by helping to increase the productiveness of agriculture, bringing in its train a greater degree of prosperity that eventually permeated both the agricultural and the nonagricultural segments of society. More specifically, the relative well-being of the era was expressed through the increased tithes, other taxes, rents, and fees accruing to the ruling groups; through the larger supplies of food produced on the vastly extended area of agricultural land; and through the oppor-

RECLAMATION OF LAND

tunities offered to the otherwise landless to occupy lands of their own.

Some of these effects were recognized in the early thirteenth century by Cesarius, abbot of the monastery at Prüm, some fifty-five kilometers (thirty-five miles) north of Trier in the Eifel region. During the previous three centuries (893–1222), he wrote, much forested land had been cleared and many estates established, thereby greatly increasing the tithes. Further, many mills had been constructed, many vines planted, and an immeasurable amount of land brought into cultivation.

The effects of bringing wilderness into the world of human culture were expressed even more clearly a century later by an observer of political affairs in the County of Holland. Philip of Leyden reported around 1350 that comital revenues from the new villages established in the former swamp wilderness of coastal Holland constituted the most important source of income for the counts. His observations are supported by the records of fourteenth-century tithe collections in the surviving comital accounts.

It was in the Middle Ages that the typically European landscape was created. These medieval patterns of rural settlement and agriculture survived with very little alteration until the early nineteenth century and remain highly visible today.

PATTERNS OF LAND USE IN THE EARLY PERIOD

Land reclamation during the High Middle Ages was an impressive undertaking, lending a flavor of growth, energy, and vitality to an entire era in much the same fashion as did the frontier experience in North America in modern times. However, to fully appreciate why reclamation was begun during the High Middle Ages and how it was carried out, it is necessary to see it in the context of the early medieval agrarian tradition from which it arose.

Land was reclaimed during the early Middle Ages, as it was later. Yet there were significant differences in the nature of reclamation. The focus in the later period was on the opening of whole new territories. In the earlier period, reclamation usually took place within territories that had long been occupied, and it was largely a matter of more intensive use of land that was already helping to sustain the population in some way. Basically it was a matter of putting more land to the growing of crops. Arable agriculture thus gained at the expense of other food-providing activities, such as livestock keeping, hunting, fishing, and gathering. The advance into true wilderness—the totally unexploited portions of the continent—did not begin in earnest until the late tenth century.

There were, in the early period, basically two types of arable agriculture. One, intensive and permanent, was based on the scratch plow and the two-field system, in which a field would be cultivated one year and lie fallow the next. The second type of cultivation was a temporary invasion of the wilderness. The slash-and-burn technique yielded a partly cleared field that could be cultivated with the hoe. After a few years, when its fertility declined, this field was abandoned to the wilderness and cultivation shifted to a newly cleared field.

The permanent fields, often known as *agri,* were most characteristic of the areas in temperate Europe that had been densely settled for a long time. These areas included the Paris basin, parts of Flanders, the middle Rhine Valley, and portions of southeastern England. In many of these areas, crops had been grown on permanent fields since prehistoric times, and during the early Middle Ages the *ager* gradually became the dominant element in the local landscape. The large estates, or *villae,* of early medieval sources were found in such areas.

Agri might be abandoned from time to time, generally as the result of war, famine, or pestilence, and then reclaimed as the local society got back on its feet. In intention, however, the creation of an *ager* was a one-time activity. It was an arduous and drastic process that eventually resulted in the complete removal of all trees, stumps, roots, and other obstacles to plowing.

At the other extreme, where population was very sparse and woodland plentiful, crop production took place not on *agri* but on temporary plots. A particular plot was reclaimed from woodland, cropped for two or three years, and abandoned, while other plots in turn were reclaimed, cropped, and abandoned. After twenty-five or more years of fallow (the abandonment period), the original plot was reclaimed once again, and the whole cycle began anew.

In this scheme, reclamation was a continuous process that was balanced out by abandonment. Further, it was only a partial process compared with the creation of permanent fields. After the large trees were girdled with a sharp instrument to kill them, the undergrowth was slashed and burned. The tools of tillage used on temporary plots, a hoe or a digging stick, were not impeded by the stumps and roots that were left behind.

RECLAMATION OF LAND

This type of minimum reclamation and tillage ranks as one of the oldest forms of crop agriculture, yet it persisted into modern times in places where people remained scarce and woodland plentiful: in some Alpine regions, parts of Corsica, the Ardennes, and Finland, to name just a few. Though this type of temporary cropping pattern has various modern names, including forest-fallow and slash-and-burn, the most appropriate here is the Middle English word "swidden."

Between the extremes of the large, intensively cultivated estates and the frontier communities without fixed fields, there was a kind of mixed-use community in which both types of tillage were practiced to some degree, along with various other food-producing activities. Most of the settled portions of Europe no doubt contained this hybrid category. (Indeed, even on the large estates the *agri* were not the only source of food.) Let us look more closely at this typical early medieval village, with its various types of land use.

Surrounding the center of such a village's territory lay its *agri*. These were normally situated close to the dwellings and their associated buildings, yards, and gardens. The remainder of a village territory was known as *saltus* or *wastina* (wasteland). It surrounded the *agri* and was the place for noncrop forms of environmental exploitation. In most of temperate Europe, the *saltus* consisted of wooded or partially wooded land, though it often was swampy or marshy land in coastal areas. Generally, the intensity of land use in the *saltus* portion decreased as the distance from the center of the village territory increased, until the imprint of human culture faded to virtually nothing at the outer fringes of the territory.

The third category of land in the early Middle Ages was the *silva* or *nemus* (wilderness). Such areas lay between and beyond existing community territories; in *silva* the imprint of human culture was slight or nonexistent. *Silva* often served as a rough boundary zone separating one settled region from another. For example, in Flanders during the early Middle Ages, the Silva Carbonaria (Charcoal Forest) acted as a border or buffer zone between Neustria and Austrasia, the two major subdivisions of Frankish territory. These and other zones of *silva* constituted the wilderness that was progressively reclaimed, colonized, and integrated into the world of human affairs during the High Middle Ages.

In the early Middle Ages soil type was one of the most important considerations governing the location of settlements with *agri*. The soils of temperate Europe often vary greatly over short distances, from light, well-drained, and sandy to heavy, moist, and clayey. The primary instrument of cultivation on the *ager* was the ard, or scratch plow, which had entered Europe from southwestern Asia and Mediterranean Europe in prehistoric times. It was of light construction, ideally suited for the light soils and dry climate of its places of origin, where the object was merely to scratch the surface of the soil. In temperate Europe, however, heavy, moist soils are very common. Because these soils need to be dug deeply and rigorously, to allow the surface to dry and to bring weed growth under control, the ard performs poorly on them. For these reasons, the *ager* of early medieval settlements was limited essentially to the loess, chalk, limestone, and sandy alluvial soils, as well as to the lighter loams on the flanks and crests of gently rolling hills—in short, to the soils that could be worked efficiently by the ard.

Because in many cases light, well-drained soils had been cultivated for centuries, perhaps even millennia, their fertility had begun to disappear. This meant that unless substantial human labor was substituted for the lost fertility, in the form of composting and fertilizing, the yield of crops cultivated on the *ager* dropped considerably. There is evidence that some yield-to-seed ratios had dropped to 3:1 or even lower by the early Middle Ages, a miserable performance by any standard. For this reason, the *ager* simply could not provide all of the calories that were needed. Indeed, in parts of Germany during the early Middle Ages, the yield of permanent fields often amounted to less than one-third of the total caloric production.

By providing what the *ager* could not, the *saltus*, as well as the streams, ponds, and lakes it contained, was extremely important to the early medieval community. It provided, first of all, the grazing, browsing, and rooting grounds for the livestock that furnished the largest proportion of the calories consumed in much of temperate Europe. Further, it supplied the game, fowl, fish, berries, fruits, nuts, and honey that rounded out what otherwise would have been a monotonous diet. Finally, the *saltus* was the local source of wood, which was a crucial commodity throughout the Middle Ages, both as fuel and as the basic raw material for a wide variety of objects, from tools to ships and houses.

The *saltus* also contributed directly to crop production. First, it was a source of fertilizer in the

 RECLAMATION OF LAND

form of sods and organic matter that could be spread on the *ager*. Second, it was in the *saltus* that medieval peasants found the land for their temporary plots.

Although the *agri* played an important role in early medieval food production, they were only one part of a complex system. Still, modern scholars often are tempted to look almost exclusively at fields or field systems. The reason for this bias is not that the permanent fields produced the overwhelming majority of calories in the average diet; they often did not. Rather, it stems from the fact that the *agri* were of pivotal importance in the relations between peasants and the ruling elites. Fields were the focal point of the manorial rents and labor services that provided the economic underpinnings of social stratification; they produced the primary taxable and storable surplus in an era characterized by subsistence agriculture. And, because of the importance of this surplus, people kept records. Most of the surviving documentation for the early Middle Ages comes from the very largest and wealthiest estates, where both the intensity of cultivation and the effectiveness of the elite's control were probably greatest. Studies of such estates are useful, but will not necessarily illuminate rural life or the nature of food production in other areas.

Outside the areas of the largest estates, the *ager* often paled in comparison with the *saltus*. In fact, most often the *ager* appeared as a rather small island in a sea of *saltus* and *silva*. Estimates of the extent of land incorporated into fields in the sixth century, for example, suggest it may have been less than 5 percent of the total land area in many parts of temperate Europe.

Permanent fields were much less crucial than *saltus* or *silva* to the well-being of the early medieval peasant. After all, raising crops on the *ager* was a highly visible activity that was carried out in plain view of everyone, which made it very difficult to avoid paying the rents and performing the labor services associated with it. In contrast, gardening, fishing, hunting, gathering, livestock keeping, and crop raising on temporary plots in the *saltus* presumably were easily concealed from the landlord class. Further, food production on permanent fields required more labor than did the subsistence strategies normally employed in the *saltus*. Thus, unless there were compelling reasons for doing so, early medieval peasants most likely did not increase their emphasis on crop production, at least in formal, fixed fields, as long as other, less visible and less labor-demanding activities could provide them with what they needed.

THE GREAT EXPANSION

Nevertheless, the consistent theme that runs through the history of medieval agriculture was the gradual shift toward arable agriculture. It amounted to an expansion of *ager* at the expense first of *saltus* and eventually of *silva*. This meant that an increasing proportion of the countryside came to be exploited by labor-intensive cultivation on permanent fields, which replaced less labor-intensive forms of environmental exploitation, not only swidden production on temporary plots but also livestock keeping, fishing, hunting, and gathering.

The major, compelling reason behind this change was population growth. Though the Middle Ages began with a sharp drop in population, the number of people is estimated to have more than quadrupled between approximately 650 and 1300. Indeed, in much of temperate Europe, population by the mid fourteenth century may have been more than six times what it was in the mid seventh century. Though it would be reckless to assume that such growth occurred without any interludes of stagnation, nevertheless, the long-term demographic trends were upward for something like seven centuries, a truly remarkable accomplishment in preindustrial times.

The primary disadvantage of such demographic growth was a proportionate increase in the demand for food and fiber. All of the subsistence strategies traditionally used in the *saltus* were highly productive for the amount of labor invested only as long as people were scarce and land was plentiful. When people became less scarce and land was plentiful, productivity began to decline. For example, swidden agriculture became less productive when the length of the fallow period was reduced and there was insufficient time for the annual leaf drop to restore the lost fertility before the next cropping phase. In addition, fishing, hunting, and gathering all became more and more time-consuming when increased demand began to deplete supplies. On the other hand, there was also a positive effect of population growth: it increased the labor supply, which made it easier to increase labor-intensive cultivation on permanent fields.

Between the late eighth and the late tenth centuries, the traditional food-providing patterns of temperate Europe began to respond to population growth by moving toward a more intensive exploi-

RECLAMATION OF LAND

tation of the land. One well-known example of this was the change from a two-field to a three-field system of crop rotation on the *ager*. A second example, of more relevance here, was the extension of the *ager* onto the plentiful, and ultimately more productive, heavy and moist soils that constituted much of the *saltus* and *silva* of temperate Europe.

Since the new soils needed to be dug deeply and rigorously, a replacement was needed for the traditional ard, or scratch plow. This necessity seems to have been recognized early on. Archaeological evidence from prehistoric times reveals a modified scratch plow with a fairly broad and flared cutting end, or share. This plow could be tilted and twisted to one side, and thereby made to dig and partially turn over some of the topsoil. However, as greater attention was paid to the heavy, moist soils of the *saltus* during the early Middle Ages, a different plow came to be used. It originated in eastern Europe early in the Christian era. Heavier, and usually wheeled, it included a coulter to cut the soil vertically, a plowshare to cut it horizontally, and a moldboard to turn it over.

Because the new plow was poorly suited to cultivating light, dry soils, it did not replace the ard but came to exist alongside it. The use of the ard died out only when the tillage of the soils for which it was so well suited came to an end. For this reason, the spread of the heavy, wheeled plow should be seen as a symptom of the expansion of crop agriculture on permanent fields into areas that had not previously been under the plow.

It is important to note that the new plow was not an isolated invention. It was part of a new system of technology that included the harrow to pulverize clods of soil after plowing, improvements in animal harnessing, and the slow switch in draft animals from the ox to the faster and more powerful horse. Together, these improvements provided the peasantry of temperate Europe with a technology uniquely suited to cultivating the heavy, moist soils of the *saltus* and eventually the *silva*.

Both the three-field system of crop rotation and the expansion of permanent fields onto the soils of the *saltus* required a considerable augmentation of labor input. The three-field system required essentially more of the same kinds of labor that were involved in the two-field system: plowing, fertilizing, planting, weeding, and harvesting. The cultivation of the heavier soils, on the other hand, presupposed not only the arduous task of reclamation, including the removal of trees, stumps, and roots, but also the use of a heavy, cumbersome, and expensive new instrument of cultivation. The new plow, with its greater traction demands, in turn required the care and feeding of more, as well as more expensive, draft animals.

Because of these heavy labor requirements, it is not surprising that the first signs of both innovations appeared in the most densely settled portions of temperate Europe. As late as the mid tenth century, Europe's population, though greater than ever before, still resided in essentially the same places it always had. The dense population in these areas both allowed and required the introduction of the three-field system and the expansion of intensive arable farming into the *saltus*. It was only later, toward the end of the tenth century, that many Europeans began to leave their homes and as colonists established new settlements in the still extensive wilderness areas between, and especially beyond, their traditional areas of settlement.

The timing of these population shifts may have depended on a number of factors, but ultimately it may well have been a series of political changes that proved to be crucial. During the ninth and early tenth centuries, a series of invasions by Arabs, Magyars, and Vikings created a security crisis in parts of temperate Europe that had known several generations of relative peace and quiet. The Vikings, in particular, penetrated into some of the very areas that a short time later were to see some of the earliest large-scale reclamation of wilderness, especially sections of northern France, the Low Countries, and Germany. The existing scattered, discontinuous settlements of these regions were vulnerable to attack, particularly since virtually all vestiges of former royal power had disappeared and there was very little chance that these communities would receive outside help. The ease with which Vikings could sail up the great rivers of northern and western Europe and launch surprise attacks demonstrates the weakness of the defenders.

These difficult conditions seem to have caused a contraction of settlement in many of the affected areas, which could be surprisingly far inland. We know, for instance, that in the Ardennes a number of villages were abandoned, with fields left untilled, after an attack in 893.

When the attacks began to decrease during the tenth century, they did so not because of any significant revival of centralized royal power but because a new set of effective defenses was organized by local rulers, many of whom went on to

RECLAMATION OF LAND

assume most of the rights, privileges, and responsibilities that at least theoretically pertained to kings and emperors. One of the privileges that the new rulers characteristically assumed was the right to the disposal of wilderness, formerly one of the regalia, or royal rights. As soon as they had consolidated political control over their territories, they began to exercise this right. A large proportion of the reclamation and colonization of the High Middle Ages took place with the active encouragement of the territorial princes of France, the Low Countries, and Germany, who proceeded to allot the wilderness under their control to groups of colonists who agreed to bring it into the realm of human affairs.

The interests of these new rulers stood in sharp contrast to those of the old landlords of the manorial system, who persisted in trying to keep peasants confined to the traditional areas of settlement and agriculture. In order to secure the needed colonists, the new rulers often drew up agreements with representatives of prospective settlers, offering them very favorable terms. In exchange for the payment of a small homestead tax and about 10 percent of all that was produced, colonists usually received full ownership of the land they reclaimed, the rights to the disposal of such land, and complete personal freedom.

In exchange for these substantial privileges, the colonists had the opportunity to carry out a lot of very hard work. Reclamation in most cases amounted to taking on mature hardwood forests with rather simple tools. A characteristic strategy was to start with a version of the swidden, or slash-and-burn, technique. If the colonists had been required to remove all trees, stumps, and roots, and to establish permanent fields prior to planting the first crops, they would have starved. By employing the oldest of reclamation techniques, slashing and burning, they could get land into production very quickly. However, this strategy should not be confused with true swidden agriculture, because the object was to open up wilderness to agriculture on permanent fields rather than to establish a balanced cycle of partial reclamations followed by long fallow periods during which woodland vegetation recovered the land.

Colonists aiming to create a permanent field would first clear a plot for swidden agriculture and then proceed to remove the stumps and roots so that the field could be cultivated with the plow rather than the hoe. Generally there were two zones of advance into the forest: swidden to the fore and *ager* following behind.

A lowland variant of pioneering swidden agriculture developed in areas where the colonists needed to remove water instead of trees. The technique was used on a very large scale in the massive peat bogs and swamps of Holland, and generally along the North Sea from Flanders to Denmark. Colonists lowered the water table of a portion of a bog by digging networks of drainage ditches about one meter deep. This was sufficient to stop peat accumulation, and to allow the surface to dry and develop a sod capable of supporting humans and their paraphernalia.

Once under way, the reclamation and colonization movement seemed to gain a momentum all its own. This was at least partially because of the population dynamic involved. When people moved from densely populated, long-settled areas to wilderness with much lower population densities, they responded to the shortage of people by marrying younger and having larger families. Thus the population growth of the long-settled areas fed even higher growth in the frontier areas. All this growth fed the army of colonists, who continued to reclaim land without any noticeable interruption until virtually all of the wilderness zones of western, central, and eastern Europe had been incorporated into the realm of human affairs.

The expansion of agriculture into the wilderness areas of temperate Europe had a profound effect on European society. It helped to break the stranglehold that parasitic landlordism had on peasant labor and productivity in the early Middle Ages. Even those peasants who did not migrate to wilderness areas benefited, since, in an effort to keep some peasants on their lands, lords began to alter some of the most stifling aspects of manorialism. For example, money payments gradually replaced inefficient labor services and payments in kind, allowing a much fuller expression of peasant productive capacity.

Another effect of the reclamation process was a tremendous increase in food production that arose from an increase in the amount of land devoted to crop agriculture and from the fact that the new lands were much more fertile than the old, often worn-out lands they supplemented or replaced. As a result, between 1046 and 1309 there were very few famines that were more than local in scale. For nearly 300 years the steady progress of reclamation helped to increase food production at a rate equal to or exceeding the rate of population growth. In fact, it was the production of agricultural surpluses during the High Middle Ages that made possible the appearance of urban life with all its trappings.

BIBLIOGRAPHY

The literature on reclamation during the Middle Ages is extremely diffuse. There are no handbooks, reference works, or exhaustive bibliographies on the topic. Most information must be gleaned from sources devoted primarily to other topics, such as archaeology, ethnography, historical geography, place-name studies, and historical documentation. The best treatments to date are on a local or regional scale, usually appearing as part of the history of a single community, rural district, or province. For example, the county histories of England contain much information on local reclamation and colonization. Similar information is embodied in the publications of local historical and archaeological societies throughout Europe. Until reclamation begins to be studied as more than a strictly local phenomenon, the scattered nature of the sources is not likely to change.

Nevertheless, a number of works provide valuable perspectives and information that can help in formulating a general picture of medieval reclamation. H. C. Darby, "The Clearing of the Woodland in Europe," in William L. Thomas *et al.*, eds., *Man's Role in Changing the Face of the Earth* (1956), though brief and somewhat dated, remains one of the few treatments of the topic in general. Richard Koebner, "The Settlement and Colonization of Europe," in *The Cambridge Economic History of Europe,* I, *The Agrarian Life of the Middle Ages,* 2nd ed. (1966), is especially valuable for the German eastward colonization movement of the High Middle Ages. Stanton W. Green, "The Agricultural Colonization of Temperate Forest Habitats: An Ecological Model," in William W. Savage, Jr., and Stephen I. Thompson, eds., *The Frontier: Comparative Studies,* II (1979), develops a model of tremendous relevance to the study of medieval land reclamation.

Ester Boserup, *The Conditions of Agricultural Growth* (1965), and *Population and Technological Change* (1981), are fundamental to any understanding of the varieties of agriculture and the kinds and degrees of reclamation associated with them. David R. Harris, "Swidden Systems and Settlement," in Peter J. Ucko, Ruth Tringham, and G. W. Dimbleby, eds., *Man, Settlement, and Urbanism* (1972), examines a particular variety of shifting agriculture. William H. TeBrake, *Medieval Frontier: Culture and Ecology in Rijnland* (1985), applies some of Boserup's perspectives to peat bog reclamation in Holland. Hans-Jürgen Nitz, "The Church as Colonist: The Benedictine Abbey of Lorsch and Planned Waldhuffen Colonization in the Odenwald," in *Journal of Historical Geography,* 9 (1983), looks at the church's involvement in German woodland reclamation.

The general agrarian context of medieval reclamation can be developed from the following studies: Marc Bloch, *French Rural History,* Janet Sondheimer, trans. (1966); Georges Duby, *Rural Economy and Country Life in the Medieval West,* Cynthia Postan, trans. (1968); Alan Mayhew, *Rural Settlement and Farming in Germany* (1973); B. H. Slicher van Bath, *The Agrarian History of Western Europe, A.D. 500–1850,* Olive Ordish, trans. (1963); the regional chapters in *The Cambridge Economic History of Europe,* I, 2nd ed. (1966).

Particularly helpful in understanding the evolution of early medieval agriculture in relation to the growth of population and the expansion of arable agriculture are Georges Duby, *The Early Growth of the European Economy,* Howard B. Clarke, trans. (1974); and Andrew M. Watson, "Towards Denser and More Continuous Settlement: New Crops and Farming Techniques in the Early Middle Ages," in J. A. Raftis, ed., *Pathways to Medieval Peasants* (1981).

A number of ecological and geographical aspects of medieval agriculture that are relevant to reclamation are treated in William S. Cooter, "Preindustrial Frontiers and Interaction Spheres: Aspects of the Human Ecology of Roman Frontier Regions in Northwest Europe" (diss., Univ. of Oklahoma, 1976), and "Ecological Dimensions of Medieval Agrarian Systems," in *Agricultural History,* 52 (1978); Walter Janssen, "Some Major Aspects of Frankish and Medieval Settlement in the Rhineland," in P. H. Sawyer, ed., *Medieval Settlement: Continuity and Change* (1976); William H. TeBrake, "Ecology and Economy in Early Medieval Frisia," in *Viator,* 9 (1978); Charles Thomas, "Towards the Definition of the Term 'Field' in the Light of Prehistory," in Sawyer, *Medieval Settlement.*

Finally, with regard to the special status of colonists in medieval reclamation schemes, see Archibald R. Lewis, "The Closing of the Mediaeval Frontier," in *Speculum,* 33 (1958); and Bryce Lyon, "Medieval Real Estate Developments and Freedom," in *American Historical Review,* 63 (1958).

William H. TeBrake

[See also **Agriculture and Nutrition; Animals, Draft; Animals, Food; Bastide; Black Death; Charcoal; Cistercian Order; Climatology; Construction: Building Materials; Demography; Estate Management; Famine in Western Europe; Food Trades; Forests, European; Grain Crops; Hunting and Fowling, Western European; Magic and Folklore, Western European; Missions and Missionaries, Christian; Pasture, Rights of; Plagues, European; Taxation, Church; Village Life; Villages.**]

RECONQUEST or *Reconquista* is the term often used in Iberian history to describe the long military struggle of Christians and Muslims that began shortly after the Muslim invasion of the Iberian Peninsula in 711 and ended with the fall of Granada to the Catholic kings in 1492. There has been endless historiographical debate as to the nature of the Reconquest: whether it was a conscious religious and ideological effort to recover from the Moors the lands once held by the Visigoths or simply the result of political and economic expediency, with little or no ideological content. The truth probably lies somewhere in between. On the one hand, after the mid eighth century a series of important developments took place. First, as early as the late eighth century, the cult of St. James spread throughout remote Galicia and Asturias. This was followed by its growing popularity beyond the region in the succeeding centuries, culminating in the succesful promotion of the pilgrimage to Compostela by the Cluniac order. Second, the identification of St. James with the war effort against Islam was highlighted in ecclesiastical writings and popular imagination by the reported appearances of the apostle riding on his white horse to the aid of Christians. Third, from the early tenth century on, the kings of Asturias proclaimed themselves heirs to the Visigothic empire, thus laying claim to all the lands once ruled by the kings of Toledo. The conjuncture of the cult of Santiago, the so-called Visigothic revival, and, later on in the eleventh century, the idea of the crusade provided the ideological foundations for the Reconquest. Many historians have argued that this description of the Reconquest, indeed the term itself, was to a large extent the outcome of ecclesiastical fabrication and did not correspond in fact to the complex relations between Christians and Moors in the Iberian Peninsula. The twelfth-century *Cantar de mío Cid* does not reveal any conscious will on the part of the Christians to reconquer the lands but rather their appetite for booty. Moreover, the Reconquest remained throughout the Middle Ages a useful political weapon for Iberian kings and, more often than not, a profitable enterprise.

BIBLIOGRAPHY

José María Lacarra, ed., *La reconquista española y la repoblación del país* (1951); Derek W. Lomax, *The Reconquest of Spain* (1978); Angus MacKay, *Spain in the Middle Ages: From Frontier to Empire, 1000–1500* (1977).

TEOFILO F. RUIZ

[See also **Alfonso I of Aragon; Alfonso X; Almoravids; Aragon, Crown of; Asturias-León; Cantar de Mío Cid; Castile; Catalonia; Cid, History and Legend of; Church, Latin: 1054–1305; Cluny, Order of; Crusades and Crusader States; Granada; Islam, Conquests of; Portugal; Santiago de Compostela; Spain, Christian-Muslim Relations; Spain, Muslim Kingdoms of; Valencia.**]

REEVE. An official in Anglo-Saxon England who assisted an ealdorman in the administration of justice. As early as the reign of Ine of Wessex (*d. ca.* 726) royal reeves (*gerefas*) served in the king's household and were subject to the king's will; failure to enforce the law brought fines or even expulsion from office. By the early ninth century they represented the king locally and their powers expanded rapidly to collecting dues and labor services, presiding over folk courts, and performing military functions. They also attempted to ensure that all accusations and complaints of injustice were heard and determined. By the tenth century they were assisting in the administration of royal manors and boroughs, enforcing royal rights and the payments of taxes, and supervising commercial transactions.

The reeves' responsibilities increased further during the middle decades of the tenth century, when they were entrusted with administering shires, presiding over shire courts, and receiving pledges for the observance of peace. This elevation of local responsibility occurred when groups of shires were put under the control of one ealdorman, who no longer could attend personally to all his traditional duties. Thus, the position of shire-reeve, or sheriff, came into being. Appointed directly by the king, some sheriffs held office for many years and some even presided over more than one shire. They received grants of land from the king, regulated the agricultural operations on royal estates, and received a share of the profits from the periodic harvests. By the eleventh century they presided over subordinate judicial sessions of hundred courts; assembled shire levies; directed military defenses against Viking incursions; proclaimed the king's peace, commands, and enactments; led posses in pursuit of criminals; assessed and collected Danegelds; and controlled most shire finances. Land forfeited to the king now was taken over by sheriffs and administered by them until disposition.

After 1066 they became an indispensable link in

the Norman chain of political command, and their powers increased even further.

The manorial reeve. The Anglo-Saxon reeve, who evolved into the sheriff, with substantial legal and police duties, after the Norman Conquest, should not be confused with the English manorial reeve on agricultural estates from the twelfth to the late fifteenth centuries. (The latter official, known in the lands of the Holy Roman Empire as *der Schultz* and on French manors as *le maire,* was the principal serf in any manorial village.)

Being the prototype of the Reeve (Reve) described in the General Prologue of Chaucer's *Canterbury Tales,* the manorial reeve was the "boss," supervisor, or foreman for the lord on his estate(s). This reeve was "appointed" by the landowner or "elected" by his agricultural and manorial specialist peers (millers, carpenters, smiths, and so on), but was actually a hereditary official, since his male ancestors had normally held the same position.

Unlike management personnel in later, industrial societies, the manorial reeve could not regulate the work schedules, duties, or areas of responsibility of those in his charge. His sole responsibility was to report infractions of traditional manorial duties to the lord's household. The reeve was indispensable to the lord, since the fines levied in manorial courts, based on the reeve's investigations, constituted an important source of the landlord's income.

The manorial reeve often lived in a two-room hut, with a wall or barrier separating his winter livestock from his family's living quarters. Though his social and economic status was clearly lower than that of the Anglo-Saxon reeve and later sheriff, his impact on a day-to-day basis in the operations of the manorial estates was crucial.

BIBLIOGRAPHY

Robert L. Reynolds, *Europe Emerges* (1961); Ronald Edward Zupko, *British Weights and Measures: A History from Antiquity to the Seventeenth Century* (1977).

RONALD EDWARD ZUPKO

[See also **Bailiff; Chaucer, Geoffrey; England: Anglo-Saxon; Estate Management; Law, English Common: to 1272; Sheriff.**]

REFECTORY, a room for eating and refreshment, especially the dining hall or chamber of a monastery, convent, or college. The refectory is almost always in direct communication with the kitchen. In a claustral monastery, it is usually adjacent to the cloister. The typical refectory is an elongated rectangle in plan; after the late twelfth century it is frequently vaulted. Along one of the long sides of the refectory is placed a pulpit or lectern for the reading of Scripture during the communal meals. Just outside the refectory a lavabo or fountain is generally provided for the ablutions of the monks or other diners.

BIBLIOGRAPHY

Wolfgang Braunfels, *Monasteries of Western Europe: The Architecture of the Orders* (1973).

GREGORY WHITTINGTON

[See also **Cloister; Monastery.**]

REFORM, IDEA OF. The terms *reformare* and *reformatio* are key words in medieval Christian parlance. Their force is essentially retrospective; though customarily translated "reform," they could more accurately be rendered as "restore" and "restoration." In classical pagan literature they could refer to a miraculous return to a previous state, for example through restoration of lost youth (Ovid, *Metamorphoses*). This notion of reform as turning back to an earlier condition is suggested also in later and purely secular usage: Rudolf I of Habsburg, on becoming emperor in the late thirteenth century, announced his intention to "restore the peace" with the formula *pacem reformare.* Usually implicit or explicit in such usage was the understanding that reform harked back to an ideal state of affairs in the past, a "golden age" of the church, the monasteries, the state, or society in general. It is only in the modern era that these terms, linked with Enlightenment notions of progress, came to be used with reference to a forward-looking transformation, or a process of building toward an ideal goal not already realized in the past. Because conceptions of the ideal era might differ, there was no consensus regarding the nature of the reform to be undertaken in medieval Christendom; concepts of reform varied widely.

The notion of reform in a specifically Christian sense was first articulated in the patristic era with reference to the individual soul. Having fallen into sin, each individual stood in need of reform. In such contexts the term "reform" came to be closely linked with "conversion." Entry into the monastic life was one way of effecting and securing a transformation of this sort; Augustine, for example, did not feel that his own spiritual recovery was assured until he was able to assume the full rigor of the ascetic life. Partly because it was the monasteries that developed the theory of individual reform, it was natural that the term should become extended within a monastic milieu to institutional transformation as well. Thus, when monks in the ninth and following centuries sought to restore monasticism to what they saw as its original vigor, they evolved a theory of institutional reform that owed much to earlier theology of personal religious life.

When the project of reform spread from the monasteries to the church at large in the eleventh century, the ideology of reform was further translated into ecclesiological language. This article, then, will focus on (1) theological notions of individual reform, particularly as they were developed in the patristic era; and (2) the ideas of reform embodied in the monastic and church reforms of the Middle Ages.

INDIVIDUAL REFORM IN THE PATRISTIC ERA

The patristic concept of reform has been unfolded by Gerhard B. Ladner, who distinguishes the idea of reform in terms of four related but distinct groups of notions. First, cosmological ideas of renewal, elaborated by Plato, the Stoics, the Neo-pythagoreans, and others, envisaged a general cyclical pattern of recurrence in which a set succession of eras would be perpetually reenacted. In extreme forms this theory maintained that not just the general eras would be repeated, but the details of individual lives as well. Frequently the assumption was that each cycle began with a golden age, from which history declined. Such ideas were incompatible with the linear conception of history found in the Bible, and in particular with Christian conceptions of freedom.

Second, vitalistic notions of renewal or renascence posited a restoration of life or of growth following a period of dormancy. The metaphor used could be vegetative, but the myth of the phoenix arising from its ashes also came into play in such contexts. The pagan renascence under Theodosius in the late fourth century, which sought to defend, revise, and revive the literature of pagan antiquity, employed such ideas. Whereas the vitalistic notion of renewal suggests a spontaneous urge, the idea of reform involves a conscious pursuit of goals.

Third, millenarian concepts of renewal, which anticipate a 1,000-year period of bliss at the end of history, derive mainly from Jewish messianic expectations (tempered by Hellenistic cosmology), and were transmitted to Christendom through the book of Revelation, especially chapter 20. Christian millenarianism has arisen in various forms: Augustine reinterpreted the millennium as the last era in ordinary Christian history, while Joachim of Fiore conceived it as the imminent and ultimate age of the Holy Spirit, which would succeed the age of the Son just as the latter had already superseded the age of the Father. Later theories of renewal (utopian, revolutionary, and progressive) have owed much to millenarian precedent. The distinguishing feature of millenarianism is its insistence that when the millennium or 1,000-year kingdom comes, there will be absolute, total perfection on earth. The idea of reform, on the other hand, maintains that imperfection will remain in earthly affairs; perfectibility is always relative, and will be realized to an extent that cannot be foreseen.

Fourth, the ideas of conversion, baptismal regeneration, and penance are closely linked with the idea of reform but not precisely identical. The effects of baptism are instantaneous and nonrepeatable; postbaptismal conversion and penance, seen as nonrepeatable during the earliest Christian centuries but later made repeatable, were turning points rather than gradual processes. Reform, on the other hand, involves a prolonged process of spiritual recovery, which may be initiated by baptism or by penance but requires multiple and repeated means (such as the Eucharist) toward its fulfillment.

Ladner therefore defines the concept of reform as "the idea of . . . free, intentional and ever perfectible, multiple, prolonged and ever repeated efforts by man to reassert and augment values pre-existent in the spiritual-material compound of the world" (p. 35).

New Testament language of renewal sometimes (for instance, in John and Titus) refers to baptismal regeneration. When Paul speaks of *anakainosis* and related concepts, however, he is referring to a sustained process of renewal that begins with conversion and baptism, and extends beyond this initial stage throughout life. The typical Latin term for this process is *reformatio*. Thus, for example, Romans 12:2 enjoins readers not to be conformed to this world but to be reformed (*reformamini,* in the Vulgate) according to the transformation that has occurred in their minds. II Corinthians 3:18 speaks of the inner person as renewed daily, reformed from glory to glory in accordance with the Creator's image. This notion of restoration according to God's image, which echoes the language of Genesis 1:26, takes on christological implications: whereas Christ *is* the image of God, human beings are made and later reformed *according to* or *in* God's image.

The Greek fathers developed these biblical conceptions in various ways, of which the notion of recovering one's likeness to God is one of the most important. Genesis referred to human beings as made in God's "image and likeness"; some of the earliest Fathers saw the body as marked by the image of God, and the soul as characterized by his likeness, the latter being more valuable than the former. Because this likeness has been obscured by an accumulation of impurities—or has, so to speak, been painted over by sin—it needs to be purified through the process of being-made-like. The Septuagint gives *homoiosis* rather than *homoioma* for "likeness," thus emphasizing process rather than state. Gregory of Nyssa in particular, taking advantage of this translation, equated the soul's likeness to God with the process of seeking him or of assimilation to him: ". . . to progress forever in seeking, and never to pause on the road up, this is truly to enjoy the desired. . . ." Thus the Greek fathers developed Paul's notion of ongoing reform within the soul as a process that extends through one's life. They convey similar perceptions in their discussion of other motifs, such as the return to paradise and the establishment of the kingdom of God.

The other central category in the Greek understanding of reform is that of deification: what God is by nature, human beings are called upon to become through grace or adoption. Irenaeus, for instance, stressed that Christ had become human so that human beings could become divine. In all such contexts the fundamental idea is one of gradual progress toward that ideal state from which Adam had fallen.

In the West the notion of reform was taken over and in some ways transformed. Tertullian frequently used the term *reformare* in the broad sense of a restoration or a return to some previous state of affairs. He held that the constant *reformatio* in nature, where all things recur and are preserved, is a sound argument for the resurrection of bodies, and that the prime exemplar of such restoration is the phoenix. His most significant contribution, though, was the notion of reform to something better than the original state (*in melius reformare*—a phrase taken over by Cyprian and by later Latin fathers). While he used *reformare* with reference to baptism, he also recognized a process of ascesis or discipline (*exercitatio*) after baptism by which the individual is purified and assimilated to God. Ambrose, building on such earlier references to reform, emphasized that reform entails more than a mere recovery: "The Lord came to reform the grace of nature, and even to increase it, so that where there was a superabundance of sin, there would be a superabundance of grace." Ambrose's distinction between a grace of nature (*gratia naturae*) and a grace of renewal (*gratia renovationis*) is expressed with special poignancy in the *Exultet* of the Easter liturgy, which refers to the happy or fortunate guilt (*felix culpa*) of Adam: The sin of Adam made it possible, through Christ's incarnation, for humankind to enjoy a higher state than Adam himself could ever have achieved without sinning.

The theology of personal reform is further developed by Augustine, whose *Confessions* is a classic account of his own reform, worked by divine effort through the mediation of friends and circumstances. From Augustine's perspective both the final resurrection of the body and the reform of the soul in this life entail an improvement on the original state (*renovatio in melius*). When the body is resurrected, it will be a spiritual body, superior to the present one; whereas Adam's body had the possibility of not dying (*posse non mori*), the resurrection body will be characterized by the impossibility of dying (*non posse mori*). So, likewise, the regenerated Christian on earth, who is in fact a predestined saint, stands higher than Adam; such an individual is distinguished by resistance to far greater temptation than Adam's, and is characterized not only by the possibility of not sinning (*posse non peccare*) but also by the impossibility of sinning (*non posse peccare*), thanks to Christ's redemptive work.

Augustine saw the reform of the soul as prefigured in the very act of God's creation. When God began to create, on the first day he fashioned spiritual matter and physical matter that were as yet unformed, and then he called them to himself (*revocante ad se creatore*) by bestowing form upon them. This process of *revocatio,* then, is the archetype of human *reformatio,* according to Augustine. The calling of both spirit and matter to God is in this respect significant: the reform of human beings is ultimately a process that includes body as well as soul, though the latter remains superior.

REFORM, IDEA OF

Like Paul and the Greeks, Augustine develops the notion of reform by referring to the Genesis language of creation in God's image and likeness. Yet he maintains that the likeness to God (traces of God, *vestigia Dei*) can be found throughout nature, while it is only in human beings that God's image is present. Unlike the Greeks, then, Augustine ranks the image above the likeness; whereas they see the likeness as pertaining to the higher element in humanity, he sees the image as that which is distinctive to humanity. An image is something begotten by that which it reproduces—as an object produces its image in a mirror, a model serves as the basis for a painting, a parent begets a child, or God the Father begets Christ. There are degrees of likeness between prototype and image; having been created according to God's image, human beings have become dissimilar to God through sin, and need to be restored to similarity through reform. Ultimately, though, the process of reform is something that God alone can accomplish: "We could deform the image of God in us, but we cannot reform it."

Augustine agrees with the Greeks in seeing the assimilation of human beings to God as a process of deification, in which we become divine by adoption and grace rather than by nature.

Augustine's theory of the City of God likewise serves to develop the notion of reform. The City of God is not equated with the institutional church, and its development through the present era until the end of time (the *procursus*) is not intended for "church reform" as that concept later evolved. What Augustine does mean to say is that the City of God consists of individuals who are themselves undergoing reform, and who will in the end restore the numbers of souls in heaven lost through the fall of the rebellious angels.

Augustine's influence on later generations ensured that his conception of reform would be perpetuated throughout the Middle Ages and beyond, even if revised. It is not surprising, for example, to find Caesarius of Arles insisting that reform involves not only recovery of pristine health (*ad sanitatem pristinam revocare*) but also conversion to better things (*converti ad meliora*). Echoes of Augustine similar to this can be found liberally dispersed through medieval theology and spiritual literature.

THE MEDIEVAL THEOLOGY OF REFORM

Ideas of reform in medieval theology and philosophy built upon this patristic foundation, but were not wholly derivative. In the early Middle Ages, the most striking variation on the notion of reform was perhaps John Scottus Eriugena's Platonic conception of the return of all things to God, who as the final recapitulation of his own creation renews all things by absorbing them back into himself. Bernard Silvester, in the twelfth century, spoke of *reformatio* (and *reformatio in melius*) both in a moral sense (for man the microcosm) and in a cosmological sense analogous to Eriugena's (for the matter of the macrocosm). Anselm of Canterbury was more traditional in his notion of the *imago Dei* obscured by sin and in need of reform or renewal. The same theme occurs in Bernard of Clairvaux, with a sharper sense of the difficulty in reform. It is a process that grace will bring to fulfillment only in heaven, even though progress toward this reform can take place on earth.

While medieval theology took over the patristic conceptions of reform, the term *reformare* (along with related words such as *renovare* and *restaurare*) accumulated further uses and nuances as well. The variety of its meanings becomes clear from a survey of usage in the works of Thomas Aquinas. Most commonly, *reformatio* for Thomas is a moral process. In various contexts he speaks of the "reformation of the soul" or "of the mind" that is achieved by grace. Repeatedly he speaks of the *reformatio imaginis,* the restoration to the soul of the image of God that has been lost by sin; following a tradition that comes from Augustine, he sees this image as consisting in the psychological trinity of memory, understanding, and will, and the process of reform affects all of these faculties. Elsewhere he uses *reformatio* in an eschatological sense. The bodies of the saints will be reformed (or restored); but because they will be glorified like Christ's body (according to Phil. 3:21), they will be reformed *in melius.* (Thomas uses the notion of *reformatio in melius* in loose as well as in traditional ways; when a man is made into a bishop, this transformation counts as a "reformation for the better.") In extension of this eschatological usage, Thomas refers also to the final *reformatio* of the whole world. The verb *renovare,* "to renew," is also important for Thomas, and has a similar range of meanings, plus a further sacramental significance: those who undergo baptism are thereby "renewed."

THE IDEOLOGY OF INSTITUTIONAL REFORM

The most important innovation in medieval ideas of reform is their extension to societies and institutions. Even Augustine, while he envisaged spiritual progress within the City of God, did not conceive of it as a process evident in historical institutions such as monasteries or the church. In the Middle Ages, particularly from the eleventh century onward, *reformatio* became a rallying cry for action. While never totally removed from its theological context, in the midst of institutional reform the term becomes an expression of ideology more than of theology. The primary documents vital for the cause of reform were *consuetudines* and other elaborations upon the monastic rule. These texts showed in minute detail how a truly reformed monastery was to be run; they did not attend to the theology of the religious life, except perhaps in passing and by implication. When reformers carried the zeal for reform out of the monasteries and into the church at large, the texts that most directly served their purposes were canons directed against specific abuses, such as simony and clerical marriage. Here, too, there was little urge to pursue theological issues per se. From themes that recur in these and similar documents, however, one can piece together a conception (if not a full-fledged theology) of reform.

Like the theologians, the reformers spoke at times about *reformatio in melius*. St. Norbert of Xanten, founder of the Premonstratensians and archbishop of Magdeburg, announced his intention to reform *in melius* the clergy of his archiepiscopal see. Jacques de Vitry, in a survey of reform movements, spoke of the Western church as daily being "reformed for the better." The reformers' endeavor was not a purgation that occurred once and for all; it was a task that required constant attention. Anticipating in this respect Luther's insistence that "the church must always be reformed," the Fourth Lateran Council required monasteries to attend constantly to "the reform of the order and of regular observance."

It is clear from many sources that both monastic and ecclesiastical reformers thought they were restoring their institutions to a state of pristine purity. Monks could hark back to either of two possible golden ages: the flourishing of eremitic monasticism among the desert Fathers, or the codification of cenobitic monasticism under St. Benedict of Nursia. The life of Bernard of Tiron speaks of the wilderness in northwestern France as becoming "like another Egypt" because of the hermits who gathered there. Early Cistercian documents, too, often speak of a return to the rigor of early desert monasticism. When reformers set out detailed norms for proper monastic observance, however, they typically saw themselves as reviving the regimen of St. Benedict. The *Regularis concordia* of tenth-century England tells how King Edgar restored (*restauravit*) monasteries that had fallen into neglect. Having driven out their wayward monks, he substituted devout ones, and at a synodal council he urged the new monks "to be of one mind as regards monastic usage, to imitate the holy and approved Fathers," and to preserve their unanimity by faithful adherence to the Rule of St. Benedict.

MONASTIC REFORM

The reform movements of medieval monasticism arose in response to various symptoms of corruption. These fall essentially into three categories: (1) negligence of monastic responsibilities, such as extending hospitality, performing requisite liturgical services, and maintaining the monastery through manual labor; (2) distraction or alienation from the monastic community, either in secular employment (such as counselor or chaplain to a secular lord) or in wanton desertion; (3) violation of common Christian morality, typically by indulgence in drunkenness, licentiousness, and other vices of the flesh.

All these forms of abuse were known, and some of them were widespread, in the early Middle Ages. The reasons for the corruption were various. Among the factors commonly cited are the Viking and other raids, which disrupted normal monastic life and made the usual discipline and regular liturgy difficult if not impossible. Poor financial conditions were sometimes blamed. Perhaps more important, many monasteries (like churches) came under lay control during the early Middle Ages, and lay proprietors could not be assumed to have the spiritual welfare of the monks at heart. The custom of entering young children in monasteries as oblates meant that there would be many in the monastery who had no particular religious calling and could not be expected to pretend that they did. From the viewpoint of the moralists, however, the central difficulty was simply tepidity, or lack of fervor, in the spiritual life. For all these reasons, monks who compared their experience of monasticism with the depictions of the early desert hermits or with the standard monastic rules (especially the Rule of St. Benedict) would find much that needed reform.

Among the earliest reform movements was that of Benedict of Aniane. Born in Aquitaine in the mid

REFORM, IDEA OF

eighth century, he fought under Pepin and Charlemagne before withdrawing to a monastery. Inclining more toward the rigors of the desert fathers than toward the moderation of Benedictine monasticism, he imposed extreme mortifications upon himself, constantly striving, as his biographer Ardo says, "after impossible things." When he founded his own monastery at Aniane around 779, he at first strove for the same kind of rigor among his monks. He fed them only bread and water, and in their simplified liturgy they at first used only wooden chalices. Within a few years, however, he changed his views, concluding that the moderation of Benedict of Nursia was preferable to the rigors of desert monasticism, at least for the monks he had in Gaul. He then applied himself with great diligence to mastering the details of the Rule of St. Benedict, and to writing the *Concordia regularum* to aid in following the Rule. Reversing his policy on liturgy, he advocated scrupulously precise observance in decorated chapels.

Placed in charge of reforming other monasteries in Aquitaine by Emperor Louis the Pious, Benedict established a reputation as one of the spiritual leaders of his time. In 817 he was the dominant figure at a conference of abbots held at Aachen, where he inspired a series of rules (*capitulum monasticum*). The first canon in this compilation specified that each abbot should ponder the Rule of St. Benedict word by word, and along with all his monks should endeavor to observe it fully. The second canon advised that every monk who could learn the rule by heart should do so. The remaining canons dealt with the peaceful solitude of the cloister, restoration of discipline and observances, and moral conversion of the individual monk. The canons insist on faithful observance of the Rule—though in fact there are several accommodations to time and place (for instance, the monks are allowed more clothes than would have been the case in Benedict of Nursia's Mediterranean climate).

In Benedict of Aniane, then, two quite different models of reform are apparent: that of scrupulous adherence to the rigorous rule of the desert, and that of flexible accommodation to the already moderate Rule of St. Benedict. While Benedict of Aniane insists on careful mastery of the Rule, he is willing to adapt it to circumstances as required.

The Cluniac reform, begun in the tenth century by Odo of Cluny and continued by a succession of distinguished abbots through the eleventh century and beyond, fits the general pattern of Benedict of Aniane's later reform. The ritual practiced at Cluny was significantly more elaborate than that of the Rule of St. Benedict: the number of psalms added to the schedule was considerable. It has been proposed that what the monks at Cluny were doing was adjusting to the needs of lay patrons, who endowed the monastery with the intention of having prayers said for their souls; the more elaborate the regimen of prayer, the more efficacious it was assumed to be. Another keynote in the Cluniac system is the freedom of the monasteries, each of which was to be independent of both lay and episcopal control, and subject only to the abbatial system within the Cluniac order. Other monasteries in the tenth century were commonly founded with such autonomy, but what distinguished the Cluniac houses was that they fought vigorously and successfully to maintain their freedom.

Third, Cluny was distinctive in that it served as the center for an elaborate network of monasteries: there were five by the mid tenth century, and by the later eleventh century there supposedly were more than 1,500, though some were tied less closely to the mother house than were others. The order extended through most of Western Europe. Like Benedict of Aniane, the reformers at Cluny endeavored to restore proper monastic discipline—not only at Cluny but elsewhere as well. Indeed, Odo's biographer tells us that he conceived of monasteries as floods of grace to the entire vicinity, aiding in the reform of secular clergy, knights, and others. Not surprisingly, Cluniacs were leaders in the peace movement of the tenth and eleventh centuries. Odo's spirituality was clearly marked by traditional motifs of reform, particularly that of return to a paradisiacal state of innocence.

Monastic life was a way of overcoming original sin and its effects through renunciation and austerity, and thereby recovering that original order of obedience from which Adam fell. At this juncture the link between individual and institutional reform becomes clearer than usual. As Benedict of Nursia surely perceived (but did not explicitly articulate), obedience is a quality of the individual that of its very nature subordinates the individual to a community (or to the head thereof), so that individual and institution are simultaneously reformed.

The Cistercian order, founded in 1098 by Robert of Molesme, corresponds in some crucial ways more to the earlier phase of Benedict of Aniane's reform. Like Cluny, the monastery of Cîteaux be-

REFORM, IDEA OF

came the motherhouse for an extended order, with nearly 350 abbeys established by the mid twelfth century. Unlike Cluny it placed primary emphasis on rigor: the ideal of upholding the Rule of St. Benedict "more strictly" (*actius*) recurs throughout the early Cistercian literature. Whereas the Cluniacs evolved an elaborate liturgy with rich settings, the Cistercians stressed simplicity of worship and of ecclesiastical architecture. While the Cluniacs were tightly organized within their system, each Cistercian house was autonomous (though subject to visitation).

The foundation of the Cistercian order is recounted in a series of documents which again shed light on the connection between individual and institutional reform. The *Exordium Cistercii* and the *Exordium parvum* are narratives telling how Cîteaux and the order came into existence as offshoots of an earlier, unreformed monastery. Both these documents emphasize the early monks' sense of urgent moral responsibility to live according to the letter of their monastic vows. They had sworn fidelity to the Rule of St. Benedict, and when they recognized that their cloister was lax in observance of this Rule they took counsel among themselves as to how they might heed the psalmist's words (Ps. 65:13 [66:14]), "I will fulfill my vows to you, vows which I made with my own lips." Until they undertook a more strenuous life in a strict monastery, they found themselves guilty of "perjury." In their "New Monastery," as they called it, they dispensed with those luxuries that were contrary to the Rule: mantles, furs, fine linen shirts, mattresses, cupboards full of dishes, and so forth. Conforming themselves thus to the Rule, "having put off the old man, they rejoiced in putting on the new" (Col. 3:9f.). For these reformers, the relationship between moral and institutional reform was clear. Foundation of a new monastery was a necessary step in the personal reform to which they felt committed. Bernard of Clairvaux, in the next generation of Cistercians, maintained that he could not have attained salvation outside the rigorous bonds of this order; the same conviction seems to have animated the founders, who saw their "perjury" as an offense that they needed urgently to redress.

Monastic reform continued beyond the twelfth century; the proliferation of new forms of religious life in the twelfth and following centuries, in particular the rise of the "apostolic life" and specifically the mendicant orders, can be seen as an extension of earlier monastic reform. Even within the monastic orders there were reforms throughout the High and late Middle Ages—except in the Carthusian order, which boasts that it has never had to be reformed because it has never been deformed. For the ideology of reform, however, the period up through the twelfth century holds special importance.

THE GREGORIAN REFORM OF THE CHURCH

When the reform papacy of the eleventh century set out to purge the church of corruption, it followed closely the example of the monasteries. Reforming popes of the mid eleventh century were in some cases monks themselves, and in other cases they had monks among their associates. Peter Damian and Humbert of Silva Candida, cardinals who aided in the campaign against simony and clerical concubinage in mid century, were both monks; Peter had been a leader in the ascetic revival of north Italy. Gregory VII, the firebrand who in his reformist zeal alienated many even within his circle of associates, had evidently been a monk; though he had not been a Cluniac, he acknowledged a spiritual kinship with Cluny, particularly in the quest for independence from secular control.

The Gregorian program can be seen as comprising two essential elements. First there was the project of moral reform, which Gregory fostered in his correspondence with individual churchmen. This component of the program was entirely traditional: popes from the late tenth century on had endeavored, vigorously if not consistently, to uproot the immorality of simony and clerical concubinage. This aspect of reform had been accentuated in legislation and judicial action by Gregory's immediate predecessors, especially Leo IX. Against simony the reform popes used the weapons of synodal legislation and trial. Against clerical concubinage there was the further expedient of encouraging clerics to live together in quasi-monastic houses (as "canons regular"), where they would be less likely to sin. For the ideology of reform this measure is highly important, because it represented a major step toward the assimilation of diocesan clergy to the monks, and thus a merger of general church reform with monastic reform. There was the further possibility of enjoining the laity (as Gregory VII did) to shun the Masses of priests who kept concubines, a measure that could easily lead toward radicalization of the laity and may have contributed to the spread of popular heresy in the later twelfth century.

More in the forefront of Gregory's reform, however, was the political component: he was determined to release the church from its bondage to lay rulers, which he perceived as a major cause of immorality. He insisted that all ecclesiastical elections must be canonical, meaning (most importantly) under clerical rather than lay control. He furthermore repudiated the practice of lay investiture, a symbolic act in which a lay ruler bestowed the insignia of office on a bishop or abbot; while this issue was less vital than that of appointment to ecclesiastical office, it nonetheless took on profound significance because investiture marked out theoretical lines of authority, and it was difficult to keep the theory from infringing on reality. A king who was allowed to bestow the insignia of office on a bishop was not likely to appreciate that bishop's autonomy as a servant of the church. Meeting resistance from Emperor Henry IV, Gregory turned radical, claiming power to depose emperors and to absolve the subjects of tyrannical monarchs (such as Henry IV) from their fealty—in addition to his absolute authority within the church. Those who argue that Gregory was essentially a radical or a revolutionary appeal to this side of his reform program; indeed, while the moral reform was essentially conventional, Gregory's conception of his relationship to the emperor was innovative, and startlingly so. Nonetheless, it was possible for him to represent himself as a conservative (a reformer in the medieval sense) by virtue of the ultimate goals of morality and autonomy that he was seeking.

Throughout the High and late Middle Ages, reform of the church remained a demand and an ongoing project. Bishops and cardinals were called on to reform themselves on account of their luxurious style of living and their inattention to their dioceses. Lower clerics were cited for simony, concubinage, pluralism (holding more than one appointment), absenteeism (absence from place of appointment), and other offenses. Monks were criticized for essentially the same offenses as in earlier centuries. The popes, who had been largely responsible for cultivating the notion of reform, and who rose to power in Christian society largely because they were recognized as effective advocates of reform, were targets of criticism. The difficulty that arose was in part a result of inadequate financing: because the popes could not pay sufficient or regular salaries to the members of their bureaucracy, graft became widespread.

By the late Middle Ages the standard call was for reform of the church "in head and members." Both within the orthodox church and among heretics, reform was a major goal throughout the later Middle Ages and into the Reformation. In most calls for reform, though, the philosophical and theological content was meager or nonexistent; reformist literature tended to be practical, and at times satirical, rather than theoretical. While reform remained a major concern of late medieval society, the theology of reform did not develop in proportion to the energy expended in movements for reform. The patristic motifs remained decisive until the end of the Middle Ages.

BIBLIOGRAPHY

On the patristic concept of reform the standard book (followed closely in this article) is Gerhard B. Ladner, *The Idea of Reform* (1959).

For monasticism generally there is a useful bibliography: Giles Constable, *Medieval Monasticism* (1976). Two concise histories of monasticism are Lowrie J. Daly, *Benedictine Monasticism* (1965); and David Knowles, *From Pachomius to Ignatius* (1966).

On monastic reform see Herbert E. J. Cowdrey, *The Cluniacs and the Gregorian Reform* (1970); Noreen Hunt, ed., *Cluniac Monasticism in the Central Middle Ages* (1971); Bede K. Lackner, *The Eleventh-century Background of Cîteaux* (1972); Louis J. Lekai, *The Cistercians* (1977); M. Basil Pennington, ed., *The Cistercian Spirit* (1970); Barbara H. Rosenwein, *Rhinoceros Bound: Cluny in the Tenth Century* (1982); Lucy M. Smith, *Cluny in the Eleventh and Twelfth Centuries* (1930); John R. Sommerfeldt, ed., *Cistercian Ideals and Reality* (1978).

On reform in the church generally, see *The Correspondence of Pope Gregory VII,* Ephraim Emerton, trans. (1932, repr. 1966); Guy Fitch Lytle and Uta-Renate Blumenthal, eds., *Reform and Authority in the Medieval and Reformation Church* (1981); Ian S. Robinson, *Authority and Resistance in the Investiture Contest* (1978); Gerd Tellenbach, *Church, State, and Christian Society at the Time of the Investiture Contest,* Ralph F. Bennett, trans. (1940); Brian Tierney, *The Crisis of Church and State, 1050–1300* (1964); Shafer Williams, ed., *The Gregorian Epoch* (1964).

RICHARD KIECKHEFER

[See also **Ambrose, St.; Augustine of Hippo, St.; Baptism; Benedict of Aniane; Benedictine Rule; Benedictines; Carthusians; Christology; Cistercian Order; Cluny, Order of; Councils, Western; Gregory VII, Pope; Gregory of Nyssa, St.; Henry IV of Germany; Humbert of Silva Candida; Investiture and Investiture Conflict; Joachim of Fiore; Monasticism, Origins; Odo of Cluny, St.; Peter Damian, St.; Simony.**]

REGIMEN SANITATIS SALERNITANUM. Mnemonic verses on a very wide range of subjects—the temperaments, fevers and other diseases, bloodletting, simple medicines, and so forth—were an increasingly common feature of the early medieval medical literature of France and Italy. Toward the end of the thirteenth century, several hundred of these seem to have been drawn together in what eventually became known as the *Regimen sanitatis Salernitanum* (a few can indeed be shown to go back to twelfth-century Salerno). It has been supposed that Arnald of Villanova made this collection about 1300 and composed a commentary upon it (printed many times since 1480), but this ascription is now generally rejected, for internal allusions appear to fix the commentary's composition in the fifteenth-century Netherlands. Nineteenth-century editors assembled more than 3,000 such verses from scattered manuscript sources into an entirely artificial collection that they imagined to represent the teaching of Salerno at its height; this too is no longer credible.

BIBLIOGRAPHY

There is still no better edition of the *Regimen* than that of Johann Christoph Ackermann, ed., *Regimen sanitatis Salerni* (1790). The English translation of Sir John Harington, first published in 1607 and reprinted as *The School of Salernum* (1920), conveys the flavor and sense of the original. The nineteenth-century's hypothetical collection and reorganization may be found in Salvatore de Renzi, *Collectio salernitana,* I (1852), 445–516, and V (1859), 1–104; see also the "Notice bibliographique" that follows the latter text, at 113–169. The original interpretation of the Salernitan origin of this poem is called into question by Karl Sudhoff, "Zum Regimen Sanitatis Salernitanum," in *Archiv für Geschichte der Medizin,* 7 (1914), 360–362, 8 (1915), 292–293, 352–373, 9 (1916), 221–249, 10 (1917), 91–101, and 12 (1920), 149–180. Sudhoff accepted the commentary as the work of Arnald of Villanova; see, however, Ernest Wickersheimer's assessment of *l'hypothèse arnaldienne,* "Autour du 'Régime de Salerne,'" in *Le scalpel,* **105,** no. 50 (1952).

MICHAEL MCVAUGH

[See also **Arnald of Villanova; Medicine, History of; Medicine, Schools of.**]

REGINALD OF CANTERBURY (*ca.* 1040–*ca.* 1109) was born and educated in France, but moved to England before 1092 and entered the monastery of St. Augustine in Canterbury. There he began writing poetry of great technical skill, especially in rhyme, but little inspiration. Besides occasional verses he wrote a Latin epic of some 4,000 hexameters on St. Malchus.

BIBLIOGRAPHY

The life of St. Malchus has never been printed. Shorter poems are in Thomas Wright, *Anglo-Latin Satirical Poets,* II (1872), 259–267. See also Max Manitius, *Geschichte der lateinischen Literatur des Mittelalters,* III (1931), 841–846.

W. T. H. JACKSON

[See also **Anglo-Latin Poetry.**]

REGINO OF PRÜM (Regino Prumiensis) (*ca.* 845–28 May 915), German Benedictine, music theorist, canonist, and chronicler. According to an early-seventeenth-century document, he was born "from very noble parents" in Altrip on the Rhine (near Ludwigshafen) and educated at the imperial monastery of Prüm, in the Eifel. Elected abbot of Prüm in 892, he was forced to resign seven years later because of political pressures. He left for Trier, where, at the request of Archbishop Ratbod (*d.* 915), he rebuilt the abbey of St. Martin, ransacked by the Danes in 882. There he compiled, between 900 and 908, his three celebrated works.

One was a tonary (*tonarius*) or catalog of liturgical chants classified according to the order of the eight musical tones or modes, to which he added a theoretical preface in the form of a letter to Ratbod (*Epistola de armonica institutione*), of which there are two versions: a shorter, earlier one (Brussels, Bibliothèque Royale Albert Ier, MS 2751, early tenth century) and an expanded, later one (Leipzig, Universitätsbibliothek, MS Rep. I.8.95, Catal. 169, tenth century), perhaps not authentic. The latter was again modified in Metz, in the early eleventh century.

A collection of canon laws (*Libri duo de synodalibus causis et disciplinis ecclesiasticis*) compiled about 906 and dedicated to Hatto I, archbishop of Mainz, was to be used as a handbook by bishops during their yearly diocesan visitations. Book I deals with ecclesiastical matters, Book II with the duties of the laity. This useful vade mecum forms the basis of later church laws and procedures.

A *Chronica,* from A.D. 1 to 906, dedicated to

REGINSMÁL AND FÁFNISMÁL

Adalbero, bishop of Augsburg (*d.* 909), was the first of its kind to be written in Germany. Despite its faulty chronology, this chronicle is particularly informative on the political affairs of the West Frankish kingdom and Lorraine from 813 to 906. It was revised and carried up to 967 by St. Adalbert, bishop of Magdeburg (*d.* 981).

Regino was essentially a man of action and a reformer. His achievements exerted a decisive influence on later medieval music theory, canon law, and historiography.

BIBLIOGRAPHY

Sources. Regino's works are gathered in the *Patrologia latina,* CXXXII (1853), with the exception of the *tonarius,* which is in Edmond de Coussemaker, ed., *Scriptorum de musica medii aevi . . .* , II (1867, repr. 1963)—very defective facsimile and transliteration of the Brussels manuscript. See also Yves Chartier, *L'epistola et le tonarius de Réginon de Prüm* (diss., Univ. of Ottawa, 1965, rev. 1983), with French trans., commentary, critical ed. of the Brussels and Leipzig MSS, and full bibliography. For Regino's collection of canon laws, see Paul Fournier, "L'oeuvre canonique de Réginon de Prüm," in *Bibliothèque de l'École des chartes,* **81** (1920).

An edition of the *Chronica* is edited by F. Kurze (1890). See also *Die Chronik des Abtes Regino von Prüm,* E. Dümler, trans. (1857).

Studies. J. Choux, "Décadence et réforme monastique dans la province de Trêves, 855–959," in *Revue bénédictine,* **70** (1960); Paul Fournier and Gabriel Le Bras, *Histoire des collections canoniques en Occident,* I (1931), 244–268; W. Hellinger, "Die Pfarrvisitation nach Regino von Prüm," in *Zeitschrift für Rechtsgeschichte,* **79–80** (1962–1963); H. Loewe, "Regino von Prüm und das historische Westbild der Karolinger Zeit," in *Rheinische Vierteljahrblätter,* **17** (1952); W. R. Schleidgen, *Die Überlieferungsgeschichte der Chronik des Regino von Prüm* (diss., Univ. of Bochum, 1974); K. F. Werner, "Zur Arbeitsweise des Regino von Prüm," in *Die Welt als Geschichte,* **19** (1959).

YVES CHARTIER

[See also **Adalbert, St.; Law, Canon: To Gratian; Musical Treatises; Political Theory, Western European; Tonary; Tones, Musical.**]

REGINSMÁL AND FÁFNISMÁL. The two Eddic poems so titled by modern editors tell the story of Sigurd's youth prior to his meeting with Brynhild. *Reginsmál* (The words of Reginn) comprises twenty-six stanzas (seventeen in the *ljóðaháttr* meter and nine in *fornyrðislag*) and nine prose inserts. It relates how Reginn's brother Otr, who was accustomed to doze by Andvari's Falls in the shape of an otter, was killed by Loki. Together with his companions Odin and Hœnir, Loki is subsequently captured by Otr's father, Hreiðmarr, and obliged to raise a ransom. He extracts the necessary gold from Andvari, but it is burdened with Andvari's curse. Treasure and curse are then transferred to Hreiðmarr, who suffers the consequences when he is killed by his covetous son Fáfnir. Fáfnir now seizes the gold and broods on it in the shape of a dragon, refusing Reginn a share. Reginn forges a special sword (Gramr) for his foster son Sigurd and urges him to kill Fáfnir. Sigurd insists on first avenging his father, Sigmund, against the sons of Hunding. He sets sail, runs into a storm, encounters Odin on a promontory, and takes him aboard; the storm subsides. Odin offers advice on battle auguries and strategies. Thereafter a great battle is fought in which Sigurd kills Hunding's three sons. Reginn proclaims his victory and praises him.

The story is continued in *Fáfnismál* (The words of Fáfnir), which comprises forty-four stanzas (thirty-five in *ljóðaháttr* and nine in *fornyrðislag*) and six prose inserts. Sigurd ambushes the serpent Fáfnir and delivers a lethal blow with his sword. Before dying, Fáfnir engages his slayer in a lengthy dialogue concerning Sigurd's identity and motive, the cursed treasure, and some mythological lore without immediate relevance. Reginn emerges from behind the scene to congratulate Sigurd and instruct him to roast the serpent's heart. As Sigurd does so, he tests the roasting meat with his finger, burns it, and thrusts it into his mouth to cool it. The taste of dragon's blood endows him with the ability to understand the speech of the birds chirping in the bush, and they advise him to kill Reginn in order to forestall his avenging of his brother Fáfnir. Sigurd promptly follows their advice. They then direct him to Gjúki's court, where he will marry the king's daughter Guðrún. Sigurd rides off, taking Fáfnir's treasure with him.

The clusters of verse that go under the headings *Reginsmál* and *Fáfnismál* combine stanzas in two meters with a considerable amount of prose. They also combine two distinguishable stories: the story of Sigurd's vengeance for his father and the story of his slaying of Fáfnir and winning of the treasure. The vengeance story in the latter part of *Reginsmál* intrudes in the middle of the treasure story. Andreas Heusler explained this situation with the hypothesis that *Reginsmál-Fáfnismál* represents a conflation of two separate poems: a "Hortlied" (Treasure poem) in *ljóðaháttr* and a "Vaterrachelied" (Vengeance poem) in *fornyrðislag*. The compiler of a lost poetic biography of Sigurd, which Heusler called the "Sigurdliederheft," combined the separate poems in such a way as to produce a chronological sequence: first the prehistory of the treasure was told, then Sigurd's vengeance for his father, and finally the conclusion of the treasure adventure. In the process of this chronological reordering, the treasure story was split in two and the vengeance story was inserted between the two parts. This arrangement in the "Sigurdliederheft" was inherited by the compiler of the Eddic manuscript (Codex Regius 2365, 4°). Heusler's solution does not work perfectly because there is a residue of *fornyrðislag* stanzas in his *ljóðaháttr* "Hortlied," but it does offer a generally attractive explanation for the cluttered transmission.

Another curious feature of *Reginsmál-Fáfnismál* is the unusual amount of prose interspersed among the stanzas. This prose was studied by Finnur Jónsson, who concluded that it could not be derived from the poems themselves. He therefore posited a lost "Sigurðar saga" used by the compiler of the Eddic collection to supplement his verse sources. The existence of such a "Sigurðar saga" has been widely accepted, but its content has been differently assessed. Hans Kuhn suggested that the tale of Sigurd's youth already existed in oral tradition as an amalgam of verse and prose. There is no evidence that the verse is older than the eleventh or twelfth century.

BIBLIOGRAPHY

Sources. An edition is Gustav Neckel, ed., *Die Lieder des Codex regius nebst verwandten Denkmälern,* rev. by Hans Kuhn (1962), 173–188. Translations include *The Poetic Edda,* Henry Adams Bellows, trans. (1923, repr. 1969), 358–385; *The Poetic Edda,* Lee M. Hollander, trans., 2nd rev. ed. (1962, repr. 1977), 216–232.

Studies. Theodore M. Andersson, *The Legend of Brynhild* (1980); Andreas Heusler, "Altnordische Dichtung und Prosa von Jung Sigurd," in *Sitzungsberichte der Preussischen Akademie der Wissenschaften,* Phil.-hist. Klasse (1919), repr. in his *Kleine Schriften,* Helga Reuschel, ed., I (1943, repr. 1960); Finnur Jónsson, "Sigurðarsaga og de prosaiske stykker i Codex Regius," in *Aarbøger for nordisk oldkyndighed og historie* (1917); Hans Kuhn, "Das Eddastück von Sigurds Jugend," in *Miscellanea Academica Berolinensia,* 2 (1950), repr. in his *Kleine Schriften,* Dietrich Hofmann, ed., II (1971); Hermann Schneider, "Verlorene Sigurddichtung," in *Arkiv för nordisk filologi,* **45** (1929); Per Wieselgren, *Quellenstudien zur Vǫlsungasaga* (1935), 246–263.

THEODORE M. ANDERSSON

[See also **Eddic Meters; Eddic Poetry; Fáfnir; Hœnir; Loki; Odin; Scandinavian Mythology.**]

REGNAULT DE CORMONT (Renard de Cormont), master architect of Amiens Cathedral in 1288, according to an inscription he installed in the nave floor in that year. Regnault succeeded his father, Thomas de Cormont, but his tenure and accomplishments are unknown. He may have assumed charge of the work as early as 1240 and is credited with the upper portions of the choir. Nothing else is known of Regnault's life or works.

BIBLIOGRAPHY

Carl F. Barnes, Jr., "Robert de Luzarches," in *Macmillan Encyclopedia of Architects,* II (1982); Amédée Boinet, *La cathédrale d'Amiens,* 5th rev. ed. (1959); Georges Durand, *Monographie de l'église Notre-Dame, cathédrale d'Amiens,* 2 vols. (1901–1903).

CARL F. BARNES, JR.

[See also **Amiens Cathedral; Gothic Architecture; Robert de Luzarches; Thomas de Cormont.**]

REICHSTAG. See **Representative Assemblies, German.**

REINFRID VON BRAUNSCHWEIG is a Middle High German courtly narrative of 27,627 lines that survives in a single incomplete copy (Gotha, Membr. II 42). The anonymous author reveals little about himself: he complains about being young and poor (ll. 2,864–2,869); is not of the nobility and knows nothing of knighthood (ll. 12,820ff.); and alludes to a ladylove, Else, in an anagram (l. 12,803). References to the Bible, classical literature and culture, and a vast body of legends and works of German literature, as well as scientific and rhetorical excursuses, indicate an extensive schooling. The author's dialect is Alamannic, and he is generally placed in the school of Konrad von Würzburg along with several other writers from the region of Lake Constance. An allusion to the fall of Acre (1291) in line 17,980 suggests a date of composition of about 1300.

The work consists of two main parts, each using different sources and genre models. In the first, based on Konrad von Würzburg's *Engelhard,* Reinfrid von Braunschweig wins a kiss in a tournament from Irkane, daughter of the Danish king, and the two fall in love. A jealous rival of the hero accuses Irkane of unchaste behavior with Reinfrid, and she can find no champion until Reinfrid learns of her distress and returns to prove her innocence in judicial combat. After their marriage a dream informs Reinfrid that a journey to the Holy Land will ensure him an heir. The second part of the work (beginning at line 14,760) presents a crusading epic followed by a series of fantastic adventures. Reinfrid and his army free Jerusalem and the Holy Land from the domination of the sultan of Babylon. With the defeated king of Persia as his companion, the hero then undertakes a series of voyages exploring the marvels of the East, many of which derive from *Herzog Ernst* or versions of the Alexander legend. Upon hearing of the birth of his son, Reinfrid sets out for his homeland but is stranded on an island, at which point the manuscript breaks off. Among the episodes presumably lost are the hero's return and recognition by Irkane and an adventure that is to explain the two lions on his coat of arms. The latter motif suggests that *Reinfrid von Braunschweig* is the oldest surviving legend of Henry the Lion, duke of Saxony.

The work was long viewed as a derivative compilation suffering from lengthy digressions and rhetorical excess. Recent studies have demonstrated a more sophisticated narrative technique, especially in the presentation of psychological processes, ethical problems, and the treatment of the fantastic. Although the relationship of *Reinfrid* to predominant genre traditions is unclear, it appears that the work's unusually frequent but careful allusions to episodes and characters in classical works of medieval German literature consciously establish a continuity of literary idealization whose function is to contrast with the actual contemporary situation, about which the author laments in the frequent excursuses that interrupt the narrative.

BIBLIOGRAPHY

Source. Karl F. Bartsch, ed., *Reinfrid von Braunschweig* (1871).

Studies. Helmut de Boor, *Die deutsche Literatur im späten Mittelalter,* III, pt. 1, *Zerfall und Neubeginn* (1962), 92–96; Wolfgang Harms, "'Epigonisches' im 'Reinfried von Braunschweig,'" in *Zeitschrift für deutsches Altertum,* **94** (1965); Beat Koelliker, *Reinfrid von Braunschweig* (1975); Hermann Schneider, "Reinfrid von Braunschweig," in Wolfgang Stammler and Karl Langosch, eds., *Die deutsche Literatur des Mittelalters: Verfasserlexikon,* III (1933).

ARTHUR GROOS

[See also **Alexander Romances; Henry the Lion; Herzog Ernst; Konrad von Würzburg; Middle High German Literature.**]

REINMAR DER ALTE (Reinmar von Hagenau) (*ca.* 1150/1160—before 1210), Austrian poet. The name "Her Reinmar der Alte" (Sir Reinmar the Ancient) appears only in manuscript C, the *Grosse Heidelberger (Manessische) Liederhandschrift,* in which it serves to distinguish our Reinmar from later poets of the same name. He was a contemporary of Walther von der Vogelweide, who eulogized him in two poems (L 82,24 and 83,1) in terms that indicate considerable unpleasantness in their relationship.

The name "Reinmar von Hagenau" is a creation of modern scholarship based on a passage (ll. 4,774–4,820) in the courtly romance *Tristan und Isolt* (early thirteenth century) by the Alsatian poet Gottfried von Strassburg. Gottfried eulogizes Reinmar there as the Nightingale of Hagenau, a leader among poets whose heir apparent is Walther von der Vogelweide. Since the Hagenau best known to modern scholars is the Alsatian city by that name, it is not surprising, though not self-evident, that Reinmar has come to be associated with that area, especially since the courtly love doctrine for which he is best known came to Austria from the West. In the absence of historical documentation, only the internal evidence provided by the poetry can serve as a basis for pursuing this issue.

There are about eighty *Töne* that manuscript sources attribute to Reinmar, fifty-two of which are preserved exclusively under his name. (*Töne* in this context means groups of stanzas in the same meter that may or may not be intended as a unified poem.) Of these eighty *Töne,* Carl von Kraus declared forty-five, including twenty-three of those attributed in the manuscripts exclusively to Reinmar, to be nonauthentic imitations of Reinmar's art. Although the conjectures of von Kraus have been effectively discredited, first and foremost by Friedrich Maurer, the image of Reinmar that von Kraus presented still dominates the scholarship of Reinmar's poetry. Yet this image is supported by only a part of the poems attested under Reinmar's name. In fact, not even all of the poems that von Kraus thought to be authentic actually corroborate his views.

Reinmar's poetry is exclusively secular love poetry, *Minnesang*. The majority of his poems—though by no means all, as von Kraus supposed—feature the faithful though unrequited lover who has come to be associated with the term "courtly love." It is for such poems (as in MFMT VI [MF 154, 32], XII [162,7], XIV [165,10], and XX [170,36]), with their seemingly endless laments about the sorrows and pains of constant yet unrewarded love service (*Minnedienst*), that Reinmar is best known. Unfortunately, there are many who know only this side of his artistry.

Quite a different view of the *minne* relationship is presented in the woman's song (*Frauenlied*) of Reinmar. Under the term "woman's song" I shall include those poems which feature the woman in a speaking role. She appears at times alone, at others in a dialogue (usually with a messenger), and at still others in a possibly original German poetic form known as the *Wechsel*. In the last, a man and a woman utter speeches that may be connected but do not clearly form an exchange.

In the *Frauenlied* it is the woman whose infatuation is most prominent in the portrayal. In some poems we hear complaints about neglect or thoughtlessness on the part of the man (as in MFMT II [MF 151,1], L [195,37], and LIII [198,4]). In others, the woman expresses the fear that her beloved may not be trustworthy or may not have her best interest at heart (for instance, MFMT IV [MF 152,25], XXVII [177,10], and XXVIII [178,1]).

More lines of woman's song are preserved in the work of Reinmar der Alte than in that of any other medieval German poet. De Boor has noted that Reinmar's *Frauenlied* is clearly influenced by the southeast German and particularly Austrian poetic tradition known as the Danubian *Minnesang* ("der donauländische Minnesang"). This tradition is attested, somewhat sparsely, for the last half of the twelfth century, prior to the time when Reinmar, according to traditional assumptions, is supposed to have arrived in Austria from Alsace. De Boor even speaks of inherited Danubian motifs ("ererbten donauländischen Motiven") in Reinmar's poetry. These features, which, in my opinion, are indeed inherited from the older Danubian tradition, appear not only in the woman's song but also in other poems by Reinmar, such as the two "Falcon Songs" (MFMT VII and XXIX [MF 156,10 and 179,3]).

Traditionally the poems by Reinmar that are most obviously Danubian have been categorized as creations of the poet's youth. This view entails a troubling problem that has apparently escaped notice, for it raises the perplexing question of how the young Reinmar could have composed poems so clearly Danubian during a period allegedly spent in faraway Alsace. According to the traditional view, Reinmar is supposed to have come to Vienna as a mature poet—indeed, as an artist already qualified to assume the position of court poet.

In all probability de Boor was quite correct in speaking of Reinmar as an heir to the Danubian poetic tradition. Reinmar was probably not an Alsatian but rather, in all likelihood, a member of the wealthy and powerful Hagenau family of Austria. As Friedrich Wilhelm pointed out, members of this family frequently signed documents for the ruling Babenberg family of Austria and generally frequented the same circles as the Babenbergs. One Babenberg, Duke Leopold (*r.* 1177–1194), is generally (and, I think, correctly) held to be the "Liutpolt" who is mourned by the widow in Reinmar's poem of lamentation (MFMT XVI [MF 167,31]).

Günther Schweikle is, in my view, equally correct in doubting that Reinmar was court poet at Vienna. On the other hand, I cannot concur in his suggestion that Reinmar was probably a wandering minstrel. The fact that none of the eighty-odd poems under Reinmar's name shows a single trace of the desire for remuneration can only mean that Reinmar did not need to be remunerated. He claims freedom from all cares except the pains of love in several of his poems (for instance, MFMT XVII,1,3–4 [MF 168,32–33] and XXV,3,1–2 [175,15–16]). Ernst Regel and Konrad Burdach, among others, interpret these verses (in my view rightly, though in a different sense) as indications of Reinmar's financial well-being, for to make such claims, even jokingly, would surely have meant to risk undermining one's position in dealing with a client who was not inclined to be generous—and such clients were numerous. Any professional entertainer who wanted to be paid had to be prepared to exert prompt and often strong pressure to that end. The work of Walther von der Vogelweide is full of insistent demands for payment.

The widow's song of Reinmar is also noteworthy in regard to the question of his station. The "Liutpolt" of this poem is only praised as a lover, and in a manner that is perhaps suitable for a Danubian widow, but not for the genre of poems in praise of deceased luminaries. In any case, the tone of the poem is not that of a poet who expects a reward for his efforts.

A final case in point is the crusade poetry of Reinmar, of which at least three clear examples are preserved (MFMT XXX–XXXII [MF 180,28; 181,13; and 182,14]), and probably a fourth (MFMT VII [MF 156,10]), which Friedrich Heinrich von der Hagen designated as a crusade poem. In these poems Reinmar pictures himself as a participating soldier, something Walther von der Vogelweide never does. Indeed, in one poem (L 124,1) in which Walther refers to himself as a needy poor man (*nôtic armman;* L 125,5), he also addresses crusading soldiers expressly as a group to which he does not belong. The viewpoint of Reinmar, the participating soldier, is the same as that of the French poet Conon de Béthune (*fl.* 1180–*ca.* 1220), as well as the German poets Friedrich von Hausen (*ca.* 1150–1190) and Hartmann von Aue (*fl.* 1180–1203), except that Reinmar's crusade songs betray a lack of enthusiasm for the cause that, to my knowledge, is unique among contemporary poets who treated this theme. Marie-Luise Dittrich has demonstrated this convincingly and conclusively in reference to the one poem (MFMT XXXI [MF 181,13]) that has traditionally been generally accepted as an authentic crusade song by Reinmar. In yet another contrast with Reinmar, Walther's crusade poems betray an intense involvement on the part of a nonparticipant. In this, Walther's position is that of the Provençal poet Marcabru (*fl.* 1128–1150).

Reinmar's poetry is not that of a man who felt the need to ingratiate himself with the wealthy and to espouse popular causes. Indeed, Reinmar—again in contrast with Walther—shows no interest in any cause or issue that is not an amorous one. As the Austrian nobleman he seems certainly to have been, he could probably afford to.

BIBLIOGRAPHY

Sources. Texts are *Des Minnesangs Frühling,* Carl von Kraus, ed., 35th ed. (1970), 197–288 (designated MF in text; numbering after MF is the same as that in all prior editions); *Des Minnesangs Frühling,* rev. by Hugo Moser and Helmut Tervooren, 36th ed., 2 vols. (1977), I, 285–403 (designated MFMT in text).

English translations, some with commentary and other information, include Angel Flores, ed., *An Anthology of Medieval Lyrics* (1962), 417–420; Frederick Goldin, *German and Italian Lyrics of the Middle Ages* (1973), 71–95; William E. Jackson, *Reinmar's Women* (1981), which concentrates on eighteen *Frauenlieder;* Frank Nicholson, *Old German Love Songs* (1907), 51–59; Margaret F. Richey, *Medieval German Lyrics* (1958), 55–58; J. W. Thomas, *Medieval German Lyric Verse* (1968), 102–106.

Studies. Karl Bertau, "Überlieferung und Authentizität bei den Liedern Reinmars des Alten," in *Zeitschrift für deutsches Altertum,* **88** (1969); Helmut de Boor, *Die höfische Literatur,* vol. II of his *Geschichte der deutschen Literatur,* 8th ed. (1969), 282–292; Marie-Luise Dittrich, "Reinmars Kreuzlied (MF 181,13)," in Werner Schröder, ed., *Festschrift für Ludwig Wolff* (1962); Annette Georgi, *Das lateinische und deutsche Preisgedicht des Mittelalters* (1969); Friedrich H. von der Hagen, *Minnesinger,* 4 vols. (1838, repr. 1963), IV, 137ff.; Alois Kircher, *Dichter und Konvention* (1973); Carl von Kraus, *Die Lieder Reinmars des Alten,* 3 vols. (1919); Friedrich Maurer, *Die "Pseudoreimare"* (1966); Volker Mertens, "Reinmars 'Gegensang' zu Walthers 'Lindenlied,' " in *Zeitschrift für deutsches Altertum,* **112** (1983); Heinz Rupp, "Reinmars Lied Nr. 12 und die Reinmar-Philologie," in *German Life and Letters,* **34** (1980); Walter Salmen, *Der fahrende Musiker im europäischen Mittelalter* (1960); Wiebke Schmaltz, *Reinmar der Alte* (1975); Günther Schweikle, "War Reinmar 'von Hagenau' Hofsänger zu Wien?" in Helmut Kreuzer, ed., *Gestaltungsgeschichte und Gesellschaftsgeschichte* (1969), "Der Stauferhof und die mittelhochdeutsche Lyrik," in Rüdiger Krohn, Bernd Thum, and Peter Wapnewski, eds., *Staufer Zeit* (1978), 245–259, and "Pseudo-Neidharte?" in *Zeitschrift für deutsche Philologie,* **100** (1981); Manfred Stange, *Reinmars Lyrik* (1977); Piet Wareman, *Spielmannsdichtung* (1951); Friedrich Wilhelm, "Zur Frage nach der Heimat Reinmars des Alten und Walthers von der Vogelweide," in *Münchener Museum für Philologie,* **3** (1917); Vickie L. Ziegler, *The Leitword in Minnesang* (1975).

William E. Jackson

[See also **Conon de Béthune; Courtly Love; Babenberg Family; Friedrich von Hausen; German Literature: Lyric; Gottfried von Strassburg; Hartmann von Aue; Marcabru; Middle High German Literature; Minnesingers; Tristan, Legend of; Walther von der Vogelweide.**]

REINMAR VON ZWETER (*ca.* 1200–*ca.* 1260), a major author of courtly didactic Middle High

German poetry (*Sangspruchdichtung*). The dates and particular circumstances of his life are uncertain and must be extracted from his work, which, with the exception of the *Leich,* consists entirely of *Sprüche* (sung didactic gnomic verse). His art is indebted to Walther von der Vogelweide.

The author's name is spelled differently in the rich manuscript tradition of his work, but Zweter rather than Zweten or Zwetel is assumed to be correct. Roethe, the editor of Reinmar's poems, suggests that the author took his name from the village of Zeutern near Heidelberg. The poet himself says: "I was born in the region of the Rhine, have grown up in Austria and chosen to live in Bohemia more on account of its lord than the country." Only a few specifically Middle German rhymes attest the origin of the poet. Around 1227 he appears to be associated with the court of Duke Leopold VI in Vienna, and after Leopold's death in 1230, with that of his successor, the last Babenberg duke, Frederick II the Warlike. In 1235 he left Vienna for the court of King Wenceslas (Vaclav) I in Prague and remained there until about 1241. According to a near contemporary, Lupolt Hornburg of Rotenburg, Reinmar died in Franconia and was buried *ze Esfeld* (modern Essfeld, near Ochsenfurt).

Reinmar's poems are contained mainly in Cpg 848 (*C*) and Cpg 350 (*D*) in Heidelberg. Besides these two principal manuscripts there are more than twenty manuscripts and fragments. Of particular interest are the grouping and skillful thematic arrangement of the poems in manuscript *D*. Roethe's edition lists 341 poems, of which 282 are judged to be authentic. In general Reinmar's *Sprüche* do not have more than one strophe, although a few show a linking of two by theme. Since Reinmar also composed the *Leich,* the total number of surviving stanzas is well over 300. The largest number of these (some 252) are written in the *Fraun Ehren Ton* (the air of Lady Honor). Two *Sprüche* are written in the *Meister Ernst Ton* (the air of Master Serious), six use the *Ehrenboten Spiegelweise* (the mirror melody of the Herald of Honor), and twenty-three use the *Minnen Ton* (the air of Lady Love). Reinmar's small number of melodies suggests that the author had a moderate musical talent, although he was considered one of the "Twelve Old Masters" by the Meistersingers in whose manuscripts the melodies and their names have survived. Some names may be Reinmar's.

Although the religious *Leich* and later poems are missing in *D,* their authenticity is uncontested. The *Leich* is devoted to the praise of divine love in the Trinity, in creation, and in the resurrection of fallen man. The poem is certainly the work of the mature author. The other *Sprüche* are arranged by theme in manuscript *D* and the modern edition: stanzas 1–22 are religious (here Reinmar's repeated praise of Mary is notable); 23–55 deal with the nature of love between man and woman; 56–124 treat ethical considerations about life in the world, courtly virtues, nobility, and moderation; 125–157 are political *Sprüche* concerning abuses and actions by Pope Gregory IX and by the clergy (125–135), poems concerning Emperor Frederick II (136–146), and the princes, courtiers, and advisers (147–157); 158–229 are didactic sentences of a general nature, mostly written after 1241 and some giving evidence of the author's advanced age (see 180: "I am in the evening of my life").

In his poems the author displays strong convictions, a stance that suits his didactic purpose. His slighter lyrical talent is perhaps more pronounced in his religious verse. Unlike others, Reinmar never begs for favors from those on whose generosity his well-being depends. In particular his keen perceptions of honor and courtly virtue remain unshaken and are his main theme. The Meistersingers called Reinmar "Ehrenbote" (Herald of Honor) or "Ehrenbote vom Rhein" (Herald of Honor from the Rhine).

BIBLIOGRAPHY

Source. Die Gedichte Reinmars von Zweter, Gustav Roethe, ed. (1887, repr. 1967).

Studies. Franz Bäuml and Richard Rouse, "Roll and Codex: A New MS Fragment of Reinmar von Zweter," in *Beiträge,* **105** (1983); Hans-Joachim Behr, "Projectionen und Verklärung: Zum Reichsbegriff Reinmars von Zweter und den Schwierigkeiten seiner Adaptation in der deutschen Germanistik," in *Mittelalterrezeption,* II (1982); Edgar Bonjour, *Reinmar von Zweter als politischer Dichter* (1922, repr. 1970); Helmut de Boor, *Die höfische Literatur: Vorbereitung, Blüte, Ausklang, 1170–1250,* 5th ed. (1953), 417–425; Gustav Ehrismann, *Geschichte der deutschen Literatur bis zum Ausgang des Mittelalters,* II, pt. 2, 2 (1935, repr. 1959), 292–294; Georg Objartel, "Zwei wenig beachtete Fragmente Reinmars von Zweter und ein lateinisches Gegenstück seines Leiches," in *Zeitschrift für deutsche Philologie,* **90** (1971), 217–231; Volker Schupp, "Reinmar von Zweter, Dichter Friedrichs II," in *Wirkendes Wort,* **19** (1969), 231–244, and "Der Kurfürstenspruch Reinmars von Zweter (Roethe Nr. 240)," in *Zeitschrift für deutsche Philologie,* **93** (1974), 68–74; Helmut Tervooren, "Ein

RELICS

neuer Fund zu Reinmar von Zweter: Zugleich ein Beitrag zu einer mitteldeutschen-niederdeutschen Literaturlandschaft," *ibid.*, **102** (1983), 377–391; E. Wögerbauer, "Wörterbuch zu Reinmar von Zweter" (Ph.D. diss., Vienna, 1952).

F. W. von Kries

[See also **German Literature: Lyric; Middle High German Literature; Minnesingers.**]

RELICS are objects associated with the saints, most particularly their bodies. In the Middle Ages the most commonly used words for relics, *reliquiae* in Latin and *leipsana* in Greek, both included "corpse" among their root meanings.

SPIRITUAL AND HISTORICAL ROOTS OF RELIC VENERATION

The attempt to gain the intercession of the saints before God through the veneration of their relics was one of the cornerstones of the piety and practice of medieval Christianity. Relics physically linked the supernatural and the natural worlds; thus, the study of relics can help map the fluctuation of the boundaries between those worlds in medieval mentality. Relics did not merely represent the power of the saints; they were the physical extension of the presence of the holy dead into this world. Those saints resided in the divine court because of the pious actions of their lives. The living therefore venerated the saints' relics in order to seek their patronage in that court. Relics provided a proximate link to the divine ruler that was well adapted to medieval concepts of justice. Saintly patronage protected the spiritual and temporal welfare of the religious communities and laypeople who served a saint through his or her relics. That patronage manifested itself most spectacularly in miracles, such as the cure of disease or rescue from physical peril. Pilgrims sought close physical contact with relics. Sometimes they employed *brandea,* pieces of cloth or other objects placed in contact with these relics, to transmit and contain their sacred power. Relics were sacred only in so far as they were the personal presence of the saints. The relics did not perform miracles; God performed them working on behalf of the saints.

EARLY MEDIEVAL VENERATION

Beginning with Ambrose and Augustine, theologians in the West justified the veneration of relics on the basis of the miraculous manifestation of God's power in them. Adoration was to be given to God alone, but the saints were worthy of lesser veneration since God had chosen to glorify the saints and to announce that choice in miracles. In the East, Basil and John Chrysostom emphasized that the blood and other relics of the martyrs served as sensible records of the sufferings of those saints and thus served as reminders for the faithful. Relic veneration was infrequently criticized in the clerical circles of Western Christendom, although Vigilantius, in the fourth century, and Claudius of Turin, in the ninth, both saw it as a form of pagan idolatry. In lay circles, however, rejection of the cult of relics was one of the standard criticisms of the institutional church voiced by dissident heretics from the followers of Arnold of Brescia (*d.* 1155) through the Lollards. In the East the iconoclasts criticized relics as well as icons, but the triumph of Orthodoxy in 843 restored both relics and icons to full favor.

The first people to be recognized as Christian saints were martyrs, and it was their relics that were the first to be venerated. The Hellenistic world had venerated the dead heroes of its own past, but pagans avoided contact with the actual bones of the dead. They used the word *reliquiae* to refer to material objects associated with those heroes, such as the lance of Achilles, and were horrified at Christians' close contact with dead bodies. The *Martyrdom of Polycarp* (156) provides the earliest certain attestation of the collection of a martyr's bones. A number of similar accounts survive from the period of persecutions, over half of which concern female martyrs. The public veneration of the martyr's bones developed in the wake of the elevation of Christianity to official status in the Roman Empire, and they seem to have satisfied pietistic needs similar to those which had previously been served by various pagan cults. Some critics, including the pagan emperor Julian the Apostate (*r.* 361–363), pointed out that there was no scriptural warrant for the cult of martyrs. Such criticism did little to stem their popularity. By the fifth century the bones of holy people who had not suffered martyrdom, such as monks and stylites, began to be accorded similar status to those of martyrs. Although women accounted for a high proportion of the martyrs whose acts were recorded in texts by their contemporaries, most of the important shrines of the early church were dedicated to male saints. The loss of status suffered by women in the church as it gained official sanction doubtless accounted for this lack of public cult offered to women.

Three sets of beliefs gave rise to the posthumous veneration of relics in late antiquity. First, they possessed, in a manner similar to living holy people, the miraculous power to cure and to settle disputes. As the *Dialogues* of Gregory the Great (*r.* 590–604) show, the focus of the belief in the miraculous slowly shifted in Western Christendom from the living to the dead with the Germanic invasions. Second, the belief that burial near the corpse of a person certain to be summoned on Judgment Day aided one's own chance of salvation caused large cemeteries to be built around the graves of the saints. Paulinus of Nola (353/354–431) congratulated himself on the size of the city of the dead that he had helped establish around the tomb of St. Felix. Third, the saints protected the cities in which they resided. Ambrose called the discovery of the bodies of Sts. Gervasius and Protasius in 385 "of use to all" in Milan and used their relics to consolidate episcopal control and communal identity. The inhabitants of Antioch refused the request of the Byzantine emperor Leo I (*r.* 457–474) to send the relics of St. Simeon to Constantinople because the "most holy body was for their city a rampart and a fortress." Burial customs did much to shape the differing emphases within the cult of relics in the Eastern and Western Roman Empires. The Greeks exhumed and moved, or, to use the technical term, translated, numerous saints' bodies. Their shrines came to be centrally located in cities. Nevertheless, miraculous action centered on holy people actually living at the time, and eventually on icons, rather than on relics. For the Latins, the relics of dead saints were the focus of the miraculous, but canon and civil laws, following the tradition of the Theodosian Code, severely limited the exhumation of dead bodies. Their shrines were located in suburban cemeteries, and objects that had come into contact with the bodies of the saints, technically known as *brandea,* were as important "relics" as were the tombs themselves. As late as the seventh century, Pope Honorius refused to remove the body of St. Agnes from her tomb and constructed a shrine three miles from central Rome.

During the Germanic invasions of the sixth century, as is evident from the works of Gregory of Tours, the graves of the holy dead outside Gallo-Roman cities served as an important defense of Christian communities against the pagan Franks. The cult of relics, however, became one of the most important tools in the synthesis of Germanic and Roman cultures. The logic of saintly patronage sustained by Gregory and his fellow bishops closely fitted Frankish notions of personal power and justice. The Frankish nobility became as eager patrons of relic cults as they did of monasticism. Relics served very practical purposes in that society. Seventh-century missionaries enthusiastically used relics in their teaching and implanted new shrines in the Saxon territories. By the eighth century, relics were included in all altars as part of their dedication throughout the West. Legal oaths were quite regularly sworn over relics. They were also included in such secular items as the throne of Charlemagne and the hilt of the mythical sword of Roland, Durendal.

During this period the cult of the saints in northern Europe was primarily focused on the relics of long-dead saints housed in religious communities. These saints were primarily Gallo-Roman or Anglo-Saxon bishops and abbots but also included martyrs whose bones had been imported from Rome. A brisk trade in relics had begun in the wake of changes in the law concerning the exhumation of the dead. (In Italy and Byzantium the cult of relics continued to be located in cities and focused on the martyrs, although more recent saints also gained popularity.) The patronage of these saints was local in nature and central to the self-understanding of the communities in which their relics resided. It would be impossible to consider the city of Tours or the monastery of Fleury without understanding the central place of St. Martin and St. Benedict as their patrons. A saint "owned" the property of the religious community in which his—or less commonly her—relics resided. The strict enforcement of the cloister and the general decline of female monasticism meant that few important shrines existed in convents. That of a male saint, Potentianus, at the abbey of Jouarre-en-Brie was an important exception.

The logic of saintly patronage in this period was based on the economy of gift exchange. The living earned the patronage of the holy dead by rendering them their service or gifts; reciprocally the saints had duties to their servants. Communities ritually humiliated the relics of a negligent saint by strewing them on the floor of the church and chanting curses over them. Relics were so central to the economic well-being of religious communities that such communities frequently attempted to buy, discover, or

 RELICS

even steal new relics. Such actions were usually justified by reference to visionary pronouncements of the saints themselves. This use of relics reflected a vision of the supernatural world as an intensely social network of intercessors who linked living Christians to their God.

AUTHENTICATION OF RELICS

Various Western ecclesiastical authorities criticized specific relics as inauthentic and the promoters of certain cults as unscrupulous. The Council of Braga (675) called the attention of bishops to possible abusive uses of relics for personal gain. Agobard of Lyons attacked those clerics who promoted the pilgrimage to the shrine of St. Firminius during an epidemic in 829 in spite of the fact that no miracles had occurred there. Radulfus Glaber disagreed with his patron, William of St. Bènigne, over the latter's presence at the installation of relics of St. Just about 1040, which both men knew to be fakes. Guibert of Nogent's *On the Relics of the Saints* (*ca.* 1120), the most celebrated example of medieval skepticism about relic veneration, questioned a number of cults, most particularly the shrine of Christ's foreskin at Charroux, on the grounds of inauthenticity. Guibert also promoted the veneration of the Eucharist, which was the physical presence of the body of Christ, as superior to the veneration of ordinary saints' relics.

The problem of authenticity was a pressing one, because technically only authentic relics were sacred, although many writers maintained that sincere veneration, in ignorance, of inauthentic relics could also be effective. Some communities included identifying inscriptions with their relics, on tablets in the case of tombs and on parchment scrolls in the case of fragments. Copies of hagiographic texts about a saint were often kept in or near the reliquary itself. Such written evidence was important because the exact identity or location of tombs in a church could be forgotten over the course of centuries. Just as relics could be faked, so written traditions about them could be forged. Adémar of Chabannes (*ca.* 988–*ca.* 1035), for instance, authored a number of texts designed to prove the apostolicity of St. Martial and thus to add prestige to his relics. In the absence of a written tradition, authors often invoked visions of the saint or other miracles that announced the holiness of a set of bones. When such were lacking, ecclesiastical authorities sometimes employed the ordeal by fire to test the authenticity of a relic. Emperor Louis I the Pious (*r.* 814–840) had to ban the application of the ordeal to relics of the True Cross because untrustworthy merchants sold pieces of petrified wood, which could pass the test. The authenticity of relics was challenged not only on the grounds of their identification with a known personage, but because of doubts about the sanctity of that person as well. Reformers in Visigothic Spain used the ordeal by fire to test relics from Arian regions. With the decline of the ordeal as a legal procedure in the later Middle Ages, some holy people, such as Juliana of Cornillon, were reknowned for their ability to discern true relics.

CHANGES IN LATER MEDIEVAL VENERATION

Between the middle of the eleventh and the middle of the thirteenth century the increasing stress on direct personal contacts between the individual and the divine in Christian spirituality inspired new types of relics. Beginning with the great reform movement large numbers of living people were viewed by their contemporaries as embodiments of sanctity in a manner not common since late antiquity. As with the martyrs, the bodies and even the penitential instruments used by these saints were highly prized. Various communities vied for the rights to the body of Francis of Assisi even before his death, while the friar who stripped the body of Dominic Guzmán for burial kept the iron chains worn by the saint as a "great treasure." King Louis IX of France willed his hairshirt to his daughter, and his body was paraded as a relic around the Capetian kingdom. The bones of such varied figures as Thomas Becket, Bernard of Clairvaux, and Louis of Anjou became celebrated for their miraculous powers. The papally supervised process of canonization, not fully established until the Fourth Lateran Council (1215), controlled who could be called saints and thus what bodies could be considered relics. The same council also passed legislation severely limiting commerce in relics. During this time relic veneration more commonly featured objects associated with Jesus and the Virgin Mary. Since their bodies were believed to have left this world, their shrines tended to center on miraculous statues or crucifixes, as was the case at the Marian shrines of Walsingham, Chartres, Montserrat, and Einsiedeln. Although objects associated with Christ and Mary, such as pieces of the True Cross, vials of the Virgin's milk, and even the Eucharist, as the real presence of Christ's body, had been regarded as important relics since the Carolingian Age, they now came to occupy a more prominent place in the popular imagination. In Byzantium, icons established a preeminent position over relics during this period.

During the fourteenth and fifteenth centuries the role of the veneration of saints in the practice of Christianity subtly changed. Records of canonization processes suggest that the perceived need for proximity to relics in order to receive a miraculous cure declined sharply, thus adversely affecting the revenues at many relics shrines. While Peter of Luxembourg, Margaret of Hungary, and others became important patrons for late medieval Christians, their physical bodies were no longer a crucial link between the natural and supernatural worlds. Those bodies nevertheless reflected divine favor. Since the lack of putrefaction was regarded as a sign of sanctity, the "uncorrupted" bodies of such saints as Catherine of Bologna were displayed, and remain today, in glass coffins at their shrines. The sweet odor of sanctity became a common attribute of saintly bodies, both living and dead. The most important shrines of this period were those dedicated to Mary and to Christ, such as Wilsnack and Loreto. At the same time the collection and display of smaller relics became ever more popular as a means of demonstrating the spiritual wealth of individuals and ecclesiastical institutions.

RELICS DURING THE REFORMATION

In the age of reform the cult of relics, like every aspect of Christianity, was vastly transformed, but not equally so in all regions of Europe. Evidence from Germany suggests that those areas which remained Catholic had been relatively more devoted to relic piety during the pre-Reformation period than those areas which became Lutheran. Humanist scholars, from John Gerson to Erasmus, unleashed a growing crescendo of criticism directed at the superstitious elements of the cult, culminating in Erasmus' biting satire on the pilgrimage to Walsingham in the *Colloquies.* The Protestant reformers rejected all forms of intercessory piety; John Calvin composed the most systematic critique in *A Treatise on Relics,* which rejected them on theological grounds and highlighted such absurdities as the multiple heads of John the Baptist enshrined in Europe. Theological opposition sometimes turned to violent iconoclasm when Protestant crowds smashed images and reliquaries in Roman Catholic churches. The need for physical manifestations of the sacred did not disappear. Where oaths were once sworn over relics, the Bible was now employed in their stead as a sacred witness in Protestant circles. The veneration of the saints, Mary, and Jesus remained popular in Catholic regions. Even there, however, the means of gaining supernatural assistance were changing. Episcopal questionnaires from Spain show that visionary appearances of the saints and of Mary slowly replaced their physical remains as the focus of intercessory prayer and devotion. This new way of envisioning the relationship between the natural and supernatural worlds has continued to be important in Catholicism down through the celebrated Marian visions of recent times.

BIBLIOGRAPHY

Peter Brown, *The Cult of the Saints* (1981); Hippolyte Delehaye, *Sanctus: Essai sur le culte des saints dans l'antiquité* (1927); A. Frolow, *La relique de la vraie croix* (1961); Heinrich Fichtenau, "Zum Reliquienwesen in früheren Mittelalter," *Mitteilungen der Instituts für österreichische Geschichtsforschung,* **60** (1952); Patrick Geary, *Furta sacra: Thefts of Relics in the Central Middle Ages* (1978); Klaus Guth, *Guibert von Nogent und die hochmittelalterliche Kritik an der Reliquienverehrung* (1970); Martin Heinzelmann, *Translationsberichte und andere Quellen des Reliquienkultes* (1979); Nicole Herrmann-Mascard, *Les reliques des saints: Formation coutumière d'un droit* (1975); Lionel Rothkrug, *Religious Practices and Collective Perceptions: Hidden Homologies in the Renaissance and Reformation* (1980); Victor Saxer, *Morts, martyrs, reliques en Afrique chrétienne aux premiers siècles* (1980); Klaus Schreiner, "Zum Wahrheitsverständnis im Heiligen- und Reliquienwesen des Mittelalters," in *Speculum,* **17** (1966), and "'Discrimen veri ac falsi': Ansätze und Formen der Kritik in der Heiligen- und Reliquienverehrung des Mittelalters," in *Archiv für Kulturgeschichte,* **48** (1966); Pierre-André Sigal, *L'homme et le miracle dans la France médiévale. XIe–XIIe siècle* (1985); Bernhard Töpfer, "Reliquienkult und Pilgerbewegung zur Zeit der Klosterreform im burgundisch-aquitanischen Gebiet," in Hellmut Kretzschmar, ed., *Vom Mittelalter zur Neuzeit* (1956), 420–439. For an excellent bibliography, see Stephen Wilson, *Saints and Their Cults* (1983), 338–344.

THOMAS HEAD

[See also **Adémar of Chabannes; Ampulla; Antiquarianism and Archaeology; Arcosolium; Beatification; Brandeum; Canonization; Chapel; Crypt; Hagiography, Western European; Martyrdom; Ordeals; Pilgrimage, Western European; Reliquary; Translation of Saints; Vernicle; Volto Santo.**]

RELIGIOUS INSTRUCTION. The growth of medieval Christianity ultimately depended on how well ordinary lay people understood and practiced their religion. Christian belief was grounded in a written, biblical revelation, but during the Middle Ages the vast majority of Christians were illiterate. By necessity church leaders had to employ means other than the written word to convey the meaning of Christianity to the laity. Oral instruction, passed on in the church and at home, became the primary method by which lay people acquired their religious education.

In the early church, where adult baptism was the rule, candidates for baptism (catechumens) received moral and dogmatic instruction in the fundamentals of Christianity from church elders. Many of the early fathers of the church wrote sophisticated manuals of theological instruction (catechisms) to train people in the beliefs and practices of the new religion. But Christian educators had to adapt their catechetical techniques to new circumstances and a new audience as the civic life of the faltering Roman Empire collapsed and public education declined in the fifth century. Missionaries preaching among the illiterate, pagan Germanic peoples faced the challenge of reducing the increasingly elaborate theology of Christianity to its most elementary points in order to win converts and instruct ill-educated believers. Drawing inspiration from the writings of the early church fathers, church leaders declared that all Christian adults should at least know the Apostles' Creed, which contained the basic tenets of Christian dogma, and the Lord's Prayer. As the prebaptismal instruction offered to catechumens disappeared during the sixth century, when infant baptism began to replace adult baptism, ecclesiastical councils and synods decreed that parents should teach their children these two fundamental elements of Christianity in the home. Godparents were especially admonished to teach these prayers to their godchildren. Occasional sermons and readings from saints' lives delivered in church by bishops or priests supplemented this basic home instruction.

Ultimate responsibility for the pastoral care of souls (*cura animarum*) fell to parish priests, who, in the role of pastor, had to ensure that their parishioners knew the rudiments of Christianity. Since the successful religious instruction of lay people depended on the pastoral competence of their priests, efforts to better educate priests in the *cura animarum* necessarily had a concomitant effect on the instruction of the laity. In this regard the Fourth Lateran Council (1215) ushered in a golden age of pastoral care. Articulating pastoral concerns already in the air, its decrees (calling for, among other things, better education for the clergy, more preaching, and annual confession for adults) inspired bishops, theologians, and canonists to compile manuals of pastoral instruction intended to aid priests in their pastoral duties. These guides—ranging from short handbooks to lengthy *summae confessorum*—circulated widely throughout Europe from the early thirteenth century onward.

Brief pastoral treatises, appended to the decrees of provincial and diocesan synods, were often made required reading for parish priests. One such treatise, *Ignorantia sacerdotum* (The ignorance of priests), promulgated by Archbishop John Peckham in the Lambeth Council of 1281, was essentially a catechetical outline for the instruction of the laity. Although English in origin, it summed up the basic religious knowledge typically required of lay people throughout Europe in the later Middle Ages. It obliged priests to explain homiletically to their parishioners four times a year the fourteen articles of faith contained in the Creed, the Ten Commandments, the two laws of the Gospel (love of God and love of neighbor), the seven works of mercy, the seven deadly sins, the seven cardinal virtues, and the seven sacraments.

In addition to this rudimentary dogmatic and moral instruction, every lay person was expected to have memorized by age seven the Lord's Prayer and the Creed. By the late twelfth century church synods added the Angelic Salutation (the Hail Mary) and the correct way to make the sign of the cross to these basic requirements. Probably without exception lay people learned and prayed these prayers in the vernacular. In many parishes the Creed and Lord's Prayer were recited by priest and people after the Sunday sermon. Diocesan legislation also generally urged lay people to know the words of baptism, if only in the vernacular, in order to baptize infants in the case of necessity.

Priests most often relied on oral instruction to teach their parishioners the basics of their religion. Sermons—hundreds of which survive—were the chief means by which catechetical instruction was passed to the people. Regular preaching to the laity was rare in the early Middle Ages, but by the late twelfth century preaching increased, partly as a result of the growth of theology in the new schools and universities, partly as an antidote to the unau-

RELIGIOUS INSTRUCTION

thorized—and sometimes heretical—sermons of wandering preachers. The regularity and proficiency with which sermons were preached varied widely; sermons delivered several times a year were probably the norm in most parishes, although some dioceses required weekly preaching by pastors. By the thirteenth century the laity enjoyed more frequent and professional preaching by the mendicant friars—especially the Dominicans (officially called the *Ordo* [Fratrum] *Predicatorum,* the Order of [Friars] Preachers) and Franciscans—whose particular mission was to spread the Gospel through preaching. Sermon topics—generally treating moral rather than dogmatic themes—ranged from explanations of the Gospels to lessons about Christian living. Exempla (edifying stories drawn from saints' lives and moral tales) made the subject matter of sermons more palatable to ill-educated audiences. Confessional interrogations were another effective method of oral instruction. Handbooks of pastoral guidance for priests recommended that they examine their parishioners' knowledge of the rudiments of faith during their annual confession and instruct them where their knowledge was lacking.

Despite the increased pastoral proficiency of the parish priest and his growing role in the education of his parishioners, the family remained a vital avenue of religious education. Children still generally received their earliest religious instruction from their parents and godparents—as they had in the early Middle Ages.

Some children acquired additional religious training through elementary education at monastic and cathedral schools (for boys), and song schools, grammar schools, chantry schools, or local parish schools (which girls also occasionally attended). Since students usually learned to read from psalters or from primers containing the Lord's Prayer, Hail Mary, Creed, and other simple prayers, they received some religious formation in their elementary education; however, schools were never the primary means for the religious instruction of the laity. Instead, their purpose was to provide servers who could recite responses at liturgies, to train future clergy, or—in the later Middle Ages—to prepare children for professional or commercial careers. They had scant effect on the religious education of the majority of lay people, who remained illiterate.

For these people, the visual arts played an important role in religious instruction. Indeed, the biblical stories, hagiographies, and moral lessons depicted in statues, icons, carvings, stained glass, and wall paintings were regarded as the unlettered man's books. Visual representations of religious subjects could pose problems, however; without verbal explanation they were often misunderstood. Mystery and morality plays, widely performed in cities and towns from the thirteenth century on, merged oral and visual methods of instruction in order to portray dramatically biblical stories and moral lessons in a manner both didactic and entertaining.

In the later Middle Ages, as literacy increased among middle- and upper-class lay people, books became another important means of religious instruction. By the thirteenth century a wealth of instructional manuals circulated throughout Europe. The majority of these were written to aid parish priests in their exercise of the *cura animarum,* but many others were specifically intended for a newly literate lay audience. Prayer books, such as the various illuminated books of hours produced for the aristocracy (best represented by the exquisite *Très riches heures* of the duke of Berry), helped stimulate private devotions, but purely didactic works were also popular. Many of these books were written in verse to aid in their memorization.

One influential treatise—the *Manuel des péchés,* written in French verse about 1260—included explanations of the articles of the Creed, the Ten Commandments, the sacraments, the seven deadly sins, and how to make a good confession. The cleric Robert Mannyng made an English translation of it (called *Handlyng Synne*) in 1303. Another widely circulated manual covering similar topics was the *Somme le roi,* compiled in 1279 from earlier manuals by the Dominican Lorens d'Orléans for Philip III of France. The *Somme,* which circulated in several versions, was translated into at least six languages, including two popular fourteenth-century English translations, the *Aȝenbite of Inwyt* (The remorse of conscience) and the *Book of Vices and Virtues.*

The *Lay Folks' Catechism,* translated into English in 1357 from a Latin catechism written for priests by Archbishop John Thoresby of York, is an example of an officially promulgated treatise intended for the instruction of the laity. Like almost all medieval instructional manuals it rehearsed the familiar tenets of Christian belief. Written in verse, it carried a forty-day indulgence for those who memorized it. The topics of these didactic works even entered popular secular literature: Chaucer's

Parson's Tale, for example, contains a discussion of the seven deadly sins and a sermon on penitence, both drawn from manuals of pastoral care. Even unlettered lay people benefited from books such as the various *Biblia pauperum* (poor men's Bibles), which contained woodcut illustrations of biblical subjects.

John Gerson (1363–1429), chancellor of the University of Paris, was the most prolific author of catechetical manuals in the late Middle Ages. Among his many works intended for the religious instruction of the laity were the *Tractatus de parvulis trahendis ad Christum* (Tract on drawing children to Christ), considered to be the first catechism intended for children; the *Opus tripartitum* (Threefold work), containing explanations of the Ten Commandments, confession, and an *ars moriendi*—a treatise on preparing for death); and *L'ABC des simples gens* (The ABC's for simple folk), a short vernacular catechism.

BIBLIOGRAPHY

Sources. Winthrop Nelson Francis, ed., *The Book of Vices and Virtues* (1942); Gustaf Holmstedt, ed., *Speculum Christiani* (1933); Robert Mannyng of Brunne, *Robert of Brunne's "Handlyng Synne,"* Frederick J. Furnivall, ed. (1862, 1901–1903); Dan Michel of Northgate, *Ayenbite of Inwyt,* Richard Morris, ed. (1866); John Myrc, *Instructions for Parish Priests,* Edward Peacock, ed., rev. by Frederick J. Furnivall (1902); Thomas F. Simmons and Henry E. Nolloth, eds., *The Lay Folks' Catechism* (1901).

Studies. Paul Adam, *La vie paroissiale en France au XIVe siècle* (1964); Émile J. Arnould, *Le Manuel des péchés: Étude de littérature religieuse anglo-normande* (1940); Henry G. J. Beck, *The Pastoral Care of Souls in South-east France During the Sixth Century* (1950); Leonard Boyle, *Pastoral Care, Clerical Education, and Canon Law, 1200–1400* (1981); Edmund K. Chambers, *The Medieval Stage,* 2 vols. (1903, repr. 1925, 1948, 1963, 1967); Étienne Delaruelle, *La piété populaire au moyen âge* (1975); Raymonde Foreville, "Les statuts synodaux et le renouveau pastoral du XIIIe siècle dans le Midi de la France," in *Cahiers de Fanjeaux* **6** (1971); Roy M. Haines, "Education in English Ecclesiastical Legislation of the Later Middle Ages," in *Studies in Church History,* 7 (1971); John T. McNeill, *A History of the Cure of Souls* (1951); Bernard L. Manning, *The People's Faith in the Time of Wyclif* (1919); Pierre Michaud-Quantin, *Sommes de casuistique et manuels de confession au moyen âge (XII–XVI siècles)* (1962); John R. H. Moorman, *Church Life in England in the Thirteenth Century* (1955); Gerald R. Owst, *Preaching in Medieval England* (1926); Francis Rapp, *L'église et la vie religieuse en occident à la fin du moyen âge* (1971); Richard H. Rouse and Mary A. Rouse, *Preachers, Florilegia, and Sermons: Studies in the "Manipulus Florum" of Thomas of Ireland* (1979); Johann B. Schneyer, *Geschichte der katholischen Predigt* (1969); Gerard S. Sloyan, ed., *Shaping the Christian Message* (1958), 3–62; Robert Ulich, *A History of Religious Education* (1968).

JOHN R. SHINNERS, JR.

[See also **Biblia Pauperum; Confession; Drama, Western European; Exemplum; Gerson, John; Manuel des Péchés; Mannyng, Robert; Missions and Missionaries, Christian; Penance and Penitentials; Preaching and Sermon Literature, Western European; Schools (various articles); Seven Deadly Sins; Très Riches Heures; Virtues and Vices.**]

RELIQUARY, a container for a relic (a bone, garment, or object associated with a saint, Christ, or a holy site). Reliquaries are preserved from the fourth century on, becoming especially popular as the cult of relics intensified after the eighth century. Usually small in size and portable, their form varies widely. Some are elaborately decorated medallions for personal wear as an amulet; another type, called a reliquary chasse (from the Latin *capsa,* coffin), resembles a gabled building. Reliquaries containing fragments of the True Cross are often cruciform, while those containing bones may take the shape of the limb (for example, an arm bone in a *brachium,* a reliquary shaped like an arm). Most reliquaries

Reliquary of Pepin with Crucifixion group in repoussé relief. Mid 9th and 11th centuries. CONQUES ABBEY TREASURY/HIRMER FOTOARCHIV, MUNICH

are made of wood, precious metals (often encrusted with gems), or ivory, since the value of the container was seen as a reflection of the value of the relic. Reliquaries either may be lidded or hinged, so that they must be opened to reveal the relic, or they may allow the object to be viewed through a grill or a rock crystal covering.

BIBLIOGRAPHY

A. Frolow, *Les reliquaires de la Vraie Croix* (1965); Kurt Weitzmann, ed., *Age of Spirituality: Late Antique and Early Christian Art, Third to Seventh Century* (1979), 630–637.

LESLIE BRUBAKER

[See also **Early Christian Art; Enamel; Relics.**]

REMIGIUS OF AUXERRE (Remigius Autissiodorensis) (*ca.* 841–*ca.* 908), Benedictine scholar and humanist, perhaps the most efficient teacher of the "Carolingian Renaissance." He studied at the monastic school of St. Germain in Auxerre under Heiric (a disciple of John Scottus Eriugena), whom he succeeded as head of the school in 876. In 893, at the request of Archbishop Fulco, he and Hucbald of St. Amand began the reorganization of the cathedral school of Rheims, previously devastated by the Normans. Upon Fulco's assassination in 900, Remigius went to teach in Paris, where he counted among his many pupils the great Odo (879–942), future abbot of Cluny. He probably died there, in or around 908.

Apart from a few letters and some homilies, Remigius' identified production consists entirely of glosses or commentaries on biblical, classical, and philosophical works. The most important are his commentaries on Genesis, the Psalms, and the Gospels, and on the *De nuptiis Philologiae et Mercurii* of Martianus Capella and *De consolatione Philosophiae* of Boethius, all of which reveal a pervasive influence of John Scottus Eriugena.

Vastly erudite but hardly original, Remigius was, above all, a philologist, mostly interested in grammatical questions bearing on etymology and hermeneutics. His merit lies chiefly in his remarkable ability to explain in simple terms the great texts of antiquity for Christian minds. As such he is rightly considered a forerunner of the Scholastic method of the twelfth century.

BIBLIOGRAPHY

The greater part of the writings printed under Remigius' name in *Patrologia latina,* CXXXI (1884), are spurious. A useful catalog of his works (both authentic and doubtful) has been compiled by Cora E. Lutz in *Remigii Autissiodorensis commentum in Martianum Capellam,* I (1962), 11–12, with full bibliographical references.

The following will update this bibliography: Pierre Courcelle, *La "Consolation de philosophie" de Boèce dans la tradition littéraire* (1967); Diane K. Bolton, "Remigian Commentaries in the *Consolation of Philosophy* and Their Sources," in *Traditio,* 33 (1977); Colette Jeudy, "La tradition manuscrite des *Partitiones* de Priscien et la version longue du commentaire de Rémi d'Auxerre" and "L'*Institutio de nomine, pronomine, et verbo* de Priscien: Manuscrits et commentaires médiévaux," in *Revue d'histoire des textes,* **1** (1971) and **2** (1972), "Les manuscrits de l'*Ars de verbo* d'Eutychès et le commentaire de Rémi d'Auxerre," in *Études de civilisation médiévale, IXe–XIIe siècles: Mélanges offerts à Edmond-René Labande* (1974), and "Israël le Grammairien et la tradition manuscrite du commentaire de Rémi d'Auxerre à l'*Ars minor* de Donat," in *Studi medievali,* **18** (1977); Claudio Leonardi, "Remigio di Auxerre e l'eredità della scuola carolingia," in Giornate filologiche genovesi, Genoa, 1974, *I classici nel medioevo e nell'umanesimo* (1975).

YVES CHARTIER

[See also **Boethius; Hucbald of St. Amand; John Scottus Eriugena; Liturgy, Treatises on; Martianus Capella; Scholasticism, Scholastic Method.**]

RÉMUNDAR SAGA KEISARASONAR. The tale of Rémundr, the emperor's son, is an anonymous Icelandic *riddarasaga* (tale of chivalry) composed around the mid fourteenth century. The work is heavily indebted for motifs to other romances, especially *Tristrams saga ok Ísöndar.*

The plot of *Rémundar saga* is set in motion when Rémundr, who is outstanding in learning and in chivalric skills, has one night an extraordinary dream. He finds himself in a strange country, where he meets and falls in love with a beautiful maiden, whom he marries. When he awakens, he finds on his finger the ring he had received from her during the wedding ceremony. Rémundr is so smitten by the woman of his dreams that he has a lifelike image fashioned of her and takes it with him wherever he goes.

He meets a king's son, Eskupart, who claims that the maiden with whom Rémundr is infatuated is none other than his own beloved. In a duel with Eskupart, Rémundr kills him, but is himself wounded when the fragmented point of Eskupart's sword becomes lodged in his skull. Before he dies, Eskupart prophesies that the wound can be healed only by the most beautiful maiden in the world. Rémundr then meets a stranger, Víðförull, who fashions a cart in which Rémundr at first sleeps at night, and then is transported, as he gradually becomes weaker. Víðförull acts as guide in the search for the maiden who must cure Rémundr. After many adventures, Rémundr reaches India, where he is healed by Elina, the woman of his dreams. She had learned of Rémundr through a dream, and had sent Víðförull in search of him.

Rémundar saga contains several analogues to *Tristrams saga.* The motif of fashioning a lifelike statue of the beloved, which the protagonist caresses, is borrowed from the Hall of Statues episode in *Tristrams saga,* as is the motif of an embedded sword fragment. The motif of a sword splinter lodged in the skull of the enemy is modified in *Rémundar saga* into a fragment from the enemy's sword that becomes embedded in the skull of the protagonist. Finally, like Tristram, Rémundr can be cured only by the woman he loves.

The author plagiarized other romances as well. The name Víðförull is known from *Mágus saga,* and persons named Eskupart appear both in *Bevers saga* and in *Gibbons saga.* The most remarkable loan or analogy is the epithet that Víðförull bestows upon Rémundr: *hinn kranki kerrumaðr*—"the sick man of the cart"—which is a variation of Lancelot's appellative "le chevalier de la charrette." There is no evidence that an Old Norse–Icelandic version of Chrétien de Troyes's *Lancelot* existed. Familiarity with the figure cannot be precluded, however, since the indigenous *riddarasögur* borrowed a kaleidoscopic array of motifs from both Western and Oriental sources. Furthermore, the name Lancelot occurs in *Breta sǫgur* and in *Ívens saga.* An analogy to the dream in which future lovers become acquainted with each other is otherwise not known in Icelandic literature but does occur in foreign works, such as the continental prose romance *Arthur de Bretagne* (*Le petit Artus de Bretaigne*).

Rémundar saga is characterized by a rhythmic, redundant prose that derives from a preponderance of participial clusters as well as synonymous and alliterative collocations. In this respect the diction of the saga approximates that of two Norwegian translations attributed to a certain Brother Robert and Abbot Robert, respectively: *Tristrams saga* and *Elis saga ok Rosamundu.* The participial and alliterative clusters in *Rémundar saga* occur especially in descriptive passages and in passages expressing heightened emotion, for example in some portions of dialogue. The author expresses a certain self-consciousness vis-à-vis his art as he exhorts his listeners to pay attention (chap. 4), or otherwise betrays his presence through interjections intended to bridge temporal and spatial gaps in the narrative (for instance, the ends of chaps. 26 and 36, the beginnings of chaps. 30 and 35). Such authorial commentary is not unusual in the late medieval Icelandic *riddarasögur.*

Rémundar saga keisarasonar is extant in eight vellum manuscripts (or fragments thereof) from the fourteenth, fifteenth, and sixteenth centuries, and in more than thirty paper manuscripts from the seventeenth century and later. The tale of Rémundr, the emperor's son, also exists in two different *rímur* versions.

BIBLIOGRAPHY

Sources. Sven Grén Broberg, ed., *Rémundar saga keisarasonar,* 4 pts. (1909–1912); Bjarni Vilhjálmsson, ed., "Rémundar saga keisarasonar," in *Riddarasögur,* V (1954).

Studies. Eyvind Fjeld Halvorsen, "Rémundar saga," in *Kulturhistorisk leksikon for nordisk middelalder,* XIV (1969); Finnur Jónsson, *Den oldnorske og oldislandske Litteraturs Historie,* 2nd ed., III (1924), 113–114; Kr. Kålund, "Kirjalax sagas Kilder," in *Aarbøger for Nordisk Oldkyndighed og Historie,* 3rd ser., 7 (1917); Einar Ól. Sveinsson, "Viktors saga ok Blávus: Sources and Characteristics," in Jónas Kristjánsson, ed., *Viktors saga ok Blávus* (1964), esp. CCII–CCVIII.

MARIANNE E. KALINKE

[See also **Bevers Saga; Breta Sǫgur; Elis Saga ok Rosamundu; Ívens Saga; Mágus Saga Jarls; Riddarasögur; Tristrams Saga ok Ísöndar.**]

RENAISSANCES AND REVIVALS IN MEDIEVAL ART

INTRODUCTION

Antique art formed a continually present and constantly active substratum in medieval culture and stood as the alternative to the expressive fantasy of that other essential heritage, the barbarian decorative tradition. From antique art the Middle

RENAISSANCES IN ART

Ages inherited a repertoire of architectural and figural styles, types, techniques, compositions, and iconographic formulas which were copied, modified, transformed, and deformed through centuries of repetition.

Against the backdrop of this extruded continuity of antique art, instances of direct and intense contact stand out as renaissances, or revivals, which distinguish themselves from the continuous medieval present by an abandonment of contemporary stylistic trends and by a deliberate return to forms from a far-distant time. Because of the availability to the Middle Ages of a rich variety of antique figural styles—Hellenistic, Aristocratic or high Roman, Plebeian or low and provincial Roman, late antique, and early Christian, as well as the styles of other medieval classical revivals—easy distinctions between instances of continuity and revival are often blurred, particularly as the latter began to lessen in intensity or were far from the centers of initial stimulation. The reuse of antique works, especially sculpture, in a medieval context (*spolia*) further complicates the problem. Scholarship has stressed the importance of identifying antique sources present in the locality of the renaissance itself as one way to clarify boundaries between continuity and revival.

Medieval artistic renaissances generally served a specific, usually political, purpose and were regularly accompanied by revivals in other areas of endeavor, such as science, literature, and lawgiving. Medieval renaissances distinguish themselves from the later Italian Renaissance rather more by the absence of any awareness of a historical gap between the medieval present and the antique past than by any supposed lesser quality of the revival styles. Medieval renaissances, which do differ in focus and intensity, divide into two types: revivals which are court-centered, that is to say, focused in place and patronage, and revivals which are period phenomena, that is, more diffused in place and patronage.

COURT-CENTERED REVIVALS

The Carolingian renaissance. The Carolingian renaissance grew from the idea of rebirth and renewal of cultural life initiated by Charlemagne and his pan-European court and developed by them and their successors. This revival turned toward Rome in part because of the sanction given by the Roman papacy to the Carolingians' usurpatious succession to power in the West in 751 and in part because of the enduring idea of Rome as representative of civilization and culture.

St. John. Miniature from the Schatzkammer Coronation Gospels. Court School of Charlemagne. Early 9th century. VIENNA, KUNSTHISTORISCHES MUSEUM, SCHATZKAMMER COLLECTION, UNNUMBERED MS, FOL. 76v

At the outset, a new script based on late antique cursive, the Carolingian minuscule, was invented to provide an ordered writing for liturgical, legal, and scientific texts newly purged and corrected on the basis of Roman models. In their turn, the new texts were to form a basis for order and learning within an expanding Carolingian society. They were, after a brief flirtation with iconoclasm (*ca.* 785–*ca.* 795), illustrated with pictures and bound in ivories carved with iconic and narrative scenes intended to convey an authority analogous to the text itself. Thus, following the bold but isolated beginning of the ornate and naturalizing Godescalc Gospels (781–783, Paris, Bibliothèque Nationale, nouv. acq. lat. 1203), Charlemagne's court artists developed two distinctive styles. Manuscripts and ivories of the so-called Ada group, such as the Lorsch Gospels (*ca.* 810) and its covers (the manuscript: Rumania, Alba Julia, Biblioteca Documentara Batthayneum, and Rome, Biblioteca, Cod. Pal. lat. 50; the covers: London, Victoria and Albert Museum, and Rome, Vatican Museum), reveal a new concern

RENAISSANCES IN ART

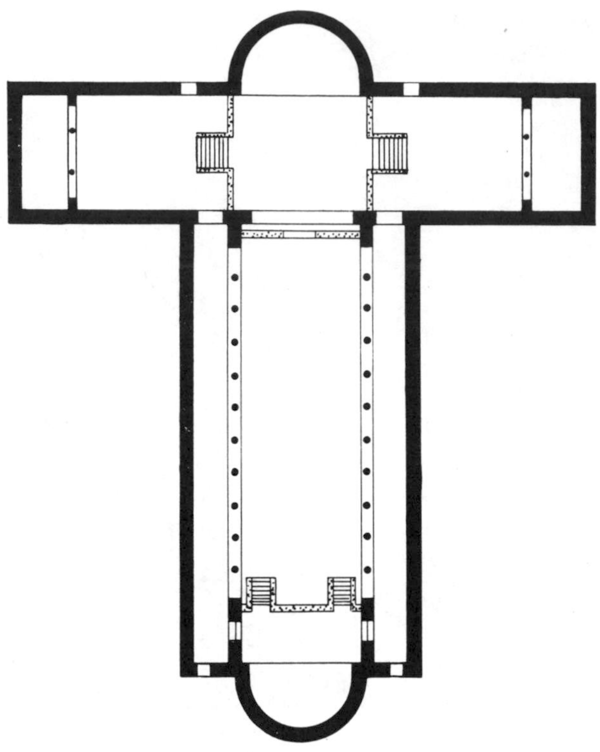

The basilica at Fulda, 819. REPRODUCED FROM EDGAR LEHMANN, *DER FRÜHE DEUTSCHE KIRCHENBAU* (1938)

for the animation of a convincingly modeled, though linearly conceived, figure within an increasingly three-dimensionalized architectural setting based on the antecedent of earlier Italian models or models from a Byzantine orbit. A still more classicizing style is found in manuscripts of the Court School group, such as the Schatzkammer Coronation Gospels (Vienna, Kunsthistorisches Museum), in which author portraits are realized in a purely painterly style set within an illusionistic landscape reminiscent of the late antique tradition. The development of these revival styles coincided with a self-conscious antiquarianism which led to a collection of Roman art and artifacts at Charlemagne's palace in Aachen and to the creation of small-scale antiquarian objects like Einhard's triumphal arch reliquary, now known only through a seventeenth-century drawing (Paris, Bibliothèque Nationale, fr. 10440).

These initial revivalist impulses formed the basis for the development of new styles (for example, those of Metz and Rheims) under Charlemagne's descendants. These later styles were also essentially court-oriented and distinguish themselves from a concurrent Carolingian "period style" present throughout the realm, a style characterized by an abstract, decorative handling of both the figure and its setting.

In architecture, the turn to Rome may have begun as early as the 760's at St. Denis, where the abbey church was rebuilt with a continuous transept in general imitation of the great T-shaped basilicas of Early Christian Rome. The architectural revival was certainly and more specifically under way by the end of the century. At Aachen itself, beginning about 792, Charlemagne constructed a palace complex (including an audience hall and a centrally planned sacral space) modeled conceptually if not formally on late antique imperial palaces, such as Constantine's in the Lateran in Rome. At Fulda, from 802 under the court-sent Abbot Ratgar (802–817), a new western apse and continuous transept, complete with T-shaped eastern crossing piers, internal column screens, and 1:4 proportions, was erected as a mausoleal setting for the relics of St. Boniface (the apostle of Germany), in clear equation with the forms of Old St. Peter's in Rome.

As in the minor arts, these early Carolingian buildings formed the basis for later developments. Early in the reign of Louis I the Pious (814–840) an ideal plan, parts of which were as classicizing as Aachen or Fulda, was developed for Carolingian monasteries. Now known through a copy (the plan of St. Gall, *ca.* 820), the schema, like Carolingian manuscripts, was intended for dissemination throughout the empire as a mechanism for order and control. Abbeys derived from this master plan, like St. Gall and perhaps Centula (St. Riquier), once must have stood across Western Europe as great, isolated architectural forms court imposed upon a landscape of vernacular building traditions.

The Macedonian renaissance. In Byzantine art, in contrast to the West, the undercurrent of continuity with the art of the classical past always remained relatively strong and the representation of the human body relatively organic. The delineation of a renaissance in Byzantium is thus more subtle. It is evidenced in the degree of physical reality and in the relation of the figure to its environment.

In the years of revitalization following the end of the iconoclastic upheaval (843), court circles of the ninth- and tenth-century Macedonian emperors initiated a broad-based revival of classical learning and humanistic expression in which the figurative arts participated. This general revival involved a deliberate searching out of classical texts (including expeditions to Alexandria and Syria), the publica-

 RENAISSANCES IN ART

tion of new, critical editions accompanied by extensive commentary, and the founding of Bardas University (863) in the Magnaura, complete with a chair of Homeric studies.

The most direct correlation between this literary and scientific return to ancient learning and the figurative arts lies in the illustration of technical treatises such as the tenth-century copy of Nicander's *Theriaca* (Paris, Bibliothèque Nationale, suppl. gr. 247). Byzantine illuminators of Christian texts, presumably working in the same ateliers as scientific illuminators, also returned to the classical and Early Christian past for inspiration. Thus seated figures, such as the St. Matthew from a tenth-century Gospels now at Mt. Athos (Stavronikita cod. 43), and standing figures, such as the five apostles on the lower register of the central panel of the mid-tenth-century Harbaville Triptych (Paris, Louvre), achieve an organic interaction between a fully comprehended anatomy and its enveloping drapery that rivals the antique itself. Indeed, the classicism is so intense that in the case of the Stavronikita image an antique Epicurus figure has been proposed as the direct model. Images such as the David and Melodia scene in the Paris Psalter (Bibliothèque Nationale, cod. gr. 137; shown at vol. 2, p. 441) and the late-tenth-century ivory showing the Entry into Jerusalem (Berlin, Staatliche Museen; shown at vol. 4, p. 492) present figures fully integrated into an illusionistically handled landscape replete with classical personifications and synecdochically rendered architectural motifs. Both of the latter are probably inspired directly by antique works; the personifications may have been inserted into the scenes for the first time in the Macedonian period.

Similarly, the apparently tenth-century development of new, Christian iconographies, such as the Anastasis type in which Christ pulls Adam out of Limbo or the bathing of the Child at the Nativity, are based on antique, pagan compositions with similar form and analogous content: Hercules dragging the dog Cerberus from the Underworld and the bathing of the child Dionysius, respectively.

Finally, the Macedonian revival of antique styles, compositions, and content that, in general terms, served the process of defining the proper image (icon) for the victorious iconodules was also occasionally applied to specific political contexts. The Joshua Roll (Rome, Biblioteca, MS Cod. Pal. gr. 431) has been associated in its iconography (Joshua as the great antetype of the victorious general) and its form (the continuous illustrated roll, or rotulus) with contemporary Byzantine conquests in the Holy Land and with the traditional imagery of triumph, the continuous narratives of the imperial triumphal columns like those of Trajan and Marcus Aurelius in Rome.

St. Matthew. Miniature from the Stavronikita Gospels, mid 10th century. Mount Athos, cod. 43, fol. 10r. PHOTO COURTESY KURT WEITZMANN

PERIOD REVIVALS

The renaissance of the twelfth century. Since its initial formulation by Charles H. Haskins in 1927, primarily as a literary and scientific revival, the concept of a twelfth-century renaissance (broadly defined as lasting from *ca.* 1050 to 1250) has been vigorously debated, modified, redefined, and even denied. In all scholarship, discussion of artistic revival in the twelfth century has played, at best, a secondary role within the larger question of the period revival for several reasons. To some extent the operative variables (low-style and provincial Roman art, *spolia,* high-style Roman and Hellenistic art, and various earlier revival styles) have not yet been fully integrated into our understanding of the revival or its chronological limits. Unlike earlier revivals, the renaissance of the twelfth century is diffused in time and in place. Antiquarian forms

RENAISSANCES IN ART

Abbot Durandus of St. Pierre. Marble relief from the cloister at Moissac, *ca.* 1100. PHOTO: WIM SWAAN

manifest themselves over large blocks of time in numerous, often unconnectable regional centers. The paucity of firmly dated monuments and the widespread absence of sufficient written records have made it difficult to understand fully the patronage and purpose of the revival. These problems aside, two separate phases of artistic revival are widely agreed upon: a Romanesque phase located primarily in southern France, Italy, and Spain and traditionally dated between about 1075 and 1140 and a Gothic phase located primarily in the Île-de-France and the Champagne and usually dated in the decades before and after 1200.

The Romanesque. In its simplest Romanesque form, the renaissance of the twelfth century has been equated with the technical revival of monumental stone sculpture, a concept that has been seriously called into question by recent discoveries and attributions for the Carolingian and Ottonian periods. In southern France, in parallel with the rise in general prosperity and literary culture, artists, particularly sculptors, began to re-explore their local antique past. Thus, at the cloister of the monastery of St. Pierre at Moissac around 1100 sculptors modeled standing figures placed in arch-enframed niches on prototypes found in Gallo-Roman grave steles. At Modena in Italy around 1100, leaders of the city proclaimed their commune independent from Tuscan overlords by appealing to the city's Roman past. Concurrently, and in the service of the city, the sculptor Wiligelmus modeled Eros figures and prophets for the duomo directly upon Roman marbles being excavated from nearby Mutina. In Campagna from the late eleventh century through the thirteenth century, artists based a series of sculptures, mosaics, and manuscript illuminations on Early Christian sarcophagus sculpture with similar iconography. In each of these instances the medieval sculptures reflect the antique heritage of the locale by turning, respectively, to provincial, low-style (Plebeian) Roman and Early Christian models. Not much later, in northern Europe, the sculptor Rainer of Huy cast a notable bronze baptismal font (1107–1118) for St. Barthélemy at Notre-Dame-aux-Fonts in Liège (shown at "Mosan Art" and "Rainer of Huy"). It is decorated with partially draped figures in high relief who twist and turn in contrapposto poses which reveal full understanding of the organic relationship between anatomy and drapery and which presuppose familiarity with high- or aristocratic-style antique models—whether Roman or Hellenistic.

Similarly, Romanesque architecture responds to a wide range of antique forms. The facade of St. Gilles-du-Gard (completed *ca.* 1140–*ca.* 1155?) long known to be somehow based on antique architectural forms, has recently been shown to reflect the composition, proportion, and details of the Roman (imperial) *scenae frons* (stage fronts) known to medieval builders through still-extant

St. Gilles-du-Gard, west facade. Mid 12th century. PHOTO: JEAN ROUBIER, PARIS

southern French examples, like the Augustan theater at Orange. In contrast, the early Romanesque abbey of Monte Cassino, now destroyed but reliably reconstructed on the basis of excavations and medieval descriptions, was rebuilt (dedicated 1071) under Abbot Desiderius on the model of the great Early Christian basilicas as part of a Rome-oriented monastic reform movement. The flight of stairs leading to an arched entry hall in front of a porticated atrium clearly recalls Old St. Peter's, while the cruciform church itself and particularly the transept forms and proportions reflect the later Old St. Paul's.

The Gothic. Evidently centered in the Île-de-France and the Champagne around the years between about 1180 and 1230, the High Gothic revival of the antique, which occurs only in the figurative arts and not in architecture, reflects a growing self-confidence in man's relationship to the natural world and parallels the rise of the French monarchy, to which it may be more directly connected than modern scholarship has supposed. Unlike the more varied Romanesque phase, the High Gothic portion of the twelfth-century renaissance seems to have turned consistently to only one style and period of the antique, namely, the high, or aristocratic, style of the early Roman imperial period. Thus, monumental column figures such as those of the Visitation Group (west portal) or the Last Judgment Portal (north transept) at Rheims Cathedral, the Cluny Museum fragment from the west facade of Notre Dame in Paris, and figures from the church of Montier-en-Der stand at ease in classical contrapposto clad in convincingly handled "wet-fold" drapery. Here, too, the style seems to have been based on examples extant in the immediate area. This same facility with the organic treatment of draped human form is also found in contemporary minor arts such as Nicholas of Verdun's Magi shrine (*ca.* 1190), now in Cologne Cathedral, and the paintings of the Ingeborg Psalter (Chantilly, Musée Condé, MS 1210?), which also yield evidence of Byzantine influence. In works like these, and in others like the fragments of a tomb from the

RENAISSANCES IN ART

The Visitation group. Central portal, west facade of Rheims Cathedral, mid 13th century. GIRAUDON/ART RESOURCE

abbey of St. Père in Chartres on which antique portrait gems are successfully imitated in stone, the antique world is met on equal terms and is assimilated into the context of a contemporary style.

OTHER REVIVALS

Each of the two great court-centered revivals of the Middle Ages themselves formed the basis for subsequent revivals.

Ottonian. The Ottonian or Saxon dynasty's (919–1024) efforts to secure its succession resulted in a politics that stressed continuity with the defunct Carolingian line and the emulation of Byzantium. Under the Ottonians, the art of antiquity was rarely approached directly. Rather, it was seen through Carolingian art and architecture, whose forms were closely imitated, and through Byzantine art, whose styles were imported. These revival elements of Ottonian art are also synthetically reflected in the development of an original Ottonian style in the figurative arts: a flexible combination of naturalism (volume, corporeality) and abstraction (stylization).

Palaiologan. The return of Byzantine rulership to Constantinople under the Palaiologoi (beginning in 1261) witnessed an intellectual revival manifested in a new consciousness for things Greek, a taste for the antique, and a new interest in the natural world. The revival of a monumental figurative style, which paralleled a revival in the other spheres, fused elements drawn from the Byzantine past (primarily the Macedonian renaissance, to a lesser extent the early Byzantine period, and, through them both, the antique) with a new power of observation manifested in the depiction of emotions and in the representation of nature.

Other revivals. In contrast to these revivals, artists of the court of Frederick II (*d.* 1250) in southern Italy turned directly to the antique as part of the emperor's conscious attempt to assert himself as the new caesar of a restored imperium.

A number of other revivals have been proposed for various periods and centers during the Middle Ages. Among them are: a revival in Rome itself under the patronage of Pope Sixtus III in the fifth century; a Byzantine revival of antique floor mosaics during the reign of the emperor Justinian in the sixth century; and a resurgence of interest in classical forms and types in eighth- and ninth-century Northumbria. In the thirteenth century the city of Venice, engaged in a quest for civic pedigree, sought to authenticate its Roman roots (in part) through a return to Early Christian and Early Byzantine forms in mosaic and sculpture. Similarly, the highly classicizing style of the Pisa Baptistery pulpit, carved by Nicola Pisano in 1259–1260, has recently been shown to be retrospective in stylistic intention and directly related to the ambitions of the city's leadership. Each of these generally more limited revivals varies in duration, scope, and intensity; taken together they further expand our understanding of the phenomenon of classical inspiration in medieval art.

SUMMARY AND CONCLUSIONS

General histories of medieval art have been structured as sequences of "high styles" (revivals) separated from one another by time gaps loosely regarded as periods of "low style" (continuity), which have received—perhaps in consequence—relatively less

 RENAISSANCES IN ART

attention. The elaboration of the depth and intensity of long-accepted court-centered renaissances like those of the Carolingians or Macedonian Byzantines and the discovery of previously unrecognized ones like those in fifth-century Rome or thirteenth-century Venice threatens the concept of a "Middle Age" by reducing it to a series of nearly contiguous revivals. This proliferation of revivals in both time and place calls attention to the need to reshape our basic period structure from a single-tiered, linear one to a double-tiered one in which a sequence of "high styles" (revivals) are arranged in time and space upon a substratum of "low styles" (continuities). This conceptual framework has already been successfully applied to the art of the early medieval period (from Constantine to Iconoclasm) in both East and West and, to an interesting extent, to Carolingian art and architecture as well. Applied to later periods of medieval art, this two-tiered construct should enhance understanding of both revivals and continuities. It should encourage greater concern for patronage and purpose and, in consequence, lead to a deeper awareness of the meaning of those now only formally understood revivals which (like the classicism of the Île-de-France of about 1200) can be isolated in both time and place. Moreover, it should yield its greatest benefits in the study of the relationship between revival and continuity in the Romanesque, where the absolute chronology of individual works of art and architecture is too often artificially determined by the present, single-tiered period structure. Indeed, only such a two-tiered conceptual framework will permit the full integration of the variable of continuity (Roman and provincial Roman styles, the use of *spolia,* and the phenomenon of revivals themselves) into our understanding of high medieval art and architecture.

BIBLIOGRAPHY

Eloise M. Angiola, "Nicola Pisano, Frederigo Visconti, and the Classical Style in Pisa," in *Art Bulletin,* **59** (1977); Albert Boeckler, "Elfenbeinreliefs der ottonischen Renaissance," in *Phoebus,* **2** (1949); Sheila Bonde, ed., *Survival of the Gods: Classical Mythology in Medieval Art* (1987); Wolfgang Braunfels, ed., *Karl der Grosse: Werk und Wirkung* (Aachen exhibition, 1965) (1965); Louis Bréhier, "La rénovation artistique sous les Paléologues et le mouvement des idées," in *Études sur l'histoire et sur l'art de Byzance: Mélanges Charles Diehl,* II (1930), 1–10; Michelangelo Cagiano de Azevedo, ed., *Roma e l'età carolingia* (1976); Marie Dominique Chenu, *La théologie au douzième siècle* (1957, 3rd ed. 1976), nine chapters of which are translated in *Nature, Man, and Society in the Twelfth Century,* Jerome Taylor and Lester K. Little, trans. (1968); Peter C. Claussen, "Antike und gotische Skulptur in Frankreich um 1200," in *Wallraf-Richartz Jahrbuch,* **35** (1973); Cäcilia Davis-Weyer, "Die Mosaiken Leos III. und die Anfänge der karolingischen Renaissance in Rom," in *Zeitschrift für Kunstgeschichte,* **29** (1966); Otto Demus, "A Renascence of Early Christian Art in Thirteenth Century Venice," in *Late Classical and Mediaeval Studies in Honor of Albert Mathias Friend, Jr.,* Kurt Weitzmann, ed. (1955), 348–361, and *Byzantine Art and the West* (1970); Paul Deschamps, "Étude sur la renaissance de la sculpture en France a l'époque romane," in *Bulletin monumental,* **84** (1925); Marie Durand-Lefebvre, *Art gallo-romain et sculpture romane: Recherche sur les formes* (1937); Albert Mathias Friend, Jr., "The Portraits of the Evangelists in Greek and Latin Manuscripts," in *Art Studies,* **5** (1927) and **7** (1929); A. Frolow, "La renaissance de l'art byzantin au IXe siècle et son origine," in *Corsi di cultura sull'arte ravennate e bizantina,* **9** (1962); Dorothy Glass, "Romanesque Sculpture in Campania and Sicily: A Problem of Method," in *Art Bulletin,* **56** (1974); Charles H. Haskins, *The Renaissance of the Twelfth Century* (1927, repr. 1957); Roger P. Hinks, *Carolingian Art* (1935, repr. 1962); Guido von Kaschnitz-Weinberg, "Bildnisse Friedrichs II. von Hohenstaufen," in *Mitteilungen des Deutschen Archäologischen Instituts: Römische Abteilung,* **60/61** (1953/1954) and **62** (1955); Dale Kinney, "Spolia from the Baths of Caracalla in Sta. Maria in Trastevere," in *Art Bulletin,* **68** (1986); Ernst Kitzinger, "Mosaic Pavements in the Greek East and the Question of a 'Renaissance' Under Justinian," in his *The Art of Byzantium and the Medieval West: Selected Studies,* W. Eugene Kleinbauer, ed. (1976), 49–63, "Byzantine Art in the Period Between Justinian and Iconoclasm," *ibid.,* 157–206, and "A Virgin's Face: Antiquarianism in Twelfth-century Art," in *Art Bulletin,* **62** (1980); W. Koehler, "Die Tradition der Adagruppe und die Anfänge des ottonischen Stiles in der Buchmalerei," in *Festschrift zum sechzigsten Geburtstag von Paul Clemen* (1926); Richard Krautheimer, "The Carolingian Revival of Early Christian Architecture," in *Studies in Early Christian, Medieval, and Renaissance Art* (1969), 203–255; Paul Lehmann, "Das Problem der karolingischen Renaissance," in *I problemi della civiltà carolingia* (1954), 309–358; Victor Lassalle, *L'influence antique dans l'art roman provençal* (*Revue archéologique de Narbonnaise,* suppl. 2) (1970); Hans Liebeschütz, "Das zwölfte Jahrhundert und die Antike," in *Archiv für Kulturgeschichte,* **35** (1953); Otto Pächt, "The Pre-Carolingian Roots of Early Romanesque Art," in *Studies in Western Art: Acts of the 20th International Congress of the History of Art,* I: *Romanesque and Gothic Art* (1963), 67–75; Svetozar Radojčić, "Die Entstehung der Malerei der Paläologischen Renaissance," in *Jahrbuch der öster-*

RENARD THE FOX

reichischen byzantinischen Gesellschaft, 7 (1958); Roberto Salvini, *Wiligelmo e le origini della scultura romanica* (1956); Willibald Sauerlander, "Art antique et sculpture autour de 1200: Saint-Denis, Lisieux, Chartres," in *Art de France,* I (1961), 47–56; H. Toubert, "Aspects du renouveau paléochrétien à Rome au début du XIIe siècle," in *Cahiers archéologiques,* 20 (1970); Warren T. Treadgold, ed., *Renaissances Before the Renaissance* (1984); Kurt Weitzmann, "The Character and Intellectual Origins of the Macedonian Renaissance," in his *Studies in Classical and Byzantine Manuscript Illumination,* Herbert L. Kessler, ed. (1971); Carl A. Willemsen, *Kaiser Friedrichs II: Triumphtor zu Capua, ein Denkmal hohenstaufischer Kunst in Süditalien* (1953).

CLARK MAINES

[See also **Aachen Palace Chapel; Anglo-Norman Art; Byzantine Art: 843–1453; Byzantine Empire; Carolingians and the Carolingian Empire; Early Christian and Byzantine Architecture; Early Christian Art; Gothic Art: Painting; Gothic Art: Sculpture; Lombard Art; Macedonian Renaissance; Middle Ages; Pre-Romanesque Architecture; Pre-Romanesque Art; Romanesque Art.**]

RENARD THE FOX. About 1174–1177 a French poet, of whom we know only his name, Pierre de St. Cloud, proposed to his audience, weary of the subjects offered them until then—chansons de geste, stories based on classical themes, Breton romances of Arthur and the knights of the Round Table, the tale of Tristan and Isolt—an account of the long and cruel war between two "barons," Renard and Isengrin. His poem marked the beginning of an immensely popular medieval work, the *Roman de Renart.* This work introduces us to a world of animals in which, unlike the fable, all the personages bear a name and conduct themselves as members of the kingdom of Noble the lion, a society modeled on the feudal world of twelfth-century France. A series of episodes in which the wily Renard is outwitted by his intended victims—Chantecler the cock, Tibert the wild cat, Tiécelin the crow—leads to the main theme, the long-standing conflict between Renard and Isengrin the wolf, Noble's constable. Before Noble and the assembled barons Renard is accused of having committed adultery with Isengrin's wife, Dame Hersent. Further accusations are launched by his numerous enemies, and after a judicial debate conducted according to the customary law of the time, Renard accepts trial by ordeal, from which he is saved only by his own alertness and rapidity in flight.

Pierre de St. Cloud's tale was quickly followed by others, called "branches" by their mainly anonymous creators. Gathered together into manuscript collections by the beginning of the thirteenth century, these tales constituted the archetype of the *Roman de Renart.* Despite its name, then, the *Roman de Renart* is not a unified composition relating a number of episodes in a logical, coherent manner, but a collection of independent stories linked essentially by the presence and the personality of Renard. The archetype comprises some eighteen branches, usually designated by the numbers they bear in the edition by Ernest Martin. They were composed in the period from about 1174 to about 1205. In them are represented all the classes of medieval society: the feudal monarchy, surrounded by prelates and its proud, quarrelsome, selfish, and arrogant nobility; the clergy, both monastic and secular; the peasantry, including both the wealthier farmers and the wretched villeins. The hero of the original branches is always Renard, who, like the heroes of the classical epics, early acquires heroic epithets describing his physical and moral attributes: Renard the Red, Renard the plotter of all wickedness.

After Pierre de St. Cloud's initial story of adultery, followed by the rape of Dame Hersent by her erstwhile lover, Renard is guilty of dastardly acts against not only most of Noble's subjects but also the king himself. His principal victim is, however, Isengrin, who, despite his superior force, is no match for his cunning and unscrupulous adversary. In branch III, chronologically the second after Pierre de St. Cloud's, Renard pretends to administer the tonsure, using boiling water, to admit Isengrin into the monastic order of Tiron, then has him fish in a freezing pond, where he is caught by the villagers and loses his tail. In branch IV, Isengrin is trapped at the bottom of a well in a Cistercian abbey, from which he escapes only after a severe beating at the hands of the monks. In branch X, Renard plays the doctor and has Isengrin flayed so that his hide may serve to cure an ailing Noble. But none of the animals is safe from Renard, except his cousin and faithful ally, Grimbert the badger.

In branch I, *The Judgment of Renard,* the most popular of all the branches, Renard is finally summoned by Noble to his court to defend himself against the accusations of his enemies. Despite a spirited defense, he is condemned by his peers to be hanged. Only by promising to make a pilgrimage to the Holy Land to atone for his many crimes does he

RENARD THE FOX

escape; but as soon as he is at a safe distance, he contemptuously casts off his pilgrim's gown and insignia, and ridicules the king. The branch concludes with an epic pursuit of Renard by Noble's vassals, led by the royal standard-bearer, Tardif the snail—a supremely ironic touch. Branches I*a* and I*b* attempt to supply sequels to I, which obviously was felt to be incomplete: in I*a* the fugitive Renard is besieged in his castle; in I*b* he seeks safety by disguising himself as an itinerant minstrel. In branch VI he defends himself against Isengrin in a judicial combat; in VIII he sets off on a pilgrimage to Rome with Bernard the ass and Belin the ram. He confesses with complacency to a long list of heinous crimes and ends up by devouring his confessor in VII; in XI he usurps Noble's throne. In branches XII and XIV Renard participates in noisy, irreverent parodies of religious offices. Finally, in branch XVII, Renard is believed to be dead; he receives a splendid funeral in which all the beasts participate, but at the last moment resuscitates and flees, carrying Chantecler with him.

In these original branches the authors often denied any serious intent, and the comic intent is usually obvious. The comic effect comes primarily from the sustained, gay, mocking parody. Pierre de St. Cloud caricatured the most revered figures of medieval French literature: Noble the lion, solemnly seated amid his great vassals, inevitably evoked the image of King Arthur presiding at the Round Table or of Charlemagne holding court on great feast days. The tale of adultery parodied the illicit loves of Tristan and Isolt, or of Lancelot and Guinevere, while the suspicious and unhappy Isengrin strongly resembles King Mark. The parody in branch II–V*a* reaches a climax in the final scene, an obvious travesty of the epic charge in which Renard is pursued by a horde of ferocious, clamorous dogs, each of which is distinguished by name, led by the baron Roenel with lance leveled for attack.

But Pierre de St. Cloud was also parodying his contemporaries, the society of the end of the twelfth century, its customs and institutions. Noble is above all a feudal monarch, and the other beasts—Isengrin the constable; Brichemer the stag, jurist and seneschal of the realm; Brun the bear; Tibert; Chantecler; Renard himself—represent the feudal aristocracy in its various aspects. When Noble convokes his barons on Ascension Day to aid him in holding his assizes, he is imitating the kings of France, who with increasing frequency from the twelfth century on assembled their court on certain feast days to hear disputes among the great vassals. In the second part of II–V*a*, Pierre de St. Cloud has the animals and barons debate at length the charge brought against Renard according to judicial procedure and principles that would be codified some forty years later in the books of customary law of northern France. Moreover, the institution of the king's court became increasingly popular under Louis VII, during whose reign Pierre de St. Cloud wrote, and certain traits in Noble, as well as certain allusions to personages and events, lead to the conclusion that it was Louis VII who inspired the portrait of Noble. The earliest poem of Renard was not just a parody; it was also a keen and deliberate satire of feudal customs and institutions, of the king of France and his subjects. Even the papal legate was not spared: the model for Monseigneur the Camel of Lombardy was undoubtedly Cardinal Pietro di Pavia, jurist and trusted counselor of Louis VII.

In subsequent branches the satirical intent comes out in the detailed descriptions of medieval life, descriptions that on close examination betray surprising realism rather than simply parody. Rarely is the satirical element completely absent, and the true meaning of the tales becomes clear only when the historical or political or social allusions are seized. No class of society is spared: the faults and errors of the monarch; the brutality, rapacity, and arrogance of the nobility; the worldliness and lack of true devotion, or the ignorance and stupidity, of the secular clergy; the laziness, gluttony, and avarice of the monastic clergy; the ignorance and animality of the peasants—all suscitate the mockery and even the contempt of our poets.

By 1250 ten more branches had completed the *Roman de Renart*. In some Renard no longer appears. In others a clearly moralizing tendency is evident. Gradually Renard ceases to be a joyous scoundrel who exposes the follies and vices of society, and becomes the symbol of ruse, falsity, and hypocrisy. By this time he had become so popular that his name had replaced the Old French generic term for fox (*goupil*), and *renardie* had been coined to convey all the undesirable notions associated with the personage.

After 1250 no new French branches appear. Instead, Renard is the hero of a series of satirical allegorical poems. In 1261 Rutebeuf composed *Renart le Bestourné*, a virulent satire against the mendicant orders, which are accused of leading Louis IX and the kingdom of France to destruction.

RENARD THE FOX

The *Couronnement de Renart,* composed between 1263 and 1270, is a political allegory of the struggle of the counts of Flanders and the old aristocracy against the growing power of the new and wealthy patrician oligarchy, aided by the Franciscans and Dominicans. After a number of amusing adventures of Renard equal in their joyous parody to the original branches, *Renart le Nouvel,* composed about 1288 by Jacquemart Gielée of Lille, becomes a bitterly satirical moral treatise on the decadence of the feudal and chivalric society, and the loss of Christian morality. Finally, in the first half of the fourteenth century appeared *Renart le Contrefait,* a vast and encyclopedic compilation in which tales of Renard are intermingled with long chapters on world history, satirical passages on the politics and morality of the period, information and notions of all sorts. By this time Renard had become a symbol, the personification of evil, of the devil.

Renard's success was not limited to France. Toward the end of the twelfth century, an Alsatian poet, Heinrich der Glîchezaere, reproduced in his *Reinhart Fuchs* the theme of branch I, the *Judgment,* combining with it several of the earlier branches and incorporating episodes of his own invention, some of them borrowed from local history, to form a complete, coherent, logical story. At times parodic, satiric, or simply comic, the poem is essentially grave, even tragic, the work of a jurist and moralist reflecting upon the problem of evil, ruse, and falsity in the world.

About the beginning of the thirteenth century, another telling of the *Judgment* (which Martin incorporated into his edition of the *Roman de Renart* as branch XXVII), *Rainardo e Lesengrino,* written in Franco-Italian, appeared in northern Italy.

Although the fables and parables of some of the leading preachers and writers of sermons, in particular Odo of Cheriton and Nicole Bozon, indicate that the personages and episodes of the *Roman de Renart* must have been well known in England, there are few traces of Renard in medieval English. In the mid thirteenth century a short poem, *Of the Vox and of the Wolf,* retold the story of Renard and Isengrin in the well, with allusions to other branches. The great English contribution to the legend of Renard came at the end of the fourteenth century with Chaucer's Nun's Priest's Tale, probably the best of the *Canterbury Tales.* This is a genial rendering of Pierre de St. Cloud's story of Renard and Chantecler. The fidelity with which certain details and even certain forms of expression are reproduced suggests that Chaucer was following the French version, and the substantial changes, mainly additions increasing the comic effect, can be attributed to the poet's talent and the demands of a later public. Finally, in 1481 William Caxton published *The History of Reynard the Fox,* his translation of a prose version of the original Flemish adaptation of the *Roman de Renart.*

It was in the Flemish and Dutch Low Countries that the cycle of Renard had its greatest and most lasting success. *Van den Vos Reinaerde* was composed in the first half of the thirteenth century. It had remarkable success in the Middle Ages and through it the best of the stories of Renard were passed down in several countries of northern Europe. The poet, or poets, followed the method used by Heinrich der Glîchezaere to produce a complete, unified, coherent story. The first part gives one more version of the *Judgment,* adding details or making alterations to give a distinctly Flemish atmosphere to the tale and heightening the satirical effect. The second part, entirely new, introduces many Flemish elements combined with many borrowings from the French branches. Although the satirical vein predominates, the poem is a joyous parody and avoids the pessimism of *Reinhart Fuchs* and the later French stories. A Latin translation by Baldwinus Juvenis appeared around 1270/1280. A century later another Flemish poet took up the *Van den Vos Reinaerde,* making some important changes and adding a new continuation; but this work, *Reinaerts Histoire,* lacked the unity and coherence, and above all the joyous good humor, of its predecessor, being instead a sustained satire of the church and clergy. From Flanders it passed to Holland, where a prose version with the title *Die Hystorie van Reynaert die Vos* was first published in 1479. The rhymed version of *Reinaerts Historie* was translated into Low German as *Reinke de Vos* and published in 1498. This version was reprinted many times during the next four centuries; in 1752 Gottsched produced a High German version that served as the model for Goethe's famous *Reinecke Fuchs,* composed in 1794. *Reinke de Vos* was also translated into Danish, Swedish, Icelandic, and English, while the Dutch *Reynaert de Vos* went through many printings until the nineteenth century. Contrary to what happened in France, where the medieval branches seem to have dropped almost into oblivion, the tradition of Renard remained very much alive through the centuries in the Low

Countries, where the joyous hero continued to personify ruse, falsity, hypocrisy, and human malice.

BIBLIOGRAPHY

Editions. Dominique Martin Méon, *Le Roman du Renart,* 4 vols. (1826); Ernest Martin, ed., *Le Roman de Renart,* I (1882); Mario Roques, *Le Roman de Renart,* 6 vols. (1948–1963); Jean Dufournet, *Le Roman de Renard* (branches I–V, VIII, X, XV) (1970).

Later allegorical poems. George Raynaud and Henri Lemaître, eds., *Le Roman de Renart le contrefait,* 2 vols. (1914); Alfred Foulet, ed., *Le couronnement de Renart* (1929); Jacob W. Muller, *Van den Vos Reinaerde,* 3rd ed., 2 vols. (1944); Wytze Hellinga, *Van den Vos Reynaerde* (1952); Georg Baesecke, *Das mittelhochdeutsche Gedicht vom Fuchs Reinhart,* 2nd ed. (1952); Rutebeuf, *Renart le bestourné,* in Edmond Faral and Julia Bastin, eds., *Oeuvres complètes de Rutebeuf,* I (1959); Jacquemars Giélee, *Renart le nouvel,* H. Roussel, ed. (1961); William Caxton, *The History of Reynard the Fox,* Norman F. Blake, ed. (1970).

Studies. Robert Bossuat, *Le Roman de Renard* (1957); John Flinn, *Le Roman de Renart dans la littérature française et dans les littératures étrangères au moyen âge* (1963); Lucien Foulet, *Le Roman de Renard* (1914); Hans Robert Jauss, *Untersuchungen zur mittelalterlichen Tierdichtung* (1959).

JOHN F. FLINN

[See also **Beast Epic; Dutch Literature; Fables; French Literature; Rutebeuf; Ysengrimus.**]

RENAUT DE BEAUJEU (*fl.* late twelfth century), also spelled Renaud, is known principally because of his romance *Li biaus descouneus* (also known as *Le bel inconnu* or *Guinglain*), which was written about 1190. Only one manuscript of it survives, Chantilly, Musée Condé, MS 472. In the work the author identifies himself as "Renals de Biauju" and dedicates the romance to a lady for whom, he says, he has already written a *chanson.* Jean Renart's *Guillaume de Dôle* cites the opening stanza of Renaut's song (preserved also in three *chansonniers* [songbooks]: Paris, Bibliothèque Nationale, MS fr. 20050, fol. 19, and MS fr. 846, fol. 78; Bern MS. 389, fol. 124), and attributes it to "the good knight Renaut de Baujieu of Rencien." This and the cryptic rubric *li alens de Challons* in the Bern *chansonnier* are the only biographical clues concerning Renaut's identity, apart from the fragmentary information in his romance.

Li biaus descouneus narrates in 6,266 octosyllabic lines the first quest of the young and unknown knight Guinglain at the court of King Arthur. He frees the blonde Esmerée, queen of Wales, by a bold kiss (*fier baisier*) while she is disguised as a dragon. He is then, however, unable to resolve the conflict between his marriage to the woman he has won (the queen) and his continuing love for the Fair Enchantress (*la Pucelle as blances mains*), who has continually protected him. The author provocatively ends his romance here, promising to restore Guinglain to his true love, the Enchantress, if his own lady will grant him her favor. Otherwise, Guinglain will remain separated from his lady forever. No sequel to *Li biaus descouneus* has so far been found.

The same plot, with slight modifications, is found in the Middle English *Lybeaus Desconus* (which was probably based upon the same French original as Renaut's version), the Italian *Carduino* by Antonio Pucci (fourteenth century), and the German *Wigalois* by Wirnt de Gravenberg (written about 1210).

BIBLIOGRAPHY

The best edition is *Le bel inconnu,* G. Perrie Williams, ed. (1929, repr. 1969). Studies include Françoise Boiron and Jean Charles Payen, "Structure et sens du 'Bel Inconnu' de Renaut de Beaujeu," in *Moyen âge,* 76 (1970); Gaston Paris, "Études sur les romans de la Table Ronde: Guinglain ou le Bel Inconnu," in *Romania,* 15 (1886); William H. Schofield, *Studies on Libeaus Desconus* (1895).

JEANETTE M. A. BEER

[See also **Arthurian Literature.**]

REPOUSSÉ, the ornamentation of metal with relief designs hammered from the back with hammers and punches. Most ancient civilizations used the process, which continued to be popular through the Baroque period in Europe. Examples include Hellenistic and Roman bronze armor, Byzantine silver religious icons, and medieval gold reliquaries.

BIBLIOGRAPHY

David Talbot Rice, *Byzantine Art,* 3rd ed. (1962), and *Art of the Byzantine Era* (1966).

MARY GRIZZARD

[See also **Arms and Armor; Icons, Manufacture of; Metalsmiths, Gold and Silver; Pre-Romanesque Art; Reliquary** (all with illustrations).]

REPRESENTATIVE ASSEMBLIES, ENGLISH. See **Parliament, English.**

REPRESENTATIVE ASSEMBLIES, FRENCH. There were assemblies of almost every conceivable type in medieval France. At the top of the hierarchy there were meetings whose membership was drawn from the clergy, the nobility, and the inhabitants of towns of nearly every part of the kingdom. During the fourteenth century they began to be referred to as assemblies of the three estates, and by the last third of the fifteenth century they were occasionally called Estates General, a term that is used to designate them today. Beneath the Estates General there were central assemblies consisting of representatives from a number of provinces, such as those which comprised Languedoil. Then there were the assemblies of the individual counties, duchies, and provinces; and finally there were meetings of yet smaller jurisdictions. Sometimes only the clergy, the nobility, or the deputies of the towns of the kingdom, a region, a province, or a smaller area assembled. In the Alps and the Pyrenees there were meetings of individual valleys. By the eve of the Wars of Religion, assemblies of the Catholic clergy had become periodic and the Protestants were developing an elaborate system of national and provincial representative institutions.

ORIGINS

Assemblies have often played prominent parts in the governance of villages, towns, and tribes, but the concept of representation had to be invented before they could be effectively employed in large territories. In ancient times the representative principle was almost nonexistent, but it appeared in the Middle Ages in Western and Central Europe. This unique European development was made possible by the emergence of the concept that an individual or group of individuals could legally represent and commit their constituents. This concept, in turn, depended upon a long-standing tradition of a ruler consulting his leading subjects and the organization of society into corporate groups such as towns, cathedral chapters, and estates.

The Franks and other Germanic tribes had frequent assemblies of the free warriors, but when they overran the Roman Empire they became so widely dispersed that these meetings were no longer practical. Under the Merovingian and Carolingian rulers, the warriors gathered in May preparatory to engaging in military campaigns, but their political and judicial functions were assumed by lay and ecclesiastical magnates, who usually met to advise their sovereign during the autumn as well as when the warriors assembled. By the tenth century the Carolingian Empire had disintegrated to the point that the lay magnates, especially, preferred to devote their energies to local interests, and the role of the assemblies declined. As a result, modern historians have generally refused to see more than a most indirect link between these assemblies and the representative institutions that were so prominent during the fourteenth century. Nevertheless, they were of importance because they contributed to the theory, which found some adherents throughout the history of the French monarchy, that ultimate authority rested with the people. "History and tradition tell us," Philippe Pot informed the Estates General in 1484, that "the kings were originally created by the votes of the sovereign people." In 1577 Claude de Beauffremont told Henry III and the deputies to the Estates General that the nobility "placed the crown on the head of the first king." Four years earlier, the Protestant jurist François Hotman had traced the history of the Estates General from the Gauls, through the Franks, and down to his own time, when he believed that the ancient French constitution had fallen into decadence. Spokesmen for the provincial estates of Auvergne, Burgundy, and Rouergue asserted equal antiquity for their assemblies; and the three estates of Navarre, though claiming less ancient origins, informed Louis XIV in 1672 that their first king "was the creation and creature of his subjects."

The decline of the Carolingian Empire led to the rise of feudalism with its system of relationships that provided a firmer basis for the development of institutionalized assemblies than had previously existed. A lord had the right to require his vassals to give him aid and counsel. To avail himself of these services, he had to summon them to meetings. Soon many vassals began to see that there were advantages in attending and claimed that it was their right to be summoned. Thus the Capetian kings often held meetings consisting of their leading nobles and prelates, but the mass of the population did not participate. In a similar fashion the dukes and counts began to summon their vassals. This practice was eventually to give rise to many, but by no means all, of the provincial and local estates. Once more, however, only the elite of society was included.

From about the beginning of the thirteenth century, the growth of towns, the increased activity of cathedral chapters, the development of far-flung monastic orders, and eventually the emergence of a sense of community among the inhabitants of some rural areas made it desirable to find means whereby groups of individuals, whether burghers, canons, monks, or peasants, could, as corporations, defend the rights of the corporate body and be represented at court in judicial, military, fiscal, and other matters. This need to invent the representative principle was met by the revival of Roman and canon law with their use of the power of attorney, through which a person could appoint someone to act for him in a court of law. It was but a single step for the new corporate groups, which were beginning to be treated as individuals, to assume the same right. Thus, chapters, towns, and other groups began to appoint proctors with varying degrees of authority to act in their name. These proctors were given formal or informal instructions as to what they should seek from the convoking authority and what concessions they could make. Unless they violated their instructions, their actions were theoretically binding on their constituents. Occasionally the convoking authority sought to have the proctors given full or unlimited powers, but corporate groups in France resisted such demands, and proctors frequently refused to act on a given matter, on the grounds that they did not have full powers or that to do so would violate their instructions.

The concept that society was divided into three estates and that this situation should be reflected in the organization of representative assemblies developed slowly. As early as 1025–1030, when feudalism was tightening its grip on France, Bishop Gerard I of Cambrai and Bishop Adalbero of Laon made separate statements dividing French society into three groups. The function of the first group was to worship; of the second, to fight; and of the third, to labor. At the time the bishops wrote, this tripartite division reflected, to a reasonable degree, the actual social situation, and it gradually became accepted. From it emerged the belief that there were three estates: the clergy, the nobility, and the third estate. With the growth of towns and the rise of lay education during the twelfth and thirteenth centuries, the third estate especially became a large, confused conglomerate consisting of such diverse groups as lawyers, merchants, artisans, and peasants. Nevertheless, the concept that society was composed of three estates persisted until the Revolution and ultimately led many of the representative assemblies that emerged to be divided into three houses, although during the Middle Ages the three estates frequently deliberated together at both the national and the provincial level.

THE ESTATES GENERAL AND THE CENTRAL ASSEMBLIES

The assemblies that met at Paris in 1302 and at Tours in 1308 have traditionally been regarded as the earliest meetings of the Estates General, but there were at least five other kinds of national assemblies during the late thirteenth and early fourteenth centuries. Some were ceremonial or military in nature; others were enlarged meetings of the king's council or separate assemblies of the clergy, nobility, or towns. These meetings were sometimes concerned with taxation, a role that even the Parlement of Paris seemed on the verge of assuming at one point. With such a wide variety of assemblies, the occasions requiring the presence of all the more important elements in society were limited. In 1302 it was Philip IV's quarrel with Boniface VIII, and in 1308 his condemnation of the Templars, that led to their summons. In the two centuries that followed, national assemblies dealt with many other political and governmental matters. The judicial, financial, and military organizations especially claimed their attention, and there were times when the deputies considered such matters as coinage, commerce, the domain, and the composition of the king's council. Usually only a brief *ordonnance* on a limited subject resulted from their deliberations, but occasionally long, comprehensive enactments emerged, such as the one of 1413 consisting of 258 articles on a wide variety of subjects.

However, the need for the crown to convoke the three estates to deal with the above matters was infrequent. So long as this was true, the estates could not become a permanent part of the institutional structure of the kingdom. They had to have at least one important function that required periodic meetings. The most likely prospect was to establish the right to vote, and perhaps to collect taxes. This became a viable possibility only when the Hundred Years War put such great demands on the royal treasury that adequate revenue could not be obtained from more traditional sources.

By the late thirteenth century the French kings

could no longer support themselves from their domain even in time of peace. To supplement their income the last Capetian and early Valois monarchs extracted money from the clergy, sought to extend the feudal aids beyond their immediate vassals to their other subjects, assessed forced loans that often were not repaid, and milked the Jews of all they could. It must have come almost as a relief when they were at war and could declare that an urgent necessity existed, a situation that, in accordance with Romano-canonical principle, justified levying a war subsidy. In some periods, as between 1315 and 1321, they used large central assemblies of various types to persuade their subjects that a levy was justified, but consent to actual taxes was neither given nor in all probability requested. To obtain the money it was necessary to go to individual magnates, towns, and local assemblies because the right of a national assembly to tax was no more accepted by provincially minded Frenchmen than was the right of the king to do so. If his need was obviously great, the king could simply summon the *arrière ban,* in which he sought to include all his subjects on the grounds that there was a universal obligation to military service, and to fine those who did not enter the army. There was little talk of the right of subjects to consent to taxes, and when they attended large assemblies, it was in theory to give their counsel and in practice to strengthen the king's hand in his local negotiations by endorsing his requests. Even with these preparations, resistance to tax collectors was strong. The king rarely extracted all he wanted from a locality, and in 1314 there was well-organized and dangerous opposition in many provinces.

Philip V made elaborate preparations for an assembly in 1321, but he was unable to extract even an admission from the secular estates that the reforms he proposed were worthy of financial support. Disgusted, he and his successors reverted to reliance on feudal obligations and various ad hoc measures; large assemblies were abandoned.

The opening of the Hundred Years War in 1337 made it imperative that the crown find an adequate source of revenue. In 1343 and again in 1345–1346, Philip VI reverted to large assemblies that had modest results because of the opposition of the people. The defeat at Crécy in 1346 awakened most Frenchmen to the seriousness of the situation. The Estates General that met near the close of the following year agreed to a substantial levy on the condition that assemblies of the individual bailiwicks determined the nature of their respective taxes and elected the tax collectors, who became known as *élus*. Nobles and clergymen were to pay as well as the members of the third estate. It seemed for a moment that a national representative assembly would become the tax-consenting institution, and that everyone would bear a share of the costs of government. Unfortunately the Black Death struck before the tax could be collected, and it carried to the grave not only a large percentage of the taxpayers but also many of the tax collectors. As a result, the anticipated revenue was not realized and the disorganized government once more reverted to negotiating with local assemblies when consent to taxation was needed. In the few instances when a large assembly was required, the crown usually convoked the three estates of Languedoc and of Languedoil. This division of the Estates General into two parts dates back to 1345–1346 and was caused by the wide cultural, historic, and linguistic differences between the two regions, as well as by the vast size of the kingdom and the dangers the deputies encountered on their travels to attend.

Meanwhile, resistance to taxation continued, but King John II's defeat and capture at the Battle of Poitiers in September 1356 caused the situation to change abruptly. The events of the four years that followed had a profound effect on both the estates and taxation. In the absence of the king, his teenage son Charles assumed the direction of the state. Meetings of the three estates of Languedoil and Languedoc became frequent, and there was at least a chance that they would become a permanent part of the institutional structure.

In October 1356 Charles won an agreement from the three estates of Languedoil that met at Paris that they would support an army of 30,000 men, but in return they insisted that he dismiss some of his leading advisers and appoint a council consisting of members of the estates. After some hesitation, Charles refused and disbanded the assembly; but when an effort to obtain money from the local estates failed, he was compelled to order the estates of Languedoil to meet in February 1357. This time the bourgeois-dominated estates voted a tax, which fell most heavily on the nobility, to support the army, and insisted that the tax be collected by *élus* whom they appointed. The *élus* in turn were to be directed by officials at Paris whom they also named. Charles acquiesced, but again the local estates would not contribute. Other meetings of the estates of Languedoil followed, but the refusal of the provinces to pay the taxes they voted caused Charles to despair. Since concessions to the radicals brought no reward, Charles broke with their leader, Étienne Marcel, the colorful provost of the merchants of Paris. In retaliation Marcel aroused the Paris mob and attacked the royal palace on 22 February 1358. Two prominent noblemen in Charles's entourage were slaughtered before his eyes. Now permanently alienated, Charles left Paris, won support in several meetings of the local estates, and directed the three estates of Languedoil to meet at Compiègne in May. This time the nobles attended in sufficient numbers to take the leadership of the estates away from the bourgeoisie and voted a 5 percent tax on their income to pay their share of the costs of raising an army. Before Charles had to employ force against the Parisians, however, Marcel's opponents in that city murdered him and some of his followers. On 2 August, two days after this event, Charles reentered his capital.

A rare opportunity for the estates to become a part of the institutional structure of the kingdom had been lost. Henceforth, Charles and his advisers sought to avoid convoking assemblies, both large and small, and to collect what taxes they needed without consent. Not only had the estates of Languedoil challenged the authority of the crown, but their consent to taxation had proved of little value because the local estates had refused to accept their verdict and had given only what they pleased. Charles did find it advisable to assemble the Estates General in Paris in May–June 1359 to reject a disadvantageous treaty that his captive father had negotiated with England and to turn to central assemblies on several other occasions, but their role henceforth was to serve as an occasional vehicle for royal propaganda.

It was, of course, one thing for the crown to regard the estates as potentially dangerous and often useless instruments, and another to collect the needed funds to support the government. The Treaty of Brétigny (1360), which marked a disastrous defeat for France, actually furthered the cause of the monarchy in this respect. Included was a provision that 3 million *écus* be paid the English in return for King John's release. Since the obligation to pay a lord's ransom was a clearly established feudal aid, John's vassals contributed with unprecedented willingness. His other subjects, however, had in the past resisted efforts to transfer the burden of feudal aids to them, but in this instance, according to the historian John Henneman, "the feudal obligations of royal vassals and the Romano-canonical principle that taxes for the common profit were justified in time of evident necessity" joined to involve all Frenchmen in a joint fiscal endeavor. For a number of years a tax would be necessary to pay the large sum involved, and this tax would be levied in time of peace, in itself something of an innovation because the French had usually been reluctant to admit that necessity could exist without war. Furthermore, consent was not theoretically required for taxes involving feudal aids or evident necessity. In some instances it might be advisable to hold a consultative central assembly for propaganda purposes or to initiate local negotiations, but the acceptance of the tax was so general that even these limitations to the crown's ability to levy the tax were rarely applicable.

Therefore, shortly after his release John unilaterally imposed the gabelle, a tax on the sale of salt, and the *aides,* a tax on the sale of wine and other products. The *élus,* who had formerly been temporary elected officials, now became royal officials who arranged for the farming of these taxes and apportioned direct taxes when they were instituted at a later date (in 1393). The jurisdiction over which they presided became known as the *élection.* There was no more need for the provincial and local estates to consent to these taxes than there was for the Estates General to do so. Local disorders and other problems did lead to some meetings, but they became less frequent even in the lands of the great magnates and in Languedoc, where the estates had cooperated more fully with the crown. Charles became king in 1364, as Charles V, and in 1369 he renewed the war with England. Payments on John's ransom ceased, but military requirements took their place and Charles continued to enjoy a comfortable income until he died. Indeed, as death approached, his conscience began to trouble him, and in September 1380 he revoked the direct tax, an act that especially benefited the nobility and peasants. Demands from the towns that the sales taxes also be suppressed became so strong that the advisers of his successor, the youthful Charles VI, felt compelled to acquiesce. The result was a brief revival of the central and local assemblies in 1380 and 1381.

In 1382 the crown reimposed the sales taxes without consent and quickly suppressed the insurrections that followed. From then until 1418 the sales tax remained the basic source of royal income. It was not sufficient, however, to meet all the requirements of the court, and in most years a new direct tax known as the taille was imposed. During this period there was a little-known assembly in 1411 that might be classified as being an Estates General, and a meeting of the three estates of Languedoil two years later. At first the estates of Languedoc fared better, but after 1393 they went into eclipse. Meetings of the estates in the great feudal duchies became less frequent. Only in Dauphiné, which was still a nominal part of the Holy Roman Empire, did the estates play a vital part in the government.

Perhaps the most surprising aspect of the history of the medieval estates is that they displayed no sign of revival during the reign of Charles VI, who was at first a minor and then, from 1392, insane. Not even the necessity to defend the kingdom against the English could be convincingly demonstrated to justify taxes until late in his reign. Yet, in spite of a mad king and the lack of any compelling reason for relatively heavy taxation, levies were annually made without consent on a larger portion of France than at any other time in its history. Indeed, it was not until well into the seventeenth century that the crown again exercised such unilateral tax powers. Royalist theorists openly proclaimed that the king could tax without consent, and the deputies who attended the estates of Languedoil in 1413 made no counterclaims despite their demand for administrative reforms and the appointment of honest officials. The Treaty of Troyes (1420), in which Charles VI recognized Henry V of England as his heir, was to be ratified by the three estates. It contained articles in which Henry swore to respect privileges of his new French subjects and to seek the "advice and consent" of the estates of both kingdoms in order to prevent future discord between the two realms; but when it came to taxation, he only engaged himself not "to impose any impositions or exactions on our [Charles's] subjects without reasonable and necessary cause, nor otherwise than for the public good of the said kingdom of France."

Only circumstantial evidence can be offered to explain why there was no widespread demand for a revival of the estates, but this evidence is most persuasive. In the reign of Charles V magnates had often been permitted to take about a third of the royal taxes collected in their lands, but under Charles VI they frequently took it all. Towns were sometimes given permission to retain part of the taxes collected within their walls. It has been estimated that a third or more of the total royal tax fell into other hands. With the magnates' own financial position depending heavily on the king's capacity to tax, it is little wonder that they did not present a united front against such exactions. Since they had large clienteles both within and without the royal government who profited from their largess, the forces favoring heavy taxes were almost irresistible.

There were, of course, some influential persons who did not profit directly or indirectly from taxation, but their silence was purchased by the growing practice of exempting them from taxation. During the fourteenth century it had seemed likely that the French would develop a system of taxation in which the priest, noble, burgher, and peasant each bore his fair share of the burden; but under the weak Charles VI especially, nobles, clergymen, royal officials, university faculties, and some towns won exemption from most taxes. With some of the most powerful persons in the kingdom profiting from taxes and others escaping paying their share, it is not surprising that there was no strong opposition to Charles VI's fiscal policies or a concerted demand that the estates give consent to the levies that were made. It was Charles's very weakness in dealing with the powerful forces in his kingdom that enabled him to exercise "absolutist" tax powers even though the crown had sunk to its lowest depths in centuries.

It is impossible to say how long this system of government would have lasted if the members of the royal family had continued to agree on the division of the spoils, for so long as the Valois princes were united, it was difficult for the opposition to be heard. Bitter rivalries began to develop, however, when Charles V and his brothers were replaced by their children. In 1407 John the Fearless, duke of Burgundy, had his first cousin, Louis, duke of Orléans, murdered. The count of Armagnac assumed the leadership of the Orleanists, and a bloody feud ensued in which John sought public support by posing as a reformer. In 1418 he seized Paris and "rescued" the mad Charles from the Armagnacs, but the following year he was treacherously murdered in circumstances that gravely implicated the dauphin Charles. Philip the Good, John's successor, felt compelled to avenge his father and made an alliance with Henry V of England, who had intervened in France several years before. Henry married Charles VI's daughter and was recognized by that mad king as his heir. France became divided into at least four parts. By the terms of the Treaty of Troyes (1420) the English were to govern Guyenne and Normandy with only token acknowledgment of the suzerainty of the Paris government; Philip of Burgundy was given a similar privilege in his hereditary lands. What remained of the territory under their control was to be administered by officials in Paris, who were for the most part Burgundian appointees. The excluded dauphin was recognized as the king's lieutenant and then, upon his father's death in 1422, when he ascended the throne as Charles VII, as king in most of the lands south of the Loire River. To win support, the rivals either taxed lightly or once more turned to the assemblies of the estates.

The dauphin Charles, who was widely believed to be illegitimate, was in an especially difficult position. In 1418 he sought financial assistance from a regional assembly at Limoges, and in 1419 and 1420 he turned to the provincial and local estates for funds. In 1421 he again altered his tactics and summoned the Estates General to meet at Clermont in Auvergne. By this act he inaugurated a fifteen-year experiment in which there were meetings of the Estates General or the estates of Languedoil on an average of about once a year. In these meetings he nearly always asked for financial assistance, but was generally voted less than he requested. The proportion of this sum to be paid by each jurisdiction in the area that had participated in the meeting was then established. The final step was to collect the promised money, and it is here that no pattern can be established for those provinces that acknowledged Charles.

Dauphiné was still part of the Holy Roman Empire. Its inhabitants did not participate in the French assemblies, and any contribution they made to Charles was voted by their own estates. The powerful counts of Foix and Armagnac kept their lands outside the sphere of royal administration. Languedoc and Rouergue attended meetings of the Estates General with reluctance when they went at all. Their presence in such assemblies did not constitute acceptance of their share of the tax. Rather, they insisted on having meetings of their own estates after these sessions, in which they generally appropriated less than their assigned share. Auvergne and other provinces in central France deputed to the Estates General more willingly, but they were equally determined to pay only the taxes they approved in their own assemblies and had no compunction in reducing the amount requested. In these areas the Estates General and the estates of Languedoil at best served as forums in which Charles and his advisers could explain their financial requirements. Once those who attended agreed that the king needed a certain amount, it was possible to put moral pressure on the provincial and local estates to vote at least a large portion of their share.

In Touraine, Poitou, Saintonge, and some other provinces where royal authority was more fully established and local loyalties were less strong, the consent of a central assembly usually sufficed to collect a tax. Even here, however, the provincial estates had to be revived to give their adherence to levies that had not been agreed to by a larger meeting.

In 1436 Charles held his last central assembly for essentially financial purposes. In that year the three estates of Languedoil met at Poitiers, voted a taille of 200,000 livres, and revived the *aides* for three years; after that period had elapsed, Charles continued to collect the *aides* in Languedoil without obtaining the consent of any type of assembly, on the pretext that they had been granted in perpetuity. In 1437 he began to determine the amount of the taille in Languedoil without consulting the central assembly, but where it was customary, he continued to summon the local estates to vote their share.

Charles held a meeting of the Estates General in 1439 to advise on whether he should make peace, but used those who attended to vote a taille of 100,000 livres in addition to a levy of 300,000 livres he had imposed on his own authority earlier in the year. Thereafter, he does not appear to have held any central assemblies of the three estates during his reign, but he continued to convoke meetings of a single order, such as the clergy, and to hold consultative assemblies that were devoid of representative elements.

Charles's abandonment of the Estates General and the central assemblies did not mean that henceforth he levied the taille at will, for the provincial and local estates continued to meet in those parts of France where they had been summoned to approve their share of the taxes voted in higher assemblies. What the new policy meant was that instead of these assemblies haggling over whether they should contribute their full share of a tax set in the Estates General or a central assembly, they now haggled over whether they should pay their share of a tax set by the king and council alone. For this reason, and because many of the provincial estates had objected to participating in the Estates General, they raised little or no protest when these meetings were discontinued. Even in those provinces where the consent of the Estates General removed the need to obtain that of the estates, there was no outcry.

It is not difficult to explain why Charles embarked on this new course. He had revived the central assemblies during the desperate days of his youth because he needed their assistance to tax. They had proved to be useful as propaganda devices to prepare the way for asking the strong provincial estates to consent to an imposition, and in some provinces they had relieved him of the need to seek consent at all. By 1436, however, Charles's prestige had grown considerably. He had made peace with the Burgundians and had regained Paris, his capital. Hence, the Estates General and the central assemblies were no longer necessary. He could persuade the strong provincial estates to vote taxes without consulting them, and he could tax the provinces where the local estates were weak without actually obtaining their permission. Henceforth meetings of the estates in the Île-de-France, Champagne, and most of the Loire Valley were exceptional.

By the early 1440's Charles felt that he was in a position to launch an attack on the best-established provincial estates. In 1443 he told the three estates of Languedoc that he had had enough of such assemblies after they had refused to vote him all that he had asked; but a few generous, well-placed bribes were enough for the estates to win friends at court who persuaded the vacillating king to relent. As the war drew to a close and the reconquest of Normandy and Guyenne brought additional revenues, Charles was in a position to cut the taille in central France by about 30 percent. At the same time, he created *élus* in Limousin and La Marche, and ordered these officials, and those of Auvergne, where they already existed, to collect the tax without convoking the estates. Once more there was little protest; the inhabitants were more impressed by the reduction in the tax than the absence of the estates. Actually, feudal lords in this region continued to make use of assemblies, and the estates occasionally met to deal with local matters.

The English had revived the estates of Normandy after the Treaty of Troyes and had made considerable use of those in Guyenne. It was Charles's intention to continue this practice after the reconquest, but when the estates of Normandy refused to give him all he requested in 1450–1451, he took advantage of the presence of *élus* and ordered them to collect taxes without convoking the estates. For some reason he reversed himself in 1458 and specifically promised not to levy taxes without the consent of the three estates. When Charles reconquered the duchy of Guyenne in 1451, his initial intention was not to tax without consent, but after the inhabitants of Bordelais had invited the English to return the following year, he revoked the privileges that he had granted and levied the *aides* on his own authority. The taille, on the other hand, was probably accorded and collected by the estates in most of the region.

It is apparent that Charles VII, unlike Charles V, did not establish a relatively uniform tax administration after defeating the English, although his victory was more complete. Part of the reason for his failure to do so must be attributed to weakness of character. It was easy to rid himself of the Estates General and the estates of Languedoil because there was little demand for them, but where the provincial estates had responded strongly to his occasional efforts to curtail their activities, he had surrendered to their desires.

Louis XI was more original and dynamic than his father, but he lacked the intellectual stability and the consistency to alter the institutional structure of the state. At the beginning of his reign he offered to permit the provincial estates to choose any tax they desired to replace the *aides* and taille, and to appoint the tax collectors. The Court of Aids and the *élus* were abolished, but he soon revoked these administrative innovations that would have seriously weakened the monarchy. He made few other changes in tax matters except to increase the taille, which fell largely on the countryside, from 1.2 million livres in 1469 to 4.6 million livres in 1481 and to remove from the towns part of their tax burden.

Louis loved to consult, and his reign was characterized by numerous assemblies of the nobles, prelates, and above all the deputies of the towns. Such meetings gave him an opportunity to obtain information from his leading subjects and, more important from his point of view, to air his own ideas. Only once did he summon the three estates of his kingdom to a meeting. The occasion was his desire to win public support for taking the duchy of Normandy from his estranged brother and providing him with the less wealthy and less exposed duchy of Guyenne instead. During the meeting, which took place at Tours in April 1468, Louis skillfully maneuvered the deputies to recommend the measures he desired, and they departed without taking any action that could have offended him.

Louis's arbitrary acts, his lack of respect for tradition and privilege, and above all his exorbitant taxes led to a strong reaction following his death. As his son, Charles VIII, was barely thirteen years of age, a struggle ensued to determine who should control the government and have custody of the young king. Louis had intended that his daughter, Anne de Beaujeu, and her husband, Pierre, should have these responsibilities; but the duke of Orléans, as Charles's nearest male relative, claimed a dominant role in the government. A number of great nobles also sought important roles, and a collegiate system of government was soon established. The Beaujeus, finding themselves thrust into the background, turned to the Estates General in the hope that the deputies would restore them to power. Their spokesman in the estates, Philippe Pot, made a brilliant speech before the estates that assembled at Tours in January–March 1484 in which he claimed that since kings "were originally created by the votes of the sovereign people," it was the duty of the estates to appoint the council during a minority. The magnates' influence in the estates was so strong, however, that the deputies would do no more than endorse the members of the existing council and urge that twelve of their number be added. Since the king and council were to choose the deputies who were to serve, the attempt of the Beaujeus to use the Estates General failed.

Louis's excessive taxation came under vigorous attack, and after considerable debate the taille was set at 1.2 million livres annually for the next two years, after which the Estates General was to meet again. In addition, Charles was voted 300,000 livres to defray his coronation expenses. At this point the unity within the estates collapsed. Each province began to try to reduce the proportion that it was to pay, although the total was only about a third of what Louis XI had levied. Once the sum assigned to a province with strong estates had been agreed upon, it was necessary to convene those estates and get their consent. It took three sessions before the estates of Burgundy agreed to pay 30,000 livres of the 45,000 livres assigned them. The estates in other provinces were equally insistent on their right to consent but fortunately more willing to contribute their share of the levy.

The Estates General was to meet again in 1486, but it was not convoked. By then the Beaujeus had obtained control of the government. Since they had been unsuccessful in their effort to use the estates in 1484, they saw no reason to risk another meeting, especially at a time when other magnates were certain to try to turn the deputies against them. Their position was especially vulnerable because they had failed to keep the taille at the 1.2 million livres set by the Estates General, although their efficiency and frugality enabled them to come close to this goal. Also, the fact that it had been necessary to get the consent of the provincial estates after the Estates General had set the size of the tax prevented the latter from becoming an effective instrument. Hence, in 1486 and thereafter, the Beaujeus sought the consent of the estates in the provinces in which they were active and imposed taxes on the remaining provinces on the authority of king and council.

The Estates General of 1484 was the first in which the bailiwicks and seneschalsies were invited to elect deputies, a procedure not utilized again until 1560. In 1506 and again in 1558 the crown reverted to the medieval practice of summoning the nobility and clergy individually, and asking the towns to send deputies. Attendance at the two meetings was less than at most of the medieval assemblies, but contemporaries nevertheless referred to them as estates. The consultative traditions of the monarchy did not die. Charles VIII, Louis XII, and Francis I during the early part of his reign held a bewildering variety of assemblies of the clergy, the nobility, the towns, and of financial and judicial officers. The actual composition of each assembly was determined by the purpose it was to serve, and therefore varied from meeting to meeting. Hence these assemblies never became institutionalized, and when the Middle Ages drew to a close, there was no national representative assembly in France.

Much has been written to explain why the Estates General did not succeed in playing a role comparable with that of the English Parliament, but of all the factors that have been suggested, the most important was the strength of provincialism in France. England was united by the Norman Conquest, and a sense of the community of the realm developed that led people to look to their central institutions, including Parliament. Provincial assemblies were never of more than minor significance and soon vanished altogether. France, on the other hand, was a much larger country with at least two distinct languages and cultures, those of Languedoc and Languedoil, to say nothing of many dialects and local differences in each of these regions. It was united for the most part because of the extinction of the great feudal families. When a province escheated or was inherited by the king, it was customary for him to recognize the rights and privileges of his new subjects and to govern them through existing institutions. Hence, the unity that was achieved was essentially in the person of the king. Probably the best opportunity for the Estates General to become firmly established occurred during the early stages of the Hundred Years War, when it became necessary to establish a permanent system of taxation. At that time local loyalties centered on the duke or count. Provincial institutions, including the estates, were at least as rudimentary as, and in most instances more rudimentary than, those of the crown. It was perhaps possible at this time to impose an Estates General over the local assemblies; but the Black Death caused the tax efforts of the Estates General of 1347 to fail, and the radicalism of the estates of Languedoil in the 1350's alienated the crown and a large segment of the nobility. As a result Charles V and Charles VI did their best to stamp out assemblies. Charles VII had a chance to make the estates of Languedoil functional, for the provincial estates in that vast region had been suffocated during the two previous reigns and were essentially as new as the central assembly; but, albeit reluctantly, he eventually opted for a decentralized system of government with provincial sovereign courts as well as provincial estates. These institutions, in turn, fostered the strong provincial loyalties that characterized late medieval and early modern France.

THE PROVINCIAL AND LOCAL ESTATES

It was at the provincial and local levels that Frenchmen realized their aspirations for self-government. The composition and procedures of the provincial estates fluctuated widely during the Middle Ages, and it was only as that period ended that even the more precocious of them began to assume a stable form.

Representative institutions first appeared in France in the south, but it was not until Philip VI decided to hold separate meetings of the three estates of the northern and southern provinces during the winter of 1345–1346 that the estates of Languedoc were born. At first seven seneschalsies were included, but by the terms of the Treaty of Brétigny France lost part of these lands and the boundaries of Languedoc were restricted to the three large seneschalsies of Toulouse, Carcassonne, and Beaucaire (later Nîmes). Between then and 1393 the crown shifted back and forth between convoking this or that estate, the three estates, and the three seneschalsies individually. In the quarter of a century that followed, all types of assemblies went into an eclipse and taxes were collected by royal officials without consent. Charles VII revived the estates of Languedoc. Gradually the estates of the seneschalsies were subordinated to those of the province and ultimately ceased to meet except on rare occasions. The three estates not only consented to taxes, but also apportioned them among the dioceses. Diocesan assemblies then divided the taxes among the towns and communities. Royal officials were almost entirely excluded from the process. Membership in the provincial estates fluctuated, but by the close of the fifteenth century it was becoming customary to permit only the twenty-two archbishops and bishops to attend for the clergy. Participation by the nobility became restricted to twenty-two barons; and by the third estate, with the inevitable exceptions, to delegations from the episcopal cities and the towns whose turn it was to stand for the other localities in their respective dioceses. Thus, the third estate came to have forty-four votes to the twenty-two each for the other estates, a not insignificant detail since the three estates normally deliberated together and voted by head. The deputies took oaths to keep their deliberations secret, and in 1559 they adopted the secret ballot to replace a show of hands. In 1523 Francis I granted the deputies immunity from arrest while the estates were in session, and in 1555 Henry II forbade the parlement of Toulouse to interfere in deputies' affairs.

The assembly of the estates of Normandy, like that of Languedoc, was largely a royal creation. In later epochs the provincial leaders looked to the charter their ancestors had obtained in 1315 as the bulwark of their liberties, but in fact the king had only promised not to tax except in cases of "evident utility or urgent necessity." Charles V and Charles VI had suppressed the estates, but they were revived during the period of English domination. Soon after the reconquest of the province, Charles VII reverted to the practice of taxing without consent, but in 1458 he reversed his position and promised to levy only those taxes which had been voted by the three estates.

During the fourteenth century, nobles, prelates, and deputies from the chapters and towns had been summoned, but by the early sixteenth century a system of indirect suffrage had developed. The seven prelates and six nobles who continued to receive personal summonses rarely attended. Instead, bailiwick assemblies were held to elect the deputies of the clergy and the nobility, and viscounty assemblies chose those of the third estate. In the provincial estates the deputies sat in a single chamber and voted by bailiwick rather than by order.

The estates of Dauphiné, Burgundy, Provence, and Brittany were primarily the creations of their feudal lords. Dauphiné passed into the hands of the royal family in 1349, but because of its special status, which included being a fief held from the emperor, its estates were not snuffed out by Charles V and Charles VI. The estates in the other three provinces also fared better than those of Languedoc and Normandy because they were not directly under the crown. Their composition and procedures were similar in many respects. In general, abbots, priors, and deputies from the chapters joined with the prelates in standing for the clergy. Nobles with fiefs made up the second estate. Attendance by the third estate was more varied. In 1488, 115 towns and communities were directed to send deputies to the estates of Dauphiné. Brittany and Burgundy were less generous. Only the towns sent deputies, but there was some representation from the adjacent counties in the latter. In Provence the third estate was composed primarily of the deputies of the *vigueries* and bailiwicks. Since the deputies usually voted by head rather than by order during the Middle Ages, the nobles were in a position to dominate the proceedings if they bothered to attend in large numbers.

The estates in these provinces often had difficulty in imposing their authority on the lesser jurisdictions in their midst. The Burgundian dukes and their estates succeeded in incorporating Auxerre, Bar-sur-Seine, Autun, and some other localities, and the estates in these small localities were allowed to die; Auxonne and Charolois managed to retain their estates long after the close of the Middle Ages, however, and Mâconnais successfully resisted the imperialistic designs of the Burgundian estates until the Revolution. Dauphiné had trouble incorporating enclaves within its boundaries, and it was not until 1558 that Gap was brought within the tax structure. In its Alpine valleys, village assemblies known as *escartons* functioned until the Revolution. Provence was never able to subject the towns of Marseilles and Arles to the taxes granted by the estates, and eventually deprived the deputies from these towns of the right to vote.

The estates of Guyenne had the greatest difficulty in imposing their authority over the subordinate jurisdictions. During much of the Hundred Years War the English and the French controlled substantial portions of the region, making meetings of the estates of the entire duchy impossible. As a result, the estates of the ten seneschalsies and financial jurisdictions called *recettes* were able to establish their autonomy. Even when meetings of the estates of Guyenne became frequent, during the latter half of the sixteenth century, this situation was not altered and consent to taxes was given at the local level. At first all three estates were active in these local assemblies, but by the close of the Middle Ages the clergy and nobility had ceased to attend the assemblies in Bordelais, Condomois, Agenais, Rivière-Verdun, and Lannes except on rare occasions, and the right to convoke these meetings had often fallen into the hands of the officials of the principal town.

There were a number of provinces in the Pyrenees that had assemblies. Of these Béarn, Navarre, Bigorre, Nébouzan, and Soule became possessions of the house of Foix-Navarre. This family governed the first two as independent states until the seventeenth century, but held the latter three as fiefs of the French crown. Two of the five, Béarn and Soule, developed two-house legislatures consisting of the nobility and clergy in an upper house, and the deputies of the towns and valleys in the lower house. Deputies elected by valleys also participated in the estates of Bigorre and Navarre. Two other provinces, Quatre-Vallées and Labourd, had come into the hands of the crown by the close of the Middle Ages. The early history of their estates is blocked from view by lack of documentation, but when their composition can be determined, only members of the third estate participated. The county of Boulogne and the Burgundian provinces in the north that passed to the Habsburgs with the death of Charles the Bold in 1477 also had estates.

At the close of the Middle Ages the estates treated thus far, with the exception of the seneschalsies of Bordeaux and Périgord, consented to direct taxes and sometimes to indirect taxes. In all, they comprised slightly over half of France. With the exception of Normandy and several sections of Burgundy, officials of the estates apportioned and collected the direct taxes they voted.

The estates also played important roles in some

other parts of France. In Bordelais, Périgord, Haute- and Basse-Auvergne, Forez, the *plat pays* of Lyonnais, and perhaps to a lesser extent in Beaujolais, the estates met frequently, had officials, voted taxes for their own purposes, and protested against royal exactions. By 1500 the first two estates had ceased to participate regularly except in Périgord and Forez, but the towns in the other provinces were active. The municipal officials of Bordeaux claimed the right to convoke the lesser towns in Bordelais; those of Clermont, the thirteen good towns of Basse-Auvergne; those of St. Flour, the towns or provostship of Haute-Auvergne; and as a minimum the officials of Villefranche-sur-Saône cast a protecting arm over the lesser communities in Beaujolais. The right of the municipal officials of a capital town to convoke the third estate was a powerful weapon that enabled local leaders to respond to any threat. Those of Clermont, especially, made full use of this privilege; and it is probable that the good towns of Basse-Auvergne met more often during the sixteenth century than any other representative assembly in France.

There was little chance that assemblies of the three estates would develop in the seneschalsy of Lyonnais because of a bitter quarrel between the clergy and the burghers of Lyons over their respective rights and privileges. Furthermore, the affluent church owned so many fiefs in the countryside that the nobility was weaker than in most parts of France. For a time it had looked as though Lyons and lesser communities might develop an assembly, but in 1427 the members of the town council decided to elect a separate deputation to the central assembly that was to meet at Poitiers because they thought they were more apt to obtain a tax reduction if they acted alone. Deserted by their natural leader, the *plat pays* apparently continued to meet. At some point between 1481 and 1525 the inhabitants became formally organized as a corporation with duly empowered syndics to act in its name. At first all the parishes sent deputies to attend the meetings, but by 1568 a system of indirect suffrage had been introduced. There was also a representative institution in Franc-Lyonnais.

There were also jurisdictions in which the estates assembled occasionally after the Hundred Years War but never became a part of the institutional structure. The estates of Bourbonnais apparently met under the auspices of the Bourbon dukes until near the end of the fifteenth century. Those of Poitou were still active in the 1460's, and met frequently between 1549 and 1553 in conjunction with the estates of Saintonge, Angoumois, Haut- and Bas-Limousin, Haute- and Basse-Marche, and La Rochelle to deal with the gabelle. The estates in these and other jurisdictions assembled occasionally until 1651 to ratify treaties, codify customs, and above all elect deputies to the Estates General.

From the standpoint of the crown, the most important duty of the estates was to vote and collect taxes; but from the standpoint of the inhabitants, the estates performed many other services. In times of trouble, as during the Hundred Years War and later during the Wars of Religion, they raised armies to protect their province, negotiated with potential invaders and even with foreign powers, and strengthened fortifications. In happier times they repaired roads and bridges, made rivers navigable, financed research and scholarly publications, and supported educational institutions. During the sixteenth century the estates of Quercy began to contribute toward the support of a university, two colleges, and six elementary schools in the province. The estates also appointed deputies to defend the interests of the province before the king and council and the various law courts. To accomplish this goal the deputies gave presents to their governor and to people of influence at court. The success of their endeavors is suggested by the fact that the increase in royal taxes between 1480 and 1560 did not keep pace with inflation. To perform the above duties the estates found it necessary to create bureaucracies, to establish archives, and to levy taxes to support their own activities as well as those of the king.

During the 1340's and 1350's the estates in each jurisdiction had appointed officials to collect a single specified tax, after which their offices had lapsed. Only when it became generally accepted that consent to taxation would be an annual affair did the estates feel the need to develop a permanent bureaucracy, and this did not occur before the reign of Charles VII. Furthermore, whatever temporary steps were taken in the mid fourteenth century were terminated when Charles V discontinued the practice of convoking the estates. Hence, the three estates of Languedoc did not appoint a permanent clerk until 1455, a syndic until 1480, and a treasurer to administer the money allocated for their use until 1522. As their administrative role increased, the estates felt the need to expand the bureaucracy and to create an archive to preserve their records, which they did in 1486. The seneschalsies also had syndics, and the dioceses developed their own bureaucracies.

The estates of Brittany had a syndic, a treasurer, and a clerk by 1526, and by 1534 they were taking steps to establish an archive. In Guyenne the bureaucracies developed at the seneschalsy level because of the weakness of the provincial estates. Here we find syndics in Rouergue by 1478, in Agenais by 1486, in Comminges by 1520, in Quercy by 1551, and in Périgord by 1552. Soon other officers were appointed, and Comminges could boast a treasurer, clerk, and archivist as well. The Norman estates developed more slowly. Until 1569 the attorney of Rouen appears to have acted as their syndic and archivist. It was probably not until 1578 that they had a treasurer and not until 1609 a clerk who did not double as a royal official. The only significant exception to the pattern of bureaucratic growth beginning around 1450 or thereafter took place in Dauphiné, which escaped Charles V's attack on the estates. Here important steps toward establishing a bureaucracy took place between 1367 and 1400.

At first it was deemed sufficient to have a syndic to act for the estates when they were not in session, but soon many of the more important provinces found it advisable also to have an executive committee or an abridged assembly that could meet quickly in case of an emergency and serve as an executive arm. The Assemblées des Commis des États appeared in Dauphiné in the late fourteenth century. At about the same time the Burgundian dukes established the Chambre des Élus, but it was well into the fifteenth century before the estates won the right to choose a majority of its members. The estates of Provence established their committee in 1480 and the estates of Béarn created the Abrégé des États two years later. The estates of Brittany, however, were reluctant to trust any group to act for them. It was not until the 1580's, when the Wars of Religion were creating so much havoc, that they established a committee, and it was abandoned when the crisis passed.

On the whole, the crown showed little concern about the development of these bureaucracies. Its own bureaucracy was inadequate in many respects, and most rulers must have been relieved to see the estates assume some of the duties of government. Quarrels over the size of the tax and various abuses were frequent, but in general the kings accepted the role of the estates from about 1460 until the seventeenth century. Certainly the estates never challenged the basic position of the kings. Occasionally a king like Louis XI or Francis I might try to limit the amount of taxes one of the provincial estates levied for its own use, but such measures proved to be temporary.

Thus the flowering of the provincial estates in France took place during the late fifteenth and the sixteenth centuries, and their direct antecedents rarely dated back to before 1418, when the dauphin Charles found it necessary to seek the support of his subjects. During this same period more towns won charters of privilege, and they became more prosperous and populous. Village assemblies and parish officials largely replaced the seigneurs and the priests in local government. The suffrage in bailiwick assemblies was increased to include the villages in places where there were no provincial estates, and there were demands for their inclusion where these estates existed. Hence the age of the "new monarchs" was also the age of the growth of self-government. The two processes went hand in hand because, as Henry VIII of England so aptly put it, "We at no time stand so highly in our estate royal as in time of Parliament, wherein we as head and you as members are conjoined and knit together in one body politic."

BIBLIOGRAPHY

Sources. Jean Masselin, *Journal des États généraux de France tenus à Tours en 1484 sous le règne de Charles VIII*, A. Bernier, ed. (1835); Georges Picot, ed., *Documents relatifs aux États généraux et assemblées réunis sous Philippe le Bel* (1901).

Studies. Joseph Billioud, *Les États de Bourgogne aux XIVe et XVe siècles* (1922); Thomas N. Bisson, *Assemblies and Representation in Languedoc in the Thirteenth Century* (1964); Léon Cadier, *Les États de Béarn depuis leurs origines jusqu'au commencement du XVIe siècle* (1888); A. Dussert, "Les États du Dauphiné aux XIVe et XVe siècles," in *Bulletin de l'Académie delphinale*, 5th ser., 8 (1914), and "Les États du Dauphiné de la Guerre de Cent Ans aux Guerres de Religion," *ibid.* and 5th ser., 13 (1922); Henri Gilles, *Les États de Languedoc au XVe siècle* (1965); John Bell Henneman, *Royal Taxation in Fourteenth-century France: The Development of War Financing, 1322–1356* (1971), and *Royal Taxation in Fourteenth-century France: The Captivity and Ransom of John II, 1356–1370* (1976); J. Russell Major, *Representative Institutions in Renaissance France, 1421–1559* (1960), "French Representative Assemblies: Research Opportunities and Research Published," in *Studies in Medieval and Renaissance History*, 1 (1964), and *Representative Government in Early Modern France* (1980).

Gaines Post, *Studies in Medieval Legal Thought* (1964); Henri Prentout, *Les États provinciaux de Nor-*

mandie, 3 vols. (1925–1927), and extract from *Mémoires de l'Académie nationale de sciences, arts, et belles-lettres de Caen,* n.s. **1–3** (1925–1926); Charles M. Radding, *The Administration of the Aids in Normandy, 1360–1389* (1973); Maurice Rey, *Le domaine du roi et les finances extraordinaires sous Charles VI, 1388–1413* (1965), and *Les finances royales sous Charles VI: Les causes du déficit, 1388–1413,* 2 vols. (1965); Antoine Thomas, *Les états provinciaux de la France centrale sous Charles VII,* 2 vols. (1879); Joseph M. Tyrrell, *A History of the Estates of Poitou* (1968).

J. Russell Major

[See also **Burgundy, Kingdom of; Charles V of France; Charles VII of France; Dauphiné; France; Gabelle; Hundred Years War; Languedoc; Louis IX of France; Louis XI of France; Political Theory, Western European; Taille, Tallage; Taxation, French.**]

REPRESENTATIVE ASSEMBLIES, GERMAN. Having first appeared in the Iberian Peninsula in the late twelfth century, representative assemblies began to emerge in other lands in Western Europe in the thirteenth century, developed in most others, including the German-speaking countries, in the fourteenth and fifteenth, and augmented their power and authority, often reaching their high point, in the sixteenth and seventeenth centuries. On the whole, there was the same general complex of reasons for these developments: the need of rulers to consult with their subjects and seek their support and money, especially for war; the desire of some or all of the politically active classes to act during emergencies, protect the common good or at least their interests, and restrain princely excesses; and the severe economic, social, political, and demographic crises of the late Middle Ages, which nearly everywhere greatly exacerbated the level of warfare, shook the foundations of government, and pitted rulers and subjects against each other. In German lands, as elsewhere, assemblies convened sometimes at the behest of rulers, sometimes on the initiative of the estates. These assemblies often evolved fitfully and slowly over several centuries before achieving a clearly delineated place in the polity, and they most commonly took the final form in three houses for the clergy, the aristocracy, and the towns. (So, too, did the English Parliament, which was tricameral inasmuch as Convocations of the Clergy constituted a third "house.") In the German lands there also arose many questions, sometimes posed only much later, about how "representative" such assemblies were. Strictly speaking, representation seems to require that a representative has the legal authority, partial or plenary, to act on behalf of another who has somehow chosen, or helped to choose, his representative. But it is always dangerous to impose on the past modern preconceptions, and a particularly tricky one is our notion of citizenship with its implied right to participate fully in political life. Until the abolition of property qualifications and the gradual introduction of universal suffrage in the nineteenth and twentieth centuries, citizenship had always been limited to a distinct minority of the adult, male population who were legally free and possessed a certain minimum amount of wealth. Only these men of sufficient leisure and income could afford the onerous responsibilities of the active political life. Whether they "represented" those subject to them (women, minors, serfs, slaves) is a question many of them would have thought curious, especially since their claims to rule in the political sphere were habitually accepted except in times of great stress. Similarly, sometimes in the High and late Middle Ages certain corporate bodies (such as cathedral chapters), estates, or parts of estates (for instance, the leading towns of a principality) unilaterally acted ostensibly on behalf of others or of the common good—both extended senses of the word "representation." Whether this kind of "representation," deputed or not, openly claimed or not, was accepted by its putative beneficiaries was another matter entirely.

But German-speaking lands also differed from the rest of Europe in several fundamental respects that affected the evolution of their representative assemblies. First, these lands constituted the bulk of the largest political unit in Europe, the Holy Roman Empire. Even if no one in it had spoken some form of Italian, Slavic, or French (as many did), the diversity of the dialects of the German majority alone compounded the problems of size and regional disparities as impediments to the creation of a significant "national" or imperial representative assembly. Size bore on the second relevant factor: the definitive failure of centralized monarchy and the triumph of the princes in the thirteenth century. The sudden death of Frederick II in 1250, after three centuries of overambitious royal efforts to devise stable rule in a vast area running from the Baltic to the Papal States and from the Rhineland to Poland, plunged all of Central Europe into a prolonged crisis of political succession and legitimate rule at every level. Furthermore, the problem of political succession, which was the single most important cause of warfare in Europe until the eighteenth century, was intensified in German lands by the prevalence of the electoral principle (the imperial throne, the kingships of Bohemia and Hungary, and all ecclesiastical principalities) and by the practice in most hereditary territories of partition among the surviving male heirs. Even in the four lay electoral principalities of the empire (the Electoral Palatinate, the kingdom of Bohemia, the duchy of Saxony, and the margravate of Brandenburg), where the custom of partition was forbidden by the Golden Bull of 1356, it survived until the sixteenth century, and in many other territories until the seventeenth and eighteenth centuries. As a result of all these conditions, observers foreign and domestic spoke of German Europe well into the fifteenth century as anarchic. The establishment of peace and order, and specifically of judicial alternatives to violence and the feud, thus commanded the stage of German political life longer and more conspicuously than in much of the rest of the Continent. The princes and city-states, to whom the task of administering justice and keeping peace had fallen by delegation or default in the High Middle Ages, were only just beginning to achieve a modicum of success in the fifteenth century. Their limited success and the inevitable conflict arising from their competing jurisdictions led the great reform Imperial Diet of 1495 to be preoccupied with establishing an Imperial Peace, an Imperial Cameral Court (*Reichskammergericht*) to enforce it, and the finances to support this system. At the local and regional level, many estates had much earlier been drawn into this maelstrom of issues revolving around stability and order; but the composite picture that emerges is as varied as the 300 or so units of effective government that finally developed.

The failure to build a strong monarchy had another repercussion. As in Italy, there was no one central figure strong enough to compel competing parties to submerge their differences and to obey his overriding will. The centrifugal tendencies of medieval politics, in which everyone was conscious of his own rights and was determined to be free from domination, thus went essentially unchecked. Although the princes triumphed over the emperor in the thirteenth century, they scarcely did so over their subjects before the sixteenth. For over 300 years some of their potential subjects—prelates, nobles, and towns—expended enormous energy on escaping subjugation to a local prince and achieving imperial status as "citizens" of the empire and hence subject to the emperor alone. Those who gained that coveted status became the backbone of the empire and looked to it to protect their independence. In retrospect, Hegel and some German Romantics argued that the empire was never meant to be a purely political organism, but rather a judicial order to guarantee the rights of all of its subjects. One does not have to be a worshiper of the centralized nation-state to recognize the self-justifying and wistful nature of this idea. More concretely, what has perplexed historians of German politics is the precise role that representative assemblies played in German political life at the national, territorial, and local levels. Did they help or hinder the development of the "state"? Were they merely particularist and narrow-minded, or did they contribute something positive to the political order? The answers to these questions depend in the end as much on one's own values as on the detailed analysis of the history of any single German representative assembly.

THE IMPERIAL DIET OR *REICHSTAG*

Although historians sometimes apply these two words to periods as early as the tenth century, they are quite misleading inasmuch as there existed no imperial representative assembly before the fifteenth century, and neither of these terms was in fact used before then. Until then the emperors or kings only "held court" (*conventus, colloquium, curia, Hoftag*) with the princes, secular and ecclesiastical, to seek their aid and counsel, adjudicate cases, confer fiefs and offices, grant and confirm rights and privileges, and celebrate on a grand scale. Sometimes others might appear or be summoned; for instance the Roman lawyers of Bologna were asked to advise Frederick Barbarossa at Roncaglia in 1158. But such people might also turn up at the daily royal court, seeking favors or justice; and in neither case can one speak of a representative assembly, even in the weakest sense. The Golden Bull contemplates the king's meeting only with the princes, and such gatherings continued down to the early seventeenth century.

The first attempt to hold a more inclusive assembly dates, however, from the later thirteenth century. Rudolf of Habsburg (1273–1291), the first king after the calamitous interregnum (1254–1273), may have toyed with such an idea to achieve the "reformation of the empire" (*reformatio imperii*), but he found too strong both regionalism and the power of the princes, to whom he ultimately delegated the task of negotiation with their own subjects and, tellingly, the crown's, "as often as it will have seemed useful to you"; and he promised furthermore to confirm their decisions. His successor, Adolf of Nassau (1292–1298), evidently inspired by developments in England, summoned a *generale parlamentum* to convene in Frankfurt in March 1295 and, when his illness necessitated a postponement, in June 1296. Representatives from the imperial cities were invited. What Adolf sought to enforce was the waning obligation of the estates, above all the princes, to obey a royal command to attend court. This issue, together with many others, resulted in a struggle with the electors ending in Adolf's deposition in 1298. The weakness of the crown had been exposed yet again. Under Louis the Bavarian (1314–1347) the electors frequently excused themselves from court, and by the fifteenth century voluntary personal attendance at court by the princes in general was the norm, although many deemed it prudent to send representatives.

Yet Rudolf and Adolf had stirred a current among the imperial cities, which began to press their claims to be consulted. The royal prerogative nevertheless remained intact. Sometimes no cities at all were invited to *Hoftage,* and sometimes nonimperial towns attended while imperial cities were ignored. The protests of the latter did not avail until 1495, after which they were regularly summoned.

Three factors, reaching back into the fourteenth century, made possible the full emergence of the *Reichstag* in the fifteenth. The first was the constitutional definition of the seven electors by the Golden Bull in 1356. These seven princes had been specified as the electors by Eike von Repgowe as early as 1224. They had divided in the double election of 1257 but then acted together in 1298 when they deposed Adolf of Nassau. The Golden Bull set them clearly apart from all other princes and laid the legal foundation for a potentially more vigorous role in the governance of the realm. The second factor that prompted the realization of that possibility was the crucial weakness or absence of most of the monarchs for over a century: Wenceslaus (1378–1400), deposed in 1400 for drunkenness and incompetence; Sigismund (1410–1437), fighting the Turks much of the time in his kingdom of Hungary; and Frederick III (1440–1493), habitually resident in his hereditary Austrian lands and away from the historic *Reich* for twenty-seven years. Under Wenceslaus the electors in the 1380's came to preside at *Hoftage* by default when the king failed to keep his word to come. In 1394, while Wenceslaus was being held prisoner in Bohemia, the electors took the critical step of unilaterally summoning the estates to an assembly. They did so as well in 1397, 1400, 1422, and the later 1420's. At the same time the practice became normal under Sigismund and Frederick III of representation of the king at such meetings rather than his personal presence.

The third factor that forced the situation was, as was almost invariably the case, war and its financial exigencies, caused by the pressures put on the empire by the Hussites and the Turks. Save for the emperor's coronation expedition to Rome, never before in the history of the empire had the estates been called upon to tax themselves on its behalf. The revolt of Hussite Bohemia against the Roman church and the Roman Empire between 1420 and 1434 in the view of many contemporaries threatened to destroy both. Cardinal Giuliano Cesarini at the Council of Basel in 1431 feared that this heresy would infect all Europe, and before they were finally defeated on the battlefield in 1434 the Hussites had invaded Prussia and advanced as far as Danzig. Europe made peace with them, only to have to turn its attention to the steady Turkish advance up the Danube Valley, culminating in the two sieges of Vienna in 1529 and 1683 and Ottoman rule of much of Hungary between those years. For two-and-a-half centuries the Habsburgs needed vast sums to protect the eastern flank of the empire, and so the *Reichstag* blossomed in the fifteenth century to debate imperial defense and its financing. By 1480, Frederick III noted, no fewer than twenty-six *Reichstage* had convened during his reign to take up the Turkish threat.

Those who were going to pay, the towns in particular, had to be invited to attend. The *Reichstag* of 1422, convened by the electors alone, devised two different systems of taxation: a direct tax on individuals later called the Common Penny (*der Gemeine Pfennig*) and a *Matrikel* system of negotiated quotas of money and troops assessed on each of the 300 or so imperial estates. The clergy and especially the towns, deeply suspicious of the princes' support of direct taxation, successfully resisted it. In 1427 it was imposed again with better results, but the 50,000 gulden garnered came mostly from the ecclesiastical states. The Common Penny of

1495–1499 yielded more than 100,000 gulden, but its starkly regressive character doomed it as the last general direct tax in imperial history. (All adult subjects of the empire, fifteen years of age or older, were assessed 1/24 of a gulden if they were worth less than 500 gulden; a half gulden if their worth ran between 500 and 1,000 gulden; and one gulden if they were Jews or were worth over 1,000 gulden.) Although the Common Penny survived in increasingly attentuated form until 1542, it was the *Matrikel* system of taxation that prevailed down to 1806.

Once the *Reichstag* came into being, more general concerns naturally came to the fore. Demands for "reform" that shook the Holy Roman Catholic Church had their effect on its secular counterpart, and the near-triumph of conciliarism in the general councils of Constance (1414–1417) and Basel (1431–1444) offered a specific political model of governance worth considering. The literature of imperial reform consistently employs the significant word *Reichskonzilien* rather than *Reichstag*. The whole movement finally found an adequate leader at the top only much later in the president of the electors, Bertold von Henneberg, archbishop of Mainz from 1484 to 1504. Despite many clashes of interest among the estates, despite Henneberg's struggles with King Maximilian I (1493–1519), who was resolved to revive a strong and personal monarchy, much was achieved in that era, the most creative in the history of the *Reichstag*. The great Diet of Worms of 1495 declared the Eternal Peace of the Empire, defined the structure of the Imperial Cameral Court largely independent of the crown, and levied the Common Penny to pay for this imperial judicial apparatus as well as imperial defense. Other *Reichstage* up to 1521 reinforced this emphasis on peacekeeping, defense, and orderly government by creating the Imperial Circles (*Reichskreise,* eventually six in number) and a supreme Governing Council of the Empire (*Reichsregiment,* 1500–1502, 1521–1530). Although the Common Penny and the *Reichsregiment* passed away, the *Reichskammergericht* and the *Reichskreise* became integral parts of the imperial government until 1806; and on balance the issues of peace, defense, and taxation were never more flexibly and imaginatively dealt with at any other time.

Nevertheless, the fact remained that insuperable diversity and centrifugal interests had long since won out, that the combined effect of all these reforms benefited the princes as the indispensable enforcers of law and order, and that no one had the power to compel all others to accept an imperfect vision of the common good. Maximilian's policies and behavior encapsulated this nexus of problems. The international wars conducted on imperial soil in Italy after 1494 deeply affronted the Germans, who (as Machiavelli observed) were too parsimonious to pay for the vindication of their honor on the battlefield. Maximilian proved incapable of convincing them that the wars in Italy and against the Turks were imperial and not merely Austrian affairs. Yet by the 1490's neither the king nor his subjects were accustomed to treating each other in sensitive, persuasive ways. When the imperial estates at the diet of 1497 incensed Maximilian by barring him from their closed deliberations "like some common burgomaster" (as he complained), he neatly exacted his revenge by keeping the assembled imperial estates waiting for him at their own expense for nearly seven months at the next *Reichstag* in Freiburg im Breisgau in 1498.

The estates were equally suspicious of each other, and with reason. By 1500 the *Reichstag* was rapidly assuming its final tricameral form of *curiae* or "colleges" of the electors, the princes, and the cities. Significantly, two of the three were princely; and although the electors enjoyed primary and separate status, this was counterbalanced by the fact that ecclesiastical and secular princes sat together in both houses, which effectively underscored what they had in common rather than pitting them against each other. Jean Bodin recognized the true nature of the empire when he characterized it as "an aristocratic principality, in which the emperor is only the first magnate." So did the cities, only twenty-four of which bothered to send representatives to the *Reichstag* of 1495. It was this division among the estates which explains the signal failure of the *Reichstag* of 1496 to agree that its legislation could not be vetoed by a mandate from the emperor, for each estate hoped that the emperor could be persuaded to reject any collective decision which violated its own interests. A stunning illustration of these niceties of politics occurred in 1523, when the imposition by the *Reichstag* of a toll on all goods moving across German borders was quashed by a mandate of Emperor Charles V, to whom the cities had offered a loan of 40,000 gulden. Finally, the cities showed their suspicions and their separateness by forming their own urban assemblies (*Städtetage*) after 1471 to discuss matters of mutual concern. No fewer than seventy-eight of these convened between 1471 and 1585.

In his need for money Charles V also turned in 1529 to the imperial knights, who were beginning to win their "liberty" in large numbers, for voluntary payments for the maintenance of the empire. These subsidies soon evolved into regular taxes, yet the imperial knights never acquired direct representation in the *Reichstag*. To ensure protection of their interests, they turned increasingly to control of the archbishopric of Mainz (both the see and the cathedral chapter) and of other Rhenish bishoprics, which they kept until 1803. One way or another, they were determined to be "represented" in return for the taxes they paid.

REPRESENTATIVE ASSEMBLIES IN THE PRINCIPALITIES: *LANDTAGE*

The development of representative assemblies in the several hundred territories of the German-speaking empire shows the greatest possible variety and complexity, which can therefore only be hinted at here. Since F. L. Carsten in 1959 published in English a detailed study of the parliaments of some of the major principalities (the Electoral Palatinate, the duchies of Württemberg, Saxony, Bavaria, and Jülich-Cleves-Berg, and the landgraviate of Hesse), it will not be necessary here to recapitulate their stories. They exhibit, however, some features in common with each other and with *Landtage* in other territories that deserve mention. First, their history does not parallel that of the *Reichstag*, which was peculiarly dominated by the princes. In their internal structure, *Landtage* ordinarily reflected more accurately the social orders of clergy, knights, towns, and sometimes peasants. Second, whereas the *Reichstag* was convoked from on high and emerged late, the territorial estates (*Landstände*) often took the initiative, as early as the thirteenth century, by concluding unions (*Einungen*) to maintain peace, restrain their princes, and if necessary assume control of the government. Third, generally similar circumstances favoring the growth of assemblies could eventuate in entirely disparate results. The duchies of Bavaria and Saxony, for example, were plagued by partitions and fratricidal wars within their ruling houses in the fourteenth and fifteenth centuries; yet on the eve of the Reformation the estates in Bavaria had carved out a large role in the government of the realm, whereas those in Saxony had not prospered. In the county of Württemberg (after 1495 a duchy), where far more peaceful conditions prevailed, the estates gathered for the first time in 1457 to deal with what was by contemporary standards a secondary matter, the presence of non-native councillors at court. Yet here the powers of the estates grew astonishingly rapidly, leading to the deposition of one duke in 1498, the expulsion of another in 1519, and the promulgation of the Treaty of Tübingen in 1514, which served as the fundamental law of the duchy down to the end of the *ancien régime*. Indeed, in 1818 Charles James Fox observed that Württemberg was the only state on the Continent with a constitution comparable to that of England.

Carsten rightly concluded from his work that Württemberg was not unique among the German states in the vitality and endurance of its representative institutions. Had he included the ecclesiastical principalities in his study, he would have come to even more positive conclusions. The bishoprics of northern Germany provide some instructive examples. In all of them the cathedral chapter emerged in the High Middle Ages not only as the elector of the prince-bishop, but also as his "senate" with full legal rights in canon law to counsel and consent in all important decisions. Although these chapters jealously guarded their rights and their preeminence among the estates, they usually also discovered that they could not go it alone and had to cooperate with the other estates.

Thus, in the bishopric of Münster a governing council of the estates, appearing as early as 1272 to control the bishops, reemerged sporadically and became a permanent part of the government in the 1570's. In Paderborn the estates deposed one bishop in 1415, foiled the attempt of the archbishop of Cologne to incorporate the principality of Paderborn into that of Cologne in the 1430's, and created a governing council in the 1490's. Despite later tensions among themselves, the estates held their place in the government and even expanded it in the eighteenth century. In contrast, the estates in the neighboring bishopric of Osnabrück did not sustain their strong start in the thirteenth century, when a governing council is attested in 1285. Here the estates in 1424 won a concession unique in all the ecclesiastical principalities: the electoral oath or "capitulation" of the bishop, elsewhere rendered only to the cathedral chapter, was to be sworn before the estates as well. Nevertheless, even though the assemblies convened yearly down to the French Revolution to assent to taxation, their will to resist was effectively broken by Bishop Ernest August I in the late seventeenth century.

The same archbishop of Cologne who had tried to take over Paderborn also forced the sudden emergence of the estates in his own lands. Dietrich von Moers ruled autocratically (from 1414 to 1463), conducted expansionistic wars, and experienced a sharp decline in revenue from the clergy, all of which delivered him straight into the hands of the estates. Upon his death in 1463 the estates in both the archbishopric and the duchy of Westphalia (held by the archbishops since the twelfth century) drew up an *Erblandesvereinigung* (union of the archiepiscopal lands) to which every archbishop was to submit. This document, which formed the constitution of the principality to 1803, regularized the judicial system, forbade alienation of crucial lands, and made the declaration of war and all taxation dependent on the assent of the estates. It reinforced the chapter's rights of consent and allowed the chapter to convene the estates and unite with them against the archbishop if necessary, which they did in 1476 to prevent the absorption of the see into the lands of the duke of Burgundy.

In some places no formally constituted assemblies ever came into being, for instance in the margravate of Baden. In others they appeared late, never acquired much strength, and disappeared early, for instance in the Electoral Palatinate and in the bishoprics of Basel, Bamberg, and Würzburg. The achievement of imperial status by the knights in all these territories in the sixteenth century is customarily given as the principal reason for the stunted development of representative assemblies here. While this may have been a critical factor in these instances, the absence of the nobility did not necessarily emasculate German representative assemblies. The knights in Württemberg also withdrew in the sixteenth century without adversely affecting the role of the other estates in the governance of the duchy. Normally peasants were not directly represented, but there were principalities where peasants constituted the only estate, although in most cases they achieved this position only in the centuries after 1500. Among these territories, which were invariably small, were the imperial abbeys of Kempten, Ochsenhausen, Rottenmünster, and Schussenried, the prince-priory of Berchtesgaden, the city-state of Rottweil, and certain districts ruled by the margraves of Baden, the bishop of Augsburg, the abbot of St. Gall, and the archdukes of Austria.

In lands of such disparateness, then, it is nearly impossible to formulate large generalizations about representative assemblies, especially if one looks beyond formally constituted parliaments to the wider world of politics within which they operated. In the prince-bishopric of Speyer, for example, no parliament ever evolved, but representative institutions did at several levels. As usual, the cathedral chapter played a decisive role in the governance of the see, but in the thirteenth century it also concluded a union with the other three collegiate churches of Speyer to act on behalf of the clergy of the diocese, including assent to taxation. This "representation," initially accepted, came to be challenged by the local clergy in the fifteenth century, who made use of their organization into rural deaneries to treat more directly with the bishops. The bishops also preferred to negotiate extraordinary taxation with the individual monasteries of the diocese and with their own peasants, who were administratively organized into bailiwicks (*Ämter*). Thus, despite the absence of a diet, the subjects of the bishops of Speyer were nevertheless well "represented."

While examining the entire structure of politics in a particular territory, not merely its representative assembly, one must avoid focusing primarily on crises and conflicts when rulers and their subjects were at odds with each other rather than working together in relative harmony, which must be the normal political order if it is to function at all. The study of quotidian politics is rather mundane, but it is a much surer guide to the political life of a people than might be suggested by a narrow focus on representative assemblies, where, because of their very nodal structure and transitory character, conflicts tended to emerge and explode. Concentration on assemblies, German or non-German, also distorts our perspective in another way. Most assemblies followed the estatist principle of organization—usually three but as many as five or as few as one—a model that easily implies the predominance of division among the estates. From this one can infer that nobles and towns, towns and clergy, nobles and clergy, and the rulers and the ruled were primarily in conflict. This was very often not the case, not only in ordinary daily political life, but in crises as well, when estates worked together for the common interest. In addition, there were also "interest groups," frequently fluctuating and transcending estatist boundaries, which often exerted a momentous impact on politics while working behind its formal structures. Finally, despite the flourishing of representative assemblies on German soil, many princes and their subjects preferred direct, individual negotiation instead of, or in addition to, formal gatherings of the estates. German rulers understood the principle of divide and rule, while those who were ruled resented the expense of time and money and feared the infringement of their particular rights by the prince or by the other estates in such circumstances. Far from being always and automatically regarded as a good thing, then, representative assemblies, in the eyes of many people in German Europe, were, like war, only the final instrument of politics.

BIBLIOGRAPHY

On the Reichstag. Heinz Angermeier, *Die Reichsreform 1410–1555* (1984); Thomas A. Brady, Jr., *Turning Swiss: Cities and Empire, 1450–1550* (1985); *Deutsche Reichstagsakten* (1867–); F. R. H. Du Boulay, "Law Enforcement in Medieval Germany," in *History,* **63** (1978); Eberhard Isenmann, "Reichsfinanzen und Reichssteuern im 15. Jahrhundert," in *Zeitschrift für historische Forschung,* **7** (1980); Peter Moraw, "Reichsstadt, Reich und Königtum im späten Mittelalter," in *Zeitschrift für historische Forschung,* **6** (1979), "Versuch über die Entstehung des Reichstags," in Hermann Weber, ed., *Politische Ordnungen und soziale Kräfte im Alten Reich* (1980), and "Organisation und Funktion von Verwaltung im ausgehenden Mittelalter (*ca.* 1350–1500)," in Kurt Jeserich *et al.*, eds., *Deutsche Verwaltungsgeschichte,* I (1983); Steven W. Rowan, "A Reichstag in the Reform Era: Freiburg im Breisgau 1497–98," in James Vann and Steven Rowan, eds., *The Old Reich: Essays on German Political Institutions, 1495–1806* (1974), "The Common Penny (1495–99) as a Source of German Social and Demographic History," in *Central European History,* **10** (1977), "Imperial Taxes and German Politics in the Fifteenth Century: An Outline," *ibid.,* **13** (1980); Georg Schmidt, *Der Städtetag in der Reichsverfassung* (1984); Ernst Schubert, *König und Reich: Studien zur spätmittelalterlichen deutschen Verfassungsgeschichte* (1979), 323–349; Joachim W. Stieber, *Pope Eugenius IV, the Council of Basel, and the Secular and Ecclesiastical Authorities in the Empire* (1978).

On the Landtage. Siegfried Bachmann, *Die Landstände des Hochstifts Bamberg* (1962); Roger Ballmer, "Les assemblées d'états dans l'ancien évêché de Bâle," in *Schweizer Beiträge zur Allgemeinen Geschichte,* **20** (1962); Peter Blickle, *Landschaften im Alten Reich* (1973); Otto Brunner, *Land und Herrschaft,* 5th ed. (1965, repr. 1973, 1984); Francis L. Carsten, *The Origins of Prussia* (1954), and *Princes and Parliaments in Germany from the Fifteenth to the Eighteenth Century* (1959); Henry J. Cohn, *The Government of the Rhine Palatinate in the Fifteenth Century* (1965), 189–201; Francis R. H. Du Boulay, *Germany in the Later Middle Ages* (1983); Lawrence G. Duggan, *Bishop and Chapter: The Governance of the Bishopric of Speyer to 1552* (1978); Robert Folz, "Les assemblées d'états dans les principautés allemandes (fin XIIIe–début XVIe siècle)," in *Recueils de la Société Jean Bodin pour l'histoire comparative des institutions,* **25** (1965); Dietrich Gerhard, "Assemblies of Estates and the Corporate Order," in *Liber memorialis Georges de Lagarde* (1970); Thomas Glas-Hochstettler, "The Imperial Knights in Post-Westphalian Mainz: A Case Study of Corporatism in the Old Reich," in *Central European History,* **11** (1978); Herbert Helbig, "Ständische Einungsversuche in den mitteldeutschen Territorien am Ausgang des Mittelalters," in *Album Helen Maud Cam,* II (1961); Gustav Knetsch, *Die landstädische Verfassung und reichsritterschaftliche Bewegung im Kurstaate Trier, vornehmlich im XVI. Jahrhundert* (1909); Marlene LeGates, "Princes, Parliaments, and Privilege: German Research in European Context," in *European Studies Review,* **10** (1980); Alec R. Myers, *Parliaments and Estates in Europe to 1789* (1975), 174–178; Reinhard Renger, *Landesherr und Landstände im Hochstift Osnabrück in der Mitte des 18. Jahrhunderts* (1968); Karsten Ruppert, "Die Landstände des Erzstifts Köln in der frühen Neuzeit: Verfassung und Geschichte," in *Annalen des Historischen Vereins für den Niederrhein,* **174** (1972); Ernst Schubert, *Die Landstände des Hochstifts Würzburg* (1967).

LAWRENCE G. DUGGAN

[See also **Austria; Bavaria; Cologne; Germany** (various articles); **Habsburg Dynasty; Maximilian I, Emperor; Palatinates; Saxony; Wittelsbachs.**]

REPRESENTATIVE ASSEMBLIES, IRISH. See **Parliament, Irish.**

REPRESENTATIVE ASSEMBLIES, SCOTTISH. See **Parliament, Scottish.**

REPRESENTATIVE ASSEMBLIES, SPANISH. See **Cortes.**

REREDOS, a screen, often decorated with a painting or paintings, tapestry, or, usually, ornate relief (often with niches for additional sculpture), placed on the wall behind an altar. Prevalent in the Gothic period, such screens were rarely produced thereafter. Use of the term is unusual after about 1550 until its reintroduction by nineteenth-century scholars.

LESLIE BRUBAKER

[See also **Altar–Altar Apparatus; Architecture, Liturgical Aspects; Predella.**]

RESCRIPTS. In its origins, the term "rescript" could denote any written answer; in Roman law, however, it had come to denote exclusively the written answer of the emperor to the request of a subject. Canon law, by imitation of the Roman law, came to restrict its meaning to that of written answers by popes to questions and petitions addressed to them. Although the earliest papal rescript is said to have been issued by Pope Siricius in 385, the form became truly significant from the twelfth century, when lawyer popes began to use it frequently, in fuller imitation of the Roman emperors, as a fundamental means to develop the law. The papal chancery contributed greatly to the technical development of rescripts.

As responses, rescripts presuppose questions or petitions for favors, dispensations, or honors. The internal form of the rescript was well defined: after summarizing the petition and the facts on which it purported to be based, the response to the query or the disposition of the request was set out. A rescript might also close with conditional clauses affecting its validity or lawfulness. Generally, a rescript would also require executors who would see to it that its provisions were carried out.

BIBLIOGRAPHY

Bernard C. Gerhardt, *Interpretation of Rescripts* (1959); Alphonse van Hove, *De rescriptis* (1936); William H. O'Neill, *Papal Rescripts of Favor* (1930).

GIULIO SILANO

[See also **Decretals; Decretum; Law, Canon; Papal Provisions.**]

RESERVATION OF THE SACRAMENT. Prior to the eighth century laymen were permitted to give themselves communion, not only when they were ill, but when there was no liturgical celebration. This fact is attested in the writings of Hippolytus of Rome, Jerome, and others. During the patristic period the eucharist was celebrated only on Sundays and feasts, at which times laymen took some of the consecrated bread and wine home with them for daily communion.

The early Christians' daily communion is thus linked to home reservation of the sacrament, which is attested by references in the writings of Tertullian, Novatian, and Jerome. Tertullian is concerned, for example, lest the body and blood of Christ be profaned in the home of a believer married to a nonbeliever, encouraging the believer to receive secretly. Bede informs us that the sacrament was still being reserved in homes in the seventh century.

In addition to home reservation, the sacrament was also kept in churches, but the practice was not general before the ninth century. In its description of the papal Mass, *Ordo romanus* I (seventh or eighth century) notes that on his way to the altar the pope was presented with a box (*capsa*) containing the sacramental bread remaining from the previous celebration. A portion of this bread was placed in the chalice before communion. So long as the sacrament was reserved in homes, however, reservation in churches was not essential even for the sick and dying. Even at the time of death a dying person might receive from the sacrament reserved in his home or at a special Mass celebrated there.

From the ninth century on, however, reservation of the sacrament in churches became the rule, but throughout the Middle Ages there was no universally accepted custom dictating the mode of conservation. *Ordo romanus* I mentions that the Eucharist was kept in a box (*capsa*) stored in the sacristy. The use of pyxes was common in Gallican lands.

In Italy, generally, the receptacles for the sacrament were reserved in the sacristy; north of the Alps they were more commonly kept on the altar along with the relics. To protect the sacrament from desecration by rodents or nonbelievers, the Fourth Lateran Council (1215) urged that the sacrament be kept under lock and key (canon 20).

Wall tabernacles, mounted in the choir or sanctuary, were common in Italy. In the northern countries tabernacles made in the forms of towers or doves were often suspended above the high altars. Due to the increasing desire to view the host during the twelfth and thirteenth centuries the custom arose in Germany of erecting large structures in the shape of towers, called Eucharist houses, in which the sacrament was kept in a moon-shaped glass container behind a grillwork. Visitors could enter the enclosure to make their devotions.

From the sixteenth century on, these various methods of reserving the sacrament in churches began to yield to the growing custom that originated in Italy of having a tabernacle permanently fixed at the center of the high altar.

BIBLIOGRAPHY

Michel Andrieu, *Les ordines romani du haut moyen âge,* 5 vols. (1931–1961); Roger Béraudy, "Reservation of the Eucharist," in Aimé G. Martimort, ed., *The Church at Prayer,* II, *The Eucharist* (1971); Bologna, Centro di Documentazione, *Conciliorum oecumenicorum decreta* (1962); William H. Freestone, *The Sacrament Reserved* (1917); Archdale A. King, *Eucharistic Reservation in the Western Church* (1965); Edmond Maffei, *La réservation eucharistique jusqu'à la Renaissance* (1942); Stephen J. P. Van Dijk and Joan H. Walker, *The Myth of the Aumbry: Notes on Medieval Reservation Practice and Eucharistic Devotion* (1957).

RONALD JOHN ZAWILLA, O.P.

[See also **Altar–Altar Apparatus.**]

RESPONSORY. The term "responsory" refers to two categories of chant sung during the Divine Office in the Latin West: (1) great responsories (*responsoria prolixa*), sung primarily during the night Office of matins, and (2) short responsories (*responsoria brevia*), sung during the day hours. The number and distribution of responsories for individual hours and nocturns differed in secular and monastic traditions and varied to some degree with specific feasts or seasons and with local uses.

The term "responsory" appeared in the fourth century and derived from its responsorial performance, that is, the alternation of a choir (singing the respond) and one or more soloists (the verses and doxology). The performance of a typical responsory in a ninth-century Frankish center consisted of a full statement of the choral respond (with its incipit intoned by the soloist), a single verse, an abbreviated statement of the respond (the so-called *repetendum*), the doxology (usually only the first half), and the *repetendum* again. However, this practice was not universal. Amalarius of Metz, for example, described a more elaborate performance practice in Rome during the same period. Furthermore, the doxology was not always performed with each respond, and some responsories had more than one verse.

Responsory texts are drawn to a large extent from the historical and prophetic books of the Old and New Testaments or from nonscriptural sources such as the lives of saints. The texts often have a close association with the lessons that precede them. The music relies largely on standard formulas and adaptation of common phrases or entire melodies. All but a few of the verses (including the doxology) use set recitation formulas, or tones, which are fairly elaborate. The responds employ three basic musical principles: (1) standard but plastic melodies adapted to different texts, (2) standard phrases arranged differently for individual texts (a process often called centonization); and (3) melodies not associated with common material. The melodic style is moderately ornate, with sections of recitation alternating with flourishes of groups of notes on a single syllable. Some responsories, particularly later ones, have long, elaborate melismas.

Responsories were also the focus of the practice of troping in the broadest sense of the term: new music (in the form of melismas) and text (as prosulas to new and old melismas) were often added to responsories. Polyphonic settings of responsories formed a central part of two of the most important repertories of early medieval polyphony: the Winchester Troper of about 1000, containing fifty-nine responsories, and the *Magnus liber organi* of about 1175 from the Notre Dame period. Other polyphonic settings of responsories were rare until the late fifteenth century, when such settings were cultivated in England. Polyphonic responsories became an important part of English music during the sixteenth century.

BIBLIOGRAPHY

Paul F. Cutter, "Responsory," in *The New Grove Dictionary of Music and Musicians,* XV (1980); Walter H. Frere, ed., *Antiphonale sarisburiense,* I (1901, repr. 1966), 3–61; René-Jean Hesbert, ed., *Corpus antiphonalium officii,* IV: *Responsoria, versus, hymni, et varia* (1970); Helma Hofmann-Brandt, *Die Tropen zu den Responsorien des Officiums,* 2 vols. (diss., Univ. of Erlangen, 1971); Helmut Hucke, "Responsorium," in *Die Musik in Geschichte und Gegenwart,* XI (1963), and "Das Responsorium," in *Gattungen der Musik in Einzeldarstellungen: Gedenkschrift Leo Schrade,* I (1973); Michel Huglo, "Antiphoner," in *New Grove,* I (1980); Thomas F. Kelly, "Melodic Elaboration in Responsory Melismas," in *Journal of the American Musicological*

Society, 27 (1974); Ruth Steiner, "Some Melismas for Office Responsories," *ibid.,* 26 (1973); Peter Wagner, *Einführung in die gregorianischen Melodien,* III: *Gregorianische Formenlehre* (1921, repr. 1962), 327–351.

LANCE W. BRUNNER

[See also **Amalarius of Metz; Antiphonal; Centonization; Divine Office; Magnus Liber Organi; Winchester Troper.**]

RESPONSUM LITERATURE, ISLAMIC. See **Fatwā.**

RESPONSUM LITERATURE, JEWISH, consists of the questions posed to eminent authorities in Jewish law requesting guidance and the replies of such authorities. Hundreds of thousands of such responsa were written, but due to the dislocations of Jewish history and the destruction of Jewish communities and libraries only a small part of the total literature has survived. Much scholarly work now going on has involved the discovery and identification of responsa materials found in manuscript collections throughout the world and their eventual publication.

Responsa literature, like other varieties of Jewish legal literature, sought to arrive at legal decisions. Unlike other legal opinions, which were somewhat abstract in nature, responsa ordinarily arose out of the interfacing of Judaism and Jews with the changing social and economic realities of everyday life. The wide dispersal of Jewish communities throughout the Middle Ages always carried with it the danger of localism, with the tone of Jewish life determined largely by factors in the immediate environment in which Jews lived. It was through the responsa literature that widely dispersed communities were able to maintain contact with one another and were exposed to the finest scholarly thinking of the age, which had widespread influence. At a time when Jews distinguished themselves as international traders, there were few caravans indeed that did not carry with them, in addition to a cargo of goods for trading, a set of questions from one rabbinic authority to another. It is of more than passing interest that even in those periods when the Muslim and Christian worlds were at war with one another, Jews living under Christian rule managed to remain in contact with Jews living under Islam and vice versa.

During the Middle Ages, Jews were ordinarily given autonomy by the governments under which they lived. Although there were variations in the status of Jewish courts, they had jurisdiction over a wide range of activities within the Jewish community. Their concern was not only within areas of religious life, but also with a variety of social, economic, and political issues within the community. Moreover, Jewish courts were asked to rule on questions that reflected the relationship between Jews and the governments under whose jurisdiction they lived. Responsa literature always dealt with requests made by one rabbinic authority to another. It was not customary for an individual Jew to address a question to a great authority who lived a considerable distance away. Rather what ordinarily occurred was that a litigant sought to press his claim before the court of his own community. Only when the local judge could not come to a satisfactory conclusion would the question be submitted to a worthy authority by the perplexed local rabbinic judge.

For the historian responsa materials often constitute a veritable gold mine of information about the medieval world. The correspondence often included much historical information noted tangentially by the author of the responsum. The date of the responsum, its place of origin, realia of dress, housing, food, and structures of community organizations are all significant data in the reconstruction of the social and religious history of the Jews in the Middle Ages. Responsa materials often have implications for general history as well. Rabbinic authors often take note of marching armies, crusading mobs, details about the reign of princes and monarchs, and particularly relationships between the church and the Jews, which have significant implications for the world of the Middle Ages outside of the Jewish community. While the primary focus of responsa is that of law rather than philosophy, there were respondents who dwelled at length on academic and philosophical issues. In time such contributions took on importance for the intellectual history of Judaism.

Goanic responsa. While responsa are known in an earlier time they began to take on major importance in the middle of the eighth century. The Babylonian geonim considered themselves as possessing hegemony over the Jewish world of the time, partly as a result of the lengthy period of creativity

RESPONSUM LITERATURE, JEWISH

that had culminated in the Babylonian Talmud. Extensive contact was maintained between Babylonia and the major centers of Jewish knowledge and culture in Spain and North Africa. At times queries were received as well from other, remote Jewish communities, whose cultural and religious institutions were in their infancy. Often questions sent to the Babylonian academies were accompanied by donations for the maintenance of those institutions as sources of scholarship for the Jewish world. There is a significant body of opinion that holds that the process of exchanging questions and answers was itself a determinative factor in establishing the Babylonian Talmud as the sole authority in the life of the Jewish community. During the era of the flowering of gaonic responsa literally tens of thousands of responsa were dealt with by the Babylonian academies, though many of them were lost over the course of time.

Unlike responsa literature at a later period, a gaonic responsum ordinarily represented the collective thinking of a group of scholars. Questions were generally addressed to the heads of the academies and then distributed to their students and disciples for study and discussion. Only after prolonged and lengthy debates were answers ultimately transmitted to questioning communities. The replies generated in the gaonic period were fundamentally different from those of a later time. In this period, before the flowering of European centers of Jewish civilization, texts were not easily available and the Babylonian Talmud was still a labyrinth into which only the most learned would venture. Often the question requested the elucidation of a talmudic term. At times it asked for a clarification of a talmudic discussion or even a matter of Jewish belief or practice. Rabbi Natronai bar Hilai, gaon of Sura from 853 to 858, authored many responsa. Among them are instructions about the proper recitation of grace after meals and comments on the structure of the Sabbath morning liturgy and the proper preparation of a mezuzah. All reflect a low level of halakhic understanding on the part of the questioners.

Some scholars believe that questions were often occasioned by the need to give appropriate responses to Karaites or perhaps Muslims or Christians with whom Jews were often joined in debate. Most of the gaonic responsa were rather succinct, sometimes even one-word answers, reflecting in part the relative simplicity of many of the questions that were posed as well as the authoritativeness of the responses that were given. If there were debates within the academies and a variety of different points of view expressed, few discordant notes were allowed to rise to the surface.

In the gaonic period, two of the most significant respondents were Sherira Gaon (*ca.* 906–1006) and his son, Hai Gaon (939–1038). Numerous collections of gaonic responsa were edited and circulated. Since, however, the editors of such collections were interested in the legal decisions per se and not in other information contained in the texts, they often excised names of places, people, and dates, as well as other similar information of historical interest.

Responsa of the rishonim. The period that followed the eclipse of the Babylonian academies had profound implications not only for the development of responsa literature thereafter but for the wider intellectual and religious history of the Jewish people as well. With the demise of the Babylonian academies there was no longer one center of religious authority to which all Jews could turn for definitive answers to perplexing problems. It was replaced by numerous independent Jewish centers, with the result that decisions were made by local political and religious leaders and not by any distant source. Questions put to local authorities could now be answered far more quickly than they had been answered when both questions and responsa had to traverse the long caravan routes. That factor alone was sufficient to stimulate increasing independence of individual centers. Even more significant, perhaps, responsa were no longer as definitive as they had been, as differences of opinion became more and more manifest among authorities. Increasingly, responsa tended to be longer and more complex in structure. The respondent sought not only to elucidate but to prove his point of view to those who would quarrel with him.

The establishment of major new centers for the study of talmudic thought brought about a change in the nature of the questions themselves. New commentaries had increasingly made the talmudic text more readily understandable to the serious student, and requests for explanations were no longer common. Every so often we note responsa dealing with theological and philosophical issues, focusing at times on the mystical element within Judaism. By and large, however, there was a narrowing of the focus in the questions that are put to respondents. The focus tended to be more and more on the specifics of the halakhah and its ability to guide people in the performance of their daily tasks. As their communities rapidly expanded from the eleventh to the fifteenth century, Jews had to define their relationship to the Christians and Muslims among whom they lived, as well as contend with the waves of hatred often directed at them and their institutions. Among the issues they were asked to deal with were their relationships to the secular authorities, quarrels within the leaderships of the communities, rights of residence, and a variety of disagreements in their conduct of business.

It was during this period that some of the most creative and brilliant personalities of Jewish intellectual history shaped the development of Jewish thought. While they were turned to largely by the Jewry of their own lands, their reputations as rabbis and scholars were such that their opinions were sought by Jews who lived in areas remote from them as well. Moreover, renowned rabbis would often consult with and counsel one another in the common effort to provide the proper rabbinic answer in response to contentious issues. The most important scholars of the time included Gershom ben Judah of Germany (*ca.* 960–1028), Solomon ben Isaac (Rashi) of France (1040–1105), Jacob ben Meir of France, known as Rabbenu Tam (1100–1171), Maimonides (1135–1204), Meir ben Baruch of Rothenburg (1212–1293), Solomon ben Abraham Adret of Spain (1235–1310), Isaac ben Sheshe of North Africa (1326–1408), and Simon ben Zemach Duran of North Africa (1361–1444). All of these respondents distinguished themselves in a variety of other ways. There were some (Rabbenu Tam and Maimonides) who had worldwide reputations as theologians and philosophers; others had major roles in the organization and administration of the Jewish community. All of them were acknowledged halakhic authorities whose mastery of the Jewish legal system was beyond any doubt. Their ability to make clear and unequivocal decisions was buttressed by the readiness of the people to follow their leadership, a function not of a hierarchy of any kind but rather of the quality of their scholarship. As a result of the far-flung contacts of Jews from around the world, what effectively came into being was a process of Jewish legislative activity that continued to grow and develop over the centuries without the elaborate structure of lower and appellate courts that had existed during the Second Jewish Commonwealth (from about 200 B.C. to A.D. 70). Despite the existence of strong traditional local custom and usage, the relative unity of halakhic norms throughout the world seems utterly remarkable. Moreover, because of the degree of self-government accorded to Jewish communities the respondents constituted a very significant element in maintaining Jewish autonomy and deepening its ability to maintain those institutions that were the key to its vitality during the Middle Ages.

In many respects, the period from the twelfth to the fifteenth century was one of the most fruitful of all periods of Jewish history—a time of intense political and economic development. It was also, however, a period of profound dislocation and distress, of pogroms and expulsions. All of those factors were dealt with by the respondents, who thus contributed greatly to the resilience of Judaism.

BIBLIOGRAPHY

Irving A. Agus, *Urban Civilization in Pre-Crusade Europe: A Study of Organized Town-Life in Northwestern Europe During the Tenth and Eleventh Centuries Based on the Responsa Literature,* 2 vols. (1965); Simḥah Assaf, *Tekufat Ha-Geonim Ve-Sifruta* (1955), 211–220; Boaz Cohen, *Kunteres Ha-Teshuvot* (1930); Menachem Elon, *Ha-Mishpat ha-ʿivri* (*Jewish law*) (1973), III, 1,213–1,277; Isidore Epstein, *The Responsa of Rabbi Solomon ben Adreth of Barcelona as a Source for the History of Spain* (1925), *The Responsa of Rabbi Simon b. Zemah Duran as a Source for the History of the Jews in North Africa* (1930), and the reprint in one volume of the two previous books, *Studies in the Communal Life of the Jews of Spain, as Reflected in the Responsa of Rabbi Solomon ben Adreth and Rabbi Simon ben Zemach Duran* (1968); Zacharias Frankel, *Entwurf einer Geschichte der Literatur der nachtalmudischen Responsen* (1865); Solomon B. Freehof, *The Responsa Literature* (1955), and *A Treasury of Responsa* (1963); Alexander Marx, "Aim and Tasks of Jewish Historiography," in *Publications of the Jewish Historical Society* (New York), **26** (1918); Joel Müller, *Briefe und Responsen in der vorgeonäischen jüdischen Literatur* (1886), and *Einleitung in die Responsen der babylonischen Geonen* (1891).

ALEXANDER M. SHAPIRO

[See also **Cairo Genizah; Gaonic Period; Gershom ben Judah; Jacob ben Meir; Jews; Judaism; Law, Jewish; Maimonides, Moses; Rabbinate; Rashi; Talmud, Exegesis and Study of.**]

RESURRECTION CYCLE. Early images of the Resurrection follow the Gospel narratives and depict only the Marys, usually two or three, arriving at the tomb. This image, which appears in the third-century baptistery frescoes of the meeting house at Dura Europos in northern Mesopotamia, perhaps was inspired by the Roman *paternalia* or family visits to the tomb. The scene received a new inflection around 400 in a version that stressed the conversation between the Holy Women and the angel and showed the tomb as obviously empty. Represented in a nave mosaic of S. Apollinare Nuovo, Ravenna, and in the Rabula Gospels in Florence, this scene dominated Byzantine Resurrection iconography and occurred frequently in the West, for example in the Drogo Sacramentary of about 850 and Duccio's *Maestà* of 1308–1311. These early images often place the Resurrection scene outdoors, and in some examples outside of a circular building or in front of a ciboriumlike structure that variously represent the Holy Sepulcher, the Church of the Resurrection, or the honorific aediculae that enclosed these sacred sites. A later example is a fresco dated between 1230 and 1237 in the Church of the Ascension, Mileševo (in present-day Yugoslavia).

Additional elements progressively crept into art to enrich and expand the tale of the Three Marys. One of the women sometimes appears at the tomb holding a censer, a detail that suggests the influence of liturgical ceremonies. The vignette of the Marys buying spice from a merchant, depicted in Romanesque sculpture at Arles, Beaucaire, and St. Gilles, France, seems to reflect the impact of popular religious drama.

As early as the seventh century, Christ himself is shown appearing to the Marys in the episode known as the Chairete (Mt. Sinai icon). The bodily resurrection of Christ was figured first in Ottonian art of the late tenth century and was handled in a variety of ways by artists of the later Middle Ages. Christ is represented standing within the sarcophagus in a plaque from the Klosterneuburg altar, stepping out of the tomb in the altarpiece by the Hohenfurth Master (see vol. 6, p. 272, for illustration), or posed in front of or atop the coffin.

Although the Resurrection continued to appear during the Gothic period in Northern Europe, Italian Trecento art displayed a particular predilection for the theme. Giotto, in his frescoes for the Arena Chapel, Padua, combined traditional elements of the Resurrection, such as the open sarcophagus, attendant angels, and sleeping soldiers, with Christ's appearance to Mary Magdalen, the *Noli me tangere*.

BIBLIOGRAPHY

Hans Aurenhammer, *Lexikon der christlichen Ikonographie,* I (1959), 232–249; Wolfgang Braunfels, *Die Auferstehung* (1951); André Grabar, *Christian Iconography: A Study of Its Origins* (1968), 123–125; Louis Réau, *Iconographie de l'art chrétien,* II, 2 (1957), 538–550; Gertrud Schiller, *Ikonographie der christlichen Kunst,* III (1971); Otto Schönewolf, *Die Darstellung der auferstehung Christi: Ihre Enstehung und ihre ältesten Denkmäler* (1909); Kurt Weitzmann, "Eine vorikonoklastische Ikone des Sinai mit der Darstellung des Chairete," in *Tortulae: Studien zu altchristlichen und byzantinischen Monumenten,* Walter N. Schumacher, ed. (1966), 317–325.

MICHAEL T. DAVIS

[See also **Chairete; Drama, Liturgical; Dura Europos; Early Christian Art; Easter; Manuscript Illumination, Western European; Noli Me Tangere; Passion Cycle; Pre-Romanesque Art.**]

RESURRECTION, ISLAMIC. Islam arose in an environment in which the idea of a future resurrection of mankind was already highly developed, and it is not surprising, therefore, that this idea should have come to occupy a central place within Muslim religious thinking. The bedrock of Muslim belief concerning resurrection is, of course, the Koran as supplemented by the second great source of revelation in Islam, *ḥadīth*. Systematic exposition of the doctrine of resurrection (*al-qiyāma*) is to be found, in briefest form, in the creed (*ᶜaqāᵓid*) composed by prominent individual theologians and, in more elaborated form, in the great theological summae and in specialized treatises on eschatology. In the summae the doctrine of resurrection was—like eschatological matters generally—treated under the heading of "received doctrine" (*al-samᶜiyāt*), to which a special section, placed at the end, was devoted.

Although the details of the events connected with the resurrection vary from exposition to exposition (not to mention the further variation occasioned by popular lore), the general outline of events is clear. The Day of Resurrection is heralded by "signs of the Hour," which include natural cataclysms, a breakdown of the moral order, devastations wrought by the beasts Gog and Magog,

RESURRECTION, ISLAMIC

the rise of Antichrist to lure Muslims from the true faith, the Second Coming of Jesus and his destruction of Antichrist, and the appearance of the Mahdi (sometimes identified with Jesus) to establish a millennial era of peace and righteousness. The resurrection is immediately preceded by a trumpet blast, which effects the dissolution of the creation into total nothingness (*al-fanāʾ*), and is itself effected by a second blast. In the interval between the two blasts, God alone exists in His original, self-subsistent state. The resurrection is thus a veritable re-creation of the world and is no more incredible than the original creation, a point that the Koran itself emphasizes in countering skepticism concerning the Resurrection.

The resurrection itself is indistinguishable from the Gathering (*al-ḥashr*) of mankind before the presence of God for judgment. Following this judgment (which is depicted by means of several different images, such as the weighing of deeds on a scale and the ordeal of crossing a narrow bridge suspended over hell), individuals are consigned to either the abode of punishment (hell) or the abode of reward (paradise). For some the abode of punishment is a temporary purgatory from which admittance to paradise is later granted. For others it is a final destination.

A future resurrection is necessitated by the intense moralism of the Koran, which links the very existence of a moral order to divine commands and divinely instituted sanctions located in the hereafter and which regards ultimate happiness as realizable only in paradise as a consequence of moral rectitude in this life. From the perspective of the Koran, all affirmation of the finality of death makes nonsense of human life and the cosmos and amounts to a denial of the existence of God. Because of the centrality that the resurrection has in the message of the Koran as the event ushering man into the hereafter and linking this life to the next, genuine skepticism concerning the resurrection (of the sort represented by the Sadducees in Judaism) has not been possible for Muslims. Those rare individuals among them in the Middle Ages who did express such skepticism in effect placed themselves outside the pale of Islam.

But within that pale, interpretations of the resurrection varied. Although they were sometimes mutually exclusive, they at least allowed their adherents to affirm with clear conscience their Muslim identity. Interpretations differed as to the degree of literalism (or symbolism) that was to be allowed in dealing with the particular images associated with the resurrection. The most important cleavage among the interpretations arose out of disagreement over the role of the body in the resurrection. The philosophers (*falāsifa*) generally embraced the Hellenic notion of the immortality of the soul and the conception of ultimate happiness as deliverance of the soul from the body and from the material world as a whole. Not wishing to reject utterly the language of bodily resurrection, they accorded it a purely metaphorical, or symbolic, character. The theologians (*mutakallimūn*), on the other hand, insisted on a real resurrection of both body and soul, or spirit. Differences arose among them over the relation between soul and spirit (*nafs* and *rūḥ:* identical or different?) and over the state of individuals in the interim between death and the Resurrection. With respect to the latter question, it became a hallmark of orthodoxy among the theologians to affirm a conscious existence of some sort during the interim. During that period the individual was interrogated by the angels Munkar and Nakīr concerning deeds done in this life and punished for wrongdoing (as a foretaste of the judgment and punishment awaiting him after the resurrection).

Among Sufis and Ismaili Shiites interpretations are to be found that may be classified under the heading of realized eschatology. For Sufi theosophists, man's ultimate fulfillment was achieved in the realization of oneness with God and the extinction of separate, individual selfhood, which together are described as a "return" to God. Since the resurrection was also treated by the theologians as a return to God, it was quite natural that the theosophists should have considered the Resurrection to be realized in the mystical experiences of the adept. Ismailis share with Twelver Shiites a belief in an earlier resurrection of the righteous, distinct from the resurrection of gathering for judgment, which inaugurates the millennial age and is effected by the Mahdi himself, who accordingly bears the title of *al-qāʾim* ('the Resurrecter'). "Reformed" Ismailism considers this resurrection to have taken place in 1164 by proclamation of Imam Hasan II; as a result the righteous are believed to have since lived esoterically in a resurrected state even while upon the earth.

BIBLIOGRAPHY

Henry Corbin, *Creative Imagination in the Sūfism of IbnʿArabi,* Ralph Manheim, trans. (1969), 199–200,

206; Majid Fakhry, *A History of Islamic Philosophy* (1970), 165–167, 314–315, 2nd rev. ed. (1983), 145–146, 282–283; Louis Gardet, "Ḳiyāma," in *Encyclopaedia of Islam,* new ed., V (1986); al-Ghazālī, *The Precious Pearl,* Jane I. Smith, trans. (1979); Imām Muslim, *Ṣaḥīḥ Muslim,* ᶜAbdul Ḥamīd Ṣiddīqī, trans., IV (1975), 1461–1528; Jane I. Smith and Yvonne Y. Haddad, *The Islamic Understanding of Death and Resurrection* (1981), 1–97, with extensive bibliography on the subject, 245–254; John B. Taylor, "Some Aspects of Islamic Eschatology," in *Religious Studies,* 4 (1968); Arent J. Wensinck, *The Muslim Creed* (1932, repr. 1966).

BERNARD G. WEISS

[See also **Islam, Religion; Millennialism, Islamic; Paradise, Islamic; Philosophy and Theology, Islamic; Purgatory, Islamic.**]

RETABLE (from the Spanish *retablo*), originally a shelf or ledge placed above an altar to hold candles, flowers, or other ornaments. By the eleventh century, however, the retable had also evolved into a low, usually unhinged carved or painted altarpiece (or later, carved central composition with painted wings) placed at the back of the altar. The earliest known examples, all from Northern Europe, are: the Lisbjerg Retable, a retable of bronze gilt and brown enamel at the National Museum in Copenhagen (*ca.* 1140); a retable of stucco in Erfurt Cathedral (*ca.* 1160); and a retable of copper gilt, most probably by a Mosan metalsmith, from St. Castor in Coblenz, now at the Cluny Museum in Paris.

Other retables, mostly painted wooden panels dating from the thirteenth century, can be found at St. Elizabeth's Church, Marburg (1290), and in museums in Berlin and Munich. Larger painted retables, some as high as fifteen feet, and dating from the fourteenth and fifteenth centuries, are found in the Cloisters collection in New York.

BIBLIOGRAPHY

Johannes Jahn, *Wörterbuch der Kunst* (1957), 18–19; Peter Lasko, *Ars sacra: 800–1200* (1972).

ROBERT K. HAYCRAFT

[See also **Altar-Altar Apparatus; Altarpiece; Gothic Art: Painting; Metalsmiths, Gold and Silver; Mosan Art; Rossello di Jacopo Franchi** (with illustration).]

REVERDIE, a dance song celebrating spring; sometimes expanded to include certain allegorical poems that have a spring setting, an amorous encounter and dialogue, and a description of the lady encountered.

Also, a rhetorical topic (*topos*) describing the coming of spring and including one or more of the following motifs: rebirth; the harmony of the universe and the love that binds it together, often grouping nature-love-harmony-music (that is, the poet's song); and an element of discord in this ideal setting, either in the lover himself or in his relationship with his lady, sometimes expressed through images of winter.

BIBLIOGRAPHY

Pierre Bec, *La lyrique française au moyen âge (XIIe–XIIIe siècles),* I (1977), 136–141; Leo Spitzer, *Classical and Christian Ideas of World Harmony* (1963), esp. 59–63; James J. Wilhelm, *The Cruelest Month: Spring, Nature, and Love in Classical and Medieval Lyrics* (1965).

STEPHEN MANNING

[See also **Troubadour, Trouvère.**]

REXACH, JUAN (*fl. ca.* 1437–1482), a Valencian artist who left several paintings in a local version of the Hispano-Flemish style, which derived from the influence of the van Eyck brothers or the Valencian painter Luis Dalmaú. Among Rexach's works is a signed St. Ursula altarpiece (1468), which was found in a church at Cubells and is now in the Museo de Arte de Cataluña, Barcelona. His crowded compositions contrast with the spacious, balanced designs of a contemporary fellow Valencian, Jacomart (Jaime Baçó).

BIBLIOGRAPHY

Chandler R. Post, *A History of Spanish Painting,* VI, 1 (1935), 54–100.

MARY GRIZZARD

[See also **Baçó, Jaime; Dalmaú, Luis.**]

REYKDŒLA SAGA (The saga of the Reykdalers) is a feud story from northern Iceland. Roughly the

REYKDŒLA SAGA

first half relates the protracted hostilities between Vémundr kǫgurr and Steingrímr Ǫrnólfsson. The quarrel is precipitated by Steingrímr's outlawing of the villain Hánefr, the foster father of Vémundr's son. Thereafter, Vémundr provokes a series of confrontations by such devices as buying timber promised to Steingrímr, seizing his oxen, inciting a half-wit to strike him with a sheep's head, abducting a bride, and making Steingrímr liable to prosecution by urging his workmen to damage another man's property. Each confrontation is patiently and skillfully settled by Vémundr's uncle Áskell, but the quarrel eventually culminates in an armed clash, in which both Steingrímr and Áskell are killed.

In the sequel, Áskell's son Skúta takes responsibility for the vengeance and succeeds in killing first two accessories to the slaying, then the slayer himself under the very eyes of his two protectors, the chieftains Þorgeirr and Eyjólfr. Þorgeirr tries unsuccessfully to have Skúta assassinated. Eyjólfr's son Glúmr (the hero of *Víga-Glúms saga*) also makes an attempt, but an accommodation is reached through the marriage of Glúmr's daughter to Skúta. Hostilities flare again and the couple are divorced. Skúta lures Glúmr into an ambush, but Glúmr turns the tables on him and Skúta escapes only by disguising himself as a shepherd. After thwarting several more attempts on his life, Skúta is eventually brought to bay and killed in his bedchamber.

St. Ursula and her virgins arriving in Rome. Detail from the St. Ursula altarpiece by Juan Rexach, 1468. FOTO MAS, BARCELONA

Reykdœla saga (which still awaits translation into English) occupies a key position in the study of the Icelandic family sagas. It has customarily been dated to the middle years of the thirteenth century, but Dietrich Hofmann has produced strong arguments in favor of a date before 1220. It may therefore be the earliest of all the family sagas, a possibility that makes it crucial to our understanding of how the sagas developed. *Reykdœla saga* is set apart by a number of special features: an absence of skaldic stanzas, a reliance on indirect discourse, a quantity of references to oral tradition, a preoccupation with conflicting versions of the tale, and a relatively undramatic and narratively unsophisticated stringing together of the district and family conflicts that make up the story. If *Reykdœla saga* is old and closer to its oral prototype than most sagas, it provides special insight into the nature of the antecedent tradition. The disparity between its ingenuous reporting and the more polished narrative of the great sagas may give us a measure of the artistic development that took place during the period of saga writing in the thirteenth century. On the other hand, it must be borne in mind that there were presumably great ranges in oral as well as literary skills. The author of *Reykdœla saga* could have managed good oral sources badly, or he could have been at the mercy of an unskilled storyteller, whose version he failed to improve. Even so, there are a few striking scenes, such as the encounter between Glúmr and Skúta (which is also included in *Víga-Glúms saga*). The most memorable character is Áskell, whose inexhaustible goodwill is hardly paralleled elsewhere in the sagas.

BIBLIOGRAPHY

An edition is Björn Sigfússon, ed., *Ljósvetninga saga með þáttum: Reykdœla saga ok Víga-Skútu* (1940); a translation into German is in Wilhelm Ranisch and Walter Heinrich Vogt, trans., *Fünf Geschichten aus dem östlichen Nordland* (1939, new ed. 1964).

Studies include Anne Heinrichs, "'Intertexture' and Its Function in Early Written Sagas: A Stylistic Observa-

Rheims Cathedral, west facade (*ca.* 1255–1290) by Bernard de Soissons. (Towers added 1305–1427.) FOTO MARBURG/ART RESOURCE

tion of *Heiðarvíga saga, Reykdœla saga,* and the Legendary Olafssaga," in *Scandinavian Studies,* **48** (1976); Dietrich Hofmann, "Reykdœla saga und mündliche Überlieferung," in *Skandinavistik,* **1** (1972); Knut Liestøl, "Reykdœla saga: Tradisjon og forfattar," in *Festskrift til Finnur Jónsson* (1928).

THEODORE M. ANDERSSON

[See also **Family Sagas, Icelandic; Víga-Glúms Saga.**]

REYNES, HENRY OF. See **Henry of Reynes.**

RHEIMS CATHEDRAL, or more properly, Notre Dame de Rheims, is the metropolitan church of the archdiocese of Rheims and the traditional site of the coronation of the kings of France. This cathedral is one of the five High Gothic cathedrals of France and one of the most imposing examples of Gothic architecture anywhere. The Gothic cathedral was begun after a fire on 6 May 1210 destroyed a ninth-century Carolingian cathedral, and it was completed in the fourteenth century. Despite the long period required for construction, the building is more unified in style than its extensive sculptural program. The architects of Rheims were Jean d'Orbais, Jean (le) Loup, Gaucher de Rheims, Bernard de Soissons, and Robert de Coucy.

BIBLIOGRAPHY

Robert Branner, "Historical Aspects of the Reconstruction of Reims Cathedral, 1210–1241," in *Speculum,* **36** (1961); Louis Demaison, *La cathédrale de Reims,* 3rd rev. ed. (1954); Hans Reinhardt, *La cathédrale de Reims* (1963); Francis Salet, "Chronologie de la cathédrale [de Reims]," in *Bulletin monumental,* **125** (1967), with extensive bibliography.

CARL F. BARNES, JR.

[See also **Bernard of Soissons; France: 987–1223; Gothic Architecture; Jean d'Orbais; Loup, Jean; Robert de Coucy.**]

RHETICIUS OF AUTUN, ST. (*fl.* early fourth century), churchman, was born into a wealthy Gallic family. He and his wife renounced their marriage and entered religious life. Appointed bishop of Autun, he gained great authority by condemning Donatists and absolving Caecilian, bishop of Carthage, at a synod held in Rome in 313. He wrote a commentary on the Song of Songs and a treatise on baptism.

BIBLIOGRAPHY

Source. "Dictum de baptismo," in *Patrologia latina,* VI (1844), 45–46.

Study. Hans Lietzmann, *A History of the Early Church,* Bertram Lee Woolf, trans., III (1950, rev. 1953, repr. 1961).

NATHALIE HANLET

[See also **Donatism.**]

RHETORIC: ARABIC, HEBREW, PERSIAN

ARABIC RHETORIC

Origins. Study of the artistic uses of language began, among the Arabs, for reasons that were in part literary, in part theological.

The cultural ferment of the early Abbasid age (*ca.* 750–850) created new poetic forms. These delighted the public with their fluency, wit, and novelty of feeling, but drew hostile or dismissive judgments from the contemporary scholars of language and pre-Islamic poetry. The old poetry, whose guardians the philologists were, was admired for its purity of language and poetic vigor. The new poetry, according to the philologists, was unreliable on the first point and diminished on the second; moreover, what it lacked in power it tried to supply in artifice. The very sensible differences between the old poetry and the new—in vocabulary, themes, adornment, and decorum—led to definition of the chief issues of debate and invited attempts at fixing values and criteria. Early opinions on such matters are reported in many books. The first systematic work of Arabic rhetoric, the *Book of Decorative Devices* (*Kitāb-al-badī*ᶜ) by the Abbasid prince Ibn al-Muᶜtazz, sprang directly from this battle of ancients and moderns: it was written (in 887/888) with the avowed aim of showing that the rhetorical ornaments, so freely used by the new poets, were at home already in pre-Islamic poetry and in the Koran.

The theological impetus came from study of the Koran. The question of what is literal and what is metaphorical is an immediate and ubiquitous puzzle of scriptural interpretation. Moreover, the doctrine that the Koran is perfect and inimitable in its suiting of word to thought, that its language is the miracle that proves Muḥammad's prophethood, invited comparison of the Koran with other texts (as in al-Bāqillānī) and prompted, despite the need to fit taste to dogma, serious study of tropical expression, figures of speech, and, ultimately, the stylistic possibilities of syntax.

In time, an eminently practical need was added to literary and scholarly interest: the clerks who manned the bureaucracy had to master elegant writing. Official letters and documents meant for public reading (patents of investiture, promises of military aid, news of victory) developed a florid style: the mannered rhetorical figures of poetry—even the conventional conceits—appeared in them. Such a style served between officials as the verbal form of ceremonial behavior, and between friends, as a social grace. Addressed to the common man it was perhaps, like royal magnificence, a way of instilling loyalty and awe.

The rhetorical tradition is indigenous. Many of the devices and criteria discussed in Arabic rhetoric have parallels in the rhetoric of classical antiquity, but there is no evidence of significant classical influence. Aristotle's *Rhetoric* and *Poetics,* although translated, had no effect on the main current of Arabic rhetoric. This is easily understood: epic and drama were unknown to Arabic literature, and nothing in Islamic public life corresponded to the forensic and deliberative oratory of antiquity. Some philosophical ideas appear here and there—such as assigning to poetic utterances a place in the classification of statements according to truth value (al-Fārābī) or the notion in Qudāma's *Critique of Poetry* that a good panegyric should praise its man for the four cardinal virtues and their combinations—but these ideas remain peripheral to the rhetorical tradition.

Rhetoric in the tenth and eleventh centuries. There was no single school of rhetorical theory until the scholastic treatment of the subject emerged with the successors of ᶜAbd al-Qāhir al-Jurjānī (*d.* 1078). Although the writers before al-Jurjānī do quote one another, their terminology varies, as does their scope and purpose. Some books deal chiefly with poetry, some, such as the *Two Crafts* (*Kitāb al-ṣināᶜatayn*) of Abū Hilāl al-ᶜAskarī (*d.* after 1010), with poetry and art prose. One tenth-century work, Ibn Wahb's *Al-burhān fī wujūh al-bayān*, is devoted exclusively to prose, with excursions into logic and the art of disputation. Besides books with a broad theoretical interest, there were compendia of *topoi* and anthologies of similes arranged according to subject matter, and critical works comparing rival poets.

The following are some of the principal areas of discussion:

1. *The moral content of poetry.* Poetry may please even when its content is morally repugnant or, in religious law, vicious. "Poetry is dissociated from religion" (Qudāma, *d.* 945). It has power to improve character: it can put heart into the cowardly, or make the niggardly magnanimous. Since literary theory completely ignored popular prose fiction and had no narrative poetry to deal with, discussion of the morality of fiction (a familiar example of this issue in European literature is in Boccaccio, *De genealogia deorum gentilium* XIV.9)

was limited to three chief topics: tropical expression, conventional motifs with the poet as subject, and hyperbole. The first two are unobjectionable, although culturally obsolete conventions are at times discouraged (as by Ibn Rashīq, *d.* 1064 or 1070, in *Al-ᶜUmda,* I. 230) because they are ridiculous, not because they are false. Hyperbole is proper to poetry according to the authors, although they do report opinions in favor of holding to the truth in panegyric (as does Ibn Rashīq, I. 98). The old maxim "in poetry, what most lies most pleases" is often quoted and understood to mean tropical (figurative) speech and hyperbole. It is illustrative of the authors' acceptance of hyperbole that Qudāma, who urges panegyrists to stress the virtues that separate man from beast, adds this proviso: when philosophers speak of the cardinal virtues they mean the middle way in each, but poetry must be extravagant.

2. *The ancients and the moderns.* Even when the new poetry was no longer looked down on, it was still by and large agreed that the ancient poets were rough but sinewy and the moderns sweet but without comparable fiber; that the ancients had power where the moderns had artifice; and that the ancients invented the motifs that the moderns, on the whole, elaborated and embellished.

3. *Decorum and style.* As in classical rhetoric (for example, Cicero's *De oratore* III.37–53), there is much discussion of the need for pure and correct language, clear expression, and a manner that suits the occasion. To achieve *jazāla,* the style that is pure and impressive, the urban poet of the Islamic age must avoid harsh, savage words smacking of unimproved bedouin life on the one side, and an anemic or marketplace vocabulary on the other. "The best vocabulary is that which a person of average education understands but would not use." Regarding clarity, "Poetry is at its worst when you have to ask what it means." Discussions of decorum include general maxims such as "To each station the speech proper to it." Poets should observe social and literary manners. One must not use ill-omened phrases in a panegyric. As al-Amidī writes (*Kitāb al-muwāzana,* 218), it is bad form to say "her lovely hand gave the hateful sign of parting," because to say that there is anything repulsive about seeing the beloved is contrary to "the way of the Arabs in poetry." It is understood that decorum changes with time: The bedouin poet Imruᵓ al-Qays could compare, in a sharply precise simile, a girl's henna-tipped fingers to a certain soft worm of white shading to pink; in a poet of the Islamic age such a simile would be in bad taste (Ibn Rashīq I.299).

4. *Invention, convention, plagiarism.* Invention means bringing forth a poetic notion (conceit, image, motif) that is not analogically derivable from a previous one. In the Islamic age, such invention is rare. A poet may "generate" (*tawlīd*) a new notion from an old one by making it more precise or more fully descriptive, by inverting it, or the like. This too is meritorious. There is much debate over the shades of literary borrowing, ranging from convention to theft. A poet, no matter how great his natural talent, must study the literary tradition or go astray (Ibn Rashīq I.197). Nor can he dispense with the store of conventions. "No writer can do without using the *maᶜānī* [ideas, motifs] of the ancients or avoid pouring his matter into the molds of those who preceded him. However, whatever he takes he must dress in his own words . . . refining its composition and embellishing its ornaments. If he does this he has a better title to it than any who used it before him" (Abū Hilāl al-ᶜAskarī, 202).

5. *Word and sense.* The authorities agree that the motifs and ideas used by the poets are easily come by; artistry depends on the words. These should suit the sense. "Hearing and understanding should, as it were, run a race and finish in a dead heat" (al-Jāḥiẓ, *d.* 869). The poet should not allow his words to distort what he meant to say, and he should not allow his desire for figures of speech to lure him into using ugly or barbarous words. ᶜAbd al-Qāhir al-Jurjānī uses the term "form of idea" (*ṣūrat al-maᶜnā*) to express the weave of thought and word. He offers the view in *Dalāᵓil al-iᶜjāz* (237) that his predecessors who attributed poetic worth to wording, not ideas, meant merely what he expressed with greater precision: that what matters is success in giving an underlying thought a particular (and particularizing) verbal form. This is not the extreme interpretation of the indivisibility of *res* and *verba,* but a lucid commonsense view of the relation of word and sense in a highly conventional lyric.

6. *Natural diction and artifice.* There is a difference between conscious rhetorical technique and manneredness (*takalluf*). Extravagant use of rhetorical devices is a mistake. According to Ibn Rashīq (I.130) Ibn al-Muᶜtazz excels because "his technique is subtle and unobtrusive, so that at times only an expert in the fine points of poetry can pick

out his devices." Theory constantly demands naturalness; implicitly it also demands technical brilliance. These two demands seem reconciled in the notion that a rhetorical device can strike the audience with its perfect fit. In an anecdote told by al-Jurjānī in his *Asrār al-balāgha,* a bedouin delivers an extremely compact sentence in rhymed prose. When this is remarked on, he asks in surprise: "How else can you say it?"

7. *Harmony and unity.* Ḥātimī wrote that "a poem should be proportionate like a body." Harmony of parts (an elusive concept) is required at various levels: harmony of sounds, symmetry of phrasing, proper attention to the subdivisions of a theme, and avoidance of incongruities in style or decorum. In poetry symmetry, or parallelism, is also served by the device of recalling in the second half of a verse, by way of repetition or antithesis, a word in the first hemistich. In a well-constructed line, the rhyme word must seem demanded by what leads up to it. All critics stress the importance of good beginnings, smooth transitions between themes (the pre-Islamic poets, it is noted, paid no attention to this), and appropriate endings. Ibn Ṭabāṭabā (*d.* 933?) demands—none of his colleagues go so far—that the whole poem must be in point of fluency like a single word, and so well organized that any switch of verses will impair it. The rhetoric books do not explicitly demand a linear development of thought, and do not (with rare exceptions) cite whole poems. Since Arabic poems may or may not have linear development, and since the theoreticians were mainly interested in general principles, not in applied criticism, these lacks are understandable. The practical explication of texts—such as al-Marzūqī's commentary on the *Ḥamāsa,* an anthology of old poems—shows more interest in the relation of one statement to the next.

8. *Rhetorical devices.* These are extensively treated. With time the lists grow longer, the distinctions more elaborate. Ibn Rashīq, for example, devotes chapters to such devices as metaphor and metonymy, simile, allusion, gnomae, paronomasia, antithesis, various forms of repetition, explication (a compact statement followed by a more detailed version), division (dealing with all members of a class or set; for example, the slain/the captives/the fugitives), hyperbole, and quotation.

9. *Euphony.* Various authors provide basic hints, such as avoid tongue-twisters and the like. Al-Khafājī (*d.* 1073) attempts to show that aesthetic response to the sound of a word depends on the relations among the consonants' points of articulation.

Rhetoric as a formal discipline. ᶜAbd al-Qāhir al-Jurjānī (*d.* 1078), in his two great works, laid the basis for the systematic study of the subject. In *The Demonstration of Inimitability* (of the Koran: *Dalāᵓil al-iᶜjāz*) he developed the stylistic analysis of syntactic patterns. His *Principles of Eloquence (Asrār al-balāgha)* is a masterpiece of the logical and psychological analysis of metaphor and related topics. Subsequent writers used a threefold division of the matter of rhetoric: the stylistic study of syntax ("meanings," or *maᶜānī*); the analysis of metaphor, simile, and analogy ("clarity," or *bayān*); and rhetorical devices (*badīᶜ*). The series of interrelated books and commentaries by al-Sakkākī (*d.* 1229), al-Qazwīnī (*d.* 1338), and al-Taftazānī (*d.* 1389) is remarkable for logical and grammatical acumen.

Art prose. Most points of rhetoric, the authors remark, apply alike to poetry, public oratory (exhortation, admonition, and so forth), and the epistolary art. There are some topics specific to prose. In rhymed prose the rhyme word should be natural and carry some weight in the text. Parallelism (of the kind familiar from the Old Testament) is demanded as a basic virtue of art prose. It is noteworthy that some authors (such as Ibn al-Athīr, I. 198) condemn mere elegant variation and demand that the parallel phrase augment the meaning. The rhythm of clauses in an extended period is discussed. A frequently treated topic is the proper length and amount of detail in a speech or epistle. According to al-Qalqashandī's (*d.* 1418) encyclopedic manual for clerks, a compressed style is best for communicating with kings, a middle style for corresponding with equals or with the "middle class of leaders," and prolixity for haranguing the people. Manuals for clerks contain many sample letters for practical study. Much rarer are principles for the overall plan of a speech or epistle. An example occurs in al-Nuwayrī's fourteenth-century encyclopedia (VII 201–202), where a fourfold division is recommended for patents of investiture and similar documents: a pious introduction; a setting forth of the circumstances that led to conferral of the office; description of the appointee and his qualifications; and exhortations to the appointee.

Andras Hamori

HEBREW RHETORIC

One important work on rhetoric and poetics has survived from the efflorescence of medieval Hebrew poetry in Spain, southern France, and Italy: the *Book of Discussion and Conversation,* written in Arabic by Moses ibn Ezra (*d. ca.* 1140). The book contains a long section on rhetorical devices, as well as hints about what a poet ought to study and what a good poem is like. All this is entirely in the Arabic rhetorical tradition. Ibn Ezra also takes up matters of Hebrew literary history: when did the Jews begin to write rhyming verse; why the Hebrew poets of Spain are so much the best; and why the Hebrew lexicon is poorer than the Arabic (a consequence, he believes, of the exile). To show that the Hebrew language has always been capable of artistic expression, he uses biblical phrases to illustrate rhetorical figures.

Ibn Ezra writes from a religious and philosophical perspective: Poetry is inferior to truth; it may be a frill ("In my youth I valued poetry because I thought it made a good impression"), a frivolous thing (wine songs), or a wicked thing ("I have never written a satire against a real person").

Several commentators used rhetorical terms to describe biblical passages. The most thoroughgoing work of this kind is a fifteenth-century catalog of the Prophets' rhetorical devices. Its author, Judah ben Jehiel (Messer Leon), was no longer in the Arabic tradition: his masters were Cicero and Quintilian.

ANDRAS HAMORI

PERSIAN RHETORIC

During the ninth and tenth centuries, Persian gained acceptance as a language of poetry and of diplomatic correspondence—at least at Iranian courts. It never seriously challenged Arabic as the language of religion, philosophy, or science, however. Persian poetry developed during this period with explosive vigor, but there is virtually no writing in Persian on poetry or the artistic use of language. When scholars of Iranian origin, such as Ibn Qutayba or (ᶜAbd al-Qāhir) al-Jurjānī, wrote on these subjects, they did so in Arabic, and took their examples from Arabic poetry. Nor were their works ever translated into Persian.

When Persian came at last to be used as a vehicle for discussing poetry as well as composing it, the works that emerged were straightforward manuals of prosody written for the instruction of courtly amateurs. The first of these to survive, and probably one of the first written, is Rādūyānī's *Tarjumān al-balāgha* (The interpreter of eloquence), which was composed sometime around the beginning of the twelfth century. The next, Rashīd al-Dīn Ṿatvāt's *Ḥadā'iq al-siḥr fī daqā'iq al-shiᶜr* (The gardens of mystery: On the niceties of poetry), did not appear until three-quarters of a century later and was largely an unacknowledged crib from Rādūyānī, with examples added and updated. Both works are limited to identifying and illustrating the arts by which poetry is adorned. They provide some insight into contemporary taste, but do not address themselves to more theoretical questions.

Far more important than either of these works is the comprehensive study of Shams-i Qays that is generally known by its short title, *Al-muᶜjam* (The compendium), which he composed during the first quarter of the thirteenth century. Shams-i Qays's book is now esteemed principally for the lengthy chapters on rhyme (*qāfīya*) and meter (*ᶜarūḍ*) that it contains in addition to the by then customary discussion of tropes and figures. It also contains a concluding section on the nature of poetic composition itself that is the first and very nearly the only examination of this question to appear in Persian. It is almost wholly derived from Arabic works, but has the virtue of making a sketch of their principal themes available to those whose knowledge of that language was weak.

Shams-i Qays's study of rhyme and meter was never superseded, and his discussion of the quiddity of poetry was never continued. A number of manuals of prosody have appeared from that time to this, all more or less extensions of Rādūyānī and Shams-i Qays.

JEROME W. CLINTON

BIBLIOGRAPHY

Arabic rhetoric. Iḥsān ᶜAbbās, *Ta'rīkh al-naqd al-adabī ᶜind al-ᶜarab* (1971); K. Abu Deeb, *Al-Jurjānī's Theory of Poetic Imagery* (1979); Al-Amīdī, *Al-muwāzana* (1961–1965); Al-ᶜAskarī, *Kitāb al-ṣināᶜatayn* (1971); Ibn al-Athīr, *Al-mathal al-saᵓir* (1939); Vincente Cantarino, *Arabic Poetics in the Golden Age* (1975), with much space devoted to Arab Aristotelianism, and some selections from the main current of Arabic rhetoric; Gustave Edmund von Grunebaum, "Arabic Literary Criticism in the Tenth Century A.D.," in *Journal of the American Oriental Society,* **61** (1941), and *A Tenth-century Document of Arabic Literary Theory and Criticism* (1950), al-Bāqillānī's analysis of the superiority of the Koran to the eloquence of poets; Wolfhart Heinrichs,

Arabische Dichtung und griechische Poetik (1969), the first half an outstanding discussion of many of the basic matters of Arabic poetic theory, and *The Hand of the Northwind* (1977), on the theory of metaphor; al-Jurjānī, *Die Geheimnisse der Wortkunst* (*Asrār al-balāgha*), H. Ritter, trans. (1959), the most profound work of its kind in Arabic; August F. M. van Mehren, *Die Rhetorik der Araber* (1853); Ibn al-Rashīq, *Al-ᶜumda* (1972); Amjad Trabulsi, *La critique poétique des arabes* (1955), a survey.

Hebrew rhetoric. Raymond P. Scheindlin, "Rabbi Moshe Ibn Ezra on the Legitimacy of Poetry," in *Medievalia et humanistica,* n.s. 7 (1976).

Persian rhetoric. Muhammad Ibn ᶜUmar al-Rādūyānī, *Tarjumān al-balāgha,* A. Atis, ed. (1949); Benedikt Reinert, "Probleme der vormongolischen arabisch-persischen Poesiegemeinschaft und ihr Reflex in der Poetik," in Gustave Edmund von Grunebaum, ed., *Arabic Poetry: Theory and Development* (1973); Lutz Richter-Bernburg, "Linguistic Shᶜūbīya and Early Neo-Persian Prose," in *Journal of the American Oriental Society,* 94 (1974); Shams al-Dīn Muhammad ibn Qays al-Rāzī (Shams-i Qays), *Al-muᶜjam fī maᶜmāyīr ashᶜār al-ᶜajam,* rev. ed., Mudarris Razavī, ed., incorporating the introduction and notes of the first edition by Muhammad ibn ᶜAbd al-Vahhab Qazvīnī, and with an introduction by the editor (1959); Rashīd al-Dīn Vaṭvāṭ, *Ḥadā'iq al-siḥr fī daqā'iq al-sḥiᶜr,* ᶜAbbās Iqbal, ed. (1930), and repr. in an edition of the *Dīvān,* Saᶜīd Nafīsī, ed. (1960). The first part of the concluding section of Shams-i Qays's work is translated in Jerome W. Clinton, "Šams-i Qays on the Nature of Poetry," in W. al-Qadi, ed., *Studia arabica et islamica* (1981), 75–82.

A. H.
J. W. C.

[See also **Arabic Literature; Arabic Poetry; Hebrew Belles Lettres; Hebrew Poetry; Iranian Literature;** and individual authors.]

RHETORIC: BYZANTINE. The Byzantines inherited from the ancient world both the practice of oratory on a variety of public and private occasions and a body of rhetorical theory that formed the staple material of elite education. So not only were Byzantine public men usually trained and experienced speakers, but Byzantine audiences were sophisticated and sensitive to the nuances of an art elaborated over more than a thousand years.

Traditionally, Greek oratory had been divided into forensic, deliberative, and epideictic oratory. The disappearance of genuine political assemblies left scarcely any occasion for deliberative oratory, and the exercise of judicial functions by officials or by the emperor himself much reduced the scope of forensic oratory. On the other hand the growing ritualization of public life and of some aspects of private life provided frequent occasions for epideictic oratory, which, from being a mere demonstration of technique, became an important medium of public communication. At the same time the Christianization of society opened up a new domain of religious oratory unknown in the ancient world.

The principal genre was panegyric. Examples survive from the period from the fourth to the sixth century, and in larger numbers from the ninth century onward. The eleventh and twelfth centuries are particularly well represented. Some of these speeches were delivered on regularly recurring occasions, for example panegyrics on the emperor at Epiphany and those on the patriarch on the Feast of St. Lazarus (the Saturday before Palm Sunday). But for the majority it is not easy to determine the occasion of their delivery. Often it will have been at an ad hoc gathering in a palace, church, or private house. Some may not have been orally delivered at all but sent in written form to their addressee. The texts of panegyrics, as of other speeches, were often circulated by the orator to friends and colleagues, by whom they were critically discussed. Collected editions of panegyrics and other speeches were often prepared by the orator himself (such as Nikephoros Basilakios in the mid twelfth century) or by an editor after his death (for example, Niketas Choniates at the beginning of the thirteenth century). Whether the panegyrist received any reward other than goodwill can rarely be determined. It probably depended on the social standing of the speaker and his subject.

The content of panegyric speeches, as of many others, usually followed closely the precepts of ancient rhetorical manuals, particularly the two treatises on epideictic oratory attributed to Menander. Thus the orator deals with the birthplace, parentage, birth, and education of his subject, then goes on to show how his actions exemplify the standard virtues of wisdom, courage, justice, and self-control. He may add a brief and laudatory reference to his physical appearance. These speeches may seem to the modern reader to be tissues of commonplaces. Yet the Byzantine hearer or reader—apart from the aesthetic satisfaction he derived from technical virtuosity—learned from minor variations and nuances, and did not expect balanced and critical judgment from a panegyrist.

Another epideictic genre much prized by the Byzantines was the funeral oration and its near relation, the monody, a kind of memorial speech delivered some time after the death of the subject. These generally follow the same structural pattern as panegyric speeches, dwelling on the virtues of their subjects rather than on their actions or their careers. The narrative or descriptive thread is often interrupted by passages of high emotion. Funeral orations are often more informative than the run of panegyrics.

Other forms of Byzantine epideictic oratory included the *prosphonetikos,* or speech of greeting, for example to an emperor returning from an inevitably victorious campaign or to a dignitary on taking up a new office; the *presbeutikos,* or speech delivered by an envoy to an emperor or to a foreign ruler; the *epithalamioi,* or marriage speech; the *eucharisterios,* or speech of thanks for some benefit received; and the inaugural speech on taking up office, and in particular the inaugural lectures of publicly appointed teachers, which often contain information on their earlier careers. During wars, good news from the front was often the occasion for a display of oratorical talent by speakers who, in the words of one of them, "spring to the platform when news arrives of the emperor's victories." Finally, there were many descriptive speeches on cities or buildings, many of which were probably not actually delivered.

In the middle and later Byzantine periods these frequent speeches, often copied and circulated widely, played a part in the dissemination of information—or misinformation—the molding of opinion, and the assertion of common ideas comparable to that of journalism in more recent times. In the course of the civil wars of the fourteenth century real political oratory, addressed to decision-making bodies, is occasionally encountered. The techniques of persuasion were known and available.

A special type of oratory is the speech of a general to his troops. None survives from the Byzantine world, though there are literary imitations of the genre in the historians. Writers on military matters emphasize the importance of these speeches and outline the ideas to be expressed in them; at least one textbook of military rhetoric survives unpublished.

Preaching had always been part of the ministry of the church. As the urban upper classes adopted Christianity, men with a classical training in rhetoric rose to leading positions in the church. Preachers like Gregory of Nazianzus, Basil, and John Chrysostom introduced into the sermon all the sophisticated elaboration of traditional rhetoric and left models which their successors strove to the best of their ability to imitate. Sermons might be moral exhortations, expositions of doctrine, explanations of ritual or cult, or comments on current events or other subjects. Many, particularly in the ninth and tenth centuries, were panegyrics on persons of the Trinity or saints, closely resembling in structure and style secular panegyrics. In general Byzantine sermons are marked by rhetorical pyrotechnics rather than by simplicity or directness. Like secular speeches, they were often circulated in written copies and so could be reused. In this way many homilies of the fathers of the church and later preachers became associated with particular church feasts, at which they were redelivered. Collections of these—*panegyrika* and homiliaries—were compiled for liturgical use. Laymen as well as clergy preached, though the practice was uncanonical. Many orators were equally at home in secular and religious oratory, examples being the emperors Leo VI (*r.* 886–912) and Manuel II (*r.* 1391–1425), Eustathios, archbishop of Thessaloniki (late twelfth century), and the layman Nikephoros Gregoras (mid fourteenth century).

There were other occasions for religious oratory. Many of the polemics against the Latins so frequent from the twelfth century are in form, and probably in fact, speeches. The polemics aroused by the Hesychast movement in the fourteenth century stimulated much oratory by clerics and laymen alike.

Few Byzantine men of letters were not public speakers. Stylized oral communication played a notable part in the formulation and spread of received ideas, and its techniques profoundly affected every branch of literature.

BIBLIOGRAPHY

Hans-Georg Beck, *Kirche und theologische Literatur im byzantinischen Reich* (1959); Albert Ehrhard, *Überlieferung und Bestand der hagiographischen und homiletischen Literatur der griechischen Kirche,* II (1938), 242–305, III (1939–1952), 523–722; Herbert Hunger, *Die hochsprachliche profane Literatur der Byzantiner,* I (1978), 63–196, and "The Classical Tradition in Byzantine Literature: The Importance of Rhetoric," in Margaret Mullet and Roger Scott, eds., *Byzantium and the Classical Tradition* (1979), 35–47; George A. Kennedy, "The Classical Tradition in Rhetoric," *ibid.,* 20–34, and *Greek Rhetoric Under Christian Emperors*

(1983); George L. Kustas, "The Function and Evolution of Byzantine Rhetoric," in *Viator,* **1** (1970), and *Studies in Byzantine Rhetoric* (1973).

ROBERT BROWNING

[See also **Basil the Great of Caesaria, St.; Gregory of Nazianzus, St.; John Chrysostom, St.; Leo VI the Wise, Emperor; Manuel II Palaiologos; Nikephoros Gregoras; Niketas Choniates; Oratory; Universities, Byzantine.**]

RHETORIC: WESTERN EUROPEAN. Rhetoric is the systematic analysis of human discourse for the purpose of identifying useful precepts for future discourse. Its roots lie in ancient Greece, but it was highly developed by the Romans. Medieval Europe inherited from Rome a thoroughly developed system of rhetoric based on the five steps commonly used in preparing and presenting a public speech (*oratio*), but Western European writers often adapted the ancient doctrines for their own purposes. The history of medieval rhetoric thus becomes one of continuity and of alterations to meet contemporary needs.

It is essential, therefore, to examine this ancient rhetorical heritage before turning to the particular developments of the Middle Ages.

ANCIENT ROMAN RHETORIC AND ITS SCHOOL BASE

The rhetorical works of such Greek writers as Isocrates, Plato, and Aristotle had virtually no influence in the medieval West. Roman rhetoric, on the other hand, had great direct and indirect influence. Marcus Tullius Cicero (106–43 B.C.), whose works proved to be the most popular medieval sources of Roman rhetorical theory, had defined rhetoric in his *De inventione* (87 B.C.) as "eloquence based on rules of art" and further declared it to be a "branch of political science." For Cicero the aim of eloquence was to persuade an audience by speech.

To accomplish this end, Roman rhetorical theory laid out a systematic plan involving a sequence of five steps. Cicero wrote seven rhetorical works, but the books most influential in the Middle Ages were his *De inventione* and the anonymous *Rhetorica ad Herennium,* for centuries universally attributed to him. His *Topica* influenced Boethius and others interested in the relation of rhetoric and dialectic. His other rhetorical works, including the more philosophic *De oratore,* had greater influence in the Renaissance and later. The *De inventione* provides these definitions of what Cicero calls the "five parts of rhetoric": (1) invention (*inventio*), the discovery of valid or seemingly valid arguments that render one's cause plausible; (2) arrangement (*dispositio*), the distribution of arguments thus discovered in the proper order; (3) style (*elocutio*), the fitting of the proper language to the invented matter; (4) memory (*memoria*), the firm mental grasp of matter and words; (5) delivery (*pronuntiatio*), the control of the voice and the body in a manner suitable to the dignity of the subject matter and style.

These five processes, Cicero says, prepare the speaker for the three types of orations named by Aristotle: deliberative, as in political assemblies; forensic, as in law courts; and epideictic or demonstrative, as on other occasions in which praise or blame is involved. In Cicero's view, rhetoric deals only with special cases (*causae*) that involve individuals, and not with general questions (*quaestiones*) of the kind that philosophers discuss.

Most of *De inventione* is devoted to the doctrine of *status* (or *constitutio*), that is, the discovery of the "issue" or point to be resolved in any controversy. Roman use of this approach apparently follows the Hellenistic writer Hermagoras of Temnos. Cicero identifies four types of issues: (1) fact conjecture (*conjecturalis*)—"Was there an act?" (2) definition (*definitiva*) or verbal description—"Was the act murder?" (3) nature (*generalis*) or quality—"Was the murder justified?" and (4) competence (*translativa*) or jurisdiction—"Is this the proper court to hear the case?"

Having determined the issue and its implications for the case at hand, the speaker can then turn to framing the six parts of the oration itself: *exordium, narratio, partitio, confirmatio, refutatio,* and *peroratio.* The *exordium* is a passage that brings the mind of the listener into a proper condition to receive the rest of the speech; its task is to make the listener attentive, docile, and well disposed. The *narratio* is an exposition of events that have occurred or are supposed to have occurred. The *partitio* makes the speech clear to the listener, either by showing what is agreed or disputed, or by providing a systematic forecast of the matters to be discussed. The *confirmatio* or proof marshals arguments in support of the speaker's case. The *refutatio* marshals arguments to disprove the case of the opponent. The *peroratio* is the end and conclusion of the speech; its three parts are a summing-up, the exciting of ill will against the opponent, and the arousing of pity and sympathy for the speaker or his case.

In all of this there is a strong interest in forensic (legal) matters. In fact, Cicero spends very little time on the other two types of speeches. Furthermore, *De inventione* is a treatment of only the first of the five "parts of rhetoric." Though he intended to write later on all five, he never did so. It is worth noting that Cicero was about nineteen when he wrote *De inventione;* clearly his book represents his basic schooling rather than any lengthy experience or reflection on his part.

The second major Roman rhetorical work associated with Cicero was the immensely popular *Rhetorica ad Herennium.* Written by an unknown author within a few years of Cicero's *De inventione,* it is so strikingly similar in tone and content that for 1,500 years it was assumed to be a work of Cicero's. During the Middle Ages it was known as Cicero's "Second Rhetoric" (*Rhetorica secunda*) or his "New Rhetoric" (*Rhetorica nova*); thus Cicero's *De inventione* was known as the "Old Rhetoric" (*Rhetorica vetus*) or simply the "Rhetoric" (*Rhetorica*). The *Rhetorica ad Herennium* is clearly from the same school background as the *De inventione.* It originally had no title, and is generally known by its prefatory dedication to one Caius Herennius, also unknown.

The work covers all five of the "parts of rhetoric." Books I and II parallel Cicero's work very closely, but book III goes on to discuss delivery and memory, and book IV is devoted to style. The fourth book, which was sometimes circulated as an independent treatise in the Middle Ages, identifies three levels of style—plain, middle, and grand—then declares that distinction (*dignitas*) is to be achieved through the judicious use of "figures" (*exornationes*). Sixty-four figures are defined, with examples: forty-five "figures of speech" and nineteen "figures of thought." (Ten of the figures of speech are placed in a special class that later theorists called "tropes": onomatopoeia, antonomasia, metonymy, periphrasis, hyperbaton, hyperbole, synecdoche, catechresis, metaphor, and allegory.) This catalog in *Rhetorica ad Herennium* IV became the standard listing of figures in the Middle Ages, influencing writers in every medieval literary and rhetorical genre from letter writing to preaching. It was often copied separately as an independent treatise on style.

The *De inventione* and the *Ad Herennium* reveal a common body of rhetorical doctrine, inherited from Hellenistic Greek sources and taught systematically in schools in the Roman republic to prepare boys for a civic life in which public oratory was a major factor. The remarkable continuity of this teaching process may be seen in the *Institutio oratoria* (*ca.* 95) of Marcus Fabius Quintilianus, written nearly two centuries after Cicero's youthful *De inventione* but describing essentially the same schooling practices Cicero had undergone. Quintilian's twelve-book *Institutio* not only includes a detailed treatment of the five parts of rhetoric but also provides a comprehensive exposition (books I and II) of the process by which the Roman citizen-orator is to be trained. The program begins with work under a *grammaticus,* with exercises in reading, listening, writing, and speaking in a variety of modes of imitation (*imitatio*). Quintilian defines grammar as "the science of speaking correctly, and of interpreting the poets." At an appropriate age work is added under a *rhetoricus,* utilizing the same learning methods in more advanced exercises (*progymnasmata*) leading ultimately to the *declamatio,* or fictitious oration.

The impact of these Roman teaching methods upon medieval culture is still not completely understood. It should be remembered that the Roman Empire exported schools along with its armies and the merchants that followed them; in some places the Roman schools lasted for some time after the collapse of the empire itself. Moreover, the "textbooks" that distilled school lore survived even longer, and hence may sometimes have been studied by medieval readers who had little sense of their original purpose.

Moreover, the basic grammar text of Donatus (*ca.* 350) and the more advanced *Institutiones grammaticae* of Priscian (*fl. ca.* 510) both testify to the survival of elementary pedagogical methods familiar to Quintilian and to Cicero before him. The English writer Bede (673–735) composed a short Latin treatise on the tropes and figures based largely on Donatus. John of Salisbury in his *Metalogicon* (1159) describes in detail his own schooling along Quintilianic lines, and similar testimony can be found in his contemporaries Hugh of St. Victor and Alan of Lille. About 1344 the Faculty of Grammar at Oxford University issued a statute directing its teachers to pursue similar methods.

It may well be that throughout the Middle Ages the basic methods of teaching language skills—language acquisition, grammar, and rhetoric—followed the general Roman pattern, whether or not teachers and students acknowledged or even recognized that fact. If that is so, then it may be hazardous for modern readers to make overly fine distinctions between "grammar" and "rhetoric" in the Middle Ages, especially in the case of writers known to have had the coordinated kind of schooling described by John of Salisbury and others. It has been demonstrated, for instance, that the Roman poet and literary theorist Horace (65–8 B.C.) in his *Ars poetica* reveals a close connection between rhetorical and literary concepts reminiscent of his schooling. The ubiquitous Roman schools, whose teaching methods were perpetuated through the survival of texts based on those methods, thus had a profound if unrecognized influence on anyone educated during the Middle Ages.

THE TRANSITIONAL PERIOD: 396–1087

During the third through fifth centuries a number of "minor" rhetorical treatises were produced that had some currency in the Middle Ages. These include works by Fortunatianus, Julius Victor, Aquila Romanus, and Sulpitius Victor. The most important of the group, for the Middle Ages, was the commentary on Cicero's *De inventione* written by Marius Victorinus, which was extremely popular from the eleventh century on and played a major role in the Ciceronian commentary tradition down through the Renaissance. The method of Victorinus—to write down each passage and then immediately add an explanatory comment before copying the next passage—was followed by most of the twelfth- and thirteenth-century Ciceronian commentators.

The first major rhetorical work with a pronounced Christian bias was the *De doctrina christiana* of Augustine, begun in 396 (books I–III) and finished in 426 (book IV), while he was bishop of Hippo in North Africa. This work is important in rhetorical history for several reasons. First of all, Augustine argues forcefully for the retention of rhetoric as a useful tool in accomplishing the church's apostolic mission of converting the world; to do this he had to argue against some contemporary views that all of pagan culture—including grammar, literature, and rhetoric—should be banished from the Christian commonwealth envisaged by Christ. In addition, he faced accusations that the sophistic oratory of his time—"empty eloquence"—proved that rhetoric was dangerous and misleading for Christians. Augustine's reply was that it would be foolish to allow only bad men to be eloquent while leaving Christ's spokesmen dumb and inarticulate. Moreover, in the fourth book he takes pains to demonstrate that the Bible itself used all three levels of style found in Roman rhetorical theory.

Augustine's vigorous defense of rhetoric, at a time when Christian fundamentalism might well have doomed Roman culture and all its parts (including rhetoric), certainly helped to preserve rhetoric for Christian use. His insistence on Cicero as the prime rhetorical theorist was another contribution. In books I–III of *De doctrina christiana* he argues that God intends all Christians to be rhetorically apostolic, that is, to be responsible for carrying God's message to their fellow men through the use of language, "the conventional signs that men show each other to express their thoughts and feelings." His theory of "sign," including some ideas only recently popular again among linguists and semioticians, states that God puts all things into the temporal world as signs to be read by men; man, too, can invent signs to show other men. Hence, mankind's tasks are first to discover the meaning of God's signs—as in the Bible, for instance—and then to invent signs so other men can share this understanding. Augustine thus presents a new doctrine of rhetorical responsibility for Christians.

Meanwhile, the practical Roman rhetorical doctrines were transmitted into the Middle Ages in two ways: by the copying of the *De inventione* and "Ciceronion" texts like the *Rhetorica ad Herennium,* and by the popular compendia (abstracts) of rhetorical doctrine written by the "encyclopedists"—Martianus Capella (*fl.* 410–427), Flavius Cassiodorus Senator (*ca.* 490–*ca.* 583), and Isidore of Seville (*ca.* 570–636).

It was apparently Martianus Capella's *De nuptiis Philologiae et Mercurii* (The marriage of Philology and Mercury) that introduced to the Middle Ages the Roman concept of the "Seven Liberal Arts": grammar, dialectic, rhetoric, geometry, arithmetic, astronomy, and music. Throughout the Middle Ages these seven were habitually divided into two groups: the trivium of arts dealing with "word" (grammar, dialectic, rhetoric), and the quadrivium of arts dealing with "number" (geometry, arithmetic, astronomy, and music). After an allegorical introduction, each of the seven arts is summarized in the form of a compendium—that is, in a précis or epitome that concentrates on the basic ideas of the art rather than on the individual contributions of particular authors. (This popular method was to produce in the twelfth century the controversy over *ars versus auctores,* the question of whether it was best to study the digested principles of an art or to utilize individual authors' views of it.) Martianus Capella's sober synopsis of the *ars rhetorica* is solidly reflective of the Roman tradition.

Cassiodorus, the second major encyclopedist of this period, has a clearly Christian purpose in his *Institutiones divinarum et saecularium litterarum* (Institutes of divine and human readings). The work is designed as a complete guide to divine and secular studies, with the seven liberal arts proposed as secular means to understanding the "knowledge diffused everywhere in Scripture." In effect, Cassiodorus canonizes the seven arts as "seven pillars of wisdom" (Prov. 9:1) and points out that in Exodus the Lord told Moses, "Thou shalt make seven lamps, and shalt set them to give light" (Exod. 25:37). Grammar is the source and foundation of liberal studies; dialectic separates true from false; and rhetoric is the science of speaking well on civil questions. Comparing the aim of rhetoric to persuade with the aim of dialectic to formulate incontestable statements, Cassiodorus cites the statement of the writer Varro that rhetoric is like an open hand, and dialectic like a closed fist. The compendium of the late classical writer Consultus Fortunatianus is his major source for the section on rhetoric, which concentrates on invention; his only references to memory and delivery refer the reader to Fortunatianus. He devotes twice as much space to dialectic. Then he introduces the four arts of the quadrivium as "sciences" dealing with number.

One important point, little understood by either medieval or modern readers, is that Cassiodorus's *Institutes* is primarily a reading guide for the Benedictine monks at his monastery of Vivarium rather than a self-contained or comprehensive statement of all the available lore on the subjects discussed. It is thus a rather meager source of information for those later readers unable to supplement it with the fuller texts on each subject.

The *Etymologiarum sive originum libri xx* (Etymologies) of Bishop Isidore of Seville was far more popular in the Middle Ages than these works of Martianus and Cassiodorus. This is important because Isidore goes a step beyond Cassiodorus, making the seven liberal arts, especially the trivium, literally "propaedeutic"—preparatory to divine or professional studies. Grammar, dialectic, and rhetoric prepare readers to handle the other arts. The different functions of the three arts thus must be distinguished carefully. Isidore sees more similarities between grammar and rhetoric than between dialectic and rhetoric. Actually, however, his treatment of all three arts is very brief, relying largely on Donatus for grammar, Cassiodorus for rhetoric, and Aristotle, Victorinus, and Porphyry for dialectic. His treatment of tropes and figures is a jumble of Donatus, Quintilian, and the *Rhetorica ad Herennium.* Isidore includes sections on medicine, law, and Scripture after his treatment of the liberal arts.

All in all, the three encyclopedists provide a rather narrow funnel for the transmission of ancient lore. Nevertheless, their later popularity indicates that their discussions shaped the knowledge of many medieval readers.

One problem inherent in the trivium was the interrelation of the three verbal arts. This was to prove a matter of controversy throughout the Middle Ages and beyond. Indeed, on this point the views of Petrus Ramus at the University of Paris in the 1540's and 1550's caused enormous controversy in his lifetime and beyond, since he argued that rhetoric should deal only with style and delivery; this argument even spilled over later into the New World at Harvard and other places. One modern scholar, Richard McKeon, has in fact argued that the whole history of medieval rhetoric can be understood in terms of the rise and fall of each of the three arts in relation to the other two, and of whether the third art was presented as logic or as dialectic.

A major figure in the medieval phase of the controversy was Anicius Manlius Boethius (*ca.* 480–524), who in addition to his famous *Consolation of Philosophy* wrote seven treatises dealing with dialectical and rhetorical subjects. He was interested not in distinguishing rhetoric from philosophy (as Cicero does in *De inventione* I.1), but in distinguishing the various arts of discourse—especially dialectic and rhetoric—from each other. His most influential rhetorical work was his *De differentiis topicis,* popularly known in the Middle Ages as *Topica Boetii.* Its fourth book, comparing rhetoric and dialectic, was often copied and circulated separately. It appears, for instance, as an independent work in the 1215 curriculum at the University of Paris.

The *Topica Boetii* deals with the difficult concept of topic (Latin: *locus* [place]), or what Boethius calls "the seat of an argument," the place from which an argument may be drawn. His preoccupation with the problems of determining the use of the *topica*—he finds, for example, that both dialectic and rhetoric use topics for inventing or discovering ideas—finally restricts rhetoric almost exclusively to invention, without regard for arrangement, style, memory, or delivery. This emphasis was to have catastrophic results for rhetoric in medieval universities like Paris and Oxford, where dialectic was judged to be a far superior means of invention; rhetoric was eliminated almost entirely from the curriculum for several centuries.

While Boethius sees many similarities between the two arts, he outlines several differences between them: dialectic deals with thesis (question without circumstances), while rhetoric deals with hypothesis (question attended by circumstances); dialectic proceeds by interrogation and response, rhetoric leads to uninterrupted discourse; dialectic employs syllogisms, rhetoric uses enthymemes; dialectic seeks to dislodge an adversary, rhetoric aims to move the mind of the hearer. The section on rhetoric in book IV provides only sketchy definitions of the three standard types of speeches, the five parts of rhetoric, and the Ciceronian six parts of an oration; three-fourths of the section is devoted to the Roman doctrine of *constitutio* or *status,* in which arguments are drawn from the four questions of fact, definition, quality, and jurisdiction. Boethius also discusses "circumstances" under seven headings that came to influence later commentary writers in rhetoric, grammar, and other fields: *quis, quid, ubi, quando, cur, quomodo, et quibus adminiculis* (who, what, where, when, why, how, with what assistance).

Boethius thus drew the battle lines for a thousand and more years of conflict between dialectic and rhetoric. It was not merely Aristotle versus Cicero but discipline versus discipline, function versus function.

After Boethius perhaps the most significant figure in the rhetorical history of the early Middle Ages is Hrabanus Maurus (780–856). He was a pupil of Alcuin (*ca.* 730–804), who had been charged by Charlemagne with the renovation of Frankish education; Alcuin is the author of the *Disputatio de rhetorica et de virtutibus* (*ca.* 794), in which he and Charlemagne discuss rhetoric and its relation to kingship. His pupil Hrabanus holds a unique position in the history of medieval rhetoric, for he was the first to enunciate in such specific terms the medieval pragmatic principle that everything ancient or modern can be used for the new Christian world order. In his major work, *De institutione clericorum* (On the education of the clergy, 819), his frequent refrain is *ad nostrum dogmatem convertimus* (we shall convert [them] to our doctrine). His method is a purposeful eclecticism. His advice for preachers takes whole passages verbatim from Augustine's *De doctrina christiana* and *De civitate Dei,* but he also uses Cassiodorus, Isidore, Alcuin, Gregory the Great, Cicero, and Quintilian. But, significantly, it is now Augustine rather than Cicero who is seen as the arbiter of rhetorical virtue.

With Hrabanus Maurus, then, there is a subtle but profound shift in attitude: the new age will make its own choices, select its own exemplars, make the past serve the present. It is this attitude that accounts for the truly medieval forms of rhetoric—the three new genres that sprang up in Europe to rival and even surpass the Ciceronian legacy from ancient times. By the early thirteenth century it is possible to see Ciceronian rhetoric as but one of four parallel rhetorical genres, the others being the *ars dictaminis* (the art of letter writing), *ars praedicandi* (the art of preaching), and *ars poetriae* (the art of verse writing). All share the preceptive intention of ancient rhetoric—that is, they offer direct advice on the composition of oral or written discourse.

SURVIVAL OF THE ANCIENT RHETORICAL TRADITIONS

It is important to remember that certain ancient rhetorical texts continued to be copied and studied throughout the Middle Ages. Cicero was the universally recognized *magister eloquentiae* for medieval writers. In the thirteenth century, for instance, Boncompagno da Signa titled one of his own works *Rhetorica novissima* to show that it surpassed even Cicero's *Rhetorica nova;* Dante places Cicero in the first rank of the unbaptized; it is only Cicero's rhetoric that appears in the new vernaculars—for example, in Brunetto Latini's *Trésor* (*ca.* 1260) and in versions by Guidotto da Bologna (before 1266) and Jean de Harens (1282).

The *De inventione* and the *Rhetorica ad Herennium* are the dominant Ciceronian texts. His *Topica* is known chiefly through the commentary of Boethius. Cicero's most mature work, the dialogue *De oratore,* written after a lifetime of legal and public service, was virtually unknown during the Middle Ages; the rediscovery of its complete text at Lodi in 1421 is in fact a part of the history of Renaissance rather than medieval humanism. Though the orations of Cicero were sometimes studied, there is little evidence of medieval interest in his other rhetorical treatises: *Brutus, Orator, De optimo genere oratorum,* and *Partitiones oratoriae.* On the other hand, his reputation was enhanced by philosophical works like *De officiis* and *Tusculanae disputationes.*

The numerous commentaries on *De inventione* and *Rhetorica ad Herennium* provide evidence of continuing interest in Cicero. In the medieval context, the existence of a "commentary" or "gloss" usually indicates the use of a book in the schools. What the master teaches, the master explains. (By the end of the fourteenth century, there are a few examples—like Luigi of Gianfigliazzi and Lorenzo Ridolfi—of nonschool commentators.) Scholars have now identified nearly 600 separate items ranging from brief notes to full-scale commentaries, of which 79 are complete explications of Ciceronian works. They find that the peak of such commentative activity lay in the period from 1080–1225, with a resurgence from after 1290 until the sixteenth century. Many of the commentaries are anonymous, identified only by their incipits, as in the case of the popular *In primis materia et intentio rethoris.* Manegold of Lautenbach (*ca.* 1030–1103) is one of the earliest known commentators; Thierry of Chartres wrote commentaries on both *Ad Herennium* and *De inventione* in addition to his more celebrated *Heptateuchon,* or defense of the seven liberal arts. A popular work of the twelfth century was by one "Alanus" (Alan of Lille?). The grammarian Peter Helias also wrote on Cicero. Later commentators include Brunetto Latini, Barolinus de Benincasa de Canulo, Guarino da Verona, Jean Poulain, and Johannes Heynlin aus Stein. The ancient commentary of Victorinus survives in thirty-one medieval manuscripts, that of Grillius in fourteen. Most medieval commentators reveal a strong interest in matters of invention: the *loci* or topics (especially in relation to the topics of dialectic) and the doctrine of *status* (*constitutio negotialis*). There is visible influence of parallel studies in both dialectic and grammar, especially in twelfth-century treatises. Not one of these hundreds of medieval works has yet been edited in complete form (though both Grillius and Victorinus are available in modern printed editions). Further research will no doubt identify even more such rhetorical commentaries, and it seems clear that the whole area is one deserving additional study.

The medieval history of Quintilian is also easily summarized. For the greater part of the Middle Ages, Quintilian was known primarily through a fragmentary text (*textus mutilatus*) of the *Institutio oratoria,* although there is occasional mention of the *Declamationes* attributed to him. The peak of interest in Quintilian seems to have occurred in early-twelfth-century France. For instance, Anselm of Bec composed an epitome of the *Institutio* that has not survived; John of Salisbury's *Metalogicon* (1159) describes the Quintilianic education plan employed at Chartres by his teacher Bernard. Otherwise there are only fleeting references, which may have been based as much on general reputation as on actual reading of his text.

The reasons for this comparative neglect are easily seen: the educational plan outlined in books I and II of the *Institutio* had been absorbed into everyday elementary education to the extent that recapitulating it was superfluous; the discurvisely treated ideas in the section on the five parts of rhetoric (books III–IX) were more concisely presented by Cicero's works; and the political climate of medieval Europe rendered irrelevant the republican concepts in the last three of Quintilian's twelve books treating the ideal orator, literature, and civic virtue. The *Institutio oratoria* was to excite the Italian humanists of the fifteenth century after Poggio Bracciolini found a complete text of the work at St. Gall in September 1416, but for the Middle Ages it was a text either ignored or forgotten.

The question of Aristotelian rhetoric is far more complex. The fate of the text of Aristotle's *Rhetorica* may seem paradoxical to the modern observer. There was enormous interest in Aristotle. William of Moerbeke organized a massive project in the 1260's and 1270's to translate into Latin all of Aristotle's works, including the *Rhetorica.* In fact, the work survives in ninety-six manuscripts. Egidius Colonna, Jean de Jandun, and others wrote commentaries on it. Yet it was virtually unused as a rhetorical text during the Middle Ages. Instead, it was treated as a book of moral philosophy, being copied most often with Aristotle's *Ethica* or *Politica;* only rarely is it found in the same volume with any other rhetorical work. Some writers on psychology plumbed book II of the *Rhetorica* for quotations on emotion.

On the other hand, the most important Aristotelian influence on medieval language usage came in the field of the *disputatio,* or formal debate employing dialectic. Records of postclassical schools indicate the continuing use of the Roman practice of *declamatio*—student exercises in which opposing speakers delivered orations on a given subject—but the major impetus for the medieval form of disputation undoubtedly came from the popularity of the Latin translations of the two key works by Aristotle, *Topica* and *De sophisticis elenchis* (On sophistical refutations).

For the next century dialectical disputation was to be found as a regular feature of elementary education along with grammar and rhetoric—until the universities preempted the subject for their curricula, relegating rhetoric and elementary grammar to the lower schools. *De sophisticis elenchis* deals with logical fallacies, while the *Topica* discusses more than 200 *loci* or topics for invention of ideas and devotes book VIII to the mechanics of debating a human opponent. This last section of the *Topica* includes consideration of the psychological factors involved in such debate; it is worth noting that in his *Rhetorica* Aristotle refers to the *Topica* nine times.

Insofar as the *disputatio* trained medieval men for the hurly-burly of verbal conflict for which Roman rhetoric had been designed, it naturally tended to displace rhetoric, at least in the scholastic environment. The evident social and intellectual utility of *disputatio,* rather than purely academic theorizings about the nature of the arts of the trivium, led to the exclusion of rhetoric from the northern universities dominated by dialectic. Beginning in 1215, Paris—"mother of universities"—required that first-year students study both the *Topica* and the *De sophisticis elenchis;* regular classroom practice was to treat a text first by an oral reading (*lectio*) of the master, followed by the raising of questions (*quaestiones*) and then the resolution of problems by disputation (*disputatio*).

Since the Parisian curricular model of 1215 shaped European universities for 500 years, disputation was to remain a major force into early modern times. This was true even in Italian universities, where the Ciceronian spirit remained a substantial influence. (It is interesting to note that in 1642 the first Harvard College commencement featured student disputations in Latin.) Whether or not disputation was labeled as "rhetorical," in practice it had much in common with rhetorical precepts. Many thousands of European men underwent years of exposure to it, with incalculable effect upon their later language habits. This too seems an area of investigation well worth pursuing.

Greek rhetoric in medieval Western Europe has been little studied to date. The school exercises (*progymnasmata*) attributed to Hermogenes (second century) were translated into Latin around 500 by the grammarian Priscian and appear in medieval library catalogs as *Praeexercitamenta.* The similar work of Aphthonius (fifth century), though popular in Byzantium, became popular in the West only after the advent of printing.

Arabic contributions consisted mainly of translated commentaries on Aristotle's works, including his *Rhetorica* and *Poetica;* Ibn Rushd, for example, has two types of commentaries on these books. The ninth-century scholar al-Fārābī wrote a gloss of the *Rhetorica* that was translated into Latin by Herman the German, himself a translator of the *Rhetorica.* Al-Fārābī also wrote another treatise (*De scientiis*) that identifies the "science of eloquence" (*kalam*) as a third art of discourse separate from grammar or logic. However, when Dominicus Gundissalinus (*ca.* 1125–1150), archdeacon of Toledo, used al-Fārābī's *De scientiis* and *De ortu scientiarum* as sources for his own *De divisione philosophiae,* he made rhetoric a part of logic. In general, the transmission of Arabic rhetorical concepts to the Latin West seems to have been plagued by problems of poor texts and even worse translations.

THE THREE NEW RHETORICAL GENRES OF THE HIGH MIDDLE AGES

Each of the three medieval rhetorical genres evolved in response to a particular set of needs. The circumstances surrounding each genre must be understood. The *ars dictaminis* appeared first, in the 1080's; the *ars poetriae* came in the 1170's; and the *ars praedicandi* began to develop about 1200.

Ars dictaminis. The application of certain ancient rhetorical principles to the special problem of letter writing was a truly medieval invention. The teachers of Cicero and other ancient Romans had made it clear to their students that the *ars rhetorica* could instruct them in all forms of human discourse, written as well as oral. Quintilian, in fact, declares that his goal for his students is *facilitas,* the ability to improvise effective discourse suitable for any situation. The Roman classroom consciously coordinated all kinds of language, whether Greek or Latin, verse or prose, spoken or written. With this linguistic background a literate Roman like Cicero could compose either eloquent epistles or eloquent orations. No special letter-writing training was deemed necessary.

This facility in composition was no longer widespread after the collapse of the Roman schools. Cassiodorus, the sixth-century minister of the illiterate Theodoric the Ostrogoth, was perhaps the last major epistolary artist on the ancient Ciceronian model; his *Variae,* a collection of his letters on a wide spectrum of subjects, provided models for many later writers. Other, less brilliant writers of the seventh to tenth centuries faced with diplomatic or legal correspondence turned increasingly to formularies that offered texts in which only the proper names needed to be supplied for a given occasion. The *Formulae Marculfi* (mid seventh century), for instance, offers 109 formulas for royal or private acts; the formulas serve a double function in that they are both types of correspondence and a written record of contractual agreements. The formulaic approach was inherently defective, however; no finite number of preset documents could cover an infinite number of possible communicative needs. At the same time the explosive growth of feudal and ecclesiastical relationships made written communication increasingly important.

No doubt informal letter-writing practices did arise to supplement formularies. It is not yet clear whether practice preceded theory in this case, but it is clear enough that the first theoretical approach to this problem came out of the famous Benedictine abbey of Monte Cassino in Italy about 1087. Alberic of Monte Cassino's *Breviarium de dictamine* and *Dictaminum radii* (or *Flores rhetorici*) are the first known treatises to apply rhetorical principles to letter writing. In particular he stresses the importance of the greeting (*salutatio*), based on "the person to whom and the person from whom it is sent." From these and other remarks it is clear that Alberic had been actively teaching his students to apply Ciceronian rhetoric to the composition of the letter (*epistola*). Alberic uses a term that came to denote the whole epistolary art when he describes his second work as *de prosaico dictamine opus*—"a work on prosaic dictamen." Significantly, the same work has a final section titled *De rithmis,* an indication that Monte Cassino was also a center of study of rhythmical patterns in prose as well as in forms like hymns, and clear evidence as well that from the beginning the new *ars dictaminis* was allied with the patterns of rhythmical prose known as the *cursus.* Some modern scholars have argued that Alberic was merely confirming already well-known concepts and practices, but in any case these two treatises are, as far as we know, the first to enunciate the principles that rapidly stabilized into a dictaminal format that remained constant for nearly 500 years.

Nevertheless it was the northern Italian city of Bologna which rapidly became a center of the dictaminal art, whose details were blocked out by such writers as Hugh of Bologna, Adalbert of Samaria, "Master A," Anonymous of Bologna, Baldwin, and Bernard of Bologna.

By 1135 what one writer calls the "approved format" of five letter parts was firmly set; it was to be seriously challenged only centuries later by "Renaissance" writers like Erasmus and Christopher Hegendorff, but letter-writing manuals on the Bolognese model were being published as late as 1550.

The adaptation of the five-part letter from the Ciceronian six-part *oratio* can be seen clearly in this comparison:

Ciceronian Parts of an Oration	Bolognese "Approved Format" for a Letter
Exordium	*Salutatio,* or formal vocative greeting to addressee; *Captatio benevolentiae,* or introduction.
Divisio	(Omitted as a separate part.)
Narratio	*Narratio,* or narration of circumstances leading to petition.
Confirmatio	*Petitio,* or presentation of requests.
Refutatio	(Omitted as a separate part.)
Peroratio	*Conclusio,* or final part.

The typical *ars dictaminis* opens with a definition of "prosaic" (for example, "speech without accountability to metrical law"), then defines the five parts of a letter. Space given to discussion of the *salutatio* (often a third of the whole treatise) reveals the importance attached to the careful recognition of the social status of addressee and sender; for instance, the *Practica sive usus dictaminis* (*ca.* 1300) of Lawrence of Aquileia lays out seven social levels from pope to heretic, while others have as many as twelve. The sensitivity is no doubt the product of the complex relationships inherent in a feudal society.

More than 300 separate treatises of the *ars dictaminis* have survived in manuscript form. All were written in Latin. The most famous authors were Italians: Guido Faba, Thomas of Capua, Boncompagno of Signa. A thirteenth-century poem,

The Battle of the Seven Arts by Henri d'Andeli, calls dictamen "that Lombard art" after the region in northern Italy where Bologna lies. There were virtually no English authors, and German writers usually imitated the Italians. Some French writers, like Jean de Meun and Pons of Provence, added a literary flavor to their otherwise standard manuals by discussing prose style at great length (which the Italians seldom did).

One striking feature of the dictaminal tradition is the habitual use of a collection of model letters (*dictamina*) as an appendix to the letter-writing manual itself. The reader thus could learn the basic principles of the five-part letter from the manual, then find hundreds of complete letters presented as models of how to use those principles. This combination of theory and practice must have been very effective, judging from the large number of such letter collections that have survived. Some writers, in fact, became more famous for their excellent model letters than for their statements of theory; Peter of Blois and Peter of Vinea are examples. Guido Faba had example letters in both Latin and Italian. He and other writers also published collections of proverbs that might be used in the introductions of letters.

One interesting feature of the dictaminal movement was the use of the *cursus,* or rhythmical prose style based on the concordance of accents in successive clause endings. An extraordinarily technical subject, it is difficult to discuss in English because it was designed for Latin. For example, the writers distinguish three main types of clausular patterns: *planus, tardus,* and *velox* (even, slow, rapid). It was once thought that the papacy had devised this complex stylistic system to prevent the forgery of its documents, but the widespread popularity of the *cursus* shows that any well-educated writer of Latin could master it fairly easily.

Although dictaminal manuals continued to appear for many centuries, the element of standardization inherent in the *ars dictaminis* sometimes led to its submergence into the *ars notaria.* That is, the notaries—the makers of formal leases, contracts, and other legal documents—were naturally interested in stabilizing the physical aspects of documents so they could be handled easily. To the extent that the letters described in the *ars dictaminis* (and exemplified in the appended letter collections) could be standardized, they came close to serving the same purpose.

All in all, the *ars dictaminis* served a useful purpose in Europe, providing a sensible, pragmatic solution to the basic problem of letter writing. It deserves further study, because it illuminates some fundamental medieval ideas about both the nature of language and the complexities of social relationships in a feudal society.

Ars poetriae. The second major medieval application of rhetoric was in the field of verse writing. Within about a century (1175 to sometime before 1280) European teachers of grammar produced six Latin works giving precepts for the composition of verse ("the future poem," as one modern scholar, Douglas Kelly, has put it).

It must be remembered that the medieval *ars grammatica* included the study not only of correctness in speaking and writing but also of poerty—what we would today call "literature." It was only natural, then, that it would be the grammar masters who taught students about past poets like Vergil and Horace, and then went on to lay down the principles for the writing of new poetry.

The six major works of this kind are Matthew of Vendôme's *Ars versificatoria* (*ca.* 1170), Geoffrey of Vinsauf's *Poetria nova* (1208–1213) and *Documentum de modo et arte dictandi et versificandi* (*ca.* 1180, rev. *ca.* 1210), Gervase of Melkley's *Ars versificaria* (*ca.* 1215), John of Garland's *De arte prosayca, metrica, et rithmica* (after 1229), and Everard the German's *Laborintus* (before 1280).

Twelfth-century grammarians, especially in France, were greatly concerned about the relation of their subject to the other two arts of the trivium, rhetoric and dialectic. The study of dialectical or logical aspects of language led to a series of treatises about what came to be called "speculative grammar" (*grammatica speculativa*), sophisticated study of such matters as the nature of meaning and the various forms of "significations" of words. The movement came to be especially strong in the thirteenth and fourteenth centuries at the universities of Paris and Oxford. The *modistae,* as their authors were called, were the precursors of modern linguists. Among the most influential were Thomas of Erfurt, Siger of Courtrai, Michael of Marbais, and Boethius of Dacia.

A parallel concern for the relation of rhetoric to grammar led to the application of Ciceronian rhetorical principles to the creation of new poetry. The *Rhetorica ad Herennium* was the major source used, partly because it includes all five parts of rhetoric and especially because it offers a lengthy treatment of figures and tropes in relation to style.

The earliest of the six works, Matthew of Vendôme's *Ars versificatoria,* is a rather loosely organized discussion of concepts drawn from both Horace's *Ars poetica* and rhetorical treatises. However, the rapid consolidation of the doctrines of the new *ars poetriae* can be seen less than forty years later in the most popular of the six treatises, the *Poetria nova* (New poetics) of Geoffrey of Vinsauf. Geoffrey's book survives in more than 100 manuscripts; Chaucer parodies him in a passage about Chantecleer in his Nun's Priest's Tale in the *Canterbury Tales;* and he is cited (by Stephen Hawes) as late as the end of the fifteenth century.

Poetria nova is divided into seven sections, several of which demonstrate a clear reliance on Ciceronian ideas. The treatise begins with general observations on the need for planning a poem in advance by finding things to say, putting them in proper order, finding the appropriate style in which to say them, remembering them, and then using voice, facial expression, and movement to present them to an audience. An inept recitation of good material, he concludes, is as bad as a beautiful recitation of bad material. Geoffrey's advice on how to plan, write, and recite poetry is reminiscent of the Ciceronian five parts of rhetoric: invention, arrangement, style, memory, and delivery.

One feature that undoubtedly helped make the *Poetria nova* so popular was Geoffrey's frequent use of verse examples. This must have made the book an extremely useful teaching tool for other grammar masters. Particularly useful was his extensive section on the sixty-four tropes and figures, taken directly from the fourth book of *Rhetorica ad Herennium.* In a remarkable literary feat, Geoffrey writes a continuous verse passage that uses all sixty-four tropes and figures—in the order they appear in the *Ad Herennium.* His book, in other words, not only gave medieval verse writers specific principles to follow but also provided good literary examples to amplify each point.

Gervase of Melkley, a contemporary of Geoffrey, also discusses in detail the relation of theory to practice. He says that writers should look equally to the advice of Donatus the grammarian, Horace the poet, and Cicero the rhetorician. (This is a useful reminder of the medieval grammar masters' continuing concern for the relation between grammatical rules, literature, and rhetoric.)

Perhaps the most ambitious of the six works in this tradition was the *De arte prosayca, metrica, et rithmica* of John of Garland (*ca.* 1195–*ca.* 1272). John's treatise, whose title might be roughly translated as *The Art of Writing in Prose, Verse, and Rhythmics,* attempts to lay out the unifying principles underlying all writing.

His book, like Geoffrey's, is divided into seven parts: the doctrine of invention (quoting both Horace and Cicero), the methods of selecting material, the arrangement and ornamenting of material (by use of tropes and figures), the parts of a letter and the vices to be avoided in letter writing, the amplification and abbreviation of material, examples of letters, and examples of metrical and rhythmical compositions (in this case, liturgical hymns).

Like the *modistae* who sought a universal grammar that could explain all language, John tried to identify a metagenre that could explain all types of writing. Though his book does not succeed in doing that, it is nevertheless an interesting example of a grammarian's attempt to get to the heart of the nature of writing. It is a book worth careful modern study, especially now that it is available in an English translation.

The movement to write arts of poetry seems to have died out around the middle of the thirteenth century. The last major treatise, Everard the German's *Laborintus,* repeats all the ideas of Vinsauf, Melkley, and Garland but comments rather cynically on the woes of teaching the subject. Everard complains that the students cannot read or count, and are so surly that it is necessary to "tame" them. Worse, he deplores the emphasis on teaching students how to disguise things with words: "When the word flourishes," he says, "the mind dries up."

Whatever the reason, Everard's is the last significant treatise in the arts of poetry applying Ciceronian rhetorical principles to verse writing. Perhaps the continuing popularity of Geoffrey of Vinsauf's *Poetria nova* helped to convince later grammar masters that no new books were needed. Nevertheless, the evidence indicates that the methods of elementary language instruction remained substantially unchanged in Europe down through the times of Shakespeare, Milton, and Rabelais, even if no further books like Geoffrey's were written during the rest of the Middle Ages.

Ars praedicandi. The third medieval rhetorical genre, the *ars praedicandi* or art of preaching, is not a medieval invention, or even a Christian one. Ultimately its roots lie in pre-Christian Jewish liturgies, with alterations made by Jesus, St. Paul, and other speakers of the New Testament period. Yet the final shape of the typical medieval sermon was apparently determined by the same twelfth-century studies of language forms that led to the dialectical *disputatio* and the grammarian's arts of poetry.

The Judaic tradition of commenting publicly on a given text had by the time of Jesus established a regular three-part reading pattern for the weekly synagogue service. A member of the congregation (a wise man, or rabbi) would read aloud a section of the Testament, explain it or otherwise comment on it, and lead a general discussion of it involving all the men present. So important was this audience factor that the authoritative Mishnah, a compilation of traditions written about 200, reminds the faithful that neither reading nor exposition could take place without at least ten men present. As a Jew, Jesus was of course intimately familiar with this pattern, and took advantage of it to speak to synagogue congregations when he began his public career (see, for instance, Luke 4:14–44).

What made the new Christian rhetorical situation so different from its Judaic predecessor, however, was that Jesus charged his followers to be "apostolic" or "evangelistic"—that is, to "teach all nations" in order to convert them to belief in the new order (Matt. 28:18). By its nature, then, the new church was obliged to be rhetorically persuasive. The career of St. Paul (3–68), especially as reported in Acts of the Apostles, shows how this mandate was carried out in the earliest days of the new church. Paul would speak in a synagogue at Corinth or Antioch, as any Jew could, then organize those who believed him into a new group (*ekklesia*) and move on to a new town. The Epistles of Paul in the New Testament are letters sent back to those new "churches" to keep up their spirits. They were read aloud and discussed in Ephesus or Colossus, repeating the pattern of the original synagogue tradition.

Jesus' own speaking furnished a model for later preachers, especially in his use of illustrative stories or parables like those of the Prodigal Son, the Good Samaritan, or the Lost Sheep. Significantly, one Gospel writer (Mark 4:33–34) says that Jesus spoke directly and plainly to his own disciples, but used parables for the general public audiences "according as they were able to understand." This distinction between expert listeners and less educated or experienced hearers was to remain a major theoretical principle throughout the Middle Ages, and still appears in preaching textbooks. The distinction was often used, for instance, to justify the use of allegory to present multiple meanings for a single statement.

Despite the obviously rhetorical responsibility of the Christian church, and despite the study lavished over the centuries on almost every other aspect of Christianity, there was only one major preceptive treatise on preaching written in the first 1200 years after the birth of Christ. The first worldwide, or ecumenical, council of the church at Nicaea in Asia Minor in 325 made each bishop responsible for preaching in his own diocese, but it said nothing about the form or nature of ecclesiastical oratory, the sermon. Pope Gregory I the Great (*ca.* 540–604) included a section on the priest as "herald" in his *Cura pastoralis* (Pastoral rule) written in 591. Yet his remarks on the problems of preaching to diverse congregations are fairly generalized, even though he does include an interesting list of thirty-six pairs of human "characters" (such as servants/masters, humble/haughty) together with brief sample sermons for each pair.

The one major work before about 1200 is *De doctrina christiana* (On Christian doctrine) by St. Augustine (354–430). Augustine, one of the four Latin fathers of the church, wrote the first three chapters ("books," in medieval practice) in 396, then the fourth in 426 while bishop of Hippo in North Africa. The first three books deal with "sign," that is, "that which is used to signify something else"; the sounds that human beings make as language, for example, are intended to be "signs" of ideas the speaker wishes to convey. Smoke is a sign of fire. Augustine argues that the whole world is a sign put before men by God so that they can understand him. Therefore, he says, men are obligated to learn how to use signs both to understand God's universe and to tell other men about what they have found, so that God's plan will be carried out. In specific terms, Augustine says this means that grammar and rhetoric must be learned so that the sign system of language will be comprehended. A man knowing how language works will then be able to understand the Bible as a set of messages from God.

The fourth book argues that rhetoric, and especially Ciceronian rhetoric, provides men with the ability to persuade others to follow God. It does not offer significantly new rhetorical concepts, but it does declare that the Bible actually uses all three levels of style described by Cicero. Augustine's strong defense of rhetoric was an extremely important factor in convincing Christians of his time that it was critical to employ the human art of rhetoric; many of his contemporaries, disgusted with pagan literature and drama, argued that more things Roman should be rejected so that a new type of Christian society could be formed. Augustine's defense of rhetoric was a turning point in this debate. Why, he asks, should Christians be so foolish as to let only evil men learn how to use rhetoric well?

Perhaps because the Ciceronian rhetoric did seem to supply whatever training a preacher would need, it was to be nearly 800 years before a specifically Christian theory of preaching appeared around 1200. A large number of sermons, in both Greek and Latin, were available for study and imitation; thus no need may have been felt for theoretical treatises.

Guibert of Nogent (*ca.* 1064–*ca.* 1125) did point out that the "four senses of interpretation" of Scripture could be used in sermons. By 1084 he had finished a lengthy commentary on Genesis, to which he prefixed a short treatise showing how these four methods of scriptural interpretation unveiled the true meanings of a text. He called his little treatise *Liber quo ordine sermo fieri debeat* (A book about the way a sermon ought to be given). The methods explained by Guibert go back to Judaic and Hellenic (especially Alexandrian) types of exegesis.

Guibert explains the "four senses" in a famous passage that was often quoted later as a brief summary of the whole approach:

> There are four ways of interpreting Scripture; on them, as though on so many scrolls, each sacred page is rolled. The first is History, which speaks of actual events as they occurred; the second is Allegory, in which one thing stands for something else; the third is Tropology, or moral instruction, which treats of the ordering and arranging of one's life; and the last is Anagogy, or spiritual enlightenment, through which we who are about to treat of heavenly and lofty topics are led to a higher way of life. For example, the word "Jerusalem": historically it represents a specific city; in allegory it represents the holy Church; tropologically, or morally, it is the soul of every faithful man who longs for the vision of eternal peace; and anagogically it refers to the life of the heavenly citizens, who already see the God of Gods, revealed in all his glory in Sion.

These four senses of interpreting a text—any text, not just Scripture—become enormously popular during the Middle Ages in literature as well as in preaching. Allegory in particular shaped popular works like Henri d'Andeli's *Battle of the Seven Arts* and *The Castle of Perseverance,* in which Humanum Genus enters the castle of Remedial Virtues; the method remained popular into the Renaissance in works like Edmund Spenser's *The Faerie Queene* and John Bunyan's The *Pilgrim's Progress*. It seems likely that the frequent use of allegory and other "senses" by preachers accustomed medieval audiences to understanding varied meanings in literature as well.

However, the basic form of the medieval sermon, the "thematic" sermon, took shape around 1200. It seems to have evolved from the same kind of twelfth-century studies of the relations among the liberal arts that led grammarians and dialecticians to seek their own new uses for language. Ciceronian ideas are very strong in the earliest formative stages of the *ars praedicandi,* though modern scholars are not yet sure about the extent to which dialectic played a part in the evolution of this new rhetorical genre. Major writers in this development of the thematic sermon were Alexander of Ashby, Alan of Lille, Thomas Chabham (Thomas of Salisbury), and Richard of Thetford.

The medieval art of preaching (*ars praedicandi*) produced more than 300 separate treatises over the next three centuries. These books are remarkably uniform in their theoretical doctrine, demonstrating that the *ars praedicandi* is a true genre with a well-developed set of principles. All tell the preacher to select a theme (a short quotation from Scripture) and to explain why it was chosen, to divide the quotation into parts—usually three—and then to develop or amplify each of the divided parts. Often each of the three parts is itself divided into three, to make a total of nine parts to be amplified.

The basic format of the medieval thematic sermon remained standard for many centuries and is still used by some preachers. It has six (sometimes seven) essential parts: (1) opening prayer for divine aid; (2) protheme (sometimes called antetheme), or introduction of the theme; (3) theme, or scriptural quotation; (4) division, or statement of parts ("members") to be discussed; (5) subdivisions, or division of divisions; (6) amplification of each member; (7) conclusion, or final prayer, or exhortation (optional).

Methods of amplification obviously become very important to the preacher once he has named his theme and then divided it into three or nine parts. Besides the four senses of interpretation, another set of methods of amplification was put forward by

Richard of Thetford (*fl. ca.* 1245) in his *Ars dilatandi sermones* (Art of amplifying sermons). Richard's "eight modes of dilation" are (1) placing a locution in place of a name, as in defining, describing, interpreting, or any other kind of exposition; (2) dividing; (3) reasoning, including syllogism, induction, example, or enthymeme; (4) using concordant authorities; (5) etymology; (6) proposing metaphors and showing their aptness for instruction; (7) the four senses of interpretation; and (8) cause and effect.

Over the centuries preachers developed a bewildering array of means to amplify the scriptural themes they chose. One popular mode was the use of authority (*auctoritas*), the quotation of some famous author (or the Bible itself) to support a point. Another was the exemplum (*exemplum*), or narrative told to illustrate an idea. Many writers suggest using the sixty-four tropes and figures from book IV of the *Rhetorica ad Herennium.* Some suggest complicated correspondences between all the parts of a sermon, so that the audience is reminded that a word or idea from point 3 occurs again in point 6, for instance.

A few writers, like Robert of Basevorn (*fl.* 1322) and Thomas Waleys (*fl.* 1349), argue that delivery is itself a way of amplification, since gesture, facial expression, and voice add emphasis to what the preacher says. For the most part, though, authors of preaching manuals ignore this aspect of the sermon to concentrate on theme, division, and amplification.

As might be expected, a whole apparatus of auxiliary works grew up around the *ars praedicandi* as preacher's aids. There were alphabetical concordances to Scripture, so that a preacher wishing to speak on a particular subject (say, adultery) could look under that word and find a list of places in the Bible where quotations about it could be located. Copies of the Bible with glosses could give him ideas about how to interpret a given passage for his congregation. There were collections of sermon outlines, and collections of complete sermons (though these were apparently for general study rather than for re-use, in contrast with the letter collections that often accompanied the *ars dictaminis*).

Collections of exempla, like the famous one ascribed to Jacques de Vitry (*ca.* 1160/1170–1240), enabled the preacher to pick out useful stories to entertain his audience while pointing out a moral lesson. Franciscan preachers were particularly well known for their ability to use popular tales to enliven their sermons.

The *ars praedicandi,* like the *ars dictaminis,* grew up to meet a particular medieval need—in this case, the need for a reliable method of oral discourse in the liturgical setting, which demanded effective rhetorical performance by the preacher every week of every month of every year. Great variety was required. The long-lasting popularity of the thematic sermon mode proves that the *ars praedicandi* met the need very well.

THE TRANSFORMATION OF MEDIEVAL RHETORIC

Ironically, it was the rediscovery of two ancient Roman rhetorical texts that helped to accelerate the decline of the three medieval rhetorical genres based ultimately on Ciceronian concepts. In 1416 the Italian humanist Poggio Bracciolini discovered in the Swiss monastery of St. Gall a complete text of Quintilian's *Institutio oratoria,* a work known to the Middle Ages only in a fragmentary form. And in 1421 Bishop Landriani discovered in Lodi, Italy, the long-lost text of Cicero's most philosophical rhetorical work, the dialogue *De oratore.* Both works appealed at once to Italian humanists exploring such concepts as civic duty, the nature of language and literature, and the relation of rhetoric to philosophy. Meanwhile, some *dictatores* (teachers of the *ars dictaminis*) in Italy had already begun to use the genre of the letter-writing manual to expand into discussions of prose style and other matters closer to literature than to dictamen. The *Ars arengandi,* the theory of secular speech, developed as early as the thirteenth century in Italy, provided a base for humanist oratory. Erasmus and others produced their own, different views on the composition of letters. By the fifteenth century, too, the great interest in ancient texts of all kinds produced a revived concern for the literary ideas of the poet Horace, which effectively supplanted the study of medieval poetic theorists like Geoffrey of Vinsauf and John of Garland; this development was further advanced when the long-neglected text of Aristotle's *Poetics* became generally circulated in the same century.

Of the three medieval rhetorical genres, only the *ars praedicandi* seems to have survived into modern times in basically the same form. Even the advent of Protestant preaching after Martin Luther's break with the Roman church in 1517 did not immediately change the form of Christian preaching. It is now clear that secular oratory did begin to influence preaching. There is, however, a good deal of current research under way on Renaissance modes of preaching, and the fate of medieval preaching concepts in that period is still not completely clear.

Western medieval rhetoric, then, reveals a fundamental aspect of the Middle Ages: the eagerness to use the past for the needs of the present. Cicero in particular was called upon as a guide for writers and speakers facing the task of creating new poems, letters, or sermons. The history of rhetoric in the Renaissance is not yet written, but the evidence so far seems to indicate that a variety of new forces came into play during the period 1450–1650—such as the advent of printing, the increasing role of popular oratory, and humanist studies of language.

BIBLIOGRAPHY

Bibliographies and texts. For a general bibliography see James J. Murphy, *Medieval Rhetoric: A Select Bibliography* (1971). For preaching manuals see Harry Caplan, *Mediaeval Artes Praedicandi: A Hand-list,* 2 vols. (1934–1936); Thomas-Marie Charland, *Artes praedicandi: Contribution à l'histoire de la rhétorique au môyen âge* (1936). For verse-writing treatises, see Edmond Faral, *Les arts poétiques du XIIe et du XIIIe siècle* (1924, repr. 1958, 1971). For the *ars dictaminis* see Noel Denholm-Young, "The *Cursus* in England," in *Collected Papers of N. Denholm-Young* (1969); Ludwig Rockinger, *Briefsteller und Formelbücher des eilften bis vierzehnten Jahrhunderts* (1863, repr. 1961).

Translations. Collections include Joseph M. Miller, Michael H. Prosser, and Thomas W. Benson, eds., *Readings in Medieval Rhetoric* (1973); James J. Murphy, comp., *Three Medieval Rhetorical Arts* (1971). Translations of individual works include Geoffrey of Vinsauf, *Poetria nova,* translated by Margaret F. Nims (1971), by Jane Baltzell Kopp, in Murphy, *Three Medieval Rhetorical Arts,* and by Ernest Gallo, *The "Poetria nova" and Its Sources in Early Rhetorical Doctrine* (1971); Geoffrey, *Documentum de modo et arte dictandi . . . ,* Roger Parr, trans. (1968); John of Garland, *Parisiana poetria,* Traugott Lawler, ed. and trans. (1974); Matthew of Vendôme, *The Art of Versification,* Aubrey E. Galyon, trans. (1980).

Studies. Ernst R. Curtius, *European Literature and the Latin Middle Ages,* Willard R. Trask, trans. (1953); George A. Kennedy, *Classical Rhetoric and Its Christian and Secular Tradition from Ancient to Modern Times* (1980), esp. 120–194; Paul O. Kristeller, *Renaissance Thought and Its Sources,* Michael Mooney, ed. (1979), esp. 106–133, 228–242; Richard McKeon, "Rhetoric in the Middle Ages," in *Speculum,* 17 (1942); James J. Murphy, *Rhetoric in the Middle Ages* (1974), and, as editor, *Medieval Eloquence* (1978).

JAMES J. MURPHY

[See also **Allegory; Aristotle in the Middle Ages; Ars Poetica; Ars Praedicandi; Cursus; Dialectic; Dictamen; Grammar; Preaching and Sermon Literature, Western European; Trivium**; and individual authors.]

RHÉTORIQUEURS, a term deriving from a nineteenth-century misreading, denotes a number of French writers who, as court dependents from about 1460 to 1530, served as official secretaries, advisers, diplomats, chroniclers, or poets, interacting with prominent political leaders and renowned musicians and artists of their day. Discredited by critical bias from the time of their successors, the sixteenth-century Pléiade poets, up to the present century in such studies as that of Henry Guy, the Rhétoriqueurs have only recently received a more impartial appraisal for their literary contributions in late medieval France. While never formally comprising a literary school, these "poëtes, orateurs et historiens" shared a common heritage bequeathed by Jean de Meun and Alain Chartier, and exhibited mutual respect through poetic exchanges and conventional tributes to each others.

Modern critics do not completely concur on the designation of Rhétoriqueurs. Nevertheless Georges Chastellain (*ca.* 1405/1415–1475) and his disciple Jean Molinet (1435–1507), affiliates of the Burgundian dukes Philippe le Bon and Charles le Téméraire, respectively, figure most prominently among the earlier generation of Rhétoriqueurs, who were attached to the different ducal courts, much like the lesser-known Jean Robertet (*d. ca.* 1503), in the service of Pierre de Bourbon, and Jean Meschinot (*ca.* 1420–1491), the poetic voice from Brittany. During the following period, one of more concentrated political and literary activity, most Rhétoriqueurs were drawn to the courts of King Charles VIII, King Louis XII, and Queen Anne de Bretagne, who subsidized such writers as Octavien de Saint-Gelais (1468–1502), Guillaume Cretin (*d.* 1525), Jean Marot (1457–1526), André de La Vigne (*ca.* 1470–*ca.* 1515), and Pierre Gringore (*ca.* 1475–1538 or 1539). The most widely acclaimed of all the Rhétoriqueurs, Jean Lemaire de Belges (*ca.* 1473–*ca.* 1525), disciple of Molinet, distinguished himself as a protégé of the Bourbon, Burgundian, and French courts.

Encompassing a wide spectrum of genres, forms, subjects, and themes, the Rhétoriqueurs' works range from panegyrics on royal births, marriages, and military victories (such as Molinet's *Faicts et dictz*) to eulogies of a recently deceased patron or mentor (Chastellain's "La mort du duc Philippe" or Robertet's "Complainte de la mort de Maistre George Chastellain"); from stylized poems extolling the Virgin (La Vigne's or Cretin's prizewinning *chants royaux*) to lengthy tributes to a patroness (Lemaire's *Couronne margaritique*); from didactic moral exposés (Meschinot's *Lunettes des princes*) to pseudoautobiographical, anticourtly narratives (Saint-Gelais's *Séjour d'honneur*); from journals relating a military expedition (Marot's *Voyage de Venise*) to histories of France from the creation of the world (Lemaire's *Illustrations de Gaule et singularitez de Troyes*); from sacrilegious parodies (Molinet's "Sermon de Billouart") to acerbic religious satires (Gringore's *Sottie du jeu du prince des sotz*).

Very likely influenced by the medieval Latin rhetorical tradition and the vernacular *Arts de seconde rhétorique* (poetic treatises that taught verse forms, rhyme patterns, and so on), the Rhétoriqueurs enthusiastically experimented with all forms of versification, the extravagant accumulation of sounds, words, and images, the adoption of verse and prose within the same text, the use of allegory and mythology for less traditional ends, the interpolation of names, foreign languages, and other texts into their creations, and all levels of equivocation. Their exploration of multiple linguistic possibilities thus reflects a consciousness of the force of poetic language.

BIBLIOGRAPHY

Cynthia J. Brown, *The Shaping of History and Poetry in Late Medieval France: Propaganda and Artistic Expression in the Works of the Rhétoriqueurs* (1985); Kathleen Chesney, *Fleurs de rhétorique* (1950); Pierre Jodogne, "Les 'rhétoriqueurs' et l'humanisme," in Anthony H. T. Levi, ed., *Humanism in France at the End of the Middle Ages and in the Early Renaissance* (1970), 150–175, and *Jean Lemaire de Belges: Écrivain franco-bourguignon* (1972); Ernest Langlois, ed., *Recueil d'arts de seconde rhétorique* (1902); Franco Simone, "La scuola dei 'rhétoriqueurs,'" in his *Umanesimo, rinascimento, barocco in Francia* (1968); Paul Zumthor, *Anthologie des grands rhétoriqueurs* (1978), and *Le masque et la lumière: La poétique des grands rhétoriqueurs* (1978).

CYNTHIA J. BROWN

[See also **Chant Royal; French Literature; Jean Lemaire de Belges.**]

RHODES (Ródhos). The most easterly of the islands of the Aegean Sea, Rhodes lies about eleven miles (almost 18 km) south of Asia Minor; the capital, Ródhos, lies about 36 degrees north by about 28 degrees east. It is some forty-five miles (72 km) in length and twenty-two miles (35 km) in width at its widest point. The island has an excellent climate and fertile soil. During the later Roman Empire, it served as the capital of the "province of the islands." In 654 Muslim pirates from Syria took the island from the Byzantines and had the remnants of the great Colossus of Rhodes carried off on 900 camels. During subsequent centuries, Rhodes remained largely in Byzantine hands, although it was subject to periodic Arab raids. In 1148 the Venetians received trading privileges there, and in 1204 it was taken by a Greek who later became a vassal of the Nicaean Empire. In 1309 Rhodes was captured by the Knights of the Hospital of St. John of Jerusalem, who maintained it as a fortress against the Turks until its capture by the Ottomans in 1522.

BIBLIOGRAPHY

George Ostrogorsky, *History of the Byzantine State,* Joan Hussey, trans. (1957, rev. ed. 1969).

LINDA C. ROSE

[See also **Chivalry, Orders of; Muᶜāwiya; Navies, Islamic; Nicaea, Empire of.**]

RHODRI MAWR (*d.* 878), Welsh ruler. Rhodri, as his epithet *Mawr*—"the Great"—suggests, consolidated much of Wales in a reign noted for its military success and cultural brilliance. Upon the death of his father, Merfyn Vrych ("the Freckled"), in 844, Rhodri assumed the throne of Gwynedd. Approximately ten years later he acquired Powys. His claim was based upon his mother, Nest, being the sister of Cyngen, the last survivor of Cadell Ddyrnllug's dynasty, who died in Rome in 856. Rhodri's marriage to Angharad, who was the sister of Gwgon ap Meurig, king of Ceredigion (Cardigan), brought him domination of Seisyllwg, the territory formed from uniting Ceredigion with

Ystrad Tywi (Carmarthen), after Gwgon drowned in 872.

Rhodri's bloodless political success at home was counterpointed by the bitter warfare he waged against Vikings and Saxons. The Danes ravaged Anglesey in 855, but the next year Rhodri fought and killed their leader, Gorm. News of this battle must have reached the court of the West Frankish king Charles the Bald (*r.* 843–877), because Sedulius Scottus (Sedulius "the Irishman"), a favorite of Charles, composed an ode celebrating a victory over the Danes and another one to Rhuaidhri (Roricus), who scholars agree was Rhodri Mawr.

Warfare ceased only for a time. Welsh chronicles record the battles of Banolau and Menegyd in 874. Then in 877 the Danes swept Anglesey on a Sunday raid and sent Rhodri fleeing to Ireland. The Annals of Ulster tell how "Rhuaidri son of Muirminn (Merfyn), king of the Britons, came to Ireland, fleeing before the Black Foreigners." Rhodri returned only to meet death in battle against the Saxons a year later.

At his death Rhodri's carefully amassed kingdom was divided among his six sons, with Anarawd taking Gwynedd and Cadell receiving Seisyllwg, where his descendants, including Hywel Dda ("the Good") ruled for generations.

During the reigns of Rhodri and his father, Merfyn Vrych, their court at Aberffraw was a center for learning and a crossroads for those traveling to and from Ireland and the Continent. Records, including genealogies and the *Historia Brittonum,* date from this period, as well as a substantial amount of native verse.

BIBLIOGRAPHY

Nora K. Chadwick, "Early Culture and Learning in North Wales," in Chadwick, ed., *Studies in the Early British Church* (1958), and "The Welsh Dynasties in the Dark Ages," in Arthur J. Roderick, ed., *Wales Through the Ages,* I (1975); Myles Dillon and Nora K. Chadwick, *The Celtic Realms,* 2nd ed. (1972), 108–116; John E. Lloyd, *A History of Wales from the Earliest Times to the Edwardian Conquest,* I, 3rd ed. (1939, repr. 1948, 1954), 323–333.

MARILYN KAY KENNEY

[See also **Historia Britonnum; Sedulius Scottus; Wales: History.**]

RHYMED OFFICES. Between the ninth and sixteenth centuries, some 1,500 newly composed liturgical offices are known. Many others remain to be discovered. The texts of nearly 1,000 were published between 1889 and 1909 in twelve volumes of *Analecta Hymnica.* Although the vast majority were destined to be sung on the appropriate liturgical date, the chants for only about two dozen have appeared in print. No published work has dealt with this repertory of texts and chants in general, although some individual offices have received attention. Thus a vast storehouse of literary, liturgical, and musical composition for the late medieval church remains unknown.

The new offices were required in the celebration of the Office Hours for saints and feasts newly instituted in this period. Some feasts were for saints already in the church Kalendar; others were for saints newly introduced or, after canonization was formalized in the twelfth century, newly canonized; some feasts were newly established, such as Corpus Christi in 1264; others were formally authorized after centuries of unofficial use, as was the Feast of the Trinity in 1316 (various sources give 1331 or 1334). A few offices were written for persons never officially recognized: one venerating the fourteenth-century English mystic Richard Rolle of Hampole can surely never have been intended for liturgical use even though it appears in the York Breviary; others, like the one to Simon de Montfort the Younger (*d.* 1265), may have been intended for use in choir once the feast was authorized. Certainly many of these new offices, or at least the vitae from which they were often derived, formed a part of the documents presented in the process of canonization. In the case of St. Stanislaus of Poland (canonized 1253), the Dominican author of the office, Vincent of Kielce, actually traveled to Rome with the commission for canonization. Offices for saints already in the Kalendar were no doubt written for some special occasion, such as the discovery of a relic, the translation of the saint, or the dedication of a new church or altar. The ravages of the Norsemen in the tenth century caused the relics of many French saints to be "discovered" and translated, with a consequent upsurge of interest in cults long dormant. Unfortunately, with our present knowledge of the repertory of the rhymed offices, and our vast ignorance as to the date or destination of the breviaries and antiphonals in which the majority of offices are to be found, it is possible to link the office with a specific author, place, or date in only a few cases. Sometimes the identification must depend on hagiographical evidence, itself often uncertain or ambiguous. For a few offices, the information is more secure, as when a rubric or a statement in the documents of canonization gives precise information. With respect to St. Thomas Becket, for example, we have the following, in the vita written by Abbot Benedict of Peterborough (*d.* 1193):

> He wrote [*composuit*] the distinguished volume on the passion and miracles of St. Thomas, and made the whole of the historia *Studens livor:* I say the whole because he noted [*insignivit*] the literary text with the chants most excellently.

The original Becket office was thus written within twenty-three years of Becket's death, by a monastic author. It was therefore probably monastic in form. Of the different office for Becket's translation in 1220 we have no similar information. Occasionally our evidence comes a great deal later. The late-fifteenth-century chronicler of Poland Jan Dlugosz says this of the office of St. Stanislaus, in existence by at least the thirteenth century:

> First, in his honour, brother Vincent of Kielce, O.P., made and wrote [*composuit et descriptsit*] the lessons, and chants with sweet and notable melody and balance and with eloquent style for performance by the church in each hour of night and day. . . . (*Liber beneficiorum dioec. Cracoviensis,* III: *Monasteria,* in *Opera omnia,* IX, 447–448)

In both of these quotations, as in other instances, the author is said to have been responsible for texts and chants, and from the words such as *edidit, compilavit, composuit,* which are used to describe the process of composition, we may conclude that it was a mixture of original composition; texts from Scripture, reminiscences, or borrowing from other hagiographic material or from existing liturgical forms such as hymns or sequences; and reworking of common formulas. In the case of the texts, these origins are often relatively easy to trace. To what extent the same processes were at work in the music is much more difficult to establish.

The word *historia* used in such quotations is a conventional term for new offices, centered as they are on the recitation of the saint's biography, or similar narrative description, as expounded in the vita that forms the basis, often verbatim, for the lessons of Matins. The word is, of course, a standard liturgical term for such lessons, especially when they are drawn from the historical books of the Bible, as they are during the summer. In different manuscripts transmitting the same office, however, the extent of the lessons frequently varies considerably. Sometimes the whole vita is distributed over the nine lessons (or twelve for monastic use); sometimes only the first sentence of the individual sections of the vita is written in the books, in which case the whole vita was surely read from some other source; sometimes nine, or twelve, consecutive sentences from the vita are distributed over the nine or twelve lessons, and if such distributions reflect actual practice, the vita was massively abbreviated, perhaps to the point of making nonsense of the story. Such distortions may have been tolerated for the sake of convenience if the vita were read complete in, say, the refectory during mealtimes. In any case, the amount of variety probably indicates the large amount of choice local church officials may have had with respect to late medieval liturgical composition. It seems unlikely that similar truncations would have been tolerated in the regular services.

On rare occasions, the newly composed lessons were rhymed, following the increasing trend in the tenth to the twelfth centuries to regularize new liturgical compositions such as sequences and tropes into strictly metrical lines with rhyme. Normally, however, it was not the lessons but the truly sung parts of the new offices that were written in poetic form. The poetic requirements were applied to all the sung items of the Office Hours, namely, the antiphons, whether for psalms, for the three major canticles (Magnificat, Benedictus, and Nunc dimittis), or for the monastic canticle; the invitatory antiphon; the responsories and their verses. Thus, in a normal new feast of the later Middle Ages, the usual distribution of poetry in the services would be as follows (poetic texts are in italic):

Vespers 1:	*antiphon(s)* and psalm(s) *hymn* Magnificat *antiphon*
Compline:	*antiphon* and psalm *hymn* Nunc dimittis *antiphon*
Matins:	invitatory *antiphon* *hymn*
nocturn 1:	3 or 6 *antiphons* with psalms 3 or 4 lessons each followed by a *responsory* and *verse*
nocturn 2:	as nocturn 1
nocturn 3:	3 *antiphons* with psalms or

RHYMED OFFICES

	1 *antiphon* with monastic canticles 3 or 4 lessons each followed by a *responsory* and *verse* Te Deum
Lauds:	5 *antiphons* and psalms hymn Benedictus *antiphon*
Vespers 2:	*antiphon(s)* and psalm(s) hymn Magnificat *antiphon*

In this scheme, however, Compline rarely has proper material and is drawn from common stocks. If celebrated during Easter, moreover, only one nocturn would be sung. The number of antiphons at Vespers varies from one to five, apparently depending on the ecclesiastical Order in which the feast was celebrated. There are thus some sixteen to thirty antiphons and perhaps a dozen responsories in each office. In a few cases, the dialogues (versicle and response) that introduce offices and lessons are rhymed, but even so they are always textually and musically separate from the antiphons and responsories that form the core of what has come to be called the rhymed office.

The texts of each antiphon, responsory, and verse normally form a single stanza of poetry, although sometimes the rhyme schemes of consecutive items are interlocked to form longer "poems." Thus, in the second nocturn of St. Calixtinus the first and second antiphons (antiphons 7 and 8 of monastic Matins) are as follows:

A7	*Qui confidens in Domino*	*a*
	minanti se palmatio	*a*
	presentare non timuit	*b*
A8	*Ruga carens et macula*	*c*
	eterna tabernacula	*c*
	ingredi meruit	*b*

Such items would be separated in the service by at least one psalm, so such larger schemes within the office must be regarded merely as literary devices.

The texts are normally drawn from the vita, a key passage being paraphrased and condensed into poetry. This process is most clear in the responsories, which often paraphrase the last sentences of the lesson they immediately follow, as, for example, in the office to St. Thomas Becket:

Lesson 2:	. . . Sed vir Dei manum suam mittens ad fortia, *exilium,* damna, *contumeliens, et* opprobria . . . nulla *prorsus* fractus *aut immutatus* injuria. *Tanta namque fuit confessoris Christi* constantia, *ut omnes coexules suos dicere videretur, quod* omne solum forti patria est.
Responsory 2:	*Thomas manum mittit ad fortia spernit damna spernit opprobria Nulla Thomam frangit injuria*
Verse:	*Clamat cunctis Thome constantia omne solum est forti patria.*

The texts of antiphons are less clearly drawn from the vita, and the texts of hymns even less so, if at all. In fact, for a number of reasons, hymns are separate from rhymed offices and will be excluded from the discussion except to demonstrate their independence. The central position of Matins, especially the lessons and responsories, in the creation of a late medieval office, whether rhymed or not, can lead to a structural division of the office into three or even four parts: items preceding Matins may in themselves complete one cycle of narrative; those after Matins, a second similar cycle; and within Matins antiphons and responsories may have interlocking parallel cycles. Thus, in an unrhymed office to St. Monica, the mother of Augustine, the biography proceeds to her death in the Magnificat antiphon of first Vespers, again in the last responsory of Matins, and again in the Benedictus antiphon of Lauds. The topics of responsories echo or complement those of the antiphons in the same nocturn:

Matins: *antiphons*
1. The infant Monica is shaped by Christ.
2. Monica teaches her children.
3. She is contemplative.

responsories
1. The infant Monica is shaped by Eloquence.
2. Monica begs Catholic illumination for her husband.
3. She is consoled and Augustine, dead in spirit, is roused a true Catholic.

The sectional nature of most offices is confirmed by the chants to which antiphons and responsories are set. It is normal practice for successive antiphons, and independently the responsories, in Matins to be arranged in serial order of the eight musical modes so that antiphon 1 and responsory 1 are in mode 1. These separate modal cycles run to mode 8, whereupon the cycle begins again, so that the ninth item is in mode 1. In monastic cycles,

RHYMED OFFICES

where there are thirteen antiphons and twelve responsories, the regularity of the last items in the sequence seems not to be so obligatory. As with the textual narrative, the items preceding and following Matins have their own independent modal cycles running as far as the number of items will permit. Hymns do not generally form a part of the modal cycles, and are thus separate from the rhymed office per se. In standard chant, invitatories occur in only a few of the available modes. This restriction is normally true of later offices, too, so that the invitatory also does not form a part of the modal cycle, although it is obvious, from a number of pieces of evidence, including its textual character as a single-stanza poem, that it must be included as a part of the rhymed office. To emphasize its special character, however, it is normally a purely formal invitation of somewhat general character, and does not fit into the narrative and biographical sequence of the other texts.

In practice, the strict modal order of the music is often broken, but in such a way that an underlying sequence is visible and must surely be accepted as representing the original arrangement. In the rare cases, such as the office of St. Dominic, where we have an authorized original version, the strict order is maintained. Normally, however, it is clear that rearrangements and reordering of the original material have taken place, perhaps with some omissions and replacements. Why these shufflings took place and who authorized them is not known. It is not impossible that some originated from practical necessity, for example because the choir could not sing the range implied by the strict modal sequence. Rearrangements of responsories may have been a consequence of rearranging the order of the lessons of Matins. It is possible that an original order may be ascertained if, for instance, the modal order in sequence coincided with a chronological presentation of the biographical narrative, but since nonchronological presentations of such material are not uncommon in the Middle Ages, this approach may not be very useful.

The number of different arrangements of a single office is sometimes very great in a widely distributed text. Comparing the patterns of arrangement, together with a more conventional analysis of text and chant, would allow, in most cases, manuscripts to be placed in related groups. The destination and date of liturgical books may be narrowed down by such means, and much information about how liturgical texts and chants were transmitted across Europe and the centuries may be revealed by such studies.

A different kind of rearrangement follows from the adaptation of a monastic office for use in a secular establishment, or vice versa. Even if it is not known from other evidence, sometimes it is possible to determine that the monastic form was the original because, for example, omissions in the modal cycle or poetic structure betray an underlying series, as when the modes run 123(4)567(8)123(4). On the other hand, monastic items added to a secular form may break the underlying series: 123(7)456(2) 781(5).

It is tempting to think of this repertory as largely a style cultivated in monasteries, and certainly most important monastic centers produced rhymed offices; but secular institutions obviously were heavily involved, and orders such as the Franciscans and Dominicans produced offices that were secular in form. The Franciscans are said, in some modern reports, to have been responsible for about 700 rhymed offices. This number is massively exaggerated. Appearances may be misleading, however, as with the office to St. Thomas Becket. Widely distributed all over Europe, the office appears more frequently in secular form, and is so printed in *Analecta Hymnica.* Its clear association with English books, mostly of the secular Sarum rite, of which many survive and are well known, reinforces its secular nature. Yet it is clear that its original form must have been monastic, since its author was Abbot Benedict of Peterborough, and since we know some of its original items, which do not appear in the secular form.

Authors, who may also be the compilers and composers of the chants, are identified for perhaps a hundred of the known offices. For the later centuries, say from the twelfth, offices that can be attributed to a particular author are scattered in time and place, so that it is not possible to speak of a school of poetry or composition. In fact, it is clear that in many cases much of an office was borrowed or adapted rather than composed. The extent of textual borrowing can now be made clearer (the author of this article has prepared a complete concordance of the poetry for publication): obviously, conventional phrases such as *duc nos ad celi gaudia* (bring us to the joys of heaven) are often reused and probably signify little in terms of deliberate borrowing. On the other hand, often quite distinctive and sometimes quite long phrases are reused, perhaps with the substitution of a proper name, in a way that must indicate specific borrowing.

The extent of borrowing of the chants is much more difficult to assess, for several reasons. First, the chants have to be found in a legible manuscript with music. Catalogs of liturgical manuscripts are notoriously deficient in this kind of information. Once found, the music has to be transcribed and presented to a computer in a form that will allow borrowings to be identified. The problems with this task are enormous and have not been solved entirely satisfactorily. Nevertheless, it is clear that the borrowings are similar to those of the texts; there are conventional motives that signify little, phrases similar enough for some relation to be suspected, and phrases identical in both pitch and notational form, so that some form of direct copying or borrowing must be accepted.

All of this textual and musical borrowing is well known, although it has not been investigated systematically, and its true extent cannot yet be assessed. Nevertheless, we may suppose that compilation of a new office involved some combination of direct copying, deliberate variation, recollection (or imprecise borrowing), adaptation of conventional formulas, and free composition. Recent theories about copying, oral transmission and aural recollection, and originality may easily be applied to this repertory.

The identification of borrowings will allow our present view of the repertory to be refined. There are a few special cases: for instance, the late-thirteenth-century prose office for Corpus Christi explicitly borrows its tunes from earlier rhymed offices, including those of Sts. Dominic, Thomas Becket, Nicholas, and Catherine, an interesting case of adapting rhymed material to prose texts. Normally, however, the most obvious and easily traceable borrowings are within the religious orders. The office of St. Francis, for example, was partly used in the compilation of offices to St. Clare and St. Anthony of Padua, and in the office of the Trinity composed by John Peckham, Franciscan archbishop of Canterbury from 1279; and the office of St. Dominic was extensively employed in the offices of the Crown of Thorns, Peter Martyr, Thomas Aquinas, an office to St. Ann by an English Dominican of the fourteenth century, and dozens of others. We may thus easily identify a Franciscan and a Dominican group. Less obvious traditions are easy to identify. Items of the office of St. Dominic reappear in the office of St. Bernward, Benedictine bishop of Hildesheim. Here, the connection appears to be that the later Benedictine office adopted much of the Dominican *opus Dei;* the adoption seems to have extended to the chant in this case.

Similar borrowings have not yet been investigated in offices of the other orders. There seems to be no relationship between the rhymed offices of St. John of Bridlington, a fourteenth-century Augustinian, and St. Augustine, or even between the rhymed offices to St. Augustine and to Monica, his mother, although one might certainly have been predicted in this case on the basis of the practice in other orders. In fact, the rhymed office to St. Monica owes more to the prose setting of her office, and Augustinian idiosyncrasies, if any, may relate to the more widely distributed prose version of his office. The relation between rhymed and nonrhymed material, especially when it involves the chant, must await the collection and analysis of much more data.

The Carmelites celebrated a number of rhymed offices, especially to the Virgin, and although borrowings are known from within and without the order, a Carmelite subgroup has not been fully established.

Similarly, no monastic subgroups have been isolated. Very many Benedictine saints were provided with rhymed offices, but the appropriate comparisons have not yet been made. One might predict, for example, that the office to St. Scholastica would borrow from that to St. Benedict, her brother. The Carthusians firmly rejected poetry and ornaments of all kinds. Although the Cistercians were renowned for similar austerity, and there was some prohibition of such frills as poetry and quite strict regulation, in the late twelfth century, of the style of plainchant, a number of rhymed offices with chant in the modern style were used in the order. An office for the *Sanctum Sudarium* (Holy Shroud) at Cadouin is found only in local Cistercian manuscripts; German Cistercian sources transmit a unique office of Corpus Christi. A number of Cistercian sources also have the office for St. Edmund Rich, a thirteenth-century archbishop of Canterbury who, like his predecessor St. Thomas Becket, was exiled in French Cistercian houses. This particular office in fact borrows wholesale from the Benedictine office to Thomas Becket; why the Cistercians should choose to venerate Edmund and not Thomas is the kind of puzzle that accompanies much of this repertory.

The Thomas Becket office itself was perhaps

more widely distributed over Europe than any other. Actually, there are several distinct but occasionally related offices, including one for the Translation and a version, unique to Canterbury, for his return from exile. The secular or monastic form of the main office is found in manuscripts from Finland to Hungary at least until the sixteenth century. In English manuscripts it is frequently erased, blacked out, or torn out as a result of the actions of Henry VIII's commissioners in the 1530's and 1540's. Only in Poland and Bohemia does the proper office seem not to have been celebrated. Here is another curious circumstance. In this case the explanation may be that the office of St. Stanislaus of Poland, celebrated also in Bohemia, displaced the Thomas office: Stanislaus, like Thomas, died protecting his church from temporal authority, and one such saint may have been sufficient. There are slight textual links between the offices of Stanislaus and Thomas. In dozens of other cases, however, the Thomas office was borrowed wholesale, sometimes when a saint was martyred in similar circumstances, or perhaps, as in the case of St. David of Wales, merely when some *auctoritas* of a religious or political nature was required.

Apart from the offices associated with religious orders, then, certain others achieved such a status that they cut across geographical and religious divisions sufficiently to establish themselves as major subgroups within the repertory. Some of the offices to the Virgin, in particular the office of the Conception, and offices to extremely popular saints, such as Catherine of Alexandria, are in this category. St. Catherine, in whose honor there exist dozens of interrelated rhymed offices, probably provided a model for numerous other female saints, such as Dorothy and Barbara. In fact, most female saints—and there are many of them, often virgins and martyrs—have numerous offices. The rites of these saints are often quite luridly descriptive, and one is inclined to wonder whether the motivation for writing such vitas and offices was altogether spiritual in every case. A study of the different types of text and the reasons for writing them would surely illuminate much about late medieval ecclesiastical literary creation.

THE POETRY

In keeping with the general trend to move gradually from prose to poetry in the tenth to the twelfth centuries, new offices of the tenth and eleventh centuries can hardly be described as rhymed, and serve only as an antecedent to the later repertory. Some are characterized only by irregularly distributed assonance, rhymed prose, or the occasional use of the metrical cursus. A few are more strictly in Classical Latin meters. The term "rhythmic(al)" rather than "rhymed" is sometimes applied. Gradually, as the quantitative style was replaced by the qualitative, irregularity was replaced by regularity in both meter and rhyme. Often, however, it is difficult to decide whether a prose text has accidental features of poetry (sometimes difficult to avoid in Latin), is very irregularly poetic, or is truly poetic, with a large number of "defective" or irregular lines. Sometimes a largely prose office includes one or two rhymed items, and occasionally even these are sufficiently irregular as to escape notice easily, as in this antiphon to St. Bertin: *Gloria sanctorum Deus accipe vota tuorum nosque tuas laudes in Bertino venerantes respice placatus nostro solvendo reatus.* Here the lines are 6-10-6-8-6-8 syllables, with rhymes clearly regular enough to be intentional.

For the period before the mid twelfth century, in the present state of knowledge, one can do little more than list offices certainly or possibly attributed to particular poets/composers. This notable repertory of offices is difficult to describe in general literary terms. The opening of the most famous office typifies the difficulty. *Gloria tibi Trinitas equalis una deitas* divides most naturally in syntax and meaning into three phrases of two words each. But splitting it after *Trinitas* creates poetry of the modern kind, with a minor amount of syntactical and semantic difficulty. The consequences of dividing the chant into two phrases rather than three are almost as significant musically. The office of the Trinity was written together with offices to Lambert and Stephen, possibly for Metz, by Archbishop Stephen of Liège (*d.* 920). The northeast area of France around Liège, the Moselle Valley, Aachen, and Metz (that is, lower Lorraine) is well known for its cultivation of literary, liturgical, and musical innovations in the Carolingian and post-Carolingian centuries. Hucbald of St. Amand (*ca.* 850–930) wrote offices to Andrew, Cilinia, Theodoric of Rheims, and Peter, of which the last survives, and he may have been responsible for the offices to Rictrude, Eusebia, and Maurontus for the abbey of Marchiennes, near Douai.

To the west, a flourishing school of literary and musical composition seems to have grown up in

RHYMED OFFICES

Normandy, but it has yet to be isolated, described, and separated from the school that apparently developed at about the same time to the south, centered on the cathedral of Chartres, in the time of Fulbert (*d.* 1028). At Mont-Ste.-Catherine, near Rouen, the monk Ainard wrote an office to Catherine, and abbot d'Ysembert was associated with offices to Nicholas and Ouen. Angerran, abbot of St. Riquier, is said to be the author of offices to Wandrille, Ausbert, Wulfran, and Valerius. Fulbert himself was responsible for writing several well-known Marian chants and offices for Giles and the local saints Cheron, Emanus, Piat, Leobinus, and Laumer. Some are prose, some are in hexameters. Farther to the south and east, the monastic centers of the Rhine Valley, extending into Switzerland, celebrated a number of new offices, many of them for local saints. Odo, abbot of Cluny (*d.* 942), wrote twelve antiphons for the monastic office of St. Martin. In the monastery of Micy, near Orléans, at the end of the century, Letald wrote the rite, and the monastic *historia* with its chants, of Julian, bishop of Le Mans. In Alsace, one may cite *histoire* for Gregory I, Hidulphus, Odilia, and Gorgonius (patron of the monastery of Gorze), written by Bruno of Egisheim, later pope Leo IX (*d.* 1054). Berno of Reichenau (*d.* 1048) is credited with offices to Ulrich and Meinrad, and Hermannus Contractus (*d.* 1054) may well have contributed to the genre. At Augsburg, Udalschalc (1124–*ca.* 1150) wrote offices to Ulrich and Afra.

A gradual movement south and west into Germany began to emerge. The cultivation of new offices continued in France and expanded to England and west and north on the Continent. In the south, however, especially in Italy, rhymed offices were not so favored. This difference between north and south was recognized by Ralph of Tongres, writing in the fourteenth century: "All nations have *histoire* of the Temporale that conform to the Roman Antiphonal; and *historie* of the Sanctorale, or saints' days, in Italian churches conform to Rome because they admit few proper saints. But Gallican, then English, and finally German churches open themselves to more proper *historie* for saints."

Other offices and supposed poets/composers are known. In the later centuries, probably fewer names of authors are known, but the attributions are more certain. Probably many more remain to be discovered. Although hardly any serious study has been devoted to the predecessors of the rhymed office, contemporary rubrics and chronicles provide evidence that the men named above were responsible not only for the texts but also for the chants.

Gradually, the fully metrical and rhymed office emerged in the late eleventh or early twelfth century. No one area or school seems to be associated with this development. One of the earliest truly rhymed offices is also one of the most extensive and elaborate: the office to St. Edmund, king and martyr, probably written at Bury St. Edmunds shortly before 1135, includes a full monastic and rhymed service for the Vigil of the Feast and for the feast itself. In the mid twelfth century, Nicholas of Clairvaux (*d.* 1179) wrote two monastic offices, to the Holy Cross and to the Virgin. From this date, the accentual and regularly rhymed text is usual.

Commonly, ordinary antiphons have four lines; antiphons *ad evangelia* (for the Magnificat, Nunc dimittis, and Benedictus) and monastic canticle antiphons are longer. In any case, the most frequent arrangement involves eight-syllable proparoxytone lines, sometimes with interspersed catalectic paroxytone lines of seven syllables. The rhyme scheme is regular. This scheme is also the standard for sequences from this period. Responsories tend to have more than four lines and are sometimes quite poetically elaborate; the verse may or may not be related to the poetic scheme of the responsory proper. Schemes such as these are common:

R	8	*a*	R	8	*a*
	8	*a*		7	*b*
	7	*b*	*	8	*a*
*	8	*c*		7	*b*
	8	*c*	V	8	*a*
	7	*b*		7	*b*
V	8	*d*			
	8	*d*			
	7	*b*			

After the verse, of course, the responsory would be repeated in part (as marked with the asterisk). In standard chant the abbreviated repeat often causes grammatical and syntactical nonsense. One would expect poetry written after the shortening of the repeat had become common practice to make the appropriate adjustment. The responsory verse, in fact, is the item of these offices that is most often in prose, even when all the remainder is poetry. This traditional retention of the psalmodic and recitational nature of the verse may go hand in hand with the retention of the conventional reciting tone to which standard responsory verses were set. Certainly, however, many offices have poetic verses set

RHYMED OFFICES

to modern chant quite far removed from a reciting tonc.

Literary conceits are not uncommon. Catalectic lines, for example, may all be drawn from well-known hymns; the first words of successive items may create the Lord's prayer or the *Ave Maria;* acrostics, alliteration, and other devices occur. Puns and wordplay, as in *Hugo iugo subiugatus* or the alternation of *auctor* and *Autor,* are ubiquitous. One of the most interesting devices is the extending of the rhyme scheme, or at lcast the vowel scheme, beyond the common limit of two syllables. When carried to extremes, as in the following verse from the office of St. Dorothy, the device becomes an affectation similar to extravagances in other cultural manifestations of certain eras.

R3	*Inclinare Dorotheam*		ea	8
	praeses studet idolis		i	7
	tunc germanis mittit eam		ea	8
	novellis apostasis		i	7
	spondet illis condonare		ae	8
	Gaze multitudinem		euiuie	7
	dolens eam iugulare		ae	8
	propter pulchritudinem		euiuie	7
V	*Sed perverse convertuntur*		euu	8
	crucem tollunt et sequuntur		euu	8
	Christum pro quo moriuntur.		uu	8
R8	*Dum sub ense prestolatur*		au	8
	mortis ictum deprecatur	oi	iueeau	8
	pro his a quibus veneratur	oia	iueeau	9
	sue necis memoria		oia	8
	ut abundent temporalibus		oaiu	9
	solvantur a mortalibus		oaiu	8
	culpis et criminalibus		aiu	8
	post hoc vivant in gloria		oia	8
V	*Expleta tunc oratione*		ioe	9
	exauditur in agone		oe	8
	Domine promissione		ioe	8

Perhaps the writing of an eight-syllable (out of eight) or six-syllable (out of seven) "rhyme," as above, is not as difficult as one might think, given long words like *multitudinem.* Often the meter is faultless. But, as these examples also indicate, the poetry often cannot be read metrically without distorting the accent:

cŭlpīs ă crīmĭnālĭbŭs.

Hypermetric syllables are quite common. Sometimes they can be eliminated by normal elision. Even in this case, however, they are commonly given a separate note in the musical setting. This is a common practice in other repertories also, indicating that poetry destined for musical performance, the normal state of affairs with much medieval poetry, was not necessarily bound by its own inherent musical laws.

Since many offices can be assigned at least to a century and a country, a good deal could be learned from this repertory about local pronunciation of Latin and the geographical distribution of vocabulary. In some cases, an author's style can easily be discerned, as with the group of offices by Christian of Lilienfeld (*d.* before 1322); examination of other Austrian offices might reveal a school of poetry. Christian also wrote treatises on poetry. To my knowledge neither these nor others refer specifically to the special features inherent in the composition of rhymed offices.

Quite apart from the literary aspects, these offices hold a vast amount of hagiographical information, sometimes very concisely, as in the example below. A good deal of this information, as far as I can judge from summaries of saints' biographies, either conflicts to some extent with, or provides information not generally recorded in, standard dictionaries (this dictionary included). In addition, the smaller of such reference works do not reflect well in their choice of entries those saints who were the choice of the Middle Ages for veneration with rhymed and proper texts and chants. There are two main reasons for this discrepancy: the cult of many saints did not survive the Middle Ages, and saints venerated in this way were often more of purely local than universal importance. In addition to offering an untapped source of hagiographical information, rhymed offices are textually interesting for many other reasons. They are full of place-names; and many of these, or the particular forms of them, are not recorded in the onomastic dictionaries, as for instance in the office to St. Imerius:

Felix Brixia que natum genuit
plus tamen Melia que patrem habuit
ad hec per omnia Cremona floruit
que sanctum tenuit.

Names of people also abound. Miscellaneous ecclesiastical information can often be extracted, as can information about other minor matters: medicine, music, architecture, for example. Vocabulary, grammar, and pronunciation could be studied from geographical and chronological points of view once the appropriate basic descriptions have been completed.

Symbolism and allegory are common, of course,

Example 1. Trinity

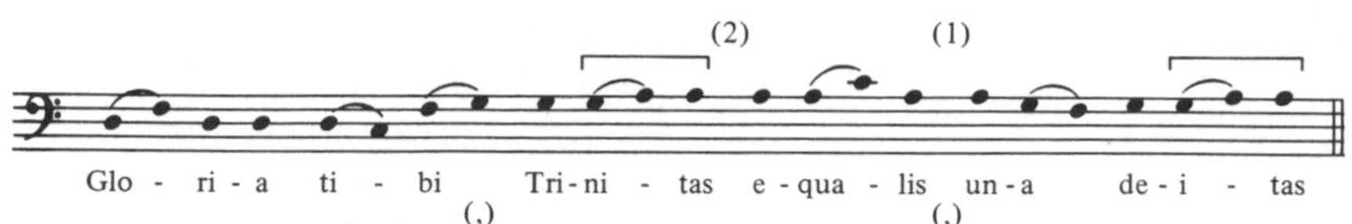

and biblical references underpin much of the narrative. For Louis IX, king of France (*d.* 1270, canonized 1297), for example, the chief office was written by the Dominican monk Arnaut of Prat between 1301 and 1306. Louis was neither cleric nor martyr, and thus the need to relate him to biblical forebears was a concern. The psalms were carefully chosen for their references to kingship, although normally assignation of specific psalms was probably not a feature of most offices; comparisons with David and Solomon are obvious. Less direct allusions depend on exegesis: lesson 6 relates Louis's generosity, and the text of the accompanying responsory, *Cum esset in accubitu/rex* . . . , derives from the Song of Songs, *Dum esset rex in accubitu suo/nardus* . . . ; the odor of *nardus* is equated with charity in exegesis.

THE CHANTS

If offices are viewed as a whole, the most obvious feature is the ordering of the modes, already mentioned. Given a range of about a tenth for each chant, in fact often exceeded, the sequential arrangement results in an overall written range of at least two octaves, and sometimes closer to three. At first thought, the unlikelihood that any choir could successfully execute such a range would seem to confirm the opinion that written pitches did not necessarily correspond to performance pitches. Frequently, in any case, modes 5 and 6 are transposed, in their written form, a fifth upward, but it is clear the transposition was not made to eliminate the flat that is normally in modes 5 and 6, since the flat often remains even in transposed versions.

On the surface, the chants of individual items usually seem to differ little from those of the standard Gregorian repertory. And no doubt the original inspiration was from that repertory. The opening of the chant for the first antiphon of Vespers for Trinity, for example, whose text has already been cited, is shown in Example 1.

If divided at (1), mandated by a rendition of the text divided into three sections, marked by commas in parentheses, the phrase conforms entirely to a standard melodic motive in mode 1 with the reciting note extended by ornament; if divided at (2), by a "modern" rendition, the whole nature of the melody is changed. The phrase is divided into balanced sections, the first of which conforms to a standard phrase in mode 1, and the second takes on the character of a triadic phrase more like mode 5. This division is emphasized by the rhyme, and by the presence of the musical rhyme *GAA* at the end of each section; this figure is the most common cadence in the other most prominent new musical style of the time, the sequence. There can be little doubt that the increase in regularity of meter and rhyme forces balanced phrases, each articulated by cadencelike figures, onto the melodies. Thus, older plainsong style, notable for its fluidity, even unpredictability, had changed into one of careful and deliberate architecture. If the poem, as is usually the case, has four lines, the new chant style will resemble a hymn, and choirs, especially if untrained, will inevitably perform in such a way as to emphasize the phrasing. We might note that, starting in the sixteenth century, the tendency was increasingly to give to all styles of plainsongs the name "hymn."

The increased articulation, the greater number of cadences, and the overall arrangement in modal order lead inevitably to a strongly sharpened sense of modal definition. Even the possibility that some phrases may be in different modes, a feature recognized in the fourteenth century by Marchettus of Padua, may strengthen the feeling of mode by lending a sense of tonal movement away from and back to the true modal center. One might conclude that the modal system had become not a way of describing and categorizing plainsongs but a prescriptive basis for composing them. But certain modes were favored; others, avoided. Mode 1 is the most common, followed by modes 5, 6, and 7, where qualities of the modern major scale are prominent; modes 3 and 4 are the least favored.

This new style emerges very clearly with respect to antiphons, especially the simpler ones, because

RHYMED OFFICES

they are set largely one note to a syllable, so that the poetic balance is reflected in the music. In responsories, however, the new style is not nearly so clear. Their texts, to begin with, are normally set with a very variable number of notes to a syllable, so that all sense of symmetry disappears. The balance, articulation, and modal definition are therefore much less noticeable. The distinction between the two styles perhaps reflects different approaches to their composition. Although insufficient analysis has been done, in antiphons it is possible to detect several procedures. Some antiphons are borrowed wholesale from earlier offices, and are often virtually identical in both pitches and notational features. In other antiphons some phrases are borrowed identically from earlier rhymed offices, while the remaining ones merely conform to the general shape of similar phrases in the same mode but are varied in degree of ornamentation, pitches, and notation. And there are phrases that seem to be unrelated to a model of any kind. These three procedures are analogous to Leo Treitler's three kinds of medieval composition: direct copying, reproduction by memory or oral recollection, and original composition. Because of the much more diffuse nature of the music of responsories, it is not yet possible to say precisely how they were composed. It seems, however, that they may have been borrowed wholesale, but with adaptations, from saints' offices of the standard Gregorian repertory at least as much as from other responsories of the rhymed repertory. This procedure of borrowing with adaptations is common in the standard repertory itself. Responsory verses in the later repertory, however, are usually newly composed and do not closely follow the Gregorian responsory tones.

Obviously, there is a great deal of melodic borrowing, as there is of textual borrowing. My impression, at the moment, is that textual and musical borrowing do not normally coincide. Texts are usually borrowed for some obvious reason, such as homage or allegory, and the simultaneous borrowing of the tune would strengthen the connection. Chants or phrases, independent of the text, must have been borrowed for similar reasons, which are rarely clear. It may be, although to assert it would be foolish in our present state of knowledge, that even apparently abstract melodic motives in chant carry with them, as they certainly do in seventeenth-century music, associations, symbols, meanings, or topoi now hidden from us: if so, the symbols are intellectual and recondite. It may be possible, for example, that certain melodic characteristics are associated with religious orders or categories of saints (for instance, martyrs or confessors) rather than with strictly verbal ideas.

Naturally, the reasons for borrowing and the methods of adaptation are of great interest for the musician. Perhaps of greater interest, however, are the newer musical styles demonstrated in some of the original compositions. Already at the end of the tenth century the presence of unfamiliar styles was recognized. Referring to Letald, for example, a report says: "In composing the office of St. Julian he did not want to depart from the likeness of old chant, lest he fabricate barbarous and inexpert melody; for it does not please me, he said, that some authors disdain to follow old melodies in every way and use newness in the musical styles that are so much different." Apart from those already mentioned, the most obviously novel features are an increase in range, so that a twelfth or more is not uncommon, incorporating both plagal and authentic versions of the mode, and melodic movement in the same direction for longer motives, giving a sense of direction to the melodies that is quite foreign to standard plainsong. Extremes of range are occasionally found (Ex. 2). Such chants must surely have been written with the abilities of specific choirs in mind. On rare occasions, the new style is clearly for the purpose of blatant word painting (Ex. 3).

Sometimes complete phrases are repeated, giving melodies a form, such as *abca,* as with certain hymns. Sometimes complete motives are repeated; the final phrases of responsories are a conventional place for this procedure to be applied in a sequential and highly organized fashion, without words. Here, then, purely abstract musical criteria are the sole determinants of the composition (Ex. 4).

Sources for the chants of perhaps half the repertory are known, although only for about a tenth of the repertory have they been transcribed so that analysis can begin. There are no doubt certain offices for which no music was ever provided, since they were written only for private recitation or reading. Musically, the repertory of rhymed offices influenced other forms. Chants from the repertory were used as tenors in motets, Mass movements, and cyclic masses, especially in the fourteenth and fifteenth centuries. In addition, texts of individual items are used in polyphonic motets and votive pieces. Many so far unidentified motet texts up to the sixteenth century, by such composers as Josquin des Pres, may eventually be located in the repertory.

Example 2. Apollonia

Example 3. Catherine (wheel)

Example 4. Theodulus

The forthcoming concordance will facilitate these researchers.

THE SOURCES

Breviaries and antiphonals from all areas of Europe from the eleventh to the sixteenth centuries contain rhymed or other proper offices. Only Carthusian books and books for the Roman curia are significant exceptions. New offices that appear in liturgical books had presumably been approved, and if they are in the proper Kalendar position, the approval must have predated the writing of the book. On the other hand, offices appended to books or inserted between, say, Kalendar and Psalter of a Breviary presumably postdate the production of the book. The important and difficult task of dating liturgical books often, therefore, depends on the dating of individual offices.

Some offices are transmitted in self-contained libelli, but most are short enough for only a few folios to be required. Rather than surviving as independent gatherings, the libelli probably have often been bound between the sections of breviaries, or have ended up as flyleaves in quite different books. Several offices bound together, such as those for Sts. Martial, Ursula, Valerius, and others in Paris, Bibliothèque Nationale, MS lat. 916, sometimes occur in manuscripts that may be described as *Officia.* In other cases, the office follows the relevant vita, in which case the chants are not usually given. Corpus Christi College (Oxford) MS 134, the "offices" of St. Oswin, contains (1) a list of relics, (2) a vita, (3) a sermon on his passion, (4) texts on his virtues and miracles, (5) the rhymed office with music, including prayers, lessons, and material for the octave, (6) a reading on St. Oswin for All Saints Day, (7) a report and sermon on his Invention (the discovery of his relics), and (8) the office of the Invention. In such a manuscript, especially if Mass items are included, we may have the material assembled for the process of canonization.

Collections of offices, often in conjunction with hymns and sequences, by a single author are known, for example in the *Liber officiorum* of Origo Scaccabarozzi of Milan (*d.* 1293), in the Austrian collection by Christian of Lilienfeld (*ca.* 1300), and in a manuscript allegedly supervised and corrected by the poet himself, Johannes of Jenstein, archbishop of Prague (*d.* 1400). The authentic and corrected version of the St. Dominic office, with the chants, is in Humbert's Codex, the manuscript prepared for the master general of the order (*ca.* 1254). Such sources presumably transmit the exact originals.

Usually, however, most sources of a single office differ from others because of the constant borrowing and shuffling already mentioned. Indeed, offices that appear at first glance to be quite distinct may share a considerable amount of material. These features often make it extremely difficult to determine exactly what a particular office is, when no single manuscript can be identified as the source,

RHYMED OFFICES

and thus it is extremely difficult to decide how an edition should be organized. It may be necessary to develop the idea of a large stock of items for a single saint from which various offices are compiled.

The idea of offices written without chants for private devotion or reading clearly gains ground from the fourteenth and fifteenth centuries. A parallel development of the same period is the Book of Hours. This book for private use consists of a series of what would be termed "suffrages" in liturgical usage proper—that is, an antiphon, perhaps with a responsory, but in any case in the Book of Hours without music, followed by a prayer or a very brief reading. Each suffrage petitions a saint, and the antiphon and responsory texts are often rhymed and drawn from a full rhymed office. Our knowledge of Books of Hours, however, is only a little more advanced than that of the rhymed offices. A striking link between the two repertories is in Cologne Historisches Archiv, MS W 28, partly edited in the appendix of *Analecta Hymnica,* **28.** This manuscript, which certainly appears to be for institutional use, has hundreds of what seem to be suffrages whose items are also found in rhymed offices. There are far more than a Book of Hours would contain, and the manuscript entirely lacks the elaborate artwork that makes the Book of Hours a visual as well as a spiritual pleasure.

In the sixteenth century the use of poetry, probably as a device to make religious texts less austere, spread to prayers, to the Psalter, and eventually to the whole Bible. Such developments, and perhaps even the Pietist poetry of the German Reformation, may be seen as the legacy of the rhymed office repertory, which itself came to an end almost completely, along with tropes and sequences, with the enactments of the Council of Trent.

BIBLIOGRAPHY

Analecta hymnica medii aevi, **5, 13, 14b, 17, 18, 24, 25, 26, 28, 41a, 45a, 48, 52** (1889–1909, repr. 1961), indexed in Max Lütolf *et al.,* eds., *Analecta hymnica medii aevi: Register,* 2 vols. in 3 (1978); Antoine Auda, *L'école musicale liégeoise au Xe siècle: Étienne de Liège* (1923); Madeleine Bernard, "Les offices versifiés attribués à Léon IX (1002–1054)," in *Études grégoriennes,* **19** (1980); Birger Gregersson, *Birgitta-officium,* Carl-Gustav Undhagen, ed. (1960); James John Boyce, "Cantica Carmelitana: The Chants of the Carmelite Office" (diss., New York Univ., 1984); Solange Corbin, "L'office en vers *Gaude mater ecclesia* pour la conception de la vierge," in Congresso internazionale di musica sacra, Rome 1950, *Atti* (1952); Yves Delaporte, "Fulbert de Chartres et l'école chartraine de chant liturgique au XIe siècle," in *Études grégoriennes,* **2** (1957); François Deléglise, "'Illustris civitas,' office rimé de saint Théodule (XIIIe siècle)," *Vallesia,* **38** (1983); John A. Emerson, "Two Newly Identified Offices for Saints Valeria and Austriclinianus by Adémar de Chabannes (MS Paris, Bibl. Nat., Latin 909, fols. 79–85v)," in *Speculum,* **40** (1965); Marcy J. Epstein, "*Ludovicus decus regnantium:* Perspectives on the Rhymed Office," *ibid.,* **53** (1978).

Zoltán Falvy, *Drei Reimoffizien aus Ungarn und ihre Musik* (1968); Andrew Hughes, "Chants in the Offices of Thomas of Canterbury and Stanislaus of Poland," in *Musica Antiqua Europae Orientalis,* VI (1982), "Modal Order and Disorder in the Rhymed Office," in *Musica disciplina,* 37 (1983), "Late Medieval Rhymed Offices: A Research Report," in *Journal of the Plainsong and Medieval Music Society,* **8** (1985), and "British Rhymed Offices: A Catalogue," *ibid.,* **10** (1987); Meryl Jancey, ed., *St. Thomas Cantilupe, Bishop of Hereford: Essays in His Honour* (1982); Charles W. Jones, *The Saint Nicholas Liturgy* (1963); Ritva Jonsson, *Historia: Études sur la genèse des offices versifiés* (1968), and "Un double office rhythmé en l'honneur de saint Germain de Paris," in *Revue bénédictine,* **79** (1969); Douglas K. Kirk, "Translatione Corona Spinea: A Musical and Textual Analysis of a Thirteenth Century Rhymed Office" (M.A. thesis, Univ. of Texas, 1980); A. Legris, "L'école normande de chant liturgique," in *Revue grégoriennes,* **7** (1922); Thomas J. Mathiesen, "'The Office of the New Feast of Corpus Christi' in the *Regimen Animarum* at Brigham Young University," in *Journal of Musicology,* **2** (1983); Kathi Meyer-Baer, "From the Office of the Hours to the Musical Oratorio," in *Music Review,* **32** (1971).

Jerzy Morawski, ed., *The Rhymed History of St. Jadwiga* (*Historia rymowana o św. Jadwidze*) (1977), and *The Rhymed History of St. Adalbert* (*Historia rymowana o św. Wojciechu*) (1978); Robert A. Ottósson, ed., *Sancti Thorlaci episcopi officia rhytmica et proprium missae in AM 241a folio* (1959); *Philippe de Mézières' Campaign for the Feast of Mary's Presentation: Edited from Bibliothèque Nationale Mss latin 17330 and 14454,* William E. Coleman, ed. (1981); Jerzy Pikulik, "Les offices polonais de saint Adalbert," in Pikulik, ed., *État des recherches sur la musique religieuse dans la culture polonaise* (1973); J. Thiriot, "L'office de saint Gorgon martyr," in *Revue St.-Chrodegang* (1920, 1921); Peter Wagner, "Zur mittelalterlichen Offiziums-komposition," in *Kirchenmusikalisches Jahrbuch,* **21** (1908), and *Einführung in die gregorianischen Melodien,* I, 3rd ed. (1911, repr. 1970), chap. 15.

ANDREW HUGHES

[See also **Antiphon; Antiphonal; Book of Hours; Breviary; Canonical Hours; Canonization; Divine Office; Fulbert of Chartres; Hucbald of St. Amand; Leo IX, Pope; Mode; Odo of Cluny, St.; Responsory; Sequence; Tropes.**]

RHYS OF DEHEUBARTH (*ca.* 1132–1197), Welsh ruler. The lord Rhys of Deheubarth was the younger son of Gruffydd ap Rhys ap Tewdwr and Gwenllian, daughter of Gruffudd ap Cynan. He succeeded to the old kingdom of Deheubarth (southwestern Wales) in 1155 and became the most powerful among contemporary Welsh princes. Rhys's early career was marked by submission to Henry II of England, but from 1164 he rapidly regained and expanded his dominion. By 1171 his dominant position was recognized by Henry, who appointed him justice of South Wales. He patronized Welsh poets and musicians and supported the Cistercian order, recently established in Wales. On the death of Lord Rhys, Deheubarth lost forever both its unity and its leading role in native politics.

BIBLIOGRAPHY

Bibliographies. A Bibliography of the History of Wales, 2nd ed. (1962), 11–14, 65, 91–106; *Bibliotheca Celtica: A Register of Publications Relating to Wales and the Celtic Peoples and Languages* (1909–); *Bulletin of the Board of Celtic Studies,* **20** (1962–1964), 126–164, **22** (1966–1968), 49–70, **23** (1968–1970), 263–283; Meic Stephens, ed., *A Reader's Guide to Wales: A Selected Bibliography* (1973), 14–16, 17–18, 31, 92.

Sources and studies. Thomas Jones, "Molawd a Marwnad yr Arglwydd Rhys: Fersiynau Ychwanegol," in *Bulletin of the Board of Celtic Studies,* **24,** pt. 3 (1971); John E. Lloyd, *A History of Wales,* II (1911, 3rd ed. 1939, repr. 1948), chap. 15 and *passim; idem* and R. T. Jenkins, eds., "Rhys ap Gruffydd," in *Dictionary of Welsh Biography Down to 1940* (1959); D. Myrddin Lloyd, "Rhys ap Gruffudd," in Gwynedd Pierce, ed., *Ein Tywysogion* (1954), 52–64; John Morris-Jones and T. H. Parry-Williams, eds., *Llawysgrif Hendregadredd,* 2nd ed. (1971), 107–114, 115–116, 206–207; J. E. Caerwyn Williams, "Aberteifi 1176," in *Taliesyn* (1976), 30–35.

RHIAN M. ANDREWS

[See also **Wales: History.**]

RHYTHM. No systematic study of the pattern of movement in time has been attempted covering the centuries of the Middle Ages. Problems with regard to specific notational and interpretative questions have directed scholars' attention repeatedly to the minutiae of specific sources, so that few scholars have even been tempted to ask broad questions concerning systematic principles governing order of sounds in time. The present article can thus be little more than an overview of theoretical and practical trends during the period from about 500 to 1500 and an attempt to repeat questions concerning problems during these centuries.

In the later Middle Ages a distinction came to be made between *musica plana* and *musica mensurata* or *mensurabilis.* Both categories referred specifically to the rhythmic dimension of music. *Musica plana* referred to the vast body of liturgical chant, or "plainsong," a repertoire of music which, in contrast to the other, was "plain" or rhythmically "unmeasured." *Musica mensurabilis,* on the other hand, referred to the growing body of polyphonic music, which was, of necessity, measured and notated rhythmically according to quantifiable temporal principles. These terms remain functional to the student of medieval music and form the basic twofold division of this article.

MUSICA PLANA

In musical treatises of classical antiquity rhythm and meter were often systematically treated, to the exclusion of other musical elements. Textual forces were the principal elements governing the flow of movement through time, and rhythm was said to be created from patterns of durations dependent on the proportions of long and short syllables. Durations based on syllable length could be endlessly varied, and thus poetic meters functioned as the organizing principle, imparting a regular pattern of repetition (the poetic foot) and a regular length to the poetic line. The classical attitude toward rhythm was systematized for the early Middle Ages by Augustine in his *De musica,* a work that treats rhythm and meter according to Pythagorean and Neoplatonic principles. In this tradition the organization of durations is rigorously proportional, with a long syllable (*longa*) receiving two rhythmic quantities (tempora) and a short syllable (*brevis*) receiving one.

Cassiodorus (*ca.* 490–*ca.* 583) and Isidore (*ca.* 560–636), basing his work on Cassiodorus, divided the science of music into three areas: *harmonica, rhythmica,* and *metrica.* While the first of these divisions was concerned with high and low sound, rhythmics investigated whether words fitted well together, and metrics identified the measure of various classical meters. In conception, then, a sequence of sounds (syllables and words) could form a rhythmic entity independent of any meter. The independence of rhythm and meter, inherited from classical antiquity and characteristic of the early Middle Ages, was articulated by Augustine when he stated that rhythm may lack meter, but meter cannot lack rhythm. Through Cassiodorus and Isidore definitions of rhythmics and harmonics find their way into medieval musical treatises. The definitions seem to have had little effect, however, in shaping the concept of rhythm in subsequent centuries, and the classical definitions have become little more than a relic of a classical past.

Changes in the character of the Latin language—particularly the spoken language—and the rise of new vernacular languages witnessed a decline in the structural significance of syllabic duration and a rise in the structural import of stress. The rise of dynamic—as opposed to agogic—accent brought about two structural principles that fundamentally shaped the character of medieval music and poetry: (1) the definition of subsections of a line by accent rather than symmetrical durations and (2) the principle of measuring a line by the number of syllables rather than by the number of feet. This fundamental change in the nature of musical time can be seen clearly in Bede's attempted analysis of Ambrosian hymns: While most hymns were written according to the principles of syllable duration, that is, iambic dimeter, Bede perceived the structural principle of the lines to be in the number of syllables.

The definition of line came to be a crucial element in practical and theoretical considerations of rhythm for the early Middle Ages. Two genres of musical compositions were dominant: hymnody and psalmody. In the former the length of line is regular even though the structure within the line is sometimes durational and sometimes accentual. Organization becomes further symmetrical as the number of lines is repeated in subsequent stanzas, as in this Ambrosian hymn:

Aeterne rerum conditor
Noctem diemque qui regis
Et temporum das tempora
Ut alleves fastidium

In musical performance each line was articulated either by a slight lengthening of its last pitch or by a slight pause or breath. The stanza was articulated by a pause and a breath. Regardless of internal stress and duration, the repetition of these eight-syllable lines created organized units of predictable length, and the organization of these lines into stanzas of four lines each imparted a regular, symmetrical organization and progression to musical time.

The organization of line and symmetry in psalmody is more complex. The essential textual structure of the psalm verse is the distich. The length of the line is unregulated by number of syllables, but the line usually contains from three to five principal stresses.

Díxit Dóminus Dómino méo:
séde a déxtris méis.
Dónec pónam inimícos túos,
scábellum pédum tuórum.
Psalm 109 (110)

The principal musical vehicle for performance of psalmody was the psalm tone, a musical entity consisting of two parts and corresponding to those of the psalm text, and which was adapted to the text according to the accentual pattern of the text at the ends of lines. As in the hymn, the line is at least partially defined by the slight lengthening which occurs at the end of lines, and by the longer pause which punctuates each verse. Unlike in the hymn, the length of line can vary from line to line, from verse to verse, and the cadential pattern of the music is organized by the accentual pattern of the text (tonic cadence) or by syllable count from the end of the line (cursive cadence). Nevertheless the regular repetition of lines and pairs of lines again gives a regular, symmetrical progression to musical time, and the temporal length of phrases equals grammatical or rhetorical units.

Concern with musical/grammatical entities and their definition by lengthenings or pauses became the focus of theoretical passages in *Musica enchiriadis* and in the *Micrologus* of Guido of Arezzo (990/999–after 1033). The writer of *Musica enchiriadis* (end of ninth century) notes that pitches at the ends of lines should be lengthened, that these lengthenings represent a kind of "measured singing" (*numerose canere*), and that these measurements are analogous to those of metrical feet. Guido refines the theory first presented in *Musica enchiriadis* by distinguishing levels of musical/grammatical organization (*pars, comma, colon, syllaba*) and by recommending that the lengthening at the end of a unit be proportional to the length of the unit itself. (For example, the lengthening at the end of a clause should be longer than that at the end of a phrase.) These passages are particularly helpful in approaching musical forms more complex than hymns and psalms (for example, antiphons and responsories), although Guido repeatedly requests that his reader search for examples in the repertoire of

RHYTHM

hymns (*ambrosiana,* as he refers to them). It must be stressed that these theoretical passages are concerned with the definition of musical/textual parts, with lines, as it were, and that they reflect the medieval concern with a clear and orderly flow of temporal entities as defined by grammatical principles. They do not represent evidence for durational organization of individual pitches.

Two further aspects of temporal flow in early medieval music require attention: variation of line length and variation of accentual meter. In such forms as the sequence the variation, the length of phrases—with each length defined by one repetition—became an important rhythmic principle:

Hic érgo génitus illibátae mátris útero, (15)
Hic víxit sólus hómo ab́sque névo*e*t síne dólo. (15)

Colúber Ádae málesuásor (9)
Quem súo non inf́écit fráude, (9)

Notker Balbulus, *Laudes deo*

The play with symmetry and asymmetry in the early medieval sequence created a rhythmic flow with a strong sense of momentum and play unique in the repertoire of monophonic song. The unpredictability of accentual patterns—particularly in the first part of sequence lines—gave the play of symmetry and asymmetry a new quality of rhythmic energy.

By the eleventh and twelfth centuries rhythmic stress rather than quantity had become the principle for organization of Latin poetic forms, particularly the hymn and the sequence. Much of the basic rhythmic energy generated at the level of syllable in earlier hymns and sequences was compromised, but a larger-scale rhythmic drive was achieved, which gave the characteristic momentum to Victorine hymns and hymn sequences and to such compositions as the *Dies irae:*

Díes iŕae, díes ílla,
Sólvet sáeclum iń favílla:
Téste Dávid súm Sibýlla.

Quántus tŕemor eśt futúrus,
Qúando júdex eśt ventúrus,
Cúncta strícte díscussúrus.

In this sequence each line consists of four rhythmic units, each of which consists of an accented and an unaccented syllable. Some modern scholars have suggested that such rhythmic verse should be performed in a somewhat measured manner, justifying the position by citing the notion of Johannes de Grocheo (*ca.* 1300) of music neither unmeasured nor measured (*non praecise mensurata*), a classification Johannes added to the traditional *musica plana* and *musica mensurabilis.* Most scholars have suspended judgment at this point in the face of inadequate practical and theoretical evidence.

The repertoire of secular monody composed in Latin and vernacular languages during the eleventh and twelfth centuries raises questions similar to those associated with rhythmic Latin sacred poetry of the same period. Some scholars have argued that the repertoire is measured; some have used Grocheo to argue that it is neither unmeasured nor measured; and some have approached the music as a repertoire following temporal principles very similar to that of plainsong. No hard evidence exists to support the rhythmic interpretations of the music, while the verse and refrain structures lend themselves well to performance with equal syllable and note values.

MUSICA MENSURABILIS

Ars antiqua. The rise of elaborate polyphonic composition in the eleventh and twelfth centuries necessitated some temporal organization beyond that associated with monophonic repertoires of the early Middle Ages. Early polyphony seems to have been performed (that is, improvised) at a very slow and deliberate tempo. The development of modal rhythm may well represent an attempt to elaborate rhythmically and melodically on the skeleton of the earlier slow, note-against-note polyphony.

The rise of new rhythmic practice in the twelfth century and the articulation of that practice in theoretical writings in the thirteenth century took place in a musical practice that was largely melismatic—that is, a style of music in which singers sang extended, elaborate melismata requiring fixed temporal determinants. The development of this theory and practice is inseparably linked to the development of rhythmic notation during the twelfth and thirteenth centuries. The conceptual basis of rhythm during these centuries was that of a recurring unit, a unit that came to be called *perfectio* in the thirteenth century. This unit is divisible by three and came to be articulated by six different "modes":

1. longa (2) + brevis (1)
2. brevis (1) + longa (2)
3. longa ultra mensuram (3)
   + brevis (1) + brevis altera (2)

4. brevis (1) + brevis altera (2)
   + longa ultra mensuram (3)
5. longa ultra mensuram (3)
   + longa ultra mensuram (3)
6. brevis (1) + brevis (1) + (brevis)

The only rational units in the system were the *brevis*—consisting of one tempus—and the *longa*—consisting of two tempora. Thus a *brevis* of two tempora (required to fill out temporal spaces in modes three and four) was called a *brevis altera,* while a *longa* extending over three tempora was called a *longa ultra mensuram.* (The grammatical background of this theory is obvious and has led certain scholars to view the rhythmic modes as developing from the metrical theory of late antiquity.) While the modal patterns remained in force once they had been set in motion, the basic patterns could be broken up or extended through two principles: *fractio modi* and *extensio modi.* By using *fractio,* a value of two or more *tempora* could be broken into smaller values; while by using *extentio modi,* a shorter value could be extended. A considerable degree of variation could thus be achieved within a system based on fixed, repeating patterns.

A very important aspect of this theory is that of rests, or *pausationes,* for the rests defined the length of a phrase (or *ordo*). An essential element in the rhythmic style of *ars antiqua* lies in the length of phrases and the organization of units therein. Like the phrases in the early medieval sequence, clausulae often contrasted phrases of symmetrical length with phrases of one or two units, more or less. The resulting rhythmic drive is clearly analogous to that found in the sequence, and the principle of varying phrase lengths may be identified as an underlying force active in medieval rhythm.

Layering of rhythmic density became characteristic in the polyphony of ars antiqua. Rhythmic density was created by the degree of activity, the number of notes per unit of time, in a given voice. The lowest voice (tenor) moved relatively slowly, usually repeating the same rhythm again and again throughout an extended section of music. The repetition of a rhythmic pattern in the tenor gave the music a rhythmic measure and pulse larger than that of the recurring mode. The upper voice (or voices), on the other hand, moved at a much faster rate, constantly elaborating the basic rhythmic unit, and, by varying the length of the phrases, constantly played with being in phase or out of phase with the repeating pattern in the tenor. The stylistic element of rhythmic density was developed further in the thirteenth century, for then each layer of music (each voice) had become progressively denser, as follows: (1) superius, very active, independent varying phrase lengths; (2) duplum, moderately active, independent varying phrase lengths, and (3) tenor, least active, repeating constant pattern. The result was a multidimensional perception of rhythmic density and a multidimensional play with time itself as different varying lengths of phrases in upper parts played against the repeating pattern of the lowest voice.

While the rhythmic system of the ars antiqua began in melismatic forms, individual notes of these forms acquired a text in the late twelfth and thirteenth centuries, the melismatic forms became syllabic, and the principal musical form of the late ars antiqua arose—namely, the motet. The formal writing of motets required a new type of notation (*cum littera*), and as the notation—and the musical style associated with the motet—developed, the theoretical basis for the rhythmic system began to unravel. The flow of the rhythmic unit began to slow under the load of texts, the *brevis* became the principal rhythmic unit, and the *brevis* in turn was subdivided into semibreves. While the fundamental rationale of the relation between *longa* and *brevis* could still be viewed as a variation of some rhythmic mode (although in fact it often was not), no theoretical basis existed for the subdivision of breves into semibreves. By the end of the thirteenth century, particularly in the so-called Petronian motet, the breve was divided into two to nine subdivisions of seemingly irrational duration.

Ars nova. The musicians of the fourteenth century began self-consciously to apply order to the rhythmic disorder of the late thirteenth century, and they called their new musical movement *ars nova.* They worked to give a consistent, systematic rationale to the subdivision of each level of rhythmic measurement. Thus, they not only solved the problem of irrational division of the breve, but gave new order and creative possibilities to all rhythmic levels. Musicians of the fourteenth century defined three levels of temporal measure in music: that of the *longa,* that of the breve, and that of the semibreve. They constructed a logical system whereby each level could be divided by two or by three and used the archaic terminology of the thirteenth century to describe these divisions; "perfect" described division by three, and "imperfect," division by two.

(For schematic description of these principles see the *Ars Nova* article.)

Complex rhythmic structures became possible in the notational system of the *ars nova* that were beyond the capabilities of the *ars antiqua*. Considerably greater variety in the rhythmic elaboration of longer values arose, and the rhythm as an element in musical structure sometimes seemed to eclipse other elements of musical structure. The technique of syncopation—the systematic displacement of normal rhythmic flow—became a standard rhythmic technique, and complex techniques such as retrograde rhythms—rhythms in which the values of the first part occur in mirror image in the second—were employed. Small rhythmic sequences were repeated throughout these compositions, functioning as motives that gave unity to a composition as a whole. Finally, large-scale repeated rhythmic patterns were employed in the tenor voice, creating an overall rhythmic structure known as "isorhythm," and the points of repetition of this macrorhythm were often articulated by rhythmic activity in the upper voices.

Rhythmic complexity reached an apex in the music of the late fourteenth century, particularly that associated with the papal court at Avignon. In addition to the excessive use of syncopation, techniques of "coloration"—wherein one set of rhythmic subdivision was substituted for another—were employed extensively, leading some scholars to refer to the repertoire as "mannered."

BIBLIOGRAPHY

Willi Apel, *The Notation of Polyphonic Music 900–1600*, 5th ed. (1953); Rudolf Bockholdt, "*Semibrevis minima* und *Prolatio temporis:* Zur Entstehung der Mensuraltheorie der Ars nova," in *Musikforschung,* **16** (1963); Lance W. Brunner, "The Performance of Plainchant: Some Preliminary Observations of the New Era," in *Early Music,* **10** (1982); John Caldwell, *Medieval Music* (1978); Richard L. Crocker, "*Musica rhythmica* and *Musica metrica* in Antique and Medieval Theory," in *Journal of Music Theory,* **2** (1958); Ursula Günther, "Die Mensuralnotation der Ars nova in Theorie und Praxis," in *Archiv für Musikwissenschaft,* **19/20** (1962/1963); Janet Knapp, "Two 13th-century Treatises on Modal Rhythm and the Discant: *Discantus positio vulgaris* [and] *De musica libellus* (Anonymous VII)," in *Journal of Music Theory,* **6** (1962); Lucas Kunz, "Beda über reinrhythmische und gemischtrhythmische Liedtexte," in *Kirchenmusikalisches Jahrbuch,* **39** (1955); J. E. Maddrell, "*Mensura* and the Rhythm of Medieval Monodic Song," in *Current Musicology,* **10** (1970); Thomas J. Mathiesen, "Rhythm and Meter in Ancient Greek Music," in *Music Theory Spectrum,* **7** (1985); Francis de Meeûs "Le problème de la rythmique grégorienne—À propos de travaux récents," in *Acta musicologica,* **28** (1956); Carl Parrish, *The Notation of Medieval Music* (1957); Fritz Reckow, "Proprietas und Perfectio: Zur Geschichte des Rhythmus, seiner Aufzeichnung und Terminologie im 13. Jahrhundert," in *Acta musicologica,* **39** (1967); Gustav Reese, *Music in the Middle Ages* (1940); John Rayburn, *Gregorian Chant Rhythm: A History of the Controversy Concerning Its Rhythm* (1964); Curt Sachs, *Rhythm and Tempo: A Study in Music History* (1953); Hendrik Vanderwerf, "Deklamatorischer Rhythmus in den Chansons der Trouvères," in *Musikforschung,* **20** (1967), "Concerning the Measurability of Medieval Music," in *Current Musicology,* **10** (1970), and *The Chansons of the Troubadours and Trouvères* (1972); William C. Waite, *The Rhythm of Twelfth-century Polyphony* (1954); Johannes Wolf, *Geschichte der Mensural-notation von 1250–1460* (1904).

CALVIN M. BOWER

[See also **Ambrosian Chant; Ars Antiqua; Ars Nova; Ars Subtilior; Cassiodorus Senator, Flavius Magnus Aurelius; Guido of Arezzo; Gregorian Chant; Hymns, Latin; Isidore of Seville, St.; Isorhythm; Johannes de Grocheo; Latin Meter; Melisma; Motet; Music, Western European; Musical Notation, Modal; Musical Notation, Western; Musical Treatises; Notker Balbulus; Plainsong, Sources of; Poetry, Liturgical; Psalm Tones; Sequence (Prosa); Tones, Musical.**]

RIB, a decorative or structural arch employed in the construction of domes and vaults. Any rib visible on the intrados of a vault is decorative regardless of its structural function in the vault. If constructed within the mass of the vaulting severies (bays), a rib may provide lateral stability. If erected prior to and serving as a stable framework on which the vaulting severies are built, ribs provide support for the severies. This construction is best typified by the rib (bed)-vaulted construction of French Gothic architecture of the thirteenth century. Timber ribs are also found in such constructions as bridges and roofs.

A rib at the apex of the intrados of a vault is termed a ridge or crown rib and is normally decorative only and laid out along the dominant horizontal axis of the vault. While an individual vault may have a ridge rib, the most common application is that of identical ridge ribs in a series of vaults emphasizing the longitudinal continuity of the apices of these vaults. The ridge rib was favored in England, especially, during the Gothic period. English examples include Gloucester Cathedral (1090–1100) and Lincoln Cathedral (late twelfth century). In France, the ridge rib of the vaulting of Ste. Chapelle, Riom (*ca.* 1380–1390), is clearly the result of English influence.

BIBLIOGRAPHY
Paul Frankl, *Gothic Architecture* (1962), 1–52.

CARL F. BARNES, JR.

[See also **Arch; Construction: Building Materials; Dome; Gloucester Cathedral; Gothic Architecture; Intrados; Vault.** Illustrations at **Romanesque Architecture and St. Philibert,** this volume.]

RIB VAULT. See **Vault.**

RICHARD I, CRUSADE AND DEATH OF. See **Crusade and Death of Richard I.**

RICHARD I THE LIONHEARTED (1157–1199), king of England from 1189 to 1199. Born 8 September 1157, Richard, the third child of King Henry II and Eleanor of Aquitaine, acquired the epithet Lionheart (Coeur de Lion) because of his courage as a warrior. Well educated like the other members of his family, he received from his mother a taste for literature, associated with troubadours, and even composed some verse.

At the death of his eldest brother, the Young Henry, in 1183, Richard became heir to all his father's possessions. Already he had been made duke of Aquitaine, responsible for controlling southwestern France. Favored by his mother, he had frequent differences with his father. He revolted first in 1173–1174. Then in 1188–1189, with the help of Philip II Augustus of France, he forced his father, old and near death, to make humiliating concessions. Acquiring by the death of his father on 6 July 1189 most of the Angevin possessions in France, Richard then went to England to be crowned on 3 September. With his life hitherto spent in France, he regarded England simply as a treasury to finance his crusading and wars. Staying there only long enough to provide for its governance, mostly by such men as the chancellor William Longchamp (*d.* 1197) and the justiciar Hugh de Puiset, bishop of Durham (*d.* 1195), he departed on 12 December and was to return for only two more months at the end of the Third Crusade. Unrivaled as a soldier and builder of fortifications, Richard was also politically shrewd, diplomatically capable, and more generous and imaginative than his father. Yet as an absentee ruler he left no imprint upon his kingdom, remaining always a foreigner to England.

Embarking at Marseilles on 7 August 1190 for the Holy Land, Richard stopped at Messina in Sicily, hoping to gain from his fellow crusader Philip II Augustus a release from his long betrothal to Philip's half-sister Alice in order to marry Berengaria, daughter of the king of Navarre. Upon Richard's payment of a handsome indemnity and some concessions of land in France, Philip granted the release. A year later, on the island of Cyprus, which he had conquered, Richard celebrated his marriage to Berengaria; their marriage was to be barren. On 8 June 1191 Richard finally arrived at Acre, soon taken by the crusaders. Feigning illness, Philip Augustus then returned to France and began to foment trouble against Richard. Meanwhile, despite some military successes against the Muslim ruler Saladin and the capture of Jaffa, Richard and his fellow crusaders were not able to retake Jerusalem. Learning of Philip's treachery and of the connivance of his younger brother John, Richard concluded a peace with Saladin that permitted the entry of Christian pilgrims into Jerusalem and assured the security of the remaining Christian lands in Syria. He then embarked for England in October 1192.

Wary of passing through France, Richard traversed the Adriatic and then set off by land through Austria and Germany. He was seized, however, by the duke of Austria, whose lord, the emperor Henry VI of Germany, was an ally of Philip II Augustus. Turned over to Henry, he remained a captive until payment of a ransom of 150,000 marks of silver. Released at Mainz on 4 February 1194, Richard was back in England by 13 March. His treacherous brother John, having been warned by Philip to "look to yourself, the devil is loosed," had fled to Normandy. In England Richard devoted himself primarily to raising money and troops for his war of revenge against Philip II Augustus. On 12 May, leaving the government in the capable hands of Hubert Walter (*d.* 1205), archbishop of Canterbury, he crossed the Channel, never to return.

For the next five years Richard campaigned against Philip II Augustus, winning each engagement and retaking all the land and castles lost. To make Normandy more secure he constructed at Les Andelys, high above the Seine, the famous Château Gaillard, his saucy castle, a marvel of engineering skill. That he should meet his death while besieging the castle of Châlus in Limoges, which belonged to a disloyal vassal, was in character. A wound in his left shoulder from the arrow of a crossbow became infected, and ten days later, on 6 April 1199, he died. The fame of Richard, as his sobriquet implies, rested solely on his military feats both on the crusades and in France.

BIBLIOGRAPHY

James A. Brundage, *Richard Lion Heart* (1974); John Gillingham, *The Life and Times of Richard I* (1973), *Richard the Lionheart* (1978), and "The Unromantic Death of Richard I," in *Speculum,* **54** (1979); Kate Norgate, *Richard the Lion-Heart* (1924); Sidney Painter, "The Third Crusade: Richard the Lionhearted and Philip Augustus," in Kenneth M. Setton, ed., *A History of the Crusades,* II (1962), 45–86; Austin L. Poole, *From Domesday Book to Magna Carta, 1087–1216,* 2nd ed. (1955).

BRYCE LYON

[See also **Aquitaine; Crusades and Crusader States: Near East; Eleanor of Aquitaine; England: Norman-Angevin; Henry II of England; John, King of England; Justiciar; Philip II Augustus; Walter, Hubert.**]

RICHARD II (1367–1400), king of England, 1377–1399, was the younger son of Edward the Black Prince. He succeeded his grandfather Edward III on the English throne on 22 June 1377. Because of his youth, power was exercised by a council. Richard first took an active role in affairs during the Peasants' Rebellion of 1381, when he courageously met with the rebels. The king began thereafter to rely upon a group of younger magnates. Richard's favorites and his policy of peace with France were offensive to a faction headed by his uncle, Thomas, duke of Gloucester. Parliament in 1386 impeached Richard's chancellor, Michael de la Pole, earl of Suffolk, and established a commission to supervise the king. Richard consulted his judges, who declared that the royal prerogative had been treasonably violated. The king attempted armed resistance, but his supporters were defeated. In the parliament of 1388, Gloucester and four other lords appellant appealed Richard's friends of treason and purged the household.

The king's wife, Anne of Bohemia, died in 1394, and the return home of her followers formed a link between John Wyclif and Jan Hus. Thus, the Lollard challenges to the dominion of the church and state, which surfaced in the Peasants' Rebellion, produced further fruit in the Hussite wars that troubled the Holy Roman Empire from 1415 to 1436. In 1396, Richard cemented a truce with France with his marriage to Charles VI's young daughter Isabelle. Richard also took part in two expeditions to Ireland in 1394 and in 1399. The king used these opportunities to develop a new retinue.

In 1397, Richard took his revenge upon his enemies. Gloucester died in custody, and a parliament dealt with two other appellants. The parliament roll was later altered to increase Richard's power. In September 1398, the king took advantage of a quarrel between the two remaining appellants to exile the duke of Norfolk and Henry Bolingbroke, the son of Richard's uncle, the duke of Lancaster. Upon Lancaster's death in February 1399, the king confiscated his lands. While Richard was in Ireland, Henry returned, and the king was unable to hold an army against him. Richard surrendered in August, and on 30 September 1399 he abdicated. He died at Pontefract Castle in February 1400, probably of forced starvation.

Richard II had a high conception of the prerogatives of kingship, which his own deposition did so much to damage. He was unstable, but he was neither the madman nor the despot that he has been pictured. Richard was a patron of poets, the remodeler of Westminster Hall—and the inventor of the handkerchief. The reign saw a renaissance of English vernacular literature after an eclipse of more than two centuries. Geoffrey Chaucer, William Langland, John Gower, Thomas Usk, and Thomas Hoccleve combined to produce a rich variety of prose and verse that achieved wide recognition.

BIBLIOGRAPHY

Caroline Barron and R. DuBoulay, eds., *The Reign of Richard II* (1971); Edmund Curtis, *Richard II in Ireland* (1927); Louisa D. Duls, *Richard II in the Early Chronicles* (1975); Anthony Goodman, *The Loyal Conspiracy*

(1971); Harold F. Hutchison, *The Hollow Crown* (1961); Richard H. Jones, *The Royal Policy of Richard II* (1968); Gervase Mathew, *The Court of Richard II* (1968); John J. N. Palmer, *England, France, and Christendom, 1377–1399* (1972); George O. Sayles, "Richard II in 1381 and 1399," in *English Historical Review,* **94** (1979); Anthony B. Steel, *Richard II* (1941, repr. 1962); George B. Stow, Jr., ed., *Historia vitae et Regni Ricardi Secundi* (1977); Anthony Tuck, *Richard II and the English Nobility* (1973).

JAMES L. GILLESPIE

[See also **Chaucer, Geoffrey; England; Henry IV of England; Hundred Years War; Peasants' Rebellion.**]

RICHARD III (1452–1485), king of England, has been painted as a villainous monster by Sir Thomas More and William Shakespeare, and this portrait has remained indelible in spite of vehement attempts to rehabilitate his character.

Richard was the youngest son of Richard, duke of York. He took little part in the struggles of Lancaster and York that culminated in the deposition of Henry VI by Richard's eldest brother, Edward IV, in 1461. At this point, Richard became duke of Gloucester, but the earl of Warwick was the dominant figure of the 1460's.

Warwick, not content, allied with Richard's other brother, George, to drive Edward IV and Richard into exile in October 1470. Richard returned with Edward the following March and commanded the vanguard in the Yorkist victories at Barnet and Tewkesbury. It is likely that Richard was involved in the murder of Henry VI in the Tower of London, which cemented his brother's triumph. Richard has also been accused of masterminding the judicial murder of his brother George in 1478; this is less likely, although the brothers were rivals for Warwick's inheritance, having married his coheiresses.

Richard's marriage to Anne Neville gave him a strong position in the north. In 1480, Edward IV appointed him lieutenant general for northern England, and Richard provided a degree of law and order not often found there. (After his accession, Richard took the lead in the establishment of the Council of the North, which continued his work.)

On 9 April 1483 Edward IV died, and Richard became protector of the realm on behalf of Edward's twelve-year-old son, Edward V. A long minority did not bode well, and Richard was exposed to the machinations of the Woodvilles, the king's maternal relatives. Richard responded by striking first. He executed the most obnoxious of the Woodvilles and secured custody of the king and his younger brother. Richard then attacked the followers of Edward IV, who might challenge his actions. Lord Hastings, therefore, followed the Woodvilles to the block, probably on 13 June, although the date and motivation are in dispute. London preachers questioned the legitimacy of Edward IV's children, and on 25 June an assembly of estates declared that Richard was the rightful king. The next day, Richard modestly acceded to the assembly's carefully cultivated desire that he assume the crown.

Richard was crowned on 6 July after his nephews had been placed in protective custody in the Tower, never to be seen again. It was—and is—thought that Richard murdered them. It is possible, however, that the deed was done by the duke of Buckingham, Richard's erstwhile supporter, who revolted unsuccessfully in October 1483. Richard tried hard to overcome his past. He worked hard to promote trade abroad, and at home he made it easier for poor suitors to obtain justice from the king's council.

The king's enemies, however, turned to the Lancastrian exile Henry Tudor, who returned from France on 7 August 1485. Richard met Henry at Bosworth Field on 22 August. Richard was killed in battle, and Henry Tudor became King Henry VII. Richard III was a hardheaded realist, but he was not necessarily an inhuman monster.

BIBLIOGRAPHY

James Gairdner, *History of the Life and Reign of Richard III,* rev. ed. (1898); Alison Hanham, "Richard III, Lord Hastings, and the Historians," in *English Historical Review,* **87** (1972), and "Hastings Redivivus," *ibid.,* **90** (1975); Paul M. Kendall, *Richard III* (1955); Dominic Mancini, *The Usurpation of Richard III,* C. A. J. Armstrong, ed. and trans., 2nd ed. (1969); James Petre, ed., *Richard III: Crown and People* (1985); A. J. Pollard, "The Tyranny of Richard III," in *Journal of Medieval History,* 3 (1977); Charles D. Ross, *Richard III* (1981); Desmond Seward, *Richard III: England's Black Legend* (1984); Horace Walpole, *Historical Doubts on the Life and Reign of Richard III* (1768); B. P. Wolffe, "When and Why Did Hastings Lose His Head?" in *English Historical Review,* **89** (1974), and "Hastings

Reinterred," *ibid.*, **91** (1976); George W. Woodward, *King Richard III* (1978).

JAMES L. GILLESPIE

[See also **England; Henry VI of England; Hundred Years War; Wars of the Roses.**]

RICHARD DE BURY (1287–1345), English bishop and chancellor, immortalized his "great delight in books" in an essay, the *Philobiblon,* completed on 28 January 1345, a month before his death. Although at first it might seem surprising that this unprecedented handbook for bibliophiles was written by a former lord chancellor of England who was also the bishop of Durham, it was actually very much in character.

Richard was the son of Sir Richard de Aungerville, a knight near Bury St. Edmunds. After his father's death the younger Richard was educated by an uncle, a rector who prepared him for Oxford. There he studied from about 1302 to 1312. Little evidence suggests that he received any advanced degree before he left to join the king's clerks, yet he was sufficiently learned to impress even Petrarch as "knowledgeable about literature" and to hold his own in conversation with the Oxford dons who surrounded his table in later years.

As a royal clerk Richard assembled England's largest private letter formulary, just as one day he would boast of England's largest episcopal library. With the successful invasion of England by Queen Isabella and young Edward III, for which he had raised money in Gascony, Richard became keeper and treasurer of the Wardrobe, keeper of the Privy Seal, treasurer of the Exchequer, bishop of Durham, and lord chancellor of England—an unbroken string of promotions from 1327 to 1335, from his fortieth to his forty-eighth year. Nevertheless, some circumstances cast doubt on his administrative ability: he remained lord chancellor for only six months; he felt obliged to secure an exemption from accounting for each office he held; and ultimately he left his personal affairs in great disorder. He distinguished himself more on royal embassies to Paris, Avignon, and Scotland.

Richard spent his final years in Durham, where he could indulge his "ecstatic love" of book collecting. Suppliants gave books to ensure his favor; mendicant clerics, acting as his agents, sent volumes from all over Europe; his own scribes filled his manors with copies. According to contemporary chronicles, Richard owned "more books than did all the rest of the English bishops"—a collection that cluttered his rooms and would have overflowed five large wagons. He preferred the ancient authors but also acquired the "subtle" and "novel" moderns.

The *Philobiblon* attempts to justify this bibliomania. Books are described as "the desirable treasure of wisdom and knowledge, which all men covet." Since wisdom is priceless, the dedicated collector "cannot serve books and mammon." Books themselves cry out against the abuses they suffer from clerical ignorance and the ravages of war. As fervently as any humanist, Richard relates his attempts to save neglected volumes from mice and worms. He concludes with a plan to use his books to establish a lending library in an Oxford college.

Richard died a month later. His final accounting could no longer be deferred, and his library was sold to pay his debts. Yet his crusade for books was not in vain, for at least forty-six surviving manuscripts of the *Philobiblon* witness its impact.

BIBLIOGRAPHY

Sources. Philobiblon, Antonio Altamura, ed. (1954), and *The Philobiblon,* Archer Taylor, trans. (1948); Noël Denholm-Young, ed., *The "Liber Epistolaris" of Richard de Bury* (1950).

Studies. Christopher R. Cheney, "Richard de Bury, Borrower of Books," in *Speculum,* **48** (1973); Noël Denholm-Young, "Richard de Bury (1287–1345) and the *Liber Epistolaris,*" in *Collected Papers of N. Denholm-Young* (1969), 1–41; Alfred B. Emden, *A Biographical Register of the University of Oxford to A.D. 1500,* I (1957), 323–326; Neal W. Gilbert, "Richard de Bury and the 'Quires of Yesterday's Sophisms,'" in Edward P. Mahoney, ed., *Philosophy and Humanism: Renaissance Essays in Honor of Paul Oskar Kristeller* (1976), 229–257; Beryl Smalley, *English Friars and Antiquity in the Early Fourteenth Century* (1960), 66–74; Christian K. Zacher, *Curiosity and Pilgrimage: The Literature of Discovery in Fourteenth-century England* (1976), 60–86, 173–177.

JOHN HOWE

[See also **Codex; Edward II of England; Libraries; Manuscript Books, Production of.**]

RICHARD OF MIDDLETON. See **Richardus de Mediavilla.**

RICHARD OF ST. VICTOR (*ca.* 1123–1173), mystical theologian of the abbey of St. Victor, Paris, and a disciple of Hugh of St. Victor. He became subprior in 1159 and prior in 1162.

Benjamin minor and *Benjamin major* are mystical works of scriptural exegesis in which Richard describes six ascending stages of contemplation to which correspond degrees of love, culminating in absorption into the Divine Beloved.

In *De Trinitate,* his most important work, Richard, like Anselm, propounds "necessary reasons" for faith. Attempting to demonstrate the reality of a Divine Cause from sense experience, he also employs dialectic and analysis of the notion of perfect love to establish the doctrine of the Trinity.

BIBLIOGRAPHY

Sources. Opera omnia in *Patrologia latina,* CXCVI (1880); *Liber exceptionum* and *Sermones centum* in *Patrologia latina,* CLXXVII (1879), 193–284, 901–1210, attributed to Hugh of St. Victor; *Liber exceptionum,* Jean Châtillon, ed. (1958); *Opuscules théologiques,* Jean Ribaillier, ed. (1967); *De quatuor gradibus violentae caritatis,* Gervais Dumeige, ed. and trans., in Brother Yves, *Épître à Séverin sur la charité* (1955); *De statu interioris hominis,* Jean Ribaillier, ed., in *Archives d'histoire doctrinale et litteraire du moyen âge,* **34** (1967), and *De Trinitate* (1958); *La Trinité,* G. Salet, ed. and trans. (1959); *Benjamin minor,* S. V. Yankowski, trans. (1960); *Selected Writings on Contemplation,* Clare Kirchberger, ed. and trans. (1957); Grover A. Zinn, *Richard of St. Victor: The Twelve Patriarchs, The Mystical Ark, Book Three of the Trinity* (1979).

Studies. Philippe Delhaye, "Les perspectives morales de Richard de Saint-Victor," in *Mélanges offerts à René Crozet,* II (1966); Gervais Dumeige, *Richard de Saint-Victor et l'idée chrétienne de l'amour* (1952); Joseph Ebner, *Die Erkenntnislehre Richards von St. Victor* (1917); Albert M. Étheir, *Le "De Trinitate" de Richard de Saint-Victor* (1939); Étienne Gilson, *History of Christian Philosophy in the Middle Ages* (1955), 634–635; Robert Javelet, "Thomas Gallus et Richard de Saint-Victor mystiques," in *Recherches de théologie ancienne et médiévale,* **29** (1962) and **30** (1963); Ralph J. Masiello, "Reason and Faith in Richard of St. Victor and St. Thomas," in *New Scholasticism,* **48** (1974); René Roques, *Structures théologiques de la gnose à Richard de Saint-Victor* (1962).

JANICE L. SCHULTZ

[See also **Exegesis, Latin; Hugh of St. Victor; Philosophy and Theology, Western European.**]

RICHARD OF WALLINGFORD (*ca.* 1292–1336), abbot of St. Albans Abbey and inventor of scientific instruments and a planetary machine. Born in Wallingford, Berkshire, England, the son of a prosperous blacksmith, he was orphaned at an early age and adopted by William of Kirkeby, abbot of St. Albans in Wallingford. He went to study at Oxford, where he took his degree in the arts. He then joined the abbey of St. Albans and was ordained a deacon in 1316 and a priest the following year. He returned to Oxford and studied theology and philosophy for the next nine years. On a visit to St. Albans upon the completion of his studies, Richard was elected abbot—the former abbot having died after Richard's arrival. Richard eventually obtained confirmation as abbot from the pope at Avignon. Returning to St. Albans, he faced a revolt of the townspeople and the burden of a heavy debt incurred by the abbey. Within the next several years he was able to clear most of the debt and to quell the local revolt. It was at this time that he contracted leprosy.

Richard's first mathematical or astronomical writings appear to have been instructions for the use of the tables of John Maudith, astronomer of Merton College from about 1310 to 1316. He next produced his *Quadripartitum,* a work of fundamental trigonometry for the solution of problems in spherical astronomy based on Ptolemy's *Almagest.* It is believed to be the earliest comprehensive medieval treatise on trigonometry to be produced outside of Spain and the Islamic world. In the years 1326–1327, while still at Oxford, Richard prepared a treatise on astrological meteorology in addition to his *Tractatus albionis.* The latter was a work on the theory, construction, and use of an instrument of his own invention, which he named the "Albion." The Albion ("all by one") consisted of an equatorium—an instrument used to determine the positions of the planets without the necessity of making calculations—together with other instruments for the calculation of eclipses. The treatise also dealt with the use of an astrolabe and a *saphea Arzachelis.* (The *saphea Azarchelis* is the Latin name for the form of universal stereographic astrolabe designed by al-Zarqālī [*d.* 1100] and further developed by ᶜAli ibn Khalaf [eleventh century]. The instrument had the same capabilities as the fixed-latitude instrument and was much more convenient for converting from ecliptic to equatorial coordinates and vice versa.) The *Tractatus albionis* had considerable influence on the sciences in Southern Europe until the sixteenth century.

While at work on the *Tractatus albionis,* Rich-

RICHARDUS DE MEDIAVILLA

ard prepared a treatise, the *Rectangulus,* on another instrument of his own invention, which he also called the "rectangulus," to be used for calculation and observation and as a substitute for the armillary sphere.

During his last period at St. Albans, Richard raised large sums that he utilized for the construction of his planetary machine or astronomical clock, which he installed in the abbey. It is the earliest mechanical timepiece of which certain knowledge exists. Wallingford's escapement preceded the invention of the verge and foliot escapement with contrate wheel. He devised a series of ingenious astronomical trains that incorporated an oval wheel to provide variable velocity for the solar motion, correcting trains for the moon and lunar phases, and eclipse attachments. The clock had an astrolabic dial and a tidal dial, and it struck the hours. An amazingly complex mechanism produced within forty years of the probable introduction of the mechanical clock on the Continent, this clock was subsequently lost in the dissolution of the monasteries in England.

BIBLIOGRAPHY

Silvio A. Bedini and Francis R. Maddison, "Mechanical Universe: The Astrarium of Giovanni de' Dondi," in *Transactions of the American Philosophical Society,* n.s. 56 (1966); Robert Gunther, *Early Science in Oxford,* II (1926), 337–370; John D. North, "Monasticism and the First Mechanical Clocks," in J. T. Fraser and Norman Lawrence, eds., *The Study of Time,* II (1975), and *Richard of Wallingford,* 3 vols. (1976); Lynn White, Jr., *Medieval Technology and Social Change* (1962).

SILVIO A. BEDINI

[See also **Astrolabe; Astronomy; Calendars; Clocks and Reckoning of Time; Clockwork, Planetary; Science, Islamic; Technology, Western.**]

RICHARDUS DE MEDIAVILLA (Richard of Middleton) (*ca.* 1249–1302/1308) was born in either England or France. Hence, the name "Richard of Middleton" assumes the answer to a long-debated and still unsettled question. He may well deserve to be called "Richard of Menneville." In fact, "Mediavilla" may even be a family name, not a place-name at all. In any case, having joined the Franciscan order at some point, Richard studied in Paris. In 1283, still a bachelor of theology, he was a member of the seven-man committee that censured Peter John Olivi. Since Olivi's 1285 letter to the same committee addresses Richard as a master, he probably became a master of theology at Paris in 1284 and continued to teach there until 1287. We do not hear of him again until 1295, when he was elected minister of the Franciscan province of France. Richard also spent some time in the company of St. Louis of Toulouse at the Castel dell'Ovo near Naples in 1296 or 1297, probably as teacher and companion, but he seems to have departed before Louis's death in August 1297. He himself died sometime between 1302 and 1308.

Richard left a substantial body of writings, all of them originally produced in the 1280's (although some were revised in the 1290's). He studied and taught during the age when Paris was adjusting to the condemnations of 1277 and was thus sensitized to the dangers of an overzealous Aristotelianism. It was also the period of the *correctorium* controversy, in which the philosophy of Thomas Aquinas was attacked by Franciscans but defended by Dominicans and others. Richard's work is notably balanced on both counts. He is true to his Franciscan education, but not narrowly so. His writings display extensive knowledge of Aristotle. Historians of science have remarked on his interest in natural philosophy and his respect for the role of experience. As for Aquinas, Richard joins his confreres in criticizing Thomas on some issues, yet sides with him instead of with Bonaventure on others.

In some respects, like Olivi, Richard stands within a developing Franciscan tradition that looks forward to John Duns Scotus. Unlike Olivi, however, Richard's views aroused no suspicion and he therefore reaped the scholarly and administrative rewards to be derived from a Parisian education. His work was widely and respectfully read by succeeding scholars. All in all, the title usually accorded him by tradition, *doctor solidus,* is quite fitting.

BIBLIOGRAPHY

Sources. Ricardus de Mediavilla, *Super quatuor libros sententiarum* (1507–1509), *Quodlibeta* (1507–1509), *Quaestiones disputatae,* q. 13, in *De humane cognitionis ratione* (1883), 221–243, *Quaestio disputata de privilegio Martini papae IV,* Ferdinando D. Delorme, ed. (1925), *Quaestio de gradu formarum,* in Roberto Zavalloni, *Richard de Medievilla et la controverse sur la pluralité des formes* (1951), 35–169, three sermons in Edgar Hocedez, *Richard de Middleton* (1925), 490–509, and one sermon in Willibrord Lampen, "Richard de Middleton," in *La France franciscaine,* 13 (1930).

Studies. In addition to Hocedez and Zavalloni, see Johannes Beumer, "Der Theologiebegriff des Richard von Mediavilla," in *Franziskanische Studien,* **40** (1958); Josef Lechner, *Die Sakramentenlehre des Richard von Mediavilla* (1925); Michael Schmaus, "Die theologische Methode des Richard von Mediavilla," in *Franziskanische Studien,* **48** (1966), and "Die trinitarische Ebenbildlichkeit des Menschen nach Richard von Mediavilla," in Heribert Rossmann and Joseph Ratzinger, eds., *Mysterium der Gnade* (1975).

DAVID BURR

[See also **Duns Scotus, John; Peter John Olivi; Philosophy and Theology, Western European: Thirteenth Century; Thomism and Its Opponents.**]

RICHER OF ST. REMI (*fl.* second half of tenth century), French chronicler. A monk of the abbey of St. Remi in Rheims, he wrote the *Historia de France,* covering the period from 885 to 995, as a continuation of the *Annales* of Hincmar. The *Historia* is in four books and stops abruptly with events in 995. It was written between 991 and 998.

BIBLIOGRAPHY

The text can be found in *Patrologia latina,* CXXXVIII (1853), 17–170, and Georg H. Pertz, ed., *Monumenta Germaniae historica; Scriptores,* III (1849), 561–657. For a French translation, see Robert Latouche, ed., *Histoire de France* (*888–995*), 2 vols. (1930–1937, repr. 1967). For biographical details, see Max Manitius, *Geschichte der lateinischen Literatur des Mittelalters,* II (1923, repr. 1976), 214–219, 730.

EDWARD FRUEH

[See also **Hincmar of Rheims.**]

RIDDA WARS. See **Islam, Conquests of.**

RIDDARASÖGUR. The medieval romances of Norway and Iceland are commonly known as *riddarasögur* (tales of knights, chivalric tales). Although usage varies considerably, literary historians apply the term *riddarasögur* to two different types of compositions: (1) works translated (mostly from the French) into Norwegian in the thirteenth century and (2) indigenous Icelandic romances composed mostly during the fourteenth and fifteenth centuries.

Although, strictly speaking, the word *riddarasögur* suggests the Old Norse–Icelandic equivalent of the French *romans courtois,* the designation has in modern usage come to embrace prose translations into Norwegian of secular works with varied content and from various languages. The *matière de Bretagne* and *matière de France* are represented in the north through translations of a number of *romans courtois* and chansons de geste. Both High and Low German heroic tales are preserved in the monumental *Þiðreks saga,* as are Latin pseudohistoriographical writings in *Alexanders saga,* a free translation of the metrical *Alexandreis* of Gautier de Châtillon (Walter of Châtillon), *Breta sögur* (a free translation of Geoffrey of Monmouth's *Historia regum Britanniae*), and *Trójumanna saga* (based primarily on Dares Phrygius' *De excidio Trojae*).

Late medieval Icelandic romances that are original compositions are also subsumed under the term *riddarasögur.* On occasion the indigenous Icelandic romances have also been called *lygisögur* (lying tales). Both designations—*riddarasögur* and *lygisögur*—are attested in medieval Icelandic literature (for example, *Bragða-Mágus saga, Flóres saga konungs ok sona hans*). Nonetheless, because of the pejorative connotation of the word *lygisögur,* and because the term is misleading, the designation *riddarasögur* is to be preferred in scholarly discussion.

The term *fornsögur suðrlanda* (tales of ancient days set in southern lands), coined by Gustaf Cederschiöld in the nineteenth century as the title for an edition of romances (both translated and original), has been adopted by some scholars. This designation has been used in contradistinction to *fornaldarsögur norðrlanda,* indigenous mythical tales of ancient days set in northern Europe.

The term *riddarasögur* will be used here to refer both to the translated and to the original Icelandic romances. "Translated *riddarasögur*" denotes the older romances derived from a specific source, or romances for which other European versions are extant. "Icelandic *riddarasögur*" denotes late medieval original compositions.

As stated above, from the standpoint of chronology as well as origin, Old Norse–Icelandic romances fall into two distinct but related categories: romances translated predominantly during the thirteenth century in Norway (but now preserved almost without exception in Icelandic manuscripts), and original romances composed during the fourteenth and fifteenth centuries in Iceland. The distinguishing features of both groups of romances are their derivative character and their prose style. The romances are indebted primarily to foreign sources but also in varying degree to the indigenous literary tradition for content, style, and form. Although almost all the sources were in verse, the translated *riddarasögur* always employ prose.

TRANSLATIONS FROM FRENCH

During his reign (1217–1263) King Hákon IV Hákonarson of Norway initiated a program of translation that was to continue into the reign of Hákon Magnússon (1299–1319). The author of *Viktors saga ok Blávus,* a fourteenth-century Icelandic *riddarasaga,* commends King Hákon Magnússon for supporting the translation of foreign romances and mentions that the king himself derived great pleasure from hearing such tales.

Literary historians have generally assumed that the first of the romances to reach the north was Thomas' *Tristan.* The *Tristrams saga ok Isöndar,* usually referred to as *Tristrams saga,* holds a unique position in the history of medieval Scandinavian and French literature; the saga is the only complete extant redaction of the Thomas branch of the Tristan legend; it is also the only romance translated in Norway for which both the name of the author and the date of the translation are preserved. According to the prologue, *Tristrams saga* was written by Brother Robert in 1226 at the behest of King Hákon Hákonarson. This translator seems to be identical with the Abbot Robert who translated *Elie de St. Gille* into Norwegian as *Elis saga ok Rosamundu.* The Anglo-Norman name suggests that Robert may have been an English monk, perhaps attached to an English foundation in Norway, such as Lyse or Hovedøya.

Other translations supply less information than *Tristrams saga* or *Elis saga* regarding the circumstances of their composition. Three works of Chrétien de Troyes reached the north: *Erec et Enide* (*Erex saga*), *Le chevalier au lion* or *Yvain* (*Ívens saga*), and the fragmentary *Le conte du graal* or *Perceval* (*Parcevals saga,* a translation of lines 1–6,518; *Valvens þáttr,* line 6,519 to the end of Chrétien's text). *Ívens saga* alone states that King Hákon Gamli (the Old) was responsible for having the romance translated. The appellation "the Old" was used to distinguish the king from his son Hákon Ungi (the Young), who died six years before his father, at the age of twenty-five, in 1257. If the reference to Hákon Gamli was indeed the work of the translator and not added by a later copyist, then we can certainly delimit the period during which *Ívens saga* originated. The other translations of Chrétien's works are silent regarding royal patronage. Nonetheless, for want of compelling evidence to the contrary, it seems plausible to assume that *Parcevals saga* and *Valvens þáttr* were also written during the reign of Hákon Hákonarson, especially because of their stylistic similarity to *Ívens saga. Erex saga* presumably also originated during the thirteenth century, although the work is unlike the other romances that are known to have been translated during this time. Major structural deviations from the French source—marked condensation, on the one hand, and two interpolated episodes, on the other—and striking dissimilarity to the style of the other translated romances suggest that the character of *Erex saga,* as we know it from extant manuscripts, is largely the work of one or more Icelandic redactors. Because of the uniformity of style and clear structure of the work, it is more reasonable to suppose that the far-reaching and complex modifications were undertaken on the basis of an already extant translation rather than introduced during the process of translation.

If there is some uncertainty regarding the genesis of the translation of two of Chrétien's romances, there is none in the case of a translation of lais commonly attributed to Marie de France and known in Norwegian as *Strengleikar.* The preface to the collection declares that King Hákon Hákonarson had ordered the translation from French of a book called *ljóða bók* (Book of lais or Songbook). The author informs us that these lais were performed on *strengleikar,* various kinds of stringed instruments; hence the title under which the Norwegian collection of lais has been transmitted. Although the translator asserts that his source was a book of lais, the collection as we know it corresponds neither to the content nor to the arrangement of the two extant manuscript collections (London, British Museum, MS Harley 978; Paris, Bibliothèque Nationale, MS nouv. acq. fran. 1104). Four of the lais have no known French originals (*Gurun; Strandar strengleikr* [Lai of the beach]; *Ricar hinn gamli* [Richard the old]; *Tveggia elskanda strengleikr* [Lai of two lovers]). Thus, the *Strengleikar* anthology is the third major compilation of lais in existence.

Among the twenty-four works collectively entitled *Les lays de Bretagne* in the manuscript B.N. MS

RIDDARASÖGUR

nouv. acq. fran. 1104 is *Le mantel,* better known by the fuller title *Le mantel mautaillié,* a work that is often classed among the fabliaux because of its ribald content—the progress of a chastity test at King Arthur's court. The Norwegian translation of this work, *Möttuls saga,* was also made by order of King Hákon Hákonarson. Comparison of the saga with extant French manuscripts of *Le mantel mautaillié* shows that the saga is marked by a type of stylistic amplification characteristic of the best of the translations, such as *Strengleikar* and *Tristrams saga. Möttuls saga* is introduced by a prologue that contains a lengthy hyperbolic portrait of King Arthur. For this there is no French source, and it has been suggested that *Möttuls saga* was the first of the Arthurian tales to be translated, that the introductory portrait of Arthur was intended to familiarize the Norwegian audience with the legendary king. Although such a theory is not implausible, use of a prologue to introduce one or more of the characters coincides with structural practice not only in the translated sagas (for example, *Tristrams saga, Parcevals saga, Erex saga*) but also in the indigenous romances (such as *Saga af Tristram ok Ísodd, Valdimars saga, Sigurðar saga turnara*). Thus, the portrait of Arthur may be nothing other than an expression of structural tendencies common to the Old Norse–Icelandic romances.

Through Hákon's program of translation, the popular French literature of the day became accessible to Norwegians. Since the events depicted in most of the translated works take place in a courtly milieu, the readers or listeners could glean information regarding behavior in a chivalric society. Hákon's interest in European literature has been interpreted as an expression of didactic intent, and the romances as a fictional King's Mirror—instruments for instructing in chivalrous behavior. To some extent such an assessment of the *riddarasögur* is valid. Nonetheless, the romances are above all a literature of fantasy and escape. That the translations were intended to amuse and divert is attested in several works (for example, *Möttuls saga, Strengleikar, Elis saga*). Authorial commentary in the later indigenous *riddarasögur* is evidence that Icelandic authors considered amusement a primary function of translated as well as original romances.

In addition to the Arthurian literature associated with Hákon Hákonarson's reign, a number of other French romances and chansons de geste were translated into Norwegian, presumably during the thirteenth century. *Flóres saga ok Blankiflúr* derives from the romance of adventure *Floire et Blancheflur.* A chanson de geste popular in many countries, *Boeve de Haumtone,* is represented in the Old Norse–Icelandic *Bevers saga.* In *Karlamagnús saga,* extant in an older and a younger redaction, are compiled translations of several chansons de geste, including *Chanson d'Otinel, Le pèlerinage de Charlemagne, Chanson de Roland,* and *Chanson d'Aspremont,* as well as Latin historiographical material, such as Pseudo-Turpin.

Several *riddarasögur* derive only indirectly from known sources, inasmuch as they correspond to no extant redaction, and may either be based on a lost version or be a re-creation of known French versions. *Flóvents saga* is a remnant of what much have been a Merovingian epic cycle. Although French, Dutch, and Italian poems about Floovant exist, the immediate source of the saga is not known. Similarly, *Mágus saga jarls* is related to the epic poem *Les quatre fils Aimon* (or *Renaud de Montauban*) and *Le pélerinage de Charlemagne,* but the saga corresponds to no extant versions. The romance of adventure *Parténopeus de Blois* is transmitted in Spanish, Italian, and English versions in addition to *Partalopa saga.* A direct source for the saga cannot be determined, however. In these three cases, an Icelandic reworking of an original Norwegian translation ought not to be precluded.

OTHER TRANSLATED MATERIAL

Several sagas fall outside the mainstream of romance translation. *Þiðreks saga,* of which a thirteenth-century Norwegian manuscript is extant, stands in a class by itself because of its Germanic content and sources. The work consists of a compilation of tales concerning Dietrich von Bern. Whether the author used a single source—written or oral—or compiled his work from different accounts cannot be determined. A few *riddarasögur* derive from Latin sources. Although a French romance about the legendary friendship of Amis and Amiles exists, *Amíkus saga ok Amílius* is a translation not from the French but of a Latin version found in Vincent of Beauvais's *Speculum historiale.* Finally, two Icelanders distinguish themselves for their translations. According to the epilogue in one of the manuscripts of *Alexanders saga* (Copenhagen, Arnamagnæan Institute, AM 226 fol.), Walter of Châtillon's epic poem was translated by Brandr Jónsson, bishop of Hólar (1262–1264). Manuscripts of *Alexanders saga* attest that the translation was undertaken at the behest of King

RIDDARASÖGUR

Magnús Hákonarson (1263–1280). *Klári saga* is attributed to another bishop, Jón Halldórsson of Skálholt (1322–1339). According to the preface, the source of *Klári saga* was a Latin metrical romance—unknown to us today—that the bishop had discovered in France.

THE TRANSLATIONS: CONTENT

It is generally assumed that the translation into Norwegian of those *riddarasögur* with more or less known sources took place in the thirteenth century and commenced with Brother Robert's *Tristrams saga.* The manuscript situation is unfortunate, however. Norwegian manuscripts are extant of only a few works, such as *Strengleikar, Elis saga,* and *Þiðreks saga.* Our knowledge and assessment of the Norwegian translations of the thirteenth century is based largely on Icelandic manuscripts, most of them several centuries and scribes removed from the original translations. The response of Icelanders to the translated romances varied. Icelandic copyists not infrequently asserted themselves as editors, freely modifying both content and structure of the manuscripts they were copying.

A striking example of editorial reworking that verges on creative writing is the text of *Ívens saga* as preserved in a seventeenth-century paper manuscript (Stockholm, Royal Library, 46 fol.). Although this text of *Ívens saga* is markedly condensed, when compared with the texts of two older vellums (Copenhagen, Arnamagnæan Institute, AM 489, 4to; Stockholm, Royal Library, Codex Holm. perg. 6, 4to), the paper manuscript nonetheless preserves from the French some readings no longer found in the vellums and others that better reflect the French source. At the same time, the paper manuscript deviates substantially from the text of the vellums in several episodes where those older manuscripts correspond to the French text.

A more extreme case of scribal independence appears to be *Erex saga,* which represents a systematic revision of an original translation. Furthermore, a copyist has interpolated two new episodes, one of which he seems to have borrowed from *Þiðreks saga.*

Another striking example of a copyist indulging in creative writing in *Elis saga ok Rosamundu.* To the text of the original translation (preserved in the manuscript (Uppsala, University Library, De la Gardie 4–7), which concludes with a reference to translator and royal patron, an Icelander has appended a continuation of eleven chapters (preserved, for example, in Stockholm, Royal Library, Codex Holm. perg. 6, 4to).

There is considerable ambiguity and uncertainty regarding the character of the original Norwegian translations. Absolute fidelity to the content, structure, and style of the sources is the exception in the Old Norse–Icelandic romances. Brother Robert and his colleagues did not "translate" in the modern sense with its connotation of fidelity. Various modifications in the *riddarasögur* vis-à-vis their sources betoken an awareness of the background and needs of the audience for whom these sagas were intended. Adaptation of the foreign material occurred by one or more means: through choice of one of several valid interpretations for an ambiguous passage; through reduction or omission of text that might have been deemed superfluous or inappropriate; through amplification for the sake of greater clarity or better motivation; through modification of details or of the sequence of details to conform to differing literary sensibilities; and through choice of appropriate stylistic ornamentation to stress significant portions of the narrative. Consequently, the *riddarasögur* retain the substance of their sources only imperfectly. The extent of the modifications, with concomitant shifts of perspective, nuance, or attitude, can vary from episode to episode in the same work as well as from saga to saga.

Our assessment of the talents of the Norwegian translators and of the works they produced is based almost exclusively on Icelandic manuscripts, sometimes several centuries younger than the original translations. Considerable evidence exists, however, to suggest that the translators followed their sources more exactly than is apparent from the oldest extant manuscripts of the *riddarasögur.* By means of late Icelandic paper manuscripts, Paul Schach has demonstrated that the text of *Tristrams saga* as we know it from Kölbing's edition is corrupt. The seventeenth-century paper manuscript of *Ívens saga* mentioned above (Stockholm, Royal Library, MS 46 fol.), although drastically abbreviated, retains passages and episodes from *Yvain* not found in the older vellum manuscripts. A recently discovered eighteenth-century Icelandic redaction of *Guiamars ljóð,* the first of the *Strengleikar,* presents conclusive evidence that the Norwegian manuscript of the *Strengleikar* (De la Gardie 4–7) could not have been the first fair copy of the translator's rough draft, as the nineteenth-century editors (Keyser and Unger) had hypothesized. At most, not even half a century could have elapsed between the translation of the lais and the production of De la Gardie 4–7, yet the Icelandic redaction contains several striking instances of agreement with the French *Guigemar* where the Norwegian redaction has lost text or has acquired corrupt readings. The above suggests that considerable discrepancy can exist between the translator's work and the text as preserved in Icelandic or Norwegian manuscripts.

Two opposing but not mutually exclusive tendencies prevail in the *riddarasögur.* On the one hand, the authors suppressed entirely or reduced considerably large portions of text from their sources, and not infrequently these are the very passages that are stylistically characteristic of the romances. Long monologues, repetitive material in the form of anticipation or summary, and authorial intrusions were condensed or exercised from the longer courtly romances. Because of their succinctness, the integrity of the lais (*Strengleikar* and *Möttuls saga*) was not impaired. On the other hand, the authors augmented portions of the narrative, and the "interpolations," together with material retained from the sources, bear the peculiar stylistic stamp of the *riddarasögur.* In consequence, even those sections of the narrative that are more or less faithful translations from the French can at times evince nuances and connotations different from those obtaining in a source. In speaking about the *riddarasögur* the word "author" is used advisedly. Because of the problematic state of manuscript transmission, we cannot be sure to whom all interpolations and excisions are to be attributed. In not a few cases a *riddarasaga* is as much the creation of a translator as of an Icelandic redactor.

THE TRANSLATIONS: FORM

By virtue of their pan-European content, the Old Norse-Icelandic romances are an integral element of the medieval European narrative tradition. Their prose form places the *riddarasögur* in a unique position, however. Although the foreign sources with few exceptions (for example, pseudo-historiographical works) employed verse form, the translators chose to transmit the material in prose. Tradition was perhaps the most cogent reason for the change of form. To be sure, skaldic and Eddic meters were flourishing, but prose had become the accepted form for extended narrative, secular as well as religious, indigenous as well as translated. The prose developed for the *riddarasögur* was, however, unlike the classical prose of the Icelandic family sagas. The translators' prose was modeled after Latin style and, to some extent, syntax. Two principles governed the courtly style of translation, or court prose (so called because of its association with the Norwegian court): elaboration and euphony. The combination resulted in a rhythmical prose characterized chiefly by amplification that was achieved through syntactic parallelism, synonymous as well as antithetic, and through tautological or synonymous collocations. These rhetorical devices are frequently accompanied—and consequently stressed—by assonance, rhyme, and, especially, alliteration; the last is the chief poetic characteristic of the *riddarasögur.* The resultant language is rhythmical as well as euphonious, and it is not unreasonable to suppose that alliteration, the dominant Norse metrical form, was chosen to compensate for the loss of the verse form.

Alliteration is an essential contextual component of the *riddarasögur.* It is used to signal important dialogue or action, to set a particular scene in relief, to introduce a character, to convey heightened emotion. Alliterative clusters are a striking mode of auditory ornamentation, and for that reason are an effective means to emphasize significant portions of narrative. As the author stresses now one scene, now another, he also imposes his sense of structure on the narrative, even as alliteration serves to conjoin phrases, clauses, or successive sentences. Extended alliteration occurs in scenes dramatically and structurally significant for the plot. At times one sound predominates, but more frequently alliterative groups in varying combinations are interlaced, or synonymous or antithetic collocations appear as part of an extended enumeration.

Despite an extraordinary homogeneity of the *riddarasögur* by virtue of their content and common repertoire of rhetorical devices, the translated romances nonetheless evince considerable diversity in the application of stylistic techniques. Alliteration in one saga stresses heightened emotion: *Ek hefi . . . vent tign minni j tyning, yndi mitt j angurssemi,* l*if mitt j* l*eidindi,* h*iarta mitt j* h*ugsott,* v*nnustu mina j* o*vin,* f*relsi mitt j* f*rijdlejsi* (I have . . . turned my honor into annihilation, my delight into depression, my life into loathing, my heart into anxiety, my sweetheart into an enemy, and my freedom into outlawry; *Ívens saga,* chap. 10). (Text is Kölbing ed.; translation, *Ívens saga,* Foster W. Blaisdell, ed. [1979].) The same effect may be

RIDDARASÖGUR

achieved in another saga by means of semantic variation and antithesis—*þá verð ek gegnum* dauðann *at ganga, þvi at hans* dauði drepr *á mitt hjarta. Hversu skal ek hér mega lengr* lífa? *Mitt* líf *skal hans* lífi *fylgja* (I must pass through death, for his death beats upon my heart. How shall I be able to live here longer? My life must follow his life; *Tristrams saga,* chap. 15)—or by participial clusters—*Nú ertu, Ísönd, mik* hatandi. *Ek em nú* syrgjandi, *er þú vilt ekki til mín koma, en ek sakir þín* deyjandi, *er þú vildir ekki miskunna sótt minni. Ek em nú* syrgjandi *sótt mína ok* harmandi, *er þú vildire ekki koma at hugga mik* (Now you hate me, Ísönd. I grieve because you will not come to me, and I die for your sake since you would not take pity on my affliction. And now I grieve and mourn my affliction because you would not come to comfort me; *Tristrams saga,* chap. 99). Scenes with similar content can differ markedly in structure and style from saga to saga, as well as within one saga. Nonetheless, the stylistic and lexical interrelationships of the *riddarasögur* cannot be denied.

ICELANDIC *RIDDARASÖGUR:* BORROWED ELEMENTS

Continental European literature was introduced to the north primarily by way of Norway. Nonetheless, had it not been for the extraordinary literary activity of Icelanders, manifested by centuries of scribal copying, editing, and re-creating of older texts, we should today have to assume that continental fiction was largely unknown in Scandinavia. Iceland played a significant role in preserving the Norwegian translations. What is more, familiarity with the *riddarasögur* had considerable impact on Icelandic literary tastes and compositions. The indigenous *riddarasögur* attest the popularity of the translated Norwegian romances in Iceland. The latter gave the impetus to the production—probably not before 1300—of an indigenous corpus of *riddarasögur,* consisting of adaptations or reworkings of extant romances (whether in written or oral form cannot always be determined), as well as original compositions patterned after the translated *riddarasögur,* and constructed of motifs and episodes borrowed from far and wide.

One of the *Strengleikar, Bisclaretz ljóð,* was adapted with insubstantial modifications as *Tióðels saga.* Thomas' version of the Tristan legend, as preserved in the Norwegian *Tristrams saga,* underwent a curious transformation in the fourteenth-century Icelandic *Saga af Tristram ok Ísodd.* The nature of the distortions of plot and characterization suggests that the author intended to parody the Tristan legend, perhaps even Arthurian romance in general. Indeed, the pervasive presence in Icelandic romances of names, motifs, and situations from *Tristrams saga* suggests that Brother Robert's translation enjoyed greater popularity and renown in Iceland than did the other translated *riddarasögur.* In both *Rémundar saga keisarasonar* and *Haralds saga Hringsbana,* major motif complexes from the Tristan legend are found, such as a sword fragment embedded in a knight's skull, a proxy wooing, a substituted bride, and a voyage for healing. Particularly prevalent are variations and analogues of the Hall of Statues episode. Reminiscences of the motif of creating an effigy of the beloved occur in *Rémundar saga keisarasonar, Þiðreks saga* (in three different subplots), *Jarlmanns saga ok Hermanns,* and the younger *Mágus saga* (also called *Bragða-Mágus saga*). As in *Tristrams saga,* a dragon fight takes place in *Flóres saga konungs ok sona hans;* as proof of his deed the protagonist cuts off a claw instead of a tongue, however. Like Ísönd, women in a number of romances are sought out for their powers of healing (*Blómstrvalla saga, Jarlmanns saga ok Hermanns, Haralds saga Hringsbana, Mírmanns saga, Nítida saga, Rémundar saga keisarasonar*).

Albeit not as generously as *Tristrams saga,* other translated *riddarasögur* contributed motifs and situations to the formation of a corpus of indigenous Icelandic romances. The chastity-testing mantle from *Möttuls saga* reappears in *Samsons saga fagra,* the author of which enlarges upon the history of the origin of the mantle. The figure of the innocent fool, for whom the eponymous hero of *Parcevals saga* is a prototype, plays a role in *Kára saga Kárasonar* and *Vilmundar saga viðútan.* Like Parceval, the hero in the latter work is reared in the wilderness. In *Bærings saga,* as in the *Saga af Tristram ok Ísodd,* the motif of the *leicht getröstete Witwe* (easily consoled widow), known from *Ívens saga,* appears. An especially popular borrowing from *Ívens saga* was the grateful lion motif. Like Íven, the protagonist in *Ectors saga, Grega saga, Kára saga Kárasonar, Konráðs saga keisarasonar,* and *Sigurðar saga þögla* comes to the assistance of a lion, and the grateful beast subsequently becomes his inseparable companion. A rustic permutation of the knight with the lion appears in the chivalric folktale *Vígkæns saga kúahirðis.*

ICELANDIC *RIDDARASÖGUR:* TYPICAL MOTIFS AND FORMS

The authors of the indigenous romances exhibit considerable awareness of their art. Not infrequently they step forward to declare their intentions and to defend their fanciful compositions. They pride themselves on having searched far and wide for interesting narratives (*Jarlmanns saga ok Hermanns, Adonias saga, Vilhjálms saga sjóðs*). They extol their compositions as an ideal form of entertainment (*Þiðreks saga, Mágus saga jarls*). The author of *Viktors saga ok Blávus* praises King Hákon Magnússon's support for the translation of foreign romances and urges his audience to seek pleasure in literature rather than in less worthy pursuits, such as dancing. Attention to a good tale is declared an ideal antidote to evil thoughts (*Sigurðar saga þögla, Adonias saga*). As if anticipating criticism, or in reply to it, the Icelanders defend their preference for fantasy (*Sigurðar saga þögla, Vilhjálms saga sjóðs*), and now and then chide their audiences for finding fault with the subject matter (*Flóres saga konungs ok sona hans, Þiðreks saga, Vilhjálms saga sjóðs*).

Icelandic authors blended apparently disparate elements culled from a variety of contemporary and older works, both native and foreign, to arrive at a new synthesis: the indigenous romance. In an effort to be cosmopolitan and to appeal to their audiences' interest in the foreign and the exotic, they sent the characters peopling their romances to the far reaches of the earth in search of adventure. The introduction of *Vilhjálms saga sjóðs* contains an extreme but not atypical synopsis of the geographical setting of more than one romance: "This story begins in England, passes on to Saxland and then to Greece, proceeds to Africa right out to where the sun goes down, thence to the great city of Ninive in the southern hemisphere and finally to the mighty Kakausi mountains at the end of the world." The Icelandic romances carry on the tradition of the continental literature that inspired their inception and composition. *Sigurðar saga þögla* is set "in the days of the famous King Arthur who ruled over the land of the Britons, which has since been called England." The author divulges that *Flóres saga ok Blankiflúr* is one of his sources of information. Similarly, in *Flóres saga konungs ok sona hans* we find an expression of indebtedness to *Þiðreks saga*.

The authors of the Icelandic *riddarasögur* were particularly fond of magic and marvelous objects, about which they gleaned information from medieval lapidaries and popular European literature. Magic stones and mirrors reveal and reflect events in distant places (*Gibbons saga, Nítida saga, Blómstrvalla saga, Nikulás saga leikara*), and confer invisibility (*Flóvents saga, Sigurðar saga þögla, Blómstrvalla saga*), while precious jewels are sources of illumination for towers and halls (*Ectors saga, Mágus saga jarls, Rémundar saga keisarasonar, Sigurðar saga ok Valbrands*). Flying carpets and mantles are a preferred mode of transportation (*Gibbons saga, Sigrgarðs saga frækna, Jóns saga leikara, Viktors saga ok Blávus*). By means of magic apples (*Dínus saga drambláta, Gibbons saga*), magic stones (*Sigurðar saga þögla*), and magic philters (*Saga af Tristram ok Ísodd, Dínus saga drambláta, Kára saga Kárasonar*) passion is induced. Some magic potions cause physical disease (*Mírmanns saga*); others cure it (*Ajax saga, Ála flekks saga*).

Both hostile and amicable fantastic creatures known from European romance as well as the indigenous *fornaldarsögur* find their way into the Icelandic *riddarasögur*. Characters endowed with extraordinary powers can raise storms (*Vilhjálms saga sjóðs, Haralds saga Hringsbana*) and restore youth (*Mágus saga*). There are many mythical creatures: werewolves (*Ála flekks saga*), dragons (*Flóres saga konungs ok sona hans, Ectors saga, Grega saga, Kára saga Kárasonar, Konráðs saga keisarasonar, Sigurðar saga þögla, Valdimars saga*), and shapeshifters (*Dínus saga drambláta, Bærings saga, Viktors saga ok Blávus*); giants (*Bærings saga, Ectors saga, Kára saga Kárasonar, Samsons saga fagra*) and dwarfs (*Nítida saga, Gibbons saga, Ectors saga*); witches (*Ála flekks saga*), trolls (*Dínus saga drambláta, Hrings saga ok Tryggva, Sigurðar saga þögla*), and berserkers (*Ectors saga*).

The heroes of these romances not infrequently manage to reach maturity against seemingly insuperable odds. They are to be exposed or killed, sometimes as a consequence of a promise to the higher powers (*Samsons saga fagra, Ála flekks saga, Sigrgarðs saga ok Valbrands, Vilhjálms saga sjóðs*). Because women are an object of desire, abduction is a favorite theme (*Dámusta saga, Jarlmanns saga ok Hermanns, Nikulás saga leikara, Sálus saga ok Nikanors*). A not uncommon figure in Icelandic romance is the Maiden King or haughty princess who treats her suitors in cruel fashion (the "König Drosselbart" motif). Nonetheless, the determined suitors usually manage to outwit and thoroughly humiliate the obstreperous ladies (*Dínus saga drambláta, Gibbons saga, Klári saga, Nítida saga, Niku-*

RIDDARASÖGUR

lás saga leikara, Sigrgarðs saga frækna, Sigrgarðs saga ok Valbrands, Sigurðar saga þögla, Viktors saga ok Blávus).

The Icelandic romances carry on the rhetorical tradition of the translated *riddarasögur*, but in more moderate form. As in the Norwegian translations, similar phraseology for similar situations predominates. The degree of stylistic embellishment varies, however, from saga to saga, and within the same work there is considerable stylistic diversity. Just as the indigenous *riddarasögur* contain an admixture of elements borrowed from foreign romance and the indigenous heroic saga, so in one saga we may come upon a blend of the rhetorically elaborate style of the translated *riddarasögur* and the more moderate diction of the *fornaldarsögur*. The focus of a scene—a knightly encounter at arms in a tournament, or a Viking skirmish at sea—and an author's stylistic inclinations largely determine phraseology and rhetorical ornamentation.

In one saga a beautiful woman may be described rather succinctly in the taciturn style associatied with classical Icelandic prose—*hann sier at kona liggur j sængine og sefur. hun et so frid at alldri sæ hann jafn fridan kuen mann* (He sees that a woman is lying in the bed. She is so beautiful that he has never seen another woman as beautiful; *Sigurðar saga turnara,* chap. 8, Agnete Loth, *Late Medieval Icelandic Romances,* V)—but a similar scene in another romance generates the embellished prose evolved by the Norwegian translators: *og j þesse sæng sa hann liggia eina jungfru so fagra og elskuliga sem alldri fyrr sidan hann var fæddr sa hann nockura hennar lika. þviat so var hun bio'rt og blòmalig riòd og ròsalig skær og skemtilig ⟨ad⟩ hann hafdi alldri slika sied. hvorke àdur nie sidan* (And in this bed he saw a maiden lying, so fair and lovely that never before in his life had he seen anyone like her. She was so bright and blossoming, ruddy and rosehued, pure and pleasant, that he had never seen her like either before or after; *Adonias saga,* chap. 6, Loth, *op. cit.*, III). Since the chronology of the late medieval Icelandic romances is highly uncertain, further analyses of style and motifs, such as that by Einar Ól. Sveinsson, of *Viktors saga ok Blávus,* are desirable.

Although some Icelanders deprecatingly dismissed the indigenous romances as *lygisögur,* as a pack of lies, the popularity of such literature of escape cannot be denied. The number of extant romances, including medieval and post-Reformation translations as well as original Icelandic compositions, has been estimated to come close to 265. In the indigenous romances the Icelanders' delight in variation is evident: ancient motifs and situations appear in ever new guises, a result of recombination and transformation. Antiquarian interest was undoubtedly responsible for many a text being copied in Iceland. Nonetheless, the preservation of Norwegian translations in late medieval vellums and post-Reformation paper manuscripts, concomitant with the transmission of names, motifs, and even entire episodes from the translated *riddarasögur* in the Icelandic *riddarasögur,* bespeaks more than passing interest or acquaintance with European literature. The assimilation of the foreign matter into native Icelandic compositions attests the lasting impact on Icelandic literature of the *riddarasögur* imported from Norway.

BIBLIOGRAPHY

Editions. Gustaf Cederschiöld, ed., *Fornsögur Suðrlanda* (1884), containing *Mágus saga jarls, Konráðs saga keisarasonar, Bærings saga, Flóvents saga* (two redactions), *Bevers saga;* H. Erlendsson and E. Þórðarson, eds., *Fjórar riddarasögur* (1852), containing *Sagan af Þorgrími kóngi og köppum hans, Sagan af Sálusi og Níkanor, Æfintýri af Ajax keisarasyni, Sagan af Valdimar kóngi;* Eugen Kölbing, ed., *Riddarasögur: Parcevals saga, Valvers þattr, Ívents saga, Mírmanns saga* (1872); Åke Lagerholm, ed., *Drei Lygisǫgur* (1927), containing *Ála flekks saga, Flóres saga konungs ok sona hans, Egils saga einhenda ok Ásmundar berserkjabana;* Agnete Loth, *Late Medieval Icelandic Romances,* 5 vols. (1962–1965), containing in vol. I, *Victors saga ok Blávus, Valdimars saga, Ectors saga,* in vol. II, *Saulus saga ok Nikanors, Sigurðar saga þǫgla,* in vol. III, *Jarlmanns saga ok Hermanns, Adonias saga, Sigurðar saga fóts,* in vol. IV, *Vilhjálms saga sjóðs, Vilmundar saga viðutan,* in vol. V, *Nitida saga, Sigrgarðs saga frækna, Sigrgarðs saga ok Valbrands, Sigurðar saga turnara, Hrings saga ok Tryggva* (texts accompanied by English résumés), and *Fornaldarsagas and Late Medieval Romances: AM 586 4to and AM 589 a-f 4to* (1977); Desmond Slay, ed., *Romances: Perg. 4:0 NR 6, Royal Library, Stockholm* (1972), containing *Amícus saga ok Amilíus, Bevers saga, Ívens saga, Parcevals saga, Valvens þáttr, Mirmants saga, Flóvents saga, Elis saga ok Rosamundu, Konráðs saga, Þjalar Jóns saga, Mǫttuls saga, Klári saga;* Bjarni Vilhjálmsson, ed., *Riddarasögur,* 6 vols. (1954)—contains I, *Saga af Tristram og Ísönd, Bevers saga, Mǫttuls saga;* II, *Ívens saga, Partalópa saga, Mágus saga jarls (hin meiri);* III, *Mírmanns saga, Sigurðar saga fóts, Konráðs saga, Samsons saga fagra;* IV, *Elis saga og Rósamundu, Flóres saga og Blankiflúr, Parcevals saga, Valvers þáttr;* V, *Klári saga, Flóres saga konungs og sona hans, Ála flekks saga, Rémundar saga* *keisarasonar;* VI, *Vilmundar saga viðutan, Sigurðar saga fóts, Tristrams saga og Ísoddar, Drauma-Jóns saga, Jarlmanns saga og Hermanns, Sarpidons saga sterka.*

Studies. Geraldine Barnes, "The *Riddarasögur* and Mediaeval European Literature," in *Mediaeval Scandinavia,* **8** (1975); Foster W. Blaisdell, Jr., "The So-called 'Tristram-group' of the *Riddarasögur,*" in *Scandinavian Studies,* **46** (1974), and "Some Observations on Style in the *Riddarasögur,*" in Carl F. Bayerschmidt and Erik J. Friis, eds., *Scandinavian Studies: Essays Presented to Dr. Henry Goddard Leach* (1965); Ingar M. Boberg, *Motif-index of Early Icelandic Literature* (1966); T. Damsgaard Olsen, "Den høviske litteratur," in Hans Bekker-Nielsen, T. Damsgaard Olsen, and Ole Widding, eds., *Norrøn fortællekunst: Kapitler af den norsk-islandske middelalderlitteraturs historie* (1965); Stefán Einarsson, *A History of Icelandic Literature* (1957); Peter Hallberg, *Stilsignalement och författarskap i norrön sagalitteratur* (1968), "Norröna riddarsagor: Några språkdrag," in *Arkiv för nordisk filologi,* **86** (1971), and "Is There a 'Tristram-group' of the *Riddarasögur?*" in *Scandinavian Studies,* **47** (1975); E. Fjeld Halvorsen, "Riddarasögur," in *Kindlers Literatur Lexikon,* VI (1971), cols. 267–274; Otto L. Jiriczek, "Zur mittelisländischen Volkskunde: Mitteilungen aus ungedruckten Arnamagnäanischen handschriften," in *Zeitschrift für deutsche Philologie,* **26** (1894); Eugen Kölbing, "Über isländische Bearbeitungen fremder Stoffe," in *Germania: Vierteljahrsschrift für deutsche Alterthumskunde,* **18** (n.s. 5) (1872); Finnur Jónsson, *Den oldnorske og oldislandske Litteraturs historie,* 2nd ed., II and III (1923–1924); Henry G. Leach, *Angevin Britain and Scandinavia* (1921, repr. 1975); Lars Lönnroth, *European Sources of Icelandic Saga-Writing* (1965); Konrad Maurer, "Islands und Norwegens Verkehr mit dem Süden vom 9.–13. Jahrhunderte," in *Zeitschrift für deutsche Philologie,* **2** (1870); P. M. Mitchell, "Scandinavian Literature," in Roger Sherman Loomis, ed., *Arthurian Literature in the Middle Ages* (1959, 5th repr., 1979); Eugen Mogk, *Geschichte der norwegisch-isländischen Literatur,* 2nd ed. (1904); Marius Hygaard, "Den lærde stil i den norrøne prosa," in *Sproglig-historiske Studier tilegnede professor C. R. Unger* (1896); *Les relations littéraires franco-scandinaves au moyen âge: Actes du colloque de Liège* (1975); Klaus Rossenbeck, *Die Stellung der Riddarasǫgur in der altnordischen Prosaliteratur* (1970); Margaret Schlauch, *Romance in Iceland* (1934); Kurt Schier, *Sagaliteratur* (1970); Einar Ól. Sveinsson, *Verzeichnis isländischer Märchenvarianten, mit einer einleitenden Untersuchung* (1929), and "Viktors saga ok Blávus: Sources and Characteristics," in *Viktors saga ok Blávus,* vol. II of Jónas Kristjánsson, ed., *Riddarasögur* (1964); Björn K. Þórólfsson, *Rímur fyrir 1600* (1934); Knud Togeby, "L'influence de la littérature française sur les littératures scandinaves au moyen âge," in Hans Ulrich Gumbrecht, ed., *Grundriss der romanischen Literaturen des Mittelalters,* I (1972); Mattias Tveitane, "Europeisk påvirkning på den norrøne sagalitteraturen: Noen synspunkter," in *Edda: Nordisk tidsskrift for litteraturforskning,* **69** (1969); Jan de Vries, *Altnordische Literaturgeschichte,* II, 2nd ed. (1967); Erik Wahlgren, *The Maiden King in Iceland* (1938).

MARIANNE E. KALINKE

[See also **Ála Flekks Saga; Alexanders Saga; Arthurian Literature; Bevers Saga; Boeve de Haumtone; Breta Sǫgur; Chanson de Geste; Chrétien de Troyes; Courtly Love; Erex Saga; Flóres Saga Konungs ok Sona Hans; Flóres Saga ok Blankiflúr; Fornaldarsögur; Ívens Saga; Jarlmanns Saga ok Hermanns; Karlamagnús Saga; Klári Saga; Konráðs Saga Keisarasonar; Lai, Lay; Mágus Saga Jarls; Marie de France; Matter of Britain, Matter of France, Matter of Rome; Mírmanns Saga; Möttuls Saga; Parcevals Saga; Partalopa Saga; Pseudo-Turpin; Rémundar Saga Keisarasonar; Samsons Saga Fagra; Sigurðar Saga Þögla; Strengleikar; Þiðreks Saga; Trójumanna Saga; Troy Story; Vilmundar Saga Viðutan; Vincent of Beauvais; Walter of Châtillon.**]

RIDDLES. The riddle, although a ubiquitous cultural phenomenon, enjoyed special popularity in the Middle Ages, developing into a literary form in both Latin and the vernaculars. The riddles that survive reflect learned as well as folk traditions and range from playful exercises in ingenuity to didactic tools. Many of them, particularly those in Latin, seem to have been employed in the schools as teaching devices, demonstrating, for instance, grammatical points or rhetorical techniques. Some riddles conveyed theological concepts and information about the physical world. Others, more akin to those of our own common experience, are simply playful, a challenge to the reader's or hearer's cleverness. Some are risqué, occasionally involving an innocent object described in terms that invite an obscene reply.

The most important influence upon the riddle genre as it developed in the Middle Ages was Symphosius, the composer or collector, sometime between the third and fifth centuries, of one hundred riddles in his *Aenigmata.* Symphosius influenced especially the Latin riddlers of England, who in turn had considerable influence on the Continent. Between Symphosius and the Anglo-Latin school comes the collection of sixty-two enigmas known as the Berne riddles, composed in Italy in the seventh century. Although Symphosius' work and

Hradčany Castle, Prague. The Vladislav Hall, by Benedikt Ried, 1493–1502. PHOTO: WERNER NEUMEISTER, MUNICH

the Berne riddles have a number of themes in common, the direct influence of the former on the latter has not been established. In England, however, Aldhelm (*ca.* 640–709/710), abbot of Malmesbury and bishop of Sherborne, who was the author of the most important Anglo-Latin collection, specifically acknowledges his debt to Symphosius. Aldhelm's one hundred hexameter *Aenigmata* are included in his prose *Epistola ad Acircium.* Not a riddle in the strict sense of presenting a puzzle to the reader, each of the *Aenigmata* is explained in its title. The subjects are meant to glorify God's creation; the answer to the final and longest riddle is, appropriately, *creatura* (creation), and the riddles serve as an important repository of details of Anglo-Saxon daily life. Other Anglo-Latin collections of note are those of Tatwine, archbishop of Canterbury (*d. ca.* 734), roughly a third of whose riddles are of a religious nature, and Eusebius, whom some identify with Hwaetberht, abbot of Wearmouth (*ca.* 680–*ca.* 747). Other collections from England survive, including a number of riddles traditionally, but erroneously, attributed to the Venerable Bede.

The collection of medieval riddles of most interest today is that included in the Old English Exeter Book. Uneven though it may be, it excels all its predecessors in literary merit. The Exeter Book riddles, the first known vernacular collection, are puzzling with respect to date as well as origin. Nineteenth-century attribution of the entire collection to Cynewulf has long since been discounted, as has the suggestion that they form even a unified group. One can say only that they were probably copied by a single scribe from various sources and that many of them date from the early eighth century, the rest later. Resemblances between the Exeter Book riddles and those of Symphosius, Aldhelm, Tatwine, and Eusebius are many, although, with the exception of a few clearly derived from Aldhelm, the evident kinship may result as much from reliance upon a common body of material—both folk and learned—as from direct influence.

Riddles as a literary form underwent a resurgence of interest during the Renaissance, as Tottel's *Miscellany* attests. In Italy and France, although not in England, the literary riddle flourished into the eighteenth century.

BIBLIOGRAPHY

The Exeter Book riddles are printed in George P. Krapp and Elliott Van Kirk Dobbie, eds., *The Exeter Book* (1936), 180–210, 224–225, and 229–243. A complete translation can be found in Paull F. Baum, *Anglo-Saxon Riddles of the Exeter Book* (1963). For texts and translations of Symphosius and Aldhelm, see Raymond T. Ohl, *The Enigmas of Symphosius* (1928) and James Hall Pitman, *The Riddles of Aldhelm* (1925, repr. 1970). For the texts of Tatwine and Eusebius, see Adolph Ebert, "Über die Räthselpoesie Angelsachsen, insbesondre die Aenigmata des Tatwine und Eusebius," in *Berichte über die Verhandlungen der königlich sächsischen Gesellschaft der Wissenschaften zu Leipzig,* **29** (1877). For the pseudo-Bede riddles, see Frederick Tupper, Jr., "Riddles of the Bede Tradition," in *Modern Philology,* **2** (1904–1905).

Studies of a general nature include D. G. Blauner, "The Early Literary Riddle," in *Folklore,* **78** (1967); Erika von Erhardt-Siebold, *Die lateinischen Rätsel der Angelsachsen* (1925); Agop J. Hacikyan, *A Linguistic and Literary Analysis of Old English Riddles* (1966); Archer Taylor, *The Literary Riddle Before 1600* (1948, repr. 1976); F. H. Whitman, "Medieval Riddling: Factors Underlying Its Development," in *Neuphilologische Mitteilungen,* **71** (1970).

MELVIN STORM

[See also **Aldhelm; Anglo-Saxon Literature; Anthologia Latina; Tatwine of Canterbury.**]

RIED, BENEDIKT (*ca.* 1454–1534), late Gothic master mason who had a long and influential career in both ecclesiastical and secular building in Bohemia, Saxony, and Silesia. Among his many projects were the Vladislav Hall in Hradčany Castle, Prague; additional work on St. Vitus Cathedral in Prague; the completion of major churches in Kutná Hora, Annaberg, and Louny; and the construction of Frankenstein Castle in Silesia.

BIBLIOGRAPHY
Götz Fehr, *Benedikt Ried* (1961).

LON R. SHELBY

[See also **Gothic Architecture; Masons and Builders; Prague.**]

RIEMENSCHNEIDER, TILMAN (*fl.* 1478–1531), one of Germany's most successful sculptors in both stone and limewood. Active in Würzburg from 1485 until the mid 1520's, he pioneered the use of monochrome unpainted wood altarpieces (Münnerstadt, 1490–1492; Rothenburg, St. Jacob's Church, 1501–1505; Creglingen, 1505–1510). Riemenschneider is also famed for his funerary effigies, especially the Monument of Lorenz von Bibra, Würzburg Cathedral (1519–1522), and the Monument of Henry II and Kunigunde, Bamberg Cathedral (1499–1513). His work is characterized by his great attention to surface description and by his refined, delicate figures.

BIBLIOGRAPHY
Michael Baxandall, *The Limewood Sculptors of Renaissance Germany* (1980), 172–190, 259–265; Justus Bier, *Tilmann Riemenschneider,* 4 vols. (1925–1978); Max Hermann von Freeden, *Tilman Riemenschneider* (1954); Kurt Gerstenberg, *Tilman Riemenschneider* (1941, 1962); Hubert Schrade, *Tilmann Riemenschneider,* 2 vols. (1927).

LARRY SILVER

[See also **Altarpiece; Retable.**]

RIGORD (1145/1150—*ca.* 1208), a monk of the royal abbey of St. Denis near Paris, is best known for his history of the reign of King Philip II Augustus of France, the *Gesta Philippi Augusti.* Born in a village of lower Languedoc, he first practiced medicine before joining the abbey in 1186. Apparently he began writing the *Gesta* before he entered St. Denis but did not complete it until the first months of 1196, when it was presented to the king. For this work Rigord acquired the title of royal chronicler (*cronographus regis francorum*), making him the first semiofficial historian of the French monarchy. In addition to the *Gesta Philippi Augusti,* Rigord also wrote a *Short Chronicle of the Kings of France,* in which he sketched the history of France from earliest, legendary times. This text survives only in fragments of a manuscript preserved at the Bibliothèque Municipale of Soissons (MS 129, fols. 130–137). He died while at work on a revision of the *Gesta.*

The Last Supper (detail). Carved altarpiece by Tilman Riemenschneider from St. Jacob's Church, Rothenburg, 1501–1505. PHOTO: WIM SWAAN

BIBLIOGRAPHY
Editions. For the text of Rigord's *Gesta,* see Henri-François Delaborde, ed., *Oeuvres de Rigord et de Guillaume le Breton,* I (1882). Delaborde, "Une courte chronique des rois de France," in *Bibliothèque de l'École des chartes,* **45** (1884), includes a partial edition of the *Short Chronicle.*
Studies. M. Daunou, "Rigord," in *Histoire littéraire de la France,* XVII (1832), 5–20; Gabrielle M. Spiegel,

The Chronicle Tradition of Saint-Denis: A Survey (1978), 56–63.

GABRIELLE M. SPIEGEL

[See also **Biography, French; Biography, Secular; Guillaume le Breton; Philip II Augustus.**]

RÍGSÞULA (The chant of Rígr) is a poem of forty-eight stanzas generally included with the *Poetic Edda,* though preserved only in a manuscript of the *Prose Edda* (*Codex Wormianus,* AM 242 fol.). It differs markedly from other Eddic poetry in being neither mythic nor heroic, nor even gnomic like the *Hávamál.* It has the form of a culture myth relating and legitimizing the divine origin of the social order. The three social classes of Germanic life are traced back to the god Rígr (a name that seems to be derived from Irish *ríg,* king). He is not included in Snorri's Norse pantheon, though the compiler of the manuscript identifies him (on unknown grounds) with Heimdall (he behaves more like Odin). *Rígsþula*'s time and place of origin have been much debated, with dating ranging from Viking Ireland to thirteenth-century Norway (the age of King Hákon Hákonarson). Whatever its origin, it is of extraordinary sociocultural interest for its descriptive details of the lives and relative prestige of the social classes in ancient Scandinavia.

In times of yore, relates the poem, the god Rígr wandered on "green paths" to visit in succession the homes of Ái the great-grandfather and Edda the great-grandmother, of Afi the grandfather and Amma the grandmother, of Faðir the father and Móðir the mother. In each home he was well received and entertained, simply in the first, elaborately in the second, sumptuously in the third. He was even welcomed into the conjugal beds, begetting sons named Thræll the slave in the first, Karl the freeholder in the second, and Jarl the earl (nobleman) in the third. Each of his sons marries a woman of suitable class and begets children whose names are clearly indicative (and amusingly so) of their respective classes. Thræll and his family are dark and shriveled, ugly and deformed: they manure the fields, herd swine and goats, dig turf, and build fences. Karl and his family are handsome and well groomed; they plow the fields, build homes and perform crafts, and spin and weave. Jarl and his family are blond and keen-eyed; they drink wine and "pass judgment," their tablecloths are of linen, and their occupation is to make war: forge weapons, tame horses, train dogs. When Jarl is grown, Rígr returns to acknowledge him by conferring on him his own name and teaching him the art of runes. Rígr's favorite is Jarl's youngest son, Konr *ungr* (young kinsman), whom he trains in the highest magic skills, including the language of the birds. A bird urges him to seek out the princes Danr and Danpr, but here the poem breaks off, no doubt by a copyist's inadvertence. It is clearly intended that Konr *ungr* is to become the first *konungr* (king). The wordplay suggests that the immediate purpose of the poem may be to glorify kingship, for which reason some have seen in it an allusion to Hákon (the high kinsman?) and his conflict with the Danes.

In spite of its didactic content, the poem is a magnificent work of art, adorned with precise and suggestive details, and building to a climax in true fairy-tale style. Its very artfulness and logical structure support the thesis of a late origin, propounded by Klaus von See, and could relate it to Snorri Sturluson's mythography. Yet its contents describe a society that need be no younger than the Viking Age. That it also confirms the divine right of kings allies its contents with the well-known concept of sacral kingship. Georges Dumézil views the poem as reflecting the tripartite structure of Indo-European society, while A. Y. Gurevich compares it to the European schema of *laboratores, bellatores,* and *oratores* (workers, soldiers, priests).

BIBLIOGRAPHY

Text, translation, and bibliography. Standard edition is Gustav Neckel, ed., *Edda: Die Lieder des Codex Regius nebst verwandten Denkmälern,* 4th ed., rev. by Hans Kuhn (1962). English translations are in Henry Adams Bellows, ed. and trans., *The Poetic Edda* (1923, repr. 1957, 1969); Lee M. Hollander, ed. and trans., *The Poetic Edda* (1928, 2nd ed. 1962). Bibliography is in *Islandica,* **13** (1920) and **37** (1955).

Studies. Georges Dumézil, "The Rígsþula and Indo-European Social Structure," John Lindow, trans., in Dumézil, *Gods of the Ancient Northmen,* Einar Haugen, ed. (1973); Jere Fleck, "*Konr—Óttarr-Geirroðr:* A Knowledge Criterion for Succession to the Germanic Sacred Kingship," in *Scandinavian Studies,* **42** (1970); A. Y. Gurevich, "Sociological Interpretations of Rígsþula," (Russian with Swedish summary), in *Skandinavskii sbornik,* **18** (1973); Einar Haugen, "The Mythical Structure of the Ancient Scandinavians: Some Thoughts on Reading Dumézil," in *To Honor Roman Jakobson,* II (1967); Klaus von See, "Das Alter der Rígsþula," in *Acta* *philologica scandinavica,* **24** (1957); Einar Ólafur Sveinsson, *Íslenzkar bókmenntir í fornöld,* I (1962).

EINAR HAUGEN

[See also **Eddic Poetry; Odin; Scandinavian Mythology; Vikings.**]

RIMBERT, ST. (*ca.* 830–888), also spelled Rembert, grew up under the tutelage of Ansgar (Anskar), whom he succeeded as archbishop of Hamburg-Bremen in 865 and whose biography, *Vita Anskarii,* he wrote shortly afterward. This biography is one of the most important of the Middle Ages, not only because it gives a great deal of circumstantial detail about its subject (such as the loss of his library to Danish pirates), based on personal conversation, but also because it is the earliest source of reliable information about the Scandinavian countries visited by Ansgar. Unlike most vitae, it is a factual biography, with little attempt to embellish its subject by references to the classics or the Bible.

BIBLIOGRAPHY

Vita Anskarii in Werner Tillmich, ed., *Quellen des 9. und 11. Jahrhunderts zur Geschichte der hamburgischen Kirche und des Reiches* (1961); Max Manitius, *Geschichte der lateinischen Literatur des Mittelalters,* I (1959), 705–707.

W. T. H. JACKSON

[See also **Birka; Denmark; Missions and Missionaries, Christian.**]

RÍMUR (singular, *ríma*), Icelandic "metrical romances."

DEFINITION

In Iceland during the fourteenth century, at a time when the writing of prose sagas was beginning to decline, there began to develop a unique kind of narrative poetry: stanzaic, usually long enough to be broken into fits or chapters, and paying strict attention to the niceties of alliteration and syllable count. These poems became very popular during the fifteenth century, which was a period more noted for the energy spent in copying manuscripts than for that devoted to creative endeavors. It is fair to say that this poetry dominated the Icelandic literary scene from the fifteenth until well into the nineteenth century, not only making an indelible mark on what might be called the Icelandic literary consciousness, but probably also playing a major role in helping to preserve intact the inflectional system of the Icelandic language.

These poems, or *rímur,* may be called metrical romances so long as it is kept in mind that they are separate in origin from the Continental romances, and that the term "romance," like the Old French *roman,* has no formal restrictions on what the authors consider suitable subject matter. The term *rímur* is probably a loan word from English, although it is not possible to determine at what time the word entered Icelandic. Old English *rīman,* "to enumerate, to recount," developed the Middle English cognate *rime,* "romance, story," which is used exactly as the Icelandic term. In *Piers Plowman* (B-text, V, 395), Sloth says, "But I kan rymes of Robin hood and Randolf Erl of Chestre." *A Gest of Robyn Hode* (fifteenth century), although traditionally classified as a ballad, has all the formal characteristics (apart from a lack of alliteration) of the *rímur,* including the meter and the division into fits. And Sir William Craigie, the premier English authority on the *rímur,* was always fond of pointing out that Coleridge's *The Rime of the Ancient Mariner* (1798) showed a spiritual affinity to its otherwise unrelated Icelandic counterparts.

HISTORY AND CHARACTERISTICS

The division between medieval and modern *rímur* has been conventionally set at 1600, largely on the basis of phonological grounds. Some seventy-five *rímur* from before this date survive (of which nearly thirty remain unpublished), and it is this period which has been the most extensively studied, especially by Björn K. Þórólfsson. The largest collection of early *rímur* (*rímnaflokkar*), thirty-three in all, is found in a vellum manuscript (AM. 604, 4to, *Staðarhólsbók*) written about 1530. Another major collection, sixteen *rímnaflokkar* (in Codex Guelferbytanus 47.2. Augusteus quarto, *Kollsbók*), was written about 1480–1490.

Subject matter. The subject matter of the early *rímur* is varied, but by far the largest number of the surviving poems are based on *riddarasögur* (sagas of knights). These are, in order of probable composition, with the number of fits indicated, and unpublished *rímur* marked with an asterisk: *Hringur og Tryggvi,* 13 (also called *Geðraunir,* and based on a saga now lost); *Dámusti,* 4; *Blávus og*

Viktor, 12; *Sigurður fótur*, 5; *Sálus og Nikanór*, 11; *Filippó*, 8 (also called *Krítarþáttur*); *Geirarð*, 8 (based on *Mágus saga*); *Herburt*, 4; *Geiplur*, 4 (based on *Karlamagnús saga*, part 7, "Af Jórsalaferð"); *Landrés*, 9 (based on *Karlamagnús saga*, part 2, "Af frú Ólíf og Landrés"); *Skikkja*, 3 (based on *Möttuls saga*); *Konráð*, 8; *Dínus*, 4; *Bragða-Mágus*, 9; *Haraldur Hringsbani*, 6 (based on a saga now lost); *Vilmundur viðutan* by Ormur, 16; **Bæringur*, 12; **Hektor*, 16; **Reinald og Rósa*, 12 (based on a saga now lost); **Mábil sterka*, 10 (based on a saga now lost); **Sigurður þögli*, 15; **Sigurður Fornason*, 3 (based on a saga now lost); **Jarlmann*, 12; **Rollant*, 6 (based on *Karlamagnús saga*, part 4, "Af Agulando konungi"); *Pontus*, 30 (based on the German folk-book *Pontus und Sidonia*); *Amicus og Amilíus*, 12 (also called *Raunaflokkur*); **Valdimar frækni*, 8; **Rollant* by Þórður, 18 (also called *Keisararaunir* and based on *Karlamagnús saga*, part 8, "Af Rúnzivals bardaga"); **Þjalar-Jón*, 16; **Vilmundur viðutan* by Hallur, 24; **Mírmant*, 12; **Oddgeir danski*, 10 (based on *Karlamagnús saga*, part 3, "Af Oddgeiri danska," and *Kong Olger danskis krønike*, published in 1534).

Closely related to the *riddarasögur* in style and subject matter and also well represented among the early *rímur* are those based on the *fornaldar sögur Norðurlanda* (sagas of the north in ancient times). These *rímur* are: *Sörli sterki*, 6; *Völsungur*, 6; *Friðþjófur frækni*, 5; *Úlfhamur*, 6 (also called *Vargstökkur* and based on a saga now lost); *Hjálmþér*, 11; *Grímur og Hjálmar*, 4 (based on a saga now lost); *Bjarki*, 8 (based on *Skjöldunga saga* and *Hrólfs saga kraka*); *Hrómundur Gripsson*, 6 (also called *Griplur* and based on a saga now lost); *Sturlaugur*, 7; *Bósi*, 10; *Án bogsveigir*, 8; **Hrólfur Gautreksson*, 5; **Ormar Framarsson*, 4 (based on a saga now lost); **Ölvir sterki Hákonarson*, 6 (based on a saga now lost); **Andri jarl*, 13 (also called *Öndrur* and based on a saga now lost); **Illugi eldhúsgoði*, 6 (based on a saga now lost); **Þórir háleggur*, 10 (based on a saga now lost); **Hálfdan Brönufóstri*, 16 (also called *Brönurímur*); **Ásmundur og Egill einhendi*, 10 (also called *Eglur*); **Hálfdan Eysteinsson*, 12; **Göngu-Hrólfur*, 20.

The *konungasögur* (sagas of kings) provide the material for four early *rímur*: *Ólafur Haraldsson*, 1 (Stiklastaðaorrusta); *Ólafur Tryggvason*, 3 (Indriða þáttur ilbreiðs); *Ólafur Tryggvason*, 5 (Svöldrarorrusta); *Ólafur Haraldsson*, 2 (Rauðúlfs þáttur).

Rímur based on the *íslendingasögur* (family sagas) are few, suggesting that there were perhaps at this time some unstated restrictions on the type of material considered suitable for these poems. Surviving are: *þrænlur*, 10 (based on *Færeyinga saga*); *Grettir*, 8 (also called *Grettlur*); *Króka-Refur*, 8; *Skáld-Helgi*, 8 (based on a saga now lost); *Hemingur*, 6. Two *rímur* exist based on Eddic material, *Lokrur*, 4 (based on the Útgarða-Loki episode in *Snorra Edda*), and *þrymlur*, 3 (based on *þrymskviða*).

The remaining *rímur* fall into three groups, none of which goes back to saga material. The largest group is based on international folktales (märchen) and is similar in style and content to the *riddararímur*: *Jón leiksveinn*, 3; *Virgiles*, 2 (also called *Glettudiktur*); *Klerkar*, 5 (also called *Klerkaspil*); **Skógar-Kristur*, 2; *Móðar*, 2; **Hermóður*, 10. Two single-fit poems are satires: *Skíði*, 1 (an account of the vagabond Skíði's dream-visit to Valhöll) and *Fjós*, 1 (a satire on a fight in a cow shed with a list of the ancient heroes who never chose such a site for combat). The third group consists of *rímur* based on exempla: **þjófar, eður Ill Verri, Verst*, 4 (based on "Af þrimr þjófum í Danmörk"); **Jónatus*, 3 (based on chapter 120 of the *Gesta Romanorum*); **Órn*, 3 (a Christian allegory based on a bestiary account of the eagle).

Rímur before 1500. Ólafs ríma Haraldssonar (Stiklastaðaorrusta) is by Einar Gilsson, *lögmaður* (chief legal official) for the north and west of Iceland, 1367–1369. The poem is preserved in *Flateyjarbók*, so it cannot be dated later than about 1390. This is the earliest *ríma*, but dating and attribution of authorship in the later *rímur* are problematical. Björn K. Þórólfsson proposed a tentative chronology in 1934, but it has not stood up well to more recent research. While most of the early *rímur* are anonymous, some are associated with named authors. This may take the form of a first name found in a poem, as with Kálfur skáld (*Völsungs rímur*, IV:49, "Vitulus vates"), Björn (*Geðraunir*, XI:59), Þorsteinn (*Hjalmþérs rímur*, XI:55), Guðmundur (*þjófa rímur*, IV:76–77), Jón (*þjalar-Jóns rímur*, I:3), or Ormur (*Vilmundar rímur*, XVI:66). The latter had been confidently identified as Ormur Loftsson (*fl. ca.* 1450), but these *rímur* have been reassigned to *ca.* 1530 and that attribution is no longer valid. The greatest controversy has raged over the authorship of *Skíða ríma*, which in the earliest traditions had been attributed to a certain Einar fóstri (*fl. ca.* 1450), although in the eighteenth century the names Sigurður fóstri

Þórðarson (*fl. ca.* 1440) and Svartur Þórðarson á Hofstöðum (*fl. ca.* 1470) were linked with the poem. While the matter is still unresolved, the otherwise unknown Einar fóstri still appears to have the best claim on the poem.

Rímur after 1500. The names of a number of *rímur* poets from the beginning of the sixteenth century have been preserved. The most important of these is Sigurður blindi. His fame as a poet was widespread and is preserved in an old verse:

Það er að segja af Sigurði blind:
samdi hann ljóð um hverja kind,
sá hann hvorki sól né vind,
seggjum þótti hann kveða með hind.

[This is said of Sigurður blindi: he composed poems on all sorts of topics, he saw neither sun nor wind, it seemed to men he composed with elegance.]

Numerous *rímur* have been attributed to him, including *Andra rímur* and *Reinalds rímur,* although none with certainty. Tradition also has it that Sigurður blindi and Jón Arason (1484–1550), the last Catholic bishop of Hólar, together composed *Hektors rímur*. Contemporary with Sigurður blindi was another blind poet, Rögnvaldur blindi. To him are attributed *Skógar-Krists rímur, Brönurímur,* and others. Even when the full name of an author is known, this is not necessarily of any help, as in the case of Árni Jónsson (*fl. ca.* 1550), who appears to have written *Hálfdans rímur Eysteinssonar,* but who is otherwise unknown. It is only in the latter part of the sixteenth century that the matter of authorship becomes less problematical. Chief among the *rímur* poets at this time is Þórður Magnússon á Strjúgi (*fl. ca.* 1580), who wrote *Fjósa ríma, Rollants rímur* (*Keisararaunir*), and *Valdimars rímur,* and whose name has been linked less certainly with others. The first five fits of *Mírmants rímur* are attributed to Andrés Magnússon (*fl. ca.* 1550). Magnús Jónsson prúði (*ca.* 1525–1591) wrote the first thirteen fits of *Pontus rímur* and his name is linked less certainly with other *rímur.* Hallur Magnússon (*d.* 1601) wrote *Vilmundar rímur,* Ormur Jónsson í Gufudal (*fl. ca.* 1600) wrote *Gögu-Hrólfs rímur,* and the historian and scholar Arngrímur Jónsson lærði (1568–1648) wrote *Arna rímur.*

Origins. The origins of the *rímur* remain obscure. What is clear is that the traditional view that would derive them from dances and ballads is no longer adequate. In many ways the emergence in Iceland of the *rímur* during the fourteenth and fifteenth centuries presents a situation parallel to the Middle English alliterative revival; while the lines of descent are clear, the exact processes by which the earlier forms developed into the latter remain a mystery. Einar Gilsson's *Ólafs ríma* gives no indication of being other than written within a well-established literary tradition. How old this tradition is, it is not possible to say. Nor do the surviving dances and ballads provide any clues to the origins of the *rímur.* Even though the most common ballad (and dance) meter is similar to the most common *rímur* meter, it is sufficiently different to make a demonstrable connection between the two varieties unlikely. Also, the narrative technique in the ballads is so different from that found in the *rímur,* which, added to the growing evidence that points to the ballads being a much later phenomenon than previously suspected, makes it more satisfactory to consider each of these types of poetry as having separate origins. Where then is one to look for the origins of the *rímur*? Much more research still has to be done before a positive response can be given to this question, but some lines of investigation look particularly promising.

Eddic poetic influences. It seems clear that the origin of the *rímur* lies in no single source but that they developed under the influence of a number of different stimuli. The art of narrative poetry was not unknown during the earliest centuries of the settlement of Iceland. The poems of the Edda share with the *rímur* two important characteristics: both groups of poems are narrative, covering a variety of topics, heroic as well as mythological, and both are stanzaic in form (as opposed to the nonstanzaic variety of Germanic heroic poetry exemplified by *Beowulf*). The *rímur* are an indigenous Icelandic tradition and are in all likelihood a direct descendant of these earlier Eddic poems, for it was in Iceland that the Eddic traditions were preserved the longest. But in diction and meter the *rímur* differ greatly from the poems of the Edda.

The most common Eddic meter is *fornyrðislag,* and the Eddic poems are singularly lacking in stylistic ornamentation through the use of *heiti* (appellations) and kennings (metaphorical expressions). From as early as the ninth century occasional poetry in the *dróttkvætt* meter survives. In the hands of the court poets, this so-called skaldic poetry became widespread and popular, developing into an elaborate, formal, occasional poetry, a type of poetry that is singularly unsuitable to narrative. Despite the individual beauties of some of the longer poems of this type, their effectiveness lies in the accumulation of detail rather than in any developed sense of narrative technique.

Vocabulary and poetic devices. If the *rímur* are closer to the Edda in terms of narrative technique, they nevertheless owe their debt to the skaldic poetry in terms of their diction, which is replete in the use of the *heiti* and kennings so favored by the skalds and which have been exhaustively catalogued by Rudolf Meissner in *Die Kenningar der Skalden* (1921). In *Rímur fyrir 1600,* Björn K. Þórólfsson uses Meissner's classification system to provide an overview of the use of *heiti* and kennings in the early *rímur.* These *heiti* and kennings have much in common with their skaldic counterparts. Thus for both types of poetry the *heiti* for gold include: *hodd,* "hord, treasure"; *seimur,* "wealth"; *taurar,* "riches." Similarly, both types of poetry share gold kennings such as *dögg Draupnis,* "the drops of the ring Draupnir"; *jötna rómur,* "the voice of the giants"; *Rínar grjót,* "pebble of the Rhine"; *sævar bál,* "flame of the sea." The early *rímur* relied heavily on *Snorra Edda* as a source for their *heiti* and kennings, but as the sixteenth century progressed, the older traditions became weakened and inappropriate kennings begin to make their appearance, some of which become established as satisfactory *rímur* kennings.

Not only did individual poets use *heiti* and kennings to ornament their verses, they could also use them as a code under which to conceal their names or the names of those for whom the poems may have been intended. This practice of *fólgin nöfn,* "concealed names," is found in some of the early *rímur,* although it becomes more frequent in later centuries. As can be seen from the so-called Icelandic rune poem, not only did the runes have names, but these names could have a wider lexical significance: the first letter of the runic alphabet, *fé,* meant both this letter and wealth, and so on. To illustrate this practice are the following two stanzas from Ormur's *Vilmundar rímur,* XVI:64–65.

Veraldar prýði og veglegt ár,	S		A
vimra mót við græði,		O	
auðurinn nógur og ísinn blár,	F		I
eignast máttu kvæði.			
Veglegt hvíld og vatna mót,	R		O
virða gamanið blíða,		M	
grátur skýja og ferðin fljót,	U		R
ferju Hárs nam smíða.			

[The ornament of the world (*sól,* "sun" = S) and the noble year (*ár,* "year" = A), the meeting place of the rivers (*Vimur* = a river *heiti*) with the sea (*ós,* "estuary" = O), sufficient wealth (*fé,* "wealth" = F) and the bright ice (*ís,* "ice" = I), you (Sofía) may have this poem.
Noble repose (*reið,* "riding" = R) and the meeting place of the waters (*ós* = O), the pleasant delight of men (*maður,* "man" = M: *maðr er manns gaman,* "man is the delight of man," *Hávamál,* 47), the weeping of the clouds (*úr,* "drizzle" = U) and the rapid journey (*reið* = R), (Ormur) made the boat of Hár (Óðinn) (= the poem).]

Meters. When it comes to the origins of the *rímur* meters, the greatest amount of uncertainty is found. By the end of the nineteenth century, Helgi Sigurðsson was able to divide these *rímur* meters into twenty-three principal divisions, and in addition to catalogue over two thousand named individual varieties of these meters.

The most common meter is *ferskeytt,* "square meter." In a survey by Björn K. Þórólfsson of sixty-one *rímur* written before 1600, 178 out of a total of 438 fits are composed in ordinary *ferskeytt,* a total that rises to 208 if certain more complicated forms of *ferskeytt* are added. *Ferskeytt* has four lines rhyming *a b a b.* The first and third lines have seven syllables, the second and fourth lines six syllables.

Grettir *höggin geysistór*
gumnum lét á ríða,
aldrei hann í kúa kór
kom til þess að stríða.
(*Fjósa ríma,* stanza 39)

[Grettir knew how to land mighty blows on men, he never went into a cow shed (cow choir) to fight.]

As in all four-line *rímur* meters there are two alliterating words in the first and third lines, one in the second and fourth. The meter can be made more complicated by the addition of internal rhymes, as in this example of *ferskeytt, aldýra* (showing full use of internal rhyme), *alhent* (showing rhymes in the first and third syllables of each line), and *tályklað* (showing rhymes in the fifth and seventh syllables of the first and third lines).

Ráðum dáðum Rósa ljós
rís í prís enn hærra,
hári kláru hrósar drós,
hálmi og málmi skærra.
(*Reinalds rímur,* XII:12)

[On account of her good counsel the beautiful Rósa

rose still higher in esteem, the woman boasts shining hair, fairer than straw or steel.]

While this meter (or one very similar to it) is found among the European vernaculars, there are various problems in attempting to link these forms to *ferskeytt,* and it seems most plausible to seek the origin of the Icelandic form in an Irish counterpart. In Irish poetry, in both Latin and Gaelic, are found meters from as early as the eighth century that bear striking similarities to *ferskeytt* (the Icelandic innovations were to have masculine rhyme in the first and third lines, and to shorten the second and fourth lines by one syllable). An example in the vernacular is found in a poem of praise to St. Columba (Columcille; in Icelandic, Kolumkilla) written about 700. The poem is said to be *laíd imrind,* "having full end rhyme"; four-line stanzas rhyming *a b a b,* each line with seven syllables, with the last word of each line alliterating with the first word of the next line.

Níbu fri coilcthi tincha
tindscan ernaigdi cassa,
crochais—níbu hi cinta—
a chorp for tonna glassa.
(Fergus Kelly, ed., in *Ériu,* **24** [1973], stanza 2)

[It was not on soft beds he undertook elaborate prayers. He crucified—it was not for crimes—his body on the green waves.]

This is similar, if not identical, to the meter found in poems such as the seventh-century *Versiculi Familiae Benchuir,* and a form identical to *ferskeytt* in syllable count is found in the Icelandic *Sancti Thorlaci episcopi officia rhythmica et proprium missæ* (*Þorlákstíðir,* from the early fourteenth century). The following stanza has the proper alliteration in lines three and four.

Hunc canoro iubilo
veneretur orbis
cecis, mutis, mutilo
medetur et orbis.
(Robert A. Ottósson, ed., stanza 28)

[The world reveres him (Þorlákur) with tuneful song, he cures the blind, the dumb, the crippled, and the world.]

Another common meter is *skáhenda,* in which thirty fits are written in the corpus surveyed by Björn K. Þórólfsson. This meter has four lines rhyming *a b c b.* Lines one and three have seven syllables and lines two and four six syllables. In lines one and three, the third and seventh syllables of each line rhyme.

Ræða skal í Rögnis sal
Róms að einu bragði
Ástir þá við auða Ná
Amilíus að lagði.
(*Amicus og Amilíus rímur,* III:30)

[I shall say in the hall of the voice (= breast) of Rögnir (Óðinn) (= poetry, the poem) that in a single glance Amilíus fell in love with the Ná (= Gná, a *heiti* for goddess) of the gold ornament (= woman).]

This meter may also have developed from Latin hymn meters associated with Ireland, especially a *rhythmus* such as the ninth-century *Rhythmus ad Deum,* although this particular poem appears to have been widely distributed in Anglo-Saxon England and on the Continent (there exists one manuscript glossed in Old High German), so that it is not possible to be sure of a direct connection between the Irish and Icelandic versions of this meter. It may be, as Vésteinn Ólason suggests, that the form entered Icelandic from Middle High German.

The other early *rímur* meters have not been fully researched. They are *úrkast* (four lines, rhyming *a b a b,* eight syllables in lines one and three, four syllables in lines two and four); *stafhenda* (four lines rhyming *a a b b,* each line with seven syllables); *samhenda* (four lines rhyming *a a a a,* each line with seven syllables—both *stafhenda* and *samhenda* follow rhyme schemes and syllable counts found widely in early Latin hymns); *braghenda* (three lines, rhyming *aaa,* the first line with twelve syllables and three alliterating words, lines two and three with eight syllables each); *stuðlafall* (three lines rhyming *a b b,* line one with ten syllables, two alliterating words, and a feminine ending, lines two and three with seven syllables each and masculine endings).

By the end of the sixteenth century new meters began to make their appearance, such as *afhending* (two lines rhyming *a a,* the first line with twelve syllables and three alliterating words, the second line with eight syllables and two alliterating words); *stikluvik* (four lines rhyming *a b a a,* lines one, three, and four with seven syllables, line two with six syllables); *gag(a)raljóð* (four lines rhyming *a b a b,* each with seven syllables).

The mansöngur. Even though the *rímur* are narrative poems, it appears to have soon become the custom to introduce each *ríma* with non-narrative material called a *mansöngur* (singular; plural, *mansöngvar*). The word *mansöngur,* "maid song," originally applied to occasional poetry addressed to women (and as such apparently provocative to nonfeminine audiences, with the result that this poetry is severely proscribed in the earliest surviving Icelandic law code, *Grágás*). By the time the term came to apply to the non-narrative introductions to the individual *ríma,* its nature had changed somewhat. Not all the early *rímur* have *mansöngvar,* and in some poems there is a substantial *mansöngur* only to the first *ríma,* with a *mansöngur* of only one or two stanzas to subsequent fits. In those instances where the *mansögvar* are absent or brief, it is not clear if this represents the original state of affairs, or if the copyists have deliberately omitted the *mansöngvar* or shortened them, a practice that is quite common in subsequent centuries. Nor is it clear why the *mansöngvar* became associated with the *rímur,* but by the middle of the fifteenth century the custom of introducing each *ríma* with a *mansöngur* is well established and continues to be a feature of the *rímur* thereafter. The early *mansöngvar* retain their links with the earlier poetry under the same name by being largely about love, although as time progresses a variety of topics become appropriate.

The tone of the *mansöngvar* varies, but common themes in the early *rímur* are the misfortunes of love and the praises of women. The *mansöngvar* most clearly demonstrate the existence in Iceland of the themes of love encountered in the continental traditions of *fin'amors.* Not only do individual *mansöngvar* lament the miseries of being in love, they may also list famous instances from the Bible and secular narratives of those who landed in misfortune as a result of love, and if a *mansöngur* is dedicated to an individual woman, the poet may take the occasion to praise the beauties of women in general. One remarkable feature of the early *mansöngvar* is the frequent reference to Ovid, bearing witness to a continuous familiarity with the Roman poet, which goes back to at least the twelfth century (*Jóns saga biskups*).

PRESENTATION OF THE *RÍMUR*

There is every reason to believe that the presentation of the *rímur* changed little over the centuries. They were never an "oral poetry" in the accepted sense of the term, for they were never composed extemporaneously. Neither were they a poetry principally to be read, however. The *rímur* were entertainments provided during the evening activities (working wool, making rope, and so on) as well as on festive occasions. They were not read, but rather chanted or *kveðið* (from *kveða,* "to recite poetry"), the melody being extended over the stanza and repeated or varied in the following stanzas according to the style or skill of the *kvæðamaður* or reciter. The reciter was unaccompanied but sometimes would be joined by a second voice, and they would then recite in harmony (*tvísöngur*). Each of the *rímur* meters had melodies (*rímnalög, kvæðalög, stemmur*) appropriate to them, and although most of the surviving *rímnalög* are in the diatonic major scales, some, which are of undoubted antiquity, are in the pentatonic, modal, and minor scales. These are likely to have had their roots in medieval secular and ecclesiastical music, but this topic has yet to be systematically researched.

Despite—or perhaps because of—the popularity of the *rímur,* they were not equally welcomed in all quarters. In *Eín ny Psalma Bók* (1589), Guðbrandur Þorláksson (*ca.* 1541–1627), bishop of Hólar, lets the *rímur* head the list of the types of poetry he finds most objectionable, poetry he hoped (vainly as it turned out) the contents of the new hymnbook would supplant.

> Finally [I prepared this book] for this reason, that they [the Icelandic people] may cease from useless versification, romances [*rímur*] of trolls and ancient heroes, love songs [*mansöngvar*], amorous verses, passionate poems, satirical and insulting verses, and other wicked and disgusting poetry, filth, slander and maliciousness, which here among the common people are a great deal more loved and practiced, God and his angels to anger, the devil and his imps to delight and serve, than in any other Christian land.

This is only the first in a series of learned and pious objections to the *rímur* over the following centuries. Yet the *rímur* continued to flourish, and it was not until the nineteenth century, when a radical change of taste was coupled with an equally radical change in economic and social conditions, that the *rímur* were eventually supplanted as the single most important literary genre and one of the favorite means of entertainment in Icelandic popular culture.

BIBLIOGRAPHY

Facsimilies. William Craigie, *Early Icelandic Rímur: MS No. 604 4to of the Arna-Magnæan Collection in the*

University Library of Copenhagen (1938); Ólafur Halldórsson, *Kollsbók: Codex Guelferbytanus 47.2. Augusteus Quarto* (1968).

Editions. Mevrouvd Petronella Maria (den Hoed) Boer, *Hemingsrímur* (1928); Finnur Jónsson, ed., *Hrólfs saga kraka og Bjarkarímur* (1904), and *Rímnasafn: Samling af de ældste islandske rimer,* 2 vols. (1905–1922), containing the following *rímur*: Ólafur Haraldsson (Stiklastaðaorrusta), Skíði, Grettir, Skáld-Helgi, Ólafur Tryggvason (Indríða þáttur ilbreiða), Ólafur Tryggvason (Svoldrarorrusta), Ólafur Haraldsson (Rauðúlfs þáttur), Þrænlur, Þrymlur, Lokrur, Völsungur, Griplur; Friðþjófur, Sturlaugur, Hjálmþér, Sörli, Grímur og Hjálmar, Úlfhamur, Geðraunir, Sigurður fótur, Skikkja, Geiplur, Landrés, Geirarð, Bragða-Mágus, Blávus og Viktor, Sálus og Nikanór, Dámusti, Dínus, Jón leiksveinn, Virgiles, Klerkar; Finnur Sigmundsson, ed., *Stakar rímur* (1960), containing *Fjósa ríma;* Grímur M. Helgason, ed., *Pontus rímur* (1961); Theo Homan, ed., *Skíðaríma* (1975); Otto L. Jiriczek, ed., *Die Bósa-rímur,* Germanistische Abhandlungen, **10** (1894, repr. 1977); Jón Helgason, ed., *Móðars rímur og Móðars þáttur* (1950); Eugen Kölbing, ed., *Amis and Amiloun. . . . Nebst einer Beilage: Amícus ok Amilíus rímur* (1884), cxvii–cxx, 189–229, 251–253, 255–256; Ludvig Larsson, ed., *Sagan och rimorna om Friðþiófr hinn Frækni* (1893); Ólafur Halldórsson, ed., *Haralds rímur Hringsbana; Áns rímur bogsveigis; Bósa rímur; Vilmundar rímur viðutan,* 4 vols. (1973–1975); Pálmi Pálsson, ed., *Króka-Refs saga og Króka-Refs rímur* (1883); Theodor Wisén, ed., *Riddara-rímur* (1881–1882), containing the following rímur: Filippó, Hebert, Konráð.

Studies. Andrés Björnsson, "Um Skikkjurímur," in *Skírnir,* **121** (1947); Björn K. Þórólfsson, *Rímur fyrir 1600* (1934), and "Dróttkvæði og rímur," *ibid.,* **124** (1950); Sir William Craigie, *The Art of Poetry in Iceland* (1937), *The Romantic Poetry of Iceland* (1950), and *Sýnisbók íslenzkra rímna,* 3 vols. (1952), containing extensive introductory material in Icelandic with an English summary in each volume; Davið Erlingsson, "Blómað mál í rímum," in *Studia islandica: Íslenzk fræði,* **33** (1974), with a summary in English; Einar Ól. Sveinsson, "Um rímur fyrir 1600 og fleira," in his *Við uppsprettturnar* (1956); Finnur Jónsson, ed., *Ordbog til de af Samfund til udg. af gml. nord. litteratur udgivne rímur samt til de af Dr. O. Jiriczek udgivne Bósarímur* (1926–1928); Finnur Sigmundsson, *Rímnatal,* 2 vols. in 1 (1966), a catalog of all the *rímur;* Hallfreður Örn Eiríksson, "On Icelandic Rímur: An Orientation," in *Arv,* **31** (1975); Helgi Sigurðsson, *Safn til bragfræði íslenzkra rímna að fornu og nýju* (1891); Hreinn Steingrímsson, "'Að kveða rímur,'" in *Scripta islandica,* **24** (1975); Shaun F. D. Hughes, "'Völsungs rímur' and 'Sjúrðar Kvæði': Romance and Ballad, Ballad and Dance," in *Ballads and Ballad Research,* Patricia Conroy, ed. (1978), and "Report on *Rímur* 1980," in *Journal of English and Germanic Philology,* **79** (1980); Jón Helgason, "Noter til Þrymlur," in *Opuscula,* V (1975); Jón Þorkelsson, *Om digtningen på Island i det 15. og 16. århundrede* (1888); Eugen Kölbing, "Beiträge zur kenntnis und kritischen verwerthung der älteren isländischen rímurpoesie," in his *Beiträge zur vergleichenden Geschichte der romantischen Poesie und Prosa des Mittelalters* (1876); Konráð Gíslason, "Forelæsninger over de ældster 'rímur,'" in Björn M. Ólsen, ed., *Forelæsninger og videnskabelige afhandlinger* (1897); Ólafur Halldórsson, "Eftirhreytur um rímur," in *Gripla,* **2** (1977); Páll Eggert Ólason, "Fólgin nöfn í rímum," in *Skírnir,* **89** (1915); Carl C. Rokkjær, "Rímur og folkeviser," in *Acta philologica scandinavica,* **26** (1963); Stefán Einarson, "Alþýðukveðskapur frá miðöldum," in *Skírnir,* **123** (1949), and "Report on *Rímur,*" in *Journal of English and Germanic Philology,* **54** (1955); Sveinbjörn Benteinsson, *Bragfræði og Háttatal* (1953); Vésteinn Ólason, "Nýmæli í íslenzkum bókmenntum á miðöld," in *Skírnir,* **150** (1976), and "Ballad and Romance in Medieval Iceland," in Conroy, ed., *Ballads* (1978).

Discography. Íslenzk rímnalög: Icelandic rímur songs, Parlaphone-Odeon CBEP 20 (1966); *Íslenzkur arfur söngva, Íslenzk rímnalög: A Heritage of Icelandic Songs, Icelandic Rímur Songs,* Odeon-EMI MOAK 17 (*ca.* 1963); *100 íslensk kvæðalög gefin út í tilefni 50 ára afmæli Kvæðamannafélagsins Iðunnar,* SG Hjólmplötur SG-122 (1979).

SHAUN F. D. HUGHES

[See also **Eddic Meters; Eddic Poetry; Fornaldarsögur; Kenning; Skaldic Poetry.**]

RINGERIKE STYLE. This style of Viking art developed from the Mammen style and flourished during the first half of the eleventh century. It is named after a group of decorated stones in southern Norway of Ringerike sandstone. The style employs disciplined clusters of tendrils with a large animal motif, or "great beast," and a snake.

BIBLIOGRAPHY

Signe H. Fuglesang, *The Ringerike Style* (1980); David M. Wilson and Ole Klindt-Jensen, *Viking Art* (1980).

JAMES A. GRAHAM-CAMPBELL

[See also **Mammen Style; Viking Art;** and illustration overleaf.]

RITUAL. The term *rituale* seems to appear after the Council of Trent with the *Rituale sacramento-*

Ringerike-style decoration on a bronze-gilt weather vane from Heggen Church, Norway, mid 11th century. UNIVERSITETETS OLDSAKSAMLING, OSLO, INV. NR. 23602

rum romanum of Cardinal Giulio Antonio Santoro (1532–1602) and the *Rituale romanum* (1614) to designate a liturgical book that had already been known in manuscripts of the tenth and eleventh centuries and that had received various names in the last centuries of the Middle Ages, such as *agenda* in Germany and *manuale* in France. In the Spanish liturgical tradition, where the term *manuale* is older, it seems rather to have designated the sacramentary.

Originally the elements destined to form the ritual were part of the sacramentary or the pontifical. In the monasteries, they were added to the collectar. Thus the Roman ritual *Avignon 101,* one of the oldest independent rituals, copied between 1363–1368, expressly states that it is an extract of the pontifical. The oldest collectar-ritual edited is that of Durham (MS A. iv.19) from the mid tenth century. Elements of the ritual had already been utilized in independent booklets (*quaterniones*) for various liturgical ceremonies (for instance, the testament of Riculfe, bishop of Elne, 915). Once constituted, the liturgical, now known as the ritual, was often completed by a small missal with Mass texts for the celebration of the sacraments in the ritual and sometimes for the principal feasts.

Prior to the thirteenth century the majority of the rituals conserved were monastic, for example (among those edited) Vallicelliana C 32, those of Rheinau, and those of Biburg in the diocese of Regensburg. In addition to properly monastic rites they generally contained the liturgy of baptism. On the other hand the *North Italian Services of the Eleventh Century* is a secular ritual from an unknown church of northern Italy.

The pastoral reform of the thirteenth century, organized by the statutes of diocesan synods and supervised by pastoral visitations, obliged every pastor to have a *manuale* containing the rites of baptism, marriage, extreme unction, and funerals (see the Parisian statutes of Eudes of Sully [*d.* 1208]). At least in the more important dioceses these manuals had a relatively stable form. In his edition of the *Manuale ad usum percelebris ecclesis Sarisburienis,* Arthur Collins takes the manuscripts into account, but reproduces the edition published at Rouen in 1543.

Medieval parish rituals do not contain the form of private penance or the rules governing sacramental practice, which were not introduced until the printed rituals of the sixteenth century.

BIBLIOGRAPHY

Walter von Arx, *Das Klosterrituale von Biburg* (1970); A. Jefferies Collins, ed., *Manuale ad usum percelebris ecclesie Sarisburiensis* (1960); Helge Faehn,

Manuale Norvegicum (1962); Adolph Franz, *Das Rituale von St. Florian aus dem zwölften Jahrhundert* (1904), and *Das Rituale des bischofs Heinrich I. von Breslau* (1912); Pierre-Marie Gy, "Collectaire, rituel, processionnal," in *Revue des sciences, philosophiques, et théologiques,* 44 (1960); Gebhard Hürlimann, *Das Rheinauer Rituale: Zurich Rh 114, Anfang 12. Jh.* (1959); Hilding Johansson, *Hemsjömanualet* (1950); Cyrille Lambot, ed., *North Italian Services of the Eleventh Century* (1931); Victor Leroquais, *Les pontificaux manuscrits des bibliothèques publiques de France,* I (1937), 53–54; Ambros Odermatt, *Ein Rituale in beneventanischer Schrift: Roma, Bibliotheca vallicelliana Cod. C 32, Ende des 11. Jahrhunderts* (1980); Knud Ottosen, *The Manual from Notmark* (1970); Jorge M. Pinell, "El *Liber horarum* y el *Misticus* entre los libros de la antigua liturgia hispana," in *Hispania sacra,* 8 (1955), esp. 95; Odette Pontal, ed., *Les statuts synodaux français du XIIIe siècle: Les statuts de Paris et le synodal de l'ouest* (1971), esp. 71; "Testamentum Riculfi," in *Patrologia latina,* CXXXII (1880), 468; A. Hamilton Thompson and U. Lindelöf, eds., *Rituale Ecclesiae Dunelmensis,* Surtees Society, CXL (1927).

PIERRE-MARIE GY, O. P.

[See also **Liturgy, Treatises on; Mass, Liturgy of the; Missal; Pontifical; Sacramentary.**]

RIURIK. See **Rurik.**

RIWĀQ (plurals, *arwiqa, rūq*) signifies a tent supported upon one pole in the middle, a roof in front of a *bayt* or tent, or a curtain that is let down upon the front of a tent. It is also the front of a *bayt* or tent, a place that affords shelter from rain, and a portico, particularly such as surrounds the courtyard of a mosque.

BIBLIOGRAPHY

Al-Fīrūzābādī, *Al-Qāmūs al-Muḥit,* III (1925), 238–239; Edward W. Lane, *An Arabic-English Lexicon,* I, pt. 3 (1867, repr. 1978), 1191–1192; Ibn Manẓur, *Lisan al-ᶜArab,* X, pt. 40 (1956), 132–134; Ibn Sīdah, *Kitāb al-Mukhaṣṣaṣ,* II (*ca.* 1900, repr. 1965), 4; al-Zabīdī, *Tāj al-ᶜArus,* Hussein Nassar, ed., VI (1969), 362–363.

GHAZI I. BISHEH

[See also **Bayt; Otaq** (with illustration).]

ROADS AND BRIDGES, WESTERN EUROPEAN. The Middle Ages was the great age of bridges. Although modern structures surpass their predecessors in size and technique, they are planned as a means of communication or, perhaps, with an eye to military strategy. Bridges in the Middle Ages were something more: they frequently were the focus of town life. It was possible, at various times and places in medieval Europe, to be born on a bridge in a lying-in hospital, to reside on a bridge and go to market there, to carry on a business, whether retailing or manufacturing or both, to attend services in a chapel, and even, in the twelfth century, to hear lectures given by masters of the University of Paris. One could grind one's grain at a mill on a bridge, retire to spend one's old age on a bridge or one could be judged by a court sitting on a bridge, and the execution of the sentence could be carried out there. Often the fortified bridgehead was the entrance to the town. At the time of the joyous entry of a lord whom the town felt obliged to honor, the bridge was decorated. In other words, the bridge was of central importance to the community, whereas roads occupied a lower place in medieval esteem.

ROMAN HERITAGE

A substantial road system and numerous bridges were inherited by the Middle Ages from the Romans in those parts of Europe belonging to the empire. These regions included present-day Italy, Spain, France, England, and portions of western Germany. It must not be forgotten, however, that the Romans in their conquests took over roads already in use. This was true of barbarian lands as well as long-civilized regions. It is not necessary to take seriously the remark of a medieval author concerning an area on the fringes of civilization: "They have no roads because they do not communicate with each other." There was a tin route across Gaul, and it has been remarked that the rapidity with which Caesar's legions marched and countermarched across Gaul proves the existence of practicable roads there before the Roman occupation. Also, a number of bridges are mentioned by Caesar, including two at Paris.

A road system developed by provincials to connect urban centers and accommodate trade could not satisfy Roman imperial needs. To assure control and defense of their dominions the Romans needed rapid access to all parts of their empire. Accordingly, they constructed paved roads to allow their

ROADS AND BRIDGES, EUROPEAN

armies to march efficiently from one end of their dominions to another. The main routes were determined in Rome by a central bureaucracy without much regard for local topography. There are a number of straight roads running long distances up and down steep slopes.

A Roman paved road was a massive affair. Statius (*ca.* A.D. 90) describes construction as beginning with furrows (ditches for draining) and continuing with hollowing out a trench, commonly one meter deep. This was filled with layers, first of sand, then slabs and blocks in cement mortar, then concrete with crushed stone and mortar, then stones in gravel concrete. Only certain Roman roads had such deep foundations or careful construction. Many were of gravel or were little more than pathways. The quantities of stone needed for a paved road were not a deterrent to construction. Labor was supplied by soldiers and maintenance was carried out by corvées supervised by local authorities.

In their preoccupation with roads the Romans seem to have considered bridges as subordinate features of a road system planned to facilitate troop movements. They built three bridges in Britain in connection with Hadrian's Wall and provided the Via Domitia across southern Gaul with several bridges. There were some timber bridges in the provinces, but the Romans could and did build magnificent stone bridges, especially in Italy, such as the Ponte d'Augusto at Narni and the Ponte Sant'Angelo at Rome. Some of the most impressive Roman bridges, for instance at Segovia and at Pont-du-Gard, were originally built as aqueducts. In Germany there were Roman bridges at Saarbrücken, Trier, and Mainz, and in Spain at Alcántara and elsewhere. In Gaul there were bridges in numerous towns.

The Roman connection between bridges and religion seems to have been minor. Some recent opinions hold that the word *pontifex* (priest) has nothing to do with the Latin word for bridge (*pons, pontis*), but is derived instead from a lost Umbrian word, so that the meaning of *pontifex* is maker of sacrifices, not bridges.

THE MEDIEVAL VIEW OF BRIDGES

There was a marked difference between the ancient and the medieval attitude toward bridges. It has been said that "whereas the Romans were road-conscious but quite prepared to cross rivers by ford, the men of the Middle Ages were essentially bridge-conscious." Medieval men substituted bridges for fords. Their view of bridges seems to have had a precedent in the pre-Roman period, for the Gauls named many a town after a bridge, such as Briva Isarae, or Pontoise (in contrast, the Romans in naming colonies preferred to commemorate their generals). Also, in Gaul at least, some of the town bridges were due to individual enterprise, like the Pont Flavien near St. Chamas (Bouches-du-Rhône).

Unlike the Romans, who believed that the spirit of the stream was unfavorable to those crossing it, medieval people were convinced that bridges were pleasing to God; and unlike the moderns, they did not consider them in a Romantic but rather in an allegorical context. A famous omen in medieval literature is the burning of Charlemagne's wooden bridge over the Rhine at Mainz, which, according to Einhard, presaged the death of the emperor. Gregory the Great tells in his *Dialogues* the story of an allegorical vision of a bridge that led from this world to heaven over the black and dingy stream of hell. The dreamer feels his foot slip on the bridge, which, in characteristically medieval form, was a foot span of minimum width unprovided with protective railings. He was rescued by good spirits, and Gregory, uninterested in the architectural aspects, explains that the vision illustrates Matthew 7:14: "Narrow is the way that leadeth unto life."

Our present-day perception of medieval bridges has been much influenced by the nineteenth-century Romantic movement with its love of legends and picturesque ruins, and its interest in the magical and supernatural. Legends of the devil as a bridge builder seem to date from the modern period. The present Pont-du-Diable (Isère) was called the bridge of St. Hugo in the fourteenth century, and the Pont-du-Diable over the Gouffre Noir of the Hérault was built in the eleventh century by two convents. On the contrary, in the Middle Ages the role of the devil as regards bridges seems to have been exclusively destructive. St. Bénézet, according to testimony at the beatification inquiry, once hurried back from a fund-raising expedition in Burgundy because he knew that the devil was scattering the stones of a pier foundation.

Bridges needed the protection of saints. On the facade of a church at Borgo S. Donnino in Italy there is a twelfth-century sculpture of the collapse of a wooden bridge. The faithful, hurrying to see the newly discovered tomb of S. Donnino, are shown falling into the river, and the saint is depicted as preserving them. To assure the duration and safety of a medieval bridge it was considered helpful to build either on it or at the end of it a chapel where Mass could be said daily and the aid of the saints invoked. On the other hand, there were not many miracles associated with bridges during the Middle Ages.

BRIDGES IN THE EARLY MIDDLE AGES

For some time after the barbarian conquest of the West the theories of government regulation continued to be the same. The barbarian law codes repeated the statements of the Theodosian Code of 438 that persons living in the neighborhood of public works, including roads and bridges, were responsible for their maintenance, and that no one was exempt from this obligation. The Carolingian kings who ruled Gaul and parts of Germany and Italy followed the Roman practice with regard to repairs. One can read between the lines of the repeated admonitions of Louis the Pious in his capitularies that his efforts to make his subjects perform public works were only moderately successful. In medieval times, as in ancient, the construction of roads and bridges, whether at new sites or repairs at the old, continued to require express authorization by government authorities.

Medieval customs with regard to bridges appeared already in Merovingian times, as, for example, in the sixth-century houses constructed along the length of a bridge at Paris and in the ninth-century mills built under the span there. Medieval views altered the legal aspects of bridge building. Public works were affected by the German concept of law as customary, an idea that inhibited the building of bridges at new sites, because nothing novel or different could be required of the inhabitants of a neighborhood. When in 821 Louis the Pious did insist that bridges should be built where they were needed, not necessarily in their former location, his tone was defensive. Tolls were considered by the Merovingian kings not as income to meet govermental responsibilities but as a suitable gift for a monastery for the good of the royal soul. Evidently, since the upkeep of roads and bridges was supposed to be provided by the local inhabitants, money was not needed for this work. This divorce between tolls and maintenance continued to plague later centuries. If tolls were merely a perquisite, there was logic in charging not only the people who crossed a bridge but the boatmen passing under it. The Carolingians attempted to stop this practice but in vain, and it continued throughout the Middle Ages. Still another typically medieval idea was the Carolingian provision that local people were privileged to pass free over the bridge, perhaps on the grounds that they made and maintained it.

The early Middle Ages saw the rise of a new and distinctively medieval concept of the role of the bridge in warfare. The modern idea is to build bridges so as to increase one's own troop mobility or to destroy them to prevent their use by the enemy. The medieval concept was somewhat different. It was to fortify and garrison the bridge to prevent the enemy from crossing over or passing under it. This strategy was used in sixth-century Italy by Belisarios and in the ninth by Charles the Bald against the Vikings. Fortified, garrisoned bridges at Treix (Trilbardou) on the Marne and at Paris on the Seine were successful in stopping them. There are numerous examples of medieval bridges proving a formidable obstacle against river traffic. Armed men on London Bridge prevented King Cnut in 1016 from passing under it; and in 1263 a mob, congregated on the bridge and armed with whatever missiles came to hand, was able to prevent the unpopular Queen Eleanor of Provence from passing underneath. It should be remembered that a medieval bridge ordinarily had only one or two archways open to river traffic, the other passages being too narrow, too shallow, or obstructed by mills, fishponds, or perhaps rocks. Even a broken-down bridge could completely block boats.

MEDIEVAL ROADS

If the people of the early Middle Ages developed some of the basic medieval ideas and practices concerning bridges, evidence indicates they built rather few of them at that time. Yet we know still less about early medieval roads. People displayed a lack of interest in roads, understandable in a civilization that had little trade. It has been claimed that Roman routes were substantially adequate for medieval purposes, but this statement must be qualified. In Britain the network of Roman roads continued to be used because it was centered on London, an important administrative center both in antiquity and in the High Middle Ages. In Italy the continuity of settlement and geographical features encouraged the use of Roman routes. It was otherwise in France, however. In Roman times the consul Agrippa (*d.* 12 B.C.) made Lugdunum (Lyons) the crossroads of Gaul, from which four routes led, one to Aquitania, one to the Rhine, one to the northern ocean, and one down the Rhône to Massilia (Marseilles). At this time Lutetia Parisiorum (Paris) was a small provincial town. Under the Carolingians the favorite royal residences were in west-central Germany, especially at Aquisgranum (Aachen or Aix-la-Chapelle), and it was only with the Capetians, who were dukes of Paris, that that city rose to prominence. France has been called the work of the French kings, and eventually all roads led to Paris. If the ancient roads had a south-north orientation through Troyes and Rheims, the Middle Ages saw an almost equal development of southeast-to-west routes along the watercourses. In addition, only 80 of 500 French towns can be traced back to ancient times; and the founding of many new ones and the popularity of pilgrimages like those to St. Martin of Tours and Mont-Saint-Michel forced the development of new routes and the abandonment of others. Of four routes through France to Santiago de Compostela only two followed Roman roads. The two new ones followed the line of Auxerre, Vézélay Limoges, Périgueux, and Pamplona, and from Lyons through Le Puy, Conques, and Moissac to Pamplona.

In most of Germany there had been no Roman roads, and the little trade from ancient times had been mostly in amber and furs. As the exchange of goods increased, new routes developed. These included Strassburg to Augsburg, Augsburg to Erfurt via Bamberg, Regensburg to Frankfurt and Fulda and Hoxter to Bremen, and east from Hoxter to Magdeburg. From Duisburg a route led through Paderborn to Bremen.

Opinion has been sharply divided as to the usefulness of the Roman roads to the Middle Ages. Some writers have contended that ancient methods were such as to assure an indestructible roadbed, and others that the Romans, by using cement, made certain of the cracking of the road and hence its early deterioration. The truth seems to be that some Roman roads continued to be practicable through the Middle Ages. In some cases, the stones forming the surface were fastened together with clamps or laid on the substructure. Many stretches of Roman roads became impassable, however, because of erosion or because the stones were carried away by local people for building purposes.

Some medieval roads, at least the narrower ones, were the property of individuals, such as lords, secular or ecclesiastical, or of convents, whereas the wider ones belonged to the king. Beaumanoir in the *Customs of the Beauvaisis* in the thirteenth century gave a classification of roads as they should be: the path, four feet wide, too narrow for carts; the *carrière,* eight feet, on which carts cannot pass; those sixteen feet wide, on which two carts can draw abreast; thirty-two feet, on which cattle can pasture without damage to property; and sixty-four feet, the road of Julius Caesar. Beaumanoir complains that the greed of men has appropriated parts of these roads, so that they are illegally narrow.

The documents show proprietors chiefly interested in asserting ownership or collecting the fines for infractions of the law (profits of "justice") on the roads or in amassing toll receipts. In the thirteenth century it was asserted that tolls were collected on them to pay for their upkeep, but those who took the tolls were inclined to see them as perquisites to which no obligations were attached. Owners were active in trying to prevent merchants from avoiding their charges by using other roads or making new ones.

Roads, like bridges, were pious works in the later Middle Ages. In the fourteenth century, Mahaut, countess of Artois, willed money for the repair of bridges, roads, and other difficult passages. In 1434 the bishop of Merseberg stated that it was God's will that he should care not only for the church but for the building of roads and bridges for poor pilgrims and others.

Charity was inadequate for the task of keeping roads and bridges in repair. In France, from the thirteenth century on, the right to collect taxes was frequently granted by the king to towns for the purpose of repairing bridges, fountains, and bad spots on the roads. Usually the towns or parishes or people living along or owning land along a road were responsible for maintenance. Thus in 1395–1396 the road between Lille and Menin had deteriorated so badly that no cart or even horse could pass in wintertime, "which is against the public good of our subjects and especially those that live near the said great road." Accordingly, eleven neighboring parishes were to determine what each should pay toward repairs. In France and in England some roads were maintained by corvées.

There were paved roads at various places, but they seem usually to have been on routes leading

ROADS AND BRIDGES, EUROPEAN

out from towns, for example from Harfleur to Orléans, or from Senlis to Verberies, and to have extended no considerable distance. Most roads were dirt roads. Too many heavily laden vehicles passing over the same spot in wet weather could produce impassable mudholes. Beaumanoir suggested that if the road became so bad that to repair it would be impossibly expensive, an area next to it should be set aside for a new road.

In most cases attempts to improve roads envisioned the removal of encroachments, restoration of boundary stones, or repairs of bad spots. Damage to roads listed by Beaumanoir included the removal from the roadbeds of stones and wood laid down to improve them. To mend a mudhole in Germany, sometimes gravel was thrown on it, but it was perhaps more usual to render roads passable with bundles of twigs and with sticks or logs. At some places in France and Germany a specified forest supplied wood for repair of a particular road. Plank roads, the equivalent of the American pioneer corduroy road, had been built across swamps in northern Germany, many even as far back as prehistoric times.

BRIDGE BUILDING: ELEVENTH THROUGH FOURTEENTH CENTURIES

There was an upsurge in bridge building beginning in the eleventh and early twelfth centuries. This occurred in England, Germany, and France. In the first two countries the ruler retained his powers over roads and bridges, while in France roads and bridges had become private property. Tolls continued to proliferate, but there was no necessary connection between their collection and road and bridge maintenance. In northern France between the year 1000 and the mid twelfth century most bridges were constructed by lay and ecclesiastical lords. Where local counts or dukes possessed well-organized fiefs in the eleventh and twelfth centuries, as many bridges were built in each of these centuries as were built in the thirteenth.

Bridge building as a pious deed. In the eleventh century, in areas as far removed as Spain and Scandinavia, bridge building was considered a pious deed aiding a soul in purgatory. In Germany at Eichstätt Bishop Gundekar II (1057–1075) promoted the building of the Old Mill Bridge (Altmühlbrücke) as a Christlike act of love for one's neighbor. In southern France bridge building was aided by the development of the idea of the bridge as a pious work. This concept had important similarities to those of the Peace of God movement, which attempted to eliminate violence against and robbery of the clergy and poor and to prohibit castle building. The public utility of the whole region was given as one reason for the erection of the bridge at Albi. The justification of bridge building as a work acceptable to God was that it saved lives in floodtime and aided the poor, for since construction was financed through charity, passage across the bridge was free to all. Fortifications on bridges conceived in this way were strictly forbidden. At the Pont-de-la-Daurade at Toulouse, at Tours, and at Regensburg in 1182 only freewill offerings were to be received from those passing over the bridge.

Bridge corporations. The idea of making the bridge a corporation (*opus pontis*) appears first in France along the Rhône and the Loire and then in England and Germany. The great advantage of this system was that the bridge as a corporation could receive gifts, administer property, and thus provide for maintenance.

Early organizations—and the most famous manifestation of the idea that the bridge is a work laying up merit in heaven—were the bridge-building brotherhoods. There seem to have been only three of these organizations, all unconnected with one another, and all in the Rhône Valley—at Avignon, Lyons, and Pont-Saint-Esprit. The earliest was founded by St. Bénézet, described in a contemporary document as "initiator and minister" of the bridge at Avignon, which was built in only eleven years, 1177–1188. His organization included both brothers and sisters, all of them laymen, who were occupied in collecting funds and acquiring and administering properties. They had nothing to do with the building of the bridge, for this was managed by the bishop and consuls of Avignon. Even in the heyday of the concept of the bridge as a pious work, initiating the great stone bridge across the mighty Rhône was insufficient to merit sainthood, and Bénézet was canonized for miracles of faith healing.

The second brotherhood of a bridge appeared at Lyons after the citizens had begun the bridge around 1180–1182, and here the brothers' responsibilities concerned construction. They seem to have been little involved in financial affairs. There were only brothers, no sisters, of the Pont-de-la-Guillotière at Lyons, and some of them were eccle-

 ROADS AND BRIDGES, EUROPEAN

siastics, although most were laymen. Lastly, at Pont-Saint-Esprit it was the citizens of the town, then called St. Saturnin, who in 1265 went to the prior of the convent of St. Pierre, lord of the town, and requested permission to build a bridge across the Rhône. The brothers (and sisters) of the bridge first appear in documents a dozen years after the bridge was started, and their duties were strictly confined to soliciting alms. They had nothing to do with construction or finances, which were administered by rectors chosen by the prior and townspeople. All three of the bridge-building brotherhoods lost control over their particular bridges at least within a century and a quarter of their founding, and those that lingered on did so to take care of the bridge hospital.

The fading of the bridge-building brotherhoods made no difference to the idea of the bridge as a pious work. Chapels and hospitals were built on or next to bridges, and the promised heavenly reward became institutionalized in the indulgence. The combination of a hospital and bridge under the same management was rare, however often they might be located in proximity one to another. On the other hand, bridge chapels frequently shared donations with the bridge. In Germany and Switzerland there were chapels on the bridge at Basel, Lucerne, Regensburg, Saalfeld, Bingen, Bruchsal, Neudenau, Esslingen, Jena, and elsewhere. Here the most honored saint was Nicholas. There were numerous bridge chapels in England and France. On London Bridge was the chapel of St. Thomas of Canterbury, on St. Ives Bridge that of St. Lawrence, St. Catherine at Ludford, and St. Mary at Nottingham. In France at Blois the patron was St. Fiacre, at Montauban St. Catherine, at Clamecy (Nièvre) St. John, at Beaugency St. Jacques, and at Romans the Virgin. Some bridges had two chapels, notably the Pont-de-la-Guillotière and the Pont-Saint-Esprit, where each had one chapel dedicated to the Holy Spirit and one to St. Nicholas. In France, bridge chapels seem to have been built where the idea of the bridge corporation existed.

Bridges and indulgences. Indulgences were issued for contributions that helped build or maintain bridges in Italy, France, Germany, and England. The earliest in France was perhaps that for the Pont-de-la-Guillotière, *ca.* 1184. The idea had reached Germany at least by 1229, when Donauwörth obtained one for its bridge, and indulgences were frequently requested in England. The idea was also used in Italy, for example in 1314 for the bridge at Ficecelo. The formula varied. In general, to those who were penitent and confessed, a forty-day indulgence in purgatory was promised. Sometimes the reward was offered to those donating labor or loaning oxen or carts for use in construction. A recurrent theme in these formulas is the avoidance of accidents and the benefit to the poor and pilgrims, but sometimes the rich and merchants were included. Perhaps the greatest number of indulgences was granted to the bridge at Coblenz. Building it had required eighty-five years, and a contemporary computed in 1500 that the sum of indulgences had reached 9,746 days and 12 hours. Nevertheless, at most places charity was inadequate, and other measures had to be used to finance bridges.

Bridges and taxation. England had an immense advantage at this time in that the corvée was in force and that the king was entitled to collect taxes. In 1097 a wooden bridge was rebuilt at London after a flood. Provision for its reconstruction was the same as under Roman law, that is, the residents of the regions near London were subject to forced labor. The Anglo-Saxon Chronicle declared that these people were "grieviously oppressed by the heavy demands made for London Bridge." Between 1110 and 1125 Henry I imposed a tax for repairs to London Bridge, but this was not the sole financial support of the structure, for in 1122 the bridge corporation owned lands, and in 1281 it sent out messengers to collect alms throughout the realm for the repair of the bridge. London Bridge was burned in 1136 and rebuilt in elm in 1163. At the time the idea of building great stone bridges was beginning to be accepted, however, and reconstruction of London Bridge (1176–1209) was begun under the direction of the bridge master, Peter, chaplain of St. Mary Colechurch. Perhaps it was a question of prestige or perhaps Londoners hoped a stone bridge would be more durable, less subject to flood damage than a timber structure. King Henry II seems to have imposed a tax on wool to finance the structure, and when Peter of Colechurch died before the end of work, King John imported to complete it Master Isembert, who had built bridges at Saintes and La Rochelle. Evidently King John's demands on citizens to build bridges were heavy, for they figure among the clauses of Magna Carta. The result was that responsibility for bridges was strictly limited to districts where the local people had customarily

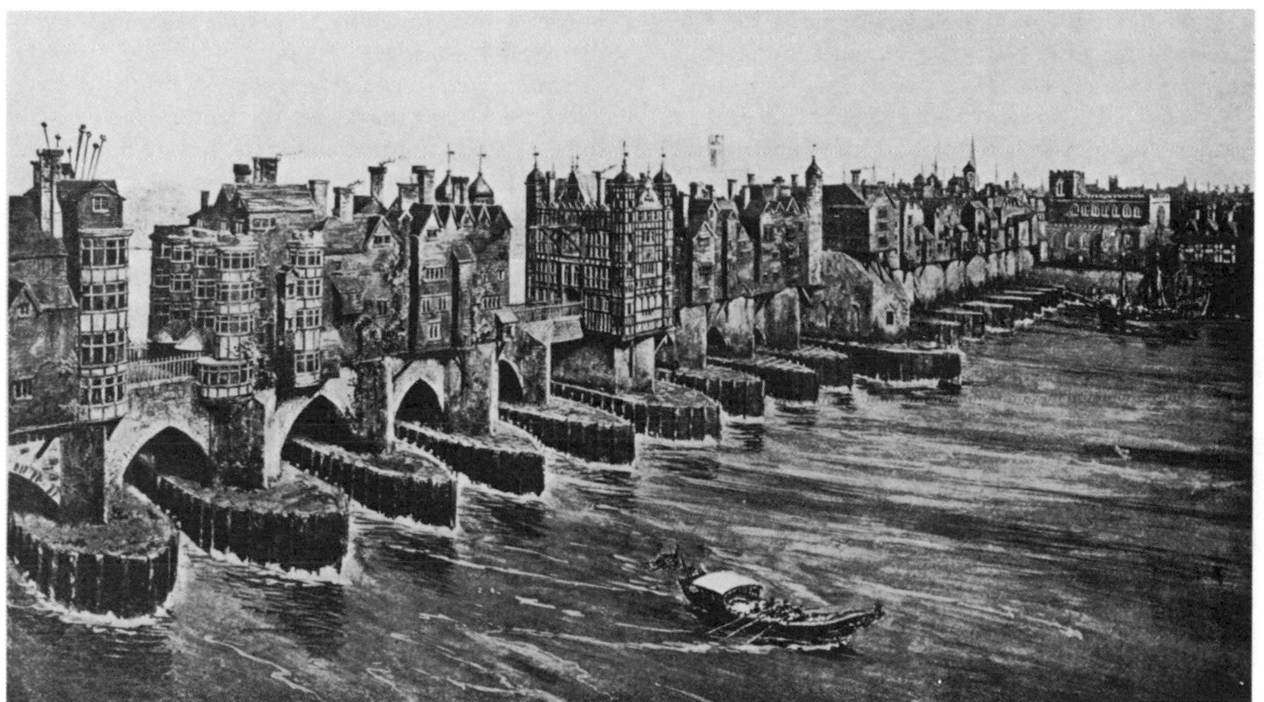

Old London Bridge as seen from the east in 1630. Note Traitors' Gate (*left*), drawbridge and Nonsuch House (*center*), and St. Magnus Church (*right*). From a model by John B. Thorp in the British Museum. REPRODUCED FROM MALCOLM C. SALAMAN, *LONDON, PAST AND PRESENT* (1916). Courtesy of The New York Public Library, General Research Division, Astor, Lenox, and Tilden Foundations

been liable. This precluded support for bridges at new sites.

In England bridges continued to be maintained through a combination of tolls, taxes, corvées, and charity. Responsibility for bridges was taken seriously by the government. For example, in 1241 the sheriff of Wiltshire was ordered to distrain the village of Hungerford to the extent of 5 marks for not keeping a certain bridge in repair, and at the same time the sheriff of Berkshire was to find out which villages were responsible for neglected bridges.

Nevertheless, charity continued, and the endowed bridges were among the more successful. The bridge at Bideford, dating from the first quarter of the fourteenth century was (and is) heavily endowed with lands. At Rochester the Romans had built a bridge over the Medway on Watling Street, but just before 1387 the span was of typically medieval construction with stone piers and a wooden superstructure. As was usual in England at that time, parishes along the riverbanks (fifty-three of them) were responsible for maintenance, but such responsibility was parceled out according to the size of the pier and the resources of the parish. Hoo, a large district, was to make two piers. But the two middle piers—the most vulnerable—required twelve parishes to keep them in repair. In 1339, 1361, and 1382 the bridge was impassable, and under these circumstances a ferry was usually substituted. When the new bridge was decided on, permission from the king was obtained to collect alms for it and to collect a toll (pontage) on the old bridge for the same purpose. Materials were donated by Sir John de Cobham and Sir Robert Knolles (famous in the French wars); they built a bridge chapel dedicated to the Holy Trinity and endowed it with a chantry and the bridge with lands. Evidently the responsibility of the parishes was allowed to lapse. (Incidentally, the wardens still retain much of the property obtained in the fourteenth century.) Here was an exception to the general trend on the Continent that more and more bridges were supported by taxes in addition to tolls. Rochester Bridge was financed by rents, alms, collection of toll, sale of produce, boat hire, fishing

 ROADS AND BRIDGES, EUROPEAN

rights, annuities, and the sale of lime. This was barely sufficient for the bridge, and in times of emergency indulgences were obtained.

The novelty (to us) that bridges could ever be considered pious works has tended to obscure the fact that during the Middle Ages there were bridges built with totally different ideas in mind. Even in the eleventh and twelfth centuries, and of course much oftener in later times, many a bridge was built for profit, defense, or convenient access, whether for local people, pilgrims, or merchants. Bridges such as that at Regensburg, where in 1182 nothing was to be given for passage except free-will offerings, eventually acquired tolls; and tolls were also collected at Tours, Albi, and Grimma, where for pious reasons the crossing had originally been gratuitous. Bridge ownership could be lucrative. At Compiègne the canons of St. Corneille had enormous difficulties in asserting their right to their bridge. A royal provost had ruined their bridge, erecting his own instead, and brazenly ignored his excommunication by the canons. Finally, in 1112, they were able to obtain from Louis VI a charter confirming them in full possession and enjoyment of their bridge with the right to build and repair it.

Defense dictated the construction by Richard I the Lionhearted of four spans at Les Andelys (Eure) in 1097 in connection with his stronghold of Château-Gailliard, and in 1388 the town of Strassburg built a bridge over the Rhine during a war with Baden, apparently for military reasons.

Construction of a bridge might mean rerouting of traffic to the advantage of the builders. The construction of the Pont Ecumant made the St. Gotthard pass practicable, encouraging the abandonment of the fairs of Champagne by Italian merchants, who then passed through Germany to the Low Countries instead. The Regensburg bridge (1135–1146) shifted trade between northern France and the Danube region to the axis Würzburg-Nuremberg-Regensburg instead of Würms-Wimpfen-Passau. A timber bridge at Laufenburg constructed in 1207 shifted traffic to the less hilly side of the Rhine, and a particularly flagrant attempt to capitalize on the diversion of trade through bridge construction was attempted by the markgraf Dietrich of Meissen in the first half of the thirteenth century. He destroyed the abbot of Pegau's bridge and founded near his castle of Groitzsch a settlement with bridges to reroute traffic between Bohemia and Nuremberg. His plans, however, were foiled by Emperor Frederick II, who destroyed his bridges.

Urban and secular support of bridges. After about the middle of the twelfth century there began to be a change in bridge builders. Before this period they had been almost entirely ecclesiastical and lay lords; afterward townsmen came to the fore. By 1162 the knights and burghers of Saumur had built a bridge across the Loire, but it eventually passed into the possession of the abbey of St. Florent. Other municipalities, however, began to take over the responsibility for bridges. In 1182 the town of Regensburg secured from Emperor Frederick I Barbarossa all rights over its bridge, and in 1188 Lübeck did the same for the bridge over the Trave. Towns acquired bridges from bishops disillusioned in their hope for profits, like those at Metz and Albi in the thirteenth century. With the increasing importance of townsmen there was less emphasis on the bridge as a pious work and more on its role as a public utility.

The twelfth century inaugurated the age of great stone bridges, including London Bridge, bridges at Saumur, Orléans, and Beaugency over the Loire, and at Avignon and Lyons over the Rhône. The thirteenth century continued the same enthusiasm for new bridges, so that where one or two at a town had been considered adequate, more were built. The increase in numbers compounded the problem of maintenance, which forced itself on the attention of the public. For example, floods washed out bridges at Paris in 1196/1197, 1206, 1280, and 1296, and the record was worse at Basel. There, floods carried away parts of the bridge in 1268, 1274, 1275, 1302, 1340, 1343, 1408, 1421, and 1424. Medieval people believed that a stone bridge was so much more durable than a timber structure that the extra initial cost was justified.

Charity, it was agreed, was a proper support for roads and bridges, but it was obvious that it was not about to provide them in the desired numbers. At the same time that St. Bénézet and his brothers of the bridge were brilliantly successful in fund-raising efforts at Avignon, collectors at Agen failed dismally to obtain donations for more than the erection of a single pier. There were several means to increase funding for public works. One was to insist that the recipient of tolls be responsible for maintenance of roads and bridges. In 1235 an imperial peace proclamation made at Mainz decreed that those who received tolls were obligated

ROADS AND BRIDGES, EUROPEAN

to keep roads and bridges in repair. In France the royal government actively intervened. For one thing, the Parlement of Paris assessed the cost of repairs against the recipient of the tolls. Convents that in the twelfth century had gladly received a gift of tolls (which the donor considered would aid his soul) willingly relinquished them after the middle of the thirteenth century. The abbess and nuns of Fontevrault in exchange for other property turned over to Charles of Valois in 1293 everything they owned between one bridgehead of the Ponts-de-Lé and the other—the tolls and justice, "together with the houses and islands and other things" they held. Maintenance was too expensive: every year it had been necessary to journey six leagues to obtain wood for the repair of the bridge. The abbess retained only free passage across the bridge for herself, the nuns, and their servants.

Generally, bridge tolls were not an effective source of revenue. It is obvious that if the structure was impassable, income necessarily ceased (except for that from boatmen passing under the bridge). Second, local people were frequently exempt from paying tolls, and last, to the end of the Middle Ages there were always bridges where the toll was diverted from maintenance to other purposes, whether to fund a hospital, furnish a dowry, or increase the income of an individual. In 1339 tolls on the Pont-Vieux at Millau were divided among the king, the viscount of Fézenzaguet, and the hospital of St. John of Jeruslaem. The inhabitants of Millau were responsible for fortifying and guarding the bridge, and they paid taxes for its repair, but they passed free over the bridge. Local people preferred paying taxes for maintenance of the bridge rather than paying tolls. At Metz townsmen were entitled to free passage across the bridges but paid a death tax to the hospital of St. Nicolas-en-Neubourg, which was in charge of maintenance. Many residents of villages near Metz came annually to the hospital to swear they were "bourgeois of the hospital" and to donate the clothes of their dead as alms.

There were always a few bridges where passage over the structure was gratuitous, as was the case at Avignon and Orléans, but the reasons these bridges were able to provide free crossing was that they were corporations owning property. The endowed bridge was a corporation with its own seal. In England, London, Bideford, and Rochester bridge corporations all owned extensive property, including houses, gardens, and meadows. In the fifteenth century the Frankfurt bridge owned real estate, in the fourteenth the Regensburg bridge possessed baths, and in 1482 at Grimma the bridge was given a share in a silver mine by the town council. The income of the bridge at Orléans came from various sources. It was entitled to a toll on the bridge on market day, charges on boats passing under the span, the solicitation of alms in the duchy of Orléans, money from the alms trunk in front of the chapel of St. Anthony, rent from a mill, and income from houses, vineyards, meadows, and other rural properties. By far the most important source of income was rents from houses, which accounted for one-half to two-thirds of revenues. The bridge at Orléans and its hospital of St. Anthony with an endowment accumulated over the years were hardly dependent on tolls, and only in an emergency, like those after the English siege of 1428–1429 and the floods of 1435, was it necessary to appeal to the king for special taxes and tolls.

In the great twelfth-century bridge at Orléans the medieval ideal of the bridge as a pious work offering free and safe crossing over dangerous waters and almost entirely supported by voluntary donations was realized. Most bridges failed to acquire an adequate endowment or in some cases lost it. The Pont-Saint-Esprit, constructed by free-will offerings, was ordered to share them with the convent of St. Pierre, and the bridge was maintained after 1328 by a salt tax called the Petit-blanc. About 1308 the Pont-de-la-Guillotière was taken away from its bridge-building brotherhood and given to a convent that promised to rebuild it in stone and at the same time hoped to turn a profit from the endowment. The venture was a fiasco. In 1320 the bridge was in such a ruinous condition that the citizens of Lyons obtained from the king of France permission for a *barra* (toll) to be collected on the bridge, at Mâcon and at other places near Lyons. When, in 1334, the town gained control of the bridge, it had been denuded of almost all its property donated by the faithful for over 150 years. The archbishop of Lyons allowed the abbey of Chassagne to retain the endowment to support the bridge hospital (a small overnight shelter) and one of two chapels, on the grounds that the latter were properly objects of charity, but the bridge was a matter of public concern, the responsibility of the commune of Lyons, to be supported by tolls and taxes.

Royal support of bridges. Governments promoted the construction of bridges and roads. For

 ROADS AND BRIDGES, EUROPEAN

example, in Germany in 1310 Emperor Henry VII allowed Regensburg to impose taxes to improve roads, bridges, and the town entrance, and in 1342 Emperor Charles IV in his capacity as king of Bohemia gave permission for taxes to rebuild the Prague bridge, severely damaged in a flood. The English kings had long insisted that local inhabitants build and maintain bridges, and they did this not only in England but on the Continent. In 1283–1285 Edward I ordered the vice-seneschal of the Agenais to convoke a regional assembly to secure support for a bridge at Agen, and in 1286 he authorized the collection of a *barra* for this purpose. The advantage of the latter charge was that it could be collected at any point, whether or not the bridge was passable. Where charity had failed, taxes were effective in financing the bridge at Agen, which was usable early in the fourteenth century.

The kings of France willingly granted the right to collect taxes for bridges and roads, and this accounts for the high level of bridge building between about 1250 and 1350. They did more, however. Philip IV the Fair in 1304 forced the unwilling people of Montauban to erect a brick bridge and to build on it three towers for the king to garrison. He made a contribution to construction, ordered neighboring communities to do likewise, and authorized a toll on strangers crossing the bridge. The royal initiative in bridge building was something new, as for several centuries this had been provided locally.

Just as roads "were the great contribution of the Romans" to the English system of internal communications, according to C. T. Flower, "so the substitution of bridges, often substantially built, for fords was the great public work" of the medieval period. This statement may also be applied to France and Germany. Before the first half of the fourteenth century almost all the great bridges had been built. The period of the Hundred Years War was not conducive to enterprises of this sort, even if the most important urban centers had not been already provided with bridges. Maintenance was the overriding concern of the last couple of centuries of the Middle Ages, and this was true in Germany and England, as well as in France.

THE SURVIVING MEDIEVAL BRIDGES

Numerous medieval bridges are still in use. Among these in Spain are the bridge of St. Martin over the Tagus near Toledo, the Puente Major over the river Minho at Orense, and bridges at Martorelli over the Llobregat and over the Ebro at Saragossa, built in 1437. In Italy the most famous medieval bridge by far is the Ponte Vecchio in Florence, but many others can be seen, like the one over the Serchio at Lucca, over the Nervia at Dolceaque, and over the Ticino at Pavia. In Switzerland, Lucerne retains two picturesque covered bridges, one of them dating from 1333. In Great Britain and France some of the most renowned spans have disappeared, while out-of-the-way and smaller bridges have outlasted their better-known contemporaries. It is still possible to see Bideford Bridge (fourteenth century), the Brig of Ayr, built before 1286, and a number of thirteenth-century bridges in southern England, but London Bridge, the pride of medieval England, is gone. In France nothing remains of the medieval Parisian bridges or the great twelfth-century spans over the Loire, with the single exception of half of the bridge at Beaugency. Many bridges of the period are still to be seen in the less frequented parts of France. Examples are the immense Pont-Saint-Esprit over the Rhône and other, shorter spans like that at Montauban and the picturesque Pont-de-Cahors with its towers still boldly rising from the bridge.

Caution must be observed before assuming that the present-day appearance of a medieval bridge is identical with its appearance when first built. Bridges are exposed not only to alterations resulting from the changes in taste and requirements of succeeding ages, but also to shifts in the streambed and to catastrophic floods. In Spain, Alcántara, originally Roman, was rebuilt by the Visigoths, and again by Halaf, son of Mahomet Alameiri, in 871, restored in 1258, and repaired in 1380. In the medieval period most bridges were of timber, whereas the vast majority of bridges surviving from the period are in stone. The most common alterations in the appearance of medieval bridges have been the widening or even removal and extensive rebuilding of the superstructure. At Albi the narrowness of the stone bridge allowed passage only to pedestrians and pack animals, but in the nineteenth century brick was added to make it wide enough for carts. Beaugency has lost not only its stone towers and chapel but also its fishpond in the fifth arch. One of the few bridges that retain the medieval silhouette is the Ponte Vecchio at Florence, where shops still line the roadway, as in earlier centuries

ROADS AND BRIDGES, EUROPEAN

they did at the Grand and Petit Ponts in Paris and at London Bridge, and elsewhere.

BRIDGE CONSTRUCTION

Medieval bridge builders had before their eyes a series of Roman examples, ranging from timber bridges, spans with stone piers and wooden roadbeds, to structures entirely of stone. The ancients used iron-tipped piles under their piers, which were in many cases of large stone blocks with an inner core of concrete. The piers were of massive bulk. Roman bridges had pointed upstream cutwaters rising to the height of the springing of the arch or to the bottom of a small flood-arch through the pier. Often the arches were of parallel courses of stone without interlocking, but it is unclear whether the purpose was to save wood by reusing a narrow centering over and over or whether it was to give elasticity or to limit collapse in case of partial crumbling. Roman arches were always semicircular, but the ancients varied the size of the arch—and therefore the springing—as required to preserve a level roadbed.

Much greater diversity can be seen in medieval attempts to solve the problems of bridge construction than characterized Roman attempts. Medieval contributions included the introduction of novel shapes for arches and cutwaters, an improvised method of founding piers, and the use of a sand-lime mortar and small stones (except where large stones were readily available from ancient structures). The medieval builders built bridges with a more substantial distance between the keystone and roadbed, which in many cases sloped upward to a midpoint, instead of being level. Upstream cutwaters might be pointed, square, or even lacking entirely. They might be low or rise to the height of the springing of the arch or to the top of the parapets. Roman arches had been semicircular, but medieval arches were semicircular, segmental, or pointed.

Several Roman ideas were taken over by the Middle Ages. Some of these were used in only a few cases, such as arch openings through the pier for floodwaters, and building arches of parallel courses of stone. In France there were flood arches through piers, as for example at Béziers (about 1200), the Pont-Saint-Esprit (second half of the thirteenth), Montauban (early fourteenth), and the Pont-Saint-Bénézet. At Avignon the date of the four arches still to be seen is in dispute. They may be either from 1177–1188 or from the fourteenth century. For some Roman practices still followed in the Middle Ages, like fastening stones with iron bars sealed in lead, an adequate supply of large, hewn stones was essential. These conditions were present at the Pont-Saint-Esprit and at the Pont-Saint-Bénézet, for at the former there was an adjacent quarry, and at the latter at least some stones were Roman. (St. Bénézet's admonition to his followers was that if stones were needed for the bridge they should go and find some.) Many medieval bridges were built of small stones, as was true at Albi. At Montauban the entire structure was made of brick, and at Toulouse a pier built before 1480 had a facing of limestone imported from the Pyrenees, but the rest of the bridge was of brick.

A point on which ancient and medieval builders were entirely agreed was the necessity of massive piers, one-third to one-half the size of the arch openings. Such piers were still being recommended by Leone Battista Alberti in the fifteenth century. One of the reasons was that the Romans, an eminently practical people, disdained mathematics as a useless abstraction, with the result that they could not calculate the minimum-sized piers necessary to support the thrusts and strains of the arches. (Even in the eighteenth century Henri Gautier complained that the method for doing so supplied to him by the mathematician La Hire was useless: it involved albegra, something no builder knew. Evidently the theoretical training of builders was approximately the same in the early eighteenth century as it had been in the Middle Ages.) Massive piers had various advantages in the eyes of medieval builders, who found that they suited the scanty nature of their financing. Also, they were practical sites for houses and shops to bring in rent to support maintenance, and they were independent of the rest of the bridge. It was possible to construct massive piers one at a time, and if the bridge was forty years abuilding, no part of the structure suffered.

Neither Roman nor medieval builders ever fully solved the problem of secure foundations. The Romans understood how to put in a cofferdam and exhaust the water before driving piles, but they were satisfied to discontinue the operation when the pile first refused the pile driver. The same problem of secure foundations plagued the Middle Ages. In the twelfth century, and perhaps as early as the eleventh, "starlings" were constructed. These

ROADS AND BRIDGES, EUROPEAN

were made of piles driven into the riverbed to a depth of perhaps half their length so as to form an enclosure. Into this pen rubble was dumped to a height above water level, beams were laid down, and on top stones were paved and the masonry built. This starling method avoided entirely the need for nice engineering expertise or the assembling of large numbers of men and of piles needed to build a cofferdam, and it was also especially suited to bridges on tidal rivers, like those at Rochester, Bideford, and London. Disadvantages of starlings included the necessity of continuous maintenance. At Orléans the driving of piles to reinforce the starlings was an annual affair, continuing from June into September. Furthermore, as the starlings became larger and the freeway diminished, so did scour (damage caused by running water) increase. Old London Bridge measured 906 feet (276 meters), but of this the nineteen piers blocked 403 feet (123 meters) and the starlings still more, so that only 245 feet (75 meters) were available for the freeway (source: the plan of George Dance the Elder, dated 1799). The result was a waterfall under each arch at high tide, and the noise was called "the roaring of the bridge." Enormous piers contributed to the maddening difficulties experienced by the people of Lyons at the Pont-de-la-Guillotière, where not only one but several piers and arches were washed out again and again. The problem was related to the gravel bottom, the shallowness of the foundations, and the constriction of the stream by dikes to protect the riverbanks, which forced the river to flow faster and deeper. However, contemporaries ascribed the overturned piers to the "harshness" of the waters. Only in the sixteenth century were builders able to solve the problem, and the present-day Pont-de-la-Guillotière dates from that period. It was because of the difficulty in founding piers that so many medieval bridges were planned so as to cross islands in the rivers. This was true at Jargeau and at Ponts-de-Cé; and at Orléans there were a market, hospital, and chapel on an island in the middle of the bridge. The Pont-Saint-Bénézet described an angle so as to cross the island Barthelasse, where the dancing referred to in the song "Sur le pont d'Avignon / L'on y danse, l'on y danse" took place.

By the middle of the thirteenth century builders were using cofferdams. There is in existence a very detailed account of the construction of one during repairs to the bridge at Albi (1408–1410). After driving two parallel rings of piles and packing clay between them to make them watertight, the men, working around the clock, exhausted the water inside by means of wooden buckets. Customarily, at this point iron-shod piles were driven into the riverbed, and on these masonry was laid. Even knowledge of how to build a cofferdam did not guarantee success, however, and in 1435 one at the Pont d'Orléans had to be abandoned, because it turned out to have been built over a spring in the river bottom.

An aspect of bridge building in which medieval people seem to have been more daring than the Romans was in the length of their arches. A Roman arch at Alcántara measured 90 feet (27 meters), and that at the Ponte d'Augusto 105 (32 meters). These lengths were exceeded by many medieval bridges: Villeneuve d'Agen (fifteenth century), 115 feet (35 meters); a semicircular arch over the Serchio near Lucca, 120 feet (37 meters); at Martorelli over the Llobregat, 122 feet (37 meters); at Orense over the Minho (perhaps fourteenth century), 123 feet (38 meters); Puente de San Martín near Toledo (thirteenth century), 140 feet (43 meters); at Céret over the Tech (1336), 149 feet (45 meters); Puente Major at Orense (thirteenth century), 159 feet (48 meters); and Vieille-Brioude (Haute-Allier) (*ca.* 1340–1822), 178 feet (54 meters). The immense length of the last may have been practicable only because its single arch was braced against two banks. For nearly 400 years, says Séjourné, it had been the largest arch in the world. (We omit from consideration the arch at Trezzo of 271 feet [83 meters], on the ground that it lasted less than forty years, from 1377 to 1416.)

Pointed and segmental arches were also medieval innovations. The most famous segmental arches of the period occur in the Ponte Vecchio at Florence (1340), where they measure 90 and 100 feet (27 and 31 meters). The earliest in France was probably at Carcassonne (1184), where they measure only one-fifteenth less than a semicircle, but they were also employed at Pont-Saint-Bénézet and the Pont-Saint-Esprit. The advantage of the segmental arch is that it allows for smaller and fewer piers in the river, thus minimizing blocking of the freeway. Few segmental arches were constructed in the Middle Ages, perhaps at least in part because of a failure to grasp the mathematics involved. The ogival arch, which is extremely stable, was very popular, although it required more arches in the river, and semicircular arches continued to be built long after the discovery of other types, to the very end of the Middle Ages.

The originality of medieval builders was displayed in novel shapes not only for arches but also for cutwaters, as well as in the invention of starlings. The Middle Ages introduced the pointed downstream (as well as upstream) cutwater and also cutwaters rising to the height of the parapets. Bridges with these features included Millau (before 1156), Carcassonne (before 1184), Orthez (before 1254), and the Pont-Notre-Dame at Entraygues-sur-le-Lot (1269). Cutwaters pointed downstream protect the piers from eddies, something square ones do not do, and those cutwaters rising to the height of the parapets meant small safety areas for the protection of pedestrians on narrow bridges lacking sidewalks. Yet neither cutwaters pointed downstream nor cutwaters rising to the height of the parapets were widely used. Square ones—or even none at all—continued to be built throughout the Middle Ages.

The question then arises as to why medieval innovations were not more widely adopted. Part of the answer must lie in the fact that over most of Europe medieval bridge building was a very parochial art. It was limited by the mediocre experience of local people and the paucity of funds. During much of the later Middle Ages, regional authorities, bishops, convents, lay lords, or townsmen living adjacent to the desired bridge initiated bridge construction, which was then carried out by contractors and workmen from the neighborhood. For example, at Agen in the years 1345–1355 all the contractors were from the neighborhood with the single exception of one from Toulouse. At Nyons (Drôme) in 1398 the town employed a builder from Romans, and at Romans in 1388 the master of the works was sent to Lyons to study plans for rebuilding the Pont-de-la-Guillotière in stone. The wardens of Rochester Bridge in the fifteenth century sent to London for advice on repairs, but all these distances were small. Rare instances of the importation of a foreigner include King John's appointment of a contractor from his continental dominions to complete London Bridge and, in Germany, the hiring of Master William of the papal court at Avignon in 1333, who with his assistants built two piers and an arch of the bridge over the Elbe at Rudnitz. In general, however, there do not seem to have been specialists in the art of bridge building. To replace an arch, frequently contracts were let with both a local carpenter and mason. In 1133 the builder of the cathedral at Würzburg also constructed the bridge across the Main. If it was common practice for masons and carpenters accustomed to cathedral construction to double as bridge builders, it would be natural for them to use the same type of arch in both structures.

Methodical maintenance was already practiced at London Bridge in the thirteenth and at Rochester and Orléans in the fourteenth century. By the fifteenth century, governments provided regular inspections at Albi, Orléans, and Ponts-de-Cé. In anxious or difficult situations, approval was required not only of masons and carpenters but of governmental officials, town officers, and the important men of the commune, as when there was doubt whether a pier foundation was sufficiently deep. The consultation with notables may not have added much to the technical knowledge available, but it did at least diffuse the responsibility.

It is beside the point to criticize medieval bridges for being asymmetrical. For example, the fourteenth-century stone bridge over the Moselle at Coblenz had fourteen arches of differing widths, and the arches of the Castelvecchio in Verona (1356) vary from 79 to 61 feet (24 to 18.6 meters). For one thing, the idea of a master arch, wider than the others, was already used by the Romans; for another, the search for a secure pier foundation necessitated placing them at irregular intervals; then changes in taste altered the shapes of arches after floods; and finally, symmetry does not seem to have entered into the medieval idea of a beautiful bridge. What rendered the bridges attractive were the handsome houses built on them and the colorful tapestries strung along the roadway on fete days.

CONCLUSIONS

A consideration of Western European roads and bridges in the Middle Ages shows many features that would be expected of an era in which there were no strong central governments and in which transportation was difficult and slow. The movement of men, materials, and ideas was inhibited, which allowed for local improvisation but failed to encourage the spread of technologically superior innovations. Also, the limitations imposed by lack of funds, resulting from the medieval methods of financing roads and bridges, contributed to this parochialism. Nevertheless, in spite of these factors, by the end of the Middle Ages certain technological improvements had been introduced, and Western Europe had been provided with a system of bridges much superior to and more extensive than what had existed in Roman times.

BIBLIOGRAPHY

Leone Battista Alberti, *Ten Books on Architecture,* James Leoni, trans., Joseph Rykwert, ed. (1755, repr. 1966); Philippe de Beaumanoir, *Coutumes de Beauvaisis,* Amédée Salmon, ed., I (1899), 367–382; M. Janet Becker, *Rochester Bridge, 1378–1856: A History of Its Early Years Compiled from the Wardens' Accounts* (1930); Marjorie N. Boyer, "The Bridgebuilding Brotherhoods," in *Speculum,* **39** (1964), "Rebuilding the Bridge at Albi, 1408–1410," in *Technology and Culture,* 7 (1966), *Medieval French Bridges* (1976), "Moving Ahead with the Fifteenth Century: New Ideas in Bridge Construction at Orleans," in *History of Technology,* **6** (1981), "Water Mills: A Problem for the Bridges and Boats of Medieval France," *ibid.,* 7 (1982), and "A Fourteenth-century Pile Driver: The *Engin* of the Bridge at Orleans," *ibid.,* **9** (1984); Frank Brangwyn and Walter Shaw Sparrow, *A Book of Bridges* (1920); Henri Cavaillès, *La route française, son histoire, sa fonction: Étude de géographie humaine* (1946); Alexandre Collin, *Le Pont des Tourelles à Orléans (1120–1760): Étude sur les ponts au moyen âge,* in *Mémoires de la Société archéologique et historique de l'Orléanais,* **26, 27** (1895); Maurice Daumas, ed., *A History of Technology and Invention,* Eileen B. Hennessy, trans. (1969), 221–226, 555–556; Virginia Wylie Egbert, *On the Bridges of Mediaeval Paris: A Record of Early Fourteenth-century Life* (1974); William Emerson and Georges Gromort, *Old Bridges of France* (1925); Cyril Thomas Flower, ed., *Public Works in Medieval Law,* 2 vols. (1915–1923); Hubert Gautier, *Traité des ponts, où il est parlé de ceux des Romains et de ceux des modernes,* 4th ed. (1765); Albert Grenier, *Manuel d'archéologie gallo-romaine,* Deuxième partie, *L'archéologie du sol: Les routes,* I (1934), continuation of Joseph Dechelette, *Manuel d'archéologie préhistorique, celtique et gallo-romaine,* 4 vols. (1908–1927); Marie-Claude Guigue, "Notre-Dame de Lyon: Recherches sur l'origine du Pont de la Guillotière et du grand Hôtel-Dieu et sur l'emplacement de l'hôpital fondé à Lyon, au VIe siècle, par le roi Childebert et la reine Ultragothe," in *Mémoires de la Société littéraire, historique et archéologique de Lyon* (1874–1875); Hans Hitzer, *Die Strasse, vom Trampelpfad zur Autobahn: Lebensadern von der Urzeit bis heute* (1971); Gordon E. Home, *Old London Bridge* (1931); Edwyn Jervoise, *The Ancient Bridges of the South of England* (1930); Erich Maschke, "Die Brücke im Mittelalter," in *Historische Zeitschrift,* **224** (1977); Karl Möhringer, *The Bridges of the Rhine: Roman, Medieval, and Modern* (1931); Frederick William Robins, *The Story of the Bridge* (1948); Louis F. Salzman, *Building in England down to 1540* (1952); Paul Séjourné, *Grandes voûtes,* 6 vols. (1913–1916); Robert Silverberg, *Bridges* (1966); Charles Singer *et al.,* eds., *History of Technology,* II (1956), 500–516, 524–527; David B. Steinman and Sarah R. Watson, *Bridges and Their Builders,* 2nd ed. (1957); Wilbur Jay Watson, *Bridge Architecture, Containing Two Hundred Illustrations of the Notable Bridges of the World, Ancient and Modern, with Descriptive, Historical, and Legendary Text* (1927); *idem* and Sarah R. Watson, *Bridges in History and Legend* (1937); Charles S. Whitney, *Bridges: A Study in Their Art, Science, and Evolution* (1929).

MARJORIE N. BOYER

[See also **Construction; Masons and Builders; Mills; Technology, Western; Travel and Transport, Western European; Vehicles, European.**]

ROADS AND COMMUNICATIONS, BYZANTINE. Roman needs to reach the eastern frontier and especially the foundation of Constantinople shaped communications in the Byzantine Empire. For more than a millennium, Constantinople was the center of land and sea routes between the eastern and western Mediterranean and between the Aegean and the Black Seas. In the Middle Ages, it dominated the road between Europe and the lands of Islam and was the main port for relations with Russia. For most of the period, it was the greatest trading and manufacturing city of the Western world. Maps, itineraries, and milestones give a detailed picture of the road system of late antiquity, but their evidence ends with the fifth century. The invasions of the Dark Ages severely disrupted communications, and routes of that period are poorly known. The Byzantines gradually restored the road system, which, since the routes were determined by geographical conditions, was based essentially on the Roman system and underwent few changes for a thousand years. Byzantine writers provide only sporadic information about the roads in their narratives of campaigns or their accounts of the imperial military highway; more detailed, though less intelligible, information appears in the writings of Arab geographers.

The main artery of the empire was the great military highway from the Balkans to Syria, best known as the route of the crusaders. It entered Byzantine territory at Belgrade (Singidunum) and led from there to Nish (Naissus), then through steep

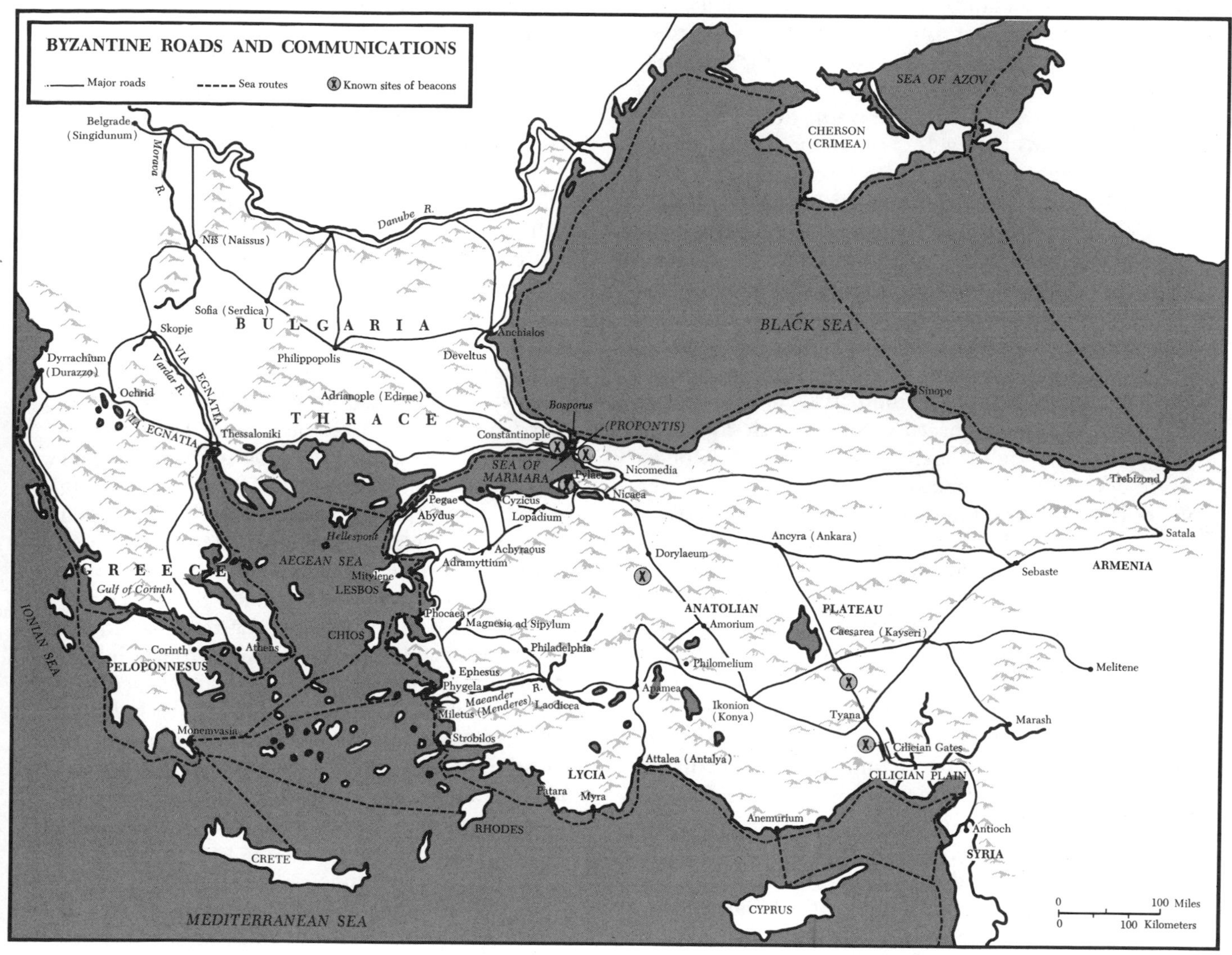

passes and forests to Sofia (Serdica), to pass the whole breadth of Bulgaria in easy stages through Philippopolis to Adrianople, then across the rolling country of Thrace to Constantinople. The journey took about a month. The route from the capital eastward crossed the Bosporus and continued through Nicomedia to Nicaea, but smaller parties usually avoided this detour by crossing the Propontis to Pylae and continuing by road to Nicaea. East of that city, the highway branched to avoid the arid steppe around the salt lake in the center of the Anatolian plateau. The southern branch, favored by emperors and the First Crusade, led through Dorylaeum, Amorium, Iconium (the later Seljuk capital Konya), and Tyana to the Cilician Gates, the narrow gorge which led to the Cilician plain and Antioch. Alternatively, to reach the eastern frontier, the highway branched at Iconium or Tyana for Caesarea (Kayseri) and led thence through the Anti-Taurus to Marash or Melitene, or northeast to Sebaste, Satala, and Armenia. The whole route was provided with stations where the emperor would stop and be met by the various thematic armies. The northern branch led east from Nicaea to Ancyra (Ankara), then southeast to Colonia and Tyana. The route through Ancyra, with its contin-

ROADS, BYZANTINE

uation to Caesarea or Sebaste and the frontier, was favored in Roman times and in late antiquity.

Numerous other routes connected the various parts of the empire and joined it with the surrounding lands. For traffic coming from Italy, the main port was Dyrrachium (Durazzo), from which numerous roads gave access to the interior. The most important in the Middle Ages, as in antiquity, was the ancient Via Egnatia, which passed through Ochrid to Thessaloniki, then along the north coast of the Aegean to Constantinople. From Durazzo, major routes also led into the Balkans, to Skopje and Belgrade, and south into Greece. The strategic location of Thessaloniki ensured its predominance as the main commercial center of the western Balkans and Greece. It stood at the junction of the Via Egnatia and the easy route which connected Central Europe through the valleys of the Morava and Vardar with Greece and continued south as the only practicable highway to Athens and the Peloponnesus. In the eastern Balkans (for much of this period the independent country of Bulgaria), a major highway followed the course of the Danube from Belgrade to the sea, with routes running south from it through several passes to Sofia, to Philippopolis, and to a major road junction around Develtus and Anchialos; from there, good routes led north to Russia, south along the coast to Constantinople and west into the interior. By all these routes, communication between the Balkans and the capital was ensured. Most roads converged on Constantinople, with some leading to Thessaloniki, the second city of the empire.

The main routes of ancient Asia Minor had led to such great Aegean cities as Ephesus and Miletus, but the foundation of Constantinople redirected most of the imperial, military, and long-distance traffic. This change did not involve the decay of western Anatolia or abandonment of its road system. It remained the richest part of the country, and its ancient routes continued in use. From the capital, this area was reached directly from Cyzicus or Pegae on the Propontis, or by a long detour through Nicaea and Lopadium. These routes converged north of Achyraous, from which roads led to Adramyttium and the Aegean coast (followed by the Second Crusade) or southward to Magnesia or Philadelphia (the route of the Third Crusade). The main highway of Roman Asia Minor led from Ephesus up the Maeander Valley to Laodicea, Apamea, and Philomelium to join the southern branch of the military highway; parts of this route were followed by the Second and Third Crusades. On the Anatolian plateau, the main centers of communication were Dorylaeum, Amorium, Ancyra, and Caesarea. In the north, the great center was Trebizond, which came into special prominence in the thirteenth and fourteenth centuries as the terminus of the caravan route from Persia.

The rough configuration of the Byzantine lands, with their many mountains, meant that as much traffic as possible went by sea, usually sailing in sight of land. Here, too, most routes converged on Constantinople. The major port of the western Balkans was Durazzo, whence vessels followed the coast and islands around the Peloponnesus to Monembasia. From there, those proceeding directly to the east steered by the Aegean islands to Chios or Samos or made for Crete and Rhodes. Small vessels bound for Constantinople avoided the long and dangerous circuit of the Peloponnesus by passing through the Gulf of Corinth and being hauled across the isthmus. They then sailed north to Thessaloniki or directly by the islands to the capital. These sea-lanes were essential for the Venetians, who later built many castles along them. Traffic to Constantinople had to pass the strongpoint of Abydus on the Hellespont, where all stopped and paid customs dues. Ships sailing north to Bulgaria and Russia followed the western coast of the Black Sea or cut across to Cherson. Trebizond attracted much of the trade of that region, with sea routes leading from it along the southern shore to Constantinople or Georgia, or across to Cherson or to the mouth of the Danube.

Shipping to the Arab lands followed the coast of Anatolia, usually touching at the large islands of Mitylene, Chios, Samos, and Rhodes, and sometimes at the ports of Adramyttium, Phocaea (later a Genoese stronghold), Phygela, and Strobilos. From there, they rounded the headland of Lycia, stopping at Patara and Myra, and turned north to Attalea (Antalya), the greatest city of the southern coast. Here, customs were collected on goods coming from the East; these were frequently disembarked here to be transported overland to the capital, avoiding the Aegean altogether. From Attalea, vessels could follow the coast all the way to the ports of Cilicia and Syria, but far more often they sailed across to Cyprus and made from there to Syria or the Holy Land.

Transport by land was notoriously slow; by sea, it was faster but less secure and impossible after the calm summer season. To respond to the frequent

ROADS IN THE ISLAMIC WORLD

attacks of the Arabs, therefore, the Byzantines needed a swifter form of communication, which they devised in a system of beacons. These were lit on high hilltops across Asia Minor from Lulon above the Cilician Gates, whence most attacks came, to Mount St. Auxentius just outside the capital. A clock at Lulon, synchronized with one in Constantinople, told the meaning of the signal by the hour in which it was given. If necessary, the imperial army would then set out along the great military highway. Arab raids were frequent, as apparently were the more peaceful visits of traders, whose activities probably account for the relatively detailed knowledge of the Byzantine road system that appears in Arab sources.

BIBLIOGRAPHY

David French, *Roman Roads and Milestones of Asia Minor* (1981); Nicholas G. L. Hammond, *Migrations and Invasions in Greece and Adjacent Areas* (1976); Friedrich Hild, *Das byzantinische Strassensystem in Kappadokien* (1977); George Huxley, "A List of *Aplekta,*" in *Greek, Roman, and Byzantine Studies,* **16** (1975); Pierre Jaubert, trans., *Géographie d'Edrisi,* 2 vols. (1836–1840); Josef K. Jireček, *Die Heerstrasse von Belgrad nach Constantinopel und die Balkan Passe* (1877); Konrad Miller, *Itineraria romana* (1916); Boris Nedkov, *La Bulgarie et les terres avoisinantes au XIIe siècle selon la "Géographie" d'al Idrissi"* (1960), in Bulgarian with French summary; William Mitchell Ramsay, *The Historical Geography of Asia Minor* (1891), hopelessly outdated and full of mistakes, but not yet replaced.

CLIVE FOSS

[See also **Anatolia; Bulgaria; Cilician Gates; Crusades and Crusader States; Geography and Cartography; Idrīsī, al-;** and individual cities.]

ROADS IN THE ISLAMIC WORLD. A major factor affecting the character of roads in the Islamic countries of North Africa and the Middle East (excluding Anatolia) was the disappearance of all wheeled transportation over the several centuries immediately prior to the rise of Islam. The development of the road system of the area during the Islamic period was actually the latter phase of a continuous evolution that began in approximately the third century.

At the root of the disappearance of wheeled vehicles was the economic advantage to be realized by using pack camels instead of oxcarts, an advantage put at 20 percent in Diocletian's edict on prices (301). The actual working out of the economic competition involved a complicated series of additional factors, however, such as the difficulty of harnessing camels to carts, the high cost of vehicles in a wood-poor area, and the social barriers existing between desert camel breeders and potential camel users in urban and agricultural areas. But despite uncertainties in the chain of causation, it is quite apparent that all but the most extraordinary vehicular traffic had vanished from the lands conquered by the Arabs in the seventh century well before the invaders arrived.

The ways in which the road system changed over time to accommodate the new transport conditions are several. The physical state of the road surface became less important once wheels were dispensed with, as did width, steepness of grades, and sharp turns. In the largely dry, unforested, and flat terrain of much of the Middle East and North Africa, these matters had already—before the wheel's disappearance—been less of a concern than they were elsewhere, and they became even less so; in addition the Roman road network fell into disrepair, though not necessarily into disuse, because repair became less urgent.

Yet when circumstances dictated, Muslim rulers and engineers demonstrated concern and ability in improving the physical state of roads. A late, detailed illustration from a Persian chronicle of the seventeenth century deals with a rainy and forested mountainous region just south of the Caspian Sea:

> The narrowness of the roads through the forests and over the mountain passes of Māzandarān makes it difficult for even a single rider to traverse them. At every step, the rider is forced to dismount because of some hazard, and it is impossible for slow-moving camels to make their way along them. . . . [To remedy this] solid bridges of stone, brick, and lime mortar were built over all the rivers that crossed the road. In the case of watercourses which carried flash floods down from the mountains, wherever the workmen thought the banks might collapse, they constructed diversionary channels lined with brick and cemented with lime mortar to take off the surplus water and lead it down to a river. Efforts were made to level the road, and wooded sections were cleared by woodcutters. Sand and gravel were brought from immense distances so that the ground on each side of the road could be sloped off in order to carry rainwater into channels and thence into the rivers; in this way, the center of the road remained dry and free from mud. Narrow stretches of the road through the forest were cleverly

widened. In some places, massive timbers were laid down, and in others, the engineers had to cut away rock, using a variety of novel techniques. (Iskandar Beg Munshī, *The History of Shah ᶜAbbas the Great,* 1,211–1,212)

In contrast with the road's physical state, other elements of route maintenance took on increased importance, notably security and provision of bridges, water supplies, and caravansaries. When towns were not conveniently at hand, stopping points were commonly constructed at intervals of one day's travel (fifteen to twenty miles, or twenty-four to thirty-two kilometers) to give safe overnight shelters for men, goods, and animals, usually in a structure built around a protected central courtyard.

The nonvehicular nature of the transport system affected urban streets as well. Although paving was not unknown, it was largely unnecessary. Careful control of road width to allow vehicles to pass and provision of large turnaround spaces for wagons in market areas were likewise unneeded. These and similar factors contributed greatly to the development of cities with narrow, winding streets and equally narrow lanes of open shops in the markets.

The main routes followed during the Islamic period differed little from those of the pre-Islamic period. (They have been summarized and schematically mapped from the Arabic geographers by Aloys Sprenger.) Since the cost of transportation by land was much greater than that by water, usable water routes took precedence over roads for long-distance trade—for example, across northern Libya, where the Mediterranean offered a better alternative, or north and south in Egypt, where the Nile was preferable. In the case of the Euphrates, water transport was very difficult upstream, so the parallel caravan route through the nearby desert remained a vital link connecting Iraq and the East with Syria and the West.

Mention of the Euphrates route and other great routes, such as the one from Baghdad across northern Iran to central Asia (called the Khorāsān Highway after that province of northeastern Iran) or the one from Yemen through Mecca to Syria in western Arabia, gives rise to not inaccurate visions of great caravans of pack animals crossing arid wastes and of pilgrims trudging toward their spiritual capital. But it should be kept in mind that most medieval Muslims were settled in villages and towns, and most road use arose from local economic activities. Animals carrying grain from village to town or bricks from kiln to building site are as typical of the influences affecting the development of the road system as the long-distance camel caravan trekking through the desert.

BIBLIOGRAPHY

Richard W. Bulliet, *The Camel and the Wheel* (1975); Iskandar Beg Munshī (Eskander Beg Monshi), *The History of Shah ᶜAbbas the Great,* Roger M. Savory, trans., II (1978), 1211–1212; Aloys Sprenger, *Die Post- und Reiserouten des Orients* (1864, repr. 1966).

RICHARD W. BULLIET

[See also **Trade, Islamic; Travel and Transport, Islamic; Vehicles, Islamic.**]

ROBBIA. See **Della Robbia: Luca, Andrea, Giovanni.**

ROBERT I OF SCOTLAND (1274–1329). Born probably at Turnberry on 11 July 1274, Robert Bruce VIII inherited his grandfather's claim to the Scottish throne and his mother's earldom of Carrick. In 1296 he and his father were in Edward I's army invading Scotland, and after the expulsion of King John Balliol they unsuccessfully petitioned for the vassal throne. In 1297, proclaiming his Scottish birth, Robert Bruce rebelled against Edward I; and although he made terms, this submission was not completed. After the defeat of William Wallace in 1298 he became one of the guardians of Scotland, ostensibly for King John. Within a year, however, he quarreled with the leadership and was superseded; and early in 1302, when it seemed that John might be restored, he made submission to Edward I, in the hope, it has been suggested, that the latter might still give the Scottish vassal throne to the Bruces. With the collapse of the Balliol cause (1304) and the death of his father, Robert Bruce doubtless became aware of his own responsibility for securing the throne that he felt was the family's right, but that the family had hitherto hoped to receive as vassals from Edward I.

In February 1306 Robert quarreled with and (in an unpremeditated act) murdered the leading Scottish patriot, John Comyn, lord of Badenoch. From that time, Robert was determined to win the throne of an independent Scotland. On 25 March 1306 he

ROBERT I OF SCOTLAND

was inaugurated as king in traditional fashion, upon a stone at Scone, but his support was modest, and on 19 June he was heavily defeated by the English at Methven. By the winter he was a refugee in the Western Isles, and after his return to Ayrshire in 1307 further disasters befell him, so that he became a hunted fugitive, while three of his brothers had been taken prisoner and executed.

After the death of Edward I (7 July 1307) and Robert's move to the north, where the English were weaker, the tide turned. By swift strikes and truces, he kept his enemies divided. At Inverurie on 23 May 1308 he defeated John Comyn, earl of Buchan, and secured control of the Inverness-Aberdeen area. By the end of that year he controlled the area as far south as the Tay and in 1309 drove the MacDougalls from Argyll. After truces (1309) and an ineffectual stay by Edward II at Berwick (1310–1311), King Robert attacked Lothian and northern England. Often he took blackmail from a whole county to refrain from ravaging it but to have freedom to march through to attack the next county; in this way the war was self-financed. Dundee and Perth fell in 1312–1313 and Edinburgh and Roxburgh early in 1314. To save the threatened key stronghold of Stirling, Edward II came north with a large army; but he suffered a crushing defeat at the hands of Robert and his much smaller force at Bannockburn on 24 June 1314.

Nonetheless this did not compel the English to sue for peace. King Robert, in addition to raiding England (where he was unable to penetrate further south than Yorkshire), then sent his only remaining brother, Edward, to lead the native Irish against the English as "king of Ireland" (1315). Edward was killed in 1318. That same year Berwick fell and was held against English siege in 1319. A two-year truce in 1320–1321 was followed by another unsuccessful English invasion in 1322, which Robert met with "scorched earth" tactics. Robert also intrigued with Thomas, earl of Lancaster, against Edward II in 1321–1322, and in 1323 with Andrew Harcla, earl of Carlisle. And in 1327, a thirteen-year truce that had begun in 1323 was deliberately broken by Robert. The weak English government, defeated in a humiliating encounter, had decided by September to make peace (completed at Edinburgh in March 1328) and recognize Robert I as an independent king. The Scots undertook to pay £20,000 and secured a marriage of Robert's son to Edward III's sister.

Robert's determination not to accept vassal status is expressed in several documents asserting the freedom of Scotland, notably the letter to Pope John XXII known as the Declaration of Arbroath (1320). His domestic policy was as successful as his war policy. He relied upon two notable captains, his nephew Thomas Randolph, whom he made earl of Moray (1312) with a huge territory, and Sir James Douglas, who was also rewarded with ample lands. In 1313 he gave notice that all who did not join him within a year would lose their lands by 6 November 1314. This probably had much to do with Edward II's invasion of 1314. Many took the hint, but even those who did not, for example the earl of Fife, had all or most of their lands restored later, the earl of Mar as late as 1327. Robert was not profligate with gifts of land to his supporters, but he did dispose of the Comyn and Balliol lands and those of the earl of Atholl. In 1326, during the long truce, he claimed that his income was inadequate, and in return for yielding the right to provision armies by "prise" (a compulsory levy of produce for which the market price was supposed to be paid) he was given an annual tenth of incomes for life. To this was added in 1328 a further tenth for three years to pay off the English. These grants were made in parliaments to which, for the first time to our knowledge, burgesses were summoned.

The deaths of Robert's brothers left a serious lack of heirs. He was twice married, but his second wife and his daughter by his first marriage, Marjory, were held prisoner in England from 1306 to 1314. In 1315 the king's brother Edward Bruce was recognized as heir presumptive, and after him Marjory, who was soon married to Walter Stewart. She died in childbirth in 1316, leaving a son, Robert Stewart, who was recognized as heir presumptive in 1318. He succeeded as Robert II only in 1371, however, since in 1324 the king had a son, David. The latter was acknowledged as heir in parliament in 1326 and was married to Joanna (Jeanne), sister of Edward III, in 1328. King Robert was by then clearly very ill with a wasting disease called "leprosy." He lived at a manor house at Cardross by Dunbarton and from there made a last pilgrimage, probably by sea, to Whithorn. He died at Cardross on 7 June 1329, a week before the pope granted to the Scottish kings the right to be crowned and anointed—full recognition of their independence.

The reign of Robert I has left the earliest surviving register of royal charters and the earliest surviving royal accounts. He was also the subject of a verse romance in Middle Scots written in the 1370's

 ROBERT II OF SCOTLAND

by John Barbour, archdeacon of Aberdeen. This poem, *The Bruce,* is our main source for the difficult years 1307–1309, although it undoubtedly overplays the appeal and the success of the king. But its substantial accuracy for the period 1312–1329 is unquestioned, and its theme of "freedom" reflects the widespread yearning that gave Robert Bruce his success.

BIBLIOGRAPHY

G. W. S. Barrow, *Robert Bruce and the Community of the Realm of Scotland* (1965, rev. 1987); *Regesta regum Scottorum,* V, A. A. M. Duncan, ed., *The Acts of Robert I, 1306–1329* (1987).

A. A. M. Duncan

[See also **Barbour, John; David II of Scotland; Edward I of England; Edward II of England; Parliament, Scottish; Scotland: History.**]

ROBERT II OF SCOTLAND (1316–1390) (*r.* 1371–1390) was the first Stewart ruler. Although his ineffectiveness has been condemned by all modern commentators, his reign is ripe for reevaluation. The son of Walter the High Steward and Marjorie, daughter of Robert I, he was declared the latter's heir in 1318 but was displaced as such with the birth of the future David II (to Robert I) in 1324. Robert nonetheless had considerable administrative experience, notably as guardian or lieutenant of Scotland during David's imprisonment in England, from 1346 to 1357. Although he crossed the king several times, becoming involved in a feeble rebellion in 1363, he eventually developed a preference for the low profile and a proclivity for conciliation and the via media. As guardian he once wrote, "For our own part we beseech you and on the part of our lord the king we firmly command and direct you."

It has been observed of Robert that there are "few medieval sovereigns about whom so little is known, and of whom it is so difficult to form any clear picture." When he succeeded at age fifty-five, on 22 February 1371, he was regarded by the nobility as, at best, "first among equals." Married twice, he had fathered at least twenty-one offspring, only four of whom "were indisputably born in lawful wedlock."

Yet Robert's reign reveals a surprising amount of activity in parliament and the general council. His *acta* reveal a greater degree of personal involvement in the affairs of the kingdom than is often allowed. In 1373 he defined succession to the crown through an elaborate entail. He showed some interest in law reform. He closely allied himself with the most powerful nobles in the land. The oft cited lawlessness that supposedly plagued his kingdom is recorded from districts controlled by his unruly sons, notably those of Alexander, earl of Buchan, "the Wolf of Badenoch." Even the exchequer was in a fairly healthy condition during Robert's active reign.

The renewal of war with England in 1378 for the first time since 1356 may have been largely beyond his control. It largely concerned the recovery of lands in the Borders still in English control. A French expeditionary force that waged the dismal campaign of 1385 under Jean de Vienne (chronicled by Froissart) was sent to assist the Scots against Richard II. The greatest casualties of the war were several Border abbeys torched by the English, who regarded Scottish adherence to Pope Clement VII as the action of schismatics. The posthumous victory of the earl of Douglas over Hotspur (Sir Henry Percy) at the Battle of Otterburn (1388) provided scant compensation.

In 1388 Robert II formally renounced his administrative powers to the general council while retaining the "dignity" of kingship; his second son (Robert Stewart, earl of Fife) was appointed guardian. This enlightened transaction illustrates the bloodless evolution of Scottish constitutionalism.

Robert spent considerable sums rebuilding the castles of Rothesay and Edinburgh. He also presided over something of a literary flowering: the works of John Barbour, most noted for his sustained poetic narrative *The Bruce,* and of John of Fordun, who produced a patriotic chronicle of Scottish history, both appeared during his reign—which was perhaps less "dismal" and "pedestrian" than modern authorities have alleged.

BIBLIOGRAPHY

William C. Dickinson and Archibald A. M. Duncan, *Scotland from the Earliest Times to 1603,* 3rd ed. (1977), 195–202; Gordon Donaldson, *Scottish Kings* (1967), 34–40; Archibald H. Dunbar, *Scottish Kings: A Revised Chronology of Scottish History, 1005–1625,* 2nd ed. (1906), 159–171; Alexander Grant, *Independence and Nationhood: Scotland 1306–1469* (1984), 178–181; Ranald Nicholson, *Scotland: The Later Middle Ages* (1974), 149, 178–179, 184–204; Thomas Thomson, ed., *The Acts of the Parliaments of Scotland,* I (1844), 181–202.

Edward J. Cowan

[See also **David II of Scotland; Scotland: History.**]

ROBERT D'ARBRISSEL (*ca.* 1047–1117), founder of the Fontevrault order, was one of the most celebrated preachers of his time. His power to move audiences of the most diverse social makeup—from lepers and prostitutes to the highest ranks of the clergy and nobility—was legendary. In an age of intense religious activity, Robert was exemplary: his reformer's zeal was linked to a profound commitment to the ideals of personal poverty and charity, as well as to a new and exalted conception of the status of women.

Born in the village of Arbrissel in Brittany, Robert was the son and grandson of local parish priests. Little is known of his youth and early intellectual formation, which seems to have involved an extended period of traveling as a wandering scholar. There followed a long stay in Paris (*ca.* 1078–1089) devoted to the literary and philosophical studies of the trivium cycle. The first signs of his religious vocation date from this time. In 1089 Robert was summoned to Rennes by the bishop, Sylvester de la Guerche, to aid the latter's attempts at clerical reform in Brittany. Robert spent four years at Rennes, where, with the title of archpriest, he campaigned zealously against ecclesiastical abuses, especially the widespread practices of clerical marriage (exemplified by his own family background) and simony. With the death of Bishop Sylvester in 1093, the reform movement came under attack, and Robert was forced to leave Rennes. He settled in Angers (where the famous poet Marbod was head of the cathedral school) and assiduously applied himself to what was to be the final phase of his studies.

During his two-year sojourn in Angers, Robert practiced a rigorous asceticism that culminated in his flight to the forest of Craon in 1095 in order to take up the life of a hermit. At first Robert pursued in solitude his strict program of mortification of the flesh combined with prayer and meditation. This prompted Yves, bishop of Chartres, to write to him, cautioning against the special dangers and temptations of such solitary devotion. Robert's purely hermitic existence was, however, soon modified by the arrival in Craon of an ever-increasing number of disciples who wished to follow his example. Having organized this group into a community of canons regular at La Roë, Robert received a donation of land from Renaud de Craon for the foundation of a monastery under the Augustinian Rule. The episcopal confirmation of this grant took place at Angers in February 1096, and Robert's status as head of the community was simultaneously recognized by Pope Urban II. According to Baudri of Bourgueil, the pope also conferred upon Robert at this time the special office of public itinerant preacher.

While Robert was at first able to combine his two official charges, by 1098 he had definitively renounced the direction of La Roë in order to devote himself exclusively to public preaching throughout northwest France. His success was such that a large number of followers accompanied him on his travels, imitating his exemplification of Christian poverty. This group included all social classes, from lepers to peasants to nobles. The preponderance of women in this context was striking. While Robert's repeated diatribes against the corrupt practices of the regular clergy certainly provoked hostile reactions among contemporaries, it was the status of his own female followers that provided his critics with their most powerful ammunition. Thus Marbod (bishop of Rennes since 1096) addressed his famous letter of reproach to Robert, condemning him not simply for having abandoned La Roë, but, most especially, for his dangerously irregular and intimate life with the women in his train.

By 1101 Robert had decided to establish his large body of itinerant followers on a permanent site, where the women would be separated from the men and a communal religious life would be strictly regulated. The site chosen was Fontevrault (Fons Evraldi) in the diocese of Poitiers, whose bishop, Pierre II, was to be one of Robert's strongest supporters. During its first years Fontevrault was governed by a provisional rule that privileged the much more numerous women of the community, by designating women as contemplatives and directing men to engage in manual labor. It was during this period (*ca.* 1101–1102) that Geoffrey of Vendôme wrote his solicitous letter, which, however, strongly criticized Robert's continuing practice of syneisaktism (the ascetic practice of living and even sleeping with women so as to provoke physical desire in order to master it).

Meanwhile, the community expanded very quickly: numerous gifts and new members were received, and an ambitious program of building was undertaken. By 1102–1103 a more formal administrative structure was required, and Robert, who had refused the title of abbot, named two women to head the nascent order. Hersende de Champagne was invested as prioress, with Pétronille de Chemillé designated as associate director. With this new organization in place, Robert began an extended series of trips throughout the west of France, during which he combined itinerant preaching with the founding of priories dependent on Fontevrault. These voyages, punctuated by periodic returns to Fontevrault, continued for the rest of Robert's life.

In 1106 Pope Paschal II issued a bull that confirmed the foundation of the order at Fontevrault and accorded it special papal protection. The ensuing nine years were a period of intense activity for Robert, whose travels took him from the Touraine to Brittany. His preaching resulted in a large number of territorial donations from the French nobility, among whom Robert's prestige became quite high, as well as from people of modest circumstances. Foulque le Jeune, count of Anjou, and Pierre II, bishop of Poitiers, were of special importance in furthering Robert's success at this time, and he was in frequent contact with both of them. It was also during this period (probably *ca.* 1110) that Robert's only surviving work was written: a letter to Ermengarde, countess of Brittany. The letter gives a sense of the content of his sermons; there is great emphasis on inner piety, spiritual purification, personal charity, and divine love and mercy.

By April 1113, when Paschal II reconfirmed the special status of Fontevrault, Hersende had died (probably during the winter of 1112–1113) and Pétronille had replaced her as prioress. For the next two years, Robert continued to travel and preach extensively. A series of charters gives evidence of the continuing expansion of Fontevrault's holdings as well as of Robert's largely successful involvement in related legal disputes. Early in 1115, however, a serious illness prompted Robert to focus his attention on the mother abbey, which needed a more formal organization to maintain itself intact after its founder's death. First, Robert obtained the explicit agreement of the members of the community to form a hierarchized double order in which the brothers would always remain subordinate to the nuns, who would have absolute control in both spiritual and temporal matters. The whole congregation would be under the jurisdiction of an abbess, and Robert obtained ecclesiastical approval of the principle that this abbess be not a virgin but a widow. There followed in October 1115 the election of Pétronille de Chemillé, Robert's personal choice, as the first abbess of Fontevrault. By the end of the year, her status had been confirmed by Pope Paschal II and by the papal legate, Gérard, bishop of Angoulême. It was only after Pétronille's election that Robert set forth a definitive and comprehensive rule for the new order: the nuns were placed under a modified version of the Benedictine Rule, while the much smaller male community, which included both clergy and laity, was governed by the Augustinian Rule.

Having thus provided Fontevrault with a stable organization, Robert spent the final year and a half of his life visiting and administering the order's priories, as well as arbitrating various ecclesiastical disputes; Pétronille often accompanied and aided him on these trips. He continued to preach right up to the end, giving his final sermon at the monastery of Bourdieux one week before his death on 25 February 1117, at the Fontevrist priory of Orsan. Shortly thereafter, his body was transported to Fontevrault, where he was buried after a public ceremony attended by an enormous crowd, which included many high ecclesiastical and secular dignitaries.

BIBLIOGRAPHY

Sources. Brother André, *Vita auctore Andrea (Vita altera),* in *Patrologia latina,* CLXII (1854), 1,057–1,078. Written between 1117 and 1120, postdating the biography of Baudri to which it refers. Brother André focuses almost exclusively on Robert's final years and death. He is unknown apart from this work and was most likely a monk and priest at Fontevrault and the companion, and perhaps the personal confessor, of Robert.

Baudri of Bourgueil, *Vita auctore Baldrico (Vita prima),* in *Patrologia latina,* CLXII (1854), 1,043–1,058. Commissioned by Pétronille and written shortly after Robert's death. Baudri was archbishop of Dol from 1107 until his death in 1130 and one of the major prelate-poets of the so-called École de la Loire.

Geoffrey of Vendôme, *Epistola* 47, in *Patrologia latina,* CLVII (1854), 181–184; Marbod de Rennes, *Epistola* 6, in *Patrologia latina,* CLXXI (1854), 1,480–1,486; Robert d'Arbrissel, *Sermo domini Roberti de Arbrussello ad Comitissam Britanniae,* in J. de Petigny, "Lettre inédite de Robert d'Arbrissel à la comtesse Ermengarde," in *Bibliothèque de l'École des Chartes,* 5 (1854); Yves de Chartres, *Epistolae* 34 and 37, in *Patrologia latina,* CLXII (1854), 46, 49–50.

Studies. Reto R. Bezzola, "Guillaume IX, le premier troubadour, et Robert d'Arbrissel, le fondateur de Fontevrault," in *Les origines et la formation de la littérature courtoise en Occident (500–1200). 2e Partie: La société féodale et la transformation de la littérature de cour* (1960), 275–316; Jean-Marc Bienvenu, "Aux origines d'un ordre religieux: Robert d'Arbrissel et la fondation de Fontevraud (1101)," in *Aspects de la vie conventuelle aux XI–XIIIe siècle. Actes du 5e congrès de la Société des Historiens Mediévistes de l'enseignement supérieur public* (1975), 119–135, and *L'étonnant fondateur de Fontevraud, Robert d'Arbrissel* (1981); René Niderst, *Robert d'Arbrissel et les origines de l'ordre de Fontevrault* (1952); J. de Petigny, "Robert d'Arbrissel et Geoffroi de Vendôme," in *Bibliothèque de l'École des Chartes,* 5 (1854); Louis A. Picard, *Le fondateur de l'ordre de Fontevrault: Robert d'Arbrissel, un apôtre du XIe siècle, son temps, sa vie, ses disciples, son oeuvre* (1932); Johannes Wilhelm von Walter, *Die ersten Wanderprediger Frankreichs: Studien zur Geschichte des Mönchtums. Teil I: Robert von Arbrissel* (1903). An appendix contains a critical text of Marbod's letter and of the great Rule of Fontevrault.

KEVIN BROWNLEE

[See also **Baudri of Bourgueil; Marbod of Rennes; Paschal II, Pope; Urban II, Pope;** and frontispiece to volume 8.]

ROBERT DE BORON (*fl. ca.* 1200), a Burgundian poet, probably born in what is today the Franche-Comté, near Montbéliard. It is likely that he was a familiar at the court of Gautier de Montbéliard. Robert composed a cycle of Arthurian romances: *Joseph d'Arimathie,* a work that identifies the Grail with the cup of the Last Supper, thereby linking biblical times with the Arthurian world; *Merlin,* a romance relating the adventures of Merlin from his diabolical conception to the crowning of Arthur; and in all probability a *Perceval,* which brings the Grail quest to fulfillment and ends with a short *Mort Artu,* the dissolution of the Arthurian world. Of the original poems only the *Joseph* and the first 504 verses of the *Merlin* are extant. But the entire trilogy was turned into prose shortly after its composition, and it was this prose cycle that constituted the point of departure for the vast Vulgate cycle of Arthurian romance.

BIBLIOGRAPHY

Editions. The verse *Joseph:* Robert de Boron, *Le roman de l'estoire dou Graal,* William Nitze, ed. (1927, repr. 1983); the prose *Joseph:* Richard O'Gorman, ed., "The Middle French Redaction of Robert de Boron's *Joseph d'Arimathie,*" in *Proceedings of the American Philosophical Society,* **122** (1978); the prose *Merlin:* Alexander Micha, ed., *Merlin: Roman du XIIIe siècle* (1979), with the 504 extant verses in the Introduction; the prose *Perceval:* William Roach, ed., *The Didot Perceval According to the Manuscripts of Modena and Paris* (1941); the entire prose cycle (Modena MS): Bernard Cerquiglini, ed., *Le roman du Graal* (1981).

Studies. Pierre le Gentil, "The Work of Robert de Boron and the *Didot Perceval,*" and Alexandre Micha, "The Vulgate *Merlin,*" in Roger Sherman Loomis, ed., *Arthurian Literature in the Middle Ages* (1959); Loomis, *The Grail: From Celtic Myth to Christian Symbol* (1963), esp. 223–248; Richard O'Gorman, "The Prose Version of Robert de Boron's *Joseph d'Arimathie,*" in *Romance Philology,* **23** (1970); Alexandre Micha, *Étude sur le Merlin de Robert de Boron* (1980).

RICHARD O'GORMAN

[See also **Arthurian Literature; Grail, Legend of.**]

ROBERT DE CLARI (*fl.* 1200–1216), a French knight, author of an Old French prose account of the Fourth Crusade. Born at Clari (Cléry-sur-Somme), he served in the crusading army under his lord Peter of Amiens and was present at the siege and sack of Constantinople in April 1204. Robert joined the emperor Baldwin's expedition to Salonika, which saw the death of Peter of Amiens. In 1205 Robert returned to France, where he dictated his history (*La conquête de Constantinople*), speaking as a witness of events dating from the calling of the crusaders by Pope Innocent III in 1198 to the death of Baldwin in April 1205. He probably relied on reports for the remainder of his narrative, which ends with the death of Emperor Henry I of Jerusalem on 3 June 1216. With other evidence lacking, we may use this date as a terminus a quo for the death of Robert himself.

The value of Robert's account is especially apparent when it is read with that of Geoffroi de Villehardouin. The two narratives complement each other in perspective and confirm each other in detail. Villehardouin's account describes what passed among the crusading leaders and what concerned the whole crusading enterprise. Robert's is given from the perspective of the *povres chevaliers* (humble knights) and dwells upon the picturesque and the particular. It is Robert who tells us of the marvels of Constantinople.

Robert is considered a reliable source, especially when he speaks from direct observation. He was not entirely objective, however. He clearly disliked Boniface of Montferrat and blamed the disaster at Adrianople on the refusal of the *hauts hommes* (leaders) to share with their troops the riches of Constantinople. He described—perhaps with irony—the taking of Constantinople as a just revenge for Greek treatment of the Trojan ancestors of the French. Otherwise, Robert, who spoke of himself only briefly and in the third person, appears as a disinterested and unpretentious observer.

BIBLIOGRAPHY

Edition and translation. Robert de Clari, *La conquête de Constantinople,* Philippe Lauer, ed. (1924); *The Conquest of Constantinople: Translated from the Old French of Robert of Clari,* Edgar H. McNeal, trans. (1936, repr. 1979).

Studies. Peter F. Dembowski, *La chronique de Robert de Clari: Étude de la langue et du style* (1963); Jean Larmat, "Sur quelques aspects de la religion chrétienne dans les chroniques de Villehardouin et de Clari," in *Le moyen âge,* **80** (1974); Albert Pauphilet, "Robert de Clari et Villehardouin," in *Mélanges de linguistique et de littérature offerts à M. Alfred Jeanroy par ses élèves et ses amis* (1928), and "Sur Robert de Clari," in *Romania,* **57** (1931).

SUSAN M. BABBITT

[See also **Chronicles, French; Crusades and Crusader States: Fourth; Villehardouin, Geoffroi de.**]

ROBERT DE COUCY (*d.* 1311) was the last of five or six architects known by name responsible for the design and construction of the cathedral of Notre-Dame at Rheims, France, between 1211 and around 1310. De Coucy may have installed the labyrinth in the nave floor that gave the names of his predecessors. His work at Rheims is unknown, and he is not identified with any other building.

BIBLIOGRAPHY

Carl F. Barnes, Jr., "Jean d'Orbais," in *Macmillan Encyclopedia of Architects,* II (1982); Robert Branner, "The Labyrinth of Reims Cathedral," in *Journal of the Society of Architectural Historians,* **21** (1962); Francis Salet, "Chronologie de la cathédrale [de Reims]," in *Bulletin monumental,* **125** (1967).

CARL F. BARNES, JR.

[See also **Jean d'Orbais; Rheims Cathedral.**]

ROBERT DE LUZARCHES (*fl.* first half of thirteenth century), first master architect of Amiens

Nave of Amiens Cathedral. Designed by Robert de Luzarches, *ca.* 1236. PHOTO: WIM SWAAN

Cathedral, in or shortly after 1218 until the mid 1230's. Robert was responsible for the design and construction of the nave of this cathedral. His work was influenced by contemporary Parisian designs, and he may have been trained in Paris. No building other than Amiens can be attributed to him.

BIBLIOGRAPHY

Carl F. Barnes, Jr., "Robert de Luzarches," in *Macmillan Encyclopedia of Architects,* II (1982); Robert Branner, "Paris and the Origins of Rayonnant Gothic Architecture down to 1240," in *Art Bulletin,* **44** (1962); Alain Erlande-Brandenbourg, "La façade de la cathédrale d'Amiens," in *Bulletin monumental,* **135** (1977).

CARL F. BARNES, JR.

[See also **Amiens Cathedral; Gothic Architecture; Regnault de Cormont; Thomas de Cormont.**]

ROBERT GROSSETESTE. See **Grosseteste, Robert.**

ROBERT GUISCARD (*d.* 1085), Norman leader in southern Italy. Son of a lesser Norman landholder, Tancred of Hauteville, he followed his elder half brothers to southern Italy in 1047. Choosing as his sphere of activity the hills of Calabria, he soon became the scourge of the region. Following his marriage (*ca.* 1050), he began rapidly to expand his holdings. In 1060 he captured Reggio and Taranto and in 1071 drove the Byzantines from Bari. Thenceforth, he styled himself duke of Apulia. The papacy watched the growth of his power with considerable concern. Pope Gregory VII thought to counterbalance Robert's threat by supporting Duke Richard of Capua but was forced to abandon this effort due to his growing involvement in the investiture controversy with Emperor Henry IV. With the death of Richard in 1078, Robert emerged as the strongest Norman leader in southern Italy. Gregory was now forced to turn to him for support against the emperor.

Guiscard had aided his younger brother, Roger, in the early stages of the conquest of Sicily, but his own concerns centered on his mainland domains and the threat of a Byzantine reconquest. During the 1070's, he became increasingly embroiled in the affairs of that empire; and, when his son-in-law, the emperor Michael VII, was deposed and died, he set up an imposter to gain papal support for an attack on Constantinople. He attacked Corfu and Durazzo (Dyrrachium) in 1082, but his progress was slowed by rebellion in Apulia. In 1083, he suffered defeat from a Byzantine army at Larissa. Before he could recover from this disaster, he had to return to Italy to drive Henry IV from Rome and rescue the pope. Gregory died at Salerno in May 1085; Robert renewed his Byzantine campaign only to die on 17 July of the same year.

BIBLIOGRAPHY

Ferdinand Chalandon, *Histoire de la domination normande en Italie et en Sicile,* I (1907, repr. 1960); David C. Douglas, *The Norman Achievement, 1050–1100* (1969); *Roberto Guiscardo e il suo tempo: Atti delle prime giornate normanno-sveve* (1975).

JAMES M. POWELL

[See also **Alexios I Komnenos; Bari; Bohemond I, Prince of Antioch; Byzantine Empire: History; Gregory VII, Pope; Henry IV of Germany; Italy, Byzantine Areas of; Normans and Normandy; Roger I of Sicily; Sicily, Kingdom of; Tancred.**]

ROBERT KILWARDBY. See **Kilwardby, Robert.**

ROBERT LE DIABLE, legendary character, the son of a demon and a duchess of Normandy. According to the tale, after a youth filled with enormous atrocities and acts of brutality, Robert finished life as a hermit and upon death was venerated as a saint. This widespread folk legend gave rise to three Old French works dating from the twelfth through fourteenth centuries: *Le roman de Robert le Diable, Le dit de Robert le Diable,* and *Le miracle de Nostre Dame de Robert de Diable.* Later treatments include an opera by Giacomo Meyerbeer (1831).

BIBLIOGRAPHY

Karl Breul, "Le dit de Robert le Diable," in *Abhandlungen hern prof. dr. Adolf Tobler . . . dargebracht* (1895); René Herval, "La légende de Robert le Diable," in *Dictionnaire des lettres françaises: Le moyen âge* (1964), 640–641; Eilert Löseth, *Robert le Diable: Roman d'aventures* (1903); Dorothy S. McCoy, "From Celibacy to Sexuality: An Examination of Some Medieval and Early Renaissance Versions of the Story of Robert the Devil," in Douglas Radcliff-Umstead, ed., *Human Sexuality in the Middle Ages and Renaissance* (1978); Gaston Paris and Ulysse Robert, *Les miracles de Nostre Dame par personnages,* VI (1881), 3–77.

RICHARD O'GORMAN

[See also **French Literature.**]

ROBERT OF COURSON. See **Courson (Courçon), Robert of.**

ROBERT OF GREATHAM (or Gretham) (*fl.* thirteenth century) was the author of two thirteenth-century Anglo-Norman verse texts, the *Miroir* (also known as the *Evangiles des domness,* or Sunday sermons) and the *Corset,* of which only a fragment survives. The former is a series of verse sermons with commentaries and interpretations. The latter is part of a manual of doctrine not unlike Peter of Peckham's *Lumere as lais* and St. Edmund's *Merure de seinte église.*

BIBLIOGRAPHY

Marion Y. H. Aitken, *Étude sur le miroir; ou, Les évangiles des domnées de Robert de Gretham* (1922).

BRIAN MERRILEES

The Annunciation to the Shepherds and the Flight into Egypt. Miniature from the *Missal of Robert of Jumièges,* 1006–1023. ROUEN, BIBLIOTHÈQUE MUNICIPALE, MS 274 (Y.6), fol. 33r

[See also **Anglo-Norman Literature; Peter of Peckham; Preaching and Sermon Literature, Western European.**]

ROBERT OF JUMIÈGES (*d.* 1055), Norman abbot of the Benedictine abbey of Jumièges (1037–1044), pre-Conquest bishop of London (1044–1051), and archbishop of Canterbury (1051–1052). He also was patron of the *Missal of Robert of Jumièges* (Rouen, Bibliothèque Municipale, MS Y. 6), which is actually a sacramentary. Robert is thought to have donated the work to the monastery of Jumièges while bishop of London. Margaret Rickert suggests the manuscript was illuminated at Ely between 1006 and 1023. Art historical analysis suggests that the manuscript fuses two well-defined styles of illumination: that of the Winchester School and the Carolingian style of Rheims.

BIBLIOGRAPHY

Charles R. Dodwell, *The Canterbury School of Illumination, 1066–1200* (1954), and *Painting in Europe, 800–1200* (1971); Margaret Rickert, *Painting in Britain: The Middle Ages* (1954, 2nd ed. 1965); Henry Austin Wilson, ed., *The Missal of Robert of Jumièges* (1896).

JENNIFER E. JONES

[See also **Anglo-Saxon Art; Manuscript Illumination, European; Pre-Romanesque Art; Sacramentary.**]

ROBERT OF MELUN (*d.* 1167), an English-born philosopher and theologian. He taught in France, perhaps as early as 1120. Certainly in 1137 he was teaching dialectic at Mont-Sainte-Geneviève in Paris, where John of Salisbury was among his pupils. Thence around 1142 he transferred to Melun and the teaching of theology. He returned to England about 1160 under the aegis of Thomas Becket, who obtained for him the election to the bishopric of Hereford in 1163. Despite this patronage, Robert originally sided with King Henry II (1154–1189) in his dispute with Becket, although he reversed his position before his death in 1167.

Robert wrote three theological treatises, of which *Sententiae* (1152–1160) is the most important. With respect to the theological controversies of his day, he fiercely opposed Bernard of Clairvaux, especially on issues in which he regarded Bernard as unwarranted in his condemnation of Peter Abelard. Indeed, Robert was a profound, although not an uncritical, student of Abelard and absorbed from his teacher the methods that enabled him to dissent from Abelard's own theses on various points. Although less influenced by the Victorines, he nevertheless regarded Hugh of St. Victor as a great luminary of French thought.

BIBLIOGRAPHY

Source. Raymond-Marie Martin, ed., *Oeuvres de Robert de Melun,* 3 vols. in 4 (1932–1952).

Studies. D. E. de Clerck, "Le dogme de la rédemption de Robert de Melun à Guillaume d'Auxerre," in *Recherches de théologie ancienne et médiévale,* **14** (1947); Charles L. Kingsford, "Robert of Melun," in *Dictionary of National Biography,* XVI (1896), 1252–1254; A. L. Lilley, "A Christological Controversy of the Twelfth Century," in *Journal of Theological Studies,* **39** (1938); David E. Luscombe, *The School of Peter Abelard: The Influence of Abelard's Thought in the Early Scholastic Period* (1969), 281–298; Raymond-Marie Martin, "Un texte intéressant de Robert de Melun," in *Revue d'histoire ecclésiastique,* **28** (1932), and "L'immortalité de l'âme d'après Robert de Melun (*d.* 1167)," in *Revue néoscolastique de philosophie,* **36** (1934); Peter W. Nash, "The Meaning of *est* in the *Sentences* (1152–1160) of Robert of Melun," in *Mediaeval Studies,* **14** (1952).

ELAINE GOLDEN ROBISON

[See also **Becket, Thomas, St.; Christology; Philosophy and Theology, Western European: Twelfth Century to Aquinas.**]

ROBERTINIANS. See **Capetian Family Origins.**

ROBIN HOOD. The picture of Robin Hood that is widely held today contrasts in many respects with that of the outlaw of medieval legend. While the modern image was fashioned by dramatists and writers during the sixteenth and seventeenth centuries, the medieval Robin Hood, who was probably the creation of itinerant minstrels, is a more elusive figure who lives principally in the early ballads and a handful of historical sources.

Although certain ballads of Robin Hood are medieval in origin, the earliest allusions to the English outlaw are found not in these but in literary and record texts. The first specific reference to Robin Hood as such occurs in the *B* version of Langland's *Piers Plowman,* composed about 1377. In that poem Sloth is represented as a priest who makes forty vows and forgets them on the morrow. He cannot say his paternoster perfectly, "But I can rymes of Robyn Hood, and Randolf erle of Chestre." After Langland's mention of the "rymes," Robin Hood was not long absent from the literary and record sources. Robin Hood's bow is mentioned in the *Reply of Friar Daw Topias to Jack Upland,* written in 1419 or 1420. In the fifteenth-century composition *How the Plowman Learned His Pater Noster,* the poor people "songe goynge homeward a Gest of Robyn Hode," while in Alexander Barclay's translation (1509) of Sebastian Brant's *Narrenschiff* "fits" of Robin Hood are again mentioned. In the fifteenth century, references to Robin Hood occur also in the record sources. In 1439 a petition to parliament called for the arrest of Piers Venables of Derbyshire, who "in manere of insurrection wente into the wodes in that County, like it hadde be Robyn Hode and his meynee." This is the first indication of the anti-heroic and unflattering references of Robin Hood that were to occur down to the seventeenth century, and to a time when Guy Fawkes and his associates could be described by Robert Cecil as "Robin Hoods."

A part in the formation of the early legend appears to have been played by the three Scottish chroniclers Andrew of Wyntoun, Walter Bower, and John Major (*d.* 1550). Andrew of Wyntoun, who wrote his *Original Chronicle of Scotland* about 1420, spoke of Robin Hood and Little John as "waythmen," or outlaws, and placed them in Inglewood and Barnsdale. Wyntoun is the only writer to name Inglewood in Cumberland, the home of Adam Bell, in this connection. Walter Bower, in his continuation of John Fordun's *Scotichronicon,* remarked that it was the foolish people who celebrated him; while John Major in his *History of Greater Britain,* which was written in the 1520's, wrote of Robin Hood as a "prince of thieves." These references suggest that Scotland, the home of certain of the Border ballads, played some part in the reception and transmission of the legend. A ship called *Robyne Hude* was at Aberdeen in 1438. The reference in Gavin Douglas' *Palice of Honour,* composed about 1501, to "Robene Hude and Gilbert with the quhite hand," a character who occurs only in the *Gest,* is worth noting and suggests that the Scottish poet was familiar with that work.

From the very start there appear to have been contradictory elements in the character of the legend. To Wyntoun, Robin Hood was an outlaw, to Walter Bower an assassin whose name could be taken as a term of abuse and whose deeds were celebrated by foolish people; yet to John Major, Robin Hood was the kindliest of robbers, "the robberies of this man I condemn, but of all robbers he was the most humane and the chief." In the fifteenth century, therefore, the nature of the legend was still far from decided and the literary background of the tales not yet complete. Friar Tuck is met for the first time only in the 1470's in a dramatized version of the story of Robin Hood and Guy of Gisborne found among the papers of John Paston, while Maid Marion was not to appear until the time of the May festivities and the Morris dances at the end of the fifteenth century. She was almost certainly by origin the shepherdess Marion of the medieval French *pastourelles.*

Like other problems connected with the English

outlaw, the date of the genesis of the legend is far from certain. The medieval ballad texts as we have them belong to the fifteenth century. These include the *Lytell Gest, Robin Hood and the Monk,* and *Robin Hood and the Potter*. The *Gest* is the central text of the Robin Hood saga and contains such well-known episodes as Robin Hood and the abbot of St. Mary's and Robin Hood meeting the king in disguise. The *Gest* was almost certainly compiled during the first part of that century and may have given rise to other stories. Yet the extant ballads may well draw on older material, including the "rymes of Robyn Hood," which were in circulation when Langland wrote in the 1370's. The proliferation of references to Robin Hood after 1377 and their complete absence before that time suggests that the tales may possibly have originated during the first half of the fourteenth century. As the *Gest* speaks of liveries and fees, which are features of bastard feudalism in the early fourteenth century, the reign of Edward II (1307–1327) has been suggested as a probable time for the composition of certain of the stories.

In an endeavor to date the origin of the tales, many historical Robin Hoods have been sought. The "outlaw hero" has rarely if ever been a purely literary creation; and the activities, suitably transformed, of the leader of some group of outlaws may lie behind the emergence of the stories in the *Gest*. It was in this way that legends grew up around modern outlaws like Jesse James and Sam Bass, and such may have been the case with the original of Robin Hood. Nonetheless, attempts to identify a historical Robin Hood have on the whole proved singularly unsuccessful. Such identifications include a Robert Hood whose name occurs on the Great Roll of the Pipe in 1228, 1230, and 1231; a follower of Simon de Montfort in 1265; and a Wakefield tenant of Edward II's reign whose activities appear at first sight to accord with the deeds of Robin Hood as described in the eighth fit of the *Gest*. Not one of these identifications can, however, be regarded as certain.

The geographical setting of the ballads can be established with greater certainty. In the early ballads and in the other sources two centers, Barnsdale and Nottingham, emerge. Yet despite the modern association of Robin Hood with Sherwood Forest, his original habitat is much more likely to have been Barnsdale, seven miles (7.5 km) north of Doncaster, in the West Riding of Yorkshire. The *Gest* does not mention Sherwood Forest as such and associates the outlaw with the Yorkshire region. In the *Gest,* Little John is told to "walke up to the Saylis," a tenement located within the parish of Kirk Smeaton near Pontefract. Doncaster and Wentbridge are also mentioned in the *Gest*. It may be that the early stories of Robin Hood reflect the activities of a group of outlaws who operated in the Barnsdale region, which was in medieval times a dangerous stretch of the Great North Road. It is also possible that the *Gest* itself was constructed from two different literary traditions, one concerned with Robin Hood in the Barnsdale region and another which described the activities of the sheriff of Nottingham some fifty miles to the south.

Much of the interest of Robin Hood as depicted in the medieval ballads comes from the image that he presented to contemporaries. To the ballad audience of the late Middle Ages, Robin Hood must have seemed a new type of hero, one very different from the aristocratic heroes of the old romances. Although claimed by modern scholars to be of both peasant and gentry origin, Robin Hood is referred to throughout the early ballads as a yeoman. The term "yeoman" was capable of bearing different meanings in the fifteenth century but generally appears to have meant someone of independent status, who may or may not have been in service. It is in this sense of someone giving honorable service that the term was customarily used in the Close Rolls, Patent Rolls, and the early Rolls of Parliament. The Robin Hood of the medieval ballads was clearly not a knight; he possessed neither title nor estate, and his followers did not belong to the aristocratic stratum of society. Yet in the episodes of the *Gest,* Robin is a figure with aristocratic manners and with certain of the virtues of the knightly class. He appears therefore to have been a new type of hero, neither gentry nor peasant, a figure influenced by the content of the romances still in the minstrel repertoire.

As a new kind of outlaw hero Robin Hood was to have descendants in many lands. He is the archetype of the "social bandit" found in several preindustrial peasant societies, and like them he has his roots in the social and economic conditions of his time. In late medieval England, the state was relatively weak, and local administration often corrupt. In such a society the "noble bandit" was thought able to redress wrongs and secure justice. The medieval tales reflect aspects of this society. Thus they refer to a period when sheriffs could be bribed and justices were retained by powerful patrons. They probably mirror the activities of real "gentry gangs" who operated in the fourteenth century. Again the figure of Robin Hood may reflect the new self-confidence, based upon the economic advance, of a large section of the English peasantry. Less certain is the suggestion that the earliest versions of the legend were a by-product of agrarian struggles over rents, services, and social status that culminated in the Peasants' Revolt of 1381. The English outlaw was not noticeably concerned with the economic exploitation of the rural population that is vividly described in several of the political poems of the time. In the *Gest* the principal victim whom he aids is a poor Lancashire knight, Sir Richard of the Lee. Although the abbot of St. Mary's was an important landlord, there is in the *Gest* no mention of the abbot extorting money from his tenants, exacting burdensome services, or compelling men to grind corn at his mill. Again the ballads do not describe those parts of the country particularly affected by the revolt. The targets of Robin Hood's criticism are the justices of the forest and of the common law, against whom grievances could have been felt by more than one section of the medieval community.

As regards the appeal of Robin Hood, the evidence suggests that in the fifteenth century the appeal of the ballads was to a wide and socially undifferentiated audience. That some members of the gentry were familiar with tales of Robin Hood is proved by the fact that in 1473 Paston kept a servant to play Robin Hood, St. George, and the sheriff of Nottingham, whom he jocularly accused of having gone off into Barnsdale. Yet before the end of the Middle Ages the appeal of the forest hero appears to have been mainly to ordinary people. For Langland it was not a knight but rather Sloth, the personification of vagabondage, who was likely to neglect his paternoster in favor of "rhymes of Robyn Hood." Robin's popular appeal is confirmed by the references in the fifteenth and sixteenth Scottish chronicles, and further evidence of it is to be seen in the numerous Robin Hood proverbs coined at a popular level during the later Middle Ages. The most famous among these is found in the early-fifteenth-century *Reply of Friar Daw Topias to Jack Upland:*

On old Englis it is said
Unkissid is unknowun
And many men speken of Robyn Hood
And shotte nevere in his bowe,

meaning that people speak of matters about which they have no personal experience. The use of Robin Hood proverbs in literary sources may suggest that by the fifteenth century the legend was capable of appealing to a literate as well as to a popular audience.

Finally, the historical character of the legend, firmly anchored as it is in the real world of the Middle Ages, must dispel the notion that Robin Hood was in origin a mythological figure. Mythological characters belong generally to a much earlier period of European history. What evidence there is suggests that Robin Hood was based upon the memory of one of a number of Barnsdale outlaws, while the association of the English outlaw with various English place-names and features, often taken as evidence of his mythological character, can be dated to periods long after the first development of what was to become one of the greatest legends of medieval England.

BIBLIOGRAPHY

For the text of the ballads, see Francis J. Child, ed., *The English and Scottish Popular Ballads,* III (1890), 39–233, which contains the *Gest* and other Robin Hood ballads; Richard B. Dobson and John Taylor, eds., *Rymes of Robyn Hood* (1976), with bibliography; and John W. Hales and Frederick J. Furnivall, eds., *Bishop Percy's Folio* (1867–1868), which gives the edition of the Robin Hood ballads in the Percy folio. William H. Clawson, *The Gest of Robin Hood* (1909), contains a good analysis of the text of the *Gest.* For the general historical background see John G. Bellamy, *Crime and Public Order in England in the Later Middle Ages* (1973).

Secondary studies of the legend include John G. Bellamy, *Robin Hood: An Historical Enquiry* (1985); D. Crook, "Some Further Evidence Concerning the Dating of the Origins of the Legend of Robin Hood," in *English Historical Review,* 99 (1984); R. H. Hilton, "The Origins of Robin Hood," in *Past and Present* (1958); J. C. Holt, "The Origins and Audience of the Ballads of Robin Hood," *ibid.* (1960), and *Robin Hood* (1982); Maurice Keen, *The Outlaws of Medieval Legend* (1961); J. R. Maddicott, "The Birth and Setting of the Ballads of Robin Hood," in *English Historical Review* (1978).

JOHN TAYLOR

[See also **Anglo-Norman Literature; Ballads, Middle English; Middle English Literature; Outlawry.**]

RODRIGO DE OSONA (*fl. ca.* 1464–1484), Spanish painter of a signed *Crucifixion* panel (1476;

The Crucifixion, with Pietà, Sts. Peter and Paul, the Guardian Angel, and St. Anne on the predella. Altarpiece by Rodrigo de Osona from S. Nicolás, Valencia, 1476. FOTO MAS, BARCELONA

Valencia, church of S. Nicolás). This artist introduced the influence of the Italian Renaissance to Valencia during his period of activity. The Italian Quattrocento style, including the use of one-point linear perspective and the depiction of classical ruins, was further developed in the paintings by his son of the same name, active in Valencia from 1504 to 1513.

BIBLIOGRAPHY

Allgemeines Lexikon der bildenden Künstler (*Thieme-Becker Künstler Lexikon*), Hans Vollmer, ed., XXVIII (1934), 466; August L. Mayer, *Geschichte der spanischen Malerei* (1922), 112–116; Chandler R. Post, *A History of Spanish Painting,* VI, pt. 1 (1935), 12, 173–267.

MARY GRIZZARD

[See also **Aragon; Valencia.**]

RODRIGO DÍAZ. See **Cid, History and Legend of.**

RODRIGO, MOCEDADES DE. See **Mocedades de Rodrigo.**

RODRÍGUEZ DEL PADRÓN, JUAN (**Juan Rodríguez de la Cámara**) (*ca.* 1390–*ca.* 1450), was born in the region of Padrón, Galicia, to a family of the minor nobility. Although little is known of his early life, apart from the possibility that he was a page in the household of John II, we do know that later he was part of the retinue of Juan Cardinal de Cervantes, and with this prelate traveled through Europe. He accompanied him to the Council of Basel, where he must certainly have come into contact with the great humanists of Germany, Italy, and France. He spent some time in Italy, and around 1440 went to Jerusalem, where he made his profession as a member of the Franciscan order. By 1442 he had returned to Spain, retiring to a monastery at Herbón.

Rodríguez is chiefly remembered as the author of the *Siervo libre de amor* (Servant freed from love, *ca.* 1442), an autobiographical and allegorical work in Castilian dealing with the author's experience of courtly love. Because of his emulation of the famed Galician poet-lover Macías, Rodríguez's reputation as an exponent of courtly love has led to a rather unbalanced interpretation of his works, in particular of the *Siervo libre.* This work, a mixture of prose and poetry, has always been considered the first of the "sentimental novels" in Spain, but recent research indicates that this classification of the *Siervo libre* as a whole is based primarily on the character of one of its component parts, the *Estoria de dos amadores* (Story of two lovers). In fact, the *Estoria* is used as a negative exemplum by the author, and the *Siervo libre* is not a defense of the values of courtly love but a recantation by an aging poet uncertain of salvation outside the bounds of orthodox Christianity. The third part of the *Siervo libre,* entirely missing from the single extant manuscript, would have shown the rejection of the worldly fame offered by courtly love, in favor of eternal salvation as a servant of God.

Rodríguez's poetry, written in the *cancionero* tradition, displays all the elements inherited from the Provençal troubadours, but is always flavored with an overriding disillusionment with the system of courtly love. Hence, we perceive a pragmatic attitude in poems such as *Diez mandamientos de amor* (Ten commandments of love) and *Siete gozos de amor* (Seven joys of love), in which the restrictive and frustrating nature of courtly love is made clear. Nevertheless, in all of his poems Rodríguez emphasizes his position as the foremost among courtly lovers and his worthiness to be remembered as the equal of Macías.

The personality of the author is further revealed in his treatises, the *Cadira del honor* (Seat of honor) and the *Triunfo de las donas* (Triumph of women). In the first he insists on the traditional and properly instituted formulas for ennoblement, and shows himself to be in sharp disagreement with the then-current proliferation of titles. The second is a contribution to the polemic on profeminism and antifeminism raging in Spain in the mid fifteenth century. Rodríguez, aligning himself with the profeminists, reveals that he considers men to be the cause of women's failings. Men, he claims, are deceivers and use the code of courtly love to their own ends, making women appear to be cruel when they act in their own defense. Thus, his complaints about the feignings of the courtly lover mark a growing disillusionment with the system of courtly love, and are a natural development from the sentiments expressed in his earlier poetry. Another treatise, the *Oriflama,* presumably dealing with heraldry, has been lost.

Love is again the subject of the *Bursario* (Pocket novel), a rendition of Ovid's *Heroides,* with new elements contributed by Rodríguez. He may also have been the author of versions of the ballads (*romances*) *Rosaflorida, El conde Arnaldos,* and *La hija del rey de Francia.*

In all his works Rodríguez displays a rather latinized syntax typical of the late Middle Ages in Spain, and a penchant for allegory and hyperbole that has obscured the true nature of his writings.

BIBLIOGRAPHY

Editions. Juan Rodríguez del Padrón, *Obras completas,* César Hernández Alonso, ed. (1982); *Obras de Juan Rodríguez de la Cámara (o del Padrón),* Antonio Paz y Melia, ed. (1884).

Studies. Gregory P. Andrachuk, "On the Missing Third Part of the *Siervo libre de amor,*" in *Hispanic Review,* **45** (1977), "The Function of the *Estoria de dos amadores* Within the *Siervo libre de amor,*" in *Revista canadiense de estudios hispánicos,* **2** (1977), and "A Re-examination of the Poetry of Juan Rodríguez del Padrón," in *Bulletin of Hispanic Studies,* **47** (1980); Dinko Cvitanóvič, *La novela sentimental española* (1973), esp. 55–120; Edward J. Dudley, "Court and Country: The Fusion of Two Images of Love in Juan Rodríguez's *El siervo libre de amor,*" in *Publications of the Modern Language Association of America,* **82** (1967); Martin S. Gilderman, "La crítica literaria y la poesía de Juan Rodríguez del Padrón," in *Boletín de filología española,* nos. 40–41 (1971), and "Toward a Revaluation of Rodríguez del Padrón and His Poem of Courtly Love, 'Siete Gozos de Amor,'" in *Hispania,* **56** (1973); César Hernández Alonso, *Siervo libre de amor de Juan Rodríguez del Padrón* (1970); Javier Herrero, "The Allegorical Structure of the *Siervo libre de amor,*" in *Speculum,* **55** (1980); María Rosa Lida de Malkiel, "Juan Rodríguez del Padrón: Vida y obra," in *Nueva revista de filología hispánica,* **6** (1952); Carmelo Samonà, "Per una interpretazione del 'Siervo libre de amor,'" in *Studi ispanici* (1961); Barbara F. Weissberger, "'Habla el Auctor': *L'Elegía de Madonna Fiammetta* as a Source for the *Siervo libre de amor,*" in *Journal of Hispanic Studies,* **4** (1980).

GREGORY PETER ANDRACHUK

[See also **Courtly Love; Ovid in the Middle Ages; Spanish Literature: Sentimental Romances.**]

ROFFREDUS DE EPIPHANIIS OF BENEVENTO (*ca.* 1170–after 1243) was a civil and canon jurist. He served as a judge in the Magna Curia of Emperor Frederick II (*r.* 1211–1250), and as an advocate in papal courts. His legal outlook was above all that of the practicing attorney. His *Quaestiones sabbatinae* are subtitled *Quaestiones de facto emergentes,* that is, questions arising from actual law cases (as opposed to theoretical discussions). His *Libellus iuris canonici* likewise attests to his practical outlook, as he exhaustively outlines the procedures of ecclesiastical courts. Roffredus is noteworthy as one of the first experts in civil law to expound on canon law. The earliest glossators had despised all non-Roman law; Roffredus was not a man to allow considerations of theoretical purity to keep him from an arena that offered so much opportunity for the practice he loved.

BIBLIOGRAPHY

Roffredus' three treatises, *Libellus iuris civilis, Libellus iuris canonica,* and *Quaestiones sabbatinae,* are printed together as *Corpus glossatorum juris civilis,* VI (1968, repr. of 1500 ed.).

Studies include Gian Carlo Caselli's introduction to *Corpus glossatorum,* a brief and illuminating analysis of his legal outlook; and Giovanni Ferretti, "Roffredo Epifanio da Benevento," in *Studi medievali,* 3 (1908–1911), a painstaking reconstruction of Roffredus' biography. See also John A. Clarence Smith, *Medieval Law Teachers and Writers, Civilian and Canonist* (1975), 41–42; Helmut Coing, ed., *Handbuch der Quellen und Literatur der neueren europäischen Privatrechtsgeschichte,* I (1973).

ELAINE GOLDEN ROBISON

[See also **Glossators; Law, Canon; Law, Civil.**]

ROGER I OF SICILY (1031–1101), great count of Sicily and count of Calabria, the youngest son of Tancred of Hauteville, was born in Normandy in 1031. Arriving in southern Italy in 1056, he joined his brother, Robert Guiscard, in the siege of Reggio di Calabria and was rewarded with the fief of Monteleone. Disappointed, he rebelled against Robert and secured the grant of half of Calabria. With the fall of Taranto and Reggio in 1060, the brothers turned next to Sicily, which Robert had already received in fief from the papacy in anticipation of its conquest from the Muslims. Robert, however, devoted most of his attention to the conquest of Apulia from the Byzantines, with the result that Roger played the leading role in the conquest of Sicily.

Ibn al-Thumna, *qāᶜid* (caid) of Syracuse, had gained control of most of the island, but he was defeated by his brother-in-law, Ibn al-Ḥawwās, near Castrogiovanni. As his support began to melt away, Ibn al-Thumna called on the Normans for aid. Already in 1060, Roger had made an abortive attack on Messina. Now, in 1061, with the support of Ibn al-Thumna, he tried again. It was only after returning to the mainland for reinforcements that he was able to capture the city. He and his brother then expanded westward along the coast toward Catania. They failed to take Castrogiovanni, but Roger pillaged as far south as Girgenti. Following the death of Ibn al-Thumna, the brothers quarreled once again. In the ensuing settlement, Roger gained joint control of all Calabria with Robert.

Muslim efforts to dislodge the Normans from Sicily were hindered by internal divisions. As a result, Roger drove the African commander Ayyub from the island and, with the support of Robert, took the city of Palermo in 1072. But the Muslims maintained a stubborn resistance in the interior and, with aid from North Africa, even carried the struggle to Calabria. It was not until the fall of Noto in 1091 that the entire island was under Norman control.

After the death of Robert Guiscard in 1085, Roger emerged as the dominant figure among the Normans in the south. In Sicily, he laid the foundation for strong central power, limiting the size of fiefs with which he rewarded his followers. Given strong Muslim resistance to conversion, he adopted a policy of toleration aimed at gaining their loyalty. He strongly supported the Latin church. Pope Urban II entrusted to him and his son the apostolic legateship for the island, placing control of ecclesiastical appointments in his hands during the critical period of reestablishment of the Latin hierarchy. By the time of his death on 22 June 1101, the foundation had been laid for the work of his son, Roger II.

BIBLIOGRAPHY

Ferdinand Chalandon, *Histoire de la domination normande en Italie et en Sicile,* I (1907, repr. 1960); David C. Douglas, *The Norman Achievement, 1050–1100* (1969); Denis Mack Smith, *A History of Sicily,* 2 vols. (1968); *Ruggero il Gran Conte e l'inizio dello stato Normanno* (1977).

JAMES M. POWELL

[See also **Normans and Normandy; Palermo; Robert Guiscard; Sicily, Islamic; Sicily, Kingdom of; Urban II, Pope.**]

ROGER II OF SICILY (1095–1154), count of Sicily from 1101 to 1130 and king from 1130 to his death in 1154. He was the son of Roger I, the great count of Sicily (*d.* 1101), and of Adelaide, who married Baldwin of Flanders, king of Jerusalem, in 1113. Roger I had conquered the island of Sicily from the Muslims in the years between 1061 and 1091. Roger II continued the policies of his father, leading an attack on Muslim North Africa in 1123 and pursuing the interests of his family in southern Italy. Following the death of his cousin, Duke William of Apulia, on 25 July 1127, Roger laid claim to his inheritance. He defeated Pope Honorius II at Benevento and gained his recognition as duke of Apulia on 23 August 1128.

In the papal schism that followed the death of Honorius, Roger supported the antipope Anacletus II, who was a supporter of a pro-Norman papal policy against Innocent II. In September 1130, Anacletus invested Roger as king of Sicily, Calabria, and Apulia. Innocent then rallied his supporters against Roger. St. Bernard of Clairvaux labeled him a usurper and tyrant. At home Roger faced rebellion. But in 1139, after the death of Anacletus, Roger was able to defeat Innocent and to reach an agreement in the treaty of Mignano on 25 July recognizing him as king of Sicily, duke of Apulia, and prince of Capua. The royal title was thus conceded but reserved to the island conquered from the Muslims.

The government created by Roger II recognized the heterogeneity of peoples, laws, and institutions within the confines of his new kingdom. The Normans had brought with them the feudal customs of northwestern France, but in Italy they confronted the centralized administrative structures of the Byzantines and Muslims as well as the highly decentralized Lombard city-states. In the scholarly debate over the nature of Roger's government, some have stressed its feudal character and others its relationship to indigenous elements, particularly to Byzantine influences. L.-R. Ménager has denied to Roger responsibility for the Assizes of Ariano, with their strong Roman legal flavor.

These discussions point to the difficulty of the problems. Clearly Roger II could not rely upon a single idiom to communicate his power to peoples of diverse cultural and religious backgrounds. His choice was to build a strong and centralized government, essentially on a Western model but incorporating offices and institutions already familiar to the peoples of the kingdom. His royal court evolved to provide both a focal point and the basic network for royal administration on the local level.

Roger's kingdom was far from secure. There was a strong realization on the part of the Normans that their conquests had been made at the expense of the Byzantine Empire and the sultanate of Mahdia and that these powers might attempt to recover them. Roger had early moved against North Africa but with no permanent success. In 1135, however, he conquered the island of Gerba to use as a base of operations, and during the 1140's he seized the coast from Tripoli to Cap Bon. Likewise he moved against the Byzantines, capturing Corfu in 1147 and raiding in the Gulf of Corinth. Roger's foreign policy had a very significant impact on the balance of power in the Mediterranean and was, at least indirectly, important to the expansion of Western European interests in the eastern Mediterranean. By the end of Roger's reign, the kingdom of Sicily had emerged as a major power.

BIBLIOGRAPHY

Erich Caspar, *Roger II (1101–1154) und die Gründung der normannisch-sciliischen Monarchie* (1904); *Convagno internazionale di studi Ruggeriani, Atti,* 2 vols. (1955); David C. Douglas, *The Norman Fate* (1976); Léon-Robert Ménager, "L'institution monarchique dans les états normands d'Italie: Contribution a l'étude du pouvoir royal dans les principautés occidentales, aux XIe–XIIe siècles" (2 parts), in *Cahiers de civilisation mediévale,* 2 (1959), and "La législation sud-italienne sous la domination normande," in *I Normanni e la loro espansione in Europa nell'alto medioevo* (Centro italiano di studi sull'alto medioevo) (1969); *Società, potere, e popolo nell'età di Ruggero II* (1979).

JAMES M. POWELL

[See also **Normans and Normandy; Roger I of Sicily; Sicily, Kingdom of.**]

ROGER DE FLOR (*d.* 1305), Italian mercenary, born at Brindisi. He was present as a Templar at the siege of Acre (1291) and later organized the Catalan Grand Company and led it in support of King Frederick II of Sicily (*r.* 1296–1337), and of the Byzantine emperor Andronikos II in Asia Minor. Fearful of Roger's ascendancy, the Palaiologoi had him murdered in April 1305. The most important primary source for Roger's life is the Catalan chronicle of Ramòn Muntaner, who fought alongside Roger.

BIBLIOGRAPHY

Henrietta M. Goodenough, trans., *The Chronicle of Muntaner,* in Hakluyt Society, 2nd ser., 50 (1921), chaps. 194, 196, 198–203, 205, 207–215; Angeliki E. Laiou, *Constantinople and the Latins: The Foreign Policy of Andronicus II, 1282–1328* (1972), 131–146; Karl Lanz, ed., *Chronik des edlen En Ramòn Muntaner* (1844).

SUSAN M. BABBITT

[See also **Andronikos II Palaiologos; Catalan Literature; Crusades and Crusader States; Sicily, Kingdom of.**]

ROGER OF HELMARSHAUSEN (*fl. ca.* 1100), goldsmith of the Lower Rhine region. "Frater Rogkerus" of Helmarshausen is mentioned as the artist who executed a *scrinium* (shrine or reliquary) dedicated to Sts. Kilian and Liborius, in a deed dated 15 August 1100. In the document Heinrich von Werl (bishop of Paderborn, 1084–1127) contracts to make payment for the shrine, as well as for a golden cross, to Thietmar I, abbot of Helmars-

Portable altar of Sts. Kilian and Liborius by Roger of Helmarshausen, *ca.* 1100. Paderborn Cathedral, Treasury. FOTO MARBURG / ART RESOURCE

hausen. It is generally accepted that this *scrinium* can be identified with the portable altar of Sts. Kilian and Liborius now at the Cathedral Treasury of Paderborn; this identification is borne out by the dedicatory inscription on the altar (in which Bishop Heinrich is cited as donor, Sts. Liborius and Kilian as recipients) and by the representations of both saints and Heinrich on the altar itself. All other attributions to Roger are made on stylistic grounds. The objects most closely associated with the Paderborn portable altar are: the portable altar of Sts. Felix and Blasius from Abdinghof Abbey (Paderborn, Franciscan Church); the gold reliquary cross from St. Dionysius, Enger (Berlin, Schlossmuseum, inv. no. 88.635); and the Gospelbook cover from Helmarshausen (manuscript: Trier, Cathedral Library, MS 139; book cover: Cathedral Treasury, no. 68). Roger's influence was appreciable not only in Helmarshausen itself, especially on the local production of illuminated manuscripts, but also in Hildesheim, where he had a far-reaching influence on goldsmithing. Roger has recently been identified with the Theophilus whose *De diversis artibus* constitutes our most important extant primary source concerning the techniques of painting, sculpture, glass painting, enameling, and goldsmithing as practiced in the early Middle Ages. The author was a monk, probably from northwestern Germany, writing in the early twelfth century, all of which data are consonant with what we know of Roger of Helmarshausen.

BIBLIOGRAPHY

Charles R. Dodwell, ed. and trans., *Theophilus: De diversis artibus* (1961); Franz Jansen, *Die Helmarshausener Buchmalerei zur Zeit Heinrichs des Löwen* (1933); Beda Kleinschmidt, "Der Abdinghofer Tragaltar: Eine Arbeit des Rogerus von Helmershausen oder des Reinbold von Paderborn?" in *Zeitschrift für christliche Kunst,* **22** (1909); Erich Meyer, "Neue Beiträge zur Kenntnis der Kunst des Roger von Helmarshausen und seines Kreises," in *Westfalen,* **25** (1940), and "Die Hildesheimer Rogerwerkstatt," in *Pantheon,* **32** (1944).

GRETEL CHAPMAN

[See also **Altar, Portable; Bells; Émail Brun; Enamel; Metalsmiths, Gold and Silver; Metalworkers; Romanesque Art; Theophilus.**]

ROGER OF SALISBURY (*ca.* 1065–1139), bishop of Salisbury and one of England's greatest statesmen. His innovative contributions still endure. Like many twelfth-century leaders, he rose from an obscure background, entered the secular clergy, and demonstrated exceptional administrative ability.

Roger was different, however, in that as a priest of Avranches in Normandy he met young Henry, the future king of England, and thus found wider scope for his talents and larger reward for his services. With Henry I he crossed the Channel to England, gained high ecclesiastical preferment, undertook major civic obligations, patronized art and learning, promoted his own relations, and endured the inevitable tensions between spiritual and temporal loyalties.

In 1101 Roger became royal chancellor and shortly afterward bishop of Salisbury. Debate about lay investiture delayed all English episcopal consecrations until 1107, but thereafter the Anglo-Norman church enjoyed remarkable tranquillity. The kingdom was also at peace, and Henry I (*r.* 1100–1135) therefore spent increasing time in troubled Normandy. In fact, he was out of Britain for more than half his long reign and always trusted Roger to rule in his absence. The bishop accepted the challenge enthusiastically and quickly introduced a more efficient bureaucratic government. Roger did not occupy a formal office or position but can be likened to a regent, or viceroy, or chief justiciar, the term used by later medieval commentators. His power was purely personal, and contemporaries rightly claimed he was "second only to the king."

Roger's expertise was particularly evident in financial and judicial administration. The Exchequer is his stellar achievement and lasting memorial. This systematic method of collecting, assaying, and accounting for the royal revenue was a significant improvement and gave England a rational fiscal apparatus long before any other European nation. The viceroy also sent royal justices on regular circuits, or eyres, to hear pleas in the countryside. This brought the reality of government to countless people and encouraged them to seek royal protection through chancery writs and formal charters.

Despite national concerns, Roger did not neglect diocesan responsibilities. In fact, it was said he devoted half the day to religious and half to secular business. He rebuilt the cathedral at Old Sarum (now destroyed) on a magnificent scale and erected mighty castles at Sarum, Sherborne, Devizes, and Malmesbury. He aided some monasteries, especially of the Austin canons, but exploited others for his own aggrandizement. By adroit patronage he created a dynasty that influenced the church for three generations. His sons were archdeacons at Salisbury; one nephew, Alexander, became bishop of Lincoln (1123–1148) and another, Nigel, gained Ely (1133–1168). Nigel's son, Richard Fitz Nigel (or Richard Fitzneale), was royal treasurer, author of *The Dialogue of the Exchequer* (*ca.* 1180), and bishop of London (1189–1198).

Roger faithfully supported Henry but did not relish the prospect of his haughty daughter and sole legitimate heir, Matilda, dowager empress of Germany, becoming ruler of England. In 1135 he therefore championed Stephen of Blois's usurpation of England's throne. Yet, in the common twelfth-century image, Roger's turn on the wheel of fortune was reaching its climax. In June 1139 King Stephen (*r.* 1135–1154) viciously turned against his aging chief administrator, cast him and his episcopal nephews into prison, demanded the surrender of their castles and wealth, and generally shifted authority from clerical administrators to self-seeking lay magnates. Several bishops, especially Henry of Winchester, condemned the king's action in a national synod, but to no avail. Roger died a broken man on 11 December (or 4 December) 1139. Many of his adherents quickly left government service, and the nation entered the trying years often later called "the Anarchy." However, the administrative procedures developed by the man some called "Roger the Great" withstood the civil strife and to this day form the basis of England's judicial and financial systems.

Although Roger's career fascinated many chroniclers, none left a full account of his life; and no personal letters or tracts have survived. Thirty-two of his charters are known, and he frequently appears attesting royal writs between 1100 and 1139. His grandnephew Richard Fitz Nigel best described his governmental work, and the principal contemporary observers were William of Malmesbury, Henry of Huntingdon, Ordericus Vitalis, John of Worcester, and the anonymous authors of the Anglo-Saxon Chronicle and the *Gesta Stephani.*

BIBLIOGRAPHY

Judith A. Green, *The Government of England Under Henry I* (1986); Charles Johnson, ed. and trans., *The Course of the Exchequer by Richard Son of Nigel* (1950); Edward J. Kealey, *Roger of Salisbury, Viceroy of England* (1972), and "King Stephen: Government and Anarchy," in *Albion,* **6** (1974).

EDWARD J. KEALEY

[See also **England: Norman-Angevin; Exchequer; Justices, Itinerant; Justiciar; William of Malmesbury.**]

ROGERIUS (*d.* 1162/1166), Italian lawyer, probably from Piacenza, who studied and taught Roman law at Bologna. Recent scholarship indicates he introduced the study of Roman law into southern France, probably at Montpellier, although Arles has also been suggested.

Rogerius' Bolognese activity is attested by thousands of glosses signed *R.* or *Rog.* in pre-Accursian manuscript commentaries to the *Code* (*Codex Justinianus*) and *Digest.* Attribution of the *Quaestiones de iuris subtilitatibus* to Rogerius would date his influence in France as early as 1141, since this work was used by the archbishop of Arles in a decision of 5 November 1141. He was also a source for *Lo Codi* (1155/1162), a Provençal abridgment of the *Code.*

Few dates are known concerning his life. The date 1158 appears in his gloss on CJ 1.17.2pr. in three manuscripts. Azo in his *Lectura codicis* (CJ 5.16.10) reports that R(ogerius) defended the rebellious Count Hugh of Baux (Provence), accused of breaking oath with Ramon Berenguer IV of Barcelona, count of Provence (*d.* 1166). The latter enjoyed the support of Emperor Frederick Barbarossa. Rogerius, arguing against his former master "B," (probably the pro-imperial Bulgarus), was able to postpone forfeiture until Frederick's final decision against Hugh at the Diet of Turin (18 August 1162). Rogerius died sometime thereafter, since Placentinus, arriving in Montpellier in 1166, refers to Rogerius as his predecessor "of recent memory."

Rogerius does not clearly belong to any school. In the great twelfth-century debate between Martinus Gosia and Bulgarus concerning equity, he sides with Bulgarus. Rogerius distinguishes between Roman equity and "modern equity." While recognizing fixed equity principles developed in antiquity (that is, by the Roman praetor), Rogerius opposes discretionary equity principles developed by Martinus and his school that would permit judges to curtail laws in accordance with personal standards of fairness. Such changes were to be left to the prince. On the other hand, Rogerius shares Martinus' modernizing tendencies, discussing current issues in Roman law terms, although his attempt in *De iure personarum* to treat serfs in Roman categories indicates he was an amateur in some contemporary legal problems.

As a legal philosopher he represents a major advance over earlier jurists, and many of his distinctions were incorporated without attribution by Azo and hence Accursius.

Rogerius' most influential work (with six extant manuscripts) was his unfinished *Summa 'Cum multae essent partes iuris'* on the *Code* (to IV.58), completed by an unknown pupil and Placentinus. Reportedly the first *Summa codicis,* it served as a model textbook for Placentinus' and Azo's *summae,* which superseded it. Unedited fragments of commentary are found on all of the three medieval divisions of the *Digest: Digestum vetus, Infortiatum,* and *Digestum novum.*

Several *opuscula* edited by Hermann Kantorowicz show the originality and subtlety of Rogerius. In his *Enodationes quaestionum* and other works he adapts the genre of *quaestiones legitimae* (confrontation and resolution of seemingly contradictory ancient texts), which was employed in the earliest glosses to harmonize texts and by Gratian to organize canon law. In the *Enodationes, Libellus de praescriptionibus,* and other shorter works, he resolves issues raised by conflicting texts in the literary form of dialogues between "Rogerius" and "Iurisprudentia." His dialogues employ a highly developed rhetoric, probably derived from French humanistic sources. Several shorter works attributed to Rogerius are now considered spurious.

BIBLIOGRAPHY

Sources. De praescriptionibus (1530), repr. in *Tractatus universi iuris,* XVII (1584), 48, and in *Patrologia latina,* CXLVI (1884), 1,485; *Quaestiones super institutis,* in Hermann Kantorowicz and William W. Buckland, *Studies in the Glossators of the Roman Law* (1938, repr. 1969), 133. Kantorowicz also edited *De iure personarum,* 279, and *Enodationes quaestionum super codice,* 281. *Summa codicis,* J. B. Palmieri, ed., in *Bibliotheca juridica medii aevi,* I(b), 2nd ed. (1914), 49–233.

For descriptions of manuscripts see Gero Dolezalek, *Verzeichnis der Handschriften zum römischen Recht bis 1600,* 4 vols. (1972); Gustav Pescatore, "Verzeichnis legistischer Distinktionen mit Angabe des Verfassers," in *Zeitschrift der Savigny-Stiftung für Rechtsgeschichte* (rom. Abt.), 33 (1912).

Studies. André Gouron, "Rogerius, *Quaestiones de iuris subtilitatibus* et pratique arlésienne: A propos d'une sentence archiépiscopale (1141, 5 novembre)," in *Mémoires de la Société pour l'histoire du droit et des institutions des anciens pays bourguignons, comtois, et romands,* 34 (1977); Carlo Guido Mor, "A l'origine de l'école de Montpellier: Rogerius ou Placentin?" in *Recueil de mémoires et travaux* (Société d'histoire du droit . . . écrit, Montpellier), 6 (1967); Bruno Paradisi, *Storia del diritto italiano: Le fonti del diritto nell'epoca bolognese,* pte. 1ª: *I civilisti fino a Rogerio* (1962); Gustav Pescatore, "Das Zeitalter des Rogerius," in *Miscellen*

(1889), repr. in *Beiträge zur Mittelalterlichen Rechtsgeschichte* (1898[?], repr. 1967).

WALTER PAKTER

[See also **Azo; Bologna, University of; Bulgarus; Corpus Iuris Civilis; Gratian; Law, Civil—Corpus Iuris, Revival and Spread; Law, French: In South; Law, Schools of; Lo Codi; Martinus Gosia; Placentinus.**]

ROHAN MASTER (*fl.* early fifteenth century), a manuscript illuminator and panel painter active in France. The Rohan Master takes his names from his masterpiece, the *Grandes heures* (*ca.* 1420–*ca.* 1425), owned in the sixteenth century by the Rohan family (Paris, Bibliothèque Nationale, MS lat. 9471). The Rohan Master's style is powerful and robust. Its crude expressiveness has led some scholars to suggest that the master was not of French origin, but it is certain that he worked in Paris.

BIBLIOGRAPHY

Millard Meiss, *French Painting in the Time of Jean de Berry: The Limbourgs and Their Contemporaries* (1974); *The Rohan Master: A Book of Hours, Bibliothèque Nationale, Paris* (MS Latin 9471), Millard Meiss, introduction, and Marcel Thomas, commentaries (1973).

WILLIAM J. DIEBOLD

[See also **Book of Hours; Manuscript Illumination: Western European; Panel Painting.**]

The dead man before God, with St. Michael repulsing a demon trying to possess the man's soul. Miniature illustrating the Office of the Dead from the *Grandes heures* of the Rohan Master, *ca.* 1420–1425. PARIS, BIBLIOTHÈQUE NATIONALE, MS. LAT. 9471, fol. 159

ROIG, JAUME. See **Catalan Narrative in Verse.**

ROJAS, FERNANDO DE. See **Celestina, La.**

ROLAND, SONG OF. Returning from an expedition into Spain in 778, Charlemagne's army was crossing the Pyrenees when attackers suddenly burst out of ambush and fell upon the rear guard. The enemy massacred a large number of Franks, plundered the baggage train, and made good their escape.

The first mention of this disaster appears in a version of the *Royal Frankish Annals* written a half-century later. The most famous account is in Einhard's *Vita Caroli Magni* (Life of Charlemagne), dated 830–833. It mentions three slain officers by name, one of whom, "Hruodlandus Brittannici praefectus" (Roland, prefect of the Breton march), is the hero now generally associated with the incident. The traditional site of the battle is near the village of Roncesvalles, Spain (Roncevaux, in French), but scholars do not agree as to where the fighting took place.

The *Song of Roland,* a French epic and one of the greatest masterpieces of world literature, provides a fanciful account of this event interspersed with much legendary material. Composed about 1100, it is penetrated with the ideas and values of the French aristocracy at the time of the First Crusade. There is considerable evidence that a Roland legend existed before this date, and an oral or a written version may have preceded the poem we know. Believed to be the oldest extant chanson de geste, the *Song of Roland* had a great influence on the French epic tradition.

The poem survives in an assonanced and in a rhymed redaction, each represented by more than one manuscript copy. During the Middle Ages, the work was translated and adapted into several languages. The Anglo-Norman text preserved in Digby 23, a twelfth-century manuscript of the Bodleian Library at Oxford, is considered to be the oldest and best version and will be the only one summarized and discussed below. The meaning of the last line in this copy, "Ci falt la geste que Turoldus declinet" (Here ends the story that Turoldus tells[?]), and the identity and role of Turoldus are much-debated questions. A number of verses are followed by the mysterious letters *AOI*.

Charlemagne's seven-year campaign in Spain has come to a climax with the siege of Saragossa. King Marsile's deceitful offer to become the emperor's vassal and a Christian divides the Franks. Roland counsels his uncle Charlemagne to carry the war to its conclusion; Ganelon pushes for accommodating the Saracens. Furious at being nominated by his own stepson to negotiate with Marsile, a very dangerous mission, Ganelon vows vengeance against Roland and conspires with the enemy to get rid of him. The traitor arranges to have Roland lead the rear guard into an ambush at Roncevaux. Roland and his friend Oliver debate whether or not to sound the oliphant to call for help. Appealing to honor and wishing to set an example, Roland refuses to blow the horn. The rear guard puts up a good fight but, in the end, is annihilated. However, Marsile's army has been decisively beaten. After sounding the oliphant, Roland dies facing the enemy. Charlemagne arrives and recognizes that his nephew died victoriously. Marsile manages to reach Saragossa, where, in a dramatic turnabout, he is reinforced by the Emir Baligant. The struggle now takes on a cosmic aspect, as the forces of Christendom are pitted against those of the pagan world. Victory hangs in the balance until Charlemagne kills Baligant in a duel. At Aachen (Aix-la-Chapelle), Alda accosts the returning emperor and, upon hearing the news of her fiancé Roland's passing, dies on the spot. Ganelon is haled before Charlemagne and accused by him of treason. The case is decided by a judicial combat. The loyal Thierry slays Ganelon's champion, Pinabel. The Franks execute the traitor and thirty of his kinsmen. Marsile's widow Bramimonde is baptized. The angel Gabriel appears to Charlemagne in a dream and summons him to new campaigns against the pagans.

Narrated in a style closely linked with the formulaic diction of oral literature but also utilizing techniques found in works intended for reading, the 4,002-verse assonanced poem is exceptionally well-structured and elevated in tone. The two story lines (Charles-Marsile-Baligant and Roland-Ganelon) are intertwined, and there are numerous contrasts and parallels, notably Roland and Oliver in the horn scenes. Using a familiar debating technique, the hero's companion-in-arms turns the tables on him by giving the same reasons he, Roland, had earlier provided for not sounding the oliphant. The archfoes Charles and Baligant are contrasted, priest-king on the one hand, diabolical tyrant on the other. Certain groups of laisses are arranged symmetrically, and hemistichs and even entire verses are repeated with little or no change, producing striking effects. Irony plays an important role, for example when Ganelon uses the equivocal word *fillastre* (stepson or poor imitation of a son) echoing Roland's choice of the term *parastre* (stepfather or unworthy father). Unity is enhanced by repeatedly opposing good and evil ("Pagans are in the wrong and Christians are in the right") and by ringing the changes on such themes as betrayal, conversion, and victory. The refrain "Halt sunt li pui" (The mountains are high) creates an atmosphere laden with foreboding. Nature responds to tragic developments; for example, a terrifying earthquake and storm precede the hero's death.

The poet enunciates certain religious ideas clearly and forcefully (Christianity is superior to all other faiths, the Franks are the Chosen People, those who die at Roncevaux are martyrs), but scholars have taken divergent views on the poem's ethos and the motivation of the main characters. Are the Franks so concerned with their reputation and honor and so consumed with revenge that their Christianity is a mere mockery? Is Roland guilty of the sin of pride? Is Ganelon without one redeeming feature? Does the poet side with Oliver in the battlefield debate? How helpful are the elucidations in such contemporary works as the Latin *Pseudo-Turpin Chronicle* and the German *Rolandslied*? Some symbolism is unmistakable (breast-beating, flowers, olive branches), but the meaning of Roland's proffered gauntlet, for instance, and of the four marble objects at Roncevaux is less clear, at least to the modern reader.

One thing is certain: the poet created unforgettable characters and a narrative that rivets the attention. Probably no other source succeeds as well in depicting the attitudes and, above all, the aspirations of the noblemen of the day.

BIBLIOGRAPHY

General. Joseph J. Duggan, *A Guide to Studies on the Chanson de Roland* (1976), is chiefly concerned with the years 1955–1974 but includes a good selection of earlier works. The *Société Rencesvals (pour l'étude des épopées romanes)* was founded in 1955 and derives its name from the form of Roncesvalles in Digby 23. One may follow trends in *Roland* scholarship by consulting the proceedings of its triennial congresses, its *Bulletin bibliographique* (since 1958), and, especially, *Olifant* (since 1973), a quarterly publication of the American-Canadian branch of this society.

Editions, translations, and glossaries. The French manuscripts of *Roland* together with several related texts including Latin and medieval French versions of the *Pseudo-Turpin Chronicle* and a modern French translation of the *Rolandslied* are transcribed in *Les textes de la Chanson de Roland,* Raoul Mortier, ed., 10 vols. (1940–1944). The critical editions of the Oxford text in widest use today are by Joseph Bédier (1937); Frederick Whitehead, 2nd ed. (1946); Gérard Moignet, 2nd ed. (1969); and Gerard J. Brault, 2 vols. (1978). All provide textual notes. Bédier and Moignet include a translation in modern French, and Brault provides one in modern English. Other English translations include those of Patricia Terry (1965), Robert Harrison (1970), Douglas David Ray Owen (1972), Howard S. Robertson (1972), and Frederick Goldin (1978). Glossaries are found in Bédier's companion volume, *La Chanson de Roland commentée* (1927, repr. 1968), and in Whitehead.

On the poem's literary aspects, see Bédier and Moignet. The most extensive treatment, however, is in Brault.

Studies. Some of the books dealing exclusively with the *Song of Roland* are Paul Aebischer, *Préhistoire et protohistoire du "Roland" d'Oxford* (1972), and *Rolandiana et Oliveriana* (1967); Prosper Boissonnade, *Du nouveau sur la Chanson de Roland: La genèse historique, le cadre géographique, le milieu, les personnages, la date et l'auteur du poème* (1923); André Burger, *Turold, poète de la fidélité* (1977); Maurice Delbouille, *Sur la genèse de la Chanson de Roland, travaux récents, propositions nouvelles: Essai critique* (1954); Joseph J. Duggan, *The Song of Roland: Formulaic Style and Poetic Craft* (1973); Edmond Faral, *La Chanson de Roland: Étude et analyse* (1934); E. F. Halvorsen, *The Norse Version of the Chanson de Roland* (1959); George Fenwick Jones, *The Ethos of the Song of Roland* (1963); Pierre Le Gentil, *La Chanson de Roland,* 2nd ed. (1967), and an English translation by Francis F. Beer (1969); Ramón Menéndez Pidal, *La Chanson de Roland et la tradition épique des Francs,* 2nd ed. (1960); Barton Sholod, *Charlemagne in Spain: The Cultural Legacy of Roncesvalles* (1966); Eugene Vance, *Reading the Song of Roland* (1970).

Iconography. Rita Lejeune and Jacques Stiennon, *La Légende de Roland dans l'art du moyen âge,* 2 vols. (1966), trans. by Christine Trollope as *The Legend of Roland in the Middle Ages,* 2 vols. (1971).

GERARD J. BRAULT

[See also **Anglo-Norman Literature; Chansons de Geste; Chivalry; French Literature; Laisse; Pseudo-Turpin; Roncesvalles; Rolandslied.**]

ROLANDSLIED, a twelfth-century German poem of 9,094 lines with end rhymes, widely known in Germany. It is extant in only one complete manuscript, P Heidelberg codex Palatinus Germanicus 112, with thirty-nine miniatures and four fragments. The author, Pfaffe Konrad (*Chunrat,* verse 9,079), a clerk possibly of Ratisbon (present-day Regensburg), translated the *Rolandslied* from a version of the French *Chanson de Roland* for Duke Henry of Bavaria at the behest of Henry's duchess. He translated it first into Latin (which he notes in verse 9,082) and then from Latin into Rhenish Middle High German. The poem was meant for a Bavarian (Regensburg) audience. The ducal couple was either, it is assumed, Henry the Lion of Bavaria and Matilda Plantagenet of England, his wife, or his uncle Henry II Jasomirgott of Bavaria and Austria and his second wife, Theodora Komnena of Byzantium. In the first instance the *Rolandslied* would be dated between 1168 and 1172; in the second, between about 1160 and 1177.

The *Rolandslied* narrates Karl and his Twelve Peers' fight against the Saracens (historically the Basques in the Pyrenees), who decimate the Frankish vanguard fighting under Roland's command at the Runzeval (Roncesvalles, Roncevaux) Pass.

The structure of the *Rolandslied* is tripartite. In verses 1–2,760 Genelun (Ganelon) betrays the Franks; in verses 2,761–6,949 the Franks are defeated; in verses 6,950–9,016 Karl is revenged.

This ultimate subjugation of pagan Spain in the *Rolandslied* takes the form of a Christian crusade against infidels. Roland, Oliver, and the majority of the Peers die because Roland, their leader, in his pride refuses to blow his horn, Olifant, while there is still time to summon help from the Frankish main contingent under Karl.

The outline of the epic and many narrative features (such as battle descriptions and individual heroism) are mainly borrowed from the *Chanson de Roland,* whereas verses 1–360 partially rest on the *Pseudo-Turpin.* In Konrad's Middle High German version the power struggle between Roland and Roland's stepfather, Genelun, who betrays Roland and the Franks to the pagans for money and glory, is described less as a private feud between two powerful lords than as a crusade to be won for God's greater glory. Roland's sword, Durendart (Durendal in the *Chanson de Roland*), which is God's finest weapon in either version, may not fall into enemy hands after Roland has killed thousands of pagans with it. In the end, although emerging victorious, Karl is desolate at the loss of his nephew. He has Genelun convicted and quartered at Aachen (Aix-la-Chapelle).

Konrad does not keep the Old French one-rhymed laisse (*tirade*) but, perhaps due to his intermediary Latin version, settles on rhymed couplets. His language is still heavily formulaic. But the tragic perspective that rules supreme in the *Chanson de Roland* is here muted by a heavy overlay of the crusade spirit, such as was preached by St. Bernard of Clairvaux. This reorientation changes the heroes into heroic martyrs eager to die in the service of Christianity.

Konrad exalts the figure of Karl by attributing supernatural qualities to him, and he casts Genelun in the mold of a Judas from the outset, thereby turning the poem into a theocratic *Karlslied.* Whereas the *Chanson de Roland* is a heroic epic, the *Rolandslied* keeps a middle course between crusade song and sermon on martyrdom.

The *Rolandslied* influenced Der Stricker's *Karl,* the *Karlmeinet,* and Wolfram von Eschenbach's *Willehalm.*

BIBLIOGRAPHY

Two critical editions, both going back to the same editorship, are available: Carl Wesle, ed., *Das Rolandslied des Pfaffen Konrad,* 2nd ed. (1963); Carl Wesle, ed. *Das Rolandslied des Pfaffen Konrad,* 2nd ed. (1967), with an introduction by Peter Wapnewski and a bibliography. Konrad der Pfaffe, *Das Rolandslied des Pfaffen Konrad: Einführung zum Faksimile des Codex Palatinus Germanicus 112 der Universitätsbibliothek, Heidelberg,* Wilfried Werner and H. Zirnbauer, eds., I (1970), II (1977). A German translation of the *Rolandslied* is by Dieter Kartschoke (1970).

Studies. Hans Helmut Christmann, "Neuere Arbeiten zum Rolandslied," in *Romanistisches Jahrbuch,* **16** (1965); Robert Folz, *Le souvenir et la légende de Charlemagne dans l'empire germanique médiévale* (1950); Karl-Ernst Geith, *Carolus Magnus: Studien zur Darstellung Karls des Grossen in der deutschen Literatur des 12. und 13. Jahrhunderts* (1977); Christian J. Gellinek, "The Epilogue of Konrad's *Rolandslied,*" in *Modern Language Notes,* **83** (1968), and "À propos du système de pouvoir dans la *Chanson de Roland,*" in *Cahiers de civilisation médiévale,* **19** (1976); Dieter Kartschoke, *Die Datierung des deutschen Rolandsliedes* (1965), and *Das Rolandslied des Pfaffen Konrad* (1971); Hans Erich Keller, "La place du *Ruolantes Liet* dans la tradition rolandienne," in *Moyen âge,* **71** (1965); Rita Lejeune and Jacques Stiennon, *La légende de Roland dans l'art du moyen âge,* 2 vols. (1966); Cola Minis, "Französisch-deutsche Literaturberührungen im Mittelalter," in *Rheinisches Jahrbuch,* **4** (1951), and "Der Pseudo-Turpin und das *Rolandslied* des Pfaffen Chunrat," in *Mittellateinische Jahrbücher,* **2** (1965); Marianne Ott-Meimberg, *Kreuzzugsepos oder Staatsroman? Strukturen adeliger Heils-versicherung im deutschen Rolandslied* (1980).

CHRISTIAN J. GELLINEK

[See also **Chansons de Geste; Charlemagne; Henry the Lion; Middle High German Literature; Pseudo-Turpin; Roland, Song of.**]

ROLANDUS (*fl.* twelfth century), canonist and theologian, the author of *Quadrifidio ciborum* and *Sententiae.* The first, written about 1150, is among the earliest commentaries on Gratian's *Concordia discordantium canonum,* expounding part II thereof, illustrating it with hypotheticals, and occasionally criticizing it. The *Sententiae,* later in date, is a markedly Abelardian theological treatise. Rolandus' own birth and death dates and birthplace are unknown.

His influence did not go beyond the Bolognese school of his day, but on the nineteenth-century rediscovery of his writings they were wrongly ascribed to the Rolandus who became Pope Alexander III and were used by modern historians to understand the pope. Today Rolandus is best seen as representative of the intellectual life of nascent Bologna.

BIBLIOGRAPHY

Rolandus, *Quadrifidio ciborum,* ed. by Friedrich Thaner as *Die Summa Magistri Rolandi nachmals*

Papstes Alexander III (1874); Rolandus, *Sententiae,* in Ambrose M. Gietl, ed., *Die Sentenzen Rolands nachmals Papstes Alexander III* (1891); John T. Noonan, "Who Was Rolandus?" in Kenneth Pennington and Robert Somerville, eds., *Law, Church, and Society* (1977).

JOHN T. NOONAN, JR.

[See also **Abelard, Peter; Gratian; Law, Canon: After Gratian.**]

ROLF, THOMAS (*fl.* 1380's), English illuminator. The Infirmarer's Roll of Westminster Abbey records a payment to Thomas Rolf in 1386/1387 for the illumination and binding of a new missal, presumably the infirmarer's. Margaret Rickert and Amanda Simpson have wondered whether Rolf may have been an illuminator of the Litlyngton Missal (Westminster Abbey, MS 37), fully accounted for 1383/1384. Despite Neil Ker, the two missals should not be confused. Rolf is otherwise mentioned only cursorily in two London records, entitled "lymnor."

BIBLIOGRAPHY

Margaret J. Rickert, *Painting in Britain: The Middle Ages* (1954, 2nd ed. 1965), 153, 244, note 22; Amanda Simpson, *The Connections Between English and Bohemian Painting During the Second Half of the Fourteenth Century* (1984), 138; Neil R. Ker, *Medieval Manuscripts in British Libraries,* I (1969), 410; Richard Marks and Nigel Morgan, *The Golden Age of English Manuscript Painting, 1200–1500* (1981), 89.

BARRIE SINGLETON

ROLL. See **Volumen.**

ROLLE, RICHARD. See **Mysticism, Christian: English.**

ROMAN DE FAUVEL. See **Fauvel, Roman de.**

ROMAN DE LA ROSE (Romance of the Rose). The *Roman de la Rose* was the most influential allegory in the European Middle Ages. Paradoxically, it is not one work but two, and the two component parts are disparate in date, authorship, length, and intellectual inspiration. Only versification, characters, and a thread of allegorical narrative bind them together.

The first 4,058 lines were written by Guillaume de Lorris around 1237. Using the classical device of a *somnium* (dream vision), the author portrays himself as dreamer-narrator-lover in a courtly dream-quest of a "rose." The romance opens with an explanation of the profound significance of dreams and with the claim that this particular vision, dreamed when the narrator was in his twentieth year and dedicated to his lady, is both new and instructive: "Ce est li *Romanz de la Rose,* / ou l'art d'Amors est tote enclose. / La matire est et bone et neuve." (This is the *Romance of the Rose,* embracing all the art of love. The matter is both good and new.) In fact, most substantive elements were derived from classical tradition (especially Ovid) or from contemporary literature (lyric poetry, romance, and perhaps playful Latin satires like the *Concilium in Monte Romarici* [Council of Remiremont, *ca.* 1150]). Even Guillaume's disquisition on love, delivered by the God of Love (vv. 2,058–2,748), condenses material from Andreas Capellanus' *De Amore.* Only Guillaume's ensemble, a sustained allegory of love's emotional turmoil, is new—an exquisitely fashioned and perceptive piece of psychological analysis.

The narrator, wandering in spring along a river, comes upon a Jardin de Deduit (Garden of Pleasure). Its high enclosing walls bear images of those whose presence would be inimical in the courtly garden: Haine (Hatred), Felonie (Treachery), Vilenie (Villainy), Covoitise (Covetousness), Avarice, Envie (Envy), Tristesse (Sadness), Vieillesse (Old Age), Li Tens (Time), Papelardie (Pope-holiness or Hypocrisy), and Pauvreté (Poverty). A small door to the garden is opened by the garden's portress, Oiseuse (Idleness), mistress of Deduit. Inside is a paradise of birdsong, and Leece (Happiness) sings to the accompaniment of musicians and jongleurs. Deduit dances with his troupe of companions Beauté (Beauty), Richesse (Wealth), Largesse (Generosity), Franchise (Open-heartedness), Courtoisie (Courtesy), Oiseuse, and Jeunesse (Youth). The narrator is invited by Courtoisie to join the dance. Amour (the God of Love), accompanied by Doux Regard (Fair Glance), watches, then follows the narrator when he strays toward a fountain perilous.

The lover enters the Garden of Deduit, Narcissus at the fountain within. Miniature from a 15th-century MS of the *Roman de la Rose*. BY PERMISSION OF THE BRITISH LIBRARY, LONDON, MS EGERTON 1069, fol. 1r

In this fountain Narcissus once had glimpsed his shadow and had subsequently died. The waters of the fountain have been seeded with love by Cupid, and two crystal stones mirror the two halves of the garden. In this mirror perilous the narrator sees a rose garden and is induced to walk toward it. But the moment he tries to pluck a rosebud of surpassing beauty from the garden, Love's arrow Beauté pierces his eye, followed in swift succession by the arrows Simplece (Simplicity), Courtoisie, Compagnie (Company), and Beau Semblant (Fair Seeming). The God of Love approaches the narrator, who accepts Love's domination and asks to know his feudal duties. Guillaume de Lorris here intervenes with the comment that the romance proper is now beginning, for "li romanz des or amende" (from this point the story gets better).

Love cautions against villainy, slander, coarseness of language, pride, and avarice. He recommends that the lover show courtesy to all, respect to women, and joyousness: that he be elegant in dress and mien; cultivate such natural talents as music, dancing, and athletics; and that he avoid promiscuity. These precepts will be helpful during the inherent trials and sufferings of love, as will Espérance (Hope), Doux Penser (Fair Thought), Doux Parler (Fair Speech), and Doux Regard.

The God of Love departs and Bel Accueil (Fair Welcome) now encourages the lover to approach beyond the spiny hedge around the rose garden. A succession of enemies threaten the lover's advance. Lurking Danger, symbol of the lady's modesty, reacts immediately, while Male Bouche (Slander), Honte (Shame), Peur (Fear), and Jalousie (Jealousy) provide further hazards. The lover withdraws despairingly. Raison (Reason) descends from her tower to advise him to abandon his adventure. The lover obstinately refuses and seeks out Ami (Friend) as a confidant and adviser. With Friend's help Danger is soothed. Franchise and Pitié (Pity) intercede, and Bel Accueil decides to renew support for the lover. That support is short-lived, however: the lover's request for a kiss is instantly denied. Bel Accueil blames Chasteté (Chastity), but relents at the appearance of Venus. At this point Guillaume again intervenes with a plea to his own lady for her favor.

Repercussions follow the first kiss. Jalousie overwhelms Bel Accueil and the lover with reproaches, citing a fear of Lecherie (Lechery) and Luxure (Abandon). Jalousie then builds a prison tower where, under guard of Danger, Honte, Peur, and Male Bouche, Bel Accueil is placed under the surveillance of La Vieille (The Old Woman). Nothing escapes the vigilance of the Old Woman's malevolent eye, which had once viewed the whole of love's dance: "el set toute la vielle dance." The first part of the romance ends thus in uncertainty (v. 4,058).

Jean Chopinel de Meun-sur-Loire (*d.* 1305) resumed the narration between 1275 and 1280 without introductory fanfare. In his continuation the lover remains intent upon his quest and, realizing that Espérance is unreliable, turns back to Raison. The latter listens to the lover's complaints and then tries to change his disposition. Puzzled by Raison's paradoxical warnings against love, the lover asks for a definition of the problem. A philosophical disquisition on love ensues in which Aristotelian naturalism rather than courtly behavior is the dominating criterion. Procreation, Nature, Fortune, wealth, power, and the four types of love are among many topics that recur within Raison's 3,000-line speech. The stylistic focus also shifts from Guillaume's courtesy to frank, and even crude, inquiry. Jean neatly anticipates future criticism of this frankness through the lover's questioning protests.

Raison responds that there is no justification for inhibition in the naming of "noble things." The male generative organs were created by God in Paradise for the worthy purpose of perpetuating the species. It is therefore no sin to name them by their true names: "ne faz je pas pechié/se je nome les nobles choses/par plein texte sanz metre gloses."

The lover recognizes the justness of the explanation, but announces that Raison's words grow tedious when he cannot forget his love. Raison leaves, and the lover runs to Ami. The latter's counsel is more pragmatic: be loyal to Love, show restraint near the castle where Bel Accueil is imprisoned, handle Male Bouche with care, and cultivate La Vieille and all other guards with gifts, bribes, and prayers. If the three guards Peur, Honte, and Danger are perceived favorable despite their external protests, the lover must seize the moment—and the rose! The wishes of Bel Accueil must always be observed, however.

The lover replies that he would prefer less hypocritical methods, especially with Male Bouche. Ami convinces him that a direct attack upon that deceitful enemy is never efficacious. The lover then inquires about alternative entrances to the castle. Ami cautions that the path of Fole Largesse (Foolish Generosity) and Trop Doner (Excessive Giving) is not accessible to anyone who is not a friend of Richesse. In a digression he explains that Pauvreté is worse than death, because its torturing effects are prolonged, while death is instantaneous. In the lover's circumstances, small, well-placed gifts will produce the best results.

Unfortunately, continues Ami, the successful conquest of a woman is only the beginning. Jean's misogyny is evident in the final portion of Ami's speech, which incorporates angry recrimination and invective from Le Mari Jaloux (The Jealous Husband) (vv. 8,426–9,390).

Doux Parler and Doux Penser reappear without their companion Doux Regard. Obediently the lover avoids the castle for the moment. He meets and is repulsed by Richesse, who tells him scathingly that he should have listened to Raison. The lover attempts to conciliate his enemies, and the God of Love decides to intervene with help. Love summons his company (enumerated in verses 10,419–10,428). He worries at the presence of Abstinence Contrainte (Forced Abstinence) and of Abstinence's inseparable companion Faux Semblant (False Seeming). He yields eventually to the argument that the second allows the first to exist, and turns to a plan of attack on the castle.

He laments the loss of Tibullus, Gallus, Catullus, and Ovid, who once spread Love's doctrines. He explains the necessity for aid to Guillaume de Lorris, who could die if his poem remained incomplete. The strengths and weaknesses of friends and enemies are assessed. Faux Semblant is permitted to join the group if his cooperation can be guaranteed.

Faux Semblant's lengthy response (vv. 10,922–11,984) permits Jean to voice scathing satire against the mendicant orders. Then the attack upon the castle begins. The allies attack from four quarters. Courtoisie, Largesse, Faux Semblant, and Abstinence Contrainte seize Le Vieille and prevail upon her to subvert Bel Accueil. La Vieille counsels the inexperienced young Bel Accueil in a long digression about life and love, youth and fortune. The lover is grateful for the cooperation of La Vieille, who, encouraged with a timely gift, arranges the lover's meeting with the Rose. Meanwhile Male Bouche has been killed, his tongue cut out by Faux Semblant, and Love's troupe has advanced so far that the lover is in sight of the Rose. Once again Danger, Peur, and Honte intervene to lock up Bel Accueil. Jean de Meun here inserts an apology to all women and good religious who may have received offense from his work. Another melee proves unsuccessful for Love's forces, and a truce is called. In the army's presence Venus now swears help and support in a joint oath with the God of Love.

Nature has heard the oath and has now returned to her forge for the unending task of recreating all species. Her plaintive mood induces her to summon her chaplain Genius for a long confession. Genius first indulges in his own diatribe against women and their indiscretions. He then listens to the confession by Nature—a didactic yet lyrical synthesis of Jean's views about the universe, Platonic and Pythagorean theory, Aristotelian naturalism, free will and determinism, cosmogony and theology. Man alone is an exception to the harmony of the universe, laments Nature. She reproaches man for his disobedience, and dispatches Genius to excommunicate all renegades who fail to fulfill Nature's precepts.

Genius disappears, the battle resumes, and Venus throws a flaming torch into the castle. Courtoisie, Pitié, and Franchise encourage Bel Accueil to facilitate the lover's conquest. The lover's hedonistic possession of the Rose is the logical conclusion to Nature's (and therefore God's) first commandment as it had been preached by Genius. Then, since the sexual act is the ultimate happiness, the lover awakes.

At Jean de Meun's conclusion the ineffable beauty of Nature has effectively eclipsed the beauty of Guillaume's Rose. Courtly idealism has been negated by irony and by gross misogyny. Social satire and philosophical digression have replaced psychological analysis. Narrative unity has been undermined by contradictory speculations. Nevertheless, Jean de Meun's romance has a unity of its own. Its purpose of scholarly *disputatio* concerning love topics binds a diversity of sources together: Abelard and Heloise, Alan of Lille, Andreas Capellanus, Aristotle, St. Augustine, the Bible, Boethius, Cato, Cicero, Claudian, Homer, Horace, Huon de Méri, John of Salisbury, Juvenal, Livy, Lucan, Ovid, Plato, Ptolemy, Pythagoras, Raoul de Houdenc, Rutebeuf, Sallust, Terence, Theophrastus, Valerius, Vergil, William of St. Amour, and others.

The heirs of the *Roman de la Rose* are legion also. An incredibly large number of manuscripts (some 300) of the work itself survive. The romance has also inspired numerous prose versions, translations, and adaptations throughout Europe. In England, Chaucer made at least a partial translation in the 1360's and later demonstrated the influence of Guillaume and Jean in all his major works. Gower's *Confessio Amantis* is a 30,000-line allegory structured entirely around a lover's confession to Genius. In the thirteenth and fourteenth centuries scores of allegorical love-narrations borrowed the symbolism of the *Roman.* Jean de Meun's antifeminism was perpetuated in Deschamps, Villon, and *Les quinze joies de mariage.* Guillaume de Deguileville condemned the whole work, while citing its influence upon his *Pèlerinage de la vie humaine.* Christine de Pizan attacked Jean de Meun's misogyny in her *Epistre au Dieu d'Amours* in 1399, thus initiating "La querelle de la Rose," in which John Gerson and Nicholas of Clamanges joined her against Jean de Montreuil and Pierre and Gontier Col. And although the *Roman de la Rose* suffered an eclipse of popularity in seventeenth-century France, it was among the first medieval works to be revived in the next hundred years. Debate about its *sen* and *conjointure* have continued ever since.

BIBLIOGRAPHY

Editions and translations. The principal editions are those of Ernest Langlois, 5 vols. (1914–1924), and Félix Lecoy, 3 vols. (1965–1970). English translations (as *The Romance of the Rose*) are by Harry W. Robbins (1962) and Charles Dahlberg (1971, 2nd ed. 1983).

Studies. Joseph L. Baird and John R. Kane, *La Querelle de la Rose* (1978); Jean Batany, *Approches du "Roman de la Rose"* (1973); John V. Fleming, *The "Roman de la Rose": A Study in Allegory and Iconography* (1969); Alan Gunn, *The Mirror of Love* (1952); David Hult, *Self-fulfilling Prophecies: Readership and Authority in the First "Roman de la Rose"* (1986); C. S. Lewis, *The Allegory of Love* (1936, repr. 1958); Maxwell Luria, *A Reader's Guide to the "Roman de la Rose"* (1982); Charles Muscatine, *Chaucer and the French Tradition* (1957); Stephen G. Nichols, Jr., "The Emergence of a Psychological Allegory in Old French Romance," in *PMLA,* **68** (1953), "Marot, Villon, and the *Roman de la Rose:* A Study in the Language of Creation and Re-creation," in *Studies in Philology,* **63** (1966) and **64** (1967), and "The Rhetoric of Sincerity in the *Roman de la Rose,*" in *Romance Studies in Memory of Edward Billings Ham* (1967); Armand Strubel, *Le Roman de le Rose* (1984); Ronald Sutherland, "The *Romanunt of the Rose* and Source Manuscripts," in *PMLA,* **74** (1959).

JEANETTE M. A. BEER

[See also **Allegory; Antifeminism; Chaucer, Geoffrey; Christine de Pizan; Courtly Love; French Literature; Guillaume de Lorris; Jean de Meun; Visions.**]

ROMAN DE RENART. See **Renard the Fox.**

ROMAN DE TOUTE CHEVALERIE. An Anglo-Norman version of the Alexander legend, but independent of the continental *Roman d'Alexandre*, the *Roman de toute chevalerie* is attributed to Thomas of Kent and was probably composed between 1175 and 1185. The *Roman de toute chevalerie* is based on English Latin sources and is itself the source of the Middle English *Kyng Alisaunder*.

BIBLIOGRAPHY

Brian Foster and Ian Short, eds., *The Anglo-Norman Alexander (Le roman de toute chevalerie) by Thomas of Kent*, 2 vols. (1976–1977).

BRIAN MERRILEES

[See also **Alexander Romances; Anglo-Norman Literature.**]

ROMAN EGYPT, LATE

LAND AND PEOPLE

Land. Separated from its neighbors by barriers of water and desert, and defined by a remarkable interplay of those factors, Egypt was always distinctive. Most of its surface is desert, with cultivation limited to a narrow strip along the Nile until the river broadens into its delta, at which point most of the land down to the Mediterranean is usable either for farming, for pasturage, or (in antiquity) for swampy crops like papyrus. Rainfall is scanty throughout the country; the climate is mild in winter, hot and dry in summer, and comparatively constant. In these circumstances, agriculture depended entirely on the Nile, and the size of harvests on the adequacy of the rise of the Nile in a given year (either too much or too little was harmful). Bad years occurred, but in normal years Egypt produced a surplus of cereals large enough to make a major contribution to feeding the rest of the empire, particularly the capitals, Rome and, later, Constantinople. The dependence on irrigation required constant attention to the extensive network of canals and basins which are a feature of the Egyptian countryside to the present time.

People. The bulk of the population of Egypt was made up of indigenous, Egyptian (Coptic) speakers. The country also contained the descendants of Greek settlers (most, but not all, immigrants in the Hellenistic period), whose relative numbers cannot be estimated, as well as smaller numbers of other groups. Many Egyptians had over the course of time learned Greek and hellenized themselves, while some Greeks had certainly become Egyptianized. The relatively clear lines which can be drawn in the third century B.C. are no longer easily visible by late antiquity, though the distinction between a hellenized upper class and the more purely Coptic lower classes is clear enough. Many of these hellenized aristocrats, however, were either of Egyptian extraction (partly or entirely) or had Egyptianized themselves substantially, and even among those who played a considerable role in the culture of the imperial court there are indications of close involvement in traditional Egyptian priestly activities.

POLITICS, GOVERNMENT, AND ECONOMICS

Political history. Deserts to the east and west have protected Egypt from invasions, and only occasionally has Nubia produced a power strong enough to threaten Egypt. The Mediterranean coast is difficult for hostile landings. Egypt was therefore largely spared the barbarian incursions that occupied so much of the empire's attention in the third century and later, though occasional raids from the desert Blemmyes, from the mid third century on, caused damage, with particular problems in the earlier and middle fifth century. There were occasional Egyptian revolts (one ill-known one around 293–294), and Egypt was the locus of the revolt of Domitius Domitianus in 297–298. On the whole, however, Egypt was politically and militarily calm. Partly for this reason it was little visited by emperors (apart from those two revolts, no visits between 284 and 337 are securely attested).

On the other hand, in the shrunken Eastern or Byzantine Empire Egypt was more important than it had been in the full Roman Empire of the second century, with its food resources and comparative wealth. It therefore played a large role in the ecclesiastical disputes of the period and, as time went on, contributed from its Greek aristocracy a significant number of influential figures in the empire. After the split of the Egyptian Monophysite church from the main body of the orthodox church following the Council of Chalcedon (451), relations between Egypt and Constantinople deteriorated. There was a revolt in the delta under Emperor Maurice (*r.* 582–602), and Egypt supported Heraklios in his revolt against Phokas in 608–609. The Persians took Egypt without great difficulty in 619 after cutting it off from the rest of the empire; it was retaken a decade later when Heraklios forced a

ROMAN EGYPT, LATE

Persian retreat. While Egypt did not, as has often been claimed, welcome the Arabs as liberators in 640–641, neither did it have the capacity for a prolonged and successful resistance without better support from the central government.

Government. Egypt is often seen as an isolated area in the Roman Empire, and it is true that the emperors notoriously sought to keep it apart to protect the security of the grain supply of Rome (and thus their own safety). But even in earlier times there were many links between Egypt and other provinces. In the fourth century and later, with the assimilation of Egyptian administration to the rest of the empire by Diocletian and his successors, the remaining barriers broke down, at least for the Greek upper class. We find members of the municipal aristocracy in imperial service as bureaucrats, and we find them (sometimes the same people) as rhetoricians and poets at the imperial court and traveling throughout the empire.

Diocletian increased the Roman military presence in Egypt and spread the available troops more evenly across a larger number of garrisons. He also provided a close link between the need for provisions of the military and the structure of the system of taxation in grain and other foodstuffs. Various emperors reorganized the civil administration into different provinces, but these changes are not likely to have made much difference to most of the population, which continued to look to the prefect, or *praeses,* as an ultimate source of justice, while ordinary concerns were handled by more local officials. The majority of the latter were local residents serving in liturgical positions for limited periods (though many of them held enough different offices over the course of time that they spent large parts of their lives in part-time government service). Many of these were part of the municipal government of the chief towns of the nomes, which had been given municipal charters by Septimius Severus at the start of the third century. Others were village-level tasks, filled by moderately prosperous farmers who lived in the villages. These unpaid and temporary jobs often involved less time than they did risk of exposure to financial ruin if some obligation to the imperial government were not met. Though imperial officials as such (career appointees) are met with often enough in the papyri, there do not seem to have been many of them in proportion to the population governed. At the local level, it was the military that was the more noticeable presence.

Economy. The Egyptian nomes retained their traditional structure, with many small villages and a central town serving as market and service center and as place of residence for the wealthier classes. Ever since Ptolemaic times the towns (*metropoleis*) had been the favored home of the propertied Greek and hellenized population, and with the municipalization of the nome *metropoleis* under Septimius Severus, a period of efflorescence of this class began. The fourth century was perhaps the acme of this stratum, the wealthier and abler members of which began, virtually for the first time, to play an important role on the Mediterranean scene as members of the elite of government and culture.

In the villages, most of the land continued to be owned by small farmers, though considerable amounts were owned by residents of the *metropoleis* and farmed by the villagers on lease, as had been the case for hundreds of years. There are some signs that such dependent relations increased in the course of the fourth and, even more, the fifth century, but the so-called "large estates" of the metropolitan aristocracy still consisted mainly of small farms dispersed over a wide area and rented out to local tenants, rather than large tracts of adjacent land. In the sixth and seventh centuries we find much more obvious dependence on the "great houses," but it seems from recent studies that this relationship involved the responsibility of the great landowners for the collection of the taxes of the peasantry who depended on them, rather than outright ownership of huge tracts by them; in effect, the system replaced much of the liturgical system of the fourth century by a more permanent set of responsibilities for the rich.

RELIGION

Egypt was famous in the Greek and Roman worlds for its animal-form divinities, but it became equally well known in the late Roman period for the vigor and violence of factional Christian strife. The Christian church got an early start in Egypt, but large-scale conversion apparently did not come until the early fourth century, after which it proceeded rapidly. The Egyptian church was much involved in the doctrinal disputes of the fourth and fifth centuries, and the bishops of Alexandria became prominent players in ecumenical councils. The most famous, Athanasius (bishop, 328–373), was often in exile for his staunch orthodoxy, and Cyril (bishop, 412–444) played a critical role in the fight against Nestorianism. The Egyptian church split after the

Council of Chalcedon (451), with the majority (largely Coptic) supporting a Monophysite view of Christ's nature; the orthodox (Melchite) church also survived in Egypt, however, and both had their own bishops of Alexandria. The conflict between the two was closely linked to imperial politics for the remainder of Byzantine rule in Egypt.

Egypt was also renowned as a primary locus of the development of monasticism, especially for the work of St. Anthony (*ca.* 250–*ca.* 350) and St. Pachomius (*ca.* 290–346), the latter of whom was a pioneer in creating a cenobitic rule for his monks. At the same time, many monks lived in the towns and villages rather than separately in monasteries, and they were frequent figures in the streets of communities.

LANGUAGE AND CULTURE

Egypt was the source of many prominent figures in the cultural life of the Roman Empire in the fourth and fifth centuries. At a local level, it witnessed a remarkable revival of Egyptian culture. The use of the earlier form of written Egyptian, called demotic (essentially a cursive form of the old hieroglyphs), had practically disappeared by the second century both from literary use and from documents. When the language was again written, it was in an alphabet derived mostly from Greek with some additions (for non-Greek sounds) from the demotic alphabet. In the fourth century, with the Christianization of the country, there was an efflorescence of writing in Coptic, both translation from other languages (especially Greek) and original composition; this revival continued for several centuries. Many entire genres are missing from what survives of Coptic literature, and in some cases we do not know if they ever existed. Theology and hagiography are prominent among the surviving remains.

Many residents of Egypt were bilingual, and some even composed in both languages, as did, for example, Dioscorus of Aphrodito in the sixth century, well known because of the discovery of his archives on papyrus. With other authors (such as Athanasius), versions of some works exist both in Greek and in Coptic, but it is difficult to know if the author wrote in both, wrote in one and translated it into the other, or had someone else do the translation. There was also some use of Latin, mainly in the imperial army and bureaucracy, but even there Greek was the main working language from day to day.

BIBLIOGRAPHY

A basic introduction to the papyrological evidence may be found in Orsolina Montevecchi, *La papirologia* (1973), with extensive bibliography. For the chronological framework, see Roger S. Bagnall and K. A. Worp, *The Chronological Systems of Byzantine Egypt* (1978). For the Nile, see Danielle Bonneau, *La crue du Nil* (1964).

On the Blemmyes, see Anna Maria Demicheli, *Rapporti di pace e di guerra dell'Egitto Romano con le populazioni dei deserti africani* (1976). The fullest account of the revolt of Domitius Domitianus is Jacques Schwartz, *L. Domitius Domitianus* (1975). See also Alan K. Bowman, "The Military Occupation of Upper Egypt in the Reign of Diocletian," in *Bulletin of the American Society of Papyrologists,* **15** (1978). On the revolt of Heraklios, see Zbigniew Borkowski, *Inscriptions des factions à Alexandrie* (1981). The classic work on the Arab conquest is Alfred J. Butler, *The Arab Conquest of Egypt and the Last Thirty Years of the Roman Dominion,* 2nd ed. by P. M. Fraser (1978).

On government, the most complete treatment is Jacqueline Lallemand, *L'administration civile de l'Égypte de l'avènement de Dioclétien à la création du diocèse (284–382)* (1964). The basic treatment of the economy of Egypt in this period is Allen C. Johnson and Louis C. West, *Byzantine Egypt: Economic Studies* (1949); for the so-called large estates, the classic work is Edward R. Hardy, Jr., *The Large Estates of Byzantine Egypt* (1931, repr. 1968), but also see the important work of Jean Gascou, "Les grands domaines, la cité et l'état en Égypte byzantine," in *Travaux et Mémoires* (College de France: Centre de recherche d'histoire et civilisation de Byzance), **9** (1985).

On religion, Ewa Wipszycka, *Les ressources et les activités économiques des églises en Égypte du IVe au VIIIe siècle* (1972), shows the church as an actor in the economic life of the community. On the rate of conversion, see Roger S. Bagnall, "Religious Conversion and Onomastic Change in Early Byzantine Egypt," in *Bulletin of the American Society of Papyriologists,* **19** (1982). For a discussion of monasticism, see Derwas Chitty, *The Desert a City* (1966); and E. A. Judge, "The Earliest Use of Monachos for 'Monk' (P. Coll. Youtie 77) and the Origins of Monasticism," in *Jahrbuch für Antike und Christentum,* **20** (1977). See also his and S. R. Pickering's "Papyrus Documentation of Church and Community in Egypt to the Mid-Fourth Century," in *Jahrbuch für Antike und Christentum,* **20** (1977).

For the cultural life of the hellenized elite, see Alan Cameron, "Wandering Poets: A Literary Movement in Byzantine Egypt," in *Historia,* **14** (1965), and "The Empress and the Poet: Paganism and Politics at the Court of Theodosius II," in *Yale Classical Studies,* XXVII (1982), 217–289. See also Gerald M. Browne, "Harpocration Panegyrista," in *Illinois Classical Studies,* **2** (1977).

For the Egyptian cultural revival, see L. S. B. Mac Coull, "Coptic Sources: A Problem in the Sociology of Knowledge," in *Bulletin de la Société d'archéologie copte,* **26** (1984).

ROGER S. BAGNALL

[See also **Athanasius of Alexandria, St.; Byzantine Church; Church, Early; Coptic Art; Copts and the Coptic Church; Cyril of Alexandria, St.; Egypt, Islamic; Melchites; Monasticism, Origins; Monophysitism; Roman Empire, Late.**]

ROMAN EMPIRE, GERMAN. See **Germany: Idea of Empire; Holy Roman Empire.**

ROMAN EMPIRE, LATE. "Not everything which has taken place among uncultured people is worthy of narration," proclaimed the fourth-century Roman historian Ammianus Marcellinus. Recently Emmanuel Le Roy Ladurie announced his lack of sympathy with this attitude: for a preindustrial society of the sort that Ammianus treated, the accomplishments of elites are less significant than those of "the enormous mass of rural humanity, enmeshed in its Ricardian feedback." By Ammianus' canon a familiar history of the late Roman Empire from the accession of Diocletian to the death of Heraklios (284–641) is possible. Ladurie points in another direction, and the purpose of the present essay is to outline the present and to envisage some future states of knowledge of this period of the Roman Empire.

THE MEDITERRANEAN WORLD

Of all the seas the Mediterranean is the most enclosed. Between the Strait of Gibraltar, its only natural opening, and the Syro-Palestinian seaboard stands a complex network of small seas delineated by islands, peninsulas, and straits. The Adriatic and Ionian seas together with the Libyan coastline form the boundary between the eastern and western halves of the basin. The narrows of Gibraltar protect the littoral from the surging tides of the Atlantic, making possible fertile deltas at the estuaries of such rivers as the Ebro, Rhône, Tiber, Po, and Nile. Behind the coastline marked by roadsteads and harbors stand the often mountainous interiors of Europe, the Near East, and Africa.

Many typical features of life in this great crossroads had evolved centuries before the accession of Diocletian in 284. Pastoralism and agriculture had long been the foundations of the economy. Since the end of the second and dawn of the first millennium B.C., Phoenician and Greek seafarers had extended urban living from its Near Eastern and lower Balkan center throughout the coastline. A composite Mediterranean urban society had emerged, fostered by the constant maritime traffic. In general, cities, which attracted much of the harvests of fields and flocks, grew up near river estuaries, natural harbors, and straits—all necessary stopping places for the small craft that seldom sailed beyond the sight of land. Behind this urban core stood villages and camps of farmers, shepherds, and overland traders. Of the three hinterlands of the Mediterranean, only the Near East (including Egypt) had been urbanized. The other two, Europe and North Africa, did not experience a noticeable urbanization until the Roman conquests of the first century B.C. and the first century A.D.

Before the time of Diocletian and Heraklios the Mediterranean world had evolved a composite society that formed the base of many state systems. Despite ethnic and linguistic differences, local communities from Gibraltar to Egypt resembled one another in the manner in which they practiced agriculture or commerce. In a typical community, town- or city-dwelling elites became patrons of the exploited rural folk. The urban elites withdrew often excessive amounts of produce from the countryside, risking the starvation of the growers, but bettering their own social and economic status as they fostered exchanges of harvests along the harbors, roadsteads, and straits of the coast. Such patronage had become and would remain for centuries a part of everyday life.

Two fundamental aspects of the Mediterranean environment of the Roman Empire are difficult to determine: the distribution of the population and the climate. In studying the latter, scholars need data that can be quantified, and the existence of this information for all but the most recent past is unusual. Of late, researchers such as Bryson and Simkin have undertaken promising investigations of volcanic eruptions of the past. Departing from the present consensus that volcanoes cast tiny particles into the stratosphere and therefore cause short-term cold spells by obscuring the sun's rays, they have posited for the northern hemisphere peaks of volcanic activity and hence cold weather north of 30° N around 800 and 1400. According to this theory, the Mediterranean of late antiquity should have experienced a rather high degree of volcanic activity and cold weather. One may seek confirmation for such a suggestion in approximately fifteen eruptions of Mounts Etna and Vesuvius between 200 and 800. Yet such information does not occur in sufficient quantity for one to speak of an overall climatic trend. For the moment it seems best to wait for more work on the history of climate, and to admit that the weather patterns to which the subjects of the rulers from Diocletian to Heraklios had to adjust remain unknown.

Similarly uncertain are the distribution and changes in the size of the Mediterranean population in late antiquity. Theories are not lacking, and from these a few fundamental assertions may be suggested. On the analogy of today's developing countries and indeed all preindustrial societies, one may assume that country folk outnumbered city dwellers by a substantial margin. Furthermore, it seems likely that the total population from Britain to Egypt and from the High Atlas to the Caucasus numbered in the millions rather than the hundreds of thousands. Yet these basic statements render little help, for historical demographers of the present day want to measure changes in a given population through the careful study of birth rates, death rates, immigration, and emigration. Data for such measurements does not exist for the late Roman Mediterranean. The peoples of this period did experience one event of importance for demographers, an outbreak of bubonic plague between 541 and 544. Transmitted from inner Africa to Pelusium in Egypt in 541, it spread throughout the lower Nile basin, the Syro-Palestinian seaboard, and the environs of Constantinople the following year; and thence to the Dalmatian coast, western Italy, Carthage and her hinterland, eastern Spain, and the Rhône-Saône corridor. For Constantinople at least the plague took the pneumonic form. Given its tendency to afflict city dwellers more heavily than country folk, its progress may reveal the most densely settled areas of the Mediterranean of the mid sixth century. Furthermore, the historian Procopius of Caesarea provides in his unusually detailed account of the plague a rather accurate estimate of the rate of deaths at Constantinople. His figures suggest a city numbering between 500,000 and 1 million before the disease struck. Yet such figures provide only the beginning of a proper reckoning of the late Roman population. Because country folk were evidently less affected by plague, the majority of the sixth-century Mediterranean escapes accurate estimation. For the present one must admit ignorance of the increase, stability, or decrease in emigration, immigration, births, and deaths among the Romans of late antiquity.

A PRECURSOR: HELLENISTIC CIVILIZATION

Between the late third and early seventh centuries the area administered by Roman authorities shrank from the entire littoral and large portions of the three interiors to the shorelines of the central and northeastern Mediterranean. The student who wishes to understand this dramatic transformation must begin not with the Roman Empire itself, but with the composite civilization that preceded it. By first studying the Hellenistic world one can gain some idea of the organization of the Mediterranean basin before the growth of Roman power, as well as some appreciation of the forces that caused the contraction of the empire in late antiquity.

Hellenistic civilization was not a monolith, but a network of kingdoms and smaller states that combined Greek and Near Eastern urban life. Its center extended from the lower Balkans to the Persian Gulf, but approximations of it could be found as far east as the Ganges basin and westward throughout the Mediterranean coastline. In the latter area the Hellenic influence was strong even in non-Greek cities such as Carthage and Rome. In its most concentrated form Hellenistic civilization endured from the death of Alexander the Great to the Roman conquest of the Mediterranean (323–*ca.* 150 B.C.). But the dominant Greco-Macedonian culture did not prevail everywhere. Even in the Near Eastern center there were dissidents. The Jews of Palestine, for instance, clung to their unique ancestral religion, while the Hamitic substratum of Ptolemaic Egypt demonstrated through revolts and the retention of the hieroglyphic script its adherence to the pharaonic past.

The Hellenistic way of life prevailed minimally or not at all in the two less sophisticated interiors of the Mediterranean. In North Africa, Hamitic-speaking nomads, mountaineers, and plains-dwellers known to the ancients as Libyans, Numidians, and Mauretanians had long confronted the Phoenician settlers, especially around Carthage. In Hellenistic times these largely rural folk came for the first time under the leadership of a strong chieftain, the Numidian Massinissa, who constructed a resemblance of a Hellenistic kingdom based at Cirta (modern Constantine) in the early second century

ROMAN EMPIRE, LATE

B.C. Less receptive to the Hellenistic way of life were the Celts, masters of most of the interior of Europe. From Cornwall to the lower Danube and from the upper Ebro basin to Central Europe these linguistic kindred of the Italic peoples fostered a common way of life amidst political disunity, especially between about 400 and 50 B.C., the age of the great La Tène culture. Evidence from the Greek observer Poseidonius of Apamea suggests that the druids, the priestly element in control of both religion and education, repelled the foreign culture of the Greeks. In any case urban civilization scarcely advanced beyond the Mediterranean coast of Europe in Hellenistic times. Celts encountered urban life chiefly through migration to the richer south—to the Po basin beginning in 400 B.C. and Galatia (in Asia Minor) in the early third century—and through mercenary service in various Hellenistic kingdoms.

THE DOMINATE

Before the Roman conquest of the Mediterranean no empire whose center was on the shoreline ventured inland more than 125 miles (200 kilometers). The western hegemony of Carthage, for instance, hugged the coast, and imperial Athens restricted her interest to the ports and passageways between the Bosporus and Sicily. Even the great Hellenistic powers, which inherited the traditions of the older land-based empires of the Near East, found it necessary to shift their interests from the interior to the Mediterranean shore. Alexandria in Egypt, Antioch in Syria, and Pella in Macedonia became the centers of power. In the early phases of their conquest of the Mediterranean the Romans did not deviate from this standard. The Greek historian Polybius of Megalopolis placed the beginning of the Roman Empire between the preliminaries of the second Punic War and the end of Rome's third conflict with Macedonia (220–168 B.C.). During this period the Roman Senate limited the theater of activity to the territories of Carthage and other Hellenistic powers. Only in the first century B.C., when the field of competition between senatorial magnates broadened, did Roman forces push significantly beyond coastal regions. Pompey the Great, Julius Caesar, and the Julio-Claudian emperors brought Roman administration and Greco-Roman culture to the interiors of the Near East, Europe, and North Africa. This unusual penetration of the hinterlands caused trouble for the empire. Twice it fell apart in crisis, in the first century B.C. and the third century A.D.. Each time, however, it recovered and for a while reigned supreme from Britain to Egypt, and from the High Atlas to the upper Euphrates River.

Administration. In the latter half of the third century a succession of Danubian soldier-emperors led the second recovery of the Roman Empire. The most successful of these was Gaius Valerius Diocles, who upon his accession took the name Gaius Aurelius Valerius Diocletianus. During his long reign (284–305) Diocletian standardized many innovations of his immediate predecessors. Since the time of Caesar Augustus, for instance, most emperors had wanted to be thought of as mere *principes* (first citizens, whence the imperial system called the Principate) rather than despots. Diocletian and his successors abandoned this pretense. *Dominus noster* (Our Lord) became the most common imperial title, and it has hence become common to call the state system they created the Dominate. The Dominate differed from its predecessor in several respects. During the Principate a single emperor ruled from Rome; only occasionally did emperors establish residence outside the capital and share power with a colleague. From the reign of Diocletian onward a multiplicity of capitals and emperors were regular features of imperial life. Diocletian created a tetrarchy, a college of four emperors. By the end of the fourth century it became common for two emperors to reign, each over one of the geographical halves of the Mediterranean basin. At times single emperors—Constantine I (306–337) and Justinian I (527–565) were the most successful—ruled the entire empire.

The troubles of the third century had forced emperors to move closer to the disturbed frontiers. Diocletian and his successors honored this tradition. Rome remained an occasional capital, but cities closer to the northern and eastern frontiers such as Trier, Milan, Ravenna, Nicomedia, and Antioch rivaled her as imperial favorites. Eventually one of these new centers, Byzantium on the Bosporus, refounded by Constantine, became the New Rome and, beginning with the second reign of Emperor Zeno (476–491), the lone center of imperial power.

The track of imperial residence is symptomatic of the transformation of the Roman Empire in late antiquity. The emperors surrounded themselves with elaborate palace bureaucracies, and delegated military and civil authority beyond the imperial capitals to generals, prefects, and their subordi-

ROMAN EMPIRE, LATE

nates. The *Notitia dignitatum,* a register of dignitaries edited for the last time in the early fifth century, describes the Roman Empire as Diocletian and his immediate successors had organized it. They first divided it into eastern and western halves, with the boundary at the Adriatic-Libyan axis. Further divisions were the four prefectures of Gaul, Italy, Illyricum, and the East, each under a praetorian prefect; twelve dioceses under *vicarii* (vice-regents); and provinces greater in number and smaller in size than those of the Principate. Amazingly enough, the Roman Empire described by the *Notitia dignitatum* extended over approximately the same territory as it had during the time of the Julio-Claudian emperors. The northwestern provinces, the interior of North Africa, the lands of the upper Tigris and upper Euphrates rivers, and the right bank of the Danube returned to imperial control. The only substantial losses were the old province of Dacia (modern Romania), which Constantine conceded to the Goths in 332, and the lower left bank of the Rhine River, which Emperor Julian awarded to the Franks in 358. The civil wars of the fourth century and the more general troubles of the fifth century, however, forced the emperors to make some administrative changes. Constantius II (337–361), Theodosius I (379–395), and Arcadius (395–408) briefly administered the African provinces from the East during civil conflicts. Their successors followed this precedent by sending military aid to the weaker West during the fifth century. The tendency of the East to administer part of the West came to fruition during the reign of Justinian I, who ruled an empire that embraced not only the old prefectures of Illyricum and the East, but those of Italy and Africa (including southeastern Spain). In Justinian's system three areas—Sicily, the lowermost Danube, and some eastern Aegean islands—stood under the special jurisdiction of the quaestor of the army. This new organization survived only a short time after Justinian's death. The rampages of the Avars in the upper Balkans, the Lombard invasion of Italy, the increased activity of the Visigoths in Spain, and especially the early conquests of Islam reduced the Roman sway by the mid seventh century to parts of Africa, fragments of Italy, the lower Balkans, Asia Minor, and the Aegean basin. As the Roman Empire contracted, the successors of Justinian devised yet another means of administering it.

The final changes in the government of the late Roman Empire reflected the evolution of the Roman army since the time of Diocletian. The *Notitia dignitatum* and other evidence illustrate the system devised by Diocletian and Constantine I. Mobile units of crack soldiers, the *comitatenses* (imperial escorts), were posted at strategic locations behind the frontiers, and *limitanei* (border guards) were located in fixed garrisons along the outer defenses of the empire. Commanded by *magistri militum* (masters of soldiers) and their subordinates, this impressive force theoretically numbered 600,000 men. Since the third century the emperors had tried to maintain a strict separation of civil and administrative authority. The masters of soldiers were to concentrate on soldiering, while the praetorian prefects saw to the army's supplies but otherwise did not intervene in military affairs. Many pressures forced the abandonment of this neatly balanced system. The *Notitia dignitatum* shows that in some minor provinces the division of civil and military power did not exist. In the Anatolian province of Isauria, for instance, the principal authority was a count who combined the functions of commander and head administrator. Such experiments, together with abundant evidence of the intervention of masters of soldiers in civil affairs, show that Diocletian's and Constantine's system could not bear the strain of everyday exceptions to administrative rules. In another respect the army of the Dominate as it was first conceived was a failure. It had been based on conscription, but in the fifth century bad management of the army's supplies was forcing soldiers to add trading and farming to their duties. Demobilization ensued, and to replace the loss of effective fighters the emperors began to rely heavily on foreign troops or small bands of hirelings. Only in the East did Constantine's army persist into the sixth century, but innovations after Justinian I's death suggest that here too it was difficult to maintain. Following the Lombard invasions of Italy, Emperor Maurice (582–602) put the empire's remaining holdings in Italy under an *exarchos* (commander). The exarchate of Ravenna was born, and the exarchate of Carthage was similarly organized. The exarch possessed both civil and military authority, and he delegated power in his territories to masters of soldiers. Beneath these stood garrisons of locally conscripted peasant soldiers whose families worked grants of land. In the exarchates, then, civil and military power were one and the same, and local conscripts who fought on and for home ground (as opposed to the conscripts of Constantine's army, who often saw service abroad) were effective soldiers. The exarchate system was evidently the forerunner of the famous *themata* (themes), which had their beginnings during the reign of Heraklios. The innovations of Maurice and Heraklios marked the end of Diocletian and Constantine's administrative system.

Economy and social structure. Most of the empire's subjects were shepherds or farmers. Since the days of the Principate an agricultural system called the Colonate had developed. The three principal administrative and social elites—senators, equestrians (knights), and curials (town magistrates)—controlled most of the arable land. They took fractions of harvests as rents from the *coloni* (cultivators), to whom they leased portions of their holdings. Taxation of the revenues from these estates was a major source of income for the imperial government. In times of stress neither the government nor the estate lords relinquished their claims to portions of the harvests, and consequently a double burden of exactions fell on the peasant majority. During the age of the Dominate, the Colonate persisted, to the advantage of the principal estate owners, the emperors, and wealthy senatorial aristocrats. Variations in the system existed throughout the empire. In North Africa, Mancian tenures (hereditary grants to developers of waste lands) persisted at least until the turn of the sixth century. In Gaul and Italy powerful senatorial families founded in the fourth century were still influential in the age of Justinian I. Their prestige attests the continuation of the Colonate in these regions. Their hold on the land, however, was not permanent. During the reigns of Justinian and his immediate successors many senatorial aristocrats fled from the disturbed West to the more stable East. Ironically enough, the East to which they fled was not a promising territory in which to construct new versions of the huge estates they had been accustomed to. Since the late fourth century the lords of Syria had complained of the patronage (that is, the protection and economic support) of peasants by military veterans. Such activity produced a triangle of competition in which the peasantry possessed the ability to bargain for more advantageous arrangements with their patrons. As a result, Syria of the fourth and fifth centuries became a land of burgeoning peasant villages. The phenomenon was present throughout the prefecture of the East by the sixth century. One may conjecture that the new independence of eastern peasants helped to make the theme system a success.

In the final analysis the health of the imperial economy depended not only on the government's capacity to extract produce from the countryside through taxation, but also on its ability to encourage commercial exchange. To foster trade all across the empire would ensure prosperity, cultural homogeneity, and a strong state system. In general, the emperors of the Dominate were inept economic managers who were more concerned with the smooth functioning of their governments than with the well-being of the trading public. Until the third century, when crisis beset the imperial economy, the principal foundations of Mediterranean-wide exchanges had been a trimetallic monetary system and the big grain fleets, which had supplied Rome from Africa, Sicily, and especially Egypt. Diocletian and his successors tried but failed to maintain both. In the latter case Diocletian's celebrated Edict on Maximum Prices (*De maximis pretiis,* 301) shows through its reckoning of trade routes and price levels that the old contacts between East and West had been revived. Furthermore, Diocletian attempted to restore the three imperial coinages, issuing a sturdy aureus (gold piece), good silver, and large bronze units called *folles* (literally: money-bags).

Soon after his abdication, however, his successor Constantine I made some innovations that rendered the economy more local than it had been during the Principate. In order to supply the New Rome on the Bosporus, Constantine diverted the grain ships from Egypt, producing at a stroke two economic zones that corresponded to the geographical halves of the Mediterranean basin. Henceforth small craft continued to ply the coasts from the Aegean and Levant to Spain, but without the East-West traffic of the big grain fleets they could not equal the volume of exchanges of the Principate. Constantine made other fateful breaks with the past. He abandoned silver as the second currency, and his successors tended to follow his lead. Furthermore, he issued a new gold coin, the solidus (literally: genuine [piece]) or nomisma. Struck at the rate of seventy-two to the Roman pound, the new issue proved to be not an exceptionally stable support of market exchanges, but a tiny piece of bullion so valuable that it could not function in the marketplace. For ordinary transactions the burden fell on the bronze currency, and Constantine and his successors evidently paid scant attention to it.

By the end of the fourth century smaller bronze

ROMAN EMPIRE, LATE

nummia (pieces) replaced the *follis*. The emperors made little attempt to regulate the ratio at which bronze was issued in relation to the solidus. By the late fifth century the value of the *nummion* had therefore plummeted amidst government-sponsored inflation. Sometime in the 480's or 490's the Vandal and Ostrogothic governments of Italy and Africa made an attempt to halt the trend toward a barter economy. For the first time since the reign of Diocletian they sponsored the issue of municipal bronze *folles* valued at forty-two and forty *nummia,* respectively. These local experiments were evidently the inspiration for the currency reforms of Emperor Anastasius I (491–518), who ordered the issue of forty-*nummia folles* beginning in 498. Anastasius' system persisted, providing at least for the Eastern Empire a measure of the stability that Diocletian and Constantine had sought.

The emperors of the Dominate drew their financial and other civil administrators and recruited many of their soldiers from a single reservoir of manpower, the citizenry. To a modern observer citizenship is nearly identical with residence. The peoples of the ancient Mediterranean had regarded it instead as a privilege, a right to possess property and hold office reserved for a minority. The Antonine and Severan emperors (96–235), however, accelerated grants of citizenship to provincial elites and veterans to such an extent that around 212 Emperor Marcus Aurelius Antoninus, nicknamed Caracalla, issued the famous Antonine Constitution, awarding the franchise to all (or nearly all) free inhabitants of the Roman Empire. By such a grant the Roman concept of citizenship approached that of a modern state, but Roman society still managed to retain its elite character. From the time of the early Principate there had existed especially in penal law a convenient if not technically exact distinction between two kinds of citizens, *honestiores* (the more honorable) and *humiliores* (the more humble). In the Severan age, just as the Antonine Constitution recognized that citizenship was no longer a rare privilege, this distinction became a new mark of social status. Diocletian and his successors accepted the Severan system. A substantial majority of the empire's inhabitants possessed the franchise. Significantly enough, however, the word *subiecti* (inferiors) became a common term for citizens in late imperial documents. Among the citizenry the *honestiores* formed an elite minority. Senators, equestrians, and other distinguished elements as far down the social scale as decurions (provincial town councillors) and military veterans were members of this prestigious group. The urban poor and peasantry, the principal supports of the Dominate, populated the ranks of the *humiliores*. Service in the Roman army was their principal means of rising to the upper level of society.

Religion and culture. In order to assure the success of their system, the emperors had not only to keep full the ranks of the army and civil bureaucracy, but also to make sure that recruits for the system were properly educated. Furthermore, they had to give direction to another dimension of life, religious fervor. In the latter realm they confronted an inherited conglomerate that had been present since the Hellenistic age. Fertility goddesses, sky gods, divine rulers, and magical forces drew the attention of many of the empire's inhabitants. Minorities, especially the Jews of Palestine and the coastal cities, clung to their distinctive convictions. In general, the assemblage of beliefs remained the same in late antiquity. The empire's inhabitants continued to observe, for instance, the cults of Near Eastern fertility goddesses and Roman emperors who had been accorded divine honors. In one respect, however, the religious outlook of Roman society changed dramatically.

Since the days of the late Republic and early Principate, the Jewish community had posed a problem for the Roman conquerors. Worship of the gods approved by the state was a means of assuring the empire's success. Yet the Jews were a distinct people, and their beliefs also had to be protected. By the time of Julius Caesar and Caesar Augustus a compromise emerged: the Jews were to retain their ancestral customs, and their leaders were to pray at intervals to their God on behalf of the health and safety of the Roman people. The arrangement endured amidst intermittent toleration and persecution for several generations. Around the end of the first century, however, the Romans suspended the compromise in the case of a heretical sect of Jews, the Christians, who by then boasted of such a mixture of converts that they could not be considered a distinct people. Persecution and perseverance ensued. At the end of the third century the Christians enjoyed a generation of relative peace in their relations with the imperial authorities. During this generation they became a strong minority, especially in the cities of the Roman Empire. In the latter years of Diocletian their acceptance at all levels of society seemed assured.

In the fourth century the Christian church be-

ROMAN EMPIRE, LATE

came an important part of the Dominate through an unexpected turn of events. Between 303 and 311 Diocletian and some of his colleagues launched the most sustained persecution the Christians ever suffered. The faithful endured, and in 311 Emperor Galerius issued an edict suspending hostilities and granting Christians roughly the same rights of worship that the Jews had received in the late Republic. As a result of this signal decree the Christians might have remained a tolerated minority, but instead they progressed to the top of Roman society in part because of the religious preferences of some of Diocletian's successors. The most influential of these was Constantine I. In the early years of his reign Constantine was evidently a devotee of Apollo Helios and Sol Invictus (the Unconquered Sun), two important sky gods who were frequently identified with one another. Yet personal religious experiences soon caused him to be at least attracted to Christianity. In 324, when he began founding the New Rome on the Bosporus, Constantine issued laws forbidding normal forms of traditional worship and aiding the construction or enlargement of Christian churches. These laws set a precedent to which Emperor Theodosius I (379–395) gave further impetus: the Christian faith began to be the official religion of the Roman Empire. In the last few weeks of his life Constantine completed his conversion to the new faith by receiving baptism from Eusebius, the Arian bishop of Nicomedia. Henceforth Christians stood on a new threshold of prestige and power.

After the time of Constantine, Christianity solidified its position in Roman society. The relaxation of imperial hostility enabled the faithful to make more visible their differences of belief and practice. Meetings convened to resolve disagreements now assumed a grander scale. The famous ecumenical councils held in various eastern cities in 325, 381, 431, 451, and 553 hardly brought internal disputes to an end, but they did serve to demonstrate the primacy of Christians, especially in the sees of Rome, Constantinople, Antioch, and Alexandria. While Christians debated among themselves, the successors of Constantine showed for the most part strong attachments to the new faith. The most influential of these was Theodosius I, who gave new direction to Constantine's laws of 324. In 380 and 381 Theodosius ordered all subjects of the empire to subscribe not just to Christian beliefs, but to the creed sanctioned by the First Ecumenical Council, held at Nicaea in 325. Ten years later he reinforced his order, forbidding all homage to the old gods of Roman society. These decrees assured a succession of orthodox emperors as the principal earthly guarantors of the new official faith.

Meanwhile, Christians made another important contribution to the imperial order. Until the fourth century Christianity had been primarily a religion of cities. Now that imperial encouragement was at hand, the faithful began to penetrate the countryside in significant numbers. The most successful of the new missionaries were monks who spread spiritual guidance and a Christianized form of education into those regions of the empire that had not yet experienced the new religion. By all of these activities Christianity became part of the Dominate, an organized church that stood alongside the military and civil administration.

When Christians became part of the establishment, they modified and yet preserved many essentials of the Roman system of education. The Bible and the church fathers were to them the core of a proper upbringing, but even before the time of Constantine they had also paid attention to the masterpieces of Greek and Latin literature. These they had studied, edited, translated, and of course interpreted. In their attention to the classics they found themselves in agreement with their principal opponents, the Hellenes (usually called "pagans"), men and women of letters whose enthusiasm for the great books extended to the traditional religious fervor expressed in them. While Christians and Hellenes debated the meaning of the *Timaeus* of Plato or Vergil's *Fourth Eclogue,* they witnessed a fundamental change in the method of transmission of both Christian and non-Christian writings. By the fourth century the methods of recording Scripture and perhaps a decline in Egypt's ability to export papyrus led to the triumph of the parchment codex (book) over the papyrus roll. The ease of consultation afforded by the codex and the competitive attention of Hellenes and Christians assured an amazing continuity of the Greco-Roman system of education. Even in its Christianized form it began with the elementary study of Greek or Latin, and culminated in sophisticated rhetorical exercises, producing magistrates and commanders who could read and write, and authors of sometimes formidable talent. The persistence of the classical mode of education was crucial to the survival of the Roman Empire. If it could reach a large part of the population, it would assure continuity of the imperial tradition for many generations to come.

VARIANTS WITHIN THE SYSTEM

By all appearances the Dominate was thus a state system of extraordinary stability. The emperors and their subordinates recruited newcomers from the poor majority, imbued them with Roman values, and coordinated the efforts of a large bureaucracy, an enormous army, and the newly established Christian hierarchy. Such are appearances, fostered by the panegyrists, poets, historians, and even church fathers who were among the beneficiaries of the system. Some of these authors probably shared the opinion of Ammianus Marcellinus regarding the lower elements of society: not all events besetting the poor were worthy of account. This way of thinking has made it difficult for historians to determine the extent to which farmers and shepherds, the majority of the population, were willing to support the system. In traditional (that is, preindustrial) societies literacy is a restricted rather than a widespread phenomenon. A recent study by R. P. Duncan-Jones of literacy in the Roman Empire has suggested that many city dwellers and probably the mass of the rural population could not read or write. How then does one determine the attitude of the country folk toward the Dominate?

At present the attempt to match clues from Roman evidence with the behavior of modern peasants is in its infancy. For the moment a better-developed field of endeavor yields information on the exploited elements of the late Roman Empire: the study of local cultures. We have the viewpoints only of the literate members of these cultures, but these privileged elements were separate from, and indeed frequently at odds with, the Roman establishment. Consequently, one can gain a sense of other leaderships that set parts of the Mediterranean population on courses not prescribed by the imperial authorities. At the time of Diocletian most of these local cultures were submerged beneath the dominant Greco-Roman way of life. By the death of Heraklios many of them had developed into states or at least chiefdoms. The local variants within the system therefore made a major contribution to the world of late antiquity.

In the Near East, cultures whose protagonists belonged to the great Hamito-Semitic and Indo-European language families had flourished before the Roman conquest and indeed before the Hellenistic age. Three of their descendants, speakers of Coptic, Syriac, and Armenian, played important roles in shaping the destinies of the region between the third and seventh centuries. For each of the three the ecumenical council held at Chalcedon in 451 was a signal event. Christians, ever anxious to spread the Gospel in other languages, had sponsored written translations of Scripture and exegesis in Hamitic Coptic and Semitic Syriac since the time of the Principate, and in Indo-European Armenian perhaps since the turn of the fifth century. The structures of these languages made possible interpretations of Christian belief that differed from those of Christians who spoke Greek or Latin. When a majority backed by the Eastern Roman government and the bishop of Rome proclaimed at Chalcedon the conviction that Jesus the Christ embodied two natures, one divine and the other human, many Armenian, Syriac, and Coptic Christians rejected the formula as a denial of the very real birth and death of the Christ, who possessed one nature. The so-called Monophysite schism, one of the most important to beset Christendom, was born. Religious, rather than political, motives inspired its proponents, but because the enthusiasm of Monophysites for their faith often led to violence, these Eastern Christians contributed to the breakdown of Roman control in their homelands. By the accession of Heraklios, Armenia, Syria, and Egypt had become doubtful parts of the Roman Empire.

While Monophysite Christians began to follow a separatist course of action within the Roman Empire, the ancient culture of the Jews was experiencing trial and tribulation at the hands of the Romans. Intermittent persecution was not new to the Jewish communities in Palestine and the cities of the Mediterranean. Ever since the great rebellions of the first and second centuries A.D., the Jews, now bereft of the Great Temple at Jerusalem, had frequently felt the wrath of the Roman authorities. The triumph of Christianity, however, brought a new turn to the old hostility, for Christian emperors transferred to law the antipathy of Christians toward the main body of Jews. The Jews reciprocated, fomenting by the time of Justinian I revolts against Roman rule and then siding with the Persians against the Romans when the former conquered Palestine in 614.

Until the beginning of the fifth century Palestine remained the center of the Jewish community. A succession of patriarchs at Tiberias directed worship all over the Roman Empire. Tiberias and Caesarea served as major centers for the Palestinian Talmud, a western Aramaic part of that great compilation of oral learning appended to the Torah. Yet around the turn of the fifth century both of

ROMAN EMPIRE, LATE

these centers of Jewish life came to an end. By the end of the fourth century the Palestinian scholars migrated to Babylonia, where a greater Talmud composed in eastern Aramaic was in progress, and the line of patriarchs presiding at Tiberias ceased in 429. As the center of Jewish activity shifted to Babylonia, the editors of the Talmud collected many bitter recollections of life under Roman rule.

By the time of Heraklios, Jewish hostility and Monophysite enthusiasm helped create a separate destiny for the peoples dwelling between the Taurus Mountains and the Nile basin. They had the assistance of relative newcomers to the cultivated lands of the Near East. Desert nomads, some of them speakers of western Aramaic and others belonging to the southern branch of the Semitic language family, had lived in inner Syria and near the Arabian coast of the Red Sea even before the time of the Principate. From the fourth to the sixth centuries the Lakhmids, clients of Persia in Mesopotamia, and the Monophysite Ghassanids, clients of Eastern Romans from about 500 in Syria, were the most visible groups. Into this frontier society was born Muḥammad of Mecca (570–632). Within his lifetime Jewish and Christian influence created a composite culture of nomads and merchants in northern and western Arabia, and classical Arabic became widely used. From these elements and the religious experiences of the Prophet came the commonwealth of Islam, which initiated the dramatic conquests of the Near East. When Heraklios died in 641, Syria, Palestine, and Egypt were in Islamic hands. The Koran, evidently redacted for the first time soon after Muḥammad's death, was the first literary masterpiece of this new culture.

While the Near East experienced this dramatic turn of fortune, the Hamitic-speaking substratum of North Africa freed portions of the southwestern Mediterranean from Roman rule. In late antiquity the Romans called the natives in this area Moors or *Afri barbari* (African barbarians). Throughout late antiquity mountaineers from the Tunisian Dorsal to the High Atlas and desert nomads plying the oases between Egypt's Thebaïd and Tripoli became increasingly troublesome presences on the fringes of Roman Africa. In succession the Romans (until 429), the Germanic Vandals (429–533), and Eastern Romans (after 533) had the unhappy task of defending especially the coastal lowlands against these marauders. Local inscriptions and the war commentaries of Procopius of Caesarea present contrasting portraits of their outlook and way of life. Procopius depicts a population attached to ancestral transhumance and old gods such as the Egyptian Ammon. On the other hand, inscriptions set up by leaders of short-lived chiefdoms that had grown up in the interior by the turn of the sixth century suggest that the first expressions of enduring independence from Roman rule were remarkably Roman in character. Around 500, for instance, there flourished one Masties, ruler of a tiny hegemony in or near the Auras Mountains of Numidia. A cenotaphic commemoration of this chieftain shows that in succession he held the Roman titles of *dux* (captain) and *imperator* (emperor).

Whether the Moors organized themselves on a Roman model or not, they contributed to the shrinkage of Roman power in Africa. By the death of Heraklios, the son of an exarch of Carthage, Roman civilization had but forty-two years to survive in North Africa. The sequel, the Islamic conquest, shows that intrusive minorities would continue to play an important role in this region, which the Arabs called *Djazīrat al-Maghrib* (the island of the West). But the native populations, particularly under the leadership of the Almoravids and Almohads, also gave direction to the Maghrib.

As the native dwellers of the Maghrib and Near East separated all or some of their homelands from Roman rule, the peoples of Europe were shaping a special destiny for the lands north of the Mediterranean coast. Of those who participated in the transformation of Europe in late antiquity, only the Celts had experienced Roman dominion for generations. The others, speakers of Iranian, Slavic, and Germanic dialects, together with members of the Turkish branch of the Ural-Altaic language family, were newcomers.

The study of the Celtic contribution to the world of late antiquity is in its infancy. Critics have recognized a revival of Celtic art forms in the late Principate as a sign of rejection of Roman civilization, but in looking for Celtic survivals after the time of Diocletian they have given undue attention to the British Isles, where the phenomenon is most noticeable. There are also signs of a revival in continental Europe. The Bacaudae, for instance, wealthy and impoverished dissidents who stirred up revolts in the northwestern provinces between the third and fifth centuries, practiced in Armorica (roughly modern Brittany) judicial sentencing in a manner that recalls the Celtic veneration of the oak. By the late fifth century the population of Armorica became more Celtic as the Bretons, fugitives from

ROMAN EMPIRE, LATE

the Anglo-Saxon invasions of England, fled Cornwall for this northwestern tip of the Continent. The signs of a Celtic resurgence are not restricted to Armorica. Throughout late Roman Gaul, for instance, there was a noticeable abandonment of Roman city names in favor of Celtic tribal names, and the system of land tenure resembled the one observed by the Celts before the Roman conquest. In Noricum (roughly present Austria) the persistence of Celtic place-names away from the well-traveled roads suggests an endurance of pre-Roman habits in these areas. Despite four centuries of Roman rule, then, the Celts apparently clung to some of their old ways of life, and laid the foundation for dramatic changes that are usually credited to other peoples.

During the Principate the Romans confronted groups of Germanic peoples dwelling in villages from the lower Rhine to the lower Danube. East of this long frontier were nomads whose domains stretched from the Crimea to the Aral Sea. Some of these, subgroups of the Iranian Sarmatians, managed to infiltrate stretches of Roman land in the Danube basin. In late antiquity the Germanic peoples, the Iranian Alani, and newcomers such as the Turkish Huns, the Turkish Avars, and the Slavic peoples continued to face the Romans in friendship or hostility, but the line of confrontation shifted to the south and west. The principal movers of this change in Europe's cultural balance were evidently the nomadic Huns and Avars, who penetrated primarily the grasslands of southern Romania and Hungary, but pushed with or before them many Alani, Germans, and Slavs. These migrated peaceably or forcibly inside Roman territory from Britain, Spain, and even North Africa to the inner Balkans. Their rural habits scarcely prepared them to maintain Roman civilization at its previous level. At best these intruders were able to construct short-lived kingdoms or hegemonies that were loosely tied to the Roman Empire. By Heraklios' time many of these experiments in government had failed. The most noteworthy survivors were the Germanic kingdoms of the Visigoths, Franks, Anglo-Saxons, and Lombards in Spain, Gaul, England, and northern Italy, respectively. Of the Slavic and Turkish invaders of the Balkans, the Bulgars were destined to construct the most enduring state, but they had scarcely begun their task in Heraklios' lifetime.

The most enduring result of the migration of northerners in late antiquity was the appearance of zones of Germanic and Slavic speech west of the Rhine and south of the Danube. The Germanic peoples were the first to produce a new literacy. In the late fourth century the Arian bishop Ulfilas devised from runes and Greek characters a Gothic script, and then translated the Bible into Gothic. Gothic missionaries spread the Arian faith and the new Bible beyond the realms of the Goths. In the meantime the day-to-day business of governing both Germanic and Roman subjects forced Germanic rulers to devise codes of law. The first of these were Latin adaptations of Roman codes, but around the turn of the seventh century one of the new monarchs of southern England, the Jutish king of Kent Aethelbert, produced the first codification written in a Germanic dialect. An impressive contribution to the civilization of Europe had begun.

ROMAN SURVIVAL AND HELLENISTIC REVIVAL

When Heraklios died in 641 the Roman Empire extended not from Britain to the second cataract of the Nile River, but from the lands behind Carthage to inner Anatolia. With all the cultural forces at work in the lands ruled by the emperors from Caesar Augustus to Diocletian, the wonder is that the Roman Empire survived at all. Historians have offered many explanations for this phenomenon. Three primary causes of endurance may be distinguished. All three were forces at work in Mediterranean society at or even before the beginning of the Roman Empire: Greek values, the Roman system of clientage, and cities.

From its beginnings the city was the core of the Roman Empire. In the developed Principate the emperors combined garrisons and hamlets in the European and African interiors in an effort to create replicas of the urban centers that had long existed on the Mediterranean coast and in the Near East. In late antiquity the contraction of Roman power and the activities of Germanic, Slavic, and Moorish peoples set urban life back in the western hinterlands, but along the Mediterranean coast and in the Near East cities old and new persisted. They did so not so much because emperors, caliphs, and kings encouraged their growth, but because overland traders and merchants continued unabated their traditional activities. Because the Near East and the Mediterranean littoral retained their urban character, the possibility of the endurance or restoration of Roman power in these areas remained strong. A recognition of this reality may be sought in the appearance of the term *Romania* in late

ROMAN EMPIRE, LATE

Roman literature. The word came to designate the Roman way of life both in and beyond the territories administered by the Roman government. One example of the persistence of Roman habits outside the empire of East Rome will suffice. The eighth-century papyri from Aphrodito (Kūm Ashqūh) in Egypt show that the early Islamic government little disturbed the Roman organization there. After the time of Heraklios the Roman Empire never did reach from the Pyrenees to the Nile River, but subsequent extensions of power in Sicily and northern Syria show that reconquests in at least the urban zone were possible.

Another important defense available to the Romans of late antiquity was an adaptation for foreign affairs of the ancient system of clientage. During the time of the republic the Romans combined military and foreign policy. They sought to reduce their allies (at first only Italian peoples) to inferior status, in part by introducing Roman prefects as commanders of the army's allied cohorts. The result of these efforts was the full absorption of the Italians into the Roman order. Following a revolt in the early first century B.C. the Italians received Roman citizenship, and their cohorts were fully integrated into the Roman army. As the Roman state stretched beyond Italy, the Romans exported overseas the related practices of Romanizing noncitizen troops and making foreigners first allies, then clients, and finally citizens. The twin foundations of the republican empire were treaties or proclamations of friendship with client kings and the recruitment of noncitizen *auxilia* (reinforcements). By the late Republic both elements could enter Roman society; client kingdoms became provinces, and soldiers in the *auxilia* received hereditary grants of citizenship upon retirement. During the Principate the emperors continued these methods of state-building until the Severan age, when the Antonine Constitution in effect erased the distinction between the *auxilia* and the citizen legions, and the buffer zone of client kingdoms (always potential provinces) reached its apogee. Thereafter the Roman Empire shrank in size, but the emperors never relinquished their efforts to recruit noncitizen units for the army and to make clients of allies.

Diocletian and his successors made some modifications in the traditional mixture of military and foreign policy. From the time of Constantine I onward Christianity became linked with the Roman government, and the emperors tried with varying success to impose the new official religion on their clients. Furthermore, they devised a slightly different method of making treaties with foreigners and recruiting them for the army. Under the new system client kings in or beyond Roman lands contributed troops called *foederati* (allies) to the Roman army on demand, and received conditional grants of land and supplies for their services. They retained their own commanders; frequently the client king was the commander-in-chief. The practice extended throughout the empire. Moorish tribesmen along the southern frontier were military clients, as were the Ghassanids of Syria. The most studied *foederati* are the Germanic peoples, whose western kingdoms were originally client states. As always, however, the Romans tried to reduce the *foederati* to an inferior status, and to introduce Roman commanders over their soldiers. By the age of Justinian I they had succeeded. Procopius of Caesarea indicates that in his time *foederati* were merely units of the Roman army rather than independent troops. Furthermore, Justinian's generals brought the federated kingdoms of the Vandals in Africa and the Ostrogoths in Italy back under Roman administration. In the long run the Roman Empire was destined to be smaller than it was under Justinian. But Justinian's successors never stopped trying to extend their conquests or at least create an outer zone of clients, and their efforts assured the survival of the civilization they sought to protect.

The third factor in the endurance of the Roman Empire was the activity of a local culture not treated in the previous survey, that of the Greeks. During the Principate Greek culture was more than a local phenomenon. It was, with the Latin ways of the Romans, the dominant culture of the empire. Yet even as it formed, this Greco-Roman composite began to suffer imbalance. From the first through the third centuries the emperors perceived the northeastern Mediterranean as a vital part of the empire, and as a result concentrated much of the state's material and human resources there. Greek men of letters who wrote during the developed Principate generally expressed satisfaction with the Roman order; Roman traditions and the thought world of the Greek East were in harmony. In the latter half of the third century, however, an imbalance became evident. An Athenian named Publius Herennius Dexippus expressed in histories that survive in fragments not only loyalty to the Roman Empire, but a vivid recollection of the attainments of classical Athens. This new accentuation of old Greek values was a foundation of the new imperial order of Constantine I. The location of a strong imperial capital in a favored region of the empire gave impetus to a process that is often called Hellenization. The growth of Greek as an official language and the emergence of a core of imperial power extending from Sicily and southern Italy to northern Syria—areas where Greek speech had flourished for centuries—are signs of this process. The empire of the *Rhomaioi* (the Romans) drew its inspiration from the imperial past, but it did so in a Greek manner.

The survival of a Greek-speaking Roman Empire in part of the urban coastline was one of the most important developments in the Mediterranean of late antiquity. Equally important were the Islamic conquest of the Near East, the appearance of Moorish chiefdoms in the Maghrib, and the emergence of the Germanic successor kingdoms in Western Europe. All of these carriers of civilization drew their inspiration from the Roman Empire. It is most common to regard the divided Mediterranean that emerged by the death of Heraklios as a new development, a foretaste of the national states that have come into being in recent centuries. One of the advantages of a survey of the late Roman Empire is that the observer can look backward rather than forward in time for precedent. In the world of late antiquity there is an element of Hellenistic civilization. A generation ago N. H. Baynes sought Hellenistic roots for the thought world of East Rome; subsequent critics, such as R. J. H. Jenkins, have given guarded approval to his perception. The present investigation of the late Roman Empire and its antecedents makes possible an extension of Baynes' interpretation. By Heraklios' time the distribution of political power and indeed the whole cultural balance of the Mediterranean were similar to those of the Hellenistic age. The Maghrib of Massinissa and Masties resembled one another; competing chiefdoms converted the interior into inexact replicas of an urban civilization. Europe of the La Tène Celts was a forerunner of Europe of the successor kingdoms; once again politically disunited peoples controlled the inner reaches from Spain and Britain to the lower Danube. East Rome and Islam competed with one another, but both made the Eastern Mediterranean once again the political and cultural leader of Eurasia. Finally, as was the case in Hellenistic times, there existed a zone beyond the eastern heartland where cities continued to flourish. As the Roman Empire contracted, then, it helped to restore an old cultural balance. After a few centuries of unprecedented direction from the West, the peoples of the Mediterranean returned to a more familiar division of leadership.

PROSPECT

The present analysis of the late Roman Empire differs from most interpretations, which equate the disappearance of emperors ruling in the West with the fall of the Roman Empire, and which see East Rome, Islam, and the Germanic kingdoms as carriers of a new order. These standard perceptions derive from Western church fathers and Eastern Hellenes, who despite their differences of belief agreed that such shocking events as the Visigothic sack of Rome in 410 augured or marked the doom of the Roman state. Of these, Augustine of Hippo Regius and the Hellene Eunapius of Sardis were the most influential. The treatise *On the City of God* enjoyed wide circulation, and the *History* of Eunapius, which proclaimed the ruin of the empire amidst the abandonment of traditional religion, found a reading public especially through an epitome composed around 500 by Count Zosimus. The attitudes of Augustine, Zosimus, and others found their way into Edward Gibbon's *History of the Decline and Fall of the Roman Empire,* still the best account of the Roman Empire of late antiquity. With the benefit of hindsight Gibbon extended his narrative to the real end of the Roman Empire in 1453, but he honored the interpretations of fifth-century critics by inserting some "General Observations on the Fall of the Roman Empire in the West" soon after his narration of the events of 476. Gibbon's version can still be found in today's textbooks. In the late nineteenth and early twentieth centuries, however, a few critics began to see a continuum rather than catastrophe in the Mediterranean of the first millennium A.D.. The most influential of these were the Viennese art historian Alois Riegl, who first used the expression *Spätantike* (late antiquity) to describe the gradual evolution of artistic styles, and the Belgian historian Henri Pirenne, who at least postponed the disruption of life until the secure establishment of the Islamic caliphates and the Frankish kingdom.

At the end of the nineteenth century Theodor Mommsen, the founder of Roman studies as they exist today, wished for a second lifetime devoted to the study of the late Roman Empire. In the last part of his *History of Rome* he envisioned a history "carried out in the large spirit and with the comprehensive glance of Gibbon, but with a more

ROMAN EMPIRE, LATE

accurate understanding of details." Despite some promising responses to Mommsen's challenge, for instance by Ernst Stein and A. H. M. Jones, such a history remains to be written. When it is composed, it will take into better account the position of the rural masses in the Mediterranean of late antiquity. In his interesting sketch of Europe's destiny between the fourteenth and eighteenth centuries, Le Roy Ladurie suggested that the country folk remained "unmoved" despite and because of wars, pestilences, and ecological imbalances. It remains to be seen whether the transformation of the Roman Empire, the rise of Islam, and the beginnings of Germanic Europe changed the lives of the peasants and shepherds of the Mediterranean world.

BIBLIOGRAPHY

Sources in English translations. Ammianus Marcellinus, with an English Translation, John C. Rolfe, trans., 3 vols. (1935–1939); III, 97; Eusebius, *The Ecclesiastical History, with an English Translation,* Kirsopp Lake, trans., 2 vols. (1926–1932), II, 317–321; William Fairley, trans., *The Notitia Dignitatum, or Register of Dignitaries,* Translations and Reprints from the Original Sources of European History, VI, no. 4 (1900); Elsa R. Graser, trans., "The Edict of Diocletian on Maximum Prices," in Tenney Frank, ed., *An Economic Survey of Ancient Rome,* V (1935), 305–421; Josephus Flavius, *Josephus, with an English Translation,* Henry S. J. Thackeray *et al.,* trans., 9 vols. (1926–1965), VIII, 547–567, IX, 271–279; *Lactantius: De mortibus persecutorum,* J. L. Creed, ed. and trans. (1984), Clyde Pharr, trans., *The Theodosian Code and Novels, and the Sirmondian Constitutions* (1952), 440, 451, 473–474; Polybius, *The Histories,* William R. Paton, trans., 6 vols. (1922–1927, repr. 1975), I, 3–9; Procopius, *Procopius, with an English Translation,* Henry B. Dewing, trans., 7 vols. (1914–1940), I, 103, 451–475, II, 73–91.

Studies. Ernst Badian, *Roman Imperialism in the Late Republic,* 2nd ed. (1968); Timothy D. Barnes, *Constantine and Eusebius* (1981), and *The New Empire of Diocletian and Constantine* (1982); Salo W. Baron, *A Social and Religious History of the Jews,* 2nd ed., II (1952), 3–321, III (1957), 3–74; Norman H. Baynes, *Byzantine Studies and Other Essays* (1955), 1–23; Jean-Noël Biraben, *Les hommes et la peste en France et dans les pays européens et méditerranéens,* 2 vols. (1975); Horst Braunert, *Politik, Recht und Gesellschaft in der griechisch-römischen Antike* (1980), 129–152; Peter Brown, *Society and the Holy in Late Antiquity* (1982), 103–152; Reid A. Bryson and Brian M. Goodman, "Volcanic Activity and Climatic Changes," in *Science,* **207** (1980); Alan Cameron, *Claudian: Poetry and Propaganda at the Court of Honorius* (1970); Gabriel Camps, "Aux origines de la Berbérie: Massinissa ou les débuts de l'histoire," in *Libyca: Archéologie-épigraphie,* **8** (1960); Jérôme Carcopino, "Encore Masties, l'empereur maure inconnu," in *Revue africaine,* **100** (1956); Max Cary, *The Geographic Background of Greek and Roman History* (1949); Centro Italiano di studi sull'alto medioevo, *Topografia urbana e vita cittadina nell'alto medioevo in Occidente, 26 aprile–1 maggio 1973,* Settimane di studio 21, 2 vols. (1974); Maria R. Cimma, *Reges socii et amici populi romani* (1976).

Frank M. Clover, "The Pseudo-Boniface and the *Historia Augusta,*" in *Bonner Historia-Augusta-Colloquium 1977/78* (1980), and "Emperor Worship in Vandal Africa," in Gerhard Wirth, ed., *Romanitas-Christianitas: Untersuchungen zur Geschichte und Literatur der römischen Kaiserzeit* (1982); Christian Courtois, *Tablettes Albertini: Actes privés de l'époque vandale [Fin du Ve siècle]* (1952), and *Les Vandales et l'Afrique* (1955); Barry Cunliffe, *The Celtic World* (1979); Alexander Demandt, "Magister militum," in *Pauly's Real-Encyclopädie der classischen Altertumswissenschaft,* suppl. XII (1970), and *Geschichte des römischen Reiches in der Spätantike,* in *Handbuch der Altertumswissenschaft,* III, 6 (late 1980's); Harold A. Drake, *In Praise of Constantine: A Historical Study and New Translation of Eusebius' Tricennial Orations* (1976); R. P. Duncan-Jones, "Age rounding, Illiteracy, and Social Differentiation in the Roman Empire," in *Chiron,* **7** (1977); Aly M. Fahmy, *Muslim Naval Organization in the Eastern Mediterranean from the Seventh to the Tenth Century* A.D., 2nd ed. (1966); Moses I. Finley, *The Ancient Economy,* 2nd ed. (1985); W. H. C. Frend, *Martyrdom and Persecution in the Early Church: A Study of a Conflict from the Maccabees to Donatus* (1965); Jean Gagé, "L'empereur romain et les rois: Politique et protocole," in *Revue historique,* **221** (1959); Peter Garnsey, *Social Status and Legal Privilege in the Roman Empire* (1970).

Edward Gibbon, *The History of the Decline and Fall of the Roman Empire,* John B. Bury, ed., 7 vols. (1896–1900); Roger Goodburn and Philip Bartholomew, eds., *Aspects of the Notitia Dignitatum* (1976); John R. Goody, ed., *Literacy in Traditional Societies* (1968); Philip Grierson, "The *Tablettes Albertini* and the Value of the *Solidus* in the Fifth and Sixth Centuries A.D.," in *Journal of Roman Studies,* **49** (1959); Johanna Haberl with Christopher Hawkes, "The Last of Roman Noricum: St. Severin on the Danube," in Charles Francis Christopher Hawkes and Sonia Hawkes, eds., *Greeks, Celts, and Romans: Studies in Venture and Resistance* (1973); Mason Hammond, "The Emergence of Mediaeval Towns: Independence or Continuity?" in *Harvard Studies in Classical Philology,* **78** (1974); Fritz M. Heichelheim, *An Ancient Economic History from the Paleolithic Age to the Migrations of the Germanic, Slavic, and Arabic Nations,* Joyce M. Stevens, trans., III (1970); Judith Herrin, "Aspects of the Process of Hellenization in the Early Middle Ages," in *Annual of the British School* *of Athens,* **68** (1973); Thomas H. Hollingsworth, *Historical Demography* (1969).

Hubert Jedin *et al.*, eds., *Handbuch der Kirchengeschichte,* I (1962, 3rd ed. 1973), and II in 2 pts. (1973–1975, 2nd ed. 1979–1983), which cover the period up to 700, trans. by John Dolan as *Handbook of Church History* (1965–); Romilly J. H. Jenkins, "The Hellenistic Origins of Byzantine Civilization: Report on the Dumbarton Oaks Symposium of 1962," in *Dumbarton Oaks Papers,* **17** (1963); Arnold H. M Jones, *The Later Roman Empire, 284–602: A Social, Economic, and Administrative Survey,* 3 vols. (1964), and *The Roman Economy: Studies in Ancient Economic and Administrative History,* Peter A. Brunt, ed. (1974); Walter E. Kaegi, "The Fifth-century Twilight of Byzantine Paganism," in *Classica et mediaevalia,* **27** (1966), and *Byzantium and the Decline of Rome* (1968); Emmanuel Le Roy Ladurie, "L'histoire immobile," in *Annales: E.S.C.,* **29** (1974); Lloyd R. Laing, ed., *Studies in Celtic Survival* (1977); Abdallah Laroui, *The History of the Maghrib: An Interpretive Essay,* Ralph Manheim, trans. (1977); Ramsay MacMullen, *Soldier and Civilian in the Later Roman Empire* (1963), "The Celtic Renaissance," in *Historia: Zeitschrift für alte Geschichte,* **14** (1965), and *Roman Social Relations, 50 B.C. to A.D. 284* (1974); John F. Matthews, *Western Aristocracies and Imperial Court, A.D. 364–425* (1975).

Harold Mattingly and Edward A. Sydenham, eds., *The Roman Imperial Coinage,* VI, Carol H. V. Sutherland, *From Diocletian's Reform (A.D. 294) to the Death of Maximinus (A.D. 313)* (1967), and VII, Patrick Bruun, *Constantine and Licinius, A.D. 313–337* (1966); Fergus Millar, *A Study of Cassius Dio* (1964), "P. Herrenius Dexippus: The Greek World and the Third-century Invasions," in *Journal of Roman Studies,* **59** (1969), and *idem et al., The Roman Empire and Its Neighbours,* 2nd ed. (1981); Arnaldo Momigliano, *Alien Wisdom: The Limits of Hellenization* (1975); Theodor Mommsen, *The History of Rome: The Provinces from Caesar to Diocletian,* 2 vols., William P. Dickson, trans. (1886), I, 6; Lucien Musset, *Les invasions,* 2 vols., 2nd ed. (1969–1971), vol. 1 trans. by Edward James and Columba James as *The Germanic Invasions: The Making of Europe, A.D. 400–600* (1975); George Ostrogorsky, *History of the Byzantine State,* 3rd ed., Joan Hussey, trans. (1969); Evelyne Patlagean, *Pauvreté économique et pauvreté sociale à Byzance, 4e–7e siècles* (1977); Henri Pirenne, *Mahomet et Charlemagne,* Jacques Pirenne, ed. (1937); Claire Préaux, *Le monde hellénistique: La Grèce et l'Orient (323–146 av. J.-C.),* 2 vols. (1978).

William M. Ramsay, *Pauline and Other Studies in Early Christian History,* 2nd ed. (1908); Pierre Riché, *Education and Culture in the Barbarian West, Sixth Through the Eighth Centuries,* John J. Contreni, trans. (1976); Alois Riegl, *Die ägyptischen Textilfunde im K. K. österreichischen Museum* (1889); Jean Rougé, *Recherches sur l'organisation du commerce maritime en Méditerrannée sous l'Empire romain* (1966); Lellia Cracco Ruggini and Giorgio Cracco, "Changing Fortunes of the Italian City from Late Antiquity to the Early Middle Ages," in *Rivista di filologia e di istruzione classica,* **105** (1977); Jeffrey B. Russell, "Celt and Teuton," in Lynn White, ed., *The Transformation of the Roman World: Gibbon's Problem After Two Centuries* (1966); Josiah Cox Russell, *Late Ancient and Medieval Population* (1958); Brent D. Shaw, "Climate, Environment, and History: The Case of Roman North Africa," in T. M. L. Wigley *et al.*, eds., *Climate and History* (1981); Adrian N. Sherwin-White, *The Roman Citizenship,* 2nd ed. (1973); Tom Simkin *et al., Volcanoes of the World* (1981); Bernt Stallknecht, *Untersuchungen zur römischen Aussenpolitik in der Spätantike (306–395 n. Chr.)* (1969).

Ernst Stein, *Geschichte des spätrömischen Reiches . . . (284–476),* I (1928), 2nd ed. in French, *Histoire du Bas-Empire . . . ,* Jean-Rémy Palanque, ed. (1959), II, *Histoire du Bas-Empire . . . (476–565),* Jean-Rémy Palanque, ed. (1949); Marinus A. Wes, *Das Ende des Kaisertums im Westen des römischen Reichs,* K. E. Mittring, trans. (1967); Edith M. Wightman, "Peasants and Potentates: An Investigation of Social Structure and Land Tenure in Roman Gaul," in *American Journal of Ancient History,* **3** (1978); Otto Friedrich Winter, "Klientelkönige im römischen und byzantinischen Reich," in *Jahrbuch der österreichischen byzantinischen Gesellschaft,* **2** (1952); Herwig Wolfram, *Geschichte der Goten von den Anfängen bis zur Mitte des sechsten Jahrhunderts,* 2nd ed. (1980); Patrick Wormald, "The Decline of the Western Empire and the Survival of Its Aristocracy," in *Journal of Roman Studies,* **66** (1976); Erich Zöllner, *Geschichte der Franken bis zur Mitte des sechsten Jahrhunderts* (1970).

Bibliographies. Ernst Stein's history, as edited by Jean-Rémy Palanque (see above), contains the best guide to the major collections of primary sources for the late Roman Empire. More recent are the periodical reviews of scholarship by André Chastagnol, "Histoire de l'Empire romain," in *Revue historique,* **249** (1973), **259** (1978), **269** (1983).

The following periodicals also contain bibliographies: *L'Année philologique* (1924–); *Archäologische Bibliographie [1981–]* (1982–), continuation of *Bibliographie zum Jahrbuch des [Kaiserlich] deutschen Archäologischen Instituts [1913–1980]* (1914–1981); *Bibliographie analytique de l'Afrique antique* (1967–); *Byzantinische Zeitschrift* (1892–); *Gnomon: Kritische Zeitschrift für die gesamte klassische Altertumswissenschaft* (1925–); *Revue d'histoire ecclésiastique* (1900–).

FRANK M. CLOVER

[See also **Alani; Ammianus Marcellinus; Augustine of**

Hippo, St.; Barbarians, Invasions of; Byzantine Empire; Church, Early; Climatology; Colonus; Constantine I, the Great; Constantinople; Councils (Ecumenical, 325–787); Demography; Dux; Exarchate; Ghassanids; Heraklios; Islam, Conquests of; Jews (various articles); Justinian I; Lakhmids; Limitanei; Magister Militum; Maurice, Emperor; Monophysitism; Muḥammad; Navigation; Nomisma; Notitia Dignitatum; Praetorian Prefect; Procopius; Rome; Sarmatians; Stratiotai; Themes; Urbanism; Vandals; Warfare; Zosimus.]

ROMAN NUMERALS. The term "Roman numerals" designates that set of symbols by which numbers were represented in literature and epigraphy during the lifetime of the Roman civilization; it presumably served as well in computation and in other fields of social intercourse. Arithmetical operations, however, were performed on the abacus (in which beads or counters on separate lines or columns would stand for units, tens, hundreds, and so on), in soil or sand, or on wax tablets. Whichever medium was used, these arithmetical operations held but a transitory usefulness, to be undone or erased after the operation. Only the results, in the form of number representations, were carried to the script of papyrus, parchment, or engraved monuments in the form known as Roman numerals.

Unaltered in their shape and in the value principle, that is by cumulative succession from higher to lower order, these numerals were inherited by Western Europe after the disappearance of the empire, and persisted as the standard usage for number representation until late in the Middle Ages. The intrusion of the Hindu-Arabic numerals shortly after the year 1100 gave rise to a dichotomy of usage in number representation and to a competition between the two systems, that of the abacists and that of the algorists. The survival and evolution of the Roman numerals after imperial times and their struggle with the Arabic numerals therefore constitutes an integral part of medieval culture throughout a full millennium.

DESCRIPTION AND ORIGIN

Roman numerals were based on a decimal system making use of separate symbols for the units, the tens, the hundreds, and the thousands. The system also included a special symbol; for the midpoint of progression in each order: V, L, and D for 5, 50, and 500. All in all, the system was complete with a mere seven symbols: I, V, X, L, C, D, M. Intermediate quantities were indicated by mere repetition of lower symbols until the next superior order. In time, however, a subtractive device crept in. It consisted in placing an inferior symbol immediately before the next superior one and reading the complex figure backward by substraction: IV instead of IIII, or XL in lieu of XXXX, and so on for 90 (XC) and 400 (CD) and 900 (CM). Although an unsophisticated scientific tradition might consider this to be only a minor inconvenience, the mixture of additive and subtractive principles in the same notation would be perceived as rather inconvenient by a more mathematically minded cultural milieu, as indeed happened.

The origins of this Roman system are still obscure, and no satisfactory explanation has been proposed for it as yet. David E. Smith's contention still holds true: "The theories of the origin of Roman numerals are for the most part untenable." This would include, among others, Priscian's theory (sixth century) all the way down to Mattheus Hostus' theory (sixteenth century). Fragmentary explanations, such as the one referring the origin of C and M to the initials for *centum* and *mille* (Priscian and Mommsen), do help to understand particular phases of the evolution but offer no sure clue as to the origin of the entire system. Karl Zangemeister's hypothesis, advanced in 1887, claiming that the origin lay in the general application of the decussate principle (crossing out by varying strokes), did not have much success. Smith concluded that epigraphy "fails to solve the problem of origins, but it shows the change in forms from century to century."

EVOLUTION

From epigraphists and paleographers we can obtain a glimpse of the evolution of the shape of Roman numerals during the medieval period. Epigraphic evidence for the earlier Middle Ages, as Jean Mallon has observed, shows that while normally the original copy of a text to be inscribed on a monument would be issued in ordinary, usually cursive contemporary script, the engraver who transferred the copy onto stone would cling to the monumental tradition of writing. With the passing of time, as the shape of letters evolved under the

 ROMAN NUMERALS

stress of cursive tendencies, monumental or epigraphic forms tended to resist change. A similar conservatism may be observed among scribes of manuscripts. The *libraria* hand could evolve in shape and ductus; but when representing numerals, the letters would tend to retain their archaic shape. This paleographic evolution reveals itself most clearly in the shapes of V(5) and in the ligature VI(6). For we see the old Visigothic V or U changing in form, but remaining in the archaic form of u for the Roman numeral representing 5; so also for the VI represented as G, which is merely a paleographic ligature of V and I. Later on, though, as will be explained, these stereotyped Roman symbols for 5 and 6 would be introduced unaltered into the Hindu-Arabic series, to replace the 5 and 6 of this system.

It is due to a similar paleographic feature that the ligature of X and L in the Visigothic hand (representing 40) came to stand independently as ꭗ for 40 among the improved Roman numerals of Spain, of which paleographic albums of Spanish script give numerous examples.

Two additional steps in the improvement of the shape of Roman numerals have been observed, principally if not perhaps exclusively in the Spanish tradition, mostly among astronomers and astrologers, of whom tenth-to-twelfth-century Spain counted a great many. A first step was in the abandonment of the problematic subtractive principle: IIII was written in place of IV, then VIIII instead of IX, also LXXXX instead of XC, or CCCC instead of CD. We can only surmise the motive behind this change: a desire to avoid confusion and error in astronomical texts and tables, where continuous or cyclical series of numbers could be visually warped by the intrusion of subtractive complexes. The corrective did not prove to be of lasting advantage. Astronomers and scribes must have soon realized that sprawling symbols like VIIII, or, at the system's most acute inconvenience, figures like LXXXXVIIII for 99, meant wastage of costly parchment and labor, in addition to increasing the likelihood that a tired scribe would commit errors.

We notice, therefore, the appearance of a new improvement of the Roman numerals that was already generalized by the end of the eleventh and beginning of the twelfth century. At first, this consisted in the use of the initial letters of the units' names to replace the most cumbersome Roman symbols, for example *q* for 4 (*quatuor*), and *n* or *no* for 9 (*novem*). Once adopted for the most cumbersome symbols, it was inevitable that the system would be extended to all the units from three to nine, making use of minuscules and majuscules to distinguish between units beginning with the same initial: *q* = 4, *Q* = 5, *s* = 6, *S* = 7. Together with the *o* = 8 and *n* = 9 or *no* = 9, the entire series of units was thus represented, including a *t* = 3. Examples of this usage are found in astronomical tables from Spain that date from as early as the twelfth century. The practice does not seem to have survived very long on account of its inherent sources of confusion: *t* for 3 could be confused with a *t* for 0 already in use in this system; similarly, since the symbol for 9 varied between *n* and *no*, it could be confused with the *o* already standing for 8 in the system, or even as an alternate form for 0, as the twelfth-century translations of al-Khwārizmī's arithmetic (*Calculation with the Hindu Numerals*) clearly attest: *t vel o sunt cifre* (*t* or *o* are cifres [zero]). It would seem reasonable to assume that it is in order to avoid some of this confusion that the figure for 8 (*o*) was eventually replaced by a clearer abbreviation of *octo* by contraction: ȣ, or sometimes ȣ, and finally a mere 8, which became the figure for 8 in the *ghubār* system based on al-Khwārizmī. The same complex of factors must be presumed to have led the early users of the *ghubār*-Spanish numerals to shift the "Hindu" form of ∧ for 8 to stand for 7 once it had been released from its original service in the Hindu-Arabic figures. For the early forms of the figure for 7 in the *ghubār* show an instability of "orientation" as between the two sequential forms of ∧ and ∨, originally standing for 8 and 7, respectively, in the Hindu-Arabic system.

How long in fact the improved Roman numerals persisted in use can only be determined after an exhaustive collation of all manuscripts that can be identified as carrying traces of this system, together with their accurate dating. But one thing already appears certain. With the rapidly growing favor shown the *ghubār* system in Spain in the twelfth century and its transmission to the Europeans through several channels during the same century, the earlier gropings toward an improvement of Roman numerals came to a swift end. Nonetheless, the latter system yielded four of five typically "Western" symbols to the *ghubār* system (such as u = 5, G = 6, ˥ = 7, and 8 = 8), which replaced the original symbols for these values in the Hindu-Arabic system.

THE ROLE OF SPAIN

The improved Roman numerals above described were never widely diffused outside of Spain. Indeed, they are so characteristic of Spain that they provide a cue to spotting a late Carolingian Latin scribe who is transcribing a Spanish model or exemplar if he regularly fails to recognize or understand these altered Roman numerals. An outstanding example is the figure for the date in a manuscript of the *Liber embadorum* of Abraham bar Ḥiyya (Savasorda) translated by Plato of Tivoli in the year A.H. 540. M. Curtze, its first editor, read the figure as A.H. 510, or A.D. 1116, thus placing it among the earliest twelfth-century translations in Spain (Abraham and Plato worked in Barcelona). Charles Haskins considered the date to be too early for the activity of Plato of Tivoli and by relating it to other astronomical data given therein corrected it to the year 540 A.H., that is, A.D. 1145, which obviously is the right date. Neither Curtze nor Haskins nor possibly the Western scribe recognized the peculiar Spanish form of X in ligature for 40, which they all read as a normal X = 10 Roman numeral. Other examples of such errors of reading involve the *q* = 4, the *q* in uncial form being taken for an *a*, or the ↄ = 7 also read as an *a*.

From manuscript evidence it becomes clear that Roman numerals evolved decisively in Mozarab and Arab learned circles in Spain, while in Latin Europe the numerals persisted unaltered through the twelfth and thirteenth centuries. We perceive here a clear reflection of the more active and notably superior level of scientific culture in the Iberian Peninsula in contrast to Frankish Europe. The creative period of Andalusian and Spanish science began to gain momentum during the caliphate of ᶜAbd al-Raḥmān III (929–931) and his immediate successors. A climax was reached in several locations under the kings of the *taifas* (1010–1095) with the work of Maslama of Madrid, al-Zarqālī of Toledo; Ibn Masarra, Ibn Juljul, Ibn Hazm of Córdoba. The Almoravid invaders who came to shore up a declining Islam in Spain (1095–1150) did not overtly oppose scientific activity; but by that time the Christian advance had made possible an osmosis of scientific interests from Andalusian circles to northern Spain, and shortly the effects were felt in continental Europe. Renowned philosophers flourished in Almoravid times: Ibn Ṭufayl (Abubacer), Ibn Bājja (Avempace), Ibn Gabirol (Avicebron), Ibn Daud (Avendauth), and even the young Ibn Rushd (Averroës). The rigorist Almohads (1150–1250), who displaced the Almoravids, assured the dominance of the fanatic Maliki jurists and the near-extinction of independent science in the Arab portion of Spain. Both Averroës and Maimonides died in exile, Averroës in North Africa in 1198 and Maimonides in Egypt in 1204. But during the active period of scientific activity the Iberian Peninsula became a crucible in which the Romano-Gothic cultural tradition was fused with the younger Arab civilization then reigning in Egypt, Damascus, and Baghdad. Among the ingredients of this fusion must be counted the systems of number representation. Roman numerals remained in use among Christians and Mozarabs. Even the Greek-Coptic numerals of Byzantine administration were known and used in Muslim Spain, as is attested by the survival of the "Fez" numerals observed by Colin and among the Mozarabs of Toledo as shown by Ángel González Palencia. Whether the presence of these Greek numerals in Spain is ascribed to the effects of Justinian's reconquest (sixth century) or, more plausibly, to the system of Byzantine administration maintained until 749/750 by the Umayyads has little direct bearing on the reality of a sturdy survival of much of the classical tradition in medieval Spain, merging with the new values in science and literature brought by the Arabs.

COMPETITION WITH THE ARABIC NUMERALS

Into the midst of this vigorous scientific activity the Hindu-Arabic numerals and arithmetic were injected during the tenth century, if not earlier. Judging from the evidence so far available, the new system did not obtain immediate acceptance among the mathematicians and astronomers of Andalusia, even less so in the administration and the marketplace. Indeed, what Gerbert of Aurillac discovered in Spain around the year 980 and brought to the schools of Europe was a mere acquaintance with the nine numerals without a zero, a clear sign that arithmetical operations with them were not grasped. Gerbert and his disciples used the numerals on the counters of their abacus without showing any understanding of the place value essential for performing arithmetical operations with them.

In Spain, however, mathematicians and astronomers seem to have been more strongly impressed with the advantages and potentialities of the Khwarizmian system. And yet, before a definite triumph was assured by the twelfth century as evidenced by

ROMAN NUMERALS

the numerous translations and adaptations of al-Khwārizmī's arithmetic into Latin during that century, a running competition seemed to take place in which the improved Roman numerals described above strove to hold their own against the simplification and allurement of the Khwarizmian system. The outcome of this competition was the emergence of the *ghubār* form of the Hindu numerals, which is basically the Khwarizmian system but carrying definite traces of the improved Roman numerals in the substitution of the "Roman" symbols of 5, 6, 7, 8, and of 0 for the original forms of al-Khwārizmī.

That the algorism (al-Khwārizmī's arithmetic) exerted some influence on the evolution of Roman numerals in Spain seems to follow from the vagaries observed, as when place value is introduced in the Roman numerals in expressions like X° = 48 and many variants of the case. Here we see that both symbols belong to the improved Roman numerals. But since the ligature X° already represented 40, the real significance of place value was not yet quite obvious. Nevertheless the impressive number of astronomical manuscripts from medieval Spain where improved Roman numerals are often used with place value attests to a certain struggle between the two systems.

On the other hand, at the time when al-Khwārizmī's arithmetic was passed to Europe in Latin translations, the nine numerals and the zero presented in these translations or adaptations all embodied the Spanish (*ghubār*) rather than the Oriental form of the Arabic numerals. Yet, at the same time that this evolution was taking place in twelfth-century Spain, we meet with a few scattered examples of manuscripts in which there appears to be a deliberate attempt to adopt the nine Hindu figures in their original (Oriental) form, save for the zero, which is here a *t* as in the improved Roman numerals of Spain. One rare example from the twelfth century is a London manuscript (British Library, Cotton Vespasian A.II) that contains in folios 27 and 40 at least three astronomical mathematical texts in the same twelfth-century hand. The three works are related either to Abraham Ibn Ezra or to Rudolph of Bruges, the disciple of Hermann of Carinthia. In the two texts ascribed to Ibn Ezra one finds the systematic usage of the Arabic numerals in their Oriental, non-*ghubār* shape. Here is a comparative table of these figures in their Oriental shape and in the form encountered in this manuscript:

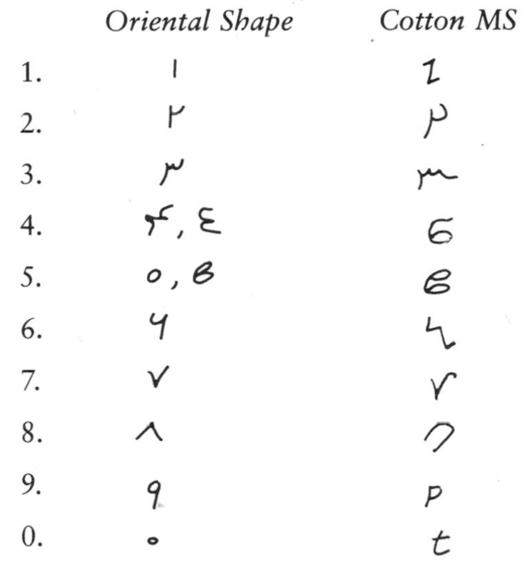

	Oriental Shape	*Cotton MS*
1.	١	[illegible]
2.	٢	[illegible]
3.	٣	[illegible]
4.	٤, ع	6
5.	٥, ϐ	ϐ
6.	٦	[illegible]
7.	٧	r
8.	٨	[illegible]
9.	٩	p
0.	٠	t

The close resemblance of the Cotton manuscript figures to the Oriental shape of Arabic numerals will not escape the observer, although this Latin scribe (for he can hardly be other than that) shows an inclination to shape some of the figures as if they were letters of the Roman alphabet, in particular the figures of 2, 3, 7, and 9. Because of the connection of these two texts with Ibn Ezra, on the one hand, and because of the absence of these figures in the middle text by Rudolph of Bruges, where only traditional Roman numerals appear, it is legitimate to assume that this attempt to introduce the Arabic numerals in their genuine form originated in the Spanish circle of learned men who consciously aimed at their European audience. In other contexts, though, Ibn Ezra is known to have made use of the Hebrew numerals based on the alphabet.

Another London manuscript (British Library, Arundel 268, fols. 75–76) shows the 2 and 3 of the Arabic numerals in their Oriental form, just as in the Cotton manuscript. The text in Arundel is that of the *Liber trium judicum* by Hermann of Carinthia in its nuclear form. (It was wrongly ascribed to Hugh of Sanctalla by C. S. Burnett.) Hermann of Carinthia's own translation of the *Introductorium maius in astronomiam* by Abū Ma^c^shar (1140) in a twelfth-century copy (Oxford, Corpus Christi College 95) contains an Oriental Arabic 3 (fol. 90v), but also an improved Roman xlo (48) in a passage (II.2) where the forty-eight constellations of Ptolemy are discussed. The Oxford codex also contains works by Daniel of Morley and William of Conches and may have been the very source from which Daniel quoted Hermann's version of Abū Ma^c^shar.

These scattered examples, therefore, seem to point to a circle composed of Ibn Ezra, Hermann of Carinthia, Rudolph of Bruges, and Daniel of Morley, to which this short-lived effort to adopt the Oriental Arabic numerals instead of the *ghubār* forms must be ascribed.

Despite the introduction of al-Khwārizmī's arithmetic with the *ghubār* numerals in the first part of the twelfth century, Latin scholars remained unimpressed by the new system, at least until the exertions by Leonardo Fibonacci of Pisa in his *Liber abaci* (first edited in 1202; revised and dedicated to Michael Scot in 1228) had made a clear case for the simplicity and advantages of the "algorism" when fully and correctly understood. Leonardo himself remained faithful to the *ghubār* form of the numerals as introduced in the twelfth century in the translations of al-Khwārizmī's work. Between the middle of the twelfth century and Leonardo's time, the old unreformed Roman numerals remained the prevalent usage in Western Europe and continued so, with less and less vigor, however, for another century after Leonardo. In detailing the learning of his Oxford cleric, Chaucer stresses that he knew his "augrim" (algorismus), as if to mark a modernist trait in the late fourteenth century.

The lessons of a protracted experience with Western scientific manuscripts from the mid twelfth to the late fourteenth century show that the Arabic numerals in their *ghubār* (Spanish) form made their way but slowly in the Latin West, even in works of science. They did not displace the Roman numerals until a full two centuries after their introduction. Moreover, many manuscripts bear testimony of a double usage, Roman and Arabic numerals being employed in the same text. The usual practice in these cases was to use Roman numerals in the text and give their equivalents in Arabic numerals in interlinear or marginal notations. The reverse also occurred but much less frequently, especially in the ealier period. The triumph of Arabic numerals, fully achieved by the beginning of the fifteenth century, consigned the Roman numerals to a merely ornamental function.

BIBLIOGRAPHY

David E. Smith, *History of Mathematics,* II (1925, repr. 1958), 54–64, provides a short, authoritative account of the origins of Roman numerals. Also useful is David E. Smith and Jekuthiel Ginsburg, *Numbers and Numerals* (1937). A broader cultural and anthropological approach yields some insights into the "natural" ways of representing numbers, although it is often of little help in solving problems of origins. Such works include Eugen Löffler, *Ziffern und Ziffernsysteme der Kulturvölker in alter und neuer Zeit* (1912); and Karl W. Menninger, *Number Words and Number Symbols: A Cultural History of Numbers,* Paul Broneer, trans. (1969), 242–246, 305.

Gottfried Friedlein, *Die Zahlzeichen und das elementare Rechnen der Griechen und Römer und des christlichen Abendlandes vom 7. bis 13. Jahrhundert* (1869), 54, provides interesting bits of historical information. He reports that the author of the *Ars geometrica* tells us that several kinds of notation had been invented according to felt needs: the *apices* of various shapes, characters drawn from the alphabet, or marks resembling the counters used by Gerbert. A detailed review of Friedlein's book appeared in J. Hoüel, "Die Zahlzeichen und das elementare Rechnen . . . ," in *Bullettino di bibliografia e di storia delle scienze matematiche e fisiche,* **3** (1870).

Whereas numismatics does not seem to hold much promise of evidence as to the origins of Roman numerals, epigraphy and paleography have much to contribute. See Jean Mallon, "Pour une nouvelle critique des chiffres dans les inscriptions latines gravées sur pierre," in *Emerita,* **16** (1948); Joaquim María de Navascués, *La era ". . . as"* (1951); Francisco J. Simonet, *Historia de los Mozárabes de España* (1967), 834; Edward M. Thompson, *A Handbook of Greek and Latin Palaeography* (1893, repr. 1964, 1966); Zacarías García Villada, *Paleografía española,* II (1923).

Other works of interest include Charles H. Haskins, *Studies in the History of Mediaeval Science* (1924), 11; José María Millás y Vallicrosa, *Estudios sobre historia de la ciencia española* (1949), 260; Richard Lemay, "The Hispanic Origin of Our Present Numeral Forms," in *Viator,* **8** (1977).

RICHARD LEMAY

[See also **Arabic Numerals; Mathematics; Paleography, Western European; Science.**]

ROMANCE OF HORN, an Anglo-Norman adventure romance written around 1170 by an otherwise unidentified Thomas. The orphaned hero, Horn, son of Aälof, king of Suddene (probably south Devonshire), is set adrift in a rudderless boat and reaches Brittany, where he grows to manhood and attracts the love of the king's daughter, Rigmel. Despite his defense of the kingdom against Saracens, Horn is banished and flees to Ireland, where once more a king's daughter falls in love with him. He finally returns to Brittany and following further adventures marries Rigmel; eventually he assumes the throne of Brittany.

The Anglo-Norman *Romance of Horn* is the source of one of the earliest Middle English romances, *King Horn,* composed around 1225. Both texts remain known for their celebration of an English hero.

BIBLIOGRAPHY

Susan Crane, *Insular Romance: Politics, Faith, and Culture in Anglo-Norman and Middle English Literature* (1986); Mildred K. Pope, ed., *The Romance of Horn by Thomas,* I (Anglo-Norman Text Society, **9–10**) (1955), and II (rev. and completed by T. B. W. Reid, Anglo-Norman Text Society, **12–13**) (1964).

BRIAN MERRILEES

[See also **Anglo-Norman Literature; Ballads, Middle English.**]

ROMANCE OF THE ROSE. See **Roman de la Rose.**

ROMANESQUE ARCHITECTURE

DEFINITION AND CHARACTERISTICS

Romanesque architecture is usually categorized, in broad terms, as the dominant architectural style of Europe from the early eleventh century to the mid twelfth century. Although generally valid, taking in most of the major monuments of Romanesque architecture, this definition, based on geographical and temporal criteria, is not sufficiently encompassing to include either the many late examples of the style that continued to be built in certain areas well into the thirteenth century and beyond or the occasional non-European structures such as those in the Holy Land. To take in all Romansque buildings, it is necessary to devise an inclusive definition based on style. This was the intent of those who initiated the concept of Romanesque architecture early in the nineteenth century in France. For them, the term was intended to differentiate architecture that employed round arches in its construction from that which used pointed or broken arches. This latter architecture retained the stylistic designation "Gothic," which, since the Renaissance, had been applied indiscriminately to all medieval architecture.

Implicit in the early definition of Romanesque was the idea, as reflected by the name itself, that round-arched medieval architecture was derived from the architecture of Roman antiquity, which employed the same form. As the study of medieval architecture advanced, however, it was realized that while many if not most Romanesque buildings were based on the semicircular arch, certain buildings, for example the cathedral of St. Lazare at Autun (Burgundy, begun *ca.* 1120), were built largely with pointed arches, and some early Gothic buildings, such as the cathedral of Notre Dame at Sens (Champagne, begun *ca.* 1140), make extensive use of round arches. Thus, more precise stylistic criteria must be advanced.

The single stylistic feature that most accurately identifies Romanesque architecture is regular bay division on both the interior and exterior of the building. On the interior of Romanesque buildings, bay division, or division into units of space, is accomplished by use of pilasters as at St. Guilhem-le-Desert (Languedoc, *ca.* 1076), attached columns as at St. Étienne, Nevers (Burgundy, *ca.* 1083–1097), or combinations of these elements as at La Madeleine, Vézelay (Burgundy, *ca.* 1120–1140), placed regularly along the nave and aisle walls of the structure. These projections are frequently connected with their counterparts on the opposite wall by ribs protruding from the intrados or inner surface of the vaults covering the spaces. On the exterior, bay division is most frequently stated by flat, strap buttresses, for example at Anzy-le-Duc (Burgundy, late eleventh century). The international acceptance of this method of articulating wall surfaces, occurring during the years 1020–1030, marks the debut of Romanesque architecture. It represents a clear break from previous architecture, in which flat, continuous wall surfaces were stressed.

While bay division is the crucial diagnostic feature of Romanesque architecture, there are other aspects that unite many Romanesque buildings. These include two dominant plan types: the echelon apse plan and the ambulatory and radiating chapel plan, extensive use of vaulting, and experimentation with wall structure. These features developed in response to common pragmatic problems faced by architects in this period of considerable church expansion and widespread church-building, a peri-

 ROMANESQUE ARCHITECTURE

La Madeleine, Vézelay, nave (1120–1140). SCALA / ART RESOURCE

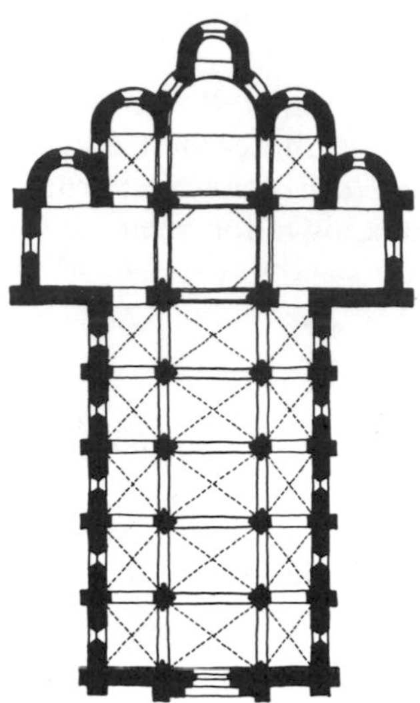

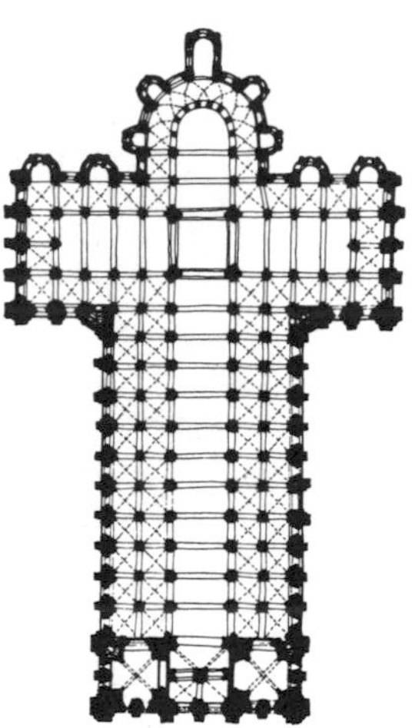

Two apse plan types of the late 11th century: Echelon plan at Anzy-le-Duc Priory (*top*); ambulatory with radiating chapels at St. Sernin, Toulouse (*bottom*). Reproduced from Whitney S. Stoddard, *Monastery and Cathedral in France* © 1966 WESLEYAN UNIVERSITY

od during which the land was covered with "a white robe of churches," according to the eleventh-century chronicler Radulphus Glaber.

The Romanesque church plan types evolved to meet the dual demands of adequate space and ease of circulation. The echelon plan, which consists of a cruciform basilica with small apses opening off the east walls of the transept and east ends of the choir aisles and a major apse terminating the choir to the east (arranged in a chevron fashion), was most commonly employed for monastic churches. For that reason, it is sometimes called the Benedictine plan. The smaller apses afforded space for the private masses by those monks who were also priests and therefore required to celebrate mass daily.

In the cases of larger monastic churches or churches that had to serve large congregations or great numbers of visitors, such as cathedrals or pilgrimage churches, the ambulatory and radiating chapel scheme was frequently adopted. In this type of plan, the aisles, flanking the choir, are joined by a semicircular passage extending around

ROMANESQUE ARCHITECTURE

the central apse. Chapels, usually semicircular in plan, radiate off this passage—the ambulatory—to provide auxiliary altar space as well as locations in which to display relics. The semicircular passage allows these chapels to be visited without disturbing activities in the central vessel of the church. The problem of plan was solved quite early in the Romanesque period. Around 1030, both plan types were fully developed and in widespread use.

Vaulting and experimentation with wall structure are closely related features. Although large-scale vaulting had been common in late Roman architecture, pre-Romanesque architecture did not regularly employ vaults over the high, central nave. Vaults were used only in the ancillary spaces of larger buildings, for example in crypts and aisles, and occasionally to cover the naves of small churches. The typical wooden roofs were fire hazards; as a result, during the Romanesque period builders sought to rediscover the large-scale masonry vaulting techniques of antiquity.

Masonry coverings require heavy supports, and, consequently, Romanesque architecture is also characterized by the use of solid, massive bearing walls and piers. The weightiness of vaults and walls made fenestration for direct illumination of the nave difficult, and wall structures had to be devised which would permit windows without a resultant decrease in wall strength. This problem led to extensive structural experimentation. The final solution was not reached until skeletal construction was achieved, and this achievement also served to introduce Gothic architecture.

SOURCES OF THE ROMANESQUE STYLE

The immediate sources for Romanesque architecture, as defined above, are three. The survival of Roman remains certainly influenced the predilection for the round arch. More specifically, superimposed arcades, such as those at the Pont du Gard (Provence), a Roman aqueduct of the first century (A.D.), suggest the arcaded interiors of Romanesque churches. Roman decorative devices—moldings, fluted pilasters, and Corinthian capitals—are also present in the vocabulary of Romanesque ornament.

A second source for the Romanesque is the pre-Romanesque architecture of northern Spain, southern France, and northern Italy dating from about 950 to 1020. While sometimes called the "first Romanesque architecture," this architecture should be seen as a source for Romanesque style and not as an early manifestation of it. Although possessing some of the features that later characterize developed Romanesque architecture, these features are nascent, never elaborated or exploited. Nor are they used with the consistency that characterizes their use after about 1020–1030. For example, many of the churches in this southern tier have barrel-vaulted naves, but the naves tend to be extremely small, scarcely wider than the side aisles of subsequent Romanesque churches and requiring minimal technical skill to construct. Even small vaults, however, require sturdy support, and the heavy walls of these pre-Romanesque buildings anticipate those of their Romanesque successors.

Another feature present in these early buildings is rudimentary bay division, examples of which may be seen at St. Martin du Canigou in the French Pyrenees (1001–1026) and Sta. Cecilia at Montserrat in Catalonia (*ca.* 957). Montserrat is particularly prophetic as the projections that achieve the bay division, along with the short segments of nave wall support to which they are attached, form simple compound piers. Infrequently, as at S. Pere at Cassérres (*ca.* 1010), also in Catalonia, the small barrel vault of the nave is crossed by ribs. Cassérres has a single rib dividing the nave into two bays.

The third major source for Romanesque architecture can be found in Ottonian architecture, the name given to architecture in the Holy Roman Empire from about 950 to 1050. Coeval with the southern pre-Romanesque architecture just discussed, Ottonian architecture differs considerably in style. Ottonian buildings are much larger than their southern counterparts and consequently are wooden-roofed rather than vaulted. In size they are closer to the major structures of the Romanesque. Ottonian buildings frequently have crypts, which are sometimes in the form of semicircular passages. Crypts were to be important in the Romanesque architecture of some regions, and an analogy may be drawn between semicircular Ottonian crypts and Romanesque ambulatories. Entrances to Ottonian churches were often elaborated with monumental, towered, multistoried complexes called westworks. An emphasis on the facade, often achieved through the use of towers, is carried on during the Romanesque period. The features, characteristic of Ottonian architecture, were, to a great extent, inherited from Carolingian buildings. Ottonian architecture can thus be seen as a link between the architecture of the Carolingian renaissance and the eleventh century.

 ROMANESQUE ARCHITECTURE

Ottonian architecture also provided the intermediary between Byzantine architecture and Romanesque architecture as certain features of Byzantine origin are introduced into Western European architectural design by their appearance in Ottonian churches. Tribunes and nave support systems which alternate columns and piers are two such features that appear in Byzantine, Ottonian, and Romanesque architecture alike.

By the early eleventh century, buildings closely related to Ottonian structures had already appeared across a broad area north of the Loire Valley in what is now northern France. Montiérender (960–992) and Vignory (*ca.* 1050), both in Champagne, are large, nonvaulted basilicas with interesting elevations. Montiérender has a three-story elevation with a tribune which opens onto the nave through paired arches. Each pair of arches is contained within a larger arch. The median support for the paired arches is a column, while laterally they rest on square piers which also support the containing arch. This results in an alternation of support as well as treatment in depth of the wall. The wall thus has a sturdy, sculptural quality, differing from the more planar Ottonian aesthetic and anticipating the Romanesque. Vignory also has a three-story elevation with paired openings forming the intermediate story. The arches are carried by similarly alternating supports, but they are not contained under a larger arch as at Montiérender. These arcades do not have tribunes behind them. Rather, they open onto the flanking aisles. The arcades are introduced at Vignory to lighten the wall as well as to animate it, giving it greater visual interest.

The abbey church of St. Remi at Rheims (1005–1049) was probably the most important of this group of churches. Built to be the largest church in Gaul, the original design was altered during construction and has since been much changed by additions, reconstructions, and restorations. The original building had a three-story elevation similar to that at Montiérender but much larger in scale. The nave was carried on supports consisting of bundles of engaged columns, again indicating a more sculptural approach to wall design. None of these engaged columns, however, rose into the upper stories of the nave elevation, so that the crucial bay division was still lacking.

In Normandy, the abbey church of St. Pierre at Jumièges (late tenth–early eleventh centuries) belongs to this group. Farther to the south, the destroyed cathedral at Orléans (from *ca.* 1012) and the cathedral of Bishop Fulbert at Chartres (begun 1020) can also be included as Ottonian derivatives.

As a result of the multiple problems facing builders in the Romanesque period and the many sources that influenced their solutions to these problems, Romanesque is a style noted for its variety. Specific solutions were favored in certain geographical areas, giving rise to regionally identifiable variants of Romanesque architecture which can best be discussed separately.

FRENCH ROMANESQUE

While the Romanesque was an international style, it is within the borders of present-day France that the style saw its fullest and richest expression with the greatest number of regional variants. Exactly where French Romanesque first appeared is a moot question. Many important buildings are no longer extant or have been much remodeled. By early in the second quarter of the eleventh century, however, buildings properly Romanesque, at least in part, existed in several regions of France, including Burgundy, the Loire Valley, and Normandy. Located approximately halfway between the two major areas of pre-Romanesque architectural development, these buildings drew on both sources.

Burgundy. Burgundy was the most architecturally active region of France in the Romanesque period. In large part this was due to the fact that Burgundy was a center of monasticism. In the eleventh and early twelfth centuries, the great abbey of Cluny, founded in the early tenth century, was at its zenith, and in 1115 the important Cistercian abbey of Clairvaux was founded by St. Bernard. While monasticism in general provided one of the major impulses in the development of Romanesque art and architecture, Cluny, in particular, was a lavish patron of architecture.

The abbey church of St. Philibert at Tournus is instructive for an understanding of Burgundian Romanesque. Its building history (*ca.* 950–1120) spanned much of the Romanesque period. Of tenth-century date is the crypt under the east end of the church. The ground level at the east end of St. Philibert, dedicated in 1019, features an ambulatory with radiating chapels that repeats the plan of the late-tenth-century crypt below. This is one of the earliest appearances of this plan type in Romanesque architecture. The nave was planned with a non-bay-divided elevation in the early eleventh century. Following 1066, however, when the nave was vaulted, bay division was created by the application

ROMANESQUE ARCHITECTURE

of attached columns to the nave wall surfaces. At the west, St. Philibert's nave is preceded by a two-story narthex of three bays. This narthex carries two towers at the extreme west. While this elevation of the western facade recalls Ottonian westworks, the decorative detailing, which consists of arched corbel tables carried on pilasters, is more closely related to southern pre-Romanesque architecture. The vaulting of both stories of the narthex also looks to southern antecedents.

Tournus is a museum of vault types employing a ribbed barrel vault in the nave of the upper narthex story, quadrant or half-barrel vaults in the aisles of the same story, groin vaults in the lower floor of the narthex and nave aisles, and transverse barrel vaults over the lower narthex aisles and the nave. A dome, carried on squinches, covers the crossing. This compendium of vault types, within one structure, clearly illustrates the experimental nature of Romanesque architecture.

The abbey of Cluny fostered two major variants of Romanesque architecture. The first was based on the now-destroyed abbey church of Cluny II, constructed from about 955 to 1010. This building was built on the echelon apse plan, partially recovered through excavation. The use of the plan at such an important monastic center must certainly have helped to establish its popularity. The church may have been vaulted with a ribbed barrel vault that helped to create bay division. The church was probably decorated with two towers to the west and a third tower over the crossing of the nave and transept. These features were repeated over a broad geographical area, but the influence of Cluny II can be seen most clearly in Burgundy. Echoes of Cluny II can be seen at St. Philibert (illustrated in this volume), St. Bénigne at Dijon (1001–1018), Charlieu (from *ca.* 1033), Chapaize (from *ca.* 1050), and La Charité-sur-Loire (from *ca.* 1125), among others.

Cluny III (*ca.* 1088–1130), at one time the largest church in Christendom but now almost entirely destroyed, was characterized by an ambulatory with radiating chapels, two transepts arranged in the shape of an archiepiscopal cross, compound supports carrying nave walls consisting of an arcade, triforium, and clerestory, and a ribbed, pointed barrel vault over the nave. These features reappear on a much smaller scale at such Burgundian churches as Paray-le-Monial (*ca.* 1100), the cathedral of St. Lazare at Autun, and Notre-Dame at Beaune (*ca.* 1150). These buildings are further allied through the use of similar decorative vocabulary. All feature ornament close to Roman decoration, such as that found on the extant city gates at Autun, and elaborate sculpted capitals, often historiated.

Cluny III, abbey church (*ca.* 1088–1130). Interior as reconstructed by K. J. Conant and T. C. Bannister. Reproduced from Kenneth John Conant, *Carolingian and Romanesque Architecture, 800–1200* (1959). COURTESY OF K. J. CONANT

Two other Burgundian monuments warrant mention: the abbey church of La Madeleine at Vézelay, an important pilgrimage site, and the priory church of St. Étienne at Nevers. At Vézelay, only the nave and narthex remain from the Romanesque church. Both date to the period 1120–1140. The nave has a two-story elevation and is covered by a series of groin vaults carried on compound supports. These are the earliest preserved nave groin vaults in France. The aisle bays also support groin vaults, and this uniformity of covering, throughout the main body of the church, parallels the almost contemporary early Gothic use of this idea.

St. Étienne at Nevers is one of the best-preserved

Notre-Dame-du-Port, Clermont-Ferrand, exterior view from the east showing lantern transept (before 1150). FOTO MARBURG / ART RESOURCE

mature Romanesque buildings. Built on the ambulatory and radiating chapel scheme, it is a three-story building with a tribune elevation and is entirely vaulted. The nave is covered by a ribbed barrel vault buttressed by the quadrant vaults over the tribunes and carried by walls supported on compound piers. The presence of a clerestory under the vaults indicates that the problem of direct lighting, as well as fireproof covering, had been solved at St. Étienne. (See illustration at "Gothic Architecture.")

Auvergne. The most clearly defined and consistent regional variant of Romanesque architecture is found in Auvergne. The major Romanesque buildings of St. Nectaire (*ca.* 1080), St. Saturnin (first half of the twelfth century), Orcival (begun *ca.* 1100), Notre-Dame-du-Port at Clermont-Ferrand (first half of the twelfth century), Issoire (*ca.* 1130–1150), and St. Julien at Brioude (twelfth century) are so similar that the description of St. Nectaire will suffice to identify the regional style.

St. Nectaire is a cruciform basilica with an ambulatory and three radiating chapels to the east. The nave features a two-story elevation consisting of a nave arcade and a tribune. Auvergnat Romanesque buildings lack clerestories to provide direct illumination of the nave. This is perhaps due less to structural timidity than to a response to the often cool climate of the region.

To the west, St. Nectaire has a two-towered entrance complex with a tribune across the interior of the facade. The church is covered by a barrel vault. Neither the wall nor the vault surface have regular protruding elements and this results in a non-bay-divided nave, typical of the region but highly atypical for Romanesque in general. The aisles, divided by bays, are covered by groin vaults. The tribunes are quadrant vaulted, providing buttressing for the high vault.

The treatment of the crossing is one of the most diagnostic features of Auvergnat style. The crossing is covered by a dome on squinches. Above, on the exterior, there is a tower over the crossing. On either side of the crossing, the aisles are raised in height to provide windows above the roofs of the transept arms. These windows, along with openings above the choir vault in the east wall of the crossing, dramatically illuminate this area of the church. The Auvergnat crossing, with raised flanking bays to either side, is called a lantern transept.

The exterior of the east end of St. Nectaire, as well as of the other related buildings, is decorated with polychrome tile work recalling Islamic ornament. The source for this decorative scheme is to be found in Spain, an area well known through pilgrimages across the Pyrenees. This use of Islamic motifs relates the Auvergnat churches to Romanesque buildings in the Velay, the area just east of Auvergne. In particular, the cathedral at Le Puy (largely twelfth century) and the chapel of St. Michel de l'Aiguilhe (twelfth-century entranceway) in the same city make extensive use of Islamic devices, including polychromy, triple-cusped arches, octagonal domed vaults, and even *kūfī* inscriptions. In this connection, it should be mentioned that the first recorded pilgrimage from France to Santiago de Compostela left Le Puy under the leadership of Bishop Godescalc in 951.

Western and southwestern France. The west of France had seen considerable architectural activity in the pre-Romanesque period. While many important churches of the tenth and early eleventh centuries have been lost, for example St. Martin I and

ROMANESQUE ARCHITECTURE

II at Tours (from *ca.* 903 and 998, respectively), and St. Nicolas and the cathedral at Angers (*ca.* 1010–1020, *ca.* 1015–1025), several structures, late Carolingian and Ottonian in style, survive. These include St. Généroux (mid tenth century), Autrèche (tenth century), and Cravant (early tenth century), all in the Loire Valley. More important is the church of St. Philibert-de-Grandlieu, which had a primitive echelon apse as early as 814–817. The extant church has a nave (*ca.* 1000) with archaic compound supports, cruciform in shape, bay division, and a wooden roof.

In the Romanesque period, this large area produced two distinct architectural styles. The first style, centered around Poitiers, is exemplified by a series of hall churches, churches in which the side aisles are roughly the same height as the nave. These churches have high nave arcades that directly carry the nave vaults with no intervening stories. In this group, ribbed barrel vaults, sometimes pointed in profile, are typical. The aisles are covered either by groin vaults or quadrant vaults. While not allowing direct illumination of the nave, the light filtering through from the exterior aisle walls is maximized by the tall nave arcades. To the east, the Poitevin group usually has an ambulatory and radiating chapels. To the west, the facade consists of a richly decorated screen which usually masks the interior configuration of the church behind. Typical examples of this group include Notre-Dame-la-Grande at Poitiers (*ca.* 1130–1145), St. Jouin de Marnes (*ca.* 1095–1130), and Aulnay (second half of the twelfth century).

The second western French group of Romanesque churches is centered in Périgord. The churches of this group are generally aisleless with radiating chapels opening directly off the apse to the east. Their most distinctive feature is their covering, which consists of a series of domes covering the building, bay by bay. These domes are carried on pendentives in the Byzantine fashion instead of on squinches in the Islamic manner. The Byzantine style was most likely transmitted to France through S. Marco in Venice (1063–1094). Included in this group are St. Étienne-de-la-Cité at Périgueux (begun *ca.* 1100), the cathedral at Angoulême (begun *ca.* 1105), Fontevrault (begun *ca.* 1115) in the Loire Valley (the northernmost example), Souillac (*ca.* 1130), and St. Front at Périgueux (*ca.* 1120), which is built on a Greek-cross plan in direct emulation of S. Marco.

Southern France. Southern French Romanesque

Angoulême Cathedral, nave (begun *ca.* 1105). © ARCH. PHOT., PARIS / S.P.A.D.E.M. / ARS, NY 1987

architecture continued the traditions of the area's important pre-Romanesque style. Throughout the Romanesque period the architecture of this region remained much less evolved than its counterpart in Burgundy, Auvergne, or Normandy, for example. In several respects, much southern French Romanesque resembles the Poitevin style, as both are characterized by the hall church format with no clerestory, naves covered by ribbed barrel vaults, and aisles often quadrant vaulted. In the south, typical examples are the cathedral at Elne (1042–1068) and St. Trophîme at Arles (*ca.* 1170–1180). Several monuments in southern France, particularly in Provence, are aisleless, as at St. Gabriel (mid twelfth century), Montmajour (*ca.* 1117–1153), and the cathedrals at Avignon (*ca.* 1140–1160) and Orange (late twelfth century).

Another distinctive feature of the Provençal group is the facade design that consists of a gable over an arch carried on columns. These facades, strongly Roman in flavor, exist at St. Restitut (twelfth century), St. Trophîme at Arles, St. Gabriel, and the cathedral at Avignon. The triple-arched facade of St. Gilles-du-Gard (begun 1130's) also recalls Roman antiquity, being particularly close to triumphal arch design. (See illustration at "Renais-

St. Étienne, Caen, west facade (*ca.* 1100). FOTO MARBURG / ART RESOURCE

sances and Revivals.") The presence of numerous Roman remains in Provence—at Arles, Nîmes, Orange, and Vaison-la-Romaine, and elsewhere—undoubtedly provided the inspiration for these facades.

Normandy. In the development of medieval architecture, Norman Romanesque plays a critical role. Not only is it one of the earliest regional variants to reach maturity, but it also anticipates much of the formal vocabulary of early Gothic architecture. By 1050, the essential features of Norman Romanesque had been defined at the abbey churches of Notre-Dame at Bernay (1017–1055), Mont-Saint-Michel (1024–1084), and Notre Dame at Jumièges (1037–1066). Norman builders used both the echelon apse, as at Bernay and in the original plan of St. Étienne at Caen (ca. 1063–early twelfth century), and the ambulatory plan, sometimes without radiating chapels (Notre Dame at Jumièges) and sometimes with them (Mont-Saint-Michel). Norman Romanesque also employed two different elevations, a three-story elevation with a triforium at the intermediate level (Mont-Saint-Michel and La Trinité at Caen, from *ca.* 1062) and a three-story elevation with a tribune (Jumièges and St. Étienne at Caen). While none of the Norman buildings originally had vaulted naves, Norman wall structure was extremely innovative. In particular, the increasing complexity of compound piers, the alternation of nave supports, and the piercing of a passageway within the thickness of the wall, at clerestory level, should be noted. This last feature, marking increased skeletonization of the wall, was critical for the advent of early Gothic design. The clerestory passage first appeared in the transepts of Bernay and Jumièges about the mid eleventh century and at St. Étienne, Caen, was extended around the entire building before the start of the twelfth century.

St. Étienne typifies the precocious character of Romanesque architecture in Normandy. Not only did it possess the above-named features, but the nave elevation, consisting of three superimposed arcades of approximately equal height, anticipates Gothic design in its reduction of masonry surface. Further, the facade of St. Étienne (*ca.* 1100) is the earliest harmonic, two-towered facade, a design which reveals the interior elevation on the exterior and which omits the upper chambers over the central portal so that the nave rises to its full height immediately inside the door. This is a rejection of the long-dominant westwork idea, still found in Normandy at Notre-Dame, Jumièges. Finally, between 1128 and 1135, the first true sexpartite rib vaults were added over the alternating supports of St. Étienne's nave, replacing the original wooden roof. Thus in 1135 St. Étienne had sexpartite vaults, alternation of support, compound piers, a harmonic, two-towered facade, an opening of the wall in elevation, and a voiding of the wall in the thickness resulting from the use of the clerestory passage. All of these features are important concepts in the vocabulary of early Gothic architecture.

Pilgrimage road churches. The above variants of Romanesque architecture are geographically defined. Interregional—even international—groups of monuments also existed, however. One of these developed along the roads that led to Santiago de Compostela in northwestern Spain, the most important pilgrimage site during this period. Five closely related buildings belonged to this group: St. Martin at Tours (second half of the eleventh century), St. Martial at Limoges (second half of the eleventh

 ROMANESQUE ARCHITECTURE

St. Étienne, Caen, nave (*ca.* 1063–after 1100). PHOTO: JAMES AUSTIN

Fontenay, abbey church, nave (*ca.* 1139–1147). © ARCH PHOT., PARIS / S.P.A.D.E.M. / ARS, NY 1987

century), Ste. Foi (St. Foy) at Conques (*ca.* 1050–1130), St. Sernin at Toulouse (begun 1077), and Santiago de Compostela (from 1075). Tours and Limoges are no longer extant. All five churches employed the ambulatory and radiating chapel system and had small apses opening off the east walls of the transept arms. All probably had two-story elevations with quadrant vaulted tribunes and ribbed barrel vaults over the naves. Aisles, doubled at Tours and Toulouse, and ambulatories were groin vaulted. As the chronologies of these buildings are not entirely clear, it is difficult to ascribe primacy to any one building in the development of this type. The pilgrimage roads, to Jerusalem and Rome as well as to Santiago, provided channels for the dissemination of Romanesque art and architecture, helping to make it a truly international style, the first in Europe since the fall of the Roman Empire.

Cistercian architecture. The architecture of the Cistercian order, developed in France, was the other interregional and international variant. Much of its development comes late in the Romanesque period, paralleling the beginnings of Gothic architecture. The Cistercians held rigid ideas, closely regulated, about architecture, and as a result, their churches are extremely close in design. Cîteaux (*ca.* 1125–1150), Clairvaux (from 1133), Pontigny (from 1140), and Fontenay (*ca.* 1139–1147) are all characterized by simple elevations of two stories. Typically, naves are covered by ribbed, pointed barrel vaults. The Cistercians favored a squared-off variety of the echelon apse plan in their early buildings but subsequently adopted the ambulatory and radiating chapel system. By decree, the buildings were void of almost all decoration.

The most important aspect of Cistercian architecture is the order's early acceptance of rib vaulting, first used in their conventual buildings—chapter houses, refectories, and others. This established a taste for a unified series of bays covered by identical vaulting units, just as the groin vaults at Vézelay had done. By the third quarter of the twelfth century, the Cistercians were commonly employing rib vaults for the covering of their churches' naves. Contemporary with the use of rib vaults in early Gothic buildings, these Cistercian vaults, as well as the order's use of the pointed arch, have resulted sometimes in the designation of Cistercian architecture as "half-Gothic."

From its origins in France, the Cistercian style spread to all corners of Europe, from Sweden to Portugal and from England to Eastern Europe.

ENGLISH ROMANESQUE

Romanesque architecture was introduced to England during the reign of Edward the Confessor (1042–1066) at Westminster Abbey (1045–1065). Prior to that, architecture in the British Isles had adhered to a non-bay-divided late-Saxon style. Although Edward's Westminster is only partially known through excavation, enough has been recovered to identify the building as a strongly Norman-influenced structure. It was the Conquest of 1066, however, that provided the major impetus for Romanesque architecture in England as numerous churchmen, brought from Normandy by William the Conqueror, sought to establish familiar surroundings in their new land. Among extant buildings in Normandy, St. Étienne at Caen and Notre Dame at Jumièges seem to have been the most important sources in this development. This is not unexpected, since those two monuments were closely linked with the Norman ruling family in an area where church and state were extremely interconnected.

In plan, English buildings employed both the ambulatory of Jumièges, for example at Norwich (begun 1096), and the echelon apse of Caen, as at Durham (begun 1093). The three-story elevation with tribune was favored, but the proportions of the three floors varied. Winchester (from 1079) and Peterborough (from 1118) had equal tripartite division of nave walls, as at Caen, while churches such as Durham had tribunes and clerestories that were reduced in height. Compound nave supports, as at Caen, were common in English Romanesque building (Durham and Norwich). At Durham there is alternation of support, which uses the Jumièges system of alternating piers with columns. The clerestory of most of these major post-Conquest buildings features the Norman clerestory passage, underlining the importance of Norman design for England. The predilection for geometric decoration and a tower over the crossing also clearly recall a Norman heritage.

There are, however, important indigenous developments in English Romanesque architecture. Included among these is the horizontal extension of many English churches manifested by the increased lengths of both naves and chevets—the western and eastern arms on either side of the crossing. This increase in length, resulting in enlarged interior space, may be partially in response to the necessities of the dual program of several English Romanesque churches that were at once cathedrals and monasteries (for example, Durham and Norwich). More important for the continuing development of medieval architecture were English experiments with rib vaulting. These began at Durham in the choir aisles (*ca.* 1096). The choir itself was rib vaulted by 1104 and the north transept arm by 1110. The south transept arm and nave of Durham were rib vaulted by 1133. While tenuous in form, these vaults clearly showed the potential of this form for covering high, wide spaces. The Durham vaults, particularly those in the choir and nave, and the rib vaults inspired by Durham, for example at St. Étienne, Caen, mark the end of Romanesque vaulting experiments and the introduction of a feature crucial to Gothic developments.

ITALIAN AND SICILIAN ROMANESQUE

Italian Romanesque architecture, while not as important in the overall development of medieval architecture as that of France or England, offers several interesting regional variants. During the Romanesque period, Italy also served as a transmitter of Byzantine architectural forms to the West through the agency of S. Marco in Venice.

Lombardy. Lombardy had formed part of the important southern tier of pre-Romanesque architecture. The small, barrel-vaulted structures of this style imparted an early interest in masonry covering to the region in the Romanesque period. While it does seem likely that rib vaults appeared in Lombardy at an early date, perhaps as early as about 1040 at Sannazzaro Sesia and certainly by the 1070's and 1080's, the importance of these vaults has been overemphasized. Their form, domed up, their geographical distance from the heartland of early Gothic in the Île-de-France area around Paris, and the lack of other features in these Lombard churches, all of which show a distinct relationship to Gothic style, argue against their importance. S. Ambrogio at Milan is a case in point.

S. Ambrogio is a large, transeptless basilica whose three eastern apses date from the ninth century. To the west, a large atrium precedes the church. The lack of a transept and the presence of a forecourt recall the strong Early Christian heritage of the Italian peninsula. Opinion differs as to the

Durham Cathedral, nave (1093–1133). PHOTO: WIM SWAAN

date of the main body of the church, but it seems likely that it dates from the last two decades of the eleventh century. The three domed-up rib vaults of the nave, although sometimes dated with the nave walls, are almost certainly a result of rebuilding after an earthquake in 1117. (By this date the choir and north transept rib vaults at Durham were in place.) Further, their form is more closely allied to early Gothic rib vaults. (See illustration at "Narthex.")

Other Lombard churches of significance include S. Sigismondo at Rivolta d'Adda (*ca.* 1100), Parma Cathedral (twelfth century), and S. Abbondio at Como (*ca.* 1063–1095), a building which while wooden roofed owes its character to a combination of Early Christian and Lombard pre-Romanesque traditions.

Central Italy. No area remained as close to its Early Christian architectural heritage as central Italy. A number of buildings in this area, while coeval with mature Romanesque structures elsewhere, are Early Christian in much of their formal character. Examples of this archaizing variant include S. Clemente in Rome (*ca.* 1100) and the Pisa

ROMANESQUE ARCHITECTURE

S. Miniato, Florence, nave (*ca.* 1062). PHOTO: WIM SWAAN

Cathedral (from 1063), neither of which have naves divided by bays. S. Clemente, in particular, is close to the flat-walled, wooden-roofed, columnar basilicas of the Early Christian period. Pisa Cathedral, while more complicated in plan and more plastic in the treatment of the walls, is, nevertheless, a building dominated by the conservative recall of a long-standing tradition.

S. Miniato al Monte at Florence (*ca.* 1062) is an interesting blend of tradition and innovation. An Early Christian basilica in most of its aspects, it has, however, rudimentary bay division in the nave created by use of compound piers, which alternate with columns—two columns flank either side of each pier—and carry diaphragm arches crossing the nave.

The eleventh-century abbey church at Monte Cassino (dedicated 1071), destroyed during World War II, was perhaps the most important building in this region. While the plan of the church depended on Early Christian antecedents, in particular Old St. Peter's in Rome, the building may have had innovative vaults constructed with pointed arches. It has been suggested that these vaults provided the inspiration for the influential pointed barrel vaults of Cluny III.

Apulia and Sicily. The impetus for the construction of Romanesque architecture in southern Italy came in the mid eleventh century with the arrival of the Norman conquerors. Despite the presence of the Normans, the Romanesque architecture of Apulia has less to do with architecture in Normandy than with indigenous Italian models, in the case of Apulia, and with Byzantine and Islamic influence in Sicily.

In Apulia, S. Nicola at Bari (mid 1080's–1196) serves as a paradigm for the regional Romanesque style. Its design is primarily a mixture of other Italian styles. The plan, contained within a rectangular perimeter wall, looks to Lombardy, as does the rudimentary bay division of the central nave divided into two bays, each consisting of three arches, and the crypt. The tripartite nave elevation, with an intermediate tribune, is closest to central Italian prototypes, such as Pisa Cathedral, although a distant echo of Normandy can perhaps be discerned. The wooden roof of S. Nicola can be related to Pisa and central Italy in general. The facade, with paired towers projecting beyond the plane of the west wall enclosing the nave and flanking aisles, vaguely recalls the porch front of St. Nicolas at Caen (from *ca.* 1083) but is closer to the Lombard design of S. Ambrogio in Milan and Parma Cathedral. Apulian Romanesque buildings based on S. Nicola at Bari include the cathedrals of Trani (from 1098), Bari (from *ca.* 1156), Bitonto (from *ca.* 1175), and Ruvo (twelfth–thirteenth centuries).

The Romanesque architecture in Sicily exudes an exotic flavor created by the mixture of local Islamic and Byzantine styles with Romanesque elements and a lingering Early Christian tradition. While Cefalù Cathedral (from 1131) clearly reflects this Sicilian eclecticism, the late Romanesque cathedral at Monreale (begun 1174) sums up the style best.

The plan of Monreale, in its general features, recalls the plan of S. Nicola at Bari and thus evokes a Romanesque style. The nave walls are planar with crisply punched, undecorated clerestory window openings. The nave walls are carried on simple columnar supports. The resultant configuration, without bay division, closely suggests Early Christian basilican architecture. Decorative motifs used on the interior are derived from both Byzantine and Muslim sources.

The elaborate system of interlocking arcades of pointed arches that decorates the exterior of the east end is ultimately Islamic in origin, although interlocked arcades of a simpler design are used also in late Anglo-Norman Romanesque decoration.

SPANISH ROMANESQUE

Spain, especially Catalonia, like Provence and Lombardy, had formed part of the important southern tier of pre-Romanesque architecture. As in those other areas, this style was a major contributing force in the development of the local mature Romanesque style. The Catalan churches of S. Pere de Roda (from *ca.* 1020), S. Vincente de Castillo at Cardona (*ca.* 1020–1040), and S. Pons de Corbera at Llobregat (*ca.* 1080) typify this development. All are solidly built masonry structures with complete bay division on the interior accomplished by compound supports carrying ribbed barrel vaults. Elevations are simple with no clear horizontal division into stories. The latter two buildings have direct illumination of the nave provided by clerestory windows. On the exterior, the churches are bay divided by flat pilasters connected at the top by arched corbel tables, a decorative motif carried over from the pre-Romanesque style. The cathedral of Seo de Urgel (1131–1175) is a late monument in the Catalan Romanesque style.

Spain also drew on other sources of inspiration in the development of Romanesque architecture. Moorish architecture, which had influenced pre-Romanesque Mozarabic Christian buildings, such as S. Miguel de la Escalada (*ca.* 912) and Santiago de Peñalba (from 919), continued to color the Spanish Romanesque in the eleventh and twelfth centuries. The strongest influence appears in the so-called Mudéjar buildings of the late eleventh century and later. These Christian buildings are partially Moorish in construction technique and style. They are built of brick, are usually wooden roofed, and make frequent use of cusped and pointed arches in their decorative schemes. S. Tirso at Sahagún (twelfth century) is one of the major monuments of Mudéjar Romanesque.

Northern Spain, crossed by the pilgrimage route to Compostela, was especially open to French architectural influence. (The church at Santiago de Compostela has already been discussed in this regard.) To a lesser extent, the Cluniac church of S. Salvador at Leyre (eleventh century), the cathedral at Jaca (mid eleventh century), S. Isidoro at León (1054–1067 and early twelfth century), and S. Martín at Fromista (late eleventh century) all show a marked relationship to French prototypes.

Late in the Romanesque period, an interesting group of distinctive churches was built in western Spain. These buildings, including the cathedrals of Zamora (1152–1174) and Salamanca (*ca.* 1200) and the church at Toro (from 1160), feature ribbed domes under complexly decorated lantern towers. Both French, particularly Poitevin, and Moorish influences are blended in these buildings with an eclecticism typical of much Spanish Romanesque architecture.

GERMAN ROMANESQUE

Germanic territory, which in the Romanesque period included present-day Holland, Belgium, and Switzerland, long remained faithful to the architectural traditions established in the pre-Romanesque period by Ottonian architecture. Well into the eleventh century and even later the dominant type of church was the wooden-roofed basilica with a simple nave elevation, no bay division, and, often, multitowered massing, including a westwork. Ste. Gertrude at Nivelles (mid eleventh century), the abbey church at Alpirsbach (*ca.* 1095), and St. Godehard at Hildesheim (1133–1172) characterize the group. The original wooden-roofed design of the abbey church at Maria Laach (1156) also follows this scheme closely, except that the nave supports have half columns placed against pilasters, creating full Romanesque bay separation. All of these buildings are decorated on the exterior by extensive use of the arched corbel tables, which had made an early appearance in the southern tier of pre-Romanesque architecture.

Cluny II was an important influence on German architecture of the Romanesque period. This holds true particularly for buildings of the Congregation of Hirsau, a congregation based on the Customs of Cluny. The churches in Hirsau itself, St. Aurelius (rebuilt beginning in 1120) and the destroyed church of Sts. Peter and Paul (1082–1091), are exemplary in this regard.

One of the most important developments in German Romanesque architecture took place at Speyer Cathedral. Originally started about 1030, Speyer was completed around 1061. It is a basilica of immense size with an overall length of approximately 435 feet (133 m) and a nave about 235 feet (72 m) long and about 45 feet (14 m) wide, almost as wide as Beauvais, the largest High Gothic church. The nave was originally wooden roofed and the nave walls had bay division, an early and rare appearance of this Romanesque characteristic in Germany. Bay division was accomplished by half

Speyer Cathedral, nave (11th and 12th centuries). PHOTO: FRANZ KLIMM, SPEYER

columns attached to the nave wall surfaces. These half columns rose into the clerestory level of the two-storied elevation, where they carried arches framing the clerestory windows. Above the windows rose a short section of wall, without bay division, carrying the wooden roof.

The nave of Speyer Cathedral was groin vaulted around 1100. To accomplish this, every other support in the nave was elaborated by the addition of a pilaster behind the half column. This created a system of approximately square double bays. While the exact date of the vaulting cannot be established, the high groin vaults at Speyer probably antedate those at Vézelay; as at Vézelay, the nave aisle was also groin vaulted, creating a uniform covering scheme. Whatever their date, the scale of Speyer's nave vaults is unprecedented, cresting at about 107 feet, the highest Romanesque nave vault ever built. The overall dimensions of Speyer's nave thus equal or surpass those of many later Gothic churches.

One group of German churches employed a plan different from the two predominant Romanesque types already discussed. The transept arms of these churches have rounded ends creating a trefoil configuration with the apse. This plan enjoyed particular popularity in Cologne, where it was used at St. Mary in Capitol (*ca.* 1040–1069), Great St. Martin (from 1185), the Church of the Apostles (begun *ca.* 1190), and St. Gereon (*ca.* 1191). While it has been suggested that the ultimate source for this plan was the Early Christian church of S. Lorenzo in Milan, an immediate source may have been the trefoil chevet east of the transept at Mainz Cathedral (first half of the eleventh century). The trefoil configuration was also popular in contemporary, nearby early Gothic monuments, such as the east end of the cathedral of Notre Dame at Tournai (*ca.* 1165) and the French cathedrals of Notre Dame at Noyon (from *ca.* 1150) and Notre Dame at Soissons (1176).

Mention must also be made of the nave at Tournai (*ca.* 1110). Originally wooden roofed, the nave features four stories—a triforium has been inserted between the tribune and the clerestory. While this piling-up of stories is anticipatory of early Gothic architecture, as can be seen in the chevet of Tournai itself, the overall character of the elevation looks back to the Ottonian tradition, as there is no bay division.

In Switzerland, the influence of Burgundy, lying immediately to the west, was strong. In particular, the influence of Cluny II can be felt in such major monuments as Payerne (*ca.* 1040–1100) and Romainmôtier (first half of the eleventh century and later).

SPREAD OF THE ROMANESQUE

While the above-mentioned countries saw the most extensive building and most important developments in the Romanesque period, the style spread much farther, affecting Christian architecture across the entire length and breadth of Europe and the British Isles and in the Holy Land, where the style was carried by pilgrims and crusaders. In general, the Romanesque architecture that developed around the periphery of the European heartland tended to reflect the style of the nearest major regional style. Thus, the architecture of the Dalmatian coast relied heavily on the Italian Romanesque. The cathedral of Zadar, for example, has echoes of Lombard and Apulian Romanesque as well as some features that seem to recall the central Italian style of Pisa. Not dedicated until 1285, Zadar typifies the late date of many of these more provincial monuments.

ROMANESQUE ARCHITECTURE

In Scandinavia, German influence is primary in the major buildings. The Romanesque parts of Roskilde Cathedral (*ca.* 1068–1088) in Denmark and Lund Cathedral (*ca.* 1135–1146) in Sweden are the most significant examples. Lund is very close in most regards to Speyer Cathedral, although some of the decoration finds its source in Lombardy, the presumed home of the architect of Lund, Master Donatus. In smaller Scandinavian masonry churches, some influence is felt from the Saxon churches of England, reflecting perhaps the presence of missionaries from the British Isles. The cathedral of Gamla Uppsala (*ca.* 1134–1150) in Sweden typifies this relationship.

While proximity to established centers was the major factor determining the particular variants of Romanesque architecture along the frontiers of Europe, there were other agents for the dissemination of the style to these regions. The monastic orders, particularly the Cistercians, carried their special brand of Romanesque with them. Cistercian churches directly dependent on French monuments can be seen in Sweden at Alvastra (*ca.* 1235–1260), in Portugal at Alcobaça (1158–1223), in Hungary at Kercz (beginning in 1202), and in Poland at such monastic churches as Lekno (1153).

The Romanesque architecture of the Holy Land was markedly French in flavor, a result of the considerable French presence there. Although much altered, the additions to the Holy Sepulcher in Jerusalem (1149) are the most important manifestations of the style. The crusaders added a transept and ambulatory with radiating chapels to the complicated extant monument. The path of influences, however, went both ways. The Knights Templars, or Poor Knights of Christ and the Temple of Solomon, a religious order set up to protect pilgrims to the Holy Land, developed a characteristic architectural style meant to recall the Dome of the Rock, next to which stood their headquarters in Jerusalem. The chief characteristic of Templars' Romanesque is the polygonal central plan. The order built churches on this plan throughout Europe. Examples include the Convento do Cristo at Tomar in Portugal (*ca.* 1150–after 1162) and the Templars' church at Laon in France (*ca.* 1160), both of which are transitional between Romanesque and Gothic.

SECULAR ROMANESQUE ARCHITECTURE

The above discussion has necessarily focused on religious architecture, inasmuch as the concept of Romanesque style was developed on the basis of church design. The contemporary domestic and military buildings are but poorly known. Very little has survived, and what does exist has usually been altered radically. Surviving buildings suggest that there were affinities between secular and religious architecture in the period, primarily the use of similar decorative motifs and a predilection for sturdy masonry construction. Domestic architecture is represented by several two and one half-story buildings which survive in heavily rebuilt form at Cluny (second half of the twelfth century), a three-story house at St. Gilles-du-Gard in Provence (late twelfth century), and the Frankenturm at Trier in Germany (*ca.* 1050), a tower house. These buildings, however, should perhaps be seen as exceptional, since most domestic architecture was of wood.

The walls surrounding the town of Vézelay, those enclosing Mont-Saint-Michel, and the crusader castle at Krak des Chevaliers in Syria (*ca.* 1200) typify military architecture constructed during the Romanesque era. At Krak des Chevaliers, there is a small aisleless chapel with a pointed, ribbed barrel vault, and the ribs are carried on attached half columns which provide bay division. The chapel is fully Romanesque in a style closely suggesting that of southern France.

BIBLIOGRAPHY

John Beckwith, *Early Medieval Art* (1964), 153–218, a general study of medieval art that contains a short but interesting section on Romanesque architecture, and a summary bibliography with further excellent bibliographical material in the footnotes. Alfred W. Clapham, *English Romanesque Architecture,* 2 vols. (1930/1934), although occasionally out of date, remains the single best study of Romanesque architecture in England. His *Romanesque Architecture in Western Europe* (1936) is a good but somewhat dated general handbook with good plans and photographs. Kenneth J. Conant, *Carolingian and Romanesque Architecture 800–1200,* 4th rev. ed. (1978), the best general textbook available, although the author shows a strong bias in favor of developments in Burgundy, with good illustrations and bibliography. Henri Focillon, *Art of the West in the Middle Ages,* Donald King, trans., I (1963), 17–101, originally published in 1938; the section on architecture in this general volume remains one of the most succinct statements about Romanesque architecture, with good bibliography.

Pierre Héliot, *Du carolingien au gothique: L'évolution de la plastique murale dans l'architecture religieuse du nord-ouest de l'Europe (IXe–XIIIe siècle)* (1966); dealing primarily with northern French architecture, this essay is critical and innovative from a methodological

ROMANESQUE ART

viewpoint. Hans Erich Kubach, *Romanesque Architecture* (1975), a lavishly illustrated volume containing excellent plans, sections, and photographs, also a convenient chronological chart and good bibliography are included; the text is idiosyncratic and possibly confusing to students. Gustav Kunstler, *Romanesque Art in Europe* (1973), largely a picture book, but the photographs are above-average in quality and adequate information is given in the extended captions accompanying the photographs. Whitney S. Stoddard, *Art and Architecture in Medieval France* (1966, rev. ed. 1972), 3–90, the best short treatment of Romanesque architecture in France. J. J. M. Timmers, *A Handbook of Romanesque Art*, Marian Powell, trans. (1976), a convenient collection of plans, photographs, and maps.

Eric G. Carlson

[See also **Apse Echelon; Basilica; Bay System; Chevet; Church, Types of; Clerestory; Cluny, Abbey Church; Construction: Building Materials; Crusader Art and Architecture; Durham Cathedral; Gothic Architecture; Krak des Chevaliers; Masons and Builders; Monte Cassino; Mozarabic Art; Mudéjar Art; Pisa Cathedral; Pre-Romanesque Architecture; Romanesque Art; S. Marco, Venice; Santiago de Compostela; Rib; Vault; Westminster Cathedral.**]

ROMANESQUE ART acquired an identity long after that of Gothic art. Recognition began with the study of sculpture. Since it was obvious that Gothic portal designs derived from examples immediately preceding them, analysis led to the Romanesque as a source for the later style. As Romanesque sculptural style was studied, it was primarily French material that was used. Even the great German scholar Wilhelm Voege, who established many of the main directions research was to follow during the later part of the nineteenth century, worked with French sculpture and based his chronology of mid-twelfth-century sculpture on French examples. It was Henri Focillon, however, who had the greatest impact on students in persuading them of the stylistic independence of Romanesque art, again using primarily French examples as normative. Since Focillon taught enthusiastic crowds, not only in France but also in the United States, his influence has been quite pervasive. It is the origin of most present general observations on the nature of Romanesque style, in spite of its bias, and is discussed below.

Another Frenchman, Georges Gaillard, was responsible for extending the system of analysis to Spanish material and for arriving at a compromise among scholars who for nationalistic reasons sought priority of date for Spain or for France. Arthur Kingsley Porter, an American, brought to the explanation of the evolution of the Romanesque at pilgrimage sites across southern France and northern Spain the evidence amassed by scholars interested in the chansons de geste.

Other scholars, particularly such Frenchmen as Robert de Lasteyrie and Marcel Aubert, held a position on the chronological evolution of the style that might be called orthodox. Porter questioned the validity of most of the accepted dates in France, Italy, and Spain, causing them to be reexamined. The orthodox manner of dating French Romanesque monuments depended on the date of Abbot Suger's reconstruction of the abbey church of St. Denis, near Paris, whose rebuilt choir was consecrated in 1144. Suger wrote an account of the work he accomplished (three treatises: *Ordinatio* [1140/1141]; *Libellus alter de consecratione ecclesiae Dionysii* [1144]; and *Liber de rebus in Administratione . . .* [1144–1149]), an invaluable aid to our understanding of the contemporary attitude toward art. Perhaps the sculptures of the facade portals, as we know them from excellent line drawings of the eighteenth century, were the first sculptures of the Romanesque style of the Île-de-France, from which the French Gothic descended. It was thought that too early a date for the sculptures of St. Sernin at Toulouse, or for the capitals of the abbey of Cluny, would not accord with the point of development reached in 1144 at St. Denis. There was an unstated necessity to make the dates of all other schools as early as possible so that a linear development could be established for the proto-Gothic style of the Île-de-France; this is the chronology Porter opposed.

The major problems of Italian Romanesque sculpture were isolated by such authors as Adolfo Venturi, Émile Bertaux, and Pietro Toesca. From an entirely different geographical direction, the Austrian scholar Josef Strzygowski brought strong consideration of material from the eastern Mediterranean and from Scandinavia, enriching the scope of further investigations. Jurgis Baltrusaïtis followed his fascination with the Near East and did research on Armenian, Georgian, and related cultures. Finally, the period since the late 1950's has seen a great increase in understanding the role of contemporary Byzantine art in terms of the creative centers of the West. The art of Islam and its relations with

ROMANESQUE ART

the countries of Christianity have also received attention, and promise additional scholarly riches for the comprehension of Europe during the eleventh, twelfth, and thirteenth centuries.

The other arts, such as mural painting, manuscript illumination, stained glass, and metalwork, practiced during this period were not distinguished by the great innovations of monumental sculpture or carving in stone. They continued traditional techniques and adapted preceding styles. Among the minor arts, metalwork proved to be the most creative medium. Consequently, in recognition of their achievements, attention will be given to several artists working with metal. More space will be allotted to the discussion of painting in this essay, but most attention will be paid to sculpture as the means through which the Romanesque artist made his greatest contributions.

ROMANESQUE SCULPTURE IN FRANCE

Characteristics. The introduction of large-scale, monumental, figurative sculpture in relief and, to a much lesser extent, of sculpture in the round was a phenomenon of the eleventh century. The life-size or larger-than-life-size portrait of an emperor in marble, bronze, or other important material had last been commissioned in the Western Roman Empire in the fifth century. Statues of goddesses and gods were illegal for purposes of worship after the fourth century. Large reliefs depicting political triumphs, devotional history, or vignettes of everyday life went out of fashion at the same time. Figurative relief of Christian subject matter never disappeared and was used throughout the period from the fifth to the eleventh century. The objects, however, were usually quite small, often tiny, in scale; precious materials were used, such as silver, silver gilt, gold, ivory, and small stones—crystal, agate, lapis lazuli, and steatite; techniques such as engraving, repoussé, champlevé, and enameling were applied. Of what remains, the most splendid examples are reliquaries, crosses, and other religious objects; secular material was destroyed because of practical necessity. The important point is that figurative art in relief sculptural techniques, although not in stone, prospered between the late empire and the rise of feudal states in Western Europe during the period of Romanesque art. By the eleventh century, society in Western Europe had reestablished certain values, aesthetic and moral, to the point that monumental relief sculpture appeared again along with the quest for the third dimension.

Romanesque art north of the Loire and east of the Garonne in France and in England comes from a tradition of painting developed in England from the tenth century on. It is characterized by great visual excitement. Produced at scriptoria and ateliers such as those of Winchester and Canterbury, manuscripts and other easily movable objects spread the style. The earliest artists of these manuscripts had favored copying the agitated line drawings developed by the Carolingian miniaturists of the school of Rheims, in which a sketch line was used to indicate mass in space in accord with the tradition of illumination as practiced in the fifth century. From a mode that had once caught the subtleties of light and shade on objects in space, the Anglo-Saxon artists shifted to a dramatic use of outline for descriptive elements to create a style of extreme liveliness, including extraordinary deformation of figurative representations. Frequently in these manuscript illustrations there is no frame other than the written text and edge of the page. Distortion, rather than articulation, of a figure is the norm. The effect is one of dynamic tension across whatever composition results, integrating not only the figured portion but also the page as a two-dimensional construction.

In contrast with this kind of art is that developed in Germany and its dependencies. Here another kind of Carolingian art was manifest along with an extraordinary conservatism among patrons, who continued the Ottonian styles of the eleventh century far into the thirteenth century. For this reason Germany did not participate so profoundly in the Romanesque experience as did the western and southern sections of Europe. Rather, the Teutonic preferences mitigated its impact as a style.

Focillon's law of the frame, that any figure or object will touch the edges or frame of whatever space is allocated, has been widely accepted. It confirms French Romanesque design principles in sculpture. The observation is suitable to sculpture used as architectural decoration or, put another way, to sculpture that subserves architectural elements, such as capitals, lintels, trumeaux, and moldings. The sculptor given a specific field fills it, usually necessitating a very strong deformation, exaggeration, or minimization. The figure is squashed, stretched, twisted, or turned to fit the space.

Among the earliest stone sculptures in Spain, France, and Italy to survive are those that seem to

ROMANESQUE ART

The Raising of Lazarus, depicted on a capital from the Panteón de los Reyes, S. Isidoro, León, late 11th century. HIRMER FOTOARCHIV, MUNICH

have been commissioned by secular authorities: the capitals in the Panteón de los Reyes, S. Isidoro, León, dated during the third quarter of the eleventh century; the capitals and reliefs of the Portal of the Counts of St. Sernin, Toulouse, late eleventh century; and in Italy about the same time, the reliefs by Master Wiligelmo decorating the facade of Modena Cathedral. The capitals were definitely used to enhance the burial locations of the aristocratic families that ordered them: the kings of León and the counts of Toulouse. The third was probably the result of a gift for the rebuilding of the cathedral of Modena by Countess Matilda of Tuscany (1046–1115), a great landowner and successful political force in central Italy at the time, and a very devout supporter of the papacy in its struggle with the German emperors. The needs of these patrons were met by a new set of artistic possibilities.

Those three examples illustrate the role sculpture can play in different ways—it can be decorative and didactic at the same time. Some of the capitals at León and Toulouse are not solely organized by acanthus leaves or other related ornament but have human figures. The figures have a significance beyond their mere appearance, since in most of these instances they represent a religious episode, presented so as to be understood historically, allegorically, analogically, or anagogically. The dual role of important Romanesque sculptures raises the question of the proper interpretation of Romanesque figural sculpture: Is it to be taken as a meaningful comment on aspects of Christian faith, or to be enjoyed for purely aesthetic reasons, or to be interpreted as a combination of each? Even in the twelfth century, the moral conscience of the age, Bernard of Clairvaux, inveighed against the meaningless excesses of contemporary art whle Abbot Suger of St. Denis in general was pleased to reach the spiritual ultimate from material manifestations, particularly art.

It is appropriate that the subject matter of the capitals at León includes the Raising of Lazarus, images of local saints, and reference to human virtues. These topics suggest a mode of salvation by personal conduct, through the sacrifice of martyrs in the faith, to the miracles of the Son of God. Romanesque public art continued these related topics throughout its existence. There was always an emphasis on "last things." The Vision of Christ in Heaven was expanded or sharpened to depict the Last Judgment and other apocalyptic events. The Spanish example and the French example did not as yet have consistent programs interconnecting their sculptures. The Italian example is more extensive and complex.

France has been organized into schools of sculpture, generally conforming to the geographical divisions set up for the classification of architecture. Not completely satisfactory, nevertheless they are Languedoc, including the pilgrimage road sites; the school of the west, referring to Saintonge and Poitou; Burgundy; Provence; Auvergne; and the Île-de-France.

Languedoc and the pilgrimage road. Stylistically, the Spanish and French sculptures along the northern road from Santiago to the Pyrenees and in the southwest, or Languedoc, of France, belong to a single tradition. There is a plausible theory that stone carvers never lost their capabilities in Spain; Arabic and Mozarabic carved architectural details are cited to prove the argument. The same

ROMANESQUE ART

theory holds for southern France. In the Pyrenees, close to the modern border, are two small parish churches—St.-Genis-des-Fontaines and St.-André-de-Sorède, whose sculptures are dated by inscription to 1020–1021. The lintels of the main portals show Christ flanked by angels or apostles in arcades. This compositional scheme can be traced through earlier ivories as far back as Early Christian or pagan sarcophagi. A long tradition of iconography and artistic convention is responsible for the earliest Romanesque sculptures, just as is the continued technical dexterity of the stonecutters.

The beveled frame of the marble altar of St. Sernin, Toulouse, possibly consecrated by Pope Urban II in 1096, has a similar composition and subject. Its style, however, shows a change, which along with that of the relief sculptures now set in the low wall separating the ambulatory from the choir, belongs to the earliest school of the Romanesque in Languedoc. It is not clear where the ambulatory sculptures of St. Sernin were first used; perhaps on the west facade, perhaps over a cloister portal, or perhaps even as a retable. There is a superb relief of Christ in a mandorla held by tiny figures in the four corners of the rectangular slab. Seated facing front, his right hand raised in a gesture of blessing, he is accompanied, on other marble slabs, by angels and archangels, each under a separate arch on colonnettes. These sculptures will be analyzed to establish in general what the Romanesque sculptural style is and in particular what its manifestations in Languedoc are.

The ambulatory figures are carved *en cuvette,* that is, the area inside the mandorla or arcade is sloped away from the figure, rather like a saucer. The sculptor handled his stone to enhance the visual effect of three-dimensional projection. The central mass of the figure is rounded at the edges as it adheres to the gently curving background. The surface plane is slightly modeled into areas that describe a draped human figure. The drapery, however, is not handled in a way to reveal human anatomy. The schematizations are reminiscent of human form as seen in three-dimensional space but are free from any necessity to show mass in space in a realistic or phenomenal way. The drapery sections are related to the artistic structure that integrates the surface. Interior descriptive lines are incised or made by carving away the stone so they exist in a kind of recess that parallels the lines, frequently making them appear doubled. The backward and forward pull between the planes, between solids and voids, and the contrast between lines and masses develop a visual tension across the composition. This forces the eye of an observer to move constantly instead of remaining stationary. This effect is most typical of Romanesque style in whatever variation or in whatever medium it may be found.

Christ in Majesty. Relief in the ambulatory of St. Sernin, Toulouse, before 1096. PHOTO: JEAN ROUBIER, PARIS

The earliest French portal with sculptures is the Porte de Miègeville, on the south side of the nave of St. Sernin, Toulouse. (See illustration at "St. Sernin.") Its style continues the basic principles established for the ambulatory sculptures and emphasizes an aggressive three-dimensional relief projection. The subject of the tympanum is the Ascension of Christ. On the lintel are the Apostles, turning upward to witness the event. In the spandrels flanking the tympanum are isolated white

The Journey to Emmaus and Doubting Thomas. Relief panels from the cloister of S. Domingo de Silos, *ca.* 11th century. PHOTO: WIM SWAAN

marble figures of St. Peter and St. James, the latter the major saint of the pilgrimage across northern Spain to Santiago de Compostela. Next in line of the great portals of this school are the Puerta del Cordero and the Puerta del Perdón on the south side of S. Isidoro, León, and finally the south transept portal at Santiago itself, the Puerta de las Platerías. The latter incorporates material from the north facade of the transept, already transposed in a jumbled way to the south side in the early twelfth century, as described in the *Pilgrims' Guide to the Way of Saint James*.

Lying slightly south of the pilgrimage road, near Burgos, is the monastery of S. Domingo de Silos. Its cloister is probably of the eleventh century. It is so beautiful it must be mentioned, although historians have not been able to do more than recognize its stylistic isolation. In addition to its early capitals and relief panels are several examples of the last phase of the Romanesque, making the two-storied cloister one of the most attractive monuments of the period.

At Toulouse are the remains of several cloisters, dismantled at the time of the French Revolution but partially saved and now displayed in the Musée des Augustins. Even more famous are the great cloister and the south entrance of the monastery of St. Pierre at Moissac. The size and uniformity of the cloister at Moissac add to its impressiveness. The columns are alternately single and double, although the capitals are double throughout. They carry historiated scenes of the Old and New Testaments, the lives of saints, and so on. Among the earliest of the sculptures are slabs placed against the piers

ROMANESQUE ART

at the corners and in the middle of each walk or side of the cloister. These are very close to the sculptures in the ambulatory of St. Sernin and concur in date. (See illustration at "Moissac.")

The sculptures of the south porch form one of the supreme achievements of Romanesque art. To the search for monumental three-dimensional relief has been added an almost exaggerated striving for intensity of expression. The tympanum subject is Christ in Glory, surrounded by the symbols of the four Evangelists and supported by the Twenty-four Elders of the Apocalypse. The trumeau below and the wall responds are scalloped. The curving edges contrast almost violently with the angularity of the crossed lines that zigzag against the trumeau and the long, uninterrupted lines of the garments of St. Peter and the prophet Isaiah as they shrink back to the outer walls of the porch, away from the entrance. On one side of the deep vaulted bay are complex reliefs in architectural frames with scenes from the life of the Virgin: most prominently the Annunciation and the Visitation facing the Parable of Dives and Lazarus (iconographically parallel to the Incarnation and the Last Judgment). Among other important sculptures related to those at Moissac are particularly those of the abbey church of Souillac (*ca.* 1120–*ca.* 1130) and of the church of Ste. Foy at Conques (completed *ca.* 1130) in the Rouergue.

School of the west. The monuments belonging to the so-called school of the west are Notre-Dame-la-Grande at Poitiers (*ca.* 1130–*ca.* 1145), St. Pierre at Aulnay, and Ste. Eutrope at Saintes (begun 1080's). The architects and sculptors put sculpture all over the facade of Notre-Dame-la-Grande so that it is a single vast composition of relief sculpture. A single subject, the Ascension of Christ, covers the facade of the cathedral of Angoulême (begun *ca.* 1105). Architects preferred to have the voussoirs of the arches of their portals or windows covered with heavily cut relief carving rather than placing the carving on tympana, trumeaux, or capitals, as in Languedoc. The general effect of their buildings is one of great visual activity and monumental scale. It is the ensemble of the display that gives distinctiveness to the school of the west rather than the specific detail.

School of Burgundy. The first major Burgundian sculptural scheme is that decorating the huge capitals which once formed the crown of the ambulatory of the abbey of Sts. Peter and Paul at Cluny (Cluny III). The Benedictine order of Cluny, the

Adoration of the Magi (top), Annunciation, and Visitation. Reliefs from the south porch of St. Pierre, Moissac, *ca.* 1115–1130. GIRAUDON / ART RESOURCE

greatest religious—and perhaps political—force of the eleventh century, apparently did not establish any uniform sculptural style in spite of its preeminence. Except for a general interest in commodious buildings and attractive and informative decoration for the cult structures, Cluny does not seem to have exercised close supervision of the other churches and structures belonging to the extensive Cluniac establishment, unlike the Cistercian order.

The motherhouse at Cluny is now destroyed; the capitals of the ambulatory have been preserved and are displayed in the Musée Ochier at Cluny. They are remarkable from any point of view. Their execution dates from before the consecration of the main apse in 1095 by Pope Urban II. The complicated program of their subjects is concerned with sets of octaves: notes of the plainsong and the virtues, accompanied by scenes of Adam and Eve. The style of carving reflects the dominant architectural preference for flat planes and a strong linear emphasis, probably taken from examples of Roman architecture surviving in the region.

The second phase of Burgundian sculpture, comparable in date, evolution, and importance with the

ROMANESQUE ART

The Ascension. Detail from the west facade of the cathedral of Angoulême, *ca.* 1136. HIRMER FOTOARCHIV, MUNICH

The Third Tone of Music. Capital from the ambulatory of the abbey church of Cluny. Before 1095. Musée Ochier, Cluny. PHOTO: WIM SWAAN

work at Moissac, is the sculptural decorations of the basilica of La Madeleine at Vézelay (1104–1120) and that of Lazarus (St. Lazare) at Autun. It was believed that Mary Magdalen had come to southern France with a group of saints from Palestine. The resting place of the relics of each became a very important pilgrimage site. It is the sculptures of the narthex that make Vézelay a modern pilgrimage site. The ground floor has three entrances. Each has a sculptured tympanum with appropriate lintel and capitals above the columns, supporting the voussoirs. The central portal has a trumeau that reaches into the lintel above. Both physically and metaphorically it connects our mundane space to the divine world. John the Baptist hyphenates the acts of mortals and saints with the Pentecost or Gift of Tongues above a splendid and crowded display of elongated apostles, angels, symbols, and Christ enthroned.

The elongation is ethereal in effect because of the narrowness of each representation, criss-crossed by elegant swirls and patterns of very thin, parallel, light lines describing the garments and their wind-blown contortions. The capitals of the nave columns, placed high against the polychromed transverse ribs, carry historiated scenes, many of them parables from the New Testament, saints' lives, and allegorical subjects. All of them are rigorously fitted to the sharp rectangular and rhomboidal shapes of the three exposed sides of the capitals.

Of equal interest and haunting beauty are the west portal tympanum of St. Lazare, Autun, on which is placed a Last Judgment, and the column capitals decorating the interior. In the Musée Rolin in Autun are the remains of a lintel that held the Fall of Man, once placed over the north transept entrance. The figure of Eve picking the apple with her left hand is stretched out in a reclining position. Slender and long, weaving through stylized vegetation, she is the most seductive woman of Romanesque art. She and the rest of the sculptures at Autun are ascribed to the school of Gislebertus, who placed his name on the tympanum of the west portal, beneath Christ's feet: *Gislebertus hoc fecit.* Nothing more is known about him; there exist no records besides his work. Hypothetically, a career in Burgundy has been worked out for him as an artist whose personal style evolved and who was a member of a shop. As usual, our knowledge of artists in the Romanesque period is severely limited to the specific and often isolated work they signed. Signatures are not rare, which suggests that although we consider the typical Romanesque artist to be anonymous, many were not during their own lifetimes.

School of Auvergne. In Auvergne, the Romanesque churches must have an effect similar to that experienced hundreds of years ago. Wild country, forests, small valleys, poor soil, and sparse population have kept the villages relatively unmolested by modern technology. For the parish churches of these villages, sculptural decoration usually is restricted, on the exteriors, to stringcourses and window embrasures. On the interior, however, series of majestic capitals surround the ambulatories and occasionally also top the wall shafts of the naves. The style is sober and related to that of the school of Languedoc: both develop strongly projecting relief; the figure stylizations for both tend to be somewhat heavy. The Auvergnat facial type cannot be confused with any other: a square jaw and face; eyes drilled so sharply and deeply they seem small and piercing.

At Notre Dame du Port in Clermont-Ferrand, over the south entrance to the church is a large composition divided into compartments by flat straps. It is rather reminiscent of the west portal of Ste. Foy, Conques, but the details of the carvings are strictly Auvergnat.

School of Provence. In southern France, or that part of it called Provence, there developed a type of sculpture more classically conceived than any other in France. Except for a few motifs that might relate to Languedoc or to monuments in Poitou, the traits of the figurative sculptures betray close interest in Roman relief work. In Provence, which was the most Roman of all Gallic provinces, many remains of Roman civilization were above ground in the twelfth century: sarcophagi; public structures such as triumphal arches, amphitheaters, theaters; the whole range of structures needed by a large and rich population. These were observed and the results were incorporated into the sculptures of the facades of St. Trophîme at Arles, the priory church at St. Gilles-du-Gard, and the cloister at St. Trophîme (dated 1180), the most prominent collections of Romanesque work. The dating of these sculptures has been most difficult. They were probably executed sometime around the middle of the twelfth century.

Pentecost relief on the tympanum, with John the Baptist on the trumeau. Central narthex portal of La Madeleine, Vézelay, *ca.* 1132. GIRAUDON / ART RESOURCE

The facades of St. Trophîme and St. Gilles have apostles standing in niches. Their scale is far greater than almost any other reliefs of the period, and each is almost free from the plane behind it. Drapery is arranged to give the impression of anatomical correctness. Nevertheless, the Romanesque principle that composition dominates over representation holds true.

Along with this classicizing type of drapery goes a vocabulary of architectural motifs appropriate to buildings of a similar source. In fact, one of the differentiating characteristics of each of the Romanesque schools is the adaptation of a rich decorative vocabulary derived from the monuments that provided the sources for their figurative styles. What remained of the past in each major geographic region is what was available to the Romanesque sculptor. He was ready to profit by searching, and he found, near to hand, what he needed for his technical development, much as Pablo Picasso and

Eve, depicted on the lintel formerly over the north transept entrance of St. Lazare, Autun. School of Gislebertus, *ca.* 1120–1132. Musée Rolin, Autun. PHOTO: JEAN ROUBIER, PARIS

Georges Braque found "primitive" sculpture in the early twentieth century.

School of the Île-de-France. The sculptures of the facade portals of the abbey of St. Denis, near Paris, as we know them from excellent line drawings of the eighteenth century, were perhaps the first sculptures of the Romanesque style of the Île-de-France, from which the French Gothic descended. Several heads purported to be from St. Denis are in the Walters Art Gallery, Baltimore, and in the Louvre. From St. Denis the atelier of sculptors could have traveled to Chartres, where they executed the sculptures of the west facade of that cathedral and created one of the masterpieces of the Middle Ages. The composition encompasses the three portals and their supporting elements. Each tympanum holds a major theme and contributes to an integrated iconographic scheme. On the right is the Incarnation with events related to the Birth of Christ and the Life of the Virgin. To the left is the Ascension of Christ. In the center, Christ in Glory raises his hand in judgment with the Twenty-four Elders of the Apocalypse as the heavenly witnesses. The capitals present a detailed set of scenes of the lives of St. Anne and the Virgin. The jamb figures are the ancestors of Christ, but the late Middle Ages took them to be the kings and queens of France.

The jamb figures are crushed into the spaces—or, more properly speaking, the widths of the columns—which continue both below and above them. They are absolutely determined by the linearity of the architecture; lines carry from the colonnette bases through the figures to the moldings around the tympana and down the corresponding side. The sculptures are totally subordinated to their architectural function. The bodies are long and narrow, almost tubelike. They are covered by a very fine network of lines. The heads, in contrast with the extreme condensation of the body, are normally proportioned. The eyes stare, unfocused; no emotion tightens the muscles of the face. The figures, caught in the embrasures of the portals, are at peace within themselves. The same serenity pervades the heads as well as the bodies of the figures in the tympana, where more space has

ROMANESQUE ART

Two Apostles. West facade of St. Gilles-du-Gard, mid 12th century. HIRMER FOTOARCHIV, MUNICH

perforce been allotted them. It would be hard to exaggerate the beauty of these sculptures and their influence on the course of art for the next 300 years in Europe.

MINOR ARTS OF THE MEUSE VALLEY

Among the earliest objects to be created using the formulas of Romanesque art and the media of metal techniques were those manufactured in the Meuse Valley of modern Belgium. No distinction was made in the Middle Ages between minor and fine arts. The man who practiced any art was essentially a craftsman, learned in his technical virtuosity but not acquainted with the higher stages of education as then set out. Socially, the artisan began to rise in the social hierarchy when the demands of his art forced him to become educated, as happened in the fifteenth century, and has continued to do so ever since. Three artists who created these objects and excelled in their crafts were Rainer of Huy, Roger of Helmarshausen, and Godefroid of Huy (Godefroid de Clair).

Jamb figures from the west facade of Chartres Cathedral, *ca.* 1145. PHOTO: WIM SWAAN

Rainer of Huy cast the baptismal font for St. Barthélemy, Liège, between 1107 and 1118. The great basin of the font rests on the backs of twelve oxen, here symbolizing the twelve apostles. Metaphorically, it depicts the "molten sea," as did the font in the Temple of Solomon as described in 1 Kings (7:23ff.). The historiated scenes around the

Reliquary of the True Cross (the Stavelot Triptych) incorporating champlevé enamel medallions by Godefroid of Huy, *ca.* 1155, and Byzantine enamels of the 11th century. NEW YORK, PIERPONT MORGAN LIBRARY

vasque are the Baptism of Crato the Philosopher and the Preaching of John the Baptist in the Desert. The cool elegance of the figures is not paralleled at all in France or England. Rainer's reliefs maintain a great deal of Ottonian quality, although he moved toward the Romanesque without completely restructuring his composition in a two-dimensional sense and creating an overall tension. His reticence perhaps is the result of the impact of Byzantine art. (See illustrations at "Mosan Art" and "Rainer of Huy.")

Roger from the abbey of Helmarshausen, on the Weser River, moved closer to the Romanesque style than did Rainer of Huy. He signed and dated the portable silver altar of Sts. Liborius and Kilian (dated 1100; Paderborn Cathedral), commissioned by Bishop Henry of Werl. It is silver embossed with precious stones, filigree, and pearls. (See illustration at "Roger of Helmarshausen.") He also probably executed the silver portable altar on which is depicted the Martyrdom of St. Blaise (at Abdinghof Abbey, Paderborn), which also has copper gilt and openwork niello.

The work of Godefroid of Huy is exemplified by the twelfth-century wings of the portable altar given to the abbey of Stavelot (from *ca.* 1150; New York, Morgan Library). They frame pieces of the True Cross, flanked by Byzantine enamels on the interior field. Godefroid's contribution consists of six medallions of champlevé enamel, copper gilt, silver gilt, engraving, embossing, and precious stones and gems. The full Romanesque style is revealed in the enamels, which have the Story of the True Cross and display the high quality of workmanship for which the Meuse region was and is famous.

ROMANESQUE SCULPTURE IN ITALY

School of Lombardy and Emilia. Modern historians have tended to accept 1117 as the date after which the sculpture of northern Italy should be placed. In that year there was a severe earthquake in the region; contemporary accounts tell of great destruction. Since complete destruction is very unlikely, it is probable that some of the extant examples are earlier. This is particularly true of the four great marble plaques on the west front of Modena Cathedral. A likely time for their execution is before the translation of the body of S. Giminiano, the titular saint of the cathedral, to the new crypt in 1106, and possibly sometime before the new church was started in 1099.

The sculptor of the reliefs of the Modena facade, Master Wiligelmo (Willcgelmus), mentioned himself in an inscription still in place. Another, accompanying plaque has a relief of Jacob Wrestling with the Angel and Truth in Combat with Fraud. The latter's style recalls work done in Languedoc, just as other pieces by Wiligelmo and his shop may be related stylistically and iconographically to work in Provence. The four historiated marble slabs placed horizontally across the facade have scenes from Genesis: the Creation of Man, the Fall of Man, the Chastisement of Man, the Labors of Eve and Adam, the Sacrifices of Cain and Abel, the Death of Abel, and Noah's Ark. Some of the edges of the plaques have been mutilated, proof they were once used in another way. Most of them retain an outer frame consisting of an arcade of round arches supported by colonettes. Borders, columns, and figures are all treated by Wiligelmo as equal in terms of relief projection. These establish the foreground plane. The figures themselves are heavy, awkward, and stumpy—proportions that enhance the third dimension. There is a great deal of empty surface left on the background plane that contrasts with the forward projection of the elements of the composition. The result is a strong, bold composition interpreting the scenes of Genesis.

In addition to these plaques, the sculptor or someone from his shop carved a set of prophets for the inner faces of the jambs. The prophets complete the iconographic scheme of thc facade, which retells the Creation and Fall of Man and his first salvation through Noah. The new salvation through Christ is foretold by the prophets on the jambs. They have the thickset proportions of the figures in the Genesis scenes, but each is enclosed by an architectural frame that seems to cramp him. This creates a contrast between figure as mass and lack of background as space. A tense but silent struggle for free movement occurs. This is typical of the Romanesque school of Lombardy throughout the twelfth century.

The south portal of the cathedral, the Porta dei Principi, opening onto a side aisle, is designed with a single range of voussoirs and a lintel, but no tympanum. The lintel has narrative scenes from the life of S. Giminiano. On the north, the corresponding Porta della Pescheria has a similar decorative arrangement. The lintel has lively scenes from Aesop's fables, though the immediate source might have been the *Roman de Renart*. The theme of the voussoirs also departs severely from customary religious iconography. It is given over to a combat between knights in contemporary armor. To permit no mistake, they bear the names of King Arthur and his knights. It has been a puzzle to students of the Matter of Britain (Matière de Bretagne), the stories of the Round Table, as to when and why this possibly earliest representation of King Arthur appeared in northern Italy. This is one reason the date of the cathedral and its parts has been so scrutinized. The answer for its presence may be that crusaders and pilgrims from the north going to embark at Bari for the Levant popularized the poetic material so much that it was honored by being placed in a prominent position over the north door at Modena. There are other twelfth-century references in the Italian visual arts to the story of Arthur. For example, the floor mosaic at the cathedral of Otranto has knights in combat, identified by inscription; the bishop's throne at the cathedral of Bari has knights on its base.

The second phase of Lombard sculpture depends on the work of the sculptor Niccolò (Nicholaus) da Verona (*fl. ca.* 1135). In contrast with Wiligelmo's style, Niccolò's figures are smaller and their appendages are in proportion to the more slender forms. More persons are in the historiated scenes, and there are more background indications of city or landscape. There are many more decorative details as well. Technically the solids are more rounded and separated from the background plane, and the moldings of the frames are multiplied and set at variance with each other in terms of smooth surface and broken surface covered with simple, broad, usually classically derived motifs.

Niccolò's most important work is at Verona. He carved the tympanum and related sculptures on the porch over the central portal of S. Zeno. (Another Niccolò and another Guglielmo executed the handsome marble reliefs of the Old Testament and the New Testament, which are placed to the left and right of the portal, respectively.) He also carved the tympanum of the cathedral of Verona. For the cathedral of Ferrara, he made his masterpiece. He inscribed his name and the date, 1135, on the work. The church is dedicated to St. George, who appears in the tympanum as a knight in armor killing a dragon with his lance. A superb composition is developed, with the horse and rider slightly off-center and a broken lance thrusting from upper left to lower right toward the dragon. The upper part of the lance projects over the moldings of the inner edge of the tympanum, as do the tip of the saint's

St. George and the Dragon, with scenes from the Life of Christ. Tympanum relief by Niccolò (Nicholaus) da Verona, Ferrara Cathedral, 1135. REPRODUCED FROM *THE ART BULLETIN*, **12**, no. 4 (1930)

head and other parts of the scene. In other words, dragon, horse, and rider are pushed in front of the frame. The background plane is left entirely neutral. The result is a tour de force.

A similar projection of form, this time a violent one, occurs in the handling of the prophets on some of the jambs on either side of the portal. The figures are placed irregularly within the circumference of the individual colonnettes. A deep conch shell backs their heads like a halo. Their feet and limbs are twisted; their arms, taut. They project such an intensity of feeling that they seem to shout the prophecies on their scrolls.

Benedetto Antelami (*fl.* 1150–*ca.* 1233), the third of the great Lombard sculptors, was responsible for the complex decoration of the baptistery at Parma. On a pulpit, conserved in the cathedral, is carved a Deposition inscribed with his name and the date 1178. At this late time, the sculptor was interested in freeing the figure from the background plane and able to do so. There are free-standing statues in rectangular niches at medium height on several sides of the polygonal baptistery. On the interior, his associates and successors placed a rich ensemble of reliefs and free-standing figures, including the Labors of the Months.

School of Tuscany. In Tuscany, figurative sculpture did not appear until the mid twelfth century. The early Romanesque architecture of the Arno Valley reflected classical Roman procedures adapted to an esthetic that was an extremely pure statement of two-dimensionality. Its forms were very linear and decorated with incrustations of white marble articulated by flat bands of dark green, almost black, stone. There was no place for relief sculpture, nor for architectural sculpture except classical moldings along cornice lines of pediments or around doorways and windows. The style changed from the eleventh-century flat walls of S. Miniato al Monte and the baptistery at Florence to the twelfth-century arcaded facades of Lucca and Pisa.

Still, relief sculpture was not used primarily as an adjunct to architecture, in contrast with the practice in France. Instead, except for the lintel, where it frequently occurs, Romanesque sculpture adorned pulpits, fonts, and other types of church furniture. The first example was carved for the cathedral of Pisa by a Guglielmo (*fl. ca.* 1159–1162), not to be confused with the sculptors of Lombardy. He translated an accurate classicizing tendency from architectural decorations, including the human figure, such as the reliefs on the columns flanking the main entrance to the baptistery, into a classicizing, awkward figure style. Guglielmo's manner of carving and his choice of motifs continued in the lower Arno area for some twenty-five years, until another sculptor again submitted to the influence of classical

Fountain house in the cloister adjoining the cathedral of Monreale, 1172–1189. PHOTO: WIM SWAAN

sculpture, this time sarcophagi of the fourth and fifth centuries. This was Biduino (*fl.* 1180–1200), who signed and dated the lintel of S. Cassiano a Settimo in 1180. Christ's Entry into Jerusalem was carved across the lintel. Biduino did at least three lintels using this subject. One is in the Cloisters collection of the Metropolitan Museum in New York. His manner, along with that of Bonnano (*fl. ca.* 1174–1186), who cast the bronze doors of the Porta di S. Ranieri of the south transept of the cathedral of Pisa (1180), lasted until a strong Byzantine influence was manifested in the early thirteenth century.

School of southern Italy and Sicily. Art in the Norman kingdom of southern Italy and Sicily was not a coherent expression of a single culture. Just as the court used the three major languages of the region—Latin, Greek, and Arabic, or the colloquial variations of them—so did the artists draw from different cultural traditions. They did not make an amalgam of them. The great cycles of mosaic decoration in the palaces and churches at Palermo were all Byzantine in inspiration, while architectural sculpture and the decorations of church furnishings were strictly Latin or Romanesque. Decorative details for walls, floors, and moldings frequently reflected Arabic taste. The magnificent abbey cathedral of Monreale, on a narrow plateau above the city of Palermo, displays the independence of each art from the other. The overall effect of the juxtaposition of styles is dazzling.

The cathedral of Monreale dates from the last quarter of the twelfth century. The Corinthian capitals of the nave are Roman antique spoils in excellent condition. In the cloister (dated 1172–1189) adjoining the cathedral to its south, twin

ROMANESQUE ART

colonnettes encrusted with strips of glass mosaic of gold, black, and red support twin capitals of white marble. Many of the more than 100 pairs are historiated with scenes from the Old and New Testaments or from more recent history: the Crusades and the donation of the cathedral to the Virgin by King William II. The fountain house is in the southwest corner; the fountain itself is a chevroned shaft topped with a bulbous mass surrounded by male and female figures performing a classical dance. Many of the capitals of the cloister walks have human figures peering through acanthus leaves, pirouetting at the corners in place of volutes, or engaged in combat. They do not seem to present metaphorical interpretations of religious or historical materials, nor does there seem to be an overall iconographic program.

On the mainland the Gospel and the Epistle pulpits of Salerno Cathedral (1153–1181) are the most interesting sculptural monuments. Other important pulpits, paschal candlesticks, and historiated reliefs are found at Sessa Aurunca, Gaeta, and the chapel of Sta. Restituta in the cathedral of Naples.

ROMANESQUE WALL DECORATIONS

Rome and Italy. Rome is phenomenally rich in twelfth-century mosaic and fresco cycles. It is also phenomenally poor in sculpture. There is no Romanesque sculpture at all unless a fountainhead now placed on the steps to the sanctuary at S. Bartolomeo in all'Isola is of the twelfth century instead of the early eleventh (the reign of Emperor Otto III), as generally believed. The frescoes and mosaics in Rome represent a revival of Early Christian prototypes. Rome was a conservative cultural focal point in the West. In spite of the loss of population since its days as the capital city of an empire, Rome remained urban. In terms of art, it was always true to its visual version of greatness. Its response to the political and economic innovations of the Romanesque period was to replay its moment of world supremacy. Since this coincided with the early Christian period, Rome preferred its own great mosaic and fresco paintings to the relief sculptures of the sarcophagi of the period. Rome was a pilgrimage center for tens of thousands of tourists or religious doing the business of the church. Nevertheless, the specific Roman revival of Early Christian mural styles was not exported. Wall decorations in the rest of Europe followed local prototypes with varying degrees of influence from contemporary Byzantine art.

During the long history of Rome, there were periods of intense activity in architecture and the embellishment of architecture, partially dictated by the political circumstances of the moment. One such period coincides with the economic prosperity brought about by the Carolingians in the ninth century. Another, in the twelfth century, came as the triumphant aftermath of the investiture conflict (1075–1122) and the power balance established among the German empire, the Norman kingdom of Sicily, and the Patrimony of St. Peter. Rome was rebuilt and furbished. Old churches were redone: S. Clemente, Sta. Maria in Cosmedin, Sta. Maria in Trastevere, and SS. Quattro Coronati; new churches were erected: S. Crisogono and S. Bartolomeo in Isola; cloisters were added to SS. Quattro Coronati and S. Paolo fuori le Mure, and campaniles were built throughout the city.

The most luxurious decorations of the twelfth century are the mosaics of the apse of S. Clemente. Their design and iconography return to Petrine and Constantinian traditions. Even the floors at S. Clemente and Sta. Maria in Cosmedin reached back to classical antiquity and were laid out in geometric patterns, with large medallions of porphyry and verde antiqua surrounded by simple interlace of small tesserae of marble and glass. These designs anticipate the type of decorative work used on floors, walls, and church furniture that was known as Cosmati from the Roman family who specialized in their fabrication after 1150.

The new, upper church of S. Clemente was built and constructed after 1110, the lower church having been abandoned after the destruction wreaked by the Normans in 1084. The nave walls of the lower church, however, retain the remains of many frescoes, some dating as far back as the early Christian period. In the late eleventh century a Roman butcher, Beno de Rapiza, is shown as the donor of a famous cycle of mural paintings of the legends of Sts. Alexis and Clement, dating from the period 1085–1115. The fact that the donor belonged to the artisan "class" marks this as one of the earliest appearances of urban nonnoble citizens as patrons of art. The growth of a commercial and artisan "class" in Rome foreshadows a similar situation in France during the thirteenth century, and the gifts by corporations of stained glass windows at Chartres and elsewhere.

The style of the frescoes of the lower church of S.

ROMANESQUE ART

Clemente seems to relate to the kind of work executed at the abbey church of Monte Cassino, the motherhouse of the Benedictine order. Its abbot, Desiderius, rebuilt the abbey church, consecrated in 1071. It was a time of great power and wealth for the abbey, spectacularly and strategically situated on the main inland road between Capua and Rome. Desiderius apparently with deliberation copied aspects of the most venerable churches in Rome: St. John Lateran and Old St. Peter's in the Vatican. Paul the Deacon's account of Desiderius' activities states that he sent monks to Constantinople to supervise the casting of bronze doors for the entrance of the church. Parts of these still exist at Monte Cassino and relate to a large series of eleventh-century bronze doors cast at Constantinople and brought to Italy. In addition, Desiderius sent for artists and materials to execute opus sectile and probably mosaic decorations. The total effect must have been much more splendid than the frescoes completed at his order for the little church of Sant'Angelo in Formis, not far south of the abbey near Capua, where, in the apse, he is shown as the donor of the church, which he offers to the Virgin and the Christ Child surrounded by archangels. The nave at Sant'Angelo in Formis, with its scenes of the Bible, and the west wall, with the Last Judgment, were done in campaigns slightly later than that of the apse. The ensemble is truly Byzantine. Only a slightly more abstract structure controls the design of the panels than would be usual in the Eastern Empire. The sinuous rhythms are somewhat broken; the range of colors is changed.

It is not necessary to trace the introduction of Byzantine elements to Monte Cassino to explain the brilliant renewal of the arts in Italy at this time. Instead, the continuing Byzantine cultural presence in the country is attested by murals in small churches in the south as well as by the vastly imposing cycles of Byzantine mosaic work at the cathedral of Cefalù, the church of the Martorana and the Capella Palatine, both in Palermo, and the cathedral of Monreale. Most of these were executed under the supervision of Greek artists and are paralleled by similar stylistic decorations in Greece and Turkey. To the northeast, Venice, the dominant cultural and economic power, served the same function. Byzantine artists executed enormous mosaic wall decorations in Venice and its dependencies. Byzantine influence would continue to penetrate Italy throughout the twelfth and thirteenth centuries. In Europe, Byzantine influence played a role for the art of painting that classical antiquity did for sculpture.

Wall decoration in Spain. In northeastern Spain many of the small churches of Catalonia have preserved their fresco decorations, particularly those of their apses. These have a lively and expressive style, vigorous and contorted, and typically Romanesque in the breakup of the forms and the resultant contrast of solid and void across the compositions, with no trace of space intruding on the figures. In spite of this strong Romanesque quality, there are murals—for example, the Catalan murals of Sta. María de Mur (now in Boston, Museum of Fine Arts)—that depend greatly on Byzantine prototypes for many of their stylizations. In the Boston murals the facial type of Christ is Byzantine, but the presentation is Romanesque.

The frescoes of S. Clemente de Tahull have been removed from their original positions and taken to the Museo de Arte de Cataluña, an excellent museum housing the great majority of Catalan twelfth-century masterpieces of painting, both mural and panel. The collection of retables or altar frontals is the richest in Europe. Panel paintings, we know from the evidence at the monastery of St. Catherine on Mt. Sinai, were executed throughout the Middle Ages, even during the iconoclastic controversy of the Eastern Roman Empire. Practically none have survived, certainly none in the West after the seventh or eighth century. The collection in Catalonia suggests what treasures have been lost. These panels usually have small scenes flanking a major figure, an age-old type of composition. These are dedicated to various saints, to Christ, or to the Virgin, accompanied by scenes from their lives. The colors tend to white, yellow, red, orange, and black. Startlingly vivid, the paintings, executed on wood covered with fine plaster as described by the German Benedictine monk Theophilus, are brilliant examples of Romanesque art.

In León, the ceiling of the Panteón de los Reyes, S. Isidoro, is covered with a masterpiece. All the vaults are painted with scenes of religious subjects. One of the most charming is the Annunciation to the Shepherds. Not nearly so much under the influence of Byzantine art as the Catalan style nor nearly so dependent on Mozarabic art for the color scheme, these frescoes are much more picturesque in detail and pleasant in narration.

Wall decoration in France. The most complete and evocative sets of frescoes in France are in the abbey church at St. Savin-sur-Gartempe, near Poi-

The Annunciation to the Shepherds. Fresco on the ceiling of the Panteón de los Reyes, S. Isidoro, León. HIRMER FOTOARCHIV, MUNICH

tiers. A few have been lost, some have faded, but all have been spared by the restorers of the nineteenth century. The church is a typical one of the West with a barrel-vaulted nave flanked by aisles that rise to the same height. Light enters from the apse and the side walls, giving a fair, even effect. The colors of the frescoes vary from yellow, yellow ocher, and red to pale green. The backgrounds are all light. In fact, one of the ways specialists have organized French frescoes has been to place all those with light backgrounds in one category and those with dark backgrounds in a second category. There are comparatively few of the latter, and all are particularly Byzantine in manner. In contrast with the collections of the Museo de Arte de Cataluña, those of the Musée des Monuments Français in Paris consist of full-scale copies, on canvas for the murals and in plaster for the sculptures. Both types of art are effectively placed in settings simulating their original locations. This makes for an easy overview of the medieval treasures of France. Nothing, however, can replace a firsthand view of the originals or of the spaces and structures originally devised for their display.

The crypt at St. Savin-Sur-Gartempe, the radiating chapels, the great apse and transept, the vault of the nave, the tribune gallery to the west, and the west porch were once covered with frescoes dating from the early to the mid twelfth century. Apparently a single atelier was responsible for the work, although several groups probably succeeded each other in the task. Very impressive are the frescoes of the Old Testament covering the nave vault in long, horizontal strips facing each other along the spine of the vault. Here scenes begin with the Creation of Man and continue to the story of Moses. The tribune over the porch presents the Passion of Christ, some of which can be seen from the nave through a wide arch. The porch has a selection of scenes from the Apocalypse. The radiating chapels have cycles dedicated to local saints. The figure proportions changed according to the distance from the observer, as, for example, the difference between figures in the vaults of the porch and of the nave.

The type of monumental painting influenced by Byzantine style is effectively displayed by the frescoes of the little chapel at Berzé-la-Ville, a priory belonging to the abbots of Cluny, whose foundation is a short distance away. Possibly St. Hugh, who

ROMANESQUE ART

sought privacy here from the pressures of his abbacy, was the patron of the artists. Originally all the walls and vaults of the upper room were covered with a rich scheme of murals. Now there are traces of scenes from the Life of Christ and figures of saints in the nave leading to a great image in the apse of Christ Enthroned in a mandorla with the twelve apostles; he is blessing St. Paul and giving a scroll and keys to St. Peter. Such an iconography shows the close relation between the reform abbey of Cluny and the papacy at Rome, an axis that spiritually dominated the West during the twelfth century. Below the Majesty of the Lord are the martyrdoms of Sts. Blaise and Lawrence, both saints in favor at Rome at this time. These frescoes, admirable for their high quality, reveal Byzantine influence in their dark backgrounds and emphasis on three dimensions. Nevertheless, in spite of the somber colors, heavy backgrounds, and inclusion of non-Western iconographic details, the frescoes have the startling, restless effects of the Romanesque style. Other frescoes of high aesthetic merit are in the churches of St. Martin-de-Vic and St. Aignan at Brinay, and in the crypt of the church of St. Nicolas at Tavant.

Other European schools of wall decoration. Monumental painting flourished elsewhere in Europe during the Romanesque period: in England, Germany, Austria, and Scandinavia. Massive destruction has taken most of the work in England; only a few scattered remnants remain to suggest the high quality that must have prevailed. Of particular note are fragments in two chapels (St. Anselm's and St. Gabriel's) of the cathedral at Canterbury. In Germany must be cited the frescoes in the abbey church at Prüfening, and in Austria those of the church of the Nonnberg, Strassburg, and of the little church dedicated to St. John at Pürgg in Styria.

MANUSCRIPT ILLUMINATION

The schools of Romanesque illumination have left a number of manuscripts sufficient to construct the history of the art, examples of which are now held for the most part in the extensive collections of the Vatican or of the state libraries of England, France, Germany, Austria, and Italy, and in private libraries in the United States, such as the Morgan Library in New York City. Romanesque style was disseminated over all of Europe, in contrast with the more local manifestations of the Ottonian, Anglo-Saxon, and Carolingian schools. Nevertheless, there were variants as a result of local condi-

The Sacrifice of Abel. Detail of fresco in the nave vault of the abbey church of St. Savin-sur-Gartempe, early–mid 12th century. HIRMER FOTOARCHIV, MUNICH

tions. Instead of royal or imperial patronage, churchmen of the Romanesque period commissioned manuscripts. Abbeys produced manuscripts for themselves, as did church schools, instead of for export as gifts for rulers ordered by lay abbots. Greater economic prosperity, increased travel, and a growing class of rich churchmen, lower nobility, and urban merchants and artisans brought new needs to the scriptorium. Education was far more available and required for progress in the church hierarchy, for the functioning of canon law, and for the efficiency of notaries in lay courts. The illuminated text, no longer solely for the divine service, was adapted to utilitarian ends.

Among the most popular books produced were large Bibles, Passionals, and Lives of Saints. The scriptoria produced other edifying tracts to be read rather than displayed, such as exegetical writings of the fathers of the church or the moralizing of contemporary intellectuals. Richly decorated Psalters, prototypes of the books of hours, were made for the use of women of high estate. These deluxe items marked the high status as well as the piety of the owner. Society during the Romanesque period had the same religious needs as in prior times, but the population was more numerous, more affluent,

ROMANESQUE ART

Angel locking the damned in hell. Miniature from the Psalter of Henry of Blois. Winchester school, mid 12th century. BY PERMISSION OF THE BRITISH LIBRARY, LONDON, COTTON MS NERO C.IV, FOL. 39r

and more desirous of books. Geographically, Romanesque manuscripts were used from England to the Latin Kingdom of Jerusalem and from Scandinavia to Sicily.

The illuminated manuscript of the Romanesque period was no longer a dominant mode of artistic creation; rather, it accepted the leads established in other media. It of course remained distinct because of the particular problems confronted by the artist: the combination of text and image, the combination of writing and ornament, and, by no means least, scale.

The traditional sites of manuscript production continued to exist throughout the period. More emerged. Rome, for example, became a center for the making of the large Bibles that were influential all over Latium and Tuscany. The style was related to that of its monumental art, both archaic and Byzantine. The focus of central Italy was the abbey of Monte Cassino. Sicily produced manuscripts much more Byzantine in iconography and style, as did the ateliers of Jerusalem; an example of the latter is the Psalter of Queen Melisende (1131–1143; London, British Museum, MS Egerton 1139; see illustration at "Crusader Art").

In Spain a remarkable series of manuscripts of the *Commentary on the Apocalypse,* by the monk Beatus of Liébana (*ca.* 776), was produced under strong Mozarabic influence. Their color was intensified by the juxtaposition of orange, red, green, and yellow, and dark blue as well. These were used as local tones to magnify the decorative impact as well as the spiritual exaltation that seems to emanate from the extreme linear stylizations of figure and setting. These books were produced throughout the eleventh century, culminating in the French Apocalypse of St. Sever (Paris, Bibliothèque Nationale, MS lat. 8878).

The very strong Anglo-Saxon schools of England, which had offered so much to the nascent Romanesque styles of painting and sculpture, were partially submerged after the Norman invasion of the island. Their strength was such that the mature Romanesque style of England returned to northern France as the source for local interpretations of the Romanesque, as, for instance, in the extensive embroidery known as the Bayeaux Tapestry. The influence also spread to the Low Countries. New centers of production in England include Bury St. Edmunds and St. Albans, in addition to Winchester and Canterbury.

The abbey of Hirsau in Germany was the center for the dissemination of the influence of Benedictine Cluny. Weingarten Abbey near Constance spread the Anglo-Saxon English style in a country already open to Byzantine art and adhering steadfastly to Ottonian precedents. Cologne, Trier, and Regensburg continued to be active and were joined by Salzburg and others. In general, however, the influence of English manuscript styles prevailed throughout Europe north of the Alps.

BIBLIOGRAPHY

The series issued by the Atelier Monastique de l'Abbaye Sainte-Marie-de-la-Pierre-qui-Vire, under the title *La nuit des temps,* must be consulted. For more than two decades Zodiac Press has published single volumes dedicated to the Romanesque monuments of the regions of France, and recently they have published volumes on Spanish subjects as well. All are remarkable for the quality of their photographs. All the arts are included. George H. Crichton, *Romanesque Sculpture in Italy* (1954), the best compendium in English available on the subject, is somewhat dated. Charles R. Dodwell, *Painting in Europe 800–1200* (1971), is an excellent, detailed, and dependable review. André Grabar and Carl Nordenfalk, *Romanesque Painting from the Eleventh to the Thirteenth Century,* Stuart Gilbert, trans. (1958), contains brilliant essays by eminent scholars, illustrated by excellent reproductions. M. F. Hearn, *Romanesque Sculpture* (1981), an up-to-date survey based on the most recent research, stresses northern monuments and slights Italy. Émile Mâle, *Religious Art in France: The Twelfth Century,* Harry Bober, ed., Marthiel Mathews, trans. (1978), is a magnificent work on the iconography of the art of the twelfth century in France. David M. Robb, *The Art of the Illuminated Manuscript* (1973), a large survey of the entire Middle Ages, has a section on the Romanesque that is very useful and an interesting counterweight to that by Dodwell, and presents a point of view no longer generally accepted concerning the early evolution of Christian art. Whitney S. Stoddard, *Monastery and Cathedral in France* (1966, 1972), though restricted to French monuments, gives a good access to contemporary international scholarship concerning the Romanesque throughout Europe and includes the minor arts. Hans Swarzenski, *Monuments of Romanesque Art: The Art of Church Treasures in North-Western Europe,* 2nd ed. (1967), a distinguished presentation of style and its development in the minor arts, particularly those of the lower Meuse and Rhine valleys, has an excellent collection of detailed photographs.

CARL D. SHEPPARD

[See also **Anglo-Norman Art; Apocalypse, Illustration of; Bayeux Tapestry; Beatus Manuscripts; Benedetto Antelami; Bible; Byzantine Art, 843–1453; Catalonia (800–1137); Cistercian Order; Class Structure, Western; Cluny, Order of; Crusader Art and Architecture; Early Christian Art; Fresco Painting; Gislebertus; Godefroid of Huy; Guglielmo da Verona; Manuscript Illumination, European; Matter of Britain, Matter of France, Matter of Rome; Metalsmiths, Gold and Silver; Moissac, St. Pierre; Monte Cassino; Mosaic and Mosaic Making; Mosan Art; Mozarabic Art; Nicholaus da Verona; Panel Painting; Pilgrimage, Western European; Pre-Romanesque Art; Rainer of Huy; Roger of Helmarshausen; St. Sernin, Toulouse; Suger of St. Denis; Wiligelmo.**]

ROMANIA. See **Romanian Principalities; Walachia/Moldavia.**

ROMANIAN LANGUAGE AND LITERATURE. The Romanian language came into being in Dacia, a territory bordered by the Danube, Tisa, and Dniester rivers and by the Black Sea. Dacia was the last province to be conquered by the Romans (in two campaigns led by the emperor Trajan, A.D. 101–106), and the first to be abandoned by them (in 271, during the reign of Aurelian). Nevertheless, Latin obliterated the indigenous language of the Thracian, Dacian, and Getian peoples and, after a few centuries, gave birth to a Romance language, which we know as Romanian. Scholars consider its survival an enigma; W. D. Elcock is one of the Romance linguists who have expressed their admiration for the persistence of Romanian. In *The Romance Languages,* he writes: "One cannot cease to wonder at the extraordinary tenacity of this Vulgar Latin of the east, so faithfully maintained by a people virtually lost to history and bereft of all that support of a Latin literary tradition which in the West counted for so much."

As to when and where Romanian first distinguished itself as a language independent from Latin, there are two theories. According to Alexandru Rosetti and Alexandru Philippide, Romanian was formed as a language during the sixth century, while other linguists and historians (Emil Petrovici, Constantin Daicoviciu) consider that its formation took place between the eighth and tenth centuries. The earliest trace of Eastern Romance ("proto-Romanian") could have been the phrase "Torna, torna, fratre," uttered by a soldier of the Byzantine army in the sixth century.

As to where Romanian was first spoken, there are also two conflicting views. Romanian scholars believe that the cradle of their language lay north of the Danube. The colonists introduced by Trajan settled in the Carpathian area and extended the influence of their language to the south and north of the mountains. Other linguists place the beginnings of Romanian south of the Danube, in Moesia and Illyricum, where Latin was implanted as early as the third century B.C. From these provinces Latin would then have been carried north by later migrations. The Romanic descendants of the Latin spoken south of the Danube are the Istro-Romanian, Aromanian (Macedo-Romanian), and Megleno-Romanian dialects that survive to this day.

The development of the Romanian language and culture was strongly influenced by the Slavic invasions of the sixth century. The settling of the Bulgarians, Serbs, Croats, and Slovenes south of the Danube, and their conversion to Christianity in the ninth century, when Cyril and Methodius translated the Holy Scriptures into Old Church Slavonic, had lasting religious and cultural consequences:

the ties of medieval Romania (Dacoromania) with Catholic Western Latinity were severed. It is a profound irony that a people with linguistic and religious foundations so fundamentally Latin (of Latin origin are the following essential terms: *creştin* < *christianum* [Christian]; *cruce* < *crucem* [cross]; *cumineca* < *comminicare* [to take communion]; *biserică* < *basilicam* [church]; *credintă* < **credentia* [faith]; *inger* < *angelum* [angel]; *crăciun* < *creationem* [Christmas]) should have adopted the Eastern Orthodox liturgy, while neighboring Poland and Hungary were to adhere to Western Roman Catholicism. Even the name by which Romanians were known in the Middle Ages underwent a Slavic influence, the German term *Wallach* becoming *Vlach*.

Until the sixteenth century, Slavonic was the language of religion and literature in the Romanian principalities, and the Cyrillic alphabet was used in written documents until the nineteenth century. It is possible that the impact of Byzantium could have changed the cultural picture, but Slavic culture acted as a buffer and a filter, passing on to the Romanians only a meager part of the rich Byzantine literary heritage: a number of religious, historical, and legal works and a few romances (*cărţi populare*). Even this scant infiltration ceased when Byzantium was conquered by the Turks. The cultural aftermath was the flight of erudite Greeks to the West. As the Ottoman forces penetrated deeper into the Balkans, Bulgarian and Serbian monks sought refuge in Walachia and Moldavia—constituted in the fourteenth century as political states by the princes Basarab and Bogdan, respectively—where they set up a monastic culture.

LITERATURE

At a time when the Occident was producing works such as the *Canterbury Tales,* the *Decameron,* and the *Libro de buen amor,* the development of Romanian literature in Moldavia and Tara Românească was limited to copying or imitating obsolete Slavonic literary works, most of them handed down in posterior copies. The few extant manuscripts from the monasteries at Putna, Voroneţ, and Cozia, and elsewhere, written in Medio-Bulgarian and Paleo-Serbian, bear testimony to Byzantine styles in calligraphy and illumination. The icons and extramural frescoes, preserved even today on the walls of Voroneţ, Suceviţa, and other Romanian monasteries, display the same imprint. The first religious Slavonic texts written in Romanian monasteries are from the late fourteenth and early fifteenth centuries: a hymn by Filotei, some sermons by Grigorie Ţamblac.

The beginnings of historiography are represented by a series of annals, from Bistriţa, Putna, and other places, and by a lost chronicle in Slavic of Stephen the Great (1457–1504), who was ruler of Moldavia. The Latin translation of this chronicle, *Chronica breviter scripta Stephani . . .* , dated 1502, is preserved in Munich, Bayerische Staatsbibliothek, codex latinarum 952. The significance of three subsequent chronicles (those of Macarie, Eftimie, and Azarie) lies mainly in the information they furnished to later Moldavian chroniclers such as Grigore Ureche.

Another chronicle, in "walachico sermone," which survives only in Balthasar Walter's Latin translation (*Brevis et vera descriptio rerum . . . Ion Michaele Moldaviae Transalpinae sive Valachiae Palatino gestarum*), celebrated the deeds of Michael the Brave, the first Romanian ruler to unite, however temporarily, the major components of modern Romania—Walachia, Moldavia, and Transylvania.

The most important Slavonic document written in Walachia during the sixteenth century is *Învăţăturile lui Neagoe Basarab către fiul său Teodosie* (The teachings of Neagoe Basarab to his son Teodosie), an ethical and practical guide on kingship whose models are Byzantine. The authorship of Neagoe Basarab, who ruled Walachia between 1512 and 1521 and built the monastery of Curtea de Argeş, was disputed for a long time, but is generally accepted today on the understanding that the monk Ioan Eclesiarh edited the text and made significant interpolations. The content of Neagoe Basarab's *Teachings* is heterogeneous. The work includes political precepts, excerpts from the Bible, from *Barlaam and Josaphat,* and from *Physiologus.* Some chapters, for example the one that deals with the ceremony of receiving foreign ambassadors (*soli*), are believed to portray Walachian court customs during the sixteenth century.

The Romanian language was probably first used in written form in the last decades of the fifteenth century, especially in the business affairs of the church. Expressions such as "idiomate valachico scriptus" or "ex valachico in Latinum versa est" from foreign documents of the fifteenth century seem to prove it; however, it took nearly a century for Romanian to replace Slavonic in chancelleries and almost two centuries in churches. The oldest surviving document in Romanian is a letter written in 1521 by the boyar Neacşu, informing Hans Benkner, the mayor of Braşov, of a Turkish raid in Walachia.

The first Romanian religious texts, *Codicele Voronețean, Psaltirea Scheiană,* and *Psaltirea Voronețeană,* preserved in copies of the sixteenth century, are fifteenth-century translations made from the Slavonic in the Maramureş region of northwestern Transylvania. For some time scholars linked their appearance to the rise of either Hussitism or Lutheranism. According to a more recent and more plausible hypothesis, these Romanian translations represent an effort made during the fifteenth century by Romanian noblemen from Maramureş to assert the independence of the Romanian Orthodox church, threatened with absorption by the Slavonic bishopric of Muncaci.

Several decades later, the deacon Coresi from Braşov printed these translations in his *Lucrul Apostolesc* (1563), *Psaltire* (1570), and *Psaltire slavo română* (1577). Between 1559 and 1581, Coresi printed other Romanian translations; *Catehismul, Tetraevangheliarul, Cazanie şi Molitvelnic, Liturghier, Pravila,* and *Evanghelie cu tîlc.* Inspired by the Lutheran movement, his typographical activity had as its ultimate aim the adoption of Romanian as the liturgical language of the national church: "It is better to utter in holy church five words with meaning than a thousand incomprehensible words in a foreign language" (*Evangheliarul românesc,* 1561). While Coresi printed mainly translations from the New Testament, his successors, Şerban, his son, and Marian printed in Orăştie a translation of certain books from the Old Testament entitled *Palia* (1582).

All these sixteenth-century religious translations, printed in Transylvania, laid the foundations of the Romanian literary language. The Maramureşean texts, archaic and dialectal in both grammar and lexicon, are heavily influenced by Slavonic syntax. The Coresian ones tend to eliminate the dialectal features and adopt a clearer style, whereas the language of *Palia,* in spite of its many Hungarian terms, is remarkably vivid and flexible.

Besides religious writings, the anonymous translators turned their attention to apocryphal literature. Their endeavor to transmit to Romanian readers the hagiographic and apocalyptic legends that enjoyed such wide diffusion in Byzantium may be judged from the *Codex Sturdzanus, Codex Todorescu,* and *Codex Martianus,* all copied in the sixteenth and seventeenth centuries. Some texts—*Legenda Sfintei Vineri, Legenda Sfîntului Sisinie, Legenda Sf. Alexie*—offer the Christian paradigm of endurance and reward for faith, while others—*Apocalipsul Apostolului Pavel, Moartea lui Avraam, Călătoria Maicii Domnului în iad,* and *Legenda Duminicii*—reveal the mysteries of the otherworld.

The translation of two treatises—*Physiologus* and *Fiore di virtù*—reveals the need for didactic literature. *Fiziologul*—a fourth-century treatise on zoology and ethics in which the characteristics of animals and birds are interpreted as religious and moral symbols—was translated from an earlier Slavonic version. *Floarea darurilor (Albinuşa)* was consecutively translated from Italian, Serbian, and Greek. Its miscellaneous contents included comparisons of virtues and vices with real and fantastic animals, and stories taken from the Bible, hagiography, Alexander's romance, and the *Gesta Romanorum.* This work stimulated the minds of many generations of readers throughout the Romanian territories over the following three centuries.

Similar interest was shown in romances (*cărți populare*), translated during the sixteenth and seventeenth centuries from Serbian and Bulgarian. The recounting of Alexander the Great's heroic deeds in the *Alexandria* was aimed at bolstering the Romanian cause for independence at a time when Michael the Brave was fighting the Turks. The vigorous defense of Christianity in *Barlaam and Josaphat* strengthened religious spirits in a country constantly exposed to the influence of other faiths. Finally, *Archirie şi Anadan* (circulating in the eighteenth century), with its condemnation of ingratitude, advanced moral values.

The interpretation of the zodiacal signs, of lightning and thunder, and of involuntary movements by the human body as ways of predicting the future is recorded in treatises such as the *Zodiac, Gromovnic,* and *Trepetnic,* some of which are probably still read by Romanian peasants.

Reputable literary historians such as Nicolae Cartojan consider that the medieval character of Romanian literature lingers on into the nineteenth century. Limitations of space preclude treatment of this issue, but Romanian literature from the seventeenth and eighteenth centuries will be briefly considered to give some idea of its increased artistic value.

The richness of the historiography that flourished in Moldavia is evident in the chronicles (*letopisete*) that were written by Grigore Ureche (*ca.*

ROMANIAN LANGUAGE

1590), Miron Costin (1633–1691), and Ion Neculce (1672–1745). Covering Moldavian history from 1359 to 1743, they were not only more objective and sophisticated than were those of their predecessors (Ureche and Costin were exposed to Latin literature while studying in Jesuit schools in Poland), but also more prone to pay attention to oral traditions. Many of their episodes (mini-novellas), which vividly describe the conflicts of interest between princes and boyars, and between Moldavians and Poles or Turks, were a valuable source for later generations of writers interested in romantic and realistic themes.

But the Moldavian who became most famous beyond his country's borders was Nicolae Milescu (1636–1708), historian, geographer, and ethnographer. His *Enchiridion sive stella orientalis occidentali splendens,* published in Paris in 1669, contains a defense of the Christian faith. His travel memoirs synthesizes then current knowledge about Russia and China, and includes picturesque details and personal reminiscences.

LANGUAGE

Basically, the language of the first written texts presents few lexical and grammatical differences from contemporary Romanian. The following fragment of the New Testament (Mark 13:19–28) from Coresi's *Evangheliar* (1560–1561), despite its awkward syntax, would be understood, without much difficulty, by most educated Romanians.

> *Zise domnul ucenicilor lui: Fulgerul ce iase de la răsărit și se iveaște pînă la apus, așa va fi și întru venitul fiiului omenesc: iuo [=unde] va amu fi trupul acolo aduna-se-vor vălturii[=vulturii]. Aciiași [numaidecît] după scîrbitul [=suferințe] zilelor acelor, soarele va întuneca și luna nu-ș va da lumina ei, și stealele vor cădea den ceriu și atunce se va ivi semnul fiiului omenesc în ceriu, și atunce vor plînge toate rudele [=generațiile] pămîntului și vor vedea fiiul omenesc vii[n]d în nuorii [=norii] ceriului cu silă [=putere] și cu slavă multă și va tremeate îngerii lui cu bucine în glasure mari, și vor aduna aleșii lui de patru vînture, den capetele ceriului pînă în sfîrșitul lor. De smochinu învățați-va pildă, cînd amu steblele [= ramurile] ei vor fi tinereale și frunza înfrunzeaște, să știți că aproape iaste de secerat. Așa și voi cînd veți vedea acealea toate, să știți că aproape iatse lîngă uși.*
> (p. 56)

This fragment will serve as a reference point for a brief discussion of the most relevant linguistic features of Romanian in general and of the language of the sixteenth-century texts in particular. As may be seen from the following words extracted from the text cited above, Romanian reduced the ten vowels and three diphthongs of Latin, distinguishable by quantitative opposition, to only five pure vowels (*a, e, i, o,* and *u*): *da* < *dare* (to give); *ceriu* < *coelum* (heaven); *fiu* < *filium* (son); *lor* < *illorum* (theirs); *aduna* < *adunat* (gathers). Besides these vowels inherited from Vulgar Latin, Romanian created two medial vowels, *ă* and *î*: *răsărit* (risen); *întru* (in). Romanian *ă* (from atonic Latin *a)* appears also in Bulgarian and is attributed to the Thraco-Illyrian substratum. The vowel *î* developed from a vowel followed by a nasal. As the word *capete* < *capita* (heads) shows, Romanian preserved the intervocalic plosives (other examples not from the above text are: *rîpă* < *ripam* [riverbank]; *muta* < *mutare* [to move]; *pleca* < *plicare* [to leave]). Other developments were the loss of final *-s* and its substitution with *-i* (*doi* < *duos; flori* < *flores* [flowers]), the palatalization of the dentals *d, s, t,* followed by yod (*zise* < *dixit* [he said]; *și* < *sic* [and]; *țeară, țară* < *terram* [earth/country]), and rhotacism, the change of intervocalic *l* to *r* (*cer* < *coelum* [sky] *soare* < *solem* [sun]). Much as in Slavic, Romanian palatalized and assibilated the final consonants followed by *i* (*știți* < *scitis* [you know]). This change plays an important role in differentiating the singular from the plural (*ales—aleși* [chosen]; *nuor, nuori,* modern Romanian *nori* [clouds]). The only phonetical borrowing from Slavonic is that of velar *h* (*duh* [spirit]).

Unlike the other Romance languages, Romanian preserved from Latin the neuter gender (*timpure, timpuri* < *tempora* [times]) and a system of three cases: nominative (*Ioana, casa*), genitive-dative (*Ionaei' casei*), and vocative (*Ioană*). The survival of both these features may be explained by the influence of Slavic languages. In addition, Romanian borrowed from Slavonic a feminine morpheme for the vocative, *-o* (*Ioano*), which coexists with the Latin one. Another peculiarity, the postposition of the article (derived from the Latin demonstratives *ille, illa*—fiu*l*, țar*a*), also present in Bulgarian and Albanian, is attributed to the influence of the Thracian substratum. Arguments against this theory are that postposition gained ground in Romanian relatively late, after the sixteenth century, and that the article is postposited in some Scandinavian languages that have no geographical contiguity with the Balkans.

As the sixteenth-century fragment shows, Romanian preserved all four conjugations (*aduna* < *adunare* [to gather]; *cădea* < *cadere* [to fall]; *zice* < *dicere* [to tell]; *şti* < *scire* [to know]) and remained faithful to the Latin tense system, as did the Western Romance languages. Besides the numerous verbs in *-i* (in the text, *ivi* [to appear] < Slav. *javiti*), a new type appeared, namely the verbs in -î: *urî* < *horrere* (to hate). As elsewhere in the Romance world, the synthetic forms of the tenses were replaced by analytical ones. A single exception is the pluperfect *cîntasem,* which continues the Latin past perfect *cantavissem* (I had sung). Moreover, influenced by the Balkan languages, Romanian uses the subjunctive—and not the infinitive—as a direct object or subject of another verb (*vreau să cînt* [I want to sing]).

Pronouns in Romanian preserved the irregular inflection. Numerals, with the exception of *sută* (hundred), are Latin, but from eleven to nineteen they are formed according to a Slavonic model: *unsprezece, doisprezece,* etc. Adverbs, prepositions, and conjunctions in Romanian were also formed from elements of Latin origin: *la* < *illac* (to); pînă < paene (until/up to) + *ad; acolo* < *eccum* + *illoc* (there); *între* < *inter* (between); *să* < *si* (subjunctive marker); *şi* < *sic* (and), etc.

In the same way as the other Romance languages, Romanian simplified the inherited Latin syntax. Prepositional markers were developed in order to indicate cases that were not differentiated by special morphemes; the accusative preceded by the preposition *pre* (*pe*), designating persons (*pe fiul lui*), is one of them.

Besides these permanent changes, the sixteenth-century texts from Maramureş reveal a number of linguistic peculiarities that arise from their dialectal and archaic nature: The monophthongization of the diphthongs *ea* and *oa* (*leage-lege* [law]; *noapte-nopte* [night]), the preservation of the nasal *n,* when preceded by yod (*întînniu* [the first]; *spuniu* [I say]), and rhotacism (*lumina* > *lumină-lumiră* [light]. The nouns belonging to the second Latin declension preserved the vocalic ending (*domnu* < *dominum* [lord]) and the neuter ending *-ure* (mod. Rom. *-uri*). New analogical preterit forms (*făcui* [I did]; *venirăţi* [you came]) are used parallel to the old ones (*feciu, venetu,* etc.), which continue the Latin *feci, venitis.* The perfect subjunctive is still preserved in a form with conditional meaning: *intrare* < *intraverim,* etc.

In the texts written in the south of Transylvania, many of these features disappear. However, some of the archaic forms were still in use during the following century. For example, the Bible published in Bucharest in 1688 includes forms with the suffix *-toriu* (*judecătoriu* [judge]) and the final *u* preserved after a consonantal cluster (*pumnu* [fist]), as well as old verbal preterit forms (*rumpse* [he broke]; *pus* [he put]). The Moldavian texts of this century present specific dialectal features: initial *f* becomes *h* (*fiu; hiu* [son]), *e* becomes *i,* and the demonstrative *acest, cest* (this one) is very frequent.

Romanian vocabulary is less conservative than its grammar. Since Romanian was isolated from the rest of the Latin world, its lexicon underwent massive influence from contiguous languages. Even in the sixteenth century, however, when the Slavonic linguistic infiltration was still very strong, the active basic vocabulary was mainly Latin. In analyzing a sixteenth-century text, Alexandru Graur pointed out that out of 94 words only 6 were not of Latin derivation. In the Gospel text a similar proportion is evident; the number of Slavic borrowings is limited: *ucenici* (apprentices); *iveaşte/ivi* (he appears/appeared); *scîrbit* (suffering); *trup* (body); *rudă* (relative); *silă* (strength); *slavă* (glory); *glasure* (voices); *sfîrşit* (end); *steble* (branches)—a total of only 11 words. Some Hungarian words also found their way into sixteenth-century texts. In later centuries Romanian received infusions of Greek, Turkish, and French words.

An article on Romanian literature should not fail to mention the unwritten folk literature, which many critics contend is the basis of the literary language. Certain ballads (*cîntece bătrîneşti* [old-songs]) reflect an ancient pastoral culture, in which life and death, wedding and burial, nature and spirit become one (*Mioriţa*). Other ballads praise sacrifice for the sake of art (*Meşterul Manole*), for one's country (*Constantin Brîncoveanu*), or for social justice (*Vartici, Toma Alimoş*).

These ballads (first published in 1852 by Vasile Alecsandri), as well as the often plaintive lyrical songs (*doine*) and the carols (*colinde*), record the spiritual and material existence of Romanians since time immemorial.

BIBLIOGRAPHY

Studies of Romanian in Western languages are not abundant. In French, see O. Densusianum, *Histoire de la langue roumaine* (1929); Alexandru Rosetti, *Brève histoire de la langue roumaine des origines à nos jours* (1973). In English, Elizabeth Close, *The Development of Modern Rumanian: Linguistic Theory and Practice in*

Muntenia, 1821–1838 (1974), covers a later period, but may be of interest to readers of this article. W. D. Elcock, *The Romance Languages,* new ed. (1975), provides useful, if brief, discussions of Romanian. In Spanish, see Iorgu Iordán y María Manolíu, *Manual de linguística románica* (1972).

In Romanian, the literature is extensive. What follows is a selection of some of the more important works. Nicolae Cartojan, *Istoria literaturii române vechi,* 3 vols. (1940–1945); Ion C. Chiţimia, *Probleme de bază ale literaturii române vechi* (1972); A. Niculescu, *Individualitatea limbü române între limbile romanice* (1965–1978); Al Piru, *Literatura romîna veche,* 2nd ed. (1962); Sextil I. Puşcariu, *Istoria literaturii române: Epoca veche,* 2nd ed. (1930); Alexandru Rosetti, *Istoria limbii române* (1968), *idem,* ed., *Istoria literaturii române, I, Folclorul: Literatura română în perioada feudală, 1400–1780,* 2nd ed. (1970), *idem.* and B. Cazacu, *Istoria limbü române literare* (1961).

OLGA TUDORICA IMPEY
MICHAEL H. IMPEY

[See also **Alexander Romances; Barlaam and Josaphat; Bestiary; Cyril and Methodios, Sts.; Greek Language, Byzantine; Latin Language; Slavic Languages and Literatures; Walachia/Moldavia.**]

ROMANIAN PRINCIPALITIES. Modern Romania attained its national independence only with the signing of the treaty of Berlin in 1878. "Romania" in the Middle Ages was a name usually designating the East Roman or Byzantine Empire, or, in the thirteenth century, the Latin Empire of Constantinople. By the fourteenth century the Romanian-speaking people, or Vlachs (from Slavonic; Latin: *Vlachi* or *Blachi;* Greek: *Bláchoi;* also English: Walachians), residing north of the Danube achieved political recognition with the organization of the principalities of Walachia and Moldavia. The Vlachs were converted to Orthodox Christianity and used the Slavonic liturgy. The Orthodox church gave shape and content to the cultural life of the Romanian principalities. For nearly 200 years Walachia and Moldavia were border districts along the frontier between Christian Europe and the Tatars and Ottoman Turks. For that reason their history is comparable to that of other turbulent border districts where regional independence was often preserved under the cover of nominal subservience to a potent neighbor and through adroit exploitation of the antagonisms of larger, more powerful states. Hungary, Poland, and the Ottoman Empire each exerted political influence and occasional suzerainty over the principalities. Dynastic rivalries within Walachia and Moldavia frequently provided the opportunity to shelter exiled claimants to the throne and for military intervention. By the early sixteenth century, Polish influence in the lands along the Black Sea was on the wane. In 1526 the Turkish army inflicted a devastating defeat on Hungary at the Battle of Mohács. Thus, the conditions that had enabled Walachia and Moldavia to preserve a measure of political independence disappeared. Thenceforth, until the nineteenth century, these principalities were dependencies of the Ottoman sultan.

Although western Walachia was organized by the Hungarian kingdom as the banat of Severin (Szörény; present-day Turnu-Severin) in the early thirteenth century, Walachia proper is not mentioned as a political entity until the Angevin-Hungarian king Charles Robert (ruled as Charles I, 1308–1342) in 1324 recognized the voivode Basarab I (*ca.* 1310–1352) as his vassal. Basarab and his descendants periodically rebelled against Hungarian tutelage, frequently with success. The reign of Mircea the Old (Mircea cel Bătrîn, 1386–1418), prince of Walachia, coincided with the emergence of Ottoman dominantion of the Balkan peninsula following the Battle of Kossovo in 1389. Mircea together with a Hungarian army held the Turks at bay at Rovine in 1395. But after the disaster that befell the Hungarian king Sigismund (*r.* 1387–1437) at Nicopolis in 1396, Mircea ultimately agreed to pay tribute to the sultan. Mircea's successors, who ruled Walachia from their principal residence at Tîrgovişte, were divided by bitter dynastic rivalry between the Danişti and the Draculişti. In general the Danişti were favored by the Hungarians the Draculişti by the Turks. The exception was the notorious Vlad III Ţepeş, (Dracula, *d.* 1476), who received support alternately from each and betrayed both.

Somewhat later in the fourteenth century, Moldavia emerged also as a frontier district of Hungarian creation. The names, precise family relationships, and regnal years of the earliest Moldavian voivodes are much disputed. The first appears to have been Dragoş (*ca.* 1347–1354), installed by King Louis I the Great of Hungary in Moldavia, the newly created march against the Tartars. A later voivode, Bogdan I (1363–1367), while nominally subject to the Hungarian crown, was virtually an independent prince. Moldavia's geographical situation exposed the principality to the expanding power of the united monarchy of Lithuania and Poland, and it submitted to Polish-Lithuanian suzerainty in 1387. The voivodes of Moldavia, whose principal residences were at Suceava and Iaşi (Jassy), frequently found themselves caught between competing Hungarian and Polish ambitions. In the aftermath of the fall of Constantinople (1453), Moldavia began to pay tribute to the Ottoman sultan. Under the voivode Stephen (Ştefan) the Great (1457–1504), Moldavia attempted to preserve its independence. With Polish encouragement Stephen joined an Ottoman campaign against Hungary and Walachia. Somewhat later he invaded Walachia with the object of expelling the Turkish-backed Walachian voivode and establishing the Danube as the frontier against Turkish advance. In this he failed. The sultan countered by invading Moldavia and sacking Suceava, but without effecting the conquest of the principality. After Stephen's death, however, Moldavia became a dependency of the Ottoman Empire.

BIBLIOGRAPHY

Emmanuel Beau de Loménie, *Naissance de la nation Roumaine, de Byzance à Étienne-le-Grand de Moldavie* (1937); Constantin C. Giurescu, *The Making of the Roumanian People and Language* (1972); Manfred Huber, *Grundzüge der Geschichte Rumäniens* (1973); Nicolae Iorga, *Histoire des Roumains et de leur civilisation* (1920, 2nd ed. 1922), English edition, *A History of Roumania: Land, People, Civilization,* Joseph McCabe, trans. (1925); Robert W. Seton-Watson, *A History of the Roumanians: From Roman Times to the Completion of Unity* (1934); Aloisio L. Tăutu, "Basarab il Grande, fondatore del primo stato romeno indipendente (1310–1352)," in *Antemurale,* **1** (1954).

JAMES ROSS SWEENEY

[See also **Banat; Barbarians, Invasions of; Bāyazīd II; Bohemian Brethren; Bosnia; Bulgaria; Crusades of the Later Middle Ages; Hungary; Indo-European Languages, Development of; Nicopolis; Ottomans; Poland; Vlachs; Vlad Ţepeş; Walachia/Moldavia.**]

ROMANOS I LEKAPENOS (*ca.* 870–948), Byzantine co-emperor. The son of an Armenian peasant, Romanos was the chief admiral (*drungarios*) of the Byzantine fleet, and in 919 he married his daughter Helena to Emperor Constantine VII Porphyrogenitos and took the title of *basileopator.* From 920 to 944 he ruled as co-emperor. He conducted the war against the Bulgars that ended in the peace of 927, and he was responsible for bringing the Mandylion to Constantinople from Edessa after capturing the latter city from the Muslims. In 922 Romanos enacted legislation protecting small landowners by restoring the right of preemption (the first right of purchase belonging to the close relatives of an individual who was selling land). Three of his sons became co-emperors, and his family in effect existed as a separate dynasty alongside the legitimate Macedonian house. Romanos was deported to the island of Prote after a coup by two of his sons, and he died there. These two sons were arrested in 945 and exiled by Constantine VII.

BIBLIOGRAPHY

George Ostrogorsky, *History of the Byzantine State,* Joan Hussey, trans. (1957, 3rd rev. ed. 1969); Steven Runciman, *The Emperor Romanus Lecapenus and His Reign* (1929, repr. 1963).

LINDA C. ROSE

[See also **Bulgaria; Byzantine Empire: Economic Life and Social Structure; Byzantine Empire: History; Constantine VII Porphyrogenitos; Dunatoi; Law, Byzantine; Mandylion; Penetes.**]

ROMANOS II (938/939–963), Byzantine emperor from 959 to 963. Romanos II was the son of Constantine VII Porphyrogenitos, to whom Constantine addressed his treatise *De administrando imperio* (On the administration of the empire). Not a strong ruler, he was heavily influenced by his wife, Theophano. During his brief rule there were a number of Byzantine military successes, including the recapture of Crete and victories against the Hamdanids. He is reputed to have been a man of great charm.

BIBLIOGRAPHY

George Ostrogorsky, *History of the Byzantine State,* Joan Hussey, trans. (1957, 3rd rev. ed. 1969).

LINDA C. ROSE

[See also **Basil II "Killer of Bulgars"; Byzantine Empire: History; Constantine VII Porphyrogenitos; Crete; Hamdanids; Theophano, Empress.**]

ROMANOS IV DIOGENES (*d.* 1072). Byzantine emperor from 1068 to 1071, Romanos secured the throne of Byzantium by marrying Empress Eudokia, the widow of Constantine X Doukas. A Cappadocian noble, he was an able general who had distinguished himself against the Pechenegs. As emperor he was involved in campaigns against the Seljuks that began well but ended in the Byzantine rout at Manazkert (1071), after a number of his troops proved untrustworthy. Romanos was taken prisoner by Alp Arslan, who treated him honorably and released him upon the signing of a treaty promising tribute, ransom, and military help to the Turks. The opposing party in Constantinople deposed Romanos upon his return to the capital. He was blinded and died soon afterward.

BIBLIOGRAPHY

George Ostrogorsky, *History of the Byzantine State,* Joan Hussey, trans. (1957, 3rd rev. ed. 1969).

LINDA C. ROSE

[See also **Alp Arslan; Byzantine Empire: History; Doukas; Manazkert; Russia, Nomadic Invasions of; Seljuks.**]

ROMANOS MELODOS, ST. (*ca.* 480–*ca.* 560), the most famous Byzantine poet and author of numerous kontakia (long metrical homilies set to music). Of Syrian origin, born perhaps in Emesa (present-day Homs, Syria), he apparently served as a deacon in Berytus (modern Beirut) in a church dedicated to the Resurrection; he arrived in Constantinople at the turn of the century.

In Constantinople, Romanos was a chanter in a church dedicated to the Virgin in the Kyros quarter, though his name is also associated with the church in Blachernae. His talent for chanting as well as for writing the kontakion (which is of Syrian origin) seems to have been propagandized by the story of his miraculous acceptance of a parchment from the Virgin, who bade him swallow it. Henceforth Romanos created works that attained great fame for their poetic excellence. Later writings attribute to him more than 1,000 kontakia, one to each saint in the church calendar; however, at present only some 88 are viewed as his creations, and of these only about 60 are completely accepted as genuine works of Romanos.

In the mid fifth century the kontakion was a metrical sermon that was probably cantillated with only the refrains actually sung. If Romanos did compose music (as is generally assumed), the original melodies have been totally lost, as there was no truly musical notation in that period. The earliest musical manuscripts with the melodies for Romanos' texts of kontakia date from the thirteenth century and contain highly elaborate and melismatic melodies that, while they may be older than the date of actual writing, still probably date from a much later period than that of Romanos' life. The transmission of the chanted tradition of the kontakia had undergone a serious change by the end of the seventh century, when the more or less full presentation of a kontakion in the morning service was reduced to its prooimion and the first stanza (*oikos*). Because of the rather lengthy texts of individual kontakia, it is reasonable to assume that the earliest melodies used for their singing may have been syllabic. By drastically curtailing the length of the text to be chanted, possibilities for a developing melismatic traditions were created.

Although some authors attribute to Romanos the authorship of the most famous kontakion in the Byzantine tradition, the Akathistos Hymn, at present most scholars no longer view him as its author, though he may have written one of the two *prooimia.* His vocabulary and poetic skills remained unsurpassed. Not long after his death Romanos was canonized as a saint, and his memory is honored in the Greek Orthodox church calendar on 1 October. By the late twelfth century his tomb was being pointed out to pilgrims visiting Constantinople, according to the Russian pilgrim Anthony of Novgorod. Theories of Romanos' Jewish origin have been questioned and are denied by the most knowledgeable specialists.

BIBLIOGRAPHY

Collections or editions of Romanos' works include *Rōmanou tou Melōdou hymnoi,* Nikolaos B. Tōmadakēs, ed., 4 vols. (1952–1958); *Sancti Romani melodi cantica,* Paul Maas and C. A. Trypanis, eds., 2 vols. (1963–1970); Romanos le Mélode, *Hymnes,* José Grosdidier de Matons, ed. and trans., 5 vols. (1964–1981); *Kontakia of Romanos, Byzantine Melodist,* Marjorie Carpenter, ed. and trans., 2 vols. (1970–1973).

Studies are José Grosdidier de Matons, *Romanos le Mélode et les origines de la poésie religieuse à Byzance* (1977); Kenneth Levy, "An Early Chant for Romanos' Contacium trium puerorum," in *Classica et medievalia,* 22 (1961); C. A. Trypanis, "The Metres of Romanos," in

Byzantion, 36 (1966); G. Zuntz, "Probleme des Romanos-textes," in *Byzantion,* 34 (1964).

MILOŠ VELIMIROVIĆ

[See also **Akathistos; Byzantine Literature; Byzantine Poetic Forms; Hymns, Byzantine; Kontakion; Liturgy, Byzantine Church; Music, Byzantine; Musical Notation, Byzantine.**]

ROME

THE MEDIEVAL SETTING

The decisive period of the depopulation of ancient Rome is thought to have been the fifth century. In 500 the Ostrogothic king Theodoric is said to have made a donation for the repair of the Palatine Palace and the city walls. His minister, Cassiodorus, complained of the collapse of public buildings such as granaries. But Rome was still a city of splendors, at least at its monumental core.

Christian Rome was at this time coming into existence; many Christian buildings were humble, but some were already costly and conspicuous. There were several main zones of Christian monuments. One was outside the walls, in nuclei where the cemetery and sanctuary area were located, within three Roman miles of the city. These contained churches, monasteries, and oratories, and the *necropoleis* themselves. Some important churches outside the walls, such as St. Peter's, S. Paolo, and S. Lorenzo, were linked with the city by colonnades. Within the walls the churches were distributed according to a pattern which reflected early Christian settlement and already bore little relation to the Christianized population of the sixth century. The twenty-five or so historic *tituli* (places of worship) were fairly evenly shared between the seven ecclesiastical regions, save for the Campo Marzio zone, with only one *titulus*. The Lateran area and that of St. Peter's contained other ecclesiastical foundations besides the churches. A few other great churches existed, such as S. Maria Maggiore and S. Croce in Gerusalemme, which were not *tituli.*

The main monumental area of the inner city was relatively unscathed in the early sixth century. However, from 459 the government had authorized the use of *spolia* (looted building materials) from decrepit temples for the construction of new public buildings. After this date *spolia* were used almost universally for constructing churches, and later they were used for all new building. The sieges of the Gothic wars were also destructive, since they involved the burning of large areas of the city and the evacuation of most of the population for an appreciable period. By the end of the century, Pope Gregory I (*r.* 590–604) had referred to the frequent collapse of ancient buildings from lack of maintenance and to the threatened failure of the aqueduct system. There were small inhabited nuclei clustered at points on the roads inside the walls leading to the greater churches outside, such as the Lateran, St. Peter's, S. Maria Maggiore, S. Lorenzo, S. Agnese, S. Sebastiano, and S. Paolo. Apart from these areas, and those inhabited by the Byzantine garrison, habitation within the walls tended to cling to the riverbanks, especially in the zones later known as Parione, Pinea, and Arenula. Large areas within the walls, such as those of the Castra Praetoria and the Baths of Diocletian, or the Esquiline and Coelian hills, became almost deserted. It was, however, a very long period before the public buildings in the monumental sector were built over entirely by churches and private dwellings. This fate gradually overtook the Stadium of Domitian, the Alexandrine Baths, and the Theater of Pompey, but the center of Domitian's Stadium (Piazza Navona, then the Agone) remained clear, and large parts of the neighboring Theater of Pompey still can be seen behind the buildings. The last public monument to be placed in the Forum was the Column of Emperor Phokas (602–610).

Augustus divided Rome into fourteen civil regions. It is maintained by some scholars (against an earlier opinion of Jordan) that after the sixth century the civil regions passed into desuetude, and that they were replaced in the ninth or tenth century by the ecclesiastical regions, whose origins probably lie in the third century. The ecclesiastical regions were used, and not the civil ones, in the early Middle Ages. However, the increase in density of population of the areas bordering the left bank of the river probably lay behind a new arrangement of the regions, first visible in the ninth century and used consistently by the twelfth. This new pattern assigned twelve regions to the left bank: no fewer than seven of these correspond to the ancient Augustan regions. Trastevere was the thirteenth region; the "Leonine City" of St. Peter's was not treated as the fourteenth region until the early modern period. One of the thirteenth medieval regions, Monti, embraced most of four of the fourteen Augustan regions; this was the eastern area of the city, whose abandoned condition later caused it to be termed the *disabitato.*

From the fifth century until the early eleventh the clerical organization of the city centered around the

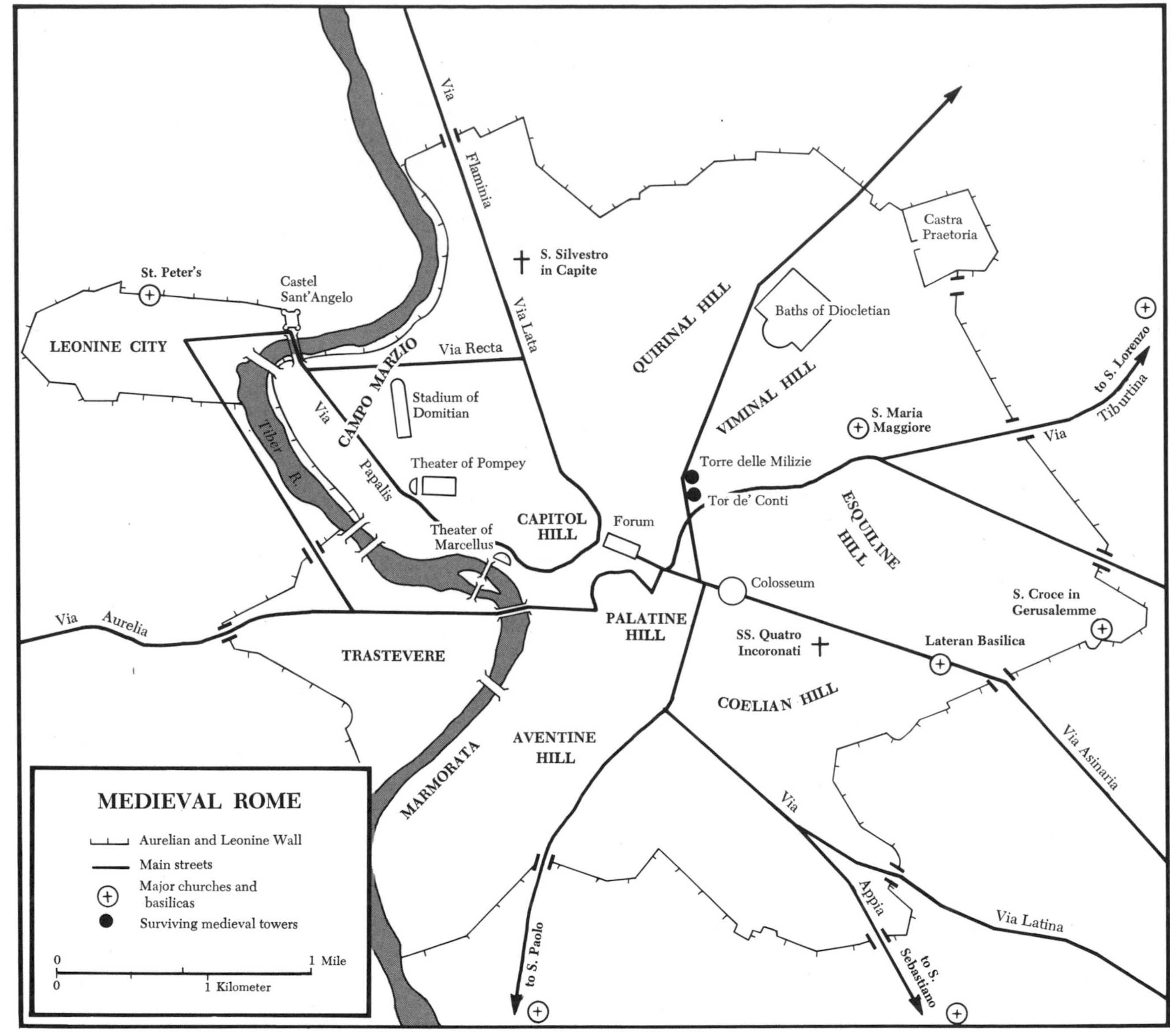

twenty-five *tituli,* each of which had its own priest. The original names of the *tituli* came from the founder or endower of the *titulus* and not from the names of martyrs or saints. More than half the *tituli* had not been built as churches but had grown up as domestic cult centers. None, naturally, were located in the ancient monumental center. Of the nontitular churches the most important were St. Peter's (which properly belongs to the category of churches serving the sanctuaries and *martyria* outside the walls) and the Lateran. The latter was a great Constantinian church with adjacent baptistery, oratories, and chapels. Annexed to it was the main administrative center of the Roman bishopric, the Lateran patriarchate, referred to from the ninth century onward as a "palace." The patriarchate was extensively rebuilt by the eighth-century popes, and it has been argued that the triclinium built there by Leo III (*r.* 795–816) was constructed in imitation of the Great Hall of the Imperial Palace at Constantinople. Such an important headquarters was bound to influence the urban pattern, and churches and monasteries were located on roads linking the Lateran with the Fora, though some of these were ancient *tituli* (for example, S. Clemente and SS. Quattro Incoronati).

St. Peter's exercised an influence even greater than the Lateran on street plan and development. Like the Lateran, St. Peter's was from the early Middle Ages surrounded by a complex of related institutions: pilgrim hostels (*xenodochia*), oratories, monasteries, and the *scholae* or compounds for foreign pilgrims. There was also a papal residence, quite elaborate from the time of Leo III, and from the ninth century a "palace" for the emperor or his representative in Rome. From an early date the money changers and vendors concerned with pilgrims trafficked within or just outside the atrium of the church. The whole *borgo* under Pope Leo IV (*r.* 847–855) and after the Muslim sack of Rome in 846 was surrounded by a wall, which enclosed the Leonine City. On the north this connected with the fortress of the Mausoleum of Hadrian (later known as the Castel Sant'Angelo). On the opposite side of the river, leading east from the terminus of Ponte Elio at the castle, the Via Papalis, also called Via di Parione, connected the Leonine City with the roads leading to the Lateran. The other main road forking out from Ponte Elio was the Via Recta, which connected with the settled area north of the Pantheon (a church from the seventh century), and the churches and settlements on the east side of the Via Lata. The other main settled area was the low-lying zone bordering the river to the northwest of the Theater of Marcellus. This zone was approached from the other bank by the bridges crossing the Tiber Island; prior to the eleventh century it seems to have been only thinly settled. Downstream from the Tiber Island the Roman port of Marmorata had been abandoned, and the medieval port of "Ripa" was by the ninth century established on the Trastevere bank.

The deaconries (*diaconiae*) of the Roman church were an important influence on settlement in the earlier Middle Ages. From the early seventh century these existed as centers for social welfare and for provisioning the pilgrims and the poor. One of the earliest deaconries, S. Maria in Cosmedin, was sited in the ancient *statio annonae,* or general center for the distribution of grain, and others were sited in or adjacent to the ancient public granaries (*horrea publica*). Church estates outside Rome were specifically assigned for the maintenance of individual *diaconiae,* whose number sharply increased during the eighth century. The deaconries tended to be placed on routes frequented by pilgrims, and this seems to have given new vitality to the area of the Fora at the turn of the eighth century. A century later the Fora were deserted, although with the exception of S. Maria Antiqua the churches built there remained. *Xenodochia,* or hospices, existed not only at St. Peter's and the Lateran but in other parts of the city.

The monasteries of the earlier medieval period were grouped principally round the three churches of St. Peter's, the Lateran, and S. Maria Maggiore. Some, however, were situated elsewhere; there were three in Trastevere, and the social role of a rich monastery like S. Silvestro in Capite, on the edge of the settled area, must have been appreciable.

The Capitol played no part in the life of early medieval Rome. A church with a monastery, S. Maria in Capitolio, was located there from the eighth century, but the place had no public function. In the eleventh century the ancient Tabularium on the east side was turned into a fortress by the Corsi family. There may have been a residence for the imperial envoy on another part of the Capitol hill; Henry IV dated some documents from the Capitol. The prefect of Rome, an official over whose appointment popes and emperors had clashed, sat in the Capitol in the early twelfth century. When the revolution of the Romans set up the first medieval Senate in 1143/1144, the insurgents began by storming and occupying the Capitol, which from then until the end of the Middle Ages was the seat of communal government. As a result, the senatorial palace was built around 1150 and S. Maria in Capitolio was reconstructed as S. Maria in Aracoeli in the mid thirteenth century. The senatorial palace was also rebuilt on a larger scale at this period. There was a market on the western side.

URBAN PATTERN AND THE ANCIENT INHERITANCE

The infrastructure of Rome suffered severely from the sixth-century collapse. Under Gregory I the Byzantine government was still nominally responsible for the aqueducts, which were in poor repair. Adrian I (772–795) repaired the Aqua Traiana, which supplied St. Peter's; the Aqua Claudia, which supplied the Lateran; the Aqua Jobia; and the Aqua Vergine, which was said to have supplied virtually the whole city. The last repair of the Trajan aqueduct seems to have been that of Nicholas I (*r.* 858–867). Later in the Middle Ages the only aqueduct to have been continuously operative seems to have been the branch of the Aqua Vergine which fed the Trevi Fountain. Most of the population, living near the river, depended either on wells or on the river itself. There is reference to an aqueduct outside the Porta Latina in 1072, and to the repair of an aqueduct which may have been a branch of the Marcia in 1179. The spring of Pope Damasus I (*r.* 366–384) supplied St. Peter's (though unreliably) from the Vatican hill itself.

A paradox of medieval Rome was the twelve-mile circuit of walls that enclosed a city which seldom exceeded 30,000 people. The repair of the walls was a major burden upon administration, even heavier after the enclosure of the Leonine City by a further circuit of walls following the Muslim attack of 846. The walls could not be manned in a full military sense, but they constituted a formidable psychological deterrent to an invader. However, a determined and well-equipped army could usually force its way into Rome, as occurred in 964, 1083, 1084, 1167, 1312, 1410, and 1417.

As is described above, the Christianization of the city gave it two focus points: the Lateran church and patriarchate, and St. Peter's. The latter proved in the long term to be by far the more potent influence on urban plan. The Lateran palace was important until the end of the twelfth century, when the reconstruction of the papal palace at St. Peter's pointed to the final victory of the Leonine City, meaning the area walled from 847 to 853. From the early Middle Ages the St. Peter's area derived added ceremonial importance from its being the site for the state entry of the emperor-elect, who entered through the Via Triumphalis, passing from the St. Peter gate to the square or the *cortina sancti Petri,* where the imperial palace was located. This counterbalanced the importance of the Lateran in the procession of the papal *possessio,* or formal possession-taking, of the see by the newly elected pope.

The collapse of habitation and organization in late antiquity led to the abandonment of a large area. To the east of the Capitol, to the south beginning at the Theater of Marcellus, to the north of the Campo Marzio, lay the largely uninhabited zone which Richard Krautheimer and others have termed the *disabitato*. The major roads, and certain gates and churches, produced islands of settlement in the *disabitato,* which also contained isolated farms and monasteries. Its predominantly agricultural character is marked as early as the pontificate of Gregory I, when Tiber flooding is said to have prevented the Romans from sowing their land. The first tentative papal effort to repopulate parts of the *disabitato* came only at the end of the Middle Ages, with a scheme of Nicholas V (1447–1455) to encourage building in the zone to the north of the Colosseum.

From the early thirteenth century the commune appointed "masters of the buildings of the city" (*magistri aedificiorum urbis*), who had power to remove abusive structures and partitions from the streets and squares (especially booths and "porticoes"), to control garbage disposal, to clean and maintain streets, to look after water supply, and to recover communal property which had been improperly occupied. The *maestri di strada* constituted an embryonic town-planning authority which had parallels in other Italian cities. At the end of the Middle Ages they began to replan streets and to tax property owners to finance new development. They were not, however, empowered to protect ancient monuments, although one or two of these (such as the Column of Trajan) received special legal protection, and the communal statutes of 1363 in theory protected others. But a special class of workmen called *effossores* worked at the exploitation of ancient buildings, and a whole district of lime burners, the *calcario* in the area of the Circus Flaminius, existed where the marbles of the ancient monuments were reduced to building lime.

In spite of their progressive looting and demolition, the buildings of ancient Rome exercised a powerful hold on the mind and imagination of the Middle Ages. The first extant Roman "guide," the seventh-century *Notitia ecclesiarum urbis Romae,* describes the ancient monuments of the city impartially with the Christian ones. The *Mirabilia urbis Romae,* probably written by Benedict, canon of St. Peter's, between 1140 and 1143, stresses the ancient monuments far more than the Christian; and the same is true of the less-well-informed *De mirabilibus urbis Romae,* composed about half a century later by the Englishman Master Gregory. The medieval literary inheritance contains a similar emphasis on the ancient monuments, most notably in the fine tenth-century poem *O Roma nobilis,* and in the early-twelfth-century poem by Hildebert of Lavardin, archbishop of Tours. But the satirical inheritance, the *invectiva in Romam,* was equally venerable: it was commonly remarked in this tradition that Roman morals were as ruined as Roman walls.

The idea of *renovatio* of the ancient world recurs in the history of Roman architecture no less than in the history of ideas. The Hellenistic revivals of the art and architecture of the seventh and early eighth centuries in Rome, the great building campaigns of the popes influenced by the Carolingian renaissance of a century later, the conservative but nevertheless classicizing architecture of the great twelfth-century churches all testify to the same persistence of classical models.

POLITICAL AND ADMINISTRATIVE HISTORY

The sieges, the forced movements of population, the destruction of many aqueducts, and the impoverishment of the surviving senatorial class all meant that by the time of the Byzantine victory over the Goths in 553 Rome was depopulated and seedy. There are no reliable population figures; the estimate of 90,000 inhabitants in the late sixth century seems overly generous, though it reflects wartime immigration. War had been renewed within twenty years of the Gothic defeat, through the Lombard invasion which by 574 had come close to isolating Rome from the rest of Byzantine Italy. Only a slim corridor over the Appenines connected Rome by way of the Via Flaminia with the exarchate of Ravenna, and this situation did not change in essentials for two centuries. Under such intense pressure much of Roman administrative and social organization collapsed. The *praefectus urbi* lingered on into the eighth century, but other lay civic offices declined or ceased to exist. The *praefectus annonae* was no longer regularly appointed, and the main burden for provisioning Rome came to be borne by the church. The same fate met the officials responsible for maintaining walls, aqueducts, and imperial palaces. The *consules ordinarii* disappeared. The senatorial class remained, if precariously; its interests were supposed to have been consulted by the emperor in the issue of the Pragmatic Sanction of 554. As an institution the Senate appears to have ceased to function by the late sixth century. The *numeri* of the Byzantine army were commanded by the *dux* or *magister militum,* and there was a sort of Greek quarter north of the Palatine hill for the Byzantine officials.

A new political balance emerged at the time of Pope Gregory I the Great. The pope never assumed formal political powers, although he frequently carried out political negotiations with the Lombards, and he used the landed resources of the Roman church to supply Rome and maintain essential services, including the care of refugees. He often adjured the government to pay its troops, but is only once said to have paid them from church funds. To finance these functions he instituted intense supervision of the landed properties of the Roman church in Italy and elsewhere by rectors, *defensores,* and so on. Natural disasters added to his difficulties. The pontificate began after severe flooding of the Tiber and a subsequent plague (the concentration of population in mainly low-lying areas near the river had made it more vulnerable to such dangers).

In the seventh century the popes suffered from continuous Lombard military pressures (the peace of 678–681 brought little respite) and also from the disadvantages of constant theological dispute with the Byzantine government. Near the end of the century the local levies of Ravenna entered Rome and used force to protect the pope from government displeasure (693–695). The Italian regionalism of this movement was to remain an important factor during the momentous events of the following century. The powers of the Byzantine military governor of the Roman duchy over the local levies known as the *exercitus Romanus* became gradually less, by comparison with the authority of the nobles who led the army, the *proceres exercitus.* An *ordo militaris* emerged among the Roman nobles. Some popes, such as Gregory II (*r.* 715–731) and Adrian I (*r.* 772–795), belonged to this noble class, just as had Gregory I before them. When the popes came to break away from Byzantine sovereignty and to appeal to Frankish power in the eighth century, they referred not only to the Roman people (*populus Romanus*) but to the "army of the Roman *res publica,*" by which they meant the particularist "Roman army" and not the army owing obedience to the Byzantine Empire.

The Lombard threat against Rome became acute in 727–728 with the seizure by King Liutprand of various towns in the Tiber Valley north of Rome. For a time he restored these, but other frontier towns on the Via Flaminia fell to Lombard forces in 739. The king met Pope Zacharias in 742 and again agreed to restore what he had seized. In 752 King Aistulf prepared to mount a final attack on Rome, causing the pope to appeal to the Franks. Even after the Frankish army had defeated Aistulf in 755, the Lombard king again attacked Rome in the following year and plundered the sanctuaries until the Franks once more dislodged him. Pro-Lombard and pro-Frankish parties appeared among the Roman notables, causing internal instability after Pope Paul I's death in 767. The last Lombard attacks on Rome were instigated by King Desiderius in 771 and 773. In the latter year Charlemagne intervened, and in 774 he entered Rome, inaugurating a long Frankish protectorate over the city.

The office of *patricius* of the Romans, offered to Charles Martel and confirmed by another pope to Pepin and his sons, was a Byzantine dignity which conferred judicial and administrative powers in Rome on its holder. For example, when Charlemagne judged the accusers of Pope Leo III in 800, he did not need any powers to pass judgment beyond those he already possessed as patrician. The Roman people acclaimed Charlemagne as emperor during the ceremony of coronation in 800.

The *optimates militiae,* the noble military leaders, had lost their direct participation in the papal elections as a result of the election decree of 769, but the Frankish government attempted to restore it to them in the *constitutio romana* of 824. The great lay nobles often took clerical orders so as to hold high offices in the ecclesiastical hierarchy; the Byzantine government had tried to forbid this practice at the time of Gregory the Great, but by the eighth century it had become standard. Under Stephen II (*r.* 752–757) the *primicerius notariorum,* one of the main officials of the Lateran patriarchate, was a certain Theodotus, who had earlier been consul and duke. Over a century later, under Adrian II (*r.* 867–872) and John VIII (*r.* 872–882), the powerful nobles who held such key posts were turning the whole machinery of the Roman bishopric to their advantage. The offices of *primicerius, secundicerius, nomenclator,* and *vestiarius* (or chief financial officers) all fell to such men. The imperial *missus* in Rome proved powerless to stop these abuses.

The late eighth and early ninth centuries were a period of prosperity in which the clergy enjoyed the Frankish donations and the revenues from their flourishing church estates. The new papal *domus cultae* proved a successful form of estate management, although an unpopular one with the Roman nobles. The direct contributions of the Frankish government and the flourishing pilgrim traffic also helped the popes to build churches, execute public works, and decorate the city as befitted the chief bishopric of the Frankish Empire. But decline followed the sack of Rome by Muslims in 846. Like many bishoprics, in the early tenth century the papacy fell under the control of local nobles; in the Roman case the ruling family was the house of Theophylact, the nobleman whose leadership enabled the Romans to defeat the Muslims at the Battle of the Garigliano in 915. His daughter, Marozia, dominated Roman politics until 932, when she and Hugh of Provence were expelled, and Rome came to be ruled by Alberic of Rome, her son by Alberic of Spoleto. Alberic ruled until his death in 954. His son, Octavian, elected pope as John XII (*r.* 955–964), was a less successful politician, whose errors led to the intervention of King Otto of Germany in Rome in 962 and to the renewal of the empire and imperial control.

For a century after the coronation of Otto I as emperor in 962, the imperial government made spasmodic efforts to keep order in Rome. As happened elsewhere in the empire, the great nobles were the real rulers, and attempts to control them through an imperial *missus* or through an imperial-appointed pope were often ineffective. Roman factions were held in check until Otto II's death in 983; a period followed in which Rome was dominated by the Crescenzi family. Otto III reestablished imperial control in 996 and tried to set up a permanent imperial government in Rome, with the help of obedient popes (Gregory V, *r.* 996–999; Sylvester II, *r.* 999–1003). After the failure of Otto III to make this policy work effectively, the noble factions again ruled the city, nominating the popes as best suited them. From 1012 to 1046 the family known as that of "Tusculum" controlled Rome, generally, until the end of the period, working in cooperation with the emperors. The influence of Romans on imperial government was shown in Emperor Conrad II's constitution of 1038, which laid down that cases in Rome and its district should follow Roman rather than Lombard law.

Roman administration during the eleventh century showed imperial and feudal influence, and also saw a gradual retreat of noble influence in papal government. Early in the century the organization of the "Sacred Lateran Palace" began to change, and the papal chancellor emerged, emancipated from the older civic Roman regional *scriniarii.* The *iudices dativi,* the lay judges, continued to sit, but the cardinals now participated in the administration of justice to laymen and clergy at the Lateran Palace. The ancient posts of judges such as the *vestiarius* and *sacellarius,* lost their former importance. The nobles continued, however, to be called to the main papal councils, both to what became known late in the century as the *curia,* and to the sittings of the papal *consistorium.* While no longer the real rulers of Rome by the 1060's, the nobles were implicitly recognized by the popes as part of the governmental system; and no systematic attempt was made by the Reform popes to reduce noble influence.

The critical point of eleventh-century Roman history was the fall of Rome to Emperor Henry IV in March 1084. Pope Gregory VII (*r.* 1073–1085) was isolated in Castel Sant'Angelo, while the emperor was crowned by the antipope, Clement III. Most of the great clerical and lay officers went over to Clement. A few weeks later the Norman army arrived, fighting nominally for Gregory VII. The German garrison was defeated and the city was fired and looted in the areas of St. Peter's, the Lateran, and the Via Lata. The Lateran quarter was so devastated that the zone surrounding the church of SS. Quattro Incoronati was still abandoned in 1116. The clergy and lay officers did not return to the city until after the ejection of Clement III from Rome in 1092; even so the partisans of Clement were active in Rome for another decade.

The treaty between the Roman people and clergy and Genoa, made in 1120, arranged for large sums to be paid by Genoa to Roman nobles as well as clerks, although the object of the treaty was a privilege to be issued by the pope in favor of the church of Genoa. Not only the nobles but the lesser Roman folk pressed for a share in the economic benefits of papal government at this time, as St. Bernard disgustedly recorded in his *De consideratione*. The separate juridic existence of the Roman people was recognized by the emperors, especially in the oaths they took in 1111, 1133, and 1155. In 1143 the Romans stormed the Capitol, then the seat of the judges and of the official known as the prefect, and "set up the order of the senators." The following year was held to be the legal date of the "renovation" of the senate, and in 1145 the pope conceded that henceforth there should be annually appointed senators or communal officials who would hold office by his authority. The Romans were also given substantial annual money payments by the pope. Their reluctance to give full acknowledgment to papal authority was shown by their welcoming the supposedly heretical Arnold of Brescia in 1148.

Roman communal independence and civic control of economic resources increased during the wars of Pope Alexander III (*r.* 1061–1073). The Romans negotiated their own naval and commercial treaties with Genoa and Pisa (1165–1174) and also vigorously opposed the economic competition of Tusculum in wool and textiles. They made the church compensate them for war losses. In 1188 Pope Clement III (*r.* 1187–1191) made a treaty with the Romans which consolidated these communal gains. The pope recovered two-thirds of the profits of the Roman mint, but was committed to some heavy annual payments to the Romans. In 1191 pope and emperor agreed to the destruction of Tusculum by the Romans. The election of a body of communal magistrates or senators was opposed by the popes, who preferred the election of a single "senator." This dispute occasioned a civil war under Innocent III (*r.* 1198–1216), who appointed a single senator from 1204. Substantial communal independence continued, however; for example, the commune controlled the mint. The aggressive attempts of the Roman commune to rule the Roman district were incompatible with the strong rule of the popes in the papal state; but Gregory IX (*r.* 1227–1241) lost control of Rome for long periods, even after he had paid large sums to placate the Romans. The war with Emperor Frederick II favored Roman opportunism, as the war with Frederick I had done in the preceding century. The climax of antipapal communal government in Rome came with the senatorship of Brancaleone degli Andalò, a Bolognese noble whose tenures of office (1252–1255, 1257–1258) saw the humiliation of popes Innocent IV (*r.* 1243–1254) and Alexander IV (*r.* 1254–1261). The Roman churches were financially exploited and sometimes even physically demolished by the Romans during this period.

There is some doubt about the importance of the popular elements in the constitution of the Roman communal government at this time. The documents suggest, though they leave room for some doubt, that under the senator there was a council of restricted size containing some notables at least; it may have been entirely selected from that class. How the council was chosen is unknown. There was also a popular "parliament" in which a general voice of approval or disapproval could be expressed. Tension periodically erupted between popular and magnate parties: in 1294 a revolution expelled the magnate regime and called in a foreign senator. One of the main aims of communal government was to assert the *iura sequimentorum*, the rights claimed by Rome over the area stretching from Corneto (Tarquinia) and Montalto in the north of the papal state to Terracina in the south. Places in this area were required to send men and material to the Roman carnival games, and to pay the salt tax.

Angevin intervention in Italy led to Angevin domination in Rome. The Romans elected Charles of Anjou senator for life in 1263, and from the time of his victories in 1266 until the eclipse of Angevin power after 1282 the city was Angevin-ruled. Angevin influence remained strong in Rome until the late fourteenth century; the nobles who governed Rome were usually drawn from a clientele of Angevin dependents. Popes Nicholas III (*r.* 1277–1280) and Boniface VIII (*r.* 1294–1303) tended to resist French and Angevin pressure, and the former issued a constitution in 1278, *super electione senatoris,* which justified the "spiritual and temporal monarchy" of the popes in Rome. It limited the Senate office to a single year and barred it to foreigners and lay noblemen. Nicholas himself accepted the position, delegating it to a series of vicars.

There were anti-Angevin movements in Rome before and during the occupation of the city by Emperor Louis of Bavaria in 1327 and 1328, and the "popular" rule in Rome of the so-called tribune Cola di Rienzo in 1347 was both anti-Angevin and antinoble in inspiration. With the exception of the brief stay of Urban V from 1367–1370, no pope was seen in Rome between 1304 and 1377. Papal absence had profound economic and probably also demographic effects; it also affected Rome as a religious center. Politically the Avignonese popes made great efforts to control their Italian lands, including Rome, but the independence of the Roman commune remained substantial. On the other hand, the power of the baronial nobility in the city was reduced. The city statutes of 1363, besides the rule of Cola di Rienzo, testify to popular influences in the government. New officials of a popular origin appear, especially "reformers" and later the "conservators," who were elected every three months and had powers over revenue. Other popular officials were the *banderesi,* the leaders of the regional militia. The senator-nobles disappeared; the senator became an imported official, the temporary head of the popular administration. The *banderesi* claimed the right to act as "executors of justice."

In the last decade of the fourteenth century Pope Boniface IX (*r.* 1389–1404) energetically attacked the independence of the commune, skillfully utilizing the enmity between popular and noble factions. In 1398 he effected a successful coup against the commune, which had permanent effects. The commune had to recognize the "full dominion" of the pope and his right to appoint communal officials. The financial independence of the commune from the papacy was also seriously compromised. The *banderesi* disappeared; the senator became a papal official; and the Roman judges came under strong indirect papal control. When it so wished, the papal government did set aside the communal statutes. Though made at a period of apparent papal weakness, Boniface IX's attack on communal liberty in Rome was successful and permanent in its effects. Although later, during the Great Schism, Rome was a prey to political disorders and subject to foreign rulers such as Ladislas of Durazzo or Braccio da Montone, the legal changes made in the city's government by Boniface IX were never reversed. The papal *signoria* of the city was from this point almost complete, and except for brief periods such as 1404–1405 the communal officials were hardly more than papal agents. By the time of John XXIII (*r.* 1410–1415) the financial administration of the city, the *camera urbis,* had become little more than a department of the papal chamber. Revolutions of baronial nobles were quite frequently to trouble the peace and security of the city during the fifteenth century, but the basis of papal rule remained untouched. When Pope Martin V (*r.* 1417–1431) entered Rome on 28 September 1420, he began a new period of the city's history, in which it was to become the showplace capital and the international financial center of its absolute papal rulers. The flight of Pope Eugenius IV (*r.* 1431–1447) from Rome in 1434, and the conspiracy of Stefano Porcari in 1452/1453, were brief parentheses which did not seriously interfere with the remaking of Renaissance Rome.

SOCIAL AND ECONOMIC HISTORY

The central part played by the Roman nobles in early medieval government of the city has already been emphasized. The class that was sometimes referred to (after the demise of the Senate as an official body) as the *Senatus,* which attended the holy liturgy in the section of the church designated as the *senatorium,* was from the later antique period until the Reform papacy of the eleventh century the real governing class of Rome. Members of this class frequently entered into minor orders, and held the key positions of the bureaucracy of the Lateran Palace, such as *primicerius defensorum, secundicerius, nomenclator,* and *vestiarius.* After the defeat of the Byzantine administration in the early eighth century the great nobles often also assumed titles which had earlier appertained to the great Byzantine officials, such as *consul et dux.* These usages were extended in the tenth century by Theophylact and his successors. Theophylact was *magister militum et vestiarius, dux et senator.* His grandson Alberic adopted the title of *princeps* as well as that of "senator of all the Romans," usages which bespoke the extraordinary domination exercised by the latter. "Senator of all the Romans" was also used by Crescentius de Nomentana at the end of the tenth century and by Romanus of the Tusculan family (later Pope John XIX, *r.* 1024–1032), in the early eleventh century.

At the time of the emergence of the papal state in the eighth century the interests of the great nobles often clashed with those of the clerical bureaucracy. These clashes were especially violent at the time of Popes Paul I (*r.* 757–767) and Stephen III (*r.* 768–772). The clerical answer to noble pressures was the reorganization of papal estates in vast *domus cultae,* which provided both a labor force and military service. The burning of these estates by the nobles in 815 indicates the threat they were felt to represent to noble power. In 824 a countercoup against the nobles was effected by Pope Paschal I (*r.* 817–824) with the help of the rural militia, the *familia sancti Petri.* After the death of Charlemagne in 814 the imperial government tended to favor the Roman nobles, and the *constitutio romana* of 824 spelled out this attitude.

In the tenth century the noble class secured even more extensive control of the government, and especially under the rule of the *princeps* Alberic the "senatorial" families carved out for themselves a stronger economic and social position in the Roman countryside, relying on the feudalization or *incastellamento* of the villages. This dominant position of the nobles in the countryside seems in the eleventh century to have formed the basis for a firmer hold of particular noble families on particular quarters of Rome. The Cenci dominated most of the city within the Tiber bend, though they had lost their control of Castel Sant'Angelo by Gregory VII's time. The Corsi had a fort on the Capitol hill; the Pierleoni (earlier a merchant family, but noble by Gregory VII's time) controlled the zone around the Theater of Marcellus, and much of Trastevere; Frangipani fortresses were located in the Forum, on the Palatine hill, and in the Colosseum. Many churches were owned and fortified by nobles in this period. In the twelfth and thirteenth centuries the progressive multiplication of "towers" and the fortification of ancient monuments produced a patchwork of fortified areas in the city, each dominated by a *consorteria* of nobles. Tor de' Conti and Torre delle Milizie are major surviving examples of the noble "towers."

The most important economic resources of Rome were the revenues of the Roman church and the income from pilgrims. Under Constantine the Roman church had not enjoyed an income in excess of that of a single rich senatorial family. By the time of Gregory I it was the richest landowner in Rome by far, absorbing many great senatorial patrimonies and holding them in mortmain. Noble families tried to recover church lands or to hold them on long leases, and they were especially successful at the time of the disintegration of the ancient church-owned *curtes* in the thirteenth century. But as late as the sixteenth century well over a quarter of the land in the Roman area was church-owned.

In the later Middle Ages the cash revenues of the Roman church accruing from sources outside Rome sharply increased. At the end of the twelfth century the income of the pope, excluding estates owned by Roman churches, income of justice and letters, and the mint, was about two thousand pounds of Provins (about 540 pounds sterling at twelfth-century exchange rates) annually. Under Boniface VIII (*r.* 1294–1303) his cash income was about 400,000 pounds of Provins (33,000 pounds sterling) annually, apart from monies going to clerks of the Roman court. This figure was little changed in 1420. It was, of course, necessary for the pope to reside in Rome for the Roman economy to enjoy the benefits of the income he attracted: for most of the fourteenth century he either was absent at Avignon or found that his revenues were much diminished by the Great Schism.

Rome was never a major center of industrial production. It was always an important communications center by land and sea, and the guilds of seamen and of merchants exporting and importing by sea are two of the earliest recorded. Control of sea routes was always vital to the city, and major treaties of the Roman commune with Genoa and Pisa (1165, 1174) were concerned with the security of the seaboard between Corneto (Tarquinia) and Terracina. Another period of concern over the control of this coast occurred under Angevin domination (1266–1282). Rome never seriously entered competition in the twelfth century for the Italian textile markets, but her wool and textile industry was important enough to provoke a bitter struggle with the nearby town of Tusculum (Tuscolo) for control of the sheep runs which converged on the Via Valeria. This hostility ended in 1911 with the destruction of Tusculum. Competition with Viterbo was a major factor in the twelfth and thirteenth centuries: the object was partly to control the agricultural resources of south Etruria and partly to dominate the grain-exporting ports of Corneto and Civitavecchia. The *iura sequimentorum* which Rome tried to impose over the district gave the city notable economic advantages, such as the salt tax.

Roman exports were low; imports, as is to be expected for a city of service industries, were high. In the mid fifteenth century goods for a value of 200,000 gold ducats (950,000 pounds of Provins) were imported annually either through the *dogana della grassa* or *dogana di Terra,* the land-customs office at Sant'Eustachio, or through the *dogana di Ripa,* the port of Rome. The food supply services were always important, which explains the great prominence in the later Middle Ages of the *bovattieri* or cattle-raising merchants, who were often also sheep farmers.

The *campsores,* money changers doing banking business, represented important elements in the Roman economy from the eleventh century. During the thirteenth century this class tended in its upper echelons to be replaced by "merchants following the Roman Court," who were often Tuscans. Though their main business was curial, their interests reached into other sectors of the Roman economy. Notaries were important in Rome at all periods. The *schola* of church regionary notaries was at first distinct from that of the public *tabelliones,* and the college of papal notaries formed part of the governing bureaucracy. By the eleventh century there was a distinction between the regional *scriniarii* and notaries of the Sacred Palace on one hand, and scriptors and notaries permanently attached to the papal writing office. In the later Middle Ages there was a college of notaries, whose office was conferred by papal (but sometimes by imperial) authority.

Settled groups of foreign faithful, who organized hostels and other charitable institutions for their countrymen in Rome, were elements in the Roman population from the early Middle Ages onward. By the ninth century there were *scholae* of Anglo-Saxons, Frisians, Lombards, and Franks. In the later Middle Ages there were equivalent institutions. The *schola Saxonum,* for example, was transformed by Innocent III into the new Hospital of Santo Spirito and linked with a new charitable order. But by the fourteenth century a new English hostel, the *Universitas Anglorum,* had been set up.

The pilgrims (*romei* or *romapeti*) were important in the city's economy, but we lack data to document their economic effects. Inns were important: the senator Brancaleone gave pilgrims the right to buy food from whom they pleased. More Romans rented out their property than resided in it in the later Middle Ages. But it may be that the economic effects of pilgrimage were felt through the charitable institutions rather than through direct payments for services. From 1300 onward the new institution of the Jubilee periodically increased the flow of pilgrims, but its effects were modest after the first because of the absence of the pope in 1350 and the schism after 1378. There was a none too successful Jubilee in 1390, followed by the unauthorized pilgrimage of the "Whites" in 1399, and by an equally unauthorized pilgrimage in 1400, which Boniface IX did not recognize as a Jubilee.

BIBLIOGRAPHY

Friedrich Baethgen, "Quellen und Untersuchungen zur Geschichte der päpstlichen Hof- und Finanzverwaltung unter Bonifaz VIII," in *Quellen und Forschungen aus italienischen Archiven und Bibliotheken,* **20** (1928–1929); Josef Benzinger, *Invectiva in Roman: Romkritik im Mittelalter vom 9. bis zum 12. Jahrhundert* (1968); Alain de Boüard, *Le régime politique et les institutions de Rome au moyen âge, 1252–1347* (1920); Robert Brentano, *Rome Before Avignon: A Social History of Thirteenth-century Rome* (1974); Paolo Brezzi, "Holy Years in the Economic Life in the City of Rome," in *Journal of European Economic History,* **4** (1975); Paolo Delogu, André Guillou, and Gherardo Ortalli, *Longobardi e Bizantini* (1980); Arnold Esch, *Bonifaz IX. und der Kirchenstaat* (1969); Herman Geertman, *More veterum: Il liber pontificalis e gli edifici ecclesiastici di Roma nella tarda antichità e nell'alto medioevo* (1975); Clara Gennaro, "Mercanti e bovattieri nella Roma della seconda metà del trecento," in *Bullettino dell'Istituto Storico Italiano per il Medio Evo e Archivio Muratoriano,* **78** (1967); Ferdinand A. Gregorovius, *History of the City of Rome in the Middle Ages,* Annie Hamilton, trans., 8 vols. in 13, 2nd rev. ed. (1903–1912, repr. 1967); Richard Krautheimer, *Rome: Profile of a City, 312–1308* (1980); Peter Llewellyn, *Rome in the Dark Ages* (1971), and "The Roman Church in the Seventh Century: The Legacy of Gregory I," in *Journal of Ecclesiastical History,* **25** (1974); Peter Partner, "The 'Budget' of the Roman Church in the Renaissance Period," in Ernest F. Jacob, ed., *Italian Renaissance Studies* (1960), 256–278, and

The Lands of St. Peter: The Papal State in the Middle Ages and the Early Renaissance (1972); Volkert Pfaff, "Die Einnahmen der römischen Kurie am Ende des 12. Jahrhunderts," in *Vierteljahrschrift für Sozial- und Wirtschaftsgeschichte,* **40** (1953); Charles Pietri, *Roma christiana: Recherches sur l'église de Rome, son organisation, sa politique, son idéologie de Miltiade à Sixte III (311–440),* 2 vols. (1976); Jeffrey Richards, *The Popes and the Papacy in the Early Middle Ages, 476–752* (1979), and *Consul of God: The Life and Times of Gregory the Great* (1980); Antonio Rota, "La costituzione originaria del comune di Roma," in *Bullettino dell'Istituto Storico Italiano per il Medio Evo e Archivio Muratoriano,* **64** (1953); Pierre Toubert, *Les structures du Latium médiéval: Le Latium méridional et la Sabine du IXe siècle à la fin du XIIe siècle,* 2 vols. (1973), and *Études sur l'Italie médiévale (IXe–XIVe s.)* (1976), 974–998; Richard C. Trexler, "Rome on the Eve of the Great Schism," in *Speculum,* **42** (1967).

PETER PARTNER

[See also **Antiquarianism and Archaeology; Cardinals, College of; Condottieri; Curia, Papal; Diaconicon; Dux; Early Christian and Byzantine Architecture; Holy Year; Italy, Byzantine Areas of; Italy, Rise of Towns in; Jews in the Papal States; Jubilee; Lateran; Lombards, Kingdom of; Magister Militum; Old St. Peter's, Rome; Papacy, Origins and Development of; Papal States; Pepin III and the Donation of Pepin; Pilgrimage, Western European; Processions; Roman Empire, Late; Schism, Great; Scholae; Spolia; Urbanism, Western European;** and individual personalities.]

ROMUALD OF RAVENNA, ST. (*ca.* 952–1027), founded a number of hermitages, mainly in central Italy, some of which eventually formed the nucleus of the Camaldolese Order. Now sometimes called an anchoritic St. Benedict, he was credited with reviving the eremitical discipline of the ancient church and giving a "law" to his hermits, who lived in communities that were usually associated with a monastery. Exhibiting a comprehensive reforming activity directed toward monasteries, communities of canons, and the laity, Romuald was one of the first to launch the campaign against simony which shook the church later in the eleventh century. Closely associated with Emperor Otto III (*r.* 996–1002), who was prevented only by death from entering one of Romuald's hermitages, he worked with the emperor to convert the Slavs with the help of disciples like Bruno of Querfurt. Romuald's feast day is 7 February.

BIBLIOGRAPHY

The chief sources for Romuald's life are Bruno of Querfurt's *Vita quinque fratrum,* in *Monumenta Germaniae historica, Scriptores,* XV, pt. 2 (1888, repr. 1963), 716–738, and Peter Damian, *Vita beati Romualdi,* Giovanni Tabacco, ed. (1957). The pioneering work on Romuald was done by Giovanni B. Mittarelli and Anselmo Costadoni, *Annales Camaldulenses,* I (1755), and Walter Franke, *Romuald von Camaldoli und seine Reformtätigkeit zur Zeit Ottos III* (1913). For further literature see Alberico Pagnani, *Vita di S. Romualdo,* 2nd rev. ed. (1967), 387–394.

KENNERLY M. WOODY

[See also **Bruno of Querfurt, St.; Camaldolese, Order of; Hermits, Eremitism; Monasticism, Origins of; Otto III, Emperor; Peter Damian, St.; Peter Urseolus, St.; Reform, Idea of.**]

ROMULUS, the name given to certain Latin fable collections. Although long thought to have been the early Roman king (from the dedication found in the *Romulus Nilantii [Romae imperator Tiberino filio suo salutem]*), Romulus was probably the pseudonym of an obscure plagiarist whose work ousted the name of the Roman freedman Phaedrus (*d. ca.* A.D. 50) and even succeeded in making the term Romulus a generic term for fable collections. The original fifth-century *Romulus* probably consisted of eighty-four fables in prose (forty-four from Phaedrus) and is now lost. The oldest extant texts inspired numerous early medieval derivatives in prose and verse, including the highly successful adaptation in elegiac verse by Gualterus Anglicus (Walter of England), chaplain to King Henry II of England, the *Novus Aesopus* of Alexander Neckam, and a lost Anglo-Latin version that gave rise to the *Fables* of Marie de France. Derivatives tend to be named after their editor or the location of the manuscript.

BIBLIOGRAPHY

Julia Bastin, *Recueil général des Isopets,* 2 vols. (1929–1930), contains the text of the *Novus Aesopus* and the version by Gualterus Anglicus; Léopold Hervieux, *Les fabulistes latins depuis le siècle d'Auguste jusqu'à la fin du moyen âge,* 5 vols., 2nd ed. (1893–1899).

GLYN S. BURGESS

[See also **Fables; Fables, French; Marie de France; Neckham, Alexander.**]

RÓMVERJA SAGA, an Old Norse, probably Icelandic, adaptation in saga style of Sallust's *Catilinae coniuratio* and *Bellum Iugurthinum* plus Lucan's *Pharsalia,* combined in such a way as to form one continuous narrative about the civil wars in the later years of the Roman Republic. Two different redactions have been preserved in fourteenth-century manuscripts. The first one stays close to the Latin originals but simplifies and tones down their rhetoric in accordance with the ideals of classical saga prose; it was probably written in the early thirteenth century and is now preserved only in fragments. The second redaction, which is complete and probably was written in the fourteenth century, presents an abbreviated and partly rewritten version of the first one, closer in style to the postclassical *riddarasögur* (sagas of courtly romance).

BIBLIOGRAPHY

Editions. Jakob Benediktsson, ed., *Early Icelandic Manuscripts in Facsimile,* XIII (1980); Rudolf Meissner, ed., *Rómveriasaga (AM 595 4°)* (1910).

Studies. Jakob Benediktsson, "Rómverja saga (sǫgur)," in *Kulturhistorisk leksikon for nordisk middelalder,* XIV (1969), 398–399; Fredrik Paasche, "Über Rom und das Nachleben der Antike im norwegischen und isländischen Schrifttum des Hochmittelalters," in *Symbolae Osloenses,* **13** (1934).

LARS LÖNNROTH

[See also **Riddarasögur.**]

RONCESVALLES. Spanish epic fragment of 100 verses found written on two worn parchment folios in a census record of 1366 in the Provincial Archives of Pamplona. The handwriting is from Navarre or Aragon of the first years of the fourteenth century. There is disagreement concerning the date of composition of the text, which is variously given as early to late thirteenth century.

Part of a Spanish epic related to the *Chanson de Roland,* the fragment contains Charlemagne's search for Roland among the dead on the battlefield. After discovering Archbishop Turpin and then Oliver, he comes upon his nephew. As he laments over Roland's body, he reviews his own early life and their many exploits together, fainting from grief at the conclusion. Duke Aymón also finds his dead son, Rynalte de Montalbán, and is mourning over his loss when summoned to revive the king.

Similar in some respects to the *Pseudo-Turpin,* the *Roncesvalles* reflects an independent Peninsular tradition of the defeat of Charlemagne's rear guard in the Pyrenees, evidenced by the lament over three bodies, the recall motif containing *Mainete* material, the presence of Rynalte de Montalbán, and the character of the *planctus* itself. All themes and motifs have counterparts in other Spanish epic texts as well as in the *romancero.*

Carelessly written, the text shows Navarro-Aragonese traits, perhaps of scribal origin. The language is highly formulaic, with a varied set of formulas much like those found in the *Cantar de mío Cid.* The assonated double-hemistich epic line resembles that of the *Cantar de mío Cid,* with the same hemistich-length preferences, 7–8–6–9, and the second himistich tends to be slightly longer than the first. There are six laisses of differing length in which the *á-e* assonance (with the paragogic *e*) is favored.

BIBLIOGRAPHY

Editions with studies. Jules Horrent, *Roncesvalles: Étude sur le fragment de cantar de gesta conservé à l'Archive de Navarre (Pampelune)* (1951); Ramón Menéndez Pidal, "*Roncesvalles,* un nuevo cantar de gesta español del siglo XIII," in *Revista de filología española,* **4** (1917), repr. in abbreviated form in his *Tres poetas primitivos* (1948).

Other studies. Jacques Horrent, "L'allusion à la chanson de Mainet contenue dans le 'Roncesvalles,'" in *Marche Romane,* **20** (1970); Martín de Riquer, "El *Roncesvalles* castellano," in his *La leyenda del Graal y temas épicos medievales* (1968); Ruth House Webber, "The Diction of the *Roncesvalles* Fragment," in *Homenaje a Rodríguez-Moñino,* II (1966), 311–321.

RUTH HOUSE WEBBER

[See also **Cantar de Mío Cid; Pseudo-Turpin; Roland, Song of; Spanish Literature, Epic Poetry.**]

RONDEAU. A musical-poetic form (from the Latin *rotundum* [round]) of the fourteenth and fifteenth centuries. It was one of the *formes fixes* of the French *ars nova* style. Its thirteenth-century prototype was a round dance song in which a soloist sang one verse of text to a phrase of music (*a*), the chorus repeated the music with their consistent refrain (*A*), the soloist then sang two verses to the first and second phrases of music (*a b*), and then the chorus responded with the full two-line refrain to both phrases of music (*A B*): *a A a b A B*. By the fourteenth century the final refrain had been added to the beginning as well—*A B a A a b A B*—and the rondeau had become an art song for solo voice with instruments.

The earliest protorondeaux appear as interpolations into the narrative romance *Guillaume de Dole* (*ca.* 1228), while others are found in later narrative works. These are typically of six or eight lines. In the fourteenth century the form was extended to lengths of eight, eleven, or thirteen lines; by the times of Guillaume de Machaut and late in the century, examples of sixteen lines appear. In the fifteenth century, a twenty-one-line form became popular—for example, in the works of Christine de Pizan and Charles of Orléans—but this was usually not set to music. Rondeau texts are generally concerned with courtly love and are often rather playful or whimsical as a result of the repetitive infixing of refrains that remain, even in the developed formal song of the *ars nova,* reminiscent of the dance. The circularity of the form seems to have inspired some tricks of composition as well. Guillaume de Machaut, in the three-part rondeau "Ma fin est mon commencement," retrogrades the melody of each part so that the music literally illustrates the text: it is the same backward as forward. An early-fifteenth-century addition to the manuscript Chantilly, Musée Condé, MS 564 (formerly 1047), presents a canonic roundeau of Baude Cordier ("Tout par compas suys composés") notated on circular staves, while his "Belle, bonne, sage" appears in the shape of a heart. In the later fifteenth century the rondeau gained popularity as a literary form increasingly disssociated from music, although such composers as Guillaume Dufay, Gilles Binchois, and others of the Burgundian school still favored it over other lyric forms.

BIBLIOGRAPHY

Willi Apel, ed., *French Secular Compositions of the Fourteenth Century,* I and III (1970, 1972); Nico J. H. van den Boogaard, *Rondeaux et refrains du XIIe siècle au debut du XIVe* (1969); Gilbert Reaney, "Concerning the Origins of the Rondeau, Virelai, and Ballade Forms," in *Musica disciplina,* 6 (1952), and "The Poetic Form of Machaut's Musical Works: The Ballades, Rondeaux, and Virelais," *ibid.,* 13 (1959).

MARCIA J. EPSTEIN

[See also **Anglo-Norman Literature; Ars Nova; Ars Subtilior; Ballade; Chansonnier; Charles of Orléans; Chartier, Alain; Christine de Pizan; Dance; Deschamps, Eustache; French Literature: After 1200; French Literature: Lyric; Guillaume de Dole; Ma Fin Est Mon Commencement; Machaut, Guillaume de; Troubadour, Trouvère; Virelai.**]

RONDELLUS, a technique of musical composition for three voices or a composition written with this technique. The *rondellus* technique, which flourished in thirteenth-century England, involved voice (or phrase) exchange—that is, the exchanged repetition of concordant phrases of music. In one type of *rondellus,* the exchange was between two voices; the third voice was a vocal or instrumental tenor that held a separate supporting melody. Another type involved the exchange of musical phrases among all three voices. The two types may be schematized as shown below:

(1) voice	1	A ...	B ...	
	2	B	A	
	3	C		
(2) voice	1	A ...	B ...	C ...
	2	B ...	C ...	A ...
	3	C ...	A ...	B ...

In his *Descriptio Cambriae* (1198), Gerald of Wales seems to describe the *rondellus* technique; Walter Odington, writing around 1300, provides a fuller discussion. The technique was employed within the musical genre of conductus, both for the terminal melismatic cauda and for the texted body of the work. It also appears in motets of English provenance.

As a generic term, *rondellus* refers to a composition written exclusively or predominantly in *rondellus* technique, producing the effect of a canon (or rota) without staggered entrances. The term also appears in some continental sources as a latinized word for rondeau.

BIBLIOGRAPHY

Luther A. Dittmer, "An English Discantuum Volumen," in *Musica disciplina,* 8 (1954); Robert Falck, "Rondellus, Canon, and Related Types Before 1300," in *Journal of the American Musicological Society,* 25 (1972); Frank L. Harrison, *Music in Medieval Britain,* 4th ed. (1980).

MARCIA J. EPSTEIN

[See also **Cauda; Conductus; Gerald of Wales; Melisma; Motet; Musical Treatises; Odington, Walter; Rota.**]

Entrance porch over the central doorway, west facade of Regensburg Cathedral. Designed by Conrad Roriczer, 1456–1477. PHOTO: WIM SWAAN

ROOD SCREEN. See **Screen.**

RORICZER, CONRAD (1410/1415–1477), illustrious member of the fifteenth-century Roriczer family of Regensburg master masons. Conrad served as designer or consulting architect for churches in Nördlingen, Eichstätt, Ingolstadt, and Nuremberg. But the focus of his career was at Regensburg Cathedral, where he was *Dombaumeister* (cathedral architect) between 1456 and 1477, while work proceeded on the nave vault and west facade.

BIBLIOGRAPHY

Lon R. Shelby, ed. and trans., *Gothic Design Techniques: The Fifteenth-century Design Booklets of Mathes Roriczer and Hanns Schmuttermayer* (1977).

LON R. SHELBY

[See also **Gothic Architecture; Masons and Builders.**]

RORICZER, MATHES (*d. ca.* 1495), a German master mason who worked at the church of St. Lorenz in Nuremberg and at Eichstätt Cathedral before taking the place of his father, Conrad, as *Dombaumeister* (cathedral architect) at Regensburg Cathedral by 1478. He is perhaps more famous as the author and publisher of two booklets on Gothic design techniques—*Büchlein von der Fialen Gerechtigkeit* (Booklet on pinnacle correctitude) and *Wimpergbüchlein* (Booklet on gablets), and a pamphlet on practical geometry, *Geometria deutsch.*

BIBLIOGRAPHY

Facsimile edition of Roriczer's *Büchlein von der Fialen Gerechtigkeit* and *Geometria deutsch* by Ferdinand Geldner (1965); critical ed. and English trans. by Lon R. Shelby, *Gothic Design Techniques: The Fifteenth-century Design Booklets of Mathes Roriczer and Hanns Schmuttermayer* (1977).

LON R. SHELBY

[See also **Architect, Status of; Construction: Engineering; Gothic Architecture; Masons and Builders; Parler Family; Villard de Honnecourt.**]

ROSARY (from the Latin *rosarium,* "rose garden," and by the fourteenth century, "collection of texts"). From patristic antiquity throughout the Middle Ages the continuous repetition of prayers, biblical passages, and related liturgical texts was a feature of Christian spirituality. To assist in counting these repetitions various devices were used, such as pebbles, knotted ropes, and beads. In the early Middle Ages the saying of groups of fifty psalms, the kyrie eleison, and paternoster were the most popular repetitive devotions, and by the twelfth century and the rise of Marian piety, the angelic salutation, Ave Maria, together with genuflections and prostrations, was added to these. According to a popular tradition reported in the work of the Dominican Alan de la Roche (1428–1475), it was St. Dominic (*ca.* 1171–1221) who, through a miraculous apparition of the Virgin Mary, invented the rosary; whatever the case, clearly the Dominicans did promote its use. But the practice existed long before St. Dominic, and the addition of the contemplation of the various mysteries of the Virgin to the saying of chaplets, groups, and psalters of Aves came long after Dominic's time and is associated especially with the Carthusians. To assist those saying the rosary, strings of beads, disks, gems, carved ivory, and other ornate objects were used. These were often called paternosters, and the London street Paternoster Row takes its name from the artisans making rosaries there. By the Late Middle Ages, many devotional rosary books and collections of sermons had been written and various religious confraternities formed, especially in Italy, to promote the use of the rosary.

BIBLIOGRAPHY

Stephan Beissel, *Geschichte der Verehrung Marias in Deutschland während des Mittelalters* (1972); *500 Jahre Rosenkrantz, 1475 Köln 1975: Erzbischöfliches Diözesan-Museum Köln, 25 Oktober 1975–15 Januar 1976* (1975); Willibald Kirfel, *Der Rosenkranz: Ursprung und Ausbreitung* (1949); G. G. Meerssemann, "Le origini della Confraternita del Rosario e della sua iconografia in Italia," in *Atti e memorie dell'Accademia patavina di scienze, lettere ed arti,* 76 (1963–1964); Gislind Ritz, *Der Rosenkranz* (1962).

ROGER E. REYNOLDS

[See also **Ave Maria.**]

ROSCELINUS (*ca.* 1050–*ca.* 1125) was a logician who taught at various cathedral schools in northern France. As is the case with most teachers of dialectic in his day, almost nothing of his writings has survived, and the facts of his life and teaching must be pieced together from the statements of others. The attitudes of these witnesses toward Roscelinus range from unsympathetic to antagonistic.

After receiving his education at Soissons and Rheims, Roscelinus became a canon at Compiègne. There, shortly before 1090, he applied his training in logic to the doctrine of the Trinity, reportedly dissolving the divine unity into three separate entities in order to avoid the problem of how the Father, Son, and Holy Spirit could be one substance and yet not all be incarnate in Christ. Roscelinus was quickly accused of teaching tritheism, and his opinion was brought to the attention of ecclesiastical authorities as well as the most famous theologian of that day, Anselm, then abbot of Bec and soon to be archbishop of Canterbury. Anselm assumed Roscelinus was referring not to three persons or relations in the Godhead, where a distinction was proper, but to three separate entites or gods who were united not substantially but only in will and power.

In defending his teaching, Roscelinus allegedly compared the Trinity to three angels and was reported to say that only custom stood in the way of speaking of three gods, erroneously claiming the authority of Lanfranc and Anselm for his opinion. The issue was temporarily resolved in a synod at Soissons in 1092, where Roscelinus recanted his position. His subsequent tendency to return to his earlier formulation, however, led Anselm to revise and complete his treatise *De incarnatione Verbi* (On the incarnation of the Word) in 1093.

Despite his trial for heresy, Roscelinus' recantation and his reputation as a logician ensured his subsequent career. He held canonries at Tours, Loches, and Besançon. At the turn of the century he was probably the most famous teacher of dialectic in the schools of northern France. His reputation and numerous students led Peter Abelard to study under him at Loches in the early years of the twelfth century. Parallel to his approach to the Trinity, Roscelinus apparently affirmed that only individuals exist in external nature and that universal concepts are verbal expressions for mental constructs.

Abelard eventually repudiated what he saw as the extreme nominalism of Roscelinus. In his *Theologia Summi boni,* written between 1118 and 1120 for his students in logic, Abelard developed his own approach to the Trinity, and in so doing ridiculed Roscelinus both as a teacher of dialectic and as an orthodox Christian on the doctrine of the Trinity. Abelard's description of the Trinity in terms of logic—that one essence and three persons were analogous in logic to one statement being simultaneously a proposition, a question (*assumption*), and a conclusion—was viewed by contemporaries as an unfortunate example.

Roscelinus apparently sent Abelard's book to the bishop of Paris to be examined for heresy, and he wrote a scathing letter to Abelard defending his own teaching and reputation. Roscelinus was thus instrumental, along with Alberic of Rheims and Lotulph of Novara, in Abelard's condemnation at the Council of Soissons in 1121 and the burning of his work.

After his letter to Abelard, the only writing of Roscelinus known to have survived, he dropped from view, and his death may have occurred a few years later. Through the comments of Abelard, Otto of Freising, and John of Salisbury, Roscelinus' name became forever linked with the position that only individuals exist and that the universal has neither objective nor subjective reality, but is only a sound or verbal expression. He has thus been traditionally viewed as the earliest and most extreme representative of nominalism.

BIBLIOGRAPHY

Anselm's *De incarnatione Verbi* and two letters concerning Roscelinus are available in English in Jasper Hopkins and Herbert Richardson, eds. and trans., *Anselm of Canterbury,* III (1976), 1–37.

Studies include François Picavet, *Roscelin, philosophe et théologien* (1911); Joseph Reiners, *Der Nominalismus in der Frühscholastik* (1910).

WILLIAM J. COURTENAY

[See also **Abelard, Peter; Anselm of Canterbury; Anselm of Laon; Dialectic; John of Salisbury; Lanfranc of Bec; Nominalism; Ockham, William of; Otto of Freising; Philosophy and Theology, Western European: To Mid Twelfth Century; Trinitarian Doctrine; William of Champeaux.**]

ROSE WINDOW, a large circular window in the terminal wall of a church which, by the design of its tracery, is said to resemble the petals of a mature rose. In a rose window the tracery is predominantly semicircular and directed toward the rim of the window. Chartres (both transept terminals), Laon (choir terminal), and Mantes (west facade) have especially fine rose windows.

BIBLIOGRAPHY

For illustrations, see Whitney S. Stoddard, *Monastery and Cathedral in France* (1966), figs. 162, 193, 220, 221, 228, and 229.

CARL F. BARNES, JR.

[See also **Glass, Stained; Gothic Architecture; Music, Western European (with illustration); Wheel Window.**]

ROSENGARTEN (also known as *Der Rosengarten zu Worms*) is a Middle High German narrative poem. It exists in several divergent versions, of which those labeled *A* and *D* by nineteenth-century scholarship are the most important. The *A* version is generally dated around 1250 and the *D* toward the end of the thirteenth century. There is no recent edition. The 1893 edition by Georg Holz contains both versions along with the fragmentary version *F.* The manuscript transmission of the *A* version derives entirely from the fifteenth century, while fragments of the other versions can be dated back into the fourteenth century.

In the *A* version Kriemhilt, daughter of King Gibeche of Worms and fiancée of Siegfried, has a rose garden surrounded by a thread. Having heard of the fame of Dietrich von Bern (Theodoric the Ostrogoth) and his heroes, she wishes to match them against the heroes of Worms. She challenges Dietrich and his men to break the thread around the garden and to trample the roses. The intruders will be met by men from the Worms court and the winner of each individual combat will receive a kiss from Kriemhilt and a wreath of roses. The challenge is grudgingly accepted by Dietrich and his men, who find it beneath their dignity. In addition to the men at Dietrich's court, Dietleib (hero of *Biterolf und Dietleib*) and the warrior-monk Ilsan join the group to make up the requisite number twelve. The battles are fought and Dietrich's men win them all. The only retardation in the almost mechanical battle narration is brought about by Dietrich's reluctance to fight Siegfried. Hildebrand manages to drive him into battle with taunts. Two of the warriors, Ekkehard and Hildebrand, refuse the queen's kiss. The monk Ilsan demands a pitched battle with a group of fifty-two knights. He defeats them all singlehandedly (killing twelve) and goes to receive fifty-two kisses and rose wreaths from Kriemhilt. His rough beard scratches and bloodies her face. "Thus should I kiss a treacherous girl," he remarks (line 376.3). The themes of this version are clearly the pride of Kriemhilt and the senselessness of blind courtly service of ladies.

The *D* version shifts the focus radically by having Kriemhilt's father, Gibeche, issue the challenge to Etzel (Attila), who then passes the challenge along to Dietrich. These changes remove most of the opprobrium attached to Kriemhilt in *A*. The parodistic element comes to the fore here and blunts some of the satire of the *A* version. The *F* version accentuates the courtly elements and places them in sharp contrast to the scenes of violence. This version exists only in fragments.

The indebtedness of the *Rosengarten* to the surviving *Nibelungenlied* is clear enough, but the discrepancies are interesting. Here Kriemhilt's father bears the name Gibeche, a name that is probably older in the heroic tradition than the Dankrat of the *Nibelungenlied;* and he is still alive. Siegfried appears here as Kriemhilt's fiancé, a role he never plays in the earlier epic.

The strophic form is also reminiscent of the

Nibelungenlied, with its four long lines rhyming *a a b b*. Each line is divided by a caesura and has four stresses in the first half-line and three in the second. This strophic form is known as the *Hildebrandston.*

BIBLIOGRAPHY

The poem has been edited by Georg Holz, *Die Gedichte vom Rosengarten zu Worms* (1893). See also Helmut de Boor, "Die literarische Stellung des Gedichtes vom Rosengarten in Worms," in *Beiträge zur Geschichte der deutschen Sprache und Literatur* (Tübingen), **81** (1959); Joachim Heinzle, *Mittelhochdeutsche Dietrichepik* (1978); Bernhard Schnell, "Eine neue Fassung des 'Rosengarten'?" in *Zeitschrift für deutsches Altertum und deutsche Literatur,* **108** (1979).

EDWARD R. HAYMES

[See also **Biterolf und Dietleib; German Literature; Middle High German Literature; Nibelungenlied; Sigurd; Theodoric the Ostrogoth.**]

ROSENPLÜT, HANS (*ca.* 1400–after 1460), the first in a line of prolific "artisan poets" of Nuremberg. Rosenplüt wrote for the pleasure and edification of the townspeople. An earnest craftsman of workaday verse, he used and established a number of literary forms (the *Priamel,* carnival play, town panegyric) that were to become vastly popular in the century to follow.

Hans Rosenplüt first appears in the Nuremberg records (kept in this town with bureaucratic zeal) in 1426. He is entered into the list of townspeople newly admitted to residency (*Neubürger*) as a day-laborer (journeyman, most likely) in the trade of chain-mail smith (*sarwürcht*). Since the language throughout his works is the Franco-Bavarian spoken in Nuremberg, we must assume that Rosenplüt immigrated from the province nearby. Only a year later, he was able to qualify as *sarwürcht* master. Yet, unable, apparently, to buy himself a house with a workshop (craftsmen lived and worked with assistants in the same house), Rosenplüt had to rent quarters outside the city gates—the "suburbs" then being places where the poorer townspeople were required to live.

While registering initially under his family name, Rosenplüt, the poet began using the name "Hans Schnepper" ("the mellifluous and loquacious one") as the kind of professional nom de plume which didactic poets were fond of giving themselves from the twelfth century on. The name befits the ready and agile manner with which Rosenplüt was able to cast almost anything into verse. Considering that writing was an avocation for him, the size of his oeuvre suggests that couplets flowed easily from his quill. It was as "Hans Schnepper," the poet, that Rosenplüt now made his reputation. Starting in 1429, the Nuremberg records refer to him exclusively by that name.

In 1430, "Hans Schnepper" was granted the status of regular burgher (*burger der reht stat*) within the city walls. He most likely attained full citizenship so quickly by marrying the widow of a deceased master (a common practice). For to engage in his trade, a master had first to become the married head of his own hearth (*aigen rauch*). His wife was expected to furnish room and board for the apprentices and journeymen.

The records indicate that Rosenplüt's chain-mail shop was not a successful one. All his life, in fact, his name is conspicuously absent from the tax rolls (real property, salt). Perhaps prompted by lack of success in his apprenticed trade (rapidly becoming obsolete), Rosenplüt—in the early 1440's—changed his profession to that of brass founder (*Rotschmied*). Here he joined a future-oriented craft, specializing in the casting of large guns, for which Nuremberg was gaining increasing fame.

Perhaps honoring his success, in 1444 the town council appointed Rosenplüt master gun keeper (*Büchsenmeister*), one of several, a salaried office he seems to have held for the rest of his life. During the 1449/1450 siege of Nuremberg by Margrave Albrecht Achilles, the town fathers posted Rosenplüt, with heavy guns, at important city gates. Through his steady employment as gun keeper, Rosenplüt's circumstances had become more secure by the 1450's. He was able to acquire (by purchase or inheritance) a house of his own, in the northwest quarter near the dairy market (*Milchmarkt*).

Rosenplüt took satisfaction in calling himself an "untutored layman." Yet like many self-taught people, he was eager to display his knowledge. He laced his verses, especially the images, with reams of information, the kind any upright Nuremberg burgher must have considered good to know. It is a "cobbler approach" to literature, expected of the didactic poet (earnest, overly florid writing, verses hammered together, as it were), something we must keep in mind when reading Rosenplüt. Following a practice first put to use by Heinrich der Teichner (didactic poet of the fourteenth century), Rosenplüt closed his major works (but not the ribald carnival plays) with a couplet rhyme on his name. Since the copyright concept did not exist, such a "signature" had to do in its place. "Rosenplüt" could not be excised without breaking up the poem's ending.

Rosenplüt's works have been preserved in over sixty different manuscripts and printed editions. While there is a core of about six manuscripts (mainly of Nuremberg provenance) that contains most of his writings, the size and complexity of the transmission (variants of the same text, spurious attributions) have, for over a century, foiled attempts to prepare a reliable edition.

The most venerable form in which Rosenplüt worked was the novelistic verse tale, centering on the subject of adultery. In demand since the days of Der Stricker (*fl.* 1220–1250), verse tales (*Mären*) are best known through Chaucer's fabliaux. While employing the stock characters of sex comedy (unfaithful wife, amorous cleric, sly servant, dimwitted suitor), Rosenplüt meant these tales to teach by negative example. Marriage was, after all, the cornerstone not only of Nuremberg's moral edifice, but—in the master's shop—of its economy.

Equally humorous—and wittier—are the host of shorter poems written by Rosenplüt, mainly salutes to wine and beer (*Weingrüsse, Biersegen*) and the so-called *Priamel.* The latter are one-stanza ditties that take about ten seemingly unrelated statements about the nature of things and people, and integrate them by means of a funny closing line. Rooted in proverbial humor and wisdom, the *Priamel* existed before Rosenplüt. But in mastering the form, he gave it immense popularity.

The same holds true for Rosenplüt's carnival plays (*Fastnachtspiele*), burlesque sketches with which the Nurembergers, carousing in taverns, entertained themselves at Mardi Gras even before Rosenplüt's time. In their open and gross lewdness (fecal, sexual), carnival plays, like Mardi Gras itself, released frustrations penned up all year in the tightly regulated life of the Nuremberg craftsman. Rosenplüt is the first author of such playlets known to us by name. Together with Hans Folz (*ca.* 1435/1440–1512), his successor, he wrote so many of them (about thirty) that Nuremberg was to become the center of this carnival play tradition for two centuries.

Not all of the carnival plays are exercises in imaginative obscenity. Taking advantage of the carnival liberties the town council permitted at his time (censorship set in soon), Rosenplüt wrote some of the few carnival plays known to deal with political topics. Most noteworthy is *Des Türken Vasnachtspil,* which attacks the "do-nothing" policy of the reigning emperor, Frederick III, by bringing his archenemy, the Turkish sultan, to Nuremberg, where the "great infidel" proclaims peace, frees the peasants, reforms the church, and restricts the authority of princes.

The pedagogic bent expected of a town poet comes fully to the fore in the many instructional verse tracts (*Reimreden*) Rosenplüt wrote on religious topics (in praise of the Virgin and various saints) and on ethical concerns (the value—before Calvin—of laboring by the sweat of one's brow). In *Reimreden* on social issues, he shows personal knowledge of the life to which the poor and disenfranchised (including the Nuremberg Jews) were relegated and pleads for improvements—within the system, to be sure. Rosenplüt never attacks the ruling town council, constituted (as in most European cities) of patrician families.

Rosenplüt devotes many of his verse tracts to political causes, a habit rare among German authors. In early decades (the first political tract dates from 1427), these are exercises in local patriotism. He defends, with indiscriminate fervor, the right of Nuremberg to govern itself as an independent imperial city and inveighs against encroaching territorial princes. His 1447 poem in praise of Nuremberg is the first such panegyric not addressed to a court. Like much of Rosenplüt's writing, this "Laudation to a City," his most popular poem, was a seminal form much favored by later poets like Hans Sachs.

In the late 1450's, Rosenplüt began to widen his perspective. Looking beyond the walls, he perceived the medieval order (always one more of faith than fact) losing its center. No security can exist for Nuremberg that does not include peace in central Europe. Like many of his contemporaries, Rosenplüt viewed the "Turkish threat" (Constantinople had fallen in 1453) as a sign of doomsday for Christian Europe. In his 1458/1459 tract *Türkenlied,* he calls on Emperor Frederick III to restore order and peace by enlisting the dormant support of burghers and peasants. His last datable work (1460) is another such political tract (addressed to Duke Ludwig of Bavaria), in which he salutes the peace agreements between territorial princes.

When Rosenplüt died in 1460 or shortly thereafter, his heir apparent as principal town poet, Hans Folz, had already begun his work. Folz was, within two generations, in turn succeeded by the great Hans Sachs. All three worked the same forms of "applied literature" (*Gebrauchsliteratur*). And beginning with Hans Rosenplüt, this notable triad of artisan poets made Nuremberg the center of German letters for one-and-a-half centuries.

BIBLIOGRAPHY

Karl Euling, *Das Priamel bis Hans Rosenplüt: Studien zur Volkspoesie* (1905); Hanns Fischer, ed., *Die deutsche Märendichtung des 15. Jahrhunderts* (1966); Adelbert von Keller, ed., *Fastnachtspiele aus dem fünfzehnten Jahrhundert,* 4 vols. (1853–1858, repr. 1965/1966); Hansjürgen Kiepe, *Die Nürnberger Priameldichtung* (1984); Rochus von Liliencron, ed., *Die historischen Volkslieder der Deutschen vom 13. bis 16. Jahrhundert,* I (1865, repr. 1966); Jörn Reichel, "Hans Rosenplüt genannt Schnepperer: Ein Handwerkerdichter im spätmittelalterlichen Nürnberg," in *Mitteilungen des Vereins für Geschichte der Stadt Nürnberg,* 67 (1980), and *Der Spruchdichter Hans Rosenplüt* (1985); Dieter Wuttke, ed., *Fastnachtspiele des 15. und 16. Jahrhunderts* (1973).

ECKEHARD SIMON

[See also **Carnival; Chaucer; Class Structure, Western; Drama, German; Folz, Hans; German Literature; Heinrich der Teichner; Mären; Middle High German Literature; Nuremberg; Stricker, Der.**]

ROSKILDE CHRONICLE (*Chronicon Roskildense*), the earliest product of Danish historiography, can be dated around 1140. The brief Latin text discusses the quarrel over who should succeed Archbishop Asser of Lund, and it mentions the triumph of Eskil, the bishop of Roskilde, in 1138 but not the murder of his rival, Ruko of Slesvig, in 1143. Though the chronicle is anonymous, the strong individuality of the author breaks through in very personal opinions and interests. A strong clerical bias, an interest in the history of the church of Roskilde, and a passionate attachment to the cause of King Niels and his son Magnus in the civil wars of 1131–1134 have led scholars to conjecture that the chronicle could be the work of Archbishop Eskil himself.

The first section (chaps. 1–9) covers the events of Danish history from Harald Klak's baptism at Mainz in 826 to Sweyn Estridsen's rise to power in 1042. The narrative is derived from Adam of Bremen's *History of the Bishops of the Church of Hamburg,* so Danish political history is coordinated with the history of the see of Hamburg-Bremen, from St. Ansgar to Bishop Libentius. In an attempt to improve upon Adam's chronology for the earliest period, the author of the chronicle confuses the sequence of events and turns Gorm the Old and Harald Bluetooth into two Gorms and three Haralds. The second part (end of chap. 9 to chap. 19) covers the period from the reign of Sweyn Estridsen to the rise of Erik III the Lamb. It is here that the author gives the freest expression to his points of view. Though he mentions very briefly that Knud the Holy had died a martyr's death and been canonized, he calls Knud's taxes "unheard of" and uses them to explain his murder. He condemns the murder of Knud Lavard but sides openly with the murderer, Prince Magnus, in the wars that followed; calls Erik II Emune (the Memorable), Knud's avenger, "a contentious man, full of anger and lies"; and rejoices at his murder by Sorte Plov, whom he presents as an instrument of the Lord. The events in this second section must have been known to the author either from the testimony of witnesses or from his own experience.

Chapter 19 ends with the statement that Bishop Ruko "usurped" the episcopate of Roskilde. The abruptness of this ending suggests that the author interrupted his account there, hoping perhaps to take it up again at a later date. A twentieth chapter has been added by what is clearly a second hand, and covers the reign of Waldemar I the Great. The very last sentence, which mentions Knud IV Waldemarsen and Waldemar II the Victorious, is possibly the work of yet another hand.

The *Roskilde Chronicle* is preserved in three manuscripts: an incomplete manuscript from the end of the thirteenth century (Kiel, Universitätsbibliothek, Codex Kiloniensis, fol. 49r–63v); a copy by Petrus Olai (*d.* 1570) in his *Collectanea* (Copenhagen, Kongelige Bibliotek, AM 107, 8° fol. 145r–159v); and a copy made around 1600 by Stephanius (Uppsala, Universitetsbiblioteket, MS de la Gardie 25–29, fol. 5–10).

BIBLIOGRAPHY

The Chronicon Roskildense is edited by Martin C. Gertz in his *Scriptores minores historiae Danicae medii aevi,* I (1917). See also Ellen Jørgensen, *Historieforskning og historieskrivning i Danmark indtil aar 1800* (1931), 25–27.

JOAQUÍN MARTÍNEZ-PIZARRO

[See also **Adam of Bremen; Denmark; Knud Lavard;**

Coronation of the Virgin altarpiece by Rossello di Jacopo Franchi, 1420. Accademia, Florence. ALINARI / ART RESOURCE

Lejre Chronicle; Missions and Missionaries, Christian; Saxo Grammaticus; Scandinavia: Political and Legal Organization; Vikings.]

ROSSELLO DI JACOPO FRANCHI (1376/1377—1457/1458), Florentine painter documented from 1404 to 1456. Rossello's mature work was profoundly influenced by that of Lorenzo Monaco (*d. ca.* 1424). His key works include *S. Blaise* (1408; Florence, Duomo); the signed *Madonna and Child with Angels* (formerly at the Straggia, now lost); the *Crucifix with Flagellants* (1414; Rovezzano, S. Michele); the *Coronation of the Virgin* (Florence, Accademia), dated by most sources 1420; and the *Madonna del Parto* (Florence, Palazzo Davanzati).

An exquisite decorator with a refined sense of form, Rossello painted softly modeled figures with gently melancholy and enigmatic faces. His work forms an important link between the art of Nardo di Cione and the Renaissance.

BIBLIOGRAPHY

Bruce Cole, *Masaccio and the Art of Early Renaissance Florence* (1980), 48–49; Richard Fremantle, *Florentine Gothic Painters from Giotto to Masaccio* (1975), 461–470; Carol Talbert Peters, "Rossello di Jacopo Franchi: Portrait of a Florentine Painter, *ca.* 1376–1456" (diss., Indiana Univ., 1981).

ADELHEID M. GEALT

[See also **Gothic, International Style; Gothic Art: Painting and Manuscript Illumination; Lorenzo Monaco; Nardo di Cione.**]

ROSSO. See **Giovanni (Nanni) di Bartolo.**

ROTA (wheel), a Latin term used to designate a type of musical composition of the thirteenth and fourteenth centuries. The rota is a canonic work with successive entrances; it is distinct from the *rondellus,* in which the voices enter simultaneously.

The practice of singing rounds probably predates the earliest written examples of the thirteenth century, as such compositions are easily improvised upon a single melodic line. The only composition specifically labeled "rota" in a manuscript source is the multiple-voice English round "Sumer Is Icumen In," although other works can be identified by their structure as belonging to the same genre. Strictly speaking, the rota differs from the true canon in that the former is built upon a static harmonic pattern of triads, while the latter is more motivic and linear.

BIBLIOGRAPHY
Frank L. Harrison, *Music in Medieval Britain,* 4th ed. (1980); Ernest H. Sanders, "Tonal Aspects of 13th-Century English Polyphony," in *Acta musicologica,* 37 (1965); Walter Wiora, "Der mittelalterliche Liedkanon," in Hans Albrecht, Helmuth Osthoff, and Walter Wiora, eds., *Kongress-bericht, Gesellschaft für Musikforschung* (1950).

MARCIA J. EPSTEIN

[See also **Music in Medieval Society; Rondellus; Sumer Is Icumen In.**]

ROTROUENGE (also *rotruenge;* Provençal: *retroncha*), a term used in trouvère and troubadour poetry for a type of lyric song with refrain. On the basis of only ten clear surviving examples, some of which show a distinctive rhyme scheme, there is no way to distinguish as a group the poems marked with this term in manuscript sources. The term may have been applied by poets as an ornamental title rather than as a descriptive one.

BIBLIOGRAPHY
Jean Frappier, *La poésie lyrique en France aux XIIe et XIIIe siècles* (1960); Hendrik Vanderwerf, "Rotrouenge," in *The New Grove Dictionary of Music and Musicians,* XVI (1980).

MARCIA J. EPSTEIN

[See also **Chansonnier; Music, Western European; Provençal Literature; Troubadour, Trouvère.**]

ROUEN. Nestled in an amphitheater of hills on the right bank of the Seine some 75 miles (120 kilometers) south of the English Channel and about 85 miles (140 kilometers) northwest of Paris along the river's winding course, Rouen was one of the most significant urban centers in medieval France because of its religious, political, and economic importance.

The city's origins can be traced to the time of Julius Caesar. It derived its name from the Celtic Ratuma or Ratumacos, which the Romans modified to Ratomagus. During the early empire it served as the chief city of the *civitas* of the Veliocasses and attained prominence during the third century as the chief city of Lugdunensis Secunda, a province that generally corresponded to the medieval duchy of Normandy.

Rouen may have been converted to Christianity by a St. Mello in the third century. It certainly had a bishop by the fourth century, and later it had an archbishop, the metropolitan of Normandy. By the thirteenth century the city contained more than thirty churches, and its skyline was dominated by the cathedral and the abbey church of St. Ouen.

The city retained its political importance after the withdrawal of the Romans. In the Carolingian period it was the site of a mint and the permanent headquarters of a count. Ravaged by the Vikings in 841, Rouen recovered to become the chief city of the lands that Charles the Simple gave to Rollo in 911. Although some of the later dukes preferred the city of Caen, Rouen's preeminence in Normandy was never challenged during the ducal period.

In 1204, when King Philip II Augustus of France took Normandy from King John of England, Rouen maintained its influence. By the reign of Louis IX, the financial Exchequer of Normandy had been moved to the city. In the thirteenth century it was one of the locations of the Norman judicial Exchequer and became that institution's permanent seat from 1302. During the Hundred Years War the English captured the city in January 1419 after a siege of twenty-six weeks. Although the conquerors imposed a punitive fine of 300,000 *écus* upon the inhabitants, they also confirmed the city's privileges, and prosperity revived. The city served as the political, administrative, and military center of English Normandy, and it was in Rouen that Joan of Arc was executed in 1431. French forces recaptured Rouen in 1449, and the city entered one of its most brilliant periods. Culturally it was a pioneer in the French Renaissance; one of the first printing presses in France was set up in Rouen in 1485. Politically the city's importance was confirmed by the reorganization of the Norman Exchequer in 1499.

During the second half of his reign, King Henry II of England granted the city communal status. The *Établissements de Rouen* lays out the form of communal government: a powerful mayor, nominated by twelve councillors and twelve aldermen but selected by the king, a group of councils with various judicial and administrative duties, citizens sworn by oath to their obligations. It served as the model for other Norman towns and was copied by a number of important towns in western and southwestern France: Tours, Poitiers, Angoulême, La Rochelle, and Bayonne among them.

The *Établissements* continued in effect after the French conquest of 1204. During the thirteenth century, however, there were increasing tensions between the dominant merchant class and the rest of the inhabitants. These tensions led to the suspension of the *Établissements* in 1292 and their replacement in 1321. A new charter provided for broader participation in the communal government, but in the 1340's townsmen complained that its provisions were not enforced. The *Harelle* of 1382, a major riot, was as much another manifestation of the social tensions within the city as it was a protest against the fiscal exactions of the French crown. After it ended, Charles VI abolished the city's communal form of government, replacing it with direct royal administration.

The economic prosperity of Rouen rested on its geographic position. Located almost midway between Paris and the sea, at a point where the Seine was deep enough to accommodate oceangoing vessels, Rouen acted as a conduit for international trade. During the tenth century it served as the emporium at which Viking booty was exchanged and operated one of the last slave markets in the West. Its merchants were known as purveyors of wine in England. Following the conquest of England in 1066, Rouen obtained privileges that strengthened its economic position. From this time of Henry I it enjoyed a monopoly of the river trade that passed through the city and virtually exclusive rights to Norman trade with Ireland. Its merchants were exempt from all customs duties in London except those on wine and great fish. By the time of Henry II, Rouen's traders were free from all other tolls and duties throughout the rest of the Angevin dominions. Under the French, trade with England naturally suffered, but it remained important, and during the English occupation of the fifteenth century, it flourished. After 1204 Rouen at first maintained its monopoly on the Seine, but this was gradually eroded in favor of Paris.

Throughout the Middle Ages, Rouen's merchants traded a range of goods, including leather, wine, grain, salt, salt fish, and paper. Its cloth sales became international by the last quarter of the twelfth century, and the *gris* of Rouen reached the shores of the Levant in the following decades. In the fifteenth century its paper merchants supplied the majority of English needs. Manufacturing and commerce fueled Rouen's economic vitality. Unlike many cities it was not dependent on a single industry but produced woolens, hosiery, hats, furniture, and glassware.

For much of the Middle Ages, Rouen was the second largest city in France. By the mid thirteenth century its population numbered between 30,000 and 40,000, and the city had spilled onto the left bank of the Seine. The Black Death and the ensuing demographic crises devastated the city. By 1380 Rouen had lost between one-third and one-half of its population. The city recovered from these catastrophes, however, and its population probably exceeded 70,000 during the first half of the sixteenth century.

BIBLIOGRAPHY

Nadine-Josette Chaline, ed., *Le diocèse de Rouen–Le Havre* (1976); A. Giry, *Les Établissements de Rouen,* 2 vols. (1883–1885); Michel Mollat, *Le commerce maritime normand à la fin du moyen âge* (1952); Michel Mollat, ed., *Histoire de Rouen* (1982).

PETER POGGIOLI

[See also **Black Death; Caen; Commune; Échevin; England; Eudes Rigaud; France; Hundred Years War; Joan of Arc, St.; John, King of England; Normans and Normandy; Paper, Introduction of; Philip II Augustus; Textiles; Trade, European; Urbanism, Western European.**]

ROUEN, USE OF. Scarcely anything is known of the use, or liturgical form, of Rouen before the Carolingian era. In the eighth century, Charlemagne ordered the introduction of the Roman chant and the Roman rite, which was carried out by St. Rémi, archbishop of Rouen. This Carolingian liturgy remained without alteration at least until the eleventh century, if one may judge from the *De officiis ecclesiasticis,* a faithful description of the Norman liturgy put together by John of Avranches, who served as archbishop of Rouen from 1069 to 1079. After this period, the Roman base was retained, but a certain number of particularities appeared, both in the calendar and in certain usages, of which several may be survivals of pre-Carolingian rites.

Many of the liturgical books of the High and late Middle Ages still exist, preserved in public libraries. The missals routinely contain the calendar for Rouen. Over the course of the centuries, various new celebrations were introduced, justified either by the devotion of the people of Rouen or by the preference of one of Rouen's archbishops, a number of whom thereby betray their origins. Thus we have feast days for various local saints—the bishops Ansbert, Ouen, and Victrice, and the abbots Wandrille and Philibert. We also have the feast of the Picard St. Firmin, introduced by Archbishop Thibaut (1222–1229), himself a Picard; the feast of St. Julien of Le Mans, where Archbishop Maurice (1231–1235) had been bishop; and the feast of St. Francis of Assisi, dear to Eudes Rigaud (1248–1275), who was a Franciscan.

In the manuscript Paris, Bibliothèque Nationale, lat. 904, there are several liturgical dramas for Christmas, Epiphany, and Easter. The canons of Rouen played in these. The manuscript Rouen Y110 contains the famous procession of the donkeys (*Ordo processionis asinorum secundum Rothomagensem usum*).

BIBLIOGRAPHY

Nadine-Josette Chaline, ed., *Le diocèse de Rouen-Le Havre* (1976); René Delamare, *Le De officiis ecclesiasticis de Jean d'Avranches, archêveque de Rouen, 1067–1079* (1923); René-Jean Hesbert, "Les manuscrits liturgiques de l'église de Rouen," in *Bulletin philologique et historique (jusque'à 1715) du comité des travaux historiques et scientifiques, 1955–1956* (1957); Henri Loriquet, *Le graduel de l'église cathédrale de Rouen au XIIIe siècle* (1907).

ANDRÉ FOURÉ

[See also **Carolingians and the Carolingian Empire; Divine Office; Eudes Rigaud; Gallican Rite; Liturgy, Treatises on; Lyonese Rite; Mass, Liturgy of the; Metz, Use of; Troyes, Rite of.**]

ROUND ARCH. See **Arch.**

ROUND TABLE, KNIGHTS OF. See **Arthurian Literature.**

ROUSSEL DE BAILLEUL (*fl.* 1071–1073) was the commander of Norman mercenaries in the Byzantine army. He was present at the Battle of Manazkert in 1071 but withdrew from the field, helping to bring about the Byzantine defeat. Subsequently (1073), he tried to establish an independent principality in Portus and then fought against Emperor Michael VII Doukas (*r.* 1071–1078) on behalf of Caesar John Doukas, whom Roussel proclaimed emperor. The Turks helped the Byzantines against Roussel and he was captured and handed over to Alexios I Komnenos, then an imperial general, in 1073, and served with him.

BIBLIOGRAPHY

J. M. Hussey, "The Later Macedonians, the Comneni, and the Angeli, 1025–1204," in *Cambridge Medieval History,* 2nd ed., IV, pt. 1 (1966), 210.

LINDA C. ROSE

[See also **Byzantine Empire, History; Doukas; Pontus.**]

RUBEN I (*d.* 1092 or 1095), the founder of the Rubenid house of Cilician Armenia. The twelfth-century Armenian historian Samuel of Ani refers to Ruben as a relative of Gagik II, the last Bagratid king of Armenia, who died in 1079; but this is probably an erroneous assertion, very likely fabricated by the Rubenids themselves in order to strengthen their claim to the throne of Cilicia. Ruben was probably a minor chieftain who had served under Gagik. He might have been related to a certain Rupenes, *strategos* of Larissa and Hellas, who lived at the beginning of the eleventh century, although this is not likely. Ruben settled in the region of Kopitara (Gobidara) in the Taurus Mountains around 1080. Unlike other Armenian chieftains in the region during this period, particularly the Het^{c}umids, who submitted to Byzantine domination, Ruben soon established himself as the leader of the anti-imperial faction.

Buried at the monastery of Kastałon, Ruben was succeeded by his son, Constantine I (1093 or 1095–1102), who consolidated and enlarged his father's holdings.

BIBLIOGRAPHY

Nicholas Adontz, "L'aïeul des Roubéniens," in *Byzantion,* **10** (1935); Ghevont Alishan, *Sissouan; ou, L'Arméno-Cilicie* (1899); Samuel of Ani, *Chronology* (in

Armenian), Aršak Ter-Mikelian, ed. (1893), *Samuelis praesbyteri Aniensis: Temporum usque ad suam aetatum ratio,* John Zohrab and Angelo Mai, eds. (1818 and 1839), and in *Collection d'historiens arméniens,* Marie F. Brosset, ed. and trans. (1874–1876, repr. 1979).

ANI P. ATAMIAN

[See also **Bagratids (Armenian); Cilician Kingdom; Het^cumids; Rubenids.**]

RUBENIDS. One of the two main families of Cilician Armenia; the first king of Cilician Armenia was a Rubenid.

Ruben I (*d.* 1093/1095), the founder of the line, is an obscure figure but was probably a member of the army of Gagik II, the last Bagratid king of Armenia. After Gagik's death (1079), Ruben, like many other Armenian chieftains and their followers, migrated and settled in the region of Gobidara in the Taurus Mountains, north of Sīs. His son, Constantine I (*r.* 1093/1095–1102), consolidated his father's holdings and gained control of the nearby fortress of Vahka.

The Rubenid barony was enlarged by Constantine's son, Tᶜoros I (*r.* 1100/1102–1129), who captured the fortress of Barjraberd and the city of Anazarba, which he made the seat of the barony. It was Tᶜoros who is traditionally said to have avenged the murder of King Gagik II by the Greeks, by killing the sons of the assassin; this may have given rise to the belief that the Rubenids were related to Gagik.

Although the Rubenids eventually became the masters of Cilicia, they did not gain a dominant role in the area until after the death in 1112 of Koł Vasil (Basil the Robber), the Armenian ruler of Kesoun and Raban in northern Syria. The early Rubenid barons were concerned mainly with consolidating their position in the Taurus but soon began expanding southward for control of the plain of Cilicia and of the principal trade routes and ports. This expansionist policy brought the Rubenids into conflict with Byzantium, which was in nominal control of Cilicia; with the Hetᶜumids, the great Armenian family whose lands lay to the west and who were loyal vassals of the Greeks; and with Antioch, the Rubenids' neighbor to the east.

Tᶜoros I pursued a cautious policy toward the Latins who were increasingly establishing themselves in the surrounding areas. Tᶜoros' brother, Leo (Baron Leo I, *r.* 1129–1138/1140), by 1135 added to the growing Rubenid holdings the important cities of Mamistra (Mamestia, Mopsuestia), Adana, and Tarsus, only to lose them to the Byzantine emperor John II Komnenos in 1137–1138. During this campaign, Leo, his wife, and his two sons Ruben and Tᶜoros were captured by the Greeks and taken to Constantinople, where Leo and Ruben died in captivity.

Tᶜoros eventually escaped and returned to Cilicia, and by 1148 had retaken the castle of Vahka and reestablished the Rubenid barony at Anazarba. During his reign Tᶜoros (Tᶜoros II, *r.* 1144/1145–1168) succeeded in keeping generally cordial relations with both the Seljuks and the Latins, whom the Byzantines tried to set against the Rubenids. But Tᶜoros was again, in 1158, overcome, in the great campaign of the Byzantine emperor Manuel I, who once more reduced Cilicia to the position of a vassal state.

Upon Tᶜoros II's death (1168), his brother Mleh invaded Cilicia, with the help of Nūr al-Dīn, the Zengid atabeg of Aleppo and Damascus, and controlled the barony for several years, backed by the threat of the atabeg's forces. But the latter's death in 1174 brought Mleh's ouster and murder by the Armenian nobility, who chose in his place Ruben III (*r.* 1175–1186/1187), the son of Tᶜoros II's brother Stepᶜanos.

Ruben III was able to deal successfully with the problem of raiding Turkoman tribes and the threatened invasion by Saladin in 1180. He was unable, however, to prevent an invasion and his own capture by Bohemond III of Antioch, who considered the growing Rubenid barony a threat to his principality. Ruben's brother Leo led other Armenian nobles in defeating Bohemond, and in either 1186 or 1187, when he retired to the monastery of Trazarg, Ruben passed the leadership of the barony to Leo.

It was under Leo I/II (baron, 1186/1187–1198/1199; king, 1198/1199–1219) that Rubenid power reached its apex. He saw the fortunes of Cilicia as being best served by a turning toward the West, and his reign was highlighted by his coronation in the name of the German emperor and the pope and the reestablishment of the Armenian kingdom in Cilicia. After Leo's death in 1219, however, the Rubenids were replaced as the royal house of Cilicia, through the marriage in 1226 of Leo's daughter Zabel (Isabel) to a Hetᶜumid prince, thus joining the two rival houses on the throne.

RUBLEV, ANDREI

Rubenid Rulers of Cilicia

Ruben I (*d.* 1093/1095)
Constantine I (1903/1095–1102)
T^coros I (1100/1102–1129)
Constantine II (1129)
Leo I (1129–1138/1140)
T^coros II (1144/1145–1168)
Ruben II (1169–1170)
Mleh (1170–1175)
Ruben III (1175–1186/1187)
Leo I/II (baron, 1186/1187–1198/1199; king, 1198/1199–1219)
Zabel (1219–1252)

BIBLIOGRAPHY

Nicholas Adontz, "Notes arméno-byzantine (VI): L'aïeul des Roubeniens," in *Byzantion,* 10 (1935); Ghevont Alishan, *Sissouan; ou, L'Arméno-Cilicie* (1899), 39–60; Claude Cahen, *La Syrie du nord à l'époque des croisades et la principauté franque d'Antioche* (1940); Sirarpie Der Nersessian, "The Kingdom of Cilician Armenia," in Robert L. Wolff and Henry W. Hazard, eds., *A History of the Crusades,* II, 2nd ed. (1969), 630–659.

ANI P. ATAMIAN

[See also **Cilician Kingdom; Cilician-Roman Church Union; Crusades and Crusader States: To 1192; He^ctumids; John II Komnenos; Lambron; Leo I/II of Armenia; Manuel I Komnenos; Mints and Money, Armenian; Ruben I; Sīs; Tarsus.**]

RUBLEV, ANDREI (*ca.* 1360–1430), the most famous artist of medieval Russia. A monk at the Trinity–St. Sergius Monastery at Zagorsk near Moscow, Rublev worked in and around this principality on royal and church commissions. Although he was evidently schooled in the Palaiologan manner of contemporary Byzantine art, Rublev was highly creative in his interpretations of both traditional iconography and style.

More is known of Rublev's career than of his personality; he was often mentioned in contemporary chronicles, in the lives of St. Sergius and St. Nikon, the first two abbots of Trinity Monastery, and in many later sources, including the lives of icon painters compiled in the seventeenth century. He was first mentioned at work on the frescoes and icons of the Annunciation Cathedral in the Moscow Kremlin in 1405, in third place after the great Greek artist Theophanes (Feofan Grek) and Prokhor of Gorodets, a Russian painter who might have been one of Rublev's teachers. In 1408 he was employed on the decorative program of the Dormition Cathedral in Vladimir, with his friend Daniil Chernyi (Chorny). The two again worked together in the Trinity Cathedral at Zagorsk, probably between 1422 and 1427, on what must have been the capstone of Rublev's career.

Old Testament Trinity. Icon by Andrei Rublev, *ca.* 1411–1427. State Tretyakov Gallery, Moscow, inv. no. 13012. PHOTO: SOVFOTO

Among Rublev's most famous preserved icons are those of the so-called Zvenigorod Deesis, found in 1918 under some firewood in a barn near the Dormition Cathedral of Zvenigorod. These icons were probably painted for a monastery in Moscow, torn down late in the seventeenth century. Although the icons have suffered greatly by their haphazard treatment, they show Rublev at his greatest. The central icon of Christ, in particular, demonstrates Rublev's individual vision of Palaiologan style. In his best-known icon, the Old Testament Trinity, Rublev again expressed a Russian rather than a Greek idea of this theme and used to great effect his famous sky blue, for symbolic and aesthetic purposes.

Although much of Rublev's work has been lost, he was venerated after his death, and his artistic innovations had a great impact on later icon painting in Russia.

BIBLIOGRAPHY
George P. Fedetov, *The Russian Religious Mind,* 2 vols. (1946–1966); H. P. Gerhard, *The World of Icons,* Irene Gibbons, trans. (1971); Victor N. Lazarev, *Andrei Rublov i iego shkola* (1966); Leonid Ouspensky and Vladimir Lossky, *The Meaning of Icons* (1969); Arthur Voyce, *The Art and Architecture of Medieval Russia* (1967).

ANN E. FARKAS

[See also **Deesis; Dionysios the Greek; Hesychasm; Hosios Lukas; Iconostasis; Icons, Manufacture of; Icons, Russian; Moscow Kremlin, Art and Architecture; Pecherskaya Lavra; Peter, Master; Prokhor of Gorodets; Russian Art; Theophanes the Greek.**]

RUDEL, JAUFRÉ. See **Jaufré Rudel.**

RUDOLF OF FULDA (*d.* 865), a monk and teacher. Active in church politics, he mediated a dispute between the pope and Otgar, archbishop of Mainz. In 836 he wrote a life of St. Leoba, a companion of St. Boniface. Between 842 and 847, Rudolf compiled a work on the miracles occurring at Fulda. He also wrote, with Meginhart, the *Translatio S. Alexandri.*

BIBLIOGRAPHY
Max Manitius, *Geschichte der lateinischen Literatur des Mittelalters,* I (1911, repr. 1974), 668–671; *Monumenta Germaniae historica: Scriptores,* II (1829), 673–681 (for St. Alexander), XV (1887, repr. 1963), 118–131 (for St. Leoba) and 328–341 (for Fulda).

NATHALIE HANLET

[See also **Fulda.**]

RUDOLF OF ST. TROND (Sint-Truiden) (*d.* 1138). Born before 1070, Rudolph studied at Liège and was a monk at Burtscheid prior to his nomination as *scholasticus* and, later (1108), abbot of the monastery of St. Trond. He was exiled for two years at Ghent and Cologne (1121–1123) and traveled twice to Rome before his death. His main work is the elegantly written *Gesta abbatum Trudonensium,* which offers valuable insights into the history and literary culture of a twelfth-century monastic milieu. Rudolph is the probable author of a number of poems and letters, as well as a lost treatise on simony. The attribution to him of a choral treatise, *Quaestiones in musica,* seems unfounded.

BIBLIOGRAPHY
Rudolf's *Gesta abbatum Trudonensium,* R. Koepke, ed., is in *Monumenta Germaniae historica: Scriptores,* X (1852, repr. 1963), 227–317; the letters are at 317–332. For Rudolf's other works, their authenticity, editions, and bibliography, see Michael McCormick, *Index scriptorum operumque Latino-Belgicorum medii aevi: Nouveau répertoire des oeuvres médiolatines belges,* pt. 3, II (1979), 222–234, 296–297. For a statistical linguistic analysis of the *Gesta* and the letters, see Paul Tombeur, *Raoul de Saint-Trond, Gesta abbatum Trudonensium I–VII: Index verborum* (1965), and *Raoul de Saint-Trond, Epistulae: Index verborum* (1966).

MICHAEL MCCORMICK

RUDOLF VON EMS (*ca.* 1200–*ca.* 1255) ranks among the most important and prolific writers of the postclassical period of Middle High German literature. Little is known about his life and background except what he tells us or what can be inferred from his works, which fall roughly in the second quarter of the thirteenth century. Rudolf mentions only his first name (Ruodolf) in acrostics or references to himself, adding in *Willehalm von Orlens* (vv. 15,628ff.) that he is a *ministerialis* of Montfort (at the eastern corner of Lake Constance.) The continuator of his *Weltchronik* calls him "Ruodolf von Ense" (v. 33,496), presumably referring to Hohenems in Vorarlberg. His surviving works are now generally placed in the following general chronology: *Der guote Gêrhard, Barlaam und Josaphat, Alexander* I, *Willehalm von Orlens, Alexander* II (fragment), and the *Weltchronik* (fragment). Earlier courtly works rejected in *Barlaam* (vv. 5, 10ff.) and a redaction of the legend of St. Eustace mentioned in *Alexander* (v. 3,289) have not survived. A more precise determination of the approximate dates of composition depends upon further considerations, such as Rudolf's specification of patrons and our presuppositions concerning his artistic development and relationships with the Hohenstaufens.

Der guote Gêrhart (6,920 verses, two manuscripts), Rudolf's first surviving work, composed about 1220–1225, is based on an otherwise unknown story transmitted to him by Rudolf von

Steinach, a *ministerialis* of the bishop of Constance, who appears in documents between 1209 and 1221. In spite of its stylistic dependence on Gottfried von Strassburg, the work strikes a new tone: its hero is—for the first time in German literature—a merchant, for whom plausible historical models have been posited. The story of Gerhard is contained within a frame: Emperor Otto I has founded the archbishopric of Magdeburg and prays to God to reveal the place in heaven that his beneficence has earned. In response to this presumption, an angel commands him to travel to Cologne and learn truly humble generosity from a patrician named Gerhard the Good. Gerhard reluctantly narrates the adventures that have won him his name. While on a business venture in the Near East he spent his entire capital in order to ransom the fiancée of King William of England and her English escorts from heathen captivity. The English knights return to England and Gerhard takes the princess with him to Cologne to await word from King William. After receiving no report, Gerhard arranges a marriage between the princess and his son, who must give her up when William appears suddenly at the wedding festivities. Gerhard transports the couple to England, where a council has gathered to resolve the presumed interregnum, declines the throne offered to him by the nobles he once freed, establishes William as king, and returns to Cologne, refusing all rewards for his good deeds. The work concludes with a return to the frame and the effect of this narrative upon Emperor Otto.

Barlaam und Josaphat (16,164 verses, over thirty manuscripts) is generally dated between 1225 and 1230 on the basis of references to Wîde (documented from 1223 to 1232), abbot of the Cistercian monastery of Kappel near Zürich, who provided Rudolf with his Latin source and whose convent advised the Middle High German adaptation (vv. 3ff., 5, 37ff., 402). The story is a christianized version of the Buddha legend that was written by St. John of Damascus (*ca.* 675–*ca.* 750), translated into Latin in the twelfth century, and then adapted frequently in nearly every medieval European vernacular. Rudolf presents the narrative in a courtly tone, sometimes distancing himself from the antiworldly orientation of his source, so that it is difficult to decide whether the hero's monastic final years are the reward for an exemplary worldly career or its transcendent goal. As in other versions of the legend, King Avenier of India, a noble pagan hostile to Christianity, has his son Josaphat raised alone in a palace in order to avert a prophecy that he will become a Christian. The hermit Barlaam gains access to the palace and, after lengthy presentation of Christian history and doctrine told in a series of fables, converts Josaphat. In order to undermine his son's new belief, King Avenier arranges a great religious debate between his wise men and an impersonator of Barlaam, who is, however, overcome by the truth and easily defeats his disputants. The king then tempts Josaphat's resolve with beautiful women, with admonitions of his filial obligations, and finally with power, by dividing the kingdom between them. Josaphat converts his people and becomes an ideal Christian monarch, whereas Avenier's fortunes decline until he finally perceives his error and becomes a Christian. After unifying the kingdom on the death of his father and then ensuring his own succession, Josaphat abdicates in order to retreat from the world and dies after thirty-five years of eremitical asceticism.

Willehalm von Orlens (15,689 verses, over thirty manuscripts) is a courtly romance notable for the apparent contemporaneity of its setting and for the exemplary behavior of its child lovers in overcoming an undermotivated and overly severe separation. The unknown French source was obtained by Johannes von Ravensburg (sometimes identified with Johannes von Löwenthal) and Rudolf's adaptation was commissioned by the Hohenstaufen governor and literary patron Konrad von Winterstetten, who died in 1243. Further references to the recent death of Count Konrad von Öttingen (documented 1223–1231 but deceased several years later as a Teutonic Knight), to Master Hesse (documented about 1230–1240), a notary of Strassburg and apparent executor of Gottfried von Strassburg's literary estate, and to an imperial peace of 1235 support a dating of 1235–1240. The work begins with a history of the hero's parents that is closely modeled on related episodes in Gottfried's *Tristan* (although the general tenor is more that of an anti-*Tristan*) and reflects a running feud between Hainaut and Brabant in the late twelfth century. The hero's father is killed in a feud with Jofrit von Brabant, who adopts the young Willehalm as his son and heir. Willehalm develops into an exemplary youth and travels to England to complete his education. King Reinher makes him the companion of his daughter Amelie, and the young couple gradually fall in love. Upon hearing that Reinher intends to marry Amelie to the king of

Spain, the lovers attempt to flee, but are captured. Willehalm's life is spared on a variety of harsh conditions, including banishment from the country coupled with the promise never to speak again unless permitted to do so by Amelie. Willehalm continues his knightly career in the service of King Amelot of Norway, fighting foreign incursions. He eventually aids the abbess Savine, sister of Reinher, who brings the steadfastly loyal Amelie to him. After being married and then reconciled with King Reinher, Willehalm becomes ruler of England. His descendant is Godfrey of Bouillon, the first ruler of Jerusalem, a motif probably added with the young Conrad IV, who was king of Jerusalem, in mind. The popularity of the story is evidenced by seven illuminated manuscripts, illustrated in an embroidery from the Marienkirche in Bergen (Rügen), a tapestry in Sigmaringen, and a painting in Castle Runkelstein (Bozen), and by its later adaptations, including one by Hans Sachs (1533).

The fragmentary *Alexander* (21,643 verses, two manuscripts and one fragment) names no patron and appears to have occupied Rudolf during several decades of his literary career. From the acrostics at the beginning of each book, *R. Alexa* . . . , it seems that ten books were originally intended. The surviving torso, which has been poorly transmitted, breaks off in Book VI and appears, on the basis of sources, style, and the reconstruction of displaced acrostics, to have been written in at least two stages. The assumption that these stages reflect a change in patronage or a pause during which *Willehalm von Orlens* was composed is unprovable but remains attractive to most scholars. Rudolf's story of Alexander the Great initially follows the *Historia de preliis* of Archpresbyter Leo (version I^2) and employs elaborate stylistic devices such as quatrains and acrostics; after verse 5,105 he follows the *Historiae Alexandri* of Curtius Rufus as his principal source and generally restricts the ornamentation of his narrative to the beginning of books. In addition to his two main sources, Rudolf also used the Bible, Pseudo-Methodius, the *Epitome* of Julius Valerius, Peter Comestor, and the *Alexandreis* of Walter of Châtillon. He cites three earlier versions of the Alexander legend, of which only that of Lamprecht of Trier has survived. Rudolf's tendency to employ and compare various sources apparently stems from his desire to write *rehte wârheit,* or "proper truth," that is, historically correct narrative with instructional value. Alexander has been idealized with this in mind, although whether he is presented ahistorically as a perfect courtly king or as the prefiguration of such a king (whose character is necessarily limited in the ultimate pattern of Christian history) is controversial. The several stages of composition and the unfinished nature of the work suggest that it remained an experiment in which such differences may not have been reconciled.

Rudolf died before finishing his last work, the *Weltchronik* (world chronicle), having reached a point in the story of Solomon (variously placed between verses 33,321 and 33,478), according to the anonymous continuator who extends the chronicle to 36,338 verses. The approximate date of the work is established by the prologue to Book V (vv. 21,556–21,740), which contains a lengthy encomium of Rudolf's patron, Conrad IV (*d.* 1254), and alludes to his father, Frederick II (*d.* 1250), as deceased. The continuator's statement that Rudolf himself died in a Romance-speaking country (v. 33,483) is frequently associated with Conrad's Italian campaign in 1251–1254, but this assumption leaves little time for the composition of the ensuing 12,000 verses. The order of the work, which was intended to span salvation and world history from creation to Rudolf's present, follows a traditional division of history into six world ages (of Adam, Noah, Abraham, Moses, David, and Christ), breaking off in the presentation of the fifth. The main sources are the Bible and the seminal *Historia scholastica* of Peter Comestor; others include Geoffrey of Viterbo's *Pantheon* and Honorius of Autun's *Imago mundi.* Although the chronicle is fragmentary, its principal theme appears to be the revelation of God's divine plan in the course of time as manifested by a sequence of exemplary figures. That this principle of history was meant to extend to, if not to culminate in, the Hohenstaufen dynasty is suggested by the apostrophe of Conrad IV at the beginning of Book V as "King of Jerusalem," thereby establishing a typological relationship between David, the prototype of the divinely instituted ruler, and Conrad. The unusual popularity of the *Weltchronik* is attested not only by more than 100 manuscripts and fragments, but also by its extensive use as a source or model for many late medieval vernacular chronicles and Bibles.

Rudolf von Ems was long considered to be an imitator of the great writers of the preceding "classical" period: Heinrich von Veldeke, Hartmann von Aue, Wolfram von Eschenbach, and especially Gottfried von Strassburg. Rudolf clearly places himself within this literary tradition, in terms of both the style and ethos of his works, as the literary reviews in *Alexander* (vv. 3,105–3,268) and *Willehalm* (vv. 2,173–2,296) attest. Nonetheless, he must also be recognized for his innovative and influential treatment of different themes, genres, and modes of presentation. While retaining the courtly tone established by the vernacular Arthurian romance in particular, Rudolf ignores this predominant genre entirely in favor of narratives from the precourtly and learned Latin tradition, the clerical narrative, the saint's legend, and historiography. Even *Willehalm,* although nominally a "romance," also exhibits the changes evident throughout Rudolf's work. The heroes tend to be paradigms of a static perfection that adversity only confirms, whether they be knights and "mirrors of princes," saints, or even merchants. The stories are placed in a particularized—even contemporary—historical and geographical setting. Rudolf's interest in themes that are both exemplary and factual, supported by Hohenstaufen patronage, becomes increasingly clear in his development toward historiographical narrative.

BIBLIOGRAPHY

Editions. Der guote Gêrhart, John A. Asher, ed., Altdeutsche Textbibliothek, LVI (1971); *Barlaam und Josaphat,* Franz Pfeiffer, ed., repr. with afterword by Heinz Rupp (1965); *Willehalm von Orlens,* Victor Junk, ed., Deutsche Texte des Mittelalters, II (1905, repr. 1967); *Alexander,* Victor Junk, ed., Bibliothek des Literarischen Vereins in Stuttgart, 272 and 274 (1928–1929); *Weltchronik,* Gustav Ehrismann, ed., Deutsche Texte des Mittelalters, (1915, repr. 1967).

Studies. Helmut Brackert, *Rudolf von Ems: Dichtung und Geschichte* (1968); Xenja von Ertzdorff, *Rudolf von Ems: Untersuchungen zum höfischen Roman im 13. Jahrhundert* (1967); Walter Haug, "Rudolfs 'Willehalm' und Gottfrieds 'Tristan': Kontrafaktur als Kritik," in Wolfgang Harms and L. Peter Johnson, eds., *Deutsche Literatur des späten Mittelalters* (1975); Wolfgang Walliczek, *Rudolf von Ems: Der guote Gêrhart* (1973); Roy A. Wisbey, *Das Alexanderbild Rudolfs von Ems* (1966); Ulrich Wyss, "Rudolfs von Ems *Barlaam und Josaphat* zwischen Legende und Roman," in Peter F. Ganz and Werner Schröder, eds., *Probleme mittelhochdeutscher Erzählformen* (1972), 214–238.

ARTHUR GROOS

[See also **Alexander Romances; Biblical Poetry; German Literature: Romance; Middle High German Literature;** and individual authors.]

RUFINUS (*fl.* late twelfth century). Canon lawyer, theologian, and archbishop, Rufinus was born in central Italy, perhaps in Assisi, sometime before 1130. He first appeared as a master of canon law at Bologna about 1150, where he is known to have taught Stephen of Tournai and perhaps also John of Faenza (Johannes Faventinus). He himself had probably been a student of Gratian at Bologna, but nothing is known for certain of his early life or education. Judging from the elegant Latin and the broad knowledge evident in his writings, he had taken full advantage of the educational opportunities available in Italy and perhaps, following in the footsteps of other Italians such as Peter Lombard and Rolando Bandinelli (later Pope Alexander III), had gone to Paris. Sometime before 1179 Rufinus was made bishop of Assisi. That year, on 5 March, he had the honor of giving the opening address at the Third Lateran Council. With the support of Peter II de Insulis, abbot of Monte Cassino, at whose request he had written the treatise *De bono pacis,* Rufinus was elected archbishop of Sorrento sometime before 1186. He died before 1192.

Rufinus is a pivotal figure in the development of canon law. His primary work, the *Summa decretorum* (1157–1159), was the most influential and widely used decretist writing until the *Summa* of Huguccio a generation later. A product of Rufinus' teaching at Bologna, the long and systematic *Summa* was both an apparatus and a gloss of Gratian's *Decretum.* Trained in theology as well as canon law, Rufinus made use of such recent products of the Paris schools as the *De sacramentis christianae fidei* of Hugh of St. Victor (*ca.* 1134) and the *Sentences* of Peter Lombard (1155–1158). In fact, Rufinus is the first author known to have used the Lombard's theological textbook. Although he had little sympathy for Roman law, he was also the first canonist to adopt the exegetical and analytical methods developed by the civil lawyers. The result was a legal text of originality, clarity, and precision that brought Rufinus lasting recognition as "the first elegant commentator and interpreter of the golden book of decrees" (*aurei voluminis decretorum elegans apparator sive expositor primus*).

Additional evidence of Rufinus' influence as a canonist is the number of detailed glosses attributed to him in manuscripts of the *Decretum* dating from the mid twelfth to the early thirteenth century. Other works by Rufinus include the treatise *De bono pacis,* largely an exposition of Augustine's *De civitate Dei,* the first recension of which, dating from between 1174 and 1180, is now lost. The second recension, written at the request of Peter de Insulis between 1180 and 1186, was mistakenly assigned by its editors to the eleventh century. Of an apparently once vast collection of sermons, only twenty-four are now extant (in Milan, Biblioteca Ambrosiana, MS C.30 Sup.). These, which include the sermon that opened the Third Lateran Council, show Rufinus to have been an eloquent and effective preacher who frequently illustrated his sermons, like his other writings, with personal references and learned citations to classical authors, especially Cassiodorus and Plato.

Rufinus was an ardent supporter of the papacy in its struggle with the emperor. Notable among the many original and influential doctrinal contributions made in his *Summa* is the important distinction made in ecclesiastical jurisdiction between *auctoritas* and *administratio,* which Rufinus applied to the relationship between pope and emperor by proposing the formula "*auctoritas papae—administratio imperatoris.*" Even when given the most moderate reading, this formula made the emperor legally the equivalent of the administrative deputy of the pope in secular affairs. In political thought, as well as on such other key legal issues as episcopal elections and the relative dignity of ecclesiastical offices, Rufinus' innovative doctrines exercised an original influence on later canonistic thought as great as that of the novel methods of his *Summa* on the development of glossatorial techniques.

BIBLIOGRAPHY

The 1726 edition of *De bono pacis* by Bernard Pez is reprinted in *Patrologia latina,* CL (1880), 1593–1638.

The authoritative work on the life and writings of Rufinus remains the introduction by Heinrich Singer to his edition of the *Summa, Die Summa Decretorum des Magister Rufinus* (1902, repr. 1963). See also Robert L. Benson, "Rufin," in *Dictionnaire de droit canonique,* VII (1965); Stephan Kuttner, *Repertorium der Kanonistik (1140–1234)* (1937), 131–133, 178–179. The sources and influence of the *Summa* are discussed in Robert L. Benson, *The Bishop Elect: A Study in Medieval Ecclesiastical Office* (1968), 56–89; Ludwig Ott, "Hat Magister Rufinus die Sentenzen des Petrus Lombardus benützt?" in *Scholastik,* **33** (1958). On Rufinus' glosses to the *Decretum* see Josef Juncker, "Summen und Glossen," in *Zeitschrift der Savigny-Stiftung für Rechtsgeschichte, Kanonistische Abt.,* **14** (1925). On the *De bono pacis* see Francesco di Capua, "Il canonista Rufino e il suo trattato *De bono pacis,*" in *Atti del III Congresso nazionale di studi romani,* II (1935); Yves M. J. Congar, "Maître Rufin et son *De bono pacis,*" in *Revue des sciences philosophiques et théologiques,* **41** (1957). The sermons were discovered, and are discussed, by Germain Morin, "Le discours d'ouverture du Concile général de Latran (1179) et l'oeuvre littéraire de Maître Rufin, évêque d'Assise," in *Atti della Pontificia accademia romana di archeologia,* 3rd ser., *Memorie,* **2** (1928).

STEPHEN C. FERRUOLO

[See also **Decretists; Deposition of Rulers; Elections, Church; Glossators; Law, Canon: After Gratian.**]

RUGS AND CARPETS. Rugs may be defined as heavy textiles made for a variety of practical purposes, and generally designed to be used in the form in which they are originally created, without cutting, tailoring, or alteration. Carpets constitute a subclass of rugs; they are usually rectangular in shape and meant to be used horizontally on flat surfaces such as tabletops or floors. Within this necessarily broad definition, rugs and carpets are created by means of a wide variety of techniques from many different kinds of materials. Both documents and surviving examples of early rugs point to the Middle East as the area where many of the techniques, styles, and uses of rugs seem to have originated, and the weaving of rugs and carpets constitutes a major aspect of the history of Islamic art.

The simplest kind of rug is made of felt—animal fibers, generally carded sheep wool, which through a simple process of compression, accompanied by application of hot water and soap, can be fashioned into thick, unwoven slabs in a variety of shapes. Felt rugs may also be made out of dyed wool, by sewing together shaped pieces of various colors, or by stitching colored felt and other materials on top of a basic slab of felt. These "mosaic" and "appliqué" techniques are found in examples from as early as the fourth or fifth century B.C. While felt rugs as an art form are undocumented in medieval Europe, they appear to have been used in the Islamic world for many centuries.

Rugs woven on a loom form the largest category of interest to the historian of art. More expensive than the relatively cheap felt rugs, woven rugs can be created by several labor-intensive techniques that produce a durable fabric with considerable opportunity for artistic expression. Woven rugs may be subdivided into flat-woven and pile-woven. The

RUGS AND CARPETS

former, less durable and requiring less material and labor, were evidently produced across the Middle East throughout the medieval period; and fragmentary examples, generally of wool, have been discovered in various archaeological sites, such as Al-Fusṭaṭ in Egypt. The simplest flat-woven rug is known as a kilim or *gilim;* it is a weft-faced plain-weave fabric in which the wefts are packed down to cover the warps, a technique also known as tapestry weave. Where wefts of different colors meet along a vertical (warp) line, they double back in the fabric; and if they are not interlocked, the fabric will show small slits along vertical lines in the design. This technique was used throughout the medieval world; it is found in the earliest medieval church tapestries of north Germany and was used by later European weavers in the famous Aubusson carpets and Gobelins tapestries.

A second type of flat-woven rug is the brocaded rug, in which designs are formed by the introduction on top of a plain-weave fabric, during the weaving process on the loom, of extra or supplementary wefts of various colors that form the design. Although a favored technique in the Middle East, where such rugs are known as *sumak* or *jijim,* brocaded rugs did not appear in medieval Europe, where embroidered rugs and carpets evidently were preferred. The embroidery technique, used in such famous medieval fabrics as the Bayeux tapestry, involved embellishing a plain-weave ground fabric by the use of colored threads and a needle, a process totally independent of the loom. Embroiderers sometimes included metallic thread or wire, other fabrics in appliqué, or even seed pearls and other nontextile ornamental material; in medieval Europe embroidery was used for royal and ecclesiastical costumes and vestments, as well as for rugs and other ornamental fabrics.

The technique most commonly associated with the terms "rug" and "carpet" is the knotted-pile. Virtually synonymous with the popular term "oriental rug," the technique of tying rows of knots on warps during the weaving of the rug is labor-intensive but produces a fabric with great durability, reactivity to light, and tremendous potential for artistic creation, as an infinite variety of patterns can be created from the tiny dots of colored yarn formed by the knotted pile. Knotted-pile rugs from the Middle East generally consist of row after horizontal row of such knots, each knot tied on two warps, with from one to eight shots of weft between each row. The knots themselves vary according to local custom, the three basic types being a symmetrical knot, and asymmetrical knots open to the left or to the right. In Spain, where in late medieval times rugs were woven in imitation of Middle Eastern prototypes, the Spanish-knot technique utilized wool knots tied on a single warp. Excavations from medieval Al-Fusṭaṭ in Egypt have yielded fragments of cut-loop pile rugs, in which small loops of weft were trimmed to create a pile.

Knotted-pile rugs sometimes had their nap trimmed to different lengths to provide a relief effect (the *maḥfūrāt* mentioned in medieval Arabic texts), and the pile could be knotted not only of wool but also of goat hair, cotton, or silk; a finely knotted fabric could be designed with very complex and curvilinear patterns, whereas tapestry-woven and brocaded rugs from the Middle East tended to favor geometric designs.

The use of fabrics as floor coverings, most often in a setting of opulence and wealth, is a custom of great antiquity, attested to by both archaeological and literary evidence. The earliest known rug woven in the knotted-pile technique is the so-called Pazyryk rug, dating to the fourth or fifth century B.C. and discovered in an ice-bound barrow grave of a nomadic chieftain in the Altai Mountains of Siberia. Scholars are divided on whether this rug was actually woven by nomads or by sedentary peoples of other cultures. Small fragments of technically similar fabrics, dating from the first millennium of the Christian era, have been found in various central Asian sites and in Mesopotamia. Flat-woven and felt rugs of various sizes and shapes also were found in the Pazyryk burial site.

Literary sources record various types of carpets in use throughout the eastern Mediterranean basin from late antiquity, although the lack of surviving examples for the most part renders the technique and design of these carpets a matter for conjecture. The great "Garden of Chosroes" carpet, belonging to the seventh-century Sasanian emperors of Iran, appears to have been a gigantic embroidery incorporating pearls and other precious materials into its design, and before its destruction by the conquering Arabs was a famous example of royal conspicuous consumption. The Koran (88:16) contains one mention of *zarābiyya,* generally translated as "rich carpets" or "silken carpets," which are promised, along with cushions, couches, goblets, and springs of fresh water, to true believers when they enter paradise.

Medieval sources indicate that carpets were in

RUGS AND CARPETS

common use throughout the Islamic Middle East, with the products of Khorāsān, Fārs, Armenia, Azerbaijan, and Tabaristan mentioned prominently in various documents. Although *bisāṭ* (plural, *busuṭ*), the generic Arabic term for carpet, appears in many medieval Islamic texts along with other terms (*muṣallayāt,* prayer rugs; *sajjāda*, prostration rugs; *zullīya,* large carpets), we have very little idea of the techniques, styles, and artistic origins of these works, as no examples whatsoever appear to have survived. The comments of Western travelers have not been any more revealing; Marco Polo mentions the beautiful carpets that he saw during his travels through the region of Konya in Asia Minor, but it is difficult, in the light of contemporary scholarship, to attribute any surviving examples of carpets to thirteenth-century Anatolia.

The evidence of heavy textiles being used for floor coverings in the West is more meager. There are two types of association attached to carpets in Europe from the High Middle Ages on: as furnishings for the altar area in churchs, and as accoutrements for the thrones of royalty. In each case, carpets are identified with sanctity, wealth, and power. Aside from these ceremonial purposes, carpets or carpetlike textiles do not appear to have been used extensively in the West until the later Middle Ages. Europe's traditions of mosaic, opus sectile stonework, and tile flooring appear to have fulfilled the functions of opulence and conspicuous consumption performed by carpets in the Middle East; and written records attest to the practicality, rather than the aesthetic values, of the straw or rushes that were scattered on the floors of medieval banqueting halls. While there are numerous surviving examples of early medieval Islamic silks imported into Europe, such as the famous tenth-century Buwayhid Suaire de St. Josse from the Pas-de-Calais, or the Holy Coat of Jesus in the Trier Cathedral, there are almost no surviving examples of the presumably more robust woolen carpets of this period in either the East or the West, with the exception of a few tiny fragments yielded up in various excavations.

It is precisely this fact that has led some scholars to assume that the earliest Islamic carpets to survive, those of the late thirteenth or fourteenth century, may be the earliest examples of knotted-pile weaving to have been accomplished in western Asia. Certainly it is curious that the documentation of oriental carpet use in Europe, which begins to appear in European paintings and written sources of the fourteenth century, is roughly contemporary with the first evidence from Islamic painting of carpets in the Islamic world, while the earliest surviving examples of carpets from medieval Islamic civilization can be dated with some confidence to the same time.

The discovery early in the twentieth century of a group of very old carpets in mosques of Konya and Beyshehir in central Anatolia led at first to the belief that the "Marco Polo" carpets of thirteenth-century Anatolia had been identified. Given the demonstrably Chinese origins of the designs on some of these early carpets, and the evidence of carpets depicted in datable Islamic miniature paintings, this early group of carpets may be more securely dated to the fourteenth century, by which time the impact of Chinese art was evident across the entire spectrum of Islamic arts in the Middle East. What is equally interesting is that the design of one of these early Konya carpets, derived from Yuan silk patterns of China, was subsequently copied in an early carpet from Islamic Spain. This again underlines the curious fact that the earliest surviving carpets appear in the Middle East and in Western Europe at about the same time, with the European examples clearly seeking to emulate the designs of prototypes woven in Anatolia.

From a stylistic point of view, these early knotted-pile carpets, products of the High Middle Ages in the Islamic Middle East and Islamic Spain, may be divided into three groups. The first consists of patterned carpets, with repeating overall designs, sometimes of Chinese origin and sometimes consisting of geometrical Islamic arabesques. The bulk of the "Konya" carpets belong to this category, as do some of the early Spanish imitations; and there is evidence from both European painting and Islamic miniatures of the use of such carpets from the fourteenth century on.

The second group of early carpets, called "animal carpets" by the German scholar Kurt Erdmann, displays heavily stylized animal forms, whose artistic genesis and symbolism have been convincingly linked with a pan-Asiatic artistic tradition. A surviving example discovered in the small Swedish parish church of Marby, datable on the basis of comparison with depictions in European paintings to the fifteenth century, shows two stylized birds flanking a tree (now in Stockholm, Statens Historiska Museet); another example, now in Berlin (Staatliche Museen zu Berlin, Islamisches Museum), depicts the combat of a dragon and a phoenix.

RUGS AND CARPETS

Fragment of a central Anatolian pile carpet with geometric pattern adapted from Chinese silks, 14th century. TÜRK VE ISLAM ESERLERI MÜZESI, İSTANBUL

The Marby rug, showing two stylized birds. Early 15th century. Statens Historiska Museet, Stockholm, inv. 17786. PHOTO: GABRIEL HILDEBRAND © RIKSANTIKVARIEÄMBETET

There are many Italian paintings of the fourteenth and fifteenth centuries showing similar carpets, now thought to have been made in Anatolia and imported into Europe via Italy's extensive trading links in the Levant. When depicted in European paintings, these carpets are often shown as floor coverings under the feet of the Madonna or before the throne of a king or pope.

The third group of carpets appearing in early paintings of both East and West, and surviving in slightly larger numbers, consists of carpets with a repeating pattern of small medallion forms. There is an increasing body of evidence suggesting that these early carpets bear designs associated with the tribal symbols of nomadic Turkic peoples known as Turkomans, who, according to Islamic historical sources, contributed importantly to the emerging Turkish political power and to the gradual dominance of Islamic culture in Anatolia. Moreover, these early carpets have many striking similarities with more recent carpets woven by Turkoman nomads in what is today Soviet Turkmenistan (Turkmen SSR). The repeating medallions, known in the central Asian Turkoman carpets as *gül* (literally, flowers), appear to serve as symbols of particular tribal entities, and many of the forms found in Anatolian carpets of the fifteenth century seem to have endured with little change in the nomadic weavings of a more recent time. Although the two main subgroups of medieval *gül* carpets are sometimes called Holbein carpets because of their

Small-pattern "Holbein" carpet from central Anatolia, early 16th century. THE TEXTILE MUSEUM, WASHINGTON, D.C., R.34.17.1

depiction in sixteenth-century paintings by the German Hans Holbein the Younger, such carpets were extensively portrayed in fifteenth-century European painting; and similar ones are depicted in Islamic paintings dating back as far as the last quarter of the fourteenth century.

In Europe rugs seem to have functioned only as carpets, being used to cover tables (hence the phrase "to put the matter on the carpet") or placed before thrones (hence the term "called on the carpet"). Smaller rugs, evidently imported in quantity, added bright color to the visual environment and by virtue of their great cost also served as status symbols. In the areas where they were created, rugs and carpets fulfilled a much wider variety of functions. The appearance of the terms *muṣallayāt* (for prayer) and *sajjāda* (for prostration) in early Islamic sources attests to the use of carpets to provide the canonical clean place required for the daily prayers. Thus carpets were commonly used in mosques—community prayer halls of the Islamic world—to which they were given as part of protected endowments (*waqf*), and where many of the oldest examples now gracing the world's great museums survived over the centuries. There is also ample evidence that pile carpets were associated with wealth and royalty in the East as they were in the West, for examples are frequently shown in connection with kings or thrones in Islamic miniature paintings from the fourteenth century on.

The making of carpets emerged as a major commercial enterprise in the early Middle Ages, according to Islamic sources. From the later Middle Ages on, carpets proved to be an important article of trade within the Islamic world and an increasingly significant aspect of East–West trade as well. If the rug production of the eighteenth through twentieth centuries in the Middle East is any indication, however, carpets were only one part, and perhaps a small part at that, of the total volume of rug production. For rugs were bound up with the social and economic order of certain nomadic and village peoples to such an extent that they were used in virtually every aspect of everyday and ceremonial life. Nomadic weavers, for example, wove sacks, bags, pillows, cushions, and purses to contain the clothing, bedding, food, and implements that were moved from place to place with the migrations of the flocks. Other rug forms evolved to serve decorative functions; early miniature paintings demonstrate that the tent bands, door surrounds, and other ornaments of the portable dwellings used by nineteenth- and twentieth-century nomadic groups in the Middle East remain largely unchanged from at least the thirteenth century. The shape and style of other rug types, such as those used for animal caparisons, have likewise changed little over the centuries. Finally, certain types of rugs were created to serve specific occasional or ceremonial purposes, as decorations for weddings, circumcisions, funerals, and other festive social or religious occasions in the Islamic or semi-Islamic societies of the rural and nomadic Middle East. An interesting comparison may be seen in the medieval Venetian custom of hanging rugs over balconies and balustrades on feast days, revealed in the paintings of Vittore Carpaccio. The difference is that in Europe rugs were a purchased commodity belonging to the very rich, while in large parts of the Middle East those small and specifically designed rugs that formed a basic and intimate part of day-to-day life were woven by those who used them.

In the late Middle Ages the rugs and carpets in common use in Europe appear to have come from what is today Asiatic Turkey, where cultural mixture and complexity have been characteristic of the society for millennia. Turkic tribal designs and those borrowed from the broader Islamic heritage with its Chinese overtones were adapted to large commercial carpets, many of which seem to have been created for the European market from the outset. In the fifteenth century we see the beginnings of the European carpet mania that led to the westward flow of thousands of carpets—first Turkish, later Persian and Indian, and finally Caucasian and Turkoman. The popularity of these works in Europe led to a demand that resulted in imitations of the Middle Eastern carpets being created not only in Spain but in England and in central Europe as well.

While the making of carpets in Europe seems to have drawn its original economic raison d'être from the popularity of oriental carpets in European markets, and while the best-known European carpet factories, such as Savonnerie and Gobelins, were founded in the baroque age by royal design establishments that rejected the oriental styles, there are evidences in late medieval Europe of a mixed tradition of European inventiveness coupled with oriental inspiration. Written sources attest to the use of carpets in the royal Muslim courts of Spain, as well as to the use of floor coverings made from the celebrated Cordovan leather. As the gradual reconquest of Spain took place, and as carpets of Turkish and possibly Moorish design were replaced by those with the styles and heraldic iconography of the new Christian nobility, the Mudéjar artisans of Alcaraz and Letur produced rugs of curious hybrid designs. In examples of the *almirante* (admiral) carpets bearing coats of arms of some of the great Spanish noble families, the European escutcheons are placed on top of a field of Turkish inspiration in a 2–1–2 arrangement identical to that of the large octagonal *gül* forms on some of the "Holbein" rugs. Whether the Spanish weavers were aware of the heraldic functions of the Turkish prototypes or not, the Spanish rugs show a symbolic as well as an artistic appropriation of their Middle Eastern models. Spanish carpets from Cuenca later substituted rondels formed of wreaths and vegetal arabesques for the prototype *güls* of the earlier Spanish rugs.

The most provocative evidence for an extensive European carpet production in the later Middle Ages, of which no actual examples have survived, is found in late medieval Flemish and northern oil painting. In the works of Van Eyck, Memling, and Metssys, among others, there are not only depictions of carpets that conform in every respect to our conceptions of Middle Eastern design, but also examples that show a much different aesthetic. Carpets such as those under the feet of the Madonna in Hubert Van Eyck's *Madonna with Canon van der Paele* of 1436 (Bruges, Groeningemuseum), or Petrus Christus' *Madonna with Saints Francis and Jerome* of 1457 (Frankfurt, Städelsches Kunstinstitut), show designs of vaguely Islamic inspiration in an unusual range of colors coupled with completely original ornaments and borders. Given the importance of textiles in general for the culture and economy of Flanders and northern Europe at this time, and the generally very high level of accuracy in depiction of objects and fabrics in the works of late medieval painters of northern Europe, it would seem wise to follow the theory of the American carpet scholar Charles Grant Ellis that there must have been a fairly extensive manufacture of luxury carpets, of unknown technique, in Flanders during the fifteenth century.

That carpets in Western Europe at this time were not confined solely to the sacred context in either use or depiction is attested by the illustrations created during the 1460's for the *Livre du cueur d'amours espris* of René d'Anjou (Vienna, Österreichisches Nationalbibliothek, Cod. Vind. 2597). In a miniature showing the sleeping King René in his bedroom with figures of Amour and Ardent Desire, two small rugs of Turkish design are on top of the woven rush matting of the chamber; each bears the octagonal *gül* form, and one shows a design virtually identical to that of nineteenth-century rugs from Turkey and the Caucasus. The admixture of Orient and Occident is further underlined by the costume of Amour, who carries a Turkish quiver and whose tunic is bordered with gold Arabic inscriptions.

The available evidence indicates that by the end of the Middle Ages, when carpet manufacture was entering a new and glorious phase in the Ottoman Empire, Cairo, and northwest Iran, and the greatest surviving masterpieces of knotted carpets were emerging from the sixteenth-century court styles of the Middle East, an actual decline in use of carpets occurred in certain parts of Europe, as the new Renaissance taste seems to have led first to a rejection of carpets in the oriental style and ulti-

Miniature from the *Livre du cueur d'amours espris* of René d'Anjou showing Turkish rugs, *ca.* 1465. ÖSTERREICHISCHES NATIONALBIBLIOTHEK, VIENNA, COD. VIND. 2597, fol. 2

mately to the creation of a large-scale European carpet industry. In Venice, and under the patronage of Cardinal Wolsey in England, import and imitation of oriental rugs seems to have continued; but the "textile internationalism" of the later Middle Ages was largely replaced by a self-conscious Europeanism in the West, in which carpets and brocaded silks of the Middle East played a much less significant role.

BIBLIOGRAPHY

Alisa Baginski and Amalia Tidhar, *Textiles from Egypt 4th–13th Centuries C.E.* (1980); Walter B. Denny, "Türkmen Rugs and Early Rug Weaving in the Western Islamic World," in *Hali,* 4 (1982); Kurt Erdmann, *Europa und der Orientteppich* (1962); Maurice Lombard, *Les textiles dans le monde musulman VIIe–XIIe siècle* (1978); Louise W. Mackie, "Two Remarkable Fifteenth Century Carpets from Spain," in *Textile Museum Journal,* 4 (1977); Robert B. Serjeant, *Islamic Textiles: Material for a History up to the Mongol Conquest* (1972); Robert Pinner and Walter B. Denny, eds., *Oriental Carpet and Textile Studies II: Carpets of the Mediterranean Countries 1400–1600* (1986); Friedrich Spuhler, "Bisāṭ," in *Encyclopaedia of Islam, Supplement,* fasc. 3/4 (1981); Şerare Yetkin, *Historical Turkish Carpets* (1981).

WALTER B. DENNY

[See also **Kilim; Tapestry Weaving; Textiles; Textiles, Islamic.**]

RUIZ, JUAN (*ca.* 1283–*ca.* 1350), author of the early-fourteenth-century *Libro de buen amor,* which, with the *Cantar de mío Cid* and *La Celestina,* is one of the most important literary works of the Spanish Middle Ages. We know nothing about Juan Ruiz, save that he tells us he was archpriest of Hita, a town situated in the valley of the Henares River near Guadalajara. Two scholars, Emilio Sáez and José Trenchs, without firm evidence have attempted to link the poet with a certain Juan Ruiz de Cisneros. Such an identification does raise interesting possibilities, since this person was born and lived much of his life in an Arabic-speaking area of Spain. The likelihood of Semitic influences at play in the *Libro de buen amor* is another of the important questions that have concerned scholars.

The *Libro* has always delighted and exasperated its readers and critics because of the sense of exuberance and joie de vivre which color its poetry and also because it has proved impossible to associate it closely with any perceived tradition or meaning. Throughout the work there are exhortations to understand the book rightly, yet such an accurate comprehension is hindered by the poet's constantly changing stance and by his tendency to parody established literary and cultural modes and practices. The textual ambiguity that results is clearly related to that concern about the distinction between the apparent and the real, and between truth and falsity, which characterizes Spanish literature until the end of the Golden Age, and which is a key problem in the *Quijote.*

The *Libro* comes down principally in three manuscripts, all late medieval copies, two of which are relatively complete. The differences between these two has led a number of scholars to speculate that one manuscript represents a rendition finished in 1330, while the other would derive from a more perfect version of the work executed in 1343.

The book begins with ten stanzas in *cuaderna vía* (the principal verse form in the work), which constitute a kind of supplicatory oration in which the poet pleads to be released from some sort of prison. Scholars are unable to agree as to whether a real jail is intended or whether the author was referring to the kind of philosophical prison of the body often used metaphorically in medieval literature. There follows immediately a long sermon in prose which appears to be constructed according to the precepts of the university sermon and which sets into place the basic antinomy between *loco amor* (impure or evil love) and *buen amor* (good love) that prevails throughout the poem. (Neither of these two sections exists in the manuscript thought to derive from the 1330 version.) Next come nine *cuaderna vía* stanzas in which the poet asks for grace to write his book and gives the reader some idea how to interpret it. Obviously these stanzas could very well have stood at the beginning of an original text. There follow several Joys (*Gozos*) of the Virgin, which have the form of a *zajal.*

The poet returns to *cuaderna vía* for a number of sections having to do with various philosophical considerations and the problem of interpretation before finally arriving at the important *Cruz* episode, which is again composed in zajalesque form. The author tells us that he suffered a crucifixion of love when his male go-between stole the baker girl Cruz away from him. The possibilities for liturgical parody here are obviously great. The poet now wends his way toward a section in which he will engage in a lengthy debate with "a tall, handsome, well-mannered man" who is the Lord Love himself. This interchange, which Roger M. Walker believes may constitute a kind of *ars amoris,* is interspersed with a number of exempla of Aesopic and other origins, as well as a fascinating parody of the Canonical Hours. After the departure of Lord Love, the author continues the discussion, this time with Lady Venus, wife of Lord Love.

Now comes one of the most interesting and perplexing sections in the *Libro:* the encounter between Doña Endrina (Lady Sloe-plum) and Don Melón de la Huerta (Sir Garden Melon? Badger? Apple?—all three meanings are possible and have been suggested). The archpriest has taken his plot here from the twelfth-century Latin elegiac comedy *Pamphilus,* and it is difficult to determine whether the author and Don Melón should be identified with one another. There follows shortly the story of the poet's strange pilgrimage in the early spring across the Guadarrama Mountains to Segovia, during which he meets the awful *serranas* (mountain girls), who are the complete opposite in physical terms of all he yearns for in a woman. The Lenten season provides a setting for a battle between the forces of restraint and sobriety embodied in Doña Cuaresma (Lady Lent) and Don Carnal (Sir Meat-season). Don Carnal is vanquished but will return in triumph in the Paschal season along with Don Amor. The magnificent entry of the latter on Easter Sunday into Toledo furnishes the archpriest a superb opportunity to parody the medieval ceremonies associated with the Palm Sunday procession and the *adventus regis*—the arrival of a royal visitor.

Now continuing according to the outline of the liturgical calendar, the poet has a couple of amorous adventures, one on Low Sunday and the other on St. Mark's Day, neither successful. In a somewhat despondent mood he asks his old retainer Convent-trotter to find a lady for him. She then approaches on his behalf a nun, Doña Garoza, whom she has served at some point. The long episode that ensues is an excellent illustration of the mood and structure of the book in that it demonstrates the poet's artistry in combining different materials, styles, and tones into an aesthetically pleasing whole. It consists of a long debate between the nun and Convent-trotter in which each underscores the points that she wishes to make with an appropriate fable. The reader senses, however, that often the moral inherent in the fable can be perceived as somewhat oblique to the argument at hand. Finally, the nun asks for and receives a description of the archpriest, which may be a kind of parody of the rhetorical portraits of lovely ladies so common in medieval literature. Scholars have suggested that the name Garoza is related to the Arabic word for bride. But we can never be sure whether the nun remains the pure bride of Christ or whether she effects a liaison with the archpriest. In the first line of stanza 1,503 the poet tells us that "the lady took me as her true love." Two lines further along, however, he says that all this was accomplished "*con Dios en limpio amor*" (through God and in pure love).

The principal episodes of the book are now finished, but the work does not end here. It continues on for more than 100 *cuaderna vía* stanzas, with a combination of minor amorous episodes, a moving but surely parodic *planctus* (traditional lament) for the death of Convent-trotter, a devotional piece, a section praising the virtues of small women, and finally another explanation as to how we should interpret the work. Tacked onto the end are yet another series of lyric poems, Joys of the Virgin, blindmen's songs, praises of the Virgin, and a prayer to adverse fortune. Even this is not the last bit of material in the book. The poet returns to *cuaderna vía* for his song of the clerics of Talavera. This section, modeled on the *Consultatio sacerdotium* of Walter Map, recounts how the clerics are discomforted by the arrival of a letter from the archbishop of Toledo ordering them to give up their concubines. Their elaborate defense of the value of their female companions provides the perfect final ending for a book concerned with the constant, if largely unsuccessful, pursuit by an archpriest of the same sort of companionship.

Criticism of the *Libro* has tended to center on several important points which have been heavily researched and hotly debated. Not surprisingly, one of these concerns whether the work really has a unified structure and, if so, what it is. Critics have attempted to determine whether the book is only a collection of poems done at various intervals during the poet's life addressing a variety of subjects, or whether something, for example the thread of autobiography or pseudo-erotic autobiography, can be seen to run throughout. The alternation of narrative and lyric with even one sermon in prose has led scholars to look for a model for the *Libro* in the Classical Latin *prosimetrum,* the Arabic *maqamat,* and the Old French *chantefable.* Although critics really have not been very successful in explaining the form of the *Libro,* it is doubtless true that the majority remain convinced they are dealing with a unified work. Closely connected to this question of form and unity is whether there really were two versions of the book, the first one dating from 1330 and amplified and expanded in 1343.

The author claims that he had a serious, didactic purpose in writing the book. Is he serious? A perusal of recent scholarship would suggest that the matter has resolved itself into a disagreement between those who see the *Libro* as a didactic work with an important element of subversive humor and those who consider it as a comic, parodic creation containing considerable didactic content. In order to answer this question it would be necessary to understand whether *buen amor* is really the love of God and holy things or the enjoyment of women. Scholars have also attempted to explain the poet's concept of love in relation to other medieval considerations on the subject.

The use of Arabic vocabulary in the poem and allusions to Moorish customs have suggested to some that it may be a *mudéjar* work—a product of the unique interaction of Christian, Jewish, and Muslim cultures that occurred in the Iberian Peninsula during the Middle Ages. Most scholars, however, while acknowledging the existence of Semitic elements and influences in the work, continue to believe that the *Libro* was conceived within the framework of Western European Christian civilization.

The *Libro* was probably widely read in the century after its composition. It is quoted in his *Corbacho* by Alfonso Martínez de Toledo and is referred to in his *Carta al Condestable de Portugal* by the Marqués de Santillana. Beyond the fifteenth century it is difficult to assess its import on the rapidly changing literary situation in Spain. That the poem continued to be known and appreciated to some degree is demonstrated by the fact that some lines from it are quoted in a book of commonplaces from the sixteenth century. Juan Ruiz has been dubbed "the Spanish Chaucer," because some readers have been struck by a similarity of tone between him and the English poet. Because of an ongoing English interest and involvement in Castilian affairs in the late fourteenth century it has even been suggested that Chaucer might have known the *Libro* and have been influenced by it.

BIBLIOGRAPHY

Editions. Jacques Joset, ed., *Libro de buen amor,* 2 vols. (1974–1975); Raymond S. Willis, ed., *Libro de buen amor* (1972), with introduction and English paraphrase.

Studies. T. J. Garbaty, "The *Pamphilus* Tradition in Ruiz and Chaucer," in *PQ,* **46** (1967); Otis H. Green, "On Juan Ruiz's Parody of the Canonical Hours," in *Hispanic Review,* **26** (1958); G. B. Gybbon-Monypenny, ed., *"Libro de buen amor" Studies* (1970); Eric G. Naylor *et al.,* eds., "Bibliography of the *Libro de buen amor* Since 1973," in *La Crónica,* 7 (1979); Colbert Nepaulsingh, "The Structure of the *Libro de buen amor,*" in *Neophilologus,* **61** (1977); Anthony N. Zahareas, *The Art of Juan Ruiz, Archpriest of Hita* (1965).

JAMES F. BURKE

[See also **Cantiga; Cuaderna Vía; Fables; Hispano-Arabic Language and Literature; Latin Literature; Martínez de Toledo, Alfonso; Santillana, Marqués de; Spanish Literature: Satire; Spanish Literature: Versification and Prosody.**]

RULING (French: *réglure;* German: *Liniierung;* Italian: *rigatura*), a configuration of horizontal and vertical lines drawn on blank sheets of a manuscript in order to guide handwriting. Prickings determined the placement of the lines. The pattern of lines and the instrument used to draw them, the number of sheets lined at one time, whether the sheets were folded or not, and whether the lines were drawn on the hair or flesh side of parchment sheets varied with time and place, and so provide clues to a manuscript's origins.

BIBLIOGRAPHY

Bernhard Bischoff, *Paläographie des römischen Altertums und des abendländischen Mittelalters* (1979) 36–37; Léon Gilissen, "Un élément codicologique trop peu exploité: La réglure," in *Scriptorium,* **23** (1969).

MICHAEL MCCORMICK

[See also **Manuscript Books, Production of; Parchment; Pecia; Prickings; Quire; Stylus; Writing Materials, Western European.**]

RUM (derived from Latin *Roma* via Greek *Rōme*). In medieval Islamic sources this term designated the Byzantine provinces of Asia Minor. After the Seljuk conquest it denoted the same territories, now under Turkish rule (Rome proper was called *Rūmīya*). The Byzantine rulers (especially after 812) regularly styled themselves "emperor of the Romans."

The borders of Rum fluctuated with the varying successes of Byzantine or Islamic armies. For much of the Umayyad period (661–750) and part of the Abbasid era up to the Seljuk victory at Manazkert (750–1071), the eastern frontier of Rum ran along the Taurus and Anti-Taurus ranges and a series of military zones from Melitene (Malatya) to Tarsus. To the northeast lay the Armenian state. Muslim raids, including several major drives aimed at taking Constantinople in the seventh and early eighth centuries, became annual affairs usually culminating with the exchange or ransom of prisoners at fixed points. The border zones, with their heterogeneous and often heterodox populations and "fighters for the faith" on both sides, exhibited an interesting cultural symbiosis.

The ethnically variegated and unevenly Hellenized population of Anatolia was subjected to steady Turkicization (still incomplete in Ottoman times) following the Seljuk conquest. Turkish tribesmen poured in and were ultimately organized by a branch of the Seljuk dynasty established at Konya (Ikonion). This city remained the seat of Seljuk authority even after the region came under Mongol overlordship (after 1243) and subsequently under direct Mongol rule (after 1277). With the collapse of the Ilkhanids and the death of the last Seljuk puppet ruler (early fourteenth century), the Turkish emirs of Rum were gradually absorbed by the house of Osman.

Muslim geographers of the ninth and tenth centuries, often working with the materials gathered by the caliphal intelligence network, were relatively well informed about the provinces and important towns of Rum: Ibn Khurdādhbih, Qudāma ibn Ja^{c}far, Ibn Rusta, Ibn al-Faqīh, al-Mas^{c}ūdī, al-Iṣṭakhrī, Ibn Ḥawqal and the author of the *Ḥudūd al-^{c}ālam.*

BIBLIOGRAPHY

E. W. Brooks, "The Arabs in Asia Minor (641–750), from Arabic Sources," in *Journal of Hellenic Studies,* **18** (1898), "Arabic Lists of the Byzantine Themes," *ibid.,* **21** (1901), and "Byzantines and Arabs in the Time of the Early Abbasids," in *English Historical Review,* **15** (1900) and **16** (1901); Claude Cahen, *Pre-Ottoman Turkey,* J. Jones-Williams, trans. (1968); Maurice Canard, "Les expéditions des Arabes contre Constantinople dans l'histoire et dans la légende," in *Journal asiatique,* **208** (1926), and "Les sources arabes de l'histoire byzantine aux confins des Xe et XIe siècles," in *Revue des études byzantines,* **19** (1961); Hamilton A. R. Gibb, "Arab-Byzantine Relations Under the Umayyad Caliphate," in *Dumbarton Oaks Papers,* **12** (1958); Vladimir A. Gordlevsky, *Izbrannye sochinenia,* I (1960), 31–218; Ernst Honigmann, *Die Ostgrenze des byzantinischen Reiches von 363 bis 1071* (1935); Mehmed F. Köprülü, *Les origines de l'empire ottoman* (1935); Guy LeStrange, *The Lands of the Eastern Caliphate* (1905, repr. 1930, 1966); Alexander A. Vasiliev, *Vizantiia i Araby,* 2 vols. (1900–1902), ed. and trans. by Henri Gregoire and Maurice Canard as *Byzance et les Arabes* (1935–1950); Speros Vryonis, *The Decline of Medieval Hellenism in Asia Minor and the Process of Islamization from the Eleventh Through the Fifteenth Century* (1971); Paul Wittek, "Deux chapitres de l'histoire des Turcs de Roum," in *Byzantion,* **11** (1936).

PETER B. GOLDEN

[See also **Akritai; Anatolia; Ghāzī; Ikonion; Ilkhanids; Khurdādhbih, Ibn; Manazkert; Mas^{c}ūdī, al-; Ottomans; Seljuks of Rum.**]

RŪMĪ (JALĀL AL-DĪN) (1207–1273). Although Rūmī is best known by that sobriquet in the West, in the East he is more commonly referred to by the titles, derived from Arabic, "Our Lord" (Arabic: *mawlānā;* Persian: *mowlānā;* Turkish: *mevlânâ*) and "My Lord" (Arabic: *mawlawī;* Persian: *mow-*

lavī), or by his name, Jalāl al-Dīn—transliterated variously as Djelaleddin, Jelal od-din, and so on.

Rūmī is without question the greatest mystical poet in the Persian language. His works have exerted a profound and enduring influence on the spiritual life of Muslims living in Turkey, Iran, Central Asia, and India, and have gained a wide readership in Europe as well, particularly during the nineteenth century. He was also the founder of a mystical brotherhood that has survived to the present day.

Rūmī was born in September 1207 at Balkh (in modern Afghanistan), into the family of a learned Muslim theologian, Bahā^ɔal-Dīn Muḥammad ibn Ḥusayn-i Khaṭībī-i Balkhī, known as Bahāɔ-i Walad. Bahāɔ-i Walad taught in Balkh and Samarkand before disagreements with the ruler of the region and with other theologians led him to emigrate to western Anatolia around 1217, to Laranda (Karaman), then to Konya, at the request of the ruling emir. The family remained there even after the death of Bahāɔ-i in 1231.

With the death of his father, Rūmī's further education, particularly in esoteric subjects, was taken in hand by one of Bahāɔ-i Walad's former pupils, Burhān al-Dīn Muḥaqqiq. Rūmī also spent several years in Damascus and Aleppo, perfecting his knowledge of traditional, exoteric subjects. On the completion of his studies, he became, like his father before him, a teacher in the madrasa at Konya.

At this point Rūmī seemed destined to follow closely in his father's footsteps as a learned doctor of theology, distinguished by his mastery of both esoteric and exoteric learning, and by his gifts as a teacher. What transformed him into a great mystical poet, and sustained him in that role throughout the remainder of his life, was a series of three spiritual unions. The first and most formative of these was with Shams-i Tabrīzī (Shams al-Dīn Muḥammad Tabrīzī), a wandering dervish of acutely critical mind who came to Konya in late 1244. When he and Rūmī met, they quickly realized that they had found in each other the spiritual mate that each had long sought. Rūmī brought Shams-i Tabrīzī into his own home, married him to his ward, and gave his whole attention to him. Indeed, he became so absorbed in Shams that he neglected his students, who responded with a jealous resentment so intense that it eventually drove the dervish away—first for some months in 1246, and then permanently in 1247. There is even evidence to suggest that the students and Rūmī's second son connived at the murder of Shams.

However disturbing Rūmī's love for Shams was to his students, for him it opened the wellsprings of a great and unsuspected poetic talent. Under the stimulation of Sham's presence, he began to compose ecstatic, mystical lyrics in continual, rushing abundance, although he had apparently shown no bent for poetry before. After the convention of mystical lovers, so total was his identification with his beloved during the composition of his poetry—particularly after Shams's disappearance, when Rūmī asserted that he had re-created Shams within himself—that he composed most of these lyrics in Shams's name; the collected volume of them is known as the *Dīvān* of Shams-i Tabrīzī. In Rūmī's words:

> Happy the moment when we are seated in the palace,
> thou and I,
> With two forms and with two figures, but with
> one soul, thou and I.
>
> (Nicholson trans., 153)

The second of Rūmī's spiritual lovers was Ṣalāḥ al-Dīn Zarkūb, an illiterate goldsmith who had nonetheless pursued spiritual learning with great diligence and had been, like Rūmī, a student of Burhān al-Dīn Muḥaqqiq. Rūmī's disciples were fiercely resentful when Rūmī designated Ṣalāḥ al-Dīn as his successor, but he was able to compel their acceptance of him, and Ṣalāḥ al-Dīn held that position until his death in 1258. He did not engender any new outpouring of poetry but seems to have continued the inspiration begun by Shams-i Tabrīzī.

Rūmī's final love, Čelebi Ḥusām al-Dīn Ḥasan, who lived with Rūmī for the ten years before the latter's death, gave a new and important direction to Rūmī's poetry. He inspired him to begin the composition of a long narrative, didactic poem in couplets, the *Mathnawī-i Maᶜnawī* (spiritual couplets), the most important spiritual-mystical work in Persian, considered by many to be second in importance only to the Koran.

Ḥusām al-Dīn served as successor to Rūmī as *shaykh* of the mystical brotherhood that took its name, Mawlawīya (Turkish: Mevlevī), from their title for Rūmī. On his death in 1283, leadership of the order fell to Rūmī's son Sulṭān Walad, who strove successfully during his long life (*d.* 1312) to gain respect for the order and to extend its influence.

Rūmī composed an enormous volume of poetry. The *Mathnawī* alone contains more than 25,000 couplets, and the 6,000 lyrics that make up the *Dīvān-i Shams-i Tabrīzī* contain another 40,000 double lines. One scholar has calculated that Rūmī must have composed a poem or its equivalent every day or two, if the whole of his poetic corpus was indeed written after his meeting Shams-i Tabrīzī. This impressive body of work, so rich and varied in its stylistic character and thematic content, is divided between two quite different genres, mystical-lyric and narrative-didactic, in each of which Rūmī achieved a level of excellence never surpassed.

Rūmī's mystical lyrics differ sharply from erotic lyric poetry, which relies heavily upon exquisite descriptions of a highly conventional and sumptuous nature. His references to the physical world are brief and suggestive, and are made in the service of the soul's perception of what is beyond nature and indescribable.

> I am not of Nature's mint, nor of the circling
> heavens
> I am not of earth, nor of air, nor of fire;
> I am not of the empyrean, nor of the dust,
> nor of existence nor of entity.
> I am not of India, nor of China, nor of
> Bulgaria, nor of Saqsīn.
> (Nicholson trans., 125)

While the *Mathnawī* retains some of Rūmī's lyric fluency, it is a learned work that makes available the fruits of his long scholarly preparation and his many years as a teacher. In it anecdote, parable, and commentary are made the means of guiding the reader down the path of spiritual perfection. The lyrics, in contrast, are stirring evocations of spiritual longing, or of enlightenment itself.

> This is love: to fly heavenward,
> To rend, in every instant, a hundred veils.
> The first moment, to renounce life;
> The last step, to fare without feet.
> (Nicholson trans., 137)

BIBLIOGRAPHY

The best edition of the *Dīvān-i Shams-i Tabrīzī* is that of Badī ᶜuᵓz-Zaman Furūzānfar, 10 vols. (1957–1968), reissued in 9 vols. (1976). There are a number of translations of poems from the *Dīvān;* the passages given above were taken from *Selected Poems from the Dīvāni Shamsi Tabrīz,* Reynold A. Nicholson, trans. (1898, repr. 1952, 1973, 1977), which includes texts along with translations. The best edition of the *Mathnawī* is also that of Nicholson, and is printed together with a literal English translation and extensive commentary, 6 vols. (1925–1940, repr. 1982). A good survey of Rūmī's life and work in English is Annemarie Schimmel, *The Triumphal Sun,* rev. ed. (1980).

Jerome W. Clinton

[See also **Dervish; Iranian Literature; Mysticism, Islamic.**]

RUNES. The word "rune" is employed by modern scholarship to denote a letter of the runic alphabet, a system of writing native to Scandinavia, England, and continental Germanic-language-speaking areas. The use of runes, attested as early as the second century, predated the introduction of the Latin alphabet among these peoples; in some places (notably Scandinavia) runic writing continued to be used alongside Latin through the late Middle Ages. More than 5,000 runic inscriptions are known today, and while many of these are obscure or stingy in their informational content, others are primary sources of inestimable value to the study of ancient Germanic and Old Scandinavian culture.

The early history of the word "rune" reveals a semantic field associated with mystery and secrecy. It is first attested in fourth-century Gothic, where *rūna* was the translation of the Greek word *mysterion,* and in Old English, Old Saxon, and Old High German it can refer to secret, private conversations, suggesting that the runes were, at least in the early period, an esoteric cultural artifact in the possession of a small elite within the tribe. In the inscriptions themselves the word occurs first in the singular on the Norwegian stone from Einang (*ca.* 400): "[Go]dagastiz drew the rune," where it is difficult to tell whether the word is used in the sense of "runic letter" or "secret message." On the other hand, the appearance of the plural ("I write runes") on the Swedish Järsberg stone (*ca.* 550) no doubt indicates the letters themselves.

Our modern English word "rune" is not directly derived from the Old English equivalent, which is to be found today only in the archaic word "roun(d)" (to whisper). Rather, the word was borrowed and reintroduced into English from the Scandinavian and Neo-Latin writings of sixteenth- and seventeenth-century antiquaries such as the Dane Ole Worm and the Swede Andreas Bureus.

The study of runic writing and runic inscriptions is known as runology. As is the case with Greek or

RUNES

Latin epigraphy, the task of the runologist is to collect, read, interpret, and publish the corpus of inscriptions, and to study the principles, methods, and conventions of the discipline, so that other scholars (historians, linguists, archaeologists, folklorists) may have access to a reliable body of source material.

NUMBER, DISTRIBUTION, AND CHRONOLOGY OF THE INSCRIPTIONS

It is not easy to establish an exact inventory of the runic inscriptions. Every year inscriptions come to light during building and road construction, church renovation, plowing, archaeological excavation, and similar activities. (In some cases these are not new finds but rediscoveries of inscriptions once known and described in the literature.) Moreover, deciding for purposes of inventory what counts as an inscription is problematical, as for example with such items as fragmentary, obscure, unreadable, or gibberish inscriptions; objects marked with but a single rune; coins and medallions from common or similar stamps; suspected forgeries; and casual literary references to objects now lost.

Bearing these uncertainties in mind, one can offer the following statistical survey:

Almost 3,000 of the over 5,000 runic inscriptions known today are of Swedish provenance, an especially remarkable statistic considering that the present Swedish provinces of Skåne, Blekinge, and Halland belonged to Denmark, and Bohuslän to Norway, during the Middle Ages. Most of the Swedish inscriptions are found on raised memorial stones, a type of runic monument that proliferated in the late Viking Age (tenth and eleventh centuries), achieving its greatest popularity in the Swedish province of Uppland, where nearly 1,200 are known. Since these rune stones are quite stereotyped, there is not as much variety in the Swedish inscriptions as the data would suggest.

The number of runic inscriptions in Norway now exceeds 1,200. About 550 of these represent recent finds from the excavation of the wharf (Bryggen) in Bergen, an archaeological surprise that has revised many of our runological notions and should serve as a warning against excessively dogmatic generalizations.

The Danish inscriptions now number about 700. Included in this figure are inscriptions from Skåne, Blekinge, and Halland (now Swedish provinces) and part of present-day northern West Germany (Schleswig).

Runic inscriptions of Scandinavian (mostly Norwegian) provenience are also found on the North Atlantic islands colonized or visited during the Viking expansion. Iceland has about fifty, most of them of late date. More than 100 have been found in Greenland, in the Faeroes, Hebrides, Orkneys, and Shetlands, in Ireland, England, and Scotland, and on the Isle of Man.

Of English runic inscriptions proper there are only about seventy-five. The German ("South Germanic") inscriptions are even fewer, numbering about fifty. Finally, some sixteen inscriptions have been identified as Frisian.

The figures cited above do not include the sporadic occurrence of runes in manuscripts, where they were used occasionally as supplementary letters or reference marks, as a means to write short messages or comments, or as the subject of antiquarian poems and treatises.

The dating of a runic inscription is rarely absolute. Most often a tentative date is assigned in accordance with an archaeological dating of the object on which the inscription is found and with a relative chronology established on the basis of internal runological evidence. The earliest runic inscription is generally agreed to be the spear blade from Øvre Stabu in Norway, dated archaeologically to the second half of the second century.

THE OLDER FUTHARK

Given the dating of our earliest inscriptions, it is reasonable to assume that the runic writing system was developed sometime during the first century following the birth of Christ. Unfortunately, there is scarcely any evidence that would shed light on this development; on the contrary, the earliest inscriptions appear in an alphabet fully formed and remarkably stable. From the first six letters of its unique ordering, this alphabet is known as the *fuþark*, or futhark, and in order to distinguish the early variety from later Scandinavian offshoots, it is convenient to speak of the Older and Younger Futharks.

The Older Futhark appears in series in a number of inscriptions (some fragmentary), and though these show minor differences in the order and shapes of a few runes, it is possible to set up a standard Older Futhark (Table 1).

There is some variation in the forms of the runes, particularly in those for **k** (ᚲ ^ ᛦ ᛉ ᚴ), **h** (ᚺ ᚻ), **j** (ᛃ ᛃ ᛃ ᛃ ᚼ ᛡ), **p** (ᛈ ᛈ ᛈ), **s** (ᛊ ᛊ ᛊ), and **ng** (◇ □ ᛜ ᛜ). A rune may on occasion appear upside down or reversed in direction, as well as in angular or rounded variants. It is thought that the angular shape is the more archaic, on the assumption that the runes were first designed to be carved on wood. (Note the avoidance of horizontal lines.)

Some inscriptions indicate that the twenty-four-symbol Older Futhark was divided into three groups of eight runes each (as indicated in Table 1), and later Scandinavian cryptic codes make use of such divisions, called *ættir* in Old Norse ("families," though some scholars would rather relate the word to the number eight). Consequently, much has been made of the possible magical significance of numbers relating to twenty-four. However, an excess of numerological enthusiasm has given such studies a bad name and made many runologists skeptical of runic number magic altogether, an unfortunate situation, since to deny that the runes were occasionally put to use in the service of magic would be foolish.

Each of the runes possessed a name that began with the sound in question (except for ᛉ [*z*], which never appears in initial position), for example **fehu* (wealth, cattle), **ūruz* (aurochs). (The asterisk denotes a conjectural form.) Unfortunately the original names must be reconstructed from late and corrupt manuscript sources and are not always clear. In the inscriptions a rune can sometimes be understood as standing for its name rather than its phonetic value.

The correspondence between the system of signs in the Older Futhark and the phonology of the language it represented is extremely close. Except for ◇ (**ng**) and possibly ᛇ (**E**), there is a one-to-one fit between phoneme and grapheme. In the opinion of some scholars, this fact suggests an independent, analytical, and sophisticated linguistic mind behind the creation of the runic alphabet. (Note, incidentally, that runic inscriptions are customarily transcribed in boldface letters while normalized versions are set in italics.)

A major problem, however, concerns the sound value of ᛇ, here transcribed **E**. This rune occurs in only about a half-dozen meaningful inscriptions, of which several are Anglo-Saxon. To these may be added the late and untrustworthy testimony of the rune names. This sparse evidence seems to indicate that the symbol ᛇ was used to write a high front vowel, perhaps of a different derivation than the /i/ represented by the **i**-rune, but undifferentiated from it by the time of our inscriptions and possibly superfluous in the runic writing system from the very beginning.

RUNES

Table 1. The Older Futhark

An alternative (and as yet unaccepted) view holds that ᛇ originally represented the vowel /ǣ/ in Proto-Germanic. It would follow that the Older Futhark was therefore created to transcribe a stage of the language much older than our earliest inscriptions.

The curious order of the runes cannot be derived from any known model and is either totally arbitrary or based on a principle as yet undiscovered. Attempts to explain it often resort to farfetched notions of religious and mystical motivation.

The conventions of runic writing permit variable direction: an inscription may read from left to right (this direction predominates as time goes on), from right to left, and even bustrophedon (alternating directions). As a rule, words or groups of words are not separated by spacing or marks of punctuation in this early period, and when the practice does arise its use is sporadic and inconsistent. Length is never marked; double letters are not written. Nasal runes are often omitted before homorganic consonants. Occasionally two runes can be merged graphically, creating a "bind-rune," for example ᛞᚨ (**d͡a**).

THE PROBLEM OF RUNIC ORIGINS

In the history of runology, no problem has received more attention than the search to explain the genesis of the runic alphabet. Nevertheless, in spite of such profound and intense scholarly investigation over the last hundred years, there is still no agreement on the answer to this fundamental question.

Once it became clear that the runes were neither an autonomous Germanic creation ex nihilo nor a direct descendant of the ancient alphabets of the Near East (Semitic, Phoenecian), there remained three possible models from which to derive the Older Futhark: the Latin, Greek, and North Italic alphabets. All of these, singly or in combination, have been put to use in the many attempts to solve the intractable problem of origins.

A pioneering treatment of the problem and a milestone of runological scholarship is Ludvig F. A. Wimmer's *Runeskriftens oprindelse og udvikling i Norden* (The origin of runic writing and its development in Scandinavia, 1874), in which the runes are derived from Latin capitals. Wimmer begins by pointing out six obvious correspondences: ᛒ, ᚲ(from Latin C), ᚺ, ᛁ, ᚱ, and ᛊ. Another ten runes are derived by slightly modifying the shape or position of the Latin letter: ᚨ, ᚠ, ᛏ, ᛗ, ᛞ, ᛚ, ᚢ, ᚾ, ᛟ, and ᚦ. The rest are problematical. Several, according to Wimmer, were created by joining two runes; thus ᛞ (**d**) from two facing **þ**-runes, ᚷ (**g**), ◇ (**ng**), and ᛃ (**j**) from two **k**-runes, and ᛈ (**p**) from two **b**-runes (which were then simplified). ᛉ (**z**) (transliterated by Wimmer and many others as **R**, since it later merged with /r/) is derived from Latin Z, ᚹ (**w**) perhaps from the runes ᛒ(**b**) or ᚢ (**u**). Wimmer is unsure of the derivation of ᛇ, to which he assigned the value /eu/, and can only suggest that it was an independent formation on the basis of another rune.

Although the tenuous nature of these last derivations has always been recognized, Wimmer's Latin theory met with immediate acceptance and the problem was considered solved. In 1898, however, in a lecture delivered before the Fifth Conference of Scandinavian Philologists, the Norwegian Sophus Bugge raised the possibility of a Greek origin of the runes. This suggestion was picked up by the Swede Otto von Friesen, whose essay *Om runskriftens härkomst* (On the origin of runic writing) appeared in 1904 and included a résumé of Bugge's lecture.

Von Friesen attempts to derive most of the runes from Greek cursive writing. According to him, only four of the runes (ᚠ, ᚢ, ᚺ, ᚱ) must come from Latin, while another five could go back to either Latin or Greek. The invention of the runic alphabet is credited to the Goths, who in migrating to the Black Sea during the third century came into contact with both Latin and Greek.

Although von Friesen defended his Greek theory in many publications (including the influential *Encyclopaedia Britannica*) until his death in 1942, it is less convincing than Wimmer's and enjoys little support today. Many of his derivations are quite strained, and his proposed route and chronology of transmission (based on the archaeological theories of Bernhard Salin) are both now considered questionable.

For most scholars today, the derivation of the runes from North Italic (formerly "North Etruscan") alphabets has many advantages over the other two theories. Inscriptions in northern Italy, particularly those of Bolzano, Lugano, and Sondrio, offer many striking parallels to runic writing, including correspondences not only in letter-forms (for example ᚨ, ᛚ, and ᚢ), but also in conventions such as variable direction of writing, lack of geminate letters, and the use of points as word-dividers.

Although North Italic had been suggested as a possible model as early as 1856, it was the Norwegian Carl J. S. Marstrander who presented the first influential scholarly statement of the theory. In 1925 he wrote an essay on the helmet from Negau (Styria), on which had been found an apparently Germanic inscription in North Italic letters. (The language of the inscription is now thought to be Latin.) His classic study, *Om runene og runenavnenes oprindelse* (On the runes and the origin of the rune names), in *Norsk tidsskrift for sprogvidenskap,* **1** (1928), argues that the runes derive from a slightly Latinized North Italic alphabet and were transmitted to Scandinavia through Bohemia by a tribe such as the Marcomanni.

The North Italic theory was forcefully restated by the Finnish scholar Magnus Hammarström, whose *Om runskriftens härkomst* (On the origin of runic writing), in *Studier i nordisk filologi,* **20** (1930), began as a review of Marstrander's essay but soon grew into a full-fledged and independent study. The North Italic theory has also been adopted in one form or another in the influential handbooks of Arntz, Elliott, Musset, and Krause.

Nevertheless, it has not gone unchallenged, for although it seems a superior thesis in its general outlines, it is vulnerable to attack in its details, and in the frustrating fact that no single alphabet in the North Italic family has yet been found which can serve as the obvious model for the futhark.

Opponents of the North Italic theory usually espouse some version of the Latin theory. Among the most interesting of these is Erik Moltke's, first drafted in an essay from 1951 and argued more fully in his *Runerne i Danmark og deres oprindelse*

(The runes of Denmark and their origin, 1976). Moltke energetically attacks Marstrander and others, pointing out that they derive their runes from a variety of North Italic scripts (as well as Latin), and questioning whether the history of alphabets permits such a method of derivation. Further, he does not believe that a model need be found for every rune; the creator of the futhark was not a slavish imitator but an independent and creative individual. Though familiar with Latin writing and inspired by Roman culture, he freely created new letters and a new order. The concentration of early finds, argues Moltke, points to Denmark as the cradle of the runes, an area in commercial contact with the Roman world (via the Rhine) but sufficiently independent to avoid succumbing completely to the Latin alphabet.

INSCRIPTIONS IN THE OLDER FUTHARK

Only about 250 of the 5,000 known runic inscriptions come from the period of the Older Futhark (second to eighth centuries). Many of them are brief, some consisting of a single word; others are garbled, misspelled, or cryptic. Moreover, in those rare cases of general agreement on the reading of a longer inscription, interpretation is difficult, since even the most straightforward inscriptions seem to presuppose a greater understanding of the cultural context than we possess. Because of these uncertainties, generalizations based on the corpus of older inscriptions must remain tentative.

Among the finds of the earliest period (second and third centuries), loose objects predominate. Typically, brief inscriptions (for example, a name) are found on jewelry, weapons, and tools. The spear blades from Øvre Stabu (Norway) and Kovel (present-day Soviet Union) carry inscriptions naming these weapons: **raunijaz** (tester) and **tilariðs** (attacker), respectively. On the third-century fibula (a kind of clasp) from Gårdlösa (Sweden) is written **ekunwod(i)z** (I, the un-raging [that is, calm] one), presumably a reference to the rune master himself and indicating a possible religious status for those who possessed the runes.

Inscriptions become more numerous in the fourth and fifth centuries. The practice of raising inscribed stones begins, primarily in Norway and Sweden. Some of these bear inscriptions celebrating the carver, such as the rune-master formula on the stone from Einang, while others are commemorative, often simply naming the dead (for example, the stones from Skåäng, Berga, Skärkind, Tanum).

A Danish gold bracteate from Sjælland, inscribed to bring good luck to the bearer, *ca.* 450–550. NATIONALMUSEET, COPENHAGEN

More interesting are memorial inscriptions such as that on the stone from Tune (Norway): "I Wiw wrought the runes in memory of Wodurid the Lord. Three daughters prepared the stone for me, Wodurid, the most noble of the heirs prepared the funeral feast."

A characteristic find of the period from about 450 to 550 are the runic bracteates, thin medallions of gold stamped with a design and an inscription in runes or runelike characters. Probably used as amulets, these bracteates were worn on a chain around the neck; the inscriptions typically consist of magical words like **alu** (protection, ale), **laukaz** (leek, fertility), **laþu** (invitation), and rune-master formulas such as "I am called Hariuha, the danger-wise [or travel-wise]; I give good luck" on a Danish bracteate from Sjælland. Many bracteate inscriptions are unreadable or uninterpretable, and it is often assumed that these are distorted renditions of runic models that the illiterate goldsmiths did not understand.

As the seventh century approaches, the stability of form and language that characterized the older period begins to dissolve. Rapid and violent linguistic changes such as umlaut (palatalization) and breaking (diphthongization) alter the close fit between the sounds of the language and the signs of the Older Futhark, and orthographical experimentation appears as a result. A group of seventh-century stones from Blekinge in southern Sweden provides most of our evidence, for example the inscription on the Björketorp stone:

> **uþArAbA sbA hAidzruno ronu fAlAhAk hAiderA ginA-runAz ArAgeu hAerAmAlAusz uti welAdAude sAz þAt bArutz**
>
> Harmful prophecy. The bright-rune sequence I conceal (or commit) here, powerful runes. (Because of) perversity protectionless (or restless), abroad is (condemned) to an insidious death, he who breaks this (monument).

Here we can observe tendencies toward umlaut, breaking, vowel reduction, and syncope. The new rune ᛡ (**A**) appears as an alternative to ᚨ, which now undergoes a change in value to /a^{n}/.

The culmination of these developments in the older period is perhaps to be found in the Eggja stone from Norway, a flat slab, dated to about 700, that was used as part of a grave. With its approximately 192 runes it is the longest inscription in the Older Futhark. In its language, however, it looks ahead to the Old Norse of the Viking Age.

ANGLO-SAXON AND FRISIAN RUNES

The use of runes in Anglo-Saxon England was limited, and only about seventy-five inscriptions survive. A mere handful of these predate the introduction of the Latin alphabet (seventh century), and after this time the Latin letters were the dominant form of writing, not only in manuscripts but also in inscriptions.

In adapting the common Germanic futhark to their linguistic and orthographical needs, the Anglo-Saxons made changes in the forms and values of some runes and added new runes where necessary. The alphabet inlaid in the Thames scramasax, a one-edged sword from the ninth century, has twenty-eight runes (Table 2). Later innovations accounted for a few additional runes, for example back variants of /g/ and /k/.

The route by which runic writing was transmitted to England has not yet been determined with certainty. There seems to be evidence of North Germanic (Scandinavian) influence as well as West Germanic (German, Frisian), and it has been suggested that both lines of transmission may have contributed to English rune-carving. The West Germanic tradition proved to be the stronger, as is

Table 2. The Old English Futhorc

ᚠ	ᚢ	ᚦ	ᚩ	ᚱ	ᚳ	ᚷ	ᚹ	ᚻ	ᚾ	ᛁ	ᛄ	ᛇ	ᛈ
f	u	þ	o	r	c	g	w	h	n	i	j	E	p

ᛉ	ᛋ	ᛏ	ᛒ	ᛖ	ᛝ	ᛗ	ᛚ	ᛞ	ᛟ	ᚪ	ᚫ	ᚣ	ᛠ
x	s	t	b	e	ng	m	l	d	œ	a	æ	y	ea

indicated by the many linguistic and orthographical links between England and Frisia.

Most of the early English inscriptions are found on movable objects, for example the deer's astragalus (anklebone) from Caistor-by-Norwich with a seemingly North Germanic inscription, **raEhan** (roe deer). Runic stones and crosses do not appear until well into the seventh century, and most of them are demonstrably Christian monuments. The memorial inscription on the Great Urswick cross (750–850) reads: **tunwini setæ æfter toroȝtredæ bekun æfter his baeurnæ gebidæs þer saulæ**—"Tunwini set up a monument in memory of his son Torhtred. Pray for his soul." The longest and most significant English inscriptions are those on the Auzon (or Franks) casket (more than 260 runes) and on the Ruthwell cross (more than 320 runes), the latter containing portions of an Anglo-Saxon poem well known from manuscripts, *The Dream of the Rood.*

The similarities between the English and Frisian runic practices are so great that for many years it was doubted whether an independent Frisian tradition existed. However, enough genuine Frisian finds have now been made to dismiss the notion that one is dealing with imported Anglo-Saxon inscriptions.

There are at last count some sixteen runic inscriptions known from Frisia. All come from the so-called "Terpen," artificial mounds in the marshy coastal landscape, and date from the sixth to the ninth centuries.

The objects are small, and the inscriptions brief. Few words other than personal names are clear. The inscription on a weaving sley from Westeremden (*ca.* 800) reads: **adugislu m(i)þ gisuh(i)ldu**—perhaps "(for) Adugisl with Gisuhild." A sword of yew from Arum (*ca.* 600) bears the runic sequence **edæboda,** interpreted as either "return messenger" or "For Ede, the messenger." The eighth-century Toorn-

Table 3. The "Danish" Futhark

ᚠ	ᚢ	ᚦ	ᚬ	ᚱ	ᚴ
f	u	þ	ą	r	k

ᚼ	ᚾ	ᛁ	ᛆ	ᛋ	ᛏ	ᛒ	ᛘ	ᛚ	ᛦ
h	n	i	a	s	t	b	m	l	R

werd comb proclaims its identity in an inscription consisting of the single word "comb."

THE DEVELOPMENT OF RUNIC WRITING IN SCANDINAVIA

The orthographic and linguistic instability evident in Scandinavian inscriptions of the seventh century testifies to a general decline in the state of runic writing and a need for reform. By the end of the ninth century, this need had been met, as the runic alphabet underwent significant changes in form and structure. Unfortunately, scholars understand these developments only imperfectly, mainly because of the paucity of inscriptions from the eighth century.

The revitalization of runic traditions in the North first becomes evident in the proliferation of rune stones in Denmark during the ninth century, for example the important "Helnaes-Gørlev" group, which despite the presence of a few older runes shows that the transition to the younger runes is complete.

The first stable alphabet produced by these runic reforms is usually referred to as the "Danish" futhark, though its use extended far beyond Danish borders. (It is also the principal alphabet of most of the Swedish inscriptions and is sometimes simply called the "normal" runes.) Almost at the same time there arose a typologically younger variant of the "Danish" runes known as the "Swedish-Norwegian" futhark, "short-branched runes," or "Rök runes" (from their appearance on the ninth-century stone from Rök in Östergötland, Sweden's most remarkable runic monument). Normalized versions of these two alphabets are shown in Tables 3 and 4.

The most striking feature of these new alphabets is surely the reduction in the number of symbols used to write a language which had actually in-

RUNES

Table 4. The "Swedish-Norwegian" Futhark

ᚠ	ᚢ	ᚦ	ᚬ	ᚱ	ᚴ
f	u	þ	ą	r	k

ᚽ	ᚿ	ᛁ	ᛅ	ᛌ	ᛐ	ᛓ	ᛙ	ᛚ	ᛧ
h	n	i	a	s	t	b	m	l	R

creased the number of its distinctive sounds (umlaut, etc.). Some scholars have therefore doubted the logic of the reform and emphasized the shortcomings of the new system.

However, it must be admitted that a number of runes in the Older Futhark were all but superfluous from the beginning, for example ᛈ **p,** ᛇ **E,** ᛜ **ng.** A further reduction was brought about by sound changes causing partial loss of /j/ and /w/, which in any event could be rendered with the runes for /i/ and /u/. The consonant system was additionally simplified by extending to the other obstruents the principle by which the **b**-rune was occasionally used in the older period to represent its voiceless equivalent, so that in the younger system not only are both /p/ and /b/ written with ᛒ, but also /t/ and /d/ are indicated by ᛏ, and /k/ and /g/ by ᚴ.

The most radical changes, however, were carried out in the vowel system. When by regular phonological development the names of the **a**-rune and **j**-rune changed from **ansuz* to *ąss* (with nasal *a*) and from **jāra* to *āra,* respectively, the sounds represented by these runes were changed accordingly, leaving for a time symbols for both nasal and oral /a/. (The nasal one eventually went over to /o/ during the eleventh century.) The old runes for /o/ and /e/ were dropped from the system, which aside from nasal /a/ consisted of only three vowel symbols, ᛁ (**i**), ᚢ (**u**), and ᛆ (**a**). Since the umlaut had increased the number of vowels in the language to nine, a single rune had to serve as a written symbol for several vowels. Though there is no widespread consistency in runic orthography, the **i**-rune usually symbolized /i/, /e/, /æ/, and /j/, and the **u**-rune /u/, /y/, /o/, /ø/, and /w/.

As a result of this reduction of runes from twenty-four to sixteen (keeping a multiple of the number eight?), a runic series like **trik** can disguise the word *dreng* (lad, warrior), and scholars find it difficult to understand the motivation of such a development, which seems to promote ambiguity. However, it is also true that while the reader's task may be made more difficult by this ambiguity, the carver's is simplified. Further, the three vowel symbols that were preserved carried a great deal of linguistic information, for example morphological distinctions in unstressed syllables. The new system is thus not so "flawed" as earlier scholars believed.

INSCRIPTIONS IN THE YOUNGER RUNES

Along with the new runic alphabets came shifts in the distribution and typology of the inscriptions themselves, the most striking of which is no doubt the proliferation of raised memorial stones. Attested mainly in Norway and Sweden during the older period, the custom of raising rune stones seems to have taken on new life in ninth-century Denmark, whence it spread again to the other Scandinavian lands, reaching its peak in the eleventh century in the Swedish province of Uppland (more than 1,200 rune stones).

A modification of the content and formulation of the inscriptions accompanied this trend. Rarely does one find the old "I-formula" ("I N.N. made the stone") or the simple noun phrase ("X's stone"). The typical, indeed stereotypical, formula of the Viking Age rune stones follows the pattern "X raised this stone in memory of Y, his father (son, etc.)."

Inscriptions in the Younger Futharks are found most densely in areas farmed by the prosperous yeoman, or *bóndi.* At the same time, they followed the routes of the Vikings and have been found in such remote places as Old Ladoga (Russia), Piraeus (Greece), and Greenland's west coast. (None of the alleged runic inscriptions found thus far in North America has been proven genuine.)

Very few of the runic inscriptions can be dated with any precision, but most can be assigned to broad chronological groupings. In Denmark the two rune stones at Jellinge and the four at Hedeby (now in northern West Germany) provide standards for dating, since they have connections to known historical figures and events.

The first and smaller of the two Jellinge stones was raised by King Gorm the Old in memory of his wife, Thyre. Next to it stands the larger, ornately decorated Jellinge stone raised by King Harald Bluetooth in memory of Gorm and Thyre, his parents:

haraltr kunukR baþ kaurua kubl þausi aft kurm faþur sin auk aft þąurui muþur sina sa haraltr ias sąR uan tanmaurk ala auk nuruiak auk tani karþi kristną

King Harald commanded this monument to be made in memory of his father, Gorm, and his mother, Thyre, that Harald who won for himself all of Denmark, and Norway, and made the Danes Christians.

Since we know that Harald introduced Christianity to Denmark around the year 960, and that he died sometime before 987, we can date the larger Jellinge stone to within a couple of decades. Similarly, the historical context of stones two and four from Hedeby, which commemorate King Sigtryg, allows us to date these inscriptions to about 940, and two further stones (one and three) from the same location refer to King Sweyn Forkbeard's siege of Hedeby around the year 982.

Though none of these dates is absolutely certain, they provide us with a framework in which to deal chronologically with other inscriptions, always remembering the pitfalls of typological and relative dating. Thus it is clear, for example, that the interesting rune stone from Hällestad (Skåne) is post-Jellinge (about 980–1000?), though we cannot identify with confidence the battle referred to in its stirring inscription:

Askill satti sten þænsi æftiR Toka Gormssun, seR hullan drottin.
SaR flo ægi   at Upsalum;
Sattu drængiaR   æftiR sin broþur
Sten a biargi   støþan runum.
þeR (Gorms Toka)   gingu (næstiR).

Askil set up this stone in memory of Toki Gorm's-son, his gracious lord.
He fled not   at Uppsala.
Warriors placed   in memory of their brother
The stone on rock   fixed with runes.
They to Gorm's Toki   were nearest.

The longest Danish inscription from the Viking Age is found on the stone at Glavendrup (Fyn). On the basis of both content and form it must be dated before the Jellinge stone:

raknhiltr sati stain þąnsi auft ala sauluakuþa uia liþs haiþuiarþan þiakn ala suniR karþu kubl þausi aft faþur sin auk hąns kuna auft uar sin in suti raist runaR þasi aft trutin sin þur uiki þasi runaR at rita sa uarþi is stain þansi ailti iþa aft ąnąn traki

Ragnhild set up this stone in memory of Alli, priest of the Sølver, high-born chieftain of the sanctuary guard. Alli's sons made this memorial after their father and his wife after her husband; but Soti carved these runes after his lord. Thor hallow these runes. May he who

RUNES

violates this stone or carries it off for someone else become a cursed wretch.

A number of Norwegian inscriptions also have historical connections. The stone from Galteland tells of a man who "died in the troop when Knut attacked England," one of many references (most of them in Sweden) to the Scandinavian expedition that resulted in the conquest of England by King Cnut the Great (about 1016). Another Norwegian rune stone (Kuli) can be dated by virtue of its reference to the Christianization of Norway, which according to the inscription had occurred twelve years earlier.

Most of the Viking Age inscriptions, however, speak of people and events otherwise unknown, giving us a glimpse into the daily life and concerns of the landowning middle class of the time. The inscriptions serve to document family relationships (and thus settle questions of inheritance), to clarify ownership and property rights, to honor the generous and the pious as well as the brave and adventurous. Many commemorative inscriptions include a prayer asking God to help the soul of the deceased in its search for paradise. Others tell of good works done toward this end. The interesting and decorative rune stone from Dynna in the Norwegian district of Hadeland provides one of many examples of bridge-building—that is, the construction of roads and causeways over marshy land, an important contribution to the early Christian church: "Gunnvor Thrydrik's daughter made the bridge for Astrid, her daughter. She was the most accomplished maid in Hadeland."

Most of Sweden's 3,000 runic inscriptions come from the eleventh century; their number alone testifies to what was obviously a period of vitality and prosperity. In content, it must be admitted, many of them merely echo the stereotyped memorial formula; however, others convey more interesting information. Again we learn of Viking expeditions, not only to the West (England), but also to the East, a traditional goal of Swedish voyagers. Thus about twenty-five stones in central Sweden commemorate men who "went with Ingvar," the leader of an ill-starred expedition to "Serkland" (an area around the Caspian Sea), an event also described in the much later and fictionalized *Yngvars saga víðförla* (Saga of Ingvar the far-traveler). The most remarkable of the Ingvar stones stands today outside Gripsholm Castle on Lake Mälar. After a commemorative text telling us that

The Dynna stone. Norway, *ca.* 1040. UNIVERSITETETS OLDSAKSAMLING, OSLO

"Tola had this stone raised in memory of her son Harald, Ingvar's brother," the inscription switches into verse:

ÞaeiR foru drængila fiarri at gulli,
ok austarla ærni gafu;
dou sunnarla a Serklandi.

They fared bravely far after gold,
and in the east fed the eagle,
they died in the south in Serkland.

Such versified inscriptions or snatches of poetry in runes appear not infrequently in the rich collection of Swedish runic monuments. They offer parallels to the better-known Norwegian and Icelandic poetic traditions preserved in manuscripts.

Not all of those who went abroad were soldiers of fortune. The eleventh century was the period in which the missionary church once and for all gained the upper hand in the struggle to convert the Swedes to Christianity, and many of the runic inscriptions provide us with documentation of this change. "Ingirun Hård's-daughter had these runes carved for herself. She wants to journey to the East, out to Jerusalem," proclaimed an inscription (now lost) near Stockholm, one of several runic references to pilgrimages. Christian prayers are common in the inscriptions of this period, and while most consist of a brief "God help his soul," a few are more unusual in their formulation, as on the Risbyle stone from Uppland: "Ulfketill and Gyi and Unni had this stone raised in memory of Ulf, their good father. He lived at Skålhamre. May God and God's Mother help his spirit and soul, grant him light and paradise."

In addition to inscribed messages, stones from the eleventh century often bear elaborate artistic decoration. Again the Swedish province of Uppland represents a focal point, for there the robust and elegant art of the late Viking Age reached its highest level of refinement. Since it was not uncommon for a carver to append his name to an inscription, we can identify many of these artists and trace their development and chronology.

RUNES IN THE LATE MIDDLE AGES

As the eleventh century came to a close, the waning of Viking activity abroad and the consolidation of the Christian church at home spelled new changes for Scandinavia and consequently for Scandinavian runology. Latin letters were introduced and used extensively in the production of manuscripts (a runic cursive was never developed). For a time runic epigraphy and Latin writing existed side by side, but by the end of the fourteenth century the runes were no longer a living tradition.

The Latin alphabet is usually held responsible for changes in the futhark during this medieval period (about 1050–1400). In particular the creation of finer distinctions in the orthography is thought to represent an adjustment to the more expressive Latin system. However, the details and extent of this alleged influence are not clear, since we lack a thorough study of late medieval runes.

Most of the new symbols were created by the addition of simple diacritical marks on already existing runes, and since the most common of these marks was a small dot or point, the new letters are referred to as "dotted runes." As early as the tenth century the rune ᛂ (**e**) appears in Denmark, and by the middle of the eleventh century ᚤ (**y**) and ᚵ (**g**) are also in use in other parts of Scandinavia. Eventually these are joined by ᛔ (**p**) and ᛑ (**d**). More vowel distinctions were achieved by contrasting long- and short-branched symbols, for example, ᛆ (**a**), ᚮ (**o**), ᛅ (**æ**), and ᚯ (**ø**).

The result was an arsenal of letters equal in number to those of the Latin alphabet, and in a few instances the close relationship between the two is demonstrated by the occurrence of runes in alphabetical rather than futhark order, leading some scholars to posit a completely dotted runic alphabet. Since, however, such an alphabet is more of a learned amalgam from various inscriptions, it is fairer to say that the dotted runes were an addition to, rather than an integral part of, the Younger Futhark of sixteen runes.

A large proportion of the objects inscribed with runes during this period are ecclesiastical in nature. Erected rune stones on ancestral property yield to flat grave slabs or sarcophagi within the church, and the traditional memorial formulas are replaced by Scandinavian equivalents of the Latin *hic jacet* inscriptions, as on the grave slab from Grenjaðarstaður, Iceland: "Hér hvílir Sigríð Hrafnsdóttir, kvinna Bjarnar bónda, Sæmunds sonar. Gud friði hennar sál til góðrar vonanar. Hver er letrið les, bið fyrir blíðri sál, syngi signað vers" (Here lies Sigrid Hrafn's-daughter, wife of farmer Björn, son of Sæmund. God grant her soul peace for good salvation. Whoever reads this inscription pray for her fair soul, sing the blessed verse). Other medieval inscriptions appear on church walls and portals, on baptismal fonts, church bells, reliquaries, and censers.

RUNES

A most distinctive chapter in the story of medieval runology is represented by the hundreds of inscribed wooden sticks found during the excavation of the wharf in Bergen, Norway, in the 1960's. Most of them date from the twelfth to the fourteenth centuries, and until this fortuitous discovery scholars were largely unaware of the extent to which runes were used for everyday communications in late medieval times. A readily available alternative to parchment, the runic sticks were used to send messages, record mercantile transactions, label goods and inventory, or simply jot down cryptic or magic words, incantations, and futharks. One of the most remarkable finds is the stick inscribed with a royal request by a Norwegian prince: "Sigurðr Lavard sends God's greeting and his own. . . . The king would like to have your ship. Concerning the weapons . . . a spear of eighteen ells of russet, which I sent to you with John Øri. Now it is my wish to request that you be agreeable in this matter. And if you do my will then you will have in return our true friendship now and always." If the ship referred to was needed by King Sverre (Sigurd's father) in anticipation of the Battle of Florvåg on 3 April 1194, then the stick can be dated almost to the day.

After the Middle Ages runes are occasionally found (often mixed with Latin letters) in parts of rural Scandinavia, for example as proprietary marks on farm implements. A number of runic calendars also date from early modern times. However, these are mere relics of a writing system no longer alive. By the end of the sixteenth century the runes had been discovered as a curious object of study by the enthusiastic antiquaries of the north, and the science of runology had begun.

BIBLIOGRAPHY

There is no complete and up-to-date bibliography of runology. The older literature is to be found in Helmut Arntz's *Bibliographie der Runenkunde* (1937), in which more than 4,000 titles are listed alphabetically by author. The ambitious plan of Wolfgang Krause to produce a multivolume *Bibliographie der Runeninschriften nach Fundorten,* a catalog of works on the individual inscriptions arranged alphabetically by the name (place of origin or find) of the inscription, has languished after two volumes: *Die Runeninscriften der britischen Inseln* (The runic inscriptions of the British Isles), Hertha Marquardt, ed. (1961), and *Die Runeninscriften des europäischen Kontinents* (The runic inscriptions of the European continent), Uwe Schnall, ed. (1973).

Select and concise bibliographies can be found in the various handbooks and surveys of runology, the best of which is perhaps the thorough and reliable *Introduction à la runologie* of the French historian Lucien Musset (1965), who made use of material left behind by the philologist Fernand Mossé. The only general introductions written in English are Ralph W. V. Elliott's *Runes: An Introduction,* 2nd ed. (1963 repr. 1971, 1980), a thin and at times speculative work stressing the English runes; and R. I. Page, *Runes* (1987). Recent handbooks in German are Klaus Düwel's lucid and balanced *Runenkunde* (1968, rev. ed. 1983), in the Sammlung Metzler series, and Wolfgang Krause's somewhat denser *Runen* (1970), in the Sammlung Göschen. Still useful for those who read Scandinavian languages is the compendium edited by Otto von Friesen, *Runorna* (1933). See also Stephen E. Flowers, *Runes and Magic: Magical Formulaic Elements in the Older Runic Tradition* (1986).

The inscriptions themselves have been edited along both chronological and geographical lines. The standard corpus of older inscriptions is Wolfgang Krause's *Die Runeninschriften im älteren Futhark* (1966), with contributions by the archaeologist Herbert Jankuhn. Norwegian inscriptions in the older futhark appear in the four volumes of *Norges indskrifter med de ældre runer,* edited by Sophus Bugge and Magnus Olsen (1891–1924), now rather out of date. A more recent reading of Norway's oldest runic monuments is contained in Gerd Høst's *Runer: Våre eldste norske runeinnskrifter* (1976). A number of other Scandinavian inscriptions from the older period are subjected to Carl J. S. Marstrander's somewhat eccentric interpretations in his *De nordiske runeinnskrifter i eldre alfabet,* which appeared in the Norwegian archaeological journal *Viking,* **16** (1953).

Two recent linguistic studies also contain brief catalogs of the relevant older inscriptions: Wolfgang Krause's posthumously published *Die Sprache der urnordischen Runeninschriften* (1972) is based on the North Germanic inscriptions of the older period, while Elmer H. Antonsen's *A Concise Grammar of the Older Runic Inscriptions* (1975) includes inscriptions in East Germanic (Gothic) and West Germanic (German) as well as Scandinavian. A basic problem with such studies is the lack of agreement on the analysis of many inscriptions from the older period; in a sense, a grammar like Antonsen's is based on a different corpus than Krause's more traditional one, since his readings and interpretations often diverge from the consensus.

Owing to the revolutionary discoveries at the Bergen wharf, the editing of the younger Norwegian inscriptions is still incomplete, but all of those known up to 1960 are collected in the first five volumes of *Norges innskrifter med de yngre runer,* edited by Magnus Olsen and Aslak Liestøl (1941–1960). Subsequent volumes are in preparation, to cover the Bergen material and other new finds. A characteristic sampling of the inscriptions from Bergen can be found in several articles by Aslak Liestøl: "Runer frå Bryggen," in *Viking,* 27 (1964), "Correspondence in Runes," in *Mediaeval Scandinavia,* 1 (1968), and "The Literate Vikings" in *Proceedings of the Sixth Viking Congress,* Peter Foote and Dag Strömback, eds. (1971), 69–78.

The standard Danish corpus of runic inscriptions was edited in two volumes (plus an index) as *Danmarks runeindskrifter* by Lis Jacobsen and Erik Moltke (1941–1942). All of the Danish inscriptions, including those found since 1942, also appear in Erik Moltke's thorough survey *Runerne i Danmark og deres oprindelse* (1976). An English translation of this work is *Runes and Their Origins* (1985).

The monumental task of publishing the Swedish inscriptions began in 1900 with the first fascicle of *Sveriges runinskrifter.* Sponsored by the Royal Academy of Letters, History, and Antiquities (Vitterhetsakademien), the volumes of Sweden's runic inscriptions have appeared at regular intervals, grouped by the traditional provinces: (1) Öland, Sven Söderberg and Erik Brate, eds. (1900–1906); (2) Östergötland, Erik Brate, ed. (1911–1918); (3) Södermanland, Erik Brate and Elias Wessén eds. (1924–1936); (4) Småland, Ragnar Kinander, ed. (1935–1961); (5) Västergötland, Hugo Jungner and Elisabeth Svärdström, eds. (1940–1970); (6–9) Uppland, Elias Wessén and Sven B. F. Jansson, eds. (1940–1958); a final volume (10) on Uppland awaits publication; (11) Gotland, Sven B. F. Jansson and Elias Wessén, eds. (pt. 1, 1962; pt. 2 [vol. 12] still unpublished); (13) Västmanland, Sven B. F. Jansson, ed. (1964); (14) Närke, Sven B. F. Jansson, ed. (1975; a second part of this volume will cover Värmland). The edition will conclude with Norrland (vol. 15), now in preparation. A useful survey of the Swedish runic inscriptions in English is Sven B. F. Jansson's *The Runes of Sweden,* Peter G. Foote, trans. (1962). An analysis of rune carving in the province of Uppland can be found in Claiborne W. Thompson's *Studies in Upplandic Runography* (1975).

The inscriptions on the European continent (German, Frisian, and East Germanic) were collected and published by Helmut Arntz and Hans Zeiss in *Die einheimischen Runendenkmäler des Festlandes* (1939). A recent gathering of the German inscriptions can be found in the dissertation of Stephan Opitz, *Südgermanische Runeninschriften im älteren Futhark aus der Merowingerzeit* (1977).

The corpus of Anglo-Saxon runic inscriptions, under the editorship of Raymond I. Page, is still in preparation. In the meantime one can find an abundance of information in Page's *An Introduction to English Runes* (1973). Elliott's handbook (see above) also treats a number of the English inscriptions. Runes in English manuscripts are the subject of René Derolez's *Runica Manuscripta: The English Tradition* (1954).

The runic inscriptions of Iceland have been published in a Danish edition by Anders Bæksted, *Islands runeindskrifter* (1942). Many other Scandinavian inscriptions from Norse colonies are treated in Magnus Olsen's "Runic Inscriptions in Great Britain, Ireland, and the Isle of Man," in Haakon Shetelig, ed., *Viking Antiquities in Great Britain and Ireland,* VI (1954) 151–233. Some of the forgeries and other allegedly Norse artifacts and runic inscriptions in North America, including the notorious Kensington stone from Minnesota, are surveyed in Birgitta L. Wallace's "Some Points of Controversy," in *The Quest for America,* Geoffrey Ashe, ed. (1971), 155–174. A complete scientific treatment of Norse archaeological evidence (genuine and otherwise) in North America is currently in preparation by the same author.

CLAIBORNE W. THOMPSON

[See also **Alphabets; Bracteates; Cnut the Great; Denmark; Hedeby; Jellinge Style; Magic and Folklore, Western European; Missions and Missionaries, Christian; Norway; Ringerike Style; Roskilde Chronicle; Scandinavia: Before 800; Scandinavian Languages; Sweden; Viking Art; Yngvars Saga Víðförla.**]

RUODLIEB, a Latin narrative poem composed in the middle of the eleventh century by a monk at Tegernsee in southern Germany. The work survives only in two badly damaged manuscripts, one of which apparently is in the author's own hand. The *Ruodlieb* is unfinished; and the existence of corrections in the text indicates that we have the first draft of a poem whose intended final length and structure cannot be determined.

The eighteen fragments of the poem that remain tell the following story. A young nobleman (later identified as Ruodlieb) is forced into exile by his enemies. After impressing the king of a foreign land (probably in Africa) with his skill as a fisherman, Ruodlieb is invited into his service. He rises to a position of importance in the court of his new lord, called only *rex maior,* the Greater King. When the country is invaded by the forces of another king, the *rex minor* or Lesser King, Ruodlieb serves as both commander-in-chief of the Greater King's victorious army and the diplomat who arranges a peace treaty afterward.

After Ruodlieb has been in the service of the Greater King for ten years, he receives a letter from his mother informing him that all his enemies are dead and asking him to return home at once. The king grants Ruodlieb the right to leave, but first offers him the choice of wealth or wisdom as a parting gift. When Ruodlieb chooses wisdom, the king gives him twelve precepts for right living.

Concealed in what seem to be merely two loaves of bread the king sends with the departing Ruodlieb a generous supply of treasure as well.

On the way home, Ruodlieb has a series of adventures that demonstrate the value of the king's advice. Contrary to one precept, Ruodlieb allows a red-haired man to join him. The redhead soon steals Ruodlieb's coat. When they reach a village, Ruodlieb follows a precept by lodging in the home of a young man with an old wife. The redhead stays in the home of an old man with a young wife. Caught making love to the woman, the redhead kills the husband. A murder trial ensues, at which the wife pleads guilty and repents. The portion of the narrative dealing with the redhead has not survived.

Continuing on his journey, Ruodlieb meets one of his nephews. They stop at a castle, where the nephew falls in love with the daughter of the mistress of the castle.

After reaching his home, Ruodlieb discovers the treasure hidden in the loaves of bread. Later Ruodlieb arranges for the marriage of his nephew and the young woman with whom he has fallen in love. The ceremony and accompanying entertainment are described. At his mother's urging, Ruodlieb himself resolves to wed. Unfortunately, the woman whom his relatives find for him is revealed to be of unsuitable character.

Now the nature of the narrative changes. Ruodlieb's mother has two dreams that portend both struggle and great success for her son. The next fragment finds Ruodlieb in front of a cave. He has just subdued a dwarf who is foretelling that Ruodlieb will defeat two hostile kings, Immunch and Hartunch, then marry Immunch's daughter. Here the story ends abruptly.

The *Ruodlieb* has importance not only as a work of literature but also as a source of information about aspects of the social and cultural life of the eleventh century, for it blends realistic portrayals of everyday life with themes drawn from folklore and saga. The use of a series of precepts as the frame for the adventures of a hero is a common feature of fairy tales. Moreover, folklorists point out that the *Ruodlieb* contains early, if not the first, literary use of such popular folk motifs as the association of redheads with evil and the role of a dwarf as the guardian of a great treasure.

The realistic elements of the *Ruodlieb* are of particular interest. The narrative includes scenes of life both at court and in a small rural village. Two types of legal proceeding are described in detail: a marriage ceremony and a murder trial. In addition, the narrative gives details about the formalities involved in sending and receiving embassies and negotiating a treaty. Much of the narrative is didactic, with Ruodlieb exhibiting proper behavior in a variety of social settings. The one instance in which he is guilty of impolite behavior occurs when he accepts payment after defeating the Lesser King and several of his ambassadors at chess. That episode is one of the earliest mentions of chess-playing in Western literature.

As a poetic narrative, the *Ruodlieb* is an example of the transformation of a classical into a Christian literary genre. Formally, it is an epic poem. Written in Latin leonine hexameters, it incorporates many themes and episodes traditionally associated with epic. The one classical work to which allusions are made is the *Aeneid.* At the beginning of the narrative Ruodlieb is compared to Aeneas; but the rest of the poem chronicles his acquisition of a heroic excellence superior to that portrayed by Vergil.

Ruodlieb's teacher is the Greater King. From him Ruodlieb learns the greater virtues of piety, clemency, and wisdom. Whereas Ruodlieb's former lords had asked him to perform deeds of vengeance, the Greater King gives different commands (III, 12–14):

> *Sis leo pugnando par ulciscendo sed agno!*
> *Non honor est vobis, ulcisci damna doloris.*
> *Magnum vindictae genus est, si parcitis irae.*

> Be a lion in battle but like a lamb when taking vengeance! It is not honorable to avenge grievous losses. The best kind of vengeance is when you spare your wrath.

The Greater King is portrayed as Christ's representative on earth. When Ruodlieb is about to leave the court, he tells his lord that "every day with you has been Easter for me" (V, 303–307). Like Christ, the Greater King provides the earthly knight with true wisdom and wealth.

The *Ruodlieb* is a bridge between two medieval literary genres. It begins as an epic in the manner of the *Aeneid;* but in emphasizing the social rather than the military prowess of the hero, the poet gives early expression to an ideal of knighthood that emerges fully in the courtly romances of the twelfth century.

BIBLIOGRAPHY

Werner Braun, *Studien zum Ruodlieb* (1962); Franz Brunhölzl, "Zum Ruodlieb," in *Deutsche Vierteljahrs-*

schrift für Literaturwissenschaft und Geistesgeschichte, **39** (1965), 506–522; Peter Dronke, *Poetic Individuality in the Middle Ages* (1970); Gordon B. Ford, Jr., *The Ruodlieb: Linguistic Introduction, Latin Text, and Glossary* (1966), *idem,* trans., *The Ruodlieb: The First Medieval Epic of Chivalry from Eleventh-century Germany* (1965); Helena Gamer, "The Ruodlieb and Tradition," in *ARV: Journal of Scandinavian Folklore,* **11** (1955); John C. Hirsh, "The Argument of Ruodlieb," in *Classical Folia,* **27,** no. 1 (1973); Dennis M. Kratz, "Ruodlieb: Christian Epic Hero," in *Classical Folia,* **27,** no. 2 (1973), and idem, trans., *Waltharius and Ruodlieb* (1984).

DENNIS M. KRATZ

[See also **Epic, Latin; Latin Literature.**]

RUPERT OF DEUTZ (1075/1080–1129), important monastic theologian, probably born near Liège. From an early age he was a monk in the Benedictine abbey of St. Lawrence in that city; he became a priest in 1106. From 1111 on, Rupert was implicated in a series of doctrinal controversies involving, among others, Alger of Liège, Anselm of Laon, Norbert of Xanten, and William of Champeaux. Thanks to the support of Frederick I, archbishop of Cologne, he was appointed abbot of Deutz (1120), where he remained until his death.

In addition to minor works (hymns, letters, and some short occasional pieces) and several saints' lives, including an updated version of the *Life of Heribert, Archbishop of Cologne,* Rupert is the author of many extensive theological treatises. Among these are the influential *On the Divine Offices,* an analysis of the theological content of the liturgy, commentaries on Scripture, including *On the Trinity and Its Works,* commentaries on John, Matthew, the Apocalypse, the Twelve Minor Prophets, and the Song of Songs, as well as one on the Rule of St. Benedict. His *On the Victory of the Word of God* treats the theology of history, while the *Anulus or Dialogue Between a Christian and a Jew* affords insight into Jewish-Christian controversy of the twelfth century. Rupert may well be the author of an unfinished cycle of poems on the investiture contest in the diocese of Liège. Of dubious ascription are some lives of saints, a *Commentary on Job,* and the *Chronicle of St. Lawrence of Liège.*

A product of the Gregorian reform, Rupert was well versed in the classics and patristics; his theological concerns and methods were deeply influenced by St. Augustine and have been characterized as conservative in comparison with those of his contemporaries, the forerunners of Scholasticism.

BIBLIOGRAPHY

The eighteenth-century Venice edition of Rupert's works, reprinted in *Patrologia latina,* CLXVII–CLXX (1854), is being replaced by modern critical editions. The following were edited by Rhaban Haacke: *Liber de divinis officiis,* in *Corpus Christianorum, series latina, Continuatio mediaevalis,* VII (1967); *De sancta trinitate et operibus eius, ibid.,* XXI–XXIV (1971–1972); and *De victoria verbi Dei,* in *Monumenta Germaniae historica, Quellen zur Geistesgeschichte des Mittelalters,* V (1970). *Anulus* is edited by Maria L. Arduini in *Ruperto di Deutz e la controversia tra cristiani ed ebrei nel secolo XII* (1979). Rupert's poems on the calamities of the church of Liège appear in H. Böhmer, ed., *Monumenta Germaniae historica: Libelli de lite,* III (1897, new ed. 1956), 624–641.

The *Chronicle of St. Lawrence* is edited by W. Wattenbach in *Monumenta Germaniae historica, Scriptores* VIII (1848), 261–279. Since the study by Hubert Silvestre, *Le Chronicon Sancti Laurentii Leodiensis dit de Rupert de Deutz* (1952), the *Chronicle* has generally been considered a later forgery. The question was reopened by John Van Engen, "Rupert Von Deutz und das sogenannte *Chronicon sancti Laurentii Leodiensis:* Zur Geschichte des Investiturstreites in Lüttich," in *Deutsches Archiv für Erforschung des Mittelalters,* **35** (1975).

For a detailed presentation of Rupert's works and the relevant bibliography, see Michael McCormick, *Index scriptorum operumque latino-belgicorum medii aevi: Nouveau répertoire des oeuvres médiolatines belges,* pt. 3, vol. II (1979), 235–264, and *idem* and P. Fransen, *Index . . . ,* pt. 3, vol. I (1977), 36–37, 66, 82–83, 135.

On Rupert's thought and biography, see Guntram G. Bischoff, "The Eucharistic Controversy Between Rupert of Deutz and His Anonymous Adversary" (diss., Princeton Theological Seminary, 1965); John H. Van Engen, *Rupert of Deutz* (1983).

MICHAEL MCCORMICK

[See also **Anselm of Laon; Divine Office; Philosophy and Theology, Western European: Twelfth Century to Aquinas; Theology, Schools of; William of Champeaux.**]

RURIK (Riurik) (*fl.* ninth century) was the Viking chieftain traditionally credited with founding the early Russian state. If the generally accepted identification of the Russian ruler Rurik with Rorik of Jutland is correct, the main outlines of his biography can be reconstructed. Rurik grew up in Friesland, which his father received from Charlemagne after losing Jutland to usurpers. As a young man, Rurik probably shared the fief of Rustringen in Friesland with his brother Harald until around 843, when the fief was withdrawn by Emperor Lothar. After a period of raiding along the coasts of France, England, and Germany, Rurik was enfeoffed with his father's original land of Jutland, which he seems to have lost quickly to usurpers.

Sometime between 854 and 856, Rurik mounted an expedition into northwest Russia, where he established himself and his men at Ladoga. According to the Russian Primary Chronicle (which incorrectly dates this event to 862), he came in response to an invitation from the people of Novgorod to the "Russes" (apparently Vikings, or "Varangians," as they are called in Russian sources) to "come and rule" over them, for they "had no law." Probably starting out as leader of a mercenary band protecting the Novgorod land, Rurik appointed his "brothers" (clansmen) and "men" to outlying towns and eventually moved his seat to Novgorod, where he built a fortress and became a genuine ruler of the Russian land, possibly sending his lieutenants as far south as Kiev. He apparently left Russia when Emperor Charles the Bald offered him his father's fief of Friesland in 873, only to die a few years later. According to the Russian chronicles, Rurik bequeathed his Russian realm to his kinsman Oleg, for his son Igor was very young. It is unlikely that this is the same Igor who succeeded Oleg in 912; perhaps he was a grandson of Rurik. In any case, Russian princes from Igor's time on accounted themselves descendants of Rurik. One such line of Rurikides supplied the grand princes and later the czars of Moscow until that line died out in 1598.

BIBLIOGRAPHY

The primary source for our knowledge of Rurik, the Russian Primary Chronicle, includes much legendary material: *Povest vremennych let,* Varvava P. (Adrianova) Peretts, ed., 2 vols. (1950), trans. into English by Samuel H. Cross and Olgerd Sherbowitz-Wetzor as *Russian Primary Chronicle* (1953). The difficulties raised by the sources are addressed in Nora K. Chadwick, *The Beginnings of Russian History* (1946), and, with different results, by N. Riasanovsky, "The Norman Theory of the Origin of the Russian State," in *Russian Review,* 7 (1947). The identification of Rurik with Rorik of Jutland, first proposed in 1836, was established by N. T. Beliaev in his "Rorik Iutlandskii i Riurik nachalnoi letopisi," in *Seminarium Kondakovianum,* 3 (1929), also published separately (1930). There is a useful treatment of Rurik in George Vernadsky, *Ancient Russia* (1943).

GEORGE P. MAJESKA

[See also **Kievan Rus: Primary Chronicle, Russian; Novgorod.**]

RUSHD, IBN (AVERROËS) (**Abū al-Walīd Muḥammad ibn Aḥmad**) (1126–1198), Islamic Spain's renowned philosopher, Islamic lawyer, physician, and astronomer, best known in medieval and Renaissance Europe for his substantial commentaries on Aristotle.

LIFE AND WORKS

Ibn Rushd was born in 1126 in Córdoba into a family of learning and culture—both his father and grandfather were distinguished Córdorban judges. Medieval Arabic sources stress his excellent training in Islamic law (*figh*) and dialectical theology (*kalām*) and refer to him as an authority on Arabic grammar and certain Arabic poets. They give less detail concerning his philosophical and scientific training, although the physician Abū Ja^cfar Hārūn al-Tajālī is mentioned as having taught him medicine and "the philosophical sciences." In 1153 he was in Marrakech engaged in astronomical observations, but the circumstances that took him there are not fully known. The year 1163 marked a turning point in his career, as it initiated his lifelong association with the Almohad court. In this year, the philosopher Ibn Ṭufayl (1105–1185) introduced him to the Almohad ruler, Abū Ya^cqūb Yūsuf, who had a genuine interest in philosophy and who was seeking someone to write commentaries on Aristotle's works. Ibn Ṭufayl recommended Ibn Rushd for this task.

Ibn Rushd's first official appointment was as a judge in Seville. In 1171 he was in Córdoba as a judge, becoming, according to some sources, chief judge there—but there are chronological uncertainties about this period of Ibn Rushd's life. He was later attached to the Almohad court, succeeding the aging Ibn Ṭufayl as chief physician in 1182. Ibn Rushd served Abū Ya^cqūb Yūsuf until the latter's death in 1184. He then served his son and successor, Ya^cqūb al-Manṣūr. Sometime after 1195, this service was interrupted: Ibn Rushd fell out of favor with his patron and was exiled; his books were burned. The reasons seem to have been mainly

RUSHD, IBN (AVERROËS)

political, the opposition of the conservative religious scholars being a factor. He was reinstated, however, resuming his services in the Almohad court and then serving until his death in 1198.

The writings of Ibn Rushd include an important book on Islamic law, *Bidāyat al-mujtahid,* and an influential medical work, *al-Kulliyyāt* (The generalities), known in its Latin version as the *Colliget.* His philosophical output (including other works on medicine and astronomy) divides into two main groups: (1) commentaries, largely on Aristotle, but also on other Greek writers; and (2) works relating to the defense of philosophy against the severe attack that the theologian al-Ghazālī (*d.* 1111) leveled against it, more specifically against the Islamic philosophers al-Fārābī (*d.* 950) and Ibn Sīnā (Avicenna) (*d.* 1037). In this connection, it should be noted that Ibn Rushd also wrote a number of treatises (now lost) criticizing al-Fārābī and Ibn Sīnā. For although he defended them against al-Ghazālī, he was also critical of some aspects of their thought.

Ibn Rushd wrote three types of commentary: the large or major commentary, where the original text is quoted and commented on sectionally; the middle commentary, an interpretive exposition, often including considerable expansions on the original; and the epitome or paraphrase, a shorter interpretive exposition. (For some works he wrote all three types of commentaries; for others two or one.) These commentaries—some of which have survived only in their Latin or Hebrew translations—range over Aristotle's entire logical *Organon* and such of his works as the *Physica, De anima, Metaphysica, De caelo, De generatione et corruptione, De sensus et sensibilius, Meterologia, De poetica,* and *Rhetorica.* They also include single commentaries on Plato's *Republic,* Porphyry's *Isagoge,* Ptolemy's *Almagest,* a treatise of Alexander of Aphrodisias on the intellect, and some of Galen's medical treatises.

The works he wrote in response to al-Ghazālī's attack on the Islamic philosophers include three closely related treatises, forming in effect a trilogy that constitutes a lengthy philosophical book. The trilogy consists of two main treatises and a very short one. The first of the two main treatises is *Faṣl al-maqāl* (whose full title translates literally as: The decisive treatise on the determination of the nature of the connection between religion and philosophy). The second of the two main treatises is *al-Kashf ᶜan manāhij al-adilla* (whose full title translates literally as: Exposition of the methods of proof regarding the beliefs of the [Islamic] religion). *Faṣl* is a defense of philosophy in terms of Islamic legal categories and includes a theory of interpreting scriptural language. The *Kashf* is in part a criticism of the theological interpretations of religious language of such Ashᶜarite theologians as al-Ghazālī and his teacher al-Juwaynī; it suggests the building of a theological system based on what Ibn Rushd conceived to be a sounder understanding of scriptural language. The very short treatise *Damīma* (Appendix) is conventionally regarded as an appendix to *Faṣl.* Internal evidence, however, strongly suggests that it is the first of the trilogy. In *Ḍamīma* Ibn Rushd argued that, contrary to al-Ghazālī's charge, the philosophers do not deny God knowledge of particulars. They only maintain that such knowledge differs from human knowledge in that it is the cause of the existence of the particular, not its effect. The detailed philosophical defense of philosophy is his *Tahāfut al-Tahāfut* (The Incoherence of "The incoherence"), a philosophical classic in its own right. It answers al-Ghazālī's *Tahāfut al-falāsifa* (The incoherence of the philosophers), quoting paragraph by paragraph almost the whole of it and commenting on it critically, at times criticizing Ibn Sīnā as well.

PHILOSOPHY

Ibn Rushd did not present his philosophy as a system. His philosophical position has to be extracted from his commentaries, more particularly from his works answering al-Ghazālī. In his religious and political philosophy he was essentially an adherent of al-Fārābī's political Platonism. But he developed this philosophy within a framework of Islamic law. In metaphysics and natural philosophy he was the most Aristotelian of the Islamic philosophers. At an early stage of his philosophical development, however, he was close to the Neoplatonic tradition of al-Fārābī and Ibn Sīnā. This is indicated by his epitome on Aristotle's *Metaphysics,* a relatively early work. In later works, for example, his major commentary on the *Metaphysics* and his *Tahāfut al-Tahāfut,* he moved away from this tradition toward a purer Aristotelianism. Thus in the *Tahāfut* he is highly critical of Ibn Sīnā's emanative scheme and the fundamental theory underlying it, namely that every existent other than God is in itself only possible, but necessary through another. But whether Ibn Rushd freed himself entirely from Neoplatonism remains an open question.

His philosophical position (even when it reflects ambiguity) is perhaps best exemplified in his criticism of Ash^carite causal theory, his doctrine of the relation of religion to philosophy, and his views on the afterlife.

Criticism of Ash^carite causal theory. Ibn Rushd's main concern in his *Tahāfut* was to answer al-Ghazālī's attack on philosophy and the occasionalist doctrine this attack embodied. For although, in introducing his own *Tahāfut,* al-Ghazālī declared that in criticizing the philosophers he would not be adopting any one particular theological stance, the occasionalism of the school of theology to which he belonged, the Ash^carite, underlay much of the book's argument. This theology denied secondary causes, attributing all changes in the world to direct divine action. It maintained that the world order has no inherent necessity, that the uniformity of nature is only a habit (*^cadā*) arbitrarily decreed by God who can disrupt it at will.

Ibn Rushd's criticism of this causal theory pervades his *Tahāfut* but is given most fully in the seventeenth Discussion, devoted entirely to the causal question. For in this discussion he responds to al-Ghazālī's statement of the Ash^carite logical and epistemological reasons for denying necessary causal connection in nature. According to this Ash^carite view, the connection between what is habitually regarded in nature as cause and effect is not necessary. One can affirm such a habitual cause and deny the effect or affirm the effect and deny the cause without contradiction. A necessary causal connection is never experienced. Perception proves only concomitance, not necessary causal connection. What appear as causes and effects are only concomitants whose uniform coexistence is decreed by God.

In answering this position, Ibn Rushd makes a number of points that he elaborates. Of these, the most central is a metaphysical argument based on his concept of real essence, which intimately relates essence to causal action. Things, he maintains, "have essences and attributes that determine the specific action of each existent and by virtue of which the essences, names and definitions of things are differentiated." If this were not the case, he then argues in effect, then all the existents would either become one existent or cease to exist altogether. For, if it is one, the question arises as to whether such an existent has or does not have a specific act (for example, whether or not fire has the specific act of burning). If the answer is that it has, then the existence of a specific act proceeding from a specific nature is acknowledged. If the answer is that it does not, then "the one is no longer one. But if the nature of oneness is removed, the nature of existence is removed and the necessary consequence is nonexistence" (*Tahāfut al-Tahāfut,* pp. 520–521).

The relation between essence and causal action is illustrated by the example of fire. Al-Ghazālī had argued that it is possible for fire to contact cotton without burning it. Ibn Rushd answers that this can happen only when there is an impediment, but this does not deprive fire of having the property of conflagration "so long as it retains the name and definition of fire." Fire, to be fire, must have the property of burning something. A denial of this is not only a denial of objective truth, but a violation of the normal way we name things and speak about them.

Philosophy and religion. In his *Tahāfut,* al-Ghazālī not only endeavored to refute the Islamic philosophers logically. He condemned them as infidels for affirming the world's eternity, for their denial that God knows terrestrial particulars, and for their denial of bodily resurrection. The charge of infidelity was a serious one in terms of Islamic law, and in *Faṣl* Ibn Rushd defends them against it. He begins, however, by raising a more general question, namely, whether Islamic religious law allows, prohibits, recommends, or commands the study of philosophy. Basing himself on certain Koranic statements, he argues that the law commands the study of philosophy. For philosophy is the proper study of nature that leads to the proof of the existence of God. This obligation, however, applies only to those who have the capacity and training to pursue philosophy, the demonstrative class, not to those capable of reasoning only on the dialectical or (as with the masses) on the rhetorical level.

Some scriptural statements are clear and unambiguous in their intent and must be accepted literally by the three classes of men, the demonstrative, dialectical, and rhetorical. In the case of other statements, it is not obvious whether or not they are to be taken literally. Error in taking them metaphorically or in the interpretation given them is permissible. A third class of statements is quite clearly open to metaphorical interpretation, but must be interpreted by each class according to its intellectual capacity. Error here again is permissible.

It is within the framework of this theory of

RUSHD, IBN (AVERROËS)

interpretation that Ibn Rushd defends the Islamic philosophers against the charge of infidelity. Their condemned doctrines relate to scriptural statements where error in interpretation is permissible. (Not that Ibn Rushd concedes that the philosophers have committed such error.) Furthermore, in practical matters, it is the consensus of the Muslim community (*al-ijmā*ᶜ) that rules on whether or not an act constitutes Islamic infidelity (*kufr*). Consensus in matters of theoretical belief, Ibn Rushd then tries to show, is impossible. In this work Ibn Rushd offers a more specific defense of each of the theories condemned by al-Ghazālī. A main theme in *Faṣl* is the harmony of philosophy and religion.

The afterlife. In *Kashf,* Ibn Rushd again takes up the question of the afterlife in detail. Belief in the resurrection of the dead, he maintains, is incumbent on all Muslims. The scriptural statements affirming it, however, must be interpreted according to individual intellectual capacities. In this work, Ibn Rushd affirms a doctrine of individual immortality. This poses a difficulty in ascertaining his real position on this question, since the theory of the intellect he develops in his commentaries precludes belief in individual immorality.

In his epitome on the *De anima,* which has survived in its Arabic original, he discusses the division of the human rational soul into the practical and the theoretical. The practical faculty deliberates in terms of concepts directly related to particular images that are generable and corruptible; it is hence likewise generable and corruptible. But what about the theoretical faculty? It also is dependent on particular images, he argues. Its function is to abstract the form from the particulars of sense. Once abstracted, the form attains a mental status. It becomes an intelligible, but an intelligible that is still dependent on particular images and is hence generable and corruptible. But whatever is generable and corruptible, Ibn Rushd argues, requires something that takes the place of form and something that takes the place of matter. In other words, the form as an intelligible, as distinct from the form in external reality, must also have "intellectual" form and matter to explain its being generable and corruptible.

The form of the intelligible, Ibn Rushd then argues, is a separate intellectual principle that is actual and is the agent that causes the potential concept in men to become actual. It is an eternal principle that acts on all men engaged in conceptual thought. The principle, though eternal, is common to men capable of abstraction. There is nothing in Ibn Rushd's statement about its eternity that suggests or allows individual immortality. If anything, it precludes it. The same applies to that which takes the place of matter. Ibn Rushd suggests that this is a pure potentiality analogous to prime matter. It is a potentiality that can become all concepts in the way prime matter is potentially receptive of all forms. Here again, this "material intellect" is common to all men, and there is nothing in Ibn Rushd's statements about it that suggests or allows individual immortality. It is true, there is hesitation and uncertainty in his discussion of this material intellect. But this uncertainty has to do with the question of its nature—whether or not, for example, this material intellect is identical with the images the soul acquires through sense perception—not with the question of individual immortality.

The problem is also encountered in his *Tahāfut al-Tahāfut.* Ibn Rushd criticizes and rejects Ibn Sīnā's doctrine of the soul's individual immortality. One of the reasons for this rejection is that such a doctrine leads to an actual infinity of souls. The actual infinite is impossible. For, like Ibn Sīnā, Ibn Rushd subscribed to the doctrine of the world's eternity and to the Aristotelian view that men have always existed in the past. If throughout the infinite past the souls surviving men's bodies retained their individuality, the number of these souls would be infinite. But if Ibn Rushd denies the possibility of an actual infinity of souls, he should also deny an actual infinity of resurrected bodies. Yet, in the final chapter of the *Tahāfut,* he affirms the doctrine of bodily resurrection.

There are two points regarding the seemingly inconsistent statements about the afterlife in the *Tahāfut* that are worthy of note. The first is that his criticism of Ibn Sīnā's theory of individual immortality occurs in those parts of the *Tahāfut* where the discussion is relatively technical, where it is clearly addressed to readers capable of following a philosophical argument. The affirmation of bodily resurrection, on the other hand, occurs in a context where the language is rhetorical, rather than philosophical. Secondly, when affirming bodily resurrection, he adds that the philosophers do not deny it, deeming its affirmation necessary as a means for governing the masses. This suggests that when Ibn Rushd affirms individual immortality, he is addressing the nonphilosopher, giving an interpretation of scriptural language on a level the nonphilosopher can understand. This is consistent with his views in *Faṣl,* rooted as they are in al-Fārābī's political philosophy, with its dictum that the nonphilosopher must not be addressed in philosophical language. Reading Ibn Rushd in this light offers a possible resolution of the difficulty.

INFLUENCE

Ibn Rushd's commentaries on Aristotle conditioned the development of Aristotelianism in both medieval Europe and the Renaissance. They stimulated the rise of Latin Averroism, although this movement did not always reflect accurately Ibn Rushd's thought. They also helped shape the intellectual climate of the Italian Renaissance. Ibn Rushd's influence extended to medieval and Renaissance Jewish thought as well. His *Tahāfut* was also translated, in the fourteenth century only partially, but fully in the sixteenth. It made available to Europe not only his own ideas, but also those of al-Ghazālī and the Islamic occasionalists.

In the Islamic East, he did not have as strong an impact as Ibn Sīnā had. Nonetheless, there is a sense in which he was the most Islamic of the Islamic philosophers, particularly when we use the term in its cultural sense. For the question of whether his philosophy is in harmony with Islam, the religion, as he claimed, is debatable. But he was very explicit in addressing himself to Islamic religious questions. Trained as an Islamic lawyer, he was also steeped in other Islamic religious sciences, such as *kalām* (theology), in the Arabic language, and in Arabic literature.

He is important, however, not only because of the great influence he exerted in the past. His writings reveal him as a powerful analytic thinker, very much a philosopher's philosopher. There is much in his writings that remains of intrinsic philosophic value.

BIBLIOGRAPHY

Sources. Editions of Ibn Rushd's works are: *Kitab al-kashf ᶜan manāhij al-adilla,* in Marcus J. Müller, ed. and trans., *Philosophie und Theologie von Averroës* (1859); *Tahāfut al-Tahāfut,* Maurice Bouyges, ed. (1930); *Tafsīr mā baᶜd al-ṭabīᶜa: Grand commentaire de la metaphysique,* Maurice Bouyges, ed. (1938–1948); *Rasāᵓil Ibn Rushd* (1947); *Talkhīṣ kitāb al-nafs,* Fuᵓād Ahwāni, ed. (1950); *Talkhīṣ mā baᶜd al-ṭabīᶜah,* ᶜUthmān Amin, ed. (1958); *Kitāb faṣl al-maqāl with Its Appendix (Ḍamīma) and an Extract from Kitāb al-kashf,* George F. Hourani, ed. (1959); *Talkhīṣ kitāb al-jadal (Middle Commentary on Aristotle's Topics),* Charles E. Butterworth and A. A. M. Haridi, eds. (1979); *Talkhīṣ kitāb al-maqūlāt,* M. M. Kassem, ed. (Charles E. Butterworth and A. A. M. Haridi, eds. and rev., 1980).

Translations. Philosophie und Theologie von Averroës (German translation of *Faṣl, Kashf,* and *Ḍamīma*), Marcus J. Müller, ed. and trans. (1859); *Die Epitome der Metaphysik des Averroës,* Simon Van Den Bergh, trans. (1924); *Traité décisif (façl el-maqâl) sur l'accord de la religion et de la philosophie,* Léon Gauthier, trans., 3rd ed. (1948); *Tahāfut al-Tahāfut (The Incoherence of the Incoherence),* Simon Van Den Bergh, ed. and trans. (1954); *Averroës' Commentary on Plato's Republic,* Erwin I. J. Rosenthal, ed. and trans. (1956); *On the Harmony of Religion and Philosophy,* George F. Hourani, ed. and trans. (1961); *Averroës' Middle Commentary on Porphyry's Isagoge and on Aristotle's Categories,* Herbert A. Davidson, trans. (1969); *Averroës on Plato's Republic,* Ralph Lerner, ed. and trans. (1974); *Averroës' Three Short Commentaries on Aristotle's "Topics," "Rhetorics," and "Poetics,"* Charles E. Butterworth, ed. and trans. (1977).

Studies. Michel Allard, "Le rationalisme d'Averroès d'après une étude sur la création," in *Bulletin d'études orientales,* **14** (1952–1954); Majid Fakhry, *Islamic Occasionalism and Its Critique by Averroës and Aquinas* (1958), and *A History of Islamic Philosophy* (1970), 302–325; Léon Gauthier, *Ibn Rochd (Averroès)* (1948); George F. Hourani, "Averroës on Good and Evil," in *Studia Islamica,* **16** (1962); Alfred L. Ivry, "Averroës on Intellection and Conjunction," in *Journal of the American Oriental Society,* **86** (1966); Jean Jolivet, ed., *Multiple Averroès* (1978); Barry S. Kogan, "Averroës and the Theory of Emanation," in *Mediaeval Studies,* **43** (1981); Muhsin Mahdi, "Averroës on Divine Law and Human Wisdom," in Joseph Cropsey, ed., *Ancients and Moderns: Essays on the Tradition of Political Philosophy in Honor of Leo Strauss* (1964); John H. Randall, Jr., "The Development of Scientific Method in the School of Padua," in *Journal of the History of Ideas,* **1** (1940); E. Renan, *Averroès et l'averroïsme* (1882); Joseph Riordan, "Form and Intellect in Averroës" (diss., Univ. of Toronto, 1961); Harry A. Wolfson, *Studies in the History of Philosophy and Religion,* Isadore Twersky and George H. Williams, eds. (1973), 1–21, 370–454.

MICHAEL E. MARMURA

[See also **Aristotle in the Middle Ages; Ghazālī, al-; Islam, Religion; Philosophy and Theology, Islamic; Sīnā, Ibn.**]

RUSSIA. See **Kievan Rus; Muscovy, Rise of; Novgorod.**

RUSSIA, NOMADIC INVASIONS OF. The Caspian–Black Sea steppelands have long attracted the pastoral nomads, both Iranian and Altaic (Turko-Mongolian), of central Asia. This interaction of the nomads with the Finno-Ugrian and eastern Slavic populations is one of the constant factors in the evolution of these peoples.

Altaic nomads, primarily Turkic, were brought to the western Eurasian steppes with the migrations of peoples associated with the formation and expansion of the Hunnic state (fourth century A.D.). A decade after the Hunnic collapse in 454, new Turkic tribes, the Oghurs, Onogurs, and related peoples, entered the region and, joining with Hunnic remnants, gave rise to the Bulgars and other confederations. In the mid sixth century, the Avars, coming from inner Asia, briefly dominated the western steppes, only to be replaced by their mortal enemies, the Turks. The latter created an empire stretching from the borders of China to the Black Sea.

An offshoot and successor state of the Turks in this territory was the Khazar Kaganate (*ca.* 650–965). Ruled, apparently, by a dynasty of Turkic origin, the Khazars continued the pattern of cooperation with Byzantium established by their Turkic predecessors. This alliance, initially directed against Sasanian Iran, continued with the appearance of the Arabs in the Caucasus. Arabo-Khazar warfare began in 652 and lasted, with brief interludes, for almost a century. Following the victory of the Umayyad general Marwān in 737, the north Caucasus became the border between the two empires.

In the late eighth to early ninth centuries, the Khazar ruling strata and elements of the leading clans and tribes converted to Judaism. The conversion, never fully elucidated in the surviving sources and still the subject of much speculation, provided a necessary autonomy in relations with Byzantium and the caliphate. Islam, Christianity, and paganism, however, continued to flourish alongside of Judaism. Atīl, the Khazar capital on the lower Volga, became a major commercial center with a large, polyglot population. Khazar government closely followed the usages of its Turk progenitor. A particular development, known to other Turkic states, was the transformation of the Kagan into a religio-sacral figurehead while actual direction of the state was placed in the hands of a deputy (called variously the *shad, yilig,* or *beg*).

Khazaria served as Byzantium's first line of defense against nomadic incursions. In the ninth century, however, its power was weakened by foreign invaders (Hungarians and Pechenegs) and internal strife (the Kabar revolt). By the tenth century, the Khazars were no longer able to contain the steppe pressures. Byzantine policy, which now sought to turn "barbarian" against "barbarian," only exacerbated the situation. In 965, Svyatoslav of Kiev, responding to Khazar attempts to curb Rus raiding via Khazaria into the Caspian Islamic lands, delivered the fatal blow. A now greatly reduced Khazaria lingered on as a Khwarizmian protectorate. More importantly, the barrier to westward steppe incursions had been removed, thus contributing to those events that culminated in the Byzantine disaster at Manazkert (Manzikert, 1071).

The Hungarians and the Pechenegs were the nomads disturbing Khazaria in the ninth century. The Hungarian tribal union, consisting of Ugrian and Oghur Turkic elements, had been pushed westward from their Uralo-Bashkir homeland by repeated assaults from the Pechenegs. The latter, a Turkic tribal union formerly located in the Kang area (Middle Syr Darya), were in conflict with the Oghuz Turks, who had entered central Asia about 775. When Khazaria weakened, the Pechenegs, under Oghuz pressure, migrated from the Volga-Ural mesopotamia and entered the Pontic steppes in the early tenth century. Here, they were used by Byzantium to check the Rus, (for instance, in the ambush and killing of Svyatoslav in 972). The ongoing Pecheneg-Rus struggle, frequently little more than localized raiding, prompted Svyatoslav's son Vladimir I (980–1015) to create a series of fortifications on his southern frontiers to contain the nomads. In 1036, however, the Pechenegs made a serious attempt on Kiev. Decisively defeated by Yaroslav (1036–1054) and still faced with Oghuz pressure, they now migrated toward the Byzantine Balkan holdings. Subsequently, in 1091, masses of them were slaughtered there by joint Byzantine-Cuman forces.

The Oghuz, involved in central Asian political turbulence and themselves under great internal pressures (in part reflected in the Seljuk movement), were also caught up in the migration of yet another mass of Turkic tribesmen from the east (the Cuman/Qun migration, *ca.* 1017–1018). While many Oghuz entered Iran under Seljuk leadership, others appeared in the Pontic steppes after 965 (they aided Svyatoslav in his Khazar campaign). More followed by the mid eleventh century, when the full impact

RUSSIA, NOMADIC INVASIONS OF

of Cuman movements was felt. The Torki (Oghuz in Rus) appear in considerable numbers in 1054–1055, just ahead of the Cuman advance. They were then defeated by the Rus and again suffered defeat in 1060. Like the Pechenegs, they migrated to the Byzantine borders (*ca.* 1064–1065). Those remaining in the steppe were joined with remnants of the Pechenegs and other nomads to form, ultimately, the Chërnye Klobuki (Russian: Black Hoods), the Turkic border guards of the Kievan princes.

The dominant steppe people from the mid eleventh century until the Mongol conquest was the Cuman/Kipchak tribal union, whose immediate antecedents are still much in dispute. The Cuman steppe (Russian: *Pole Polovetskoe*; Persian: *Dasht-i Qipchāq*) extended from the Danube to Kazakhstan. Although they periodically raided Byzantine lands, supported the Asenids in the creation of the Second Bulgarian Empire, and helped Georgia to withstand the Seljuks, they most frequently enmeshed themselves in the domestic squabbles of their closest neighbors, the Rus. Warfare here, however, complicated by a variety of marital and military alliances, tended to be on a small scale and never assumed the aspect of a life-and-death struggle. Rus political fragmentation was almost matched in Cumania. The efforts of Konchak khan and his son Yurii to unite the Cuman subconfederations in the late twelfth and early thirteenth centuries were undone by the Mongol conquest in 1237. The Mongols reorganized the Cumans (now called Tatars), but the latter quickly Turkicized the resultant Golden Horde.

Some Cumans fled to Hungary, where they settled in regions that now bear their name. Others were sold on the steppe as military slaves in the Islamic world, where they seized power from the Ayyubids (Egypt/Syria) and formed their own state (in 1250), that of the Mamluks.

BIBLIOGRAPHY

Sources. Primary sources for these peoples cover a wide range of sources: Arabic, Armenian, Chinese, Georgian, Greek, Hebrew, Iranian (Middle Iranian, New Persian, and others), Latin, Old Slavic, Syriac, and Tibetan. Some of the Arabic sources for the earliest period are collected and analyzed in Tadeusz Lewicki, *Źródła arabskie do dziejów Słowiańszczyzny,* 2 vols in 3 (1956–1977); and Boris N. Zakhoder, *Kaspiiskii svod svedenii o vostochnoi Evrope,* 2 vols. (1962–1967). Byzantine sources for the entire period are exhaustively discussed in Gyula Moravcsik, *Byzantinoturcica* (1958). Syriac sources are covered in Károly Czeglédy, "Monographs on Syriac and Muhammadan Sources in the Literary Remains of M. Kmoskó," in *Acta orientalia hungarica,* 4 (1954). References to the individual sources and translations (where they exist) may be found in the monographs and articles listed below.

General works. Károly Czeglédy, *A nomád népek vándorlása napkelettől napnyugatig* (1969), trans. by Peter B. Golden as "From East to West: The Age of Nomadic Migrations in Eurasia," in *Archivum Eurasiae Medii Aevi,* 3 (1983); Krzysztof Dąbrowski, Teresa Nagrodzka-Majchrzyk, and Edward Tryjarski, *Hunowie europejscy, Protobułgarzy, Chazarowie, Pieczyngowie* (1975); Peter B. Golden, "Imperial Ideology and the Sources of Unity Amongst the Pre-Činggisid Nomads of Western Eurasia," in *Archivum Eurasiae Medii Aevi,* 2 (1982); Petr V. Golubovskii, *Pechenegi, torki i polovtsy do nashestviya tatar* (1884); Josef Marquart, *Osteuropäische und ostasiatische Streifzüge* (1903); Gyula Németh, *A honfoglaló magyarság kialakulása* (1930); S. A. Pletneva, "Pechenegi, torki i polovtsy v yuzhnorusskikh steppiakh (Trudy volgo-donskoi arkheologicheskoi ekspeditsii)," in *Materialy i issledovaniya po arkheologii SSSR,* 62 (1958); Denis Sinor, *Introduction à l'étude de l'Eurasie Centrale* (1963).

The Khazar period. Mikhail I. Artamonov, *Istoriya khazar* (1962); W. (V. V.) Barthold and Peter B. Golden, "Khazar," in *Encyclopedia of Islam,* new ed., IV (1978); Imre Boba, *Nomads, Northmen, and Slavs* (1967); Douglas M. Dunlop, *The History of the Jewish Khazars* (1954); Peter B. Golden, *Khazar Studies: An Historico-Philological Inquiry into the Origins of the Khazars* (1980), and "Khazaria and Judaism," in *Archivum Eurasiae Medii Aevi,* 3 (1983); S. A. Pletneva, *Ot kochevii k gorodam* (1967), and *Khazary* (1976), trans. into German by Alexander Häusler as *Die Chasaren* (1978); Ananiasz Zajączkowski, *Ze studiów nad zagadnieniem chazarskim* (1947).

The Pechenegs. Gyula Czebe, "Turco-byzantinische Miszellen, I: Konstantinos Porphyrogenitos' De Administrando Imperio 37, Kapitel über die Petschenegen," in *Kőrösi Csoma-Archiv,* 1 (1921–1925); Petre Diaconu, *Les Petchénègues au Bas-Danube* (1970); Akdes N. Kurat, *Peçenek tarihi* (1937); C. A. Macartney, "The Pechenegs," in *Slavonic and East European Reivew,* 8 (1929–1930); Gyula Németh, *Die Inschriften des Schatzes von Nagy-Szent-Miklós* (1932); Omeljan Pritsak, "The Pečenegs: A Case of Social and Economic Transformation," in *Archivum Eurasiae Medii Aevi,* 1 (1975); D. A. Rasovskii, "Rus i kochevniki i epokhu Svyatogo Vladimira," in *Vladimirskii sbornik v pamiat 950–letiya kreshcheniya Rusi* (1938).

The Oghuz (Torki) and Chërnye Klobuki. Peter B. Golden, "The Migrations of the Oğuz," in *Archivum Ottomanicum,* 4 (1972); S. A. Pletneva, *Drevnosti Chërnykh Klobukov* (1973); D. A. Rasovskii, "O roli Chernykh Klobukov v istorii drevnei Rusi," in *Seminar-*

ium Kondakovianum (Institut imeni N. P. Kondakova, *Annaly*), **1** (1927), and "Pechenegi, torki i berendei na Rusi i v Ugrii," *ibid.*, **6** (1933); Vasilii G. Vasilevskii, *Vizantiya i pechenegi*, in *Trudy V. G. Vasilevskogo*, I (1908).

The Cumans. V. V. Barthold, "Ḳipčaḳ," in *Enzyklopaedie des Islam*, II (1927); Petre Diaconu, *Les coumans au Bas-Danube aux XIe et XIIe siècles*, Radu Creţeanu, trans. (1978); German A. Fedorov-Davydov, *Kochevniki Vostochnoi Evropy pod vlastyu zolotoordynskikh khanov* (1966); Peter B. Golden, "The *Polovci Dikii*," in *Euchasterion: Essays Presented to Omeljan Pritsak*, in *Harvard Ukrainian Studies*, **3–4** (1979–1980), and "Cumanica I: The Qıpčaqs in Georgia," in *Archivum Eurasiae Medii Aevi*, **4** (1984); Josef Marquart, *Über das Volktum der Komanen*, in Willi Bang-Kaup and Josef Marquart, *Osttürkische Dialektstudien*, in *Abhandlungen der königlichen Gesellschaft der Wissenschaften zu Göttingen*, Philologisch-historische Klasse, n.s. **23/1** (1914); Karl H. Menges, *The Oriental Elements in the Vocabulary of the Oldest Russian Epos, the Igor Tale* (1951); Omeljan Pritsak, "The Polovcians and Rus'," in *Archivum Eurasiae Medii Aevi*, **2** (1982); D. A. Rasovskii, "Les Comans et Byzance," in Congrès International des Études Byzantines, IV, *Actes* (1935), and "Polovtsy," in *Seminarium Kondakovianum*, **7–11** (1935–1940).

PETER B. GOLDEN

[See also **Avars; Bulgaria; Golden Horde; Huns; Khazars; Kievan Rus; Mamluk Dynasty; Mongol Empire; Turkomans; Volga Bulgars.**]

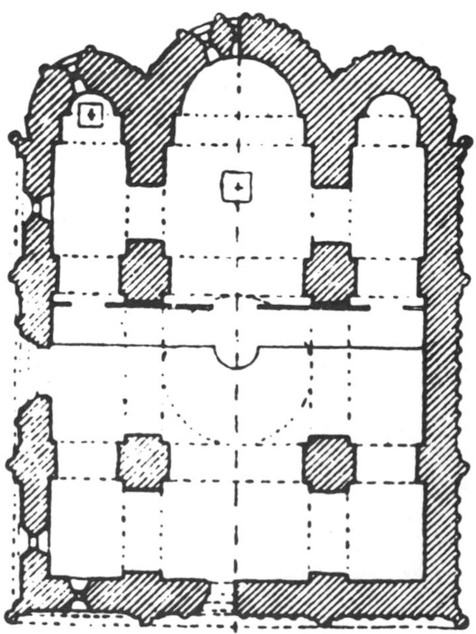

Cathedral of St. Dimitri, Vladimir, 1197, showing ground plan typical of a four-pier, cross-in-square church. ALL DRAWINGS REPRODUCED FROM *RUSSKOE ZODCHESTVO* (1953)

RUSSIAN ARCHITECTURE. Medieval Russian architecture is best understood in terms of a subtle interplay between Russian national traditions and Byzantine influences. This is true for both secular and ecclesiastical buildings. As is often the case in northern countries, wood was the normal material for buildings in the native tradition. The basic element was the *klet*, a peak-roofed cube-shaped hut of unplaned logs laid horizontally and notched at the corner joints in the manner of the American log cabin. This was the form of the simplest peasant hut and the basic element of the houses of the well-to-do, which were essentially combinations of *klet*s added onto each other. In towns such log buildings were often built with two stories, the lower story serving business purposes (and sometimes as a stable), with the upper story, reached by a covered outside stairway, serving domestic needs. Well into the seventeenth century such wooden buildings of various sizes remained the rule, particularly in central and northern Russia. The use of stone in secular buildings, apparently begun in the late tenth century, was restricted to princely and episcopal palaces, monasteries, and rare governmental buildings throughout the medieval period; stone buildings tended to mimic the wooden architecture. Stone walls around the major towns became common from the thirteenth century; brick urban fortifications appear only from the fourteenth century on and are based on Polish and German prototypes.

The Christianization of Russia around 989 brought Byzantine building techniques to Russia and initiated a broad building campaign to supply the country with houses of worship. Churches were to become the primary medium of Russian architectural creativity in the Middle Ages. While the villages began by building wooden churches such as had apparently existed in Russia before its official conversion, the major cities built more durable church buildings. The first of these was the Desyatinnaya, the "tithe church" in Kiev, founded by Grand Prince Vladimir, the "Christianizer of Russia," around 990. This (presumably) domed, triple-apsed, cross-in-square brick building (long since destroyed) was essentially a Byzantine structure. This is not surprising since written sources note that many of the major churches of the southern part of the Russian state were built by Byzantine architects. Indeed, most of the eleventh- and twelfth-century churches that have survived in this area, such as the Transfiguration Cathedral in Chernigov (*ca.* 1036)

RUSSIAN ARCHITECTURE

and the Dormition Church of the Caves Monastery (Pecherskaya Lavra) near Kiev, completed 1078, show only minor variations from the standard Constantinopolitan style of the period. Perhaps more regularly than was the case in Constantinople, ambulatories were attached to the usual domed, triple-apsed, cross-in-square structure. Even the huge cathedral of St. Sophia in Kiev built by Grand Prince Yaroslav the Wise (begun about 1037) is, under analysis, only a large Byzantine building of this style with the individual elements multiplied rather than enlarged to create a church of the necessary size. Similarly, the mosaic and fresco decorations of these churches betray the hand of Byzantine artists and their careful native students in both their programs and technique.

It is only in the northern part of the Kievan Russian state, farther removed from Byzantine contacts, that Russian influences begin to assert themselves clearly in ecclesiastical architecture. The great northwest Russian city of Novgorod presents the most obvious examples of the russification of Byzantine architectural style. Most notable of the features that graft themselves onto the Byzantine architectural style here is a tendency to verticality rarely encountered on Byzantine territory. While the standard ground plan of the middle-Byzantine cross-in-square church, with its triple apse and four piers supporting the central dome (or six piers to give an extra set of bays in the west) seems to have become a permanent feature of Russian church architecture, the vertical proportions change. Novgorodian church buildings are much taller for their size than their Byzantine, and often their Kievan, counterparts; tall church buildings seem to be a mark of Russian church architecture. One notes this penchant for vertical line in comparing the mid-eleventh-century cathedral of St. Sophia in Novgorod with the Sophia Cathedral built in Kiev at almost the same time. The verticality of the Novgorod cathedral, apparently designed by Russian architects, is emphasized by the use of narrow external buttress pilasters running from ground level to vault springings and reflecting the internal structural divisions of the edifice. The drums that support the domes are elongated too, further raising the profile of the church. Finally, one should note that even the domes seem to be subjected to vertical stress and begin their peculiarly Russian development from the Byzantine hemispheric shape through a slightly elongated shape with a pointed top ("helmet domes") of eleventh-century Novgorod to the eventual onion-shaped dome of the later Middle Ages. In twelfth-century Novgorod churches the external pilasters are joined by arches mirroring the building's vaulting, which now sometimes supports flat roofs; the walls between these buttress pilasters give the impression of curtain walls pierced by rows of narrow windows. The main churches of the Yuriev (1130) and St. Anthony (1117) monasteries show these tendencies clearly.

Cathedral of St. Sophia, Novgorod, south facade. Mid 11th century.

The twelfth century also saw the birth of a composite style of church architecture in the evolving northeast part of the early Russian state, the Vladimir-Suzdal principality, to which the Russian capital was removed in that century. A certain harmony and delicacy, and perhaps an architectural maturity, pervade the churches of this school in their treatment of the traditional Byzantine cross-in-square plans. The flat external pilasters noted in Novgorodian architecture are molded into slender engaged colonnettes, while the arched walls between them are framed in diminishing recessed arches, as are the single windows in each bay that copy their shape. The height of the facades of the buildings is visually deemphasized by the introduction of a band of blind arcading at half-height supported by short engaged colonnettes resting on carved consoles. The drums of the tall cupolas are

RUSSIAN ARCHITECTURE

Cathedral of St. Dimitri, Vladimir, south facade, 1197.

pierced with windows in recessed arch frames copying the shape of those in the facades. Engaged colonnettes and arches tie the drum windows together, while the simple borders at the top of the drum become complex belts of transition to the dome. Engaged colonnettes, some reaching from the ground to the semidomes, lighten the mass of the apses. Most startlingly, stylized limestone bas-relief figures are introduced on the facades, often in carpetlike profusion, adding the textural warmth so notoriously lacking in the stark facades of Novgorod, which are relieved only by the sets of recessed arches framing the doors in Romanesque fashion. Excellent examples of this style are the church of the Virgin's Protection on the Nerl River (1165) and the cathedrals of St. Dimitri (1197) and of the Dormition (1189) in the city of Vladimir, as well as the Yuriev-Polski Cathedral (1234).

The Mongol conquest of Russia in 1240 stopped all stone building in the Russian state, save in the northwestern areas, where Novgorod (and its satellite state of Pskov) preserved a measure of autonomy. There the spirit of innovation and experimentation that had created the earlier Novgorodian architectural style evolved in new directions, possibly inspired by trade contacts with the West. The traditional cross-in-square four-pillared church evolved into a domed square building with a high gable on each side, either sharply peaked (Transfiguration, 1374), or formed by triple arches diminishing in height at the corners (St. Theodore Stratelate, 1361). The already smaller side apses disappear while the central apse grows and becomes the complete sanctuary area. Bold bas-relief motifs and brickwork designs are strategically located on the facades to break the earlier Novgorodian architectural starkness. Free-standing bell cotes, an earlier northwest Russian development, are occasionally integrated into the architectural design of the church buildings.

In the rest of Russia, all building is of wood for almost a hundred years after the Mongol invasion. The wooden church architecture of thirteenth-century Russia has its roots in the native architecture of the log *klet* discussed earlier. Since the size of the *klet* is determined by the length of the available timber to be laid horizontally, larger churches are formed of groups of attached rectangular *klet*s, most simply in a line, later forming a cross. Eventually the central square formed by the *klet*s gives way to an octagon built of horizontal logs, effectively expanding the floor space by using eight walls the length of the timbers, rather than four. The persistent urge toward verticality seems to dictate continuing the octagon up to a tall pinnacle crowned by an onion-shaped dome carrying a cross, giving the church a towerlike appearance (the so-called "tent churches"). Subordinate *klet*s can be added to the sides, with further *klet*s attached to them as sanctuary, congregational areas, or vestibules opening into the central octagonal element. The floor level is usually raised well above the ground because of snow and is reached by a large covered outside stairway, such as is found in secular architecture. The stairway often leads into a wraparound covered porch that unites the disparate units into a single architectural entity. Transitions between the various elements are softened by the use of receding ogee-shaped wooden gables. Shingle-covered onion domes on narrow necks and intricately carved wooden cornices and balustrades add visual interest to the ensemble.

The slow rebirth of stone architecture in fourteenth-century northeast Russia demonstrates the

RUSSIAN ARCHITECTURE

Wooden tower ("tent") church at Panilova, west facade, 1600, reflecting earlier stage.

earlier loss of technical masonry skills and of innate architectural aesthetics as well as the clear influences of the popular wooden church architecture. The masonry walls are thicker than need be for the weight they bear. The traditional four piers supporting the central dome are closer to each other, diminishing the central space of the building, and are not reflected in the external pilasters that continue to divide the facades into three equal bays. The external transition from the springing of the vaults to the base of the cupola drum is treated as a series of receeding ogee-shaped *kokoshnik* gables that mimics, but does not mirror, the internal corbeling which supports a drum of smaller diameter than the space enclosed by the central piers. Good examples of this style are the Dormition Cathedral in Zvenigorod (1400), the Trinity Church of the Trinity–St. Sergius Monastery (1422) at Zagorsk, the cathedral of the Moscow Andron-

Dormition Cathedral at Zvenigorod, north facade (reconstruction), 1400.

ikov Monastery (1427), which has been restored to its original form, and the original core of the Moscow Kremlin's Annuncation Cathedral (1489). The graceful curved lines of the *kokoshniki,* so natural in wood, have been copied in the unfriendly medium of stone; by the same token, the receding corbel by means of which the tall drum rests on the central pillars recalls the supports of the central octagonal tower element in the more elaborate wooden churches. Variations on such square churches roofed with pyramidally arranged receding vaults crowned with a bulbous cupola on a tall, narrow drum continued to be built throughout the sixteenth century, particularly in the provinces, although in Moscow as well (Old Cathedral of the monastery of the Virgin of the Don, 1593). Even more noticeable in the sixteenth century is the tendency in provincial church architecture to imitate in stone and brick the tall, gradually narrowing octagonal towers of wooden churches. The Moscow area boasts two excellent examples of this style, both votive churches, the Ascension Church in Kolomenskoe (1532), which even reproduces the elevated wrap-around porch and irregular roofed outside stairways of the wooden churches, and the much-photographed church of St. Basil on Red Square (1560). The latter, while at first sight a confusing amalgam of disparate elements, is, in reality, a central tower church surrounded by eight tower chapels decorated in different fashions and crowned by variations of the bulbous onion dome. Much of the color so striking in the building is, like the enclosed wrap-around porch, seventeenth-century work.

Such extreme examples of the infiltration of the popular wooden architecture into masonry style seem to stand in opposition to an official style most successfully expressed by the major churches of the Moscow Kremlin, the Dormition (1479) and Arkhangelsky (1509) cathedrals, a style that attempted to restore the "high"-style architecture of pre-Mongol northeast Russia. Based on the traditional four- or six-piered, triple-apsed, five-dome plan of earlier Russian architecture, these "neo-Vladimirian" buildings were built as monastery churches or as cathedrals during the sixteenth century. The harmonious proportions of the earlier architecture of the Vladimir principality, however, found little favor in these later large churches. They tended to be overly tall and dominated by long narrow drums supporting massive onion domes disproportionate to their drums (the early-sixteenth-century churches of the Kremlin of Rostov-on-the-Klyazma, the cathedral of the Novodevichy Monastery in Moscow, 1524). It was probably the massive heaviness of such buildings with their misproportioned cupolas that inspired the seventeenth-century reaction of the light, playful, and asymmetrical style that might be called "native Russian baroque."

BIBLIOGRAPHY

General studies. The most comprehensive presentations of medieval Russian architecture are in Igor E. Grabar, ed., *Istoriya russkogo iskusstva,* 6 vols. (1909–1916), and in the first four volumes of Grabar, V. N. Lazarev, and V. S. Remenov, eds., *Istoriya russkogo iskusstva,* 13 vols. in 16 (1953–1968). There is a German translation of the first six volumes of the latter work, *Geschichte der russischen Kunst* (1957–1970). Mikhail Alpatov and Nikolai Brunov, *Geschichte der altrussischen Kunst,* 2 vols. (1932), and Hubert Faensen and Vladimir Ivanov, *Early Russian Architecture* (1972), are highly recommended; the latter includes stunning plates. An excellent short survey is Pavel A. Rappoport, *Drevnerusskaya arkhitektura* (1970). See also the relevant chapters in George H. Hamilton, *The Art and Architecture of Russia,* 3rd ed. (1983). Cyril Mango, *Byzantine Architecture* (1976), is particularly useful for its treatment of early Russian architecture in the larger Byzantine context; and a good presentation of Russian architecture before the Mongol conquest is Nikolai N. Voronin and Mikhail K. Karger, "Arkhitektura," in Boris D. Grekov *et al.,* eds., *Istoriya kultury drevnei Rusi,* II (1951).

Specific studies. On medieval Russian fortification architecture, see V. V. Kostochkin, *Russkoe oboronnoe zodchestvo kontsa XIII–nachala XVI vekov* (1962). The basic study of the architecture of medieval Kiev is Mikhail K. Karger, *Drevnii Kiev,* 2 vols. (1958–1961). On Novgorodian architecture see his *Novgorod Velikii: Arkhitekturnye pamyatniki* (1966) and his shorter *Novgorod the Great: Architectural Guidebook,* K. M. Cook, trans. (1973). An excellent study of the architecture of medieval northeast Russia is Nikolai N. Voronin, *Zodchestvo severo-vostochnoi Rusi XII–XV vekov,* 2 vols. (1961–1962). Two useful studies on wooden architecture are S. Zabello *et al., Russkoe dereviannoe zodchestvo* (1942), and G. I. Mekhova, *Russkoe dereviannoe zodchestvo* (1965); the latter has an English summary.

George P. Majeska

[See also **Bochka; Early Christian and Byzantine Architecture; Hagia Sophia (Kiev); Kokoshnik; Moscow Kremlin, Art and Architecture; Papert; Pecherskaya Lavra; Peter, Master; Vladimir, St.**]

RUSSIAN ART. The history of Russian art begins with the adoption of Orthodox Christianity under Grand Prince Vladimir of Kiev in 988. Preceding this, archaeological remains of the Slavs, in the form of simply built settlements and graves which sometimes contained jewelry and other metal ornaments, testify to a native Slavic art. Literary evidence, like the medieval Russian chronicles written down after the introduction of Christianity, also contain information about pagan art in Russia. The Laurentian Chronicles state that Vladimir erected idols to pagan gods in the year 980 "on the hills outside the castle with the hall; one of Perun, made of wood with a head of silver and a mouth of gold." In 922, an Arab traveler in Russia saw idols in the shape of wooden uprights with beads, and Thietmar von Merseburg (975–1018) saw in his travels among the Slavs a wooden shrine carved with images of pagan gods. These pagan works of art were destroyed or abandoned after Christianity

RUSSIAN ART

became the official religion of Russia. Yet this pagan artistic heritage probably affected certain aspects of Russian medieval art and architecture—the use of wood for building, the custom of decorating churches with exterior reliefs, the preference for small churches, and the taste for color and ornament typical of Russian icon painting.

Medieval Russian culture can be divided into two broad periods separated by the Mongol invasion in the thirteenth century. Preceding the Mongol invasion, Kiev was the earliest cultural center but by the eleventh century was superseded by principalities like Novgorod and Suzdal in the north. Suzdal fell before the Mongols in 1238 and Kiev was laid waste in 1240; Novgorod and Pskov, however, remained independent during the thirteenth and fourteenth centuries. In the late fifteenth century, the great prince of Moscow freed his domain from the Mongol overlords, and other principalities were annexed to form a centralized state that came to replace Constantinople as the capital of Orthodoxy.

Early on, Byzantine artisans were brought to such places as Kiev to help build and adorn new churches. These craftsmen were responsible for creating the first examples of medieval art and architecture on Russian soil and for training native workmen in the new religious idiom. The oldest preserved monumental decorations are the mosaics and frescoes in the church of St. Sophia in Kiev, built by order of Yaroslav the Wise between 1037 and 1067, to commemorate his victory over the pagan Pechenegs. St. Sophia became the seat of the metropolitan and the coronation church, and its architecture and interior adornment became models for later Russian churches.

The decorative scheme follows a Byzantine program, with three horizontal zones symbolizing three stages in the relationship between God and man. At the top, in the dome, can be seen a magnificent bust of Christ Pantokrator. In the apse, the Virgin Orant fills the upper part of the great curving shell, above the scene of the Liturgical Eucharist. On the lowest zone are figures of church fathers, saints, and other figures who had contributed to the church. The mosaics of St. Sophia have been related stylistically to Greek mosaics of the earlier eleventh century, like those of Hosios Lukas at Phocis in Greece. However, some Russian variants are visible in the frescoes. On the west wall of the nave, for instance, there is a composition of the Enthroned Christ surrounded by Prince Yaroslav, his wife, and his

St. Sophia, Kiev. View into the apse showing mosaic and fresco decoration including the Virgin Orant, 1043–1046. PHOTO: TASS FROM SOVFOTO

children. In the towers, scenes of the Hippodrome in Constantinople, along with hunting scenes, were probably painted as late as 1113–1125, in the reign of Vladimir Monomakh. Such representations were no doubt inspired by examples of Byzantine secular painting, but they were surely intended to glorify the Russian great princes rather than the Byzantine court. Such scenes might have inspired the frescoes in the churches of the Moscow Kremlin at the very end of the fifteenth century, when the role of the ruler was once again thought to be an appropriate theme for religious art. The latest preserved mosaic decoration in Russia comes from the church of the Archangel Michael, established in Kiev by Great Prince Svyatopolk Izyaslavich in 1108. This church has been destroyed and most of the mosaics are lost, but the remaining fragments show a technique and style different from those of St. Sophia and comparable to Greek work of the late eleventh century. Presumably, these mosaics were the creation of

RUSSIAN ART

St. George and the Dragon. Fresco from the church of St. George at Staraya Ladoga, *ca.* 1167. COURTESY OF PHAIDON ARCHIVES

another group of artists who had come to Russia from the Byzantine world.

In the city of Novgorod, where the prince vied for power with the *veche* or city council, art had its own peculiar flavor. In addition to Byzantine elements derived from Kiev and directly from the Greek world, contacts with Europe and the emergence of local artists combined to produce several varieties of native art. The churches of Novgorod and its vicinity were often commissioned by the local prince, a relative of the great prince of Kiev, but bishops, boyars, and merchants might also have churches erected. The church of St. George at Staraya Ladoga, a suburb of Novgorod, was decorated around 1167 to commemorate the defeat of Swedish invaders by the prince of Novgorod. St. George, a favorite saint among the Russian people, was here apparently considered the protector of the ruler, whom the saint delivered from evil. A prominent feature of the fresco decoration is a large representation of St. George shown as a conqueror of evil forces symbolized by the dragon. Along with an interest in decorative patterns and ornamental lines, the painting shows an elegance and grace that must have been inspired by familiarity with Byzantine art. Yet the presence of Slavonic inscriptions indicates that Russian artists worked here. A completely different style of painting appeared in the church of the Savior on the Nereditsa, near Novgorod, built as a royal commission and completed in 1199. This church was destroyed during World War II, but photographs show strongly and simply painted frescoes imbued with powerful emotion.

The third great artistic center in pre-Mongol Russia was the principality of Suzdal, founded in the twelfth century by Vladimir Monomakh and ruled by his successors until the Mongol invasion. In the beautiful stone churches, with relief sculptures carved on the exterior surfaces, it is perhaps possible to detect a remnant of pagan wood-carving traditions, along with influences from contemporary Romanesque Europe and the Caucasus. Frescoes in the church of St. Dimitri in Vladimir, built by Great Prince Vsevolod III in 1194–1197, present a powerful contrast with the contemporary painting in the church of the Savior on the Nereditsa near Novgorod. Vsevolod was educated in Byzantium, and his ideas of rulership were imperial. His earthly majesty was paralleled by the aristocratic figures of saints and apostles in the fresco of the Last Judgment. These exquisitely painted images could have been attendants in a heavenly court, far removed from the humble and sorrowful figures in the Nereditsa frescoes.

In pre-Mongol Russia, monumental church decoration in the form of frescoes and mosaics seems to have been more significant in both the artistic and religious sense than icon painting. This conclusion may be somewhat biased, since few icons have survived from this early phase of Russian medieval art. Yet it does seem true that icons played a less important role in religious ritual than they were to do later, when the development of the iconostasis focused attention upon icons and blocked from view much of the wall decoration. Nevertheless, it is interesting that the most revered icon in Russia dates from this early period, the Mother of God of Vladimir, a miracle-working icon considered to be the protector of all Russia throughout its history until the Revolution. This most sacred icon was not Russian in origin but was imported from Byzantium, probably one of two icons ordered by Great Prince Mstislav I of Kiev about 1131. Although much of this icon's surface has been lost during its long and adventurous life, enough of the original painting survives in the faces to show the delicate

The Last Judgment (detail), showing angels and six apostles. Fresco in the church of St. Dimitri (Demetrius), Vladimir, *ca.* 1195. COURTESY OF PHAIDON ARCHIVES

and sophisticated modeling of planes which had been mastered by its Greek creator. The theme celebrates the love of mother and child and thus found a powerful affinity with Russian attitudes. Although the image of Divine Motherhood, of a mother sorrowful at the coming sacrifice of her son, is Byzantine, it became one of the most beloved themes in Russian religious art. (See illustration at "Eleousa.")

The Russian icons of pre-Mongol times have been classified by scholars according to the cities or schools in which they were produced, and while there is some disagreement about the place of origin and the date, the locally made icons demonstrate the emergence of native tastes and traditions that would come to fruition in later centuries. Several icons, ascribed by Lazarev to a workshop in Novgorod directed by a Greek master, were produced in the twelfth century. The so-called Ustiug Annunciation and the head of an archangel belong to this group from Novgorod. Another icon, the Virgin of the Sign (Virgin Orant), was also painted in the late twelfth or early thirteenth century, although scholars differ about its city of origin. The aristocratic figure of this Virgin contrasts with the rather stocky Virgin in the Ustiug Annunciation, and these differences are probably to be associated with different cities, just as the monumental art of each principality was distinctive.

Although Novgorod and Pskov managed to retain their independence from the Mongol overlords of Russia, these cities also suffered from the disturbed political situation throughout the land. With the political tumult came disruption of the artistic life. Aside from Novgorod and Pskov, and some recently discovered icons from northern Russia, there is little evidence for continuity in icon painting, and even the two northern cities demonstrated a disruption in church building and decoration during the thirteenth century. But the fourteenth century marked a rebirth of culture in Russia, with increased contacts with Western Eu-

RUSSIAN ART

The Ustiug Annunciation icon. Novgorod school, 12th century. STATE TRETYAKOV GALLERY, MOSCOW

rope and Byzantium, with struggles against the Mongols, and with new religious attitudes expressed in part through art. In the history of Russian medieval art, the fourteenth century shines forth as the most significant period, when important changes led to the finest works of art ever created in Russia.

The innovations in fourteenth-century art can be most easily observed at Novgorod, where many examples have been preserved. From literary testimony, Moscow must have been an important artistic center as well, for it was during this time that the city began to become the chief political center of Russia. No monumental art of this period, however, has been preserved in Moscow; nevertheless, it is probably correct to suppose that the turning point discernible in Novgorod during the 1330's was part of a much wider development in Russian art.

The frescoes in the few churches of Pskov and Novgorod built in the early fourteenth century were closely linked to earlier medieval art, but a set of bronze gates ordered by Archbishop Basil (Vasily) in the 1330's for St. Sophia in Novgorod shows a new style inspired by the Palaiologan art of Byzantium. This new style had no doubt been introduced into Russia by Isaiah the Greek and his assistants, who, according to the Chronicle of Novgorod, decorated in 1338 the now lost church of the Entry into Jerusalem, commissioned by Archbishop Basil. The Palaiologan style was characterized by tall, elegant, slender figures with small heads and intricately fluttering drapery; the frescoes of about 1360 in the church of St. Michael of the Skovorodsky Monastery in Novgorod are vivid instances of Palaiologan art.

Greek influence must have been apparent in Muscovite art as well; the metropolitan Theognostes, a Greek from Constantinople imported Greek artists to paint the court church of the Mother of God in 1344, and the Chronicles refer to Greek and Greek-trained painters, as well as Greek icons, in Moscow; but not until the late fourteenth century does the artistic evidence support the literary.

During the late fourteenth and early fifteenth centuries, two great artists shaped the course of art in Russia. One was a Greek, Theophanes (Feofan Grek), who traveled from Constantinople to Novgorod, where he was working in 1378; later he was in Moscow and, from 1395 on, employed by the court. The other was a Russian, Andrei Rublev, first mentioned in literary sources around 1400. From the existing works of art that can be attributed to Theophanes, the magnitude of his gifts is obvious. He might have influenced Rublev, for the two worked together in 1405 in the cathedral of the Annunciation in the Moscow Kremlin. But even if Rublev was by then a mature artist who had little to learn from Theophanes, the Greek painter represented the culmination of Byzantine art in Russia, which Rublev was to transform into a purely Russian art.

Theophanes was described in a letter written by a Russian monk, Epiphanius the Wise, in 1415, as a scholar and philosopher as well as a versatile and gifted painter skilled at human figures and panoramic murals. According to Epiphanius, Theophanes worked freely without using models; he was to be seen "walking to and fro, talking with visitors and pondering wise and lofty thoughts in his mind." His versatility, education, and manner of working would have been at home in Italy, but he must have been a most unusual figure in Russia, where the artist was often a devout and humble monk.

Christ Pantokrator. Detail from the fresco by Theophanes the Greek in the dome of the church of the Transfiguration, Novgorod, 1378. PHOTO: TASS FROM SOVFOTO

Theophanes' preserved frescoes are in Novgorod, in the small church of the Transfiguration, commissioned by a boyar, built in 1374, and painted in 1378. The fresco of Christ and the scene of the Old Testament Trinity symbolize the height of Palaiologan style and show the artist's ability to paint freely and spontaneously. Loosely brushed in, these frescoes seem to bring the worshiper face to face with a miracle—the vision of Christ hovering overhead, or the appearance of angels to Abraham and Sarah in anticipation of the manifestation of the Trinity in the New Testament. Theophanes' manner has an emotional intensity that might have been influenced by hesychasm, a religious movement in the Byzantine world. But his frescoes also reflect the artist's great intelligence and genius, as well as his sophistication. His icons are similarly expressive, such as the large painting of the Mother of God from the Deesis tier of the iconostasis in the Annunciation Cathedral of the Moscow Kremlin, where Theophanes was employed in 1405. Here the full-length, aristocratic figure of the Virgin is emotionally subdued; all feeling is concentrated in the supplicating gesture of her hands, which epitomize her pity and concern for sinful man. While most of the original surface has disappeared, the silvery blue highlights typical of Theophanes' palette are still visible.

The iconostasis, it should be noted, seems to have developed about this time, and perhaps partly under Theophanes' influence, into the elaborate division between the sanctuary and the nave of the church. George Fedotov has connected this structure with a new emphasis in religious practice resulting from the Mongol invasion, when the worshiper was frequently cut off from church ritual. At any rate, the complex architectural framework into which icons were fitted came into use from the fourteenth century on, and the iconostasis in time supplemented or superseded the fresco decoration in churches. Instead of, or in addition to, the paintings on the curving walls of the church,

RUSSIAN ART

Icon of Christ from the Zvenigorod Deesis, early 15th century, probably by Andrei Rublev. State Tretyakov Gallery, Moscow, inv. no. 12863. PHOTO: NOVOSTI FROM SOVFOTO

the worshiper's gaze was focused on the high, flat, shimmering iconostasis arranged in three, four, or five ranks. While the religious symbolism of the iconostasis was derived from that of the monumental frescoes, the aesthetic impact was quite different, and the worshiper was no longer able to see all aspects of the ritual.

Andrei Rublev was a monk at the Trinity–St. Sergius Monastery near Moscow, founded by St. Sergius of Radonezh. Rublev worked in and around Moscow, on princely and church commissions, as a painter of frescoes and icons. His frescoes of the Last Judgment, in the Dormition Cathedral at Vladimir, were part of the redecoration of that church ordered by the Muscovite ruler in 1408. Several years earlier, in 1405, Rublev had been employed at the Annunciation Cathedral in the Moscow Kremlin, where Theophanes was the chief artist. In both churches, Rublev worked together with Daniil Chernyi (Chorny), a monk and friend; the two collaborated again some years later when they were called to decorate the Trinity Cathedral in the Trinity–St. Sergius Monastery. Many icons have been attributed to Rublev on the basis of style and literary evidence, and still more have been lost through the centuries. The poorly preserved icons from the so-called Zvenigorod Deesis, discovered in Zvenigorod in 1918, were probably painted by Rublev. The icon of Christ from this group, if contrasted to the fresco of Christ by Theophanes in the Transfiguration in Novgorod, demonstrates the strength and purity of Rublev's artistic vision. He was quite familiar with the latest trends in Byzantine art, for the proportions of his Christ, with the small head, swelling neck muscles, and curve of the hair, resemble Palaiologan examples. But unlike Theophanes' Christ, who seems to have coalesced momentarily into visible and material human form, Rublev's Christ is tranquil, serene, and almost but not quite tangible, indeed almost unearthly. This Christ appears to be "here," but—like a dream image—he is a fleeting vision belonging more to the world of the spirit than to the world of the flesh. Rublev's Christ is thoroughly Russian rather than Byzantine Greek, and is perhaps the manifestation of the artist's personal religious experience.

Rublev's most famous icon is his Old Testament Trinity, variously dated 1411 or 1422–1427, and created for the Trinity Cathedral in the Trinity–St. Sergius Monastery. This theme must have received special attention by Rublev, since it was a particular devotion of St. Sergius (*d. ca.* 1320), who had founded the monastery. Sergius was a simple and saintly monk who had experienced visions of the Trinity, and Rublev must have attempted in his icon to symbolize Sergius' belief as well as his vision of the presence of God in all Persons of the Trinity. While following the traditional model for this theme of the miraculous appearance of three angels to Abraham and Sarah, Rublev simplified and clarified every aspect of composition and color until the icon had become a clear symbol of the Trinity. In his version of this theme, Theophanes had concentrated upon the miraculous vision of the Old Testament event, whereas Rublev emphasized the three Persons of the Trinity, whom he distinguished through gesture and color. Unlike Theophanes' silvery tints, Rublev used strong yet delicate tones. His famous blue, rather than traditional white, colored the angels' robes, to suggest the heavenly nature of the three as well as their unity. (See illustration at "Rublev, Andrei.")

Many details of Rublev's life have yet to be

RUSSIAN ART

The Annunciation. Icon from the Trinity–St. Sergius Monastery, Zagorsk. Moscow school, late 14th century. STATE TRETYAKOV GALLERY, MOSCOW

The Four Saints: Paraskeve (Anastasia?), Gregory of Nazianzus, John Chrysostom, and Basil the Great. Pskov school, late 14th century. State Tretyakov Gallery, Moscow. PHOTO: NOVOSTI FROM SOVFOTO

discovered. To judge from his art, Rublev was deeply religious, contemplative, and sensitive to color and form. His works became a standard for later Russian painters, particularly when, in the reign of Ivan IV the Terrible, the Stoglav or Council of One Hundred Chapters set forth principles to be followed in the production of icons. Artists were admonished to reproduce the icons of Rublev and other ancient models. Duplicate versions of the Old Testament Trinity continued to be made through the seventeenth century.

The period when Rublev was active, the late fourteenth and early fifteenth centuries, was the acme of Russian icon painting; various schools developed in different cities of Russia. An icon of the Annunciation, Moscow School, late fourteenth century, shows the elegant and complex composition typical of Palaiologan examples of this theme, which attempt to capture a specific instant in the holy event. On the other hand, Novgorod icons of this time are simpler, stronger, and more graphic than those of Moscow; Novgorod artists favored red instead of gold for the backgrounds. A famous icon of St. George, Novgorod School, late fourteenth century, depicts the popular Russian saint astride a gleaming white horse against a bright red background. Icons of Pskov were typically dark and rich in color, and the figures were usually shown with brooding expressions, as can be seen on a panel with four saints from this period. All these icons show the influence of Palaiologan art, albeit translated into a native idiom, but they also demonstrate local traditions and tastes which defined the artistic workshops in each city of Russia.

From the middle of the fifteenth century on, the history of Russian art is largely the history of Moscow, which eventually encompassed all of Russia. Muscovite art of the later fifteenth century was a courtly art, aristocratic in style, and meant to serve the few rather than the many. Iconography often grew complex and thus remote from the comprehension of the ordinary worshiper. After the fall of Constantinople in 1453, and during the reign of Ivan III (1462–1505), Moscow came

RUSSIAN ART

to be thought of as the Third Rome, the heir to the Byzantine tradition. At the same time, the main source of artistic inspiration—the Byzantine world—was largely lost to Russia after the former's conquest by the Turks; other sources had to be discovered. These sources were sometimes native and sometimes foreign. Although Ivan III employed Italian architects, the full impact of the Renaissance was never felt in Russia. Muscovite art of the late fifteenth through seventeenth centuries was aesthetically rather sterile but philosophically interesting; apparently there was no substitute for the crucial role that contact with the Byzantine court had played in Russian culture.

The reinterpretation of Russian medieval art, based on new political and religious ideas, began under Ivan III and was elaborated by later czars during the sixteenth and seventeenth centuries. A new artistic attitude was first presented in the Annunciation Cathedral in the Moscow Kremlin, where the frescoes of Ivan III are in the process of being uncovered. Along with conventional subjects, secular portraits and themes from Revelation appear. The intention of this new program of decoration seems to have been to express the new importance of the Russian czar as political and religious ruler, with a sacred line of descent from earlier Russian and Byzantine monarchs. This idea was more fully developed during the next two centuries.

Even peripheral churches, like the church of the Nativity of the Mother of God, in the St. Therapont (Ferapontov) Monastery in northern Russia, might be adorned in courtly Muscovite fashion; despite its remoteness, this monastery was a place of retreat for important Muscovites, and Dionysios the Greek (*ca.* 1440/1450–1505), the most famous Muscovite artist of the time, was responsible for the decoration of the church. The frescoes here are peopled with aristocratic, elegant, and richly garbed figures; new and complex iconographic themes are introduced. Dionysios' icons, and those of other Muscovite artists of the later fifteenth century, are also complex in iconography and frequently decorative. While Rublev's icons were very familiar to these painters, his simple and deep religiosity was foreign to them. The icons of the later fifteenth century are nervous and perturbed in their emotional impact, or spiritually empty.

The medieval style continued to be the Russian form of expression until Peter the Great forcibly introduced Western art into the country at the beginning of the eighteenth century—just as Byzantine art had once been transplanted into Russian soil. The role of this long, uninterrupted medieval tradition played an important part in shaping basic concepts of art in Russia, although the influence of medieval art on later periods is often underestimated or ignored by scholars. Icons were made until the Revolution, and even later, folk painters, like those of Palekh, preserved many icon-painting traditions in their depictions of secular folk themes. More subtle influences shaped the very manner in which art was conceived of in Russia, a manner appropriate for religious art but transferred to secular art. For instance, there was often a disinterest in the aesthetic aspects of art alone, because it was believed that art should serve some purpose beyond mere pleasure. This belief is most obvious in the emergence of realism during the later nineteenth century but surfaced again during revolutionary times. Symbolism was an acceptable trait of Russian art, symbolism in the sense that a painted image could be understood to refer to a nonvisible reality, as in icons. The fanaticism with which artistic theories were developed and defended in Russia, particularly during the years before and after the Revolution, borders on religious fervor, and the most modern painters, like Kazimir Malevich (*d.* 1935), can be considered the last of the icon painters, whose religious symbols have been stripped of all reference except for their color and form. Finally, the arts in Russia were always closely interrelated—a phenomenon often noted by scholars but perhaps not sufficiently understood as a remnant of the medieval attitude that all the arts—painting, architecture, sculpture, literature, and music—exist to serve God.

BIBLIOGRAPHY

The most thorough survey of medieval art in Russia, with an extensive bibliography, was written in Russian (but also published in German): Igor E. Grabar *et al.*, eds., *Istoria russkogo iskusstva,* 13 vols. in 16 (1953–).

See also Alexsandr Anisimov, *Our Lady of Vladimir,* N. G. Yaschwill and T. N. Rodzianko, trans. (1928); Samuel H. Cross and Olgerd P. Sherbowitz-Wetzor, *The Russian Primary Chronicle: Laurentian Text* (1953); Albert S. Cook, "Ibn Fadlan's Account of Scandinavian Merchants on the Volga in 922," in *Journal of English and Germanic Philology,* 22 (1923); George P. Fedotov, *The Russian Religious Mind,* 2 vols. (1946–1966); George H. Hamilton, *The Art and Architecture of Russia,* 2nd ed. (1975); Robert Holtzman, ed., "Thietmari Merseburgensis Episcopi Chronicon," in *Monumenta Ger-*

maniae historica: Scriptores, IX (1935); Victor N. Lazarev and Otto Demus, *U.S.S.R.: Early Russian Icons* (1958); Victor N. Lazarev, *Feofan Grek i iego shkola* (1961), *Andrei Rublov i iego shkola* (1966), *Old Russian Murals and Mosaics,* Nancy Dunn, trans. (1966), and *Russkaia srednevekovaia zhivopis* (1970); Robert Mitchell and Nevill Forbes, trans., *The Chronicle of Novgorod: 1016–1471* (1914); Aleksandr L. Mongait, *Archaeology in the U.S.S.R.,* M. W. Thompson, trans. (1961); Leonid Ouspensky and Vladimir Lossky, *The Meaning of Icons* (1969); Arthur Voyce, *The Art and Architecture of Medieval Russia* (1967).

ANN E. FARKAS

[See also **Byzantine Art; Byzantine Church; Deesis; Dionysios the Greek; Hesychasm; Hosios Lukas; Iconostasis; Icons, Manufacture of; Icons, Russian; Kievan Rus; Moscow Kremlin, Art and Architecture; Novgorod; Palaiologoi; Pecherskaya Lavra; Peter, Master; Prokhor of Gorodets; Rublev, Andrei; Theophanes the Greek; Thietmar von Merseburg.**]

RUSSIAN ORTHODOX CHURCH. Numerically the largest branch of Eastern Orthodox Christianity, established as an ecclesiastical province of the patriarchate of Constantinople in 988/989, and "autocephalous" (administratively independent) since 1448.

ORIGINS

Christian missionaries from both East and West were active among the Russians (Greek: hoi Rhōs; Slavic: Rus) since the ninth century. The original Russian state (Greek: Rhōsla; Latin: Russia) was centered in the cities of Kiev and Novgorod and ruled by a dynasty of Varangian, or Scandinavian, origin, but the population was East Slavic. The presence of a bishop, sent from Byzantium, among the Russians is signaled as early as 867. The gradual penetration of Christianity made possible the conversion of Princess Olga, regent of the Kievan state. Olga accepted baptism in 957 and was then received at the court of Constantinople. Her grandson, Prince Vladimir, having hesitated between several religious options (Islam, Judaism, Western Christianity)—as described in a famous account of the Russian Primary Chronicle—chose Byzantine Christianity and made it, in 989, the official religion of the state. He also married the sister of Byzantine emperor Basil II.

As in the case of similar conversions of barbarian nations in the early Middle Ages, the motivation was not only religious but also cultural and political. The Russian Chronicle contains a candid account of the amazement felt by Vladimir's envoys when they visited the cathedral of St. Sophia in Constantinople and acknowledged—both aesthetically and intellectually—the spiritual superiority of Byzantine Christian civilization over their ancestral paganism.

Under Vladimir's son, Prince Yaroslav (1036–1054), Kiev developed into a new center of Slavic Christianity. The building of a cathedral dedicated to St. Sophia (the Wisdom of God) by Yaroslav, and the adoption by the newly founded Monastery of the Caves (Pecherskaya Lavra) of the Studite monastic rule, clearly indicate that the young Russian church was following the Byzantine model in all essentials. The mosaic decoration of the new cathedral—still preserved today—was performed by Greek masters and presents one of the best examples of eleventh-century purely Byzantine art.

The establishment of Christianity in Russia was greatly facilitated by the already existing Slavonic translations of Scriptures and liturgical texts. These translations, initiated by Sts. Cyril and Methodios during their Moravian mission (863), had been preserved and developed in Bulgaria. They were made available to the Russians, particularly from Ochrid, the major center of Slavic Christian civilization in the late tenth century. Original ecclesiastical literature soon also appeared in Kiev. Metropolitan Hilarion (Ilarion), who in 1051 became the first native head of the church, is the author of a famous *Sermon on Law and Grace.* He compared the baptism of Russia by Vladimir with the conversion of Emperor Constantine in the fourth century. Also going back to the eleventh century are the vitae of Sts. Boris and Gleb, two sons of Vladimir, assassinated by their brother Svyatopolk and venerated as martyrs for Christian nonviolence. The twelfth and thirteenth centuries witnessed the appearance of a developed local literature, which includes such documents as sermons and prayers by Cyril, bishop of Turov, and the hagiographical texts included in the Primary Chronicle, and the *Paterikon* (a collection of monastic lives) of the Kievan Monastery of the Caves.

The existence of such writings by local ecclesiastics, composed in the Slavic language, indicates the rapid acceptance among educated Russians not only of Christianity itself, but also of basic cultural patterns inspired by the Byzantine legacy. However,

RUSSIAN ORTHODOX CHURCH

there is also ample evidence of pagan survivals in wide provincial areas, where the influence of the church could initially be only quite superficial.

The earliest canonical structure of the church in Russia has been the subject of some controversy. The first solid evidence exists only for the year 1039, when a Greek metropolitan, Theopemptus, arrived in Kiev. The absence of sources for the period 989–1039 has led some historians to speculate about a possible canonical dependence of Kiev upon Rome (Baumgarten), or Ochrid (Priselkov). Today scholars believe that the personal ties between Vladimir and the Byzantine imperial house and the consistent loyalty to Constantinople shown in the Chronicle make it impossible to envisage that the early Russian church could pay canonical allegiance to any center other than Byzantium. The absence of a metropolitan in Kiev before 1039 is easily understandable: Russia was seen by the Byzantine patriarchate as a vast mission field ministered to by bishops directly dependent upon the patriarch, without the permanent structure of a regional primacy.

After 1039, however, the existence of a "metropolitanate of Kiev and all the Rus" can be solidly ascertained. The establishment of a regional metropolitan, invested with the task of consecrating all the local bishops, implied a degree of autonomy. However, Byzantium held a firm administrative grip on the young church. With only a few exceptions, the primate was always a Greek, appointed from Constantinople. Greek ecclesiastics occasionally occupied some positions not only in the capital but also in the provinces. The two well-known exceptions to the rule were the Russian metropolitan Hilarion, who occupied the see of Kiev for a brief period under Yaroslav (1051), and Clement Smolyatich (1147–1155), elected metropolitan under the pressure of the grand prince Izyaslav and considered a schismatic by Constantinople.

Throughout the eleventh and twelfth centuries the major provincial cities of the decentralized Kievan state saw the establishment of dioceses and grew into important ecclesiastical centers. Originally inspired by Byzantine architecture, cathedral-building became a local focus of creative activity: St. Sophia in Novgorod (1045–1052), Transfiguration in Chernigov (*ca.* 1036), St. Sophia in Polotsk (1044–1066) are only some of the most eminent examples of the earliest period. The settling of what was then northeastern Russia and the establishment of new cities saw the building in Vladimir of the Dormition Cathedral (1158–1189) and St. Dimitri (1194–1197), of the Dormition Cathedral in Rostov (1162), as well as such Architectural jewels as the church of the Pokrov-on-the-Nerl, a princely palace chapel (1165). This early Russian architecture, though inspired by Byzantine models, shows great local originality.

By the thirteenth century there existed in Russia two groups of dioceses, one group located to the west and the other to the northeast of Kiev. The western region (frequently identified in Byzantine documents as Little Russia) included the dioceses of Halich, Vladimir-in-Volhynia, Peremyshl, Lutsk, Turov, and Kholm. The northeastern group, gradually developing throughout the fourteenth century and identified as Great Russia, was composed of the dioceses of Novgorod, Vladimir-on-the-Klyazma, Rostov, Suzdal, Ryazan, Tver, Kolomna, and Perm. In addition, the three dioceses of Chernigov, Polotsk, and Smolensk were shifting between the two groups. The dioceses of Pereyaslavl, Belgorod, and Yuryev existed only intermittently. A new diocese, that of Sarai, was established in the fourteenth century in the residence of the Tatar khan on the Volga River. The incumbents of all these dioceses were consecrated by the metropolitan of Kiev.

THE MONGOL INVASION AND DIVISIONS IN THE METROPOLITANATE

The Mongol, or Tatar, conquest of 1237–1242 transformed Russia into a western province of an Asian empire with its capital in Karakorum, Mongolia. The province, also known as khanate of Kipchak, was administered by a subordinate Mongol khan residing in Sarai. Kiev was sacked in 1240 and ceased, for a century, to be an urban center of any importance. To replace the Greek metropolitan of Kiev, who disappeared in the catastrophe of 1240, Grand Prince Daniel of Galicia (in whose principality Mongol control was weak) nominated a Russian, Cyril, who, in 1248–1249, received canonical confirmation from the patriarchate.

This appointment of a native to the position of head of the Russian church was probably facilitated by the fact that Constantinople was, since 1204, under Latin occupation, and the patriarchate, exiled in Nicaea, had neither the personnel nor the power to impose a Greek candidate, as was done continuously in the past.

One of the aspects of the Mongol occupation of Russia was its tolerance toward all religions and, particularly, the Orthodox church. While Russian princes needed the formal approval of the khan in assuming their positions and were liable to heavy taxes and other forms of exaction, the church was formally tax-exempt, which contributed greatly to its growing economic prosperity. Furthermore, the metropolitan of Kiev and all the Rus remained an appointee of Byzantium (the imperial center and the patriarchate returned to Constantinople in 1261)—a minor political power but strategically located and entertaining good relations with the Mongols. Thus, the head of the Russian church could not only enjoy a form of diplomatic immunity but even act as a permanent ambassador of the Byzantine imperial government in Mongol-controlled territories. Even as the western parts of the former Kievan realm achieved independence from the Mongols (Galicia-Volhynia), or fell under the control of the grand principality of Lithuania, and later Poland, the church remained the single administrative structure that symbolized, and partially realized, the unity of the whole of Russia.

The acceptable modus vivendi achieved by the church within the borders of the Mongol Empire stands in sharp contrast with the growing animosity felt by Eastern Christians toward the West. Indeed, the sack of Constantinople by the crusaders (1204) was soon followed by successive invasions of the Novgorod territories in northwestern Russia by crusading Swedes and Teutonic Knights, aiming at integrating pagans—but also Orthodox Russians—into Latin Christendom. Both were repelled by Alexander Nevsky, prince of Novgorod (1240–1242). Significantly, that prince pursued a policy of appeasement toward the religiously tolerant Mongols and eventually became grand prince of Vladimir-on-the-Klyazma with Mongol approval. The fact that Alexander was seen not only as a national hero but also a saint of the Orthodox church illustrates the popular anti-Latin trend provoked in both Greek and Slavic lands by the crusades, making eventual reconciliation between East and West much more difficult.

Throughout the thirteenth and the fourteenth century the Byzantine patriarchate remained fully conscious of the importance of its huge northernmost province of Russia. In a flexible but consistent manner, it succeeded in preserving its administrative control in the midst of troubled times. Flexibility was shown particularly in the alternation of Greek and Russian appointees to the see of Kiev, an alternation that was broken only at the end of the fourteenth century for reasons explained below. Here is a list of metropolitans for the period:

Joseph, a Greek (1237–1240)
Cyril, a Russian (1242–1281)
Maxim, a Greek (1283–1305)
Peter, a Russian (1308–1326)
Theognostos (Feognost), a Greek (1328–1353)
Alexis, a Russian (1354–1378)
Cyprian, a Bulgarian (1375–1406)
Photios, a Greek (1408–1431)
Isidore, a Greek (1436–1441)

While preserving the title of Kiev, the metropolitans rarely kept residence there for any significant length of time. Already Cyril had transferred the center of his activities to the northeast, in the grand principality of Vladimir, headed by Alexander Nevsky. His Greek successor, Maxim, traveled personally to Sarai, or Golden Horde, residence of the khan, and died in Vladimir (1305). However, it was the particular lot of Peter—originally a nominee of the prince of Galicia—to establish his permanent residence in the heretofore insignificant city of Moscow, in the principality of Vladimir. After Peter's death Moscow became the ecclesiastical—and, soon, political—capital of Russia. Metropolitan Alexis would even assume temporarily the regency of the principality.

The shift of the metropolitan's residence—in spite of the fact that he was preserving the traditional title of metropolitan of Kiev—led to understandable discontent in the ecclesiastically underadministered southwestern principalities. Attempts were made from 1303 to create a separate metropolitanate of Galicia. These attempts received episodic support from Constantinople. Other, more significant attempts were made by the powerful grand prince of Lithuania, Olgerd (1345–1377), a fierce competitor of Moscow for political leadership in the former Kievan realm. Resenting the pro-Muscovite policies of metropolitan Alexis, Olgerd succeeded in convincing the authorities of Constantinople to appoint a separate metropolitan of the Lithuanians, Roman (1355–1362), who, once in Russia, claimed the see of Kiev. Eventually, however—particularly under the auspices of the patriarch of Constantinople, Philotheos (1364–1376)—the metropolitanate was reunited again: Metropolitan Alexis showed himself to be not only a national leader but also a shrewd diplomat, traveling repeatedly to the Golden Horde and even healing Taidula, the widow of Khan Ubek.

After the death of Alexis (1378), the metropolitanate went through a period of divisions and major troubles. Patriarch Philotheos, adopting since 1370 a policy of evenhandedness between Lithuania and Moscow, appointed a Bulgarian monk, Cyprian, to succeed Alexis, even before the latter's death (1376). Feared in Moscow as a pro-Lithuanian agent, Cyprian was repeatedly prevented from occupying his see. The Muscovite government pushed its own candidates for a new metropolitanate of Great Russia (Mityai, then Pimen), separate from Kiev. However, the cause of Cyprian, which implied the permanence of a single metropolitanate of Kiev and all Russia, including both Muscovite and Lithuanian-held territories, eventually triumphed (1389), and he occupied his see in Moscow.

Meanwhile, major shifts on the political map of Eastern Europe were taking place. In 1380, at the Battle of Kulikovo, the Muscovites succeeded in shaking Mongol control. In 1386, Jagiełło (Jogiala), son of Olgerd and grand prince of Lithuania, married Jadwiga of Poland, obtaining the Polish crown for himself, reuniting under it both Poland and Lithuania, and personally converting to Roman Catholicism. The southern and western principalities of the old Kievan realm, although remaining Orthodox in the vast majority of their population, would henceforth find themselves within the confines of a Western-oriented monarchy. It was inevitable that they would develop different cultural and national forms. Moscow alone remained as the bulwark of Byzantine Orthodoxy in Eastern Europe.

Following the death of the Greek metropolitan Photios (1431), the successor appointed by Constantinople was another Greek, Isidore. The reason for this break in the alternation between Greek and Russian metropolitans was due to the active preparations for a council of union with the Western church. The Constantinopolitan authorities imposed upon the reluctant Russians a committed supporter of the plan. Isidore indeed became an active participant in the Council of Ferrara-Florence (1438–1439) and a signatory of its decree. He was promoted to the rank of cardinal by Pope Eugenius IV. However, upon his return to Moscow in 1441 he was first interned, then allowed to escape to the West.

In 1448 Russian bishops elected a new metropolitan, Jonas (Iona), without referring to Constantinople. Soon after these events, Byzantium fell to the Turks (1453), and the Muscovite ecclesiastical independence became de facto permanent. In Polish-held Kiev, another metropolitan "of all Russia," Gregory Bolgarin, was appointed in 1458 by the Uniat ex-patriarch, now a refugee in Rome. In 1470, however, Gregory, abandoning the Roman communion, affiliated himself with the Orthodox patriarchate of Constantinople. The latter, under Turkish rule, had rejected all forms of union with Rome. Thus, by the end of the fifteenth century, there were two Orthodox metropolitans of all Russia, in Muscovite and in Polish-held territories. Both Jonas and Gregory claimed the title of Kiev. However, Jonas' successor, Theodosius, was appointed metropolitan of all Russia, without the title of Kiev, thus implicitly renouncing claims over Little Russia, which, in later centuries, increasingly developed its own Ukrainian identity.

The historical fate of the two metropolitanates presents quite a contrast. The growth of Muscovy into a vast empire would lead to the assumption by the metropolitan of Moscow of the title of patriarch. The title would be granted to him by the patriarch of Constantinople himself, visiting Moscow in 1589. Meanwhile, in 1596, the metropolitan of Kiev would accept union with Rome at the council of Brest-Litovsk. Since the majority of the population opposed the union, major religious strife would become one of the tragic aspects of Ukrainian history.

SPIRITUAL AND CULTURAL TRENDS

Following the pattern adopted by Byzantine missions elsewhere, Christianity was taught to the Russians on the basis of literal translations of Greek texts—Scripture, liturgy, canon law, patristic literature—into Slavic. In contrast to the Western barbarian nations, converted to Latin Christianity, Russians—and other Eastern Slavs—were not required to learn a classical language. As a result, they had no access to texts inherited from the civilization of antiquity, but were exposed to ecclesiastical literature almost exclusively. The system had the major advantage of encouraging the rapid indigenization of the Christian faith through worship in an understandable language, but the refinements of Byzantine theology and the literary sophistication of the Greek ecclesiastical hymnography were frequently lost in the translations.

In spite of these limitations, Russian Orthodoxy can only be seen as a continued development of traditions originating in Byzantium. This element of continuity was enhanced by a characteristically nervous concern of the medieval Russians to preserve the very letter of the texts received "from the Greeks." This concern would acquire a particular significance in Muscovy, after the fall of Constantinople, when the Russians would become self-conscious of their new role as sole guardians of Orthodoxy, and it would lead to crisis in the sixteenth century and schism in the seventeenth: the books were in obvious need of corrections, but the church possessed no criteria by which the corrections could be seen as accurate.

The two areas where medieval Russians were able to develop creatively the traditions of Christian Byzantium were monastic spirituality and religious art.

The founders of Kievan monasticism had already introduced those traditions in Russia in the eleventh century: St. Anthony brought from Mt. Athos the principles of anchoritic life, while St. Theodosius introduced in the Monastery of the Caves in Kiev the Constantinopolitan cenobitic Rule of St. Theodor of Studios. In northern Russia St. Sergius of Radonezh (*ca.* 1314–1392) initiated a movement inspired by the spirituality of the desert (known in the East as hesychasm), but also comparable, in its activism and energy, with the Cistercian movement in the West. St. Sergius belonged to a milieu interested in books, theology, and contacts with Byzantium. According to his vita, while still in his boyhood he miraculously learned how to read. Having chosen to retire to the forest for permanent prayer, he dedicated his first chapel to the Trinity. Later, he received, directly from the patriarch of Constantinople, a recommendation to establish a monastic community. The result was not only the foundation of his central monastery, Holy Trinity, but also that of dozens of other communities, headed by Sergius' disciples. These monastic centers, built in the forests, soon attracted peasant villagers and thus began the economic development of the Russian north. St. Sergius himself became a major national figure. While refusing the rank of metropolitan (1378), he blessed the army of Grand Prince Dmitri before his successful battle against the Mongols (1380).

In the circle of Sergius' friends, a particular place belongs to a younger contemporary, St. Stephen of Perm (1340–1396). Having learned Greek in Rostov—where Greek traditions were strong and where the episcopal see was presumably occupied by a Greek—Stephen became a missionary to the Zyrians, a Finnish people living in the region of Perm. Following the example of Byzantine missionaries, he invented a Zyrian alphabet, translated scriptural and liturgical texts from the Greek, and, eventually, became the first bishop of Perm. As the single major erudite of his time, he was also called to publish a theological refutation of the Strigolniki, an anti-institutional sect, possibly related to the Bogomils and Western Cathars.

Close to the circle of St. Sergius, one finds also the two major creators of the artistic revival which, in Russia, followed patterns received from Byzantium but which also proved, by itself, to be one of the best in the late Middle Ages: Theophanes the Greek, and his Russian pupil, Andrei Rublev. The career of Theophanes started in Constantinople, but his finest frescoes in Novgorod and Moscow are the only ones preserved. Rublev, a monk at St. Sergius' monastery, is the creator of the famous icon of the Trinity and of other great works preserved at his monastery as well as in Moscow and Vladimir.

The monastic movement initiated by St. Sergius, and also the development of Muscovy into a stable nation-state, inevitably implied that, as in all medieval societies, the church would be a rich landowner. Already tax-exempt during the Mongol period, the church continued to receive donations, particularly to assure its prayers for the departed. On the other hand, canon law prohibited the alienation of church lands, since they were "given to God." The moral and social problems created by ecclesiastical and, particularly, monastic wealth were the occasion for a fierce debate between two schools of thought, both inspired by St. Sergius. The debate involved two understandings of the church's role in society.

On the one hand, a leader of the monastic hermitages located in the far north, "beyond the Volga," St. Nil Sorsky (1433–1508), defended monastic poverty. A disciple of the Byzantine hesychasts, he considered that the only purpose of monasticism was in "mental prayer" and a purely spiritual witness to society. Wealth, and particularly the use of servile labor, was, in his opinion, incompatible with the monastic state. Nil also opposed formal canonical rigorism in clerical discipline and promoted charity in dealing with heretics (Strigolniki, and later Judaizers). His opponent, St. Joseph of Volotsk (1439/1440–1515), defended the legitimacy of ecclesiastical and monastic wealth on the ground that the church was to maintain an active role in society: without independent revenues, it could not run schools, hospitals, and hospices. Joseph's concepts included the conviction that Muscovy, following the Byzantine example, would remain a Christian medieval society, in which the church would occupy a central position. Some representatives of his circle were also inspired by the Western models of a strong, independent church and an inquisitorial attitude toward heretics.

In a series of councils meeting in the early sixteenth century, the Josephite view triumphed. It also received the initial support of the grand princes, who trusted the political loyalty of Joseph's disciples. Josephite clergy presided over the building-up of a Russian national church, which under Metropolitan Makarii (1542–1563) canonized a great number of Russain saints and held, in 1551, a general council known as the Council of One Hundred Chapters, or Stoglav, at which disciplinary and liturgical rules were standardized.

CHURCH AND STATE

From Byzantium, the Orthodox Russians received not only the Christian faith but also the principles of a political ideology: the Christian version of the Roman imperium. As defined since the Roman emperors Constantine and Justinian, this ideology implied an alliance between the ideally universal Roman Empire (with its center now transferred to the New Rome, Constantinople) and a universal Orthodox church. The system was believed to have been established by God himself, with both the empire and the church fulfilling their respective and inseparable functions in his name. Justinian had labeled it as "symphony" between the empire and the priesthood. Improperly characterized as caesaropapism by many historians, this symphony did not imply absolute imperial authority in matters of faith (such matters could only be settled through difficult conciliar procedures, as illustrated by the numerous doctrinal disputes, lasting centuries), but presupposed imperial responsibility for all organizational aspects of the church and active participation of the emperor in the task of maintaining and spreading the true Christian faith.

As the empire was gradually reduced in size and political influence, nation-states replaced the imperial structure. However, during the medieval period, these states always gave token allegiance to the idea that the New Rome was the center of the Christian world. Occasionally, Bulgarian and Serbian rulers assumed themselves the title of emperor of the Romans. The Russians were never politically a part of the empire but considered themselves—as did the other Orthodox Slavs—a part of what has been called the Byzantine Commonwealth. The Russian church remained loyal to the jurisdiction of the patriarch of Constantinople until 1448, whereas Bulgarians and Serbs had created their independent patriarchates much earlier. The name of the emperor of Constantinople was commemorated in Russian churches and, as late as 1393, the patriarch of Constantinople demanded that such commemoration not be interrupted, because the emperor was "the autocrator of the Romans, that is, of all Christians."

During the early Kievan period and the time of Mongol occupation, the Greek metropolitan of all Russia, appointed by the Byzantine emperor and patriarch, was largely independent of local Russian princely politics and can probably be considered the most powerful personality of the land. His position changed once he began to be chosen by the Russians themselves (1448). As a national religious leader he became very dependent upon the power of the Muscovite grand prince. Yet the latter, even after the disappearance of the Greek empire, never assumed the title of Roman emperor. Although in 1472 Ivan III married the niece of the last Byzantine emperor and signs of Byzantine kingship began to be used by the Muscovite rulers, when Ivan IV was crowned in the next century, he took the title only of "czar of all the Rus."

It is then that, among Josephite clergy, Moscow began to be designated as the Third Rome, the last and ultimate refuge of the Orthodox empire. The concept was never officially endorsed by either state or church. Indeed, by the sixteenth century, the idea of a world Christian empire had become anachronistic. The Middle Ages were over and Muscovy had no possibility or intention to follow medieval Byzantine or Roman patterns in every respect. In terms of the relations between state and church, the Byzantine "symphony" was abandoned. Whereas the Byzantine emperor was at least in principle subject to ecclesiastical law, the Russian czars acted with total arbitrariness. The ideology of the Third Rome was occasionally used by them to spur nationalistic messianism, but the spiritual content of the Eastern Christian tradition was really preserved not in political institutions but rather in monastic retreats, by the remaining disciples of Nil Sorsky. It is that tradition which eventually proved to be, in the modern age, the most valid Christian witness in the midst of the secularized Russian society.

BIBLIOGRAPHY

The most comprehensive treatment of the Russian church is Evgenii E. Golubinskii, *Istoriya Russkoi tserkvi,* 2 vols. in 4 and an atlas (1901–1917); Anton V. Kartashev, *Ocherki po istorii Russkoi tserkvi,* 2 vols. (1959); and Makarii, Metropolitan of Moscow, *Istoriya Russkoi tserkvi,* 3rd ed., 12 vols. (1883–1903). For a Roman Catholic perspective, see Albert M. Amman, *Abriss der ostslawischen Kirchengeschichte* (1950). General introductions in English are Andrei N. Muravev, *A History of the Church of Russia,* R. W. Blackmore, trans. (1842); H. Y. Rayburn, *The Story of the Russian Church* (1924); and Nicolas Zernov, *The Russians and Their Church,* 3rd ed. (1964). For a cultural view of medieval Russia with particular sensitivity to religious problems, see the first part of James H. Billington, *The Icon and the Axe* (1966).

The best treatment of spirituality in medieval Russia is by Georgii P. Fedotov, *The Russian Religious Mind,* 2 vols. (1946–1966). See also Igor Smolitsch, *Russisches Mönchtum: Enthstehung, Entwicklung und Wesen* (1953).

For a vision of Russia against the general background of Byzantine foreign policy and missions, see Francis Dvornik, *Byzantine Missions to the Slavs* (1970); Franc Grivec, *Konstantin und Method, Lehrer der Slaven* (1960); and Dimitri Obolensky, *The Byzantine Commonwealth: Eastern Europe, 500–1453* (1971). A very thorough study of the church in the Kievan period is Andrzej Poppe, *Państwo i kościól na Rusi w XI wieku* (1968).

On the fourteenth century, see John Meyendorff, *Byzantium and the Rise of Russia: A Study of Byzantine-Russian Relations in the Fourteenth Century* (1981).

The history and the implications of the Muscovite religious ideology are discussed by many authors; see particularly Aleksandr S. Arkhangelsky, *Nil Sorsky i Vassian Patrikeev: Ikh literaturnye trudy i idei v Drevnei Rusi* (1882); Nataliya A. Kazakova and Yakov S. Lure, *Antifeodalnye ereticheskie dvizheniya na Rusi XIV nachala XVI veka* (1955); Fairy von Lilienfeld, *Nil Sorskij und seine Schriften* (1963); Vasilii Malinin, *Starets Eleazarova monastyra Filofey i ego polaniya* (1901); George A. Maloney, *Russian Hesychasm: The Spirituality of Nil Sorsky* (1973); William K. Medlin, *Moscow and East Rome: A Political Study of the Relations of Church and State in Muscovite Russia* (1952); John Meyendorff, "Une controverse sur le rôle social de l'église," in *Irénikon,* **28–29** (1955–1956); Hildegard Schaeder, *Moskau das dritte Rom,* 2nd ed. (1957); Alexandr A. Zimin and Yakov S. Lure, *Poslaniya Iosifa Volotskogo* (1959).

John Meyendorff

[See also **Byzantine Church; Caesaropapism; Cyril and Methodios, Sts.; Hesychasm; Kievan Rus; Metropolitan; Muscovy, Rise of; Nil Sorsky, St.; Ochrid; Pecherskaya Lavra; Philotheos; Rublev, Andrei; Russian Art; Russian Architecture; Sergius of Radonezh, St.; Theophanes the Greek.**]

RUTEBEUF, a thirteenth-century French poet, author of fifty-six extant pieces written from approximately 1248 to 1277. Little is known of his life other than his sufferings spoken of in his personal poems or *complaintes.* Although perhaps originally from Champagne, Rutebeuf lived most of his life in Paris. He authored one of the first French miracle plays and the first with the word "miracle" in its title, *Le Miracle de Théophile,* but also wrote for diverse audiences. Rutebeuf's works present a wide variety of noncourtly themes and genres, including hymns to the Virgin Mary, as well as fabliaux. In his satirical pieces the poet attacks the religious orders, especially the mendicants, while writing more kindly verses on Parisian university students. The poems on Rutebeuf's own suffering tend to be those most read in the twentieth century. Among medieval poets he is frequently compared to the fifteenth-century François Villon; among later poets, to the nineteenth-century Paul Verlaine.

BIBLIOGRAPHY

Sources. Rutebeuf, *Le miracle de Théophile,* Roger Dubuis, trans. (1978); *Oeuvres complètes de Rutebeuf, trouvère du XIIIe siècle,* Achille Jubinal, ed., 3 vols. (1874–1875); *Oeuvres complètes,* Edmond Faral and Julia Bastin, eds., 2 vols. (1959–1960); *Poèmes de l'infortune et poèmes de la croisade,* Jean Dufournet, ed. (1979); *Poésies traduites en français moderne,* Jean Dufournet, trans. (1977).

Studies. Germaine Lafeuille, *Rutebeuf* (1966); Nancy Freeman Regalado, *Poetic Patterns in Rutebeuf: A Study in Noncourtly Poetic Modes of the 13th Century* (1970).

Thomas E. Kelly

[See also **Drama, French; Fabliau and Comic Tales; Miracle Plays; Troubadour, Trouvère.**]

RUTILIUS CLAUDIUS NAMATIANUS (*fl.* first half of fifth century). In October 417, Rutilius Claudius Namatianus, a pagan Gallic aristocrat and former master of offices and prefect of the city of Rome, left Rome to journey by sea to his home province. He described the journey in the fragmentarily transmitted elegiac poem *De reditu suo,* whose excellence is out of proportion to its ostensible subject. Written with a deft and epigrammatic touch, the poem includes a hymn to the eternity of Rome—poignant given the recent sack of the city by the Goths—invectives against the Jews, monks, and Stilicho, praise of various friends, and a description of a local pagan festival.

BIBLIOGRAPHY

Sources. Rutilius Claudius Namatianus, *De reditu suo sive Iter Gallicum,* Ernst Doblhofer, ed., 2 vols. (1972–1977). An English version is available in Charles H. Keene, ed., and George F. Savage-Armstrong, trans., *De reditu suo libri duo: The Home-Coming of Rutilius Claudius Namatianus* (1907).

Studies. Alan Cameron, "Rutilius Namatianus, St. Augustine, and the Date of the *De reditu,*" in *Journal of Roman Studies,* 57 (1967); Francesco Corsaro, *Studi Rutiliani* (1981).

DANUTA SHANZER

[See also **Alaric; Latin Literature; Querolus; Roman Empire, Late; Visigoths.**]

RUUSBROEC, JAN VAN (Ruysbroeck) (1293–1381), Flemish mystic and prior of a monastery at Groenendael, near Brussels. He expressed his mystical experiences and his views on moral and social duties in the most important of his prose works, *Die chierheit der gheestelike brulocht* (The adornment of the spiritual espousals, *ca.* 1350). His teachings had a great influence in the Netherlands in the fifteenth century, and parts of his work were translated into Latin, extending his influence to other European mystics.

BIBLIOGRAPHY

Willem Hendrik Beuken, *Ruusbroec en de Middeleeuwse mystiek* (1946); *Jan van Ruusbroec: Leven, werken* (1931).

SEYMOUR L. FLAXMAN

[See also **Church, Latin: 1305–1500; Flanders; Mysticism, Christian: Low Countries.**]

RYE. See **Grain Crops, Western European.**

SAADIAH GAON (Saᶜadya ibn Yūsuf al-Fayyūmī) (882–942). Saadiah Gaon, as he is commonly called, was born in the Fayyum region of Egypt, and despite apparently modest circumstances received an unusually broad education, both Jewish and "secular." He was immediately recognized as an outstanding scholar by the "Babylonian" Jewish community of Iraq when he settled there in Baghdad in 922. In 928 he was appointed gaon or principal of the talmudic academy of Sura, and thus officially became one of the leading spiritual figures of Babylonian and world Jewry. However, Saadiah's position and independent spirit brought him into conflict with the then exilarch, the officially recognized political leader of Babylonian Jewry, and Saadiah was forced into involuntary retirement for some five years. In office and out, Saadiah maintained an unusually creative and influential career, writing in practically all the literary and scholarly genres of his day.

Already as a young man of twenty, Saadiah pioneered in composing a dictionary in Hebrew, *Sefer ha-agron* (Nehemya Allony, ed. [1969]), which he later translated into Arabic. The grammatical and poetic concerns there exhibited are manifested in two other studies of a philological and linguistic—as well as polemical—sort, and in a wealth of Hebrew religious poems. Many of Saadiah's piyyutim and other poems are found among the fragments of the Cairo genizah collection, as are many of his rabbinical responsa. Saadiah was a stylistic innovator in rabbinic literature, among the first to write in Arabic, and the first to treat particular topics in separate, logically ordered monograph fashion. Pioneering too was Saadiah's compilation of a *siddur* (written in Arabic), a comprehensive communal prayer book; and an Arabic translation and commentary to the Bible. Though the commentary is extant only in fragmentary form, Saadiah's translation (*Tafsir*) acquired an enduring place among Arabic-speaking Jews.

Saadiah's involvement in nontraditional Jewish learning is most apparent in two works written in Arabic: a commentary to the mystical *Sefer yezirah* (Book of creation); and an original philosophical treatise, his magnum opus, *The Book of Doctrines and Beliefs* (or *Beliefs and Opinions*) (*Kitab al-amānāt wa-l-ᵓiᶜtiqādāt*). In the commentary, Saadiah demonstrates his skills as a mathematician and astronomer, and his familiarity with Neopythagorean number theory and symbolism; while in the philosophical work he refers to these and many other fields, including that of music theory. His wide erudition is particularly evident in *Doctrines* in his discussion of diverse creation theories, those held by Plato, Aristotle, and other Greek thinkers, as well as by Hindu, Persian (Zoroastrian), and Muslim theologians. The intellectual vitality of tenth-century Baghdad is reflected in Saadiah's composition, though his purpose is partisan, to defend and promote the "traditional" (that is, Rabbinic) Jewish faith, both in its broad principles and in its specific commandments. Ironically, the compositions of the Muᶜtazila, the Islamic rationalists, serve as his model for this purpose, both stylistically and, to a lesser degree, substantively. Like them, he is concerned primarily with establishing the createdness of the world and the oneness and goodness of its creator, and in asserting man's freedom and the rationality of his faith alongside God's omniscience and omnipotence; though unlike the Muᶜtazila, Saadiah does not adopt atomism or occasionalism. Saadiah's approach is nondogmatic for the most part, and in the attempt to integrate rabbinical beliefs and an ultimately Greek philosophy, an attempt that characterizes much of medieval Jewish philosophy, Saadiah is again a pioneer.

BIBLIOGRAPHY

A comprehensive biographical summary and bibliography is in *Encyclopaedia judaica,* XIV (1972). For a complete biography, still best is Henry Malter, *Saadia Gaon: His Life and Works* (1921, repr. 1942, 1969). The rich bibliography there has been supplemented by Aron Freimann in *Saadia Anniversary Volume,* published by the American Academy for Jewish Research (1943), 327–339. While most of Saadiah's extant work was published in the last century, in recent times two English translations of his philosophical work have appeared: a complete translation by Samuel Rosenblatt, *The Book of Beliefs and Opinions* (1948), and an abridged translation by Alexander Altmann, *The Book of Doctrines and Beliefs* (1946), repr. in *Three Jewish Philosophers* (1960). Joseph Kafaḥ has also written a new Hebrew translation and a revised critical Arabic edition of this work (1970), complementing the classic and continually popular Hebrew translation of 1186 by Judah ibn Tibbon.

ALFRED L. IVRY

[See also **Apocalyptic Literature and Movement, Jewish; Bible; Exegesis, Jewish; Gaonic Period; Hebrew Language, Jewish Study of; Hebrew Poetry; Jewish Communal Self-Government: Islamic World; Jews in the Middle East; Judaism; Philosophy and Theology, Jewish: Islamic World; Schools, Jewish; Talmud, Exegesis and Study of.**]

SABĪL (Arabic, "way," "path," whence Turkish *sebil*), a sheltered public fountain established by a pious donor, usually on an urban street. Such fountains were particularly characteristic of Mamluk and Ottoman cities. The earliest example to survive into this century, in the ᶜAmāra quarter of Damascus, was dated 1077/1078. Already in 1150/1151 the Qaṣṭal (water tower) al-Shuᶜaybiyya in Aleppo was attached to a madrasa.

The fully developed type consisted of a roofed chamber containing a reservoir or basins fed through pipes from an aqueduct; passersby drew water through grilled windows. In fifteenth-century Cairo it became customary to place an elementary school (*kuttāb*) above the *sabīl,* whether freestanding or not; the first known instance was in the madrasa complex of the sultan al-Nāṣir Faraj before 1409/1410.

In İstanbul the *sebil* was a primary focus for development of the "Turkish baroque," constituting some of the most elegant examples of eighteenth- and nineteenth-century Ottoman architecture.

BIBLIOGRAPHY

Godfrey Goodwin, *A History of Ottoman Architecture* (1971), 379, 381–382, 388–389, 393, 403; Ernst Herzfeld, "Damascus: Studies in Architecture," in *Ars islamica,* **9** (1942), 42, fig. 28, and **10** (1943), 30–32, fig. 45; *Matériaux pour un corpus inscriptionum arabicarum,* pt. 1, *Egypte: Le Caire* (1894–1903), 230, 411–412, and pt. 2, *Syria du Nord: Alep,* I (1955), 222–224, and II (1954), pls. LXXXVI–LXXXVIII; *Répertoire chronologique d'épigraphie arabe,* VII (1936), 203–204.

ESTELLE WHELAN

ŠĀBUHR I (Shapur) (*d.* 270 or 273), Sasanian king of Iran. He assisted his father (or possibly his elder brother), Ardešīr I, founder of the dynasty, to overthrow the Parthian Arsacids; he is shown on coins as co-regent and was crowned *šāhan-šāh* (king of kings) probably in 242. His son Hormizd reigned one year and was succeeded by another son, Bahrām I.

Successful wars against Rome characterize Šābuhr's reign: in 243 the Roman emperor Gordian III advanced against the Persians, who were at first on the defensive, but the tide turned and Gordian fell, by treachery or in battle, in 244. Philip the

Arab, his successor, sued for peace and paid Šābuhr a huge ransom. Rome continued to press its influence in Armenia, so Šābuhr attacked about 256, devastating Dura Europos, the Roman outpost on the Euphrates, and conquering Antioch. Masses of Roman soldiers and Syrian civilians, including many Christians, were exiled to Iran and resettled there or forced to work on construction projects. Valerian marched against Iran but was captured at Edessa about 260. In the following decade, the desert trading city of Palmyra, a Roman ally, expanded briefly under Queen Zenobia, but was finally crushed by Rome after Šābuhr's death. In the east, the Sasanian Empire stretched as far as Tashkent and the Punjab, at least for a time, and Indian tribes called *Zuṭṭ* in the Arabic sources, perhaps remote ancestors of the Gypsies, were exiled into Iran proper; in the west, Iran held lands from Georgia in the north to Syria and Cappadocia.

The western captives built Šābuhr cities and palaces whose names celebrate his triumphs: Pērōz Šābuhr (Victorious is Šābuhr), Wuzurg Šābuhr (Great is Šābuhr), Gundēšābuhr (Cohort of Šābuhr), Weh Antiok Šābuhr (Better than Antioch is this city Šābuhr has built), and Bīšābuhr or Bishapur (Noble is Šābuhr). Some of these cities had primarily Christian populations and soon became bishoprics of the growing church of Persia; Bishapur, in the Sasanian home province of Pārs (Fārs), was a royal residence with palaces adorned with Bacchantic mosaics and Iranian equestrian reliefs; the baths and fire temple at the same site testify to the enjoyment by the early Sasanians of Greek luxuries in an Iranian setting. Šābuhr saw his conquests as a revival of Achaemenian glory, and, perhaps, as revenge for the destruction Alexander the Macedonian had wrought centuries before. In a great inscription in Greek, Parthian, and Middle Persian on the walls of the Achaemenian building now called the Kaᶜba-yi Zardušt (the Kaᶜba of Zoroaster) at Naqsh-i Rustam, Šābuhr recorded both his conquests and the names and offices of the administrators of his vast realm. In chiding the Romans for having "lied" and "done harm" to Armenia, he perpetuates the religious attitude to politics of his Achaemenian predecessors. The royal bas-reliefs celebrate royal triumphs in a manner directly imitating those of Ardešīr I, though the prototypes go back to the ancient Elamites: at Bishapur, the king's mount tramples the dead Gordian and confronts the kneeling supplicant Philip; Valerian kneels at Naqsh-i Rustam, within sight of the ruins of Persepolis, which Alexander had destroyed. In a cave at Bishapur is a statue of Šābuhr in the round, carved out of a pillar of living rock, unique for the Sasanian dynasty but finding precedent in Achaemenian art.

Šābuhr I sought to advance the interests of the Zoroastrian faith: according to the ninth-century Pahlavi *Dēnkard,* the king ordered writings of the Religion on medicine, astronomy, and physics, which were said to have been "dispersed" to Rome and India, to be collected and incorporated into the Avesta, the Zoroastrian sacred scripture. The priest Kartīr, who was to attain immense power under subsequent monarchs, began his career in Šābuhr's reign and may have led this effort to strengthen the "good religion" with the attainments of foreign learning. (It is possible that Kartīr did this to counteract the cosmopolitan and scientific appeal of Mani's teachings.) But the king extended toleration to other faiths, probably to Kartīr's great displeasure. Mani, who received his enlightening vision in the year of Šābuhr's coronation, attached himself to the court and presented a compendium of his teachings in Middle Persian (probably translated from Aramaic), the *Šābuhrāgān,* to the king, whom he accompanied on military campaigns. Christians deported from the west by Roman authorities were allowed to practice their faith peacefully, and the Jewish leader Samuel was so loyal that he refused to mourn fellow Jews killed in the Persian conquest of Caesarea-Mazaca; Persian law was also declared law unto the Jews as well. Military reversals and the rise of Christianity as the state religion of Rome probably influenced subsequent monarchs to adopt a more severe attitude toward foreign faiths and cultures, particularly Christianity.

BIBLIOGRAPHY

Cambridge History of Iran, III, pts. 1 and 2, Ehsan Yarshater, ed. (1983); Arthur Christensen, *Iran sous les Sassanides,* 2nd ed. (1944).

JAMES R. RUSSELL

[See also **Ardešīr I; Avesta; Bishapur; Christian Church in Persia; Denkārd; Fārs; Gundēshāpūr; Kaᶜba of Zoroaster; Kartīr; Manichaeans; Naqsh-i Rustam; Šāhanšāh; Sasanian Art, Culture, History; Zoroastrianism.**]

ŠĀBUHR II (Shapur) (*d.* 379), Sasanian king of Iran, reigned A.D. 309–379, longer than any other monarch of the dynasty. Crowned in childhood after the death of his father, Hormizd II, he was early supported by the nobility, but later asserted autocratic power. His reign is characterized by the extension of Sasanian domains in the west and by severe persecution of religious minorities, particularly Christians.

According to Eusebius, Constantine warned Šābuhr II in a letter not to persecute the Christians, for God had sent victory over their earlier tormentor, Valerian, to the Persian monarch's own ancestor, Šābuhr I. Even if the above is merely pious legend, Šābuhr II must have been aware of the new, official sanction of Christianity in the Roman Empire and of the threat to Iran of a potential fifth column in its large Christian population in Khūzistān and Iraq. The Arsacid vassal-kings of Armenia in the northwest had accepted Christianity a generation before, and Iran sought to uproot the new faith and to exploit conflicts between the *naχarar* nobility and the Armenian throne. In 339, when Christians refused to pay double war taxes for Šābuhr's campaigns against Rome, the "great persecution" began that was to last the remainder of his reign.

After inconclusive clashes with Rome and operations against the Chionite nomads on the eastern frontier, Šābuhr, having made allies of the latter, attacked Rome again, capturing Amida in northern Mesopotamia in 359; the Roman emperor Julian the Apostate was mortally wounded in a counterattack in 363, and Iran acquired Nisibis and other areas, particularly in Armenia. It has been suggested recently that a bas-relief at Bishapur depicts Šābuhr's subsequent political coups in Armenia. Šābuhr apparently resettled large numbers of captives of various nations in Iran, and persecution engulfed Jews and Manichaeans. But in the former case repression was generally rare and seems to have been provoked by a popular messianic movement and other disturbances. Zoroastrian orthodoxy was championed by the *mōbadān mōbad* Ādurbād ī Mahraspandān, who underwent the ordeal of having molten brass poured over his chest in witness of the faith. Many religious precepts (*andarz*) are ascribed in post-Sasanian compilations to him. Šābuhr's death was followed by a violent and rapid succession of various pretenders.

BIBLIOGRAPHY

Guitty Azarpay, "Bishapur VI: An Artistic Record of an Armeno-Persian Alliance in the Fourth Century," in *Artibus asiae,* **43** (1981–1982); S. P. Brock, "Christians in the Sasanian Empire: A Case of Divided Loyalties," in *Studies in Church History,* **18** (1982); *Cambridge History of Iran,* III, pt. 1, Ehsan Yarshater, ed. (1983), 132–141; *The Complete Text of the Pahlavi Dinkard,* Dhanjishah M. Madan, ed. (1911), 454.3; Georg Hoffmann, trans., *Auszüge aus syrischen Akten persischer Märtyrer* (1880, repr. 1966); Jérôme Lebourt, *Le christianisme dans l'empire perse sous la dynastie,* 2nd ed. (1904); Pᶜawstos Buzand, *Patmutᶜiwn Hayotᶜ* (1968); Robert C. Zaehner, *Zurvan: A Zoroastrian Dilemma* (1955), 11–12.

JAMES R. RUSSELL

[See also **Armenia, History of; Bīshapur; Byzantine Empire: History; Christian Church in Persia; Chosroids (Mihranids); Hepthalites; Jews in the Middle East; Manichaeans; Mōbadān Mōbad; Sasanian Culture; Sasanian History; Zoroastrianism.**]

SAC AND SOC. In England during the tenth and eleventh centuries, sac and soc (sake and soke, *sacu* and *sócn*) denoted private jurisdiction over ordinary cases at law. We do not know exactly what cases it covered. It certainly comprised everyday offenses, such as fighting, wounding, and fornicating. The lords who had this jurisdiction took charge of stray cattle. Clearly beyond their authority lay the truly serious crimes—arson, robbery, manifest theft, and slaying by stealth—as well as other cases that the law chose for special attention, including attacks upon homes, planned assaults, harboring outlaws, and charges of theft where the accused wished to prove that he purchased in a lawful market. But we cannot tell just where the line was drawn. Sac and soc may have been limited to petty justice, or may have come to more than that. Even thieves may have been justiciable under this authority, when their guilt was not "manifest" through arrest by hot pursuit, or even manslayers if they had used no stealth.

In the late eleventh century many lords had sac and soc. Most lords of manors may have possessed the right; the Domesday Book (1087) lists fifteen who had it in western Kent alone. A jurisdiction so widely distributed may have developed from the ancient "house-peace," the power of a householder to keep order among his dependents. Yet the *Leges Henrici* (*ca.* 1115) maintained that sac and soc must always be granted by the king, and many royal grants survive to show that practice answered in some measure to this theory. The effect of such grants was mainly administrative and financial. The lord who had a private court presided over it and received the money penalties it imposed, but he was not its judge or legislator.

The earliest grant of sac and soc is from 956. How common the jurisdiction may have been at that time and how old private jurisdiction may have been, we do not know. Two centuries later, in the twelfth century, sac and soc became obsolete. Private justice did not then fail, but vast changes in the law brought new concepts and vocabulary. Sac and soc long continued to be mentioned in charters and confirmations, but their meaning became uncertain.

"Soke" (*sócn*) was used alone, elliptically, for sac and soc, but by itself it had several other senses. It meant jurisdiction in general, on any level, and the right to profits of justice. It meant asylum and protection, duty of attendance, and district. In the earliest centuries of English history it may have denoted all the standard obligations of the rank-and-file freeman to the king: the duty to render him foodstuffs and fodder, to plow his field and mow his meadow, to carry his supplies and guard his person, to fight under his banner, to attend the folkmoots, and whatever else. Where traces of this ancient system survived in the eleventh century, the obligations were administered through the territorial hundreds, and the freemen who remained responsible for them were called "sokemen."

BIBLIOGRAPHY

A short account of sac and soc and its known history are in Frank M. Stenton, *Anglo-Saxon England* (1943, 3rd ed. 1971), 492–502. The subject was investigated by Henry Adams, "The Anglo-Saxon Courts of Law," in his *Essays in Anglo-Saxon Law* (1876). A different interpretation was proposed in Frederic W. Maitland, *Domesday Book and Beyond* (1897, repr. 1970), 80–107, 258–292. Much of our understanding derives from the *Leges Henrici* and from the commentary of its recent learned editor: L. J. Downer, ed. and trans., *Leges Henrici primi* (1972), esp. 104–127, 427–430.

The subject is concisely reviewed, with attention also to the diverse senses of *sócn* and the significance of other terms that are joined with sac and soc in royal grants, in Florence E. Harmer, *Anglo-Saxon Writs* (1952), 73–85. For the theory that *sócn* in one of its senses stood for the common obligations of freemen to the king, see G. W. S. Barrow, *The Kingdom of the Scots* (1973), chap. 1; Ralph H. C. Davis, ed., *The Kalendar of Abbot Samson* (1954), xxxii–xlvii.

DONALD W. SUTHERLAND

[See also **Asylum, Right of; Domesday Book; England; Feudalism; Henry II of England; Hundred (Land Division); Law, English Common: To 1272; Outlawry.**]

SACHSENSPIEGEL. The *Sachsenspiegel* (Saxon mirror), a work famous in the history of German law and institutions, is a compilation of German customary law dating from the early thirteenth century. It is evidence that although German law in the Middle Ages was divided into numerous local customs, a complete fragmentation of German law did not take place. The *Sachsenspiegel* helped to standardize German customary law in part because the laws it contained were systematically collected within one lawbook. It therefore became a convenient source of law, and ultimately it contributed to the standardization of German medieval law generally. It also was the most important German lawbook up to the time the German civil code was promulgated in the late nineteenth century (coming into force 1 January 1900).

The person who compiled and organized the laws contained in the *Sachsenspiegel* was the Saxon judge and knight Eike von Repgowe (1180/1190–after 1233), who also, some scholars believe, may have written the first world chronicle in the German vernacular, the *Sachsische Weltchronik* (Saxon world chronicle), in 1230–1231. Eike was commissioned to compile these laws by Count Hoyer von Falkenstein (bailiff of Quedlinburg), whom he served as a vassal and to whom he dedicated his work. There is, however, no evidence demonstrating or disproving the theory that Eike ever received an official state commission to compile these laws. The laws contained within the *Sachsenspiegel,* as its name indicates, are Saxon laws. Thus it was not intended to comprise all the laws of all of Germany—with the exception that it does include laws from northern Swabia. Although Eike originally wrote the *Sachsenspiegel* in Latin (1221–1224), none of these manuscripts have survived. What we do possess is the later vernacular Low German (*Niederdeutsch*) version, which dates from 1224–1227. The fact that the *Sachsenspiegel* was a compilation of Saxon customary laws and that it was written in Low German indicates that it was intended to be used in northern Germany. Technically, the Saxon laws it contains are the laws of the Eastphalians (the East Saxons), and not those of the Westphalians (the West Saxons). The language of the *Sachsenspiegel* is unencumbered by German expressions peculiar to certain regions of northern Germany and thereby is free from the influence of local dialects.

Much like the rest of Europe, Germany came under the influence of Roman law. The reception of Roman law in Germany was made easier because for the most part the Germans were not unified politically, and their legal systems were both numerous and localized. The German stronghold that most steadfastly resisted Roman legal influence was Saxony, and this resistance was due to the fact that Saxony already possessed a uniform code of law embodied in the *Sachsenspiegel.* This is not to say that the *Sachsenspiegel* is completely free from extracultural elements, however; although there is no traceable Roman legal influence in this lawbook, there is evidence that canon law (Gratian's *Decretum, ca.* 1140) was utilized as a source, and there are numerous references derived from the Bible. Other sources include works written by St. Augustine, Isidore of Seville, and Peter Comestor.

The *Sachsenspiegel* itself is divided into two distinct parts, both of which present their laws in a systematic way. The first part comprises Saxon territorial or customary law (*Landrecht*). It is broken down into sections that deal with laws of inheritance and the family, rules for legal procedure (constitutional law), criminal law, law for the maintenance of the public peace (*Landriedenrecht*), and public law. In all, there are eight categories of customary law. The second part of the *Sachsenspiegel* comprises the feudal law (*Lehnrecht*) of Saxony as it existed and was applicable in the early thirteenth century.

Eike produced an expanded version of the Low German *Sachsenspiegel* in the 1230's. An abridged and final version appeared in 1270, several decades after his death. There were also a number of glosses written on the *Sachsenspiegel,* notably one about 1325 by Johann von Buch, a judge in Brandenburg, who referred in his text to Roman law. Buch's gloss laid the foundation for glosses written in the fourteenth and fifteenth centuries, especially that of Nikolaus Wurm late in the fourteenth century.

Even though the *Sachsenspiegel* makes no mention of laws that apply to towns or their governments, this lawbook became the model for many German municipal codes. It influenced the so-called Dutch *Sachsenspiegel* (fourteenth century) compiled in Utrecht, the Görlitz lawbook (*ca.* 1300), the Breslau *Landrecht* (1356), and the assessor's lawbook for the city of Berlin (1397). It also influenced the laws of the city of Magdeburg. The effects of the *Sachsenspiegel* were evident as well in southern Germany, because here both the *Deutschenspiegel* (1265–1268) and *Schwabenspiegel* (1275–1276) came under its influence. The importance of the *Sachsenspiegel* in German history is also evident in its description of the election of the German king: It defined who were the seven electors who chose the German king, and stated that only they had the power to depose him. It therefore presumed an elective, not hereditary, basis for kingship.

Despite the widespread significance of the *Sachsenspiegel,* it fell under the disfavor of the papacy, particularly because it specified that the pope had no authority to interfere with either territorial or feudal law in Germany, and thus claimed that its jurisdiction was beyond his reach. In order to defend the papal position, Pope Gregory XI in 1374 condemned fourteen articles of the *Sachsenspiegel* in his bull *Salvator humani generis.*

It should also be mentioned that the *Sachsenspiegel* is famous in its own right, not only for being one of the oldest European lawbooks but also because two manuscripts of it are illuminated with considerable detail. They are the Heidelberg (1300–1315) and Dresden (*ca.* 1350) manuscripts. A third illuminated manuscript, the Meissen text (1290–1295), is now lost. The lasting worth and popularity of the *Sachsenspiegel* are demonstrated by the fact that in the first quarter-century of printing it was, in addition to the Bible, among the earliest books to be printed (at Basel in 1474).

BIBLIOGRAPHY

An edition is Karl August Eckhardt, ed., *Sachsenspiegel: Land- und Lehnrecht,* in *Monumenta Germaniae historica: Fontes iuris germanici antiqui,* n.s. I (1933, 3rd ed. 1973).

Studies include Helene Bindewald, "Studien zur Entstehung der Sachsenspiegelglosse," in *Deutsches Archiv für Erforschung des Mittelalters,* **15** (1959); Conrad Borchling, ed., *Das Landrecht des Sachsenspiegels nach der Bremer Handschrift von 1342* (1925); Karl August Eckhardt, *Rechtsbücherstudien,* II and III (1931–1933, vol. II repr. 1970), and *Sachsenspiegel,* IV, *Eike von Repchow und Hoyer von Falkenstein* (1966); Alexander Ignor, *Über das allgemeine Rechtsdenken Eikes von Repgow* (1984); Guido Kisch, *Sachsenspiegel and Bible* (1941); Karl Kroeschell, "Rechtsauszeichnung und Rechtswirklichkeit: Das Beispiel des Sachsenspiegels," in *Vorträge und Forschungen,* **23** (1977); Hans-Georg Krause, "Der Sachsenspiegel und das Problem des sogenannten Leihezwangs . . . ," in *Zeitschrift der Savigny-stiftung für*

Rechtsgeschichte: Germanistische Abteilung, **93** (1976); Malcolm Letts, "The Sachsenspiegel and Its Illustrators," in *Law Quarterly Review,* **49** (1933); Rolf Lieberwirth, "Eike von Repchow und der Sachsenspiegel," in *Sitzungsberichte der Sächsischen Akademie der Wissenschaften zu Leipzig* (phil.-hist. classe), **122,** 4 (1982); Walter Möllenberg, *Eike von Repgow und seine Zeit* (1934); Erich Molitor, "Der Gedankengang des Sachsenspiegels . . . ," in *Zeitschrift der Savigny-stiftung für Rechtsgeschichte: Germanistische Abteilung,* **65** (1947); Hermann Schadt, "Zum Verwandtschaftsbild und der Weltalterlehre des Sachsenspiegels . . . ," in *Frümittelalterliche Studien,* **10** (1976); Karl Schilling, *Das objektive Recht in der Sachsenspiegel-Glosse* (1931).

THEODORE JOHN RIVERS

[See also **Eike von Repgowe; Elections, Royal; Law, German: Post-Carolingian; Schwabenspiegel.**]

SACK, a measure of capacity for dry products throughout the British Isles that was used principally for wool and grain. The wool measure generally weighed 364 pounds (165.107 kilograms), a capacity equal to 2 weys, 13 tods, 52 cloves, or 26 stone of 14 pounds, each of which equal 1/12 last. Occasionally it was 350 pounds (158.756 kilograms), or 28 stone of 12.5 pounds each. The grain measure generally contained 4 heaped bushels (about 1.80 hectoliters). Locally it was employed for the selling at wholesale of apples, ashes, charcoal, coal, and flour.

RONALD EDWARD ZUPKO

[See also **Weights and Measures, Western European.**]

SACK, FRIARS OF THE. Also called Friars of the Penitence of Jesus Christ, they were a short-lived but excellent example of the prestige of the mendicants in the thirteenth century. The sources disagree on the beginnings of the order, but it probably originated near Hyères in Provence, perhaps formed by a Franciscan splinter group. In 1251 the friars assembled in the first general chapter. Twelve houses then existed, at least ten of them in Provence. At this general chapter the bishop of Toulon gave them the Rule of St. Augustine as a code of life, and Alexander IV confirmed it in 1255.

The rapid expansion that occurred between 1256 and 1274, with Sack houses established at such population centers as Narbonne, London, Norwich, Rheims, Oxford, Barcelona, Montpellier, Saragossa, Perpignan, Toulouse, Worms, Orléans, Lincoln, Bristol, Strasbourg, Cambridge, Poitiers, and Asti—in that order—attests to great popular respect and patronage. St. Louis, for example, supported foundations at Paris, Caen, and Rouen, and James I of Aragon (1213–1276) assisted a house at Játiva. By 1274 the Friars of the Sack possessed at least 111 houses, 50 of them in France and 18 in England, with the rest scattered across Western Europe. The order had few houses in German lands, none in Scandinavia, and no convents of women.

Constitutions very similar to those of the Dominicans seem to have governed those houses, and like the other mendicant orders the Friars of the Sack devoted themselves primarily to preaching to the people in urban centers. In preparation for this ministry they studied at the universities of Montpellier, Paris, Oxford, Bologna, Cologne, and Cambridge. They supported themselves by begging.

The Second Council of Lyons in 1274 forbade all mendicant orders, excepting the Franciscans, Dominicans, Carmelites, and Augustinian Friars, to receive new members, to found new houses, to alienate their properties, or to preach and hear confessions. This legislation had the effect of abolishing the Friars of the Sack, because, unable to recruit, the order was doomed to extinction. The friars were encouraged to enter other orders, and as their properties were abandoned, they reverted to the Holy See to be sold, the proceeds theoretically to be applied to the Crusades or charitable purposes. Since scholars have uncovered no economic nor moral difficulties within the order in 1274, it has been assumed that the Friars of the Sack fell victim to the hostility of the secular clergy directed toward all the mendicants and to the rivalry between the powerful Dominicans and Franciscans and the smaller, weaker orders.

After 1274 the Friars of the Sack declined rapidly in numbers and houses. Those who wished to do so were allowed to end their days in their own convents. A few did so, but many seem to have entered other orders. The last Friar of the Sack is attested at Marseilles in 1316. When other religious houses or corporations acquired Sack houses, the papacy often stipulated that the new owners accept the remaining Sack friars with the property. No particular religious order benefited from the dissolution.

BIBLIOGRAPHY

R. Ignatius Burns, S.J., "The Friars of the Sack in Valencia," in *Speculum,* **36** (1961), is useful for one part of Spain. Richard W. Emery, "The Friars of the Sack," *ibid.,* **18** (1943), contains full documentary references and is the best modern treatment; his "A Note on the Friars of the Sack," *ibid.,* **35** (1960), updates his earlier study. G. Giacomozzi, O.S.M., *L'ordine della Penitenza di Gesù Cristo* (1962), offers the Sack constitutions. David Knowles and R. Neville Hadcock, *Medieval Religious Houses, England and Wales* (1953), gives information on the English houses.

BENNETT D. HILL

[See also **Councils, Western (1215–1274); Dominicans; Franciscans; Mendicant Orders.**]

SACRAMENTARY, the book used in the early medieval Western church that contained primarily prayer texts for the Mass and secondarily texts for other sacramental and liturgical rites, such as ordination, baptism, penance, benediction, and exorcism. Usually sacramentaries did not include Mass lections, ceremonial directories, and musical texts, which were kept separately in other types of liturgical books.

Before sacramentaries were compiled, there existed *libelli missarum.* These were booklets with one or more gatherings of folios with the variable prayers used in the Mass, such as collects, offertories, prefaces, and post-communions. These *libelli* seem to have lacked the canon of the Mass, which the celebrant probably knew by heart. The best-known representative of these *libelli,* the *Sacramentarium Veronense* or Leonine Sacramentary (Verona, Biblioteca Capitolare, codex LXXXV [*ca.* 600]; Italy outside Rome), is now classed as a sacramentary, but its structure shows it to have been copied from collected *libelli.* The prayers are arranged according to the civil calendar and were compiled probably from material available in Rome. For the Gallican rite there exists evidence of a similar *libellus,* now in a Karlsruhe manuscript (LB Aug. CCLIII [630–640]; probably Burgundy), with the so-called Masses of Mone. And for the Old Spanish rite of the Visigothic church, there is a *libellus* in an ancient Spanish manuscript now at Verona (Biblioteca Capitolare, codex LXXXIX [*ca.* 700]).

For clerics with poor memories there perhaps came into existence another *libellus* with the Roman canon of the Mass, although no ancient manuscripts are extant. Nonetheless, such books apparently existed, for in some codices of ninth-century Roman sacramentaries, the text of the canon precedes the sets of Mass prayers.

Even while the *libelli missarum* were being used, there came into being a more ample type of Mass book, the sacramentary, which contained not only the variable prayer texts for the Mass but also the canon, various blessings, and the like. The variable prayer sets were arranged according to the liturgical year: in Gallican-rite territories, beginning with Advent; in Rome, with Christmas.

There are two major types of Roman-rite sacramentaries, manuscripts of which all have varying degrees of Gallican-rite overlay. The first is the Gelasian type, mistakenly attributed to Pope Gelasius I, although it certainly postdated him by at least a century. This form of sacramentary was made for presbyteral churches in Rome. The Gelasian sacramentaries are further subdivided into two types. The *Reginensis* type is so called because it is found in the manuscript Vatican Reginensis latinus 316 ([mid eighth century]; Chelles). Here the Mass sets are divided into three sections: those for the temporale or cursus of the liturgical year, the sanctorale or yearly cursus of saints' days, and daily and miscellaneous masses, into which the canon of the Mass had been squeezed. The eighth-century Gelasians are so called because the many manuscripts of this type date to the eighth century and reflect an eighth-century compilation. Unlike the *Reginensis* type, the eighth-century Gelasian sacramentaries have their Mass sets for the temporale and sanctorale mixed. Among the many manuscripts of this type is the Gellone Sacramentary (Paris, Bibliothèque Nationale, MS nat. lat. 12048 [late eighth century]; Meaux), especially famous for its illustrations and decorations.

The Gregorian type of Roman sacramentary is ascribed to Pope Gregory I, but probably was compiled some twenty-five years after his death. Again, there are several major subtypes of this sacramentary: The Lateran type or *Sacramentarium Hadrianum* was brought into the Carolingian realm by Charlemagne, who had asked Pope Adrian I for a copy of a "pure" Roman sacramentary. Its primary example is Cambrai, Bibliothèque Municipale, MS 164 (811–812; Cambrai). The *Paduensis* type, so called because its chief manuscript exemplar is in a codex from Padua (Biblioteca Capitolare, MS D. 47, [mid ninth century]; scriptorium of Lothar), was compiled between 650–680 for use at St. Peter's in Rome and has Gelasian borrowings. The Gregorian of Aniane, formerly referred to as the Gregorian Sacramentary with Alcuin's Supplement, is now recognized to have been largely compiled and supplemented by Benedict of Aniane. This type of sacramentary was made when it was found that the *Sacramentarium Hadrianum* sent to Charlemagne by Pope Adrian was inapplicable to the transalpine situation and lacked many of the favored texts of the indigenous Gallican and Visigothic liturgies. This sacramentary, supplemented with these texts together with materials from the eighth-century Gelasians, was taken back to Rome by the tenth century and accepted there as the authentic Roman sacramentary, providing the model on which the Roman missal would eventually be based. Among the most famous illuminated manuscripts of this type are the Raganaldus Sacramentary (Autun, Bibliothèque Municipale, MS 19 [*ca.* 845]; Marmoutiers) and the Drogo Sacramentary (Paris, Bibliothèque Nationale, MS 9428 [820–probably post 844]; Metz).

Besides sacramentaries of the Roman rite, there were sacramentaries for the other major rites in the West. (1) Gallican-rite sacramentaries of the very early Middle Ages have been called missals by modern authors because they contain Mass texts. But basically they are, like their Roman counterparts, collections of variable Mass prayers, the canon, and other material for the administration of sacramental and liturgical rites. Among the best known of these are the *Missale Gallicanum vetus* (Vatican, Palatinus latinus 493 [various parts written eighth century]; France), *Missale Gothicum* (Vatican, Reginensis latinus 317 [early eighth century]; probably Autun), *Missale Francorum* (Vatican, Reginensis latinus 257 [mid eighth century]; Corbie-Paris-Soissons triangle), and the Bobbio Missal (Paris, Bibliothèque Nationale, MS lat. 13246 [eighth century]; northern Italy). (2) Old Spanish and Mozarabic-rite Mass texts are found in the *Liber missarum de toto circulo anni* (Toledo, Biblioteca Capitolare, MS 35.3 [ninth century]; Toledo) and the *Liber misticus* (Toledo, Biblioteca Capitolare, MS 35.4 [ninth/tenth century]; Toledo), where they are mixed with texts for the Office. (3) Milanese-rite sacramentaries still exist in a number of manuscripts, most of which date to the late ninth century and beyond. Although these sacramentaries have distinctive Milanese traits, they clearly have undergone Roman influence. Moreover, they have elements reminiscent of missals: the addition of Mass lections or references thereto. (4) Celtic-rite sacramentaries are extremely rare, the Stowe Missal (Dublin, Royal Irish Acad. D. II. 3 [early ninth century]; Tallaght?) being the best known. But even in this missal there are Roman-rite intrusions.

In the late ninth century, prayers beyond those of the Mass sets came to be added to the eucharistic liturgy. These prayers for vesting, *apologiae,* and for use during other parts of the Mass, together with brief directions as to their use in the eucharistic celebration, were kept originally in *libelli* or *ordinaria missae* and were subsequently incorporated into sacramentaries.

By the eighth century there came into being the missal, which contained all of the material necessary for a priest to say Mass, including the eucharistic prayers taken from the *libelli* and sacramentaries. The earliest examples seem to have originated in central and southern Italy and then were taken north. It was not, however, until the twelfth and thirteenth centuries that they supplanted sacramentaries and became popular north of the Alps.

BIBLIOGRAPHY

Antoine Chavasse, "L'organisation générale des sacramentaires dits grégoriens," in *Revue des sciences religieuses,* **56** (1982) and **57** (1983); Jean Deshusses, "Les sacramentaires: État actuel de la recherche," in *Archiv für Liturgiewissenschaft,* **24** (1982); Jean Deshusses and Benoit Darragon, *Concordances et tableaux pour l'étude des grands sacramentaires,* 3 vols. in 7 (1982–1983); Antoine Dumas and Jean Deshusses, eds., *Liber sacramentorum Gellonensis,* 2 vols. (1981); Miquel S. Gros i Pujol, "Les misses dels folis preliminars de l'Oracional hispànic de Verona," in *Miscel·lània litúrgica catalana,* **1** (1978); Odilo Heiming, ed., *Liber sacramentorum Augustodunensis* (1984); José Janini, *Liber missarum de Toledo* [*y libros místicos*], 2 vols. (1982–1983); Eric Palazzo, "Les sacramentaires de Fulda (X[e] et XIe siècles): Determination du groupe et lignes de recherches" (diss., Paris, 1986); Richard W. Pfaff, *Medieval Latin Liturgy: A Select Bibliography* (1982), 72–79; Roger E. Reynolds, "The Portrait of the Ecclesiastical Officers in the *Raganaldus Sacramentary* and Its Liturgico-canonical Significance," in *Speculum,* **46** (1971), "Image and Text: A Carolingian Illustration of Modifications in the Early Roman Eucharistic *Ordines,*" in *Viator,* **14** (1983), and "Image and Text: The Liturgy of Clerical Ordination in Early Medieval Art," in *Gesta,* **22** (1983); *Le sacramentaire grégorien,* Jean Deshusses, ed., 3 vols. (1971–1982); Cyrille Vogel, *Medieval Liturgy: An Introduction to the Sources,* W. Storey and N. Rasmussen, trans. (1986).

ROGER E. REYNOLDS

[See also **Antiphonal; Benedictional; Collectarium; Evangeliary; Gospelbooks; Lectionary; Manuscript Illumination, European; Mass, Liturgy of the; Pontificals; Psalter.**]

SACRAMENTARY, ILLUMINATION OF. Because of their liturgical importance, sacramentaries were often elaborately decorated. The opening pages, important because they introduce the heart of the Mass, were frequently written in elaborate and ornamental script and framed. Painted initials commonly opened other important passages within the text; these initials were often historiated and contained images of the celebration of the Mass or the relevant feast. One early example, the Drogo Sacramentary (Paris, Bibliothèque Nationale, lat. 9428), produced in Metz between 850 and 855, is written entirely in gold, with numerous framed text pages and forty-one historiated initials illustrating the pericopes of the Mass and feasts. (See illustration at "Initials.")

Another common image is that of Christ in Majesty, surrounded by Evangelist symbols or the angelic host—for example, the ninth-century Coronation Sacramentary of Charles the Bald (Paris, B.N., lat. 1141) and a mid-twelfth-century sacramentary from Florence (New York, Pierpont Morgan Library, MS 737). Other common liturgical miniatures include images of St. Gregory inspired by the Holy Ghost as he composes the formulas used in the Mass. In addition, miniatures recording the feasts were often incorporated.

BIBLIOGRAPHY

Robert G. Calkins, *Illuminated Books of the Middle Ages* (1983); Victor Leroquais, *Les sacramentaires et les missels manuscrits des bibliothèques publiques de France*, 4 vols. (1924); John Plummer, *Liturgical Manuscripts for the Mass and the Divine Office* (1964).

LESLIE BRUBAKER

[See also **Evangelist Symbols; Initials, Decorated and Historiated; Majestas Domini; Manuscript Illumination, European; Mass, Liturgy of the; Missal; Pre-Romanesque Art.**]

SACRAMENTS. See individual listings.

SACRISTY, a room in or near a church, usually near the sanctuary, for the storage of liturgical vessels, vestments, and other valuable property, sometimes including the church treasury and library. The sacristy is used by the clergy to vest themselves and to prepare for services. Derived from the early Christian diaconicon or secretarium, the sacristy sometimes doubles as the prothesis, the chapel for the preparation and storage of the eucharistic host and wine. In larger churches double sacristies are sometimes provided, one for the canons and the other for attendants and the lesser clergy.

BIBLIOGRAPHY

Peter F. Anson, *Churches: Their Planning and Furnishing* (1948); Richard Krautheimer, *Early Christian and Byzantine Architecture* (1975); John B. O'Connell, *Church Building and Furnishing* (1955).

GREGORY WHITTINGTON

[See also **Architecture, Liturgical Aspects; Diaconicon; Early Christian and Byzantine Architecture.**]

Fatimid luster bowl bearing Sa^c^d signature, 11th century. COURTESY OF THE SMITHSONIAN INSTITUTION, FREER GALLERY OF ART, REG. NO. 36.2, Washington, D.C.

SA^c^D, an artist/potter, possibly also the name of an atelier, of the Fatimid period in Egypt. At least fifty pieces bearing his signature exist, most of them lusterware. Among the finest is a bowl in the Freer Gallery in Washington, D.C., and another in the Victoria and Albert Museum, London. Although it has been argued that *sa^c^d* is not a name but a benediction, this is gramatically untenable; "happiness" is spelled *sāᶜadeh* and occurs on some ceramics related to *saᶜd* pieces, suggesting cognizance of the distinction. By stylistic analogy with textiles of the reign of al-Mustanṣir (1036–1094), the *saᶜd* group of ceramics may be dated to the eleventh and twelfth centuries. Related pieces of Syrian provenance have also been noted.

BIBLIOGRAPHY

ᶜAbd al-Raᶜūf ᶜAlī Yūsuf, "Khazzafūn min al-ᶜaṣr al-fātimī wa al-sālībihum al-fannīya," in *Majallah Jāmiᶜat al-Qāhirah Kullīyat al-Ādāb* (Bulletin of the Faculty of Arts, Cairo University), **20**, pt. 2 (1958), 173–279; Esin Atil, *Art of the Arab World* (1975), 42–43; Aly Bahgat and Félix Massoul, *La céramique musulmane de l'Égypte* (1930), 51–58, pls. VIII–XIII, F; Gaetano Ballardini, "Note sui 'bacini' romanici e in particolore su alcuni 'bacini' orientali in San Sisto di Pisa," in *Faenza,* **17** (1929), 113–121; Nancy P. Britton, *A Study of Some Early Islamic Textiles in the Museum of Fine Arts, Boston* (1938), 59 and fig. 51; Marilyn Jenkins, "Saᶜd: Content and Context," in *Richard Ettinghausen Memorial Volume* (College Art Association Monograph Series) (1987); Arthur Lane, "Sung Wares and the Saljuq Pottery of Persia," in *Transactions of the Oriental Ceramic Society,* **22** (1946–1947), 26–27, and *Early Islamic Pottery* (1947, 4th rev. ed. 1958), 21–22; Edward W. Lane, *An Arabic-English Lexicon,* I, pt. 4 (1872), 1,361–1,363.

JOHN CARSWELL

[See also **Ceramics, Islamic; Lusterware.**]

SAFFĀḤ, ABŪ 'L-ᶜABBĀS AL- (*ca.* 725–754), the first Abbasid caliph, was born in al-Ḥumayma, a village in Al-Sharāh (ancient Edom). His father, Muḥammad, was recognized as designated successor to Abū Hāshim, grandson of ᶜAlī ibn Abī Ṭālib, the fourth caliph (656–661), and of the slave Khawla al-Ḥanafīya. His mother was Rayṭa bint ᶜUbayd Allāh, whose grandfather had been governor of Yemen for ᶜAlī and whose brother Ziyād would become governor of Yemen, and later Medina, for al-Saffāḥ. Abū al-ᶜAbbās may have been chosen to succeed Muḥammad because he was descended from Arab nobility on both sides, whereas his brother Abū Jaᶜfar (later al-Manṣūr), for example, was the son of a concubine. His brother Ibrāhīm was designated to succeed Muḥammad on the latter's death in 742/743. The Umayyad caliph Marwān II, upon learning of this, had Ibrāhīm arrested and imprisoned in Ḥarrān. In August/September 749, Ibrāhīm died (murdered, according to Abbasid propaganda, but possibly a victim of plague).

The revolt in Khorāsān, managed for the Abbasids by Abū Muslim, was now well under way. Rather than await arrest in al-Ḥumayma, Abū 'l-ᶜAbbās proceeded secretly with a small group of relatives and retainers to Al-Kufa, where he would be proclaimed caliph. He had with him a document to prove that Ibrāhīm had designated him the leader of the movement; however, Abū Salama, the Abbasids' chief agent in Iraq, hid the group for over a month and would not produce them in public. He may have feared to disappoint those who expected an Alid candidate, or at least wished to have the approval of all the Hāshimīya (partisans of the line of Abū Hāshim) before proclaiming Abū 'l-ᶜAbbās. By one account, he even tried to assassinate Abū 'l-ᶜAbbās when the latter pressed him to go public.

At last, Abū 'l-Jahm, an agent of Abū Muslim's, forced Abū Salama's hand by conducting some Khorāsānī chiefs to Abū 'lᶜAbbās to hail him as caliph. On 28 November 749, Abū 'l-ᶜAbbās mounted the minbar of the mosque of al-Kufa with his uncle Dāwūd ibn ᶜAlī, to proclaim his caliphate publicly. He promised to raise the Kufans' stipends, and called himself al-Saffāḥ—literally, the shedder of blood, referring both to his promise to avenge Alid and Abbasid martyrs and to the host who slaughters generously to feed his guests (and hence to his promise of generosity). It was not a regnal title, and during his lifetime he was usually referred to as Abū 'l-ᶜAbbās. Dāwūd then appealed to Alid sympathy, declaring that there had been no true successor (*khalīfa*) to the Prophet save ᶜAlī ibn Abī Ṭālib.

The battle on the Greater Zāb (25 January 750) ended hope for the Umayyad dynasty. Al-Saffāḥ made his capital in southern Iraq, first at Al-Hāshimīya, then at Al-Anbār. He presided over the liquidation of nearly the whole Umayyad house and the beginning of the liquidation of the Abbasids' former co-conspirators, such as Abū Salama and his chief agents; however, he would not move against Abū Muslim. Most characteristically Abbasid institutions (such as the classical vizierate, administrative reliance on non-Arab clients, the city of Baghdad) appeared only under his brother Abū Jaᶜfar al-Manṣūr, the successor he designated.

Al-Saffāḥ died in Al-Anbār 9/10 June 754, of smallpox. He was the first caliph to possess 2 million dinars, but he was also reputedly generous.

Some sayings and couplets of his survive as testimony of his reputation for eloquence.

BIBLIOGRAPHY

Akhbār al-dawla al-ᶜAbbāsīya, ᶜAbd al-ᶜAziz al-Dūrī and ᶜAbd al-Jabbār al-Muṭṭalibī, eds. (1971); al-Balādhurī, *Ansāb al-ashrāf,* III, ᶜAbd al-ᶜAziz al-Dūrī, ed. (1978); Claude Cahen, "Points de vue sur la 'révolution ᶜabbāside,'" in *Revue historique,* 230 (1963); Jacob Lassner, *The Shaping of ᶜAbbāsid Rule* (1980); S. Moscati, "Abū 'l-ᶜAbbās al-Saffāḥ," in *The Encyclopaedia of Islam,* new ed., I (1960); Moshe Sharon, *Black Banners from the East* (1983); al-Ṭabarī, *The History of al-Ṭabarī,* XXVII: *The ᶜAbbāsid Revolution,* John A. Williams, trans. (1985).

CHRISTOPHER MELCHERT

[See also **Abbasids; Alids; Caliphate; Kufa, Al-; Manṣūr, Abū Jaᶜfar ᶜAbd Allāh Ibn Muḥammad al-.**]

SAFFARIDS, a dynasty of Iranian origin that ruled in the eastern provinces of the Iranian world in the latter part of the ninth century, and, for the subsequent six centuries, was a local power in the province of Sīstān, straddling the modern political boundary between Iran and southwestern Afghanistan, with a capital at Zaranj.

Unlike other local lines of autonomous and semi-independent governors who arose in various peripheral areas of the Abbasid caliphate as the central authority of the caliphs in Baghdad waned, and who were usually of landholding, aristocratic origin, the Saffarids were of plebeian, artisan stock, from the remote province of Sīstān, where caliphal control had long been weak and where religious sectarianism was significant. The founder of the line, Yaᶜqūb ibn Layth (*d.* 879), had been a coppersmith (*ṣaffār*) until he emerged as local emir in Sīstān and embarked on a career of military conquest in 861. Troops flocked to his standard, and within eighteen years he built up a vast, if evanescent, military empire. In the east he carried Islam into the pagan areas of the Afghan-Indian borders; in the west he conquered eastern and southern Persia, overthrowing the line of Tahirid governors in Khorāsān in 873, and penetrated almost to Baghdad itself. When he died six years later he left a powerful military force to his brother and successor, ᶜAmr, who is said to have started life as a muleteer or stonemason. ᶜAmr defeated various rivals for power in Khorāsān and made himself influential at the caliphal court itself; but his downfall resulted from his great ambition to annex the lands north of the Oxus, Transoxiana, held by another Iranian family, the Samanids. The caliphs saw in the Samanids a check on ᶜAmr's activities and rejoiced when he was defeated in northern Afghanistan in 900; ᶜAmr was captured by the Samanids and sent to Baghdad for eventual execution.

The dynamic, expansionist phase of the Saffarids thus came to an end, and their empire shrank to a local principality in Sīstān, led by a series of less competent rulers. In 911 the Samanids made Sīstān into a tributary province of their own empire; but local patriotic sentiment was strong, and a member of the Saffarid family was soon reinstalled, apparently aided by the prestige of his forebears. Under such emirs as Aḥmad ibn Muḥammad and his son Khalaf, Sīstān flourished in the tenth century, and the reputation of the emirs as enlightened patrons of literature and the religious sciences spread far beyond their province. Khalaf was not able to withstand the imperialist power of the Ghaznavids of eastern Afghanistan, however, and his principality was occupied by the great warrior-sultan Maḥmūd, who in 1003 incorporated Sīstān into his vast empire.

Sīstān remained under Ghaznavid control for some forty-five years, until that empire in turn was pushed back into eastern Afghanistan and northern India by the emergent Seljuk Turkish power. The tenacious Saffarids now came under Seljuk suzerainty (after 1048). The Seljuks tended to leave them largely undisturbed, and one of the emirs, Tāj al-Dīn Naṣr, ruled there for over sixty years (1103–1167), at times serving his suzerains militarily. In the later part of the twelfth century the Saffarids became subject to the new power that had arisen in the eastern lands, that of the Ghurids. Sīstān was devasted by the Mongol invasions in the thirteenth century, but the Saffarids survived this as well as the disturbances caused by the incursions of Tamerlane (Timur Leng). The history of the later Saffarids is obscure and is known only from a local history of Sīstān, supplemented by the information of numismatics; but the emirs apparently persisted almost to the end of the fifteenth century, when Sīstān, increasingly a backwater of the Iranian world, lost most of its political and economic significance.

The early Saffarids, Yaᶜqūb, ᶜAmr, and their immediate successors, were a catalytic force in the disintegration of the Abbasid caliphate, which, by the tenth century, had little direct political power beyond Iraq, though its moral and spiritual authority was still great. Culturally, the emirs of the later ninth and tenth centuries are of considerable importance for the development of New Persian literature, for Persian language and literature had been eclipsed by the Arab conquest. Yaᶜqūb, unable to understand the prevalent genre of eulogistic poetry in Arabic, is said to have demanded of his court minstrels that they produce verse in Persian in his praise; certainly New Persian emerged at this time as a subtle and vigorous vehicle for both poetry and prose. A century or so later the emir Khalaf ibn Aḥmad is said to have commissioned a hundred-volume Koran commentary.

The military force forged by Yaᶜqūb and ᶜAmr is significant for the evolution of military organization in the Islamic world. Its nucleus was a body of local vigilantes which had grown up in Sīstān to combat sectarianism, but Yaᶜqūb, as his policies extended beyond the confines of his native province, actually incorporated these sectarian elements into his army. He also began the purchase of Turkish military slaves to supply the cavalry for his army, a policy that was at this time becoming widespread in eastern Islam. The prestige of Yaᶜqūb and ᶜAmr enabled them to set new standards of discipline and competence within their forces, for which contemporary historians—in general hostile to the Saffarids as parvenus and challengers of caliphal authority—give them due praise.

BIBLIOGRAPHY

Sources. Malik Shāh Ḥusain, *Iḥyāᵓ al-mulūk* (1966); *The Tarīkh-e Sistān,* Milton Gold, trans. (1976).

Studies. C. E. Bosworth, *The Islamic Dynasties: A Chronological and Genealogical Handbook* (1967), 103–105, *Sīstān Under the Arabs: From the Islamic Conquest to the Rise of the Ṣaffārids* (1968), and "The Ṭāhirids and Ṣaffārids," in *The Cambridge History of Iran,* IV, Richard N. Frye, ed. (1975); Theodor Nöldeke, *Sketches from Eastern History,* John Sutherland Black, trans. (1892, repr. 1963), 176–206.

C. E. Bosworth

[See also **Abbasids; Afghanistan; Caliphate; Emir; Ghaznavids; Ghurids; Iran; Iranian Languages; Iranian Literature; Koran; Mongol Empire; Samanids; Seljuks; Tahirids; Tamerlane; Transoxiana; Yaᶜqūb ibn Layth.**]

SAGA (plural, *sǫgur* or, after the thirteenth century, *sögur*), originally an Icelandic word connected with the verb *segja* (to say) and cognate with English "saw" (a saying). It has no technical literary sense in Old Icelandic and may be applied with equal justification to a long story, a version of some event or sequence of events, a report, or an opinion on a particular item of information. Modern scholars have specialized the term to describe any of a number of Icelandic prose narratives written in the medieval period. The earliest extant sagas date from the late twelfth century, but sagas continued to be composed and copied by hand well into modern times.

The sagas range from historical narrative (dealing with past or contemporary events) to egregious fictions. They consequently fall into a variety of subgenres. The main classifications, in roughly chronological order, are kings' sagas (*konungasǫgur*); bishops' sagas (*biskupa sǫgur*); family sagas, also called sagas of Icelanders (*Íslendingasǫgur*); legendary or mythic-heroic sagas (*fornaldarsögur*); and romances (*riddarasögur*). In individual cases the generic features may of course be mixed. Thus *Egils saga* is classified as a family saga but has much in common with the kings' sagas. In the later period, native *fornaldarsögur* and foreign *riddarasögur* so interpenetrated one another that a distinction becomes meaningless. Purely fictional adventure tales are sometimes called *lygisögur* (lying sagas). Literarily preeminent are the family sagas of the thirteenth century, and unspecified references to "the sagas" usually envisage this group.

BIBLIOGRAPHY

For a discussion of the validity of generic distinctions, see the debate conducted by Lars Lönnroth ("The Concept of Genre in Saga Literature"), Joseph Harris ("Genre in Saga Literature: A Squib"), and Theodore M. Andersson ("Splitting the Saga") in *Scandinavian Studies,* 47 (1975). On saga types in general, see Theodore M. Andersson, "The Icelandic Sagas," in *Heroic Epic and Saga,* Felix J. Oinas, ed. (1978), 144–171; and Paul Schach, *Icelandic Sagas* (1984).

Theodore M. Andersson

[See also **Bishops' Sagas; Egils Saga Skallagrímssonar; Family Sagas, Icelandic; Fornaldarsögur; Norse Kings' Sagas; Riddarasögur.**]

SAHAK, ST. (*d.* 437/439), last patriarch of Armenia from the Gregorid house. The dates of his pontificate are disputed, but Armenian sources give it as lasting from 387 until his death, although he was deposed by the Sasanians in 427/428 and replaced by two Syrian prelates. Sahak was allowed by the Persian authorities to return to his domain of Aštišat in Tarōn around 432, but he does not seem to have regained the full jurisdiction of the patriarchate.

Like the other members of the Gregorid house, Sahak played a major role in the affairs of Armenia, serving as ambassador to both the Persian and the Byzantine court, and negotiating with the *naχarar*s in an attempt to prevent the downfall of the Armenian Arsacids in 428. He also maintained the Gregorid link with the Mamikonean house, to which he gave in marriage his only child, Sahakanuyš, and which inherited all his domains.

The ecclesiastical activities of Sahak were likewise extensive, and included his fight against heretical sects in Armenia. The canons subsequently incorporated into the official Canonbook of the Armenian church may not be his, but he undoubtedly corresponded with the Byzantine bishop Akakios (Acacius) of Melitene. This correspondence led to the answering Tome of the patriarch Proclus. Sahak's letter rejecting the writings of Theodore of Mopsuestia as heretical was eventually reused as the basis of the Second Council of Constantinople (Council of "The Three Chapters") in 553.

For Armenia, Sahak's most important contribution was his active support of St. Maštocᶜ in his creation of the Armenian alphabet at the beginning of the fifth century, and his continuing patronage of the first school of translators, which provided Armenia with the scriptural texts in its own language necessary for its religious autonomy, and which laid the foundation for the original works whose rapid and extensive development made the fifth century the golden age of Armenian literature.

BIBLIOGRAPHY

Nersēs Akinian, *Kᶜnnutᶜiwn S. Sahaki veragruac kanonneru ew Hayocᶜ ekełecᶜakan tarin Ē. daru skizbə,* I (1950); Gérard Garitte, *La Narratio de rebus Armeniae* (1952); René Grousset, *Histoire de l'Arménie dès origines à 1071* (1947), 169–178, 181–187; *Kanonagirkᶜ Hayocᶜ,* V. Hakobyan, ed., I (1964), 363–421, 623–626; Malachia (Maghak'ia) Ormanian, *Azgapatum,* I (1912), 255–326; Maurice Tallon, *Livre des lettres* (1955), 9–77.

NINA G. GARSOÏAN

[See also **Armenia: History of; Armenian Alphabet; Armenian Church, Doctrines; Armenian Literature; Armenian Saints; Arsacids; Councils, Ecumenical; Gregorids; Mamikonean; Maštocᶜ, St.; Naχarar; Sasanian History.**]

ŠĀHAN-ŠĀH (Middle Persian, meaning "king of kings"), Iranian title, from Old Persian *χšāyaθiya χšāyaθiyānām,* borne by all the Achaemenian kings together with other titles, especially *χšayaθya vazraka* (Middle Persian: *wuzurg šāh,* great king). The latter title was most common under the Arsacids, but in the later Parthian period the title *MLKYN MLKA* (Aramaic ideogram for *Šāhan-šāh*) is also found, as attempts were made to strengthen and centralize royal authority.

The Sasanian kings adopted the title (ideogram in inscriptions: *MLKAn MLKA;* Zoroastrian Book Pahlavi: *MLKAᵓn' MLKA*); "great king" became the designation of subordinate kings, as of Mesene, Sakastan (Sīstān), and Armenia, with the ruler of the latter often next in line for the Sasanian throne. In inscriptions, the king of kings was styled *MNW ctry MN yzdᵓn kē čihr az yazdān* (whose seed is from the gods); Ammianus Marcellinus, who in the fourth century reproduced the Persian title as *saansaan* (19.2.11), noted that the Iranian king (Šābuhr II, here associated with the previous Arsacid dynasty), was regarded as a god (23.6.5–6), *frater Solis et Lunae* (brother of the sun and moon; 17.5.3).

In Iran the symbols of the king's superiority over other dignitaries of the realm are the Kayanian *χwarrah* or *farr* (Avestan: *χvarənah-*), the divinely bestowed, visible glory or fortune of kingship; the beribboned diadem (compare with Armenian loanwords from Middle Iranian: *patiw,* honor, royal diadem; *psak,* diadem); and the supreme God, Ohrmazd.

For just as Ohrmazd (Avestan: Ahura Mazdā) was regarded in Zoroastrianism as the ordainer of the world and sovereign over the lesser divinities of his creation, so the Sasanian king was the supreme temporal lord. In the bas-relief investiture scene of the first Sasanian king, Ardešīr I, in the cliffside at Naqsh-i Rustam below the tombs of the Achaemenians, Ohrmazd as a man on horseback hands the royal diadem to Ardešīr, likewise mounted and of the same size, facing him. The hooves of the king's mount crush the overthrown Parthian, Ardawān V; Ormazd's horse tramples the evil spirit Ahriman. The Achaemenians had claimed legitimacy "by the will of Ahura Mazdā" (Old Persian: *vašnā Aura-*

mazdāha), and the human figure in a winged ring on their reliefs probably represents Ahura Mazdā.

The Sasanian king's power was not, in fact, absolute; the priesthood and nobility exercised considerable power, particularly in the middle period of the dynasty. The Zoroastrian priestly hierarchy seems to have been organized on the model of the monarchy: the office of the high priest, *mōbadān mōbad* (chief magus of chief magi), who was the coronant, was styled after *mōbadān mōbad.* In other cultures under Iranian influence, the title of "king of kings" is reflected: the Hebrew God is called *melex malxē ha-məlāxīm* (king of the king of kings); and titles such as *išxan išxanac*ᶜ (prince of princes) are found in Christian Armenia centuries after the fall of the Sasanian dynasty.

BIBLIOGRAPHY

Michael Back, *Die sassanidischen Staatsinschriften* (1978), 20, 281ff.; *Cambridge History of Iran,* Ehsan Yarshater, ed., III, pt. 2 (1983), esp. 683–698; Roland G. Kent, *Old Persian* (1953), 181. See also the Pahlavi text *Sūr Saxwan,* pars. 9–10, in Jāmāspjī M. Jamasp-Asana, *Pahlavi Texts* (1913), 157.

JAMES R. RUSSELL

[See also **Ammianus Marcellinus; Archon Ton Archonton; Ardešīr I; Arsacids; Iranian Languages; Mōbadān Mōbad; Parthians; Šābuhr II; Sasanian Culture; Shāhnāma; Zoroastrianism.**]

SAHN, Arabic word for a courtyard, usually open but sometimes roofed, whether of a house or of a religious building such as a mosque, madrasa, or *khānqāh.* The incorporation of the *sahn* into most architecture of the Middle East, secular and religious, and the concomitant emphasis on the interior at the expense of the exterior, is one of the most characteristic features of Islamic architecture.

BIBLIOGRAPHY

K. A. C. Creswell, *Early Muslim Architecture,* 2 vols. (1932–1940), and *Muslim Architecture of Egypt,* 2 vols. (1952–1959); George Michell, ed., *Architecture of the Islamic World* (1978).

BERNHARD O'KANE

[See also **Alhambra; Eyvān; Islamic Art and Architecture; Khānqāh; Madrasa; Mosque.**]

ST. ANDREWS, Scotland's leading church center in the Middle Ages and the site of the nation's first university, established in the fifteenth century. The original name, Cennrigmonaid (head of the king's mound), yielded, perhaps by the twelfth century, to the name of the church dedicated to *Sanctus Andreas,* whence—by direct borrowing, through Middle Scots *Androis*—St. Andrews (not Andrew or Andrew's).

Later tradition ascribed the foundation of the abbey of Cennrigmonaid (an abbot is mentioned in 747) to a King Angus, possibly Oengus, king of Picts (*ca.* 729–761). Northumbrian influence was strong, and relics of Andrew the apostle may have been brought from Hexham. At a later date the reformed Culdee observance was adopted at the abbey. By 1100 at Kilrymont (church of the king's mound) most of the revenues of the abbey had been secularized, despite many generous gifts to St. Andrew's shrine by Queen Margaret; her institution of the Queen's Ferry for pilgrims shows the popularity of the shrine. Archaeology has revealed a rich sarcophagus, and a shrine cross-shaft and cross-slabs, all from the period 800 to 1100 and testifying to the church's wealth. From at least the tenth century there was a bishop (probably also abbot), who enjoyed a precedence among bishops and hence was called "bishop of the Scots." His cathedral was probably the reliquary church built in the 1070's and surviving as St. Rule's Church.

Royal efforts from about 1115 to found a cathedral priory of Augustinian canons were completed in 1144, though the proposed transfer of Culdee revenues was successfully resisted and the Culdee minster was slowly transformed into the collegiate church of St. Mary of the Rock, which in the thirteenth century claimed a share in electing the bishop. But the Augustinians dominated the great cult center of St. Andrew, adapting St. Rule's and building the cathedral, which was consecrated 5 July 1318, an ambitious building on the grand scale, the largest church in Scotland, originally 391 feet (119 meters) long. The priory was the wealthiest religious house in Scotland.

The bishopric remained vacant from 1093 to 1107, and thereafter the two bishops sought to give obedience to York and Canterbury, resulting in disputes with the crown. From 1124 the Scottish kings fought off the claims of the archbishops of York to obedience from the bishops of St. Andrews as the key to subordination of the whole Scottish church to York—evidence of the unofficial primacy of St. Andrews. Requests to the pope for archiepiscopal status were unsuccessful, but in 1192 the Scottish sees, including St. Andrews, were declared "special daughter" of Rome "with no one in between" (*Cum universi*). Thereafter the bishopric was the most prestigious in Scotland, the bishop taking a leading role in investing and, from 1331, crowning and anointing the king; in 1472, in controversial circumstances, metropolitan status was granted.

In 1410, probably because of difficulties at the University of Paris, teaching at university standard began at St. Andrews, and by 1413 the foundation of the university was complete, because of the interest of Bishop Henry Wardlaw. In 1450 Bishop James Kennedy founded a college (St. Salvator's), and the colleges of St. Leonard (1512) and St. Mary (1538/1539) followed, providing a secure financial basis for teaching. In its early days the university was strongly anti-Wycliffite. Arts was always the strongest faculty, but the cathedral priory also acted as a faculty of theology and flourished; there are traces of the teaching of law and medicine.

The town of St. Andrews was granted burghal status as the bishop's burgh by David I (*r.* 1124–1153), who sent a Fleming from Berwick to be its reeve or provost. Other early inhabitants have English names. The town flourished with seaborne trade in the twelfth and thirteenth centuries, and the stages of its growth are revealed by its morphology; the medieval plots survive, and the structures of some surviving houses include fragments of late medieval date. Although of relatively lesser economic importance after about 1300, St. Andrews retained a town oligarchy independent of church influence and hence produced one of the earliest organized Protestant churches in Scotland.

BIBLIOGRAPHY

David McRoberts, ed., *The Medieval Church of St. Andrews* (1976).

A. A. M. DUNCAN

[See also **Augustinian Canons; David I of Scotland; Paris, University of; Picts; Scotland.**]

ST. ANDREWS MS. See **Wolfenbüttel, Helmstedt MS 628.**

ST. BARTHOLOMEW, MASTER OF (*fl. ca.* 1445–*ca.* 1515), Cologne painter, probably of Dutch origin, and named for the *St. Bartholomew Altarpiece* (Munich). Also active (trained?) as a manuscript illuminator, his works include the *Hours of Sophia von Bylant* (1475, Cologne). Many works, including his *Thomas Altarpiece* (*ca.* 1499, Cologne), were commissioned for Carthusian cloisters, especially in Cologne, leading to the hypothesis that the master was either a monk or a lay brother. He is noted for an uneasy mixture of decorative, jewel-like gold with descriptive Netherlandish verisimilitude in sculpturesque shrine arrangement.

BIBLIOGRAPHY

Mechthild Andreae, "Der B.-meister Gewandstudien zur Chronologie seiner Werke" (diss., Innsbruck, 1963); Rainer Budde, *Köln und seine Maler, 1300–1500* (1986), 134–158; *Der Meister des Bartholomäus-altares/Der Meister des Aachener-altares: Kölner Maler der Spätgotik* (exhibition catalogue) (1961); *Herbst des Mittelalters* (exhibition catalogue) (1970), 47–49; Paul Pieper, "Miniaturen des Bartholomäus-meisters," in *Wallraf Richartz Jahrbuch*, **15** (1953), "Das Stundenbuch des Bartholomäus-meisters," *ibid.* and **21** (1959); Rolf Wallrath, "Der Thomas-altar in Köln," *ibid.*, **17** (1955); Frank G. Zehnder, *Late Gothic Art from Cologne* (1977), 86–107.

LARRY SILVER

[See also **Carthusians; Manuscript Illumination, European;** and illustration overleaf.]

ST. CECILIA MASTER (*fl. ca.* 1280–1310), Florentine painter, close follower of Giotto, named after a panel depicting *St. Cecilia Enthroned with Scenes from Her Life* in the Uffizi at Florence. Three

St. Bartholomew between Sts. Agnes and Cecilia. Central panel of the St. Bartholomew altarpiece from the church of St. Columba, Cologne, after 1500. Now in the Alte Pinakothek, Munich. FOTO MARBURG / ART RESOURCE

St. Cecilia Enthroned with Scenes from Her Life. Panel painting of the first half of the 14th century, now in the Uffizi, Florence, no. 449. ALINARI / ART RESOURCE

scenes from the life of St. Francis, *The Healing of Giovanni of Ylerda, The Confession of a Woman Raised from the Dead,* and *The Liberation of Pietro of Alifia,* in the upper church of S. Francesco at Assisi, have also been attributed to him. His style indicates that he might have influenced or been influenced by Riminese painting as well.

BIBLIOGRAPHY

Bernard Berenson, *Italian Pictures of the Renaissance: Florentine School,* 2 vols. (1963); Richard Fremantle, *Florentine Gothic Painters* (1975); Richard Offner, *A Corpus of Florentine Painting,* I, section 3 (1931); John White, *Art and Architecture in Italy, 1250–1400* (1966), 141–142.

ADELHEID M. GEALT

[See also **Assisi, San Francesco; Fresco Painting; Giotto di Bondone; Gothic Art: Painting; Panel Painting.**]

ST. CHAD, BOOK OF (Lichfield Gospels). Written about the second quarter of the eighth century, this manuscript (since the tenth century at Lichfield Cathedral) was once thought to be connected with St. Chad, or Ceadda, who was educated at Lindisfarne under Aidan, served as bishop of York, and died in 672 as bishop of Lichfield.

The illuminated Gospelbook, written on vellum in Insular majuscule, is incomplete. It begins with the Gospels of Matthew and Mark, but ends abruptly at Luke 3:9. The richness of the decoration and the large size (12.3 × 9.4 in; 308 × 235 mm) indicates that it probably was an altar book used in the Mass. It is likely too that it was displayed open during special religious observances. The book is probably the oldest manuscript in liturgical use to this day, since the bishop of Lichfield, when admitted to office, takes an oath upon the codex.

The original scope of the manuscript can be inferred from the magnificent decoration of the Gospel of Luke; each Gospel must have contained an Evangelist portrait, a four-symbols page, a carpet page, and at least one incipit page. Although the prefatory matter is now missing, it would have also contained Jerome's letter to Pope Damasus I (*Novum opus*) explaining his translation, Eusebius' letter to Carpianus on the use of canon tables, and Eusebian canon tables, which are a concordance to Gospel passages arranged under decorated arches in columns.

The remaining illuminations consist of an incipit page to Matthew, initials LI (*Liber generationis*); a second incipit page to Matthew, initials XPI (*Christi autem*); an Evangelist portrait of a standing St. Mark with his symbol, the lion; an incipit page to Mark, initials IN (*Initium*); an Evangelist portrait of St. Luke with his symbol, the calf; a page with the four symbols of the Evangelists; a carpet page with inset cross and tightly packed patterns of animal interlace; and an incipit page to St. Luke, initial Q (*Quoniam*).

The date and place of origin of the manuscript are uncertain. A ninth-century Latin inscription indicates that Gelhi traded his best horse for the book and then offered it to the church of St. Teilo in Wales. The book arrived at Lichfield in the tenth century.

BIBLIOGRAPHY

Jonathan J. G. Alexander, *Insular Manuscripts: 6th to the 9th Century* (1978), 48–50; Françoise Henry, *Irish Art in the Early Christian Period* (1965); Thomas D. Kendrick, *Anglo-Saxon Art to A.D. 900* (1938, repr.

St. Luke. Miniature from the Book of St. Chad (Lichfield Gospels), 8th century. COURTESY OF THE DEAN AND CHAPTER, LICHFIELD CATHEDRAL. PHOTO: COURTAULD INSTITUTE OF ART, LONDON

1972); Neil R. Ker, *Catalogue of Manuscripts Containing Anglo-Saxon* (1957), 158; Elias A. Lowe, *Codices latini antiquiroes,* II (1972), no. 159; Patrick McGurk, *Latin Gospel Books from A.D. 400 to A.D. 800* (1961), 7–19, 31; Carl Nordenfalk, *Celtic and Anglo-Saxon Painting* (1977), 76–83; Thomas H. Ohlgren, ed., *Insular and Anglo-Saxon Illuminated Manuscripts: An Iconographic Catalogue* (1968), 17–18; Melville Richards, "The 'Lichfield' Gospels (Book of 'Saint Chad')," in *The National Library of Wales Journal,* **18** (1973); Margaret J. Rickert, *Painting in Britain: The Middle Ages,* 2nd ed. (1965), 10, 16–17; O. Elfrida Saunders, *English Illumination,* I (1928), 12.

THOMAS H. OHLGREN

[See also **Aidan of Lindisfarne; Anglo-Saxon Literature; Canon Table; Carpet Page; Evangelist Symbols; Gospelbook; Initials, Decorated and Historiated; Lacertine (with illustration); Lindisfarne Gospels; Vellum.**]

ST. DAVID'S, on the tip of the southwest peninsula of Wales, was and still remains the seat of a bishopric, and its patron David (or Dewi) is the patron saint of Wales. A religious community of St. David's existed from at least the eighth century, and bishops of Mynyw (Menevia), its early medieval name, are noted from 831. In the twelfth century the community attempted to secure archiepiscopal status for its bishop. Despite a long fight against the archbishopric of Canterbury, which expected obedience, it was ultimately unsuccessful, and the case effectively lapsed after 1203. It is nevertheless clear that St. David's was a place of major importance in Welsh ecclesiastical affairs, despite its isolated position: the Welsh Annals (*Annales Cambriae*) were written there from the late eighth century; King Alfred of England called the monk Asser from St. David's to his court in the late ninth century; it was attacked many times by the Vikings in the tenth and eleventh centuries; William the Conqueror journeyed to St. David's in 1081 on his first entry into Wales; Rhigyfarch, a son of Bishop Sulien, voiced a lament for his countrymen at the coming of the Normans in the late eleventh century.

The foundation was supposedly established by St. David at "Rosina Vallis" as a model of ascetic practice, according to the eleventh-century hagiographic tradition. Members of his monastic community were known as *aquatici* (water drinkers). There is no early evidence of the site or community, although the St. David's annalist (of the late eighth century or later) would place his episcopate around the year 604. His cult was known in Wales at least as early as the eighth century and in Ireland by about 800. There are early Christian burials (not precisely datable) at sites in the neighborhood. The relationship of Rosina Vallis to the present site of St. David's is unclear, but current opinion is that the original foundation was made in the vicinity of the present church, in a sheltered valley two miles from a natural harbor on the coast.

BIBLIOGRAPHY

James Conway Davies, ed., *Episcopal Acts and Cognate Documents Relating to Welsh Dioceses, 1066–1272,* 2 vols. (1946–1948); Wendy Davies, *Wales in the Early Middle Ages* (1982); Michael Richter, *Giraldus Cambrensis* (1972).

WENDY DAVIES

[See also **Asser; Gerald of Wales; Wales: History.**]

ST. DENIS, ABBEY CHURCH. The church of St. Denis, north of Paris, is on the supposed site of the martyrdom and burial of the patron saint of France. An oratory may have been built in the Merovingian period, and a large Carolingian church was consecrated in 775. The present church was built partly in the twelfth century (west facade complex, including narthex, as well as the ambulatory and radiating chapels at the eastern end of the choir) and partly in the thirteenth century (upper part of choir, transept, and new nave). The twelfth-century work was carried out in the 1140's under the famous Abbot Suger, who left a record of his accomplishments, and is celebrated as the "first Gothic church." The west facade, mutilated and heavily restored, established the standard for French church facades: triple portal, twin towers, rose or wheel window. The use of pointed arches and ribbed vaults in the choir, plus the contiguous radiating chapels, is the chief feature of Suger's ambulatory. The thirteenth-century work is in the pure Court Style of St. Louis, or Rayonnant style.

BIBLIOGRAPHY

Robert Branner, *St. Louis and the Court Style in Gothic Architecture* (1965); Carolina A. Bruzellius, *The Thirteenth-century Church at St-Denis* (1986); Sumner McK. Crosby, *L'abbaye royale de Saint-Denis* (1953), "Abbot Suger's St.-Denis: The New Gothic," in *Romanesque and Gothic Art* (Acts of the Twentieth Internation-

 ST. GALL, MONASTERY AND PLAN

al Congress of the History of Art, I) (1963), and *The Royal Abbey of Saint-Denis from Its Beginnings to the Death of Suger,* Pamela Z. Blum, ed. (1987); Erwin Panofsky, *Abbot Suger on the Abbey Church of St.-Denis and Its Art Treasures,* 2nd ed. (1979).

CARL F. BARNES, JR.

[See also **Ambulatory; Arch; Chapel; Choir; Gothic Architecture (with illustration); Narthex; Nave; Pre-Romanesque Architecture (with plan); Suger of St. Denis; Tower; Transept; Vault.**]

ST. GALL, MONASTERY AND PLAN OF. While its origins may be traced back to the year 612, the monastery of St. Gall in present-day northeastern Switzerland was a minor foundation until the ninth century. In 818, Emperor Louis the Pious placed it under imperial protection, abrogating the jurisdiction of the bishop of Constance, at the request of Abbot Gozbert (816–837). Under a number of notable abbots, including Gozbert, Grimald (841–872), and Hartmut (872–883/884), the monastery increased in wealth and importance throughout the ninth century. It reached the height of its prosperity under Abbot Salomon (890–919) and ranked among the foremost artistic and educational centers of the Carolingian renaissance.

Among the legacies of the medieval monastery is a library that resides on site to this day. It contains one of the richest surviving collections of early medieval texts and includes one document that is truly unique: the Plan of St. Gall. Dating from the third decade of the ninth century, formed of five separate pieces of parchment sewn together, and measuring approximately 45 by 31 inches (113 cm by 78 cm), the Plan is the only major architectural drawing to survive from the period between the fall of Rome and the thirteenth century. It was drawn in the scriptorium of Reichenau and dedicated to Abbot Gozbert of St. Gall, but was never actually executed. Its ground plans (in red ink) and explanatory inscriptions (in brown ink) depict an entire monastic compound, including numerous individual buildings. Among them are two churches; a square cloister and an abbot's house; dormitories for monks, guests, and paupers; kitchens; workshops; stables; gardens; a brewery and winery; an infirmary; and even a house devoted specifically to therapeutic bloodletting.

The importance of the Plan is uncontested, but almost every other issue associated with it is subject to dispute. Debate continues on such fundamental topics as the scale and proportions of the Plan; whether it was copied from a lost prototype, and if so, with what fidelity; and whether it embodies decisions of the monastic reform councils of 816 and 817 or reflects the thinking of a particular individual. Despite these uncertainties, the Plan remains a crucial document for numerous aspects of early medieval culture.

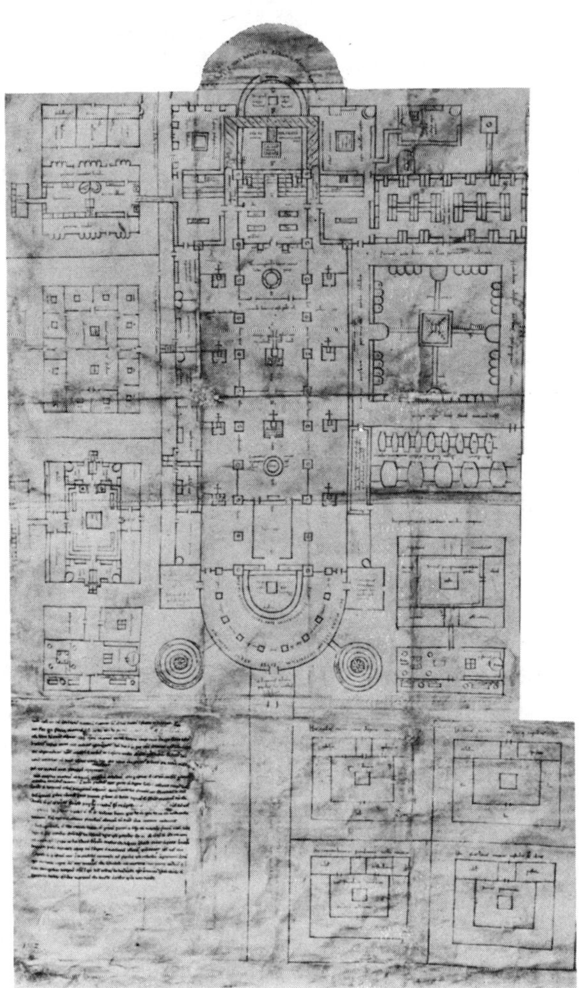

The Plan of St. Gall (detail showing church and cloister), *ca.* 820–830. ST. GALLEN, STIFTSBIBLIOTHEK

BIBLIOGRAPHY

Hermann Bikel, *Die Wirtschaftsverhältnisse des Klosters St. Gallen* (1914); James Midgley Clark, *The Abbey of St. Gall as a Centre of Literature and Art* (1926); Johannes Duft, ed., *Studien zum St. Galler Klosterplan* (1962); Walter Horn and Ernest Born, *The Plan of St. Gall,* 3 vols. (1979), with extensive bibliography; Georg Thürer, *St. Galler Geschichte: Kultur, Staatsleben und*

Wirtschaft in Kanton und Stadt St. Gallen von der Urzeit bis zur Gegenwart, I (1953), 101–125.

EDWARD A. SEGAL

[See also **Bay System; Carolingians and the Carolingian Empire; Church, Types of; Gall, St.; Monastery; Pre-Romanesque Architecture; Renaissances and Revivals in Medieval Art.**]

ST. JOHN LATERAN. See **Lateran.**

ST. MARK'S, VENICE. See **San Marco, Venice.**

ST. MARTIAL SCHOOL, the name given to repertories of sacred music from the ninth through twelfth centuries preserved in manuscripts originating in Aquitaine that had been collected at the abbey of St. Martial in Limoges in south-central France by the thirteenth century. Several of the manuscripts were written at St. Martial, and others at various churches in Limoges. St. Martial, however, was not an isolated center of musical activity.

In the sixth century, a church dedicated to St. Peter was built on the site of the tomb of St. Martial, who had founded a Christian community at Limoges around 250 and was its first bishop. The clerics who served the cult of St. Martial for the pilgrims to his tomb were specifically designated as the servants of St. Martial. In 848, that group of clergy adopted the Benedictine Rule, and thus the abbey was founded. In the same year, a church was begun beside St. Pierre-du-Sépulchre, which was dedicated to the Savior, but was also designated the abbey church of St. Martial. These were the principal churches for the cult, and the monks' cloisters were attached to them. Subsequent enlargements of the church of the Savior, to accommodate decorations of the saint's tomb and pilgrims to it, were consecrated in 1028 and 1095. Beset by financial troubles in the mid eleventh century, the abbey appealed to Cluny, requesting to become its dependent, and in 1063 did so. Thus, the survival of the monastery was assured.

Accompanying the establishment of the abbey was a flourishing school of musical composition active in Limoges and Aquitaine and devoted to the adornment of all the major feasts of the church year. The types of sacred musical composition pursued in Aquitaine may be divided into two groups that are also separated chronologically. Between about 900 and 1100, the main emphasis was on music for the Mass: Ordinary and Proper items, including sequences and proses, tropes for Mass items, and processional antiphons. In the first half of the twelfth century a new form became popular: the rhymed, rhythmical versus with its double, the *Benedicamus domino* versus. Many of these versus are set with polyphonic music, and they are accompanied in the sources by polyphonic settings of some of the proses from the earlier repertory and some newer strophic proses.

The bulk of the manuscript sources are preserved in the Bibliothèque Nationale in Paris, which purchased most of them from the library of the abbey of St. Martial in 1730. These include fonds latin, MSS 776, 778, 779, 887, 903, 909, 1084, 1086, 1118, 1119, 1120, 1121, 1132, 1133, 1134, 1135, 1136, 1137, 1138, 1139, 1154, 1338, 3549, 3719, and nouvelles acquisitions 1177 and 1871. Four other manuscripts have been identified as important sources for the Aquitanian repertories: Apt, Basilique Ste. Anne, MSS 17 and 18, and Wolfenbüttel, Herzog-August-Bibliothek, Gudiani lat., MS 79, which are tropers; and London, British Library, add. MS 36881, which contains monophonic and polyphonic versus. The music is noted in Aquitanian point notation, which employs few neumes of more than three notes. The neumes are heighted around a single line, or, in manuscripts written after 1100, on a staff with three to five lines.

Most of the earlier sources are divided into *libelli,* each containing one type of piece. Tropes of the Proper items of the Mass, tropes of each of the Ordinary items of the Mass, proses, sequence melodies, untroped melodies for each of the Ordinary items, alleluias and offertories with their verses, and processional antiphons are grouped separately, each group ordered according to the liturgical year if appropriate. In addition, Paris, Bibliothèque Nationale, fonds latin, MS 1154, contains an important repertory of lyric texts with music from the ninth century. Stylistically, the monophony is similar to contemporary plainsong.

At the end of the eleventh century, Aquitanian composers turned to the new versus. Aside from the entertainment of the monks themselves, these pieces were likely used as conductus to introduce lessons at matins and the Mass, and perhaps to introduce choral musical items such as the Gloria and the Credo. The *Benedicamus domino* versus were used as substitutes for the dismissal formula of the Office. Many of the texts can be assigned to a specific feast on the basis of internal evidence, the most popular being Christmas. The sources are less organized than the earlier ones. Generally, monophonic and polyphonic pieces are grouped together, and, in Paris, Bibliothèque Nationale, fonds latin, MS 1139, the *Benedicamus domino* versus are collected, but elsewhere other means of organization (for example, according to the kalendar) are not discernible. In the earliest layer of the repertory (Paris, Bibliothèque Nationale, fonds latin, MS 1139, fols. 32–39 and 48–79; MS 3719, fols. 23–32), the polyphonic pieces are written in successive notation, that is, one voice is noted above the first stanza, the other above the second stanza of the text. Subsequent sources use score notation.

The melodic styles of both the monophonic and polyphonic versus are similar. The texts are set in syllabic style for the most part, ornamented with cadential melismata, sometimes very elaborately; often the melismata consist of a single figure developed sequentially. The upper voices of the polyphonic pieces are only slightly more florid than the lower voices and generally move in contrary motion to them. Many pieces include elaborate cadential melismata for both voices in a note-against-note texture. The polyphonic settings of the newer rhythmic proses share these characteristics, although their cadential melismata are less elaborate. The upper voices of the settings of the older proses are more florid. Two pieces that have the *Benedicamus domino* versicle as the text of the lower voice and a rhymed versus in the upper voice have attracted much attention as precursors of the motet. Although they are polytextual, and the upper voice is much more florid than the lower, as in the thirteenth-century motet, the term motet was originally applied to pieces adapted from substitute clausulae, and consequently it is inappropriate to use it retrospectively for the two St. Martial pieces. The more descriptive term, double-texted *Benedicamus domino* versus, is preferable.

BIBLIOGRAPHY

Sources. Analecta hymnica medii aevi, VII (1889), XX (1895), XXI (1895), XLVb (1904), XLVII (1905), XLIX (1906). Bryan Gillingham, "Saint-Martial Polyphony—A Catalogue Raisonné," in *Gordon Athol Anderson: In Memoriam* (1984), I, contains a list of manuscripts of the Aquitanian repertoire.

Studies. Willi Apel, "Bemerkungen zur den Organa von St. Martial," in *Miscelánea en homenaje a Monseñor Higinio Anglés* (1958–1961), I; Barbara Marian Barclay, "The Medieval Repertory of Polyphonic Untroped 'Benedicamus Domino' Settings" (diss., UCLA, 1977), I, 94–207; Jens Bonderup, *The Saint Martial Polyphony: Texture and Tonality* (1982); Richard L. Crocker, *The Early Medieval Sequence* (1977); Sarah Fuller, "The Myth of Saint Martial Polyphony: A Study of the Sources," in *Musica disciplina,* **33** (1979); James Grier, "Transmission in the Aquitanian Versaria of the Eleventh and Twelfth Centuries" (diss., Toronto, 1985); Michel Huglo, "Aux origines du Tropaire-Prosaire," in *Nordiskt kollokvium 4 i latinsk liturgiforskning* (1978), trans. as "On the Origins of the Troper-Proser," in *Journal of the Plainsong and Medieval Music Society,* **2** (1979); Günther Schmidt, "Strukturprobleme der Mehrstimmigkeit im Repertoire von St. Martial," in *Musikforschung,* **15** (1962), with Bruno Stäblein's comments, "Zur Übertragung des Benedicamus-Tropus 'Omnis curet homo,'" *ibid.,* and Schmidt's reply, "Zur Übertragung früher Mehrstimmigkeit, besonders des Benedicamus-Tropus 'Omnis curet homo,'" *ibid.,* **16** (1963); Leo Treitler, "Transmission and the Study of Music History," in International Musicological Society, Congress (12th, 1977, Berkeley), *Report,* Daniel Heartz and Bonnie Wade, eds. (1981), and "Observations on the Transmission of Some Aquitanian Tropes," in *Aktuelle Fragen der Musik-bezogenen Mittelalterforschung: Texte zu einem Basler Kolloquium des Jahres 1975* (1982).

JAMES GRIER

[See also **Aquitaine; Benedicamus Domino; Benedictine Rule; Clausula; Cluny, Order of; Conductus; Motet; Neume; Tropes.**]

ST. MARY'S ABBEY, DUBLIN. Despite legends attributing its foundation to the tenth century, either by the Dublin Norse or by Máelsechnaill (Malachy) II, king of the Uí Néill, St. Mary's was almost certainly founded as a monastery by the reformist congregation of Savigny (Normandy) in 1139. It followed Savigny in its submission to Cistercian rule in 1147. In a bull of Pope Anastasius IV of 1154, St. Mary's is listed as a daughter house of Combermere, near Chester, which had been founded in 1133, though no documents surviving from St. Mary's show evidence of such a connection. In 1156, by decree of the abbot of Savigny, St. Mary's was made subject to the abbey of Buildwas in Shropshire, a relationship that persisted for generations.

The site of the abbey itself was on the north side of the river Liffey near the present-day intersection of Mary Street and Capel Street, at which the remains of the twelfth-century chapter house still stand. The core of the abbey's lands extended northward to Clonliffe and Portmarnock and were much augmented by donations from the great Anglo-Norman families after the invasion of Ireland in 1170. The bulk of its lands were in Dublin and within the English Pale, but some were as far away as Connacht.

Throughout most of its history, the abbey is notable for its English connections. Its charters were repeatedly confirmed by English kings, and all its abbots from the beginning of the thirteenth century were Anglo-Norman or English. It stands in sharp contrast to its Irish Cistercian rival, Mellifont, which was formally reprimanded by the Cistercian chapter for admitting only Irish speakers. Because it remained so firmly within the English sphere of influence, St. Mary's is paid scant attention in the native annals, but along with its own daughter house at Dunbrody, County Wexford, it has left the only important Irish cartularies. Many early records may have been destroyed in a fire in 1304. The abbey was dissolved in 1539, with some monetary provision being made for the abbot and monks.

BIBLIOGRAPHY

John T. Gilbert, *Chartularies of St. Mary's Abbey, Dublin*, 2 vols. (1884); A. Gwynn, "The Origins of St. Mary's Abbey, Dublin," in *Journal of the Royal Society of Antiquaries of Ireland,* **79** (1949); C. Ó Conbhuí, "The Lands of St. Mary's Abbey, Dublin," in *Proceedings of the Royal Irish Academy,* **62** (1962).

DANIEL FREDERICK MELIA

[See also **Cartulary; Cistercian Order; Dublin; Ireland; Uí Néill.**]

ST. PATRICK'S PURGATORY, site of the pilgrimage, supposedly in 1153, of an Irish knight named Owein to a cave on Station Island (County Donegal, Ireland). Owein's vision of hell and paradise, and the pardon of his sins, is the subject of an immensely popular legend dealing with the "otherworld." An English monk, H. (probably Henry or Hugh of Saltrey), learned the story from one Gilbert of Louth, who is supposed to have gotten it from Owein himself. H. of Saltrey's *Tractatus de purgatorio sancti Patricii,* which gives a definitive form of this legend associated with a popular place of pilgrimage, served as a model for numerous versions in Latin and in the vernacular. The most important vernacular version is the Old French poem *Espurgatoire saint Patrice,* generally ascribed to Marie de France.

BIBLIOGRAPHY

Editions include Thomas Atkinson Jenkins, ed., *Espurgatoire seint Patriz: An Old French Poem . . .* (1894, repr. 1974), and *The Espurgatoire saint Patriz of Marie de France, with a Text of the Latin Original* (1903, repr. 1974); Cornelius M. van der Zanden, *Étude sur le Purgatoire de saint Patrice* (1927), 45–86. See also Howard R. Patch, *The Other World, According to Descriptions in Medieval Literature* (1950, repr. 1970), 114–116.

PETER F. DEMBOWSKI

[See also **Anglo-Norman Literature; Espurgatoire St. Patrice; Irish Literature: Voyage Tales; Marie de France; Purgatory, Western Concept of.**]

ST. PETER, LITURGY OF, a form of eucharistic celebration consisting of a translation into Greek (and later into other Eastern languages) of the Latin Mass placed in the context of Eastern liturgies. It is to be distinguished from the *missa greca,* frequently found in early medieval Latin manuscripts, in which the ordinary chants of the Latin Mass (Gloria, Credo, Sanctus, and Agnus Dei) are translated into Greek.

Over the centuries there has been considerable debate as to when and where the Liturgy of St. Peter was composed—Antioch, Rome, southern Italy, Illyricum, Macedonia, Thessaloniki—but the prevailing theory, which was proposed by H. W. Codrington, places it in south-central Italy. The Latin text of the canon from which the Liturgy of St. Peter was first translated was probably not earlier than the ninth century, although there are clear reflections of older traditions such as those found in the Bobbio Missal, Gallican-rite sacramentaries, the Gelasian Sacramentary of the eighth century, and Milanese-rite sacramentaries. The earliest translation, probably more like a Greek gloss on the Latin text, was made for the use of Greek-speaking priests. It was subsequently revised, probably in the latter part of the tenth century, according to the Gregorian Sacramentary, thus resulting in two major versions, the original and the Gregorian. The whole of the translated Latin Mass, including the ordinary, was then adapted to Eastern liturgical requirements along the lines of the Greek Liturgy of St. Mark. From the eleventh century on, there was great elaboration on this liturgy, which was certainly used by Greek-speaking clergy and monks in southern Italy. This mixed Latin-Greek liturgy eventually spread to the Georgians on Mt. Athos, to Macedonia, and to Jerusalem, where it was translated into Armenian.

BIBLIOGRAPHY

Humphrey W. Codrington, *The Liturgy of St. Peter* (1936); Jean Michel Hanssens, "La liturgie romano-byzantine de Saint Pierre," in *Orientalia christiana periodica,* **4** (1938); M. Biskup, "Influssi della liturgia di San Pietro sui messali glagolitici croati," in *Ephemerides liturgicae,* **90** (1976); Cesare Alzati, "Tradizione bizantina e tradizione latina nella liturgia sancti Petri attraverso il simbolo niceno-costantinopolitano," in *Vita religiosa morale e sociale ed i concili di Split (Spalato) dei secc. x–xi: Atti del Symposium internazionale di storia ecclesiastica, Split, 26–30 settembre 1978* (1982).

ROGER E. REYNOLDS

[See also **Mass, Liturgy of the; Sacramentary.**]

ST. PETER'S, ROME. See **Old St. Peter's, Rome.**

ST. PHILIBERT, TOURNUS, the major monument of Burgundian First Romanesque architecture, is particularly important for its innovative, and presumably early, use of stone vaulting. The relics of Philibert were brought to Tournus in 875, and by 937 the monastery was important enough to have been attacked by the Hungarians. A major fire of 1007/1008 probably provides a date for the beginning of the present building.

Architecturally, the most significant parts of the church are the two-story narthex and the nave. The groin vaults of the narthex's lower floor are usually dated to the first half of the eleventh century because of their simplicity and rudeness. If the vaulting was completed by 1020, when an altar was dedicated there, the Tournus narthex would be one of the earliest vaulted structures in France.

Also interesting for the history of vaulting are the transverse barrel vaults of the nave. Supported on high, cylindrical piers, these vaults are an almost unique solution to the problem of lateral vault thrusts. The unusual nature of the nave vaults makes them difficult to date, although they were probably completed by the dedication of the church in 1120. Structurally brilliant but aesthetically disturbing, the Tournus experiment had little, if any, influence on later buildings.

St. Philibert, Tournus, showing the transverse barrel vaults of the central nave and groin vaults in the side aisles, 10th–12th centuries. GIRAUDON / ART RESOURCE

BIBLIOGRAPHY

Clement Edson Armi, *Saint-Philibert at Tournus and Wall Systems of First Romanesque Architecture* (1976); Georges de Mire, *Saint-Philibert de Tournus,* text by Jean Vallery-Radot (1955).

WILLIAM J. DIEBOLD

[See also **Romanesque Architecture; Vault.**]

ST. SERNIN, TOULOUSE, one of the most representative and best preserved of the great pilgrimage churches of Romanesque France. The church was begun in 1077 or in 1082/1083 and probably was

The Ascension. Relief on the tympanum and lintel of the Porte de Miègeville (south portal) of St. Sernin, Toulouse, after 1118. PHOTO: JEAN ROUBIER, PARIS

substantially complete when Pope Calixtus II dedicated an altar on 19 July 1119. Part of St. Sernin was built by Raymond Gayrard. The church contains very significant examples of Romanesque sculpture.

BIBLIOGRAPHY

Marcel Aubert, *L'église Saint-Sernin de Toulouse* (1933); Kenneth J. Conant, *Carolingian and Romanesque Architecture, 800 to 1200* (1959), 98–99; Marcel Durliat, "La construction de Saint-Sernin de Toulouse au XIe siècle," in *Bulletin Monumental,* **121** (1963).

CARL F. BARNES, JR.

[See also **Church, Types of; Gayrard, Raymond; Romanesque Architecture.**]

ST. VERONICA, MASTER OF (*fl. ca.* 1395–1415), an anonymous painter, named for his *Veronica* panel (Munich, Alte Pinakothek). The most important artist working in Cologne between Master Wilhelm and Stephen Lochner, he painted standing, slender, fine-featured figures, often accompanied by tiny, incorporeal, floating angels, in rich, softly modeled colors against decoratively tooled gold grounds. He is one of the artists of the International Gothic style. Other works include *Crucifix with Saints* (Cologne), *Man of Sorrows with Saints* (Antwerp), a multifigured *Calvary* (Cologne), and a half-length *Madonna with Pea Blossom* (*ca.* 1410; Nuremberg, Cologne).

BIBLIOGRAPHY

Rainer Budde, *Köln und seine Maler, 1300–1500* (1986), 38–43; Otto Förster, "Um den Meister der Veronika," in *Wallraf-Richartz Jahrbuch,* **19** (1957); Paul Pieper, "Zum Werk des Meisters der Heiligen Veronika," in *Festschrift für Gert von der Osten* (1970); Heribert Reiners, *Die Kölner Malerschule* (1925), 31–41; Klaus H. Schweitzer, *Der Veronikameister und sein Kreis* (1935); Alfred Stange, *Deutsche Malerei der Gotik,* III (repr. 1969), 50–67; Frank G. Zehnder, "Der Meister der heiligen Veronika," in *Vor Stefan Lochner* (1974), exhibition catalog, *Late Gothic Art from Cologne* (1977), 30–35, and *Der Meister der hl. Veronika* (1981).

LARRY SILVER

[See also **Cologne; Gothic Art: Painting; Gothic: International Style; Panel Painting.**]

St. Veronica with the *sudarium* and child angels. Panel painting by the Master of St. Veronica from the church of St. Severin, Cologne, early 15th century. Now in the Alte Pinakothek, Munich, no. 11866. FOTO MARBURG / ART RESOURCE

ST. VICTOR MS (Paris, Bibliothèque Nationale, latin 15139) is a composite manuscript of unknown origins, formerly owned by the Paris abbey of St. Victor and, in the fourteenth century, by St. Quentin. Folios 255 to 293 contain a collection of music copied around 1250–1275 but composed around 1200–1250, most of it related to the Notre Dame tradition. Included are several unique conducti, some with texts related to specific political events (*O tocius Asie, Gaude felix Francia, Scysma mendacis*), eleven organa that represent a late stage in the history of the genre, and forty clausulae, to most of which motet text incipits have been appended, making this a unique witness to one phase in the history of the motet. Also added are two music treatises, in French and Latin, the former one of the earliest known of such texts in the vernacular.

BIBLIOGRAPHY

Robert Falck, "New Light on the Polyphonic Conductus Repertory in the St. Victor Manuscript," in *Journal of the American Musicological Society,* **23** (1970), and *The Notre Dame Conductus* (1981); Heinrich Husmann, "Das Organum vor und ausserhalb der Notre-Dame-Schule," in *International Musicological Society: Bericht über den neunten internationalen Kongress, Salzburg 1964,* I (1964), 25–35; Friedrich Ludwig, *Repertorium organorum recentioris et motetorum vetustissimi stili,* I, pt. 1 (1910, repr. 1964), 139–157; Yvonne Rokseth, "Le contrepoint double vers 1248," in *Mélanges de musicologie offerts à M. L. de la Laurencie* (1933); Jürg Stenzl, *Die vierzig Clausulae der Handschrift Paris, Bibliothèque Nationale, latin 15139 (Saint Victor-Clausulae)* (1970); Ethel Thurston, ed., *The Music in the St. Victor Manuscript, Paris lat. 15139* (1959).

EDWARD H. ROESNER

[See also **Clausula; Conductus; Motet; Notre Dame School; Organum.**]

STE. CHAPELLE, PARIS, the Court Style palace chapel built for King Louis IX (St. Louis, *d.* 1270) of France and one of the most famous buildings in the world. The origin of the Ste. Chapelle is found in two different areas: the tradition of two-story royal private chapels, of which that of Charlemagne at Aachen and that of Louis XIV at Versailles represent early and late examples; and the desire for a special monument to illustrate royal piety.

In 1239 Louis purchased from Baldwin II, Latin emperor of Constantinople (*r.* 1228–1261), for the sum of 135,000 pounds, the relics of the Passion, parts of which were then in Venice as pledge for a loan to Baldwin. The relics arrived in Paris in one shipment from Venice on 18 August 1239 and in a second shipment from Constantinople on 14 September 1241. Ownership of these most sacred objects clearly inspired Louis to build a suitable shrine to house them, but it is unknown when this decision was made. Construction may have begun as early as September 1239, when the first shipment of relics was transferred to St. Denis for safekeeping and the twelfth-century royal chapel of St. Nicolas was destroyed. The first recorded mention of the new chapel is in a document issued by Pope Innocent IV on 24 May 1244. A "charter of foundation" issued by Louis in January 1246 suggests that construction, including stained glass, was then complete or nearly so. The chapel was formally dedicated on 26 April 1248. After Louis' death it was reported that the chapel itself cost 40,000 pounds, and the shrine containing the relics cost an additional 100,000 pounds.

The architect of the Ste. Chapelle is unknown. A tradition going back to the sixteenth century (Paris, Bibliothèque Nationale, fonds français, MS 16,886) attributes the building to Pierre de Montreuil, but this cannot be proved. Robert Branner has proposed Thomas de Cormont, second architect at the cathedral of Amiens, as architect of the Ste. Chapelle because of similarities of details in the two buildings.

Whoever its architect, Louis himself, although only 25 in 1239, when the relics were purchased, must have determined that his Ste. Chapelle would be, in Branner's words, "a reliquary of monumental size." The intention was that the building reflect in its physical lavishness the significance of the materials it was to protect and honor. Innocent IV spoke of its "workmanship surpassing its materials," and in 1323 Jean de Jandun praised "the choice of its radiant colors, the images standing out against a gold background, the transparency and brilliance of its windows, its altar frontals, and its reliquaries sparkling with precious stones."

The Ste. Chapelle is novel neither by its plan nor by its construction, but by its lavishness and decoration. It inspired copies in architecture (the Ste. Chapelle at St. Germer-de-Fly) and in the other arts, most notably the miniatures of the Psalter of Louis IX (Paris, Bibliothèque Nationale, MS lat. 10525). Despite destruction (1780–1782) of its attached two-story treasury, crowding by later buildings, and extensive and heavy-handed restoration (1837–1863) by Duban, Lassus, Boeswillwald, and Viollet-le-Duc, the Ste. Chapelle stands as one of the most characteristic examples of the architectural creations of the Court Style of Louis IX.

BIBLIOGRAPHY

Robert Branner, *St. Louis and the Court Style in Gothic Architecture* (1965), 56–84, with complete bibliography, "The Painted Medallions in the Sainte-Chapelle in Paris," in *Transactions of the American Philosophical Society,* n.s. **58** (1968), and "The Sainte-Chapelle and the *Capella Regis* in the Thirteenth Century," in *Gesta,* **10** (1971); Peter Brieger and Philippe Verdier, *Art and the Courts: France and England from 1259 to 1328,* I (1972), 8–27; Louis Grodecki, *Sainte-Chapelle,* 3rd ed. (1979), with excellent bibliography and summary of the stained glass.

CARL F. BARNES, JR.

[See also **Amiens Cathedral; Glass, Stained (with illustration); Gothic Architecture; Innocent IV, Pope; Latin Empire of Constantinople; Louis IX of France; Relics, Western European; Reliquary; St. Denis, Abbey Church; Thomas de Cormont.**]

SAINTS' LIVES. See **Hagiography.**

SAJJĀDA. See **Rugs and Carpets.**

ṢAKR IBN ḤARB. See **Abū Sufāyn ibn Ḥarb ibn Umayya.**

SALADIN (Ṣalāḥ al-Dīn Yūsuf ibn Ayyūb) (1137/1138—1193), famous Muslim war leader best known for his victory over the crusaders in the Battle of Ḥiṭṭīn (1187), his recovery of Jerusalem for Islam, and his defensive struggle against the Third Crusade.

Saladin belonged to an ambitious Kurdish family which had its roots in the area of Dwin, Armenia, but rose to prominence in Iraq and Syria. In 1138 his father, Ayyūb, and uncle, Shīrkūh, remaining in control of the castle of Takrīt, the birthplace of Saladin, entered the service of the powerful Syrian leader Zangī. In 1146, following the death of Zangī, Ayyūb joined the forces of Damascus, while Shīrkūh remained in the service of Zangī's famous successor, Nūr al-Dīn. In 1154 the two brothers plotted together to surrender Damascus to Nūr al-Dīn, helping him to become the strongest Syro-Mesopotamian leader to wage the holy war (jihad) against the crusaders. The prestige and influence Ayyūb and Shīrkūh enjoyed at the court and in the army of Nūr al-Dīn were helpful in the promotion of the career of Saladin, his brothers, and his cousins.

Although some Arab chroniclers emphasize the religious and meditative elements in Saladin's early upbringing, he was committed to a military career. In 1152 he joined his uncle Shīrkūh at Aleppo and was allotted a military fief (*iqṭāᶜ*) of his own. His performance must have been meritorious, because in 1156 he was placed in charge of the security forces of Damascus. Returning to Aleppo, he was appointed as aide-de-camp, serving as liaison officer between Nūr al-Dīn and his commanders, "never leaving the sultan whether on the march or at court" (Abū Shāmah, *Kitāb al-Rawḍatayn*). In that capacity Saladin acquired firsthand practical experience in the art of ruling a feudal military organization.

Saladin's successful bid for political power came as a consequence of the significant part he played during the three expeditions of the Syrian troops to Fatimid Egypt, led by Shīrkūh. In the first expedition, Saladin's organizational talents helped Shīrkūh to extricate his expeditionary corps from a critical situation at Bilbays (fall 1164), caused by a counteroffensive of the joint Egyptian and crusader army. In the second expedition, Saladin distinguished himself in the victorious Battle of al-Babayn (18 April 1167), and in a heroic defense of Alexandria (spring and summer 1167) against the combined forces of the Egyptians and the crusaders. In 1168/1169 Saladin once again accompanied his uncle to Egypt. This time Saladin not only contributed to the rescue of Cairo from the crusaders but helped Shīrkūh to seize control over the degenerate Fatimid caliphate by killing its treacherous vizier, Shāwar (18 January 1169). By then Saladin's reputation was firmly established, so that on 26 March 1169, following the sudden death of Shīrkūh, he was acclaimed by his Kurdish relatives and supporters as commander-in-chief of the Syrian expeditionary army; his appointment as vizier of the Fatimid caliphate was but a formality.

In this new capacity, Saladin further demonstrated his political and military talents. By launching a program of fiscal, economic, administrative, and military reforms, including the rebuilding of the Egyptian naval forces, he transformed the country of the Nile into a resourceful logistic base. By defeating crusader attacks (against Damietta in 1169, and against Alexandria in 1174) and by organizing successful military operations against the Ayla, the Yemen, Nubia, and North Africa, Saladin enhanced his reputation of being an aggressive military leader. By squelching several rebellions, by assigning his close relatives and Kurdish supporters to sensitive judicial, fiscal, and military functions, and, in September 1171, by suppressing the heterodox (Shiite) caliphate of the Fatimids, Saladin emerged as a dynamic head of a nascent Ayyubid power, defying the authority of Nūr al-Dīn himself.

In the fall of 1174, exploiting a political vacuum created by the deaths of Nūr al-Dīn (15 May 1174) and of the crusader king, Amalric (11 July 1174), Saladin succeeded in taking Damascus. This expansionist move provoked resentment on the part of the descendants of Nūr al-Dīn and those of Zangī, with Aleppo and Mosul serving as the main centers of opposition. Although ostensibly always committed to the struggle against the crusaders, during the subsequent twelve years Saladin focused his military and political attention on fighting his Muslim rivals in northern Syria, upper Mesopotamia, and eastern Anatolia. His efforts were finally rewarded with the submission of Aleppo (11 June 1183) and of Mosul (3 March 1186).

After organizing the political and administrative structure of his extensive feudalistic state, Saladin could turn his undivided attention to the problem of the crusaders. In the spring of 1187 he fielded a powerful army, an impressive array of about 12,000 cavalrymen with possibly as many auxiliary troops and irregulars, to respond militarily to the renewal of hostilities caused by a provocation on the part of the irresponsible and aggressive Reginald of Châtillon, master of Kerak and Shawbak in Transjordan. On 4 July 1187, following an imaginative tactical penetration of crusader territory, Saladin achieved a great victory over the Christian foe in the battle of Ḥiṭṭīn. The bulk of the crusader army was virtually eliminated on the spot. The majority of the crusader warriors not killed in battle were led into captivity. Among the captives was King Guy of Lusignan. Others, like Reginald of Châtillon and all Templar and Hospitaler knights, were executed in cold blood, in an act of vengeance for their persistently aggressive provocations against Islam. Only a handful of crusaders escaped the massacre to reach shelter behind the walls of the coastal fortress of Tyre.

Depleted of effective military protection, crusader territories became an easy prey of Saladin's dynamic and enthusiastic army. In less than two months after the Battle of Ḥiṭṭīn, all the major ports south of Tripoli with the exception of Tyre and Ascalon were in Muslim hands. This was also the fate of virtually all the inland towns and castles south of Tiberias. Only Shawbak and Kerak in Transjordan and a few formidable castles in the north, such as Belvoir (Kawkab), Safad, and Belfort, managed to hold out. On 5 September 1187 Ascalon surrendered in exchange for the release of King Guy from captivity. On 2 October 1187 Saladin reached the apex of his political and military career by receiving the surrender of Jerusalem. In sharp contrast to the bloodbath staged by the crusaders at the time of their conquest of Jerusalem (15 July 1099), Saladin treated the surrendering Christian defenders and residents of Jerusalem with unusual magnanimity.

In spite of the tremendous political, ideological, and lasting propaganda resulting from the liberation of the Holy City, Saladin was not destined to expel the crusaders from the lands of Islam. His numerous conquests during the years of 1188 and 1189 notwithstanding, three crucial fortresses on the Syrian littoral remained in the hands of the crusaders: Antioch, Tripoli, and Tyre. In August 1189 King Guy's revitalized army, with fresh reinforcements from Europe and assisted by a Pisan squadron, launched an expedition from Tyre directed against Acre, the ensuing siege of which set the stage for the Third Crusade (1189–1191).

Although the elite garrison of the refortified Acre, the Egyptian fleet, and Saladin's field army were at the peak of their morale and physical strength, they proved no match for the multitude of land and naval forces Europe eventually threw into the Battle of Acre. While the heroic and ultimately tragic resistance of the besieged garrison and the relentless, hazardous, and physically strenuous exercise of direct, personal command by Saladin eventually contributed to the defeat of the Christian plans to reconquer Jerusalem, the Third Crusade inflicted crippling blows on the status of the Muslim leader.

By the time of the capitulation of Acre on 12 July 1191, and the ensuing slaughter of its defenders by Richard the Lionhearted, Saladin's feudal army had lost its earlier enthusiasm for sustaining his struggle against the crusaders. His fleet was utterly destroyed by Italian naval might; and Egypt's resources, which for over two decades had supported his ambitious expansionist policies, became strained to the utmost. Under these circumstances, on 2 September 1192, after having experienced a number of humiliating encounters with Richard the Lionhearted, Saladin decided to sign a three-year truce. By its terms, Jerusalem remained in the hands of Saladin, but the Kingdom of the Crusaders, which only five years earlier was on the brink of total extinction, reestablished itself on the Syro-Palestinian coast to generate for another century debilitating attacks against the Muslims. Shortly after the signing of the truce, on 4 March 1193, Saladin passed away in his beloved Damascus, victim of a brief illness which his exhausted body was unable to overcome.

In assessing the significance of Saladin's career, one should distinguish between his historical achievements and failures and an idealized image of his personality bequeathed to posterity by his ardent supporters and advisers. Among his foremost achievements one should emphasize the suppression of the Fatimid caliphate, the reestablishment of the hegemony of orthodox (Sunni) Islam in Egypt, and the foundation of the Ayyubid regime in Egypt, Syria, and upper Mesopotamia. One should note, however, that a few years after Saladin's death the supremacy of his own sons was replaced by that of his dynamic brother al-ᶜĀdil and his descendants. More disappointing yet was Saladin's failure to finish off the crusaders. Still, all these successes and failures appear to have faded away in the resplendence of his recovery of Jerusalem for Islam.

Because of that feat he has been immortalized by posterity, eliciting lasting admiration from the Muslims and respect from the Christians. And, as liberator of Jerusalem, he has been chosen by Muslim moralists to serve as a "model prince," credited with many edifying personal traits such as piety, humility, generosity, and chivalry. His historical and semilegendary personality continues to attract the attention of modern historians and historical novelists.

BIBLIOGRAPHY

Andrew S. Ehrenkreutz, *Saladin* (1972); R. Stephen Humphreys, *From Saladin to the Mongols* (1977); Stanley Lane-Poole, *Saladin and the Fall of the Kingdom of Jerusalem* (1898); Malcolm C. Lyons and D. E. P. Jackson, *Saladin: The Politics of the Holy War* (1982); Hannes Möhring, *Saladin und der Dritte Kreuzzug* (1980); Percy H. Newby, *Saladin in His Time* (1983); D. S. Richards, "The Early History of Saladin," in *Islamic Quarterly,* **17** (1973).

ANDREW S. EHRENKREUTZ

[See also **Aleppo; Alexandria; Ayyubids; Crusades and Crusader States: Near East; Crusades and Crusader States: To 1192; Damascus; Dwin; Egypt, Islamic; Fatamids; Ḥiṭṭīn; Jerusalem; Jihad; Kurds; Mosul; Richard I the Lionhearted; Shī^ca; Sunna; Sunnite; Syria; Vizier; Warfare, Islamic.**]

SALIMBENE (1221–after 1287), Franciscan preacher and writer whose *Chronicle* is one of the principal narrative sources for the history of Italy, and to a lesser extent of France, in the thirteenth century. Born in Parma, named Balian, but known to his family and friends as Ognibene, he was the son of Guido de Adam, a wealthy and influential figure in Parma, as well as an experienced crusader, and Inmelda de Cassio, also from a noted family of Parma. Except for one document that attests his presence at Ferrara on a certain day in 1254, the only source for Salimbene's life is his *Chronicle,* which he interspersed with autobiographical fragments.

Ognibene received a sound education in letters. Then, at age sixteen, while the Franciscan minister-general Elias of Cortona was visiting Parma, he joined the Franciscan order. It was not uncommon to make such a religious commitment—St. Francis had died only a bit over a decade before—but neither was it uncommon for families, especially parents, to react strongly against such a move. His oldest brother, Guido, was already a Franciscan; another brother, Nicholas, had died; and so his decision threatened to leave his father without a male heir. His father protested directly to Emperor Frederick II, who intervened with a letter to Brother Elias asking him to return the young man. But the Franciscan order retained him. After completing his first year in the order at Fano and Iesi, Ognibene met an elderly friar who had been the last man received into the order by St. Francis. This friar advised him that Ognibene was a presumptuous name, since only God is all good, and renamed him Salimbene, for the good move, or jump, he had made into the religious life. Along with his new name, Salimbene thus also had a new genealogy, going directly back to St. Francis; in the *Chronicle* he seems pleased that he and his brother Guido had dismantled their patrimony. The Franciscan order was their new family.

Salimbene next studied Scripture and theology at Lucca, where, among other people, he met Frederick II. At Siena he became a subdeacon and met Bernard Quintavalle, St. Francis' first convert, and Hugh of Digne, from whom he learned of the teachings of Joachim of Fiore. While at Pisa in 1243, he was again pressured to leave the religious life by his father, this time via the newly elected Innocent IV, a native of Parma and a distant relative of the de Adam family. But Salimbene stayed and became a deacon. He moved on to Cremona and then to Parma, and when that city was besieged by imperial troops, he went to France, where he held private talks with Innocent IV at Lyons. At nearby Villefranche he met John of Plano Carpini, recently returned from his mission to the Tatars. Then he went to Troyes, Provins, Paris, Auxerre, and Sens, where at the Franciscan convent he made the acquaintance of King Louis IX. His travels in 1248 and 1249 took Salimbene to several places in Provence and to Genoa, where he was ordained a priest. During the same period he received permission to preach directly from the order's new minister-general, John of Parma. Following another trip to France he returned to Parma, then settled at Ferrara for seven years (1249–1256). Over the next thirty years Salimbene seems to have divided his time among the Franciscan convents of Reggio Emilia, Modena, Bologna, Rimini, Faenza, Ravenna, and Monfalcone. The final entry in the *Chronicle* is dated 1288, although there are pages missing from the end of the manuscript, meaning that it might have continued beyond that date. We thus presume that Salimbene was still alive in 1288 but we do not know when he died.

In the *Chronicle* there is mention of other writings by Salimbene, but none of these is extant: a book denouncing the misdeeds of Frederick II, a compilation of Roman history from Augustus to the Lombards, a book on Pope Gregory X, a *Book of Pests* in imitation of Patecchio, a *Book of the Prelate* against Brother Elias, a work on the correspondences between the lives of Jesus and St. Francis, and a tract on the prophet Elijah. The text of the *Chronicle* is contained in a unique, mutilated manuscript, Vat. lat. 7260, believed to be an autograph.

Salisbury Cathedral, 1220–1265. PHOTO: WIM SWAAN

Salimbene worked on the *Chronicle* in the latter part of his life; for the beginning sections of his text, going back as far as 1168, he relied on a chronicle by Sicard of Cremona. For most of the work, though, his main source was himself: his own experiences, his extensive travels, his encounters with famous and influential people. It is a book devoid of grand organizing themes and reflections on the theology of history. Instead it is a chatty, gossipy book full of anecdotes, portraits, and descriptions, down to details about the food and wine he consumed in the course of his travels. The *Chronicle* successfully combines this personal vision with a sense of the earthiness of early Franciscan spirituality and of the combativeness of northern Italian urban politics.

BIBLIOGRAPHY

Sources. George G. Coulton, *From St. Francis to Dante: Translations from the Chronicle of the Franciscan Salimbene (1221–1288)* (1907, 2nd ed. 1972); *Cronica fratris Salimbene de Adam,* in Oswaldus Holder-Egger, ed., *Monumenta Germaniae historica: Scriptores,* XXXII (1905–1913, repr. 1963); *The Chronicle of Salimbene de Adam,* Joseph L. Baird *et al.,* eds. (1986); *Salimbene de Adam: Cronica,* Giuseppe Scalia, ed., 2 vols. (1966).

Studies. Robert Brentano, *Two Churches: England and Italy in the Thirteenth Century* (1968); Rosalind B. Brooke, *Early Franciscan Government* (1959); R. Manselli, "Adam, Ognibene," in *Dizionario biografico degli italiani,* I (1960); Nino Scivoletto, *Fra Salimbene de Parma e la storia politica e religiosa del secolo decimoterzo* (1950).

LESTER K. LITTLE

[See also **Franciscans; Francis of Assisi, St.; Frederick II of the Holy Roman Empire, King of Sicily; Innocent IV, Pope; Joachim of Fiore; John of Plano Carpini; Louis IX of France.**]

SALISBURY CATHEDRAL. Sometimes called the purest English Gothic cathedral, Salisbury epitomizes the clean, uncluttered lines of the Early English style. Built on a virgin lowland site after the transfer of the see from the hilltop fortress of Old Sarum in 1220, the cathedral and cloister were under construction until the 1280's. The sprawling, graceful complex, dominated by a spire added in the mid fourteenth century, is set within a verdant close made famous by the Romantic views of John Constable. The design was probably made by Master Elias of Dereham, a canon with architectural skills, and construction was probably overseen by Nicholas of Ely.

BIBLIOGRAPHY

John Britton, *Cathedral Antiquities,* II (1836); Nikolaus Pevsner, *Wiltshire* (1963), 350–393; Gleeson White, *The Cathedral Church of Salisbury* (1896); Robert Willis, "Minutes of Lecture on the Architecture of Salisbury Cathedral," in his *Architectural History of Some English Cathedrals,* II (1972–1973).

STEPHEN GARDNER

[See also **Cathedral; Chapter House; Cloister; Gothic Architecture; Nicholas of Ely; Old Sarum.**]

SALISBURY, USE OF. See **Sarum Use.**

SALJUQIDS. See **Seljuks.**

SALMAN UND MOROLF. See **Solomon and Marcolf.**

SALOMO OF CONSTANCE (*ca.* 860–919/920). Salomo III succeeded his uncle, Salomo II, as bishop of Constance. He was essentially a prince of the church and patron of literature, especially at St. Gall, rather than a writer. He did assemble, with his brother Waldo, the *Formulae Salomonis* (*ca.* 800), a collection of letters, documents, and poems, and he wrote a few poems of consolation to friends.

BIBLIOGRAPHY

Carmina, Paul von Winterfeld, ed., in *Monumenta Germaniae historica: Poetae latini aevi carolini,* IV (1899), 296–314; *Das Formelbuch des Bischofs Salomo von Konstanz aus dem neunten Jahrhundert,* Ernst Dümmler, ed. (1857); Max Manitius, *Geschichte der lateinischen Literatur des Mittelalters,* I (1913), 595–597; Ulrich Zeller, *Bischof Salomo III* (1910).

W. T. H. JACKSON

[See also **St. Gall, Monastery and Plan of.**]

SALT TRADE. While the physiological requirement of animals for salt is still disputed, it is agreed that animals want salt and will go to considerable trouble to get it. This needs only the qualification that carnivorous animals and humans who subsist mainly on meat (for example, Eskimos and the Plains Indians of North America) obtain an unusual quantity of salt in their normal diet and lack correspondingly the normal craving for salt. The same may have applied to the early inhabitants of Europe, although archaeological evidence indicates that they were salt eaters long before they emerge in recorded history.

Salt was widely available in the seafaring cultures of the ancient Greeks in peacetime, although not among their inland neighbors, with whom they traded salt for slaves. The typical Mediterranean saltworks was a series of low-walled enclosures, made on low-lying land along the shore, into which the sea was periodically admitted and left to evaporate under solar heat. It is probably such a saline that the early king of Rome, Ancus Marcius (641–616 B.C.), according to the historian Livy, established at the mouth of the Tiber. Trails for the transport of salt from such sites of production, which became very numerous, have sometimes been cited as the first roads and the basis of modern systems of communication on land.

Not all saltworks were on the seashore, nor was solar evaporation everywhere available. Inland springs were exploited, where significantly saline, as at Aussee (Salzkammergut, Austria), where quantities of Roman coins have been found, and at Reichenhall (Bavaria), which is said to have been laid waste by the barbarian invasions of the fifth century. Both of these have been centers of salt production into the twentieth century. But both Aussee and Reichenhall are in northern Europe, where solar evaporation is not practical. They produced salt by boiling.

Most of the early Mediterranean saltworks have vanished without a trace, but those of northern Europe have left traces, in the form of *briquetage*, ceramic fragments of peculiar forms that are thought to be the remains of ceramic dishes and primitive furnaces used in salt production. Examination of *briquetage* at Nauheim (Hesse) and Schwäbisch-Hall (Württemberg) has led archaeologists to consider them prehistoric salines. *Briquetage* has been found at no less than 126 sites around the famous German salt town of Halle and, indeed, has now been discovered so widely throughout northern Europe that it is possible to speak of regional or "national" styles of *briquetage*. Nor is its occurrence restricted to inland sites. The most numerous deposits have been found all along the coasts of northern Europe, where seawater was boiled for salt.

GROWTH OF THE SALT INDUSTRY

Literary evidence of the saltworks of Western Europe, in nearly all cases, is first revealed in ecclesiastical records. This is not surprising, since the same can be said of most other aspects of medieval history. It is remarkable, however, that so many monastic settlements appear in the vicinity of saltworks—Salins (Franche-Comté) is said to have been surrounded by ten monasteries. Salt making appears to have been an early monastic industry. Some saltworks were under the control of officials of the regular clergy, and most of those controlled by lay governments were assigned in fief to churches or monasteries. In the course of time lay authority asserted, or reasserted, control; but at the very least the religious establishment retained a bewildering variety of rights and privileges. At the productive saline at Lüneburg (Lower Saxony), the "pans" (the meaning of which had evolved from a physical object in which the salt was boiled to a share of the salt) were at one time distributed among the local nobility (42½ pans), private owners (71¼ pans), charitable foundations (69 1/12 pans), and "foreign" charitable foundations (31⅝ pans), including the interests of seven monasteries. As late as the seventeenth century a historian of the saltworks at Wieliczka (Poland) described the claims of "monasteries, castles, bishoprics, cathedrals, churches, and other foundations [as] nearly insupportable."

Occasionally the church produced genuine entrepreneurs in salt. Such were several bishops of Salzburg. After its destruction by Hunnish or Germanic invaders, the Bavarian saline at Reichenhall disappears from the record, to reappear in the records of the bishop of Salzburg, who controlled a number of pans. By the end of the twelfth century salt springs were being exploited at Berchtesgaden, a scarcely accessible area twenty-four kilometers (fifteen miles) to the south. This was not authorized by the bishop and led to a controversy over property rights which escalated into one between church and state, and finally between pope and emperor. The contest, involving threats of force, falsification of documents, and the like, was resolved in 1198 with a new division of interests and with the passing of control of much of the area (but not Berchtesgaden) from the bishop to the duke of Bavaria.

By 1300 Reichenhall saline was in decline, but the bishop had transferred his interest to the mountains just south of his capital, where there had been evidence of salt, possibly even a small mine. The saltworks at Hallein, however, was based on springs and drainage waters from the adjacent mountain, Dürrenberg, which were carried to the town below for boiling. It was the principal economic asset of the principality of Salzburg and remained so until the eighteenth century, when it fell victim to nationalistic restrictions promulgated by Austria and Germany against the importation of salt from this independent enclave; but through the Middle Ages Hallein remained prosperous. Hallein had access by water to the trade of the Danube basin, and its productivity seems to have been limited only by the size of this market. By the fourteenth century the (now) archbishop of Salzburg shared control with several monasteries, with the nobility, and with members of the rising middle class (burghers), but he recovered control and even limited production (44 million to 55 million pounds [20 to 25 million kilograms] per year) to maintain the price. Altogether the saline at Hallein appears to represent one of the most prolonged success stories in the history of European industry.

In the sixth century Cassiodorus mentioned salt as the chief article of Venetian commerce, and salt was to become the economic base of this first successful trading state in medieval Europe. In the tenth century the source was still as close as Murano, but by the twelfth century it had moved to Chioggia, and then to more distant places: Cervia (south of Ravenna), and then Alexandria, Cyprus, and the Balearic Islands, expanding with the Venetian empire. It also contracted with it. Pisa was in the trade by the thirteenth century, importing salt from Sardinia, and then Genoa, with salt imported from Hyères (Provence).

A new era began in the fourteenth century with greatly increased consumption of salt in an area of low productivity—the North Sea. This was occasioned by the introduction of salted herring, an "invention" attributed to a Dutchman, Willem Benckels. Dried fish had been preserved by salting from ancient times; now fresh fish could be preserved long enough for shipment in barrels to inland points of consumption. The quantities of salt used were up to a third of the weight of the fish, by a conservative estimate.

Much of the salt used in the North Sea area was initially obtained from England, where seawater was boiled along the coast; from Holland, where salt was obtained by burning coastal peat, which was strongly impregnated with it; and from Lüneburg, the only source of strong brine in inland north Germany. The former two sources declined in the fourteenth and fifteenth centuries as Dutch peat was exhausted and the English were both exhausting the wood used as fuel and turning to economic concentration on the textile industry. Lüneburg continued to flourish, coming under the control of merchants of Lübeck, who became the principal suppliers of salt to the salt-poor Baltic region.

About 1370 salt production became important on Bourgneuf Bay, south of the mouth of the Loire and the northernmost seacoast where solar heat was adequate for the economic evaporation of seawater. Toward the end of the fifteenth century, Saintonge, at the mouth of the Gironde, became equally, and then more, important. The product, called "bay salt," was criticized as dirty, as indeed it was, being scraped up from the bottom of pans made of earth. But at the end of the Middle Ages bay salt was the principal source of supply for northern Europe. Its rival, and subsequent successor, was salt from the Mediterranean coasts of France (including Hyères), from Spain, and from the Atlantic coast of Portugal. Peccais, the area around Aigues-Mortes, became, and remains today, a center of sea-salt production. Setúbal, near Lisbon, was to become in the seventeenth century one of the greatest salt-producing centers in Europe. And it has been claimed that profits from the saltworks of the Mata, on the Spanish coast, were more important than Queen Isabella's jewels in supporting the explorations of Columbus.

THE ECONOMICS OF SALT

Salt had long been a basis for taxation, "a convenient article for fiscal management," as a Chinese author called it. Although Matthias Schleiden, writing in 1875, noted that neither ancient Greece nor Rome had salt taxes and drew the conclusion that the tax was characteristic of "despotic" governments, the matter was more complicated. Russia and England had no salt tax before the seventeenth century, but both had salt duties, that is, a tax on imported salt. Since both were importers of salt, the supposed lack of a tax is hardly significant. For quite different reasons, Venice did not have a tax. It had profitable monopolistic arrangements for both the acquisition and the sale of salt.

China could have been the model for salt taxes in Europe, but it is very unlikely that the Europeans were that well acquainted with China. Although salt seems not to have been significant in the revenues of Rome, the Romans ultimately made salt a state monopoly, to assure supply, thus establishing an appropriate technical and economic model; and they left unchanged systems of salt taxation that existed in Hellenistic states which they inherited. Still, European taxes and monopolies appeared centuries later, and in most cases as war measures. In medieval Europe, where war was more or less perpetual, the salt tax became equally permanent (it was terminated in France only in 1945 and in Italy two decades later).

The French pioneered in salt taxation, which became so important that it took over the name, gabelle, which had previously been applied to all taxes. Charles of Anjou (1226–1285), youngest son of Louis VIII, instituted a salt tax in Provence to finance his conquest of the Kingdom of Naples. King Philip V, whose father had acquired the Peccais salines in 1291, instituted a provisional salt tax in 1317. With the outbreak of the Hundred Years War in 1337, warehouses were established in each province to which the producer on penalty of confiscation had to deliver his salt at a fixed price. The fourteenth century saw a succession of repeals and reimpositions of the salt tax but ended with its permanent establishment in 1386.

The history of the salt tax in France is complicated, as indeed it is elsewhere, by being parallel to the history of the formation of the state itself. Thus there are separate histories of the salt tax in most of the principalities which ultimately became part of France. The intention then was to levy the tax uniformly on all of the provinces, but as the French nation was being put together it became necessary to accommodate to existing practices. Brittany long had no tax; and there was one rate for Normandy, where seawater continued to be boiled for salt, and another for eastern France, where salt was supplied from brine wells. In the sixteenth century some regions incorporated into France were able to bargain for exemption from the gabelle and became *pays exempts;* others purchased exemption and became *pays rédimés*. It was worth it, for the price of salt was sometimes over a hundred times the cost of production, and everyone was required to purchase a fixed amount. It was indeed "a convenient article for fiscal management."

There can have been few more complex measures in the history of government than the French gabelle; even at the apogee of centralization a *petit gabelle* existed in the region supplied by Mediterranean salines, where the rate was about half that in areas subject to the *grande gabelle,* that is, all of the rest of the country with the various exemptions noted. The Isle of Ré, a salt-producing center, was declared *province étrangère* to facilitate its foreign trade. Evasion was widespread, and persistent smuggling inspired countermeasures of ever-increasing severity. By the seventeenth century they ranged from the galleys to death (for armed contraband).

Most of Europe imitated the French gabelle, but half-heartedly. In Spain, Ferdinand and Isabella decreed death by shooting with arrows for violation of the salt laws. But it is not clear that many suffered this penalty. England had become a salt importer by 1303, when the first duty was imposed on imported salt, and the subsequent accumulation of laws required a book of 361 pages to list them in 1707, a bulk of legislation which seems to have had no counterpart in enforcement. In Austria, where the problem centered on the protection of "native" salt against that of the principality of Salzburg (that

SALT TRADE

is, the salt of Hallein), the crown sought a solution in the encouragement of its own salines at Aussee and Hallstatt. Here the crown was, on the whole, benevolently involved; indeed, it has been said that concern with the saltworks contributed more to the definition of regalian rights in Austria than those rights contributed to the regulation of the salt industry.

Beyond these strongly centralized states there were almost as many governments as there were saltworks, and attempts to establish regalian rights were hamstrung by the fact that many saltworks were older than the governments. The emperor Henry IV had preempted one-third of the production of Kloster Sulz in 1064, but because of the increasing fragmentation of the empire and the transitory character of its salt resources (small salines tended to be moved about, in search of stronger brine), the application of regalian rights did not get much beyond that. Halle, the most famous salt town in Germany (although less productive than Lüneburg), was assigned by Emperor Otto I to the local church. By the thirteenth century it had gravitated to the archbishop of Magdeburg. In 1263 it was decided, with some finality, that only four of the numerous springs at Halle would be exploited. The archbishop's share was defined as a monetary payment, but with less finality. A renewal of disagreement among the various interests in the early fifteenth century led the adversaries to call in both the emperor and the pope, and in 1414, following a series of edits (*Reichsacten*), interdicts, and bans, to an agreement for the payment of 13,000 gulden. During this conflict the *Pfännerschaft* emerged, a monopolistic aristocracy who were often dubbed the "salt Junkers," as well as the Halloren, a kind of labor union which was for centuries to add a third factor to the contest over the control of the salt resources of Halle.

TECHNOLOGICAL IMPROVEMENT

The most severe obstacle to the economic production of salt was the cost of fuel, which was universally wood; and the decline of the sea-salt boiling industry along the coasts of northern Europe reflects the problem. It was first evident in England, where salt making was nearly abandoned on the coast, although it survived on a small scale in Cheshire, where there were rich brine springs. The British sea-salt industry was to rise again in the sixteenth century, with the adoption of coal as fuel, but on the Continent inconvenience and prejudice minimized the use of coal through the eighteenth century.

The emergence of the French Atlantic coast as a center of salt production in the fourteenth century represents one response to the wood shortage. The region lay between the sunny Mediterranean and northern latitudes where solar salt making was clearly impractical (not that it was not periodically tried). And the salines of Bourgneuf Bay and Saintonge were the site of a significant improvement in the traditional method of sea-salt production which made them viable, and indeed leading, sources of salt for about two centuries. The improvement, which aimed at taking advantage of the sunniest season and avoiding its opposite, took several forms but most typically consisted of the admission of seawater only once a year, at the spring high tide, to a reservoir from which it was admitted to a series of conventional earthen enclosures of decreasing size until the last, where a layer of deposited salt was collected every day. In some cases, where the terrain permitted, the sequence of pans was arranged in a cascade, thus obviating the necessity of dipping or pumping from one to another.

In the inland saltworks improvement took other forms, for they continued to depend on wood as fuel. The fortunes of the strong brine saline at Lüneburg had been favored in the twelfth century, when its sovereign, the redoubtable Henry the Lion, destroyed the rival saltworks at Oldenslohe. In the fourteenth century its principal proprietors, now the merchants of Lübeck, connected Lüneburg by canal to the Elbe, facilitating the shipment not only of salt, but apparently of wood, for the supply was maintained; but there improvement stopped. It appears that an arrangement of fifty-four boiling houses, containing four small lead pans each, persisted from 1262 until 1789; and wood was still in use as fuel at the latter date.

The improvers at the salines of the Salzkammergut were more persistent. These were sources of rich brine, not from springs but from artificially flooded pits into what were in fact deposits of rock salt complexly intruded into ordinary rock. Such an operation was called a *Schöpfwerk*. Some time after the margrave of Steirmark began, in the twelfth century, to divest the Cistercians of control of the saltworks at Aussee, the *Schöpfwerk* was improved by installing in the ever-deepening pit wooden boxes into which the rock was placed and covered with water (an operation so hazardous that a nineteenth-century observer reported a church to be installed at the pit mouth, where one could commend his soul to God before entering). From this *Sinkwerk,* as it was called, the resulting strong brine was drained by gravity to the site of the boiling houses, at the foot of the mountain, where some water transportation was possible. The example of Aussee was followed at Hallein, at Hall, where the duke of Tyrol took control at the beginning of the fourteenth century, and at Hallstatt, where the Austrian emperors involved themselves more or less permanently in the fifteenth century.

As the forests around these saltworks were decimated, the proprietors constructed distant boiling houses and sometimes abandoned the original site altogether, but they also constructed flumes extending into the mountains, along which wood was brought. In the sixteenth century Hallstatt was to deliver brine to a lower saltworks at Ischl, through a wooden pipe, and then both were connected to boiling houses on Lake Traun, some twenty miles (thirty-two kilometers) from Hallstatt, forming a little "industrial complex" which in part still exists.

Farther east, where Europe was even more forested, we hear of no wood shortage, as for example at Wieliczka and Bochnia, near Cracow, which were major sources of revenue for the Polish crown—as well as for the nobility and the usual spectrum of ecclesiastical interests. Thanks to the recordkeeping mandated by royal interest, we have some history of the management of Wieliczka, from the fifteenth century, and encounter an international group of specialists, including Frenchmen, Germans, Italians, and Jews, as well as Poles.

A far greater problem was posed to those who suffered not only from a shortage of wood but from a lack of strong brine. These combined disadvantages ended sea-salt making in northern Europe, except for a few places such as Normandy, where seawater was concentrated by dipping it up and casting it in a shower over a designated area of beach. Ultimately the upper layer of sand from this area was swept up, leached, and boiled for salt. The viability of this dubious process is certified by its use as a major source of supply in mid-nineteenth-century Japan, but in Europe it remained unique to Normandy. The inland salines of central Europe, however, survived, in part through subsidies in support of self-sufficiency, but also in part through innovation. The history of some of these salines exhibits a prodigious effort at improvement, mainly in the direction of preconcentration of brine, that is, in increasing its concentration to the point that it could be economically boiled down with wood.

Excavation at the prehistoric saline at Nauheim (now Bad Nauheim, a popular health spa) has shown the original saltworks to have been virtually identical to the seashore saltworks where brine was simply boiled down in clay pots, but another ancient German saltworks, at Schwäbisch-Hall, seems to show through excavations made in 1939 an early attempt at preconcentration. As reconstructed, this process appears to have involved the exposure of brine in open tanks from which porous clay "wicks" protruded, thus accelerating atmospheric evaporation. It was this technique to which the German saltmakers were to apply their ingenuity.

In the sixteenth century we read of the *Lepperwerk,* a wooden trough carrying a pile of bundles of straw over which weak brine was circulated manually until atmospheric evaporation produced the desired concentration; and before the end of that century we find the *Lepperwerk* replaced by the *Gradierwerk,* an open, roofed structure packed with a mass of black thorns over which brine was circulated by pumps. Part, if not all, of this innovation very probably belongs to the Middle Ages, as so many of the inventions once known only through the printed "machine books" of the sixteenth century have now been found in the writings of fifteenth-century Italian virtuosi. The apparent technological renaissance of the sixteenth century owes much to the invention of the printing press, a fifteenth-century invention.

The most thoroughly mechanized saltworks would appear to have been that at Salins (Franche-Comté), the two brine pits and four boiling pans of which already existed in the eleventh century. It belonged to the house of Bourgogne-Chalon but became in the fifteenth century a prize contested by the dukes of Burgundy and a group of monopolistic proprietors. There were twenty-eight officials at this saltworks in 1421. When it suffered a loss of brine in 1469 (due to the intrusion of sweet water) its recovery, in consequence of a parade of relics of St. Anatole through the works, was commemorated in a tapestry, parts of which still exist. It shows horse-driven "pumps" consisting of barrels on an endless chain which dipped them into the brine pit. As described by L. Gollut in 1592, Salins was a showplace of mechanization, with pumps, siphons, and a complex system of troughs carrying brines of varying strength, and even devices which rang bells to signal some malfunctioning in the system. It is not likely that none of this existed before 1500; siphons had been known since antiquity and the endless chain pump had been known at least as early as 1430, when it appeared in the *De ingeniis* of Mariano Taccola.

ROCK SALT

Today salt mines (usually artificially flooded, for technical reasons) supply most of Europe, which abounds in subterranean deposits. Rock salt was not unknown in antiquity. Greek writers had mentioned the exploitation of the "salt mountain" at Cardona in the Spanish Pyrenees. Yet it remained more a curiosity than a source of salt even in the early nineteenth century. Rock salt also approached the surface in Transylvania, where the cellars of houses were sometimes excavated into it. The neglect of these sources, far richer than those on which Europe depended, during the Middle Ages presumably owed something to their remoteness and the consequently magnified problem of transportation; but not all rock-salt sources were so remote. Excavations at Hallstatt in the 1870's led to the discovery that the venerable saltworks there, which exploited concentrated brine, contained within its depths miner's tools and even the bodies of several unlucky miners. It had once been a mine, which was apparently flooded in antiquity. The Hallstatt saltworks emerges in recorded history as a source of brine only in the thirteenth century. The saltworks of Wieliczka seems to have been a mine when it was first made known, about the same time, but it was in the process of being flooded and was known in the Middle Ages as a brine source; again we are impressed by the difficulty of transportation, for Poland, which possessed in this saltworks one of the richest in Europe, was a major importer of salt through its Baltic ports. Still it is remarkable that rock salt was unimportant in the medieval economy; visitors to the few known rock-salt sites in Europe in the early nineteenth century found little production but an abundance of guards. One wonders to what extent the insignificance of this source through the Middle Ages and beyond may have been due to the threat it posed to the elaborate and time-honored system of salt provision, and especially of taxation, in Europe.

BIBLIOGRAPHY

Robert P. Multhauf, *Neptune's Gift: A History of Common Salt* (1978), with an extensive bibliography. See especially E. A. Ancelon, "Historique de l'exploitation du sel en Lorraine," in *Mémoires de l'Académie nationale de Metz,* 3rd ser., 7 (1877–1878); Herbert Klein, "Zur älteren Geschichte der Salinen Hallein und Reichenhall," in *Vierteljahrschrift für Sozial- und Wirtschaftsgeschichte,* **38** (1949); Matthias J. Schleiden, *Das Salz* (1875); Heinrich R. von Srbik, *Studien zur Geschichte des österreichischen Salzwesens* (1917); and the large number of articles by Walter Carlé cited in Multhauf. See also Beatrice Hopkinson, "Archaeological Evidence of Saltmoulding at Important European Saltsites and Its Relationship to the Distribution of Urnfielders," in *Journal of Indo-European Studies,* 3 (1975); Harald Witthöft, "Struktur und Kapazität der Lüneburger Saline seit dem 12. Jahrhundert," in *Vierteljahrschrift für Sozial- und Wirtschaftsgeschichte,* **63** (1976).

ROBERT P. MULTHAUF

[See also **Trade, European; Trade, Regulation of.**]

SALTAIR NA RANN (The Psalter of the Quatrains), a Middle Irish poem (probably late tenth century) on sacred history from the creation of the world to the Day of Judgment. Its name derives from the Irish practice of composing poems of 150 units—in this instance, 150 cantos made up of varying numbers of quatrains—in imitation of the 150 psalms of the Psalter. In fact, the poem in its extant form contains 162 cantos—150 on sacred history (7,788 lines) to Christ's Resurrection, constituting the body of the poem, and twelve other cantos (605 lines) by way of an epilogue. Recent scholarship identifies as an interpolation that part of canto 12 (lines 2,345–2,380 of Stokes' edition) which lists Irish and foreign kings said to have been reigning in 988, although there is disagreement about its date of composition.

The full poem occurs uniquely in Oxford, Bodleian Library, MS Rawlinson B 502, folios 19–40 (a manuscript of Leinster origin, *ca.* 1120). Neither the manuscript ascription at the head of the poem to "Oengus Céli-De" (Oengus the Culdee) nor a quatrain in the epilogue where the author professes to give his name—"I am Oengus céle De" (line 8,009)—can be prudently accepted as evidence that the poem was composed by the well-known Oengus mac Oengobann the Culdee, who composed the *Félire Oengusso* about 800. Beyond this there is no general agreement about the identity of the author. According to one theory the poem was composed by Oengus, a monk of Cluain Eidneach (Clonenagh, County Leix), in the second half of the ninth century; according to another, by Airbertach mac Coisse of Ros Ailithir (*d.* 1016). The majority of scholars simply accept a tenth-century date, based mainly on linguistic evidence.

Although the *Saltair* is structured according to the chronology of the Six Ages of the World—from Adam to the Day of Judgment—the selection and arrangement of events and people suggest that the poet's primary purpose was to sketch the history of God's providential plan for mankind's salvation as he effected it through Old Testament Jewish history and finally through Christ. Thus the *Saltair* proper treats of: Creation, the Fall of the Angels, Hell, Paradise, the Temptation and Fall of Adam and Eve, the main historical events of Genesis and Exodus, Samuel, Saul, David (at great length), Solomon, the lesser kings, and the prophets, ending with the Babylonian Captivity (cantos 1–135). Cantos 136–141 give an overall view of God's providence as manifested to various Old and New Testament figures. Cantos 142–150 treat of Christ: his Nativity, Infancy, Apostolate, Death, and Resurrection. The epilogue begins with a prayer for divine forgiveness (canto 151), followed by an exhortation to repentance based on the appeal of God's providence. The remaining cantos (153–162) describe the signs and events which will occur during each of the nine days before the Day of Judgment.

For his historical matter and chronology the poet of *Saltair na Rann* basically followed the Bible, but he also greatly embellished and expanded his narrative with apocryphal and cosmological matter. The full extent of his dependence on such matter has yet to be determined; for the section on Adam and Eve (cantos 4–12) he relied mainly on the apocryphal Greek *Apocalypsis Mosis* and the *Vita Adae et Evae,* both perhaps already combined with other matter in a single Latin text; for the signs before judgment he used the *Apocalypse of Thomas*.

BIBLIOGRAPHY

Editions. Whitley Stokes, *The Saltair na Rann: Anecdota Oxoniensia* (1883); David Greene and Fergus Kelly, *The Irish Adam and Eve Story from Saltair na Rann,* 2 vols. (cantos 4–12), with commentary by Brian O. Murdoch (1976).

Studies. John Carey, "Cosmology in *Saltair na Rann,*" in *Celtica,* **17** (1985); James Carney, "The Dating of Early Irish Verse Texts," in *Éigse,* **19** (1983), esp. 184–187, 207–216; James F. Kenney, *The Sources for the Early History of Ireland: Ecclesiastical* (1929, repr. with addition 1966), 736–737; Gearoid Mac Eoin, "The Date and Authorship of Saltair na Rann," in *Zeitschrift für celtische Philologie,* **28** (1969/1961), and "Observations on Saltair na Rann," *ibid.,* **39** (1982).

PÁDRAIG P. Ó NÉILL

[See also **Airbertach mac Coisse; Airdena Brátha; Apocrypha, Irish; Celtic Languages; Irish Literature: Religious; Sex Aetates Mundi.**]

SALVATORIS HODIE. This Advent conductus in three voices is perhaps the most celebrated of the repertory of the *Magnus liber* from around 1200. By the witness of Anonymous IV, we know that *Salvatoris* was composed by Magister Perotinus. *Salvatoris* is named a second time by Anonymous IV when he is discussing the composition of the *Magnus liber organi.* The third volume of the *Magnus liber* is, he writes, that of the three-voice conductus with melismata, and *Salvatoris* is named first as an example of that genre. The musical sources confirm the evidence of Anonymous IV to a remarkable extent, as *Salvatoris* stands first in four of its five extant sources. This confirms both the special status of *Salvatoris* within the repertory of three-voice conductus and the importance of Perotinus in the creation of the more modern parts of the *Magnus liber* repertory.

BIBLIOGRAPHY

Robert Falck, *The Notre Dame Conductus* (1981), 241; F. Reckow, "Conductus," in Hans Eggebrecht, ed., *Handwörterbuch der musikalischen Terminologie* (1973).

ROBERT FALCK

[See also **Anonymous IV; Conductus; Magnus Liber Organi; Melisma; Perotinus.**]

SALVIAN OF MARSEILLES (*ca.* 400–after 480), born in northern Gaul, possibly at Cologne, he traveled south during the 420's with his wife, Palladia, and daughter, Auspiciola, and became a monk at Lérins; by *ca.* 430 he had moved to Marseilles, where he served as a priest. Salvian was learned in both classical and religious literature, and his surviving works, written in good rhetorical Latin, include nine personal letters; *Ad ecclesiam,*

SAMANID ART

Samanid ceramic bowl with epigraphic decoration. Nishapur or Samarkand, 10th century. THE METROPOLITAN MUSEUM OF ART, NEW YORK, ROGERS FUND (65.106.2)

written about 435; and his most famous work, *De gubernatione Dei,* written in the early 440's. This last work gives valuable insight into the state of Roman society in Gaul, Spain, and Africa during the fifth century. In it Salvian attributes the barbarian successes to divine punishment of the sinful Romans.

BIBLIOGRAPHY

Sources. Karl Halm, ed., *Monumenta Germaniae historica: Auctores antiquissimi,* I, 1 (1877); Franz Pauly, *Corpus scriptorum ecclesiasticorum latinorum,* VIII (1883); Salvian, *On the Government of God,* Eva M. Sanford, trans. (1930), *The Writings of Salvian, the Presbyter,* Jeremiah F. O'Sullivan, trans. (1947).

Studies. Nora K. Chadwick, *Poetry and Letters in Early Christian Gaul* (1955); Eligius Dekkers, ed., *Clavis patrum latinorum,* 2nd ed. (1961), nos. 485–487; Eleanor S. Duckett, *Latin Writers of the Fifth Century* (1930); Martin von Schanz *et al., Geschichte der römischen Litteratur,* IV, pt. 2 (1920, repr. 1959), 523–528.

RALPH WHITNEY MATHISEN

SAMANID ART AND ARCHITECTURE. The Samanids were a Persian dynasty that ruled Transoxiana (western Turkistan) and Khorāsān (eastern Iran) from 875 to 999. Much of our information about Samanid art, especially pottery, is the result of excavations conducted at Nishapur, the provincial capital of Khorāsān. Other important ceramic finds were made at Samarkand (Afrasiyab), a principal city of the Samanid kingdom. Among the architectural remains, primarily domestic structures uncovered at Nishapur and heavily fortified mud-brick palaces excavated in Transoxiana, the most singular and best preserved Samanid monument is the mausoleum in Bukhara, the Samanid capital.

The mausoleum at Bukhara, which is dated before 943, is the burial place for several members of the Samanid dynasty. Constructed of baked brick, the building is square in plan and has a monumental entrance on each side. It is crowned by a large dome that is framed by four smaller domes. The most striking aspect of this structure is its use of baked brick, arranged in patterns, to decorate both the interior and the exterior. This employment of patterned brickwork, rather than stucco as at contemporary Nishapur, is an important innovation that was further developed in Ghaznavid and Seljuk architecture.

The extensive ceramic finds from Nishapur and Samarkand, predominantly plates and bowls, provide the most cohesive documentation of Samanid art. This pottery is best known for its slip-painted earthenware, in which the decoration is painted in colored clay slip, usually on a white ground, and then covered with a transparent lead glaze. Some of the finest examples of these wares are those in which elegant Kufic Arabic inscriptions, generally aphorisms or standardized good wishes, are the sole means of decoration. Another prominent type of ware made in this period at Nishapur, though apparently not at Samarkand, is decorated with stylized humans, animals, and birds.

BIBLIOGRAPHY

Vasily V. Barthold, *Turkestan down to the Mongol Invasion,* 4th ed. (1977); Kurt Erdmann, "Afrasiab Ceramic Wares," in *Bulletin of the Iranian Institute,* 6 (1946); Oleg Grabar, "The Earliest Islamic Commemorative Structures, Notes and Documents," in *Ars orientalis,* 6 (1966), 17, and "The Visual Arts," in *Cambridge History of Iran,* IV, R. N. Frye, ed. (1975); W. Hauser *et al.,* "The Īrānian Expedition, 1937," in *Bulletin of the Metropolitan Museum of Art,* 33 (1938); Arthur Lane, *Early Islamic Pottery* (1958), 17–19; Galina Pugachenkova, *Iskusstvo Turkmenistana* (1967); L. Rempel, "The Mausoleum of Isma^c^il the Samanid," in *Bulletin of the American Institute for Persian Art and Archaeology,* **4** (1936); Lisa Volov, "Plaited Kufic on Samanid Epigraphic Pottery," in *Ars orientalis,* **6** (1966); Charles Wilkinson, *Nishapur: Pottery of the Early Islamic Period* (1973).

LINDA KOMAROFF

[See also **Brick; Bukhara; Ceramics, Islamic; Dome; Ghaznavid Art and Architecture; Ghaznavids; Iran, History; Islamic Art and Architecture; Nishapur; Samanids; Samarkand; Samarkand Ware; Transoxiana.**]

SAMANIDS. An Iranian dynasty that ruled western central Asia (Russian Turkistan) and parts of eastern Iran and Afghanistan from 875 to 999, although efforts to restore the dynasty continued until 1005. The origins of the family are unknown, and attempts to connect the name with the Sanskrit word *śramana* (Buddhist monk) or the *thamanioi* (an Iranian tribe mentioned in classical sources) are unconvincing. More likely the name is associated with a village called Saman located near Balkh in present-day Afghanistan, although some Arabic and Persian sources place the village near Samarkand. By some authors the Samanids are said to have descended from the noble Sasanian family of Bahrām VI Čōbēn, while others claim a Turkish origin. All sources agree, however, that Saman accepted Islam from the hands of Asad ibn ʿAbd-Allāh al-Qasrī (or Qushairī), the Umayyad governor of Khorāsān (723–727). Saman named his son after Asad, but we hear nothing about the Samanids except a brief notice that Asad served under Ṭāhir, general of the Abbasid caliph al-Māʾmūn, and when Asad died his four sons were given districts to rule in the government of the province of Khorāsān about the year 819. This marked the beginning of Samanid power in the east.

The eldest son, Nūḥ, received Samarkand to rule; Aḥmad, Farghānā; Yaḥyā, Shāsh (modern Tashkent); and the youngest, Ilyās, Herat. Although the governorship of Khorāsān changed hands frequently, the brothers were repeatedly confirmed in their posts, and when Nūḥ died in 841 or 842, apparently without issue, both Aḥmad and Yaḥyā were appointed to administer Samarkand. Yaḥyā died in 855, and the administration of Shāsh was assumed by Aḥmad, who appointed one of his own sons, Yaʿqūb, to rule Shāsh, and another, Naṣr, to rule Samarkand. Thus the lines of Nūḥ and Yaḥyā were replaced by the family of Aḥmad. Ilyās died in 856; his son Ibrāhīm succeeded him in Herat, but he was then made commander of the army of Khorāsān by the governor, Muḥammad ibn Ṭāhir, and was defeated by Yaʿqūb ibn Layth. After fleeing to Nishapur, the capital of Khorāsān, he surrendered to Yaʿqūb and was taken prisoner; thus ended the line of Ilyās.

In 875 the caliph separated all of the territory north of the Oxus (Amu Darya) River from Khorāsān and gave that area to Naṣr to govern. Thus a precedent was set by dividing Khorāsān into two parts. Naṣr appointed his brother Ismaʿīl his deputy in the town of Bukhara in the same year. Disputes broke out between the two brothers, one source suggesting that Ismaʿīl sought the support of a representative of the governor of Khorāsān, Rāfiʿ ibn Harthama, against his brother, another that Ismaʿīl refused to send tax money to Samarkand. In any case, Ismaʿīl defeated and captured his brother, but he set him free and officially continued as his brother's viceroy in Bukhara until Naṣr died in 892. It is with Ismaʿīl that most Muslim historians date the real beginning of the Samanid dynasty.

The caliph had sent a patent of investiture for all of Khorāsān, including the domains of the Samanids, to ʿAmr, brother of Yaʿqūb ibn Layth, after the latter's death, so a conflict was inevitable between ʿAmr the Saffarid and Ismaʿīl. After skirmishes a battle was fought near Balkh, south of the Oxus River, in 900, and ʿAmr was defeated and captured. He was then sent to the caliph in Baghdad, who ordered him executed, while Ismaʿīl received investiture as ruler of all of Khorāsān, as well as the provinces of Tabaristan south of the Caspian Sea, Seistan to the south, and Isfahan in the west. But Ismaʿīl had to conquer these territories from local princes, since the real power of the caliph had ceased to exist and local rulers only paid lip service to caliphal commands. An army sent against Tabaristan defeated the local ruler Muḥammad ibn Zayd, who was executed. But the general of the Samanid army revolted, and Ismaʿīl personally had to lead an army against his general, Muḥammad ibn Hārūn, who fled into the mountains. The revolt was crushed. Isfahan and Seistan, however, were never conquered by Ismaʿīl, whose capital was Bukhara. In central Asia, Ismaʿīl ended the independence of a number of small states, incorporating them into the Samanid domains as vassals. For example, Khwarizm submitted to Ismaʿīl but the local dynasty continued to rule; a Samanid governor was installed in the northern part of Khwarizm, while the local dynasty held court in the south. The frontiers of the Samanid state were expanded to include Talas (or Ṭarāz) to the north, and there the borders of the Samanid state were made safe from raids of nomadic Turks, while Muslim missionaries spread among the tribes. Several sources, however, claim that because of this new security the defensive walls around the oases of Samarkand and Bukhara were allowed to decay and were not repaired, opening them to easy capture.

Isma^cīl did not pay taxes to the caliph, but he and his successors sent gifts to Baghdad and placed the name of the caliph, as well as the Samanid ruler, on coins minted in the Samanid domains. The names of both were also mentioned in daily prayers. The Samanids took the title emir, which at that time meant something like viceroy of the caliph, who himself was emir of all the Muslims. Isma^cīl was well liked by his subjects, and many stories of his justice and piety are recorded in the sources. He became sick and after a long illness and died in November 907. He was succeeded by his son Aḥmad, who was also known for his piety.

Aḥmad conquered most of Seistan by 911 after many battles, but members of the Saffarid family still held the allegiance of much of the population, and this province always presented problems for the Samanids. Tabaristan revolted under a Zaydi leader of the Shiite sect of Islam, and before Aḥmad could move against Tabaristan he was assassinated in his sleep by his slaves. Some sources claim that he was killed because he always took the advice of Muslim learned men and had made Arabic the official language of court whereas his father had accorded that privilege to Persian. Aḥmad was killed in January 914 and was succeeded by his son Naṣr, a boy of eight years.

Naṣr was surnamed Sa^cīd (the Fortunate), and he was fortunate in having as his chief minister Abū ^cAbd-Allāh al-Jaihānī, a famous geographer and learned man. Naṣr was at the outset faced by a revolt in Samarkand of an uncle of his father, a younger brother of Isma^cīl, Isḥāq ibn Aḥmad, who struck his own coins. After a series of battles Isḥāq was defeated and captured, but then several of Naṣr's own brothers revolted. They too were suppressed, and Naṣr could turn his attention to Tabaristan and Seistan. After initial successes, however, both provinces, for the most part, regained their independence. Naṣr showed partiality to heretical Ismailis who propagated their beliefs in the Samanid domains, so some of his chief followers plotted against him. But Nūḥ, son of Naṣr, persuaded his father to abdicate, and he died shortly afterward, in 943.

The reign of Naṣr represented the high point of Samanid rule, for poets, scholars, and statesmen flourished at the court in Bukhara. The Persian poet Rūdakī was one of the literary men who made Bukhara a center of learning and culture. A large library was also established there and was later used by such savants as Ibn Sīnā (Avicenna), who praised it highly. The Samanid court was modeled after the caliph's court, with a palace school for court slaves, and the system of training them became a model for later dynasties, even as late as the Janissary system of the Ottoman Empire. In Bukhara, as in Baghdad, Turkish slaves eventually took power into their own hands, and the Samanid emir, just as the caliph, became a puppet. The prime minister (vizier) was the most important official after the Samanid ruler, although later the commander of the army of Khorāsān, south of the Oxus, who was also governor of that area, came to rival the Samanid ruler in power. The central bureaucracy, with ten ministries, had a similar organization in Khorāsān, and presumably elsewhere in the Samanid state, which, as noted, also contained nearly independent vassal states. But the well-organized bureaucracy continued to exist after the fall of the Samanids and was copied by later rulers, especially Turkish dynasties.

Nūḥ, like his father, had to suppress revolts, including one by his own uncle Ibrāhīm, as well as in the vassal states of Khwarizm and Chaghāniyān (present Tadzhikistan). More important was the rise of a powerful new dynasty in the west, the Shiite Buyids, who were the greatest threat to Samanid rule in Khorāsān and western Iran down to the end of the dynasty. The reign of Nūḥ was stormy, but both the bureaucracy and the literary splendor of the court at Bukhara continued under his rule, with two competent viziers, Bal^camī and ^cUtbī, holding the office in turn for many years. Nūḥ died in 954 and was succeeded by his son ^cAbd al-Malik, who ruled until 961.

Under ^cAbd al-Malik it was clear that the Turkish military establishment had become the real power in the kingdom. Unfortunately for the Samanids, the Turks were not united, and internal conflicts for power split them into factions. At the death of ^cAbd al-Malik one group of Turks under Alptigin tried to place the son of ^cAbd al-Malik on the throne but failed when another faction succeeded in raising his brother Manṣūr to be ruler. Alptigin then went to Ghazni, where he ruled independently of the Samanids and laid the foundations for the future Ghaznavid state.

All of the Samanid rulers were Sunni Muslims who followed the Hanafi school of law, and, although the emir Naṣr had supported Ismaili missionaries, his successors persecuted them. At the court, Islamic scholars were patronized, as were the literati, and many books were written defending Sunni orthodoxy against heresy. It was under the later Samanids that many Turkish tribes in central Asia were converted to Islam, and the frontiers of the domain of Islam were moved to the east of the Samanid state. Many warriors for the faith left central Asia to fight in India and the Byzantine Empire in the west. This depleted the Samanids of fighting men and left them a prey to the newly converted Turkish state to the east, that of the Qarakhanids.

The last emirs of the Samanid dynasty ruled only because the populace supported the tradition of having a ruler from that family. Otherwise, as noted, the rulers were puppets of the military establishment, although the other centers of power, the bureaucracy and the religious leaders, did exercise influence on the military. Samanid possessions in western Iran were lost to the Buyids, while Seistan was ruled by the Saffarids, and Ghazni and other areas were independent of Bukhara even though the local rulers maintained a nominal subordination to the Samanid court.

Conflicts among factions of the Samanid government invited the Qarakhanid Turks to invade the Samanid domains. Many of the vassal princes of the Samanids in the east submitted to the Qarakhanids, and in the spring of 992 Bughrā Khān entered Bukhara, but he soon became ill and died. Nūḥ ibn Manṣūr, the Samanid emir, then returned to Bukhara, but his territory was reduced to the areas around Bukhara and Samarkand, since all of the land south of the Oxus River was taken by the Ghaznavid rulers. In 999 the Qarakhanid ruler Naṣr captured Bukhara and put an end to the Samanid dynasty. A brother of the last emir tried to regain the throne by guerrilla warfare against the Qarakhanids, but, although he was successful in a number of encounters, he was killed in 1005 and Iranian control of central Asia passed to the Turks.

BIBLIOGRAPHY

Vasily V. Barthold, *Turkestan down to the Mongol Invasion,* 3rd ed. (1968); Richard Frye, *The History of Bukhara of Narshakhi* (1954), and *Bukhara: The Medieval Achievement* (1965); *The Taʾrīkh-i-Guzīda of Hamd Allāh al-Qazwīnī,* Edward G. Browne and R. A. Nicholson, eds. and trans., 2 vols. (1910–1913).

RICHARD N. FRYE

[See also **Abbasids; Alptigin; Bahrām VI Čōbēn; Bukhara; Buyids; Emir; Farghānā; Ghaznavids; Iran; Isfahan; Ismāᶜīlīya; Janissary; Maʾmūn, al-; Nishapur; Qarakhanids; Saffarids; Samarkand; Shīᶜa; Sīnā, Ibn; Sunna; Umayyads; Vizier; Yaᶜqūb ibn Layth; Zaydis.**]

SAMARITANS. Though we have no precise data about population figures during the Byzantine period, the impression given by the sources is that Samaritans in Palestine formed a very dense and numerous population in the fifth and sixth centuries. At the end of the fifth and throughout the sixth century Samaritans were a source of serious troubles for the Byzantine rulers of Palestine. They rebelled at least four times: In 484, under Zeno the Isamrian (*r.* 474–491), they killed the bishop of Neapolis (Shechem), Terbinthius, and declared themselves independent, crowning their leader, Justus, king. The revolt was crushed, and for the first time a church was then erected on Mount Gerizim. At some point under Emperor Anastasios (*r.* 491–518), the Samaritans destroyed the local Byzantine garrison and gained control of Shechem. Under Justinian I (*r.* 527–565) there was a serious uprising in 529. The Samaritans gained control of the whole of Samaria and proclaimed Julianus, the leader of the revolt, king. They then became masters of a great part of the north of Palestine, from Caesarea to Tiberias, taking Bet She'an as well. After the revolt was crushed the Samaritans were forbidden access to Mount Gerizim, on which five churches were then built. The last reported revolt occurred in 556, during which the commander of the Byzantine army in Palestine was killed at his residence in Caesarea.

Sources on Samaritans under early Muslim rule in Palestine are very few and sometimes conflicting. The Samaritan chronicles tell almost nothing about this period, except names of their high priests and some details on persecutions with often contradictory and unexact chronologies. The Samaritans seem to have taken part in the Byzantine defense against the Muslim invasion in 634. According to al-Balādhurī taxes imposed on them were particularly high, five dinars per adult male (as against one to three dinars on other non-Muslims). There are reports on Samaritan communities outside Samaria as well, especially in Ramle, where according to the tenth-century geographer Ibn Ḥawqal there were 500 tax-paying Samaritans. Muslim sources of the period report that they were divided into two sects, the Dustāniyya (Dositheans) and Kūshāniyya (who were probably the "regular" Samaritans, *kūthīm* in Jewish sources). During the ninth century, the Samaritan chronicles report, they had to endure terrible persecutions by the Muslims, and their lands were declared the caliph's property. Apparently their conditions improved under Ismaili rule, both Qarmaṭians and Fatimids. A genizah letter mentions a Samaritan as tax collector in Palestine, around 1060. Characteristically, there is a total lack of any evidence in the medieval period of any connections between Jews and Samaritans.

BIBLIOGRAPHY

E. N. Adler and M. Séligsohn, "Une nouvelle chronique samaritaine," in *Revue des études juives,* **45** (1902); Michael Avi-Yonah, *The Jews of Palestine: A Political History from the Bar Kochba War to the Arab Conquest* (1976), 241–254; Stanley J. Isser, *The Dositheans* (1976); Henri Lammens, *Le Califat de Yazid Ier* (1921), 379–382; John Macdonald, "Samaritans," in *Encyclopaedia judaica,* XIV (1971); James A. Montgomery, *The Samaritans* (1907, repr. 1968), 110–137; Adolf Neubauer, *Chronique samaritaine* (1873); Andrew Sharf, *Byzantine Jewry from Justinian to the Fourth Crusade* (1971).

MOSHE GIL

[See also **Jews in the Middle East; Palestine.**]

SAMARKAND (ancient Marakanda), city of Transoxiana, now capital of Uzbek SSR.

It is difficult to place a date on the founding of Samarkand, although it is reputed to have been established as a frontier outpost in the mid sixth century B.C. by Cyrus the Great as protection against incursions by central Asian nomads. However accurate this report may be, the city is commonly perceived as being on the very edge of the Persian orbit, out in the no-man's-land that separates the Iranian world from inner Asia. The city was known to Europe in classical antiquity as the capital of Sogdiana and was captured by Alexander on his campaign into India. But while Samarkand for much of its early history drifted in and out of the political influence of Persia, and very occasionally that of China, locally it was usually dominated by Turko-Mongol elements. Its importance, not only for Persia and China but for medieval Europe as well, is that of location: it was an important stop on the East-West trade route, one of the last major outposts for the merchant traveling east before reaching the Jaxartes and entering the vast and sparsely populated inner Asian steppe.

Conquered by the Arabs in the early eighth century, Samarkand became one of the easternmost outposts of Islam and, along with Bukhara, one of the foremost cities of *Mā warā' al-Nahr* (the land beyond the river). At first part of the Umayyad and Abbasid empires, as localism prevailed over the theoretically united Islamic empire, Samarkand came to be ruled by a succession of dynasties. During the Iranian revival under the Samanids in the tenth century, Samarkand became a flourishing center of both Islamic learning and neo-Persian artistic and literary activity, rivaled, particularly in the former respect, by her sister city, Bukhara. Following the collapse of the Samanids in the late tenth century, Samarkand passed from one Turko-Muslim dynasty to another, first dominated by the Ghaznavids, then, in quick succession, the Qarakhanids, the Seljuks, and ultimately the Khwarizmshahs. It was these last who provided Genghis Khan (*d.* 1227) with a *casus belli* by molesting Mongol envoys, and Samarkand, though it escaped the absolute annihilation that was the lot of cities such as Merv or Nishapur, did suffer conquest and occupation by the Mongols. It was eventually incorporated into that part of the Mongol realm ruled by the descendants of Chagatay Khan (*d.* 1242). The conquest apparently took quite a toll on the city: fourteenth-century travelers lamented that the city which they saw was only a shadow of what pre-Mongol Samarkand must have been, although even in ruins the city impressed them.

By the mid fourteenth century Chagatay control of Transoxiana had been replaced by local anarchy, out of which Tamerlane (Timur-i Leng [1336–1405]), a local chieftain with hazy Chagatay connections, emerged victorious and established Samarkand as his capital. Although in his subsequent career in the Near East, Russia, and India he was responsible for unprecedented and unparalleled horrors, Samarkand flourished again under Tamerlane's reign. No expense was spared to transform his half-ruined capital into a showcase: captive craftsmen and artisans from the lands he conquered were transported back to Samarkand and set to work on building projects. It is this period that contributed the better part of the impressive Islamic architectural work that still distinguishes the pre-Soviet city.

BIBLIOGRAPHY

The best general works on central Asian history are still the classic studies of Vasily V. Barthold, particularly *Turkestan down to the Mongol Invasion*, H. A. R. Gibb, trans. (1958). Still the standard work, although unfashionably narrative, is René Grousset's *The Empire of the Steppes*, Naomi Walford, trans. (1970). Of more recent vintage is Luc Kwanten's *Imperial Nomads* (1979). Finally, although anecdotal and with no scholarly pretensions at all, Wilfred Blunt's *Golden Road to Samarkand* (1973) is a wonderfully engaging account of the history of the city.

RALPH HATTOX

[See also **Abbasids; Genghis Khan; Iran, History; Khwarizmshahs; Mongol Empire; Samanids; Seljuks; Tamerlane; Transoxiana; Umayyads.**]

SAMARKAND WARE, the ninth- and tenth-century slip-painted, lead-glazed earthenware pottery of eastern Iran. The slip was used both for coating the body and for the decoration; the colors ranged from white, yellow, and brown to purple. Designs were aniconic, generally calligraphic, or with geometric motifs. (See illustration at "Ceramics, Islamic.")

BIBLIOGRAPHY

Arthur Lane, *Early Islamic Pottery* (1947); Charles K. Wilkinson, *Nishapur: Pottery of the Early Islamic Period* (1973).

VENETIA PORTER

[See also **Ceramics, Islamic; Nishapur; Samanid Art and Architecture.**]

SAMARRA. The second great capital of the Abbasid caliphate. It was situated along the Tigris some sixty miles (ninety-seven kilometers) north of Baghdad. The city was founded by the caliph al-Mu^ctaṣim (*r.* 833–841) in 835 and continued to serve the Abbasids as the administrative center of their realm until the caliph al-Mu^ctaḍid (*r.* 892–902) returned to Baghdad in 892.

Two years after becoming caliph in 833, al-Mu^ctaṣim left his palace in the Mukharrim section of East Baghdad in search of a new capital. The most apparent cause for this venture was the hostility of the city population to the caliph's Turkish guard, a regiment that he had introduced, and on which he had increasingly come to rely. The caliph thought of alleviating the situation by establishing an administrative center in a less settled area of the city, and even just beyond the city, but he ultimately decided to leave Baghdad altogether. This was a momentous step, for in doing so, he gave up a strategic and geographic location that could not be duplicated. Following the course of the Tigris, the caliph ordered preliminary soundings at several sites, but for a variety of reasons, each was found unacceptable. In the past, the Abbasid caliphs preferred to develop their administrative centers a short distance from a commercially important settlement. The site ultimately chosen by al-Mu^ctaṣim along an expansive plain, did not, however, offer any commercial, geographic, or even strategic advantages. It was ten miles from the nearest town of any importance and thirty miles from Uqbarah, which lay in the center of a fertile and commercially relevant district. Why the caliph should have chosen this place to build a major city is difficult to ascertain.

The foundation lore suggests that the site of the new capital had been settled at various periods going back to the most ancient of times, and that it had previously been considered for settlement by the Abbasids. It is thus reported that Samarra was built for Sam (Shem), the son of Noah, in postdiluvian times, thereby also explaining the etymology of the name. Other statements indicate it to be an ancient city of the Persians. Regarding the Abbasids, there is a tradition that al-Saffāḥ (*r.* 750–754), the founder of the dynasty, was disposed to build at Samarra before he settled near al-Anbār. Similarly, it is said that his successor, al-Manṣūr (*r.* 754–775), actually began construction at Samarra but abandoned the effort in favor of Baghdad. Hārūn al-Rashīd (*r.* 785–809) reportedly built a palace at Samarra opposite the ruins of a great Sasanian monument, and he is credited as well with digging the Qāṭūl canal, where the original settlement of later times was established. There is also a legend which explains that al-Mu^ctaṣim built his city in fulfillment of an ancient prophecy.

Samarra, like Baghdad, was formed by the successive occupation of a variety of sites within a very wide general area. However, unlike the built-up area of the older capital, whose width and length were of nearly equal dimensions and densely occupied, Samarra was characterized by a series of somewhat more isolated settlements extending like a ribbon for some twenty miles along both banks of the Tigris, and bounded by the Qāṭūl to the east and the north, the Yahūdī to the south, and the Isḥāqī to the west. There were in addition centers of lesser occupation outside the perimeter of the city proper and on the west bank.

The original plans to build at the junction of the Qāṭūl and Tigris were shelved because the terrain was found unsuitable, and the land was not sufficient to meet the caliph's needs. A second parcel of land was then purchased near the village of al-Matīrah. This was an open expanse devoid of buildings and inhabitants except for a single monastery. The site was called Surramanraᵓa, but this name soon gave way to Samarra, the name which came to indicate the greater urban center which developed all around.

Al-Muᶜtaṣim built three palaces, of which the most famous was the Jawsaq al-Khāqānī, whose ruins remain today. Extensive dwellings were also built for the caliph's retinue and army, as well as a viable economic infrastructure to handle supply and services. A market area was thus built surrounding a Friday mosque. The task of construction required the formation of a large and diversified labor force recruited from among the skilled and unskilled workers of the surrounding areas and regions still further removed.

In addition to considerable archaeological evidence, knowledge of Samarra is derived primarily from the geographer and historian Yaᶜqūbī, who preserves a detailed topographical account describing the general localities of the city in relation to one another. His description is, however, terse and offers little information which suggests clear patterns of change within the areas described. It is therefore difficult to construct a detailed chronological history that illustrates shifting patterns of settlement. Some general patterns are nevertheless evident.

Samarra was subject to meticulous planning. Careful attention was devoted to the placing of various ethnic groups in set quarters which were arranged in several thoroughfares running almost the entire length and breadth of the city. In particular, it was necessary to separate elements of the military from the general populace. The Turks were kept apart from all the other elements of society save for their neighbors, the Farāghinah, but precautions were taken here as well so as to keep the two groups from intermingling. The extent of their physical isolation was reinforced by a series of unprecedented measures in an effort to guarantee their social isolation as well. Slave girls were imported to provide wives for the Turkish contingents, who were not permitted to marry other women, nor were they permitted to divorce. This marital regulation was unique, if indeed it was ever fully observed. The physical isolation of the Turks was to be complete. Each military settlement was situated at some distance from the markets and hence the general populace. It was, however, impossible to keep large areas of settlement isolated from basic services. The settlements were thus provided mosques, bathhouses, and markets called *suwayqāt,* which were, in effect, distributive outlets dealing in basic commodities, specifically, foodstuffs such as grains and meat and other unspecified necessities.

The main thoroughfare of al-Muᶜtaṣim's city was the "Great Road" (*shāriᶜ al-aᶜzam*), called al-Sarījah. This road extended the entire length of the city. With later extensions it ran some 20 miles (32 kilometers) and was reported to have been 300 feet (91 meters) wide at one point. The part of the road which still exists, although somewhat narrower (240 feet or 73 meters), nevertheless testifies to dimensions that were indeed staggering. The great government buildings, the Friday mosque and the city markets were all situated along al-Sarījah. It was throughout the entire history of the city the main line from which most of the city's traffic radiated toward the Tigris and inland. A description of the locations that bounded al-Sarījah and the other thoroughfares of the city is found in Yaᶜqūbī. To summarize him: Moving inland from the river, the first two thoroughfares contained the major institutions of the city. The next five contained no public buildings, no commercial center, and, with the exception of a group of public officials occupying the extremity of the Abū Aḥmad Road, no Arab settlement. They were heavily occupied by military contingents. The great roads all ran the length of the city. The absence of similar thoroughfares bisecting the width of the city suggests a deliberate effort to discourage traffic between the major sections of settlement. Considering also the absence of major markets in the five inland sections, it is clear that Samarra was essentially a series of military camps kept separate from one another.

Al-Muᶜtaṣim also developed the west bank of the Tigris. The area across the river had a certain bucolic quality and was characterized by some twelve villages situated along major water channels. The evidence would seem to indicate a flourishing agriculture, including excellent cash crops. The taxes earned on the west bank properties appear to represent some 60 percent of the entire tax base for the city. In addition the caliph established pleasure palaces, gardens, and parks for his convenience. His effort was emulated by various of his retainers, thereby driving up real-estate prices for west bank properties.

Following the death of al-Muᶜtaṣim, Hārūn al-Wāthiq (*r.* 842–847) became caliph. The city grew substantially, with a particular emphasis on the development of new palaces and commercial facilities on the east bank. The new caliph, seeking an identity of his own, moved his residence to a newly constructed palace along the Tigris, which he named, after himself, al-Hārūni. The market areas were enlarged and the port facilities expanded as part of an energetic program that included the refurbishing and strengthening of already existing structures. The new development affected only the first two sections inland from the water; the other five sections retained their character as military settlements. The third caliph at Samarra, Jaᶜfar al-Mutawakkil (*r.* 847–861), initially resided at his predecessor's palace along the Tigris shore, while his three sons were given new palaces of their own. One of these palaces, known as Balkuwārā, was situated on a new location to the southeast. More significant were the developments taking place along three of the inland thoroughfares, areas hitherto reserved exclusively for military occupation.

On an expansive area at the limit of the section called al-Ḥayr, the caliph undertook the construction of a second Friday mosque to replace the earlier building of al-Muᶜtaṣim. The new mosque was an enormous structure leaving no doubt that it was intended not to supplement but to replace the earlier place of worship, which was subsequently leveled. Since the new mosque was to serve the entire population of Samarra (which resided for the most part along the first two thoroughfares inland), three major traffic areas had to be constructed along the width of the urban area. Each artery was reported to have been about 150 feet (46 meters) wide so as to handle the enormous traffic. Each artery was flanked by rows of shops, representing all sorts of commercial and artisanal establishments. The arteries were in turn connected to ample side streets containing the residences of the general populace. The approaches to the mosque were settled by members of the scribal corps, generals (without troops?), notables, and others. For the first time commercial establishments and public buildings were allowed beyond the Great Thoroughfare. The result was a second market district and area of civilian settlement that altered the balance between civilians and the military. The new settlement also put a strain on the existing water supply. Previously, water was brought by pack animals. Now, feeder channels which flowed year-round were extended from the river. Although the new development may not have affected the character of occupation in old areas, Samarra increasingly took on the features of a fully integrated city and less those of a military camp (*askar*).

Pinched in by a rising tide of humanity, al-Mutawakkil undertook an ambitious building project five miles north of the city limits. He began to build a new palace precinct called al-Jaᶜfariya al-Mutawakkilīya. In addition to the caliph's palace, there were residences for his sons, fiefs for various scribes, the military, and elements of the general populace. A magnificent Friday mosque was built to serve the worshipers. The Great Thoroughfare was extended from the outer limits of Samarra. Feeder channels that brought drinking water flanked both sides of the road. In a short time the area between al-Mutawakkil's center and the original settlement at Samarra was filled in with a continuous line of occupation. The growth of al-Mutawakkilīya required the development of yet another major market area to provide services and supplies. The markets were, however, kept distant from the military and government areas so as to preserve some semblance of security. The vast project did not take into consideration the enormous costs as well as certain technical problems. When the caliph was murdered, the entire complex was abandoned. His successor, al-Muntaṣir (*r.* 861–862), returned to the older settlement at Samarra. The development of al-Mutawakkilīya was to be the last great building scheme in the general area. In 892 Samarra was abandoned by the caliph al-Muᶜtaḍid. The city declined rapidly thereafter.

BIBLIOGRAPHY
Ernst Herzfeld, *Geschichte der Stadt Samarra* (1948), gives references to previous publications dealing with the history and excavations of the city. See also Keppel A. C. Creswell, *Early Muslim Architecture*, II (1940); and J. M. Rogers, "Sāmarrā: A Study in Medieval Town Planning," in Albert H. Hourani and S. M. Stern, eds., *The Islamic City* (1970), 119–155.

JACOB LASSNER

[See also **Abbasid Art and Architecture; Abbasids; Baghdad; Caliphate; Hārūn al-Rashīd; Iraq; Islamic Art and Architecture; Manṣūr, Abū Ja**ᶜ**far** ᶜ**Abd Allāh Ibn Muḥammad al-; Mu**ᶜ**taṣim, al-; Mutawakkil, al-; Saffāḥ, Abū al-**ᶜ**Abbās al-; Urbanism, Islamic World; Ya**ᶜ**qūbī, al-.**]

SAMPIRUS OF ASTORGA (*fl.* early eleventh century), presbyter of León and notary of King Alfonso V, was bishop of Astorga from 1035 to 1040. As notary he wrote the chronicles of the kings of León, covering the reigns of Alfonso III the Great through Ramiro III (866–982). Sampirus concentrated on the military campaigns against the Moors, family politics, and the establishment of the church. The chronicles were continued by Pelagius of Oviedo.

BIBLIOGRAPHY
An edition of Sampirus' *Chronica* is in Enrique Florez, ed., *España sagrada,* XIV (1749), 438–477. See also Max Manitius, *Geschichte der lateinischen Literatur des Mittelalters,* III (1931, repr. 1973), 439–440.

NATHALIE HANLET

[See also **Asturias-León (718–1037); Chronicles; Historiography, Western European.**]

SAMSONS SAGA FAGRA (Tale of Samson the Fair, also called *Samsonar saga fagra*) is a fourteenth-century Icelandic saga that contains a skillful native blend of mythical-heroic and romantic elements. Borrowings from *Möttuls saga* and possibly from Saxo Grammaticus are mingled with analogues to *Beowulf, Grettis saga,* and Breton lais. Only two vellum manuscripts of the saga are extant, both from the fifteenth century, and at least forty-one paper manuscripts are known to exist in five different countries.

This rapidly paced narrative deals with Samson, the son of Artús (Arthur), king of England, who falls in love with Valentína, the daughter of Garland, king of Ireland, and hostage at the court of Artús. After she is sent home to her country, Kvintalín, seducer of women, lures her into the woods by means of his harp. Ólympía, once the foster-mother of Samson, saves Valentína, tricking Kvintalín by sending him first a dog and then a cat, changed by means of a thread tied about their necks into the likenesses of beautiful women. Samson's search for Valentína takes him to Bretland, where he kills Kvintalín's mother, a troll, in an underwater battle. Thinking Valentína dead, Samson becomes engaged to Ingína, daughter of Earl Finnlaug in Bretland, but she later thinks the same of Samson and marries Valentína's father. A magnificent stag is used by Kvintalín and Grélant the dwarf to lure Samson into a trap, but Samson captures them, wakes Valentína from a magic sleep, and forces the two evildoers to go on a quest for marvelous treasure. After an interlude concerning the literal-minded hero (Sigurðr, abandoned in the land of giants as in infant by his father, king of Glæsivellir, but later identified by his ring), Kvintalín and Grélant carry out their charge, killing Sigurðr and stealing his bride-to-be in the process. The saga ends happily with numerous marriages.

No *rímur* versions of this saga prior to 1600 are extant, although four different *rímur* from the seventeenth through twentieth centuries are known to exist.

BIBLIOGRAPHY
Erik Julius Björner, ed., *Nordiska kämpa dater* (1737); R. W. Chambers, *Beowulf: An Introduction to the Study of the Poem,* 3rd ed. (1959); Jürg Glauser, *Isländische Märchensagas* (1983), 195, 285–287; Finnur Jónsson, *Den oldnorske og oldislandske litteraturs historie,* III, 2nd ed. (1924). 108–109; William W. Lawrence, *Beowulf and Epic Tradition* (1928, repr. 1961); *Samson Fríði og Kvintalín Kvennaþjófur* (1905); Margaret Schlauch, *Romance in Iceland* (1934); Finnur Sigmundsson, *Rímnatal,* I (1966), 412–413; Bjarni Vilhjálmsson, ed., *Riddarasögur,* III (1961), 347–401; John Wilson, ed., *Samsons saga fagra* (1953).

PETER JORGENSEN

[See also **Beowulf; Grettis saga Ásmundarsonar; Lai, Lay; Möttuls saga; Rímur Saxo Grammaticus.**]

SAMUIL OF BULGARIA (*d.* 1014). Following the Byzantine conquest of eastern Bulgaria in 971,

Samuil and his three brothers (the Cometopuli or Kometopouloi—sons of a Count Nicholas) revolted in Macedonia in 976. They quickly gained control of Macedonia and began expanding into Bulgaria. Within ten years the three brothers were dead (the most important of them, Aaron, being killed by Samuil in 986), and Samuil was sole ruler. His state was centered in western Macedonia around Lakes Prespa and Ochrid. At Ochrid, Samuil re-established the Bulgarian patriarchate. In 986 and 991 he repulsed Byzantine attacks.

Civil war in Byzantium allowed Samuil to further expand his state. By 997 he held all Macedonia, Bulgaria, Thessaly, Epiros, and Albania. He was also overlord of the rulers of Duklja (modern Montenegro), Raška, Trebinje, Zahumlje, and part of Bosnia. In 997 he was crowned czar of Bulgaria. In 1000 or 1001 Basil II launched his counteroffensive, which against strong resistance conquered all Samuil's state by 1018. Samuil died during this war of a stroke in 1014, after Basil II had captured and blinded 14,000 Bulgarian troops. Samuil's successor, his son Gabriel Radomir, was murdered in 1015 by Aaron's son, John Vladislav, who succeeded to the throne.

BIBLIOGRAPHY

John V. A. Fine, Jr., *The Early Medieval Balkans* (1983).

JOHN V. A. FINE, JR.

[See also **Basil II "Killer of Bulgars"; Bosnia; Bulgaria; Byzantine History; Ochrid.**]

SAN MARCO, VENICE. Begun in 1063 by Doge Domenico Contarini (1042–1071) to replace the original Venetian shrine of the Apostle Mark, whose relics were brought from Alexandria in 829, S. Marco was juridically the doge's chapel, and also an apostle's martyrium. Its cruciform, five-domed design reproduced the imperial church of the Holy Apostles in Constantinople. Its interior decoration also was byzantinizing, the work of a long-lived Venetian mosaic industry founded by artisans imported from Constantinople in the 1080's. S. Marco was enlarged in the twelfth and thirteenth centuries, and its new exterior was encrusted with architectural marbles and statuary (including the famous bronze horses) looted from Constantinople in 1204.

BIBLIOGRAPHY

D. Buckton, ed., *The Treasury of San Marco, Venice* (1984); Friedrich Wilhelm Deichmann, ed., *Corpus der Kapitelle der Kirche von San Marco zu Venedig* (1981); Otto Demus, *The Church of San Marco in Venice* (1960), and *The Mosaics of San Marco in Venice,* 2 vols. (1984); Guido Perocco, ed., *The Horses of San Marco, Venice,* John and Valerie Wilton-Ely, trans. (1979); Fulvio Zuliani, *I marmi di San Marco* (1969).

DALE KINNEY

[See also **Bertuccio; Byzantine Art, 843–1453; Early Christian and Byzantine Architecture; Pala d'Oro; Venice;** and illustration overleaf.]

SAN PEDRO, DIEGO DE (*fl. ca.* 1470–*ca.* 1506), Spanish writer. Little is known of his life, except that he spent twenty-nine years in the service of Juan Téllez-Girón, count of Ureña, was active in the time of the Catholic monarchs, and in mid career frequented court circles.

His first work, *La Pasión trovada,* which exists in two distinct redactions, was the earliest long versified narrative of the Passion in Spanish, and, despite numerous later rivals, remained up to the nineteenth century the most popular. It is remarkable both for its moving simplicity and for its rejection of noncanonical material (although it does borrow ideas and techniques from the Pseudo-Bonaventure's *Meditationes vitae Christi*). His two sentimental romances, *Arnalte y Lucenda* (written *ca.* 1481) and *Cárcel de amor* (composed between 1483 and 1492), enjoyed enormous success, *Arnalte* being translated into Italian, French, English, and Flemish, and *Cárcel* into Italian, French, English, and German. In *Arnalte* the hero relates to the author the story of his unhappy love for Lucenda. The tale is to some extent marred by the less than impeccable behavior of the hero, by some near-farcical moments, and by the irrelevant inclusion of two substantial poems, a panegyric of Queen Isabella and the first long Spanish poem on the Seven Sorrows of the Virgin. *Cárcel de amor* tells a similar story, but Leriano and Laureola are portrayed as the perfect lover and the perfect lady. The author intervenes in the action, much use is made of letters, there are no comic moments or digressions, and the romance concludes not with complaints but with the dying Leriano's defense of women and love. From 1496 on, it was regularly reprinted with the inferior continuation by Nicolás Núñez.

San Pedro's elaborate rhetorical style, which, es-

Mosaic (*ca.* 1260–1265) above the Porta S. Alippio of San Marco depicting the church as it appeared in 1204. ALINARI / ART RESOURCE

pecially in *Cárcel,* concentrates rather than dilutes his ideas, was imitated in Spanish and in translation, and undoubtedly contributed to the development of Spanish Renaissance prose. His prose *Sermón* (written between *ca.* 1485 and *ca.* 1490) is an important, if semijocose, exposition of the doctrines of "courtly love," while his impressive verse *Desprecio de la fortuna* (composed between 1498 and 1506) was inspired by personal misfortune and a rereading of Boethius, and breaks away from later medieval clichés on the subject. He produced also a quantity of lyrics (printed in the *Cancionero general*) noteworthy for their polish, ingenuity, and variety of meters and styles.

BIBLIOGRAPHY

Diego de San Pedro, *Obras completas,* I, *Tractado de amores de Arnalte y Lucenda and Sermón* (1973), II, *Cárcel de amor* (1971), Keith Whinnom, ed., and III, *Poesías* (1979), Keith Whinnom and Dortohy S. Severin, eds., and, with Nicolás Núñez, *Prison of Love,* Keith Whinnom, trans. (1979); Keith Whinnom, *Diego de San Pedro* (1974).

KEITH WHINNOM

[See also **Cancionero General; Spanish Literature.**]

SANʿA (**Ṣanʿāʾ**), a city in the center of the Yemen highlands (from 1962, capital of the Yemen Arab Republic). Because of its strategic location, Sanʿa was an important military and commercial center.

Throughout the seventh, eighth, and early ninth centuries, the city was ruled by provincial governors sent by the Prophet, the orthodox caliphs, and the Umayyads and Abbasids. By the middle of the ninth century, Abbasid provincial rule was compromised by frequent administrative changes and incompetent governors. The head of a local dynasty, Ya^cfūr (Yu^cfir) ibn ^cAbd al-Raḥmān al-Hiwali, took note of this instability, and by 847 he had ousted the last of the Abbasid governors, establishing Yafurid rule over San^ca. Although independent, the Yafurids acknowledged the Abbasid caliphs and received diplomas of investiture from them.

In the later ninth century the rule of the Sunni Yafurids in San^ca was challenged by two other powers: the Zaydi (Zaydid, Zaydite) imams and the Fatimids. From 900/902 San^ca changed hands several times between the Zaydis and the Yafurids. The city then fell under the sway of the Fatimid *da^cwa* (propaganda mission) and remained for a short period under the authority of the Fatimid imams. During that time the Yafurids and the Zaydis formed an alliance against the Fatimids, but by 906 their relations were once again hostile. From 915 the Yafurid leader As^cad ruled unchallenged; after his death in 944, internal feuding caused a decline, and the dynasty came to an end in 998.

For the next half century, San^ca remained in a state of virtual chaos. In 1047 the Ismaili Sulayhids, a vassal dynasty of the Fatimids, took the city. By 1064 San^ca and its environs were firmly in Sulayhid control and the city became their capital. For the next twenty years, the Sulayhids waged continuous battle against the Najahids and the Zaydis for control of the city. By 1068 they had soundly defeated the Najahids, but the Zaydis would persist as a threat.

San^ca did not remain the Sulayhid capital for long. When the mother of the Sulayhid "ruler" al-Mukarram Aḥmad died, he handed control of the state over to his wife, Arwā. She moved the capital to Dhu Jibla in 1088, leaving San^ca in the hands of governors.

In 1098, San^ca fell to a new local dynasty, the sultans of Hamdān. They were not one but three families of the Hamdān region. The first of these families, the Banū Hātim, ruled until 1116. In that year, the city fell under the rule of the Banu 'l-Qubayb. Their control lasted only until 1139, when another Banū Hātim clan took control of the city, holding it until the beginning of Ayyubid rule.

The Ayyubids ruled San^ca through governors from 1174 to 1229. In a situation typical of the political history of San^ca, the Zaydis exploited the internal fighting among the family to challenge the Ayyubid hegemony. Throughout the early thirteenth century, the Ayyubids and Zaydis fought for both San^ca and the territory to the north. Ultimately, the Ayyubid al-Mas^cūd Yūsuf made peace with the Zaydis, leaving the city and moving south. During one of his yearly visits to San^ca in 1221, he granted the city to the Rasulid Badr al-Dīn Hasan, who declared his independence. This inaugurated perhaps the most politically brilliant period of its history. The Rasulids originally held San^ca as a fief but soon received their deeds of investiture directly from the Abbasid caliph. The high point of Rasulid rule in the Yemen came under the long reign of al-Muẓaffar Yūsuf (1249–1294), but after his death the Rasulids slowly lost control of the city.

In 1323, the Zaydi imam besieged the city. With the exception of occasional Tahirid incursions and periodic tribal uprisings, the Zaydis ruled unchallenged in San^ca until 1515, when Mamluk troops entered the city.

BIBLIOGRAPHY

The most detailed history of San^ca available in English is to be found in R. B. Serjeant and Ronald Lewcock, eds., *Ṣan^cā^ɔ: An Arabian Islamic City* (1983). See in particular the article by G. Rex Smith, "The Early and Medieval History of Ṣan^cā^ɔ," which includes a discussion of the historiography of medieval San^ca as well as extensive bibliographic references in the notes.

PAULA SANDERS

[See also **Arabia, Islamic; Yemen; Zaydis.**]

SANAHIN. The monastery of Sanahin in northern Armenia, founded at the site of a ruined fourth- or fifth-century church, is first mentioned in manuscripts in the early tenth century. It was one of the most celebrated religious and cultural centers of Armenia from the tenth to the thirteenth century. According to the eleventh-century historian Stephen of Tarōn, 500 monks were housed there and at the Hałbat Monastery nearby.

The large complex constructed within the towered walls in successive stages includes three churches, two *gawit^c*s (large vaulted halls), a library, an academy, a bell tower, χač^ck^cars (stelae), mausoleums, and other smaller structures.

The oldest surviving structure is the church of St. Astuacacin, erected in 934 by Armenian monks who had fled from Byzantium. St. Astuacacin is a

Florentius and his disciple Sanctius toasting each other upon completion of their work. Miniature from a Bible of Valeránica, 960. LEÓN, COLEGIATA DE SAN ISIDORO, COD. 2, fol. 514r

small domed-hall church with four corner chambers. Four animal reliefs are on spandrels of the central arches, and a church model is carved on the left of the apse.

The church of Amenap'rkič^{c} (the Redeemer), a larger hall church with two-story chapels in the four corners, was erected around 966 by Queen Xosrovanoyš for the salvation of her sons, the princes Smbat and Kiwrikē. Their images are carved on the east wall. Dressed in princely garb, they hold a model of the church.

Two different types of large *gawit*^{c}s are attached to the church, one commissioned by Archimandrite Yovhannēs in 1181, and the second, an unusual portico-like structure in basilican form, by Prince Vač^{c}e Vač^{c}ut^{c}ean in 1211.

The library (1063) erected by Princess Hranoyš, with niches for storing manuscripts, has an advanced constructional system using masonry arches to support the stone vaults.

The round chapel of St. Grigor (1061) has a quadrilobe plan inscribed in a circle. Other structures include the gallery-like academy associated with Grigor Magistros, and the bell tower (thirteenth century), one of the first of its kind, erected by Vag with two stories and an attic.

BIBLIOGRAPHY

Architettura medievale Armena: Roma-Palazzo Venezia, 10–30 giugno, 1968 (1968), an exhibition catalog; Sirarpie Der Nersessian, *Armenian Art,* Sheila Bourne and Angela O'Shea, trans. (1977); O. Ghalpakhtchian and Adriano Alpago-Novello, *Il complesso monastico di Sanahin (X–XII sec.)* (1970); Varaztad Harouthiounian and Morous Hasrathian, *Monuments of Armenia* (1975); Joseph Strzygowski, *Die Baukunst der Armenier und Europa,* 2 vols. (1918); T^{c}oros T^{c}oramanyan, *Nyut^{c}er Haykakan Čartarapetut^{c}yan Patmut^{c}yan,* 2 vols. (1942–1948).

LUCY DER MANUELIAN

[See also **Archimandrite; Armenia, History of; Gawit^{c}; Grigor Magistros; Hałbat.**]

SANCTIUS (*fl.* mid seventh century), a scribe, and perhaps an illuminator, at the monastery of Valeránica (Castile, Spain). He signed the large, densely illustrated Bible, completed in 960 (León, Colegiata Real de San Isidoro, cod. 2). He is pictured at its end toasting Florentius, whom he acknowledges as "master."

BIBLIOGRAPHY

John Williams, *Early Spanish Manuscript Illumination* (1977).

JOHN WILLIAMS

[See also **Florentius; Manuscript Illumination, European; Mozarabic Art.**]

SANCTUS, the part of the eucharistic prayer (the anaphora) in the Latin Mass that follows directly after the Preface. The text is adapted from Isaiah 6:3, "Sanctus, sanctus, sanctus" (Holy, holy, holy) and Matthew 21:9, "Benedictus qui venit" (Blessed is he who comes). The text is invariable throughout the year and is therefore classified as part of the Ordinary.

Most Eastern liturgies contained some form of the Sanctus from early on. Its use in the West, however, cannot be conclusively documented before around 400. The Benedictus and Hosanna may not have been part of the original chant in the Mass and, according to Jungmann, seem to have been added between the fourth and sixth centuries, probably in Gaul.

The Sanctus was conceived as the people's song in response to the Preface and was sung in the early church by all those present. By the ninth century, performance began to be gradually relegated to a trained choir. There are references to organ accompaniment by the twelfth century. References to the use of the bell signal begin to appear in the thirteenth century in conjunction with the elevation of the host, but by the end of the fourteenth century there is a reference at Chartres to the use of the bell during the Sanctus. Sanctus bells were common in English churches by the sixteenth century.

Peter J. Thannabaur has undertaken the most thorough study of the monophonic Sanctus. His extensive catalog in *Das einstimmigen Sanctus,* although not exhaustive, contains 231 melodies. Most of these were restricted to local repertories and only a handful had international currency. Melodic style is, in general, moderately ornate, with melismatic flourishes particularly on the words "sanctus" and "hosanna." Structural clarity achieved through varied patterns of melodic repetition and parallelism is a feature of most melodies; their careful construction and melodic focus place them in a different stylistic realm than the earlier "Gregorian" styles associated with the Mass Propers. Scholars have traced vestiges of the ancient congregational practice in Sanctus XVIII of the Vatican edition, in part owing to its simple, syllabic style. Peter Thannabaur has challenged this hypothesis, suggesting that the simple setting was a simplification of a more elaborate model now lost.

The Sanctus was the focus of rhetorical embellishment and intensification through tropes (that is, expansion with new music and text) and prosulas (addition of text to melismas). Systematic study of these additions has not been undertaken. Of the melodies that Thannabaur has catalogued, over one-third have some form of trope or prosula. In all, he counts 239 texts, a number of which have been edited by Blume and Bannister.

Polyphonic settings of the Sanctus begin to appear in the twelfth century. Twenty-eight settings up to around 1300 are edited by Max Lütolf, and most of these include trope and prosula texts. During the fourteenth century the preference shifted to setting untroped texts. By the second half of the fifteenth century, the polyphonic cyclic Mass (which linked the five principal items of the Ordinary through common musical material) had become the main large-scale form of composition. At this time and throughout the Renaissance the Sanctus was usually divided into five contrasting sections (Sanctus—Pleni—Hosanna—Benedictus—Hosanna), at times forming a cycle within the larger cycle.

BIBLIOGRAPHY

Clemens Blume and Henry Merriott Bannister, eds., *Tropen des Missale im Mittelalter,* I: *Tropen zum Ordinarium Missae* (Analecta hymnica medii aevi, XLVII) (1905), 303–369; Paul Cagin, *L'euchologie latine,* I: *Te Deum ou illatio?* (1906); Lucien Chavoutier, "Un Libellus Pseudo-Ambrosien sur le Saint-Esprit," in *Sacris erudiri,* **11** (1960), 180–191; Richard Crocker, "Sanctus," in *New Grove Dictionary of Music and Musicians,* XVI (1980); Michel Huglo, "La tradition occidentale des mélodies byzantines du Sanctus," in *Der kultische Gesang der abendländischen Kirche,* Franz Tack, ed. (1950); Joseph A. Jungmann, *The Mass of the Roman Rite,* Francis Brunner, trans., II (1955); Kenneth Levy, "The Byzantine Sanctus and Its Modal Tradition in East and West," in *Annales musicologique,* **6** (1958–1963); Max Lütolf, *Die mehrstimmigen Ordinarium Missae-sätze vom ausgehenden 11. bis zur Wende des 13. zum 14. Jahrhundert,* 2 vols. (1970); Peter Josef Thannabaur, *Das einstimmige Sanctus der römischen Messe in der handscriftlichen überlieferung des 11. bis 16. Jahrhunderts* (1962), and "Sanctus," in *Die Musik in Geschichte und Gegenwart,* Friedrich Blume, ed., XI (1963).

LANCE W. BRUNNER

[See also **Mass, Liturgy of; Tropes to the Ordinary of the Mass.**]

SANDALJ HRANIĆ KOSAČA (*d.* 1435), Bosnian noble who inherited his holding from his uncle Vlatko Vuković and who created what was for all practical purposes an independent principality within the Bosnian state, encompassing Hum (which roughly coincided with modern Hercegovina) and the region of the Upper Drina, Tara, and Piva rivers. Sandalj was influential in Bosnia, playing a leading role in various councils held on Bosnian affairs and in events that caused the various changes on the Bosnian throne between 1395 and 1420. In 1396 he married Hrvoje Vukčić's niece, Jelena, whom he divorced in 1411 to marry Jelena, sister of Stefan

Lazarević of Serbia. Thereafter he maintained close ties with Serbia.

Initially supporting Ladislas of Naples against Sigismund in their civil war, Sandalj worked to keep Bosnia independent from Hungary. In 1410, however, he was forced to recognize Sigismund. He participated in the murder of Pavle Radenović in 1415, which led to war with Pavle's son Radoslav Pavlović. An alliance with the Turks enabled Sandalj to emerge from this conflict with a satisfactory peace in 1420. In the 1430's he supported Radivoj against King Tvrtko II. A member of the Bosnian church, Sandalj also tolerated Catholics and Orthodox.

BIBLIOGRAPHY

John V. A. Fine, Jr., *The Bosnian Church* (1975), and *The Late Medieval Balkans* (1987).

JOHN V. A. FINE, JR.

[See also **Bosnia; Bosnian Church; Hungary; Serbia; Stefan Lazarević.**]

SANSON DE NANTEUIL (*fl.* mid twelfth century), an Anglo-Norman poet who translated into octosyllabic verse the *Proverbs of Solomon* around 1150 for Alice de Condet of Horncastle (Lincolnshire). The *Proverbs* are preserved in London at the British Library (MS Harley 4388).

BIBLIOGRAPHY

M. Dominica Legge, *Anglo-Norman Literature and Its Background* (1963).

BRIAN MERRILEES

[See also **Anglo-Norman Literature.**]

SANTIAGO DE COMPOSTELA, cathedral city and pilgrimage center in northwestern Spain. The city dates from the discovery in the first half of the ninth century of what was presumed to be the tomb of the Apostle James the Greater. His body, according to tradition, had been brought to that area for burial after his martyrdom because during his lifetime he had christianized the region through his preaching. Shortly after the discovery of the tomb a small church was built over it at the order of Alfonso II of Asturias. St. James was declared the patron saint of Spain, and a new episcopal see for the region was established there and given precedence over the one in the nearby ancient Roman city of Iria Flavia.

The tomb immediately became an important pilgrimage center, and at the end of the ninth century the original church was replaced by a much larger one, which was destroyed by al-Manṣūr when he captured and razed the city in 997. Construction of the present church was begun around 1075 or 1078, and it was consecrated in 1211. In its original, Romanesque form it was typical of the large, galleried pilgrimage churches whose ambulatories and radiating chapels enabled large numbers of worshipers to both see the relic of the saint and participate in the Mass.

In the twelfth and thirteenth centuries the city was one of the most important spiritual centers of Western Christendom, attracting thousands of pilgrims every year. It served Christians as a counter to the Muslims in the Iberian Peninsula and at the same time it was a vivid symbol of the independence of the Spanish church from Rome.

BIBLIOGRAPHY

Kenneth John Conant, *The Early Architectural History of the Cathedral of Santiago de Compostela* (1926); Paula Gerson *et al.*, *The Twelfth Century Pilgrim's Guide to Santiago de Compostela: Translation and Critical Edition* (1988); Edwin Mullins, *The Pilgrimage to Santiago* (1974); Walter F. Starkie, *The Road to Santiago* (1957); John Williams, "'Spain or Toulouse?' A Half Century Later Observations on the Chronology of Santiago de Compostela," in International Congress on the History of Art, 23rd, Granada, 1973, *Actas,* I (1976).

JERRILYNN D. DODDS
ROBERT J. SNOW

[See also **Church, Types of; Manṣūr, Ibn Abī ᶜĀmir al-; Pilgrimage, Western European; Pilgrim's Guide; Romanesque Architecture.**]

SANTIAGO DE COMPOSTELA, SCHOOL OF, the repertory of devotional music for St. James preserved in the *Codex Calixtinus,* also known as the *Liber sancti Jacobi,* in the Biblioteca de la Catedral, Santiago de Compostela, in northwestern Spain.

The *Codex Calixtinus* contains primarily material on St. James and his cult. Complete texts and music of the Proper items of the Offices and Masses for the vigil and feast day and a troped Mass end the first section of the book. The texts are attributed to Pope Calixtus II (*d.* 1124), hence the designation Calixtinus. At the end of the book, polyphonic pieces in two voices have been added. They include conductus, *Benedicamus Domino* versus, four responsories for matins of the feast day to the last of which a prose is appended, the kyrie from the troped Mass, the gradual and an alleluia from the Mass for the feast day, another kyrie trope, and three settings of the *Benedicamus Domino*. Three monophonic pieces conclude the manuscript. In addition, second voices were added to two conductus in the monophonic portion of the manuscript: *Jacobe sancte tuum,* also among the polyphony with the same music, and *In hac die*. The polyphonic pieces are attributed to ecclesiastical and scholarly figures of the eleventh and twelfth centuries, mostly French. These attributions and that to Calixtinus are thought to be false, included to add presitge to the collection, which is dated by the prosopographical evidence around 1140. The manuscript was intended to promote the cult of St. James as practiced at Compostela. The existing codex, copied in the twelfth century, is not the original since another copy (Barcelona, Archivo de la Corona de Aragón, MS Ripoll 99), made in 1173, was not copied from it. The polyphony is unique to the existing Compostela copy.

The monophonic repertory of the codex is identical in style to contemporary plainsong, from which many melodies are borrowed. The original melodies are important as examples of twelfth-century plainsong composition. The polyphonic conductus, *Benedicamus Domino* versus, and the prose are similar in style to pieces of these types from the contemporary Aquitanian repertory: mildly florid settings of the text embellished with occasional cadential melismata; mostly note-against-note texture, although the upper voice is slightly more florid than the lower. The kyrie trope *Rex immense pater pie* also exhibits these characteristics. Those pieces with liturgical tenors lean toward the style of *organum purum* of the Notre Dame repertory of around 1200. The lower voice holds the notes of the plainsong while the upper voice provides an elaborate counterpoint. The repertory of the codex shows the influence of contemporary French styles.

BIBLIOGRAPHY

Richard H. Hoppin, *Medieval Music* (1978); Wolfgang Osthoff, "Die Conductus des Codex Calixtinus," in Martin Ruhnke, ed., *Festschrift Bruno Stäblein zum 70. Geburtstag* (1967); Peter Wagner, ed., *Die Gesänge der Jakobusliturgie zu Santiago de Compostela* (1931); Walter M. Whitehill *et al.*, eds., *Liber sancti Jacobi: Codex Calixtinus,* 3 vols. (1944).

JAMES GRIER

[See also **Austurias-León; Benedicamus Domino; Conductus; Gradual; Kyrie; Notre Dame School; Pilgrim's Guide; Responsory; Tropes to the Ordinary of the Mass.**]

SANTILLANA, MARQUÉS DE (Iñigo López de Mendoza, 1398–1458), Castilian Spanish literary and political figure. He was often at odds with his king, John II of Castile, and with the prime minister, Álvaro de Luna, the cruel power behind the throne. Married to Catalina de Figueroa, he spent most of his early adulthood traveling through Spain, fighting the Moors, collecting books and manuscripts, training a private army, and plotting the downfall of Álvaro de Luna, who was finally beheaded in 1453. His other life, as a poet, scholar, and humanist, is probably more significant. The author of subtle yet earthy poems, *serranillas* (a Spanish version of the French pastourelles), he also wrote long narrative and philosophical poems such as *Comedieta de Ponza* and *Diálogo de Bías contra Fortuna*. Dante, Petrarch, and Boccaccio influenced his work. His *Prohemio e carta* (Letter to Don Pedro, constable of Portugal) is an intelligent attempt to trace a brief history of Western medieval poetry in Spain, France, Portugal, and Italy.

BIBLIOGRAPHY

D. W. Foster, *The Marqués de Santillana* (1971); Rogelio Pérez-Bustamante, *El marqués de Santillana* (1983).

MANUEL DURAN

[See also **Castile; Catalan Literature; Pastourelle; Spanish Literature.**]

SARĀY, a Persian term used also in Turkish to describe a large and sumptuous building or a complex of buildings, particularly a palace. The word is also used in phrases, such as *sarāy-i baqa,* the mansion of eternity—that is, the "next world"—and *sarāy-i fanī,* a transient abode of this world, such as a well-built and large structure serving as an inn and con-

Christ's Entry into Jerusalem. Miniature by Sargis Picak from the Gospel of Queen Mariun, 1346. JERUSALEM, ARMENIAN PATRIARCHATE, MS 1973, fol. 114

taining storage and work areas as well as shops for traveling merchants.

An imperial *sarāy*, depending on the wealth and power of the ruler, may have resembled a small city. The Topkapi *sarāy* of the Ottoman sultans in İstanbul, built between the 1470's and the end of the nineteenth century, formerly contained about one hundred large and small buildings and many gardens.

BIBLIOGRAPHY

Fanny Davis, *The Palace of Topkapi in İstanbul* (1970); J.-C. Garcin *et al.*, *Palais et maisons du Caire,* I, *Époque mamelouke: XIIIe–XVIe siècles* (1982), and II, *Époque ottomane: XVIe–XVIIIe siècles* (1983); Oleg Grabar, *The Alhambra* (1978).

ÜLKÜ Ü. BATES

[See also **Islamic Art and Architecture.**]

SARDICA. See **Serdica.**

SARGIS PICAK (also Pidsak, Pitsak, meaning "wasp," the nickname from his meticulous drawing of a wasp) (*fl.* 1301–1353), Armenian priest, scribe, and manuscript illuminator who worked in the Cilician kingdom of Armenia, mainly at the monastery at Drazark.

The last representative of the Cilician school of painting, he is the best among its fourteenth-century miniaturists: artists whose style is coarser than that of their twelfth- and thirteenth-century predecessors. Interested mainly in decorative effects and line, Sargis sometimes crowds his compositions with two-dimensional figures against a ground of different colors (*Gospel of Queen Mariun,* 1346; Jerusalem, Armenian Patriarchate, MS 1973).

This prolific painter of scores of manuscripts is represented presently by more than thirty works—mainly Gospels—at libraries in Erevan, Venice, Jerusalem, Tübingen, and New York (*Menologium,* 1348; Pierpont Morgan Library, M. 622).

BIBLIOGRAPHY

Sirarpie Der Nersessian, *Manuscrits arméniens illustrés des XIIe, XIIIe, et XIVe siècles de la Bibliothèque des Pères Mekhitharistes de Venise,* 2 vols. (1937), 137–166, *The Chester Beatty Library: A Catalogue of the Armenian Manuscripts,* 2 vols. (1958), 35–38, 181–182, *The Armenians* (1969), 153, *Études byzantines et arméniennes,* 2 vols. (1973), I: 419, 560, 601, 605, 666–667, 691–692, and *Armenian Art,* Sheila Bourne and Angela O'Shea, trans. (1977, 1978), 161–162; Bazalel Narkiss, ed., *Armenian Art Treasures of Jerusalem* (1979), 81–87; Avedis Krikor Sanjian, *A Catalogue of Medieval Armenian Manuscripts in the United States* (1976), 28, 520–562.

LUCY DER MANUELIAN

[See also **Armenian Art; Cilician Kingdom.**]

SARMATIANS (Greek: Samátai; Latin: Sarmati, Sarmatae), an Iranian tribal confederation in the Ponto-Caspian steppes, first attested by Polybius (*ca.* 160 B.C.). Its relationship to the Sauromatai, noted by Herodotus and others, remains problematic. By late antiquity, "Sarmatian" had become a generic term for various Iranian nomadic tribes of western Eurasia. These included the Siraces, Iazyges,

Roxolani, Antae, Alani, and Aorsi-Asi. Their only linguistic descendants are the Ossetians of the north Caucasus.

The original habitats of these nomads, from whom the Scythian-Saka tribes had previously emerged, lay in central and inner Asia. Their migrations to Europe were initiated by internal conflicts and warfare between China and the Hsiung-nu, which brought about the displacement of weaker tribes westward. Sarmatian expansion to the West was usually tied to the arrival of new Iranian elements from the East.

The Sarmatians appear to have taken over the leadership of the Iranian nomads of the Ponto-Caspian steppelands as early as the fourth century B.C., but it is in the second century B.C., with the arrival of the Roxolani (pressured westward by the Aorsi), that they become prominent in the sources. They involved themselves in the affairs of the Greek Bosporan kingdom, which they increasingly iranized while themselves absorbing many Hellenistic elements. And they were drawn into the web of Roman interests here from the first century B.C. through the second century A.D. The Iazyges (*ca.* 20 A.D.), later followed by the Roxolani (third through fourth centuries), migrated to the Hungarian plain. These Sarmatians, like their eastern kinsmen, were subsequently swept up by the pan-nomadic Hunnic empire.

The Aorsi (Chinese: Yen-ts'ai) were largely subsumed by the Alans in the mid first century A.D. With the entry of the Goths into the Pontic steppes around 200, the Alans, who dominated the Sarmatian union, became closely tied to them. The appearance of the Huns around 350 and their conquest of the Goths in 375 brought about the flight of some Alans to the West. Others were incorporated into the Hunnic empire. The Hunnic conquest ended the Sarmatian confederacy. Some elements were absorbed by the Turkic nomads who entered Europe with and after the Hunnic advance. Substantial pockets of Iranians (termed Alans or As) survived, however, in the Caucasus and trans-Volga steppes, playing important roles in the Khazar kaganite and the Mongol empire. Isolated groupings also entered and settled in Western Europe.

The social structure of the Sarmatians, governed by royal clans, was typical of the other cattle-raising nomads of western Eurasia. One notable exception was the important role of women in Sarmatian government, religion, and even military operations. An interesting innovation in the martial arts introduced to the steppe by the Sarmatians was the use of heavily armored cavalry.

BIBLIOGRAPHY

Vasilii I. Abaev, *Osetinskii yazyk i folklor,* I (1949); Bernard S. Bachrach, *A History of the Alans in the West* (1973); János Harmatta, *Studies in the History and Language of the Sarmatians* (1970); Anatolii M. Khazanov, *Ocherki voennogo dela Sarmatov* (1971); Yulian A. Kulakovsky, *Alany po svedeniyam klassicheskikh i vizantiiskikh pisatelei* (1899); Ellis H. Minns, *Scythians and Greeks* (1913); Michael Rostovtsev, *Iranians and Greeks in South Russia* (1922, repr. 1969), *The Animal Style in South Russia and China* (1929), and *Skythien und der Bosporus* (1931); Dmitrii B. Shelov, ed., *Voprosy skifosarmatskoi arkheologii* (1952); E. I. Solomonik, *Sarmatskie znaki severnogo Prichernomor ya* (1959); Tadeusz Sulimirski, *The Sarmatians* (1970); Max Vasmer, *Die Iranier in Südrussland* (1923); George Vernadsky, "Der sarmatische Hintergrund der germanischen Völkerwanderung," in *Saeculum,* **2** (1951), and "Eurasian Nomads and Their Impact on Medieval Europe," in *Studi medievali,* 3rd ser., **4** (1963).

PETER B. GOLDEN

[See also **Alani; Caucasia; Huns.**]

SARRACINUS (*fl.* tenth century), a scribe who, together with Vigila and Garsea, wrote the large conciliar manuscript (the Albeldense Codex) in the Castilian monastery of Albelda in 976. The manuscript, which is now in the Escorial (Biblioteca del Monasterio, Cod. d.I.2), has illustrations in the style known as Mozarabic, some of them depicting a council and a scribe at work.

BIBLIOGRAPHY

Jesús Domínguez Bordona, *Spanish Illumination,* I (1929), 18–19; John Williams, *Early Spanish Manuscript Illumination* (1977).

JOHN WILLIAMS

[See also **Mozarabic Art.**]

SARUM CHANT. The liturgy celebrated in the diocese of Sarum or Salisbury was not a distinct rite like the Mozarabic and Ambrosian rites but, rather, a local use, descended like most diocesan uses from the hybrid Gallican-Roman liturgy of the Carolingian period. The chant of the Sarum use was thus a subrepertoire or dialect of Gregorian chant, the standard Carolingian chant repertoire. The special significance of Sarum chant relative to other dialects of Gregorian chant is due to the following:

(1) Organized in the thirteenth and fourteenth centuries, the Sarum use was considered especially well arranged, up-to-date, and beautiful. It was said to have been admired even on the Continent, and it certainly influenced the formation of other English and Scandinavian diocesan uses. It thus played a seminal role in the development of medieval English liturgy, a role that might otherwise have been played by Canterbury. However, Canterbury Cathedral, being staffed by Benedictines, followed a monastic rite that could not readily be adopted in cathedrals staffed by secular canons, as most of them were. These cathedrals looked instead to Sarum, whose liturgical influence can clearly be seen in some other uses, such as that of Hereford.

(2) But the Sarum use was not only the most seminal use of medieval England. By the sixteenth century it was also the most widely celebrated in England, as more and more churches simply adopted it outright. Thus, the Sarum chant served as the basis for much of the English polyphonic music that has survived.

(3) Because of its wide diffusion, the Sarum chant is by far the best preserved of all the medieval English chant traditions. Indeed, more sources of Sarum chant survive than of all the other English diocesan repertories together, whereas some of the other uses barely survived the great destruction of liturgical books that took place during the Reformation.

(4) Thus, because of its medieval importance and because the other traditions are so poorly preserved, considerable interest in medieval English liturgy in some quarters of the Anglican church has—since the nineteenth century—naturally focused attention on the Sarum use and its chant. It is, therefore, better known, more completely published, and more widely studied than any other diocesan use from anywhere in medieval Europe. Work remains to be done, however, particularly in the area of comparative study of the melodies with those of other English and Continental uses.

The oldest complete Sarum chant book is a twelfth-century gradual (Salisbury Cathedral MS 149), containing the texts of the proper Mass chants but not the melodies. It represents the period when the see was still headquartered at Old Sarum. The oldest manuscript that includes melodies (Exeter Cathedral MS 3515) antedates the canonization of St. Thomas of Canterbury in 1173. An early-thirteenth-century manuscript (London, British Library, Additional MS 12194), written about the time the see moved to the newly built cathedral at New Sarum, was published in facsimile by W. H. Frere. Music is also found in a thirteenth-century missal (Manchester, Rylands Library, Crawford MS lat. 24), which formed the basis of a textual edition by John W. Legg. Printed editions of the Sarum gradual were issued at Paris down to 1532, the last missal in 1557.

As might be expected, the gradual shows strong affinities with Norman French traditions, particularly that of Rouen. Influence of the earlier Saxon tradition is difficult to assess, but it was probably minimal. Recent study shows the Sarum melodic tradition to have developed from the Norman into a dialect with its own peculiar traits, such as a tendency to avoid repeated notes and semitone motion and to fill in ascending skips of a third.

The Sarum kyriale generally included nine or ten pieces for each item of the Mass ordinary, with many prosulae for the Kyrie but few other tropes beyond the *Spiritus et alme* for the Gloria in the Mass of the Virgin. A wider selection of tropes and some motets occurs in a thirteenth-century manuscript (Paris, Bibliothèque de l'Arsenal 135). A manuscript from Dublin (now Cambridge University MS Additional 710) contains a typical kyriale, a good sequentiary, and the Sarum consuetudinary; the music was published in facsimile by René Hesbert.

The Sarum antiphonal, with the proper chants for the Office, was printed only once, in 1519–1520. A facsimile edition assembled from several incomplete earlier manuscripts was published by Frere. There were many editions of the breviary, however, and of a hymnal commentary known as the *Expositio Hymnorum*. The order of chants for Mass and Office throughout the year is outlined in the ordinale, which Frere edited from an early-fourteenth-century manuscript. The manuscript contained many marginal additions. Not long after it was copied it was supplanted by the New Ordinal, which survives in many manuscripts and all the prints. From the New Ordinal was compiled the processional, though many processional chants were already given in the graduals as far back as the thirteenth century. Some printed editions are famous for having a complete set of woodcuts depicting the arrangement of ministers and personnel, which differed on each liturgical day.

The Sarum customary, consuetudinary, and tonary were all published by Frere along with the ordinal. The tonary is particularly extensive and detailed; as a nationalistic touch, it presents for each mode an antiphon taken from the proper Office of St. Thomas of Canterbury.

The increasing number of chapel and college choirs after the thirteenth century fostered a tradition of musical excellence that continues to this day; it also promoted considerable composition of polyphonic music, relatively little of which survived the Reformation. Renewed interest in the medieval rites since the nineteenth century has prompted a number of publications in which the monophonic chant melodies (sometimes only the psalm tones) are adapted to modern English texts.

BIBLIOGRAPHY

Sources. Madeleine Bernard, *Répertoire de manuscrits médiévaux contenant des notations musicales,* III (1974), for Arsenal MS 135; Arthur Jefferies Collins, *Manuale ad usum percelebris ecclesiae sarisburiensis* (1960); Francis H. Dickinson, *Missale ad usum insignis et praeclarae ecclesiae Sarum* (1861–1883, repr. 1969), with music; Walter H. Frere, *Graduale sarisburiense* (1894, repr. 1966), for facsimiles of British Library, Add. 12194 and the Kyriale Lansdowne 462, *The Use of Sarum,* 2 vols. (1898–1902, repr. 1969), and *Antiphonale sarisburiense* (1901–1925, repr. 1966); Frank L. Harrison, ed., *The Eton Choir Book,* 3 vols. (1956–1961); William G. Henderson, ed., *Processionale ad usum insignis ac praeclarae ecclesiae Sarum* (1882, repr. 1969); René Hesbert, *Le tropaire-prosaire de Dublin* (1966); Andrew Hughes and Margaret Bent, eds., *The Old Hall Manuscript,* 2 vols. in 3 (1969–1973); *Hymnarium sarisburiense cum rubricis et notis musicis* (1851); John W. Legg, ed., *The Sarum Missal* (1916, repr. 1969); William Maskell, ed., *The Ancient Liturgy of the Church of England,* 3rd ed. (1882), for the Ordo Missae and those of Bangor, York, and Hereford; Francis Proctor and Christopher Wordsworth, *Breviarium ad usum insignis ecclesiae Sarum,* 3 vols. (1879–1886, repr. 1970); Richard Pynson, *Processionale ad usum Sarum 1502* (1980); Frederick E. Warren, trans., *The Sarum Missal in English,* 2nd ed. (1913); Christopher Wordsworth, *Ceremonies and Processions of the Cathedral Church of Salisbury* (1901), for the processional text based on Salisbury MS 148, and *Ordinale Sarum sive directorium sacerdotum* (1901–1902).

Studies. Terence Bailey, *The Processions of Sarum and the Western Church* (1971); Elizabeth A. Cain, "English Chant Tradition in the Late Middle Ages: The Introits and Graduals of the Temporale in the Sarum Gradual" (diss., Harvard, 1982); Nigel Davison, "So Which Way Round Did They Go?: The Palm Sunday Procession at Salisbury," in *Music and Letters,* **61** (1980); Edward G. Duff, *Notes on the Sarum hymni cum notis, Antwerp, 1541* (n.d.); Walter H. Frere, "The Newly-found York Gradual [now Oxford, Bodleian Library, Lat. lit. MS b. 5]," in *Journal of Theological Studies,* **2** (1901); Helmut Gneuss, *Hymnar und Hymnen im englischen Mittelalter,* 2 vols. (1968); Frank L. Harrison, "Music for the Sarum Rite: MS 1236 in the Pepys Library, Magdalene College, Cambridge," in *Annales musicologiques,* **6** (1958–1963), *Music in Medieval Britain,* 4th ed. (1980), and "Sarum, Use of," in *Die Musik in Geschichte und Gegenwart,* XI (1963); René Hesbert, "The Sarum Antiphoner: Its Sources and Influence," in *Journal of the Plainsong and Mediaeval Music Society,* **3** (1980); David Hiley, "The Norman Chant Traditions: Normandy, Britain, Sicily," in *Proceedings of the Royal Musical Association,* **107** (1980–1981); C. E. Hohler, "Some Service-books of the Later Saxon Church," in David Parsons, ed., *Tenth-century Studies* (1975), 60–63, 227–228; Edward C. Ratcliff, *The Booke of Common Prayer of the Churche of England: Its Making and Revisions* (1949); Dora H. Robertson, *Sarum Close: A History of the Life and Education of the Cathedral Choristers for 700 Years* (1938); Christopher Wordsworth, *Notes on Mediaeval Services in England with an Index of Lincoln Ceremonies* (1898).

PETER JEFFERY

[See also **Gallican Rite; Gradual; Gregorian Chant; Music in Medieval Society; Rouen, Use of.**]

SARUM USE. The liturgical practices of the church of Salisbury (Sarum) constitute a use or a system for carrying out the Roman liturgy. A study of the Sarum books tends to center around the large number of rubrics that describe the manner in which the services are to be performed. The peculiarities of Sarum are less apparent in terms of the actual formulas and the general structure of the liturgy, but distinctive details of this sort illustrate the extent to which Sarum was allowed to develop independently.

The diocese of Sarum was formed in 1075, and in 1091 the constitutional framework of the rite was set down by St. Osmund in his *Institucio.* This document lists the duties of the residents of the cathedral church. It also makes provision for those canons whose obligations in their own parish churches required their absence from the choir in the cathedral church.

In the early thirteenth century St. Osmund's constitutional instructions were incorporated in the consuetudinary, along with liturgical instructions that constantly had to be adapted to accommodate new feasts and changes in the observance of old ones. Many specific instructions concerning the performance of the services involve a full cathedral choir or altars dedicated to saints. These could apply only to the cathedral church, but instructions concerning the ranks of feasts, for example, were directed to all churches and monasteries under Sarum's influence. The influence was often reciprocal when churches and monasteries in other dioceses were involved: Sarum's incorporation of the feast of the Transfiguration appears to have been modeled after the celebration in the English Benedictine monasteries, which in turn followed a Cluniac tradition. The dioceses of York and Hereford, however, had their own uses, which developed independently of Sarum.

The various Sarum books that pertain to the Divine Office have elaborate rubrics. At matins, the first in each series of antiphons, lessons, and responses would be sung or read in the lower orders of the choir, and the rest in each series would ascend successively to the higher orders. However, the lessons and responses on All Saints' Day would descend accordingly. When the classes of feasts became more numerous, each class had to have its own details for this scheme, and on many feasts these directions would be written on a *tabula* after prime.

The Ordinary of the Mass left less room for deviation from the Roman rite. However, non-Roman practices were used: the hymn "Veni creator" with Kyrie and Pater noster at the foremass; "Munda me" instead of "Lavabo" at the washing of hands. Furthermore, a veil was hung in the presbytery during Lent and lifted while the Gospel was read.

The development of the calendar also affected the processional. The hour in which the processions took place depended upon the classes of feasts, and the individual feasts determined whether the procession should go outside the church or to stations within the church. The Sarum books, which were printed up to the time of the Reformation, maintain the dual application of elaborate ceremonies to the specific features of the cathedral church and to the general features of the church bodies under Sarum's influence.

BIBLIOGRAPHY

Terence Bailey, *The Processions of Sarum and the Western Church* (1971); Edmund Bishop, *Liturgica historica* (1918, repr. 1962), 211–237, 276–300; Arthur Jefferies Collins, ed., *Manuale ad usum percelebris ecclesiae sarisburiensis* (1960); William Cooke and Christopher Wordsworth, eds., *Ordinale Sarum sive directorium sacerdotum* (1901–1902); Francis H. Dickinson, ed., *Missale ad usum insignis et praeclarae ecclesiae Sarum* (1861–1883, repr. 1969); Walter H. Frere, ed., *Graduale sarisburiense* (1894, repr. 1966), *The Use of Sarum,* 2 vols. (1898–1901, repr. 1969), and *Antiphonale sarisburiense,* 6 vols. (1901–1924, repr. 1966); William G. Henderson, ed., *Processionale ad usum insignis ac praeclarae ecclesiae Sarum* (1882, repr. 1969); Joseph A. Jungmann, *The Mass of the Roman Rite,* Francis Brunner, trans. (1951–1955); Archdale A. King, *Liturgies of the Past* (1959), 280–326; John W. Legg, ed., *The Sarum Missal* (1916, repr. 1969); R. W. Pfaff, *New Liturgical Feasts in Later Medieval England* (1970); Francis Procter and Christopher Wordsworth, eds., *Breviarium ad usum insignis ecclesiae Sarum,* 3 vols. (1879–1886, repr. 1970).

JONATHAN BLACK

[See also **Antiphon; Canonical Hours; Divine Office; Gradual; Kyrie; Mass, Liturgy of the; Missal; Processions; Sarum Chant.**]

SASANIAN ART. The monuments of the Sasanian period (*ca.* A.D. 224–651) come from the area that now includes Iran, Iraq east of the Euphrates River, parts of Armenia and Georgia, and, in the east, a small portion of Afghanistan adjacent to Iran. This extensive area remained under the control of the Sasanian dynasty almost continuously until the beginning of the Islamic era in the seventh century. The works of art that are preserved fall into several categories: rock reliefs in Iran; stucco and mosaic decoration of royal and princely dwellings in Iran and Iraq; silver-gilt vessels from the Transcaucasian region of the Soviet Union (Abkhazia, Georgia, and Soviet Azerbaijan), Iran, Afghanistan, and the Perm region, north of the Caspian Sea, in the Ural Mountains. In the minor arts, there are some glass vessels and large numbers of stone stamp seals. Although coins are not included in this survey, they are particularly important for the study of Sasanian art because they provide one of the criteria for establishing the date of the surviving monuments.

Sasanian silver-gilt plate depicting Pērōz I hunting ibexes. Qazvīn, Iran, 5th century. THE METROPOLITAN MUSEUM OF ART, NEW YORK, FLETCHER FUND, INV. NO. 34.33

The kings appearing on the coins wear crowns that, at least until the end of the fifth century, changed with each succeeding reign. The coins are inscribed with the names of the rulers, and the images can therefore be compared to representations on rock reliefs, silver plates, and seals, providing evidence for the identification of the royal figures.

In the following description of the monuments, the material is divided into three chronological periods: the third through the fourth century, the fifth to the early sixth century (531), and the sixth through the seventh century. The remains are unequal in quantity and quality; the first and last periods are richly documented, while the art of the fifth to the early sixth century is still largely unknown because there are few monuments that can be dated with certainty.

THIRD AND FOURTH CENTURIES

During the third and fourth centuries the Sasanian Empire rose to become a major power in the Near Eastern world. Political and religious institutions were established, and permanent boundaries in the east and the west were defined. These events are reflected in the earliest Sasanian works of art. Most important are a series of huge rock reliefs illustrating dynastic themes: the investiture of the king by various Zoroastrian divinities (Ohrmazd, Nahid, Mithra); the king and members of the royal family; military victories and enthronement scenes. The reliefs were commissioned by most of the Sasanian kings of the third and fourth centuries, and they are largely in the province of Fārs, in southwestern Iran, the homeland of the dynasty. Only the two latest reliefs belonging to this first period, those of Šābuhr II and III (*r.* 309–379; 383–388) and Ardešir II (*r.* 379–383), are in west-central Iran at the site of Taq-i Bostan. A development is apparent in the composition and style of the sculptures executed during this period. The crowded, low-relief battle and victory scenes of the first Sasanian king, Ardešīr I (*r. ca.* 224–*ca.* 240), at Fīrūzābād and Salmas are followed by works executed in a more sculptural style. This trend continues under Ardešīr's son, Šābuhr I (*r. ca.* 240–270/273). The figures are in high relief, and fluttering windblown drapery gives definition and greater naturalism to the body forms. The military victories of Šābuhr I in the west brought an influx of Roman prisoners to Iran, and their presence explains the distinctive design of certain reliefs at Bishapur commemorating the victory and capture of the emperor Valerian in 260. The successors of Šābuhr continued to illustrate themes of victory and divine investiture in their reliefs. One enthronement scene can be attributed to Bahrām II (*r.* 274/276–293) on the basis of the crown type, and two others, badly worn, attest to the popularity of this motif in the third century. (See illustration at "Naqsh-i Rustam.")

The reliefs at Taq-i Bostan differ from those in Fārs. One is original in form, carved in a deep arched niche in the rock face. Within the niche, two kings, Šābuhr II and Šābuhr III (according to the accompanying rock-cut inscription), are represented. Šābuhr II holds out to his son, Šābuhr III, the ring of investiture. Both figures are carved on the upper part of the back wall, in high relief. Neither the smoothened side walls nor the area beneath the figures' feet is decorated in any way. On an adjacent rock carving of Ardešīr II, the investiture scene is on the standard smoothened surface of the cliff face. The king, his feet resting on a dead enemy, the Roman emperor Julian, is accompanied by two figures, Mithra and another male, perhaps the god Ohrmazd, holding the royal ring. The execution of both reliefs at Taq-i Bostan is inferior to the carvings in Fārs. The figures are stiff and rigid in pose, and the natural contours of the body are obscured by the unrealistic, linear rendition of the drapery.

The earliest Sasanian silver-gilt vessels have, in contrast to the rock reliefs, few illustrations of Sasanian monarchs. Only one example, a two-handled cup of the third century from Zargveshi, in Georgia, has a representation of a royal figure. Enclosed within circular medallions are the busts of Bahrām II, his wife, and his son. A number of other plates and bowls of Iranian provenance are decorated with portrait busts of noble and princely personages within similar circular frames. Two third-century silver plates from the Transcaucasian region illustrate a different theme. On each, an Iranian noble or prince is depicted hunting. The first royal personage to appear on a silver plate in a hunting scene is Šābuhr II. From his reign until the end of the period, no persons other than the king appear on the silver plates, and the hunt becomes the standard royal theme. The vessels are invariably in the form of an open circular plate with a low ring foot. Generally, the weapon is a bow, and the quarry consists of live animals placed before the galloping horse and dead animals beneath the feet of the royal mount.

Greco-Roman influence is apparent in the composition and style of the rock reliefs and silver vessels and is evident too on the small seals and gems. The greatest number illustrate human busts (priests, officials, and members of the royal family), often carved with exquisite naturalism. The Middle Persian inscriptions give names and titles of officials or, alternatively, pious words and phrases. Plant and animal motifs also occur on the seals, which are largely bezels, originally mounted in rings or set in pendants.

Architectural decoration from this early period is limited to remains excavated at the palace of Šābuhr I at Bishapur in southwestern Iran. These include stone building blocks with relief scenes of horsemen and standing figures as well as large sections of mosaic pavements. The latter were probably designed and, to some extent, executed by prisoner craftsmen brought back by Šābuhr's victorious armies from the west.

FIFTH TO SEVENTH CENTURY

In the early fifth century the Sasanian kingdom suffered from a series of political, social, and economic disasters. Invasions of Huns (Hephthalites) on the eastern borders of Iran disrupted the military balance of power, and a social revolution (Mazdakite movement) within Iran as well as a period of severe drought leading to widespread famine resulted in internal chaos. Remains from this period of Sasanian rule are few and the dates of the monuments disputed. There are no dynastic rock reliefs, which may indicate that this type of proclamatory monument had, with the establishment of the Sasanian royal house, ceased to be meaningful. Only a few examples of the royal silver plates with hunting scenes can be placed with confidence in this period. Seals are numerous. The designs illustrate a departure from the classic naturalism of the earlier centuries and an increasing trend toward stylization in the representation of human and animal forms. Pierced and decorated ellipsoids are common shapes.

The only significant architectural remains attributed to the fifth and early sixth centuries are a series of noble or princely buildings at Kish, in central Iraq. Molded stucco plaques having a variety of figural, plant, and geometric designs embellished the walls of the buildings. The motifs are abstract and decorative rather than realistic or even naturalistic in style and design. Particularly interesting are a series of royal busts about half life-size. Somewhat smaller busts of females are impossible to identify with certainty. Both male and female figures are fully frontal, formal representations. The king wears a crown similar but not identical to that of Bahrām V Gor (*r.* 420–438).

The latter part of the sixth century and the beginning of the seventh century was a period of particular prosperity within the lands under Sasanian rule. Economic and social reforms and aggressive military tactics led to the enrichment and expansion of the kingdom. A single rock relief at Taq-i Bostan is dated to this time, although there is some disagreement about the identity of the king, Pērōz (*r.* 457–484) or Xusrō I (*r.* 531–579). The reliefs, carved on the back, side walls, and outer face of a deep arched niche, may have been executed at different times. The large complex is adjacent to the reliefs of Šābuhr II and III and Ardešīr II. On the back wall of the niche the sculptures are in high relief, arranged in two registers, one above the other. In the upper register are three figures facing outward, their feet resting on low plinths. The king is in the center. On his right is the goddess Anahita, holding, in one hand, a ewer from which water flows, and, in her other hand, a ring of investiture. Balancing her, on the other side of the king, is the bearded figure of the god Ohrmazd, grasping a ring of investiture toward which the king reaches with his right hand. Beneath these sculptures is an armored horseman sometimes identified as the king. Perhaps the most interesting scenes are those carved on the two side walls. Both are royal hunts; in one, the animals hunted are boars, in the other, deer. These reliefs provide a unique illustration of courtly life at the end of the Sasanian period. Considerable attention is given to the representation of dress, weapons, musical instruments, and other equipment of the hunt.

A number of silver-gilt vessels can be attributed to the last century of Sasanian rule. The royal hunt remains the official theme on the plates, but the increasing repetition of the crown types as they appear on the coins makes the identification of the kings and, consequently, the dating of the vessels difficult. An unusual gold, glass, and rock crystal plate at the Bibliothèque Nationale in Paris has a representation of the king enthroned, a motif that appears on the royal silver plate only at this late period. During the sixth and early seventh centuries there is a significant increase in the types of silver vessels produced. Vases, ewers, and lobed and oval bowls become common for the first time. On some examples there are illustrations of persons other than the king. The decoration also includes cult, mythological, and ceremonial subjects as well as a variety of plant, animal, and geometric motifs. A few gold vessels are part of a treasure found at Malaya Pereshchepina in the Ukraine.

A reflection of the increasingly bureaucratic state is the quantity of seals and stamped clay sealings that have survived. In general the quality of the carving is low, the designs sketchy and schematic. Common shapes are domes and cabochons.

The major architectural remains attributed to the sixth and seventh centuries are from Ctesiphon, the administrative capital of the empire, in central Iraq. Molded stucco is the predominant type of decoration, although fragments of paintings and mosaics were recorded by the excavators. The subjects of the stuccos are the same as those from Kish: plant and animal designs as well as figural scenes, including hunts and ceremonial banquets. Stucco also decorated the walls and columns of a villa, probably of late Sasanian date, at Tepe Hissar (Damghan) in northern Iran.

It is difficult to trace a clear development in the arts during the Sasanian period because of the scarcity of the monuments and the absence of securely dated material. There are indications of considerable Western influence both at the beginning and at the end of the period. Eastern forms and motifs became popular late in the period and are clearly reflected in the metalwork. The imprint of Sasanian art on neighboring countries is illustrated by the persistence of Sasanian royal imagery in the medieval art of the West and the presence of Sasanian themes in the art of Sogdian and Khwarizmian Central Asia.

BIBLIOGRAPHY

General. Kurt Erdmann, *Die Kunst Irans zur Zeit der Sasaniden* (1943, repr. 1969); Robert Göbl, *Sasanian Numismatics* (1971); Prudence O. Harper, *The Royal Hunter: Art of the Sasanian Empire* (1978); Vladimir G. Lukonin, *Persia,* II (1967). See also *The Cambridge History of Iran,* III, pts. 1 and 2, Ehran Yarshater, ed. (1983).

Rock reliefs. Shinji Fukai and Kiyoharu Horiuchi,

Taq-i-Bustan, I–II (1969–1972); Roman Ghirshman, *Bîchâpour,* I (1971); Ernst Herzfeld, "La sculpture rupestre de la Perse sassanide," in *Revue des arts asiatiques,* 5 (1928).

Silver. Kurt Erdmann, "Die sasanidischen Jagdschalen," in *Jahrbuch der Preuszischen Kunstsammlungen,* 57 (1936); Prudence O. Harper and P. Meyers, *Silver Vessels of the Sasanian Period,* I (1981); Iosif A. Orbeli and Kamilla V. Trever, *Sasanidsky metall* (1935), in Russian.

Architectural decoration. Jurgis Baltrušaitis, "Sāsānian Stucco: A., Ornamental," in *A Survey of Persian Art* . . . , Arthur U. Pope, ed. (1938), I, 601–630; Arthur U. Pope, "Sasanian Stucco: B., Figural," *ibid.,* 631–645.

Seals. Adrian D. H. Bivar, *Catalogue of the Western Asiatic Seals in the British Museum: Stamp Seals,* II, *The Sassanian Dynasty* (1969).

PRUDENCE OLIVER HARPER

[See also **Ardešir I; Bahrām V Gōr; Bishapur; Ctesiphon; Fārs; Fīrūzābād; Hephthalites; Mazdakites; Naqsh-i Rustam; Šābuhr I; Šābuhr II; Taq-i-Bostan; Xusrō I Anōšarwān; Zoroastrianism.**]

SASANIAN CULTURE

GEOGRAPHY AND CITIES

From A.D 226 to 651, the Persian Sasanian dynasty dominated the lands roughly corresponding to present-day Iran and Iraq. On the west, the river Euphrates was the traditional border between the empire of the caesar of Rome (so called even after the *Hromaioi* and their Rōmania were Byzantine Christians only; the Islamic term *Rūm* perpetuates this ancient view of the division of the world) and the realm of the "king of kings" (Pahlavi: *šāhan-šāh*). To the northeast, the Oxus separated the easternmost province of Iran (Xurasan, "East") from the ethnically Iranian principalities (Chorasmia, Sogd) and Iranian, Turkic, and other nomadic groupings (for example, the Sakas, Huns, and Hephthalites) to the north. Here, too, the sense of an absolute boundary persisted into Islamic times: the northern lands were called "what is beyond the river" (*ma wara' an-Nahr*). The borders of the Sasanian state broadly approximated those of the Arsacid predecessors of the dynasty, and, like the Arsacids, the Sasanians on several occasions laid claim to Anatolia and Syria, and even Palestine and Egypt, with the justification that the Achaemenians had ruled these lands. As under the Arsacids and Achaemenians, the largely non-Iranian but extremely fertile and economically vital region of Mesopotamia remained the administrative center of the Iranian state.

The Sasanians inherited also the problems of their predecessors. Cyrus had met his nemesis beyond the Oxus among the Massagetae; the Parthian Arsacids were severely weakened by the incursion of the Sakas into Drangiana, which later bore their name as Sakastan, modern Sīstān; and Iran late in the fifth century was to be held hostage to the Hephthalites. In the northwest, Armenia remained a crucial buffer state with leanings toward Rome, though it should be emphasized that, despite the conversion of the Armenians to Christianity beginning early in the fourth century, their Monophysite national church and local dynasts (*naχarars*) resisted political or cultural subjugation to Byzantium. Closest to the Sasanian heartland of Pars (Greek: Persis; modern Fārs) was the province of Khūzistān, many of whose inhabitants still spoke Elamite (Elymaean, or Khuzi); the province had a large Aramaic-speaking and later Arab population and became a center of Christianity.

The Iranian plateau is high and largely inhospitable: the seasons are severe, and the terrain is mountainous, with two great deserts, the Dasht-i Kavīr and the Dasht-i Lūt, covering a large portion of the center of the country. The heart of Iran was not then (and is not now) its most heavily populated region, though sites such as Shiraz and Isfahan have been continuously inhabited for millennia. The larger cities were on the periphery of the empire, or in areas of mixed population. There were a number of populous towns in Khūzistān, the site of ancient Susa; in the Sasanian period, several of these boasted Christian bishoprics. Although crowned at the temple of Adur i Anahid of Staxy (Stakhr), near ancient Persepolis in Fārs, the Sasanian kings ruled from their traveling encampments (as shown by mint marks on coins) or from several capital towns, the largest and most important of which was Ctesiphon, near ancient Babylon.

The name of the city goes back to the Arsacids and may mean something like "main fortress" (Middle Iranian: *diz bun*), though this conjecture presents philological problems. The majority of the population were speakers of Aramaic: Jews, Christians, and pagans who worshiped the gods of the Babylonian pantheon. (Priests of the latter kept alive the knowledge of cuneiform writing down to the mid-Sasanian period.) The city was a patchwork of ethnically and, in some cases, architecturally distinct districts as much divided as linked by the canals that coursed through it. The Iranian kings, who regarded urban life as alien and contemptible, maintained a walled hunting preserve adjacent to the royal palace. Not only was the capital vulnerable to Roman attack, but the populace were often hostile to their Iranian overlords because of religion or harsh taxation. Christians welcomed the invading Arabs in the seventh century with palm branches.

In the northwest, the old Median capital of Ectabana (Hamadan) was an important Sasanian town, but its central fortified area is still inhabited, so excavations have been meager. Ray, ancient Ragha, near modern Tehran, continued to be the main trading stage south of the Caspian Elburz range, as it had been for millennia. It is possible, indeed, that this is the same town called Zorastrian Ragha in the catalogue of Iranian lands in the first chapter of the *Vīdēvdāt* (Vendīdād), one of the sections of the Zoroastrian sacred text, the Avesta. But the name is a general one meaning "hillside" that could have been applied to a place farther east. It also should be noted, perhaps, that few merchants ever followed the famous "silk road" all the way to China. The great medieval voyages of Giovanni Carpini (from 1245 to 1247), Marco Polo (from 1271 to 1295), and others have, perhaps, contributed to this misconception. Most merchants traversed only sections of the long route, that is, from Hamadan to Ragha; goods were exchanged many times, and Sasanian imposts exacted, before they reached Europe.

In the northeast, the provincial capital of Khorāsān was Nev Šābuhr or Abarshahr (medieval Nishapur), a very small town compared to the city of Islamic times; in the southeast, Zarang (Drangiana) was the administrative center of Sīstān. Many other towns, some of which were for most of the period outside the empire, are listed in a ninth-century Pahlavi work, *Šahristaniha i Eran* (Provincial capitals of Iran). The empire controlled Sogdia, with its great and ancient capital, Samarkand, only sporadically. Buddhism flourished in the Iranian-speaking lands of Bactria, despite Sasanian campaigns to suppress it. Sasanian maritime trade with South Asia was extensive, but, although there were several harbors on the coast of Fārs, it was, again, a non-Iranian region, Maisan or Mēshān (Greek: Mesene) in southern Mesopotamia, whose ports linked sea and river trade.

There are a number of reasons for the very limited urbanization of Sasanian Iran. First, it was difficult even in the Mediterranean world, where the sea allows for relatively inexpensive shipment, to feed large cities. Rome is the dazzling exception that can blind us to the general reality. In the Byzantine period, large urban centers shrank or disappeared entirely, and the model of the ancient city was also abandoned; there is, rather, a convergence of urban types in Iran and Byzantium. Iranian cities were limited in size by natural scarcity of resources, and, one imagines, by strategic considerations: capital was better invested in the massive bridges that still serve towns of Fārs and Khūzistān, or in the network of the loyal Zoroastrian priesthood-*cum*-bureaucracy, and the army, than in cities that were peripheral or alien. The sort of large-scale agriculture needed to support a big city was impossible for most of Iran, where navigable rivers are very few, and where water resources are scarce and subterranean canal systems (*ganats*) are very expensive to maintain. Many cases in law recorded in the Sasanian *Madayan i Hazar Dadistan* (Book of a thousand judgments) deal with ownership of, and access to, water resources. There is also, of course, cultural bias: the Iranians had no Athens to which they might turn as to a model of the ideal human polity. The Iranian prophet, Zarathustra (Zoroaster), preached a pastoral vision, and in the Persian national epic, the *Shāhnāma* (*Šah-name*; Book of kings), the invention of writing, that most urban art, is attributed to demons.

Zoroastrian cosmography and cosmology shaped the Sasanians' understanding of the world and their place in it. According to the Avesta, the material world is divided into seven climes or *kesvaran,* each of which is inaccessible by mundane means to the other six. The central clime, which men inhabit, is Xvanira, derived from an Avestan term that probably means something like "wheel of the sun." At the center of this clime is Eran Vej, the Iranian expanse, birthplace of Zarathustra and ancient homeland of the Iranians. Though Pahlavi books describe the place in mystical terms, it was believed by the western Iranians to have been in the vicinity of Media/Azerbaijan, though it probably meant originally a region of southern Siberia. The Avestan cosmos is geocentric, and various mountains or mountain ranges in the central clime are accorded religious and cosmic significance: from the Cagad i Dadig, the Lawful Peak, springs the Bridge of the Separator to Heaven, which souls of the newly deceased must traverse; the waters of the goddess Anahita flow down from Mount Hukairya; the 360 windows of the sun encircle Mount Terag.

NATIONAL POLICIES

The Sasanians identified the peoples of their day with the names found in the Avesta: for example, the Tuiryas, an ancient Iranian tribe who were foes of the nascent faith of Zarathustra, were considered to have been the same people as the contemporary Turks of Central Asia, who were, accordingly, called Turan. Iran was identified with Xvaniras, and the major foreign nations were, according to al-Birūnī, equated with the other six *kesvaran*. Iran itself was divided into four quadrants called by the names of the points of the compass (except for the cold and dark north, regarded by Zoroastrians as the inauspicious region of the destructive spirit Ahriman; the northwestern quadrant was called the region of the Azerbaijan (*kust i Adarbadagan*). This administrative division was applied by Xusrō I Anošarwān to offices previously held by a single nobleman, but it existed under the Parthians, and the concept at least can be traced to pre-Achaemenian Mesopotamia. The Sasanians extended this fourfold division to embrace the entire earth: Iran, Rome, Turan, and China. Iran was, ultimately, destined to rule the other three, thereby bringing peace and order to the world of the wise lord, Ohrmazd (Avestan: Ahura Mazdā).

Zoroastrian cosmography perhaps influenced the attitudes and policies of the Iranians toward subject peoples and foreign states. From ancient times the Iranians had regarded themselves as "noble" (Old Iranian: *arya-*, whence the name Iran); others were base and dangerous: a mythical bird in the Avesta, Camrus, eats non-Iranians, *an-airya-*, like grains of corn. The whole world was thus divided in the Sasanian period into Eran and Aneran; as the king of kings (*šāhan-šāh*) claimed to rule over both, Aneran within the empire presumably embraced the non-Zoroastrian religious communities: Jews, Syriac and Greek Christians, Buddhists (in the northeast and east), and Semitic pagans.

RELIGIOUS POLICIES

Certain peoples have not been clearly defined, and were perhaps of ambiguous or changing status even in that period. There were rare persecutions of foreigners of alien faith, such as the Jews, whose religion the *Dēnkard* (Acts of the religion), a Zoroastrian *summa theologiae* compiled in the ninth century, traces back to the Ahrimanic dragon Azi Dahaka, and taxation of non-Zoroastrians was always harsher than for those of the "good religion." Zealots like the third-century high priest Kartīr persecuted alien faiths indiscriminately. But Iranian-Jewish relations were most often cordial. The *resh-galuta* (chief of the Diaspora), the leader of the community responsible directly to the court, was sometimes a personal friend of the king of kings. The Sasanians seem to have denied toleration to Iranians who adopted alien faiths, or to communities whose political allegiance to the crown was suspect.

The early Sasanians tolerated and even encouraged Mani and his followers, but after the execution of the "apostle of Light" by Bahrām II in 277, Manichaean communities seem to have been forced into flight beyond the Oxus, where their faith flourished among Persian exiles and local Sogdians and others down to the ninth century A.D. and later. In the fourth century, Šābuhr II responded to Christian proselytism among Iranians and to stirrings of extraterritorial loyalty toward newly Christianized Rome with severe repressions that have come to be known in Christian annals as the "great persecution." In the mid fifth century, Yazdgard (Yazdagird) II attempted to reimpose Zoroastrianism upon Christian Armenia, perhaps regarding the Armenians as apostates rather than as bona fide foreigners. But this is not provable, for prohibitions against observance of the Sabbath were enforced at the same time, and the Jews had never practiced Zoroastrianism before adopting their present faith.

The Zoroastrian church also tried hard to eradicate *dew-yasnih*—"worship of the demons," that is, non-Zoroastrian Iranian paganism—and there are references to the destruction of temples called *nisemag i dewan* (abodes of the demons). It is not certain what these were, though it has been suggested that they included temples of the late Achaemenian and Arsacid periods that contained statues of the Zoroastrian *yazata*s (supernatural beings worthy of worship), such as Anahita. But the Sasanians were not averse to depicting the *yazata*s on rock reliefs; it seems unduly harsh, therefore, for them to have referred to cult images as demons, even if they believed demons came to dwell in statues. It is as likely that the reference is to Buddha images: the word *but* has come to mean "idol" in New Persian. There is also evidence that the Sasanian Zoroastrian hierarchy strove to impose uniformity and subordination to central authority among the various

SASANIAN CULTURE

Zoroastrian communities of the empire: in the *Letter of Tansar,* a document attributed to the high priest under the first Sasanian king, Ardešīr I, a scared fire at the court of King Gusnasp of Ṭabaristān is seized and allowed to grow cold because it was not established according to proper—that is, Persian—rites. Ṭabaristān is in the Caspian region, where, under the rule of refractory and independent-minded local dynasts, worship of the *dews* also flourished. Tansar's policy appears to have served state interests in general, whatever his spiritual convictions may have been.

Although Zarathustra preached his vision to all the world, the Sasanians appear not to have proselytized among aliens, for all their zeal in preserving the "good religion" among those whom they considered Eran—Iranians. There is much ambiguity on this point, and the evidence is variously interpreted by proponents and critics of conversion in the tiny surviving community of Zoroastrians today, where by tradition one can be initiated into the faith with the ceremony of the tying of the sacred girdle (*kusti*) only if born of a Zoroastrian father. The Avesta records a number of instances of propagation of the faith in Turan, the direst enemy of Iran, and Pahlavi texts mention the conversion of non-Iranian household servants and others to the Zoroastrian faith. The same texts recommend that non-Iranians be barred from the study of the faith, in words that recall, perhaps, the rabbinic injunction to "set a fence around the Torah." It is possible that the intention was to guard against misinterpretation by those not grounded in the practice of the Mazdean religion. Mani and, later, Mazdak seem to have drawn much of their teaching from Zoroastrian dualist doctrine while corrupting or abandoning the rituals, purity laws, and life-affirming ethical practices without which the "good religion" is but a dry husk of speculative theory. It is noteworthy that Mani's teachings were intentionally supranational, incorporating such figures as Jesus Christ and the Buddha, while Mazdak appealed to the lower classes of the empire.

SOCIAL THEORY

It would seem, therefore, that the Sasanians limited the propagation of Zoroastrianism in order to preserve tranquillity within their borders, much as the later Islamic dynasties, notably the Ottoman Turks, allowed tolerated minority religions to exist within strict bounds while preventing apostasy from Islam by their Muslim subjects. Within the Zoroastrian community, the king of kings was regarded as the "first among men," favored by Ormazd with the *kayan χwarrah,* the divine glory once held by Zarathustra's own royal patron, Kavi Vishtāspa. Like their Indian cousins, the ancient Iranians divided society into three social orders: the warriors (Pahlavi: *artesdaran*), including the king; the priests (*asronan*); and the husbandmen (*vastaryosan*). A fourth class of artisans (*hutuxsan*) was added, probably when the Iranians first encountered the complexities of urban life. With their characteristic obsession for symmetry and order, the Sasanians correlated the three main fire temples of the empire with the three old social orders (*pesagan*); the Arsacid temple of Adur Burzen Mihr in subjugated Parthia was, just as predictably, assigned to the lowly class of the husbandmen.

Sasanian coins, most of which are silver drachmas—one day's wage—express the dynasty's vision of the world order. On the obverse is the *imago clipeata* of the king with his unique crown, surrounded by a ring of pearls probably representing *χwarrah.* On four sides of the ring are crescent moons and stars representing the cardinal points. (The astral symbolism is old; it seems to have entered Islam through the Sasanians.) The realm stands at the center of the world. On the reverse is a fire altar with the sacred flame, representing the religion and priesthood. The altar appears to be superimposed upon a royal throne (*taxt*), possibly to symbolize the unity of purpose of state and faith; two armed men often flank the altar, perhaps to represent the army of Iran and, thereby, the common people (in Old Persian, *kara-* means both "army" and "populace"). Contemporaries understood well the symbolism of the Sasanians and used it: Armenian and Georgian Christians represented the cross in a ring, beribboned or above a pair of wings, in imitation of Sasanian iconography, and one Georgian prince reproduced the entire reverse of the Sasanian coin type, but with the cross instead of the fire upon the altar.

Although Christians were permitted to serve the state in positions of importance and authority, as bankers, physicians, and ambassadors, and high clergymen were sometimes close to court, the Zoroastrian clergy served the government most directly. Priests served as magistrates and tax collectors. They ran state-sponsored trading firms. They administered charitable funds and bore the title *driyosan jadagow* (advocate of the poor), a title adopted by the Armenian Christian clergy in the

SASANIAN CULTURE

fourth century. These funds were established through pious endowments to support periodic feasts in honor of the departed, called *gahanbars*. (It has been suggested that the *gahanbar* is the origin of the later Islamic *waqf*.) Education, too, was in their hands: they administered the *frahangistan*, or secular academy, and the *erbadistan*, the priestly seminary. Noblemen of established landowning families served as high officials: in the fifth century Mihranarseh, the *wuzurg framadar* (great commander), that is, prime minister, built a bridge near Firūzābād out of his own funds, and left a dedicatory inscription. We know something of the villages he owned and of the careers of his sons.

Laws of inheritance were designed to ensure familial stability and the maintenance of wealth "until *frasegird*," that is, the end of days, when evil will have been wholly banished from the world. The practice of next-of-kin marriage (Avestan: *χvaetvadaθa-*), however repugnant it may have seemed to many, served at least to keep wealth within a family and to preserve blood lines unsullied. Property included slaves, termed *uzdehig* or *ansahrig*—"exiled" or "landless": many small farmers were forced by taxes or famine to become indentured servants on the great estates of the high nobility. By the sixth century the situation had become desperate enough for Mazdak to find a vast following; and Xusrō I, after suppressing the heresiarch and his movement, sought to augment the numbers of freedmen with small holdings of land, the *azadan*.

EVERYDAY LIFE

Little is known of the everyday life of the average inhabitant of the Sasanian Empire. If a farmer, he was expected to wear dark blue garments over the white sacred undershirt (*sabig*, now called *sudra*), over which he tied the *kusti*. He rose at dawn, resisting the temptations of the demon of sloth, Busasp (Avestan: Busyasta-), washed, recited his prayers in Avestan, and worked until noon, when the main meal of the day was taken. Zoroastrianism requires of its adherents scrupulous public and personal cleanliness; washing was done with bull's urine (*gomez*, which is a mild antiseptic containing ammonia), sand, and water. Though in sickness the peasant had no access to the surgeons and Greek doctors of the royal court, there were abundant herbal cures and *nirang*s, sacred formulas recited to drive off the demons of disease. In Mesopotamia, magic bowls were used by simple folk of various faiths to keep evil influences away from the home. The bowl contained an incantation, usually in Aramaic, which ran in a spiral from the rim to the center of the bowl. The curious and perhaps conceited demon who read the text was lured to the middle, and the bowl was clapped over him.

Life, though hard, was not all drudgery for the Sasanian farmer: the Mazdean faith, unlike its successor in Iran, is cheerful. Except during their monthly confinement, women enjoyed considerable liberty; festivals were frequent; and rich and poor alike enjoyed the special *gahanbar* foods. Iranians cherished music and the recitation of the heroic epics of the past. (In Armenia, Christian clerics shouted themselves hoarse in fruitless condemnation of such entertainments, which kept alive the glow of an older way of life.) At death, the body was exposed to be eaten by birds and wild animals. For three days, the soul hovered around its old home, considering its thoughts, words, and deeds; then the soul ascended to judgement on the rays of the rising Sun of the fourth day. The dry bones were sometimes collected in ceramic or stone ossuaries (Pahlavi: *astodan*). Stone ossuaries from Iran sometimes bear inscriptions; the ceramic variety from Central Asia have Dionysian and other scenes. (In Armenian texts, Dionysus is equated with Spandaramet (Avestan: Spenta Armaiti), the divinity who presides over the earth and underworld.)

Noblemen attended the *frahangistan* in their youth, learning the martial arts, writing, and the teachings of the "good religion." They were expected to excel at horsemanship, archery, and hunting, such activities being considered a man's chiefest delights—although in the Pahlavi text *Xusrō ud rēdag* (Xusrō and his boy), the page of gentle birth opines that the best of mounts is that of the bedchamber. Hunting scenes and alluring dancing girls are favorite subjects on the fine silver bowls and ewers produced by the court and given as favors to men of rank. Between warring, hunting, and managing his estates (there is a short Pahlavi text on how to write letters of greeting, condolence, and so on), the nobleman feasted. It was customary to recline on a *taxt*, one elbow supported by a pile of five or seven pillows, the other hand holding a bowl or rhyton of wine. (Sasanian Iran produced various vintages, known by the names of the provinces from which they came.) Ammianus Marcellinus (*ca.* 330–*ca.* 396) informs us that the Persians of his day were dry of complexion, slender, abstemious, cruel, superstitious, oversexed, and tough,

SASANIAN CULTURE

but their banquets were voluptuous: meat dishes were cooked with nuts and apricots, and sweet pastries were prized. After dinner, an elaborate set speech might be recited. A sample text from the ninth century, after the fall of the empire, is recorded. The health of the king is given, and then, in a somewhat incongrous but feeling interpolation, the wish is expressed that the sovereignty of Iran be soon restored.

SCIENCE AND TECHNOLOGY

Much expense and effort were devoted to the digging and maintenance of canals in Iraq and of underground watercourses (Pahlavi: *kahas*; New Persian: *qanāt*) on the Iranian plateau, and there are several legal decisions recorded on the division of water resources. Zoroastrianism enjoins upon man the furtherance (*abzōn*) and cultivation (*ābādīh*) of the world of Ohrmazd: an Avestan proverb in the *Vīdēvdāt* declares, "He who sows corn (*aša*) sows Righteousness (*Aša*)." The Good Religion also forbids pollution of the sacred creations, notably earth and water, so the practices of the devout anticipate to an extent modern ecology.

Wheeled transport does not seem to have been greatly developed; the terrain favored beasts of burden, and a hybrid camel with the virtues of both the Arabian and Bactrian breeds was used. Horsemanship was an art at which the Iranians had excelled from ancient times, in war as in hunting, and the Sasanian Avesta, according to the Pahlavi *Dēnkard,* included a treatise on horses comparable to the Byzantine *Hippiatrica.* In connection with cavalry tactics, it may be noted that the Sasanians also possessed something like the mysterious Greek fire; Ammianus Marcellinus calls it "Median oil." The Persians also dispatched merchant fleets to the southern seas (one recalls the exploits of Sindbad the sailor: compare Pahlavi: *Zīndaq bād,* "May he live long!").

The *Dēnkard* includes a section on the various kinds of medicine: mantric, herbalist, and chirurgical. Disease was regarded as an assault of the demons of Ahreman, and this seems to have contributed to a theory of infection that was coupled with the Greek doctrine of the internal balance of humors. Various sources mention both Persian and Greek doctors whose special skills were required by the Byzantine and Sasanian courts.

Sasanian silk weaving was justly famed and imitated. The characteristic beaded roundels enclosing men or beasts may still be seen on the altar cloths of Western Europe, and in Japanese brocade (influenced by T'ang, which had absorbed much of the culture of Iranian Central Asia). A fabulous, jewel-encrusted carpet, the "Spring of Xusrō," hung in the Khonastān, the audience hall of Xusrō II at Ctesiphon. Cut into small squares, it was used to pay the invading Arab armies. Some writers report that atmospheric effects could be reproduced in the throne room, to awe visitors, but it is not known how this was done.

The royal horoscope, *Zīq ī šahriyārān,* charted the fortune of each king, and it was thought that major religious, political, and religious changes occurred at conjunctions of Saturn and Jupiter, that is to say, about once every twenty years. Major cataclysms were expected every time this conjunction moved through all four astrological triplicities. Interest in astrology perhaps contributed to a fatalism expressed in the Zurvanite teaching, and in the attitudes of such early New Persian writers as Ferdowsī (Firdawsī, *ca.* 940/941–1020). When the black-clad Arab horde was within view of the white palace of Ctesiphon, the Iranian guards cried "The demons have come!" as though a prophecy had come true; then they fled.

Although tendentious historians of Islam have regarded the Arab conquest as the consequence of Iranian corruption, backwardness, and injustice (the ruinous and enervating wars between Iran and Byzantium in the early seventh century undoutedly contributed to the dissolution of the state), Sasanian culture not only survived in Iran but exerted a formative influence on Islamic culture. The Zoroastrian religion itself ceased to be influential only with the physical devastation of the Mongol conquest of Iran in the thirteenth century, although Islam had become the religion of the majority in the ninth and tenth centuries, precipitating the flight of many Zoroastrians to India, where they became the founding fathers of the modern Parsi community. Unlike many lands conquered by the Arabs, Iran never adopted the Arabic language, though many scholars, like al-Ṭabarī (839–923) or Ibn al-Muqaffa[c] (*ca.* 720–756/757), were masters of Koranic learning and Arabic style; in the Persian language itself, the Sasanian heritage still lives.

BIBLIOGRAPHY

For a general treatment of the various aspects of Sasanian culture, see the relevant articles in *The Cambridge History of Iran,* III, pts. 1 and 2, Ehsan Yarshater, ed. (1983). See also Mary Boyce, trans., *The Letter of*

Tansar (1968); Arthur Christensen, *L'Iran sous les Sassanides* (1936, 2nd ed. 1944); Henry Corbin, *Spiritual Body and Celestial Earth: From Mazdean Iran to Shi'ite Iran* (1977), 2–23; Nina G. Garsoïan, "Sur le titre de *Protecteur des pauvres*," in *Revue des études armeniennes*, n.s. **15** (1981); J. Hampel, *Medizin der Zoroastrier im vorislamischen Iran* (1982); G. Lazard, "*Pahlavi, Parsi, Dari*: Les langues d'Iran d'après Ibn al-Muqaffa[c]," in C. E. Bosworth, ed., *Iran and Islam: In Memory of the Late Vladimir Minorsky* (1971), 361–391; Michael G. Morony, *Iraq After the Muslim Conquest* (1984); J. Naveh, and S. Shaked, *Amulets and Magic Bowls: Aramaic Incantations of Late Antiquity* (1985); James R. Russell, *Zoroastrianism in Armenia* (forthcoming), chap. 10.

James R. Russell

[See also **Ardešīr I; Armenia, History of; Avesta; Christian Church in Persia; Ctesiphon; Dēnkard; Jews in the Middle East; Kartīr; Letter of Tansar; Manichaeans; Mazdaites; Mōbadān Mōbād; Nestorianism; Nishapur; Pahlavi Literature; Šābuhr I; Šābuhr II; Šāhan-šāh; Shāhnāma; Xusrō I Anōšarwān; Xwadāy Nāmag; Zarvanism; Zoroastrianism.**]

SASANIAN HISTORY, the period of a ruling dynasty in Iran, from about A.D. 224 to 651. The Sasanians followed the Parthian or Arsacid dynasty and ruled until the Arab conquest of Iran in the mid seventh century. In their historical records, the Sasanians portrayed themselves as the restorers of order and unity to Iran. They summarily dismissed the period 331 B.C.–A.D. 224, from Alexander's conquest until the beginning of their own rule, as a dark age, in which Iran had been divided into several petty, mutually hostile principalities. Similarities between the Sasanians and the Achaemenids (*ca.* 550–331 B.C.), who shared a common origin in the southwestern province of Fārs (Persis), have suggested to many a renewal of pre-Alexandrian Iranian traditions. Moreover, certain classical authors (Herodian, Dio Cassius, Ammianus Marcellinus) interpreted the Sasanians' reunification of the Iranian world as part of a conscious attempt to reestablish the Achaemenid empire. This renewal, however, had already been initiated by the Arsacids. The latter had traced their lineage back to the Achaemenids and revived the title *šāhan-šāh* (king of kings), and thus appear to some extent to have emulated the earlier dynasty. Consequently, despite the efforts of the Sasanians to discredit their predecessors, their own assumption of power in about 224 did not mark a sudden break with the immediate past. On the contrary, in style, customs, and conditions, Sasanian Iran undoubtedly bore a marked resemblance to the Iran of Arsacid times.

The origins and early history of the Sasanians are uncertain. No conclusive dates have yet been established. Since Theodor Nöldeke proposed his widely accepted chronology in 1879, at least two plausible alternatives have been advanced. Moreover, most descriptions of the rise of Ardešīr I, founder of the dynasty, include an abundance of legend. According to the majority of sources, Sāsān was the name of Ardešīr's grandfather. All accounts agree that Ardešīr was related (by birth or adoption) to Pāpak, the ruler of Fārs and nominal vassal of the reigning Arsacid, Ardawān V (*ca.* 213–*ca.* 224). Ardešīr himself became ruler of Fārs in about 216 and assumed control of Pāpak's capital at Iṣṭakhr (Stakhr). Around 224, Ardešīr was able to defeat and kill Ardawān. He then proceeded to subjugate almost all the Arsacid dominions and adopted the former Arsacid winter capital of Ctesiphon as the main capital of the new Sasanian Empire.

After his victory over Ardawān, Ardešīr assumed the title *šāhan-šāh*. He is described in inscriptions as "king of kings of Iran"; his son and successor, Šābuhr I (*ca.* 240–270), and all later Sasanian monarchs, are called "kings of kings of Iran and Non-Iran." A number of local rulers and noble families appear to have accepted Ardešīr's suzerainty. He himself installed members of his own family over other areas, a practice that was followed by his successors. Since each of these rulers was "king" of his own region, the title "king of kings" was an accurate description of the Sasanian monarch's position.

From about 230 on Ardešīr and his son, Šābuhr I, resumed the military struggle against the Roman Empire that they had inherited from the Arsacids. Among their successes were the capture of Hatra, and later of Antioch, whose bishop and other prisoners were resettled within the Sasanian domains. About the year 259, Šābuhr took the Roman emperor Valerian captive, a triumph celebrated in rock reliefs.

The conflict with the Romans and their Byzantine successors continued throughout Sasanian history. Despite almost constant strife, the borders of the two empires changed little over the centuries. This was largely because both empires faced recurrent threats on other fronts. It was also due in part

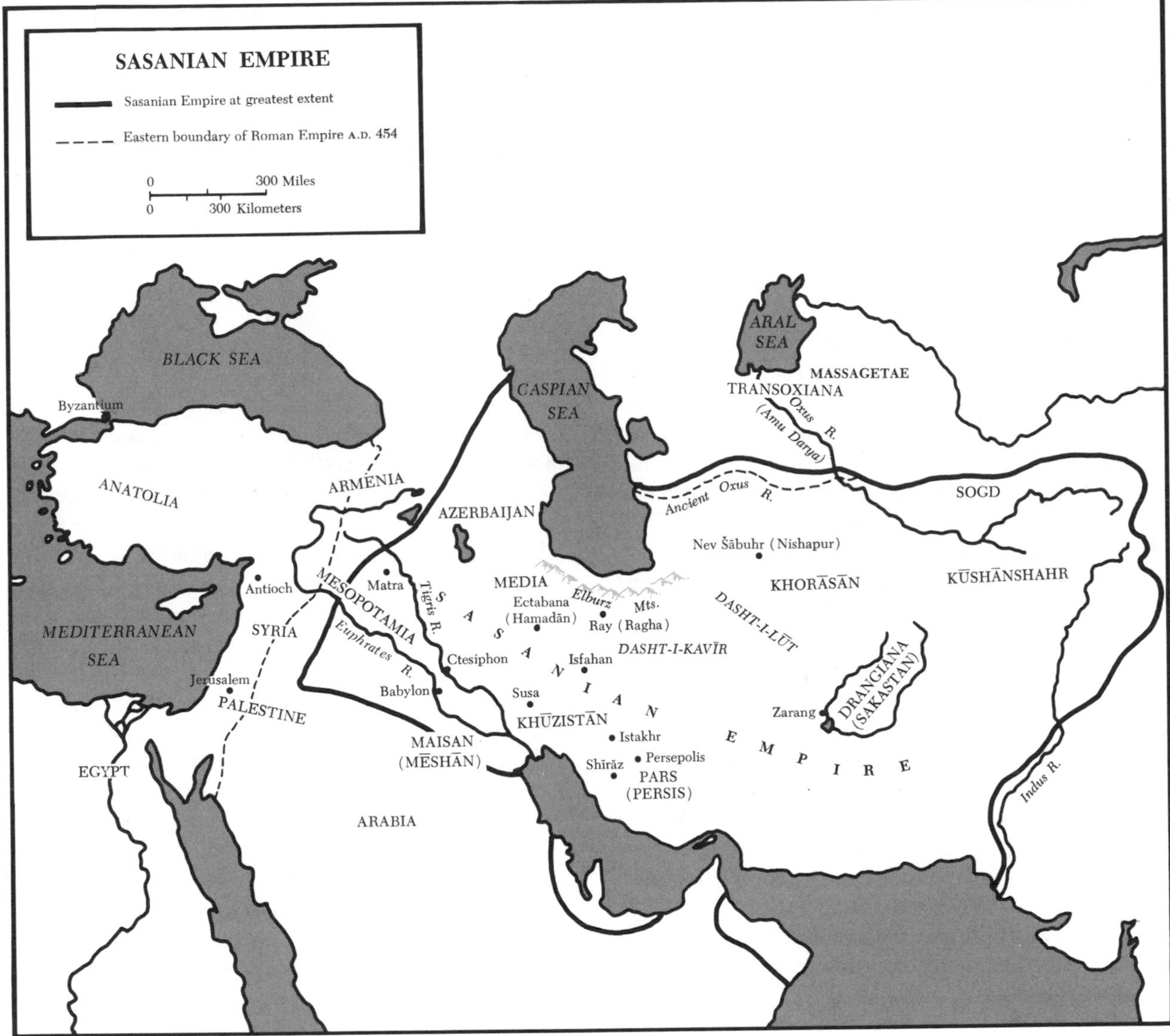

to the resilience of "buffer" principalities that arose on their borders and were usually affiliated with one or other of them. In time, both empires tended to absorb these principalities and to establish fortified cities on their frontiers instead. Two Christian Arab kingdoms resisted this trend longer than most. These were the Ghassanids of the Syrian Desert and the Lakhmids of Al-Ḥīra, vassals of the Byzantines and the Sasanians, respectively. Xusrō II, for reasons that are unclear, put an end to the power of the Lakhmids in 602; the ease with which the Arabs were able to overrun the Iranian plateau four decades later has been attributed in part to this action.

Throughout the Sasanian era, divine legitimacy for kingship was considered the prerogative of the Sasanian family. No other claimant, as will be illustrated by the case of Bahrām Čōbēn, could gain the lasting allegiance of the priests and nobles. Despite his divine right, the monarch could neither ascend nor maintain his throne without the support of these two groups. He was therefore bound to uphold their separate and privileged status, which was sanctioned by the Avesta. In order to win their approval, the monarch was required to demonstrate his capacity for kingship before his accession. Traditionally, therefore, the heir to the throne was appointed to administer a major region, such as Kūshānshahr or Armenia. He was also scrutinized for signs of divine grace and fortune (*χvarənah*;

New Persian: *farr*), which the rightful Sasanian monarch was believed to possess. The king's nature was thought to consist of fire, and the *farr,* which constituted the charisma of Iranian kingship, was often represented in iconography as a shaft of light or a nimbus of fire.

One respect in which the Sasanians differed markedly from their predecessors was in their establishment of a state church. The Zoroastrian religion, as it had come to be practiced in western Iran by the third century, was transformed under them into an officially sponsored institution, closely tied to the Sasanian ruling dynasty. This process was begun in Ardešīr's reign by a priest named Tansar or Tōsar, who was apparently responsible for the establishment of a single canon of Avestan texts. The priest Kartīr, whose activities dominated the reigns of Šābuhr I, his sons Hormizd I (270–271) and Bahrām I (271–274), and the latter's son Bahram II (*r.* 274–293) achieved much more. This energetic figure left an account of his career in a series of four rock inscriptions. His proselytizing missions both inside and outside Iran, and his persecutions of Jews, Buddhists, Hindus, Manichaeans, and two other (probably Christian) sects, indicate the growing authority of the Zoroastrian church to the exclusion of all other religious organizations. Moreover, Kartīr's close association with the Sasanian monarch anticipates the later office of *mōbadān mōbad,* the head of the Zoroastrian church.

Following the death of Bahrām II in 293, his son, Bahrām III, succeeded him as king. The son's rule lasted only a short while, however, for an uncle, Narses (Narseh)—who had previously ruled in Armenia—deposed him that same year. In 298, Narses concluded a forty-year truce with the emperor Diocletian and, in the Treaty of Nisibis, restored most disputed territories to the Romans.

Narses' son, Hormizd II (*r.* 302–309), was succeeded, after a brief struggle, by Šābuhr II (*r.* 309–379), an infant. Until Šābuhr II reached maturity, the priests and nobles took advantage of his youth to assert their own strength. Once Šābuhr himself had taken command, however, a high degree of centralization was achieved in the Sasanian Empire.

Control of Armenia had long been disputed between the Roman Empire and Iran. An Arsacid dynasty founded there in A.D. 66 paid allegiance sometimes to the Sasanians and sometimes to the Romans. At the end of the reign of Narses, the ruling Armenian Arsacid adopted Christianity; after the conversion of Constantine I, closer ties with the Roman Empire soon developed. Breaking the peace concluded by Narses, Šābuhr II marched into Armenia, which was partitioned as a result. The Sasanians, who gained the larger portion, retained the Arsacid dynasty there as vassals, until in 428 Bahrām V dethroned the reigning Arsacid and replaced him with an Iranian ruling lord (*marzpan*).

Šābuhr II sanctioned the persecution of confessional groups to which the established church declared itself hostile. The taxes exacted from Christians were doubled; this provoked a revolt, which was severely suppressed. Jews and Manichaeans also suffered. Šābuhr's condoning of such intolerance reflects the complete identification by this time of the Sasanian monarchy with the Zoroastrian church. It is likely that the church hierarchy was also approaching its fullest development. The title *mōbadān mōbad,* a parallel to *šāhan-šāh,* was probably already in use to designate the head of the church. This individual performed coronations, made religious appointments, and held the highest judicial authority in the realm. The *mōbadān mōbad* presided over the lesser *mōbad*s, one of whom was appointed over each district. These *mōbad*s performed judicial functions and apparently also registered commercial transactions. Beneath each *mōbad* were the ordinary priests (*moghān*). A specialized group of priests, known as *hērbadān,* appear to have been in charge of the fire temples. Their precise functions, however, are unclear. Eventually, the title *hērbadān hērbad,* perhaps purely honarary, evolved as a counterpart to the *mōbadān mōbad.*

Among the second privileged social category, the nobility (*āzādān,* literally "the free-born"), four ranks may be distinguished: the *šahrdārān,* local dynasts, often Sasanian princes; the *vāspuhragān,* relatives of the ruler; the *buzurgān,* heads of the leading families; and the *āzādān* (used here in a specialized sense), the lesser "village-owning" nobility. The leading families were required to send a representative to the court, where some obtained hereditary positions. Other families acquired hereditary tracts of land. All members of the aristocracy were obliged to contribute to the treasury, to furnish troops, and to fight in times of need.

Šābuhr II's long reign was followed by the short one of Ardešīr II (379–383). Within four years, Ardešīr was deposed by the nobility. Šābuhr II's son, Šābuhr III, came to the throne in 383, but died or was murdered in 388. His successor, Bahrām IV, was also murdered. There is little information to elucidate the causes of this series of depositions and murders. They probably indicate the existence of factions among the priesthood and nobility.

In 399 Bahrām's son, Yazdgard (Yazdagird) I, came to the throne. Yazdgard's reign (399–420) was chiefly noted in the Sasanian historical tradition for his apparent leniency toward the Christian communities. Despite periods of persecution and the consequent production of a considerable literature in Syriac known as the Acts of the Martyrs, Christianity continued to thrive in Sasanian Iran. Its Nestorian form was particularly widespread. Some Sasanian monarchs, moreover, appear actively to have favored the Christians. Since the Zoroastrian priesthood had virtual control over the written word, such monarchs were represented in literature as wicked or ineffectual; Yazdgard I received the sobriquet "the Sinner." By contrast, those rulers who acted in accordance with the priests' wishes earned themselves flattering accounts.

Yazdgard's son Šābuhr IV was murdered soon after his accession. The nobles, despising Yazdgard's other son, Bahrām, then raised to the throne a Sasanian from a collateral branch of the family, Xusrō. Bahrām, however, asserted his claim by marching to Ctesiphon with a group of his Lakhmid supporters. In 420, he became Bahrām V, the Bahrām-i Gōr (Bahrām the Wild Ass) of the Iranian epic tradition, in which he appeared in many legends. According to the *Shāhnāma,* for example, he was required before his accession to prove his fitness for kingship by ordeal. The crown was placed on the throne, to which two raging lions were chained. Bahrām battled with the lions and succeeded in taking possession of the royal insignia. This was interpreted as a sign that he was truly endowed with the *farr.*

By the fifth century, the Sasanian bureaucracy was fully developed. Mihrnerseh, the leading administrator under Yazdgard I, Bahrām V, and Yazdgard II, held the office of *vuzurg-framadār,* or chief civil official. This title may sometimes have been synonymous with *hazārbad* (chiliarch) and *dar-andarzbad* (court councillor). The bureaucracy was probably drawn largely from the lower ranks of the priesthood (*moghān*) and nobility (*āzādān*). It included not merely secretaries (*dabīrān*), but also astrologers, physicians, poets, musicians, and other court officials.

An ancient feature of Indo-Iranian culture, which in the Iranian world had eventually found written expression in the Avesta, was its division of society into three categories: the priests, the warriors, and the agriculturalists. By the fifth century, the development of a complex administration had demanded the addition of a fourth: that of the secretaries. This category was situated below the priests and nobles, but above the agriculturalists, whose category was itself expanded to include also craftsmen and merchants. The practical implications of this concept of social stratification for "Avestan" society are not known; in the later Sasanian period, however, each category had its own administration with its own head. A man was born into the category to which his father had belonged; movement from one category to another was considered a violence against the social order. Many Muslim thinkers continued to feel the relevance of this perception of society as four strata; its best known formulation in the Islamic period is that of Nāṣir al-Dīn al-Ṭūsī (1201–1274).

In 438, Bahrām's son Yazdgard II came to the throne. His reign saw the rise of a serious challenge from the east. The identities of the various peoples who threatened the eastern Sasanian borders at different times are not certain. The group faced by Yazdgard were probably the Hephthalites, who, according to Chinese sources, originated in Central Asia, and moved into Bactria in the fifth century. Yazdard II was obliged to move his capital eastward to Nishapur, a city founded by Šābuhr II, in order to combat this threat.

When Yazdgard died in 457, the succession was contested by two of his sons, Hormizd and Pērōz. Hormizd acceded but was deposed by Pērōz, who had the support of the Hephthalites. During his reign, however, Pērōz's relations with the Hephthalites deteriorated, and in 469, he was defeated and captured by his former allies. He was released on condition that he render an onerous tribute; until this was paid, his son Kawād was retained as a hostage. Hostilities with the Hephthalites continued, and in 484, Pērōz was killed in battle. Pērōz's brother Balāš was elected by the nobles as his successor. Peace was established with the Hephthalites, again in exchange for a heavy tribute. In 488, however, the nobles deposed Balāš and, probably with Hephthalite support, raised Kawād to the throne.

Kawād I's heretical tendencies led to his deposition by the aristocracy in 496 and the elevation of his brother Zāmāsp to the throne. Kawād managed to escape, however, and took refuge with his earlier benefactors, the Hephthalites. They again furnished him with an army, and about 498 he was reinstated.

In 531, Kawād was succeeded by his son, Xusrō I (*r.* 531–579). In Islamic sources, Xusrō is depicted as the epitome of a wise and just ruler. He is known as Anōšarwān-i ᶜĀdil (the Immortal-Souled, the Just). Islamic *belles lettres* contain numerous anecdotes praising his equity and sagacity, and record his purported conversations with his equally celebrated, probably legendary, minister Buzurgmihr.

During Xusrō's reign, an undercurrent of social discontent manifested itself in a movement led by Mazdak, probably a Zoroastrian priest with Manichaean leanings. According to the (tendentious) Islamic sources, Mazdak's vision included the common ownership of property and the sharing of women. Both notions would have been deeply disturbing to the priests and nobles. At an unknown date, Xusrō had Mazdak executed and was apparently able to suppress his supporters.

The disturbance caused by Mazdak and his followers had demonstrated the need for reform. Xusrō completed a cadastral survey begun by his father and instituted a revised system of taxation. A fixed sum was to be exacted from each area, based on the average of several years' harvests. This replaced the previous procedure of annual assessment. The priests, nobles, secretaries, and other government officials were exempt from personal taxes; for the rest, the amount due was regulated according to their means. As a result of Xusrō's reforms, the treasury could calculate in advance the income it would receive. A modified version of this system remained in operation in Islamic times.

Anxious to restore full authority to the monarchy, Xusrō decreased the powers of his two leading servants, the *vuzurg-framadār* and the commander-in-chief of the army. The functions of the former were divided between several high officials, while the latter was replaced altogether by four military commanders (*spāhbadān*), each appointed over a quarter of the realm. Moreover, Xusrō introduced salaries for the less wealthy nobles, who had previously been required to serve in the army without recompense. This was a major innovation. It not only decreased the powers of the large landowning aristocracy, who were able to maintain private armies, it also created a firm bond between the lesser nobility and the monarchy.

In 540, Xusrō was ready to resume the war against the Byzantines. His successes led to the conclusion of a fifty-year peace in 561, according to which the Byzantines were to pay tribute to the Sasanians. With the help of the Turks, who had appeared in Transoxiana, the Hephthalites were finally defeated about 557, and their territories divided between the allies. South Arabia, too, became a Sasanian dependency.

Xusrō was famous for his patronage of scholars. In his reign, Iran enjoyed increased contact with the intellectual and cultural traditions of the Greek and Indian worlds. When the Byzantine emperor Justinian I closed the philosophical academy at Athens in 529, some of the last Neoplatonists sought refuge at Xusrō's court. Translations were made into Pahlavi not only from Greek, but also from Sanskrit. The latter included a collection of animal fables, the *Panchatantra,* which was later translated from Pahlavi into Arabic by Ibn al-Muqaffaᶜ (*d.* 756/757), under the title *Kalīla wa-Dimna.*

Hormizd IV, who succeeded his father, Xusrō, in 579, was immediately faced with threats on all fronts. The most urgent of these was again to the northeast, where the Turks, now with the Hephthalites as their subjects, had invaded. Hormizd sent his general Bahrām Čōbēn, a member of the Arsacid family, against the enemy. Bahrām defeated the Turks about 588–589. After further successes, Hormizd became apprehensive of his general's power and sought to remove him. Bahrām responded by launching a major rebellion and attempting to usurp the Sasanian throne for himself. Hormizd was captured, blinded, and eventually executed. In 590 his son, Xusrō, fled to the Byzantine court. Both Xusrō and Bahrām Čōbēn approached the Byzantine emperor Maurice (*r.* 582–602) for aid. Maurice decided in favor of Xusrō and equipped him with an army. Xusrō marched against Bahrām, who fled to the Turks and was assassinated the following year.

Xusrō II's reign (591–628) saw a series of ambitious military campaigns against the Byzantines. Profiting from the internal disorders in Byzantium that followed the assassination of Maurice in 602, Sasanian forces penetrated deeper into Byzantine territory than ever before, taking Jerusalem in 614 and Egypt in 619. These successes, however, were ephemeral. In 622, the emperor Heraklios inflicted a decisive defeat on the Sasanians. Abandoning his gains, Xusrō retreated to Ctesiphon in 627. A year later he too was assassinated. His son, Kawād II, made peace with Heraklios but died within a year.

A series of very short reigns ensued until 632,

when Xusrō II's grandson, Yazdgard III, came to the throne. Since the removal of the Lakhmids in 602, the Sasanians had found themselves less able to resist raids by the Arabs. Yazdgard's minister and commander, Rustam, tried to rally the Sasanian forces against the growing Arab threat but suffered defeat and death at the battle of Al-Qādisīya in 636. Ctesiphon fell to the Arabs in 637, and Yazdgard fled. The Arabs' victory at Nihāvand in 642 gave them access to the whole of the Iranian plateau, marking the beginning of the Islamic era for Iran. Unable to find any support, Yazdgard died at the hands of an assassin in 651.

Islamic civilization was greatly enriched, and indeed partially formed, by the Sasanian heritage. The importance of Sasanian Iran in the development of later Islamic institutions, and the absorption of pre-Islamic Iranian elements into Islamic sectarianisms, have long been recognized. The Sasanian monarchs themselves captured the imagination of Islamic writers and rulers. Some later dynasties in Iran, such as the Samanids, proudly traced their lineage back to them. Others, such as the Buyids, adopted their titles and other trappings of kingship. The Iranians were believed to possess an inherent genius for kingship, which had found its most perfect embodiment in the Sasanians.

BIBLIOGRAPHY

The major general works in Western languages are Arthur Christensen, *L'Iran sous les Sassanides,* 2nd rev. ed. (1944); and *The Cambridge History of Iran,* Ehsan Yarshater, ed., III (1983). More specialized works include Franz Altheim and Ruth Stiehl, *Ein asiatischer Staat: Feudalismus unter den Sasaniden und ihren Nachbarn* (1954); Nina V. Pigulevskaia, *Les villes de l'état iranien aux époques parthe et sassanide* (1963); Martin Sprengling, *Third-century Iran: Sapor and Kartir* (1953); Geo Widengren, *Der Feudalismus im alten Iran* (1969).

Translations of relevant source materials include Firdawsī, *Le livre des rois,* Jules Mohl, ed. and trans., 7 vols. (1876–1878); Mario Grignaschi, trans., "Quelques spécimens de la littérature sassanide conservés dans les bibliothèques d'Istanbul," in *Journal asiatique,* **254** (1966); *La montée des Sassanides et l'heure de Palmyre,* Jean Gagé, trans. (1964); Al-Ṭabarī, *Geschichte der Perser und Araber zur Zeit der Sasaniden,* Theodor Nöldeke, trans. (1879, repr. 1973); al-Tha^cālibī, *Histoire des rois des Perses,* Hermann Zotenberg, ed. and trans. (1900, repr. 1963); *The Letter of Tansar,* Mary Boyce, trans. (1968).

LOUISE MARLOW

[See also **Afghanistan; Albania; Ardešīr I; Armenia: History of; Azerbaijan; Bahrām V Gōr; Bahrām VI Čōbēn; Bishapur; Byzantine Empire: History; Christian Church in Persia; Chosroids (Mihranids); Ctesiphon; Fārs; Georgia, Political History; Ghassanids; Gundešapur; Hephthalites; Iran; Iraq; Islam, Conquests of; Jews in the Middle East; Kartīr; Lakhmids; Manichaeans; Marzpan; Mazdaites; Mōbadān Mōbad; Naqsh-i-Rustam; Nestorianism; Nishapur; Pahlavi Literature; Parthians; Šābuhr I; Šābuhr II; Šāhan-šāh; Samanids; Shāhnāma; Spāhbad; Syrian Christianity; Xusrō I Anōšarwān; Xusrō II Abarwēz; Xwadāy Nāmag; Zoroastrianism; Zurvanism.**]

SASSETTA (Stefano di Giovanni) (*ca.* 1390/1400–1450). One of the great artistic geniuses of his age, the Sienese painter Sassetta produced work that was wholly original and personal while remaining true to the Sienese tradition. A member of the Sienese painting guild by 1428, Sassetta had a number of important commissions, which survive today in fragmentary condition. His first documented commission (completed 1426) was the altar for the wool merchants' guild (Arte della Lana), of which five predella panels survive. His earliest surviving work is the so-called *Madonna of the Snows* (1430–1432), now in the Contini Bonacossi Collection, Florence. The now-dismembered polyptych for the high altar of S. Francesco, Borgo San Sepolcro (commissioned 1437, completed 1444), is his greatest surviving work. The front, depicting *St. Francis in Ecstasy,* now in the Berenson Collection, Settignano, Villa I Tatti (Florence), is a marvel of detailed naturalism fused to an eccentric vision that places meaning and spiritualism above mundane reality. St. Francis is transformed into an archetypal vision, well within the traditions of the fourteenth century but in no way repetitious of it. Seven of the eight scenes depicting the life of St. Francis that once formed the back are today in the National Gallery, London; and one is in the Musée Condé, Chantilly. They are marvels of a delicate miniature style, fusing realism and abstraction in a particularly genial fashion. Sassetta's sense of delicacy and poetry absorbed the lessons of Duccio and made those earlier Sienese traditions viable for several new generations of fifteenth-century Sienese painters.

BIBLIOGRAPHY

Bernard Berenson, *A Sienese Painter of the Franciscan Legend* (1909); Enzo Carli, *Sassetta e il maestro dell'osservanza* (1957); Bruce Cole, *Sienese Painting in the Age*

St. Francis in Ecstasy. Panel painting by Sassetta from the high altar of S. Francesco, Borgo, now in the Berenson Collection, Villa I Tatti, Florence, 1444. SCALA / ART RESOURCE

of the Renaissance (1985); John Pope-Hennessy, *Sassetta* (1939).

ADELHEID M. GEALT

[See also **Gothic, International Style; Panel Painting.**]

SASUNCᶜI DAWITᶜ. See **David of Sasun.**

SAVA, ST. (1175–1235). Born Rastko, the youngest son of the Serbian (Raškan) ruler Stefan Nemanja (*r. ca.* 1168–1196), he ran away to Mt. Athos in 1192, becoming a monk under the name Sava. In 1196 Nemanja abdicated and soon thereafter joined him; together they renovated Hilandar (Khilendar), making it the Serbian monastery on Athos, with a Rule written by Sava. Throughout the Middle Ages it remained a major Serbian cultural center. In 1208 Sava returned to Serbia, bearing his father's body. Having made peace between his warring brothers Stefan and Vukan, he became abbot of Studenica (where Nemanja, whose biography he wrote, was buried). He remained abbot until 1217, when, protesting Stefan's close relations with Rome, he returned to Athos.

In 1219 Sava visited Nicaea. After he recognized the Nicene bishop as the ecumenical patriarch, Nicaea recognized Serbia as an autocephalous church with its own archbishop. Sava became Serbia's first archbishop (1219–1233). He established roughly ten suffragan bishoprics, uniting under his jurisdiction the Serbian lands of Hum and Zeta, which contributed to centralizing the Serbian state. He directed the translation from Greek of Serbia's first canon-law code, promulgated at a council held at his seat of Žiča (1221).

While returning from a pilgrimage to Palestine, after resigning as archbishop in 1233, Sava died in Bulgaria in 1235. Buried at Mileševo in 1237, he was soon canonized as a saint. His cult became important among Serbs and was associated with various subsequent Serbian movements. His relics were widely believed to work miracles until the Turks destroyed them in 1595.

BIBLIOGRAPHY

John V. A. Fine, Jr., *The Late Medieval Balkans* (1987).

JOHN V. A. FINE, JR.

[See also **Athos, Mount; Byzantine Church; Serbia; Stefan Nemanja; Stefan Prvovenčani.**]

SAVIGNY, an abbey and monastic congregation. The inception of Savigny was a manifestation of the revitalization of the monastic life and of the new religious orders of the twelfth century. Savigny was founded by the hermit-preacher Vital of Tierceville on lands given him in 1105–1106 by Ralph of Fourgères, a vassal of the count of Mortain. The site was in the forest of Savigny in the southwestern corner of Normandy on the Breton frontier. About 1112 the first conventual buildings were erected. Under the second abbot, Geoffrey (1122–1139), landed endowments began to flow to Savigny, and between 1127 and 1191 sixteen foundations were made in France and thirteen in England (all of the latter before 1154). A total of fifty monasteries of monks and nuns of France, England, and Ireland eventually derived from Savigny, the most famous of which were Aulnay near Bayeux, Vaux-de-Cernay near Paris, and Furness in Lancashire, England. The moral prestige of St. Bernard of Clairvaux prompted the fourth abbot, Serlo (1140–1158), to seek the union of the Congregation of Savigny with the Cistercian order, and with the support of Pope Eugenius III (*r.* 1145–1153) the union was achieved at the General Chapter of 1147. Although some Savigniac practices, such as the acceptance of tithes and parish churches, violated Cistercian ideals, the congregation was allowed to retain them after this union, with the ultimate result that good discipline in the Cistercian order itself weakened.

Most Savigniac abbeys were located in frontier or march areas or in politically disputed territory, where the monks served as a stabilizing influence. They also played an important role in the agricultural development of their regions, felling trees, draining swamps, and bringing the land under cultivation. Close relations between patrons and monasteries often continued for many decades, to their mutual spiritual and economic advantage. Charter evidence reveals that many gifts to the monks were actually disguised loans to benefactors, and Savigny served as a banking house for the local nobility.

The enormous flow of gifts and the profits from agriculture and banking made possible the construction of a new abbey church. Begun in 1173 and consecrated in 1220, the church contained a nave measuring 247 feet (75 meters) and a transept measuring 150 feet (46 meters), thus making it cathedral-like in proportions and the largest church building in western France. This church, elaborately decorated in the High Gothic style in the later Middle Ages, was severely damaged by Calvinist attacks in September 1562 and almost totally destroyed during the French Revolution, when monastic life ended.

Savigny produced men of outstanding piety, such as Abbots Vital and Geoffrey and the monks Haimo and Peter of Avranches, who were recognized as saints in the twelfth century; renowned writers and preachers, such as Abbot Serlo; and able administrators, such as the distinguished English lawyer and judge Stephen of Lexington, who ruled as abbot from 1229 to 1243, when he was elected abbot of Clairvaux.

BIBLIOGRAPHY

Archives Nationales Sér. L, 967–978, contains 1,084 charters and other documents relating to the abbey of Savigny in the period 1117–1491. About 121 of these documents are discussed by Marguerite-Paule Guilbaud, "Catalogue des Chartes Mancelles de l'abbaye de Savigny conservées aux Archives Nationales," in *Annales de Bretagne,* **69** (1962). The other basic sources are Claude Auvry, *Histoire de la Congregation de Savigny,* 3 vols. (1896–1898), a lengthy seventeenth-century pious and didactic history. Earlier sources include Étienne Baluze, "Chronicon Savigniacense," in *Stephani Baluzii tutelensis miscellanea nova ordine digesta . . . ,* I (1761), 326–329; *Gallia Christiana,* XI, 540–554; *Acta Sanctorum,* Januarius 1–15 (1863), 389–390.

The most useful modern treatments of Savigny are Jacqueline Buhot, "L'abbaye normande de Savigny, chef d'ordre et fille de Cîteaux," in *Le moyen âge,* **46** (1936); Bennett D. Hill, "The Beginnings of the First French Foundations of the Norman Abbey of Savigny," in *The American Benedictine Review,* **31** (1980), "The Counts of Mortain and the Origins of the Norman Abbey of Savigny," in William C. Jordan *et al.,* eds., *Order and Innovation in the Middle Ages: Essays in Honor of Joseph R. Strayer* (1976), and *English Cistercian Monasteries and Their Patrons in the Twelfth Century* (1968); Francis R. Swietek and Terrence M. Deneen, "The Episcopal Exemption of Savigny, 1112–1184," in *Church History,* **52** (1983), and Swietek and Deneen, "Pope Lucius II and Savigny," in *Analecta Cisterciensia,* **39** (1983). For the relations of one important feudatory with Savigny, see Gerald W. Day, "Juhel III of Mayenne and the Lay Attitude Toward Savigny in the Age of Philip Augustus," in *Analecta Cisterciensia,* **36** (1980).

Two studies treat aspects of the literary works of Abbot Serlo: André Wilmart, "Le recueil des discourse de Serlo, abbé de Savigny," in *Revue mabillon,* **12** (1922); and Michel Pigeon, "Marie dans l'oeuvre de Serlon de Savigny," in *Cîteaux: Commentarii cisterciensis,* **26** (1975). For the thirteenth-century English abbot of Stanley who became abbot of Savigny, see Dom Bruno Greisser, "Briefformular aus dem Kloster Savigny," in *Cistercienser-chronik,* **63** (1956), and the same scholar's "Stephen Lexington, Abt von Savigny," in *Cistercienser-chronik,* **67** (1960).

There is important material on the architecture of Savigny in Marcel Aubert, *L'architecture cistercienne en France,* I (1943), 216–217; and J. Durand de Saint Front, "Brève histoire de l'abbaye de Savigny," in *Memoires de Société archéologique et historique de l'arrondissement de Fourgères,* 3 (1959).

BENNETT D. HILL

[See also **Benedictine Rule; Cistercian Order.**]

SAVOY, COUNTY OF. Ammianus Marcellinus was the first writer to employ the word "Sapaudia," referring thereby to that region of Transalpine Gaul bounded on the north and west by Lake Geneva and the Rhône, on the south by the Dauphiné, and on the east by the Graian and Pennine Alps. In Charlemagne's division of his empire at Thionville in 806, however, the term "Saboia" is used to indicate only the part of Sapaudia roughly corresponding to the "Savoy proper" of today: the Lake Le Bourget basin south to Montmélian and the Isère Valley from Montmélian to the confluence with the Arc. This, along with the valleys of the upper Isère (Tarentaise) and of the Arc (Maurienne), formed the medieval county of Savoy.

Sapaudia had been settled since the seventh century B.C. by a Celtic people known as the Allobroges, and it may have been via Savoy and the Savine-Coche Pass (near the modern Mont Cenis) that Hannibal made his famous Alpine crossing in 218 B.C. The Romans conquered the whole region in the second century B.C.; and with the conquest of the rest of Gaul, Savoy became an important thoroughfare for legions arriving from Italy, either from Susa via the Maurienne or from Aosta via the Tarentaise. Christianity reached Vienne and Lyons in the second century, then spread among the inhabitants of the Alps. The massacre of the christianized Theban legion in the Valais, perhaps in 302, furnished the earliest martyrs, in whose honor many churches were built (notably St. Maurice d'Agaune, in 515). Vienne became the metropolitan for sees founded in the fourth century at Geneva, Belley, and Grenoble, which included Savoy proper. In 420 the future archbishopric of Tarentaise was established at Moûtiers; in 575 Maurienne was separated from the see of Turin with a bishop at St. Jean.

In 443 the Roman general Aëtius allowed the Burgundians to settle in Sapaudia as foederati charged with defending the passes to Italy. In the sixth century the Burgundians were conquered by Merovingian Franks and later became part of the Carolingian empire. Charlemagne's presence in Savoy is recalled in the *Song of Roland,* whose dying hero affirms that it was in "the vales of Moriane" (Maurienne) that Charles gave him the famous sword Durendal. With the breakup of the Carolingian empire in the ninth century, Savoy became part of the kingdom of Transjurane Burgundy, stretching from the Saône to the Valais, which lasted until the death of Rudolf III (993–1032).

During this period the region was ravaged by Saracens based in Provence and by Magyars penetrating from Helvetia. The kings proved unequal to the tasks of defense, which became the burden of local warlords (who often profited by enlarging their private holdings and building up military followings). Rudolf III sought to counter the growing power of the lay magnates and to help episcopal sees to rebuild after the invasions by granting to some bishops the counties in which their seats were located. The county of Savoy, however, remained in the hands of a certain Count Humbert (later surnamed "White Hands"), along with the Valle d'Aosta and much else in the territory between Italy, Lake Geneva, and Vienne.

Humbert (*d.* 1048) was a major figure at the court of Rudolf III; and in 1032 he supported the accession of Emperor Conrad II to the throne of Burgundy, which thus returned to the Holy Roman Empire. Humbert also held the counties of Chablais and Maurienne, which, together with the march of Susa, acquired in the next generation, provided the future House of Savoy with control over both approaches to the three major passes in the western Alps (Great St. Bernard, Little St. Bernard, Mont Cenis) and laid the foundations for economic and political prosperity in the future.

Until the thirteenth century the rulers of Savoy were often called counts of Maurienne, and their seat was at Montmélian on the frontier between the Dauphiné and Savoy. Chambéry was acquired in 1232 and its castle in 1295. The establishment of permanent organs of government there (Chambre des Comptes, *ca.* 1300; resident council in 1329) made Chambéry the capital of the medieval Savoyard state. Savoy was always a part of the kingdom of Burgundy while the latter existed. After the twelfth century this "kingdom" came to be known as the "kingdom of Arles and Vienne," but this, too, was only a theoretical entity. Whatever authority inhered in it was subsumed in the titles of the Holy Roman Empire, which is why so few emperors even bothered to come to Arles to be crowned.

In the thirteenth century comital dominions were organized into *bailliages,* of which Savoy (including Tarentaise and Maurienne) was one, with the bailli's seat at Montmélian. By the mid fourteenth century this *bailliage* contained seventeen castellanies and two judicatures within which itinerant justices circulated annually. The chief regional officer was the castellan, whose seat was the comital fortress in a given district. Many nobles enjoyed full judicial authority over their tenants, as did the bishops of Tarentaise and Maurienne originally, but the counts succeeded in reducing such rights very considerably by 1400.

General statutes (in 1379 and 1430) and central administrative offices (chancellor, 1330; treasurer general by 1358) aimed at integrating Alpine territories not originally part of Savoy into a centrally organized whole. But general assemblies were usually regional in membership except for the count's entourage. The first assembly with non-nobles clearly present was held in Piedmont in 1285. By 1374 at least two such "parliaments" had been held there with deputies from both sides of the Alps, but the earliest parliament in Savoy was in 1388. Major steps in the growth of medieval Savoy were taken with the addition of the Pays de Vaud in 1263, Bresse in 1285, Faucigny in 1355, Nice in 1388, Genevois in 1401, and Piedmont (long ruled by a cadet line) in 1418. Amadeus VIII (1391–1451) was the first duke of Savoy (1416), and his reign marks the apogee of the medieval Savoyard state. Savoy had always been an imperial fief in theory, the counts (then dukes) enjoying the legal rank of princes of the Holy Roman Empire. The principality achieved semi-legal independence in the Treaty of Cateau-Cambresis in 1559, following the end of the Habsburg-Valois wars; and in the Treaty of Utrecht (1713), the sovereign princes of Savoy were raised to royal rank, first as kings of Sicily, then from 1720 as kings of Sardinia.

The Savoyard intra-alpine zone contains many low-altitude valleys with mild climates penetrating to the interior of the mountain chains, giving relatively easy access even to pastures above the tree line ("alps"), where butter, cheese, and livestock were produced. Abundant resources in upland regions, together with patterns of semi-independent communal ownership, sometimes made for greater prosperity there than in lower valleys, despite the profits of trade and travel benefiting the latter. Savoy had much land suitable for cereal crops and vineyards, forest products, and some mining (iron, silver). The growth of a bourgeoisie in Savoy was fostered by franchises given even to small towns. Between 1195 and 1343 over 200 charters were granted to some 67 localities in Savoyard dominions (excluding the Piedmont), of which a dozen were in the county of Savoy; but only Chambéry may have had as many as 2,000 people by 1331.

Monastic culture in Sapaudia was disseminated by Benedictines from St. Maurice d'Agaune and from San Michele and Novalesa in the Val di Susa, but few early foundations survived the invasions. Revival came in the eleventh and twelfth centuries with new houses and the reform of older ones: Cistercians reformed Aulps and Hautecombe and founded Tamié and Le Beton; Augustinians reformed Abondance, St. Maurice, and the Great St. Bernard hospice and founded Sixt; La Grande Chartreuse implanted Carthusians at Vallon, Reposoir, Pomiers, St. Hugon, and Aillon. After 1250 the mendicant orders also appeared. As a center of lay culture medieval Savoy has no special distinction, but Pierre II's castle-building (1250–1268) figures in the history of military architecture, and Amadeus VI's castle at Ripaille became proverbial for luxury and *bonne chère*. Georges de Aquila, a pupil of Giotto, worked in Savoy under Amadeus V and VI, as did Jean Sapientis and Jacomo Jacquerio under Amadeus VIII, whose patronage led to the formation of an "école savoyarde" in manuscript illumination. Amadeus VIII also commissioned the first official chronicles of the House of Savoy (Orville, 1417–1419). And Martin le Franc, author of *Le champion des dames,* lived at the court of Savoy after 1440, as did the composer Guillaume Dufay for seven years between 1433 and 1455.

BIBLIOGRAPHY

René Avezou, *Histoire de la Savoie* (1949); Robert H. Bautier and Janine Sornay, *Les sources de l'histoire économique et sociale du moyen âge,* I (1968); Félix Bernard, *Les origines féodales en Savoie et en Dauphiné* (1969); L. Blondel, "L'architecture militaire au temps de Pierre II de Savoie," in *Genava,* **13** (1935); Mario Chiaudana, *La finanza sabauda nel secolo XIII,* 3 vols. (1933–1938); Francesco Cognasso, *I Savoia* (1971); Eugene L. Cox, *The Green Count of Savoy* (1967), and *The Eagles of Savoy* (1974); Marie-José, *La maison de Savoie,* 3 vols. (1956–1962); Jean Y. Mariotte *et al., Atlas historique de la Savoie, du Genevois, et de la Bresse* (1970); Ruth Mariotte-Löber, *Les chartes de franchises des comtes de Savoie* (1973); Henri Ménabréa, *Histoire de la Savoie* (1958); Henri Onde, *L'occupation humaine dans les grands massifs savoyards internes* (1942); Charles W. Previté-Orton, *The Early History of the House of Savoy, 1000–1233* (1912).

EUGENE L. COX

[See also **Bailli; Burgundy, County of; Castellan; Dauphiné.**]

SAXO GRAMMATICUS (*fl.* 1185–1208), author of the *Gesta Danorum.* He does not give his name, but he presents himself as "the humblest" of Archbishop Absalon's men and talks about his father and paternal grandfather's service at arms as though the reader could be assumed to have heard of his family. In his brief history of Denmark written shortly after 1185 (*Brevis historia regum Dacie*), Sven Aggesen states that he will not write at length about Sven Estridsen's sons because his comrade (*contubernalis*) Saxo is at work putting down their story in a more elevated style and in greater detail. This reference, coupled with one in Absalon's testament, in which he leaves some money to his *clericus* Saxo and charges him with the delivery of two books to the monastery of Sorø, allows us to place Saxo's career in the second half of the twelfth century and the first decades of the thirteenth. He may have been a canon at Lund, but this is not documented. He was certainly a member of Abalson's retinue or *hirð*.

Absalon commissioned the *Gesta Danorum,* but the work must have been completed after his death, for it is dedicated to his successor, Anders Sunesen, who was archbishop of Lund from 1202 to 1222. The preface refers to Waldemar II the Victorious' crossing of the Elbe and capture of Hamburg and Lübeck, which may have taken place in 1208, before Waldemar became king. A terminus ante quem is provided by the conquest of Estonia in 1219, which the work does not relate.

The full text of Saxo's work is known to us only from an edition printed in Paris in 1514 by Jodocus Badius Ascensius, which had been prepared by the Danish scholar and reformer Christiern Pedersen. There are also four manuscript fragments, the most important of which was discovered in Angers in 1863. The Angers fragment consists of four pages in quarto and can be dated back to the first quarter of the thirteenth century. It contains numerous stylistic variants in the form of interlinear or marginal glosses and is thought by many scholars to be part of Saxo's own working copy of the *Gesta Danorum* at an early stage. The Paris edition and the other manuscript fragments represent a later redaction. There are compendia of Saxo's work and long quotations from its text in various chronicles and histories written in the later Middle Ages and early Renaissance.

The scope of the *Gesta Danorum* is the widest possible; the first nine books are dedicated to the legendary prehistory of Denmark, beginning with the reigns of dynastic and toponymic personifications such as Dan and Skjold. Books I–IV give a survey of the kings who ruled Denmark before the birth of Christ; Book V describes the reign of Frotho the Peaceful, contemporary of the Savior and the *Pax Augustana.* The legendary section goes on to cover the heroes of the Migration Period (Ingeld and Starkad) and of the Viking Age (Ragnar Lodbrog). Historiography proper begins at the end of Book IX with a muddled account of the struggle for the throne in ninth-century Denmark; though the narrative is unreliable as to the facts, the characters are historical and belong to the period in question. The last seven books constitute an often confused selective account of Danish history from the reign of Harald Bluetooth to that of Cnut VI Waldemarsen. Saxo's narrative of the Waldemar period (Waldemar I to Cnut VI: Books XIV–XVI) is that of an eyewitness.

Gesta Danorum is a late but splendid specimen of a medieval historiographic genre, the *historia ab origine gentis,* by means of which scholars from Cassiodorus and Jordanes through Bede, Paul the Deacon, and Widukind of Corvey had attempted to give historical legitimacy to the new barbarian kingdoms of their times by providing them with an antiquity comparable to the Roman. Though a latecomer to the genre, Saxo was fully aware of its requirements and acquainted with its earlier masterpieces: he refers to Bede, Paul the Deacon, and Dudo of St. Quentin, historians of the Anglo-Saxons, Langobards, and Normans, respectively.

In his prologue, Saxo acknowledges three main kinds of sources: (1) narrative poems in the vernacular, which cannot mean exclusively Old Danish poetry now lost, but must include West Norse Eddic and skaldic compositions; (2) the treasures of antiquarian information gathered by the Icelanders, whose industry he praises highly, though he does not say in what form this information was accessible to him; (3) the testimony of Absalon, which was abundant and constantly available to him.

It is very difficult to approach Saxo's sources in general, since they bring up very different kinds of problems. The sources of the legendary books can only be understood by applying the methods of analysis of traditional narrative and folktales to the history of fictional genres in Viking-Age Scandinavia. The sources of Saxo's properly historical books, however, should be treated primarily as sources of information. Most often Saxo elaborates on the language of his source and rearranges the order of events so extensively that it is difficult to recognize specific sources for individual parts of the

SAXO GRAMMATICUS

Gesta Danorum. Adam of Bremen's *History of the Bishops of the Church of Hamburg* and Sven Aggesen's Danish history are constantly used, but there are hardly any verbal similarities or echoes left in Saxo's text; we know that he used them because of the facts, interpretations, and errors he shares with them.

Saxo's prose is remarkable for the correctness of its grammar and for its consistently classical diction (for instance, *pontifex* for *episcopus, sacras preces decurrere* for *horas legere*). Stylistically it derives from the Latin of the third and fourth centuries A.D. and has as its models the works of Valerius Maximus and Justinus, but Saxo takes the florid, bombastic tendencies of this style to extremes otherwise unknown in medieval Latin. Variation and the intensive use of syntactic parallelism are characteristic of his prose, though they are applied more sparingly in the last seven books. Here and there a few medieval features can be found in his writing: consecutive use of *quod,* occasional use of the medieval locative, a small number of nonclassical idioms (for instance, *pontem iacere* for *pontem facere*). Verbal echoes of his Latin models can be found in every page of the *Gesta Danorum.*

The prose narrative is interspersed with passages in verse, rendering monologues, dialogues, and other forms of direct speech. Most if not all of these are translations from vernacular poetry. The debate in verse between Hadding and his wife (I, viii, 18–19) is a Latin version of the well-known argument between Njǫrðr and Skaði in the *Snorra Edda* (*Gylfaginning,* chap. 23). Saxo's contribution to medieval Latin poetry is often ignored by students of this field, though Peter Dronke emphasizes the high quality of some of his verse compositions. Saxo could versify in a great variety of classical meters: elegiacs, adonics, glyconics, sapphics, iambic trimeter, and many more, all strictly quantitative forms, with no concessions to the medieval taste for rhythmic poetry. His master in metrical studies was Martianus Capella, whose encyclopedic allegory, *The Marriage of Mercury and Philology* (*ca.* 400), Saxo read and assimilated.

The classical standards implicit in Saxo's work do not prove that he was directly or exclusively inspired by the culture of late antiquity, because these standards were a pervasive feature of the twelfth-century renaissance. Saxo was well acquainted with one of the leading figures of the movement, the poet Walter of Châtillon, whose *Alexandreis* he quotes. But then Saxo himself was a brilliant representative of the period: he saw the history of his country through Roman lenses and projected Roman historical and social categories onto early Danish institutions, calling the king's men *comites* or *familiares;* noblemen *magnates, optimates,* and *nobiles;* the peasants *plebei;* and clerks *scribae.* A more personal feature of his vision is the surprising lack of religious fervor: he not only fails to emphasize sacred history, missions, and church history but argues that issues of belief must often yield to strategic and political considerations. He usually takes the side of the monarchy in clashes between state and church. His account of the pagan gods of Scandinavia is crudely euhemeristic.

In the legendary books, the sequence of stories about the various kings and their reigns combines two catalogs of early kings of Denmark, known in the terminology created by Axel Olrik as the older and younger dynasties or lists of the Skjoldungs. The older list is centered on the figure of Hrolf Kraki, who personifies the heroic values of the earlier legends; the younger list, built around the Ingeld-Starkad episode, treats its kings as statesmen rather than heroes. These books include many small episodes only loosely related to the central actions. Brief and insubstantial accounts of certain kings suggest that the author was trying to do justice to unfamiliar names in the lists. Among these less important narratives, a few great legends dominate the sequence:

- I. The story of King Gram and Princess Gro (a courtship and marriage story); the life of King Hadding, a Viking brought up by giants and later taught by Odin.
- II. The life and feats of King Frode, a Viking son of Hadding; the idyll between Regner, prince of Sweden, and Hadding's daughter Svanvit; the story of Hrolf Kraki and his champion Bǫðvar Bjarki.
- III. Hother and Balder's rivalry over Nanna; the story of Hamlet up to the murder of Feng (Hamlet's revenge).
- IV. Hamlet's subsequent adventures; the story of Wermund and Offa and of the latter's duel at the Eider.
- V. Reign of Frode the Peaceful; the story of his minister, Eric the Eloquent.
- VI. Ingeld and Starkad.
- VII. Life and deeds of Haldan, a great-grandson of Ingeld; bridal guests of four young heroes: Øder and Sigrid, Alf and Alvilda, Hagbard and Signe, Haldan and Gurid; the youth of Harald Hildetand and his apprenticeship with Odin.
- VIII. Harald Hildetand at Bravalla; the death of Starkad; the story of Ermanaric (the Ostrogoth as

SAXO GRAMMATICUS

Danish king); King Gorm and the expeditions of Thorkel Adelfar to Utgardha Loke.

IX. The story of the Viking king Ragnar Lodbrog and his sons.

There are two basic sources for the stories of these books: Danish tradition and Icelandic novels (the early legendary sagas of the twelfth century). In his important early study of Saxo's materials, Axel Olrik introduced a third possible source: legends and stories of Norwegian origin communicated to Saxo by native informants. The evidence for Norwegian narratives in the *Gesta Danorum* is weak and insufficient, however, so that the role of this third source remains a polemical issue in modern scholarship.

A new factor emphasized by Paul Herrmann is Saxo's individual contribution as narrator and often as interpreter of the legends. A complex story such as that of Hamlet's revenge may be analyzed into a number of motifs or episodes which, in turn, may be traced back to different literary or folkloristic backgrounds. The combination of these elements into one story owes much to the model of the Icelandic *fornaldarsaga,* but certain classical touches and the relative complexity of the narrative sequence, which is not as loosely episodic as in vernacular legendary fiction, point to Saxo's own hand in the composition.

A new and much-debated approach to the interpretation of Saxo's legends has been formulated by Georges Dumézil. Working from the perspective of the comparative history of religions, he comes to the conclusion that the first nine books of the *Gesta Danorum* contain several secularized and epicized myths; the story of Hadding, for example, would be a late version of the life of the god Njǫrðr, a myth transformed into a Viking novel. Dumézil's views conflict with the sense of generations of Saxo scholars that the author of the *Gesta Danorum* did not understand his vernacular sources well, and often treated them with an excessively free hand.

The historical books are organized as follows:

X. Gorm the Old; Harald Bluetooth; Sweyn (Svend) I Forkbeard; Knud (Cnut) I the Great; Hardeknud, Sweyn Estridsen, and Magnus the Good.

XI. Sweyn II Estridsen; Harald III Hen; Knud the Holy.

XII. Olaf I the Hungry; Erik I the Kind-hearted.

XIII. Niels; the murder of Knud Lavard, earl of Slesvig, and its repercussions.

XIV. Erik II the Memorable; Erik III the Lamb; the civil wars between Sweyn III Eriksen (Grathe), Knud III Magnusen, and Waldemar Knudsen; the reign of Waldemar I the Great.

XV. Waldemar I the Great: last years and death.

XVI. Knud VI Waldemarsen.

There is a lack of proportion in the treatment of the various reigns: Book XIV is longer than all the other historical books put together and covers the civil wars and Waldemar the Great's expeditions against the Wends of Pomerania in great detail. Danish relations with Henry the Lion, duke of Saxony, and with Emperor Frederick I are also dwelt on. The chief source of information here was undoubtedly Absalon, whose career as military leader and guardian of the Danish coasts is given greater prominence than his dignity as bishop of Roskilde and later archbishop of Lund. Absalon's behavior in battle is described more often and with higher praise than that of the king himself. On the few occasions in which clashes between Waldemar and Absalon take place, Saxo is squarely on the side of the bishop.

As a historian, Saxo is extremely unreliable: he changes the chronology of his sources, quotes legend as fact, and confuses homonymous characters with each other. In Book XIV there is a gross chronological distortion on account of which events of 1175–1177 (the expedition to and siege of Stettin; Absalon's fight against the Wends at Grønsund) are placed as if they had occurred in 1171. On most subjects, his sources (Adam of Bremen, Sven Aggesen, the Danish chronicles) can be consulted directly with greater profit. Nevertheless, he remains an irreplaceable source of information on the expeditions of Rugen, Pomerania, and Norway, on Waldemar the Great's foreign policy, and on the Danish institutions of the Waldemar period.

Sven Aggesen's reference to Saxo writing about the sons of Sven Estridsen, together with the simpler style of the historical books, have justified the long-held belief that Books X–XVI were written first, though not necessarily in their present order, and that the more ornate legendary books were added later. Though this is still the view of many scholars, the opinion is also heard of late that the varying complexity of style does not depend on the earlier or later date of composition of a given book, but on its particular subject; the figures of the legendary part may have required a more grandiose presentation. A recent study of the *Gesta Danorum* by Kurt Johannesson, however, stresses the unity of the work, which is read as a Platonic allegory, carefully organized into four groups of four books, illustrating the natural virtues of courage, temperance, justice, and prudence, and as a symbolic account of the rhetorical, strategic, and legal arts and their development.

BIBLIOGRAPHY
Standard edition is *Saxonis Gesta Danorum,* Carl Knabe and Paul Herrmann, eds., rev. by Jørgen Olrik and Hans Ræder, I (1931), text, with Prolegomena by Olrik, II (1957), glossary by Franz Blatt. English translations are *The History of the Danes,* 2 vols., Peter Fisher, trans., Hilda Ellis Davidson, ed. (1979–1980); and *Danorum regum heroumque historia, Books X–XVI,* 3 vols., Eric Christiansen, ed. and trans. (1980–1981).

Studies. Peter Dronke, *Medieval Latin and the Rise of European Love-Lyric,* I, *Problems and Interpretations* (1965), 243–247; Georges Dumézil, *Du mythe au roman: La saga de Hadingus et autres essais* (1970), trans. into English by Derek Coltman as *From Myth to Fiction: The Saga of Hadingus* (1973); Karsten Friis-Jensen, ed., *Saxo Grammaticus: A Medieval Author Between Norse and Latin Culture* (1981); Paul Herrmann, *Erläuterungen zu den ersten neun Büchern der dänischen Geschichte des Saxo Grammaticus,* II, *Die Heldensagen des Saxo Grammaticus* (1922); Kurt Johannesson, *Saxo Grammaticus: Komposition och världsbild i "Gesta Danorum"* (1978); Alf Önnerfors, "Philologische Marginalien zu Saxos Hamlet-Sage," in Dietrich Schmidtke and Helga Schüppert, eds., *Festschrift für Ingeborg Schröbler zum 65. Geburtstag, Beiträge zur Geschichte der deutschen Sprache und Literatur,* (1973); Axel Olrik, *Danmarks Heltedigtning,* 2 vols. (1903–1910), trans. into English by Lee M. Hollander as *The Heroic Legends of Denmark* (1919); *Saxostudier: Saxo-kollokvierne ved Københavns universitet,* Ivan Boserup, ed. (1975); Inge Skovgaard-Petersen, "Saxo, Historian of the Patria," in *Medieval Scandinavia,* 2 (1969); Joseph Svennung, "Eriks und Götvars Wortstreit bei Saxo," in *Arkiv för nordisk filologi,* 56 (1941).

JOAQUÍN MARTÍNEZ-PIZARRO

[See also **Adam of Bremen; Baldr; Cnut the Great; Denmark; Fornaldarsögur; Historiography, Western European; Knud Lavard; Latin Literature; Odin; Roskilde Chronicle; Scandinavia; Scandinavian Mythology.**]

SAXO, POETA. See **Poeta Saxo.**

SAXON ARCHITECTURE is the architecture of England from the seventh century down to the generation after the Norman Conquest. The architectural history of Saxon churches rests on fragmentary remains, thin written records, and archaeological evidence whose interpretation is comparatively recent. Aspects of its development, even its unity as a style, are matters for debate. A serious problem concerns the question of dates. Because firm dates are so often lacking, a relative chronology has been made by assigning dates, or subperiods such as *A* (600–800), *B* (800–950), *C* (950–1100), to specific constructional features, often without a critical eye to their value as chronological criteria, or without casting an eye to continental relationships. Conditions which produced specific churches are often just as obscure.

It is likely that the programs of Saxon churches reflect the political and ecclesiastical geography of the period. Saxon England was marked by separate kingdoms, by a system of lay patronage in the church, and by different spheres of ecclesiastical observance and regulation. Hence, the layout of churches responded to special circumstances, and not to uniform custom. The closely associated monasteries at Wearmouth (Monkwearmouth) and Jarrow, for example, were not laid out according to any consistent plan. Diversity of architectural style had its counterpart in a remarkable group of men who reorganized the Saxon church from the mid seventh century onward: Archbishop Theodore of Tarsus, a scholar from Asia Minor schooled in the Greek church; Abbot Hadrian of Canterbury, a learned monk of North African origin; Benedict Biscop, a Saxon nobleman with extensive continental travels; Wilfrid, the contentious bishop of York and student of the religious customs of Italy and Gaul. Their church buildings were dependent on a wider network of influences than the native insular tradition could supply.

Evidence for identification and interpretation of Saxon churches survives in churches and parts of churches from the seventh to eleventh centuries. There are a number of constructional features generally accepted as evidence of Saxon workmanship. These include distinctive patterns of quoining such as "long-and-short" quoining or "side-alternate" quoining, stripwork paneling on church towers, openings for windows and doorways cut straight through the wall and lined with large slabs called through stones, double belfry openings, and triangular headed windows. By far the greatest number of surviving churches are simple two-cell buildings with squared chancels. The main vessel is usually much longer and taller in proportion to its

St. John's, Escomb, from the southwest, showing side-alternate quoining, *ca.* 650–800. REPRODUCED FROM H. M. TAYLOR AND JOAN TAYLOR, *ANGLO-SAXON ARCHITECTURE* © 1965 Cambridge University Press

width. The covering is wood, and the pavement in some cases is cement with pounded bricks. The cellular program was expanded in churches where the central vessel opens through doorways or arches on either side to chambers or groups of chambers known as porticuses. There is a substantial body of literary and structural evidence to show that from early times parts of churches and their adjuncts, especially west towers, were often of more than one story. Reemployed Roman stone, brick, and title are common, an indication that Saxon builders used existing Roman structures as quarries.

Timber was the building material of the pagan Saxons and of places where the influence of Irish Christianity was strongly felt. Bede contrasts the *more Scotorum* at Iona and at Lindisfarne with stone building elsewhere. More attention has been paid to problems of the seventh and eighth centuries than to earlier or later periods. Scholarship, reflecting the bias of Bede, has divided church building of the seventh century between south and north: the southern or Kentish type of building being due to the Roman mission of St. Augustine and the slightly later northern or Northumbrian type to the missions introduced by Benedict Biscop and Wilfrid.

The plans of early Saxon churches in Kent are in large measure recoverable. The Kentish group forms a constellation around Augustine's abbey at Canterbury, founded in 597. The plans of three churches, Sts. Peter and Paul, St. Mary, and St. Pancras, all aligned on a common east-west axis, and all of the same period, survive. The main vessel of Sts. Peter and Paul was rectangular, with an apse at the east separated from the nave by a chancel arcade of three arches. On the north and south sides of the nave were porticuses. These rooms, according to Bede, were used for services and for the burial of eminent persons connected with the foundation. This plan and program are repeated at Rochester, Lyminge, Reculver, and at Bradwell-on-Sea (Essex), which dates after 653. The walls at Bradwell survive to their full height.

The northern churches date from the last quarter of the seventh century, when the Roman mission had established its authority over the Irish-converted areas of Northumberland. There are important remains at Wearmouth and Jarrow, Ripon and Hexham, and Escomb. Biscop's churches at Wearmouth and Jarrow, now much altered, were the artistic and intellectual lights of the age. The stone construction and stained-glass work at Wearmouth were carried out by masons and glazers brought from Gaul. The crypts at Ripon (Yorkshire) and Hexham (Northumberland) are the remains of the churches built by Wilfrid (*d.* 709). His biographer states that at Ripon, and in the later minster at Hexham, were built stone churches with crypts, apsidal ends, and small stone altars which had illuminated Gospelbooks laid upon them. Escomb, a parish church by the middle Wear, is perhaps the most complete Saxon church now standing. The main vessel measures 13.20 meters (43.5 feet) long × 4.40 meters (14.5 feet) wide × 7 meters (23 feet) high. Escomb originally had a north porticus entered from the chancel. Now, there is an increasing number of scattered churches for which an early date and porticus have been claimed. Archaeological evidence of Winchester, Glastonbury, and Deerhurst (Gloucestershire) suggests that the south-north schools are not so sharply defined as formerly thought.

There is a small group of pre-Conquest churches known to have had aisles. Hexham had a main vessel carried by columns, and galleries over the aisles. At Jarrow, Canterbury Cathedral, and Cirencester (Gloucestershire), the aisles were not continuous passages but were broken up by transverse walls, thus forming a series of separate rooms attached to the sides of the main vessel. Brixworth (Northamptonshire) is one of the most complete large-scale churches of this type still standing. It has a proposed date of mid eighth century. No build-

SAXON ARCHITECTURE

ings can be attributed with certainty to the period between 800–950 or the time of the Danish wars. A ninth-century date for the hall crypt at Repton (Derbyshire) has been suggested, but almost without exception the churches of this period have perished.

The monastic revival of the late tenth century led to the rebuilding of many churches, but of these, the greater Saxon churches, we have almost no trace due to later medieval rebuilding. Indeed, the terms "Greater Saxon" and "Later Saxon" connote only an architectural style. The corpus of major buildings in this period must for the moment begin with the Old Minster at Winchester—the most completely known plan of this group. Others include St. Dunstan's Abbey of Glastonbury, Sherborne (Dorset), North Elmham (East Anglia), Stow (Lincolnshire), Great Paxton (Hunts), and St. Augustine's at Canterbury. The monastery and cathedral at Canterbury are known respectively from Wulfric's rotunda and from a description by Edmer the Precentor. Lesser churches of the time between the Danish attacks and the Norman Conquest are most common in Yorkshire and in the districts adjacent to quarries which extend from Gloucestershire through Northamptonshire into Lincolnshire. They are represented by a large number of fragments incorporated into later work and by a smaller, but still considerable, number of churches with cellular plans and towers, such as Earls Barton, Barton on Humber, Barnack, Sompting (Sussex), and Bradford on Avon (Wiltshire). The final period of its history, the "overlap" period, consists of those buildings after the Norman Conquest but still in the Saxon style. The study of this material has consisted largely in the identification of distinctive constructional and decorational features not used by the Normans.

Western tower of All Saints Church, Earls Barton, Northamptonshire, *ca.* 935. PHOTO: A. F. KERSTING, LONDON

BIBLIOGRAPHY

Bede's Ecclesiastical History of the English People, Bertram Colgrave and Roger A. B. Mynors, eds. (1969); Martin Biddle, "Excavations at Winchester, 1969: Eighth Interim Report," in *The Antiquaries Journal,* **50** (1970); G. Baldwin Brown, *The Arts in Early England,* II (1925); Bridget Cherry, "Ecclesiastical Architecture," and Rosemary Cramp, "Monastic Sites," in David M. Wilson, ed., *The Archaeology of Anglo-Saxon England* (1976); Alfred W. Clapham, *English Romanesque Architecture Before the Conquest* (1930); Margaret Deanesly, *The Pre-Conquest Church in England,* 2nd ed. (1963); E. Dudley C. Jackson and Eric G. M. Fletcher, "Porch and Porticus in Saxon Churches," in *Journal of the British Archaeological Association,* 3rd ser., **19** (1956); Meyer Schapiro, *Late Antique, Early Christian, and Mediaeval Art: Selected Papers* (1979), 243–248; Frank M. Stenton, *Anglo-Saxon England,* 3rd ed. (1971); Harold M. Taylor, *Anglo-Saxon Architecture,* I–II (1965), III (1978); Geoffrey Webb, *Architecture in Britain: The Middle Ages* (1956); Dorothy Whitelock, *English Historical Documents, c. 500–1042* (1955).

Two annual publications which carry reviews of excavations and bibliographies of all writing on the Anglo-Saxons are *Anglo-Saxon England,* Peter Clemoes, ed., and *Medieval Archaeology.*

PETER HUENINK

[See also **Anglo-Saxons, Origins and Migrations; Augustine of Canterbury; Bede; Canterbury; Canterbury Cathedral; England: Anglo-Saxon; Westminster Abbey.**]

SAXON DYNASTY. The Saxon dynasty, also known as the Liudolfingians or Ottonians, governed Germany from 919 to 1024. They were the descendants of Duke Liudolf (*d.* 866), who was responsible for the defense of eastern Saxony, where his family lands were situated. As the power of the Frankish monarchy weakened, Liudolf's son, Otto (*d.* 912), used this military command and his familial ties to the Carolingians to assume the leadership of the entire tribe and to extend his authority to Thuringia. The Franks and Saxons elected Otto's son, Henry I (*d.* 936), as king in 919. He and his son, Otto I the Great (*r.* 936–973), retained the Saxon duchy for themselves, defeated the Magyars (Battle of Lechfeld, 955) and Slavs, checked the other dukes' striving for independence, and attached Lorraine and northern Italy to Germany. Otto's imperial coronation in 962 symbolized Germany's emergence as the dominant power in Europe. Otto II (*r.* 973–983), who tried unsuccessfully to conquer southern Italy, and Otto III (*r.* 983–1002), who perceived himself as a Roman emperor rather than as a German king, were the son and grandson of Otto I. The last member of the dynasty, Henry II (*r.* 1002–1024), the founder of Bamberg, was the grandson of Otto I's brother, Duke Henry of Bavaria.

BIBLIOGRAPHY

Robert Holtzmann, *Geschichte der sächsischen Kaiserzeit (900–1024)* (1955); K. J. Leyser, *Rule and Conflict in an Early Medieval Society: Ottonian Saxony* (1979).

JOHN B. FREED

[See also **Carolingians and Carolingian Empire; Germany: 1138–1254; Germany: Stem Duchies; Otto I the Great, Emperor; Otto III, Emperor; Saxony.**]

SAXONY. The Roman geographer Ptolemy reported that around A.D. 150 the Saxons were living north of the Elbe in western Holstein. There are an increasing number of references after the late third century to Saxons raiding the British and Gallic coasts and enlisting in the Roman army. The Saxons' maritime raids culminated in the conquest of Britain in the middle of the fifth century. By 350 they were also pressing on the Roman frontier east of the lower Rhine. In the sixth and seventh centuries they expanded to the south, and by 700 they had occupied all of what became their tribal territory, roughly the area between the Eider in the north and the Unstrut in the south and from east of the Rhine to the Elbe-Saale.

Scholars have long argued whether this phenomenal expansion of a small tribe was the result of conquest or of a peaceful alliance with other tribes, in which the name of one member was applied to the entire confederation. Specialists in early Saxon history, citing the ninth-century saga of the tribe's origins, have contended that the Saxons conquered their neighbors, and that the original Saxons then formed the almost castelike nobility of the enlarged tribe. Historians who have compared the Saxons with other Germanic tribes have dismissed the saga as an unreliable later invention and have maintained that the tribe's unique confederate and republican structure was the product of a peaceful union of smaller entities.

The tribe was divided in the eighth century into three provinces: Angria on the Weser and Westphalia and Eastphalia to the west and east of the Weser. These provinces were subdivided into seventy or eighty smaller units (*Gau* in German, *pagus* in Latin), headed by princes who led the men of their district into battle and who presided at the *Gau* courts. There was no kingship (an institution that arose among the other Germanic tribes out of the need for military leadership during the period of migrations); rather, sovereignty resided in an annual tribal assembly, which met at Marklo on the Weser and which had the power to make war and peace, to select the princes, and to choose a duke by lot from among the princes to lead the tribe in wartime. These tribal assemblies were allegedly attended by the princes along with twelve nobles, twelve freedman (*frilingi, ingenuiles, liberti*), and twelve serfs (*lati, liti, serviles*) from each *Gau*. Such an assembly would have had approximately 3,000 members, and it has been suggested by Karl Jordan recently that the provinces rather than the *Gaue* were represented. The presence of the freedmen and serfs at the assembly is explained by the fact that it was not only a political body but also a court and cultic center.

The Saxons had the most rigid social structure of any Germanic tribe. The wergild of a noble was 1,440 schillings, six times that of a freedman and eight times that of a serf. It was a capital offense for a man to marry a woman from a higher estate; marriage to a woman of a lower estate had no legal validity.

The loose tribal organization and the pro-Frankish attitude of a faction of the nobility explains why the Saxons were unable to stop the Frankish conquest in thirty-three years of intermittent fighting (772–804). Some of the Saxons had been Frankish tributaries in the sixth century, but as the power of the Merovingians declined they ceased to make these payments. After 720 the Carolingian mayors sought to reestablish this relationship and supported the labors of Anglo-Saxon missionaries, who had been working in Saxony with little success since the late seventh century. Charlemagne began the actual conquest in 772. He divided Saxony into counties in 782 and appointed Saxon nobles as counts, an indication that they had recognized the futility of further resistance. It has also been suggested that the nobility's dominance was being threatened by an internal revolution of the freedmen and serfs and that the nobles welcomed incorporation into the Frankish realm and conversion, as devices to preserve their position. In any case, Christianization was a prerequisite for inclusion in the empire. Mass conversions had started in the late 770's, and in 782 Charlemagne issued a capitulary that made the belief in witchcraft, the robbing of churches, the murder of clerics, and cremation capital offenses.

These measures sparked a revolt led by the Westphalian noble Widukind. It was suppressed, and 4,500 Saxons are said to have been executed at Verden. This bloodbath revived the revolt, which ended only in 785 with Widukind's submission and baptism. The fighting had been confined largely to Westphalia and Angria, but in 792 the war started again in Nordalbingia and ended only in 804, after 10,000 Saxons had been deported. Even before the fighting was over, Charlemagne issued, with the approval of the Saxon nobility, a capitulary (797) that ended Saxony's special status as a conquered province. By the end of his reign Charlemagne had established dioceses in Bremen, Minden, Munster, Osnabruck, Paderborn, and Verden. The bishoprics of Halberstadt, Hamburg, and Hildesheim were founded by Louis the Pious. It is noteworthy that a separate Saxon ecclesiastical province that might have unified the tribe was not created; the new dioceses were assigned instead to the metropolitan sees of Cologne and Mainz.

To secure their conquest, the Carolingians constructed army roads through Saxony, especially from the lower Rhine and the Main to the Weser. Castles and large imperial estates were located along these arteries. In addition, the Carolingians promoted land reclamation and Frankish settlement, particularly in eastern Saxony.

Although the Frankish conquest ended Saxony's independence and tribal government, it strengthened the nobility's position. Charlemagne's codification of Saxon tribal laws, the *Lex Saxonum* of 802, recognized the nobles' special status. They were the chief beneficiaries of Christianization, since the church provided them with another instrument to exert their lordship. The Frankish and Saxon nobles intermarried, and Einhard was able to report that the two peoples had become one. This rapid assimilation of the nobility helps to explain why the Saxons could assume the leadership of Germany a century later. At the same time the position of the freedmen and serfs declined. The emperor Lothar was able to win their support against his brother Louis the German during the Stellinga Revolt (841–843) by promising the lower estates a restoration of their preconquest rights. This uprising was also a last pagan reaction against Christianity.

Saxony remained, however, a remote province of the empire, and Louis the German's visit in 852, except for Arnulf of Carinthia's brief stay at Corvey in 889, was the last time that a Carolingian set foot in the land. As the power of the East Frankish monarchy declined, the Liudolfingians assumed the leadership of the tribe. They were the descendants of a Count Liudolf, who had founded in the late eighth century the monastery of Brunshausen. His grandson Duke Liudolf (*d.* 866) was charged with the defense of eastern Saxony, where the family lands were situated. As the Viking and Magyar threat grew, Liudolf's son, Otto (*d.* 912), used this military command and his familial ties to the Carolingians to extend his authority throughout Saxony. After Margrave Burchard of Thuringia was killed by the Magyars in 908, the Thuringians also accepted Otto's leadership. Otto's son, Henry, acquired extensive estates in Westphalia, thus broadening the base of his power, through his marriage to Mathilda, the great-granddaughter of Widukind, and thwarted Conrad I's attempt in 913 to deprive him of Thuringia.

Henry's election as king in 919 made Saxony's history virtually identical with that of Germany for a century, since the Liudolfingians retained the duchy for themselves. Until Otto III's reign the kings visited the Saxon palaces, bishoprics, and monasteries more frequently than those in the remainder of the country. Otto I stayed, for example, at least twenty-three times in Magdeburg and seventeen times in Quedlinburg, compared to his twelve sojourns in Frankfurt and nine in Aachen. The Saxon clergy provided a disproportionate share of the German episcopate. Twenty-seven Hildesheim cathedral canons became, for instance, bishops between 919 and 1024. Saxony was the crown land of the dynasty.

Henry made a nine-year truce with the Magyars in 926. He used the peace to fortify the monasteries and to build additional castles, garrisoned by peasant warriors, and promoted the fortresses' subsequent economic development by requiring courts and markets to be held in fortified places. In 928/929 the Germans defeated the Elbian Slavs, made them tributary, and built castles at Brandenburg and Meissen. Henry felt secure enough in 932 to stop the payment of tribute to the Magyars, and in 933 he halted their retaliatory raid on Riade on the Unstrut.

Henry had been content to collect tribute from the Elbian Slavs as a token of his overlordship, but after his accession to the kingship Otto the Great sought their conversion and the annexation of their territory. This is revealed by his foundation of the monastery of St. Maurice's in Magdeburg as a mission center in 937 and the appointment of Hermann Billung (*d.* 973) and Gero (*d.* 965) as margraves along the lower and middle Elbe, respectively. They extended German control as far as the Peene River in the north and the Bober in the south. By 948 the east Elbian Slavs were sufficiently pacified for bishoprics to be established in Brandenburg, Havelburg, and Oldenburg. The capstone of Otto's eastern policy was the foundation in 968 of the archbishopric of Magdeburg and its suffragan sees of Meissen, Merseburg, and Zeitz (transferred to Naumburg in 1030). The weakness of Otto's program was that little effort was made at German colonization. As late as 1100 there were only forty parishes at best in the large diocese of Meissen (there were about eight hundred in 1300), a good indication that the area was sparsely populated and the Slavs only nominal Christians. The harshness of German rule provoked a revolt among the Slavs in 983, and all the newly conquered territories, except for the region between the Saale and upper Elbe, were lost until the twelfth century.

During his absences in Italy, Otto I was represented in Saxony by Margrave Hermann. This vicariate formed the basis of the Billung duchy of Saxony, whose actual authority was largely confined to Lower Saxony. The Billungs were transformed, however, from the king's representatives into tribal spokesmen as the Liudolfingians' own ties to Saxony became tenuous. Otto III's eastern policies, culminating in the establishment of the archbishopric of Gniezno in 1000, aroused considerable resentment; and the Saxons never regarded the last member of the dynasty, Henry II, as a Saxon. Hermann's son, Duke Bernhard I (*d.* 1011), made Henry's confirmation of the Saxons' rights a condition for their recognition of Henry's election as king. Henry's alliance with the pagan Ljutizi (Lyubitzi) against the Polish duke, Bolesław Chobry, further antagonized the Saxons; and in 1019/1020 Henry had to suppress a revolt by Bernhard's sons.

The latter incident was symptomatic of the changing relations between the monarchy and the duchy in the eleventh century. The Saxon magnates, clerical and lay, were trying to create their own hereditary lordships through an accumulation of counties, advocacies, fiefs, and allods. Their rival ambitions often clashed. The tension was particularly acute in Lower Saxony, where the Billungs opposed the efforts of Archbishop Adalbert of Bremen (1045–1072) to acquire all of the counties in his diocese. The kings became involved because they supported the bishops against their lay rivals and because they were developing their own royal territory in eastern Saxony and Thuringia, where silver had been discovered near Goslar in 968. This was especially true of the Saxon kings' successors, the Salians, who, though descended from the Saxon dynasty on the female side, had no extensive estates at their accession. Goslar, where Henry II had built a palace, became Henry III's favorite residence. Much of this domain was lost during Henry IV's minority, and he set out to regain and enlarge it after he attained his majority. He built castles, garrisoned by Swabian ministerials, and imposed heavy obligations on the free peasantry. The nobility and peasantry of eastern Saxony, led by Otto of Northeim (*d.* 1083), whose own lands on the upper Weser were affected by Henry's policy of recuperation, rebelled in 1073. Henry finally crushed the revolt in 1075.

The Saxons' opposition to the monarchy was then subsumed in the larger battle between Henry and Pope Gregory VII. Unlike in Swabia, ecclesiastical reform was never a major issue in Saxony, except for some of Henry's episcopal adversaries, most notably Bishop Burchard of Halberstadt

(1059–1088) and his nephew and successor, Herrand (1090–1102), who introduced the Cluniac customs into Saxony; but the pope's excommunication of the king for investing the royal candidate as archbishop of Milan provided a religious justification for reviving the revolt. Eastern Saxony, in particular, provided the antikings with their chief support after 1077. After Burchard's death Henry reached an understanding with his Saxon opponents, except for such diehards as Herrand. They recognized Henry as king but did not accept his antipope; on his part Henry did not try to enforce his royal rights in Saxony. Not surprisingly, the Saxon princes showed little hesitation in joining Henry V's revolt against his father in 1104.

The last of the Billung dukes died in 1106, and his allods were divided between his sons-in-law, the Ascanian Count Otto of Ballenstedt (*d.* 1123) and the Welf Henry the Black (*d.* 1126), who obtained the Billungs' chief castle of Lüneburg. Henry V granted the duchy itself to Count Lothar of Supplinburg, a hitherto relatively unimportant nobleman. Lothar acquired, however, extensive allods, including Brunswick, through his wife, Richenza, a granddaughter of Otto of Northeim. The emperor's mistreatment of Pope Paschal II in 1111 and his attempt to procure the inheritance of the last count of Weimar-Orlamünde in 1112 turned the Saxons against him in the closing phase of the Investiture Conflict. Lothar decisively defeated the imperial forces at Welfesholz in 1115, and Henry was never again able to assert any authority in Saxony. Lothar, for example, installed Conrad of Wettin (*d.* 1157) as the margrave of Meissen in 1123 over Henry's objections. The Billungs had never exerted any influence in the selection of the margraves. Lothar secured the crown in 1125 by engaging his daughter and heir, Gertrude, to Henry the Proud (*d.* 1139), the son of the duke of Bavaria, Henry the Black.

As emperor, Lothar was once again able to draw on the resources of Saxony, where he promoted the development of the royal domain. He determined the future of the German-Slavic borderlands by enfeoffing Albrecht the Bear (*d.* 1170), the son of Otto of Ballenstedt, with the Nordmark (later the Altmark) in 1134. Albrecht inherited the neighboring Slavic principality of Brandenburg in 1150. On his deathbed Lothar conferred Saxony itself on his son-in-law, Henry the Proud. King Conrad III tried to deprive Henry the Proud of the duchy by giving it to Albrecht, but in 1142 Conrad recognized Henry's son, Henry the Lion (*d.* 1195), as duke.

As the heir of several Saxon dynasties, Henry tried to weld his inheritance into a compact territorial state. Although his ducal position gave him the right to maintain the peace throughout Saxony, he made no attempt, as was once believed, to revive the tribal duchy. Henry devoted particular attention to Nordalbingia, where he seized the county of Stade from the archbishop of Bremen in 1144, participated in the Wendish Crusade of 1147, and procured the right from Frederick I Barbarossa in 1154 to invest the bishops of the reestablished sees of Mecklenburg, Oldenburg, and Ratzeburg. He refounded the city of Lübeck at a better site in 1159 and invested a native Slavic prince in 1167 with what later became the grand duchy of Mecklenburg. At the height of his power Henry governed a territory, secured by approximately 400 ministerial families, stretching from the North and Baltic seas to the Harz. Brunswick, where he erected his famous statue of a lion as a symbol of his power, served as his chief residence. Henry's fatal mistake was to forget that his position depended on his alliance with his cousin Frederick. When Henry rejected the emperor's request for military assistance in 1176 unless Frederick granted him the advocacy of Goslar, Barbarossa became responsive to the complaints of the Saxon princes, whose own territorial ambitions had been thwarted by Henry. After complicated legal proceedings, Henry was deprived of the duchies of Saxony and Bavaria in 1180 but was permitted to keep his allods, especially Brunswick and Lüneburg.

Henry the Lion's only grandson, Otto (*d.* 1252), surrendered the Welf allods to Frederick II in 1235 and received them back as an imperial fief. Otto's sons split the new duchy into the duchies of Brunswick and Lüneburg. The latter formed the nucleus of the later kingdom of Hanover.

The downfall of Henry the Lion destroyed the last vestiges of the tribal duchy. The Westphalian section of the diocese of Cologne and the entire diocese of Paderborn were granted as a duchy to the archbishop of Cologne. The remainder of the duchy was conferred on Count Bernhard of Anhalt (*d.* 1212), the younger son of Albrecht the Bear. Since Bernhard's older brother Otto had obtained the more important part of the Ascanian inheritance, Brandenburg, Bernhard lacked the resources to enforce his ducal rights. Bernhard's power was largely confined to the areas around Lauenburg on the lower Elbe and Wittenberg on the middle Elbe, and in 1260 his grandsons divided these Ascanian lands into the separate duchies of Saxe-Lauenburg and Saxe-Wittenberg. The latter was recognized in the Golden Bull of 1356 as the electorate of Saxony. When the last duke of Saxe-Wittenberg died without an heir in 1422, the emperor Sigismund enfeoffed Frederick IV of Wettin, margrave of Meissen, whose family had also obtained Thuringia in 1249 (finally in 1264), with the vacant electorate as a reward for his assistance in fighting the Hussites. The name Saxony was then gradually applied to all of the Wettins' domains, especially those east of the Saale. The modern kingdom of Saxony was thus largely composed of territory that had never formed part of the old tribal duchy.

BIBLIOGRAPHY

There is no general history of the old tribal duchy, in either German or English. What appear to be general histories by Rudolf Kötzsche and Walter Schlesinger, are actually histories of the Wettin lands and therefore not included here.

Lutz Fenske, *Adelsopposition und kirchliche Reformbewegung im östlichen Sachsen* (1977); Hans Joachim Freytag, *Die Herrschaft der Billunger in Sachsen,* in *Studien und Vorgarbeiten zum historischen Atlas Niedersachsens,* 20 (1951); Robert Holtzmann, *Geschichte der sächsischen Kaiserzeit* (1941 and later eds.); Karl Jordan, *Heinrich der Löwe* (1979), and "Sachsen und das deutsche Königtum im hohen Mittelalter," in *Historische Zeitschrift,* **210** (1970); Walther Lammers, ed., *Die Eingliederung der Sachsen in das Frankenreich* (1970), and *Entstehung und Verfassung des Sachsenstammes* (1967); Georg Schnath, *Geschichte des Landes Niedersachsen,* 2nd ed. (1973).

JOHN B. FREED

[See also **Arnulf; Carolingians and Carolingian Empire; Charlemagne; Einhard; Germany; Henry III of Germany; Henry IV; Henry VI; Magyars; Merovingians; Ministerials; Otto I the Great, Emperor; Otto III, Emperor; Saxon Dynasty; Wergild; Widukind of Corvey.**]

SCALACRONICA, a fourteenth-century Anglo-Norman chronicle by Sir Thomas Gray of Heton (*d.* 1369), most of it written while he was imprisoned in Edinburgh Castle between 1355 and 1357. The work synthesizes earlier history in the manner of the *Brut,* but it is chiefly important for its description of English-Scottish border events that occurred during the lifetimes of Gray and his father. The chronicle ends in 1362.

BIBLIOGRAPHY

A partial edition is *Saalacronica . . . : A Chronicle of England and Scotland from 1066 to 1362,* Joseph Stevenson, ed. (1836). A partial translation is *Scalacronica: The Reigns of Edward I, II and III,* Sir Herbert Maxwell, trans. (1907).

BRIAN MERRILEES

[See also **Anglo-Norman Literature; Brut, The; Chronicles.**]

SCANDINAVIA: BEFORE 800. The early Middle Ages in Scandinavia are prehistoric in the sense that the written evidence is very limited. Archaeology may confirm that significant events occurred, but their exact nature and dates are difficult to establish. "Early medieval" Scandinavia refers to the first Christian centuries (*ca.* 1000–1250), when narrative history was first recorded. In terms of our knowledge, Scandinavia in the pre-Viking era (before 800) is in the Dark Ages.

In the present article, the modern names "Denmark," "Norway," and "Sweden" are used, although the formation of these states occurred in the eleventh century. Each country will be considered in terms of its present frontiers, except that south Schleswig, now part of Germany, is included in Denmark. Iceland, though a Scandinavian state, will not be described, as the Norse migrations to the island did not begin until the late ninth century.

INTRODUCTION

Scandinavia was little known or understood by ancient writers. The earliest reference to peoples of Scandinavian origin was in the work of Pytheas of Massilia (Marseilles), now lost (composed about 310 B.C.) but described in the *Geographia* of Strabo (*ca.* 63 B.C.–*ca.* A.D. 24). Pytheas' most noted observations concerned "Thule," thought to have been Norway or Iceland. The Teutones were also referred to by Pytheas; after they and the Cimbri invaded the Roman Republic at the end of the second century B.C., Roman interest in them quickened. Among the Roman writers who took note of the Germanic peoples are Julius Caesar, Livy, Pliny the Elder, and Tacitus.

Pliny, in his *Naturalis historia* (*ca.* A.D. 77), was the first to use the name "Scadinavia" (IV, xiii, 96, 1942 ed. by Horace Rachman) and may have been the first to describe the Danes when he called the North Sea "Codanus Bay," though it is more likely

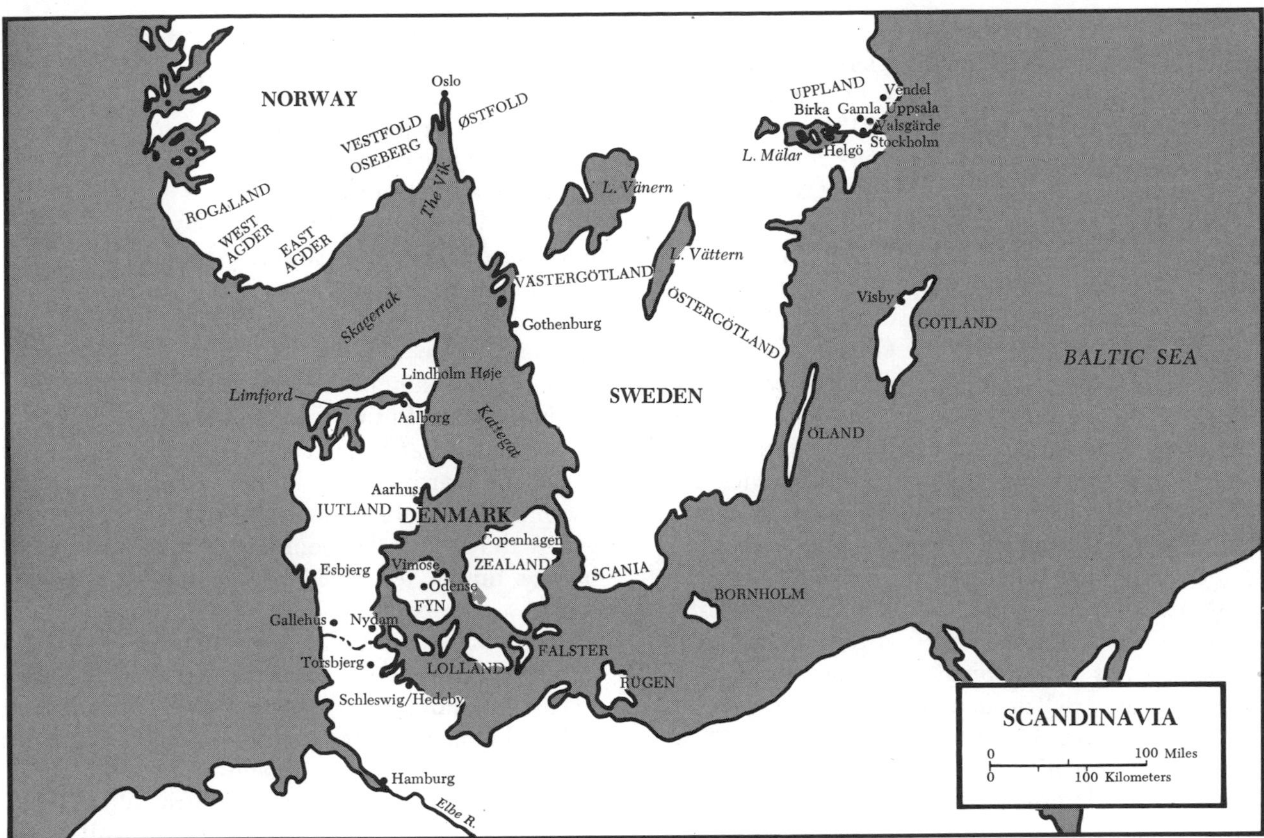

that this was a corrupt rendering of "Scadinavia." Furthermore, there is, separate from "Scadinavia," an island called "Scandia." "Nerigon" is still another island, and some scholars have seen in this name the first mention of Norway.

Tacitus' *Germania* (*ca.* A.D. 98) is the single most valuable account of the early Germans to survive from antiquity. Its details concerning Germanic, and by extension Scandinavian, material culture have been generally confirmed by archaeology. Tacitus was the first to name the Suiones or Swedes (chap. 44), and was the author of the claim that Sweden was the first unified Scandinavian kingdom. He also referred to the "Sithones" (chap. 45), and noted that they were ruled by women. (This legend of an Amazon state in the Baltic Sea area survived as late as the account of Adam of Bremen in the eleventh century.) The Old Swedish name for the Finns, *Kvaenir* (women; modern Swedish: *kvinnor* [*cf.* English "queen"]), makes reasonably certain the identification of the Sithones with the Finns. Tacitus' "Fenni" (chap. 46), who were wild and without weapons or crops, most certainly were the Lapps.

Ptolemy, writing in the second century of the Christian era at Alexandria, using Pliny, Strabo, and Erastosthenes of Cyrene as sources, constructed a geography that in the fifteenth and sixteenth centuries was the basis of "Ptolemaic" maps. The Jutland Peninsula and the isle of Scandza are clearly observable on these, but Norway and Sweden are missing, as they were unknown to Ptolemy.

Jordanes' *Getica*, written about 550, allegedly as an epitome of a great work in twelve books by Cassiodorus (a work now lost), quotes Ptolemy (book II) at length, giving very little that is new, but he is the first author to mention the Danes: "The Suetidi [Swedes] are of this stock [referring to other peoples] and excel the rest in stature. However, the Dani, who trace their origin to the same stock, drove from their homes the Heruli, who lay claim to preeminence among all the nations of Scandza for their tallness" (III, 23–25; Mierow translation).

Jordanes' statement takes on considerable importance in view of the emphasis placed on the Heruli (Eruli) by Procopius (*fl.* 550). In his *Gothic Wars* (books VI, XIV and XV especially, and *passim*), Procopius describes their manners and customs, and clearly considers them to be inhabitants of Scandinavia. He also refers to the Danes.

Still another sixth-century author writes about Scandinavia. Gregory of Tours (538/539–594/595) in his *History of the Franks* refers to an incident involving Chlochilaichus, a Danish pirate king who attacked the Frankish coast (Friesland?) about 516 but was defeated by a certain Theoderic (III, 3). This Chlochilaichus is the Hygelac of *Beowulf;* the historical authenticity of some details of the Anglo-Saxon story is confirmed by Gregory.

It is apparent that other Europeans were gaining a new appreciation of Scandinavia, and especially that they had become aware of the Danes. The theory that the Danes migrated from Sweden and drove the Heruli from their homeland is an attractive one, but it cannot be proven by archaeological evidence, for the material remains, though exhibiting local variation, are nonetheless remarkably uniform. Danish archaeology of the Migration Period indicates, if anything, that when Angles and Jutes migrated to Britain in the fifth century, no one filled their place. Great hoards of weapons of the third and fourth centuries have been found in Denmark, which suggests great conflicts; but there are few corresponding archaeological materials, other than gold hoards, that can be used as evidence of a later struggle between Heruli and Danes.

Similarly, the movement of peoples in central Sweden in the Migration Period, and especially the Swedish conquest of the Goths, is wrapped in a cloak of legend and fantasy. The only possible approach, then, to the virtually insuperable problems of this evidence is to consider in detail the archaeological materials.

The four classes of archaeological evidence in Scandinavia are settlement sites, graves, votive offering and field discoveries, and "loose finds," a grouping for objects not clearly belonging to one of the other three classes.

DENMARK (400–600)

Danish archaeologists divide their nation's prehistoric Iron Age into periods that are arbitrarily two centuries in length: the Pre-Roman (Celtic) Iron Age, Early and Late (400–200 B.C. and 200–1 B.C.); the Roman Iron Age, Early and Late (A.D. 1–200 and A.D. 200–400); the Germanic Iron Age, Early and Late (400–600 and 600–800); and the Viking Age (800–1000). Thus, beginning the prehistory of Denmark in the sixth century to conform to the first written mention is not in accord with the current Danish system of dating. That system may distinguish objects as "early Germanic" but not attempt a more precise date. It is reasonable, therefore, to include some fifth-century materials.

Settlements. Datable settlements are not towns or even villages, but isolated farmsteads. Oksbøl, northwest of Esbjerg in southwestern Jutland, is the site of remains of two houses at right angles to each other. One of the houses is about 125 feet (38 m) long and 16 feet (5 m) wide, a size characteristic of the Germanic longhouse, and is divided into three distinct rooms. In this case the most westerly room contains the hearth (the central room is usually the site of the hearth in this kind of house). The central room in the Oksbøl house was probably the manger. A third, easterly room has no traces of use. A bronze fibula, to which archaeologists have assigned a date based upon its style of ornament, is the basis of assigning the Oksbøl houses to the fifth or sixth century. Other settlement sites include one in east Jutland near Kolding and two on the island of Bornholm. The east Jutland site, called Traelborg (slave's fort), preserves a type of house with curvilinear walls that is best known in the Viking Age earthworks of the Trelleborg type. The walls' configuration indicates that principles of ship construction were used in preparing the roof of the house and that the sides of the house were supported by inclined posts. At one of the Bornholm sites, Sorte Muld, a single dwelling consisted of two wings at right angles to each other, together with a separate building for weaving and baking (an oven and loom weights were discovered there). The house appears to have been constructed of wattle and daub. Thus houses of the sixth century in Denmark do not conform to any uniform pattern in appearance, design, method of construction, or materials used.

Graves. Graves from the Early Germanic Iron Age in Denmark are found infrequently in comparison with graves of the Early Iron Age (the Late Iron Age in Denmark commences with the Germanic period). This corresponds to the near absence of discovered settlement sites. Danish archaeologists and historians are reluctant to ascribe this situation to depopulation by migration. They claim that a change in burial custom, by which grave goods were virtually eliminated, makes the identification of graves of this period extremely difficult. They also point out that many more treasure hoards have been found, and argue that this demonstrates Denmark's continuous occupation. But why are there so few settlement sites? Did the patterns of settlement also change radically? The most reasonable interpretation is that Denmark was indeed depopulated, that its people were very unsettled, and that the region was occupied by a succession of related but distinct tribal groups. The material cultures of these peoples would have been similar, but they did not stay in any one place long enough to leave an impression on the landscape.

Graves in northern Jutland are usually cremation graves under low mounds, with or without a circle of stones around the base. The grave goods are generally poor, consisting of earthenware pots or jugs. An inhumation grave with impressive funerary gifts is known from Himmerland (Gudumholm). It is a woman's grave containing a necklace of glass and amber beads, silver-embossed bronze fibulae, utensils of clay and wood, and an iron knife. This and a similar, less richly endowed woman's inhumation grave were made in naturally occurring hills but without a grave mound. The fibulae make possible the relative dating. Elsewhere in Jutland there are other graves with datable remnants of fibulae but with few other grave goods.

In the Danish islands, graves clearly datable to the Early Germanic Iron Age are rare. A number of these are inhumations—for example, at Bilidt on the Roskilde Fjord (Zealand), where there is an interment in a Stone Age kitchen midden (a refuse pile consisting chiefly of oyster shells), and some noteworthy women's graves, as at Kvarmløse near Holbaek, where a burial contained a necklace of glass beads, a wooden bucket with metal mounts, two silvered fibulae, and a small gold trinket. Fyn and Bornholm have interments of similar character. In general, both inhumations and cremations can be found among Danish graves of the Early Germanic Iron Age. There is too little material evidence to compare the relative popularity of the two customs. In northernmost Jutland, cremation predominates; in Zealand, inhumation graves oriented north-south.

Pottery and jewelry are the most common grave goods. Fibulae are often of two types: one with a rectangular head and triangular (in cross section) foot; the other with the head in the form of a cross, its arms terminating in faceted knobs, and its foot with the features of an animal's head. Graves with weapons are extremely rare throughout Denmark, except on the island of Bornholm, where one- and two-edged swords, spearheads, axes, shields, and harnesses have been found. These weapons are comparable with weapons in deposits (votive offerings), which are fairly abundant in Denmark.

Votive offerings. The most important bog deposit of the Early Germanic Iron Age was made at Kragehul, near the west coast of the island of Fyn. It is typologically comparable with the great deposits found at Torsbjerg and Nydam in southern Jutland and at Vimose (west of Odense) on Fyn, belonging to the Late Roman Iron Age (*ca.* 200–300), although it is not nearly as large. The objects, many of which had been deliberately damaged, were found at the bottom of an ancient pond that had dried out and become covered with peat. They included swords (long two-edged spathas with rectangular or hourglass-shaped hilts); wooden scabbards with bronze edging and chapes (the metal piece at the bottom of the scabbard, which keeps the sword from making a hole in it); spearheads and their wooden shafts; bows and arrows of iron and bone; shields; and toilet articles such as combs. No fibulae were found. A number of objects (spear shafts especially) were carved with runes.

At Nydam in Angeln (Nydam II), in the same area as the discoveries of Roman Iron Age weapons and a boat, archaeologists have recovered about 100 fragments of sword scabbards, including decorative devices, chapes, and edging. A comparable find at Porskaer (east-central Jutland) produced seventy sword chapes of similar character, bits of harness, and toilet articles. Several other sites in Denmark have provided smaller numbers of related items.

Chapes are particularly important in providing dates for the finds. In the Kragehul deposit some are *U*-shaped, similar enough in style to other European examples dated by associated coin evidence to provide a time-frame of the late fifth or early sixth century.

If weapons of the period were to be found in graves, we would know what kinds might have been used by an individual warrior and be able to determine whether some men were armed only with sword and shield, lance and shield, or bow and arrow, or who might wear a coat of mail or helmet. But as weapons have survived only in bogs (except on Bornholm), our knowledge of military organization is largely conjectural.

The long two-edged sword (spatha) seems to have been in general use in the Early Germanic period; the shorter one-edged sword, while known elsewhere on the Continent at the same time (the

Frankish scramasax), is absent from Danish finds until the seventh century.

Spears are of two types: one with a narrow head, the other with a shorter, wider, leaf-shaped head. The bow and arrow continued in use; and presumably the battle ax, which is common in the Viking Age (and known from the Roman period), was also in use in the Germanic Age. Defensive weaponry (shields, chain mail, and helmets) has not survived in clearly datable examples. Shield bosses indicate that the shield had a vaulted construction.

The most distinctive group of Denmark's Early Germanic Iron Age votive offerings is its treasures of gold. These number 300 to 400, and almost all belong to the Early Germanic era—few are attributed to the Late Roman Iron Age or later than the beginning of the seventh century. The greatest of these treasures are the golden horns of Gallehus.

The two horns were found separately in 1639 and 1734, a few paces from each other, and quite by accident, at Gallehus in the Tønder district of southern Jutland (now a few miles north of the German border). They were presented to the Danish kings and were housed with the royal collections until stolen and melted down in 1802. Drawings and learned treatises, however, provide allegedly accurate descriptions. The horn found in 1639 had a length of 28 inches (71.1 cm); the circumference of its mouth was 12 inches (30.5 cm). It had a smooth inner shell of pure gold and eleven outer rings of the same metal, decorated with figures (engraved and in relief) believed to portray scenes significant in Germanic mythology and religion. The horn found in 1734 was shorter, although its exact dimensions are not known. It bore a runic inscription: "ek hlewagastir holtijar horna tawido" (I, Laegest, Holt's son [or the forester], made the horn). The form of the runic letters and the ornamentation on the horns are the basis of assigning a fifth-century date to them. The literature interpreting their symbolic representations is substantial.

Less well-known or notorious than the golden horns, and less problematic, are some other golden hoards of Denmark's Early Germanic Iron Age. The hoards are found throughout Jutland and the islands, with the greatest number of discoveries made on Fyn (southwest coast), the Stevns district of Zealand (its southeasterly peninsula), and on Bornholm, a distribution that suggests merchant activity. Jewelry and ingots (a medium of exchange) constitute the bulk of the hoards; and among the former, necklaces, arm-rings, and rings are common. Fibulae, pendants, and coins also occur, along with bracteates and *guldgubber* (often translated "gold fogies" or "granddads"). The ingots are often in the shape of tubes that have been bent into rings, so that they might be clipped at a future time as the need arose for gold of a certain weight. The largest such hoard was found at Broholm in southeastern Fyn, and weighed about 9 pounds (4 kg).

The most spectacular objects in Danish (and Swedish) hoards are gold necklaces. A substantial number have been found, including three very large examples from Fyn (Hjallese), the island of Falster (Hannenov), and Øland in the Limfjord (north Jutland). Five others have been unearthed at Fraeer (north Jutland). There have been finds elsewhere in Jutland, near Aarhus and Ribe, but the phenomenon is present throughout Denmark. The largest Danish gold ring is a girdle from Stevns. It is a twisted or spiral rod that flattens at the hips and gradually widens at the front to form two great triangular plates, nearly joined, that are simply but exquisitely ornamented. It is reasonable to conclude that such jewelry was not meant to be worn by human beings but was dedicated to the gods, or was believed to possess divine powers. One is reminded of the "holy ring" on which the Danish king Guthrum swore peace to Alfred the Great in 878, and of the "ancient iron sword that served as the image of Ares" in Herodotus' account of Scythian religious practice (*Historia,* book IV). It may be that so few Scandinavian pagan idols have survived because they were of wood, or because they were deliberately destroyed. Or are we contemplating the gods themselves when we see the gold necklaces? Were the gold horns themselves divine?

The gold bracteates may have owed part of their popularity to supernatural powers with which their bearer invested them. They are thin gold disks stamped on one side only with figures or ornament, and sometimes with runes. Each has an eyelet by which it might have been attached to clothing. Six types are recognized; as a group they are all dated to the period 450–650 and are a Scandinavian, not merely a Danish, phenomenon. (They are also found in England and on the Continent.) Of the 760 known bracteates, 623 were found in Scandinavia; of these not quite half are Danish. They vary in size from 1 to 5 inches (2.5 to 12.7 cm). The most common types, labeled *A, B, C,* and *D* by nineteenth-century Swedish numismatists, clearly show a gradual barbarization of Byzantine prototypes, which are fourth-century gold medallions with the emperor's image stamped on them—medallions that had been presented to Germanic chieftains as a sign of imperial favor.

A bracteates, imitations that are closest to the Byzantine prototypes, feature a man's bust, often ludicrously exaggerated, surrounded by bands of geometric ornament. *B* bracteates have indistinct human figures accompanied by symbols (and sometimes by runes) crowding the entire disk, which is usually about half the size of the *A* bracteate. *C* bracteates vary in size, but the largest of them are the largest yet found. At the center of the disk a mounted warrior is portrayed. Banding of the type found on *A* bracteates is sometimes present, but the ornament is vinelike rather than geometric. *D* bracteates (chiefly from Norway) never have human figures and are decorated exclusively with animal ornament.

The *guldgubber* are similar to the bracteates in that they presumably were worn on clothing (some are pierced with eyelets). They are thin rectangles about 1 inch (2.5 cm) high decorated with a figure or figures having anthropomorphic characteristics that are thought to portray the gods. Sometimes male and female figures are juxtaposed in an amorous embrace, and it has been suggested that they are dancing. The *guldgubber* are dated to the period 500 to 700 on the basis of Swedish finds; more than fifty examples are known from Denmark.

Silver hoards are rather scarce in Denmark's Early Germanic Iron Age (as gold is scarce in the Viking period), but silver has been found in Zealand (Høstentorp), Lolland (Hardenberg), and Jutland (Simmersted). Most of the silver in these hoards is chopped, mangled, or lump silver, but there are also fibulae and coins.

Commentary. The Early Germanic Iron Age in Denmark was an era of substantial upheaval and change. The strong cultural influence of the Roman Empire continued; but the settlements, so extensive in the Roman era, virtually disappeared. The bog deposits were likewise a continuation of a custom evident in the third century, and thus form the basis of claims that the people of Jutland were not forced to leave their homes. At present it is argued by Danish archaeologists that the migration of the Danes, presumably from Sweden, occurred in the early third century, and that the bog deposits (Thorsbjerg, Nydam I, Vimose) were made by the victorious original inhabitants, who kept the Danes in Scania and Zealand, and prevented them from conquering Fyn and Jutland. If the things deposited in the bogs belonged to the victors—that is, were the products of the original inhabitants of the region—continuity could easily be explained. But unless religious considerations were overpowering, the victors would have needed their weapons for future engagements and would have hallowed them for their ancestral associations. If the bog deposits are the goods of the vanquished Danes, how shall we distinguish them? We do not know. Therefore the bog deposits cannot be used to date the invasions, particularly in view of the continuation of the custom until the sixth century, and because we do not know positively to whom they belonged. On the other hand, the absence of fibulae from the Kragehul find is fair evidence that the victors deposited selectively from the goods of the vanquished. If the goods had belonged to the victors, jewelry probably would have been included.

DENMARK (600–800)

There is less material evidence for the Late Germanic era than for the Early Germanic era. Even the great hoards of gold are lacking. Graves, often with weapons (in contrast with the virtually weaponless graves of the previous two centuries), are found in quantity only on Bornholm. In northern Jutland there is a very large cremation field, Lindholm Høje, where the individual graves are surrounded by boat-shaped enclosures of stones. The grave goods at this site are poor, however.

Settlements. There are virtually no discoveries beyond Lindholm Høje, located on the Limfjord in northern Jutland. It has been suggested that this is due to the imperfect archaeological investigation of modern Danish cities, and that settlements of the Germanic and Viking periods will be found under them. Hedeby, the first Danish town, which prospered in the ninth and tenth centuries, is near but not under the site of the modern city of Schleswig. Lindholm is near but not under modern Aalborg, which rises on the opposite shore of the Limfjord. It is true that the villages of Denmark have not been thoroughly excavated. But it is also true that there were no towns of any importance whatsoever before the twelfth century. The lack of settlement sites is indicative of a lack of settlements.

Graves. Lindholm Høje's well-placed location on the trade route from the North Sea to the Kattegat maintained the site's prosperity for several hundred years, well into the Viking period. The graves at this site, numbering about 700 (excavated), were preserved by drifting sand, undoubtedly present even while the cemetery was still in use, as some graves were dug in it over preexisting ones. Most of the graves are cremations, but there are some sixth-century inhumations. Many of the graves of the pre-Viking period are enclosed by stones arranged in circles, triangles, squares, and ovals, and toward the end of the period the "ship settings" (*skibssaetninger*) become dominant. These are cremation graves with the stones arranged in the form of a boat. Most of the burials, regardless of the shape of the enclosure, are poor in the quality of their grave goods. But it is apparent that the custom of including animals (especially dogs and horses)—a practice widespread in graves of east-central Sweden at the same time—has been introduced here.

In other cemeteries in Jutland, cremation and inhumation exist side by side; grave mounds also continued in use. Examples of eighth-century burials include some from Ris Fattiggaard in northernmost Jutland (Vendsyssel), cremations; Øsløs, in north-central Jutland adjoining the Limfjord (Vester Han), a cremation burial in a mound; Laastrup (north-central Jutland east of Hobro), an inhumation in a stone-lined pit; and Løvel Vandmølle (north of Viborg), where a mound built in the Roman Iron Age was employed again.

Mixed funerary practice also prevailed in the Danish islands. Many island graves have no distinguishing surface characteristics. However, important finds have been made at Kyndby near the Ise Fjord on Zealand, where a pair of rich burials have been unearthed. A woman's grave contained the bones of two dogs, sheep, and pigs; a bronze sieve; and a necklace of glass beads and amethysts. Her husband's grave contained the remains of one dog, sheep and pig bones, a sword, a shield, and a knife. Another warrior's grave found on the island of Møn (off Zealand's southeast coast) is similarly furnished. These Zealandic graves are nonetheless quite rare and can represent only a fraction of what remains to be discovered, if the graves are there to be found. On Bornholm, on the other hand, there are many cemeteries of the period, mostly in the southeastern part of the island. The burials are usually inhumations, and the deceased often are provided with weapons. Melstad, Lousgaard, and Baekkegaard are the largest cemeteries, the latter with more than 160 graves.

Commentary. Danish archaeologists continue to insist that the absence of discoveries is not a sign of "weakness, isolation, or the lack of communication with foreign lands," as Johannes Brøndsted put it; rather, interments without a grave mound or memorial, or without grave goods (making dating difficult), are responsible for the image of poverty and scant population that Denmark presents at this period. Only Bornholm, which was probably independent in the seventh and eighth centuries, has well-furnished graves. Indeed, it would be difficult to imagine a country as fertile as Denmark having been unoccupied for 400 years. It also seems that there was no migration of Slavs into the region, but they may have come close—into the area of the lower Elbe, where Charlemagne confronted them in the late eighth century. The wars of Justinian I, together with the Slavic migrations, probably halted the flow of gold to the north. It is possible that the major trade routes from the Baltic to the North Sea avoided Denmark for the most part, by using the Limfjord as the principal conduit. The most plausible explanation for the paucity of discoveries in Denmark is that cremation burials without grave goods, in a society of simple farmers, left little archaeological record. If the Danes had arrived by 600 A.D., they must also have caused some disruption of the community.

SWEDEN (400–800)

Swedish scholars do not insist on archaeological subdivisions that are arbitrarily two centuries in length. Their Iron Age is divided into three eras: the Early Iron Age (400 B.C.–A.D. 50), the Middle Iron Age (50–400), and the Late Iron Age (400–800). The Late Iron Age is further divided as the result of popular tradition. The years from 400 to 550 are known as the Golden Age and the subsequent centuries as the Vendel period, after a cemetery north of Uppsala that has yielded treasures of a legendary character.

Settlements. Three types of settlement site are known: hill forts, isolated farmsteads, and villages. The hill forts are especially numerous on the islands of Gotland and Öland. Torsborg on Gotland is very large, more than 1 mile (1.6 km) in circumference, but the best known are Gråborg and Ismantorp on Öland.

Ismantorp (probably constructed in the fifth century) is a circular earthwork about 410 feet (125 m) in diameter with limestone walls reaching 16.5 feet (5 m) in height at some places. The center of the earthwork is empty; the foundations of eighty-eight houses vary in size but are mostly rectangular and follow the course of the wall. Four zones or quarters can be distinguished with a stretch of the imagination, should one care to compare Ismantorp with the Viking Age earthworks of Denmark known as Trelleborgs (Ismantorp, however, has nine entrances, while Trelleborg has four). The houses in the interior of the "fort" may not be contemporary with the wall—another similarity to Trelleborg-type earthworks. Gråborg, the other well-known Öland site, is an irregularly circular fortification about 689 feet (210 m) in diameter with walls 30 feet (9 m) high. The fort was used as a place of refuge from the fifth to the seventeenth century. It is probable that Gråborg was built in the Golden Age and was regularly used until the end of the Viking Age.

The remains of about 2,400 houses have survived on Gotland and Öland because their foundations were constructed of earth and stones (limestone). The largest houses are about 197 feet (60 m) in length. The best-known examples constitute a whole village or estate. Four or five units, each with its group of buildings—there were twenty-four buildings in the settlement—were found at Vallhagar on Gotland, and include dwelling houses and barns of a Migration Period farming community.

Another settlement site of great importance is at Helgön, on an island in Lake Mälaren, some 9 miles (14 km) from Birka, the earliest Swedish town, which flourished in the ninth and tenth centuries. Helgön was probably the forerunner of Birka and disappeared in response to the latter's growth, or Birka may have arisen as Helgön declined. Since 1956 a large number of imported and native wares dating from the fourth century on have been found, with the greatest concentration of objects from the Vendel period. The best-known finds are a small Buddha from about 600, a bronze ladle from Egypt (also seventh century), and a bishop's crozier from Ireland. Finds of glassware have been dated to the period from 400 to 800. Most of these were unearthed from a group (among several such groups similar to the Migration Period farms at Vallhagar) of eight buildings that seem to have formed an independent unit—the abode, perhaps, of a family, a "trading company," or even a missionary outpost for which there is no literary record.

Graves. The Uppland district of east-central Sweden around Lake Mälaren abounds in graves of fantastic richness. There are three large burial mounds at Gamla Uppsala (sixth century) identified with the Yngling family immortalized in the ninth-century poem *Ynglingatal;* nearby at Vendel are fourteen graves of men from a single family interred over a period of nearly 400 years (*ca.* 600–1000). At Valsgärde, in the same district, are fifteen similar graves dating from the seventh to the late eleventh or early twelfth century. There are additional notable examples.

Gamla (Old) Uppsala, located a few kilometers from the modern university town, figures prominently in the folklore of medieval Sweden. Adam of Bremen, in book IV of his *Gesta Hammaburgensis ecclesiae pontificum* (*ca.* 1075), described the pagan temple there with its golden chain and images of Thor, Odin, and Frey; the first Christian cathedral was allegedly built on its site. South of the wooden memorial church (a museum) that exists there now are three mounds (also mentioned by Adam) arranged in a southeast-northwest line. The largest mound is about 197 feet (60 m) in diameter. The two outer mounds, which were excavated in the nineteenth century, were found to be cremation burials with modest (surviving) grave goods of the period 500–550. Aun, Egil, and Adils, three of the Yngling kings, are, according to tradition, buried here.

North of Uppsala is the enormously important cemetery at Vendel, which has given its name to the whole period. There is a large mound there, called Ottar's Hill, that contains a sixth-century cremation like those at Old Uppsala. The *Ynglingatal* states that King Ottar fell at Vendel. But Ottar's Hill is of minor importance as a grave compared with the boat burials discovered in 1881 at Vendel churchyard. These inhumations, all of males (fourteen or more in number) accompanied by boats up to 33 feet (10 m) in length, are among the richest such graves from the early Middle Ages, although none can compare with the Sutton Hoo ship burial (England, seventh century), to which they are typologically and spiritually related. The body of the deceased was placed in the stern of the boat, along with his weapons (sword, shield, spear). Four of the warriors were supplied with bronze helmets decorated with ornamental plaques that are significant in the study of Scandinavian religious traditions. In the bows of the vessels, glassware and other typical grave goods, such as a riding harness, were found. Horses, dogs, and the remnants of foodstuffs (meat) were also discovered. But the Vendel cemetery appears to have been desecrated at an early date—perhaps immediately after the interments—to signify a safe passage, to prevent haunting, or simply for loot. Parallels to this kind of robbery are found in the archaeological record of every culture. We are insufficiently informed of the nature of Scandinavian religion to draw any inferences from the plundering of the Vendel graves.

The boat burial is a phenomenon characteristic of Uppland in the sixth through eighth centuries. The Vendel graveyard is bounded on the east by the Vendel Brook, which joins the Fyris Brook to become the Fyris River and empty into Lake Mälar. Gamla Uppsala is in a bend of the combined stream, and the modern city of Uppsala is somewhat south. The fifteen boat graves that were discovered at Valsgärde in 1928 are north of Gamla Uppsala on a low ridge along the Fyris River. Ulltuna, 2 to 2.5 miles (3–4 km) south of the modern city, is another such site; it has three boat graves (discovered in 1854) dated to the seventh century. At Tuna, on the shores of Lake Mälar, nine boat graves were discovered. A remarkable feature of these graves is that they contain little gold, whereas the mounds at Gamla Uppsala, and Ottar's Hill at Vendel, though cremations, show signs of having contained the metal. It has been suggested that this demonstrates the royal nature of the mound burials, whereas the boat graves would appear to be the tombs of wealthy farmers of the district.

The fifteen graves at Valsgärde are similar in content to those at Vendel, although only five are from the period before 800. Valsgärde grave number 8 is one of the richest. The vessel in which the deceased was interred is about 33 feet (10 m) long. The warrior's body was placed amidships and covered by two large round shields decorated with iron fittings. (In other Valsgärde graves the dead is placed in the stern.) Near the body were his sword, axe, knives, helmet (similar to those at Vendel, and decorated with bronze plaques), harness, drinking horn, and glassware. In the bow of the boat were spears, kitchen utensils, and gaming pieces. The remains of animals (dog, horse) were found in the grave outside the perimeter of the vessel.

Another feature of the Valsgärde cemetery is nearby cremation graves (with few surviving grave goods), almost solely of women. These contemporary burials may be of the wives or serving women of the more "distinguished" men buried in their boats. On the other hand, there is a group of eight boat burials at a site in central Sweden (Västmanland), called Tuna-Badelunda, which are all women's graves. Dated to the Vendel and Viking periods, they surrounded a grave with numerous gold objects and bronze imported wares belonging to a female who ostensibly lived in the fourth century. Cremation graves nearby are almost exclusively of men. The pattern characteristic of Valsgärde has been reversed here.

Votive offerings, hoards, and loose finds. The most striking feature of the Swedish Migration Period archaeological record is the enormous hoards of gold that have been unearthed, most notably on the Baltic islands of Gotland and Öland. There are five categories of finds: (1) collars of gold tubing decorated with filigree and granulation, (2) bracteates, (3) gold fogies—the thin gold ornaments also found in Denmark, (4) sword pommels and scabbard mounts, and (5) Byzantine lightweight solidi, minted largely for Theodosius II (408–450), Leo I (457–474), Zeno (474–491), and Anastasius (491–518). About four-fifths of the approximately 500 gold solidi that have been found in Scandinavia have been recovered on the Baltic islands—half of them on Gotland.

The gold collars are best known in three examples that constitute the largest gold articles now surviving from Scandinavian antiquity (after the golden horns of Gallehus). One from Öland, found at Torslunda (Färjestaden), consists of five gold tubes, each surrounded by a series of rings grouped three-one-three and arranged in a regular pattern. The interstices between the rings and between each tube are decorated with delicate granulation and filigree work. Two other examples, from Västergötland, have three (Ålleberg) and seven (Möne) tubes, respectively. The techniques of execution are quite similar. Filigree and granulation, with figures of animals and faces of men, fill the spaces between the tubes. The collars each weigh about 2 pounds (1 kg).

The heaviest of the gold hoards that have come to light in Sweden was discovered in 1774 (at Tureholm, Södermanland) and has been dispersed. It weighed more than 26 pounds (12 kg). A large collar with incised half-moon ornamentation survives from the find; its construction is different from the tubular collars in that it consists of a single massive gold ring to which a half-ring or demi-lune is attached by two widely separated clasps of finger-ring size. The collar terminates at the back in twisted gold knots that made it nonadjustable, whereas the tubular collars could be opened or closed.

Another hoard, the second largest found in Sweden (at Timboholm, Västergötland, in 1904), contained 15 pounds (7 kg) of gold. There were two large bars or ingots and twenty-six unadorned rings strung into two chains. There were no collars, other jewelry, nor ornaments of any sort.

The pictorial stones of Gotland. Pictorial stones represent a class of evidence found nowhere else in Scandinavia. Most of their engravings date to the period 400 to 800, although some probably were made later. All are memorials or commemorative stones, but almost none was placed over a grave. Their importance in the history of Germanic art and religion is immense.

There are about 250 examples. They are limestone, on the average 7 feet (2 m) in height. Three periods of their development were distinguished by Sune Lindqvist, the leading twentieth-century student: the fifth, eighth, and eleventh centuries. The Sanda stone is characteristic of the first period. It is a tall, smooth slab engraved and embellished with colors. The sides of the stone are slightly concave, then flare at the top, which is somewhat convex. The decoration is simple. The edge of the stone's face is ornamented with a band of spiral and interlace, and there are isolated geometric (sun?) symbols above a representation of a rowboat (evidence that the sailing ship was unknown in Scandinavia at this time?).

The eighth-century stones are substantially different. The sides are straight and rise from the base to form a triangle. Near the top the sides flare sharply and then the head of the stone becomes an arch. The overall impression is phallic. The decoration of the stones is more complex than in the earlier examples, with recognizable scenes from mythology (and many others that cannot be interpreted). The Ardre stone is a good example (at one time it was a paving stone in a church floor, and it is somewhat damaged). In the upper third of the picture there is a warrior on an eight-legged horse—presumably Odin riding on Sleipnir—and to the left of this a house with three front entrances, which may represent Valhalla with its 540 doors. Below this is a scene that is presumably within the house. In the central third of the picture, a ship under full sail is displayed; this kind of representation is invaluable in view of the failure of sails and ship's rigging to survive in grave finds (such as the ninth-century Oseberg and Gokstad burials in Norway). In the lower third of the picture are scenes that supposedly represent deeds of the god Thor. The entire face of the stone is framed by a boldly drawn spiral-and-interlace design.

Another such stone is from Tjängvide. Here the images are the same as in the upper two-thirds of the Ardre stone: Odin on his horse, Valhalla, and a ship with eight sailors (Ardre has six) under full sail. The lower scenes are missing, and the stone itself may be a fragment with the Thor representations lost.

Commentary. The contrast that Sweden provides to Denmark in the Migration Period is not so great as the vastly more numerous treasure hoards might indicate. For the most part, Gotland and Öland have the greatest number of hoards and of settlement sites. The island of Bornholm provides most of the Danish evidence from the period. We may conclude that the three islands were part of the same cultural, if not political, province, and that their economic activity was appreciably greater than that of the mainland. The graves in Sweden are for the most part as poor as those of Denmark, with the exception of the boat burials of Uppland. It is to Norway and Norwegian graves that one must turn to get a fuller picture of conditions in the fifth and sixth centuries. The Swedish archaeological materials tantalize, but provide few answers to questions. How did the Uppland kings acquire their power? What was their relationship with the peoples and kings of other districts or with the Upplanders themselves (such as the men buried at Vendel)? What connections did Uppland have with the Gotlanders and Ölanders? Uppland was more prosperous, and certainly more densely populated, than most other areas of Sweden. Why this was so is not known, but the advantage of Lake Mälar, as an avenue of communication, was undoubtedly a contributing factor.

NORWAY (400–800)

A country with a coastline as long as that of Norway (about 1,500 miles [2,400 km]) would be expected to have fostered a number of cultures, livelihoods, and political entities, and it did to a certain extent; but the similarities in patterns of culture outweigh the dissimilarities, even in the Migration Period.

The chronology and terminology employed by Norwegian archaeologists are somewhat different from those employed by the Danes and Swedes. The Roman Iron Age extends from the first to the fourth century; the subsequent era, 400–600, is the Migration Period; and the period from 600 to 1000 is called the Late Iron Age. In Norwegian archaeology, fifth- and sixth-century materials are well represented, but nonetheless constitute only about 20 percent of all Norwegian Iron Age artifacts, which are vastly more abundant later on.

Settlements. In contrast with Denmark and the mainland of Sweden, there are substantial numbers of homesites in Migration Period Norway, most of them concentrated in the southwestern part of the country. The houses are rectangular—the Germanic longhouses usually—with exterior walls made of earth and debris, but without interior divisions. The houses average 65 to 100 feet (20 to 30 m) in length, and often are about 27 feet (8 m) wide, but examples up to 300 feet (91 m) in length are known. The houses are not grouped in villages, but are either isolated farmsteads or at most groups of up to five dwellings. Often the houses are surrounded by stone fences that enclose up to twenty-five acres of pasture and farmland.

Another kind of settlement site is the roughly circular encampment in which a group of houses is arranged radially around a central, open place. These complexes are found in Rogaland on the west coast, and farther north. Their use is unknown, but they resemble Ismantorp on Öland, and the ground plan has certain affinities with the later Danish Trelleborgs. They may be barracks, used only in times of crisis, or they may have a connection with Scandinavian religious practice. They do not seem to have been cattle barns, nor do they exhibit other usual signs of habitation.

Another settlement site of importance is in Telemark, a district of southern Norway southwest of modern Oslo. In the mountainous interior of the province, at Mogen near Lake Møsvatn, are the remains of a house built by hunters. The walls were constructed of earth. The roof was probably of turf, since the postholes of the roof supports show that they were substantial. Overall the building measured about 26 feet by 40 feet (8 m by 12 m). A large number of loose finds were made at the site, including imported glassware and locally made ironwares, and there was a big heap of rubbish by the front door (on the eastern end) consisting largely of reindeer bones. The site may represent an encampment of trappers seeking reindeer hides; their tastes nonetheless were influenced by the cultural life of the coastal regions. This is in contrast with a fourth-century settlement site on the west coast near Ålesund (at Skjonghelleren), where the hunters and trappers lived in a huge cave by the sea and had no need for iron or imports of any sort. They lived in the Iron Age in terms of time, but not in terms of technology. By the Migration Period, although there was no extensive immigration or movement of peoples, the whole of Norway had been influenced by cultural impulses coming from the south. This is particularly evident in the graves, which show close contact with the Rhineland and Frankish territory.

Graves. The graves from the fifth and sixth centuries are both cremations and inhumations. One characteristic type is cist graves (stone-lined pits) in western Norway, in which artifacts are particularly plentiful. These include weapons (sword, shield, spears), toilet articles (knives, tweezers), and the remnants of the deceased's clothing of wool, silk, or linen. The district of West Agder, the southernmost point of Norway, is the site of the Snartemo find, which contained swords inlaid with gold and silver, gold finger rings, imported bronzes, and glassware. Other graves, both men's and women's, have similar imported wares, although products of native origin outnumber them. Gold bracteates also occur in such burials along with fibulae of cruciform shape. The overall impression is that the native inhabitants had a considerable interest in imports, which they often imitated. The originals were obtainable, but the local products conformed more to native tastes.

In the seventh and eighth centuries, graves became a more prominent feature of the landscape. Circular grave mounds, often 20 feet (6 m) in height and up to 100 feet (30 m) in diameter, arranged in small (family?) groups, contain either cremations or inhumations, and both male and female graves are of this sort. Imported bronzes, pottery, and glassware have now vanished. But weapons, harnesses, tools, and domestic animals (horses, dogs, oxen) are much more common. At Morgedal in Telemark, more than 200 objects of iron, one-eighth of them blacksmith's tools and the remainder the products of a smith's forge, were recovered from a man's grave (the grave may be of Viking Age date, however). There were weapons, axes, riding harnesses, locks, and agricultural implements in the Morgedal grave. Many other graves of the period contain farm implements; hoes, sickles, scythes, and plowshares are most common.

Gold hoards. By far the greatest number of Migration Period gold hoards are found in southeastern and southern Norway, and in the southwest as far as Sogn. East and West Agder and Rogaland (the most southerly parts) are the richest districts. In a census made in 1956, for example, Rogaland had forty-four discoveries with 192 objects, with a total weight of more than 6.5 pounds (3 kg). Those hoards, which are datable through Roman coins, were made no later than the middle of the sixth century, as the largest number of issues are those of Theodosius II, Leo I, Zeno, and Anastasius (as in the Swedish hoards). Hoards from Sletner (Østfold) and Stavigjordet (Akershus) in the vicinity of Oslo are rich in bracteates, especially of the *D* type. Gold collars similar to the one found at Thureholm in Sweden have been found at Øksendal in Romsdal and Heskestad in Rogaland. In sum, the Norwegian hoards are little different in character, but smaller in weight, from the great treasure hoards of Sweden.

Commentary. Norway in the Migration Period was clearly in the mainstream of Scandinavian development, although it is chiefly along the southern coast that the influence of the Gallo-Roman export industries is apparent. Norwegian native taste was similar to that in Denmark and Sweden, and the cultural unity of southern Scandinavia was strengthened by contact between the three regions. On the other hand, no significant migration or depopulation can be observed from a study of the finds. On the contrary, the well-equipped graves of the Migration Period indicate that an unusual degree of prosperity prevailed. In eighth-century graves the increase in weaponry, together with large quantities of agricultural implements, shows that agricultural expansion was taking place. Warfare and tribal disharmony would have accompanied this, and the need for new arable lands and military problems at home forced many to settle abroad. This redirected the sphere of Norwegian economic activity away from the Rhineland (industries) and toward the British Isles.

CONCLUSION

The decline of Rome in the fifth century was the primary reason that Scandinavia remained relatively obscure for the next three centuries. Had the Roman imperial power continued in the West, the Germanic peoples who had migrated into the empire would undoubtedly have borne northward Christian and Roman civilization far earlier than the ninth century, when Carolingians began to penetrate Scandinavia. The archaeological evidence presented above shows that there were very lively connections with central, western, and southern Europe in the centuries prior to the Viking era. Had the Roman emperor Augustus not chosen to retreat from Germany after the Teutoburg defeat in A.D. 9, and had the limes not been fixed on the Rhine-Danube frontier, it is probable that Scandinavia would have enjoyed the same fate as Britain. The failure of the empire to deal with the Germanic problems of the second and third centuries, and the collapse of the dynasty of Theodosius in the fifth century, threatened to isolate Scandinavia economically. The Hunnic expansion after 433 undoubtedly created a barrier that was catastrophic to Danish societies. The migration of the Angles to Britain in the fifth century, for example, can be explained as a response to the baleful problems caused by Hunnic disruption of the economic life of Jutland. The great bog finds of Denmark could be a product of this turmoil. The wealth of Sweden in the same period is indicative of a reorientation of trade routes from the Black Sea northward. Only when the Frankish kingdom was revitalized by Pepin the Short could the state of economic decay into which Denmark had fallen be changed in favor of missionary, merchant, and piratical activity.

Scandinavians in the sixth through eighth centuries did not lose the taste for imported wares that characterized their Roman Iron Age, as the archaeological record clearly shows. The best example is in weaponry, where the short one-edged sword was replaced everywhere by the longer, two-edged spatha, in use in the late imperial armies. One can see the influence of Gallo-Roman material culture in imports, the art of metalworking, animal ornament, and tableware (drinking sets). That many of the imported wares were copied by local craftsmen and altered to native taste in no way diminishes their standing as representative of Roman culture. The gold bracteates, though often crude, are nonetheless an attempt to emulate Rome. Just as Charlemagne imitated Byzantium in building his palace at Aachen, on a lesser scale Scandinavians were copying Rome in their own material culture. The principal barrier to the Scandinavians' absorption into the heritage of the Roman Empire was their lack of a written literature. As farmers, cattlemen, and hunters, they also lacked cities, and even towns, a further bar to the development of literacy.

It is usually argued that Scandinavian paganism was a hindrance to the spread of Christian Roman culture to the north. If Christianity had not had political implications (conquest by overzealous missionaries, an entrenched aristocracy among the heathen), a gradual but genuine conversion could have developed from the subtle influence apparent in burial customs (for example, the disappearance of grave goods), the mythology of Odin (who resembles Jesus in several respects—in particular a shamanistic one), the iconography of the gods, and the appearance of cult buildings (churches) to replace open groves. Unfortunately, Scandinavia's Christian neighbors could not appreciate these changes, but the archaeological evidence proves that they had occurred. Denmark was undoubtedly evangelized by cultural influences, while Norway had to suffer the political and religious tyranny of St. Olaf. In Sweden, preaching was required for conversion. Norway and Sweden could not respond to the benefits of the cultural mission because the Viking Age intervened to mask the conversion of Scandinavian native culture that had begun in the Migration Period. In the Viking Age, vigorous Scandinavians became more eager to acquire the material benefits of their neighbors, which they had enjoyed for many centuries. In sum, Scandinavia had never been isolated, and had absorbed more of Roman civilization than might be supposed.

BIBLIOGRAPHY

For an introduction to the scholarship on Scandinavia see Gunnar Ekholm, *Forntid och fornforskning i Skandinavien* (1935); Peter Glob, *Denmark,* Joan Bulman, trans. (1971); Anders Hagen, *Norway,* Elizabeth Seeberg, trans. (1967); Ole Klindt-Jensen, *Denmark Before the Vikings,* Eva Wilson and David Wilson, trans. (1957), and *A History of Scandinavian Archaeology,* G. Russell Poole, trans. (1975); Haakon Shetelig and Hjalmar Falk, *Scandinavian Archaeology,* E. V. Gordon, trans. (1937); Mårten Stenberger, *Sweden,* Alan Binns, trans. (1962).

The standard survey for Denmark is Johannes Brøndsted, *Danmarks Oldtid,* III, *Jernalderen,* 2nd ed. (1960). For Sweden see Sune Lindqvist, *Svenskt forntidsliv* (1944); Oscar Montelius, *The Civilisation of Sweden in Heathen Times,* Rev. F. W. Woods, trans. (1888, repr. 1969).

Nordisk kultur, 30 vols. (1936–1956), contains articles in Danish, Norwegian, and Swedish dealing with various aspects of the period, such as population, religion, folklore, art, commerce, and literature.

The principal pan-Scandinavian journal is *Acta archaeologica* (1930–). The Danes publish *Skalk* (1957–), a popular journal in simple format. Other Danish journals are *Aarbøger for nordisk oldkyndighed og historie* (1866–1985); *Kuml* (1951–); *Nationalmuseets arbejdsmark* (1928–). The principal Norwegian journals are *Viking: Tidsskrift for norrøn arkeologi* (1937–); *Bergens Museums Årbok* (1883–1947); *Stavanger Museums Årbok;* and *Universitetets Oldsaksamlings Årbok* (published by Universitetets Samling av Nordiske Oldsaker, Oslo).

In Sweden most archaeological monographs have been published by the Royal Society of Letters, History, and Antiquities (Kungl. Vitterhets Historie och Antikvitets Akademien), especially in its *Handlingar,* 90 vols. (1789–1954). Swedish journals include *Fornvännen: Journal of Swedish Antiquarian Research* (in Swedish with English summaries) (1906–); *Meddelanden från Lunds universitets historiska museum;* and *Tor* (1948–).

Quarto- and folio-sized monographic series also exist, the most important of which is the Danish *Nordiske fortidsminder* (1890–). No volume has appeared since 1957, however, and it has presumably been replaced by *Nationalmuseets skrifter.*

National histories include Johannes Brøndsted, *De aeldste tider indtil år 600* (1962); Sten Carlsson and Jerker Rosén, *Den svenska historien,* I (1966); Anders Hagen, *Vårt folks historie,* I (1962); and Thorkild Ramskou, *Normannertiden, 600–1060* (1963).

SIDNEY L. COHEN

[See also **Adam of Bremen; Barbarians, Invasions of; Birka; Bracteates; Denmark; Fibula; Gotland; Gregory of Tours, St.; Jordanes; Migration and Hiberno-Saxon Art; Norway; Procopius; Snorri Sturluson; Sutton Hoo; Sweden; Vikings.**]

SCANDINAVIA: AFTER 800. See individual countries.

SCANDINAVIA: POLITICAL AND LEGAL ORGANIZATION. Certain generalizations are possible about the ways in which the early Scandinavian communities organized themselves with a view toward maintaining stability, security, and prosperity. Separate treatment is necessary for Iceland, which differed from the mainland states in being a new and nonmonarchical society. All the Scandinavian nations were converted to Christianity between about 950 and 1100.

The kingdom of Denmark comprised Jutland and the major islands, Fyn and Sjælland, along with the numerous lesser isles; across the Øresund were Skåne, Halland, and Blekinge (these three provinces, now Swedish, are referred to collectively as Skåneland), and, out in the Baltic, Bornholm. (Blekinge and Bornholm cannot have acknowledged Danish sovereignty before the tenth century.) Sweden consisted of sparsely populated Småland in the southeast, flanked to the north and west by Östergötland and Västergötland (collectively Götaland); and then the lands around the great inland sea, Mälaren, stretching from the Baltic across to Värmland on the Norwegian marches. The central provinces (with Uppland as the most important) are referred to as Svealand, inhabited by the Svear, who gave their name to Sweden as a whole (Old Swedish [OSw]: *Sveariki, Svidhiod*). Farther north lay Hälsingland and Medelpad and inland to the northwest the province of Dalarna. Proper colonization of the northernmost territories did not begin until the end of the period. The major Baltic island of Gotland acknowledged Swedish suzerainty in the course of the Viking Age.

The kingdom of Norway included a southeastern coastal province, Ranríki (now Swedish Bohuslän), which went as far south as the mouth of the Göta River (which thus formed a boundary between Norway and Danish Halland). Strictly speaking, the name Norway was not applied to the country north of Namdal, though the inhabitants of Hálogaland, the great region stretching north from there to Finnmark, came early to regard themselves as Norwegians. Inland from there are Jämtland and Härjedalen, which are now Swedish but owed allegiance to Norway for most of the Middle Ages. The island communities in the Faeroes, Shetland, Orkney, Hebrides, and Man were either predominantly Norse or firmly under Norse control, and they all looked, or came to look, on the Norwegian king as their overlord.

These major groupings came about in the Migration Age and early Viking Age, part of a long and continuing process of consolidation by coercion and consent. But throughout the period under consideration the monarchies remained federations of provinces.

ORGANIZATIONAL UNITS

The common unit in the Danish islands and Skåneland, in Götaland, and in southeastern Norway was the *herred* (district; plural, *herreder;* Swedish [Sw]: *härad;* Old Norse [ON]: *herað;* Old Danish [OD]: *hæræth*). In west Norway and Trøndelag the unit was the *fylke* (ON: *fylki*). In Jutland it was the *syssel* (plural, *sysler;* ON: *sýsla;* [OD]: *syslæ*), but the division into seven *sysler* in north Jutland appears primary in relation to the corresponding division in south Jutland. In Svealand the unit was the *hundare,* replacing the earlier *hund.*

The first element of *herred* is reckoned to be *herr* (multitude; armed host), but the meaning of the second element is uncertain. *Fylke* is from *folk* (warrior-band; people). *Syssel* implies administrative activity and denotes an area in which an officer appointed by some higher authority functioned. Swedish *hund* and *hundare* are related to "hundred" and doubtless meant a unit supplying 100 (or 120) men for war service.

The later levy organization was usually fitted into these divisions, but sometimes it created new units of its own. With the introduction of Christianity there seem to have been concerted public efforts to build a main church in the *herred* or its equivalent, probably to replace the central cult-site that existed earlier. Subsequently parishes came into being, often but not invariably coincident with secular divisions. Sometimes the parish came to form a secular as well as ecclesiastical unit.

Many units seem to have been too big for effective collaboration and administrative enforcement, and there is a regular division into quarters of the Danish and Swedish *herreder,* for example, and of the *fylke* of west Norway (but not those of Trøndelag, which were smaller). *Hundare* in Svealand were divided into halves, quarters, and eighths. Elsewhere—on Gotland, for instance—there was division into thirds and sixths.

In Denmark and Sweden the common unit above the *herred* (*syssel, hundare*) is the *land* (region). Denmark, for instance, had thirteen *land* units. Sizes varied: three *herreder* made up the *land* of Blekinge, for example; eighteen that of Östergötland; four, eight, and ten of the earlier *hund* made up Fjädrundaland, Attundaland, and Tiundaland, the main *lands* of Swedish Uppland. In Norway a variety of terms were used for such older larger groupings. A distinctive one is *lǫg* (laws; law-province), as in Þrœndalǫg (modern Trøndelag). Another name that came into use for Swedish and Norwegian law-provinces was *lagsaga* (law-speaking), because of the recital of laws at the great provincial assemblies.

The law-provinces themselves may represent still larger combinations. As a law-province, Västergötland covered its own thirty-two *herreder* along with the six of the Dalsland *land* and a solitary *herred* otherwise linked with Småland. Ancient Þrœndalǫg contained eight *fylke* and had its central assembly at Eyrathing (Øreting). At some stage Namdal, Hálogaland, Nordmøre, and Romsdal were combined with it. This expanded federation assembled on the Frosta Peninsula, while Eyrathing continued to serve as the assembly for Trøndelag proper, though, like other assemblies, it acquired wider importance as the main place for ratification of a new king's right to reign. In Denmark a new king had similarly to be accepted and hailed at only the three most important assemblies, at Viborg (north

Jutland), Ringsted (Sjælland), and Lund (Skåne). Skara, the central assembly in Västergötland, became the "assembly of all the Götar." Mora äng was the site of a joint assembly of the three *lands* of Uppsala, where a new king of Sweden had to be publicly accepted before making his progress (his *eriksgata*) to the other provincial assemblies.

What made a unit a unit—from the sixth of a *herred* to a law-province covering as much as one-third of a nation—was the *thing,* a common assembly on a fixed site where regular public meetings were formally held. The participants deferred to a common body of legal rules, customary or prescribed. They met under religious auspices, and an assembly had a special "sanctity" (compensation was increased, for example, for injury suffered at the assembly). *Herred* assemblies in Denmark might meet as often as every eighth day, and the regional assembly (modern *landsting*) once a month. In Iceland the thirty-nine local assemblies met for combined judicial and political purposes only for four to seven days each spring, with a brief autumn meeting of one or two days at which no provision was made for hearing lawsuits. The Icelandic Althing met for a fortnight every summer (outside dates 18 June–7 July), and an annual meeting was the general rule for the great law-provinces of the mainland. Gulathing (west Norway) and Frostathing met at the end of June, while the Uppsala assembly met about the vernal equinox until a reorganization put it back to a date in late January or February. Except in Iceland, it seems to have been theoretically possible to summon ad hoc assemblies at any level.

It is thought that assemblies were originally "all-things," that is, attended by all free able-bodied men of the community in question. Major assemblies, however, tended to become representative gatherings, doubtless for reasons of practical expediency and under the influence of royal policy. Thus, in the eleventh and early twelfth century, the Gulathing was attended by about 400 men of the yeoman class, selected by the *fylke*-quarter assemblies; after 1164 the number was reduced to 264. In Iceland the Althing could be attended by all free men, but the law required a minimum attendance of one in nine of a chieftain's "thingmen."

SOCIAL STRUCTURE

The staple of the social order throughout the north was the free householder, the yeoman (ON: *búandi, bóndi;* plural, *búendr, bœndr*). There were gradations depending on whether he lived on inalienable inherited land or owned his land in person or had other capital. He was of less account if he was a tenant or cotter, and men in service were also of lower status. Freedmen were of still less significance, and in theory slaves had no personal rights at all. Women, minors (twelve was once the age of majority, later sixteen), and incapable people had legal but generally not political rights. Regulation of local affairs depended on consultation and agreement among the superior free men, but free speech was not solely their prerogative and their numbers and relative influence were bound to fluctuate. Some tolerable social balance appears to have been maintained at least down to the twelfth century.

The yeomen, especially those on inalienable land, were firmly enmeshed in family ties, with formal acknowledgment of kinship over at least five generations the legal norm. One line of male descent stood separate, the dynasty from which the supreme leaders were drawn. Any man in this male line might be considered for the national kingship, but to be entrusted with the king's paramount duties of leadership in cult and war he had to be accepted by the people at their assemblies. But the yeomen could also put him down if he failed to bring prosperity and success, just as they could treat him as a criminal if he broke their law. He was more their king than they were his subjects. In the twelfth century, under church influence, considerations of primogeniture and legitimate birth began to convert Scandinavian kingship into hereditary monarchy of a more familiar kind, though the elective principle remained a vital constitutional issue, not least in Sweden. Salving and crowning then also became final confirmation of a reign's legitimacy.

Members of the acknowledged dynasty had the title *konungr* (king). It was freely used in the Viking Age and only became restricted to national monarchs in the eleventh century. Some independent ruling dynasties stuck to the title of *jarl* (earl, in Orkney, for example), but later this was used of the king's mightiest lieutenant, for whom, later again, *hertogi* (duke) was adopted on the German model.

It was the free men at their assemblies who took public council, made public decisions, and gave judgment in lawsuits. The king was a guest at their assemblies, but he inevitably acted as an initiator, arbiter, and executor. The overlap of authority meant that various leaders and officers existed intermediary between king and people. There was gradual movement, doubtless beginning long before the Viking Age, toward royal appointments in place of hereditary or elected local headmen.

From among the yeomen were drawn the lawmen (*lǫgmenn*) and law-speakers (*lǫgsǫgumenn*), experts who remembered the laws, recited them at assemblies, applied them in the courts, and framed new rules. Norwegian assemblies seem generally to have been led by a group of such men, and assemblies in Skåneland were similarly led by a group of "seniors" (OD: *aldunga*). In Götaland and Svealand the provinces had individual lawmen as their leaders, and the Icelanders had their single lawspeaker. Lawmen spoke on behalf of the whole assembly in discussions with kings and other outsiders. The great men of a region or province, and the king too, would naturally take an interest in the office of lawman (though it might continue in one family for generations). By around 1200 the lawmen in Norway were royally appointed justices. About 1200 the lawman of Västergötland came of a mighty family from outside the province.

Birth, wealth, marriage alliances, personal qualities, patronage, and royal favor might all play a part in establishing and maintaining men as local leaders. In Västergötland each *herred* and *herred*-quarter had a headman (*härads-, fjärdingshövding*). They may once have been communally appointed, but around 1200 they appear as prefects and justices acting on behalf of the king. In Denmark each "levy unit" had a locally resident "commander" (*styræsman*) who must have had more say in communal affairs because of his status. Local leaders in Norway were often untitled and are to be found among the "company commanders" (*sveitarhǫfðingjar*) of levy forces and the "best" yeomen, *viri boni et discreti,* who might be summoned to attend councils of the realm.

In the earlier part of the period a superior class of Norwegian leader had the title *hersir.* Its exact meaning is uncertain (the first element is *herr,* as in *herred*), but it does not seem to imply direct dependence on royal authority in the same way as does the title of *lendr maðr* (landed man), a local magnate who also had revenues from king's land and acted as a kind of lord lieutenant in his district. The laws distinguish these men sharply from the free yeomen—their rights are double in cash and other terms—but some precautions were taken to stop them from throwing their weight about in assemblies and lawcourts. The office often passed from father to son but it remained in the king's gift. There were perhaps 100 or so *lendir menn* in Norway in the eleventh and twelfth centuries, but by the thirteenth century there were fewer than a score; these became equated with barons and had the makings of a select aristocracy. District administration was put in the hands of fifty-odd *sýslumenn* (sheriffs), appointed by the king and answerable to him. A *lendr maðr* might be given control of a *sýsla* but there was nothing blue-blooded, permanent, or hereditary about the job. In Denmark and Sweden, on the other hand, a larger class of petty nobility existed, and district affairs were largely in their hands.

MONARCHY AND CENTRALIZATION

From the earliest time few areas can have been without a king's agent of some kind. Estates belonging to the crown lay scattered about the countryside and were each looked after by a royal steward (*ármaðr, bryti*). Kings also had important officers (*fógeti,* bailiff) in the townships that came into existence in the eleventh century. In several regions, primarily in Svealand, evidence of ancient (pre-900) royal control by a kind of "plantation" policy has been seen in numerous farms all with the name Husaby. These places, evidently with characteristically big or specialized buildings (*hús*), belonged to the monarchy and were apparently run both as farms and as depots for the supplies contributed by the locality. Some of them may also have had significance as strongholds and rallying points. In any case, the king's officer resident in a Husaby would inevitably have his finger in local affairs, and many such farms have cult- and assembly-places close by.

The most effective centralizing influence was the need for cooperation in organizing wider security: coast guard, beacon-watches, collecting and passing information, building roads, bridges, and forts. Such matters required an overall command such as the king naturally exercised. In the tenth and eleventh centuries all the monarchies developed the *le(i)dang* (ON: *leiðangr*), a levy system geared to naval warfare and movement by sea. Responsibility for providing manned and equipped vessels was imposed either on existing district units or on new divisions—*skipreide* (ON: *skipreiða*) in Norway, *skeppslag* in Roden and other parts of Svealand, and *skiben* in Denmark. These were subdivided into the units that provided the single oarsman-soldier, fractions with names like *har* (thole) and *hamna* (oarlock) in Sweden, *hafnæ* (shipboard station) in Denmark, *manngerð* (man-provision) in Norway.

Le(i)dang obligations rested primarily on coastal regions, but throughout mainland Scandinavia they became the basis of national taxation when service and supplies came to be converted into forms of cash payment in the twelfth and thirteenth centuries. In Denmark and Sweden ships lost importance as fighting units and greater emphasis was placed on cavalry and fortifications. Mounted service and provision of cap-a-pie armor and a squad of men-at-arms then bought exemption from the national *le(i)dang* taxation, and gave rise to a comparatively large class of privileged landowners, with titles of knight and squire, who, as a self-conscious and feudal-like nobility (Danish [D]: *frælse;* Sw: *frälse,* literally "freedom"), played a vital political role from the thirteenth century on.

Like other great men, a king had his own soldiers and servants, a retinue which from about 1000 came to be called the *hirð* (from Old English *hired,* "household, familia"). Members of this bodyguard were once generally called *húskarlar,* later mostly *hirðmenn.* It was an honor to belong to this corporation, which was united by mutual obligations as well as by their individual vows of loyalty sworn to the king. They were led by a marshall (*stallari*) and other ranks and offices came into being with time. The *hirð* was doubtless a mixed bunch of adventurers (including foreigners) and men of prominent families from different parts of the country. Many of them did not stay permanently in the retinue but retired to their estates to act as *lendir menn* or in other capacities as king's officers. They remained *handgengnir menn,* men who had done homage and were tied by personal bonds to the king, and could be used to implement policies that were supra-provincial. At the same time the king's personal retinue gave him a well-armed, competent, and devoted military nucleus which was important in warfare against a foreign enemy and generally put him at an advantage against internal opposition. The *hirð* might have a decisive influence when succession to the crown was at issue.

Early kings lived on progress for much of the time, visiting their estates to eat up their revenues, staying with local magnates, maintaining a presence at local assemblies, presiding at great religious festivals, supervising defenses, and organizing campaigns. From the eleventh century they generally preferred fewer fixed residences, often living in the growing townships. A more settled and fastidious court life then developed. The senior members of the *hirð* had formed a natural group of royal advisers, and now the chief secular and clerical members of the court formed a kind of privy council (ON: *ráð*); the king generally had most influence on their selection. As a more formal council of state (ON: *ríkis ráð*), and tending to be more and more aristocratic in composition, such a body became an almost indispensable element in medieval government, particularly influential at times of interregnum and when the sovereign was a minor.

Kings could always summon their *handgengnir menn,* but in the twelfth century they took the initiative in organizing larger kinds of national assemblies when some political step appeared to require wide sanction and particular solemnity. Those summoned were the king's men and the nobles, bishops and other important clergy, and often, but not invariably, a group of the "best" yeomen from each law-province or diocese. Such nascent parliaments had most influence in the thirteenth century, especially in Denmark where the nobility made this kind of assembly (the so-called *danehof*) an institution for the protection of their interests against the crown. After that the functions of such gatherings were largely engrossed by the developing councils of state mentioned above.

ICELAND

Iceland was settled in the period from about 870 to 930 by men whose families originated in southwest and west Norway. They must have brought with them ideas of public assemblies, the rights of free men, and the need for a common law, but they came in miscellaneous groups with heads of households, sometimes men of titled rank, as their natural leaders. But they were in unusual circumstances. First, they came gradually and with mixed experience to an uninhabited country; they were less fixed in the rigidities of family ties and long-standing local customs than the mainland populations. Second, differentiation in living conditions, which was not great anywhere in the north, started smaller and developed more slowly in Iceland than elsewhere. Third, since their island was remote in the Atlantic, they had no problems of external defense and hence no need for war leaders or fiscal burdens on a national scale.

By 930 the Icelanders had agreed on a constitution for the whole community, marked by the adoption of a fixed national assembly (Althing). The constitution did not envisage sovereignty vested in one dynasty and exercised by a king but rather an oligarchy of equal chieftaincies. These were called *goðorð,* an abstract from *goði* (plural, *goðar*), the chieftain's title, which means "man having some public relationship to gods, a kind of priest." (We have no reliable information about chieftains' priestly functions apart from their duty to hallow assemblies. The word *goði* is otherwise known only from Danish runic inscriptions, where it appears emphatically to mean "cult leader.") A *goðorð* could be inherited, transferred temporarily, bought, and sold. It might be owned by more than one person, though only one man could function as *goði* at any one time.

The national assembly contained deliberative and judicial organs. The chieftains, each with two advisers, sat and voted in the *lǫgrétta* (law council), where they made and mended laws and took other public decisions on behalf of the whole population. They also elected the law-speaker, whose main duties were to act as chairman of the *lǫgrétta* and as president of the whole Althing and to know the laws by heart and recite one-third of them each year, with annual repetition of those dealing with assembly procedures. He was initially elected for three years and could be reelected. The chieftains did not play a direct part in the judicial process, but they had rights and duties of nomination (especially of judges) and of a supervisory and executive kind in their localities and at the assemblies.

We know the constitutional arrangements best in the shape they were given by a reform from about 965. Until then there were thirty-six *goðar* but now there were to be thirty-nine. They with their followers were allotted in threes to a local assembly site where the spring meeting (*várþing*) and the autumn meeting (*haustþing, leið*) were held. The country as a whole was split into Quarters (now usually denoted by the compass points), and each Quarter had three assembly sites—except the north, which had four. This division was then applied to the Althing, where four Quarter courts were established and various makeweights introduced so that the three extra chieftains from the north did not disturb the balance.

The constitution expected everyone in the country to have an "assembly attachment," if not directly then through a responsible householder, who had to be "in thing with," that is, the follower of, a chieftain. Chieftain and thingman were bound by mutual contract, and technically the former could reject his follower and the latter shift his allegiance at will. The system seems to have required no fixed tolls or subsidies in the early period (there may have been a cult tax in pagan times) and probably survived by a balancing of gifts and services. The only formal taxation known in early Iceland was the tithe (introduced in 1096 or 1097). This could and did benefit some laymen inasmuch as all churches were private property and most clergy privately employed, so that the tithe shares designed for maintaining the church building and the priest passed to the man who owned them both.

Parochial divisions were made in the twelfth century, following the introduction of the tithe. An older form of division, probably originating in the settlement period and finally adopted on a national scale, was into *hreppar* (communes; singular, *hreppr*). These were largely independent of assembly and parish organization. They became regularized as groups of at least twenty adjacent farms of prescribed value. A committee of five drawn from the householders had general charge of local affairs. They superintended marks of ownership, for example, and organized autumn sheep gathering; they arranged the compensation payable to a member of the commune hit by catastrophes such as fire and livestock disease; they saw to the distribution of the tithe-quarter and other gifts intended for the poor. All the householders of a *hreppr* came together three times a year and extra meetings could be called. They could also set up their own court (*hreppsdómr*), which had recognized judicial authority in matters relating to poor relief.

Given the nature of the *goðorð,* disintegration of the system seems inevitable. Energetic, ambitious, and rich chieftains would attract followers from others less well-endowed, not least those whose authority was diluted by division of *goðorð* ownership. Concentration of *goðorð* as a result of gift and purchase would reinforce the concentration that must also have come about naturally by marriage alliance and inheritance. These processes must have operated from the start, but a reasonable balance of power seems to have been maintained until the end of the eleventh century. Thereafter they gained momentum, and in the thirteenth century five or six families owned all the *goðorð* in the country. They produced leaders who tended to behave like lords and to treat their thingmen as subjects. Rival leaders then made armed bids for sovereignty, variously backed or opposed by the Norwegian king and Norwegian prelates, inspired by what at the time were normal ideas of hierarchical unity and a supreme governor. Finally, in 1262–1264, the Icelanders agreed to pay tax to the Norwegian king. For a short time they were ruled by an Icelander with the title of *jarl,* thereafter by governors (usually with the title *hirðstjóri*). District administration was put in the hands of *sýslumenn* appointed by the crown. The *hreppar* gradually came to have the nature of administrative units within the *sýsla.*

Greenland was settled from Iceland around 985, and the colony survived there until the fifteenth century. The Greenlanders seem to have had assemblies and chieftains on the Icelandic model. They agreed to pay tax to the Norwegian crown sooner than the Icelanders did (1257–1261), and thereafter had an administration based on the *sýsla.*

LAW CODES

The chief recordings of law (none in manuscripts earlier than the twelfth century, most from the thirteenth century and later) are as follows. From Denmark we know a code for Jutland (with Fyn and Langeland), and private texts for Sjælland (and other islands) and for Skåneland (with Bornholm). We have full texts for the Frostathing and Gulathing law-provinces of Norway, fragments only for Eidsifathing (north of Oslo) and Borgarthing (the southeast provinces). From Sweden we have law-texts, variously interrelated, for Västergötland, Östergötland, Småland, Södermanland, Västmanland, Uppland, Dalarna, Hälsingland, and Gotland. Icelandic laws are known in some twelfth-century fragments and two big thirteenth-century collections (as a whole referred to as *Grágás*). They are more comprehensive than the mainland laws. The major areas covered by the extant Scandinavian texts are Christian practice; assault, injury, and homicide; marriage and family law; inheritance; land law; labor law; contracts and commerce; slaves and manumission; levy organization; and wergild. Municipal laws and maritime laws exist in special collections.

The king came to have more and more authority as a supreme judge and source of law. The peace of the country at large came to be regarded as his peace, and he was owed reparation if it was violated. All the mainland laws acknowledge the king's right to receive fines for a variety of offenses. The king's overriding interests could produce edicts that had the force of national lawgiving. A similar effect stemmed from an idea of lèse majesté which is evident in Denmark in the twelfth century and in Sweden in the thirteenth. Swedish laws have sections on *eþsörisbrot* (sworn-oath offenses), crimes which, while unpunished, meant that the king was failing to keep the oath he swore on his accession to maintain law and order.

Nevertheless justice remained for a long time essentially the affair of the yeoman class. Free people and their property were held to enjoy a natural right of immunity from molestation and injury. This was conveyed by the Old Norse abstract *helgi* (inviolability, immunity), or with specific reference to the person (ON: *mannhelgi;* OD: *manhælgh*); the adjective *heilagr* (inviolable; in which one has exclusive right); and the verb *helga* (invoke or impose a state of inviolability). (These words are related to the English "holy," but what religious connotation they had in the legal sphere is uncertain.) This normally accepted right could be automatically forfeited as the result of a trespass on the immunity of someone else. Retaliation immediately provoked by such a trespass was not normally counted illegal.

Breach of immunity often meant physical damage of some kind; it could always mean damage to self-esteem and social esteem, and this damage extended to the family at large. The degree of family commitment is reflected in the preserved wergild lists. A natural and respected way of redressing the balance was to take blood vengeance, not necessarily on the offender but on another member of his kindred, preferably one of more worth. Feuds of this kind usually resulted sooner or later in private settlements, normally with a third party as arbitrator. (There was scope for the king or his agents to enforce and provide arbitration.) We have some formulas for establishing truce and a final peace after such a settlement. In the west Norse world an individual's *réttr* (right) was also fixed by law as a sum payable as personal satisfaction in case of certain offenses, separate from compensation or other penalty. In Norway this right varied with the class, but in Iceland one sum was payable for every free person, chieftain and laborer alike.

The alternative to private (family) action was to attempt to get an offender publicly condemned by charging him with his offense before the assembly of the community. All assemblies must have started with equal judicial authority, but it gradually became accepted that courts of regional assemblies were superior to those of districts, and those of law-provinces superior again; and in the monarchies, king or council came to count as the ultimate authority, even in some cases with power to pardon.

In Iceland, "fining" cases had to be taken to a spring assembly court; more serious cases might go there or straight to the appropriate Quarter court at the Althing. Cases undecided locally could be taken to the Althing, while cases deadlocked in Quarter courts could go before the Fifth Court, a kind of supreme court which could be set up at the Althing in accordance with a law passed soon after 1000. In Iceland, as elsewhere, cases passed to a superior court only when no clear-cut verdict was given; a dissatisfied litigant had no right of appeal in the ordinary way.

There was much variety in legal procedures and the following is merely a generalized summary. It was necessary to make an offense common knowledge by publishing it as soon as possible before qualified witnesses. In some places an ad hoc gathering might be called to the scene of the offense (ON: *ǫrvarþing,* arrow-thing, with an arrow used as a summoning token). Otherwise such witnesses and any eyewitnesses and earwitnesses of the offense would be formally required by the prosecutor to attend an assembly or court after a specified interval. The accused was also summoned in person, again before witnesses, to be present to answer the charge. Accusations were then repeated in public at the assembly and a court established (if not already in being) to hear the case; in some places the court might meet at the accused person's home. In most mainland communities factual notoriety and personal identification might be easily established; it was more complex in Iceland, where a prosecutor had also to know about his opponent's chieftain and assembly and sometimes his particular neighbors.

Individuals were expected to conduct their own cases but it was permitted, generally or exceptionally, to transfer the pleading to someone else (usually obligatory when women and minors were principals). Accepted means of prosecution proof were: admission of guilt; eyewitnesses and earwitnesses (not much used because of the emphasis on establishing notoriety); confirmatory evidence (for example, bloodstained bedclothes, stolen property, and later, documents); and chiefly the prosecutor's own statement given under oath and supported by men of suitable standing who substantiated, also under oath, not so much the facts of the case as the integrity of the prosecutor. Procedural witnesses had to be produced at every stage. A defense might hinge on denial, on justification, or on procedural error in the prosecution. The means of defense chiefly prescribed was the defendant's denial under oath backed by witnesses where relevant and, regularly in mainland Scandinavia, by compurgators in numbers that varied with the seriousness of the accusation (from one to as many as three dozen).

The laws usually made it clear where the burden of proof lay—most often it was the defendant who had the right to clear himself—and then the procedure allowed for no reply or argument. If it was not already prescribed, then a court might make a kind of preliminary judgment as to which side should produce the proof. For much of the period (but not in Iceland) ordeal by hot iron was prescribed as a means of defense in certain cases, a form of proof introduced under Christian auspices and finally abolished in the thirteenth century. Dueling was accepted as a legal way of resolving disputes, at least in pre-Christian times: it does not seem to have been looked on as a form of ordeal.

Oath-helpers were in all probability at first drawn from the kin of the man they swore for. A family element remains in some forms of the prescribed groups of co-swearers, but they may also include more neutrally selected members. In some regions a standing panel (OD,OS: *næfnd*) came into being, appointed to act throughout an assembly, or for a year or longer at a time, and with functions like those of a jury concerned as much with investigating the facts of the case as with endorsing the standing of the antagonists. Compurgation hardly figures in Icelandic law, probably because of the social conditions of the settlement. A prosecutor there had generally to empanel five or nine householders of qualified status who were closest neighbors of the man accused or of the scene of the offense as prescribed. This panel (*kviðr*) confirmed by majority vote each step in the prosecution as it was presented before the judges and so substantiated the charges made against the accused. To defend himself he had to get a verdict from members of the same panel agreeing that, on the facts he presented, he was cleared.

It is probable that originally all assembly members sat in judgment, and they remained collectively responsible when the verdict was actually left to the lawmen and other local leaders with whatever coadjutors it was customary or expedient to have. In Iceland thirty-six judges sat in the courts at spring assemblies, nominated equally by the local *goðar,* and apparently thirty-six also in the Quarter courts at the Althing, each nominated by the holders of the thirty-six "ancient" *goðorð* (those in existence before about 965). Judges everywhere had small discretion since the laws generally prescribed the means and burden of proof and the penalty to be imposed. Verdicts were formally announced, and wide publicity was given to guilt, especially when the community at large had an interest in exacting the penalty.

Penalties were: fines; enslavement, temporary or permanent; conditional loss of immunity (as for example in Denmark, where a man might lose his *manhælgh* but only in relation to his prosecutor and only within certain limits of corporal punishment; or in Iceland, where the compoundable outlawry, *fjǫrbaugsgarðr,* meant loss of goods and banishment for three years); and outright loss of immunity, the penalty of the full outlaw (ON: *skógarmaðr,* forest man), all of whose property and rights were forfeit, whom no one could help without breaking the law, and whom anyone could kill with impunity and sometimes reward. Some offenses entailed fines to the king; crimes of lèse majesté usually had exile and forfeit of lands as their consequence; treason carried the death penalty. Flogging and mutilation were typical punishments for petty thieving, hanging for more serious theft. Death by stoning, suffocation, or drowning was meted out to witches and warlocks. Execution of judgment was primarily the responsibility of the prosecutor, but it was not always easy and in case of default in cash payment, for example, further cumbersome legal process was usually required. Popular opinion and local leaders might be expected to lend aid, and it became more and more the province of king's officers to seek out and punish the guilty.

BIBLIOGRAPHY

Nils Ahnlund, *Jämtlands och Härjedalens historia,* I (1948); Johannes Brøndum-Nielsen and Poul J. Jørgensen, eds., *Danmarks gamle Landskabslove,* 8 vols. (1933–1961); Aksel E. Christensen, *Vikingetidens Danmark* (1969); Andrew Dennis *et al.*, trans., *Laws of Early Iceland: Grágás,* I (1980); Vilhjálmur Finsen, ed., *Grágás,* 3 vols. (1852–1883, repr. 1974); Peter Foote and David M. Wilson, *The Viking Achievement: The Society and Culture of Medieval Scandinavia,* 2nd ed. (1980); Finn Gad, *The History of Greenland,* I, *Earliest Times to 1700,* Ernst Dupont, trans. (1970); Ólafur Halldórsson, *Grænland í miðaldaritum* (1978); Knut Helle, *Konge og gode menn i norsk riksstyring ca. 1150–1319* (1972); Åke Holmbäck and Elias Wessén, eds., *Svenska landskapslagar,* 5 vols. (1933–1946); Jón Jóhannesson, *A History of the Old Icelandic Commonwealth,* Haraldur Bessason, trans. (1974); Rudolph Keyser *et al.*, eds., *Norges gamle Love indtil 1387,* 5 vols. (1846–1895); Erik Kroman and Stig Juul, eds., *Danmarks gamle Love; paa Nutidsdansk,* 3 vols. (1945–1948); *Kulturhistorisk leksikon for nordisk middelalder,* 22 vols. (1956–1978); Laurence M. Larson, trans., *The Earliest Norwegian Laws, Being the Gulathing Law and the Frostathing Law* (1935); Thomas Riis, *Les institutions politiques centrales du Danemark, 1100–1332* (1977); Carl J. Schlyter, ed., *Samling af Sweriges gamla lagar,* 12 vols. (1827–1877); Jens P. Trap, ed., *Danmark,* XIII, *Færøerne* (1968); Hugo Yrwing, *Gotland under äldre medeltid* (1940).

PETER FOOTE

[See also **Denmark; Iceland; Law, Swedish; Norway; Snorri Sturluson; Sweden; Vikings; Wergild.**]

SCANDINAVIA IN ARABIC SOURCES. At the time that Arab power was being consolidated on the Iberian Peninsula and was simultaneously expanding into the steppes north of the Black Sea, Scandinavian pirates and traders were beginning to move into the same regions. It was inevitable that the two groups should come into contact with each other, although there is no evidence that their relations were other than cautious or openly hostile. To the Arabs the Scandinavians were *al-Madjūs* (Magians, infidels), *ar-Rūs* (the Rus), *Warank* (Varangians), or *al-Urmān* (the Northmen). The period of contact lasted from the late eighth to the twelfth century. Most of the Arabic sources on Scandinavia from before 1500, selections from more than fifty writers, were collected by A. Seippel and translated into Norwegian by H. Birkeland. These extracts, uneven as they are in terms of originality and reliability, can be divided into three groups: geographical treatises, historical accounts, and travel narratives. The following writers, presented in chronlogical order, represent the most significant independent accounts.

ᶜUbayd Allāh ibn ᶜAbd Allāh ibn Khurdādhbih (*d.* 912/913) of Baghdad is the first to mention *ar-Rūs,* whom he describes as a subgroup of *aṣ-Ṣakāliba* (the Slavs). They are traders in furs and swords; they pay tribute to the emperor in Constantinople and the ruler of the Khazars; and their goods often come to Baghdad.

Aḥmad ibn Abī Yaᶜḳūb ibn Wāḍiḥ al-Yaᶜqūbī, (*d.* 897) says that *al-Madjūs,* also known as *ar-Rūs,* raided Algeciras and Seville in 843/844. This is the first Arabic account of an expedition that had set out with 150 ships and earlier plundered Toulouse.

Aḥmad ibn ᶜUmar ben Rusta (*fl.* 903), writing in

Isfahan, gives one of the most extensive descriptions of an *ar-Rūsīya* settlement thought to be either Novgorod (Hólmgarður) or Tmutarakan (modern Taman' in Krasnodar Krai, on the Black Sea). The Rus, under a leader called Khāḳan-Rūs (Kagan Rus), are traders who have no agricultural settlements but many towns (trading centers; compare the Old Norse word for Russia, *Garðaríki* [land of settlements]). They wear gold armbands, have fine swords, are always eager for combat, sacrifice to their gods with ritual hangings carried out by shamans (*seiðmenn*), and bury their important men in grave chambers, sealing up a favorite concubine with the corpse.

Ahmad ibn Fadlān (*fl.* 922) was sent as emissary to the king of the *aṣ-Ṣakāliba* (here the Volga Bulgars) in 921/922. As part of his general description of the country, he gives a long account of *al-Rūsīya.* They are tall, blond, and heavily tattooed, and are never without their swords and knives. Their women wear torques of gold and silver. They are the filthiest of God's creatures, are inordinately fond of *nabīd* (here ale or mead), and worship posts and stakes. Poor men at death are put in a boat and burnt, but for a rich man a more elaborate funeral is held. Ibn Faḍlān witnessed one of the latter, and his account is the most detailed description of a pre-Christian Scandinavian ship burial.

Abū 'l-Ḥasan ᶜAlī ibn al-Ḥusayn al-Masᶜūdī (*d.* 956), the first Arab historian, has a great deal of general information about *ar-Rūs* and their campaigns in the region of the Caspian Sea and the Sea of Azov (912/913), and their depredations on the Iberian Peninsula.

Ibrāhīm ibn Yaᶜūb of Tortosa was a Jewish merchant who made a trip through Germany and into Russia in 973 and whose narrative is preserved by al-Bakrī. Ibn Yaᶜūb says the Rus are divided into various groups and speak a Slavic lingua franca.

Muḥammad ibn Isḥāḳ ibn abī Ya'ḳūb al-Nadīm (*fl.* 987) describes a message sent from a king in the Caucasus Mountains to the king of *al-Rūsīya* written on wood. He gives an example of what can only be runic writing, but the original has been obscured by later copyists.

Aḥmad ibn Muḥammad ibn Miskawayh (*d.* 1030) describes the capture of Barda, the chief town of Caucasian Albania, by the *ar-Rūs* in 943.

Muḥammad ibn Aḥmad Abu 'l-Rayḥān al-Bīrūnī (*d. ca.* 1050) is the first to use the term *Warank* for people who live north of the *ar-Rūs.*

Abu ᶜUbayd Abd Allāh ben ᶜAbd al-ᶜAzīz al-Bakrī (*d.* 1094) recounts the ravages of *al-Madjūs* in Andalusia in 843/844, and their sacking of Nakūr (modern Imzourene, between the rivers Rhīs and Nekor in the Rif) in 858, an event that took place during the famous raiding voyage of Björn and Hafstein.

Abū ᶜAbd Allāh Muḥammad al-Idrīsī (*d.* 1165) wrote a geographical description to accompany a silver planisphere he had made at the request of Roger II, the Norman king of Sicily. The account shows considerable familiarity with northern Europe and is the first to mention Iceland (rather than *Tūlī* [Thule]), Norway, Denmark, and Finland by name.

Muḥammad ibn abī Bakr al-Zuhrī (*fl.* 1150) mentions the lands of *al-Urmān* in Greater Armenia, but the references are obscure.

ᶜUmar ibn al-Ḥasan ibn Diḥya (*d.* 1235), a writer noted for his unreliability, gives the supposed account of a journey to the land of *al-Madjūs* by Yaḥyā ibn Ḥakam al-Bakrī al-Ghazāl (*d.* 860). This narrative, and in particular al-Ghazāl's poetic repartee with Nūd, queen of the *al-Madjūs,* is based on his historical journey to Constantinople in 839/840 and his brilliant social success in the court of Emperor Theophilos and Empress Theodora.

ᶜIzz al-Dīn ibn al-Athīr (*d.* 1233) wrote a world history in which he recounts that in 795/796 Alfonso II, king of Galicia, campaigned with help from the king of the Basques and the neighboring *al-Madjūs.* Melvinger argues that this reflects a reliable tradition of Viking attacks in Spain from as early as 745. Also given are accounts of the raids of the *al-Madjūs* on the Iberian Peninsula in 844/845 and 859/860, the capture of Barda by *ar-Rūs* in 943, and the siege of Sidon in 1110 by the crusaders (among whom were Sigurður Jórsalafara Magnússon, king of Norway).

BIBLIOGRAPHY

William Edward David Allen, *The Poet and the Spae-wife: An Attempt to Reconstruct Al-Ghazal's Embassy to the Vikings* (1960), also in Viking Society for Northern Research, *Saga-book,* **15** (1960); Harris Birkeland, *Nordens historie i middelalderen etter arabisken kilder,* Norske Videnskaps-Akademi i Oslo, Skrifter, Hist.-Filos. Klasse, 2 Scriffer, 1954, **2** (1954); I. Hrbek, "Der dritte Stamm der Rūs nach arabischen Quellen," in *Archiv orientální,* **35** (1957); James E. McKeithen, "The Risalah of Ibn Fadlan: An Annotated Translation with Introduction" (diss., Indiana Univ., 1979); Arne Melvinger, *Les premières incursions des Vikings en Occident d'après les sources arabes* (1955); Muhammad ibn Muhammad al-Idrīsī, *La Finlande et les autres pays baltiques orientaux,* O. J. Tallgren-Tuulio and Aarne M. Tallgren, eds. (1930); Alexander Seippel, *Rerum normannicarum fontes arabici,* 2 vols. (1896–1928); H. M. Smyser, "Ibn Fadlan's Account of the Rus with Some Commentary and Some Allusions to *Beowulf,*" in Jess B. Bessinger and Robert P. Creed, eds., *Franciplegius: Medieval and Linguistic Studies in Honor of Francis Peabody Magoun, Jr.* (1965).

SHAUN F. D. HUGHES

[See also **Athīr, Ibn al-**; **Bīrūnī, al-**; **Idrīsī, al-**; **Khurdādhbih, Ibn**; **Kievan Rus**; **Mas^cūdī, al-**; **Muscovy, Rise of**; **Vikings**; **Volga Bulgars.**]